February 14–17, 2012
Lisbon, Portugal

Association for
Computing Machinery

Advancing Computing as a Science & Profession

IUI'12

Proceedings of the 17th International Conference on
Intelligent User Interfaces

Sponsored by:

ACM SIGART and SIGCHI

Supported by:

Microsoft Research, IBM Research, National Science Foundation, & Interaction-Design. org

Association for
Computing Machinery

Advancing Computing as a Science & Profession

The Association for Computing Machinery
2 Penn Plaza, Suite 701
New York, New York 10121-0701

ISBN: 978-1-4503-1048-2 (Digital)

ISBN: 978-1-4503-1370-2 (Print)

Additional copies may be ordered prepaid from:

ACM Order Department
PO Box 30777
New York, NY 10087-0777, USA

Phone: 1-800-342-6626 (USA and Canada)
+1-212-626-0500 (Global)
Fax: +1-212-944-1318
E-mail: acmhelp@acm.org
Hours of Operation: 8:30 am – 4:30 pm ET

ACM Order Number 608120

Printed in the USA

IUI 2012 Chairs' Welcome

It is our great pleasure to welcome you to the 2012 ACM International Conference on Intelligent User Interfaces – IUI'12 and to Lisboa, Portugal. Starting in 1993, IUI is now on its 17th edition and has established itself has the premier venue for reporting outstanding research and development on intelligent user interface. The IUI series continues to be the principal forum for the meeting of the Human-Computer Interaction (HCI) and the Artificial Intelligence (AI) communities. This gives rise to unique, creative, interdisciplinary contributions. This year's meeting showcases those topics, with works covering innovations in mobile interfaces, collaboration technology, affective interfaces, multimodal interfaces, pen interfaces, haptic and gesture interfaces, multi-touch interfaces, speech interfaces, gaze-based interfaces, tabletop interfaces, health applications, entertainment applications, adaptive narratives and theater, sports and in-vehicle applications, geographic applications, social media interfaces, educational interfaces, sketch recognition, human-robot interfaces, personalization and assistive technologies, end-user programming, ubiquitous and smart environments, location-aware interfaces, recommender interfaces, persuasive interfaces, web-based interfaces and agent-based interfaces.

Building on previous years' success, the IUI 2012 call for papers attracted 134 full paper submissions and 78 short paper submissions. To ensure the highest possible quality we assembled a team of 48 senior program committee members and 367 reviewers. This guaranteed that every submission had at least three reviews plus one meta-review. This was followed by a rebuttal phase, keeping the procedure started two years ago. We believe that this process has guaranteed the highest quality possible for this year technical program and we would like to thank all the senior program committee members and reviewers for their hard work in making sure the most relevant works were selected. Through this very thorough review process we were able to accept 18 full papers, 15 short papers and 16 poster presentations, meaning an acceptance rate of 13% for full papers, 16% for oral presentations and 23% for combined oral and poster presentations.

In addition to the full and short papers presentations and poster presentations, IUI will also feature a Demonstrations session for which 18 submissions were accepted from a total of 26 submissions

This year, the IUI programme includes three notable invited speakers sharing their innovative work and experiences with the conference participants: Alex 'Sandy' Pentland from the MIT Human Dynamic Lab, Christopher Bishop from Microsoft Research and Takeo Igarashi from the University of Tokyo.

In order to foster the growth of the community, IUI 2012 will feature for the first time in the IUI series a Doctoral Consortium. Its success can be measured by the 12 high quality submissions received. Doctoral Consortium students will also be able to exhibit their work to the main conference audience in the poster session, thus promoting their insertion into the IUI community. We would also like to thank the conference sponsors and supporters that made it possible to provide financial support for Doctoral Consortium attendees and other students participating in the conference.

Nine full-day workshops will take place at IUI 2012 covering diverse trending topics in the IUI area: Activity Context Representation: Techniques and Languages; Developing Intelligent User Interfaces for e-Accessibility and e-Inclusion; Context-awareness in Retrieval and Recommendation (CaRR 2012); 3rd Workshop on Semantic Models for Adaptive Interactive Systems (SEMAIS); Scent and Scensibility; User Modeling from Social Media; 2nd Workshop on Interacting with Smart Objects;

2nd Workshop on Location Awareness for Mixed and Dual Reality (LaMDa'12); 1st International Workshop on Ubiquitous Personalization (UP'2012).

IUI 2012 continues and extends the cooperation with the ACM Transactions on Interactive Intelligent Systems (TiiS). Besides the streamlined processing of journal submissions based on IUI 2012 papers, IUI 2012 will feature a special session where authors of recently accepted articles for the ACM TiiS will spotlight key contributions of their work. It is our conviction that it will benefit greatly every member of the IUI community. We would like to thank Anthony Jameson and John Riedl, the Editors in Chief of TiiS, for their cooperation.

The organisation of IUI 2012 is a team effort and, besides the contributions of all Chairs and the Program committee members, a team of volunteers worked very hard to make it a reality. We are very grateful to everyone who helped managing the different aspects of the conference and contributed to its success. We would like to extend our thanks to Daniel Kim of Red Whale for assisting with the Conference web site, and Lisa Tolles of Sheridan Printing Company for the preparation of the proceedings.

Finally, we acknowledge the support of the ACM through its special interest groups SIGART and SIGCHI. We also wish to thank our corporate supporters RedWhale Software, Microsoft Research and IBM Research, and the institutional support of the National Science Foundation.

We hope that you find this an innovative and interesting program, and that the conference will provide you with the opportunities to meet other researchers and practitioners with whom you can share ideas and cooperate in the future. We're looking forward to see you in Lisboa!

Carlos Duarte
and Luís Carriço
IUI'12 General Chairs

Joaquim Jorge, Sharon Oviatt,
and Daniel Gonçalves
IUI'12 Program Chairs

Table of Contents

Session 4: Designing Narratives & Theater

Session 5: Personalization, Search & Usability

Session 6: Social Computing & Media

Session 7: Smart Infrastructure

Poster Presentation

Demonstration Session

Doctoral Consortium

Workshops

IUI 2012 Conference Organization

General Chairs: Carlos Duarte *(University of Lisbon, Portugal)*
Luís Carriço *(Universiy of Lisbon, Portugal)*

Program Chairs: Joaquim Jorge *(INESC-ID, Portugal)*
Sharon Oviatt *(Incaa Designs, USA)*
Daniel Gonçalves *(INESC-ID, Portugal)*

Workshops Chairs: Andreas Butz *(University of Munich, Germany)*
Per Ola Kristensson *(University of St. Andrews, UK)*

Demonstrations Chair: Nadir Weibel *(University of California San Diego, USA)*

Doctoral Consortium Chairs: Nuria Oliver *(Telefonica Research, Spain)*
Mauro Cherubini *(Telefonica Research, Spain)*

Local Arrangements Chairs: André Falcão *(University of Lisbon, Portugal)*
António Ferreira *(University of Lisbon, Portugal)*

Treasurer: Lawrence Bergman *(IBM Watson Labs, USA)*

Steering Committee Chair: Angel Puerta *(RedWhale Software, USA)*

Steering Committee: W. Lewis Johnson *(USC/ISI, USA)*
Mark Maybury *(MITRE, USA)*
Doug Riecken *(CCLS Columbia University, USA)*
Candace Sidner *(BAE Systems, AIT, USA)*
Robert St. Amant *(North Carolina State University, USA)*

Senior Program Committee: Christine Alvarado *(Harvey Mudd College, USA)*
Elisabeth André *(Augsburg University, Germany)*
Sumit Basu *(Microsoft Research, USA)*
Mark Billinghurst *(HIT Lab NZ, University of Canterbury, New Zealand)*
Oliver Brdiczka *(Darmstadt University of Technology, Germany)*
Jose Campos *(Universidade do Minho, Portugal)*
Pedro Campos *(University of Madeira, Portugal)*
Joyce Chai *(Michigan State University, USA)*
Teresa Chambel *(LaSIGE, University of Lisbon, Portugal)*
Fang Chen *(NICTA, Australia)*
Phil Cohen *(OGI/OHSU, USA)*
Cristina Conati *(University of British Columbia, Canada)*
Nuno Correia *(New University of Lisbon, Portugal)*

Senior Program Committee (continued):

Maria Francesca Costabile *(University of Bari, Italy)*
Allen Cypher *(IBM Almaden Research Center, USA)*
Danyel Fisher *(Microsoft Research, USA)*
Manuel Fonseca *(INESC-I/IST/UTL, Portugal)*
Bernd Froehlich *(Bauhaus-Universitaet Weimar, Germany)*
Tiago Guerreiro *(INESC-I/IST/UTL, Portugal)*
Tracy Hammond *(Texas A&M University, USA)*
Stacy Hobson *(IBM, USA)*
Antonio Krüger *(DFKI GmbH, Germany)*
Tessa Lau *(IBM Almaden Research Center, USA)*
Joseph LaViola *(University of Central Florida, USA)*
James Lester *(North Carolina State University, USA)*
Henry Lieberman *(Massachusetts Institute of Technology, USA)*
Wendy Mackay *(INRIA, France)*
Louis-Philippe Morency *(University of Southern California, USA)*
Christian Mueller *(German Research Center for Artificial Intelligence, Germany)*
Petteri Nurmi *(University of Helsinki, Finland)*
Nuria Oliver *(Telefonica R&D, Spain)*
Philippe Palanque *(ICS-IRIT, Université Paul Sabatier, France)*
Cecile Paris *(CSIRO/ICT Centre, Australia)*
Fabio Paternó *(CNR-ISTI, Italy)*
Catherine Pelachaud *(University of Paris 8, France)*
Beryl Plimmer *(University of Auckland, New Zealand)*
Rui Prada *(INESC-ID and Instituto Superior Técnico-UTL, Portugal)*
John Riedl *(University of Minnesota, USA)*
Thomas Rist *(University of Applied Sciences Augsburg, Germany)*
Dave Roberts *(Open University, UK)*
Teresa Romão *(FCT/UNL, Portugal)*
Carolyn Rose *(Human Computer Interaction Institute, Carnegie Mellon University, USA)*
Metin Sezgin *(MIT CSAIL, USA)*
Manas Tungare *(Virginia Tech / Google, USA)*
Min Wu *(Oracle, USA)*
Massimo Zancanaro *(FBK-irst, Italy)*
Michelle Zhou *(IBM Almaden Research Center, USA)*
Ingrid Zukerman *(Monash University, Australia)*

Program Committee: Matt Adcock *(CSIRO, Australia)*
Aaron Adler *(BBN Technologies, USA)*
Ana Afonso *(Universidade de Lisboa, Portugal)*
Wolfgang Aigner *(Vienna University of Technology, Austria)*
Jason Alexander *(Lancaster University, United Kingdom)*
Dzmitry Aliakseyeu *(Philips Research Europe, The Netherlands)*
Margarita Anastassova *(CEA, LIST, Laboratoire d'Interafaces Sensorielles, France)*
Adrienne Andrew *(University of Washington, USA)*
Pierre Andrews *(Università degli Studi di Trento, Italy)*
Liliana Ardissono *(University of Torino, Italy)*
Carmelo Ardito *(Università degli Studi di Bari, Italy)*
Kenneth Arnold *(MIT, USA)*
Ernesto Arroyo *(MIT, USA)*
Daniel Ashbrook *(Nokia Research Center Hollywood, Georgia Institute of Technology, USA)*
Nikolaos Avouris *(University of Patras, Greece)*
Daniel Avrahami *(Intel, University of Washington, USA)*
Seok-Hyung Bae *(KAIST, Republic of Korea)*
Alok Baikadi *(North Carolina State University, USA)*
Brian Bailey *(University of Illinois-Urbana, USA)*
Rafael Ballagas *(Nokia Research Center, USA)*
Tiffany Barnes *(The University of North Carolina at Charlotte, USA)*
Barbara Rita Barricelli *(Università degli Studi di Milano, Italy)*
Paulo Barthelmess *(Adapx Inc., USA)*
Christian Bastien *(Univ. Paul Verlaine – Metz, France)*
Scott Bateman *(University of Saskatchewan, Canada)*
Eric Baumer *(Cornell University, USA)*
Joerg Baus *(German Research Center for Artificial Intelligence, Germany)*
Russell Beale *(University of Birmingham, UK)*
Michel Beaudouin-Lafon *(Université Paris-Sud, France)*
Karin Bee *(Augsburg University, Germany)*
Nikolaus Bee *(Augsburg University, Germany)*
Andrew Begel *(Microsoft Research, USA)*
Gordon Bell *(Microsoft, USA)*
Victoria Bellotti *(Palo Alto Research Center, USA)*
Lawrence Bergman *(IBM T.J. Watson Research Center, USA)*
Shlomo Berkovsky *(CSIRO, Australia)*
Michael Bernstein *(Massachusetts Institute of Technology, USA)*
Sven Bertel *(Bauhaus-Universität Weimar, Germany)*
Sumithra Bhakthavatsalam *(Adapx, USA)*
Sourav Bhattacharya *(Helsinki Institute for Information Technology HIIT, Finland)*

Program Committee (continued):

Jeffrey Bigham *(University of Rochester, USA)*
Fernando Birra *(Faculdade Ciências e Tecnologia/UNL, Portugal)*
Pradipta Biswas *(University of Cambridge Computer Laboratory, England)*
Roland Blach *(CC Virtual Environments, Fraunhofer IAO, Germany)*
Rachel Blagojevic *(University of Auckland, New Zealand)*
Marco Blumendorf *(TU-Berlin, DAI-Labor, Germany)*
Matthias Böhmer *(German Research Center for Artificial Intelligence, Germany)*
Jared Bott *(University of Central Florida, USA)*
Matt-Mouley Bouamrane *(University of Manchester, United Kingdom)*
Mohamed Bourimi *(University of Siegen, Germany)*
Chris Bowers *(University of Birmingham, UK)*
Gregor Broll *(DOCOMO Euro-Labs, Germany)*
Andrea Bunt *(University of Manitoba, Canada)*
Paolo Buono *(Università degli Studi di Bari, Italy)*
Robin Burke *(DePaul University, USA)*
Margaret Burnett *(Oregon State University, USA)*
Giuseppe Carenini *(University of British Columbia, Canada)*
Mark Carman *(Monash University, Australia)*
Luis Carriço *(Faculty of Sciences, University of Lisbon, Portugal)*
Stefania Castellani *(Xerox Research Centre Europe, France)*
Sandro Castronovo *(DFKI, Germany)*
Marc Cavazza *(University of Tesside, United Kingdom)*
Eva Cerezo *(University of Zaragoza, Spain)*
Daniel Cernea *(University of Kaiserslautern, Germany & Linnaeus University, Sweden)*
Duen Horng Chau *(Carnegie Mellon University, USA)*
Beenish Chaudry *(Indiana University, USA)*
Zebin Chen *(Microsoft, USA)*
Jilin Chen *(Palo Alto Research Center, USA)*
Chi-Hua Chen *(National Chiao Tung University, Taiwan)*
Shiwei Cheng *(Zhejiang University, China)*
Lynn Cherny *(Adobe, Inc., USA)*
Mauro Cherubini *(Telefonica Research, Italy)*
Keith Cheverst *(Lancaster University, UK)*
Yoram Chisik *(University of Baltimore, USA & Madeira Interactive - Technologies Institute, Portugal)*
Eric Choi *(National ICT Australia, Australia)*
Jason Chuang *(Stanford University, USA)*
Cagla Cig *(Koc University, Turkey)*
Alexis Clay *(ESTIA, France)*
Nathalie Colineau *(CSIRO - ICT Centre, Australia)*
Christopher Collins *(University of Ontario Institute of Technology, Canada)*

Program Committee (continued):

Dan Cosley *(Cornell University, USA)*
Nadine Couture *(LIPSI-ESTIA, France)*
Danielle Cummings *(Texas A&M University, USA)*
Raimund Dachselt *(University of Magdeburg, Germany)*
Aba-Sah Dadzie *(The University of Sheffield, UK)*
Florian Daiber *(DFKI GmbH, Germany)*
Ionut Damian *(Augsburg University, Germany)*
José Danado *(NTNU, Norway)*
Chi Tai Dang *(University of Augsburg, Germany)*
Randall Davis *(MIT, USA)*
Nadja De Carolis *(University of Bari, Italy)*
Alexander De Luca *(Ludwig-Maximilians Universität München, Germany)*
Marco de Sá *(Yahoo! Research, USA)*
Frederic Dehais *(ISAE, France)*
Matthias Deller *(TU Kaiserslautern \ DFKI GmbH, Germany)*
Xiaoming Deng *(Institute of Software, Chinese Academy of Sciences, China)*
Debayan Dhar *(Indian Institute of Technology, India)*
A. Eduardo Dias *(Faculdade de Ciências e Tecnologia - Universidade Nova de Lisboa, Portugal)*
Paulo Dias *(IEETA - University of Aveiro, Portugal)*
Jonathan Diehl *(RWTH Aachen University, Germany)*
Anke Dittmar *(University of Rostock, Germany)*
John Dowding *(Adapx, Inc., USA)*
Steven Drucker *(Microsoft Research, USA)*
Carlos Duarte *(Universidade de Lisboa, Portugal)*
Henry Been-Lirn Duh *(National University of Singapore, Singapore)*
Elizabeth Dykstra Erickson *(ACCESS Systems Americas, USA)*
Achim Ebert *(University of Kaiserslautern, Germany)*
Gary Edwards *(Lockheed Martin Adv Tech Labs, USA)*
Patrick Ehlen *(AT&T Labs Research, USA)*
Julien Epps *(National ICT Australia, The University of New South Wales, Australia)*
Elisabetta Farella *(DEIS - University of Bologna, Italy)*
Michael Feld *(German Research Center for AI (DFKI), Germany)*
Mirko Fetter *(Otto-Friedrich-Universität Bamberg, Germany)*
Rebecca Fiebrink *(Princeton University, Microsoft Research, University of Washington, USA)*
Martin Field *(Texas A&M University, USA)*
Frederico Figueiredo *(Nokia Siemens Networks, INESC-ID, Portugal)*
Siska Fitrianie *(Delft University of Technology, The Netherlands)*
Morten Fjeld *(Chalmers University of Technology, Sweden)*
Peter Forbrig *(University of Rostock, Germany)*
Kenneth Forbus *(Northwestern University, USA)*

Program Committee (continued):

Ana Fred *(Instituto de Telecomunicacoes, Portugal)*
Jochen Frey *(DFKI GmbH, Germany)*
Jill Freyne *(CSIRO, Australia)*
Enrique Frias-Martinez *(Telefonica Research, Spain)*
Doron Friedman *(The Interdisciplinary Center, Israel)*
Krzysztof Gajos *(Harvard University, United States)*
Xuefei Gao *(University of Illinois at Urbana-Champaign, USA)*
Daniel Gatica-Perez *(Idiap Research Institute, Switzerland)*
Sven Gehring *(German Research Center for Artificial Intelligence, Germany)*
Melinda Gervasio *(SRI International, USA)*
Werner Geyer *(IBM T.J. Watson Research, USA)*
Yolanda Gil *(University of Southern California Information Sciences Institute, USA)*
Roland Goecke *(University of Canberra, Australia)*
Gloria Gomez *(Oceanbrowser Ltd, New Zealand)*
Dorian Gorgan *(Technical University of Cluj-Napoca, Romania)*
Raphael Grasset *(ARTIS-GRAVIR/IMAG INRIA, France)*
Paul Gross *(Washington University in St. Louis, USA)*
Anne Gross *(Fraunhofer IESE, Germany)*
João Guerreiro *(INESC-ID, Instituto Superior Técnico, Portugal)*
Chris Gunn *(CSIRO, Australia)*
Gholamreza Haffari *(Monash University, Australia)*
Martin Halvey *(University of Glasgow, United Kingdom)*
Michael Harrison *(School of Computing Science, Newcastle University, England)*
Kirstie Hawkey *(Dalhousie University, Canada)*
Dominikus Heckmann *(DFKI, Germany)*
Niels Henze *(University of Oldenburg, Germany)*
Eelco Herder *(L3S Research Center, Germany)*
Wilko Heuten (*OFFIS, Germany)*
DJ Hoets, *(Flipside, The Netherlands)*
Paul Holleis *(DoCoMo Euro-Labs Munich, Germany)*
Christian Holz *(Hasso Plattner Institute, Germany)*
Aaron Houssian *(Philips Research, Delft University of Technology, The Netherlands)*
Hao-Wei Hsieh *(University of Iowa, USA)*
Jochen Huber *(TU Darmstadt, Germany)*
Stephane Huot *(Univ Paris-Sud, CNRS, INRIA, France)*
Amy Hurst *(Carnegie Mellon University, USA)*
Tim Hussein *(University of Duisburg-Essen, Germany)*
Aulikki Hyrskykari *(University of Tampere, Finland)*
Francisco Iacobelli *(Northeastern Illinois University, USA)*
Netta Iivari *(University of Oulu, Finland)*

Program Committee (continued):

Shamsi Iqbal *(Microsoft Research, USA)*
Pourang Irani *(University of Manitoba, Canada)*
Linda Jackson *(Michigan State University, USA)*
Christophe Jacquet *(Supélec, LIMSI-CNRS, France)*
Anthony Jameson *(German Research Institute for Artificial Intelligence (DFKI), Germany)*
Krystian Ji *(National ICT Australia, Australia)*
Michael Johnston *(AT&T Labs Research, USA)*
Arne Jonsson *(Linköping University, Sweden)*
Christophe Jouffrais *(CNRS, Univ. of Toulouse, France)*
Kshitij Judah *(Oregon State University, USA)*
Sasa Junuzovic *(Microsoft Research, USA)*
Marko Jurmu *(University of Oulu, Finland)*
Gerrit Kahl *(German Research Center for Artificial Intelligence, Germany)*
Edward Kaiser *(Adapx, USA)*
Donald Kalar *(NASA Ames Research Center, USA)*
Ece Kamar *(Microsoft Research, USA)*
Slim Kammoun *(IRIT, CNRS & University of Toulouse, France)*
Eser Kandogan *(IBM, USA)*
Ashish Kapoor *(Microsoft Research, USA)*
Sarvnaz Karimi *(NICTA, The University of Melbourne, Australia)*
Nikolaus Karpinsky *(Iowa State University, USA)*
Judy Kay *(University of Sydney, Australia)*
Patrick Gage Kelley *(Carnegie Mellon University, USA)*
Aisling Kelliher *(Arizona State University, USA)*
Peter Khooshabeh *(University of California, Santa Barbara, USA)*
Sung-Hee Kim *(Purdue, USA)*
Jonghwa Kim *(University Augsburg, Germany)*
Felix Kistler *(Augsburg University, Germany)*
Thomas Kleinbauer *(Monash University, Australia)*
Andrea Kohlhase *(Jacobs University Bremen, Germany)*
Nicolas Kokkalis *(Stanford University, USA)*
Regis Kopper *(University of Florida, USA)*
Matthias Kranz *(Technische Universität München, Germany)*
Sven Kratz *(University of Munich, Germany)*
Per Ola Kristensson *(University of St Andrews, United Kingdom)*
David Krum *(Institute for Creative Technologies, USA)*
Alexander Kulik *(Bauhaus-Universitaet Weimar, Germany)*
Rohit Kumar *(Raytheon BBN Technologies, USA)*
A. Kumaran *(Microsoft Research India, India)*
Andrew Kun *(University of New Hampshire, USA)*
Mary LaLomia *(Philips Medical, USA)*
Shyong Lam *(University of Minnesota, USA)*
Rosa Lanzilotti *(University of Bari, Italy)*
Luis Leiva *(Universitat Politècnica de València, Spain)*

Program Committee (continued):

Céline Lemercier *(Université de Toulouse, France)*
Raimondas Lencevicius *(USA)*
Barbara Leporini *(ISTI – CNR, Italy)*
Bruno Lepri *(FBK, Italy)*
Ian Li *(Carnegie Mellon University, USA)*
Chunyuan Liao *(FXPAL, USA)*
Ilaria Liccardi *(INRIA, Université de Paris-Sud, France)*
Brian Lim *(Carnegie Mellon University, USA)*
Thomas Lin *(University of Washington, USA)*
Agnes Lisowska Masson *(University of Fribourg, Switzerland)*
Shixia Liu *(Microsoft Research Asia, China)*
Wenyin Liu *(City University of Hong Kong, China)*
Markus Löchtefeld *(German Research Center for Artificial Intelligence (DFKI), Germany)*
Joern Loviscach *(Fachhochschule Bielefeld (University of Applied Sciences), Germany)*
George Lucchese *(Texas A&M University, USA)*
Christopher Lueg *(University of Tasmania, Australia)*
Kris Luyten *(Hasselt University, Expertise Centre for Digital Media, Belgium)*
Michael Lyons *(Ritsumeikan University, Japan)*
Leilah Lyons *(University of Illinois at Chicago, USA)*
José Macías Iglesias *(Universidad Autónoma de Madrid, Spain)*
Allan MacLean *(Image Semantics Ltd, UK)*
Rui Madeira *(ESTSetúbal/IPS, IMG/CITI/FCT/UNL, Portugal)*
Jalal Mahmud *(IBM Research – Almaden, USA)*
Apostolos Malatras *(University of Fribourg, Switzerland)*
Alessio Malizia *(University Carlos III, Spain)*
Stefan Marti *(Samsung, MIT Media Lab, USA)*
Masood Masoodian *(The University of Waikato, New Zealand)*
Judith Masthoff *(University of Aberdeen, UK)*
Davide Mazza *(Politecnico di Milano, Italy)*
Emanuela Mazzone *(University of Central Lancashire, UK)*
David McGee *(Adapx, Inc., USA)*
Marilyn McGee-Lennon *(University of Glasgow, United Kingdom)*
Joanna McGrenere *(University of British Columbia, Canada)*
Gerrit Meixner *(German Research Center for Artificial Intelligence (DFKI), Germany)*
Helen Meng *(The Chinese University of Hong Kong, China)*
Takashi Miyaki *(Karlsruhe Institute of Technology, Germany)*
Jesus Molina *(Universidad de Murcia, Spain)*
Kyle Montague *(University of Dundee, Scotland)*
Florian Mueller *(RMIT University, Australia)*
Michael Muller *(IBM T.J. Watson Research, USA)*

Program Committee (continued):

Cosmin Munteanu *(National Research Council Canada, Canada)*
Dianne Murray *(Indep. Consultant, UK)*
Mirco Musolesi *(University of Birmingham, United Kingdom)*
Lennart Nacke *(University of Ontario Institute of Technology, Canada)*
Luciana Nedel *(Universidade Federal do Rio Grande do Sul, Brazil)*
Jeffrey Nichols *(IBM Research, USA)*
Hugo Nicolau *(INESC-ID, IST, UTL, Portugal)*
Sylvie Noël *(Communications Research Centre, Canada)*
Marcus Nyberg *(Ericsson Research, Sweden)*
Amy Ogan *(Carnegie Mellon University, United States)*
Alex Olwal *(Royal Institute of Technology (KTH), Columbia University, MIT Media Lab, USA)*
Stefan Oppl *(Johannes Kepler Universitaet Linz, Austria)*
Tihomir Orehovacki *(University of Zagreb, Croatia)*
Daniel Ortiz-Martínez *(Instituto Tecnológico de Informática, Universidad Politécnica de Valencia, Spain)*
Shimei Pan *(IBM Research, USA)*
Yue Pan *(School of Informatics & Computing, Indiana University, USA)*
Nadia Pantidi *(University of Nottingham, The Open University, UK)*
Oscar Pastor *(Universidad Politecnica de Valencia, Spain)*
Sharoda Paul *(GE Global Research, PARC, Penn State, USA)*
Celeste Paul *(University of Maryland Baltimore County, United States)*
Heiko Paulheim *(Technische Universitaet Darmstadt, Germany)*
Thomas Pederson *(IT University of Copenhagen, Denmark)*
Adam Perer *(IBM Research, USA)*
Mark Pfaff *(Indiana University – Indianapolis, USA)*
Matthai Philipose *(Microsoft Research, USA)*
Martin Pielot *(OFFIS Institute for Information Technology, Germany)*
Jeffrey Pierce *(IBM Research, US)*
Emmanuel Pietriga *(INRIA, University Paris-Sud, France)*
Catherine Plaisant *(University of Maryland, USA)*
Ondrej Polacek *(Czech Technical University in Prague, Czech Republic)*
Benjamin Poppinga *(OFFIS - Institute for Information Technology, Germany)*
Manoj Prasad *(Texas A&M University, USA)*
Nitendra Rajput *(IBM Research, India)*
Jamie Rasmussen *(IBM Research, United States)*
Pei-Luen Patrick Rau *(Tsinghua University, China)*
Martin Raubal *(ETH Zurich, Switzerland)*
Janet Read *(University of Central Lancashire, England)*
Tim Regan *(Microsoft Research, UK)*
Andreas Riener *(Johannes Kepler University Linz, Austria)*
Michael Robin *(Adapx, USA)*

Program Committee (continued):

Jennifer Robison *(North Carolina State University, USA)*
Michael Rohs *(University of Munich, Germany)*
Mario Romero *(Georgia Institute of Technology, USA)*
José Rouillard *(Laboratoire Trigone, France)*
Jonathan Rowe *(North Carolina State University, USA)*
Tom Rowlands *(CSIRO, Australian National University, Australia)*
Natalie Ruiz *(National ICT Australia Ltd, Australia)*
Murat Russell *(TAMU, USA)*
Antti Salovaara *(Helsinki Institute for Information Technology, HIIT, Finland)*
Carmen Santoro *(ISTI-CNR, Italy)*
Arvind Satyanarayan *(Stanford University, United States)*
Thomas Schlegel *(Technical University of Stuttgart, Germany)*
Dominik Schmidt *(Lancaster University, UK)*
Michael Schmitz *(DFKI GmbH, Germany)*
Bjoern Schuller *(Technische Universitaet Muenchen, Germany)*
Doree Seligmann *(Avaya Labs, USA)*
Shilad Sen *(Macalester College, USA)*
Yanir Seroussi *(Monash University, Australia)*
Ricky Sethi *(UC Riverside, USA)*
Frank Shipman *(Texas A&M University, USA)*
Sajad Shirali-Shahreza *(University of Toronto, Canada)*
Candace Sidner *(Worcester Polytechnic Institute, BAE Systems AIT, USA)*
Adam Sporka *(Czech Technical University in Prague, Czech Republic)*
Robert St. Amant *(North Carolina State University, USA)*
Oliver Staadt *(University of Rostock, Germany)*
Rainer Stiefelhagen *(Universität Karlsruhe (TH), Germany)*
Oliviero Stock *(FBK-IRST, Italy)*
Simone Stumpf *(City University London, UK)*
Fred Stutzman *(Carnegie Mellon University, USA)*
Xiao Hua Sun *(IBM Research China, China)*
Petra Sundström *(SICS, Mobile Life Centre, Sweden)*
Aurélien Tabard *(IT University of Copenhagen, Denmark)*
Ronnie Taib *(National ICT Australia, Australia)*
Federico Tajariol *(University of Franche-Comté, France)*
John Tang *(Microsoft Research, USA)*
Craig Tashman *(Georgia Institute of Technology, USA)*
VinhTuan Thai *(National University of Ireland, Ireland)*
Feng Tian *(Institute of Software, Chinese Academy of Sciences, P.R. China)*
Sabine Timpf *(University of Augsburg, Germany)*
Caglar Tirkaz *(Sabanci University, Koc University, Turkey)*
Elaine Tozman *(ACM, CAS, Canada)*
Polly Tremoulet *(Lockheed Martin Advanced Technology Laboratories, USA)*
Jennifer Trich Kremer *(WellPoint, Inc., USA)*

Program Committee (continued):

Manfred Tscheligi *(University of Salzburg - ICT&S, CURE-Center for Usability Research & Engineering, Austria)*
Simon Tucker *(University of Sheffield, United Kingdom)*
Recep Sinan Tumen *(Koç University, İstanbul, Turkey)*
Rogier van Dalen *(University of Cambridge, United Kingdom)*
Jan Van den Bergh *(Hasselt University, Belgium)*
Egon van den Broek *(Center for Telematics and Information Technology, University of Twente, The Netherlands)*
Keith Vander Linden *(Calvin College, USA)*
Radu-Daniel Vatavu *(University Stefan cel Mare of Suceava, Romania)*
Keith Vertanen *(Montana Tech of The University of Montana, USA)*
Jesse Vig *(University of Minnesota, United States)*
Markel Vigo *(University of Manchester, United Kingdom)*
Juergen Vogel *(SAP Research, Switzerland)*
Gualtiero Volpe *(University of Genova, Italy)*
Johannes Wagner *(University Augsburg, Germany)*
Julie Wagner *(INRIA, Univ Paris-Sud, CNRS, France)*
James Wallace *(University of Waterloo, Canada)*
Stephen Wan *(CSIRO, Australia)*
Robert Wang *(Massachusetts Institute of Technology, USA)*
Xiaoyu Wang *(Vis Center, UNC Charlotte, United States)*
Yang Wang *(NICTA, University of New South Wales, National ICT Australia, Australia)*
Jingtao Wang *(University of Pittsburgh, USA)*
Hongan Wang *(Institute of Software, Chinese Academy of Sciences, China)*
Nadir Weibel *(University of California San Diego, USA)*
Stephan Weibelzahl *(National College of Ireland, Ireland)*
Jackie Wheeler *(IBM, USA)*
Lynn Wilcox *(FX Palo Alto Lab, USA)*
Wesley Willett *(University of California, Berkeley, USA)*
Andrew Wilson *(Microsoft Research, USA)*
Marco Winckler *(LIIHS-IRIT, France)*
Stephan Winter *(The University of Melbourne, Australia)*
Maria Wolters *(University of Edinburgh, United Kingdom)*
Huahai Yang *(IBM Almaden Research Center, USA)*
Tet Yap *(University of New South Wales, National ICT Australia, Australia)*
Koji Yatani *(Microsoft Research Asia, China)*
Tom Yeh *(University of Maryland, College Park, USA)*
Chuang-wen You *(Research Center for Information Technology Innovation, Academia Sinica, Taiwan)*
R. Michael Young *(North Carolina State University, USA)*
Nelson Zagalo *(University of Minho, Portugal)*
Xiaolong (Luke) Zhang *(Pennsylvania State University, USA)*

IUI 2012 Sponsors & Supporters

Event Sponsors:

SIGART

ACM Special Interest Group on Artificial Intelligence

SIGCHI

ACM Special Interest Group on Artificial Intelligence

Corporate Supporters:

RedWhale Software

Microsoft Research

IBM Research

Institutional Supporter:

National Science Foundation

In Cooperation With:

Interaction-Design.org

Probabilistic Pointing Target Prediction via Inverse Optimal Control

Brian D. Ziebart
Carnegie Mellon University
Pittsburgh PA USA
bziebart@cs.cmu.edu

Anind K. Dey
Carnegie Mellon University
Pittsburgh PA USA
anind@cs.cmu.edu

J. Andrew Bagnell
Carnegie Mellon University
Pittsburgh PA USA
dbagnell@ri.cmu.edu

ABSTRACT
Numerous interaction techniques have been developed that make "virtual" pointing at targets in graphical user interfaces easier than analogous physical pointing tasks by invoking target-based interface modifications. These pointing facilitation techniques crucially depend on methods for estimating the relevance of potential targets. Unfortunately, many of the simple methods employed to date are inaccurate in common settings with many selectable targets in close proximity. In this paper, we bring recent advances in statistical machine learning to bear on this underlying target relevance estimation problem. By framing past target-driven pointing trajectories as approximate solutions to well-studied control problems, we learn the probabilistic dynamics of pointing trajectories that enable more accurate predictions of intended targets.

Author Keywords
Cursor prediction, probabilistic inference, continuous control

ACM Classification Keywords
H.5.2 Information Interfaces and Presentation: Miscellaneous;

INTRODUCTION
Pointing at targets is a fundamental task in graphical user interfaces for selecting icons, menus, buttons, and other graphical elements. An understanding of pointing task performance has been of key importance for designing user interfaces for efficient use. Card *et al.* [9] showed that target pointing tasks via computer mouse and joystick follow Fitts' law [12], which was previously proposed for physical pointing task completion times. Under this law, pointing at a target of width W at distance D, has an average task completion time T of:

$$T = \alpha + \beta \log_2 \left(1 + \frac{D}{W}\right),$$

where α and β are empirically estimated parameters. From it, the contributing factors to pointing task difficulty can be more abstractly attributed to the pointing task distance (D) and the target precision requirement ($\frac{1}{W}$).

Over the past 15 years, human-computer interaction research has investigated how the virtual nature of target pointing in graphical user interfaces can be leveraged to outperform the performance implied by Fitts' law. Since interactions through graphical user interfaces are quite prevalent, small improvements in task efficiency, even at the millisecond scale, can have substantial aggregate benefits. Further, for the population of users with physical motor impairments, reducing pointing task difficulty can make otherwise inaccessible applications accessible.

A number of pointing facilitation approaches have been developed and analyzed that decrease the effective target distance and/or alter the required target precision of the pointing task. Specifically, approaches have been introduced that:

- Restrict pointing to selectable targets, skipping over non-interactive portions of the user interface [14];
- Adjust the dynamics (control-display gains) for pointing motions to more quickly gravitate to and then linger within intended targets [19, 29, 7, 2, 15];
- Dynamically move candidate pointing targets closer to the current pointing location [5];
- Enlarge candidate pointing targets to make selecting them easier [23];
- Employ larger cursor activation regions to require less than single-pixel precision to select targets [16, 13, 20, 10]; or
- Generate haptic responses to cursor control that serve as an additional indicator of target precision thresholds [28, 11].

Unfortunately, the successes of these approaches have not extended to settings where multiple targets are in close proximity to one another [4], which is common in many graphical user interfaces. McGuffin and Balakrishnan identify the key limitation as the inability to reliably predict users' intended targets [24]. Without this ability, too many potential targets must be considered by the interaction technique for it to be effectively employed. They posit that improvements in desired target prediction would increase the effectiveness of any of the previously developed pointing facilitation techniques [24]. This makes target prediction a key machine learning problem for improving human-computer interactions in graphical user interfaces.

We introduce a new approach for predicting the desired target of a partial pointing motion using predictive inverse optimal control [31, 30]. The approach assumes that previously observed pointing motions are approximate solutions to a control task. The state-action costs of this control task that best explain those observed pointing motions are learned in terms of velocities, accelerations, and jerks (changes in acceleration). Using Bayesian reasoning for the target prediction task, larger probabilities are assigned to potential targets for which a partial trajectory is an efficient solution to the learned control task. We evaluate the approach to show its applicability for supporting pointing facilitation techniques.

REQUIREMENTS AND PREVIOUS APPROACHES

We begin by identifying the features required for a target prediction system and reviewing the previously developed techniques for target prediction.

Prediction Requirements for Pointing Facilitation

Four key characteristics for a pointing prediction system to be useful in support of pointing facilitation are:

- **Belief-based reasoning:** Pointing facilitation techniques have different target prediction certainty requirements for their benefits when employed on the intended pointing target to outweigh the detriment when applied to the incorrect target. For example, introducing large control-display gain for movement towards the most likely target may only be net beneficial when target certainty is high, while smaller gain modifications may provide net benefits at much lower levels of target certainty. Accurate probabilistic target predictions are needed to support this risk sensitivity.
- **Real-time efficiency:** Pointing tasks in graphical user interfaces are typically completed in fractions of a second. A pointing target prediction system must therefore be able to provide quick predictions on the order of tens of milliseconds to be useful in practice. This requirement eliminates many sophisticated machine learning techniques that are less computationally efficient.
- **Personalization and context awareness:** Users' pointing trajectories can differ greatly based on differences in capabilities (including motor-skill impairments), input devices, and contextual situation. A pointing target prediction system should take these individual and contextual differences into account, customizing to the particular user's patterns of usage in different situations.
- **Application independence:** The layout of selectable target locations and the sequences of targets selected differ substantially between the user interfaces of different applications. A target pointing prediction system should be able to generalize across these application differences.

Many different approaches have been developed for this prediction task [25, 18, 21, 3, 22]. However, we will argue throughout this paper that those approaches have lacked important properties required for supporting pointing facilitation systems, or have been too simplistic to provide accurate predictions in the general cursor target prediction setting.

Classification Prediction Approaches

Interaction techniques have been the main focus for many of the previously published papers on pointing facilitation. Relatively simple methods based on target proximity or current pointing motion are often employed by these contributions to select the target or targets upon which to apply those interaction techniques. Unfortunately, these simple target relevance estimation methods perform poorly in user interfaces with many possible targets located in close proximity, such as those in Figure 1.

Figure 1. A set of 25 potential pointing targets (tool icons) in close proximity from the GNU Image Manipulation Program. The nearest tool icon to the cursor position, particularly early in the pointing motion, is often not the intended target.

Early work specifically devoted to pointing target prediction treats the prediction task as a classification problem using properties of the motion trajectory state sequence as input. For example, Lane *et al.* [21] provides short-cuts for selecting predicted targets and base target predictions primarily on the distance to each potential target. Though probabilistic techniques have been employed, *e.g.*, using a multinomial distribution for targets conditioned on velocity, acceleration, and motion curvature characteristics [25], they have been in support of target classification rather than belief-based prediction. In contrast to our inverse optimal control approach, aggressive discretization of motion characteristics is needed limit the amount of data required to estimate model parameters and for predictions to remain computationally efficient.

Regression-Based Extrapolation Approaches

Many techniques for predicting the intended target of a partial pointing motion formulate the problem as a continuous-valued regression task. Asano *et al.* [3] employ a simple linear regression from the peak velocity of the trajectory to the total distance[1] to the endpoint:

$$\left|\left|\mathbf{s}_T - \mathbf{s}_1\right|\right|_2 = \alpha\, v_{\max} + \beta + \epsilon_i, \tag{1}$$

where $\mathbf{s}_t = \begin{pmatrix} x_t \\ y_t \end{pmatrix}$ and $v_{\max} = \max_\tau \left|\left|\mathbf{s}_\tau - \mathbf{s}_{\tau-1}\right|\right|_2$.

Predictions are made by extrapolating according to the learned regression coefficients, α and β. The parameters are fit to the demonstrated trajectory data using maximum likelihood estimation. The standard linear regression model assumption that any errors in the model's predictions ϵ_i are Gaussian distributed (Equation 1) is employed. The

[1] We denote the Euclidean distance with the norm $||\mathbf{v}||_2 = \sqrt{\sum_{i=1}^n v_i^2}$.

extrapolated prediction of the final cursor position under the trained model is then:

$$\mathbf{s}_T = \mathbf{s}_t + \frac{\mathbf{s}_t - \mathbf{s}_1}{||\mathbf{s}_t - \mathbf{s}_1||_2} (\alpha\, v_{\max} + \beta) .$$

The maximum velocity has also been previously employed as an indicator of the halfway point of a cursor trajectory [18].

A more sophisticated approach [22] is based on the observation that in idealized motion, the jerk (*i.e.*, the third derivative of position) is minimized. Under this model, the velocity is assumed to be a quadratic function of the distance traversed to the intended target location. Predictions are performed by fitting the quadratic function to the partial trajectory, and then extrapolating the point at which the velocity returns to zero, as shown in Algorithm 1.

Algorithm 1 Quadratic extrapolation for predicting pointing targets from a partial pointing trajectory.

Input: A partial trajectory, $\mathbf{s}_1 \ldots \mathbf{s}_t$, up to time step t.
Output: Trajectory endpoint prediction $\mathbf{s}_T = (x_T, y_T)$.
1: Fit a quadratic function with parameters $\alpha_2, \alpha_1, \alpha_0$ to the partial trajectory's total distance.
2: Obtain the second root of the quadratic equation: $d_T = \frac{-\alpha_1 - \sqrt{\alpha_1^2 - 4\alpha_0\alpha_2}}{2\alpha_2}$.
3: Apply the correction multiplier γ based on the fraction of predicted trajectory distance completed: $d'_T = \gamma\, d_T$ (see [22] for details).
4: Predict $\mathbf{s}_T = \mathbf{s}_1 + d'_T \frac{\mathbf{s}_t - \mathbf{s}_1}{||\mathbf{s}_t - \mathbf{s}_1||_2}$

However, apart from the correction multiplier (Step 3 of Algorithm 1), this prediction model is incapable of using previously observed trajectories to improve future target predictions. This makes it particularly ill-suited for personalizing to the different capabilities and usage patterns of individuals.

The Gaussian assumption of target prediction errors in these regression-based approaches imposes symmetry constraints on prediction beliefs. Namely, points that are reflections across each of the predicted Gaussian's principal axes have the same probability density. When the regression models' errors differ from Gaussian distributions, the Gaussian assumption leads to models with much higher uncertainty than warranted. The approach we present in this paper provides a less restrictive posterior target distribution by employing Bayesian inference methods for target inference.

INVERSE OPTIMAL CONTROL POINTER FORECASTING

We employ computationally efficient inverse optimal control techniques to learn from and predict target-based pointing motions. At a high-level, our approach has three main elements:

1. It re-casts the discrete cursor pointing task from a control perspective with continuous states and actions;
2. It employs a probabilistic inverse optimal control technique [30] to model observed pointing trajectories given the intended pointing target; and
3. It leverages Bayes' rule to obtain posterior probabilities of a partial cursor trajectory's intended target.

Crucially, the combination of these three elements provides a powerful parametric learning approach that is computationally efficient for real-time use. We elaborate upon these three elements of our approach in the remainder of this section.

Continuous Control Representation of Pointing

We take a control perspective to modeling pointing motions in which the objective is to invoke control actions that direct the pointing motion to the origin. To facilitate this perspective, we project the original trajectory into a new axis system where the x-axis is aligned with the origin-to-target direction and the y-axis is orthogonal, as illustrated in Figure 2a. Under this projection, discrete cursor locations (in pixels) are treated as continuous-valued. As we shall see, this provides computational advantages. Additionally, to later obtain model parameters at reasonable scales, we equate one unit of distance in this new projection to 100 pixels of screen distance.

Using this coordinate system, we view the instantaneous state of motion at timestep t as:

$$\mathbf{s}_t = [x_t\ y_t\ \dot{x}_t\ \dot{y}_t\ \ddot{x}_t\ \ddot{y}_t\ \dddot{x}_t\ \dddot{y}_t]^{\mathrm{T}} .$$

The higher-order changes related to position correspond to common physical dynamics. They are the velocity ($\dot{x}_t, \dot{y}_t$), the acceleration ($\ddot{x}_t, \ddot{y}_t$), and the jerk (*i.e.*, change in acceleration, $\dddot{x}_t, \dddot{y}_t$):

$$\begin{pmatrix} \dot{x}_t \\ \dot{y}_t \end{pmatrix} = \begin{pmatrix} x_t - x_{t-1} \\ y_t - y_{t-1} \end{pmatrix} \quad \begin{pmatrix} \ddot{x}_t \\ \ddot{y}_t \end{pmatrix} = \begin{pmatrix} \dot{x}_t - \dot{x}_{t-1} \\ \dot{y}_t - \dot{y}_{t-1} \end{pmatrix}$$
$$\text{and} \begin{pmatrix} \dddot{x}_t \\ \dddot{y}_t \end{pmatrix} = \begin{pmatrix} \ddot{x}_t - \ddot{x}_{t-1} \\ \ddot{y}_t - \ddot{y}_{t-1} \end{pmatrix} . \quad (2)$$

Importantly, when actions, $\mathbf{a}_t$, are viewed as the velocities specifying changes in position between consecutive timesteps, the state dynamics follow a linear relationship:

$$\mathbf{s}_{t+1} = \mathbf{A}\mathbf{s}_t + \mathbf{B}\mathbf{a}_t + \epsilon_t, \quad (3)$$

where the optional noise term, ϵ_t is assumed to be drawn from a zero-mean Gaussian distribution with variance Σ. We denote the distribution of next state under this model of dynamics as $\tau(\mathbf{s}_{t+1}|\mathbf{s}_t, \mathbf{a}_t)$.

Inverse Optimal Control for Prediction

The next element of our approach is the construction of a probabilistic model of complete cursor motion sequences given each motion's target location. This perspective allows us to employ inverse optimal control techniques from machine learning, which attempt to find the costs of a control process that makes demonstrated behavior (close to) optimal [17, 8, 26, 1, 27]. We leverage the maximum entropy variant of inverse optimal control [31, 30], which provides a state-conditioned probability distribution $\hat{\pi}$ over control actions (*i.e.*, cursor movements) $\mathbf{a}$ that is recursively defined as:

$$\hat{\pi}(\mathbf{a}_t|\mathbf{s}_t) \propto e^{-Q(\mathbf{s}_t, \mathbf{a}_t)}, \quad (4)$$
$$V(\mathbf{s}_t) = \operatorname*{softmin}_{\mathbf{a}_t} \{\text{cost}(\mathbf{s}_t) + Q(\mathbf{s}_t, \mathbf{a}_t)\} \quad (5)$$
$$Q(\mathbf{s}_t, \mathbf{a}_t) = \mathbb{E}_{\tau(\mathbf{s}_{t+1}|\mathbf{s}_t, \mathbf{a}_t)} [V(\mathbf{s}_{t+1})|\mathbf{s}_t, \mathbf{a}_t] , \quad (6)$$

where $\text{cost}(\mathbf{s}_t) \triangleq \mathbf{s}_t^{\mathrm{T}} \mathbf{M} \mathbf{s}_t$ is a quadratic cost function, and the value terms, $Q(\mathbf{s}, \mathbf{a})$ and $V(\mathbf{s}_t)$, are future cumulative expected costs. The *softmin* is a smoothed interpolation of the *minimum* function: $\text{softmin}_x f(x) = -\log \int_x e^{-f(x)} dx$. From this perspective, the recurrence of Equations 5 and 6 can be viewed as a probabilistic relaxation of the Bellman criteria for optimal control [6]; it (probabilistically) selects actions with smaller expected future costs in Equation 5 and recursively computes those future costs using the expectation over the decision process's dynamics in Equation 6. The $\mathbf{M}$ matrix contains the model's cost parameters. Parameter values are chosen so that the predictive control distribution $\hat{\pi}$ matches quadratic state properties of demonstrated behavior $\tilde{\pi}$ in expectation ($\mathbb{E}_f[g(x)] \triangleq \int_{x \in \mathcal{X}} f(x)\, g(x)\, dx$):

$$\mathbb{E}_{\hat{\pi},\tau}\left[\sum_t \mathbf{s}_t\, \mathbf{s}_t^{\mathrm{T}}\right] = \mathbb{E}_{\tilde{\pi},\tau}\left[\sum_t \mathbf{s}_t\, \mathbf{s}_t^{\mathrm{T}}\right]. \tag{7}$$

This set of constraints ensures that the trajectory's dynamic properties are maintained by the control policy estimate, $\hat{\pi}$. For example, the relationship between target-relative position (x) and target-directed velocity ($\dot{x}$) is important for characterizing target-directed motion.

When the state-transition dynamics are linear (Equation 3), the recursive relation of Equations 5 and 6 have closed-form solutions that are quadratic functions and the action distribution (Equation 4) is a conditional Gaussian distribution. This enables efficient $\mathcal{O}(T\ \dim(s)^2)$ time computation for time horizons T and much larger continuous state/action spaces than could be computed as discrete state/action spaces.

We make use of the probability distribution over each partial trajectory, $\mathbf{s}_2, \ldots, \mathbf{s}_t$ $(t \leq T)$, given the initial state $\mathbf{s}_1$ and target G:

$$\prod_{\tau=1}^{t} \pi(\mathbf{a}_t|\mathbf{s}_t, G) = e^{-\left(\sum_{\tau=2}^{t} \text{cost}(\mathbf{s}_\tau^G)\right) - V(\mathbf{s}_t^G) + V(\mathbf{s}_1^G)}, \tag{8}$$

where super-scripting the states with the target G makes the target-dependent projection explicit. Equation 8 prescribes larger probabilities to trajectories that efficiently reduce the future expected cost. A derivation and detailed algorithms for efficiently computing the policy and learning the model parameters appear in the Appendix.

Bayesian Target Prediction

We employ the learned trajectory model to estimate target probabilities. Using the probability distribution for a partial trajectory given a target location (Equation 8), we employ Bayes' rule to find the probability distribution of a target location G from a set of target locations $\mathcal{G}$ given a partial cursor trajectory. The posterior distribution,

$$P(\text{target } G | \text{partial trajectory } \mathbf{s}_1, \ldots, \mathbf{s}_t) = \frac{\prod_{\tau=1}^{t} \pi(\mathbf{a}_t|\mathbf{s}_t, G) P(G)}{\sum_{G' \in \mathcal{G}} \prod_{\tau=1}^{t} \pi(\mathbf{a}_t|\mathbf{s}_t, G') P(G')}, \tag{9}$$

assigns higher probabilities to targets towards which the partial trajectory efficiently makes progress.

This Bayesian formulation leverages a flexible **prior distribution** over targets $P(G)$ that reflect an initial belief for the next target without current cursor trajectory information. This distribution can be based on relevant contextual information, such as current application, target selection history, time of day, *etc.* However, as our focus in this work is on leveraging available cursor trajectory data to predict pointing targets, we simply assume a uniform prior distribution over possible targets, $P(G) = \frac{1}{|\mathcal{G}|}$.

The linear inverse optimal control approach we employ provides additional computational benefits for calculating these posterior probability distributions. Naïvely computing the posterior target distribution for a pointing motion of length t would entail calculating the quadratic value functions for each possible target, requiring $\mathcal{O}(|\mathcal{G}|t\ \dim(s)^2)$ time total for a set of potential targets $\mathcal{G}$. Instead, using simple projections of the state into different target-based reference frames, a single value function computation is needed and computing the posterior for each target is independent of the the time horizon t. We detail these efficient projections in the Appendix.

EXPERIMENTS

We employ a dataset of collected pointing trajectories to analyze and evaluate pointing target prediction approaches.

Collected Cursor Trajectory Data

Our dataset consists of cursor trajectories from 20 non-motor-impaired individuals that are frequent computer users captured at 100Hz. Each individual performed 300 different **target selection tasks** using computer mouse input devices. Each task requires moving a cursor from an origin point to a target click location—a circle—that the user selects via a button click to complete the task. Target locations were selected at random from the computer screen space subject to being 200 pixels away from the pointing task's starting point.

Figure 2a shows the x and y positions of trajectories from the 20 individuals on one task. The trajectories originate in the southwest corner of the plot and terminate in a small target click circle at the origin. Figure 2b and Figure 2c show how the trajectories vary over time in the x and y positions. As a pre-processing step, we discard any timesteps with no movement. These predominantly appear at the beginning of trajectories and correspond to the time that users seem to spend visually processing and responding to the pointing task.

As shown in Figure 2, a great deal of variability exists between trajectories, illustrating the sub-optimality of human control on pointing tasks. One particular trajectory in Figure 2 takes significantly more timesteps of motion to reach the target location and complete the task than other trajectories. Even more anomalous deviations are shown in Figure 3, where users slide their cursor along the outer borders of the window while completing the task (presumably due to losing track of the cursor and moving it to try to locate it). More subtle anomalies are: missing the boundary of the click target when the mouse button is pressed, responding slowly to the targeting task, and having the cursor in motion at the beginning of the targeting task.

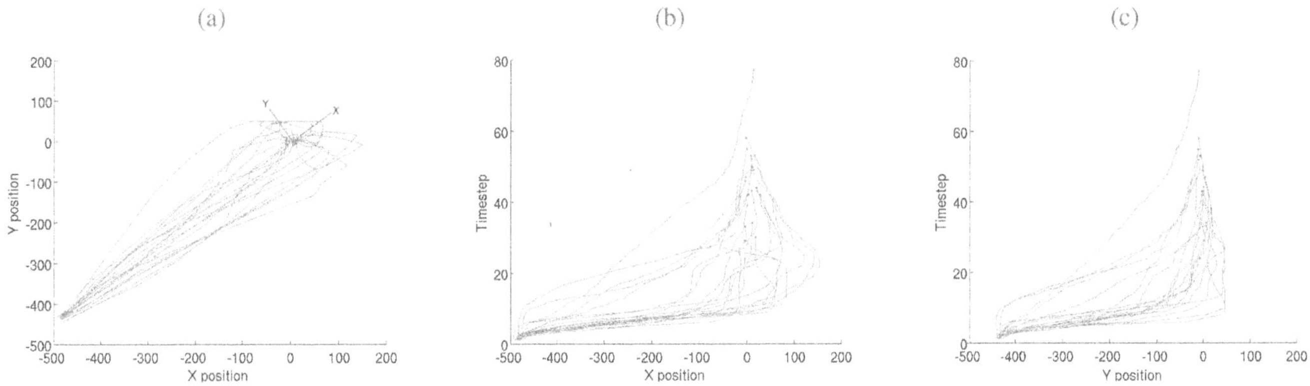

Figure 2. Cursor trajectories from 20 different users between the same pair of endpoints shown in space (a) and as a function of time (with each timestep representing 10 milliseconds) in each dimension (b, c). The target-based rotated axis frame is also shown in (a).

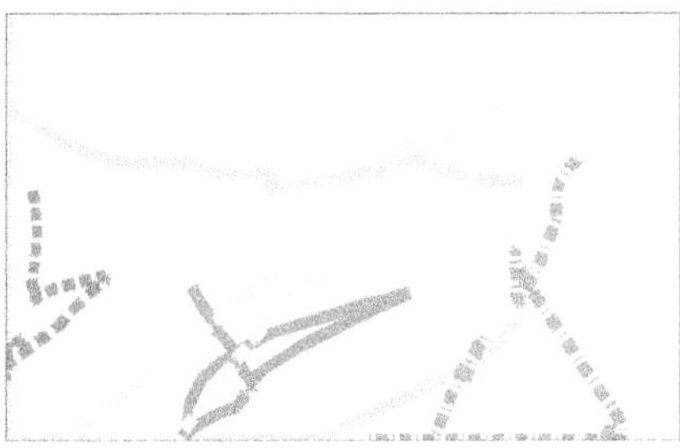

Figure 3. Five highly anomalous cursor trajectories that are very inefficient in reaching the ultimate target location.

To conservatively address the many sources of errors present in collected cursor pointing data, we discard the least task-efficient half of the cursor trajectories from each pointing task. We believe that many of the discarded trajectories can be useful sources of information for modeling cursor movements with additional pre-processing to appropriately remove properties of different errors. However, our point of emphasis in this paper is on the techniques for modeling and predicting pointing movements, so we instead use the more conservative dataset that does not require more sophisticated pre-processing.

Experimental Setup and Compared Approaches

We employ the cursor trajectories from 50 pointing tasks as training data to fit each model's parameters and employ the cursor trajectories from the remaining 250 cursor trajectories to evaluate the predictive performance of each model.

The target prediction models that we compare are:

- **Current position:** A simple baseline that predicts that the current position will be the pointing target.
- **Velocity extrapolation [3]:** The maximum velocity regression approach (Equation 1) with parameters fit from the training data set.
- **Quadratic extrapolation [22]:** The quadratic extrapolation algorithm (Algorithm 1) fit to each partial trajectory.
- **Inverse optimal control** The inverse optimal control approach using maximum causal entropy.

We obtain probabilistic predictions from the current position and regression-based approaches by assuming that prediction errors are distributed according to a 2-dimension Gaussian:

$$\mathbf{s}_T \sim N(f(\mathbf{s}_1, \ldots, \mathbf{s}_t), \Sigma(\mathbf{s}_1, \ldots, \mathbf{s}_t)),$$

where f is the regression mean estimation function and Σ is one of 11 covariance matrices estimated from the training set of cursor motions. The covariance matrix employed is selected based on an estimate of the motion trajectory's progress using: its duration for the *current position* model; the location where the maximum velocity occurs in the motion sequence for the *velocity extrapolation* model, or the estimated quadratic for the *quadratic extrapolation* model.

Model Fitting

We analyze each model's fit to the training data in this section. We begin with the assumptions made by the extrapolation approaches: (1) correlation between maximum velocity and target distance; and (2) a quadratic fit to the trajectory's velocity as a function of distance.

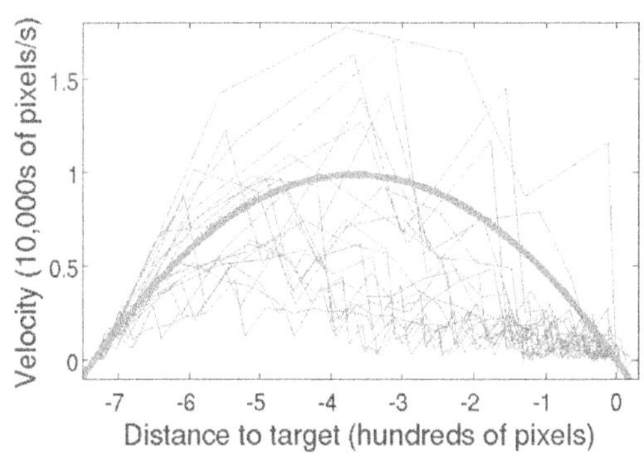

Figure 4. Velocity and position of movement in the target-oriented axis (with target at 0) for 20 participants cursor motions (thin blue lines). The quadratic function (smooth red line) fits the average of these motions very nicely, even though the individual motions deviate greatly from the idealize quadratic.

The variability in pointing movement velocities in Figure 4 is typical across tasks; trajectories reach the target by following a wide range of velocity patterns with differing maximum

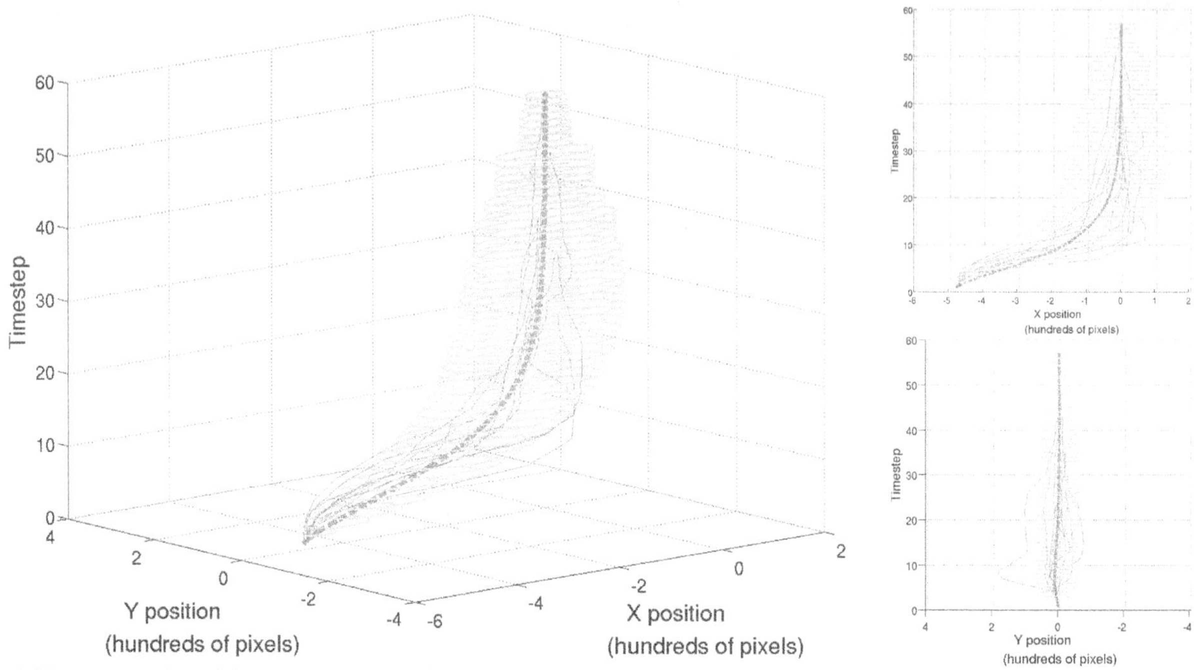

Figure 6. Three perspectives of demonstrated trajectories (thin blue lines) in x and y position over time along with the mean (thicker red line) and 95% confidence region (green ovals) of the predictive maximum causal entropy model at each point in time.

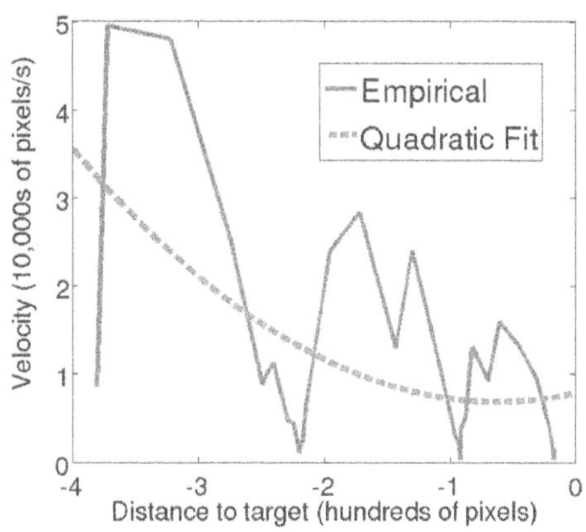

Figure 5. Velocity and position of movement in the target-oriented axis. The trajectory appears to have been decomposed into three sequences of small movements towards the target position. This composition confounds the quadratic model, which no longer predicts any endpoint (*i.e.*, the quadratic has no real roots).

velocity. Unfortunately, this introduces a large degree of uncertainty in the velocity extrapolation model obtained by regression from maximum velocity to target distance.

The average of our collected trajectories very closely fits the idealized motion quadratic (Algorithm 1), as shown in Figure 4. However, individual trajectories deviate greatly from the idealized quadratic. Indeed, for 3.1% of trajectories, no prediction is provided by the quadratic fit because the quadratic is convex (as shown in Figure 5) rather than concave. Many other quadratic fits, though concave, do not provide accurate target distance predictions. This becomes increasingly prevalent when fitting the quadratic function using only a small portion of the motion sequence.

The inverse optimal control model's fit to a set of demonstrated pointing trajectories in Figure 6. The prediction is conditioned on the starting point and the target location. The 95% confidence intervals of the prediction are adjusted based on the varying trajectory durations; completed trajectories are treated as being known at the target center. Though the confidence intervals generally do not contain 95% of the demonstrated trajectories due to the model being a simplified abstraction of a user's control-feedback loop, the model provides a reasonably good fit to the demonstrated trajectories.

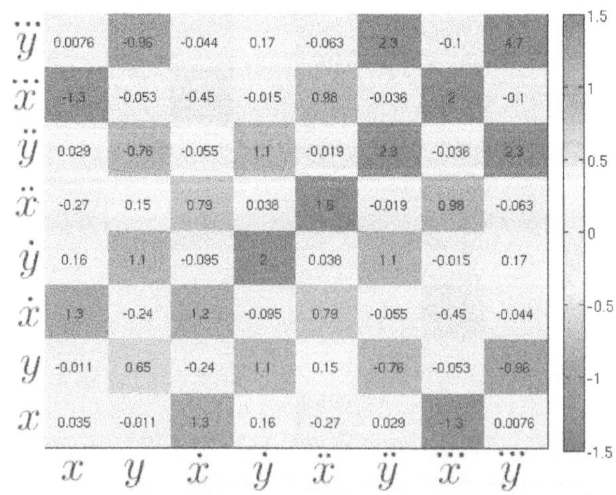

Figure 7. Heat map for the quadratic cost coefficients of matrix M learned by the inverse optimal control approach. Positive values correspond to costs while negative values can be interpreted as rewards.

A heat map of the learned quadratic parameter matrix M of the inverse optimal control model is shown in Figure 7. Each entry of the heat map is a cost coefficient corresponding to a combined quadratic term. For example, the $x\dot{x}$ term penalizes velocities that are away from the target location ($x < 0$ and $\dot{x} < 0$ or $x > 0$ and $\dot{x} > 0$) with coefficient 1.3. Along the diagonal (bottom left to top right), the cost coefficients are all positive, penalizing deviations away from zero. In particular, large higher-order dynamics (accelerations and jerks) are heavily penalized. The diagonal (xx, yy, $\dot{x}\dot{x}$, $\dot{y}\dot{y}$, $\ddot{x}\ddot{x}$, and $\ddot{y}\ddot{y}$) is similarly positive. This primarily supports the stability of the trajectory by penalizing the reinforcement of growing dynamics. Note that the heat map has a checkerboard pattern; high magnitude coefficient weights are primarily associated with same-axis combinations.

Pointing Target Prediction

We evaluate each trained model's performance in predicting each pointing motion's target given only a partial pointing trajectory. Though our collected dataset only involves a single target location, we introduce a set of closely grouped targets around the true target and ask: *How well could we predict the actual target?* Our assumption is that additional irrelevant targets do not significantly alter pointing trajectories compared to single-target pointing tasks.

We employ a challenging set of closely clustered targets to assess predictive performance: a 9-by-9 grid of potential targets spaced apart by 50 pixels. This type of configuration has previously been identified as difficult for target prediction [4]. The specific setting we employ is similar to, but larger than, the array of tool icons shown in Figure 1.

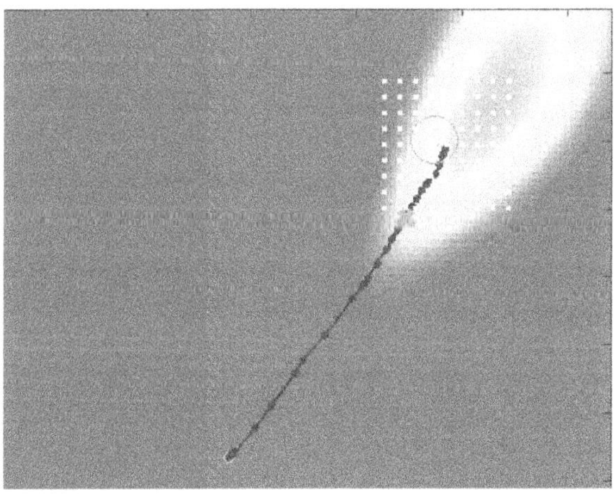

Figure 8. The likelihood function of all target locations (each pixel on the screen) given a partial trajectory (the black line up to the "X"). The initial point is denoted as a small green circle and the final target region is denoted as a larger circle. Each pixel of the figure represents 10 pixels of monitor space.

Our evaluation procedure is best described using Figure 8 for reference. Note that the task target in Figure 8 is contains six prediction task targets, making this a particularly difficult prediction task. Also in the figure, the likelihood function of the inverse optimal control approach, $P(\mathbf{s}_2, \ldots, \mathbf{s}_t|\mathbf{s}_1, G)$, is shown for each potential target point throughout the screen given one particular partial cursor trajectory (the black line up to the red "X"). Unlike regression-based approaches, that this likelihood function is not constrained to be Gaussian, which allows a great deal more flexibility than linear regression-based techniques. Target predictions for a specific set of targets—the 81 white points in the figure—are made by evaluating the likelihood function at each potential target position and normalizing after weighting by the prior probability (uniform for our experiments). For the regression-based models, we evaluate the target probability only at each target location and appropriately re-normalize the distribution.

We measure predictive performance using the classification error (*i.e.*, the frequency with which the model's most probable target is not the true target), and the log-loss of the pointing motion's true target G^*,

$$-\frac{1}{N}\sum_{i=1}^{N}\log_2 \hat{P}(\text{target } G^{i,*}|\mathbf{s}_1^i, \ldots \mathbf{s}_t^i).$$

The latter measures the amount of uncertainty of the intended target under each model's predictive probability distribution. This can be interpreted as the amount of information (in bits) needed to distinguish the true target from the others under a target prediction system's predictive belief. When the target is known with certainty, 0 bits are required, and when the distribution is most uncertain (a uniform distribution over 81 targets), $log_2\ 81 = 6.65$ bits are required. Though improvement of a pointing facilitation technique's utility to a user is the ultimate evaluation metric for a pointing prediction method, that evaluation measure is highly dependent on the pointing facilitation technique employed. Log-loss is the natural measure for belief-based predictive performance that should be useful in improving pointing facilitation techniques.

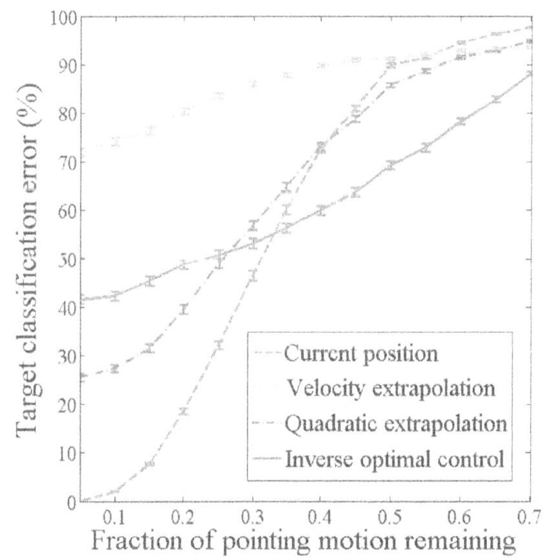

Figure 9. Mean target prediction classification error as a function of the amount of pointing trajectory remaining (in terms of time) with 95% confidence intervals.

Our evaluations are shown in Figure 9 and Figure 10 as functions of the fraction of the cursor trajectory remaining at the point in time that the prediction is made, ranging from 5% to 70% remaining—beyond which, no model performs particularly well for this task. It is important to note that the predictive model does not know what percentage of the trajectory has been completed.

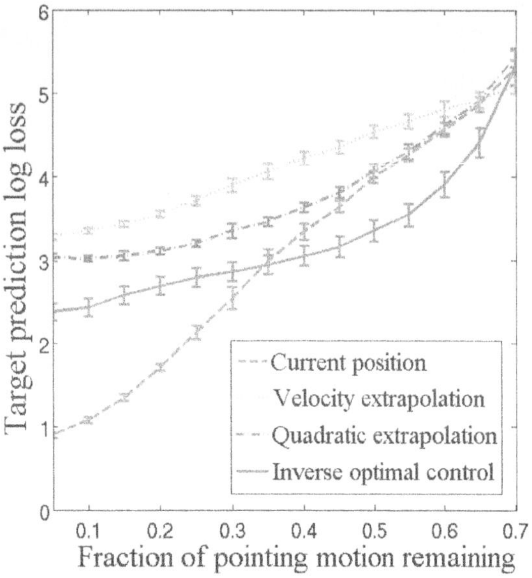

Figure 10. Target prediction log loss as a function of the amount of pointing trajectory remaining (in terms of time) with 95% confidence intervals.

For both measures, the *current position* model provides high-quality predictions when the fraction of pointing motion remaining is small. Indeed, when 95% of the motion is completed, essentially only selecting the target remains, and the *current position* assumption provides 100% accuracy. However, while that assumption biases the model to have good performance in the almost-completed-task region, significantly fewer classification errors are obtained with the *quadratic extrapolation* model when at least 50% of the pointing motion remains and by the *velocity extrapolation* model when at least 60% of the pointing motion remains. However, neither extrapolation method significantly outperforms the *current position* model under log-loss, presumably because log-loss penalizes these models for predictions based on the highly variable maximum velocities and quadratic fits that may be anomalous, as illustrated in Figure 4 and Figure 5.

The *inverse optimal control* model provides significant performance improvements over the three other models when large portions of pointing motion remain. Specifically, with between 40% and 60% of the motion trajectory remaining, it is more than twice as accurate for target classification than all other models and is only significantly outperformed in log-loss by the *current position* model when 30% or less of the pointing motion remains to be completed. We believe that the predictive performance characteristics of the *inverse optimal control* model will prove to be more beneficial for selecting appropriate pointing facilitation techniques because accurate predictions earlier in the pointing motion have the potential to provide greater benefits than later, when the motion has essentially reached the target. Understanding to what degree the *current position* model's superior performance when small amounts of pointing motion remain results from inherent bias of the model's assumption or whether the *inverse optimal control* approach can be improved to provide similar performance is an important question for future research.

DISCUSSION

We began this paper by discussing key requirements needed by a pointing target prediction system to support pointing facilitation techniques. We introduced an inverse optimal control approach that outperform previously developed techniques in critical early portions of pointing motions when predicting intended pointing targets and satisfies the requirements we discussed. Importantly, it learns parameters closely associated with motion dynamics, making it applicable to a wide range of settings. While training the model is relatively slow and computationally expensive, making predictions is fast and can be accomplished in real-time for moderate numbers of targets (*e.g.*, less than 200). Though we focused on aggregate modeling of cursor trajectories from a group of users, the approach we presented is well-suited for learning quadratic cost coefficients for each user or populations of users with similar patterns of usage—an important focus for improving computer accessibility. Additionally, contextual information can be easily incorporated into the prior target distribution in this approach.

We conclude by emphasizing that the performance of our approach in this paper should serve as a starting point. We employed a relatively simply set of statistics to base our model on in this paper—quadratic statistics of positions, velocities, accelerations, and jerks. We expect improved performance can be realized by augmenting these with linear and/or time-dependent statistics of the pointing motions. Many other opportunities exist for further improving the approach. For example, viewing pointing trajectories as mixtures of behaviors (such as some steady movements and some overshooting/correcting movements) may be beneficial for leveraging the less efficient trajectories that were discarded in the analyses of this paper while remaining computationally efficient for real-time prediction tasks. We plan to investigate these extensions and the incorporation of this predictive approach with specific facilitation techniques in future work.

ACKNOWLEDGMENTS

We thank Jin-Hyuk Hong for providing cursor pointing data, source code, and useful discussions, as well as the National Science Foundation's Quality of Life Technology Center and ONR MURI grant N00014-09-1-1052 for support of this research.

REFERENCES

1. Abbeel, P., and Ng, A. Y. Apprenticeship learning via inverse reinforcement learning. In *Proc. International Conference on Machine Learning* (2004), 1–8.

2. Ahlström, D., Hitz, M., and Leitner, G. An evaluation of sticky and force enhanced targets in multi target situations. In *NordiCHI '06: Proceedings of the 4th Nordic Conference on Human-Computer Interaction*, ACM (New York, NY, USA, 2006), 58–67.

3. Asano, T., Sharlin, E., Kitamura, Y., Takashima, K., and Kishino, F. Predictive interaction using the Delphian desktop. In *Proceedings of the 18th annual ACM symposium on User Interface Software and Technology*, ACM (2005), 133–141.

4. Balakrishnan, R. "Beating" Fitts' law: virtual enhancements for pointing facilitation. *International Journal of Human-Computer Studies 61*, 6 (2004), 857–874.
5. Baudisch, P., Cutrell, E., Robbins, D., and Czerwinski, M. Drag-and-pop and drag-and-pick: Techniques for accessing remote screen content on touch-and pen-operated systems. In *Proceedings of the 13th IFIP TC13 Conference on Human-Computer Interaction (INTERACT)* (2003), 57–64.
6. Bellman, R. A Markovian decision process. *Journal of Mathematics and Mechanics 6* (1957), 679–684.
7. Blanch, R., Guiard, Y., and Beaudouin-Lafon, M. Semantic pointing: improving target acquisition with control-display ratio adaptation. In *Proceedings of the SIGCHI Conference on Human Factors in Computing Systems*, ACM (2004), 519–526.
8. Boyd, S., El Ghaoui, L., Feron, E., and Balakrishnan, V. Linear matrix inequalities in system and control theory. *Society of Industrial and Applied Mathematics 15* (1994).
9. Card, S., English, W., and Burr, B. Evaluation of mouse, rate-controlled isometric joystick, step keys, and text keys for text selection on a crt. *Ergonomics 21*, 8 (1978), 601–613.
10. Chapuis, O., Labrune, J., and Pietriga, E. Dynaspot: Speed-dependent area cursor. In *Proceedings of the 27th International Conference on Human Factors in Computing Systems*, ACM (2009), 1391–1400.
11. Dennerlein, J., and Yang, M. Haptic force-feedback devices for the office computer: Performance and musculoskeletal loading issues. *Human Factors 43*, 2 (2001), 278–286.
12. Fitts, P. The information capacity of the human motor system in controlling the amplitude of movement. *Journal of Experimental Psychology 47*, 6 (1954), 381–391.
13. Grossman, T., and Balakrishnan, R. The bubble cursor: enhancing target acquisition by dynamic resizing of the cursor's activation area. In *Proceedings of the SIGCHI Conference on Human Factors in Computing Systems*, ACM (2005), 281–290.
14. Guiard, Y., Blanch, R., and Beaudouin-Lafon, M. Object pointing: a complement to bitmap pointing in guis. In *Proceedings of Graphics Interface 2004*, Canadian Human-Computer Communications Society (2004), 9–16.
15. Hurst, A., Mankoff, J., Dey, A., and Hudson, S. Dirty desktops: using a patina of magnetic mouse dust to make common interactor targets easier to select. In *Proceedings of the 20th Annual ACM Symposium on User Interface Software and Technology*, ACM (2007), 183–186.
16. Kabbash, P., and Buxton, W. The "prince" technique: Fitts' law and selection using area cursors. In *Proc. of the ACM CHI Conference on Human Factors in Computing Systems* (1995), 273–279.
17. Kalman, R. When is a linear control system optimal? *Trans. ASME, J. Basic Engrg. 86* (1964), 51–60.
18. Keuning-Van Oirschot, H., and Houtsma, A. Cursor displacement and velocity profiles for targets in various locations. In *Proceedings of Eurohaptics* (2001), 108–112.
19. Keyson, D. Dynamic cursor gain and tactual feedback in the capture of cursor movements. *Ergonomics 40*, 12 (1997), 1287–1298.
20. Kobayashi, M., and Igarashi, T. Ninja cursors: using multiple cursors to assist target acquisition on large screens. In *Proceeding of the Twenty-Sixth Annual SIGCHI Conference on Human Factors in Computing Systems*, ACM (2008), 949–958.
21. Lane, D., Peres, S., Sándor, A., and Napier, H. A process for anticipating and executing icon selection in graphical user interfaces. *International Journal of Human-Computer Interaction 19*, 2 (2005), 241–252.
22. Lank, E., Cheng, Y., and Ruiz, J. Endpoint prediction using motion kinematics. In *Proceedings of the SIGCHI Conference on Human Factors in Computing Systems*, ACM (2007), 637–646.
23. McGuffin, M., and Balakrishnan, R. Acquisition of expanding targets. In *Proceedings of the SIGCHI Conference on Human factors in Computing Systems*, ACM (2002), 57–64.
24. McGuffin, M., and Balakrishnan, R. Fitts' law and expanding targets: Experimental studies and designs for user interfaces. *ACM Transactions on Computer-Human Interaction (TOCHI) 12*, 4 (2005), 388–422.
25. Münch, S., and Dillmann, R. Haptic output in multimodal user interfaces. In *Proceedings of the 2nd International Conference on Intelligent User Interfaces*, ACM (1997), 105–112.
26. Ng, A. Y., and Russell, S. Algorithms for inverse reinforcement learning. In *Proc. International Conference on Machine Learning* (2000), 663–670.
27. Ratliff, N., Bagnell, J. A., and Zinkevich, M. Maximum margin planning. In *Proc. International Conference on Machine Learning* (2006), 729–736.
28. Wall, S., and Harwin, W. Quantification of the effects of haptic feedback during a motor skills task in a simulated environment. In *Proc. Second PHANToM Users Research Symposium* (2000).
29. Worden, A., Walker, N., Bharat, K., and Hudson, S. Making computers easier for older adults to use: area cursors and sticky icons. In *Proceedings of the SIGCHI Conference on Human Factors in Computing Systems*, ACM (1997), 266–271.

30. Ziebart, B. D., Bagnell, J. A., and Dey, A. K. Modeling interaction via the principle of maximum causal entropy. In *International Conference on Machine Learning* (2010), 1247–1254.

31. Ziebart, B. D., Maas, A., Bagnell, J. A., and Dey, A. K. Maximum entropy inverse reinforcement learning. In *Proc. AAAI Conference on Artificial Intelligence* (2008), 1433–1438.

APPENDIX: MAXIMUM CAUSAL ENTROPY LINEAR QUADRATIC REGULATION

We describe the maximum causal entropy approach to inverse optimal control and its efficient algorithms for the setting with linear dynamics and quadratic cost functions.

Formulation of the probability distribution

The distribution over actions we employ in this work (Equation 4) and the recursive relation defining its variables (Equation 5) are obtained by maximizing the causal entropy,

$$H(\mathbf{a}||\mathbf{s}) = \mathbb{E}_{\hat{\pi},\tau}\left[-\sum_{t=1}^{T} \log \hat{\pi}(\mathbf{a}_t|\mathbf{s}_t)\right], \tag{10}$$

subject to the constraints of Equation 7 [30]. We refer the reader to the previous paper introducing the general maximum causal entropy approach for a better understanding of the robust predictive guarantees that it provides.

Linear dynamics case

In the case of linear dynamics, the recurrence values (Equation 5) are quadratic functions of the form:

$$Q(\mathbf{a}_t, \mathbf{s}_t) = \begin{bmatrix} \mathbf{a}_t \\ \mathbf{s}_t \end{bmatrix}^{\mathrm{T}} \begin{bmatrix} \mathbf{C}_{a,a} & \mathbf{C}_{a,s} \\ \mathbf{C}_{s,a} & \mathbf{C}_{s,s} \end{bmatrix} \begin{bmatrix} \mathbf{a}_t \\ \mathbf{s}_t \end{bmatrix} + \begin{bmatrix} \mathbf{a}_t \\ \mathbf{s}_t \end{bmatrix}^{\mathrm{T}} \begin{bmatrix} \mathbf{F}_a \\ \mathbf{F}_s \end{bmatrix}, \text{ and}$$

$$V(\mathbf{s}_t) = \mathbf{s}_t^{\mathrm{T}} \mathbf{D} \mathbf{s}_t + \mathbf{s}_t^{\mathrm{T}} \mathbf{G}.$$

Expanding the definitions of Equation 5 and 6, we have:

$$\begin{aligned} Q(\mathbf{a}_t, \mathbf{s}_t) &= \mathbb{E}_{\tau(\mathbf{s}_{t+1}|\mathbf{s}_t,\mathbf{a}_t)}[\mathbf{s}_{t+1}^{\mathrm{T}} \mathbf{D} \mathbf{s}_{t+1} + \mathbf{s}_{t+1}^{\mathrm{T}} \mathbf{G} | \mathbf{s}_t, \mathbf{a}_t] \\ &= (\mathbf{A}\mathbf{s}_t + \mathbf{B}\mathbf{a}_t)^{\mathrm{T}} \mathbf{D} (\mathbf{A}\mathbf{s}_t + \mathbf{B}\mathbf{a}_t) + \mathrm{tr}(\mathbf{D}\Sigma) \\ &\quad + \mathbf{a}_t^{\mathrm{T}} \mathbf{B}^{\mathrm{T}} \mathbf{G} + \mathbf{s}_t^{\mathrm{T}} \mathbf{A}^{\mathrm{T}} \mathbf{G} \\ &= \begin{bmatrix} \mathbf{a}_t \\ \mathbf{s}_t \end{bmatrix}^{\mathrm{T}} \begin{bmatrix} \mathbf{B}^{\mathrm{T}}\mathbf{D}\mathbf{B} & \mathbf{B}^{\mathrm{T}}\mathbf{D}\mathbf{A} \\ \mathbf{A}^{\mathrm{T}}\mathbf{D}\mathbf{B} & \mathbf{A}^{\mathrm{T}}\mathbf{D}\mathbf{A} \end{bmatrix} \begin{bmatrix} \mathbf{a}_t \\ \mathbf{s}_t \end{bmatrix} \\ &\quad + \begin{bmatrix} \mathbf{a}_t \\ \mathbf{s}_t \end{bmatrix}^{\mathrm{T}} \begin{bmatrix} \mathbf{B}^{\mathrm{T}}\mathbf{G} \\ \mathbf{A}^{\mathrm{T}}\mathbf{G} \end{bmatrix} + \text{const, and} \\ V(\mathbf{s}_t) &= -\log \int_{\mathbf{a}_t} \exp\{-(\mathbf{a}_t^{\mathrm{T}} \mathbf{C}_{a,a} \mathbf{a}_t + 2\mathbf{a}_t^{\mathrm{T}} \mathbf{C}_{a,s} \mathbf{s}_t \\ &\quad + \mathbf{s}_t^{\mathrm{T}} \mathbf{C}_{s,s} \mathbf{s}_t + \mathbf{s}_t^{\mathrm{T}} \mathbf{F}_s + \mathbf{a}_t^{\mathrm{T}} \mathbf{F}_a)\}\, d\mathbf{a}_t + \mathbf{s}_t^{\mathrm{T}} \mathbf{M} \mathbf{s}_t \\ &= \mathbf{s}_t^{\mathrm{T}} (\mathbf{C}_{s,s} + \mathbf{M} - \mathbf{C}_{a,s}^{\mathrm{T}} \mathbf{C}_{a,a}^{-1} \mathbf{C}_{a,s}) \mathbf{s}_t \\ &\quad + \mathbf{s}_t^{\mathrm{T}} (\mathbf{F}_s - \mathbf{C}_{a,s}^{\mathrm{T}} \mathbf{C}_{a,a}^{-1} \mathbf{F}_a) + \text{const}, \end{aligned}$$

Thus the set of update rules for the quadratic functions are: $\mathbf{C}_{a,a} = \mathbf{B}^{\mathrm{T}}\mathbf{D}\mathbf{B}$; $\mathbf{C}_{s,a} = \mathbf{C}_{a,s}^{\mathrm{T}} = \mathbf{B}^{\mathrm{T}}\mathbf{D}\mathbf{A}$; $\mathbf{C}_{s,s} = \mathbf{A}^{\mathrm{T}}\mathbf{D}\mathbf{A}$; $\mathbf{F}_a = \mathbf{B}^{\mathrm{T}}\mathbf{G}$; $\mathbf{F}_s = \mathbf{A}^{\mathrm{T}}\mathbf{G}$; $\mathbf{D} = \mathbf{C}_{s,s} + \mathbf{M} - \mathbf{C}_{a,s}^{\mathrm{T}}\mathbf{C}_{a,a}^{-1}\mathbf{C}_{a,s}$; and $\mathbf{G} = \mathbf{F}_s - \mathbf{C}_{a,s}^{\mathrm{T}}\mathbf{C}_{a,a}^{-1}\mathbf{F}_a$.

Parameter Estimation

The model parameters in matrix $\mathbf{M}$ are fit from demonstrated state sequences. The likelihood of the demonstrated trajectories under the action distribution, Equation 4, is a convex function of those free parameters. This guarantees that standard gradient-based techniques will converge to the choice of parameters that best explains the demonstrated trajectories. The gradients have an intuitive interpretation: they are the differences of the optimization constraints (Equation 7),

$$\nabla_{\mathbf{M}} L = \mathbb{E}_{\tilde{\pi},\tau}\left[\sum_t \mathbf{s}_t\, \mathbf{s}_t^{\mathrm{T}}\right] - \mathbb{E}_{\hat{\pi},\tau}\left[\sum_t \mathbf{s}_t\, \mathbf{s}_t^{\mathrm{T}}\right]. \tag{11}$$

These values can be directly obtained from the Gaussian distribution of state over time. Namely, if $\mathbf{x}$ is normally distributed with mean μ_x and covariance matrix Σ_x, $\mathbb{E}[\mathbf{x}\mathbf{x}^{\mathrm{T}}] = \mu_x \mu_x^{\mathrm{T}} + \Sigma_x$.

The parameters can then be optimized by iteratively applying the gradients of Equation 11 with a decaying learning rate, η, *e.g.*, $\mathbf{M} \leftarrow \mathbf{M} + \eta\nabla_{\mathbf{M}}$. However, in practice, an exponentiated update, $\mathbf{M} \leftarrow e^{\log \mathbf{M} + \eta\nabla_{\mathbf{M}}}$, preserves a useful property (positive semi-definiteness) of the $\mathbf{M}$ matrix, aiding optimization.

Efficient State Projections

Computing the target posterior requires repeated calculation of state values, $V(\mathbf{s}^G)$, and cumulative trajectory costs, $\sum_{\tau=2}^{T} \mathrm{cost}(\mathbf{s}_\tau^G)$ for different goals (Equation 9). Naïvely, computing the cumulative trajectory costs is computationally expensive, requiring $\mathcal{O}(t|\mathbf{s}|^2)$ time. However, due to the linearity of the cost function, previously computed cumulative costs can be re-used.

Consider the transformation of a cost function from an initial goal G to a new goal G' using rotation matrix $\mathbf{R}_G^{G'}$ and translation vector $\Delta_G^{G'}$:

$$\begin{aligned} \sum_{\tau=1}^{t} \mathbf{s}_\tau^{G'\mathrm{T}} \mathbf{M}\, \mathbf{s}_\tau^{G'} &= \mathbf{M} \cdot \sum_{\tau=1}^{t} \mathbf{s}_\tau^{G'} \mathbf{s}_\tau^{G'\mathrm{T}} \\ &= \mathbf{M} \cdot \sum_{\tau=1}^{t} (\mathbf{R}_G^{G'} \mathbf{s}_\tau^G + \Delta_G^{G'})(\mathbf{R}_G^{G'} \mathbf{s}_\tau^G + \Delta_G^{G'})^{\mathrm{T}} \\ &= \mathbf{M} \cdot \mathbf{R}_G^{G'} \left(\sum_{\tau=1}^{t} \mathbf{s}_\tau^G \mathbf{s}_\tau^{G\mathrm{T}}\right) \mathbf{R}_G^{G'\mathrm{T}} + t\mathbf{M} \cdot \Delta_G^{G'} \Delta_G^{G'\mathrm{T}} \\ &\quad + 2\mathbf{M} \cdot \mathbf{R}_G^{G'} \left(\sum_{\tau=1}^{t} \mathbf{s}_\tau^G\right) \Delta_G^{G'\mathrm{T}}. \end{aligned}$$

Thus, with the previously computed quadratic and linear sums for projection G, only matrix operations independent of the time horizon t are needed. This reduces the $\mathcal{O}(t\ \dim(s)^2)$ time computation to $\mathcal{O}(\dim(s)^2)$ time.

Towards Online Adaptation and Personalization of Key-Target Resizing for Mobile Devices

Tyler Baldwin
Department of Computer Science and Engineering
Michigan State University
East Lansing, MI, USA
baldwi96@cse.msu.edu

Joyce Y. Chai
Department of Computer Science and Engineering
Michigan State University
East Lansing, MI, USA
jchai@cse.msu.edu

ABSTRACT
Software (soft) keyboards are becoming increasingly popular on mobile devices. To attempt to improve soft keyboard input accuracy, key-target resizing algorithms that dynamically change the size of each key's target area have been developed. Although methods that employ personalized touch models have been shown to outperform general models, previous work has relied upon laboratory-based offline calibration to collect the data necessary to build these models. Such approaches are unrealistic and interuptive, and it is unlikely that offline calibration can be applied in a realistic usage setting, as hundreds or thousands of touch points are necessary to build the models. To combat this problem, this paper explores the possibility of online adaptation of key-target resizing algorithms. In particular, we propose and examine three online data collection methods that can be used to build and dynamically update personalized key-target resizing models. Our results suggest that a data collection methodology that makes inference based on vocabulary and error correction behavior is able to perform on par with gold standard personalized models, while reducing relative error rate by 10.4% over general models. This approach is simple, computationally inexpensive, and calculable via information that the system already has access to. Additionally, we show that these models can be built quickly, requiring less than one week's worth of text input by an average mobile device user.

Author Keywords
key-target resizing, online adaptation, personalization

ACM Classification Keywords
H.5.2 Information Interfaces and Presentation: User Interfaces—*Input devices and strategies*

INTRODUCTION
In recent years, software keyboards (*soft keyboards*) have been a popular input method for mobile devices. There are several advantages of software keyboards over hardware keyboards, such as their ability to change on the fly or to be hidden to free up space for other widgets. However, they can also be more error prone than their hardware counterparts, due to factors such as touch point uncertainty [11] and lack of true tactile feedback [4].

To help combat these problems, smarter keyboard technology has been developed. One such technology that has been implemented on currently available mobile devices such as the Apple iPhone[1] is *key-target resizing* [6]. Key-target resizing algorithms dynamically change the size of each individual key on a soft keyboard as the user types, based on a model of the language and of user typing behavior. By doing so, they can more accurately guess the intent of the user and improve overall typing performance. Because the constant changing of key sizes is potentially distracting to users [8], key-target resizing algorithms do all of their changes "under the hood", and do not show the key changes to users.

Previous work on key-target resizing [6, 7] has learned a general model of typing behavior offline by aggregating the touch points of several users. However, a few studies [8, 19] have pointed to the fact that key-target resizing algorithms could be improved by building personalized touch models that focus on the typing behavior of a single individual. Because mobile devices are often associated with one individual only, this has the potential to provide users with a customized experience that produces better overall performance.

Unfortunately, one key aspect of touch model personalization has not been addressed: how do we get the data necessary to train the models? In order to build a training set, we need to know which key the user intended to hit for each touch point recorded by the system. In order to know this intent, previous work collected data in controlled laboratory studies where user intent was dictated. Unfortunately, this type of offline calibration is too unrealistic and interuptive for real-world deployment, as building a touch model may require several thousand touch points, and we cannot expect the average user to participate in such a long calibration phase. One ideal alternative would be to automatically collect the needed data from a user's daily usage of the device. Such a method would not only allow personalized models to be built without an overt collection phase, but would also allow the models to continuously adapt to user behavior. Although promising,

[1] www.apple.com/iphone/

no previous work has addressed this aspect of automated data collection and online adaptation. It is the goal of this paper to explore this idea.

To accomplish this, this paper examines several interrelated questions. We first examine how well a system can determine the fidelity of data that is captured from natural user interaction. That is, we wish to examine whether the system is able to determine user intent automatically with high enough accuracy to build robust models of personal behavior. It is likely that models that assign intent too liberally will introduce too much noise to build accurate models, while those that are too conservative will collect data too slowly to be useful. In this work, we propose several data assessment models to examine the tradeoff between the speed of model building and the amount of noise introduced by data collection.

In order to test the data collection methods proposed herein, we train key-target resizing algorithms using the data collected by each of the proposed methods and compare them to general touch models built from aggregate data and personalized models trained on gold standard data. This gives us insight into the extent to which models trained on noisy, automatically collected data can approach the theoretical gains of personalized models, and whether they are able to outperform general models built in the laboratory. Our results suggest that a data collection methodology that makes inference based on vocabulary and error correction behavior is able to perform on par with gold standard personalized models, while reducing relative error rate by 10.4% over general models.

In the next few sections, we present related work and the general formulation of key-target resizing algorithms as implemented here and in previous work. We then introduce three data-assessment methods that can be used online to build personalized key-target resizing models on the fly. To assess data fidelity we collect a dataset of natural, unscripted mobile device text input. The last few sections analyze and evaluate the presented methods.

RELATED WORK

There are two main streams of previous work: key-target resizing and touch point modeling.

Source-channel key-target resizing was introduced by Goodman et al. [6]. They conducted a user study that compared a keyboard using key-target resizing to a static keyboard in which no resizing was performed. Users had to complete several rounds of testing, in which they were given a phrase to type on the keyboard. After a small phase of a few rounds to give users time to get used to the keyboard and experimental setup, users were asked to complete several rounds on both the static and target-resizing keyboards. To simplify calculation of error rates, users were not allowed to correct their input mistakes. Their results suggested that a keyboard with key-target resizing could reduce input error rates by a factor of 1.67 to 1.87.

More recent work by Gunawardana et al. [7] introduced key anchoring into the key-target resizing framework. One potential problem with the key-target resizing formulation is that it may make certain keys difficult to hit. For certain sequences with high language model probabilities, the system may expand the size of the most likely keys to such a degree that the hit area of adjacent keys is very small. Because the algorithm does not show the resizing to the user, they may not realize that this has occurred. To alleviate this problem, key anchoring ensures that the areas directly at the center of the keys are always associated with that key, helping to ensure that there is always a selectable region for each key.

Two studies have examined the role of personalized data on key resizing. In the first, Himberg et al. [8] dynamically changed the size of keys on a 9-key number keyboard based on the touch points of the current user. Unlike the key-target resizing algorithms discussed above, Himberg et al. showed these changes to the user. Although no empirical results are given, user feedback was generally positive.

A more recent study by Rudchenko et al. [19] has examined the role of personalization in key-target resizing empirically. This study compared personalized and general models on the same dataset, and found that personalized models resulted in a 21.4% relative reduction in error rate.

Previous studies of touch behavior have identified several factors that may lead to variance and inaccuracies in attempts at acquiring a target on a touchscreen keyboard. These include such factors as the presence or absence of tactile feedback [4, 10], user's fingers occluding the target area [21], the "fat finger" problem [2], the angle at which users' fingers hit the touchscreen [12], and differences in how users perceive and model their touch behavior [12].

The extent to which each of these factors influences touch performance is likely to vary between users. Given the same device, a user with a small finger size may be nearly unaffected by fat finger issues or occlusion, while one with a large finger size may be heavily affected by them. Users may also have different mental models of how the system evaluates touch points (e.g., believes system registers touch point near the top of the finger press vs. the center) that may lead them to systematically miss the intended target [11]. Overall, the accumulation of these factors has the potential to lead to substantial differences in touch behavior between users, devices, and interfaces.

KEY-TARGET RESIZING

In this section we outline the source-channel key-target resizing formulation used in this work. Our implementation of the key-target resizing algorithm closely follows previous work [6, 7].

The common formulation of modern key-target resizing work is presented by Goodman et al. [6], who derive a probabilistic model of typing behavior, based on a noisy channel formulation. Their reasoning is as follows: when a user attempts to type a sequence of characters on a soft keyboard, the system receives this as a series of touch points. To translate these touch points into the intended character sequence we must calculate the most likely character sequence given the touch points:

$$\arg\max_{c_1,...,c_n} P(c_1, ..., c_n | t_1, ..., t_n) = \arg\max_{c_1,...,c_n} P(c_1, ..., c_n) P(t_1, ..., t_n | c_1, ..., c_n) \quad (1)$$

where $t_1, ..., t_n$ is the sequence of touch points typed by the user and $c_1, ..., c_n$ is a sequence of corresponding characters. The probability $P(c_1, ..., c_n)$ is the language model, which captures how likely the sequence $c_1, ..., c_n$ is to occur in the language. This probability can be calculated as:

$$P(c_1, ..., c_n) = P(c_1) * P(c_2|c_1) ... * P(c_n|c_1 ... c_{n-1}) \quad (2)$$

Because this is difficult to estimate from corpora, the Markov assumption is often made here that a given character in the sequence is only dependent on the previous $n-1$ characters:

$$P(c_i|c_1, ..., c_{i-1}) \approx P(c_i|c_{i-(n-1)}, ..., c_{i-1}) \quad (3)$$

The second probability we must estimate, $P(t_1, ..., t_n|c_1, ..., c_n)$, models user touch behavior. To estimate this touch model probability, a simplifying assumption is made that, given a character, the current touch point is not dependent on previous touch points:

$$P(t_1, ..., t_n|c_1, ..., c_n) = P(t_1|c_1) * P(t_2|c_2) ... * P(t_n|c_n) \quad (4)$$

This sequence-based formulation could potentially change any part of the sequence on the fly. That is, when new characters are typed by the user the algorithm may examine the sequence and decide that a different sequence is now more probable, resulting in a change in previously displayed characters. Initially, this seems like a preferable characteristic for the keyboard to have, since the introduction of new evidence may make the user's intent more clear. However, users may examine the text field only periodically [18], and they may not expect previous characters they have written to change. To combat this, the probability calculation can be transformed into a calculation of the most probable letter, rather than the most probable sequence [7]:

$$\arg\max_{c_i} P(c_i|t_i) = \arg\max_{c_i} P(c_i|c_{i-(n-1)}, ..., c_{i-1}) P(t_i|c_i) \quad (5)$$

This makes the best local decision each time a key is entered by the user, based on the current context.

Touch Model Training

To reiterate, in equation 5 there are two probabilities we must estimate: the language model and the touch model. Since language model training has been studied in many other areas of research (e.g., speech recognition and machine translation), we will adopt previous approaches in training our language model here. In this paper, we are more concerned with the touch model.

In order to train a touch model for key-target resizing, each data point in the training data must have, at minimum, 2 things: the (x, y) coordinates of the touch point and the key which the user intended to hit. Each time a user attempts to type a character, the system has access to the (x, y) touch point that the user selected. It knows which key it registers as selected by the user, via whatever process (key-target resizing or otherwise) it uses to determine this. It does not know, however, which key the user actually *intended* to hit, which may or may not coorespond to the key that it registered as selected.

Laboratory-based experiments [6, 7] have attempted to get around this by following the text copying experimental paradigm commonly used to compare keyboard layouts [14]. Using this setup, users are given an experimenter-defined phrase and asked to enter it on the device "as quickly and accurately as possible". This setup attempted to minimize between session differences in order to evaluate different systems and keyboard layouts. By dictating the text that the user must write, the experimenters also dictate their intent. This allows the experimenters to associate every touch event, even those that select the incorrect key, with an intended key. In this way the carefully constrained text copying method can be used to build generalized touch models. Personalized models can also be built and evaluated for the people who participate in the study, but not for the general population.

To attempt to develop personalized models for a wider audience, Rudchenko et al. [19] proposed a typing game as a means to collect personalized data. Although this method is able to collect data for those users who choose to download and play the typing game, this is likely to be a small percentage of the total user population. This leaves the problem that we wish to examine in the current work, that of building a personalized training set to allow online adaptation for every user, as of yet unaddressed.

DATA ASSESSMENT METHODS

This work proposes to examine the utility of 3 different methods for automatic data assessment. These methods allow a system to collect touch model training data online from natural usage, allowing the system to adapt to each user's typing style dynamically. The proposed methods use varying degrees of inference to associate touch points produced by the user with an intended key. Once the method collects a sufficient amount of data, this data can be used to learn a personalized touch model. Each of these methods considers different levels of processing to attempt to manage the trade off between the amount of data considered to be available for training and the amount of noise introduced by the data collection procedure.

Conservative Method. The conservative method makes very little inference about the fidelity of the data; it only includes data that the user explicitly provides fidelity judgments on. Unfortunately, users do not provide fidelity judgments often. The only point at which user's fidelity judgments are overt is during editing operations. Consider the following input stream (backspace characters are represented by the $<$ character):

$$wring <<< ong$$

In this example, the user mistypes "wrong" as "wring", and uses the backspace key to correct it. In doing so, the user provides us with eight touch points for training: five points from before the edit operation and three after. We can assume that the three letters typed after the edit operation were the intended characters for the three characters that were deleted. This gives us six points with their intended key. We see that the first attempt to type the character *o* was interpreted by the system as an attempt to type the letter *i*, and that the first attempts to type *n* and *g* were successful. A small amount of inference tells us that we can probably trust that the first two characters, *w* and *r*, were also correctly interpreted by the system. After all, if they were not, the user would have had no reason to stop the editing operation mid-word and would have instead changed the other incorrect characters.

However, not all editing operations result from a user mistyping. For instance, a user may chose to rephrase their input or discard their current contribution and restart the entire dialogue turn. These cases do not represent typing mistakes, and treating them as such would add noise to the data. To test whether an editing operation is performed for purposes of error correction, the conservative method compares the final string committed by the user to the string that would be produced by substituting in the deleted keystrokes. For instance, in the above example we compare *wrong* to *wring*. If all substitutions between the two strings are between adjacent keys on the keyboard this case is considered to be an error correction attempt, and the data is trusted by the conservative method.

Because edit operations are undertaken on a comparatively small percentage of the input stream, the conservative model throws out the majority of the data. By doing so, it attempts to trade the speed at which we can build a personalized model for the percentage of those characters that we return whose intent was correctly determined. In other words, it sacrifices recall to improve precision. By focusing on high precision, we minimize the amount of noise in our training data, which is critical for building accurate models, but because we only use a small percentage of the data, we must see a large amount of data before a useful model can be built.

Character-Level Method. The character-level method is the converse of the conservative method, in that it is extremely liberal in deciding what data we can trust. This method assumes that the user is careful about what they type and is prone to proofreading their text input and correcting mistakes. If this is the case, then we can trust that all input that is not involved in an edit operation was interpreted correctly by the system. This may not be an unreasonable assumption, as previous work has reported that corrected errors greatly outnumber uncorrected errors [22]. All characters that were involved in an edit operation are handled in the same manner as in the conservative method, and all characters that are not are assumed to have the intent ascribed to them by the system. In doing so, we are able to include almost every single character from the input stream in our training data.

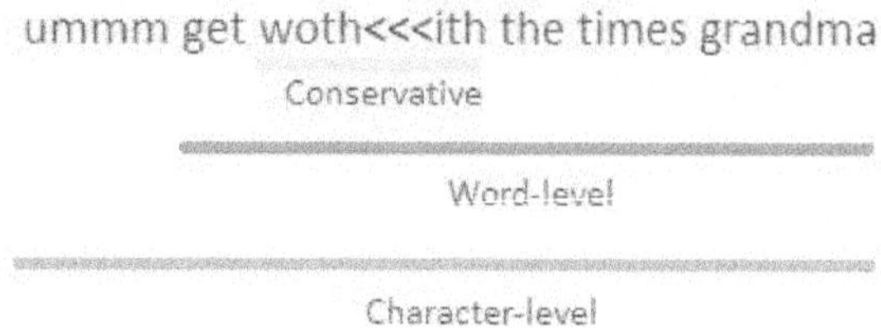

Figure 1: An example utterance showing which keypresses are retained by each of the three proposed inference methods.

The character-level method makes the opposite tradeoff from the conservative method, sacrificing precision for recall. This allows personalized touch models to be trained fast, but the accuracy of these models may suffer as a result. The success of such a model is likely to be effected by both the user's cognitive input style and the domain. Some users may be more prone to proofreading and correcting their errors and some domains may encourage users to proofread more carefully than others.

Word-Level Method. The word-level method attempts to find a middle ground between the conservative and character-level methods. In the word-level method we again handle words involved in edit operations as we did in the conservative model. We also follow the logic of the character-level model to assume that most of the data not edited by the user was correctly interpreted by the system. However, the word-level model only trusts those words that it knows; that is, it only considers words that are in its internal vocabulary to be correct, while disregarding touch points from words it is not familiar with. For characters not found in words such as spaces and punctuation, the word-level method acts like the character-level method, trusting the system's prediction. The assumption made by the word-level method is that character strings that it is unfamiliar with are more likely to be typing mistakes than those that it knows. Although there is still the possibility of real-word spelling errors [17, 9], removing out-of-vocabulary words is likely to help reduce noise in the data.

The three methods outlined above are hierarchical; all information captured by the conservative method is captured by the word-level method, and all information captured by the word-level method is also captured by the character-level method. Figure 1 shows an example of the information captured by each method for one dialogue turn in our dataset.

EMPIRICAL STUDIES AND EVALUATION

We examined the proposed data assessment methods in two separate ways. In the first round of evaluation, we examine how quickly personalized touch models can be built using each collection method, and how much noise each collection method adds to the data. To determine the effect of each method on the final touch model, in the second round of evaluation we build personalized touch models on the data collected via each method and compare the performance of key-target resizing using these touch models with general and gold standard personalized models. To enable these evaluations we first need a dataset of natural user input which associates touch points with user intents. Because no dataset of this type is currently available, we collected our own. Our data set is described in the next section.

Data Set

In this section we describe the data collection methodology used to acquire a dataset to evaluate the assessment methods outlined above. As noted previously, the primary means of data collection in previous key-target resizing studies was via a text copying procedure in which user intent is dictated by the experimenter. However, because typical mobile device text input tasks such as web search and text messaging require little to no text copying, we felt that this data collection methodology may not accurately reflect real usage behavior, and would be inappropriate for a study of online data assessment. The methods used previously are also problematic because they suppressed error correction behavior, which is likely to be an important point of inference for online adaptation methods. Additionally, as key-target resizing algorithms do not have an effect on the interface seen by the user, different methods can be compared on the same data, removing the problem of consistency across collection sessions. We thus chose to collect a dataset using a more natural text message-like chat methodology, where users are free to dictate their own intent.

For each round of data collection, two participants were asked to chat with one another using a simple mobile device messaging program. Users were asked to converse for a span of one hour, and were told that they could converse about whatever topic(s) they wished. To ensure that users were able to converse continuously the entire time and to more accurately simulate typical interaction, the participants were asked to come in pairs of friends or other individuals that are comfortable conversing for extended periods of time. An experimenter was on hand to ensure that participants were able to converse for the full hour and to suggest topics if necessary. Users were asked not to converse in any other way except via the device, and were separated from one another by an opaque screen to remove any visual feedback. Users were allowed to use any body orientation (e.g., sitting vs. standing) and typing style (e.g., one thumb, two thumb, etc.) they wished but were asked to be consistent throughout the study.

To collect data we used our own keyboard implementation based on an existing open-source keyboard[2]. Because we did not have data to train key-target resizing algorithms prior to the data collection phase, we could not provide users with a keyboard that performed resizing during data collection. Previous work [7] attempted to simulate perfect key-target resizing during data collection by simply registering a key press that was within one key's distance from the intended key to be correct. Since this method requires that the experimenter dictate the user's intent, it could not be used in this work. Instead, the keyboard used during data collection for this study did not dynamically resize keys, and instead used static key mappings that associated a fixed region with an individual key at all times.

Although we wished to make the data collection methodology as close to natural input as possible, a few controls were implemented for consistency and simplicity. Like many previous studies [20, 22], we restricted the user's error correction ability to only allow error correction via the backspace key, the most common error correction method [1]. Users were not allowed to move the cursor, select text, or to cut, copy or paste text and the system did not offer any additional text entry aids, such as automatic word completion or tactile feedback.

In order to build a gold standard for evaluation, user intent must be determined. There are 3 typing scenarios which must be considered [16]:

1. The system interpreted the user's keypress correctly.
2. The system interpreted the keypress incorrectly and the user corrected the mistake (*corrected errors*).
3. The system interpreted the keypress incorrectly and the user did not correct the mistake (*uncorrected errors*).

When the system interprets the user's keypress correctly, the intent of the user is simply the key registered by the system. If the user makes a mistake and then corrects it, intent should be determinable by examining their error correction actions. However, in the case of uncorrected errors, only the original author knows for sure which key they intended to hit. To discover the intent of uncorrected errors, users were shown the transcript of their conversation immediately after the data collection session and asked to correct the mistakes in the text. Because we only wish to handle cases in which users mistyped due to finger position rather than spelling knowledge, users were asked to correct typographic errors, but not cognitive ones [13].

Unlike with uncorrected errors, the intent of corrected errors can be discovered by examining the user's editing operations. To discover corrected mistakes, human annotators examined transcripts of the full input stream, including backspace characters. Cases in which the annotators were confident about the user's intent were marked accordingly, while cases in which annotators were unable to confidently discover the intent of a keypress from the input stream (e.g., unsure if error was typographic or cognitive), were marked as unknown and not considered during evaluation. Although many mistakes could likely have been discovered automatically by inference methods such as the conservative method outlined above, these methods are unlikely to catch all mistakes, necessitating the use of human annotators.

In order to examine the effects that device differences play in training key-target resizing algorithms, we used two different devices in our study. The two devices used were the

[2]http://developer.android.com/resources/samples/SoftKeyboard/

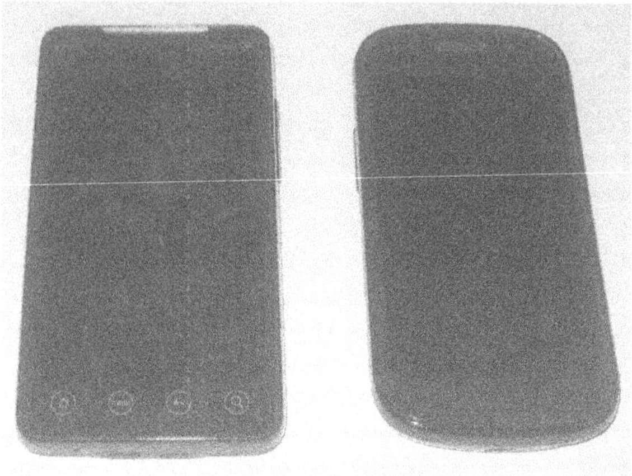

Figure 2: Side-by-side comparison of the two mobile devices used in this study, the HTC EVO(left) and the Google Nexus S (right).

	Average
Messages Length (chars)	24.7 ± 22.4
Messages Sent Per User	141 ± 67
Total Keystrokes	5097 ± 1111
Text Keystrokes	4126 ± 963
Backspace Keystrokes	642 ± 268

Table 1: Statistics of the chat dataset

HTC EVO[3] and the Google Nexus S[4]. These devices were chosen because they have similar features in terms of operating system, memory and processing power, but differ in the dimensions of the screen and device, which is likely to have an effect on typing behavior. The two devices are shown in Figure 2.

A total of 8 users (3 female) participated in the study. Participants ranged from age 20-25. Three users owned or had previously owned mobile devices with soft keyboards, but no participants had experience with the devices used in the study[5].

Table 1 shows some data statistics. As shown, users hit an average of 5097 keystrokes over the course of the hour. Of these, about 80.9% were keystrokes that made a character appear in the text field; the other keystrokes were backspaces and keyboard modification keys such as "shift". The backspace key was hit an average of 642 times. Dialogue turns averaged about 25 text characters each, although there was significant variation between users. This is relatively short compared to previous studies of text messaging; one recent large-scale text messaging study [3] reports an average length of 50.9 characters per message.

[3]http://www.htc.com/us/products/evo-sprint

[4]http://www.google.com/nexus/

[5]The dataset is available at: http://links.cse.msu.edu:8000/KTRData/KTRData.zip

Evaluating Collection Speed and Accuracy

Each data assessment method was run on the input streams of each user and compared to gold standard logs to determine precision and recall. Results are shown in Table 2.

The first column in the table shows the precision of the static model that was used by the system during data collection. This represents the case in which no attempts are made to discover the intent of or filter out data we are uncertain about. If we simply trust the intents provided by the system we obtain precision of 0.930. Put another way, the naive approach in which we build a dataset that reflects how the system currently acts produces about 7% noise, on average. Because we trust every point seen by the system, the recall of the static model is always 1. However, it is important to note that the cases in which we are regarding as noise are likely to be some of the most critical cases to model. That is, since we wish to improve overall performance, it is imperative that we can discover cases in which the system did not act optimally and adjust accordingly.

As shown, the conservative method had the lowest recall of all methods, as expected. On average, the conservative method captures a little over 12% of all data typed by the user, meaning that it would require over 8 times as much data as a perfect collection method that knew the intent of every keypress. As expected, the average precision of the conservative method was good, with an error rate of under 1%.

The results of the word and character level methods show more promise for timely data collection. On average, the character level model was able to capture 90.7% of the data with an accuracy rate of 98.2%. In comparison, the word level method captured about 10% less data than the character level, while reducing error rate by an absolute 0.7% (38.9% relative reduction). However, it is unclear from this analysis what effect this difference in error rate will have on systems trained from this data and how significant this reduction in error rate is relative to the reduction in collection rate. This will be examined in more depth in the next section.

The numbers in Table 2 also highlight some important between user differences. The overall input error rate of each user varied, from as low as 3.5% to nearly 13% in one instance. Because non-error related editing operations are disregarded by all methods, users that used many restarts or other editing operations not related to error correction (e.g., user 8) had lower overall recall rates.

Evaluating Personalized Key-Target Resizing on Noisy Data

To evaluate the collection methods in a real-usage scenario, we used the data collected by each method to train key-target resizing algorithms. To train the language model we used interpolated kneser-ney smoothed [5] 7-grams estimated from about 1 million characters from text messaging data from the NUS SMS Corpus[6]. The touch models were bivariate Gaussians trained using maximum a posteriori estimation. An exponential weighting factor was optimized on the training data to balance the contribution of the language and touch models.

[6]http://wing.comp.nus.edu.sg:8080/SMSCorpus/

User	None	Conservative		WordLevel		CharacterLevel	
	Precision	Precision	Recall	Precision	Recall	Precision	Recall
1	0.934	0.990	0.152	0.989	0.828	0.986	0.904
2	0.952	0.989	0.093	0.994	0.812	0.986	0.959
3	0.909	0.992	0.186	0.997	0.834	0.995	0.897
4	0.965	0.987	0.098	0.997	0.904	0.997	0.948
5	0.958	0.988	0.094	0.997	0.812	0.988	0.947
6	0.928	0.984	0.125	0.996	0.773	0.977	0.915
7	0.871	0.996	0.148	0.957	0.819	0.943	0.921
8	0.908	0.994	0.054	0.964	0.652	0.963	0.711
Average	0.930	0.991	0.123	0.989	0.812	0.982	0.907

Table 2: Precision and Recall for the 3 data collection methods for all users.

Because the size of key anchors must be empirically learned from data which may add a confounding factor to our analysis of touch model behavior, key anchoring was not implemented.

To compare key-target resizing models built using different collection methods, we can evaluate the models offline, using a process somewhat similar to the simulation procedure introduced by Gunawardana et al. [7]. Given a transcript of touch points, we can calculate the prediction that the system would have made had it been running a given key-target resizing algorithm when the user input that point. The output of the algorithm can then be compared to the gold standard, allowing comparison of methods without having the user type on separate keyboards utilizing different touch models. This allows us to control for between session differences.

Leave-one-out cross validation was used for evaluation. Because context is important to key-target resizing, we held out one full dialogue turn as a testing instance for each round, rather than one single button press. To better compare to previous work and to account for the limited amount of data, key-target resizing was only evaluated on keys that appeared on the alphabetic keyboard (English alphabet characters, period, comma, and spacebar). During data collection users were allowed to switch to a keyboard which contained numbers and additional symbols; these keypresses were included in the context seen by the key-target resizing algorithm, but not considered for evaluation.

A total of seven different data collection methods were examined. Two methods use aggregate data from other users, while the other five methods explore personalization with training data sets extracted via different data assessment methods. These methods differ only in the dataset used to train the touch model. The methods are as follows:

- **Aggregate Methods:**
  - *General Method.* An implementation of the typical non-personalized methods used in previous work. This method uses aggregate gold standard data from all other users to train the touch model.
  - *Device-specific Method.* Similar to the general method, but only uses gold-standard aggregate data from a single device rather than from both devices.
- **Personalized Methods:**
  - *No Filtering Method.* Baseline method that assumes that every keypress was interpreted correctly by the static model during data collection. Uses every keypress (by the current user) to train the model.
  - *Conservative Method.* Trains the touch model on the dataset extracted using the conservative inference method described previously.
  - *Word-level Method.* Trains the touch model on the dataset extracted using the word-level inference method described previously.
  - *Character-level Method.* Trains the touch model on the dataset extracted using the character-level inference method described previously.
  - *Gold Standard Method.* Trains a personalized model using gold standard (human annotated) intents.

Table 3 shows keystroke error rate for all runs and all users. As shown, the general method performs fairly well with an average error rate of 4.8%. Surprisingly, the device specific method does not significantly outperform the general method, suggesting that the differences between devices (for different users) may not be significant or systematic enough to effect error rate. However, it should be noted that this represents a small study of only two devices, so this result should be thought of only as a preliminary examination of between device differences. Furthermore, to truly examine the effect of device on typing behavior would require the study to control for user, which was not done here.

The conservative method performed significantly worse than all other personalized methods, included the unfiltered method. There are two factors that are likely to contribute to this result. The most significant factor is simply a lack of data. Because the conservative model only captures about 12% of the data, it only has a few hundred keypresses to examine given the current dataset, spread among all keys. This is likely to be too sparse to train accurate models. In order to see the true effect of the conservative method without data concerns would likely require data collection times of 5 to 10 hours per user, which is out of the scope of this study. The other factor that may have effected the conservative method is the distribution of points that it collects. Because it only retains points

	Aggregate Methods		Personalized Methods				
User	General	Device Specific	No Filtering	Conservative	Character-Level	Word-Level	Gold Standard
1	4.8%	5.1%	5.2%	10.4%	3.7%	3.8%	4.3%
2	4.8%	4.2%	4.7%	10.4%	3.9%	3.8%	3.6%
3	7.9%	7.7%	9.6%	12.6%	7.4%	7.1%	7.0%
4	2.2%	2.2%	2.7%	10.1%	2.0%	2.0%	2.3%
5	2.6%	2.4%	3.5%	9.7%	2.5%	2.0%	1.9%
6	5.1%	5.5%	6.7%	12.6%	6.2%	4.8%	4.6%
7	4.4%	4.5%	5.6%	11.1%	4.4%	4.6%	4.5%
8	5.7%	5.8%	6.5%	24.4%	6.3%	6.4%	6.2%
Average	4.8%	4.7%	5.6%	12.2%	4.5%	4.3%	4.3%

Table 3: Keystroke error rate for each user using touch models trained on data collected using a variety of methods.

involved in an error correction operation, it is likely to collect a dataset that suggests that the original system had a much higher error rate than it actually did, potentially skewing the data towards erroneous cases.

The character-level method outperformed the general model by a small but statistically significant (McNemar's test, $p < 0.01$) margin. The average error rate of the character-level model was an absolute 0.3% (relative 6.3%) lower than the general model. The word-level model performed best overall, with a average error rate of 4.3%. This represents a 0.5% reduction in absolute error rate in comparison to the general model, or a 10.4% relative reduction. Noteably, the word-level model performed just as well on average as the gold standard model, suggesting that it is possible to build models on automatically extracted training data that compare favorably to models trained in controlled settings.

DISCUSSION

Although the reduction in error rate as a result of personalization may seem small, it is in fact pretty significant. Because the character input rate of text entry is high, a small reduction in error rate can lead to significant performance improvements, and the differences in systems will quickly become apparent under heavy usage conditions. An early study of soft keyboard text entry [15] reported text entry rates of 28 words per minute for inexpert users on the QWERTY keyboard. At this rate, the 0.5% absolute difference between the error rates of the word-level and general models would mean that the general model makes one additional mistake for every 1.4 minutes of continuous input.

It should be noted that the error rates reported here for both general and personalized models are generally lower than those reported by other key-target resizing work, although the few studies that have given error rate measurements thus far have not been entirely consistent with one another. Gunawardana et al. report error rates between 8% and 12% on different test sets, but do not give individual user error rates. Rudchenko et al. [19] report error rates between 5%-21% from various users. Goodman et al. only report error rate ratios, not raw error rates.

We believe that there are several factors that may have led to these error rate discrepancies. Most notably, the differences in data collection methodology likely had a non-negligible effect. The static keyboard used in data collection for this study may have caused users to change their typing behavior to be more conservative, resulting in error rates that are lower than true error rates. Similarly, the permissive "perfect" key-target resizing methods used in previous work likely had the opposite effect, which may have lead to overestimated error rates. Additionally, allowing users to see when they have made a mistake and allowing error correction operations may have had an effect on overall accuracy, as users may more actively adjust to improve performance. However, despite the discrepancy in value, this work still validated the findings of previous work, in that general key-target resizing outperformed static key targets and personalized key-target resizing outperformed general models.

The word-level model was able to achieve performance on par to the gold standard model, while still retaining a high percentage of data during data collection. It may at first seem suprising that the word-level model can perform as well as, or for some users slightly better than, the gold standard model. It is important to note that the gold standard is only the reference upper bound for evaluating the accuracy of data collected by the three approaches. Since key-target resizing includes both the language model and the touch model, and the relative weights applied to balance the effects of these two models, the gold standard may not always lead to the best performance in key-target resizing.

Thankfully, the word-level method can be performed simply using information that is already available to the system. Since the system must interpret each key touch, it certainly has access to the stream of keypresses input by the user, which is sufficient to handle those cases involved in an error correction operation. It should also have a readily available internal dictionary, as this is necessary for other text entry aids offered by mobile devices, such as automatic word completion and spelling correction. With this information already at hand, a system should be able to perform the word-level data collection method with minimal overhead.

As mobile device text input is frequent, we feel that the high retention rate of the word-level method should be more than sufficient to make training online personalized models practical. However, it is as of yet unclear how long the data collec-

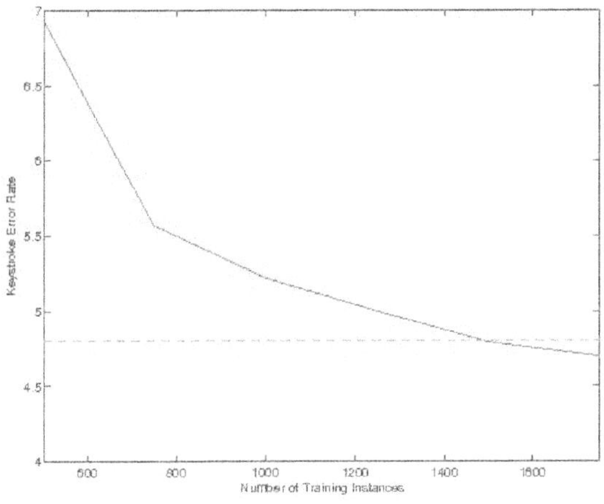

Figure 3: Average performance of personalized models trained on datasets of various sizes.

tion process must be carried out before accurate personalized models can be trained; no previous work has given concrete numbers about how much data is needed to train personalized models that outperform general models. To estimate this, we varied the amount of training instances available to the word-level model and examined error rate. Results are shown in Figure 3.

The dashed line in Figure 3 represents the average error rate of the general model. As shown, the results suggest that a surprisingly low amount of data is necessary to reach comparable performance. On average, about 1500 keypresses were necessary in order to meet the performance of the general model. The 81.2% average retention rate (recall) of the word-level collection method means that the user must type about 1850 characters for the system to capture enough data to build a model that performs at least on par with the general model.

Given this, we can use data from previous studies of mobile device usage to estimate how long data collection would take for an average user. A study of text message usage by Battestini et al. [3] suggests that the average text message is 50.9 characters in length and the average text message user sends about 7 text messages per day, for an average rate of around 356 characters per day from text messaging alone. This means that using the word-level method a system could get enough data to train a personalized model in 5.2 days of normal usage. We feel that this is a reasonable amount of overhead to incur to train a personalized model.

CONCLUSION

This paper examines the previously unexamined problem of online adaptation of key-target resizing touch models. In order to train touch models for key-target resizing algorithms, a system must have training data that associates the key that a user intends to hit with the touch point that they selected. Because the true intent of each keypress made by a user is unknown to the system in natural usage scenarios, some amount of inference must be applied to collect data online. This work introduced and analyzed three data collection methods that used varying degrees of inference to overcome this data collection hurtle.

To facilitate our experiments, we collected a dataset of unscripted mobile device chat conversations. Using this data, we examined the tradeoff between precision (accuracy) and recall (data retention rate) for each collection method. A conservative approach that only drew inference from user error correction operations was found to introduce less than 1% noise, but was only able to retain 12.3% of data input by the user. The two methods that made additional inference about keypresses not involved in error correction were able to capture over 80% of the data, while still keeping the overall amount of noise in the dataset to under 2%.

To examine the effect that each data collection procedure had on the final key-target resizing models, the training datasets extracted by each method were used to build personalized touch models, and the error rates of systems employing these touch models were compared. Our results suggest that a data collection methodology that makes inference based on vocabulary and error correction behavior is able to perform on par with gold standard personalized models, while reducing relative error rate by 10.4% over general models. This approach is simple, computationally inexpensive, and calculable via information that the system already has access to. Additionally, we show that these models can be built quickly, requiring about 5.2 days worth of text input by an average mobile device user.

Although in this work we present personalized touch models as an alternative to general models built on aggregate data, there may be some benefit to a combined approach. Most notably, because the distribution of character usage is not uniform, personalized models will be able to learn accurate touch models for some characters much faster than others. A hybrid approach that combined personalized and aggregate touch models may be able to improve overall performance and reduce the time it takes for a personalized model to show gains. We leave this interesting avenue of exploration to future work.

REFERENCES

1. Arif, A. S., and Stuerzlinger, W. Predicting the cost of error correction in character-based text entry technologies. In *Proceedings of the 28th international conference on Human factors in computing systems*, CHI '10, ACM (New York, NY, USA, 2010), 5–14.

2. Balakrishnan, R., and MacKenzie, I. S. Performance differences in the fingers, wrist, and forearm in computer input control. In *Proceedings of the SIGCHI conference on Human factors in computing systems*, CHI '97, ACM (New York, NY, USA, 1997), 303–310.

3. Battestini, A., Setlur, V., and Sohn, T. A large scale study of text-messaging use. In *Proceedings of the 12th international conference on Human computer interaction with mobile devices and services*,

MobileHCI '10, ACM (New York, NY, USA, 2010), 229–238.

4. Brewster, S., Chohan, F., and Brown, L. Tactile feedback for mobile interactions. In *Proceedings of the SIGCHI conference on Human factors in computing systems*, CHI '07, ACM (New York, NY, USA, 2007), 159–162.

5. Goodman, J. A bit of progress in language modeling. *Computer Speech and Language 15* (2001), 403–434.

6. Goodman, J., Venolia, G., Steury, K., and Parker, C. Language modeling for soft keyboards. In *Eighteenth national conference on Artificial intelligence*, American Association for Artificial Intelligence (Menlo Park, CA, USA, 2002), 419–424.

7. Gunawardana, A., Paek, T., and Meek, C. Usability guided key-target resizing for soft keyboards. In *Proceedings of the 15th international conference on Intelligent user interfaces*, IUI '10, ACM (New York, NY, USA, 2010), 111–118.

8. Himberg, J., Häkkilä, J., Kangas, P., and Mäntyjärvi, J. On-line personalization of a touch screen based keyboard. In *Proceedings of the 8th international conference on Intelligent user interfaces*, IUI '03, ACM (New York, NY, USA, 2003), 77–84.

9. Hirst, G., and Budanitsky, A. Correcting real-word spelling errors by restoring lexical cohesion. *Nat. Lang. Eng. 11* (March 2005), 87–111.

10. Hoggan, E., Brewster, S. A., and Johnston, J. Investigating the effectiveness of tactile feedback for mobile touchscreens. In *Proceeding of the twenty-sixth annual SIGCHI conference on Human factors in computing systems*, CHI '08, ACM (New York, NY, USA, 2008), 1573–1582.

11. Holz, C., and Baudisch, P. The generalized perceived input point model and how to double touch accuracy by extracting fingerprints. In *Proceedings of the 28th international conference on Human factors in computing systems*, CHI '10, ACM (New York, NY, USA, 2010), 581–590.

12. Holz, C., and Baudisch, P. Understanding touch. In *Proceedings of the 2011 annual conference on Human factors in computing systems*, CHI '11, ACM (New York, NY, USA, 2011), 2501–2510.

13. Kukich, K. Techniques for automatically correcting words in text. *ACM Comput. Surv. 24* (December 1992), 377–439.

14. MacKenzie, I. S., and Soukoreff, R. W. Phrase sets for evaluating text entry techniques. In *CHI '03 extended abstracts on Human factors in computing systems*, CHI EA '03, ACM (New York, NY, USA, 2003), 754–755.

15. MacKenzie, I. S., and Zhang, S. X. The design and evaluation of a high-performance soft keyboard. In *Proceedings of the SIGCHI conference on Human factors in computing systems: the CHI is the limit*, CHI '99, ACM (New York, NY, USA, 1999), 25–31.

16. Matias, E., MacKenzie, I. S., and Buxton, W. One-handed touch typing on a qwerty keyboard. *Human-Computer Interaction 11* (March 1996), 1–27.

17. Mays, E., Damerau, F. J., and Mercer, R. L. Context based spelling correction. *Inf. Process. Manage. 27* (September 1991), 517–522.

18. Paek, T., Chang, K., Almog, I., Badger, E., and Sengupta, T. A practical examination of multimodal feedback and guidance signals for mobile touchscreen keyboards. In *Proceedings of the 12th international conference on Human computer interaction with mobile devices and services*, MobileHCI '10, ACM (New York, NY, USA, 2010), 365–368.

19. Rudchenko, D., Paek, T., and Badger, E. Text text revolution: A game that improves text entry on mobile touchscreen keyboards. In *Proceedings of PERVASIVE* (2011).

20. Soukoreff, R. W., and MacKenzie, I. S. Metrics for text entry research: an evaluation of msd and kspc, and a new unified error metric. In *Proceedings of the SIGCHI conference on Human factors in computing systems*, CHI '03, ACM (New York, NY, USA, 2003), 113–120.

21. Vogel, D., and Baudisch, P. Shift: a technique for operating pen-based interfaces using touch. In *Proceedings of the SIGCHI conference on Human factors in computing systems*, CHI '07, ACM (New York, NY, USA, 2007), 657–666.

22. Wobbrock, J. O., and Myers, B. A. Analyzing the input stream for character- level errors in unconstrained text entry evaluations. *ACM Trans. Comput.-Hum. Interact. 13* (December 2006), 458–489.

Multimodal Interaction Patterns in Mobile Local Search

Patrick Ehlen
AT&T
San Francisco, CA, USA
patrick.ehlen@att.com

Michael Johnston
AT&T Labs Research
Florham Park, NJ, USA
johnston@research.att.com

ABSTRACT

Speak4it™ is a mobile search application that leverages multimodal input and integration to allow users to search for and act on local business information. We present an initial empirical analysis of user interaction with a multimodal local search application deployed in the field with real users. Specifically, we focus on queries involving multimodal commands, and analyze multimodal interaction behaviors seen in a deployed multimodal system.

Author Keywords

Multimodal, Speech, Gesture, Location-based, Search.

ACM Classification Keywords

H.5.2. [Information Interfaces And Presentation]: User Interfaces - Input devices and strategies (e.g., mouse, touchscreen);

General Terms

Algorithms, Design.

INTRODUCTION

Local search has often been used as a test bed application for assessing multimodal interface techniques and processing models. The MATCH system [8] enabled users to interact using speech and digital pen input to search for restaurants and other businesses in several major U.S. cities. Multimodal local search and navigation was one of the key domains for the SmartKom Mobile prototype [13], and the City Browser in-car prototype [5]. The AdApt system provided a multimodal interface for searching for apartments in Stockholm [6]. Oviatt demonstrated that a multimodal real estate search task led to higher task performance and user preference for multimodal over unimodal interfaces on a dynamic map [9]. And QuickSet [3] used a related task of laying down features on a map.

Thanks to a number of technical advances—including the capabilities of mobile computing devices such as smartphones and tablets, availability of high-speed mobile networks, and availability of speech and language processing capabilities in the cloud—it is now possible to give people true multimodal interaction for daily use. To our knowledge, Speak4it is the first commercially deployed mobile local search application to support true multimodal interaction where users can issue commands that integrate simultaneous inputs from speech and gesture (Fig. 1).

Figure 1. Speak4it

As a multimodal interaction platform in the wild, Speak4it provides us with an opportunity to revisit observations from earlier systems, many of which never left the prototype phase—or even the laboratory—and were evaluated using paid test subjects. We may ask whether findings of early prototypes hold true in a deployed multimodal handheld system used in people's daily lives. For example, evaluation of the MATCH system [1] found that 26% of commands were multimodal, 59% were speech-only, and 15% were pen-only, roughly parallel with results in Oviatt's study [9] where 19.2% were multimodal in a map-based task. But does this finding extend to a similar multimodal local search application deployed in the field, where users have genuine intentions and information needs rather than carrying out scripted scenarios in a lab?

Some other questions addressed by prior studies of multimodal prototype systems include: How does language use differ when people use unimodal voice input versus multimodal input? Does one method foster a style of speech that is more compact or less syntactically complex? Do paralinguistic behaviors like disfluencies or sentence planning restarts differ in frequency for multimodal input versus voice-only? Does allowing spatial gesture input in conjunction with speech reduce the number of spatial clauses people include in their spoken search queries?

We first present the Speak4it application and describe its capabilities. We then present some quantitative and qualitative empirical results from examination of Speak4it logs and analyze multimodal user interaction in this deployed multimodal system.

MULTIMODAL INTERACTION

Speak4it allows people to search for businesses in the U.S. by using traditional text search queries, querying by voice (unimodal), or querying by voice while gesturing with a finger on a map (multimodal). On launching the app, users see a map of their local area, and click a "Speak/Draw" button to initiate a multimodal query. They can search for businesses based on the name of the business, category, or associated keywords. For example, if a user presses the 'Speak/Draw' button and says, "coffee shops," the system will display nearby coffee shops. Users can explicitly state a location, as with, "real estate attorneys in Denver," or "Starbucks near the Metropolitan Museum." They can pan and zoom the map view using drag and pinch gestures, or use spoken commands to navigate, such as saying "San Francisco" to display that city.

The system also supports multimodal commands where the location is specified by drawing on the map [1, 3, 5, 6, 13]. Users can make point, area, and line gestures (Fig. 2). For example, the user can say, "French restaurants here" in conjunction with a point or area gesture. For a point gesture, the system returns the French restaurants closest to the point. For an area gesture, results within the area are returned. Users can also search for businesses along a specific route by drawing a line gesture—perhaps saying "gas stations" while drawing a path (Fig. 2, Right)—and the system will return gas stations closest to that gesture.

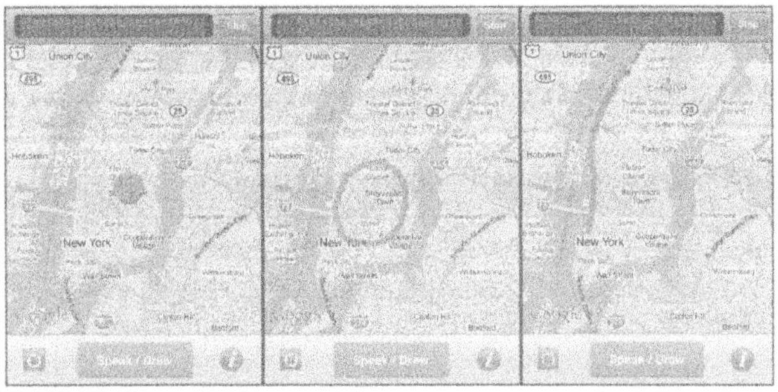

Figure 2. Speak4it gesture inputs

As a cloud-based multimodal speech system, Speak4it integrates simultaneous collection and processing of multiple streams of input data, and delivers those streams to a server that combines behaviors from different types of user signals into a single semantic interpretation (see [4] for more technical details). While voice-controlled local search exists in other smartphone applications, this method of providing simultaneous multimodal search input is unique to Speak4it, so people are not accustomed to this mode of interaction. Because it was added to Speak4it with a release update, users needed to be educated about the multimodal feature and how to use it. We provided this education in three places: (1) text on the update description that informed users of the new input method; (2) a video and text on the website demonstrating the capability; and (3) a "tip" box that popped up in the application that described the input method with an example.

Though Speak4it was designed for widespread use among ordinary smartphone users, it was also designed as a research application to gather data on real-life multimodal interaction, run experiments on aspects of the interface, and log data relevant to performance and user interactions. Server-side data related to speech, gesture, and multimodal integration are logged, as are user actions on the client. Spoken queries are transcribed from audio and annotated by a team of professional transcribers.

MULTIMODAL BEHAVIORS

With the ability to gather data on multimodal user interaction from real people using Speak4it in the wild, we wanted to revisit some observations made by earlier experimental multimodal systems to see if users' behaviors in our deployed system followed similar patterns. In particular, we wanted to assess whether users' speech behaviors might differ between unimodal (speech-only) and multimodal (speech+gesture) interactions. To do so, we extracted query data at random from Speak4it logs, omitting queries from devices known to belong to researchers on our team, resulting in 27,211 queries as a sample for analysis. We divided these data into two sets: unimodal speech queries, where users only spoke but did not provide touch input, such as "coffee shops on Market Street in San Francisco"; and multimodal queries, where users spoke a query and also made some sort of touch gesture on the map, such as "Mexican restaurants around here" combined with tracing an area on the map. Speak4it also accepts keyboard text input, but those queries were excluded here. Descriptive statistics of these two data sets are summarized in tables 1 and 2. We used Welch's t-test to assess the significance of differences in means between two groups of unequal sizes and variances in all mean comparisons. We'll report our findings, and then offer a discussion and interpretations of the data.

	Unimodal Qs	Multimodal Qs
Mode Frequency	96.94 %	3.06 %
Spatial Referents	21.24	10.58
Deictic Referents	0.87	20.79
"Me" References	0.93	0.84

Table 1. Comparison of unimodal and multimodal query frequency percentages

Mode Frequency. A first question to ask about a multimodal system is, if multimodal input capability exists, will people use it? When users were asked whether they would prefer to use multimodal input on one map-based interactive system, 95% responded that they would [10]. But in that same system, only 19.2% of user speech was expressed multimodally, most of which related to spatial location commands.

In our sample of Speak4it data, we found even fewer instances of multimodal interactions with the map, with people using multimodal queries only slightly more than 3% of the time. Within these multimodal queries, 36.51% used point gestures, 62.01% used area gestures, and 1.48% used line gestures.

Spatial Referents. Gesture is a felicitous way to convey spatial information. When that information can be conveyed by gesture rather than speech, we might expect to see fewer spatial references in multimodal queries. In the Speak4it data, we found spatial references in 21.24% of unimodal queries, in line with results from prior analyses [4]. But only 10.58% of multimodal queries contained spatial references, indicating that gesture was being used to replace spatial references. Still, for one in ten multimodal queries users appeared to provide redundant or supplemental spatial information to speech, for example saying "Kotobuki Sushi Laguna Hills" while using an area gesture to delimit a more specific area within Laguna Hills. While deictic references like "here" were present in only 0.87% of unimodal queries, people used deictic references in 20.79% of multimodal queries. And references to "me" (as in, "Walgreens near me") were rare in both unimodal and multimodal queries, at 0.93% and 0.84%, respectively.

Utterance Length and Complexity. Several studies have observed that people who are allowed to interact multimodally form utterances that are both shorter and less complex than similar content expressed by voice alone, both in human-human [2] and in human-computer [11] interactions. Search queries tend to be short in general, but we compared the difference in sample means for words per query in utterances of each input type. We found no statistical difference between unimodal [2.67 words] and multimodal [2.69 words] queries (p = 0.386). And while many metrics have been devised to assess utterance or sentence complexity, most correlate well enough with simple word count that it can be used as a proxy metric [12]. By that metric, we may also infer no difference in utterance complexity between unimodal and multimodal.

	Unimodal	Multimodal	p
Utterance Length	2.6733	2.6887	*n.s.*
Fillers	0.0025	0.0024	*n.s.*
Restarts	0.0456	0.0228	< 0.001

Table 2. Comparison of unimodal and multimodal query behaviors

Fillers and Restarts. Users who must plan more complex utterances may utter more disfluencies, such as using filler words like "um," "ah" or "er," and to exhibit utterance planning-related errors in the form of false starts or stuttered repeats. From counts of these in the transcriptions, we found the mean number of filler words per query to be small, with no difference between unimodal (0.0025) and multimodal (0.0024) (p=0.488). However, the number of false starts and repeats were higher for unimodal (0.0456) compared to multimodal (0.0228) ($p < 0.001$).

DISCUSSION

Now we offer a brief discussion of a couple observations that differed from expectation. Specifically, we'll discuss the low frequency of multimodal interactions, and the lack of difference in utterance length and complexity between unimodal and multimodal queries.

Mode Frequency. Oviatt [10] states, "just because users prefer to interact multimodally is no guarantee that they will issue every command to a system multimodally." Our observation that users only query multimodally 3% of the time certainly supports that claim. But why such a low number of multimodal interactions? One explanation may be that our efforts at alerting and educating users about the multimodal functionality were insufficient. Tests of earlier multimodal prototypes were often preceded by a tutorial or at least an informal demonstration by experimenters. MATCH used a dynamic help routine that showed users how multimodal queries could be issued [7]. One could speculate that smartphone users are busy people who are not likely to read the text that describes updates to applications, do not visit websites for those applications and view videos about how to use them, and dismiss "tip" boxes as soon as they appear, instead preferring to use the application in whatever way comes naturally. While we believe multimodal interaction is in fact very natural, in this case its usage paradigm may not be clear to people.

Another explanation for the low multimodal use rate is that our implementation of multimodal interaction could be flawed in a way that causes it to be unnatural or inconvenient for people to use. For one, our multimodal interaction paradigm conflicts with the existing paradigm that users have become accustomed to in their interactions with maps on smartphones: gestures on the map are meant to manipulate and navigate the map, not refer to it. We attempt to allow the multimodal paradigm to work side-by-side with the existing paradigm by providing the existing gesture-for-navigation paradigm when people are not speaking, and switching to a gesture-as-reference paradigm only when users press the "Speak/Draw" button. This overlays a transparent grid on the map to draw on. But maybe the existing interaction paradigm is just too strong to override, or users may simply consider this method of multimodal input too inconvenient, as it requires two hands (one to hold the phone and one to draw).

A final explanation is that multimodal input may not be suited for the domain of local business search on a smartphone. Users know their smartphones are equipped with GPS devices, and they usually look for businesses near their current location. So providing spatial information with gestures on a map may not be a convenient feature. Even in the case of unimodal voice search, we find people specifying locations in their queries only 20% of the time. The other 80% of the time they expect the location to be determined either by GPS or by the current view of the map [4]. So we might interpret this 20% as an upper bound of the percentage of queries where users feel they need to specify a location at all, whether by voice or gesture. The multimodal 3% of all queries could be viewed as 15% of queries where users even feel the need to specify a location, bringing it closer to the 19.2% seen in Oviatt's study [10].

Utterance Length and Complexity. While other studies of multimodal interaction report a decrease in utterance length and complexity for multimodal interactions, in this case we see no difference in utterance length between unimodal and multimodal utterances, and infer no difference in complexity when measured by word count. One explanation for the difference in this case is that local search query language may already differ from ordinary speech in a way that is very similar to the way people speak when they interact multimodally. Oviatt [11] observed that language in unimodal and multimodal interactions differ in a particular way: Unimodal queries were often issued as fully-formed utterances, such as, "Add an open space on the north lake to b—include the north lake part of the road and north," while multimodal queries tended toward *telegraphic speech*, such as, "Open space." But 13 years on, users may now be very practiced in using this type of telegraphic speech for search queries, and the majority of unimodal queries also use this same type of speech. And again, the fact that spatial information is often inferred from other factors may play a role here. The lack of complexity in utterance planning would also account for the failure to see any difference in disfluency behaviors between the two modes.

CONCLUSION

We sought to revisit observations on multimodal interaction from studies of prototype systems, and asked whether some of those observations persist for users interacting with a multimodal local search system in their everyday lives. Many observations remain true in a deployed local search system: People interacting multimodally use fewer spatial referents and more deictic referents than they do when querying with unimodal speech. But a couple findings differ from prior studies: Multimodal queries in our system did not exhibit much evidence for the advantages of verbal economy and reduced planning effort observed before. We also report low adoption of a multimodal map interaction paradigm on a smartphone, and discussed some reasons why that may be for this particular application.

Where do we go from here? First we will conduct a more in-depth analysis of the inertia that works against multimodal adoption in this application, and determine whether our adoption rate is due to lack of understanding or poor design choices. Implementing an online dynamic help system that demonstrates multimodal interaction, as used in MATCH [7], might be a good first step. Another step is to survey existing users or conduct a usability study to highlight issues with interaction as it was designed here. Another task may be simply to wait and see whether these observations change over time, as more data may yet tell a different story.

ACKNOWLEDGMENTS

Thanks to Jay Lieske, Brant Vasilieff, Diamantino Caseiro, Junlan Feng, Clarke Retzer, Srinivas Bangalore, Claude Noshpitz, Barbara Hollister, Remi Zajac, Mazin Gilbert, Barbara Hollister, and Linda Roberts, and anonymous reviewers for their comments.

REFERENCES

1. Bangalore, S. and Johnston, M. Robust understanding in multimodal interfaces. *Computational Linguistics 35*, 3 (2009), 345-397.
2. Clark, H. H. & Krych, M. A. Speaking while monitoring addressees for understanding. *Journal of Memory and Language, 50*, 1 (2004), 62-81.
3. Cohen, P. R., Johnston, M., McGee, D., Oviatt, S.L., Pittman, J., Smith, I., Chen, L., and Clow, J. Multimodal interaction for distributed interactive simulation. In M. Maybury and W. Wahlster (eds.) *Readings in Intelligent Interfaces*. Morgan Kaufmann Publishers, San Francisco, CA, 1998, 562-571.
4. Ehlen, P. and Johnston, M., Location Grounding in Multimodal Local Search. *Proc. of ICMI-MLMI, 2010.*
5. Gruenstein, A., Orszulak, J., Liu, S., Roberts, S., Zabel, J., Reimer, B., Mehler, B., Seneff, S., Glass, J., and Coughlin, J. City Browser: Developing a conversational automotive HMI. In *Proc. CHI 2009.*
6. Gustafson J., Bell, L., Beskow, J., Boye, J., Carlson, R., Edlund, J., Granström, B., House D., and Wirén, M. AdApt—A multimodal conversational dialogue system in an apartment domain. In *Proc. ICSLP 2000.*
7. Hastie, H.W., Johnston, M. and Ehlen, P. 2002. Context-sensitive help for multimodal dialogue, *Proc. ICMI'02.*
8. Johnston, M., Bangalore, S. Vasireddy, G., Stent, A., Ehlen, P., Walker, M., Whittaker, S., Maloor, P. MATCH: An architecture for multimodal dialogue systems. In *Proc. ACL 2002*, 376-383.
9. Oviatt, S.L. Multimodal interactive maps: Designing for human performance. *Human Computer Interaction, 12* (1997), 93-129.
10. Oviatt, S.L. Ten myths of multimodal interaction. *Communications of the ACM, 42*, 11 (1999), 74-81.
11. Oviatt, S.L., DeAngeli, A., and Kuh, K. Integration and synchronization of input modes during multimodal human-computer interaction. In *Proc. of CHI 1997.*
12. Szmrecsányi , B.M. On operationalizing syntactic complexity. *7es Journées internationales d'Analyse statistique des Données Textuelles*, 2004, 1031-1038.
13. Wahlster, W. *SmartKom: Foundations of Multimodal Dialogue Systems*. Springer-Verlag, New York, 2006.

In-Vehicle Driver Recognition Based on Hands ECG Signals

Hugo Silva
IT/IST-UTL
Av. Rovisco Pais 1
1049-001 Lisbon, Portugal
hsilva@lx.it.pt

André Lourenço
DEETC/ISEL-IPL
R. Cons. Emidio Navarro 1,
1959-007 Lisbon, Portugal
alourenco@deetc.isel.ipl.pt

Ana Fred
IT/IST-UTL
Av. Rovisco Pais 1
1049-001 Lisbon, Portugal
afred@lx.it.pt

ABSTRACT
We present a system for in-vehicle driver recognition based on biometric information extracted from electrocardiographic (ECG) signals collected at the hands. We recur to non-intrusive techniques, that are easy to integrate into components with which the driver naturally interacts with, such as the steering wheel. This system is applicable to the automatic customization of vehicle settings according to the perceived driver, being also prone to expand the security features of the vehicle through the detection of hands-off steering wheel events in a continuous or near-continuous manner. We have performed randomized tests for performance evaluation of the system, in a subject identification scenario, using closed sets of up to 5 subjects, showing promising results for the intended application.

Author Keywords
User Identification, Biometrics, Customization, Vehicles, ECG.

ACM Classification Keywords
H.3.4 User Profiles and Alert Services; H.5.2 Information Interfaces and Presentation (e.g. HCI); K.6.5 Security and Protection

General Terms
Measurement, Algorithms, Security, Experimentation.

INTRODUCTION
Current automotive technologies go far beyond the mechanical aspects, to which the sector is historically bounded to. From automated diagnosis, to interaction with the vehicle, nowadays it is frequent to find advanced electronic systems even in the most affordable models, assuring a variety of functions. Within this evolution, an important focus has been given to the in-vehicle experience, which includes, among others, customization of settings such as mirror, seat, and steering column position, and driving safety improvement using user profile dependent information [1, 4, 8]. Determining the identity of the driver is a major building block in this process, and the search for novel, non-intrusive ways of obtaining that information has been a widely studied topic by both academia and industry.

In this paper, we propose a method and system that enables the identification of the driver, using information extracted from electrocardiographic (ECG) signals collected between both hands. Our approach uses a custom sensing apparatus, which allows data acquisition through non-intrusive techniques, while being easy to integrate in the vehicle. The hardware was especially designed to be fitted to the steering wheel, however it can also be integrated into other components with which the driver naturally interacts with. We compare different ECG representations, focusing real time applications, together with a simple classification method, to determine the identity of the driver, and evaluate them on real world data.

We have performed cross-validation randomized tests for performance evaluation of the system, in subject identification using limited size groups of subjects, with promising results for the intended application. The rest of the paper is organized as follows: we present an overview of the current state-of-the-art in the field; then describe the proposed approach; afterwords we summarize the experimental results; and finally we outline the main findings and conclusions.

STATE-OF-THE-ART
Driver identification is amongst the research challenges in the smart vehicles research arena. Current approaches still rely on traditional biometric techniques, such as interaction with the vehicle, fingerprint, speech recognition, video, and/or a combination of the previous. A comprehensive overview of the state-of-the art in the field can be found in a feature article by [3] and references therein, where the authors provide an extensive motivation to the problem and describe the existing solutions. Initial work focused on behavioral patterns extracted from the interactions between the subject and the vehicle to determine the identity. Biometric approaches have started to be looked into, more recently, and are mainly based on standard modalities, such as voice, fingerprint, iris, and face recognition, with the corresponding readers integrated into several components of the vehicle.

In the overall, approaches proposed so far exhibit either latency or user interface limitations. Behavioral interaction techniques are interesting, as they use information available from the natural interaction between the driver and the standard controls of the vehicle. These also require the subject to actually use the vehicle for a period of time (e.g. techniques based on pedal pressure and steering wheel information), therefore introducing a recognition latency. Fingerprint requires a good contact between the finger and the reader; camera based systems require proximity between the user and the sensor, and are greatly dependent on environmental factors such as luminosity; speech recognition techniques require the user to vocalize expressions to the car. Our work is focused on ECG signals, which are permanently available, and can be captured using non-intrusive acquisition interfaces.

PROPOSED APPROACH

We propose a system capable of complementing the current driver recognition systems landscape, using information extracted from ECG signals collected from sensors integrated in the steering wheel. Figure 1 depicts the architecture of the proposed system, which allows the recognition of multiple drivers; the use of the system comprises two stages: enrollment and identification.

In a first interaction with the vehicle, an enrollment stage is required where the user adjusts his/her presets, and registers them in the vehicle's memory (DB), together with the representative ECG templates. In subsequent uses of the system, the users only need to identify themselves by holding the steering wheel, so that the system can collect the ECG, check it against the templates stored in the database, and determine the identity of the user; if the user is legitimately accepted, a control signal is issued to the vehicle's Human Machine Interface (HMI) and from there propagated to the corresponding subsystems.

The sensor has a differential operating principle, with a virtual ground, enabling the use of only two contact leads, which has proven to perform adequately for raw signal acquisition and simplifies the setup when compared to standard 3 or more lead-setup [11]. The chosen leads provide extended usability, can be either dry Ag/AgCl electrodes or electrolycras. The signal conditioning circuitry only enables the ECG acquisition when the subject has each hand in contact with one of the acquisition leads; it includes a pre-amplifier with total gain of 1000, and an analog band pass filtering between the 1-30Hz bandwidth. Data acquisition and processing is performed through the vehicle's HMI.

Besides the acquisition simplicity, the processing requirements are extremely lightweight, further enhancing the positive aspects of our system. Our proposal is targeted at the transmission of a control signal to the vehicle, with the purpose of enabling automatic customization of settings such as driving post adjustments (e.g. seat and mirrors), infotainment system presets, or even limiting the use of the vehicle (e.g. maximum acceleration and speed), according to the perceived driver. Our system is also prone to further enhance the security features, as it is based on a vital sign. Due to the proposed acquisition method, it can provide insight on aspects such as hands off the steering wheel. Furthermore, if combined with ECG analysis algorithms, it can also be used for the detection of medical events.

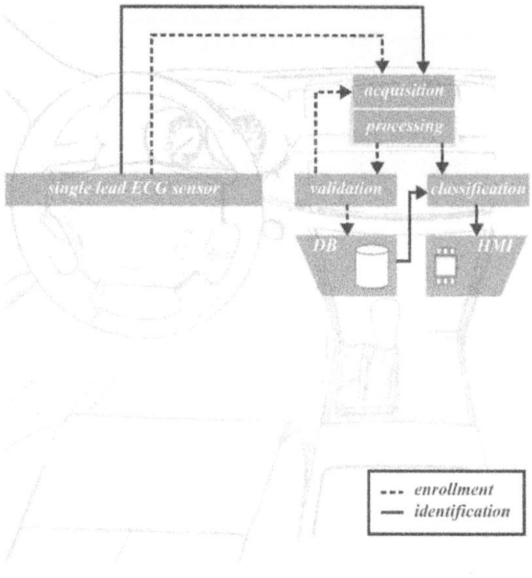

Figure 1. Overall architecture of the proposed system depicting the user enrollment authentication sequences.

METHODOLOGY

Several authors have shown the potential of ECG signals as a biometric trait [6, 10, 9]. A key element in most approaches is the discriminative content of the cardiac cycles, which are comprised by a set of notable moments, known as P-QRS-T complexes (Figure 2 (a)). These are typically detected taking the R-spike as a reference, given that it is expressed as a high-amplitude peak with a low-latency inflection, thus being easily recognizable. Figure 2 depicts ECG signals collected from four different subjects; (a) and (c) show the full heartbeat cycle collected with dry Ag/AgCl electrodes, while (b) and (d), only show the RS-T portion for data collected with electrolycras. We can observe that both electrode materials provide a similar signal detail level; furthermore the RS-T portions of all the signals exhibit noticeable differences among subjects.

Our work targets real-time applications. Instead of using the full P-QRS-T, we introduce a novel approach based on the RS-T segment enabling the implementation of single-beat dependent, being more efficient both on the temporal and spatial domains. Our R-peak detection block is based on the algorithm by [2], and the heartbeat waveforms segmented from the raw signals are taken as representative templates of the driver's ECG. For identification, we use a 1–NN classifier, in which the class label w_{x_u} assigned to an unknown sample x_u, is assumed to be the class w_{x_i} of the training sample x_i, that is more similar to x_u. We chose the Euclidean distance as similarity metric, and a distance matrix describing similarity between training and test set samples was computed. A rejection band can be used to discard impostors.

Tests were performed on signals collected at the hands and finger level using dry Ag/AgCl electrodes and electrolycras as interface with the skin. Figure 3(a) shows the experimental apparatus; dry Ag/AgCl electrodes were placed at the thenar eminence, and electrolycra strips were placed at the index and middle finger. This setting was devised to be similar, in terms

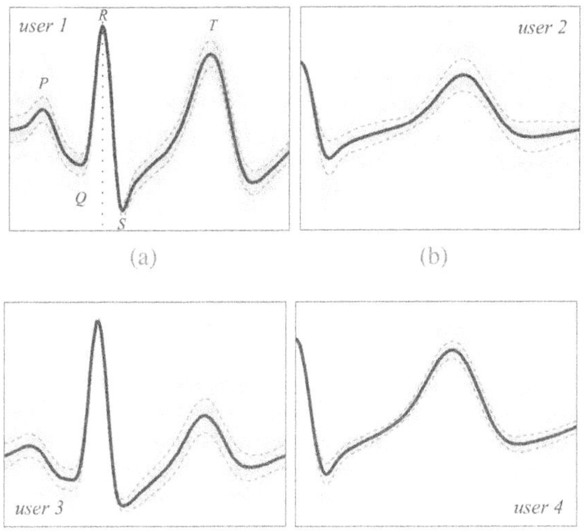

(a) (b) (c) (d)

Figure 2. Normalized ECG waveforms obtained at the hand palms and fingers using dry Ag/AgCl electrodes and electrolycras for 4 different subjects. The solid black lines represent the average of several segmented heartbeats (depicted in gray lines), while the dashed lines represent standard deviation. On the left, P-QRST-T segments are shown, while on the right only RS-T segments are presented. (a) ECG waveform of one subject with the P-QRS-T complexes annotated; (b)-(d) P-QRS-T and RS-T representations for three other subjects.

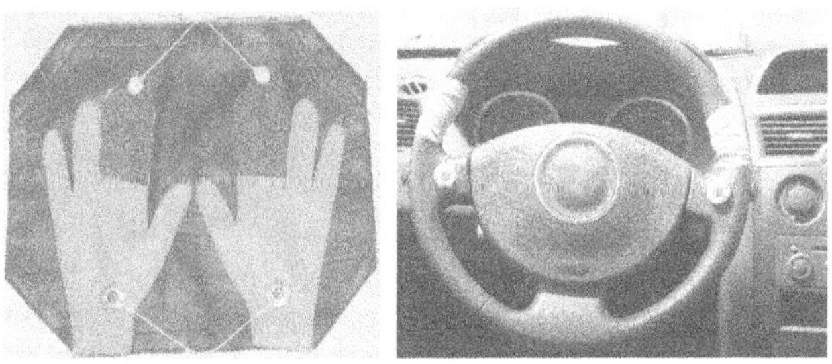

(a) (b)

Figure 3. Experimental setup for data acquisition (left), and prototype steering wheel setup fitted with ECG sensors (right).

of anatomical locations, to the regular grasp of the steering wheel; Figure 3(b) depicts a prototyped setup, where the electrodes are fitted to a car setting. In a real-world deployment, the sensors can either be integrated directly in the steering wheel, or fitted to a cover that is applied over it.

Given the context of the vehicle, with which only a limited set of drivers interact, we chose to perform the experimental evaluation on limited sets of users; from all the users involved in the study, random combinations were evaluated, ranging the number of users in each subset between 2-5. We evaluated the performance in a user identification scenario, using both the full P-QRS-T segment, and also the novel proposal based only on the RS-T segment. For each user subset size, 30 groupings were randomly selected, and for each grouping 30 runs were performed for different variations of the training and test data. In each run, the available database is randomly divided into two exclusive sets: a training set with 30% of the patterns, and a test set with the remaining 70% of the patterns.

Table 1. Performance Evaluation in terms identification error based on mean and standard deviation over cross-validation runs.

Users	Ag/AgCl		Electrolycra	
	P-QRS-T	RS-T	P-QRS-T	RS-T
2	$1.66\% \pm 2.28$	$2.40\% \pm 3.96$	$5.61\% \pm 6.38$	$6.80\% \pm 6.31$
3	$3.29\% \pm 4.06$	$4.74\% \pm 5.49$	$7.15\% \pm 5.71$	$10.55\% \pm 8.13$
4	$5.37\% \pm 5.09$	$7.14\% \pm 5.65$	$13.05\% \pm 7.25$	$16.10\% \pm 8.01$
5	$7.26\% \pm 4.02$	$10.44\% \pm 4.65$	$12.03\% \pm 5.89$	$16.29\% \pm 7.18$

RESULTS

A total of 32 healthy volunteers (25 males and 7 females), with an average age of 31.1 ± 9.46 years participated in the experiment, where they were asked to rest their hands as indicated on the device. Data was acquired during a period of approximately 1m30s, using a bioPLUX research [7] acquisition system. The files with raw ECG data were pre-processed in order to create a database with all the heartbeat waveforms; the database size was limited by the lowest amount of heartbeat waveforms for all users, in order to guarantee a balanced number of samples among users. Table 1 outlines the experimental evaluation in terms of mean identification error and standard deviation over each user subset size and using the 30 runs. Each row corresponds to a different user subset size, which ranges between 2 and 5 users; columns present the results for the whole P-QRS-T segment and for the proposed RS-T segment based approach, grouped by the type of electrodes used (Ag/AgCl, electrolycras). Figure 4 presents a graphical representation of the results; dark solid lines represent the RS-T segments based approach, while gray dashed lines represent the P-QRS-T approach. Electrolycras are distinguished from the dry Ag/AgCl electrodes by square and round markers, respectively. Superimposed error bars illustrate the standard deviation across the runs.

Results show that the dry Ag/AgCl electrodes outperform electrolycras in the application scenario addressed by our work, nonetheless the later still provide admissible results for subsets of 2 users. In the overall, the cases where the full heartbeat waveform with the P QRS-T complexes is used, exhibited the best performance; however the mean results for the RS-T segment based approach, are within the confidence intervals of the P-QRS-T approach, and present acceptable deviations. Using dry Ag/AgCl signals, for the subsets of 2 users a 0.74% deviation among them was found, while for the subsets of 5 users it reached 3.18%. These results are within the confidence intervals of what is reported in the ECG biometric literature, for chest and finger signals, which for identification results are in the order of $\sim [5-10]\%$ respectively [6, 10, 9, 5]. As shown in Table 2, our method shows results above average when compared to the results reported in literature for driver recognition, with the advantage that ECG signals are more easily collectable in a continuous manner. Due to the operating principle of the sensors and to the fact that it is a widely used signal for clinical diagnostics, this system enables other in-vehicle applications such as security enhancement via the detection of hands-off the steering wheel events and cardiac assessment.

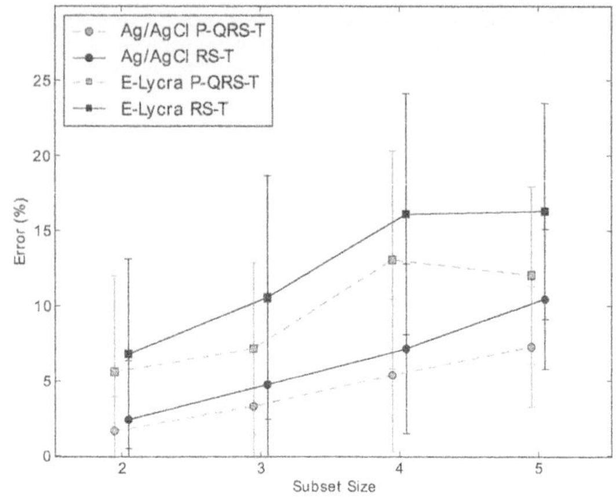

Figure 4. Identification error for the different variations of the acquisition method and the heartbeat waveform segment used for classification.

Table 2. Identification accuracy for other approaches.

Method	ECG V_2	ECG Fingers	Speech	Driver Behavior
Error	$\sim 3\%$	$\sim 5\%$	$\sim 3\%$	$\sim 30\%$

CONCLUSION

Smart vehicles tend to increasingly integrate high levels of automation and technologies, and part of the research has focused on driver recognition using non-intrusive techniques. Our work introduces a new modality to the in-vehicle driver recognition landscape, which is based on ECG signals collected at the driver's hands or fingers, through sensors integrated on the steering wheel.

The envisioned application scenario is the automated customization of vehicle settings according to the perceived driver, although the system also enables other applications. The proposed approach comprises the signal acquisition, pre-processing, and classification blocks, with the purpose of identifying a subject within a limited group of enrolled users. Given that a common daily use vehicle has a limited set of subjects that operate it, experimental results have focused on the performance evaluation in the identification considering groups containing between 2-5 users. We have evaluated the accuracy considering the full P-QRST-T complexes from the heartbeat waveform, but we also introduced a novel test based only on the RS-T segment.

Experimental evaluation were performed on real-world data collected both with dry Ag/AgCl electrodes and electrolycras, and results revealed that the P-QRS-T provides lower classification error due to the additional discriminative content; in the best case a $1.66\% \pm 2.28$ classification error was achieved for groups of 2 users. Nonetheless, with a marginal decrease in performance, the RS-T segment based approach is able to provide an adequate compromise solution, given that it has a lower temporal and spacial complexity; for groups of 2 users, this approach has revealed an error of $2.40\% \pm 3.96$. In the overall, tests have shown promising results for the proposed approach, exhibiting accuracy levels above the average found in state-of-the-art literature in the area of driver recognition for soft biometric modalities. Future work will focus on further validation of the system and testing the feasibility in other application topics such as in-vehicle security and health parameters monitoring.

ACKNOWLEDGMENTS

This work was partially funded by grants SFRH/BD/65248/2009 and SFRH /PROTEC/49512/ 2009 from Fundação para a Ciência e Tecnologia (FCT), by the National Strategic Reference Framework (NSRF-QREN) under contract #3475, and by the DEETC/ ISEL, whose support the authors gratefully acknowledge.

REFERENCES

1. BMW. Electronic seat adjustment with memory function. http://www.bmw.com/com/en/insights/technology/technology_guide/articles/seat_memory_function.html.
2. Engelse, W. A. H., and Zeelenberg, C. A single scan algorithm for QRS-detection and feature extraction. *Computers in Cardiology 6* (1979), 37–42.
3. Erzin, E., Yemez, Y., Tekalp, A. M., Ercil, A., Erdogan, H., and Abut, H. Multimodal person recognition for human-vehicle interaction. *IEEE Multimedia 13*, 2 (2006), 18–31.
4. Ford Motor Company. MyKey technology overview. http://media.ford.com/pdf/081006_MyKeyFinal.pdf.
5. Israel, S., Irvine, J., Cheng, A., Wiederhold, M., and Wiederhold, B. ECG to identify individuals. *Pattern Recognition 38*, 1 (2005), 133–142.
6. Lourenço, A., Silva, H., and Fred, A. Unveiling the biometric potential of Finger-Based ECG signals. *Computational Intelligence and Neuroscience* (2011).
7. PLUX. http://www.plux.info/biopluxresearch, 2011.
8. Rydstrom, A., Brostrom, R., and Bengtsson, P. Can haptics facilitate interaction with an in-vehicle multifunctional interface? *IEEE Transactions on Haptics 2*, 3 (July 2009), 141–147.
9. Shen, T. *Biometric Identity Verification Based on Electrocardiogram*. PhD thesis, University of Wisconsin, 2005.
10. Silva, H., Gamboa, H., and Fred, A. Applicability of lead v_2 ECG measurements in biometrics. In *Med-e-Tel Proc.* (2007).
11. Silva, H., Lourenço, A., Lourenço, R., Leite, P., Coutinho, D., and Fred, A. Study and evaluation of a single differential sensor design based on electro-textile electrodes for ECG biometrics applications. In *Proc. of the IEEE Sensors Conf.* (2011).

Performance Comparisons of Phrase Sets and Presentation Styles for Text Entry Evaluations

Per Ola Kristensson
School of Computer Science
University of St Andrews
St Andrews, Fife, United Kingdom
pok@st-andrews.ac.uk

Keith Vertanen
Department of Computer Science
Montana Tech of the University of Montana
Butte, Montana, USA
kvertanen@mtech.edu

ABSTRACT
We empirically compare five different publicly-available phrase sets in two large-scale ($N = 225$ and $N = 150$) crowdsourced text entry experiments. We also investigate the impact of asking participants to memorize phrases before writing them versus allowing participants to see the phrase during text entry. We find that asking participants to memorize phrases increases entry rates at the cost of slightly increased error rates. This holds for both a familiar and for an unfamiliar text entry method. We find statistically significant differences between some of the phrase sets in terms of both entry and error rates. Based on our data, we arrive at a set of recommendations for choosing suitable phrase sets for text entry evaluations.

Author Keywords
Text entry, phrase sets, crowdsourcing, keyboards

ACM Classification Keywords
H.5.2. Information Interfaces and Presentation: User Interfaces—Input devices and strategies

General Terms
Experimentation, Standardization

INTRODUCTION
Text entry methods are typically evaluated using a transcription task (sometimes called a copy-task). In this task participants are instructed to write stimulus phrases as quickly and as accurately as possible. Until recently there was no widely agreed upon standard set of phrases for use in text entry evaluations. As a consequence, different researchers tended to choose different text sources. For example, in a study of speech interfaces "text was drawn from an old western novel" [3]. In a study of device-independent text entry methods "phrases were extracted from the fortune cookie database delivered with Red Hat Linux 5.2" [1]. In a study on optimized keyboards "test sentences were randomly selected from news" [8]. MacKenzie and Soukoreff [4] helped improve the situation by contributing a standard set of 500 phrases.

However, does the choice of phrase set actually matter? This question has been discussed a number of times in the recent text entry literature. MacKenzie and Soukoreff [4] raise the issue of external and internal validity of phrase sets and argue that phrase sets should be standardized. Paek and Hsu [5] follow up on MacKenzie and Soukoreff's argument of the importance of using representative phrase sets and propose a method for sampling representative phrase sets from large bodies of text. Recently, we released a new phrase set based on genuine mobile emails that have been validated for memorability [7]. We argue in [7] that this set's real-world data and demonstrated memorability should increase both internal and external validity in text entry evaluations.

We believe the choice of phrase set *may* matter for the following reasons:

Reproducibility Text entry experiments that use non-standard phrase sets often end up being unreproducible since text sources used for stimuli cannot be located (e.g. text from an unnamed western novel).

Study heterogeneity Empirical measurements from different text entry studies are sometimes compared in systematic reviews. If researchers use different phrase sets they introduce a potential confound making meta-analyses more difficult.

Internal validity In an experiment it is critical that manipulation of the independent variable (the text entry method) is the only major source of variation in the measured dependent variables (typically entry and error rates). Factors that may pose threats to internal validity include phrases that are hard to remember and phrases that contain arcane punctuation or auxiliary symbols.

External validity The relative performance of the text entry methods should ideally also hold when users are composing their own text outside the laboratory. However, a phrase set that is not representative of the text that end-users are likely to write may potentially generate misleading results.

Researchers have so far primarily concentrated on the trade-off between internal and external validity (e.g. [4, 7]), and on how well the phrases model the text end-users are likely to compose (e.g. [2, 4, 5, 7]). In this paper we instead focus on the actual empirical performance implications of phrase sets and presentation styles. We carried out two experiments. Both of these experiments used an identical study design with one between-subjects independent variable (phrase set) and one within-subjects independent variable (presentation style).

Phrase set	Examples
MACKENZIE	fish are jumping great disturbance in the force I took the rover from the shop
MOBILEEMAIL	Is she done yet? How are you? We are all fragile.
AAC	let me see that that's the way its always been where is the restroom
NGRAM	Ref: Tie Line Access because it did not members, you may want
SMS	Like a personal sized or what How do you plan to manage that ya i know liao got loophole

Table 1. Example phrases from the five different phrase sets.

Phrase Sets

We investigated five phrase sets which were selected based on the criterion that the set, or the source for the set, must be publicly available (this ruled out the children's phrase set [2] and the Twitter and Facebook n-gram phrase sets [5]). Table 1 shows some example phrases from each of the phrase sets.

MACKENZIE This phrase set was released by MacKenzie and Soukoreff [4] in 2003. It contains phrases with no punctuation and limited capitalization. 500 phrases, 2713 words, 14305 characters.

MOBILEEMAIL This phrase set was released by Vertanen and Kristensson [7] in 2011. This phrase set contains phrases drawn from genuine mobile emails in the Enron email corpus. The phrase set release contains several subsets. We used the subsets `mem1-mem5` which had been verified to be memorable. 200 phrases, 1073 words, 5253 characters.

AAC A publicly available collection of short conversational messages designed by Augmented and Alternative Communication (AAC) specialists.[1] 952 phrases, 3843 words, 17169 characters.

NGRAM This phrase set was released by Peak and Hsu [5] in 2011. It consists of 4-grams sampled from the Enron email corpus. 500 phrases, 1998 words, 11282 characters.

SMS We created this phrase set from the National University of Singapore SMS corpus.[2] We used their publicly released SMS corpus dated June 20th, 2011.[3] The dataset contained noise and many of the original SMS messages were unintelligible. We filtered the data to include only messages that satisfied two criteria. First, every word in a message had to exist in a large word list. We created the word list by merging Wiktionary, Webster's dictionary provided by Project Gutenberg, the CMU pronouncing dictionary and GNU aspell. Second, a message must consist of 21–74 characters and 4–14 words. These thresholds mirror the minimum and maximum number of characters and words occurring in the MOBILEEMAIL phrase set. 769 phrases, 5442 words, 25261 characters.

[1] `http://aac.unl.edu/vocabulary.html`
[2] `http://wing.comp.nus.edu.sg/SMSCorpus/`
[3] `smsCorpus_en_2011.06.20.xml`

Phrase set	MEMORIZE	TRANSCRIBE
MACKENZIE	69.9 (22.0)	68.6 (22.1)
MOBILEEMAIL	70.1 (17.3)	66.7 (16.9)
AAC	88.0 (25.7)	83.8 (28.4)
NGRAM	67.1 (17.6)	64.6 (20.5)
SMS	62.7 (18.0)	61.0 (16.7)

Table 2. Mean entry rates (wpm) in the familiar text entry method experiment (standard deviations in parentheses).

Presentation Styles

Normally in a transcription-based text entry evaluation, participants can see the stimulus phrase while entering the text. While this avoids an explicit memorization step, it also somewhat lowers participants' entry rates [6]. We therefore decided to also investigate two presentation styles:

MEMORIZE Participants were shown a phrase and asked to try to remember it. After clicking a button, the phrase disappeared and participants typed the phrase from memory. Participants were told to type as much as they could remember.

TRANSCRIBE Participants were presented with a phrase but the phrase remained visible throughout the text entry task.

EXPERIMENT 1: FAMILIAR TEXT ENTRY METHOD

We recruited 225 participants via Amazon Mechanical Turk. We restricted the task to workers resident in the United States. Participants were randomly assigned to one of the five phrase sets. We ensured that each phrase set had an equal number of 45 participants. Each participant was given a random subset of phrases selected from the participant's assigned phrase set.

Participants were presented with a phrase and asked to type it as quickly and as accurately as possible. The session was divided into two parts. The first part consisted of 25 phrases that were presented using one presentation style, either MEMORIZE or TRANSCRIBE (described in the previous section). The second part consisted of 25 phrases that were presented using the other presentation style. The order of the presentation styles was balanced across the participants.

Results

We removed workers who provided obvious garbage responses. After this removal, we had 50 phrases from 225 participants, 11250 phrases in total.

Entry Rates

Entry rates were measured in words-per-minute (wpm), with a word defined as five consecutive characters. Timing was measured as the interval between the first key press and the last key press. Table 2 provides a summary of the entry rates. Participants wrote faster in MEMORIZE (mean = 71.6 wpm, sd = 22.0 wpm) than in TRANSCRIBE (mean = 68.9 wpm, sd = 22.6 wpm). Repeated measures analysis of variance using an initial (unadjusted) significance level of $\alpha = 0.05$ revealed a

Phrase set	MEMORIZE	TRANSCRIBE
MACKENZIE	1.7% (3.4%)	0.2% (0.5%)
MOBILEEMAIL	2.1% (5.9%)	0.2% (0.5%)
AAC	1.1% (2.4%)	0.4% (0.7%)
NGRAM	3.3% (2.3%)	0.6% (0.6%)
SMS	5.5% (6.0%)	0.5% (0.8%)

Table 3. Mean error rates (CER) in the familiar text entry method experiment (standard deviations in parentheses).

significant difference for presentation style ($F_{1,220} = 29.009$, $\eta_p^2 = 0.116$, $p < 0.001$).

We also found significant differences between the phrase sets ($F_{4,220} = 8.982$, $\eta_p^2 = 0.140$, $p < 0.001$). Tukey HSD *post hoc* tests showed that the AAC set resulted in significantly faster entry rates than all other sets. No other differences in entry rates between the sets were significant. There was no significant interaction between presentation style and phrase set ($F_{4,220} = 1.194$, $\eta_p^2 = 0.021$, $p = 0.314$).

Error Rates

Error rates were measured as character error rate (CER). CER is the minimum edit distance between the participant's written response text and the stimulus phrase, divided by the number of characters in the stimulus phrase. Table 3 provides a summary of the error rates. The error rate was higher in MEMORIZE (mean = 2.7%, sd = 4.5%) than in TRANSCRIBE (mean = 0.4%, sd = 0.6%). A repeated measures analysis of variance using an initial (unadjusted) significance level of $\alpha = 0.05$ showed this was a significant difference ($F_{1,220} = 70.877$, $\eta_p^2 = 0.244$, $p < 0.001$).

We also found significant differences between the phrase sets ($F_{4,220} = 7.569$, $\eta_p^2 = 0.121$, $p < 0.001$). We found a significant interaction between presentation style and phrase set ($F_{4,220} = 6.629$, $\eta_p^2 = 0.108$, $p < 0.001$). We therefore split the dataset by presentation style and performed two separate between-subject ANOVAs with appropriately adjusted significance levels to guard against the risk of over-testing the data. For the MEMORIZE presentation style there was a significant difference between the phrase sets ($F_{4,220} = 7.215$, $\eta_p^2 = 0.116$, $p < 0.0001$). Tukey HSD *post hoc* tests showed that the SMS phrase set resulted in significantly more errors than the MOBILEEMAIL, MACKENZIE and AAC phrase sets. No other differences in error rate between the phrase sets were statistically significant. For the TRANSCRIBE presentation style the differences between the phrase sets were not significant after adjustment of the significance level to guard against over-testing ($F_{4,220} = 3.397$, $\eta_p^2 = 0.058$, $p = 0.01$).

Total Task Time

We also investigated the total task time between the MEMORIZE presentation style and the TRANSCRIBE style. In MEMORIZE, the total task time was measured from when participants were exposed to the phrase to be memorized to the point when they had completed writing the phrase. In TRANSCRIBE, the total task time was measured from when they were exposed to the phrase to the point when they had completed writing the phrase. We found that MEMORIZE resulted in longer total task times (mean = 10.0 s, sd = 5.3 s) than TRANSCRIBE (mean = 7.0 s, sd = 3.3 s). The difference was statistically significant ($F_{1,220} = 199.0$, $\eta_p^2 = 0.474$, $p < 0.001$). In other words, participants had a higher entry rate when they memorized a phrase beforehand. However, they also spent more time performing each task.

Worker Demographics

Before the text entry task, we asked workers a number of questions about themselves. 71% of our participants were female with an average age of 33. The vast majority were native English speakers (93% native speakers, 5% advanced, and 2% moderate/beginners). 56% of workers reported using a laptop, 43% a desktop, and 1% a mobile/tablet device.

EXPERIMENT 2: UNFAMILIAR TEXT ENTRY METHOD

The previous experiment investigated performance differences when participants used their familiar full-sized keyboards. However, in practice most text entry evaluations are conducted using text entry methods that are unfamiliar to participants. We investigated if an unfamiliar text entry method would change the results. In experiment two, participants entered text by pushing buttons on the ATOMIK on-screen keyboard [8]. It has been established that optimized on-screen keyboards have a long learning curve [8]. Thus, even though we could not control the exact pointing device used by our workers, their overall task time in a short experiment would be dominated by the visual search task [8].

The method was identical to the first experiment except for the following. We recruited 150 participants via Mechanical Turk. Each phrase set had an equal number of 30 participants. Participants wrote ten phrases in each presentation style.

Results

As in experiment 1, we removed workers who provided obvious garbage responses. After removal, we had 20 phrases from 150 participants, 3000 phrases in total.

Entry Rates

Entry rates were measured as in experiment one. Table 4 provides a summary of the entry rates. Entry rate was slightly faster for MEMORIZE (mean = 10.0 wpm, sd = 2.7 wpm) compared to TRANSCRIBE (mean = 9.7 wpm, sd = 2.5 wpm). Repeated measures analysis of variance showed that this difference was statistically significant ($F_{1,145} = 5.426$, $\eta_p^2 = 0.036$, $p = 0.021$). As shown in Table 4, faster entry in MEMORIZE held for all phrase sets except for the SMS set.

We found that there were statistically significant differences between the phrase sets ($F_{4,145} = 3.6$, $\eta_p^2 = 0.09$, $p = 0.008$). Tukey HSD *post hoc* tests showed that the AAC

Phrase set	MEMORIZE	TRANSCRIBE
MACKENZIE	10.0 (2.3)	9.6 (2.4)
MOBILEEMAIL	9.2 (2.2)	8.7 (2.2)
AAC	11.5 (3.4)	10.8 (2.9)
NGRAM	9.8 (2.2)	9.4 (2.0)
SMS	9.6 (2.6)	10.0 (2.4)

Table 4. Mean entry rates (wpm) in the unfamiliar text entry method experiment (standard deviations in parentheses).

Phrase set	MEMORIZE	TRANSCRIBE
MACKENZIE	4.3% (5.8%)	1.5% (2.5%)
MOBILEEMAIL	5.1% (6.5%)	1.7% (2.5%)
AAC	4.9% (8.0%)	1.6% (2.8%)
NGRAM	4.9% (5.0%)	1.1% (1.9%)
SMS	10.8% (10.9%)	1.7% (3.1%)

Table 5. Mean error rates (CER) in the unfamiliar text entry method experiment (standard deviations in parentheses).

phrase set resulted in significantly faster entry rates than MOBILEEMAIL. No other differences in entry rates between the phrase sets were statistically significant. There was no significant interaction between presentation style and phrase set ($F_{4,145} = 1.659$, $\eta_p^2 = 0.044$, $p = 0.163$).

Error Rates

Error rates were measured as in experiment one. Table 5 provides a summary of the error rates. The error rate was higher for MEMORIZE (mean = 6.0%, sd = 7.8%) compared to TRANSCRIBE (mean = 1.5%, sd = 2.7%). Repeated measures analysis of variance showed this difference was statistically significant ($F_{1,145} = 51.759$, $\eta_p^2 = 0.263$, $p < 0.001$). In MEMORIZE, the error rate was markedly higher for the SMS phrase set compared to the other phrase sets.

There was a significant interaction between presentation style and phrase set ($F_{4,145} = 3.493$, $\eta_p^2 = 0.088$, $p = 0.009$). We therefore split the dataset by presentation style and performed two separate between-subject ANOVAs with appropriately adjusted significance levels to guard against the risk of over-testing the data. For the MEMORIZE presentation style there was a significant difference between the phrase sets ($F_{4,145} = 3.821$, $\eta_p^2 = 0.095$, $p = 0.006$). Tukey HSD *post hoc* tests showed that the SMS phrase set resulted in significantly more errors than all other phrase sets. No other differences in error rate between the phrase sets were statistically significant. For the TRANSCRIBE presentation style the differences between the phrase sets were not significant ($F_{4,145} = 0.209$, $\eta_p^2 = 0.006$, $p = 0.933$).

Total Task Time

Total task times were measured as in experiment one. Total task times were longer for MEMORIZE (mean = 47.1 s, sd = 53.1 s) than for TRANSCRIBE (mean = 44.5 s, sd = 19.0 s). However, the difference was not statistically significant ($F_{1,145} = 0.339$, $\eta_p^2 = 0.002$, $p = 0.561$).

DISCUSSION AND RECOMMENDATIONS

Our MEMORIZE condition provides empirical evidence that the MACKENZIE, AAC and NGRAM phrase sets are indeed memorable by users. Previously we only knew this for the MOBILEEMAIL phrase set. Further, we found that the MEMORIZE presentation style resulted in consistently higher entry rates than the traditional TRANSCRIBE presentation style. However, this came at the cost of slightly higher error rates and somewhat longer task times.

The phrase set by MacKenzie and Soukoreff [4] has been popular for text entry evaluations since its release in 2003. Given that two new phrase sets have recently appeared that may be more suitable in certain situations, such as mobile text [7] or special use-cases [5], it is reassuring that the MacKenzie and Soukoreff [4] phrase set provides similar performance.

We caution against using the SMS phrase set since it was significantly more error prone than the other sets. We believe this was due to the strange language, abbreviations, and sentence fragments in this set. This is supported by comments made by workers at the end of the experiment (e.g. "The ones spelled incorrectly were the hardest", "Bad grammar! Nonsensical!"). In addition, we caution against using the AAC phrase set since it resulted in significantly higher entry rates than the other sets. We believe this resulted from the set consisting almost entirely of simple, short, and familiar phrases which avoided proper names, unusual vocabulary, and difficult grammar. This probably led to faster typing due to factors such as motor memory and ease of memorization.

Based on our data we recommend text entry researchers first consider using either the MACKENZIE or the MOBILEEMAIL phrase sets. Both of these sets perform similarly in terms of entry and error rates for both the familiar and the unfamiliar text entry methods we tested. For mobile text entry methods it may be worth using the MOBILEEMAIL phrase set since it has higher external validity given that it is based on genuine mobile emails. We hope researchers will consider these recommendations when evaluating new text entry methods.

ACKNOWLEDGEMENTS

This work was supported by the Engineering and Physical Sciences Research Council (grant number EP/H027408/1) and the Scottish Informatics and Computer Science Alliance.

REFERENCES

1. Isokoski, P., and Raisamo, R. Device independent text input: a rationale and an example. In *Proc. AVI 2000*, ACM Press (2000), 76–83.
2. Kano, A., Read, J. C., and Dix, A. Children's phrase set for text input method evaluations. In *Proc. NordiCHI 2006*, ACM Press (2006), 449–452.
3. Karat, C.-M., Halverson, C., Horn, D., and Karat, J. Patterns of entry and correction in large vocabulary continuous speech recognition systems. In *Proc. CHI 1999*, ACM Press (1999), 568–575.
4. MacKenzie, I. S., and Soukoreff, R. W. Phrase sets for evaluating text entry techniques. In *Ext. Abstracts CHI 2003*, ACM Press (2003), 754–755.
5. Paek, T., and Hsu, B.-J. P. Sampling representative phrase sets for text entry experiments: a procedure and public resource. In *Proc. CHI 2011*, ACM Press (2011), 2477–2480.
6. Soukoreff, R. W., and MacKenzie, I. S. Metrics for text entry research: An evaluation of MSD and KSPC, and a new unified error metric. In *Proc. CHI 2003*, ACM Press (2003), 113–120.
7. Vertanen, K., and Kristensson, P. O. A versatile dataset for text entry evaluations based on genuine mobile emails. In *Proc. MobileHCI 2011*, ACM Press (2011), 295–298.
8. Zhai, S., Sue, A., and Accot, J. Movement model, hits distribution and learning in virtual keyboarding. In *Proc. CHI 2002*, ACM Press (2002), 17–24.

Towards Providing Just-in-Time Vocabulary Support for Assistive and Augmentative Communication

Carrie Demmans Epp[1], Justin Djordjevic[1], Shimu Wu[1], Karyn Moffatt[1,2], Ronald M. Baecker[1]

[1] Technologies for Aging Gracefully Lab
University of Toronto
{carrie, justin, shimu, ron}@taglab.ca

[2]School of Information Studies
McGill University
karyn.moffatt@mcgill.ca

ABSTRACT

Many people cannot communicate effectively with those around them. The causes vary but several tools and strategies can support their communication. These tools, which collectively fall under the banner of Assistive and Augmentative Communication (AAC), are rarely adaptive. Of those that are, few provide context-based or just-in-time vocabulary support to users even though the proliferation of smartphones makes this possible. To meet this need, we developed four algorithms to retrieve relevant vocabulary from Internet-based corpora. We used discourse completion tasks to evaluate each algorithm's ability to identify appropriate vocabulary across a set of specific contexts. The results indicate that our approach identifies appropriate context-specific words that complement general AAC vocabularies: when combined with a typical base vocabulary, the algorithms outperformed the support provided by the base vocabulary alone. They did this by adding small targeted vocabularies.

Author Keywords

AAC, Vocabulary Support, Adaptivity.

ACM Classification Keywords

H.5.m [Information interfaces and presentation (e.g., HCI)]: Miscellaneous;

General Terms

Algorithms, Experimentation, Performance

INTRODUCTION

Many people face challenges when trying to communicate with others through speech. For some this challenge is due to a lack of familiarity with the language. For others, the challenge can be attributed to medical conditions that limit their communicative abilities. This includes people who have experienced brain trauma that has resulted in aphasia (a language disorder that can disrupt reading, writing, and speaking). Regardless of the cause of communication challenges, many tools and strategies can be employed to support communication. They are called Assistive and Augmentative Communication (AAC).

Considerable effort has been invested in developing computerized AAC, resulting in a number of commercial offerings (e.g., DynaVox[1]). Though differing in complexity and the range of features offered, these devices typically provide language support in the form of words and phrases organized into categories.

As AAC users have a range of communicative abilities, use varies with some users merely glancing at the device as a prompt, and others composing full sentences to have the device speak on their behalf. Regardless of how the device is used, a frequent challenge is efficiently navigating the hierarchy of categories to find needed words.

Historically, AAC devices used proprietary hardware, but, developers are increasingly adopting smartphone platforms (e.g., Lingraphica's Smalltalk[2]), providing designers with new opportunities, including the ability to provide adaptive communication support that exploits the user's context to offer more targeted language support.

One such AAC, MyVoice[3], uses location tracking to provide context-sensitive support to its users. MyVoice can support the accomplishment of simple tasks, such as ordering a tea at a coffee shop [2], but it currently requires that users predict all of their communicative needs. That is, the user (or a caregiver) must first create a location (by marking it on a map) and then must assign words and phrases to that location. This approach suffers from two major drawbacks: (1) it is time-consuming and onerous to manually create these location-based categories, and (2) it is not readily adaptable to unexpected situations or unplanned locations.

To address this gap, we developed four algorithms based on information retrieval techniques to automatically generate location-specific vocabularies, by identifying keywords from Internet-accessible corpora. Though these algorithms have been used in information retrieval tasks [11], they have yet to be validated for providing communication support. We, thus, evaluated them using a discourse completion study to see if they augment communication support when

[1] http://www.dynavoxtech.com
[2] http://www.aphasia.com/slp/product_smalltalk.aspx
[3] myvoiceaac.com

combined with a base AAC vocabulary. All four algorithm-augmented vocabularies outperformed the base vocabulary on its own, substantiating their use as a source of vocabulary for just-in-time (jit) support.

RELATED WORK

Even though communication is dependent on context [3], the use of context in AAC is underexplored. Patel and Radhakrishnan used location to refine the ordering of the words presented on an AAC device [10]. Wisenburn used speech recognition to determine the user's context and refine the provided vocabulary [12]. This support, like that provided by Kim et al. [5], can reduce search time. However, both require the pre-existence of collections of words and phrases in the user's AAC device. Thus, they are limited when adapting to emerging needs.

To provide vocabulary that meet emergent needs based on newly encountered contexts, we must first find and retrieve the relevant vocabulary. Some work has tried to do this using large pre-existing vocabularies that were created by domain experts [7,8]. However, it is limited because only pre-entered words can be used. Information retrieval and computational linguistics have potential for improving AAC vocabularies [7], and some information retrieval algorithms have shown promise in identifying relevant vocabulary for a specific location when evaluated with humans [13].

We are evaluating the use of these algorithms for providing communication support. If they can provide vocabulary that supports communication based on a theme (e.g., wage negotiations), or a location (e.g., the local gym) users will no longer need to predict their communicative needs.

ALGORITHMS

To provide AAC users with jit support in unexpected situations, we apply four algorithms to Internet-accessible corpora. Because many of the needs that users encounter could be location dependent, we explore the use of generic and location-specific corpora for providing topic-sensitive vocabulary. For all four algorithms, the contents of corpora are first obtained, by collecting the raw HTML from the specified corpus' website. The desired text-based content of the page is then isolated. After which, it is processed by one of the below algorithms to generate collections of vocabulary items (words or phrases).

Website Algorithm

The website that is associated with a location or theme is the corpus. For example, www.cdc.gov could be used as the corpus for illness. Starting at the homepage, all text-based documents that are linked from the page are retrieved. This is repeated for all linked documents until a link depth of three is reached.

Nouns are identified using the Natural Language Tool Kit (NLTK).[4] Potential phrases are identified by recursively subdividing the document until single words remain. Using the nouns and potential phrases that were identified in the previous step, a standard information retrieval frequency count with the removal of stop words algorithm [4] is applied. The resulting words and phrases are sorted based on their frequency count: the word with the highest score is placed at the top of the list and the word with the lowest score is placed at the bottom of the list.

Review Sites Algorithm

This algorithm uses the reviews and comments from multiple review websites[5] as a corpus to which a standard frequency count with stop word removal is applied.

The NLTK is used to identify items in the list that have the same lemma. These items are combined into one entry by replacing them with their lemma and summing their scores. For example, *sitting* and *sat* share a common lemma of *sit*. If both words are in the corpus with scores of 1 and 3, then *sit* is added to the vocabulary list with a score of 4.

Next, a frequency count of all phrases within the corpus is performed, where a phrase is an n-gram of size 2, 3, 4, or 5. The list of phrases is sorted by frequency count. It is then appended to the list of words, and the log of the corpus size is used to reduce noise by discarding items with scores below this threshold.

Dictionary Algorithm

The term frequency – inverse document frequency (tf-idf) algorithm [11] is applied to dictionary websites'[6] entries; each entry is treated as a document. Using Carpena et al.'s relative location of words method [1] to identify clustered words, we process content from about.com. The clustered words are combined with the tf-idf output to form a word list. A phrase list is created by applying Justeson and Katz's collocation identification method [14] to the about.com article, and frequency counts are computed for each of the identified phrases. The median score of each list is then used as a threshold: only entries with scores greater than or equal to the median score are retained.

Idioms between one and eight words in length are retrieved from idioms.thefreedictionary.com. The list of phrases is appended to the idiom list. This is then appended to the word list.

Wikipedia-USF Algorithm

The Wikipedia[7] page for a topic or location and the University of South Florida's (USF) Free Association Database [6] are the corpora; it contains information about how closely people associate one word with another.

[4] http://www.nltk.org

[5] www.blogto.com, www.yelp.com, www.google.com/places, www.chickadvisor.com/home.html, www.urbanspoon.com/choose, www.restaurantica.com, ourfaves.com

[6] ww35.thefreedictioanry.com, idioms.thefreedictionary.com, thesaurus.com

[7] http://www.wikipedia.org

The nouns within the first sentence of the Wikipedia article are identified using the NLTK. The nouns, their associated words, and their free-association scores are retrieved from the USF database and added to the noun list. A list of potential phrases is identified by recursively sub-dividing the article into phrases until each phrase has a length of 1. Additional phrases are identified from the titles of links within the Wikipedia article.

A frequency count with stop word removal is performed for each entry in the word and phrases lists. The frequency counts and USF scores are then normalized and the two lists are combined and ordered using these scores.

METHODOLOGY

To evaluate how well communication is supported by the algorithms, we performed a modified discourse completion study [9] where we asked participants to use words generated by the algorithms when responding to a situation. Participants were given the option of using words that were not provided by the algorithms when one of the words that they needed to respond had not been supplied. Participant input was restricted in this way because it more closely resembles the worst-case system usage scenario, where the user cannot communicate beyond the support provided by the AAC. This provides lower bounds on the performance of these algorithms in supporting human communication.

We evaluated each of the algorithms with 4 contexts, consisting of 2 themes and 2 locations. Each participant was presented with three discourse completion tasks per context. Each context had one discourse that required the participant to make a request or to express a level of agreement with someone and correct a misunderstanding in the case of a disagreement. The discourses generalize to situations where these forms of communication occur; they were based on those found in the linguistics literature and were piloted with 6 people to ensure that they made sense and were representative of situations one normally encounters. We used a local movie theatre and restaurant as locations since people commonly frequent these types of places and must interact with others when there. The themes we used were illness and shopping since these are universal experiences.

During the study, each participant underwent training. The discourse completion tasks were then presented using a repeated Graeco-Latin square design (the algorithms were the first set and the context order of presentation was the second set). The presentation order of individual discourse tasks was randomized within each context.

Combined Algorithm	*M*	*SD*	*t*(63)	*p*[1]
Review Sites*	4.00	2.65	2.66	0.020
Dictionary*	3.89	2.30	3.58	0.001
Website*	4.14	2.61	2.48	0.031
Wikipedia-USF*	4.13	2.92	2.42	0.037

Table 1. T-test results comparing the combined vocabularies to the base vocabularies (M = 5.07, SD = 2.35).

[1] Bonferroni corrected p-values * significant results

Participants read the situation and were given access to the words they were to use when composing their response once they indicated they were ready to respond. If a word was missing, participants could substitute words from the list or add a placeholder before submitting a response. Participants were asked to enter the word when they submitted responses with a placeholder. This process was repeated for each of the discourses until all 48 discourse completion tasks had been performed using the algorithm-generated vocabulary lists; tasks were divided equally across the four contexts.

Since we aimed to evaluate the algorithms' effectiveness at supporting communication for many populations, we chose to evaluate the algorithms using expert English language users with no communication impairments. We recruited people who could read, write, listen, and speak without the use of aids; this population was the best proxy for all of the targeted users and they could understand the text-based situations without the need for additional support.

RESULTS

Sixteen participants (8 male, 8 female) were recruited through postings on bulletin boards and online forums. They ranged in age from 20 to 56 (median = 33.5). All participants were fluent English communicators: 13 spoke English at home and 11 were native speakers. All participants were educated to at least the high school level and 10 had completed a university degree in English.

To assess communication support we considered two measures that indicate the amount of support provided by the vocabularies: vocabulary coverage and communicative goal achievement. Vocabulary coverage is the number of words, from the participant's response, that were not provided by the vocabularies. Communicative goal achievement is the ability of the vocabulary to provide the words needed to achieve the participant's goal even if words that the participant added were not provided by the algorithm were left out. For example, responding to a server with 'water', 'just water please', 'or a glass of water please' would all result in the server bringing a glass of water.

Vocabulary coverage: we performed a series of paired t-tests with Bonferroni correction comparing each algorithm-augmented vocabulary to the base on its own. In all cases, the combined vocabularies required significantly fewer additional words to support communication than the base vocabulary did on its own (Table 1). The algorithm-generated vocabularies were also used more extensively than the base (Table 2).

Communicative goal achievement: using a 2-way ANOVA, the algorithms had no significant effect on the achievement of communicative goals ($F_{3,255} = 1.50$, $p = 0.21$, $\eta^2 = 0.01$), but there was a difference between individuals ($F_{63,255} = 3.27$, $p < 0.01$, $\eta^2 = 0.52$).

Vocabulary	*Average Size (as M (SD))*	*Average % Used (as M (SD)*
Review Sites	20.3 (6.8)	30.6 (10.8)
Dictionary	30.0 (16.8)	22.0 (8.1)
Website	31.8 (2.9)	21.6 (6.6)
Wikipedia-USF	34.0 (0)	21.3 (8.1)
Base	209.0 (0)	4.1 (1.8)

Table 2. The average size of each vocabulary, in number of words, and percentage of each vocabulary that was used across all themes and locations (the base vocabulary was static).

DISCUSSION

The algorithms were able to augment the base vocabulary to provide additional support that helped participants communicate. That participants used 12–45% of the algorithm-generated vocabularies in their responses compared to at most 6% of the base vocabulary further shows their usefulness, especially if you consider how few words were added by the algorithms (no more than 53).

The base vocabulary was largely unused, but it supported communication by providing re-usable phrases. In general, it supported the participants who chose to be polite by providing greetings, politeness markers, and stereotypical phrases (e.g., *Do you have*). The inclusion of such items in context-specific vocabularies is inappropriate because they could be used in many contexts, and they can be accessed through the base vocabulary with relative ease.

Some participants' achievement of communicative goals was better supported than others. These participants were more direct and used simple greetings and politeness markers, such as *thank you* and *hello,* rather than indirect requests. This implies that additional adjustment should be made to vocabularies when supporting people whose natural conversational style is less direct.

CONCLUSIONS AND FUTURE WORK

People who have limited communicative abilities require vocabulary support to communicate with those around them. Unfortunately, their needs cannot always be predicted. To augment the support that AAC provides, we evaluated four algorithms that were based on information retrieval techniques to find contextually relevant words.

All four algorithms provided additional support, implying that we can save human resources by using them to build on demand vocabularies for use in AAC. We are now developing a feature for a MyVoice inspired AAC; this feature incorporates these algorithms to provide jit support so that users can interact with those around them. We can then evaluate these algorithms with our target populations.

ACKNOWLEDGEMENTS

The Natural Sciences and Engineering Research Council of Canada and Google funded this work.

REFERENCES

1. Carpena, P., Bernaola-Galván, P., Hackenberg, M., Coronado, A., and Oliver, J. Level statistics of words: Finding keywords in literary texts and symbolic sequences. *Physical Review E 79*, 3 (2009).
2. Demmans Epp, C., Campigotto, R., Levy, A., and Baecker, R. MarcoPolo: Context-Sensitive Mobile Communication Support. In *Proc. FICCDAT: RESNA/ICTA 2011*, RESNA (2011).
3. de Jong, T., Specht, M., and Koper, R. A Study of Contextualised Mobile Information Delivery for Language Learning. *Educational Technology & Society 13*, 3 (2010), 110-125.
4. Jurafsky, D. *Speech and language processing: an introduction to natural language processing, computational linguistics, and speech recognition.* Pearson Prentice Hall, Upper Saddle River N.J., 2009.
5. Kim, G., Park, J., Han, M., Park, S., and Ha, S. Context-Aware Communication Support System with Pictographic Cards. In *Proc. MobileHCI '09*, ACM Press (2009), 1-2.
6. Nelson, D.L., McEvoy, C.L., and Schreiber, T.A. *University of South Florida word association, rhyme, and word fragment norms.* 1998.
7. Newell, A., Langer, S., and Hickey, M. The rôle of natural language processing in alternative and augmentative communication. *Natural Language Engineering 4*, 1 (1998), 1-16.
8. Nikolova, S., Ma, X., Tremaine, M., and Cook, P. Vocabulary Navigation Made Easier. *Proc. IUI '10*, ACM Press (2010), 361-364.
9. Nurani, L.M. Methodological Issue in Pragmatic Research: Is Discourse Completion Test A Reliable Data Collection Instrument? *Jurnal Sosioteknologi 5*, 9 (2009), 667-678.
10. Patel, R. and Radhakrishnan, R. Enhancing Access to Situational Vocabulary by Leveraging Geographic Context. *Assistive Technology Outcomes and Benefits 4*, 1 (2007), 99-114.
11. Salton, G. and McGill, M.J. *Introduction to Modern Information Retrieval*. McGraw-Hill Inc., New York, NY, USA, 1986.
12. Wisenburn, B. and Higginbotham, D.J. An AAC Application Using Speaking Partner Speech Recognition to Automatically Produce Contextually Relevant Utterances: Objective Results. *Augmentative and Alternative Communication 24*, 2 (2008), 100-109.
13. Yatani, K., Novati, M., Trusty, A., and Truong, K.N. Analysis of Adjective-noun Word Pair Extraction Methods for Online Review Summarization. In *Proc. IJCAI 2011*, Morgan Kaufmann (2011), 2771-2776.
14. WordHoard - Finding Multiword Units. http://wordhoard.northwestern.edu/userman/analysis-multiwordunits.html#justesonfilter.

Mobile Texting: Can Post-ASR Correction Solve the Issues? An Experimental Study on Gain vs. Costs

Michael Feld[1] **Saeedeh Momtazi**[2] **Farina Freigang**[1] **Dietrich Klakow**[2] **Christian Müller**[1]

[1]German Research Center for Artificial Intelligence, Saarbrücken, Germany
firstname.lastname@dfki.de

[2]Spoken Language Systems, University of the Saarland, Germany
firstname.lastname@lsv.uni-saarland.de

ABSTRACT

The next big step in embedded, mobile speech recognition will be to allow completely free input as it is needed for messaging like SMS or email. However, unconstrained dictation remains error-prone, especially when the environment is noisy. In this paper, we compare different methods for improving a given free-text dictation system used to enter text-based messages in embedded mobile scenarios, where distraction, interaction cost, and hardware limitations enforce strict constraints over traditional scenarios. We present a corpus-based evaluation, measuring the trade-off between improvement of the word error rate versus the interaction steps that are required under various parameters. Results show that by post-processing the output of a "black box" speech recognizer (e.g. a web-based speech recognition service), a reduction of word error rate by 55% (10.3% abs.) can be obtained. For further error reduction, however, a richer representation of the original hypotheses (e.g. lattice) is necessary.

Author Keywords

Speech recognition, error correction, automotive, messaging

ACM Classification Keywords

H.5.m. Information Interfaces and Presentation: Misc.

General Terms

Experimentation, Measurement, Performance

INTRODUCTION

Embedded, mobile speech recognition has evolved from simple voice commands ("*Call Anna*") to relatively natural speech input for certain domains ("*Where is the next Pizza place?*"). The next big step will be to allow completely free input as it is needed for messaging like SMS or email. Unconstrained dictation is the hardest form of automatic speech recognition (ASR) and remains error-prone, especially when the environment is suboptimal, because background noise is present or because the user can for some reason not fully concentrate on speaking. Unfortunately, in mobile scenarios this is mostly the case [5]. In the first place, this is an issue of optimizing the ASR engine, which can be done by taking enough of the right training material and by eliminating "nuisance attributes" from the recognition process. Following the post-ASR correction paradigm, we consider ASR as a black box, which cannot be optimized either because we already did our best or because we haven't got access to it. While post-correction can be applied in a number of mobile domains, the main application scenario we have in mind is dictating (and editing) text message while driving. Here, the black box scenario is very likely. Car manufacturers are in the process of moving from owned on-board ASR solutions for off-board third party services such as Vlingo [12]. Why? First of all, ASR development is costly. Then, innovation cycles of the product (car) need to be further decoupled from the much shorter cycles of value added components (such as infotainment). And finally, the bandwidth of mobile Internet has become wide enough to off-board services.

Obvious means for correcting errors that we know from personal computers at home will not be immediately applicable here, because in mobile situations, a number of constraints apply. On the other hand, correcting speech recognition errors by adding another speech recognition step bears the danger of ending up in cascading errors that frustrate the user [11]. [6] looked for modalities that are optimal for drivers using a combination of eye gaze and speech commands. However, independent from the ergonomics of the interaction, we should add some intelligence to the process, which helps reducing the number of necessary interaction steps as much as possible. In this article, we tackle the latter issue. Particularly, we address these questions: What factors do affect the performance of the error correction for the in-car domain? What methods can be used to improve it? Using a given ASR, what is the upper boundary of accuracy that can be achieved using these methods? And finally, how much user interaction is needed and how is it related to the performance?

RELATED WORK

Previous work on post-ASR correction using a single speech recognizer hypothesis focused on language models (LM) trained with statistical and other methods and relatively little training data. In all cases introduced in the following, ASR has been treated as a complete black box – the only clue given for the input string was the word sequence produced by the recognizer. The different approaches commonly employed LMs. [10] introduced a correction method using a back-off LM in order to allow domain specific tasks. [3] produced a LM consisting of two components: a word n-gram model accounts for lexical information and a maximum entropy language model (MELM) capturing higher level syntactic and semantic knowledge. In a similar study, [4] proposed a semantic-oriented approach. Here, lexico-semantic patterns (LSP) have been used that combined linguistic entries with semantic types in form of part-of-speech tags to capture constituents of utterance hypotheses. [7] developed a two-structured LM, comprised of syntactic-semantic and lexical information, as well as grammatical knowledge. Our model accounts for lexical information combined with either lexicographical or phonological similarities. Deletion and insertion errors where handled with the help of fertility models in the first three approaches, whereas our model so far includes deletions only. [13] target dialog systems with post-ASR confidence ratings based on both acoustic features, word lattice, and LM. [10] achieved a WER reduction of 14.9% using Sphinx-II for ASR and a LM trained on TRAINS-95 dialogue data for the transportation domain. However, the initial WER was rather high (42% respectively 35%). [3] improved an initial WER of 27% by 4%. They used LG-Elite and ByVoice ASR in an in-vehicle telematic domain. [4] used the same ASR and domain knowledge but also trained with the TRAINS-95 dialogue system and obtained a 6.28% WER-improvement. [7] employed data from the Saplen corpus to train different knowledge domains like fast food and Air Travel Information Service (ATIS). With these models they used the HTK ASR, which resulted in an overall 8.5% WER-improvement from a baseline of 23.88%.

POST-ASR ERROR CORRECTION APPROACHES

Fig. 1 illustrates the dialog system underlying this study. After activation, the user can speak a sentence, which is then displayed on a screen. Using one of several modalities such as touch, a central multi-functional device or short robust speech commands, an erroneous word can be selected, in which case a non-scrollable list of alternatives pops up. The user can select an alternative, choose the word to be deleted, or cancel the correction. The insertion of words is currently not implemented. Alternatively, on the main screen, the user can toggle between full sentence alternatives using left and right controls. When done, the user accepts the sentence. Given the "black box" scenario described above, one question immediately comes into mind: Where do the alternatives come from? The remainder of this paper is dedicated to this problem. Thereby, the term *interaction steps* refers to the number of individual input turns by the user, e.g. button presses. Hence, switching to the next sentence alternative is one interaction, selection a wrong word and then choosing an alternative is another two interactions.

Sentence Alternatives (DASA, WASA). Sentence alternatives, if provided by the ASR, can be used in multiple ways: for sentence-level correction (Directly Applied Sentence Alternatives, DASA) and to derive word alternatives (Word Alternatives based on Sentence Alternatives, WASA). Our WASA generator aligns all sentence alternatives with the (potentially incorrect) reference sentence on character-level using Needleman/Wunsch algorithm (using a score of 1 for match and -1 for mismatch and gaps) [9]. Then, words in the alternative are mapped to the words in the reference sentence depending on the characters they span in the alignment. It is possible that multiple words in the alternative are mapped to a single word (insertion) or that a single word in the reference

Figure 1. Simplified view of the underlying dialog system. A) user dictates a sentence, B1) user selects alternative sentence, B2) user selects a word that is wrong and chooses an alternative word (using a minimal distraction modality which is not described here), C) user accepts the sentence by choosing "Send".

spanned multiple words in the source (deletion). The alternatives for a single word then correspond to the words from all sentence alternatives mapped to that word (minus duplicates). Word alternatives are ordered by the scores of the corresponding sentence alternatives from which they were obtained. If the number of alternatives was larger than the number offered to the user, the best n were displayed according to this metric. This method heavily relies on support from the recognizer and does not consider further domain-specific knowledge.

Language Model (LM). The second word alternative generator implemented does not require additional input beyond the sentence. Rather than that, it works solely on the context of the word and employs a pre-trained language model. The motivating idea is that the information about knowing which word is wrong, combined with the fact that the immediate context (the word before and after it) are then most likely correct, could be sufficient extra information for a statistical method. It is unclear, however, to what extend LM-based approaches depend on domain-specific training data. In our experiments described below, we therefore compared *in-domain* and *out-of-domain* LM variants. In any case, LM should be able to predict the words that can appear in the position of the wrong word reported by the user. This prediction is done based on the Bayes classifier scenario: First, the probability of each vocabulary term conditioned on the surrounding words is calculated. Typically, in the statistical language modeling, an n-gram model and specifically a trigram model is used to predict the present word based on the two previous already seen words. In our language model, two words in the immediate context are also used to calculate the probability of the present word. However, contrary to the normal recognition task which runs the LM simultaneously with the recognition, this LM is used after the recognition step and as a result, the model knows about all sentence's words, not only the predecessor words. Hence, the words before and after the present word are used for calculating the probability: $\hat{w}_i = \text{argmax}_w P(w|w_{i-1}, w_{i+1})$, where $\hat{w}_i$ is the word to be predicted as an alternative for the present word; w is the vocabulary word, and w_{i-1} and w_{i+1} are the previous and next words respectively. Similar to the normal trigram model, a smoothing technique is required to overcome the problem of unseen histories in which a bigram model is used as the back-off model for smoothing. Based on our experiments on the development set, using only the previous word for the bigram model performs better than using only the next word. Therefore, the previous word is considered as the backoff model while Kneser-Ney smoothing is applied. In the Bayes classifier, the best word which has the highest probability is selected as an alternative for the wrong word. In our model, since a list of alternative words is required, we further rank the vocabulary terms in the ascending format of this probability. Finally, top n words are selected as the best alternatives for the current position.

Lexicographical and Phonological Similarities. If the ASR has made an error, it is likely that the correct word is phonologically very close to the word reported as incorrect. Although the LM can have a good prediction based on the surrounding words, it does not take the actual word into account. This way, it is much more likely to suggest alternatives that are semantically or syntactically close to the word to be replaced, instead of those with similar acoustic features. While the correct word may still be among the top 50 alternatives sorted by LM probability, the limit for alternatives in our scenario require that the LM suggestions be re-ranked based on a metric that takes such similarity to the current word into account. We tested two such re-ranking schemes in our evaluation: A *lexicographical* and a *phonological* comparison. Both use a basic Levenshtein metric to sort alternatives by their distance to the original word. While the lexicographical method works on the written word in alphabetic characters, the phonological scheme works on the IPA phonetical representation, which is obtained using the *CMU Pronouncing Dictionary* [2].

EXPERIMENTAL SETUP

The input for the evaluation consists of a pre-processed text corpus (see below), which represents the message the user wants to send. In the next step, an ASR is applied which (at minimum) outputs one transcription for each input sentence. Each sentence is then processed like a human would do with a system as it is described here, until either it is completely correct or the remaining errors cannot be fixed using the options provided. Modules generating the alternatives have access to the sentence in its current state, and – if available – any extra information from the recognizer. They do not know the correct version of a respective sentence, but they may be trained on external data prior to the experiment. For word-level correction, the word alternatives module is queried for options for each wrong word. If the correct solution is among them, it is selected. The size of the alternatives list is one of the main parameters in the following analysis. The two measures applied are *word error rate* (WER) of the original and processed sentences, as well as *interaction steps* (IS). It is important to note that interactions are counted even if they don't lead to an improvement, because the system has to expose the same level of knowledge as the user: If the user has to click a wrong word to see whether the correct alternative is available, the system should too.

The corpus is a custom collection of publicly available material from a popular microblogging service ("MB corpus"). 51 users were selected with a total of 63,841 short sentences (average 8.6 words/sentence and 4 characters/word) in English, with a special preference for automotive, traffic and traveling topics (some users indeed seemed to be writing while driving). All sentences were post-processed by regular expressions designed to remove artifacts and transform the output into a format resembling dictated speech. E.g., small numbers were changed to their written form, common abbreviations were spelled out, etc. A subset of 940 sentences was selected manually. Three native American English speakers read each sentence. The eval set consists of 482 sentences while the remainder of the corpus is used as training (63,383) and development (458) set for the *in-domain* LM. The development set is used to study the smoothing parameters. The training data consisted of 452,137 word tokens and 27,361 word types. Additionally, we trained an *Upper-Boundary* model directly on the eval set used as recognizer input. It measures the upper boundary performance that can be achieved with any LM training data based on the recognizer output.

The out-of-domain model was trained on the *Blog06* corpus created by the University of Glasgow [8]. It is a collection of homepages and permalinks from blogs monitored over an 11 week period from Dec 2005 to Feb 2006. The collection contains 3,215,171 pages. Since blog documents are user created, we found that this dataset is close to our application yet larger and more generic than the in-domain LM. We tested two recognizers: the *SAPI 5.3*-based recognizer included in Windows 7 (R_{WIN}) and the end-user version of *Dragon Naturally Speaking 10* (R_{DRAG}). R_{WIN} provides sentence alternatives and scores, while the R_{DRAG} only provides the transcription. Neither of the two recognizers was adapted to the speaker beforehand, i.e. both used generic US English models. Additionally, we created a "pseudo" recognizer (R_{PSEUD}) that takes the correct transcript and replaces random words in a controlled fashion. We tested a number of parameters in different combinations. The first goal was to find out how much the initial error rate could be improved if the number of IS would not play a role (i.e. find an upper boundary for the method). The second goal was to see how the error rate would change if a tolerance level with respect to the maximum number of IS was defined.

RESULTS

With the R_{WIN} recognizer, our baseline is the initial WER of 18.4% (and stddev of 21.8). Different degrees of improvement can be achieved using Directly Applied Sentence Alternatives (DASA) correction, Word Alternatives based on Sentence Alternatives (WASA), and LM. For each method, the number of top alternatives that are checked for the correct word is varied, starting from a low number that requires few IS because it can fit on a single screen without the user having to page or scroll, and moving towards a number (we chose 50) that models optimal performance. In addition, the maximum number of alternatives generated for LM and ASR was 50 respectively 20. For the LM method, we also compared the different training sets and ranking schemes. We omitted ranking tests for WASA because we can assume that all of the ASR's alternatives are already ordered w.r.t. similarity to the word to be corrected. On the lowest, but also least costly alternatives setting (5), the improvement in WER absolute percent is 4.8 for DASA, 5.6 for WASA, and 1.8 for LM using *in-domain* training. The corresponding numbers for the highest setting (50) are 9.4, 20.2, and 3.7. While the LM achieves a notable improvement, its "upper boundary" (6.5) still falls behind the methods that are based on extra information from the ASR. On the other hand, the performance only slightly decreases for the out-of-domain model (3.2 with 50 alternatives). In the cases where the number of displayed alternatives is smaller than the number of available alternatives (e.g. 20 vs. 50), a lexical or phonological re-ranking was performed. The phonolgical ranking almost always outperformed the lexical ranking, although the difference was not decisive ($< 1\%$). These results, as well as all others in this section, are statistically significant based on a two-tailed paired t-test at the level of $p\text{-}value < 0.01$.

The R_{DRAG} ASR has a lower initial WER, and so the effects are less visible, but still significant. Because it offers no sentence alternatives, only the LM-based correction method could be applied. Apart from that, it shows the same trends at 1.7 (in-domain), 4.2 (upper-boundary) and 1.51 (out-of-domain). The R_{PSEUD} recognizer was created to see if there was a relationship between ASR errors and difficulties of the two alternative generators. It is very likely that "real" recognizers make errors with seldom or difficult words, which are tough cases for the correction as well. Our observations appear to confirm this, as the same LM achieves a greater improvement on the artificial (evenly distributed) errors.

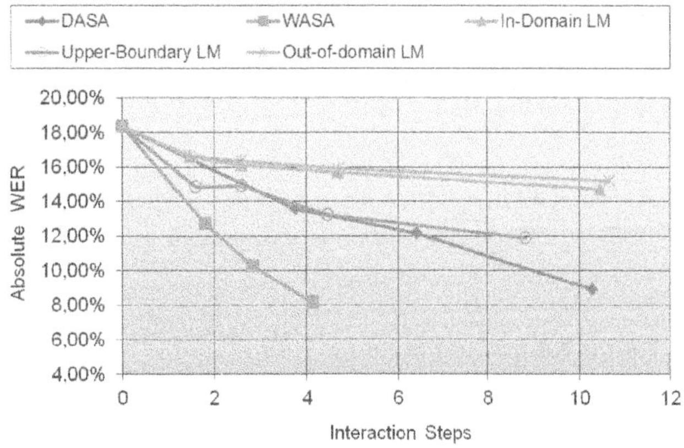

Figure 2. Tradeoff between interaction cost and correction performance. Marks correspond to the number of alternatives provided, which are 0, 5, 10, 20, and 50 (the upper limit is imposed by the ASR used).

Fig. 2 shows the IS' respective cost corresponding to the major experiments using R_{WIN}. For the LM conditions, the phonological ranking was selected. Recommendations in published standards [1] indicate that approximately five word alternatives can be displayed legibly on a 7" screen, so we counted an additional IS for each "page switch" the user would have needed to do. From the chart it can be seen what the improvement in WER for a given maximum number of IS may be. For example, if we allow four IS, the LM will provide a performance improvement of approximately 2.5% abs. However, if the ASR provides sentence alternatives, the improvement would be 10% abs. if WASA is used to generate word alternatives from them, and it requires approx. 4.1 IS.

CONCLUSIONS

This study presented a number of options how to deal with speech recognition errors in a scenario where user interactions are particularly costly and ASR configuration is limited. The approaches were compared in terms of performance, but also in terms of required interaction and with respect to their ASR feature requirements. The experiment suggests that an advanced ASR provides both the best overall accuracy as well as a good interaction/performance trade-off, but it also shows that post-correction matters: A purely LM-based approach, which requires no ASR insight, can still result in a solid performance increase of 3.7% abs. WER. While this is the biggest improvement the LM could achieve in our test, it requires approx. ten user interactions per sentence. If she commits only 2.6 interactions, which is more realistic in driving situations, the same method results in a gain of 2.6% absolute.

REFERENCES

1. ISO/TR 16352: Road vehicles – Ergonomic aspects of in-vehicle presentation for transport information and control systems, 2005.
2. Carnegie Mellon University. The CMU Pronouncing Dictionary, 2007.
3. Jeong, M., Jung, S., and Lee, G. G. Speech recognition error correction using maximum entropy language model. In *Proc. of INTERSPEECH 2004* (2004).
4. Jeong, M., Kim, B., and Lee, G. G. Semantic-oriented error correction for spoken query processing. In *Automatic Speech Recognition and Understanding (IEEE Workshop)* (2003), 156–161.
5. Jiang, X., Ma, M., and Chen, C. Speech recognition on mobile devices. In *Proc. WMMP 2008*, Springer (2010).
6. Kern, D., Mahr, A., Castronovo, S., and Müller, C. Making use of drivers' glances onto the screen for explicit gaze-based interaction. In *Proc. of AutomotiveUI-2010*, ACM (2010), 110–113.
7. López-Cózar, R., and Callejas, Z. ASR post-correction for spoken dialogue systems based on semantic, syntactic, lexical and contextual information. *Speech Communication 50*, 8-9 (2008), 745–766.
8. Macdonald, C., and Ounis, I. The trec blogs06 collection: Creating and analysing a blog test collection. Techn. rep., U.Glasgow, 2006.
9. Needleman, S. B., and Wunsch, C. D. A general method applicable to the search for similarities in the amino acid sequence of two proteins. *J. Mol. Biol. 48*, 3 (1970).
10. Rigger, E., and Allen, J. F. A fertility channel model for post-correction of continuous speech rec. In *Proc. of ICSLP* (1996), 897–900.
11. Vertanen, K., and Kristensson, P. Parakeet: A continous speech recognition system for mobile touch-screen devices. In *Proceedings of IUI 2009* (2009).
12. Vlingo Corporation. Vlingo Mobile, 2010.
13. Zhang, R., and Rudnicky, A. I. Word level confidence annotation using combinations of features. In *Proc. Eurospeech 2001* (2001).

Style by Demonstration: Teaching Interactive Movement Style to Robots

James E. Young[1,2], Kentaro Ishii[2,3], Takeo Igarashi[2,3], Ehud Sharlin[4]
young@cs.umanitoba.ca, kenta@ayu.ics.keio.ac.jp, takeo@acm.org, ehud@cpsc.ucalgary.ca

[1]University of Manitoba, Winnipeg, MB, Canada
[2]JST ERATO, Tokyo, Japan
[3]The University of Tokyo, Tokyo, Japan
[4]University of Calgary, Calgary, AB, Canada

ABSTRACT
The style in which a robot moves, expressed through its gait or locomotion, can convey effective messages to people. For example, a robot could move aggressively in reaction to a person's actions, or alternatively react using a set of careful, submissive movements. Designing, implementing and programming robotic interfaces that react to users' actions with properly styled movements can be a difficult, daunting, and time consuming technical task. On the other hand, most people can easily perform such stylistic tasks and movements, for example, through acting them out.

Following this observation, we propose to enable people to use their existing teaching skills to directly demonstrate to robots, via *in-situ acting*, a desired style of interaction. In this paper we present an initial style-by-demonstration (SBD) proof-of-concept of our approach, allowing people to teach a robot specific, interactive locomotion styles by providing a demonstration. We present a broomstick-robot interface for directly demonstrating locomotion style to a collocated robot, and a design critique evaluation by experienced programmers that compares our SBD approach to traditional programming methods.

Author Keywords
social human robot interaction, programming by demonstration, style by demonstration, tangible user interfaces, locomotion style, qualitative evaluation

ACM Classification Keywords
H.5.2 [Information Systems] Information Interfaces and Presentation: User Interfaces – Input devices and strategies

General Terms
Algorithms; Design.

INTRODUCTION
When designing robots that enter people's everyday environments it is important to look beyond utility and functionality and to explicitly consider *style*: the "expressive movement," way in which an action or behavior is performed [11]. People care a great deal about the style of objects and technologies that they possess, and a design can directly affect a person's interaction experience and satisfaction with things, including robots [26, 37]. We argue that people will desire their robots to be stylish, attractive and pleasing similarly to how they desire an attractive table, wristwatch, or car. This insight, we believe, adds an important style and design layer to the more-traditional utility and goal oriented human-robot interaction (HRI) approach. In this paper, we focus on the style of basic locomotion-based robotic interaction, but we believe that our approach can scale beyond this fundamental layer.

Figure 1. Style by demonstration: (left) a person uses a broomstick interface to show the robot a specific style of interactive movement (in this example, *follow politely*), and (right) the robot mimics the demonstration to follow politely.

Previous research shows that simple movement patterns by purely abstract entities lead people to construct intricate stories, personalities, and emotions [17]. Thus we point out the importance of considering the style of a robot's interactive locomotion movement as a key interaction layer, arguably as crucial to HRI design as a robot's physical form. We view interactive locomotion *style* as the manner in which a robot moves around a space in real-time reaction to a person. This stylistic locomotion can provide the robot with a body-language vocabulary, allowing it to interact with people in stylistically-appropriate ways in different tasks and settings. For example, a robot can present itself as being confident when approaching a task, or perhaps confused and unsure of its understanding, via upbeat or hesitant movements respectively. A robot which may endanger people can warn them to keep away by moving in aggressive, jerky movements, or a servant robot can inform people of its aspiration to serve by politely and humbly walking slowly behind them.

Advanced programming is generally required to enable robots to perform even simple tasks in the real world (e.g., pick up objects or follow a person), in part because robot actions must interactively respond to dynamic and unpredictable environments and people in real time. In many such real-world HRI tasks the style of the resulting robotic actions tends to reflect programming intrinsic task-completion- and efficiency-oriented approach [36]. To create robots that not only perform their tasks, but also act with specific style, for example, an aggressive, timid, or careful fashion, further complicates the HRI design and implementation challenge.

We propose a novel social human-robot interaction technique we call style-by-demonstration (SBD) as a means to enable people to directly design the style of interactive robot movement by providing an exemplar. This ueses in-situ physical acting to bypass traditional programming. Teaching in general is a skill that people are intimately familiar with from everyday interaction with other people, part of humanity's social stock of knowledge [2]. Teaching movement style via acting can be an intuitive and powerful method for showing a robot the style of how to perform a task. Our approach takes advantage of these existing teaching skills in order to empower people and to alleviate the difficult task of programming the style of interactive robotic movement behaviors. Programming-by-demonstration was previously explored in robotics (e.g., [10]), but as far as we know only targeted the fulfillment of a goal-oriented task. Our proposed SBD is unique in its focus on teaching the *style* of the interactive robotic behavior, rather than a set of actions leading towards an explicit task goal.

In this paper we present the design and implementation of an SBD system which enables people to teach a robot how it should interact with a person, specifically, the interactive style of the robot's locomotion. Our prototype is based on a robot-on-a-broomstick tangible interface (Figure 1) and we realized the learning by adapting and expanding an existing animation-only SBD system (*Puppet Master*, only for animated entities [38]). To evaluate our system our paper includes a design critique performed by experienced programmers who compared our SBD systems with traditional programming techniques. Overall, we believe that our SBD technique offers a new insight on how social human-robot interaction can be designed using in-situ style demonstration and acting. We believe that systems similar to ours will be increasingly important as robotics and human-robot interaction (HRI) advances, and as more people with no programming background integrate robots into their social work and domestic environments.

RELATED WORK

There has been extensive work that shows how people attribute simple geometric shapes such as triangles, circles, and points with intentionality, personalities and gender based solely on the style of their movements around a screen [8, 17, 21, 29, 34]: for example, as an aggressive male *triangle* trying to corner a female *circle* [17]. Further, much of Disney's success at creating believable characters has been attributed to their realization that a character's movement style is critically important [32]. This has been an area of interest, for example as with one animated entity which performs scripted actions such as "pick up a glass" or "knock on a door" in a "neutral," "shy," or "angry" fashion [1]. This paper builds on these extensive past efforts, and attempts to adapt them to the field of HRI.

Style work perhaps most similar to ours is that which considers robot behavior in proximity to people. Although this primarily targets practical engineering, mobility and vision challenges [5, 23] or goal-centric predictive models [6], others looked at how close a robot should be to a person for comfort [35] and how a robot should follow naturally [12] (i.e., copying a path versus shortest route). Our work continues this research direction by developing a technique that allows users to easily teach robots how to interact in a desired style.

The most direct method employed for the creation of interactive robotic behavior is to explicitly program the behavior model, defining how the robot should react in particular situations (e.g., as with [4]). This is also true for the related problem of programming interactive animated characters such as those found in video games [3, 20] – such autonomous characters must also solve real-time interactive behavior problems, and so techniques from animation are highly relevant for robotics. While the programming approach results in satisfactory behaviors, it is generally inaccessible to the non-technical end-users who will want to customize their robots' behaviors.

Programming by demonstration is a mature field of research that has been applied to such applications as programming GUI operations [25] and animation, for example, for interactive collision avoidance and planning [7], or for the direct control or static playback of animations [18]. Many such approaches require synthesis from extensive example databases that require large amounts of technical-user pre-processing [8, 22]. For robots, similar approaches are used to teach navigation routes [20], moving or posing in a human-like fashion by copying interactive behavior (not learning it) [23], or performing specific physical tasks [13, 16, 24, 27]. Overall, these approaches target a particular task goal, movement, or plausibility of physical motion such as realistic walking or collision avoidance. Our work is unique in that it does not attempt to teach the steps needed for achieving a specific goal, nor how to copy a specific interaction flow, but rather concentrates on teaching the high-level *style* of interactive behavior, recognizing interactive style as its main focus in a manner detached from a specific task goal.

Some programming-by-demonstration robot systems [10, 28] enable the creation of stylistic and expressive motions, but these result in static movements only and are not interactive to a person's input. Other work incorporates prescripted style and emotion into their learning interfaces [24], but these are statically used to represent algorithmic states, and are not learned from demonstration. Yet other work focuses on understanding how people teach each other to inform how to design robot-teaching interfaces [33]. However, as far as we know there is no previous work on explicitly teaching a robot interactive style.

Overall, while programming by demonstration is widespread in robotics and the importance of robot movement style is evident, our work is as far as we know the first to explicitly focus on the creation of *interactive* and *stylistic* robotic behaviors (i.e., *stylistic locomotion*) via demonstration, and the first to directly explore how such style can be interactively embedded within a robot's locomotion path.

STYLE-BY-DEMONSTRATION INTERACTION

Here we introduce our interaction design for robotic locomotion style-by-demonstration (SBD). Our SBD system has two phases, *demonstration* and *generation*. During *demonstration*, the user provides an example of how the robot should be interacting with the person in a desired style (a paired motion). Both paths are given simultaneously in real time: the user is demonstrating the robotic movement style in-situ, reacting to an actual person's movement, providing the robot with an exemplar of what it should react to, and in what style it should react (Figure 1).

After *demonstration*, in the *generation* phase the robot incorporates the learned reactionary characteristics into real-time interaction: the person moves freely as before but now the robot is autonomously interacting and reacting to the person's movement with its newly acquired and appropriated styled movement style (Figure 1). In our system, the robot's movement model is entirely contained in this learning: no prior robot movements or path following algorithms are included.

A Broomstick Interface for Teaching Movement Style

One leading goal in developing our new interface was to enable the user to focus on desired motion style rather than on the mechanics of moving the robot. In this case, the robot we use is an iRobot Create (Figure 2), a disc-like robot that moves via a 2-wheel-plus-caster base (preventing it from moving sideways) and rides close to the ground. We ruled out directly tracking a person's natural movements for demonstration as they would likely be too expressive and contain motions and nuances not reproducible by the robot. Further, the small size and height of our robot makes it impractical for a person to grab and move directly (i.e., will likely require crawling). Rather we suggest using a replica of the robot as an interaction metaphor supporting the in-situ demonstration of movement style.

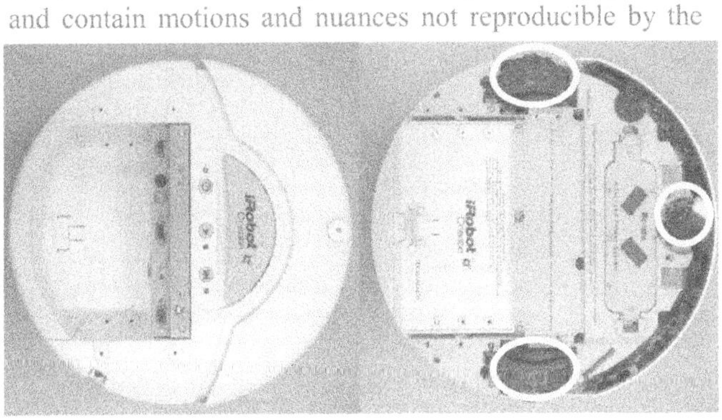

Figure 2. iRobot Roomba, with underside view: two-wheel base and coaster highlighted.

To implement our approach we developed a broomstick tangible-user interface (TUI) that connects directly to an iRobot Create, allowing the user a direct yet valid method of demonstrating style, encapsulating the robot's movement properties and constraints [14, 15]. This further focuses on the robot's particular embodiment, enabling the person to experience the interaction through the robot's capabilities, and forcing them to adhere to them [9]. Our design ensures the user's demonstrated motions will be later reproducible by the robot, and at the same time communicates the mechanical movement constraints to the user as they engage in the movement demonstration. This immediate tactile feedback reduces indirection between the input device and ultimate output, improving usability [19, 30].

We use a regular aluminum broomstick attached to the robot (Figure 1, Figure 3, Figure 9) via a two-axis swivel, allowing the stick to be freely moved (but not twisted) without moving the robot. A user can turn the robot by tilting the broomstick left or right, or twisting it, during movement. The robot's wheel motors have been disconnected (gears removed) to reduce friction and force required to push the robot. The result is a natural and familiar mechanism allowing the user to demonstrate interactive locomotion style to the robot.

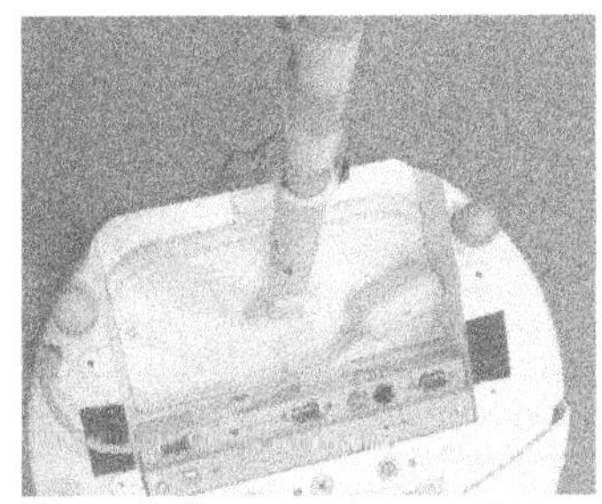

Figure 3. Broomstick mounting.

During the demonstration phase, one person walks naturally in the space (for the robot to react to) while the user maneuvers the broomstick interface to demonstrate a following movement style to the robot (Figure 1, left side). When demonstration is finished, a completely autonomous (non-broomsticked) robot enters the space and follows the person using the movement style that was demonstrated (Figure 1, right side). Communication with both the broomsticked and non-broomsticked robots is handled via Bluetooth, and both robots' and person's locations are tracked using Vicon camera motion-tracking (Figure 4). IR-reflective markers were affixed to the robots and person's shoes, with the person's location approximated as the midpoint between shoes. Note that the user manipulating the broomsticked robot is not being tracked directly, but rather their demonstrated movement style is tracked continuously through the broomsticked robot.

ALGORITHM

We adapted and extended an existing animation-only algorithm called Puppet Master for demonstrating stylistic mo-

Figure 4. The interaction space, tracking cameras highlighted.

tion to animated characters [38]. Puppet Master is an SBD platform for creating paired, style-oriented behaviors; instead of being used for robots, however, the original Puppet Master targets unconstrained animated characters.

Puppet Master is based on the notion of stylistic and interactive locomotion paths: the way the character moves to interact with a counterpart character [38]. As explained above for robotic SBD, Puppet Master has both *demonstration* and *generation* modes. After *demonstration* the real-time relationships between two animated characters are examined via their relative positions, orientations and velocities, all over an interaction history. For *generation* Puppet Master then uses a pattern patching approach for real-time output of the autonomous animated interactive character to employ the reactive style as demonstrated [38].

Puppet Master is a pattern matching algorithm that runs at relatively high speed (40hz [38]) to achieve interactivity, and uses heavy smoothing and frequency-analysis filtering to maintain coherent results. First, for *demonstration*, users provide an example of one animated character interacting with another using the locomotion path only, e.g., one character stalking another; this was previously accomplished using a digital tabletop system with tangible pucks for simultaneous character manipulation [38]. Then, during *generation*, Puppet Master searches the training set for locomotion paths similar to the real-time state, to inform ongoing character movements. Thus, the animated character output is a patch-work of training data pieces (Figure 5). Training-data is searched every time step to incorporate ongoing real-time user input, and uses a window of data (1s) compared against a window moving over the training

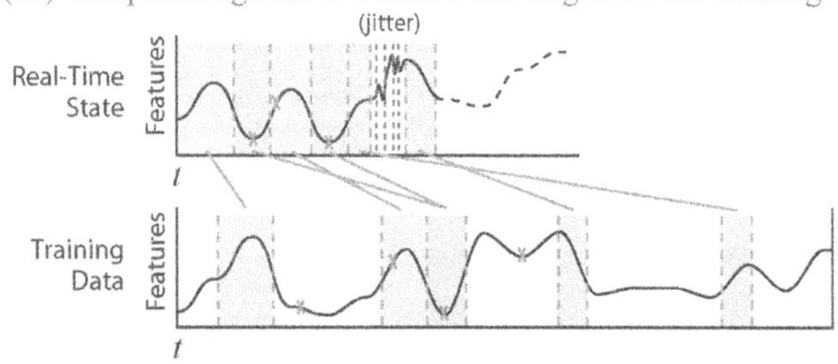

Figure 5. Real time entity is a set of patches from the best-match training data (illustration only). All dimensions of training and output for both the leader (human, in our work) and the reactor (robot) characters are summarized into a single curve for clarity. The red "x"s denote discrete auxiliary action events.

data set: this history is important to maintain higher-level movement coherency, e.g., one entity circling the other.

Here we explain the comparison metric. First, locomotion paths are distilled into defining scalar features: velocity, turning amount (left or right), relative look direction (one looking at the other), and relative position (e.g., behind and to the left of the other). These features form a vector at each time point that can be compared. The best-match training data is selected by minimizing the Euclidean distance between the real-time window of data and the moving window over the training data.

The best-match training cannot be copied verbatim to character output as the features generally conflict, e.g., the required movements to match target velocity (from the best match) may contradict the relative position. Puppet Master attempts to compromise by balancing the demands from the various features.

A problem with the Puppet Master algorithm is movement jitter, where the character will appear to vibrate rapidly in a way not consistent with the training data. This happens when the best-match source training data changes rapidly between conflicting source locations, when their match scores are similar; thus, rather than using coherent patches from the training data, in these instances only very small slices are used: this phenomenon is denoted in Figure 5. Puppet Master's solution was to a) heavily smooth the robot motions to filter the jitter and b) use frequency analysis to re-introduce the appropriate training movement detail that was lost in the filtering. This provided an improvement but the results were still not satisfactory to users [38].

The summary provided here was for the purpose of explaining the background to the Puppet Master platform; important details were omitted for brevity and we recommend those wishing to implement this work to refer to the original Puppet Master papers.

Adaption to Robots

When we applied the animation-only Puppet Master algorithm to robots we quickly found that it was not successful in generating reasonable stylistic robotic motion due to the hard movement and speed constraints posed by real robots. The animation Puppet Master freely modified the output movement (i.e., smoothed and exaggerated or tweaked) where necessary to best match the desired overall result; for example, an animated character could easily be moved a little sideways or turned while moving toward an appropriate relative location or orientation. Robots, however, work on irregular surfaces and must adhere to real constraints such as movement speed or physical design. Robots cannot be moved as freely as the animated characters, and we found that in our case the robot could not move as required to match the Puppet Master algorithm output; problems include the robot's acceleration and deceleration delays, and in our case the platform's inability to move sideways.

Thus, the result of our initial algorithm adaption was that the robot lost both the movement detail (or texture) and the relative-to-human position prescribed by the Puppet Master algorithm. Overall, the resulting reactive movement style was unconvincing and our attempts to reduce the algorithm from the animation's 40 Hz [38] to 20 Hz to better reflect the robot limitations had no observable improvement.

Our solution was to thoroughly revise the adopted Puppet Master algorithm. We applied rudimentary frequency analysis grounded in the robot's movement capabilities, balancing overall robot-human localization (low-frequency) and movement texture (high-frequency component). We used a kinematic model of the iRobot Create – describing the robot's movement capabilities and constraints (Figure 6) – to produce both the high and low frequency components in terms of robot commands: the results are movements guaranteed to be reproducible by our robot. We used this model (Figure 6) by solving for robotic movement commands (*velocity* and *turning radius*) given a target $\Delta x, \Delta y,$ and $\Delta\theta$ (difference in look direction) using simple trigonometry: $r = \Delta x + \frac{\Delta y}{\tan\theta}$, $vt = \theta r$ where r is turning radius and vt is distance or velocity multiplied by time.

First, we use the kinematic model to solve for the robot command that will move it to a given Puppet Master target state (Figure 7a,b). This is the *low-frequency* component of the desired movement as it changes relatively slowly over time, which places the robot in the desired area and orientation. However, as the robot cannot instantly keep up with the moving target over time, the texture (or details) of the desired movement are lost. Second, we find how the robot can reproduce the exact desired path (Figure 7c), by solving for the delta movement (change in direction, and location) rather than the target location. This maintains the high-frequency component, but drift in the robot's imperfect movements means that the robot soon loses its relative localization: the *low frequency* component.

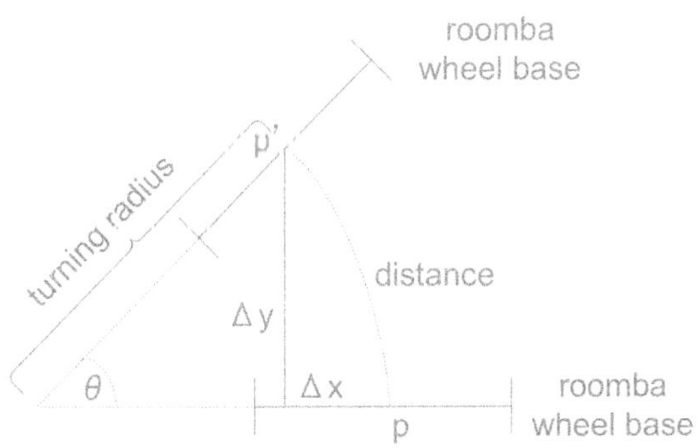

Figure 6. The Roomba movement capabilities, showing the relationship between its control scheme of setting *velocity* (distance / time) and *turning radius* and the resulting Δx and Δy.

Finally, we combine the above two components by using a weighted average of the two resulting robot commands, the velocity and turning radius Figure 7d. Focusing on the high-frequency component results in better texture retention but more location drift, and a focus on the low-frequency component has the opposite effect. We use a 70/30 high/low-frequency balance, selected through experimentation. The intuition is that existing high-frequency robot movements which tend to move away from the target location are slightly modified by the algorithm to correct their direction, while movements that are already directed toward the overall target are generally unchanged. Figure 8 details the overall process. During *demonstration*, input is fed directly into the Puppet Master base algorithm. For *generation*, the Puppet Master output is filtered through the kinematic model as a form of frequency analysis, and both outputs are weighted to produce the final robot command.

We believe that our solution is a unique method for filtering a desired movement against robot capabilities while focusing on the balance of texture and locomotion, and can be used for the general problem of applying unconstrained animation behaviors to the rigid constraints of real robots.

We further propose that our algorithm could be applied to different robot morphologies simply by using the proper kinematic model. This is not necessarily for locomotion paths only, but for any movement path, e.g., an arm path or head movement path. If a robot system is given an unpredictable movement path without look-ahead capabilities, it can apply our method to adopt the path while focusing on maintaining style if it has a kinematic model which enables it to: a) calculate the closest possible fit to reproducing that path (via a kinematic model) and b) calculate the shortest-path route to a far absolute target. These can be combined as explained above for real-time dynamic robot motion. Thus, we believe that our system can be extended and used to demonstrate movement style to robots that are more complex, with more degrees-of-freedom than the platform currently used.

Integrating Stylized Auxiliary Actions

In addition to the above algorithm enabling the demonstration of stylized movement to robots, we explored whether

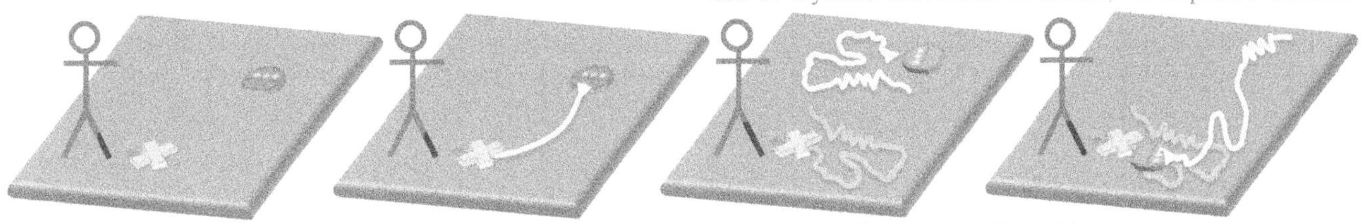

(a) robot and target state

(b) solve for robot to reach target state in one time step (if possible)

(c) target state over time forms path, solve for robot to reproduce texture

(d) combine movements, tend toward target location over time

Figure 7. The algorithm robot-movement frequency analysis principle.

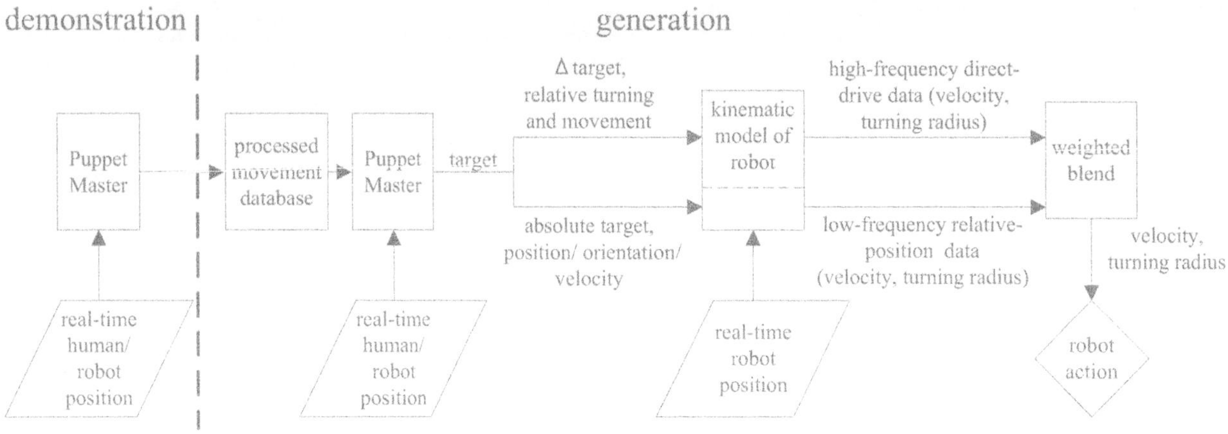

Figure 8. The algorithm data-flow and processing, and how Puppet Master connects to the real-time robot data.

the algorithm can be extended beyond movement, to support stylizing any discrete robot actions. Our presented extension allows the user to teach the robot the *appropriate times* during interaction in which it should make *happy* or *unhappy* sounds in relation to the overall behavior style. To support the teaching of auxiliary actions by the user, we augmented the broomstick with two buttons (Figure 9) so that the person can trigger the robot sounds (happy or sad) during demonstration. The buttons are wired into a modified Phidget Remote wireless FOB clicker and standard Phidget interface kit.

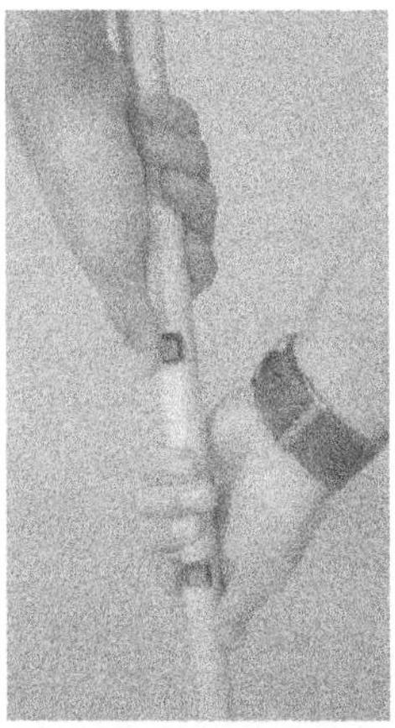
Figure 9. Broomstick-Roomba interface, with mounted buttons.

The main purpose of this extension goes beyond sound, but rather aims at exploring the scalability of the SBD algorithm and interface to any robotic actions which are not necessarily derivative of locomotion paths. Algorithmically and interaction-wise, the current robot sounds can be replaced by any discrete pre-programmed robotic action such as taking a photo, facial expressions, discrete gestures, or speech. Following, our SBD approach could be used to teach a robot the difficult-to-define problem of *when* to perform such discrete actions.

Algorithmically, we accomplished auxiliary actions by associating the demonstrated actions with the existing training data on the time axis, such that the data is marked with the action at the appropriate time: a visualization of how the timings are superimposed on the training data is given in Figure 5. Then, as particular training data is used to construct output during generation, the associated actions are included in the robot output.

EXPERIENCED-PROGRAMMERS DESIGN CRITIQUE

While the fundamental premise of our work is that SBD provides a new interaction mechanism that allows untrained users to easily design stylized robotic movement, we focus this design critique on a more preliminary question: how does SBD differ from more-traditional programming methods? We recruited experienced programmers and asked them to create interactive robot behaviors both programmatically and using our SBD broomstick interface. These participants were qualified enough to create interactive behaviors using programming, and can engage the SBD interface the same as any other person, giving them a unique comparison vantage point and providing us with an analysis of the trade-offs and benefits of each. This further enables us to reflect on a more acute question: if an expert were to design a robotic interactive style, will they still find advantages in SBD compared to the more structured programming methodologies?

We expect that these demanding and insightful technical users would inform us on a group of users that can be viewed as a worse-case subset: those with high and critical expectations of what the robot should do. Arguably, if experienced programmers who can design robotic behaviors via programming find our SBD approach advantageous, regular users lacking such expertise and training will also be able to benefit from the SBD method.

For our design critique we recruited four experienced programmers from our graduate-student lab. Our participants were three male / one female and did not have prior exposure to our work. The programmers were asked to create stylized robot movement behaviors via two conditions: 1. programming using Java code, and 2. creating the same stylized movement behaviors using our broomstick SBD tangible interface, and to reflect on their experiences with both. This design critique was primarily exploratory, and thus our main analysis method was to provide initial qualitative detailed descriptions of the reflections as themes to portray the experiences and opinions of the participants (following an evaluation method described in [31]): we see this as a precursor to direct more formal experiments.

Study Design and Procedure

We selected four stylized robot movement behaviors, a polite follow (*polite*), a robot stalking a person (*stalker*), a robot that is happy to see the person (*happy*), and a robot that is attacking a burglar (*burglar*).

For the programming condition we provided a robot-simulation prototyping test-bench and an API for reading the robot and person's locations and providing real-time commands; Figure 10a shows the output screen with robot, person (happy face), and an arrow handle for manual control. After initial explanation, programmers were given two hours to create the four behaviors.

Following the programming condition, participants created the same stylized movement behaviors using the broomstick SBD interface, where they were allowed to demonstrate stylized movement behavior, and observe it repeatedly for as long as they wished before moving on to the next, and could re-train a behavior if they were not satisfied with the result (Figure 10b). This phase was video-taped.

Post-study we interviewed (unstructured) the participants regarding their overall experience.

Results

All participants took the full two hours to program their stylized movement behaviors, and all were able to create their behaviors in the time given, although one programmer stated that they would require a great deal more time to implement proper "nuanced behaviors." For SBD, all programmers were observed to "act the characters," making faces, laughing, etc. Table 1 shows SBD demonstration attempts and length (seconds). The "total time" listed is the duration of creating all behaviors using SBD, from start to finish, including observation, thinking, brief discussion, and retraining time.

When asked which they preferred, direct programming or programming by demonstration, all programmers articulated a set of trade-offs rather than preference, for example, "the programming spoke to the scientist in me, and the other, the broomstick demonstration, spoke to the non-scientific part of me."

The programming approach was touted as being more accurate and kept the programmer "in control" in comparison with the demonstration. Because of this, one person stated that they felt like they had "a lot more power to do something creative." However, control is not easy or complete; one programmer noted "when you're programming something you have to anticipate ... what kind of situations can come up and how [the robot] should react ... that's not a natural way of doing things." The programmers made statements highlighting the difficulty of the direct programming condition. For example, general programming difficulties still exist: it's "hard to debug the program even though I have the simulated environment," "even when I program I don't know exactly what is going to happen," and "when I see problems, I still don't know why it happens."

Table 1. Demonstration times in the SBD condition; only three are shown (of four) as one participant requested not to be video-taped, and we did not record the data directly

Behavior	programmer 1	programmer 2	programmer 3
Polite follow – tries	2	1	1
time	44 s	31 s	24 s
Stalker – tries	1	1	1
time	65 s	46 s	31 s
Attacking burglar – tries	1	1	1
time	51 s	44 s	25 s
Happy to see you – tries	2	1	1
time	40 s	37 s	24 s
total time	14 m 49 s	8 m 52 s	7 m 40 s

Programmers mentioned that by focusing on style during programming the "types of things [they were] trying to express were more nuanced, more complicated behaviors" than the "easily expressed things like sine waves" that they are used to creating in interactive characters (referring to the approach to smooth animation). One programmer noted that doing the programming before demonstration helped to highlight the sheer difficulty of the real-time problem, and helped them to appreciate the demonstration system.

a) Programming test-bench. b) Demonstrate and observe cycle for broomstick SBD

Figure 10. Participants were given two hours with the test bench to program the *polite*, *stalker*, *happy*, and *burglar* behaviors. Following, participants used the broomstick SBD interface to create the same behaviors, one at a time.

Programmers noted that the SBD broomstick interaction is much faster and easier than direct coding. By using the demonstration system they "did not have to think technically or analytically," and could more-easily program movement styles. As such "there is a huge time-saving potential here." One reason cited for the broomstick's success is that people are very skilled at "understanding changing situations on an instant-to-instant basis and [can] essentially make up [their] own behaviors on the fly." However, several programmers pointed out that SBD cannot be perfect as they are "at the mercy of the system" and their "demonstration is just a small part of the bigger thing." They are "relying on its interpretations of [their] intentions, rather than on [their] actual intentions. There is no way to directly convey intentions," for example, they could not specify hard constraints such as "stay away from the corner."

We asked the programmers to provide an informal design critique of our broomstick interface. One programmer mentioned that the robot can be difficult to turn quickly; however, this programmer tried to train the robot to turn much-more quickly than the real robot could perform. That is, although the interface is limiting, its restrictions are in accordance with the movement capabilities of the real robot. Another, who has professional game development experience, said that he thinks of the robots as non-player-characters in a game where he would not consider using SBD as-is for entities at the forefront of the. However he felt that there is real potential for SBD for side-line entities. Another participant pointed out that the inherent inaccuracy of the demonstration system is not necessarily a problem, as perhaps the broomstick can be used to capture a rough behavior and serve as a medium fidelity prototyping method for behaviors that can be later programmed more thoroughly. Programmers also provided suggestions on how to mix the pure demonstration approach with more logical components, for example, to enable demonstrators to explicitly specify which components are important, or give them easy-to-understand variables to tweak when observing the result (e.g., as tangible knobs or a hand-held interface).

Two programmers noted that the physical energy required to demonstrate stylized movement using the SBD broomstick (in the large space) was more exhausting than the act of programming. They mused about the use of a remote controller to reduce the fatigue problem, although they both admitted that a remote controller would result in an interaction that would likely be less immersive and affording less expressiveness in comparison to the TUI broomstick. One participant suggested a tabletop TUI system as way to keep direct movement while lowering the effort required.

Discussion

The primary purpose of our design critique was to leverage the expertise of programmers and their unique perspective to analyze our SBD approach, particular interface and implementation. We believe that the detailed feedback from the programmers provides unique insight that will be valuable for the continued development and evaluation of SBD robotic interfaces.

Our design critique supports the general SBD idea and approach, suggesting that it is applicable and valid even for experienced programmers. As shown in Table 1, all participants managed to complete the creation and evaluation process in less than 15 minutes, substantially less than the 2 hours taken for programming. Obviously, we expect the SBD benefits to be dramatically stronger for users without extensive programming experience or abilities, where the SBD approach may be the only method that would enable them to design stylized robot movement behaviors

Beyond the time-efficiency results, we highlight the level of emotional engagement which emerged: the programmers using SBD readily acted and got into the characters, using their entire body to express movements, for example, laughing and making facial expressions to match what they were demonstrating. Thus, even for technical users who have an understanding of the nature of the robot, our results help support the idea that programming style to robots via demonstration leverages their innate social understanding and skills, and they employ emotional interaction similarly to how they would with a person.

One of the benefits of our evaluation study was that the participants, like any other person, benefited from the social stock of knowledge [2] that makes the SBD demonstration familiar and comfortable, and further had the benefit of technical understanding of the problem and the required expertise to solve it using programming. Their feedback improved our understanding of the accuracy / control versus time / ease trade-off. We observe that programming may enable people to be creative in ways that demonstrating does not, and that the complexity of the programming approach means that it still leaves a layer of uncertainty and mystery for experienced programmers, despite the extra control, which the SBD approach may help alleviate.

Further, our participants proposed to combine the programming (more control) and demonstration (easier to do) approaches, for example, by using the demonstration as a prototyping tool, or by including easy-to-understand parameters or conditions modifiable by the demonstrator.

Many of the participants' observations help us to better-understand the limitations of demonstration, for example, that there is potentially no optimal solution as machines cannot understand a person's intentions, only their actions, and this interpretation is subjective to the demonstration-learning interface and algorithm. We point out, however, that people suffer from the same problem as these robots: people cannot know others' intentions, only what can be deduced from interaction. Regardless, this suggests that we should aim to better understand the particular biases introduced by any given algorithm, and how this relates to target applications and usage scenarios.

Overall, this critique helped to verify the applicability of SBD for interactive robot behaviors and our particular interfaces, and provided insight into the trade-offs between SBD and traditional programming.

CONCLUSION AND FUTURE WORK

In this paper we presented the idea of teaching robots *interactive, stylistic locomotion* by *demonstration*. We detailed our technical solution, introduced a novel robot-broomstick interface, and detailed our robotic evolution of an animation-based algorithm. Finally, we presented a design critique that helped us gain insight into the benefits and limitations of SBD in relation to traditional programming.

One deficiency of this research to date is the lack of a formal extensive study on the use of SBD for robots, the efficiency of the broomstick TUI, as well as the quality of the underlying robot SBD algorithm. The design critique presented in this paper serves as an important, but still preliminary step toward such a thorough evaluation.

Another issue for consideration is the concern that perhaps people may not be skilled at acting out how they want the robot to behave. That is, while people know what they like or what they want, they may not be able to demonstrate it in a manner which portrays their intent. Puppeteers and actors take years of training to develop these abilities.

In the longer term we are planning to explore the scalability of both our SBD approach and our current algorithm to more elaborate robotic expressions. For example, can we use a similar algorithm to simply demonstrate to a robotic teacher surrogate how to move its arms sternly, or enthusiastically? Can it be used to demonstrate to robotic service provider, say a waiter, how to collect dishes apologetically? We expect that designing style by demonstration can be mapped to other, more complex applications, and integrated closely with other robot programming approaches.

SBD provides a new language, a new vocabulary, which people can use to communicate and program robots: with existing methods, users who cannot program will be ignorant of how to teach their robot the desired style.

With the continued advance of technology robots are expected to share more and more of our physical and social spaces. Robot acceptance will be based as much on a robot's style of interaction as on their goal oriented task performance. Providing simple, well situated tools that will enable non-technical people to show their robots in what style to act can become an important layer of future efforts of integrating robotic interfaces in our everyday environments. We believe our style-by-demonstration approach presented here is an important early step in this direction.

REFERENCES

1. AMAYA, K., BRUDERLIN, A., AND CALVERT, T. Emotion from motion. In *Proceedings of Graphics Interface 1996. GI '96, Toronto, Canada, May 22–24, 1996* (1996), Canadian Human-Computer Communications Society, pp. 222–229.
2. BERGER, P. L., AND LUCKMANN, T. The social construction of reality: a treatsie in the sociology of knowledge. Anchor Books, 1966.
3. BLUMBERG, B. M., AND GALYEAN, T. A. Multi-level direction of autonomous creatures for real-time virtual environments. In *Proc. SIGGRAPH '95* (1995), ACM, pp. 47–54.
4. BREAZEAL, C., AND SCASSELLATI, B. A context-dependent attention system for a social robot. In *Proc. IJCAI '99* (Stockholm, Sweden, 1999), IJCAI Press, pp. 1146–1151.
5. BYERS, D., AND JENKINS, O. C. HRI caught on film 2: Hands-free human-robot interaction. In *Proc. HRI '08* (NY, USA, 2008), C. Bartneck, Ed., ACM.
6. CHUEH, M., JOSHI, S., YEUNG, Y. L. A., AND LEI, K. P. Towards a mobile-robot following controller using behavioral cues. In *Proc. ICIT '06* (USA, 2006), IEEE, pp. 150–157.
7. DINERSTEIN, J., EGBERT, P. K., AND VENTURA, D. Learning policies for embodied virtual agents through demonstration. In *Proc. IJCAI '07* (2007), IJCAI Press, pp. 1257–1262.
8. DONTCHEVA, M., YNGVE, G., AND POPOVIC, Z. Layered acting for character animation. *ACM Trans. Graph. 22*, 3 (2003), 409–416.
9. DOURISH, P. Where the Action Is: The Foundation of Embodied Interaction. MIT Press, MA, 2001.
10. FREI, P., SU, V., MIKHAK, B., AND ISHII, H. curlybot: designing a new class of computational toys. In *Proc. CHI '00* (NY, USA, 2000), ACM, pp. 129–136.
11. GALLAHER, P. E. Individual differences in nonverbal behavior: Dimensions of style. *Journal of Personality and Social Psychology 63*, 1 (1992), 133–145.
12. GOCKLEY, R., FORLIZZI, J., AND SIMMONS, R. Natural person-following behavior for social robots. In *Proc. HRI '07* (NY, USA, 2007), ACM, pp. 17–24.
13. GRIBOVSKAYA, E., AND BILLARD, A. D. Combining dynamical systems control and programming by demonstration for teaching discrete bimanual coordination tasks to a humanoid robot. In *Proc. HRI '08* (NY, 2008), ACM, pp. 33–40.
14. GUO, C., AND SHARLIN, E. Exploring the use of tangible user interfaces for human-robot interaction: a comparitive study. In *Proc. CHI '08* (2008), ACM, pp. 121–130.
15. GUO, C., YOUNG, J. E., AND SHARLIN, E. Touch and toys: new techniques for interaction with a remote group of robots. In *Proc. CHI '09* (2009), pp. 491–500.
16. HALBERT, D. *Programming by Example*. PhD thesis, University of California Berkeley, 1984.

17. HEIDER, F., AND SIMMEL, M. An experimental study of apparent behavior. *American J. of Psychology 57* (1944), 243–259.

18. IGARASHI, T., MOSCOVICH, T., AND HUGHES, J. F. As-rigid-as-possible shape manipulation. *ACM Trans. Graph. 24*, 3 (2005), 1134–1141.

19. ISHII, H., AND ULLMER, B. Tangible bits: Towards seamless interfaces between people, bits and atoms. In *Proc. CHI '97* (1997), ACM, pp. 234–241.

20. KANDA, T., KAMASIMA, M., IMAI, M., ONO, T., SAKAMOTO, D., ISHIGURO, H., AND ANZAI, Y. A humanoid robot that pretends to listen to route guidance from a human. *Auton. Robots 22*, 1 (2007), 87–100.

21. KASSIN, S. M. Heider and Simmel (1944) revisited: causal attribution and the animated film technique. *Review of Personality and Social Psychology 3* (1982), 125–150.

22. LEE, J., AND LEE, K. H. Precomputing avatar behavior from human motion data. In *Proc. SCA '04* (Aire-la-Ville, Switzerland, Switzerland, 2004), Eurographics Association, pp. 79–87.

23. LIEM, M., VISSER, A., AND FROEN, G. A hybrid algorithm for tracking and following people using a robotic dog. In *Proc. HRI '08* (2008), ACM, pp. 185–192.

24. LOCKERD, A., AND BREAZEAL, C. Tutelage and socially guided robot learning. In *Proc. IEEE/RSJ IROS '04* (USA, 2004), vol. 4, IEEE, pp. 3475–3480.

25. MAULSBY, D. L., WITTEN, I. H., AND KITTLITZ, K. A. Metamouse: specifying graphical procedures by example. In *Proc. SIGGRAPH '89* (NY, USA, 1989), ACM, pp. 127–136.

26. NORMAN, D. A. Emotional Design: Why We Love (or Hate) Everyday Things. Basic Books, NY, 2004.

27. OTERO, N., ALISSANDRAKIS, A., DAUTENHAHN, K., NEHANIV, C., SYRDAL, D., AND KOAY, K. Human to robot demonstrations of routine home tasks: exploring the role of the robot's feedback. In *Proc. HRI '08* (NY, 2008), ACM, pp. 177–184.

28. RAFFLE, H. S., PARKES, A. J., AND ISHII, H. Topobo: a constructive assembly system with kinetic memory. In *Proc. CHI '04* (NY, USA, 2004), ACM, pp. 647–654.

29. SCHOLL, B. J., AND TREMOULET, P. D. Perceptual causality and animacy. *Trends in Cognitive Sciences (TRENDS) 4*, 8 (Aug. 2000), 299–309.

30. SHARLIN, E., WATSON, B., KITAMURA, Y., KISHINO, F., AND ITOH, Y. On tangible user interfaces, humans and spatiality. *Personal and Ubiquitous Computing 8*, 5 (2004), 338–346.

31. STRAUSS, A., AND CORBIN, J. *Basics of Qualitative Research: Techniques and Procedures for Developing Grounded Theory*. Sage Publications, Thousand Oaks, London, New Delhi, 1998.

32. THOMAS, F., AND JOHNSTON, O. *The Illusion of Life: Disney Animation*, first hyperion ed. ed. Disney Editions (Walt Disney Productions), 1981.

33. THOMAZ, A. L., AND BREAZEAL, C. Teachable robots: Understanding human teaching behavior to build more effective robot learners. *Artificial Intelligence 172* (2008), 716–737.

34. TREMOULET, P. D., AND FELDMAN, J. Perception of animacy from the motion of a single object. *Perception 29*, 8 (May 2000), 943–951.

35. YAMAOKA, F., KANDA, T., ISHIGURO, H., AND HAGITA, N. How close?: model of proximity control for information-presenting robots. In *Proc. HRI '08* (NY, USA, 2008), ACM, ACM, pp. 137–144.

36. YANCO, H. A., AND DRURY, J. L. Classifying human-robot interaction: an updated taxonomy. In Proceedings of the IEEE International Conference on Systems, Man and Cybernetics, 2004. SMC '04, The Hague, The Netherlands, October 10–13, 2004 (Oct. 2004), vol. 3, IEEE, pp. 2841–2846.

37. YOUNG, J. E., HAWKINS, R., SHARLIN, E., AND IGARASHI, T. Toward acceptable domestic robots: Applying insights from social psychology. *Inagural Issue of the Int. J. Social Robotics. January 2009 1*, 1 (2009).

38. YOUNG, J. E., IGARASHI, T., AND SHARLIN, E. Puppet master: Designing reactive character behavior by demonstration. In *ACM SIGGRAPH / EG SCA '08.* (Germany, 2008), EG Press, EG Association, pp. 183–191.

PhysicsBook: A Sketch-based Interface for Animating Physics Diagrams

Salman Cheema
University of Central Florida
Orlando, FL
salmanc@cs.ucf.edu

Joseph J. LaViola Jr.
University of Central Florida
Orlando, FL
jjl@eecs.ucf.edu

ABSTRACT

We present PhysicsBook, a prototype system that enables users to solve physics problems using a sketch-based interface and then animates any diagram used in solving the problem to show that the solution is correct. PhysicsBook recognizes the diagrams in the solution and infers relationships among diagram components through the recognition of mathematics and annotations such as arrows and dotted lines. For animation, PhysicsBook uses a customized physics engine that provides entry points for hand-written mathematics and diagrams. We discuss the design of PhysicsBook, including details of algorithms for sketch recognition, inference of user intent and creation of animations based on the mathematics written by a user. Specifically, we describe how the physics engine uses domain knowledge to perform data transformations in instances where it cannot use a given equation directly. This enables PhysicsBook to deal with domains of problems that are not directly related to classical mechanics. We provide examples of scenarios of how PhysicsBook could be used as part of an intelligent tutoring system and discuss the strengths and weaknesses of our current prototype. Lastly, we present the findings of a preliminary usability study with five participants.

Author Keywords

Sketch-based User Interfaces, Sketch Recognition, Mathematical Sketching, Inferring User Intent

ACM Classification Keywords

H5.2 [Information interfaces and presentation]: User Interfaces. - Graphical user interfaces.

General Terms

Algorithms, Human Factors

INTRODUCTION

Sketch-based interfaces capture the ease of using pen and paper to communicate ideas while simultaneously leveraging the power of computation. Such interfaces have been used for tasks such as 3D modeling [8], musical score creation [6], and website design [16]. We are interested in the application of sketch-based interaction in physics and mathematics domains. Both teachers and students often sketch diagrams while solving problems or demonstrating concepts. When students are asked to solve physics/mathematics problems, their solutions usually follow a general pattern. They start from a problem statement, and usually begin by drawing a diagram and annotating it with the information provided in the problem statement. Common annotations for physics diagrams include shape labels, arrows indicating vector quantities and the scale of motion. Students then go through a series of mathematical steps to arrive at an answer, typically a function or number. On paper, the answer itself does little to impart intuitive knowledge to a student. Students have to rely on their imagination to visualize how their answer would affect the scenario presented in the question. Figure 1 illustrates such a scenario.

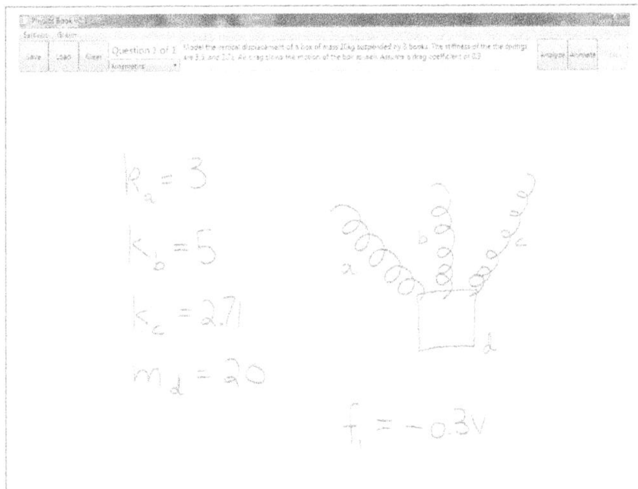

Figure 1. An example scenario where a student wants to model the vertical displacement of a box suspended by three springs and affected by air drag. Using PhysicsBook, the student can view the vertical displacement by sketching the system as shown and viewing the graph during animation.

A sketch-based tutoring system promises a natural mode of interaction, while leveraging the power of computation to animate the sketch. To this end, it is vital to develop an understanding of the entire problem-solving process, including the statement of the question, the mathematical steps in the solution and any sketched diagrams along with their annotations.

Our research goal is to construct a sketch-based physics tutoring system that integrates such knowledge and uses it to facilitate student learning. We envision it to have the following feature set:

1. *Natural Interaction*: Allow students to solve a problem as they would using pen and paper.
2. *Robust Recognition*: Distinguish between mathematical steps in a given problem's solution and any diagrams that students may have sketched.
3. *Reasoning*: Should be capable of high-level reasoning about diagrams and the mathematical steps in a student's solution . This can be done by integrating a sufficient level of physics knowledge into the system. Such reasoning allows inference of intent behind a sketch and can be used to provide error feedback and hints to students.
4. *Feedback*: Allow students to view how the values of physical quantities vary during animation. Graphing is an important tool in this respect. Step by step feedback and error highlighting may also be used for knowledge scaffolding [24].
5. *Seamless Animation*: The tutoring system should be able to animate the diagrams in a student's solution, given any granularity of input. Triggering the animation should be seamless and natural. Students should be able to interact with and manipulate the animation of sketched diagrams, by use of hand-written mathematics and/or gestures.

With these goals in mind, we have developed PhysicsBook, a prototype sketch-based system that lets users write down the solution to a physics problem in a natural manner, including mathematics and free-form drawings. Using the answer to a problem, PhysicsBook animates the drawing to indicate whether the solution was correct. Existing interaction techniques such as mathematical sketching and the MathPad^2 system [13], were used as a starting point in the design of PhysicsBook. However, PhysicsBook goes well beyond these ideas because it does not require mathematical definitions of how objects should animate as functions of time. Instead, by integrating knowledge of classical mechanics and its related concepts, PhysicsBook is able to construct animations for a range of physics problems, with just the sketched diagram and a minimum amount of mathematics needed to solve the problem.

RELATED WORK

Sketch Recognition

Understanding of free-form sketches is a hard problem because of variation in symbols and notation in different domains. Paulson et al. [20] describe techniques for recognizing and beautifying several low-level sketch primitives. Patel et al. [19] have conducted a statistical analysis to select the most appropriate ink features for distinguishing between shapes and text in sketches. Hammond and Davis have developed LADDER [7] which allows a user to specify sketch recognition rules in a domain independent manner. Users can describe sketch primitives and some high level semantics for individual domains in text form, which is then used to generate domain specific recognizers. User perception of sketch recognition has been explored by Wais, Wolin, and Alvarado [23], who draw some very important lessons for sketch-based systems in general.

Higher level sketch-based applications have also been developed for a variety of contexts. MathPad^2 [13] provides a method for integrating written mathematics with animation of hand-drawn sketches. It is a domain independent system, where users must specify all aspects of animation through mathematics. PenProof [9] is a pen-based geometry theorem proving system that can infer correspondences between geometric constructs and proof steps. CogSketch [5] is an open domain sketch analysis system, which enables conceptual labeling of sketches. ChemInk [18] is a sketch recognition system for chemical drawings that uses conditional random fields to deliver good recognition accuracy. None of these applications have intelligent tutoring in physics as their motivation.

Physics Tutoring Systems

Traditionally, physics tutoring systems have relied on WIMP interfaces. A representative example is the Andes Physics Tutoring System [22], which provides step by step guidance in problem solving. The use of WIMP interfaces has several drawbacks. Students cannot write down their solutions in a natural manner as if using pen and paper. Tutoring systems in general must utilize some understanding of a given problem and its solution, in order to provide feedback. An advantage of sketch-based tutoring systems is the promise of a more natural mode of interaction. Compared to WIMP based interfaces, they can also incorporate sketch understanding techniques to provide better feedback/animation mechanisms.

While no sketch-based tutoring system of sufficient capability exists for physics, several researchers have made strides toward one in recent years. Alvarado [2], Oltmans [17] and Kara [11] have demonstrated systems for sketch understanding in the domains of computer aided design, mechanical design and vibratory systems. These tools can recognize and animate relevant diagrams but none of these allow users to write down mathematics that can influence animation. Newton's Pen [14] is a simple pen-based tutoring system for statics that does not allow free-form drawing or the use of written mathematics in animation.

Steps toward integration of mathematics and sketched physics diagrams, in order to generate animation have been taken by Cheema and LaViola [3, 4]. In particular, [3] investigates the use of Mathematical Sketching [10, 12] as an interaction mechanism for physics tutoring, enabling animation of simple diagrams with different granularities of input. This system employs sketch correction mechanisms for ensuring correct animation. However, it is limited to basic concepts related to motion such as the use of position, velocity, acceleration and force variables defined as functions of time. Additionally, it does not support implicit association of written mathematics nor allows the use of diagram annotations to infer the user's intent. The use of such annotations is extremely important to problem solving in physics [21, 27]. One major advantage of PhysicsBook over [3] is the use of data transformations that allow it to deal with instances where the given problem solution cannot be directly used for animation.

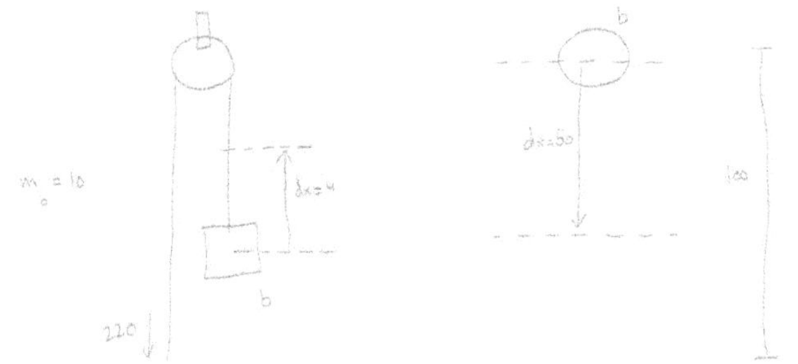

(a) Work done by pulley (b) Change in potential energy during freefall

Figure 2. A set of sample problems selected from a physics textbook.

Lastly, several commercial tools are also available that let users construct animations for physics concepts. Representative examples include Algodoo [1] and Working Model 2D [25]. Such tools can create animations but they do not let students work out a given problem and then directly associate the answer with a diagram to do the animation. In such tools, a student would solve the problem in a notebook and then have to separately reconstruct the diagram using the tool to perform the animation.

CHALLENGES IN UNDERSTANDING USER INTENT

The goals outlined in the introduction imply the need for core components to do three main tasks: Recognition, Inference and Animation. For sketch understanding, the most important tasks are Recognition and Inference. A recognizer accepts a sketch as input, containing both diagram and mathematics and generates a collection of primitive components which are then analyzed to infer correlations between the recognized diagram, its annotations and the mathematical equations in the solution. An important aspect of this process is the inference of intent in ambiguous cases. This encompasses understanding and beautification of approximate sketches and the use of annotations to gain a deeper understanding of the given problem. Techniques for beautification of sketches have been described for low-level primitives by [20] and for limited cases of higher level primitives by [3].

The challenges in sketch understanding can be highlighted by examining a set of questions from a physics textbook. In figure 2(a), a box of mass 10kg is lifted to a height of 4m by applying a force of 220N over an ideal pulley. The student is asked to find the work done on the box. A possible diagram in this case includes a circle denoting the pulley, with straight lines indicating wires. An arrow labeled with a numeric quantity can be used to indicate the force and an arrow sketched between two dotted lines can indicate change in displacement. It should be noted that this representation is not unique. The wire over the pulley could have been sketched as a single line passing over the circle, instead of as two separate line segments. Also, the student has indicated that the circle at the top is to serve as the pulley, by drawing an overlapping square to act as the hinge.

Similarly, Figure 2(b) depicts a scenario where a ball of mass 15kg is dropped from a 100m height. The student is asked to find the change in gravitational potential energy of the ball after it has fallen 50m. Note that the distance scale drawn to the right side of the sketch is redundant. The sketch contains sufficient information for animation without it. Yet, students commonly associate redundant information with a sketched diagram, in order to keep track of given information. The use of dotted lines and an arrow to indicate different levels of displacement here is common with Figure 2(a). Both examples highlight the importance of developing a semantic understanding of annotations for the animation of different classes of physics diagrams. It should also be noted that in both problems, some information is missing (e.g., the student did not indicate weight).

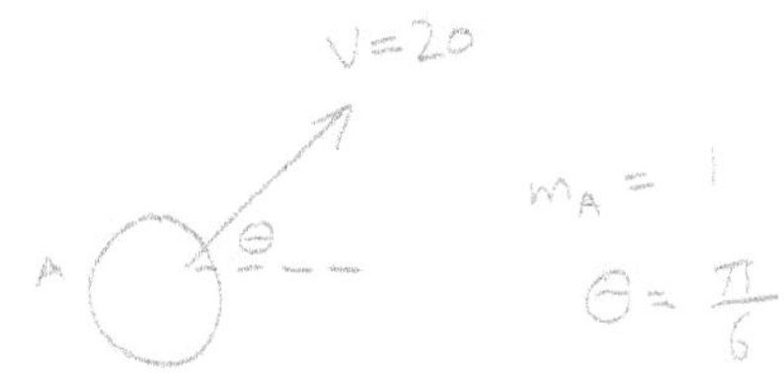

Figure 3. A soccer ball of mass 1kg is kicked with a velocity of 20m/s at an angle of $\frac{\pi}{6}$ with the horizontal. Find maximum height achieved by the ball.

Figure 3 presents a simple projectile problem that asks for the maximum height of a kicked soccer ball. A student sketches a circle to indicate the ball, and annotates it with an arrow to indicate initial velocity. The arrow is further supplemented by a dotted line that indicates the initial angle of the trajectory with the horizontal axis. Equations indicating values for mass and horizontal angle are also included. The representation contains enough information for an animation, but at the same time, there are no annotations indicating the highest point of the trajectory. This could be added in the form of a dotted line or an arrow to indicate the maximum displacement in vertical direction. This example also highlights the use of two annotations (arrow and dotted line) to define a vector quantity.

These examples highlight some of the challenges of sketch understanding for the domain of classical mechanics problems. There are often multiple ways of drawing a diagram to accomplish the same task. Students can annotate and label the diagram with arrows, dotted lines, symbols, numbers and even equations. Similar annotations carry different meaning in relation to different sketched shapes, and in relation to problem type. The information contained in sketched diagrams may be incomplete or even redundant in some cases. Such scenarios can be confusing from a recognition standpoint. Lastly, user sketches may be approximate in nature. For example, consider the problem shown in Figure 2(a). The wire to the right side of the pulley does not actually touch the square. An incorrect animation will result if the inference subsystem cannot link it to the shape properly.

A recognition system for a sketch-based physics tutor must be able to meet these challenges, in order to generate a good understanding of the problem. An understanding of a student's written solution (containing mathematics and diagram) can be used to provide hints and highlight errors, while facilitating animation. Furthermore, the use of sketch-based interfaces should allow the students to integrate the answers to assigned problems into the animation process, in order to see if a given answer causes an intuitively correct animation.

PHYSICSBOOK INTERACTION MODEL

In PhysicsBook, users sketch diagrams and write mathematics with a stylus on a tablet computer. Users can make associations between mathematical expressions and recognized sketch primitives by selecting mathematical expression(s) with a 'Lasso' gesture and then tapping a recognized item. The recognition system does real-time recognition of mathematics and can provide feedback for recognized mathematics. However, viewing of real-time feedback is disabled by default[1]. Users can trigger sketch recognition after they finish solving the problem. This approach is taken due to the finding by [23], who discovered that users prefer to trigger sketch recognition after they are done with drawing. Math recognition is conducted in real-time because of its usefulness in implicit associations processing. The system can recognize the following diagram primitives: convex shapes (circles, polygons), springs, wires and simple pulleys. After recognizing primitive components, the system attempts recognition of diagram annotations: arrows, distance scales, horizontal and vertical axes (dotted lines), and displacement level indicators (dotted lines with an arrow indicating a transition). Each primitive component's attributes (e.g. mass, spring stiffness, etc) are assigned initial values based on its appearance and annotations. This allows user input to be flexible because the system does not require the full mathematical description of all initial conditions and can provide a good animation given any granularity of input.

For each annotation, the system tries to infer its label by means of a proximity check. Labels can be symbolic, numeric or equations. Numeric labels are assumed to denote the magnitude of a physical quantity. The related variable in such cases is established by inferring user intent behind the annotation. For example, in Figure 2(a), the arrow indicating the force acting on the pulley has a numeric label. Taken in isolation, it indicates a vector quantity with a magnitude of 220. Taken in context of the pulley, PhysicsBook can reason that the arrow denotes a force acting on the free end. On the other hand, if an annotation's label is symbolic, the system attempts to infer the related equation by finding a match within the mathematics written down by the user. If an equation is associated with a label, it is evaluated to yield the variable in question. Users can alter initial values by writing down mathematical expressions to reflect proper initial conditions and associating them with diagram primitives. A 'Lasso' gesture is used to select mathematical expression(s). The association is completed by tapping the desired component. Existing associations can be viewed by hovering the stylus over a component.

Mathematical expressions can either be constant expressions (e.g. $m_A = 25$) or equations (e.g. $v_x = k\sin\theta$). Vector quantities can be specified either in terms of x and y component equations or as a single vector equation. If x and y components are not specified in an equation, we use physics domain knowledge to determine if the variable on the left-hand side of the equation is a vector or a scalar. For example, if a user writes $v_2 = v_1 + at$, the system can infer that since the variable v is often used to indicate the velocity of a moving body, the user has written down an expression for velocity. In cases, where the variable itself does not provide a hint, the parameters of the equation are examined to infer whether the quantity is vector or scalar. For example, if a user writes down $z = v_1 + gt$, PhysicsBook will be able to infer that v_1 has been used as a parameter instead of $\|v_1\|$, therefore z should be a vector quantity. PhysicsBook can deal with equations including both numeric (e.g. $f_1 = -0.5v_A$) and symbolic parameters (e.g. $f_1 = -\mu v$ where $\mu = -0.5$). By integrating physics domain knowledge, the system also avoids erroneous associations. An example of an erroneous association is trying to associate an equation specifying momentum with a spring. Illogical cases such as these are ignored by PhysicsBook.

Recognition errors or actual mistakes can cause incorrect animation that conflicts with a user's intuition. A 'Reset' mode is provided that lets users debug and correct existing equations and associations. This allows users to experiment with different initial values and gain better insight into the working of underlying concepts. Users can also view a real-time graph of several attributes of a given component. In keeping with our goal of natural interaction, the system preserves existing associations along different system modes. If users wish to alter part of an equation that is already associated with a component, they do not have to make the association again.

SYSTEM DESIGN

PhysicsBook has three main subsystems: Recognition, Inference and Animation. A sketch containing mathematics, diagram(s), and annotations forms the input to PhysicsBook. This sketch is recognized to yield diagram primitives, which are then analyzed and correlated with their annotations. Users can manually make associations between recognized diagram primitives and mathematical expressions. The end result is an animation. The animation subsystem also includes functionality for viewing a realtime graph of one or more interesting attributes of individual diagram components.

Sketch Recognition And Inference

A sketch is acquired as a collection of digital ink strokes, each of which is a sequence of 2D points. We use the IStraw algorithm [26] to enumerate all cusps in each ink stroke. For recognition of mathematical expressions, we use StarPad, which is based on [28]. StarPad can recognize mathematical expressions and provide feedback in real-time. Recognition results are displayed next to hand-written expressions. When a user triggers sketch recognition, primitives such as shapes, wires, springs and pulleys are recognized first. Next, annotations such as arrows, distance scales and displacement indicators are detected. The third step consists of finding labels for recognized primitives and annotations. The final step links related labels and equations with their corresponding sketched

[1]Users can enable it via a settings window

primitive. Figure 4 shows examples of the sketch primitives that can be recognized by PhysicsBook, while Figure 5 shows the annotations that can be applied to recognized sketch primitives.

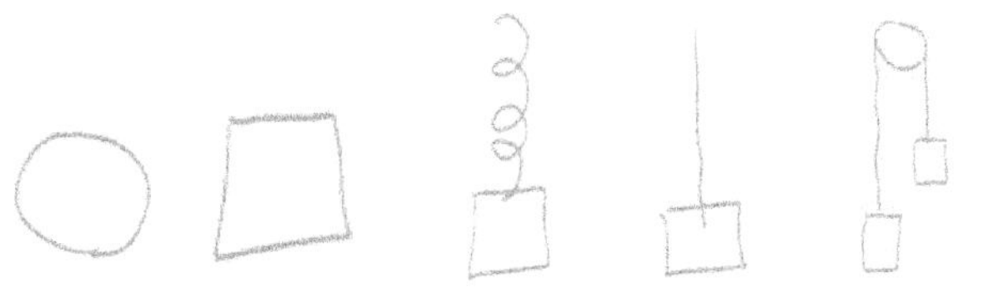

(a) Circles (b) Polygons (c) Springs (d) Wires (e) Pulleys

Figure 4. Examples of diagram components that can be recognized by PhysicsBook.

For recognizing circles, polygons, wires and springs, we based our algorithms on [3]. However, we modified the circle recognition algorithm to use the variance in average radius about the centroid of an ink stroke, instead of the variance in average angle subtended at the centroid (as suggested by [3]). The advantage to this approach is to have a more human readable threshold value supporting a much higher recognition accuracy. Any shapes that overlap each other are set aside as composite primitives. After the recognition of simple primitives, the system tries to recognize composite primitives. Currently, pulleys are the only supported composite primitive in PhysicsBook. They consist of a circle overlapped with a rectangle. The rectangle indicates the hinge of the pulley and serves to disambiguate pulleys from being recognized as other shapes.

(a) Arrows (b) Axes (c) Displacement Indicators

Figure 5. Examples of annotations in PhysicsBook that can be applied to recognized diagram components.

Implicit Associations

The function of the inference subsystem is to take recognized diagram primitives and annotations, to infer associations between them and establish initial values for variables which are then used for animation. Algorithm 1 shows the workflow for this module. First, labels and related equations are inferred for recognized annotations. Next, the relationships between annotations and sketch primitives are inferred implicitly, based on their spatial proximity. After this, labels and equations for sketched primitives are found. Lastly, equations corresponding to associated labels are found and associated with appropriate sketch primitives implicitly. This eliminates the need for users to associate all required initial conditions with the diagram manually. Implicit mathematical associations, formed in this manner, are then analyzed to extract information related to the initial state of sketch primitives.

Algorithm 1 Pseudo code for Recognition and Inference subsystems

---

Require: InkStrokes
  $Primitives \leftarrow RecognizePrimitives(InkStokes)$
  $Annotations \leftarrow RecognizeAnnotations(InkStokes)$
  for all Annotation $A_i \in Annotations$ **do**
    Try to find and associate label
    Find and associate related equation
    Find primitive with which this annotation is associated
  end for
  for all Primitive $P_i \in Primitives$ **do**
    Try to find and associate label
    Find and associate related equations from written equations
    Associate related equations from annotations
    Assign initial values to attributes
  end for

Data Extraction from Implicit Associations

After an association has been made (either implicitly by the inference subsystem or explicitly by the user), the system has to infer the actual value of the quantity denoted by the association. Annotations denoted by arrows indicate vector quantities. Arrows can have dotted lines associated with them to indicate the angle with vertical or horizontal axes. By examining arrow labels, in combination with associated angle and axis annotation, the system is able to infer any of the following vector quantities: velocity, force, momentum, acceleration.

Displacement indicators (an arrow drawn from one dotted line to another dotted line) are useful to indicate the direction of motion. They also indicate the starting and ending levels for the motion of a moving body. If an equation specifying the exact amount of displacement is specified, they also serve as distance indicators (useful to map distance in pixels to real world units). During the data extraction phase of inference, displacement indicators for each sketched shape are found (if they are part of the sketch) and associated. These are fundamentally important from an animation perspective. They indicate the correct starting and ending levels of motion from a user's perspective. Therefore, if the associated answer is incorrect, the shape will not move the requisite distance, making it obvious to the user that there is something wrong with his/her solution. In other words, by drawing displacement indicators, users explicitly indicate the limits of expected motion, which is extremely useful as the system does not have to guess them.

Animation

PhysicsBook uses a customized 2D physics engine based on concepts described in [15]. The physics engine includes standard functionality such as collision processing, application and resolution of different types of forces and an incremental position update mechanism. However, unlike a typical physics engine used in video games, it supports recognized sketch primitives as inputs. Additionally, it provides entry points for hand-written mathematics that can be associated with the physical properties of components in the physics engine, altering their animation behavior. Any such mathemat-

Algorithm 2 Position update mechanism for each shape

Require: Shapes, Associations
  for all Shape$S_i \in Shapes$ **do**
    if Equation $E_{position}(S_i) \in Associations$ **then**
      $Position(S_i) \leftarrow Evaluate(E_{position}(S_i))$
    else if Equation $E_{velocity}(S_i) \in Associations$ **then**
      $Velocity(S_i) \leftarrow Evaluate(E_{velocity}(S_i))$
      $Position(S_i) \leftarrow Integrate(Velocity(S_i))$
    else
      Compute $\Sigma Forces(S_i)$
      $Acceleration(S_i) \leftarrow \frac{\Sigma Forces(S_i)}{Mass(S_i)}$
      $Velocity(S_i) \leftarrow Integrate(Acceleration(S_i))$
      $Position(S_i) \leftarrow Integrate(Velocity(S_i))$
    end if
  end for

ical equations are evaluated at runtime, as needed, to yield scalar or vector values which are used to generate an animation that is concordant with a user's intent. It should be noted that the modified behavior caused by associated mathematics may or may not be intuitively correct. This serves as a feedback mechanism to the user indicating whether there is a mistake in his/her solution.

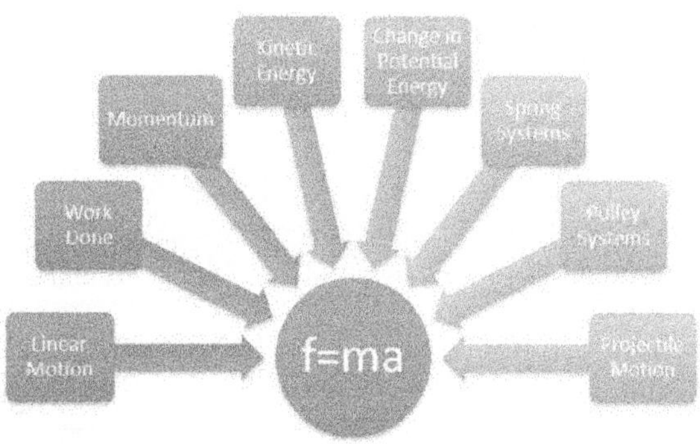

Figure 6. Figure showing physics concepts that are related to $f = ma$. Some of these concepts can be used directly as input to the animation system. For others, we incorporate data transformations that are invisible to a system user, giving much more functionality.

Algorithm 2 shows the steps taken to update the position of a shape in each animation frame. It shows that users can specify their own equations for forces, velocity, position, and acceleration directly which can augment or even replace the standard update mechanism of the physics engine. This scheme is highlighted in Algorithm 2 which shows that if a user directly specifies the position update equation for a shape, then the system's regular flow is bypassed entirely. Alternatively, if a velocity equation is specified, the system does a single integration step to update the position. If position or velocity equations are not specified, then the net force on each shape is computed, followed by the acceleration. Two integration steps are then required to update the position. Individual forces acting on a body may also be governed by associated mathematical equations, which can affect the Compute $\Sigma Forces(S_i)$ step in Algorithm 2. The advantage to using an open-ended approach like this is that it keeps the design of the animation system flexible, while allowing users freedom to associate their own equations with several physical aspects of components, which in turn enables the animation of a variety of physics problems.

Variable	Transformed To
Force	Self
Acceleration	Self
Velocity	Self
Position	Self
Spring Stiffness	Self
Wire Tension	Self
Momentum	Velocity
Work Done	Displacement
Change in Potential Energy	Displacement
Kinetic Energy	Velocity

Table 1. Variable that can be associated with diagram components in PhysicsBook. The table shows the transformation performed for each variable.

Variable Transformations

PhysicsBook allows users to animate problems from a range of physics domains related to classical mechanics. These are all concepts related to $f = ma$ (See Figure 6). However, the physics engine used for animation only accepts associations that affect simple attributes of diagram components (e.g., position, displacement, velocity, force, acceleration, and mass). Concepts that are indirectly related to $f = ma$ (e.g., work done, kinetic energy, and potential energy) must be transformed into one of the acceptable inputs, before animation can proceed. This is a deliberate design choice to keep the animation system simple, while enabling the animation of a large range of problems. Table 1 shows the list of variables which can alter animation behavior in PhysicsBook. It also highlights the transformed variable if the original variable cannot be used directly. For example, kinetic energy cannot directly affect a shape's attributes in the physics engine. However, using its formulation, the magnitude of velocity from a shape's kinetic energy can be derived as

$$K_e = \frac{1}{2}mv^2 \Longrightarrow ||v|| = \sqrt{\frac{2K_e}{m}}.$$

Coupled with an arrow annotation that indicates the direction of velocity, we can map kinetic energy to the velocity of a shape. Similarly, an annotation indicating the direction of motion (can either be an arrow or a displacement indicator) can be used in conjunction with an expression denoting the work done or change in gravitational potential energy for animation. In either of these cases, the system will infer the magnitude of required displacement for the annotated diagram component using one of the following equations:

$$W = F_1.\Delta x \Longrightarrow ||\Delta x|| = \frac{W}{||F_1||}$$

$$P_e = mg.\Delta h \Longrightarrow ||\Delta h|| = \frac{P_e}{m||g||}.$$

This mechanism for transforming variables is useful because it allows us to extend our animation subsystem to concepts that are related to $f = ma$ (See Figure 6) but not covered

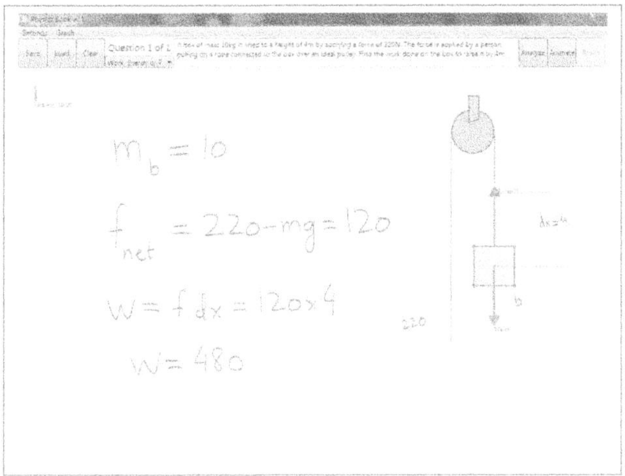

Figure 7. Example scenario where a box of mass 10kg is lifted to a height of 4m by applying a force of 220N. The force is applied by a pulling on a rope connected to the box over an ideal pulley. The student is asked to find the work done on the box as it is raised by 4m.

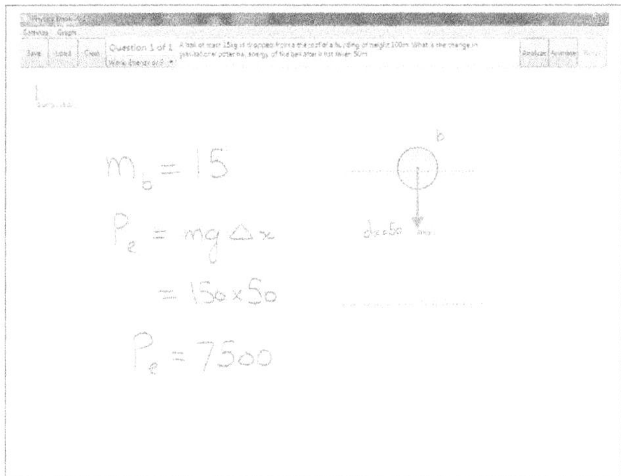

Figure 8. Example scenario where a ball of mass 15kg is dropped from a the roof of a building of height 100m. The student is asked to work out the change in gravitational potential energy of the ball after it has fallen 50m.

by any of the allowed inputs to our physics engine. It should be noted that in order to fully support related concepts, data transformations alone are not sufficient. The transformations described here highlight the fact thats diagram annotations play a key role in enabling animation for each of these instances. In all three instances described, transforming the variable yields only the magnitude of the transformed quantity. In order to get the direction for each of them, the system needs an arrow annotation to be drawn by the user.

This also illustrates the importance of diagram annotations for a sketch-based intelligent tutoring system. Diagram annotations are a natural interaction mechanism that is frequently used by students when working with pen-and-paper. Annotations allow our system to implicitly associate initial values based on their proximity to sketched primitives, freeing the user from having to make the association explicitly. Lastly, annotations aid our system in variable transformations, allowing it to guess the correct direction for vector quantities that have to be transformed from concepts that are not directly related to $f = ma$.

EXAMPLE SCENARIOS

Work Done by Force Acting through a Simple Pulley

Figure 7 represents a scenario that involves a box being pulled upward by means of a pulley. The information given to a student is the mass of the box and the magnitude of the force acting on the pulley. The student is asked to find the work done on the box when it has risen by 4m. The student sketches a circle to represent the pulley, along with an overlapping square to indicate the pulley's hinge. A square represents the box, while line segments represent the wire going over the pulley. From the given information, the student determines that the work done on the box is $W = 480J$.

To verify the answer, the student decides to animate the sketch with the solution as input. Upon analysis, the pulley system and box are replaced with corrected diagram components (wires, pulley, hinge and square). The dotted lines are interpreted by the system to indicate the start and endpoints of movement. The direction of the arrow helps to distinguish the starting level from the ending level. The label for the arrow ($dx = 4$) is interpreted to indicate that the distance between the two dotted lines is to be taken as 4m. The box is assigned the label 'b', and the equation indicating mass ($m_b = 10$) of the box is associated implicitly. The student selects the equation pertaining to the solved answer ($w = 480$) by using the 'Lasso' gesture and completes the association by tapping the square. After this, the student triggers the animation.

If the computed value is correct, the box will move exactly 4m. If it is incorrect, then the box will come to rest either before or after reaching the end level. An incorrect animation will therefore provide the student with feedback about possible errors in the solution. Notice that the student worked out the answer as he would on paper, and only associated the minimum amount of required information. The equation for mass was associated implicitly. Additionally, the system was able to determine the beginning and endpoints of motion from the displacement indicator. No equations were written down to specify how the box's position should be updated per frame update.

Change in Gravitational Potential Energy During Free-Fall

Figure 8 represents a simple projectile problem. A ball of mass $m = 15$kg is dropped from a known height. The student is asked to determine the change in gravitational potential energy after the ball has fallen 50m. The student sketches a circle to represent the ball, and annotates the diagram with two horizontal dotted lines to indicate starting and ending levels for motion. An arrow is sketched between the two levels to indicate direction of displacement. From the given information, the student determines that the change in potential energy of the ball is $P_e = 7500J$.

To verify the answer, the student again decides to animate the sketch with the solution as input. Upon analysis, the ball is replaced by a circle. The dotted lines are interpreted by the

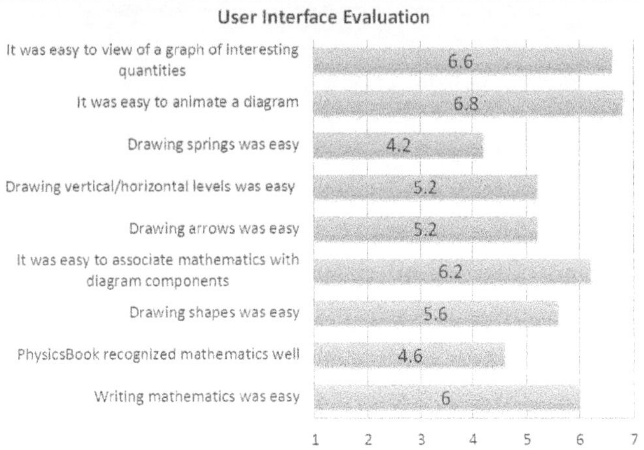

Figure 9. Mean participant ratings of individual aspects of PhysicsBook's user interface. Each of these questions required participants to respond using a 7-point Likert scale, where 1 was the most negative answer and 7 was the most positive answer.

system to indicate the starting and ending points of movement. The direction of the arrow distinguishes the starting level from the ending level, while also indicating the direction of motion. The label for the arrow ($dx = 50$) is interpreted to indicate that the distance between the two dotted lines is to be taken as 50m. The circle is assigned the label 'b', and the equation indicating mass ($m_b = 15$) is associated implicitly. The student selects the equation for potential energy ($P_e = 7500$) with the 'Lasso' gesture, associates it by tapping the circle, and triggers the animation.

The system will use the association to derive the magnitude of displacement and by utilizing the arrow annotation that depicts the direction of motion, will be able to construct the required displacement vector. If the derived change in potential energy is correct, the ball will move exactly 50m. If it is incorrect, then the ball will come to rest either before or after reaching the end level.

USER EVALUATION

We conducted a small-scale user study to get preliminary feedback about the perceived usefulness of PhysicsBook. Our goal in this study was to allow participants to experience the entire workflow of PhysicsBook. We chose two example scenarios that exposed participants to the potential of PhysicsBook.

Subjects and Apparatus

We recruited five participants (2 female and 3 male) from the University of Central Florida for an informal evaluation of PhysicsBook. The participants ages were between 22 and 28 years. Three participants had studied physics at the university level. Each participant took 15 to 20 minutes to complete the experiment tasks. The experiment was conducted on a HP Compaq TC4400 tablet computer equipped with an Intel Core 2 T5600 processor and 2 gigabytes of memory. The screen resolution was set to 1024x768 pixels. The tablet was placed on a table for the experiment. Participants sat down and used the stylus to interact with the tablet.

Experiment Procedure

Upon arriving for the experiment, each participant was given an introduction to PhysicsBook. This included instructions on how to draw shapes, springs, wires and pulleys. Participants were shown how to use the different annotations and how to associate mathematical expressions with recognized components of the diagram. They were also shown how to delete parts of the diagram by using the 'Scribble-Erase' gesture. Lastly, they were given an overview of the graphing functionality built into PhysicsBook.

For the experiment itself, each participant was given the solutions to two physics problems. The participant had to write out the given solution using PhysicsBook. The problems chosen for the experiment are shown in Figures 1 and 8. As PhysicsBook is not robust enough for a full user evaluation, we chose this controlled mode of interaction to get a preliminary idea of the effectiveness of the usage model for PhysicsBook and to measure the perceived usefulness of different components of the system. After the experiment, participants were asked to fill out a questionnaire that required them to rate PhysicsBook on a variety of metrics such as perceived difficulty in drawing the various diagram components, annotations, writing mathematics and making associations.

Results

Figure 9 shows participants' ratings of individual aspects of PhysicsBook's user interface. On the whole, participants responses seemed to indicate that they were able to draw diagram components and annotations in an easy fashion. The two notable exceptions are with respect to drawing springs and the ability of PhysicsBook to recognize mathematics well. The perceived difficulty of drawing strings is due to the fact that springs are easy to confuse with the 'Scribble-Erase' gesture in PhysicsBook. This led to poor performance and frustration among participants while drawing springs. As for the ability of PhysicsBook to correctly recognize handwritten mathematics, we suspect that the poor rating is due to our design choice where we hide the realtime recognition results for recognized mathematics. This approach was adopted in line with the findings of [23] who established that users prefer to trigger recognition once they complete an entire sketch. Our preliminary study seems to indicate that while this is true for the diagram part of the solution in physics problem solving, the participants in our study preferred to get realtime feedback about the handwritten mathematics. We plan to further investigate this aspect of user experience in the future with a larger set of participants. Figure 10 shows participants impressions of PhysicsBook's overall usefulness. It shows that despite the early stage of the prototype, participants felt positively about the potential usefulness of PhysicsBook.

DISCUSSION AND FUTURE WORK

Currently, the capability of PhysicsBook to animate a given problem is limited to select cases in domains related to classical mechanics. While we can associate and utilize mathematics written by a user, the system has limitations in sketch understanding and animation. From an animation perspective, it is important to know the starting and ending points of motion for each shape. Currently, we attempt to infer these points

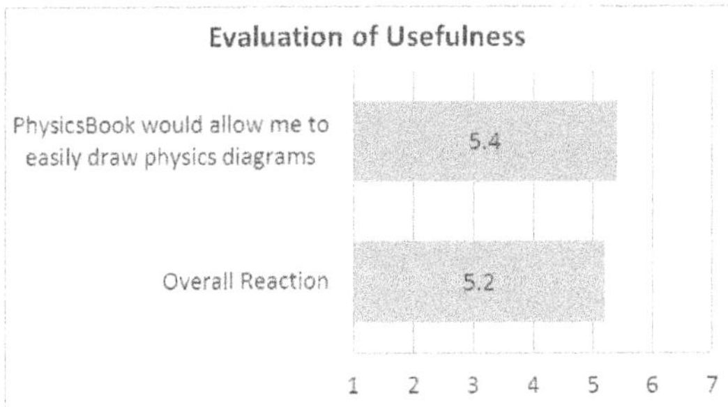

Figure 10. Mean participant rating of PhysicsBook's overall perceived usefulness. Both of these questions required participants to respond using a 7-point Likert scale, where 1 was the most negative answer and 7 was the most positive answer.

by the use of annotations and spatial reasoning. In problems related to potential and kinetic energy, we have demonstrated the usefulness of dotted lines combined with arrows to delineate displacement levels. However, the accurate determination of the beginning and end of motion in different contexts will be needed to expand the animation capability of our system. To this end, we plan to construct a database of solved problems whose analysis will yield insight into useful new annotations for sketch understanding. Such a database will also be useful for the discovery of inference rules for improvement of our inference module. Any new annotations and inference rules will enrich current functionality in terms of animation and sketch understanding, while allowing us to expand the range of problems that can be animated.

Most problems in physics require students to compute the answer in the form of a quantity at some point of interest. For example, a momentum problem may require students to compute momentum of one or more objects after an elastic collision. It is difficult to determine such points of interest in our current implementation. We can only use horizontal/vertical dotted lines to infer starting or ending points of motion. It is also not clear if such understanding can be derived from just the diagram and its annotations. We plan to utilize natural language processing techniques in the future to extract information from the problem statement itself, in order to achieve a better understanding of the solution.

Lastly, we use a customized monolithic physics engine to do animation. In its present form, it can only accept force, acceleration, mass, velocity and position as direct inputs. By using data transformations, we have expanded its capability to include concepts such as work, energy and momentum. It is unclear how much further we can extend its capabilities by using data transformations. In any case, the use of a monolithic animation system is limiting and bound to increase system complexity as the domain of diagrams becomes larger. In the future, we may utilize a framework that contains a series of animation modules tailored to different problem categories. Such an architecture will allow us to expand the range of physics concepts which can be animated significantly while keeping the design of each animation module manageable.

In addition to the constraints outlined above, we were forced to ask ourselves some interesting questions during the development of PhysicsBook.

1. What is a sufficient set of primitives and annotations that can be used to model a large set of problems in physics?
2. In some cases, the animation proceeds very quickly. Is there a practical lower limit on the duration of animation that impacts its usefulness in terms of facilitating learning?
3. If such a lower limit exists, how can we manipulate animations with durations below the limit to ensure their usefulness?
4. Is it possible to animate any given problem in a physics textbook? We believe that in reality, many physics problems can be animated with the proper software support but there may be an equally large number of problems for which the proper software support mechanism is unknown. Determining how to animate such problems is a challenging research question.

CONCLUSION

We have presented PhysicsBook, a prototype system that can recognize and animate sketched physics diagrams. PhysicsBook uses a customized physics engine for encoding domain knowledge that allows it to develop an understanding of physics problems that require a student to work out force(s), acceleration, velocity, displacement, position, or mass. Users can associate their own equations with the diagram by using a simple gesture set. In order to extend the capabilities of the animation system to branches of physics related to $f = ma$, we have designed a framework that can perform the necessary data transformations required to convert given variables to one of the acceptable inputs for our animation system. Use of data transformations in this fashion overcomes a limitation with previous approaches where users were forced to specify all aspects of animation mathematically. Our preliminary usability evaluation indicates a strong interest in the use of animations involving solutions to physics problems. Although there is more work required to reach our goals for a sketch-based physics tutoring system, we believe the PhysicsBook prototype is a solid foundation toward providing natural interfaces for physics understanding.

ACKNOWLEDGMENTS

This work is supported in part by NSF CAREER award IIS-0845921 and NSF awards IIS-0856045 and CCF-1012056. We would also like to thank the members of the ISUE lab for their support and the anonymous reviewers for their useful comments and feedback.

REFERENCES

1. Algodoo, 2011. `http://www.algodoo.com/wiki/Home`.

2. Alvarado, C. A natural sketching environmant: Bringing the computer into early stages of mechanical design. Master's thesis, MIT, 2000.

3. Cheema, S., and LaViola, Jr., J. J. Applying mathematical sketching to sketch-based physics tutoring software. In *Proceedings of the 10th international*

conference on Smart graphics, SG'10, Springer-Verlag (Berlin, Heidelberg, 2010), 13–24.

4. Cheema, S., and LaViola, Jr., J. J. Towards intelligent motion inferencing in mathematical sketching. In *Proceedings of the 15th international conference on Intelligent user interfaces*, IUI '10, ACM (New York, NY, USA, 2010), 289–292.
5. Forbus, K., Usher, J., Lovett, A., Lockwood, K., and Wetzel, J. Cogsketch: Sketch understanding for cognitive science research and for education. *Topics in Cognitive Science* (2011).
6. Forsberg, A., Dieterich, M., and Zeleznik, R. The music notepad. In *Proceedings of the 11th annual ACM symposium on User interface software and technology*, UIST '98, ACM (New York, NY, USA, 1998), 203–210.
7. Hammond, T., and Davis, R. Ladder, a sketching language for user interface developers. *Computers and Graphics 29*, 4 (2005), 518 – 532.
8. Igarashi, T., Matsuoka, S., and Tanaka, H. Teddy: a sketching interface for 3d freeform design. In *Proceedings of the 26th annual conference on Computer graphics and interactive techniques*, SIGGRAPH '99, ACM Press/Addison-Wesley Publishing Co. (New York, NY, USA, 1999), 409–416.
9. Jiang, Y., Tian, F., Wang, H., Zhang, X., Wang, X., and Dai, G. Intelligent understanding of handwritten geometry theorem proving. In *Proceedings of the 15th international conference on Intelligent user interfaces*, IUI '10, ACM (New York, NY, USA, 2010), 119–128.
10. Jr., J. J. L. Advances in mathematical sketching: Moving toward the paradigm's full potential. *Computer Graphics and Applications, IEEE 27*, 1 (2007), 38 –48.
11. Kara, L. B., Gennari, L., and Stahovich, T. F. A sketch-based tool for analyzing vibratory mechanical systems. *Journal of Mechanical Design 130*, 10 (2008), 101101.
12. Laviola, Jr., J. J. *Mathematical sketching: a new approach to creating and exploring dynamic illustrations*. PhD thesis, Providence, RI, USA, 2005. AAI3174634.
13. LaViola, Jr., J. J., and Zeleznik, R. C. Mathpad2: a system for the creation and exploration of mathematical sketches. *ACM Trans. Graph. 23* (August 2004), 432–440.
14. Lee, W., de Silva, R., Peterson, E. J., Calfee, R. C., and Stahovich, T. F. Newton's pen: a pen-based tutoring system for statics. In *Proceedings of the 4th Eurographics workshop on Sketch-based interfaces and modeling*, SBIM '07, ACM (New York, NY, USA, 2007), 59–66.
15. Millington, I. *Game Physics Engine Development (The Morgan Kaufmann Series in Interactive 3D Technology)*. Morgan Kaufmann Publishers Inc., San Francisco, CA, USA, 2007.
16. Newman, M. W., Lin, J., Hong, J. I., and Landay, J. A. Denim: an informal web site design tool inspired by observations of practice. *Hum.-Comput. Interact. 18* (September 2003), 259–324.
17. Oltmans, M., and Davis, R. Naturally conveyed explanations of device behavior. In *Proceedings of the 2001 workshop on Perceptive user interfaces*, PUI '01, ACM (New York, NY, USA, 2001), 1–8.
18. Ouyang, T. Y., and Davis, R. Chemink: a natural real-time recognition system for chemical drawings. In *Proceedings of the 16th international conference on Intelligent user interfaces*, IUI '11, ACM (New York, NY, USA, 2011), 267–276.
19. Patel, R., Plimmer, B., Grundy, J., and Ihaka, R. Ink features for diagram recognition. In *Proceedings of the 4th Eurographics workshop on Sketch-based interfaces and modeling*, SBIM '07, ACM (New York, NY, USA, 2007), 131–138.
20. Paulson, B., and Hammond, T. Paleosketch: accurate primitive sketch recognition and beautification. In *Proceedings of the 13th international conference on Intelligent user interfaces*, IUI '08, ACM (New York, NY, USA, 2008), 1–10.
21. Purcell, E. J. E. J. *Calculus with analytic geometry / Edwin J. Purcell*, 3d ed ed. Addison-Wesley, 1978.
22. Vanlehn, K., Lynch, C., Schulze, K., Shapiro, J. A., Shelby, R., Taylor, L., Treacy, D., Weinstein, A., and Wintersgill, M. The andes physics tutoring system: Lessons learned. *Int. J. Artif. Intell. Ed. 15* (August 2005), 147–204.
23. Wais, P., Wolin, A., and Alvarado, C. Designing a sketch recognition front-end: user perception of interface elements. In *Proceedings of the 4th Eurographics workshop on Sketch-based interfaces and modeling*, SBIM '07, ACM (New York, NY, USA, 2007), 99–106.
24. Woolf, B. P. *Building Intelligent Interactive Tutors*. Morgan Kaufmann Publishers Inc., San Francisco, CA, USA, 2009.
25. Working model 2d, 2011. `http://www.design-simulation.com/wm2d/index.php`.
26. Xiong, Y., and LaViola Jr., J. J. Technical section: A shortstraw-based algorithm for corner finding in sketch-based interfaces. *Computers and Graphics 34* (October 2010), 513–527.
27. Young, H. D., and Freedman, R. A. *University Physics with Modern Physics*, 12th ed ed. Englewood Cliffs, N.J. : Prentice-Hall, 2008.
28. Zeleznik, R., Miller, T., Li, C., and Laviola, Jr., J. J. Mathpaper: Mathematical sketching with fluid support for interactive computation. In *Proceedings of the 9th international symposium on Smart Graphics*, SG '08, Springer-Verlag (Berlin, Heidelberg, 2008), 20–32.

A Learning Support Tool with Clinical Cases Based on Concept Maps and Medical Entity Recognition

Manuel de la Villa[1], Fernando Aparicio[2], Manuel J. Maña[1], Manuel de Buenaga[2]

[1]Dpto. Tecnologías de la Información
Universidad de Huelva
21819 Palos de la Frontera. Huelva, Spain
{manuel.villa, manuel.mana}@dti.uhu.es

[2]Grupo de Sistemas Inteligentes
Universidad Europea de Madrid
28670 Villaviciosa de Odón. Madrid, Spain
{fernando.aparicio, buenaga}@uem.es

ABSTRACT
The search for truthful health information through Internet is an increasingly complex process due to the growing amount of resources. Access to information can be difficult to control even in environments where the goal pursued is well-defined, as in the case of learning activities with medical students. In this paper, we present a computer tool devised to ease the process of understanding medical concepts from information in clinical case histories. To this end, it automatically constructs concept maps and presents reliable information from different ontologies and knowledge bases. The two main components of the system are an Intelligent Information Access interface and a Concept Map Graph that retrieves medical concepts from a text input, and provides rich information and semantically related concepts. The paper includes a user evaluation of the first component and a systematic assessment for the second component. Results show that our proposal can be efficient and useful for students in a medical learning environment.

Author Keywords
Learning-based interaction; health informatics; visual information retrieval; ontologies; semantic interoperability; software systems in medicine; concept-based learning.

ACM Classification Keywords
H.5.1. [Information Interfaces and Presentation]: Multimedia Information Systems – Hypertext navigation and maps

General Terms
Experimentation; Human factors; Measurement; Reliability

INTRODUCTION
The abundance of medical information available through the Internet is well known. Predominant users looking up medical issues (such as diseases or treatments) and physicians in the early stages of learning have similar behaviour, as observed in [19]; they face several drawbacks among which are [24]: 1) lack of experience and domain knowledge to perform a proper search; 2) lack of awareness about the medical terminology found.

Concept maps [28] and mind maps [4] are graphical tools providing a graphic representation of knowledge that can easily be understood by others. These maps have been widely used in educational activities with different purposes, e.g., in medical education [10,11,12], where the maps have proven to provide several advantages. On the other hand, for a novice physician the task of preparing maps can be a struggle due to lack of expertise and knowledge.

In this scenario, we consider the design of a tool that would help clinicians access the meaning of medical concepts and display concept maps automatically drawn from knowledge sources. The use of this tool would allow the teacher to define the paths of access to information followed by the students and avoid dispersion in the search.

One of the most widely used tools in recent years to standardize and automatically share distributed knowledge bases consists of ontologies. Ontologies play an important role in Artificial Intelligence and Computer Science in general for different purposes such as Knowledge Management, Data Integration and Decision Support [2]. Ontologies are also a key component to enable the semantic-driven information access and, more specifically, in the annotation process of Web pages with ontology-based meta-data, which are increasingly used in the Semantic Web context [27]. There are plenty examples of ontologies in the biomedical field. After analysing some of these knowledge sources, we finally selected Freebase, UMLS and Medlineplus. A PubMed search engine has also been integrated.

The tool presented in this paper comprises two main components accessible through a Web interface, with the aim of providing an interface which helps users to understand a clinical case and interrelate most relevant medical concepts, through concept recognition and semantic graph visualization. Both components provide user services based on Freebase data: one of them is an Intelligent Information Access system that retrieves the Freebase topic's names (symptoms, treatments and diseases) in order to annotate concepts from an input clinical text and shows rich information about these concepts [1], while the other is a visual interface that leverages the discovered concepts as input to generate a corresponding concept map graphical visualization.

The rest of the paper is structured as follows: first, we review related work, about concept map and mind map approaches, about biomedical Ontologies and a state-of-art review to map-based interfaces and ontology-based graphic interfaces. Next, we broadly detail the computer tool developed, how the concepts are identified and enriched semantically, how the concept graph is built and a sample user case. Furthermore, we shows the initial outcomes of an evaluation experience in usability with students and a systematic evaluation by the visual interface. Finally, we discuss the main conclusions and future improvements to be undertaken.

RELATED WORK

Recent studies state the positive impact of clinical information-retrieval (IR) technology on physicians and medical students. In [30], the empirical studies currently published are reviewed and appraised from the point of view of how its use influences physicians, according to an assessment scale. It compiles, among others, papers stating that IR contributes to continuing education or technologies that ease access to updated medical knowledge at point of care with different purposes (to meet information needs, deal with questions, support decision making, etc.)

In [36] is assessed the effect of clinicians' use of IR systems (IRS) on performance and concludes that a significant improvement in the quality of answers provided by clinicians to typical clinical issues was associated with using IRS.

In previous work, we have presented some prototypes of IRS in the biomedical domain, as in [3] and [26].

Concept map and Mind map approaches

Concept maps [28] and mind maps [4] are graphic tools that have both been widely applied in educational activities with different purposes. Both provide a graphical representation of knowledge that can easily be understood by others, consisting of 2-dimensional graphics used to represent knowledge comprised of concepts connected by directed arcs encoding relationships between the concept pairs. Although the two approaches have similar characteristics and promote active learning, their design and preparation differ in some fundamental ways. While concept maps are focused on a set of topics, usually enclosed in circles or rectangles in a hierarchical manner (most general at the top), mind maps are non-linear and reflect what can be thought about a single topic [38].

Concept mapping is widely used to enable individuals at many different levels -from elementary school students to scientists- to construct new knowledge and externalize knowledge in a human-usable form, helping to share and compare that knowledge to further human learning and understanding. A main advantage of using concept maps in the knowledge acquisition process is that the graphic presentation of knowledge enables domain experts to quickly evaluate the represented parts of the knowledge. Examples of using this approach in medical education can be found, for instance, in [10], where some concept map studies with medical or healthcare students on nursing, dentistry and veterinary courses are reviewed, concluding with four concept maps of main educational functions: promoting learning, providing additional resources, providing feedback to students and conducting assessment.

Mind maps are also used in medical education [e.g. 11, 12], although the difficulty in using mind maps for revision is that it often takes a fair amount of time to design them and there are many topics to be covered in medicine. In preparation for exams, it would be very difficult for a student to make a good mind map for every topic. Furthermore, the non-linearity of this kind of graphic representation hinders computer-automated creation.

Knowledge visualization [5] is a new field that is only recently receiving attention from the research. It is defined as the use of visual representations to transfer knowledge between at least two persons. As we said in introduction, ontologies are widely used to standardize and automatically share distributed knowledge bases.

The similarities between ontologies and concept maps, given the hierarchical relationships established among classes in the ontology and, therefore, their instances or topics, allow a very straightforward way to transform knowledge from one technology to the other (e.g. [7, 37]).

Biomedical Ontologies

Biomedical Ontologies, as mentioned in [18], are increasingly used to tackle annotation tasks in biomedical research, enabling better integration of data and promoting translational discoveries. However, due to the large number of ontologies and the heterogeneity of formats, both deciding which ontologies are to be used and testing those selected can become costly tasks in terms of time.

Some examples of ontologies are GO (Gene Ontology), MeSH (Medical Subject Headings), FMA (Foundational Model of Anatomy), GALEN, UMLS (Unified Medical Language System), SNOMED-CT (Systematized Nomenclature of Medicine - Clinical Terms) and many others.

Biomedical ontologies may include a wide range of medical concepts, basic information such as the type or class they belong to and how they are related (e.g. symptom / disease / treatment). A formal description can be found in [15] where the following ontological constituents are identified: Classes (abstract or specific concepts), Relations (association between concepts), Functions, Formal axioms (always true sentences) and instances (topics).

Knowledge sources merged in our computer tool are UMLS (to retrieve concept synonyms and translations), Medlineplus and Freebase (used in the annotation process and also supplying descriptive and semantic information on recognized concept) and PubMed (as a scientific publication search engine for each annotated or semantically related concept).

As mentioned above, in this submission we will focus on the role played by Freebase, as it is involved in all features of the tool: annotation process and concept extraction, descriptive and semantic information retrieval, graphic generation of concept maps and results presentation through a Web interface. We chose Freebase for its domain-independence, ease of data access, open nature of published data and information reliability, making this knowledge source especially interesting for its adaptation to other fields. Freebase provides a data access mechanism called Metaweb Query Language, MQL [25], which can be remotely executed through different APIs and easily adapted to different programming languages.

Map-based Visual Interfaces

The value of an information system is conditioned by the quality and quantity of the information provided, but also by the facility and usability in the access to specific information. Moreover, access to a graphic overview may reduce the cognitive demand experienced when exploring large unfamiliar information spaces [9].

Several experiments try to assess the utility of using concept maps as containers of information and knowledge in the learning process, compared to traditional methods. One empirical study [6] compared a concept map interface with traditional web pages and reported that a concept map leads to higher accuracy in search performance than a web page. In [20]'s study, students using a concept map-based information display in a web-integrated e-portfolio system were shown to be more effective at organizing content and understanding the aggregated content than those using a web page-based system. As noted in the previous section, the graphical representation of concept maps serves as an effective visual aid to learning processes. But not only that, as recent studies extend the use of maps from mere knowledge representation towards mapping as graphic interface, exploiting their semantic and topological features to browse and aggregate multiple knowledge and resource domains. An overview of several approaches in the use of maps as visual interface is therefore justified.

In the educational field, [33] explored visualization tools for knowledge representation in digital library applications and asserted that concept maps have great potential because they can serve as visual outlines, and such knowledge representation can also engage both learners and instructors in active collaborative learning. [32] takes a teachers perspective on the usefulness of computer-generated mind maps as a graphic interface for presenting, organizing and navigating web-based course content and files. Responding to the rapid rise of freely available educational content, [9] adopt Compendium, a mind mapping and argumentation tool, to develop a graphical 'pick and mix' learning design toolbox to enable teachers to create, adapt and share learning activities.

In the information retrieval field, [21] introduced *VisSearch* as a web search environment combining concept mapping and data mining techniques. [35] suggested an alternative visual interface for knowledge repository and retrieval, based on concept maps, and have incorporated it into a standard web browser to help the user construct concept maps with multimedia components. [23] introduces *Visual Concept Explorer*, an automatic concept map generator with knowledge from medical ontologies and thesauri, and discusses how automatically generated concept maps are different from manually generated and how different applications and learning opportunities might be created.

Other concept-based and bi-dimensional proposals may be considered different perspectives on concept maps, such as tree maps, tag clouds and knowledge-based graphs.

Tree Maps are flat representations of two-dimensional hierarchical data structures, which optimize the visual space fully occupied [34]. A variant of this type consists of self-organizing semantic maps [22], based on Kohonen maps. The areas are proportional in size to the frequency of concepts and can be grouped into different colours/categories. Terms that co-occur most frequently are placed in nearby areas. The hyperbolic tree variant adds an important feature, the use of interactive mechanisms of the visual representations. They try to solve the problems related with visual overexposure, so the users may expand and contract the different types of nodes, thus minimizing the amount of information displayed by the Interface. The advantages of hyperbolic structures have been subject to numerous studies [31].

The Tag Cloud or 'tag clouds' model is a simple cloud-shaped visual interface of weighted lists of keywords (relevant concepts) that has become popular since the emergence of social software applications.

One step further, we can find systems able not only to support manual drafting of concept maps, but also to generate them automatically.

Graph-based interfaces based on ontologies

Visual Dictionaries.

One of the most frequent applications of ontologies in visual interfaces is a Thesaurus. Within this type we find

Snappy Words[1] or *Visual Thesaurus*[2]. From a dictionary (usually WordNet or similar), these tools group synonyms into synsets through lexical and semantic relations, revealed graphically by a concept map, where the initial node is the concept sought, from which its definition is derived and leaving edges that express semantic relationships with new nodes or concepts.

Search engines.

Google Wonder Wheel[3] proposes new searches based on user experience and relationships between concepts which might be the ones you originally wanted to search for, or simply give you more options to gain more information, using a graph in half screen, while updating the other half with the most relevant documents for the selected terms.

A similar metaphor is used by *Yahoo Correlator*[4], which extracts and organizes information from text, and searches for related names, concepts, places, and events to your query. *WikiMindMap*[5] builds a mental map from the information you find on a concept in the Wikipedia. It could be considered as a dynamically and automatically generated interface to browse Wikipedia.

SemRep

An interesting approach is presented in [14]. They build a system that takes as input a list of semantic predications produced by UMLS SemRep[6], from a set of documents on a specified disorder topic. The output is a conceptual condensate (a concept map in graphic format) containing only those predications that represent key information in the input documents. There are links to the original text that generated the propositions. The core of the method is a transformation process that condenses and generalizes the input predications, which use semantic information from the UMLS and frequency of occurrence of concepts and relations in the input predications.

COMPUTER TOOL DESCRIPTION

Medical concept recognition

The proposed system pre-processes a set of medical terms compiled into lists, which are then used by the Gazetteer component of the ANNIE system included in the GATE[7] distribution (General Architecture for Text Engineering software). To obtain the Freebase Topic names of *Disease or medical condition*, *Treatment* and *Symptom* Types, we use simple MQL queries parameterized with the Type identifier (see Table 1).

We also pre-processed Medlineplus topics published in XML files[8] and these were incorporated to the annotation task, improving the processing speed compared with the previously developed client service which was connected to the OBA service of NCBO using its 'Medlineplus Health Topics' ontology. However, annotation with this ontology is still functional.

Semantic and rich content

Once entities (concepts) were detected, we decided to allow the users to run searches from corresponding data sources with a pattern "*concept*", looking for Freebase Topics containing the entity string, following the scheme already outlined in Table 1.

We then developed another set of configurable MQL queries with the purpose of displaying descriptive information (text and image) and semantic information related to the concept, which may either have been recognised in the text or extracted from the subsequent search process. A query sketch can be found in Table 2.

Graph building

Users have the chance to highlight a concept and discover related information relevant for the diagnosis. The user chooses to view the graph for a concept (a disease) and queries are performed on the term, both UMLS and Freebase.

- Freebase query: We use Freebase API, which provides the MQL query mechanism (see Table 3) for the information we need, specifically: Treatment, Causes, Risk Factors, Prevention Factors, Symptoms and celebrities.

MQL QUERY	
[{ "type": **FREEBASE_TYPE_ID**, "name~=":"*", **OTHER_FILTER_DATA** }]	
TYPE	FREEBASE_TYPE_ID
Disease or medical condition	/medicine/disease
Medical Treatment	/medicine/medical_treatment
Symptom	/medicine/symptom

Table 1. Freebase MQL query scheme for Topic names retrieval.

- UTS (UMLS Terminology Services) query, which includes a Web Service API, remotely via the Internet, accessing and retrieving information from UMLS lexical and semantic resources.

[1] http://www.snappywords.com
[2] http://www.visualthesaurus.com
[3] http://www.google.com/landing/searchtips/engineers.html#wonderwheel
[4] http://sandbox.yahoo.com/Correlator
[5] http://www.wikimindmap.org/
[6] http://skr.nlm.nih.gov/
[7] http://gate.ac.uk
[8] http://www.nlm.nih.gov/medlineplus/xml.html

MQL QUERY

```
[{
"type": FREEBASE_TYPE_ID,
"id": FREEBASE_TOPIC_ID,
"name":null
TOPIC_ARTICLE TOPIC_IMAGE
SEMANTIC_PROPERTIES
}]
```

TYPE	PROPERTY	FREEBASE_TYPE_ID
Disease	Symptoms	/medicine/symptom
	Treatments	/medicine/medical_treatment
Treatment	Side effects	/medicine/symptom
	Used To Treat	/medicine/disease
Symptom	Symptom of	/medicine/disease
	Side effect of	/medicine/medical_treatment

Table 2. Freebase MQL query scheme to recover rich information related with the concept selected by the user (identified with its FREEBASE_TOPIC_ID)

UTSprovides the following information: Concept preferred name, CUI (Concept Unique Identifier, Definition, Synonyms and translations of the term to French, German, Spanish, Italian and Portuguese. The information retrieved in this phase is schematized in (Figure 1).

When all necessary information is retrieved, we construct the graph (Figure 2) using the library JUNG [29].

The initial concept is shown in the centre of the graph, with edges to nodes representing Sets Treatments, Causes, Risk Factors, Symptoms and Celebrities who have had the disease, each with a distinctive icon.

Initially, each set is shown compressed to avoid overloading the interface and the user decides which group to expand.

MQL QUERY

```
[{
"type": "/medicine/disease",
"name": SEARCH_STRING,
TOPIC/ARTICLE /TOPIC/IMAGE
"symptoms":[],
"treatments":[],
"/medicine/disease/notable_people_with_this_condition": [],
"/medicine/disease/risk_factors": [],
"/medicine/disease/causes": [],
"/medicine/disease/prevention_factors": []
}]
```

Table 3. Freebase MQL query scheme to recover information related with the concept selected by the user to build the concept map

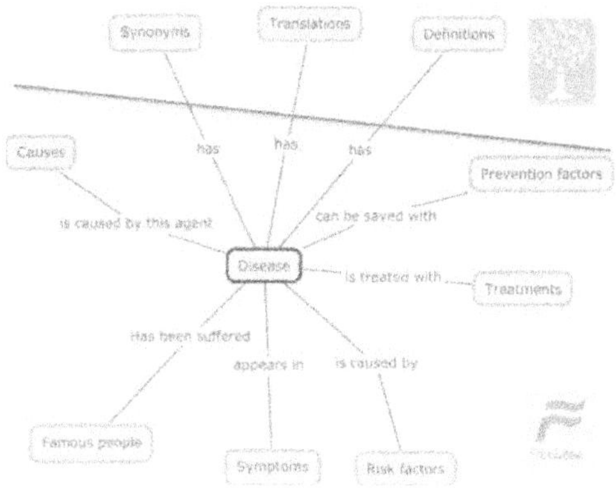

Figure 1. Concept map with the knowledge and sources the graph uses

At this point, the interface lets the user zoom and pan, changing node layouts, expanding group nodes (showing in detail, e.g., a new node for each risk factor associated with initial condition) to view the information associated with each node in the different ontologies that we use, adding terms from one node to the search string, and so on.

Use case

To illustrate tool usage we have selected one case from NCCSTS archives, widely referenced in medical education (e.g. [13, 17]) and part of the educational references highlighted by the medical faculty of UEM University.

The NLP processing of selected case[9] outcomes concerning different terms of interest (such as stroke, hemiparesis, blood pressure, Triglycerides, Cholesterol, HDL or LDL) provides a prior idea to solve the learning questions proposed. Tool behaviour after processing the case's

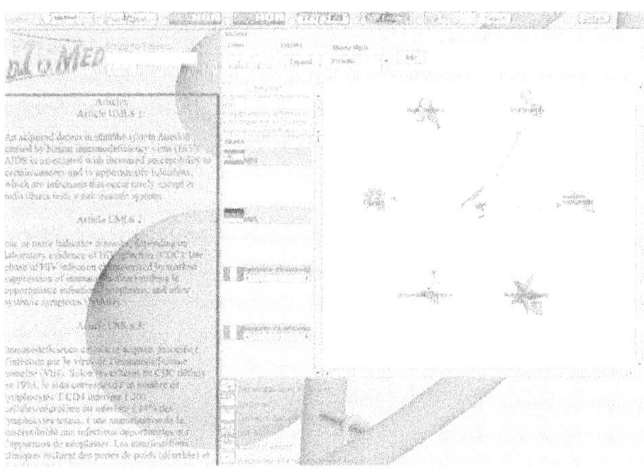

Figure 2. Application interface after graph building

[9] "A Case of Cerebrovascular Accident" by David F. Dean, "Copyright held by the National Center for Case Study Teaching in Science, University at Buffalo, State University of New York. Used with permission." http://sciencecases.lib.buffalo.edu/cs/collection/detail.asp?case_id=344&id=344

abstract is shown below, as a small fragment of the case presentation. Medical entities recognised and the corresponding sources are shown in a table that can be sorted and filtered by both. The initial output can be seen in Figure 3a. It is also possible to apply the same procedure to the full text. Simply using this brief abstract, the computer tool is able to provide supporting information on the proposed learning questions, which roughly concern the significance of ischemia and infarction, the risk factors or warning signs of stroke and relationships among these disorders with the brain and nervous system.

The key term is 'stroke', from which we can infer knowledge about some of the learning questions. Probing deeper into the Freebase diseases information, a set of symptoms, treatments and risk factors can be found connected with the resulting diseases (Acute Stroke, Cerebellar stroke syndrome, Heat Stroke, Ischemic Stroke and Watershed stroke). Each of these semantically related terms are provided through the tool, except the risk factors, which are hyperlinked to the source's topic. Figure 3b shows the stroke disease information retrieved from Freebase. Finally, we decide to view the graph associated with 'stroke' (Fig. 3c) where the node with treatments for stroke is expanded.

USER STUDY AND EVALUATION RESULTS

Following [16], there are three aspects that might be evaluated to assess the usability of a user interface: *effectiveness*, *efficiency* and *satisfaction*. In this section we present two complementary experiments carried out in order to measure effectiveness and user satisfaction in a medical learning environment. The working hypothesis is that using jointly supporting information on the recognised concepts in a clinical case with a map graph will help students of medicine to understand this clinical case.

The first experiment presented is a formal usability study with 34 users in a controlled environment. The aim of this experiment is twofold. On the one hand, the effectiveness of the tool in assisting students of medicine to understand a clinical case was assessed. On the other hand, the usability of the interface was evaluated assessing participants' subjective perception.

The second experiment is a systematic evaluation of the suitability of map graphs. In this case, a collection of 300 clinical cases was used to construct their concept map graphs. The user value of these graphs is measured in terms of *recall* and *novelty*. The former is the proportion of medical concepts present in a case represented in their map graph. The latter is the proportion of new concepts in the graph, i.e. concepts which are not present in the clinical case but have a relationship with some of them.

In conclusion, the experimentation will provide answers to the following questions:

(1) Does the entity recognition and related information provision improve learning effectiveness?

(2) Do the map graphs improve learning effectiveness?

(3) Is the proposed user interface usable?

This section deals with the experiment design to answer these questions and the results obtained. An analysis and discussion of these results will be also shown.

User oriented evaluation

A tool evaluation was carried out based on a learning activity with second-year medical degree students from the School of Biomedical Sciences at the Universidad Europea de Madrid. This activity focused on the tool's capacity for medical entity recognition and access to rich information from these entities retrieved from different sources (Freebase, MedlinePlus and PubMed).

The use of the tool, and the sources previously selected by teachers, enable us to prepare and delimit the students' access paths to the information needed in order to resolve the questions of a proposed examination in the tool assessment scenario. This information control is not possible when the same activity is performed using unrestricted Internet access.

Activity design

To perform the learning activity, framed in the case-based learning style, it was used a clinical case[10] that has served as the basis for the development of an exam with 10 multiple choice questions about the case study. The exam questions (Table 4 shows an example of this type of questions) served to gauge the students' learning with an objective qualification.

All 60 students participating voluntarily in the activity were divided into two groups. The purpose of this division was to compare the learning activity outcomes when the tool is exclusively exploited against a free search on Internet.

Members of the group that solved the exam using only the information gathered through the tool, consisting of 34 students, were anonymously asked to fill out a self-perception Likert questionnaire (on a scale from 1, strongly disagree, to 5, strongly agree).

The questionnaire was divided into a set of 5 usability questions (UQ) and 2 questions related to their perception of learning support provided by the tool (LQ).

Results

Students who employed the tool got better average qualifications in the objective examination (78.53% correct answers) than students who used unrestricted Internet searches (76.92% correct answers). In particular, the use of

[10] http://path.upmc.edu/cases/case223.html

Mitral regurgitation:
a.- Is the less common valvulopathy in the general population
b. - Has no relation with the cardiac problem presented by our patient
c. - May justify the mitral regurgitation
d. - Has a higher prevalence in women than in men

Table 4. Test question example.

the tool enabled students to obtain higher success rate in 6 of the 10 questions. This result indicates that the use of the tool is, at least, as effective in accessing information of interest as an unrestricted access via Internet in order to perform the same learning activity. This result is very positive, because it allows the teacher to define the paths of access to information followed by the students and avoid dispersion in the search, without losing effectiveness compared with a search that offers all existing Internet resources to the students.

Students' self-perception when they use the tool is mostly positive on all questions. Figure 4 shows how most of the students consider each of the questions related to the tool usability positively, with more than 60% of them strongly agreed or agreed with the proposed tool. It may be concluded that students believe that: the tool interface is nice (UQ1), it is easy to find the information required (UQ2), they feel comfortable using the tool (UQ3), the speed is reasonable (UQ4) and it is easy to use (UQ5).

Figure 5 depicts the students' self-perception results in relation to the learning support provided by the tool versus an unrestricted search on the Internet. Over 58% believe that the tool has helped them to extract relevant information about the case study (LQ1), and more than 60% believe that the tool has helped them by reducing the time needed to understand the case study (LQ2).

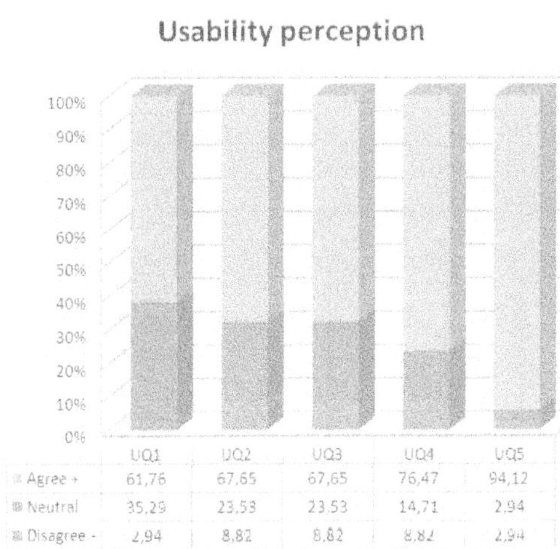

Figure 4. Students' usability self-perception

Systematic evaluation

To evaluate the concept map-based visual interface, we performed a systematic evaluation approached in two different ways. The first approach try to measure the ability of the tool to provide medical concepts in the graph, in relation to the original concepts annotated in the source document (as *recall* in information retrieval). The second approach is based on the fact that we are building a tool to support constructivist learning. We measure *novelty*, the tool's ability to discover and show us new relevant information related with the source document.

The corpus used in the systematic evaluation was the same as in the user-oriented one, a clinical cases corpus, the well-known *University of Pittsburgh Online Case Studies*[11], a compilation of formatted pathology cases for online viewing, usually employed to support case-based learning in diagnostic pathology. We randomly extracted almost 300 documents from the corpus, filtered initially by their size (there are documents composed only by a pair of sentences and several images).

The evaluation process includes several steps. We start an annotation process over the corpus with Metamap (only with SNOMED CT vocabulary source) to identify selected kinds of medical concepts (semantic types such as diseases, findings, etc., relevant types for diagnosis).

Then, to simulate the performance of our visual interface, we query Freebase ontology for all the information needed to build the concept map. This includes symptoms, causes, risk factors, treatments and prevention factors.

Although the percentage of initially annotated diseases in case studies is low, we obtained a recall result of *0,620* (Table 5).

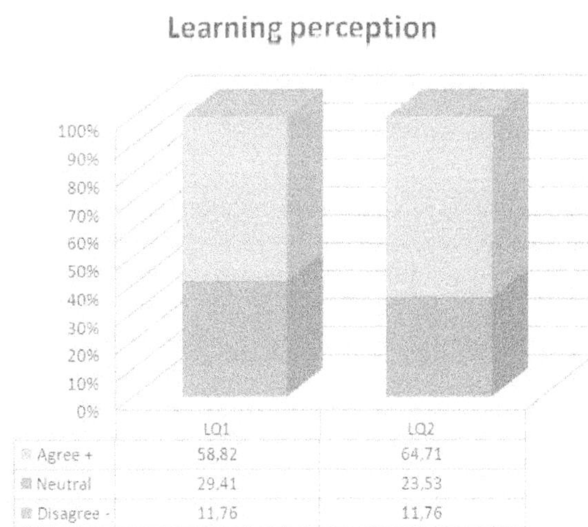

Figure 5. Students' learning self-perception

[11] http://path.upmc.edu/cases.html

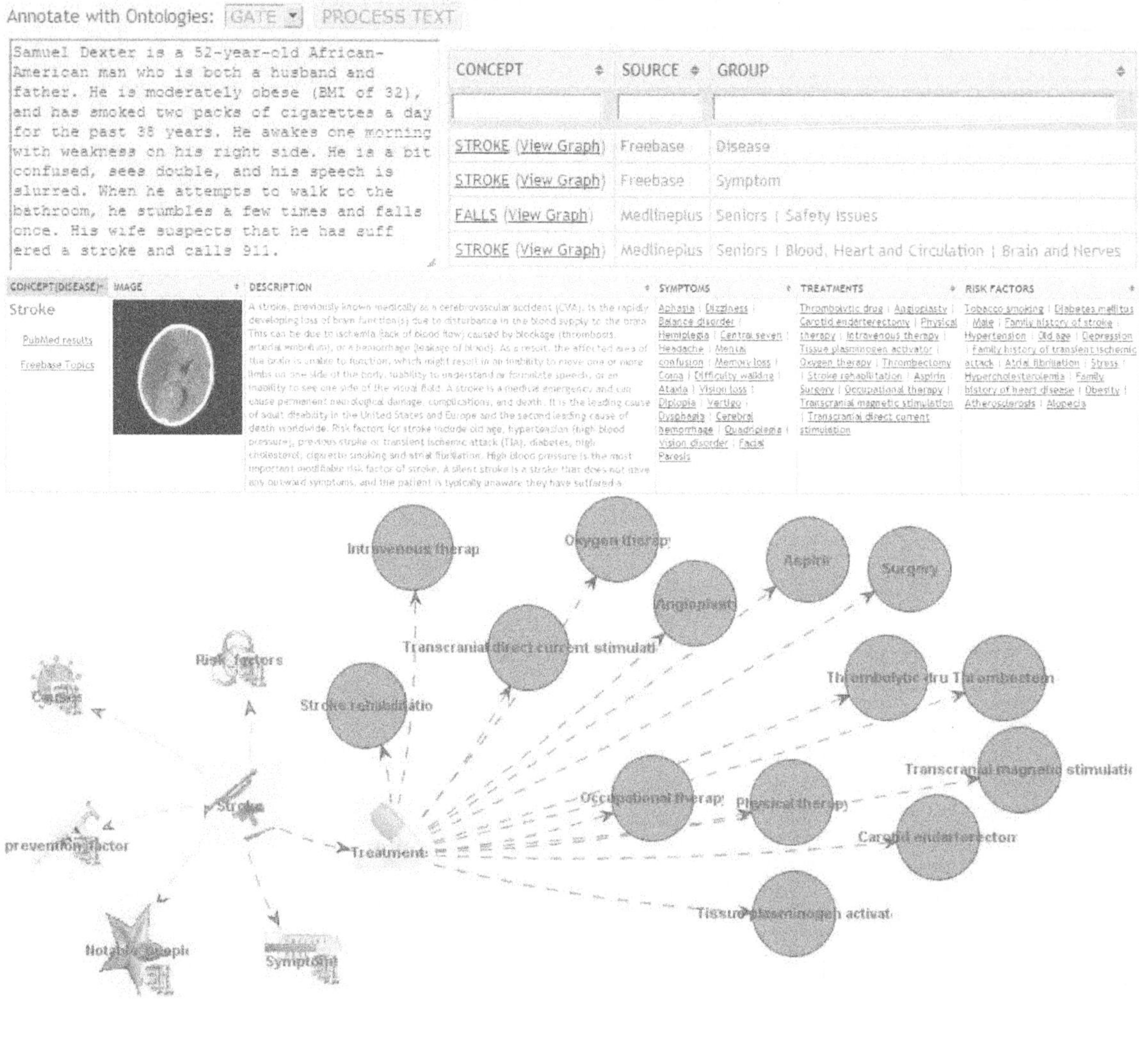

Figure 3. Initial system output after processing the NCCSTS case abstract (Top). Stroke disease information retrieved from Freebase (middle). Stroke graph with treatments node expanded (bottom).

This means that a general-purpose ontology such as Freebase is able to identify most of the diseases that appear in the medical case. It is important to take into account that there are diseases considered as part or symptom of another disease. These are not related in Freebase, and not retrieved. Furthermore, we only considered the initial definition of the case, not the more completed diagnostic file. This would have easily improved the results.

The second part of the systematic evaluation is centred on measuring the tool's capacity to discover new concepts, semantically related to the initial annotated item. It gauges how our system reveals new relevant information based on the knowledge stored in ontologies validated by professional experts.

N# docum.	Concepts annotated (avg.)	Concepts retrieved (avg.)	Recall
277	5,532	3,353	0,620

Table 5. Recall results for systematic evaluation.

As Table 6 shows, for every initial document, on average, the system is able to show more than 30 new elements that support the diagnostic process.

Causes (rev./doc.)	Prevention factors	Risk	Symptoms	Treatments	Novelty
4,783	1,054	10,874	13,711	9,444	0,389

Table 6. Novelty results for systematic evaluation.

$$Novelty(corpus) = \frac{\sum_{corpus} \frac{Cr_{Freebase}}{Ca_{SnomedCT} + Cr_{Freebase}}}{N\#\, documents} \quad (1)$$

In the previous formula, $Cr_{freebase}$ refers to the number of concepts retrieved from Freebase and Ca_{Snomed} to the number of concepts initially annotated with UMLS in the medical cases corpus. The value for novelty (0,389) is really promising.

CONCLUSIONS AND FUTURE WORK

The growing number of medical resources available on Internet entails an increasing demand by consumers for interfaces that facilitate the simplified finding and comprehension of all this information. In this communication we have presented a tool that incorporates emerging technologies to promote the sharing of different biomedical knowledge resources and helps to represent this information in a human and machine usable way, such as ontologies and concept maps. The tool comprises two modules, an intelligent information access system and a visual interface for the automatic graphical presentation of concept maps, mainly linked through information retrieved from Freebase.

One of the most widespread application fields of concept maps is education and, more specifically, health education. In addition, there is a recent working trend in education based on the idea that the knowledge acquired by students through an active role is better fixed in their minds and longer term. Considering these aspects, two types of assessment were carried out. One of them (user oriented) was conducted through a learning activity whose objectives were to contrast the results of our tool compared to an unrestricted search of all Internet available resources, when medical students in higher education were faced with an exam resolution related to a clinical case study, and measure student's self-perceptions about the aid provided by the tool and its usability. Another one (systematic) was designed to measure the annotation results using Freebase ontology on a clinical cases corpus, which has also been the source selected to prepare the learning activity, compared to the coverage provided by MetaMap.

The results achieved in the examination related to the case study indicate that, at least, the tool is not a burden to performing the learning activity compared with a search of all Internet resources. However, the tool has an essential advantage for teachers because it allows pre-selection of the knowledge sources accessible to students. The students' perception is good or very good in both usability questions and those related to the assistance provided, which is promising and encourages us to further develop and improve the tool on those issues where the maximum value was not achieved. The systematic evaluation development has enabled us to get an initial idea of the tool coverage and capacity of our concept maps to represent adequate medical knowledge, indicating the need for further progress in order to improve these results.

Therefore, in future work we plan to focus our efforts on enhancing all the available features in the tool: usability of the interface, expansion and improvement of the annotation process and enrichment of the information and concept mapping. We would also like to expand the user experience evaluation, including a new strategy involving a group of teachers with new self-perception surveys designed to measure the tool's capacity to support teachers in active learning methodologies.

ACKNOWLEDGMENTS

This work was partially funded by the Spanish Ministry of Science and Innovation (TIN-2009-14057-C03-01), Spanish Plan E and the European Regional Development Fund (FEDER).

REFERENCES

1. Aparicio, F., Buenaga, M., Rubio, M., Hernando, M. A., Gachet, D., Puertas, E., & Giráldez, I. TMT: A scalable platform to enrich translational medicine environments. *Proc. IADIS e-Society (2011)*, 401-405.
2. Bodenreider, O. Biomedical Ontologies in Action: Role in Knowledge Management, Data Integration and Decision Support. *IMIA Yearbook of Medical Informatics* (2008), 67-79.
3. Buenaga, M. de, Gachet, D., Maña, M., de la Villa, M., Mata J.:Clustering and Summarizing Medical Documents to Improve Mobile Retrieval. *MobIR '08*
4. Buzan, T., Buzan B. (1993) *The Mind Map book*. BBC Books.
5. Cañas, A.J., Carff, R., Hill, G., et al. Concept Maps: Integrating Knowledge and Information Visualization. En S.-O. Tergan y T. Keller, eds., *Knowledge and Information Visualization*. Springer Berlin Heidelberg, (2005) 205-219.
6. Carnot, M. J., Dunn, B., Cañas, A. J., Graham, P., Muldoon, J. 2001. Concept maps vs. web pages for information searching and browsing. http://www.ihmc.us/users/acanas/Publications/CMapsVSWebPagesExp1/CMapsVSWebPagesExp.htm
7. Chen C-M., Peng C-J., y Shiue J-Y. Ontology-based concept map for planning personalized learning path. *IEEE Conference on Cybernetics and Intelligent Systems*, IEEE (2008), 1337-1342.
8. Conole, G. Using Compendium as a tool to support the design of learning activities. Chapter Ten, in A. Okada, S. Buckingham and T. Sherborne (Eds) *Knowledge cartography – software tools and mapping techniques*, Springer (2008).
9. Cribbin, T., Chen, C. A study of navigation strategies in spatial-semantic visualisations. *Proc. of the 9th HCI International* (2001), 948-952.

10. Daley, B.J., Torre, D.M. Concept maps in medical education: an analytical literature review. *Medical Education 44*, 5 (2010), 440-448.

11. D'Antoni, A., Zipp, G., Olson, V., y Cahill, T. Does the mind map learning strategy facilitate information retrieval and critical thinking in medical students? *BMC Medical Education 10*, 1 (2010), 61.

12. D'Antoni, A., Zipp, G., y Olson, V. Interrater reliability of the mind map assessment rubric in a cohort of medical students. *BMC Medical Education 9* (2009), 19.

13. Dionisio, J. D. N., Dahlquist, K. D. Improving the computer science in bioinformatics through open source pedagogy. *ACM SIGCSE Bulletin* (2008) 40, 115–119.

14. Fiszman, M., Rindflesch, T. C., and Kilicoglu, H. Abstraction Summarization for Managing the Biomedical Research Literature. *Proc. Workshop on Computational Lexical Semantics, HLT-NAACL* (2004), 76-83.

15. Gruber, T. R. (1993). A translation approach to portable ontology specifications. *Knowl. Acquis.,* 5(2), 199–220.

16. Hearst, M.A. *Search User Interfaces*. Cambridge University Press (2009).

17. Jiang, H., Ganoe, C., Carroll, J. M. (2010). Four requirements for digital case study libraries. *Education and Information Technologies*, 15, 219–236.

18. Jonquet, C., Musen, M. A., Shah, N. H. (2010). Building a biomedical ontology recommender web service. *J Biomed Sem*, 1 Suppl 1, S1.

19. Kienhues, D., Stadtler, M. & Bromme, R. Dealing with conflicting or consistent medical information on the Web: When expert information breeds laypersons' doubts about experts. *Special Issue: Solving Information Based Problems: searching, selecting and evaluating information. Learn Instr* (2011)

20. Kim, P., Olaciregui, C. The effects of electronic portfolio-based learning space on science education. *Brit J Educ Technol* (2008) Vol. 39, 4, 700–714

21. Lee, Y.-J. VisSearch: A collaborative Web searching environment. *Comput Educ* 44 (2005), 423-439.

22. Lin, X., Soergel, D. y Marchionini, G. 1991. A Self-organizing Semantic Map for Information Retrieval. *Proc. ACM Int. SIGIR 1991.*

23. Lin, X. Automatically-generated Concept Maps as a Learning Tool. *WASET 2010*, 66.

24. Luo, G., Tang C. On Iterative Intelligent Medical Search. *Proc. ACM SIGIR* (2008) 3-10.

25. Meyer, S. M., Degener, J., Giannandrea, J., & Michener, B. (2010). Optimizing schema-last tuple-store queries in graphd. *Proc. ACM SIGMOD'10*, 1047–1056.

26. Millán M., Muñoz A., de la Villa M. and Maña M.J. A Biomedical Information Retrieval System based on Clustering for Mobile Devices. *Revista SEPLN*, nº 45 (2010), 255-258

27. Motik, B., Maedche, A., and Volz, R. (2002). A Conceptual Modeling Approach for Semantics-Driven Enterprise Applications. En R. Meersman & Z. Tari (Eds.), *On the Move to Meaningful Internet Systems 2002: CoopIS, DOA, and ODBASE* (Vol. 2519, 1082-1099). Springer Berlin Heidelberg.

28. Novak, J.D. Learning, Creating, and Using Knowledge: Concept Map as as Facilitative Tools in Schools and Corporations. *Routledge* (2010).

29. O'Madadhain, J., Fisher, D., Smyth, P., White, S., and Boey, Y. Analysis and visualization of network data using JUNG. *J Stat Software* (2005) 1-35.

30. Pluye P., Grad R.M., Lynn G.D., Stephenson R. Impact of clinical information-retrieval technology on physicians: A literature review of quantitative, qualitative and mixed studies. *Int J Med Inform* (2005) 74, 745-768.

31. Rao, R., Lamping, J. Visualizing Large Trees Using the Hyperbolic Browser. *Proc. ACM CHI 1996.*

32. Ruffini, M. F. (2008). Using e-maps to organise and navigate online content. *EDUCAUSE Quarterly*, vol. 31 (2008), 56–61

33. Shen R., Richardson R., Fox E.A. Concept maps as visual interfaces to digital libraries: summarization, collaboration, and automatic generation. *IVIRA 03.*

34. Shneiderman, B. 1992. Tree visualization with tree-maps: 2-d space-filling approach. *ACM T Graphic*, v. 11 (1992) 92-99

35. Weideman, M., Kritzinger, W. Concept Mapping - a proposed theoretical model for implementation as a knowledge repository. *Working paper from the "ICT in Higher Education" research project.*

36. Westbrook J.I., Coiera E.W., Gosling A.S. Do online information retrieval system help experienced clinicians answer clinical questions? *J Am Med Inform Assn*. Vol. 12, Num. 3 (2005)

37. Willemsen, A.M., Jansen, G.A., Komen, J.C., et al. Organization and integration of biomedical knowledge with concept maps for key peroxisomal pathways. *Bioinformatics 24*, 16 (2008) 21-27.

38. Zipp, G.P., Maher, C., & D'Antoni, A.V. Mind Maps: Useful Schematic Tool for Organizing and Integrating Concepts of Complex Patient Care in the Clinic and Classroom. *Journal of College Teaching & Learning 6*, 2 (2009), 59-68

PedConnect: An Intelligent Assistant for Teacher Social Networking

Jihie Kim, Yu-Han Chang, Sen Cai and Siddharth Jain
University of Southern California/ Information Sciences Institute
4676 Admiralty Way, Marina del Rey, CA 90292
{jihie, ychang, sencai, siddarth}@isi.edu

ABSTRACT
Social networking has gained immense traction in many areas, including teaching and learning. Networking sites for teachers aim to facilitate teacher communication and information sharing, but fall short of their potential. In order to support more effective use of online resources and better communication among teachers, we develop a suite of new user modeling and recommendation capabilities within a middle school teacher networking site. We foster collaboration among novice and experienced teachers when they share similar interests, enabling new mentoring relationships, and promote the use of relevant educational resources. We illustrate our approach with an implemented system called PedConnect that analyzes user activities and presents intelligent suggestions for collaboration and resource use.

Author Keywords
User profiling; teacher social networking; topic modeling.

ACM Classification Keywords
H.5.2 [Information Interfaces and Presentations]: User Interfaces – User interface management systems; I.2.0 [Computing Methodologies]: Artificial Intelligence.

General Terms
Human Factors, Algorithms.

INTRODUCTION
Two challenges face educators today: shrinking resources and proliferating digital content. Some social networking sites for teachers facilitate teacher communication and information sharing. The Middle School Portal 2: Math and Science Pathways (MSP2, http://msteacher2.org) is a Ning based social networking site for middle school math and science teachers (see Figure 1). Such sites can help teachers maintain professional support and integrate new digital teaching methods and materials, without costly workshops and professional development courses.

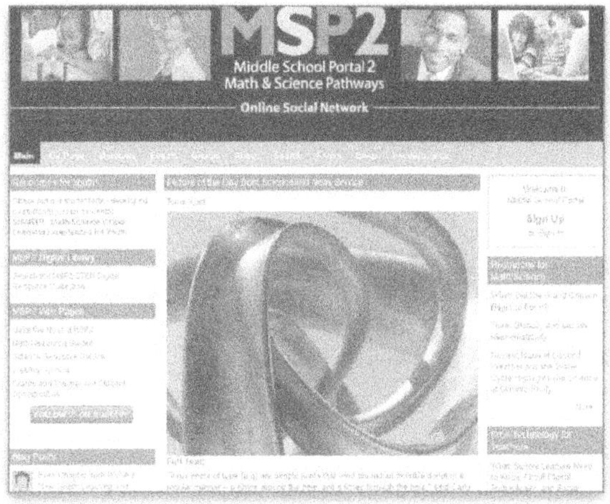

Figure 1. MSP2: Social networking portal for middle school science and math teachers.

A major shortcoming of current social networking systems is their inability to assist teachers in navigating both the static content and dynamic social landscape of online communities. While search functionalities are supported in many sites, as the amount of related online resources grow, teachers need to be able to filter them with respect to their own individual interests and pedagogical characteristics.

Another issue is lack of communication. Although the sites provide opportunities for teachers to collaborate and communicate within and across different school districts using online forums, blogs, and wikis, most of the participants remain silent. Among 1900 members on MSP2, only 10% are active. More than 70% of users who did not get their first question answered never came back to the forum. Although the MSP2 site has a few active users assisting novice teachers, they are not fully effective in guiding interactions since they cannot keep track of all the individuals. Teachers need intelligent services that that keep track of participant interests and needs, and connect them to resources or potential advisors within the social network site.

This paper describes a new teacher assistant called PedConnect that uses an integrated approach for modeling user interests and providing assistance. The approach combines many sources of information, including forum and blog data, external topic ontologies, resource metadata, and user inputs, and generates interest models for typical teacher tasks and subject topics. Such interest models are used to promote participation in forums, connect teachers to others who can potentially answer their questions, and suggest relevant educational resources.

RELATED WORK

There have been several efforts to develop recommender systems in social networking sites. For example, Guy et al. [8] connects people who possibly have an existing relation over social network. Our work focuses on discovering mentorship among potentially unacquainted people, and modeling information seeking or providing activities than analyzing relational properties. Other work provides item recommendations based on user interests, including educational needs of children [2]. As many of our educational resources have metadata that describe the content of the resources, we were able to make use of the terms in generating richer models and relating them to contributions made by individual users.

In forum analysis research there have been efforts to find experts or rate user reputations [3]. The quality of forum posts are analyzed and compared against reputations. In contrast, our work focuses on analyzing topic mentorship in terms of information sharing behavior in the forum, and connecting potential mentors to help seekers. Harper et al.'s work [9] described the difficulty of inviting users to participate in forums, suggesting that invitations worded to stress the social nature improved participation; this work may provide us with useful ways to tune the wording of PedConnect's suggestions and invitations. Many papers from past IUI conferences are also relevant here, such as [7] describing a unified system for browsing and searching.

APPROACH

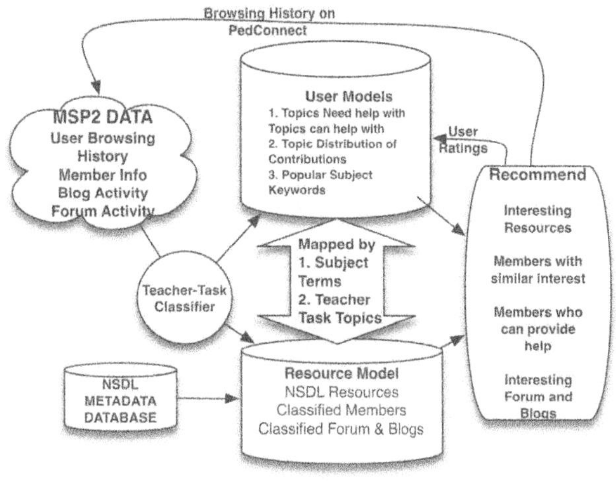

Figure 2. PedConnect: Connecting teachers to forums, resources and other participants.

User Topic Interest Modeling

Modeling Task Interests and Mentorship

We first model teacher interests using typical teacher tasks. We found most discussions within the site are about such teacher tasks and can be used to identify mentors and mentees in each topic. We derive the teacher task categories from teacher handbooks [5,6,10] and profile questions used by the MSP2 site [11]. Table 1 lists the categories. After a few iterations of annotations, the kappa-values [4] for inter-annotator agreement are rather high (> 0.9).

In generating models for individual users, several different sources of information are integrated to automatically calculate the degree of interest and mentorship in each area. The first source is user answers when they register: The user can specify which areas he needs help on and which areas he can help with. Another source is forum and blog contributions. More answers or comments on a topic area increase the degree of mentorship for that topic. Likewise, questions on a topic area increase the degree of help needed by the user on the topic. PedConnect also provides an interface for users to explicitly modify or add his/her interests. Using this information, mentor/mentee levels for each area for each user are calculated as follows:

For user i and topic j, the topic mentor/mentee levels are:
$T_{ij} = w_1$*(Profile answer for tag j) + w_2*(User selection of tag j) + w_3*(Normalized forum/blog contribution on tag j)

The mentor/mentee levels for each user are updated as the user makes new contributions or changes his/her interests. If the topic mentor/mentee level is greater than a threshold then the user is classified as a mentor/mentee in that area. We plan to explore machine learning approaches as we collect more user feedback.

Tags	Description	Kappa
activity	After class activities	0.95
assessment	Assessment/Testing/ Examinations/Evaluation	0.98
assignment	Homework/Assignment	0.96
communication	Communication with Students outside classroom	0.95
curriculum	Curriculum/Class Component/ /Supplemental Materials	0.96
demo	In-class Knowledge demonstration	0.94
discipline	Discipline, learning environment	0.99
it	Integrating Technology	0.91
parent	Involving parents and caregiver	1.00
special	Special Needs students	0.98

Table 1. Teacher Task Topics and Annotation Kappa

Modeling Subject Areas

We also model users based on their interest in Math and Science subject areas. First, we collect the domain concept terms in the National Science Digital Library math and science ontology [12]. We then we enrich the term set by retrieving relevant NSDL resources and extracting the additional domain terms used in resource metadata. We exploit the rich 'description' metadata in NSDL in generating the term lists that is used for representing subject interests. For each user, we keep track of term frequencies in his/her forum and blog contributions. The terms searched by the user are also included in modeling subject interests. As we remove old data over time, the term list reflects the most recent interests of each user. PedConnect recommends resources based on this term list.

Promoting Forum Participation

Figure 3. PedConnect: 'Interesting Discussions' View

Using the above mentor/mentee levels for each topic, the system identifies recent discussions that the mentors can participate in. Potential discussion participants are determined by matching inferred user interests with inferred discussion topics. When topic mentors log into the system, PedConnect shows discussions where their contribution would be helpful under the "Interesting Discussions" tab (Figure 3).

Promoting Communication among Teachers

Figure 4. PedConnect: 'Your Questions' View

PedConnect promotes communication among peer teachers in two ways. First, when the user logs into the system, under the "Your Questions" tab, for each question posted by the user, potential helpers who can respond to his/her questions are shown (Figure 4). These users share similar interests and have been answering related questions. Second, PedConnect recommends interesting discussions or other user's questions in order to get the current user involved (Figure 3).

Promoting Resource Usages

Figure 5 shows the resource tab of PedConnect. By matching the subject terms of resource descriptions with the popular keywords in the users' conversation history, the most relevant resources are selected and presented to the user. The interface also allows the user to make changes to their profile subject terms if necessary.

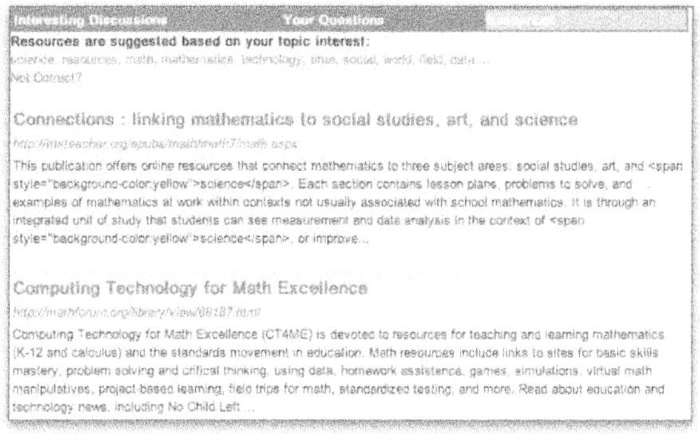

Figure 5. PedConnect: 'Resource Recommendation' View

PRELIMINARY RESULTS

Prediction of forum participation

We use existing MSP2 data from 2008-2011 in evaluating our user topic model and forum recommendation. For each discussion thread, we produce a ranked list of potential participants, ordered by their degree of topic match against the initial post. We use the actual discussion participants subsequent to the initial post as a proxy for labeling "correct" user recommendations, i.e. a user that would have participated in the thread, had the user been recommended to be a participant. This rough approximation underestimates the likelihood of participation, since actual participation was done without the PedConnect suggestions, and most users simply do not browse through all the possible discussion threads to discover threads where they could participate.

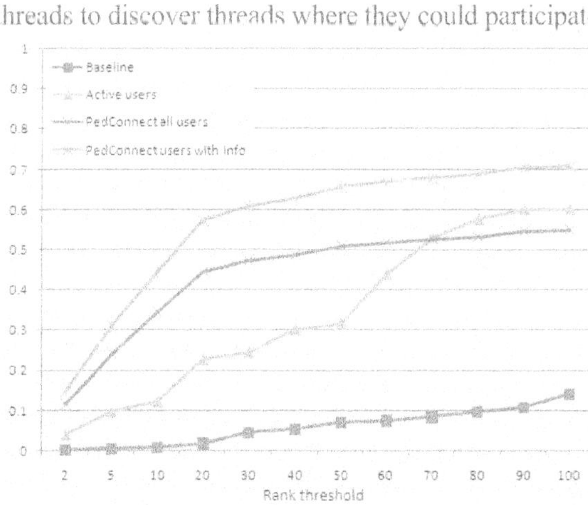

Figure 6: Recall for forum participation prediction

We calculate the recall based on the top results in the list based on some threshold. For example, assume we choose a threshold of 10. We look at the actual set of participants, and calculate the percentage of those participants who appear within the top 10 users in PedConnect's recommended list. The precision is harder to evaluate, as many users with matching topic interests do not often participate, potentially because they were not aware of the discussion. Figure 6 shows the results for different thresholds of top N users. It shows two recall scores for PedConnect: one that includes scores for all users, even those without any data, and one that only includes scores for users who have interacted with MSP2 in some way, such as a post or blog item. We compare these curves with two other methods: a baseline where users are recommended with a random rank, and one heuristic based on a list ordered by a user's activity level. We expected this heuristic to do quite well, since active users are likely to participate in many discussions.

We do not plot the precision since it is misleading for the reasons already described, e.g. at the threshold of 30, with the recall above 0.6, the precision is less than 0.1. That is, only 2 or 3 of the 30 are "correct." However, we may very well expect that many of the "incorrectly" recommended people might actually have participated in the thread, had they been made aware of the discussion.

PedConnect performed significantly better than others due to its use of the context information (discussion topic). Further, if we remove users for whom we don't have any information i.e. no profile answers and no mentor/mentee classification, the algorithm improved further. This shows that the more information we have about a user, the better we can predict whether the user is likely to participate in the discussion or not.

Initial User Feedback

Feature	Question category	Avg. Rating
Interesting Discussion	Is the task topic prediction accurate?	4
	Will you be able to help this discussion?	3.5
	Is the discussion topic prediction accurate?	3.3
	Is this discussion relevant to your interests?	4.3
Resource Recom-mendation	Is this math & science interest prediction accurate?	3.3
	Are the recommended resources relevant to your interests?	4.3
	Are recommended resources useful?	3.3
Search Engine	Are discussions relevant to the topics?	3.75
	Are the recommended resources relevant to the topics?	3.5

Table 2. A summary of the user feedback.

Two teachers participated in the initial study and were asked to rate the results' usefulness/relevancy/likelihood on a scale of 1-5 (Not at all, Slightly, Moderately, Very, Completely). For each question category, 2-3 items were presented for evaluation. Table 2 summarizes average ratings over each category, which contains 4-12 questions. The averages range between Very and Moderately. They liked the PedConnect concept and expected that the system will encourage participation. "I like what I see and think that it will encourage participation."

CONCLUSION AND FUTURE WORK

We presented PedConnect, which assists social networking by promoting user interactions and resource usage. The system integrates diverse information from the social networking site and leverages the availability of rich metadata about educational resources. We identify user topic interests and mentorship using their participation in forums and blogs. We propose several different ways to promote user participation and user interactions using the topic interests and mentorship. The technique is applied in an important domain area, where successful networking and recommendations has the potential to greatly improve education by empowering teachers with knowledge from online peers, mentors, and resources. We will continue with this approach by integrating more sources of information to expand the user profiles, improve profile accuracy, and automatically model interests that potentially change over time. We will also investigate alternative ways to promote participation. The system is fully integrated with MSP2 and will be deployed in the coming months, and we will begin evaluation of user behavior in the deployed system.

ACKNOWLEDGMENTS

This material is based upon work supported by the National Science Foundation under Grant No. 1044427.

REFERENCES

1. Anderson, R.E. Social impacts of computing: Codes of professional ethics. *Social Science Computing Review 10*, 2, (1992).
2. Brusilovsky, P., L.N. et al., Social navigation for educational digital libraries. *Procedia Computer Science* 1,2 (2010).
3. Chen, B., Tseng, B., Yang, J., Guo, J. User Reputation in a Comment Rating Environment. In *Proc. KDD 2011*.
4. Cohen, J., A coefficient of agreement for nominal scales, *Educational and Psychological Measurement*, 20 (1960).
5. Danielson, C., et al. *Implementing Framework for Teaching in Enhansing Professional Practice* (2009).
6. Fredericks, A. D. *The Teacher's Handbook: Strategies for Success*. Rowman & Litlefield Education (2010).
7. Freyne, J., Smyth, B., Farzan, R., Brusilovsky, P., Collecting Community Wisdom: Integrating Social Search & Social Navigation. In Proc. *IUI 2006*.
8. Guy, I., et al., Do you know?: recommending people to invite onto your social network, In Proc. *IUI 2009*.
9. Harper F., et al., Inviting Users To Participate in Online Discussions. In Proc. *IUI 2006*.
10. Klein, M. B. *New Teaching and Teacher Issues*. Nova Science Publishers, 2006.
11. MSP2. The Middle School Portal 2 Math and Science Pathways, http://www.msteacher2.org/, 2011.
12. NSDL. The National Science Digital Library, http://nsdl.org, 2011.

An Adaptive Solution for Intra-Operative Gesture-based Human-Machine Interaction

Ali Bigdelou* **Loren Arthur Schwarz*** **Nassir Navab**
Computer Aided Medical Procedures (CAMP)
Technische Universität München, Germany
{bigdelou,schwarz,navab}@cs.tum.edu
* Joint corresponding and first authors.

ABSTRACT
Computerized medical systems play a vital role in the operating room, however, sterility requirements and interventional workflow often make interaction with these devices challenging for surgeons. Typical solutions, such as delegating physical control of keyboard and mouse to assistants, add an undesirable level of indirection. We present a touchless, gesture-based interaction framework for the operating room that lets surgeons define a personalized set of gestures for controlling arbitrary medical computerized systems. Instead of using cameras for capturing gestures, we rely on a few wireless inertial sensors, placed on the arms of the surgeon, eliminating the dependence on illumination and line-of-sight. A discriminative gesture recognition approach based on kernel regression allows us to simultaneously classify performed gestures and to track the relative spatial pose within each gesture, giving surgeons fine-grained control of continuous parameters. An extensible software architecture enables a dynamic association of learned gestures to arbitrary intra-operative computerized systems. Our experiments illustrate the performance of our approach and encourage its practical applicability.

Author Keywords
Gesture-based Interaction; Operating Room; Inertial Sensors

ACM Classification Keywords
H.5.2 Information Interfaces and Presentation (e.g. HCI): User Interfaces; J.3 Life and Medical Sciences: Health

INTRODUCTION
The operating room (OR) is a highly complex environment and surgical staff often work under high pressure. For assistance, various types of computerized medical systems are used in the OR, for instance to visualize volumetric patient data. However, when interacting with such devices during surgery, surgeons face challenges. Sterility regulations restrict the use of classical mouse-driven or touch-based user interfaces and control terminals are often required to be spatially separated from the main operating site [15]. Interventional workflow might not allow the surgeon to leave this site and, while handling medical instrumentation, the surgeon might only have very limited freedom of movement. Typical solutions include delegating physical control over computerized systems to less-skilled assistants [10, 15]. This increases the amount of verbal communication, raising the chance of misunderstandings. The added level of indirection can also adversely affect precision and lead to inefficiency [15].

We propose a touch-free user interface solution that gives surgeons direct control over computerized systems by means of gestures. Our approach learns gestures from examples given by a surgeon who can freely define movements that fit best a particular interventional scenario and personal habits. Gestures are captured using a few wireless inertial sensors on the surgeon's arms that can easily be integrated into garment. The sensors make our system independent of cameras, enabling robust gesture recognition in the presence of critical OR conditions, including difficult lighting, cluttered backgrounds and occlusions by staff and equipment. Using our adaptive and extensible software architecture allows an easy assignment of learned gestures to functions of arbitrary medical devices without any programming. Moreover, the framework enables dynamically changing the assignment of gestures to target systems based on current workflow stages. In the collaborative OR setting, the proposed approach can also be used to distribute control, based on intra-operative roles, by attaching wireless sensors to multiple persons, each controlling distinct features with personalized gestures.

As opposed to typical gesture-based user interfaces that either give users *categorical* or *spatio-temporal* control [12, 16], our method combines both concepts. Surgeons can select discrete functions of the target system, as their gestures are automatically recognized and classified (*categorical* control). At the same time, their particular arm movements in space are used to precisely adjust continuous parameters related to the selected functions (*spatio-temporal* control).

Consider the following medical application scenario. During minimally-invasive aortic repair procedures, a stent graft is inserted through an artery into the aorta to exclude an aneurysm from blood circulation. Positioning the stent graft is guided by imaging modalities that combine intra-operative X-ray views and tomographic patient scans [5]. For the complex task of inserting the stent graft, a hypothesized surgeon would like to control the visualization himself, instead of instructing an assistant. Knowing that his right hand is occupied during catheter insertion, the surgeon trains the gesture recognition system on three gestures he performs with his left arm. He uses a circular movement for browsing slices in the tomographic scan, a vertical movement for zooming and a horizontal movement for translating the image. During an actual intervention, the surgeon needs to adjust the visualization while inserting the stent graft. To activate gesture recognition, he pronounces a voice command and starts tracing a circle with his left arm. The system immediately recognizes the intended browsing functionality. Having found the region of interest, the surgeon keeps his arm still and moves it back and forth for fine adjustment. To increase the zoom factor, he then moves his arm horizontally. The image is scaled in proportion to his arm movement. Another voice command stores the current setting and deactivates gesture control. The surgeon can now continue inserting the stent graft without accidentally modifying the visualization with his movements.

For recognizing and tracking gestures from inertial sensor data, we present a method that builds upon dimensionality-reduced gesture models, created from the training sensor data for every gesture of interest. We compare using Principal Component Analysis (PCA) and a manifold learning technique for dimensionality reduction. Given previously unseen sensor measurements, the method directly predicts the performed gesture and the relative pose within the gesture by means of a discriminative kernel regression mapping. The generality of our approach allows an application to other domains with similar characteristics, although the focus of this work is on the OR environment.

In our experiments, we evaluate the proposed method in the exemplary scenario of controlling a medical image viewer. Quantitative experiments show that the proposed method can simultaneously recognize up to 18 gestures to a high accuracy from as little as four inertial sensors. The promising results of the usability study encourage a practical application of our method in the operating room.

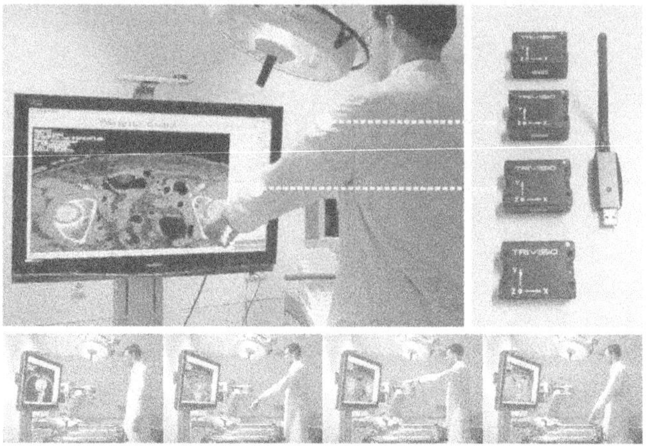

Figure 1. Gesture-based control of a medical image viewer application. Four wireless inertial sensors *(top right)* are placed on the person's arms underneath the blouse. In this example, a vertical arm gesture is used to brows the slices in a volumetric dataset.

Related Work

Using gestures for human-machine interaction has been studied intensively and surveys are available, e.g. [14, 20]. Different modalities are used to capture gestures, e.g. pens [24], cameras or sensors. The operating room scenario has been targeted by several authors, e.g. [17, 10, 21, 23]. For instance, a stereo camera setup is used in [10] for tracking the hand of a surgeon and thereby controlling the mouse pointer on a screen. In [17], a medical image viewer can be controlled by hand gestures, tracked with two video cameras. Recent Time-of-Flight cameras, measuring the depth of a scene in realtime, are employed in [21] for a similar purpose. Such vision-based systems face challenges in realistic OR environments, where optimal lighting and line-of-sight between the surgeon and the cameras cannot always be ensured.

Capturing gestures by means of inertial sensors attached to the surgeon's body is a promising alternative, circumventing the restrictions of camera-based systems. In addition, wireless sensors enable a surgeon to perform gestures independent of his location and orientation within the OR. Previous research on gesture recognition using wearable inertial sensors includes [16, 13, 25, 22, 7]. In [16], short hand gestures are measured using accelerometers and evaluated for their usefulness in controlling home entertainment devices. In [25] the authors fuse accelerometer and electromyogram signals and recognize hand gestures using Multi-stream Hidden Markov Models. The authors present an HMM-based gesture recognition approach. Hand gestures, such as quick up-down movements or circles, are recognized in [13] based on a Dynamic Time Warping (DTW) mechanism. The authors of [22] and [7] recognize the suitability of *orientation* sensors for gesture recognition, as opposed to pure accelerometers. We also employ this type of device and bring the sensors into the operating room environment.

Multi-modal interfaces which combine input streams from various input sources rely on an underlying software architecture. In [11, 19], the authors propose a modular framework for combining multiple input devices for controlling arbitrary devices. Furthermore in [3], Bogdan et al. extend this idea proposing a high level modeling approach enabling the inexperienced end-users to customize the interaction interface. To smoothly integrate our gesture recognition approach in the OR, we exploit a similar concept and explain how the main aspects of the OR domain, such as surgical workflow and collaboration, can be considered in this model, to provide users with a customizable context-aware interaction framework.

Compared to the aforementioned vision and sensor-based methods, the main contributions of our gesture-based interaction method can be summarized as follows:

- Gestures can be defined freely according to the requirements of a particular interventional scenario. By demonstrating an example per gesture to the system, surgeons do not have to adhere to a pre-defined set of movements that might interfere with their hand usage during surgery.

- Gestures are not only recognized for triggering discrete actions, e.g. "click the mouse" (*categorical* control [12, 16]), but simultaneously allow tracking the movements within a gesture for fine-tuning continuous parameters, such as the size of a displayed image (*spatio-temporal* control).
- Our gesture recognition method creates dimensionality-reduced gesture models from training sensor data and directly predicts the current gesture and the relative pose within the gesture from previously unseen sensor measurements using a discriminative kernel regression mapping.
- The underlying software architecture enables dynamically associating learned gestures to features of arbitrary target systems, taking into account different workflow stages. Additionally, interaction tasks can be distributed between multiple users in the collaborative OR environment.

Paper Organization

We introduce our sensor-based gesture recognition method, followed by outlining the underlying software framework. We then turn to practical application aspects of the system. Before concluding, we present our experimental evaluation.

INERTIAL ORIENTATION SENSORS

To recognize and track gestures, we rely on inertial sensors that measure their orientation with respect to the earth reference frame. Senors of this type are internally comprised of an accelerometer, a gyroscope and a compass that are combined by means of sensor fusion [7]. As opposed to pure accelerometers, orientation sensors exhibit relatively low levels of noise and drift. Orientation sensors are particularly suitable for gesture-based human-computer interaction, as different body poses generally result in different sensor measurements (see Figure 2). Pure accelerometers depend on body movement for extraction of characteristic signal patterns. In our implementation, we used wireless orientation sensors that are approximately 2cm × 2cm × 3cm of size and allow for 8-10 hours of battery-based, wireless operation. We use the quaternion values provided by each of the sensors, avoiding problems of other representations, such as gimbal lock.

GESTURE RECOGNITION METHOD

We propose a simple and effective method for gesture recognition and tracking based on orientation sensor data. The method consists of an offline training phase, where gesture models are learned from sensor data for all considered gestures, and an online phase, where the models are used to recognize gestures from previously unseen sensor data.

Modeling Gestures

In our work, a gesture is, at the same time, categorical and spatio-temporal [12]. A user performs a gesture to invoke a particular function of the target system and to control this function in a fine-grained, continuous manner. The gesture recognition method therefore has two goals: (1) to recognize which gesture a user is performing and (2) to identify the relative spatial pose within that particular gesture. To this end, we define a gesture to be an arbitrary movement including one or both arms that has a temporal extent and encompasses many

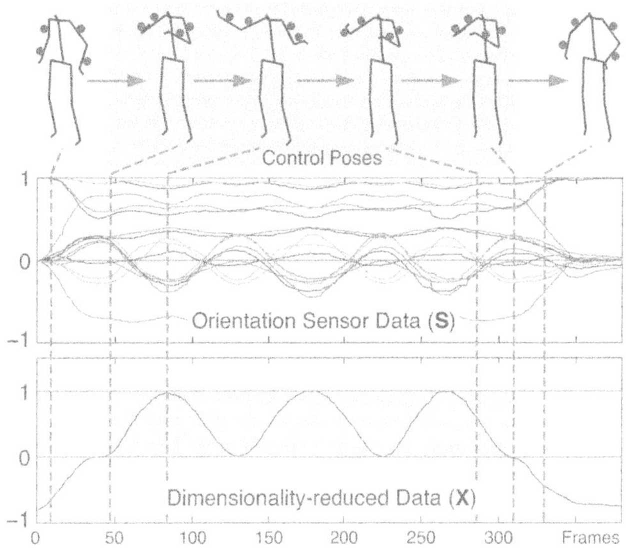

Figure 2. Selected body poses for a zooming gesture with indicated inertial sensors (*top*), highlighted in a stream of orientation sensor data (*middle*) and the corresponding dimensionality-reduced signal (*bottom*). The resulting one-dimensional value between 0 and 1 serves to control arbitrary parameter values.

smoothly-varying poses. We refer to all poses actually intended for controlling the target system as *control poses* (see Figure 2). We assume that *control poses* are preceded and followed by introduction and termination movements, such as raising and lowering an arm, that are not directly used for control. In the example shown in Figure 2, a user chooses a horizontal movement of both arms for zooming a virtual object. As soon as he starts raising his hands, the intended gesture is recognized and the zooming function is activated. When the user reaches the *control poses* in front of his body, his exact hand movement is used for controlling the zoom parameter of the virtual object.

Learning Gestures

In the training phase, our method learns prior models of gestures from sample inertial sensor data. Let $\mathbf{S} = \{\mathbf{s}_1, \ldots, \mathbf{s}_n\}$ be a dataset of n sensor measurements for N gestures of interest. Each vector $\mathbf{s}_i \in \mathbb{R}^d$ represents a particular body pose and consists of four quaternion values per sensor (i.e. for four sensors, $d = 16$). The known gesture labels for the training data are denoted by $\mathbf{C} = \{c_1, \ldots, c_n\}$, with $1 \leq c_i \leq N$. Using a dimensionality reduction technique, we construct a one-dimensional intermediate representation $\mathbf{X} = \{x_1, \ldots, x_n\}$ from the training sensor data, such that every $x_i \in \mathbb{R}$ corresponds to one $\mathbf{s}_i$. For most effectively capturing the movement characteristics of distinct gestures, we separately process the sensor data $\mathbf{S}^c = \{\mathbf{s}_i \in \mathbf{S} | c_i = c\}$ for each gesture c. The resulting dimensionality-reduced datasets $\mathbf{X}^c$ are then normalized such that, for each gesture, the *control poses* map to the range $[0, 1]$ (see Figure 2). This can be simply achieved by truncating the datasets $\mathbf{X}^c$ at their beginning and end. Concatenating all gesture-specific sets then gives $\mathbf{X} = \{\mathbf{X}^1, \ldots, \mathbf{X}^N\}$. Note that, for every index $1 \leq i \leq n$, the training dataset contains a triplet $(\mathbf{s}_i, c_i, x_i)$ of a sensor vector, its gesture label and the corresponding one-dimensional value.

Our method does not build upon a particular type of dimensionality reduction technique. However, given the non-linear nature of human motion data, manifold learning techniques can be a reasonable choice [6]. These methods, e.g. Laplacian Eigenmaps [1], can embed high-dimensional data in an arbitrary lower-dimensional space while maintaining the local spatial structure of the data. In our experiments, we compared employing Laplacian Eigenmaps and PCA.

Recognizing and Tracking Gestures

The dimensionality-reduced intermediate representation $\mathbf{X}$ allows us to translate movements for the learned gestures into a continuous, one-dimensional signal that can be used for adjusting arbitrary user interface parameters. After training, we are given new, previously unseen sensor measurements $\mathbf{s}_t$ at any time t. Our aim is to determine the intermediate representation $\hat{x}_t \in \mathbb{R}$ corresponding to $\mathbf{s}_t$ and to identify the performed gesture $\hat{c}_t$, $1 \leq \hat{c}_t \leq N$. For this purpose, we define an out-of-sample mapping that projects arbitrary sensor measurement vectors to the dimensionality-reduced representation $\mathbf{X}$. Using non-parametric kernel regression, we predict the value $\hat{x}_t$ for a sensor vector $\mathbf{s}_t$ as

$$\hat{x}_t = f(\mathbf{s}_t) = \sum_{i=1}^{n} \frac{w_i(\mathbf{s}_t)}{\sum_{j=1}^{n} w_j(\mathbf{s}_t)} \cdot x_i. \qquad (1)$$

In this summation, the estimate $\hat{x}_t$ is combined from the known projections $x_i \in \mathbf{X}$ of the sensor vectors $\mathbf{s}_i \in \mathbf{S}$ in the training data. Each value x_i is weighted in proportion to the similarity between its corresponding sensor vector $\mathbf{s}_i$ and the new sensor measurement $\mathbf{s}_t$. Dividing by the sum of all weights ensures that the summation is a convex combination and $\hat{x}_t$ lies within the range of values in $\mathbf{X}$. The weights are given by a Gaussian kernel $w_i(\mathbf{s}_t) = \mathrm{k}(\mathbf{s}_t, \mathbf{s}_i) = \exp(-\frac{1}{2}\|(\mathbf{s}_t - \mathbf{s}_i)/\sigma\|^2)$ with a width σ derived from the variance of the training sensor data $\mathbf{S}$. Using the weights, we also determine the current gesture index $\hat{c}_t$ as

$$\hat{c}_t = c_{k_t}, \quad \text{where} \quad k_t = \arg\max_i w_i(\mathbf{s}_t). \qquad (2)$$

Here, the index k_t identifies the sensor measurement in the training data that is most similar to $\mathbf{s}_t$ and thus has the largest weight. The gesture label corresponding to this training sensor vector is used as an estimate for $\hat{c}_t$. As Equation 1 only depends on the current sensor measurement $\mathbf{s}_t$, it does not take into account previous observations or recognized gestures. However, such temporal information can increase the robustness of the gesture recognition method with respect to noise and outlier sensor measurements. We therefore propose to modify the kernel regression-based weighting scheme and replace the weights $w_i(\mathbf{s}_t)$ with

$$\bar{w}_i(\mathbf{s}_t) = w_i(\mathbf{s}_t) \cdot \exp(-\frac{1}{2}((i - k_{t-1})/\sigma)^2). \qquad (3)$$

In analogy to k_t in Equation 2, k_{t-1} identifies the sensor measurement in the training data with the largest weight in the previous time step $t-1$. Multiplying $w_i(\mathbf{s}_t)$ with the exponential term essentially centers a Gaussian at this sensor measurement. This way, when computing the convex combination in Equation 1, sensor vectors around the best-scoring vector at time $t-1$ are favored at time t.

FRAMEWORK FOR GESTURE-BASED INTERACTION

In the following sections, we propose a software architecture for implementing a customizable, gesture-based interaction framework and show how we integrate the gesture recognition approach described above as a component.

Architectural Requirements

In order to smoothly integrate a gesture-based interface into a target application, a proper underlying architecture needs to be used during implementation of a gesture-based interaction framework. Such a framework should be reusable and extensible, since gestures can be used to control different kinds of features in a wide range of intra-operative systems. For example, in the envisioned scenario outlined before, an intra-operative image viewing application lets the surgeon select a patient profile, load the relevant preoperative image data, and change the viewing parameters, e.g. current slice number, zoom and pan, to find the region of interest [9].

Moreover, the used architecture also should be customizable, both in the sense of defining gestures, as well as in mapping gestures to target features. Although a wide range of body movements can be defined as gestures, selecting an appropriate subset of gestures is strongly dependent on the usage context. Usually this kind of knowledge is not available in advance. For instance, as highlighted in the introductory scenario, there are situations during a clinical intervention, in which the surgeon requires to change some settings of an intra-operative system with just one of his hands, since the other hand is occupied holding a medical tool.

Framework Implementation

In order to achieve the desired reusability, extensibility and customizability, we propose a framework with a component-based architecture. In this model, components expose their functionalities to the framework as sets of properties, methods and events. We define four main kinds of components in this framework: *sensor* components, *gesture recognition* components, *target* components and *demultiplexer* components. Examples are given in Figure 3.

Sensor components

The interface to the inertial orientation sensor hardware is encapsulated in sensor components. Each instance of this component is representing a sensor and consists of properties which contain the latest orientation data.

Gesture Recognition Components

Our implementation of the gesture recognition approach is contained in this type of component. This component has two sets of properties, input data and the recognized output. The value of the input data properties are updated directly based on recent sensor values. The number of input properties and the used dimensionality reduction technique are specified in a configuration file which can be used to customize the framework. The recognized output properties are $\hat{c}_t$, the index of the current detected gesture, and $\hat{x}_t \in [0, 1]$.

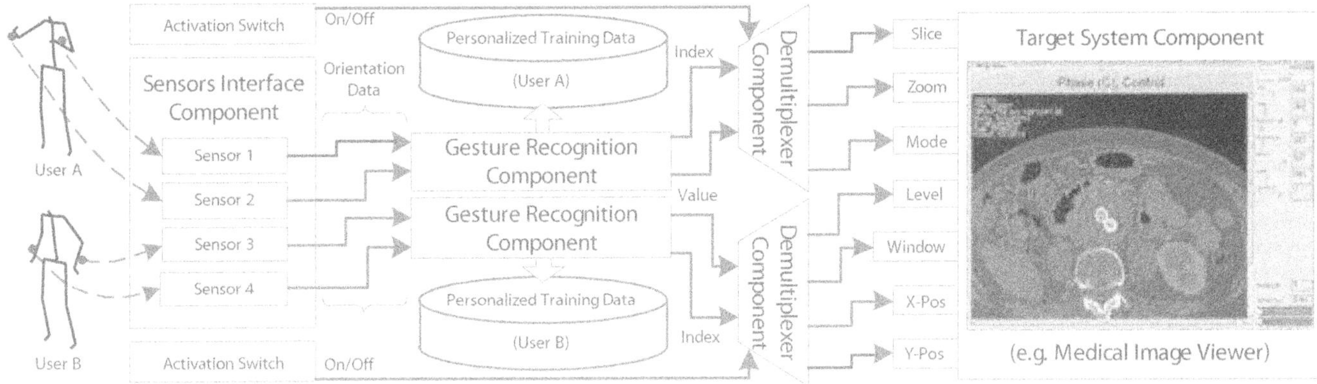

Figure 3. An exemplary component graph containing four sensor components, two gesture recognition components and their corresponding demultiplexer components and a target component. This is an exemplary collaborative domain scenario, with two users controlling a medical image viewer application. Each of the gesture recognition components is using an individual, personalized training dataset.

Target Components

Components of this type wrap the interface required to control a specific intra-operative target application. In order to control a new application with the proposed gesture-based interaction framework, a specific target component needs to be implemented. Applications could be software or hardware systems which provide a proper programming interface. Using the proposed model, the framework can access both, functions and parameters of the target application. Functions (e.g. load, save, close, etc.) can be implemented as a method within the target component and can be triggered with an event. Parameters can be encapsulated as a component property which stores a numeric or logical value and reflects a specific setting of the target system (e.g. visualization mode, zoom level, horizontal scroll, etc.).

Demultiplexer Components

These components act as a switch between the gesture recognition components and target components and forward the recognized gesture value to the relevant property of the target component. As an input, a demultiplexer component receives the recognized gesture index ($\hat{c}_t$) and the current relative pose ($\hat{x}_t$) from a gesture recognition component. For each of the trained gestures, the demultiplexer component has a separate output channel. The current relative gesture pose ($\hat{x}_t \in [0, 1]$) is routed to the relevant output channel, based on the recognized gesture index ($\hat{c}_t$). Furthermore, using its activity property, the data flow can be enabled or disabled.

Bindings and Data Flow

In order to flexibly set up the connections between recognized gestures and features of the target components, we further extend the proposed component-based framework with the pipeline data flow model, as shown in Figure 3. Since the components and their properties are known to the framework, we develop a binding mechanism to create a connection between properties exposed by different components at runtime (late binding). A binding can be either directional or bi directional. Once such a binding is defined, the framework propagates values of all the changed properties in the defined directions. This guarantees that if a property value changes in one component, all the dependent properties in the other components are be updated. The framework synchronizes the update process using an internal clock.

Customizing System Behavior

The pipeline model, including the list of composed components and their interconnections, is stored in an XML configuration file. Parsing the configuration file at runtime, the framework creates the required set of components, as well as the defined bindings between them. With this approach, the behavior of the system can be completely customized, as required for the specific usage scenario, without extra programming. For instance, one can specify which gesture changes the current slice number property of the medical image viewer application by specifying a binding between the demultiplexer and the medical image viewer component. The pipeline model can be visually displayed to the users as a graph (Figure 3). Components can be presented as the nodes of the graph and bindings as edges. Such a graphical representation can provide the end users with a visual programming interface, allowing them to customize the system behavior at runtime.

GESTURE-BASED INTERACTION IN PRACTICE

In this section, we discuss practical aspects and possibilities of the proposed gesture-based interaction framework.

Gesture Commands

Categorical gestures are typically used to command binary features (e.g. loading data, flipping an image). On the other hand, spatio-temporal gestures are more appropriate for parametric features where a value is controlled (e.g. zoom factor). However, often the interface of a target system contains a combination of binary and parametric features. The user may require to select a zoom tool before specifying the zoom value, or a pan tool has to be selected before panning in the image. Since the proposed approach has characteristics of both categorical and spatio-temporal gesture recognition methods, it can be used to set multiple parametric features of a target system without using additional techniques to switch between different modes. For example, two different gestures can be defined as horizontal and vertical movement of the right hand in front of the body. The first gesture can be assigned to controlling zoom while the second gesture is used to browse slices. In this scenario, a user can fine-tune these parameters simply by moving his hand accordingly.

Activating and Deactivating Control Flow

In order to prevent that movements similar to the trained gestures are considered as gestures, we propose using an additional switch which controls the activity of the gesture-based interface. As shown in Figure 3, this switch can be used to enable and disable the activity of the demultiplexer component. Such a switch can be physically implemented using different techniques. In our study, we examined two different implementations, one using a voice recognition module and the other using a wireless handheld switch. Note that these activation modes are not the focus of our work and the selected options are thus straightforward. Furthermore, once the user finds the proper value of a continuous parameter using its corresponding gesture, the gesture-based interface should provide a method to store the selected value. The aforementioned two exemplary implementations were also used for this functionality.

Hardware Issues

In order to develop an interaction method based on orientation sensors, hardware related issues, such as noise and drift, need to be addressed. We reduced the noise effect by applying a mean filter with a window of 10 frames (equivalent to 200ms) to the output of the gesture recognition method. This introduces a short delay; however, the effect is ignorable. Drift causes an incremental inaccuracy in the sensor measurements. To compensate this effect in our experiments, we periodically reset the boresight direction of the sensors.

Context-Awareness

Reducing the number of gestures increases the usability and reduces the duration of the training phase [4]. However, in complex domains there are many features of a system which might be necessary to access. To reduce the number of gestures as much as possible and still provide necessary control over the target system, a proper understanding of the usage workflow is necessary. At each workflow stage, usually only a limited number of settings are required. By defining a separate configuration file for each workflow stage, the proposed gesture framework can use the same set of the gestures to apply different settings in each workflow stage.

The operating room is a collaborative domain in which multiple users interact with shared resources to achieve a common goal [18, 8, 2]. In such scenarios, the interaction with the target system may be distributed between different human roles. Since each orientation sensor can be identified uniquely, the proposed framework can be rewired to support multiple-user gesture interfaces [18, 8]. For example, the main surgeon may need to browse the medical images, while the anesthetist is checking different live signals on the screen. Each of these users may separately interact with the system, while the same system is processing the sensors, detecting the gestures and propagating commands to the target features (Figure 3).

EXPERIMENTS AND RESULTS

The following sections present the results of our quantitative experiments and our qualitative user study. We used four Trivisio Colibri Wireless inertial orientation sensors, placing two on each arm of our test subjects, as suggested in [22]. The system was implemented in C++ and tested on a 2.5 GHz Intel Core 2 Duo machine with 4 GB of memory.

Quantitative Experiments

For a quantitative assessment, we recorded a dataset of 21 arm gestures, performed by one person in 12 repetitions per gesture. Considered gestures included movements of one or both arms, such as dragging an imaginary slider in front of the body, tracing out circles or waving. The experiments were performed on the recorded dataset of 10^6 frames in a batch mode to allow for systematic cross-validation. For each run, we used three of the 12 repetitions per gesture for training and three other repetitions for testing.

Gesture Recognition Rates

In order to quantify how precisely our method is able to recognize gestures, we determined the percentage of correctly classified frames for different settings. We varied the total number of gestures the method is trained and tested on and used different variations of the method, as discussed previously. Results are shown in Figure 4. For every number $n_g \in \{4, 6, 8, 10, 12, 14, 16, 18\}$ of considered gestures, 10 automatic experiments were performed, each time randomly selecting subsets of n_g gestures for training and testing out of the available 21 gestures. For each choice of n_g, the average classification rate over the 10 experiments thus indicates the performance to be expected with a random selection of gestures. The maximum and minimum for each value of n_g can be achieved with an optimal and inappropriate set of gestures, respectively. Optimality in this case refers to a minimal overlap between gestures to be recognized simultaneously. As can be seen in Figure 4.a), using Laplacian Eigenmaps for dimensionality reduction results in a similar recognition behavior to using PCA. In both cases, 95% of frames are correctly classified when 4 gestures are considered, with a decrease to 85% for 18 simultaneously learned gestures. For any value of n_g, accuracy decreases by 2-3% without the smoothness modification (Equation 3).

Processing Speed

Figure 5.a) illustrates the computational performance of the gesture recognition method for all settings of n_g. The choice of PCA or Laplacian Eigenmaps for dimenisonality reduction does not have an impact on processing speed, as these methods are applied offline. Most computationally intensive is the kernel regression step that, in each frame, passes through all frames of the training dataset. The training dataset grows from 1,000 (for $n_g = 4$) to 8,000 frames (for $n_g = 18$). On our machine, the method allows for very high frame rates above 1,000 frames per second, even for 18 gestures. Performance is slightly lower when the smoothness modification is enabled. In practice, processing speed is thus only limited by the acquisition rates of the inertial sensors, typically 60-120 Hz. These results highlight the feasibility of deploying our

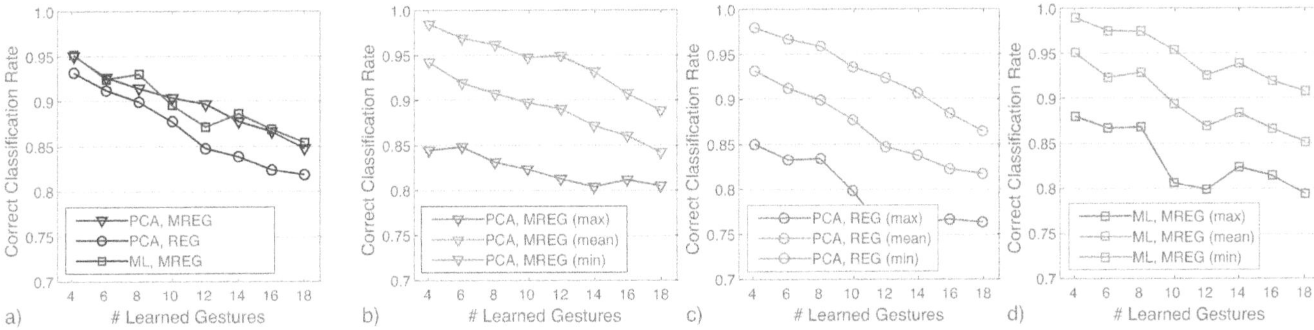

Figure 4. Correct gesture classification rates for various numbers of simultaneously learned gestures (n_g) and different method options (PCA: principal component analysis, ML: manifold learning, MREG: regression with smoothness modification, REG: plain kernel regression). a) Average rates for all experiments and 3 method settings. b)-d) Maximal, average and minimal rates for each of the 3 settings. Maxima indicate rates for an optimal, non-overlapping choice of gestures.

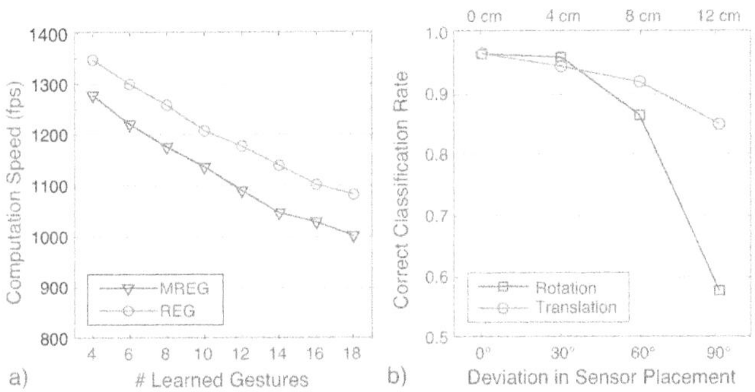

Figure 5. a) Processing speed in frames per second (fps) for different settings of n_g using kernel regression with smoothness modification (MREG) and plain kernel regression (REG). b) Sensitivity of gesture recognition to incremental deviations in sensor placement.

method on portable devices with limited processing capabilities, such as smartphones.

Sensitivity to Sensor Placement

In order to evaluate how sensitive our method is to an exact placement of the sensors, we recorded an additional dataset with a subset of 8 gestures, varying the position of the sensors on the person's arms. Starting with a training sequence of all 8 gestures and the sensors in a reference position, we tested on sequences with incremental rotational and translational deviation of the sensors. Translation was changed to 4, 8 and 12 cm (along the arms) from the reference position, rotation (around the arm axis) was changed to approximately 30, 60 and 90 degrees. Figure 5.b) shows that gesture recognition is more sensitive to rotational deviation than to translations. However, rotations up to 30° and translations up to 4 cm almost do not affect recognition rates. We argue that rotational deviations close to 90°, where recognition rates drop below 60%, are not to be expected under typical usage conditions. The results also imply that the sensors can be taken off and on, e.g. to continue work on another day, without new training.

Influence of Training Dataset Size

As a short training phase is desirable for the users [16], we evaluated the behavior of our method with respect to a varying number of repetitions per gesture in the training data. We recorded a dataset of 8 gestures with an increasing number of repetitions, ranging from 1 to 8. The sequence with 8 repetitions was taken for testing, while training on the other sequences, one by one. Apparently, training on a single repetition per gesture cannot sufficiently account for typical variation when performing a gesture multiple times. However, gesture recognition rates matched those displayed in Figure 4 for two repetitions per gesture, without additional improvement up to the case of 7 repetitions per gesture. We argue that performing two repetitions per gesture for training is not a significant burden, considering that the system only rarely needs to be re-trained.

User Study

We conducted a series of user studies to evaluate the usability of our proposed approach. In our test setup (Figure 1), we used a medical image viewer application as the target system. This application lets the user load and browse medical volumetric image data. We used a subset of 8 different gestures, each assigned to one of the main features of the image viewer, including slice number, zoom factor, view position, brightness, contrast, etc. For allowing users to activate and deactivate gesture control, we implemented two exemplary techniques: a voice recognition module reacting to the commands "start" and "stop", and a hand-held wireless switch.

Test Session

Ten test subjects participated in our study with an average age of 28 years, three of them female. The test subjects all were pursuing or hold a degree in biomedical engineering. Thus, the subjects were educated to develop intra-operative systems and have a very good understanding of the OR and medical scenarios. Among them, 4 were senior master students, 4 PhD students and 2 post-docs. After providing basic instructions to each participant, we recorded training data for every gesture with three repetitions. After 15 minutes of free exploration of the system by the users, we asked them to perform a well-defined test task, consisting in locating an aortic stent in a loaded CT dataset and navigating to its bifurcation. This task is based on a real activity within aortic stent implantation surgery, where the surgeon needs to localize the implanted stent for validation. The used dataset has been acquired at our university hospital and was anonymized accordingly.

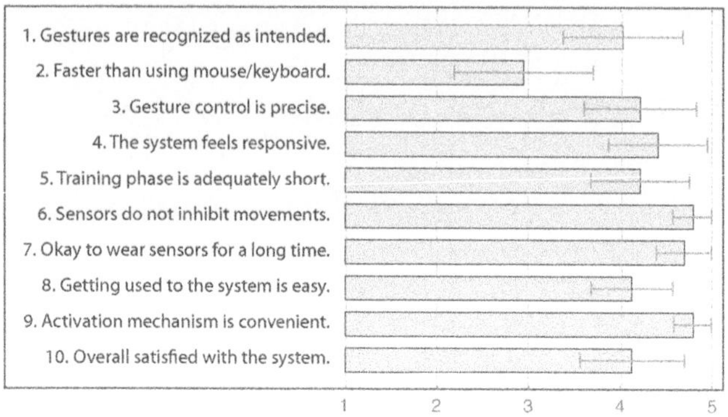

Figure 6. Average results of the usability survey for 10 testing subjects. The values indicate subjective consent to the phrases given on the left, on a scale from 1 (*strongly disagree*) to 5 (*strongly agree*). Standard deviations for each item are shown.

For evaluation, we also provided the users with the correct values for all parameters. To reach the target values, the users had to use the trained gestures. The procedure was performed twice per participant, once using voice recognition and once the hand-held switch to activate and deactivate gesture control. We measured the time the users took to complete the task for each of the methods and computed the deviation of each of the parameters from the target values. At the end, the users were asked to fill a questionnaire.

Qualitative Results

As illustrated in Figure 6, our gesture-based interface has received positive feedback. The results show that the sensors are not inhibiting the usual movement of the users and could be worn for extended periods of time. Furthermore, most of the users agree on the responsiveness and precision of the proposed system. The more skeptical response to the speed comparison with respect to using keyboard and mouse (question 2) can be explained with the fact that the participants have a bias towards using familiar classical interfaces in WIMP environments. During our study, we noticed that users liked especially being able to move freely within the room. Regarding the activation, eight of the ten participants preferred the hand-held wireless switch over the voice recognition system. This might be due to the fact that users feel faster response and more direct control over the system, using a switch compared to the voice command. In both approaches, the participants achieved an acceptable accuracy in setting the target parameter values. Using the voice command method, users reached the expected parameter values with a deviation of 2% of the respective parameter range. For the hand-held switch, precision was within 4% of the parameter range. This gave enough freedom to the users to accurately control the target application. Moreover, initial experiments in a real operating room environment provided encouraging results and show that the proposed gesture-based interface has good usability factors for an applicability in practice.

DISCUSSION

Gesture-based interaction in the OR has been explored in several studies, e.g. [15], where the authors point out the clear need for touch-less interaction in the OR based on interviews with surgeons. We found a similar interest from surgeons to whom we demonstrated our prototype. Several medical professionals observed and experienced our system, including a neurosurgeon and a trauma orthopedist, with 1 and 3 year(s) into their residency, as well as a minimally invasive abdominal surgeon and a vascular surgeon, both with more than 20 years of experience. In a qualitative feedback, the surgeons pointed out their interest in this interaction method and their ability to see this solution as a possible UI for the OR.

In terms wearing inertial sensors, it is important to note that, during their preparation, surgeons have to undress completely and wear specific sterile OR clothing. Adding ergonomic, small sensors will thus not be an additional burden in general. This might be different in cases such as radiology, where doctors only wear a cover on top of their usual clothing.

While novel depth imaging modalities, such as the Kinect, are a straightforward option for gesture-based interaction, we argue that inertial sensors are more suitable for the OR scenario. Surgeons typically alternate interaction among multiple devices distributed in the OR, e.g. patient monitoring systems or imaging devices, such as ultra-sound or X-ray. At each moment, the surgeon looks at a different display based on personal requirements. With a Kinect solution, one device would have to be added per display to capture gestures. The presented concept can be exploited to interact with different devices without any line-of-sight problems. Inertial sensors also do not limit the surgeon in moving within the OR. In addition, each sensor has a unique ID, allowing an easy distribution of sensors over multiple persons.

In our customizable gesture recognition approach, the surgeon has the freedom to define gestures as desired. Obviously, gestures that are too similar cannot be distinguished by the system. In the current setup, we asked the users to perform gestures that have a minimal mutual overlap. However, future work will include an automated method which measures the quality of the training dataset and alerts the surgeon in case of gestures that are too similar to be differentiated.

CONCLUSION

We have presented a gesture-based interaction solution for the OR based on wireless inertial sensors. Our approach allows surgeons to define a personalized set of gestures in a training phase that best fits particular requirements. Apart from automatically recognizing performed gestures from the sensor data, our method simultaneously tracks the relative pose within each gesture, allowing the surgeon to control continuous, smoothly varying parameters. The proposed software framework enables a dynamic association of learned gestures to arbitrary target systems. In our experimental validation, we showed that gestures are recognized with high correct classification rates, even when 18 gestures are learned simultaneously. Our presented smoothness modification for kernel regression decreases the sensitivity to outlier sensor data and, thus, improves gesture recognition rates. In this work, we have considered the OR as the main application scenario. However, we believe that our approach, with minor modifications, can also be applied to other collaborative workspace domains that can be characterized by a workflow model.

REFERENCES

1. Belkin, M., and Niyogi, P. Laplacian eigenmaps for dimensionality reduction and data representation. *Neural Computation 15*, 6 (Feb 2003), 1373 – 1396.
2. Bigdelou, A., Sterner, T., Wiesner, S., Wendler, T., Matthes, F., and Navab, N. OR specific domain model for usability evaluations of intra-operative systems. *International Conference on Information Processing in Computer-Assisted Interventions* (2011).
3. Bogdan, C., Kaindl, H., Falb, J., and Popp, R. Modeling of interaction design by end users through discourse modeling. In *Proceedings of the 13th international conference on Intelligent user interfaces*, IUI '08, ACM (New York, NY, USA, 2008), 305–308.
4. Cabral, M. C., Morimoto, C. H., and Zuffo, M. K. On the usability of gesture interfaces in virtual reality environments. *Latin American conference on Human-computer interaction* (2005).
5. Demirci, S., Manstad-Hulaas, F., and Navab, N. Quantification of aortic deformation after EVAR. *SPIE Medical Imaging* (2009).
6. Elgammal, A., and Lee, C. The role of manifold learning in human motion analysis. *Human Motion Understanding, Modeling, Capture and Animation* (2008).
7. Ferscha, A., Resmerita, S., Holzmann, C., and Reichör, M. Orientation sensing for gesture-based interaction with smart artifacts. *Computer communications 28*, 13 (2005), 1552–1563.
8. Freudenthal, A., Studeli, T., Lamata, P., and Samset, E. Collaborative co-design of emerging multi-technologies for surgery. *Journal of Biomedical Informatics 44* (2011), 198–215.
9. Gallo, L. A glove-based interface for 3d medical image visualization. *Intelligent interactive multimedia systems and services 6* (2010), 221–230.
10. Graetzel, C., Fong, T., Grange, S., and Baur, C. A non-contact mouse for surgeon-computer interaction. *Technology and Health Care 12*, 3 (2004), 245–257.
11. Gray, P., Ramsay, A., and Serrano, M. A demonstration of the openinterface interaction development environment. In *Symposium on User Interface Software and Technology (UIST)*, UIST '07 (2009).
12. Gustafson, S., Bierwirth, D., and Baudisch, P. Imaginary interfaces: spatial interaction with empty hands and without visual feedback. *Symposium on User Interface Software and Technology (UIST)* (2010), 3–12.
13. Hartmann, B., and Link, N. Gesture recognition with inertial sensors and optimized dtw prototypes. *IEEE International Conference on Systems Man and Cybernetics (SMC)* (2010), 2102–2109.
14. Jaimes, A., and Sebe, N. Multimodal human-computer interaction: A survey. *Computer Vision and Image Understanding 108*, 1-2 (2007), 116–134.
15. Johnson, R., O'Hara, K., Sellen, A., Cousins, C., and Criminisi, A. Exploring the potential for touchless interaction in image-guided interventional radiology. *ACM Conference on Human Factors in Computing Systems* (2011).
16. Kela, J., Korpipää, P., Mäntyjärvi, J., Kallio, S., Savino, G., Jozzo, L., and Marca, S. Accelerometer-based gesture control for a design environment. *Pers Ubiquit Comput 10*, 5 (2006), 285–299.
17. Kipshagen, T., Graw, M., Tronnier, V., Bonsanto, M., and Hofmann, U. Touch-and marker-free interaction with medical software. *World Congress on Medical Physics and Biomedical Engineering 2009* (2009), 75–78.
18. Kockro, R. A., Stadie, A., Schwandt, E., Reisch, R., Charalampaki, C., Ng, I., Yeo, T. T., Hwang, P., Serra, L., and Perneczky, A. A collaborative virtual reality environment for neurosurgical planning and training. *Neurosurgery 61* (2007), 379–391.
19. Lawson, J.-Y. L., Al-Akkad, A.-A., Vanderdonckt, J., and Macq, B. An open source workbench for prototyping multimodal interactions based on off-the-shelf heterogeneous components. In *Proceedings of the 1st ACM SIGCHI symposium on Engineering interactive computing systems*, EICS '09, ACM (New York, NY, USA, 2009), 245–254.
20. Mitra, S., and Acharya, T. Gesture recognition: A survey. *IEEE Transactions on Systems, Man, and Cybernetics, Part C: Applications and Reviews 37*, 3 (2007), 311–324.
21. Soutschek, S., Penne, J., Hornegger, J., and Kornhuber, J. 3-d gesture-based scene navigation in medical imaging applications using time-of-flight cameras. *Computer Vision and Pattern Recognition Workshops* (Apr 2008).
22. Urban, M., Bajcsy, P., Kooper, R., and Lementec, J. Recognition of arm gestures using multiple orientation sensors: Repeatability assessment. *Intelligent Transportation Systems* (2004), 553–558.
23. Wachs, J. P., Stern, H., Edan, Y., Gillam, M., Feied, C., Smith, M., and Handler, J. A real-time hand gesture interface for medical visualization applications. *Applications of Soft Computing* (2006), 153–162.
24. Wobbrock, J. O., Wilson, A. D., and Li, Y. Gestures without libraries, toolkits or training: a $1 recognizer for user interface prototypes. *Symposium on User Interface Software and Technology (UIST)* (2007), 159–168.
25. Zhang, X., Chen, X., Wang, W.-h., Yang, J.-h., Lantz, V., and Wang, K.-q. Hand gesture recognition and virtual game control based on 3d accelerometer and emg sensors. In *Proceedings of the 14th international conference on Intelligent user interfaces*, IUI '09, ACM (New York, NY, USA, 2009), 401–406.

Unistroke Gestures on Multi-Touch Interaction: Supporting Flexible Touches with Key Stroke Extraction

Yingying Jiang[1] Feng Tian[1,3] Xiaolong Zhang[2] Wei Liu[1] Guozhong Dai[1,3] Hongan Wang[1,3]
[1]Intelligence Engineering Lab, Institute of Software, Chinese Academy of Sciences, Beijing, China
{jyy, tf}@iel.iscas.ac.cn
[2]The Pennsylvania State University
lzhang@ist.psu.edu
[3]State Key Lab. of Computer Science, Institute of Software, Chinese Academy of Sciences, Beijing, China
water_wei@263.net
{dgz, wha}@iel.iscas.ac.cn

ABSTRACT
Gesture inputs on multi-touch tabletops usually involve multiple fingers (more than two) and casual touchdowns or liftoffs of fingers. This flexibility of touch gestures allows more natural user interaction, but also poses new challenges for accurate recognition of multi-touch gestures. To address these challenges, we propose a new approach to recognize flexible multi-touch stroke gestures on tabletops. Based on a user study on multi-touch unistroke gestures, we develop a gesture recognition method by extracting key strokes embedded in flexible multi-touch input. Our evaluation study result shows that this method can greatly improve the recognition accuracy of flexible multi-touch unistroke gestures on tabletops.

Author Keywords
Multi-touch interaction, flexible gesture inputs, unistroke gesture recognition.

ACM Classification Keywords
H.5.2. [**Information Interfaces And Presentation**]: User Interfaces – *Interaction styles*; I.5.4. [**Pattern Recognition**]: Applications – *Signal processing*.

INTRODUCTION
Multi-touch interaction has become more and more ubiquitous. Devices with multi-touch functions support touch-based inputs, either by fingers or by hands. When interacting with devices with small interaction surfaces (e.g., mobile phones), users largely rely on gestures produced by one or two fingers. When interacting with large display devices (e.g., tabletops), however, users often apply gestures that involve multiple fingers [11] and casual touchdowns or liftoffs of fingers. Devices that can tolerate multiple fingers and casual touchdowns and liftoffs of fingers offer more flexible and natural user interaction. However, this flexibility also leads to the difficulty in accurate gesture recognition.

Currently, many gesture recognition algorithms are based on stroke gestures (e.g., scrolling). Compared with other gestures, such as static hand shape gestures, stroke gestures are produced by the movement of fingers or hands, and can express richer meanings. Thus, they have been widely used in pen- and touch-based computing [2, 3, 10]. However, existing methods on stroke gesture recognition can hardly support flexible multi-touch stroke gestures that consist of multiple strokes by multiple fingers that are on and off the surface frequently.

In this paper, we present a method to recognize flexible multi-touch unistroke gestures. As the basic gesture type, a unistroke gesture only consists of one stroke. In multi-touch interactions, a multi-touch unistroke gesture may have multiple strokes produced by different touch points (e.g., multiple fingers), but can be essentially represented by a key stroke that is extracted from multiple strokes by considering the spatial relationship of these strokes.

Figure 1 shows the idea of key stroke with three gestures to draw a circle: one finger only (the first row), two fingers (the second row), and one finger with casual hand touch on the screen surface (the third row). Here, each row has four figures to show fingers involved (the leftmost), sampled touch points and their links based on temporal adjacency (the second from the left), multi-touch strokes color-coded based on input fingers (the second from right), and extracted key strokes (the rightmost). The gesture by one finger only is a unistroke, so no extraction is necessary. The key strokes in other two multi-touch gestures are extracted by removing temporally overlapping points (see more details in later sections).

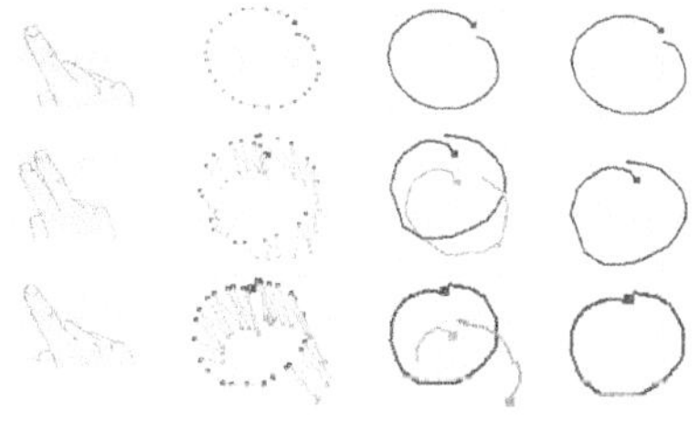
(a)
(b)
(c)

Figure 1. Different drawing styles of a unistroke circle.

RELATED WORK

Multi-touch gesture recognition has been researched in recent years to extend simple touch gestures. Roudaut et al. [4] developed a method to recognize different thumb gestures (e.g., rolling, sliding). Westerman [8] proposed a recognition approach that can track and distinguish different fingers. Holz et al. [1] explored a method to improve gesture recognition accuracy by using fingerprints to deduce finger posture and user ID. Wilson et al. [9] used the shape of the hand contact area, rather than just the point by finger, in gesture design. Li [3] allowed searching by drawing stroke gestures on touch screen mobile devices. Currently, stroke gesture recognition algorithms are largely about the recognition of unistroke gestures [2, 3, 10].

While these multi-touch gesture recognition and stroke gesture recognition algorithms usually work well, they are weak when processing complex finger gestures that involve multiple fingers and the casual touchdown and liftoff of fingers. Some research [11] has shown that users prefer more flexible gestures that are not limited to one or two fingers and allow more casual movement of hands and fingers.

In summary, existing methods on multi-touch gesture recognition cannot effectively process stroke gestures with flexible touch inputs, which are important to natural user interaction with large-screen devices (e.g., tabletops). Our goal here is to address this problem with a multi-touch unistroke gesture recognition method.

MULTI-TOUCH UNISTROKE GESTURE RECOGNITION

To our knowledge, our work is the first of its kind that explores the methods to recognize multi-touch unistroke gestures with flexible touch inputs. Our work included three components: a user study to establish basic understanding of flexible multi-touch unistroke gestures, the development of multi-touch unistroke gesture recognition algorithms, and the evaluation of our approach.

User Study

Intuitively, although multiple fingers are involved in flexible multi-touch gesture inputs, the movement of these fingers may not be totally independent. Rather, they should move in a coordinated way, as shown in Figure 1b. To know better about the movement of multiple fingers, we conducted a user study to collect data about the finger movement in multi-touch stroke gestures on tabletops.

Subjects, Apparatus, and Procedure

Twelve graduate students (9 male and 3 female) were recruited to perform gestures on a touch table. None of the participants was familiar with tabletop interaction before the study. The touch table used in the study was produced by VR VISION [7], and was based on Laser Light Plane Illumination (LLP) technique.

In the study, a subject was first given five minutes to get familiar with the multi-touch screen by trying a demo provided by Touchlib [6]. Then, the subject was asked to draw five types of gestures: line, circle, triangle, rectangle, and multiline. Each gesture was repeated four more times. The subject was told to choose whatever ways she or he liked. Furthermore, to collect a subject's natural drawing style, we provided no visual feedback of gesture input.

Figure 2. A scene of data collecting.

TouchLib was used to detect finger blobs and store blobs to files. The processes of producing gestures were observed and recorded with an upfront camera, as shown in Figure 2.

Results

By analyzing the collected data, we found that almost one-third (32%) of gestures were drawn by more than one finger. However, the movements of multiple fingers involved in gestures are synchronized: the shapes (strokes) drawn by these synchronized fingers were often similar.

We further measured the similarities of multi-touch strokes by comparing the widths, heights and distances of stroke pairs in the same multi-touch gesture. The mean of the *heightRatio* of stroke pairs (the ratio of heights of bounding boxes of two strokes in a stroke pair) is 1.112 (SD = 0.517), the mean of the *widthRatio* (the ratio of the widths of two strokes) is 1.046 (SD=0.526), and the mean of *distRatio* (the ratio of the distance between two synchronized points to the average distance of all synchronized points) is 1.000 (SD = 0.346). From the results, we can see that during the drawing process, the height and width of two synchronized strokes were similar, and the distances between synchronous fingers tended to be stable.

Multi-Touch Unistroke Gesture Recognition

Suppose the sampled touch points be represented as $\{(id_1, x_1, y_1, t_1), \ldots, (id_i, x_i, y_i, t_i), \ldots, (id_N, x_N, y_N, t_N)\}$, id_i indicates the finger index of the ith touch point, (x_i, y_i) is the coordinates, t_i is the time, and N is the number of touch points. The key stroke S consists of a sequence of points and AddPt(x,y) would append a point with the coordinate (x, y) to S.

A conventional recognition algorithm will take all touch points as the key stroke:

$$\mathrm{AddPt}(x_i, y_i),\ 1 \le i \le N$$

Thus, casual touchdowns or multiple finger inputs may affect the recognition results.

Our approach to recognize a multi-touch unistroke gesture includes three steps (Figure 3). First, touch inputs are sampled. Second, a key stroke is extracted from multi-touch inputs. Third, a unistroke gesture recognizer is adopted to identify the type of a gesture. Conventional gesture recognition approaches mentioned above can be regarded as a special case of our approach, without the step of key stroke extraction.

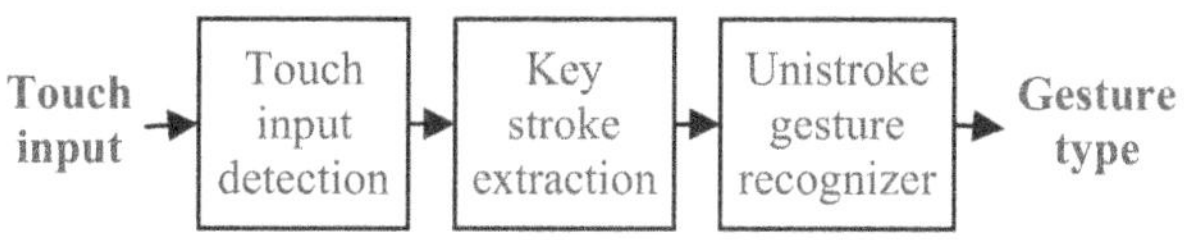

Figure 3. Recognition of multi-touch unistroke gestures.

Key stroke extraction can be done in many ways. In our research, we explored three techniques.

Removing temporally overlapped points: this technique eliminates temporally overlapped, redundant strokes by only keeping the touch point detected earlier when multiple touch points are detected at the same time:

$$\mathrm{AddPt}(x_i, y_i),\ (i=1)\,\mathrm{or}\,(1<i\le N,\ t_i\,!=t_{i-1}).$$

Taking the centroid of temporally overlapped points: this method takes the centroid points of temporally overlapped points to compose the key stroke:

$$\mathrm{AddPt}\left(\underset{t_i=t_j, j\in[1,N]}{ave}(x_j),\ \underset{t_i=t_j, j\in[1,N]}{ave}(y_j)\right),\ 1\le i\le N$$

Averaging adjacent points: this method averages adjacent points to reduce the influence of flexible inputs on the recognition:

$$\begin{cases}\mathrm{AddPt}(x_i, y_i) & (i=1)\,or\,(i=N)\\ \mathrm{AddPt}\left(\dfrac{x_i+x_{i+1}}{2}, \dfrac{y_i+y_{i+1}}{2}\right) & 1<i<N\end{cases}$$

Evaluation

To understand the effectiveness of our approach, we conducted an experiment. We implemented the three key stroke extraction methods and integrated them with TouchLib [6] (touch point sampling) and $1 recognizer [10] (unistroke recognizing). We also implemented a recognition method without key stroke extraction as the baseline condition. Our study compared these four methods in recognizing flexible multi-touch unistroke gestures.

Subjects, Apparatus, and Procedure

Twelve graduate students were recruited (7 male and 5 female). Five of them had participated in the aforementioned user study. They were all right-handed. We used the same touch table in the user study. Similarly, we provided no visual feedback to subjects' inputs and users were told to perform gestures naturally.

We collected data for 16 unistroke gestures that have been also used in the research to evaluate the $1 recognizer [10] (Figure 4). Each subject had ten trials. In each trial, the subject was asked to finish all 16 gestures one by one. In total, we collected 1920 touch gestures (16 × 10 × 12).

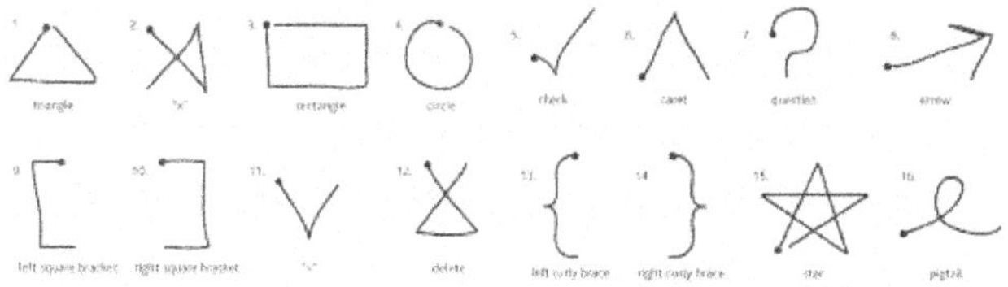

Figure 4. Unistroke gestures used in the study.

We then used four methods to recognize gesture inputs. Here, we label four methods as T1 (no key stroke extraction), T2 (removing temporally overlapped points), T3 (taking the centroid of temporally overlapped points), and T4 (averaging adjacent points).

Results

We first examined the error rates when different numbers of templates are used. As shown in Figure 5, the error rates of four techniques (T1-T4) decrease as the training samples increase, and the error rates of T2, T3 and T4 are lower than that of T1 consistently.

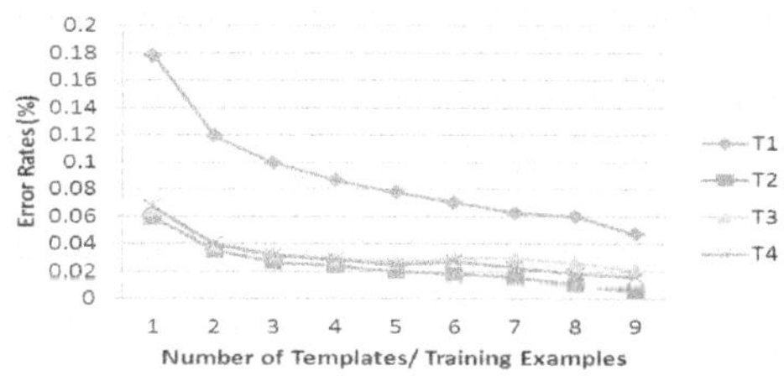

Figure 5. Recognition error rates with training data.

With just one training sample, the error rate of T2, T3 and T4 are 5.94% (SD=0.050), 6.58% (SD=0.053), and 6.74% (SD=0.052) respectively, while the error rate of T1 is 17.81% (SD=0.074). One-way ANOVA shows that the performance differences among four methods are statistically significant ($F_{3,60}$=15.387, p<.001). Post-hoc analysis (Tukey HSD) indicates that T2, T3 and T4 are significantly better than T1 (p<.001). One-way ANOVA does not show significant differences among T2, T3, and T4 ($F_{2,45}$=.108, p=.897).

We also examined the error rates of four methods on top N matching (N = 1, 2, and 3). Figure 6 shows the results of the Top-1, Top-2, and Top-3 with one training template. Here, "candidates" refers to possible gesture classes, and "top-n candidates" are the first n gestures returned from recognition algorithms based on their recognition confidence scores. As shown, T2, T3 and T4 outperform T1 in all cases.

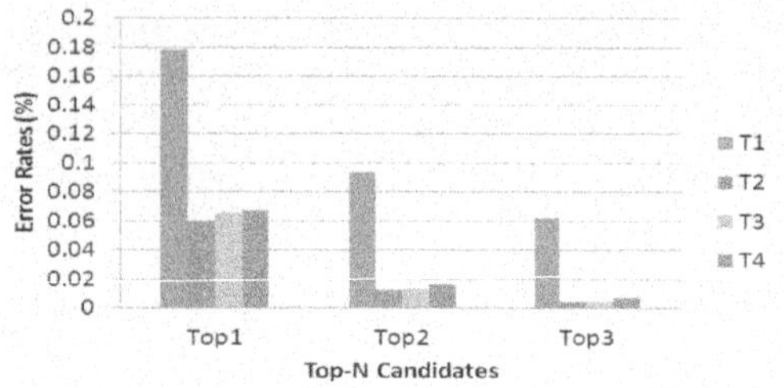

Figure 6. Recognition error rates with top-N candidates.

Figure 7 shows the recognition results of all 16 gestures. As shown, T2, T3 and T4 are better than T1 across all gestures. The gestures with more recognition errors are mainly caused by misclassification of similar gestures, such as gesture No. 5 (the check sign) and gesture No. 11 (the letter v) in Figure 4.

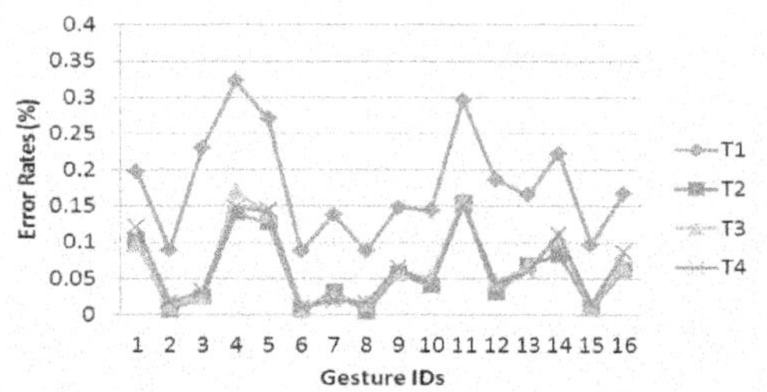

Figure 7. Recognition error rates of different gestures.

As for the time efficiency, when one template is used for each gesture, the average time for T1, T2, T3, T4 are 5.99ms, 5.86ms, 5.89ms, and 5.92ms respectively. When more templates are used, the time needed increases. No significant difference was found among four methods.

DISCUSSION AND CONCLUSION

The results of our evaluation study show that our approaches to recognize multi-touch unistroke gestures are more accurate than the traditional method. This is because key stroke extraction is considered before the application of the stroke recognizer. The three key stroke extraction methods we proposed yield comparable performances, and are all better than the conventional method. Thus, our approach can better support flexible multi-touch unistroke gestures that involve multiple fingers and casual touchdowns or liftoffs of fingers.

It should be pointed out that the recognition accuracies of all four methods used in our experiment are lower than the results reported in other studies, such as [10]. This is largely related to poorer gestures produced by our subjects because of two reasons. First, our data were collected on a tabletop, rather than pen devices in other literature. Tabletop gestures are more flexible than pen gestures. Second, our data collection process provided no visual gesture feedback while other studies usually offered such feedback. Thus, our subjects obtained fewer visual cues in evaluating and correcting their gestures. In this sense, our results are not directly comparable with others.

Accidental and deliberate multiple touches may exist in one system. One way to distinguish them is to include both our algorithm and multi-touch gesture algorithm in the system. Then, those deliberate multi-touch gestures will score higher in the multi-touch algorithm than in our algorithm, while unistroke gestures will score higher in ours than in the multi-touch one. For those ambiguous gestures, we can either use learning algorithms to ask users to specify what result is intended and remember the result, or use other methods, such as [5], to disambiguate different types of gestures automatically.

In summary, we have explored a method to recognize flexible multi-touch stroke gestures. Our studies show that using key stroke extraction can greatly improve the recognition of flexible multi-touch unistroke gestures involving multiple fingers and complex finger behaviors. In the future, we will extend our work by further extending our algorithm for *multi-stroke* gestures, *multi-user* gestures, and small screen devices.

ACKNOWLEDGEMENT

This research is supported by the National Key Basic Research and Development Program of China under Grant No. 2009CB320804 and the National Natural Science Foundation of China under Grant No. 61100151,61170182, and U0735004.

REFERENCES

1. Holz, C. and Baudisch, P. The generalized perceived input point model and how to double touch accuracy by extracting fingerprints. In CHI 2010, 581-591.
2. Li, Y. Protractor: A fast and accurate gesture recognizer. In CHI 2010, 2169-2172.
3. Li, Y. Gesture Search: A Tool for Fast Mobile Data Access. In UIST 2010, 87-96.
4. Roudaut, A., Lecolinet, E. and Guiard, Y. MicroRolls: expanding touch-screen input vocabulary by distinguishing rolls vs. slides of the thumb. In CHI 2009, 927-936.
5. Schwarz, J., Mankoff, J. and Hudson, S.E. Monte carlo methods for managing interactive state, action and feedback under uncertainty. In UIST 2011, 235-244.
6. TouchLib. http://www.nuigroup.com/touchlib/
7. VR VISION. http://www.vrvision.cn/index.asp
8. Westerman, W. Hand tracking, finger identification, and chordic manipulation on a multi-touch surface. PhD thesis, University of Delaware, 1999.
9. Wilson, A.D., Izadi, S., Hilliges, O., Garcia-Mendoza, A. and Kirk, D. Bringing physics to the surface. In UIST 2008, 67-76.
10. Wobbrock, J.O., Wilson, A.D. and Li, Y. Gestures without libraries, toolkits or training: a $1 recognizer for user interface prototypes. In UIST 2007, 159-168.
11. Wobbrock, J.O., Morris, M.R. and Wilson, A.D. User-defined gestures for surface computing. In CHI 2009, 1083-1092.

Continuous Recognition of One-Handed and Two-Handed Gestures using 3D Full-Body Motion Tracking Sensors

Per Ola Kristensson, Thomas F.W. Nicholson, and Aaron Quigley
School of Computer Science
University of St Andrews, St Andrews, United Kingdom
{pok,tfwn,aquigley}@st-andrews.ac.uk

ABSTRACT

In this paper we present a new bimanual markerless gesture interface for 3D full-body motion tracking sensors, such as the Kinect. Our interface uses a probabilistic algorithm to incrementally predict users' intended one-handed and two-handed gestures while they are still being articulated. It supports scale and translation invariant recognition of arbitrarily defined gesture templates in real-time. The interface supports two ways of gesturing commands in thin air to displays at a distance. First, users can use one-handed and two-handed gestures to directly issue commands. Second, users can use their non-dominant hand to modulate single-hand gestures. Our evaluation shows that the system recognizes one-handed and two-handed gestures with an accuracy of 92.7%–96.2%.

Author Keywords

Gesture recognition, motion tracking, wall-sized displays

ACM Classification Keywords

I.5.5 Pattern Recognition: Implementation—Interactive systems

General Terms

Experimentation, Human Factors

INTRODUCTION

3D full-body motion tracking sensors enable users to interact with TV sets and wall-sized displays using their own body. However, an open research question is how to efficiently interact with displays at a distance using such sensors. In this work we use the Microsoft Kinect 3D full-body motion tracking sensor to design a bimanual continuous gesture interface that recognizes one-handed and two-handed gestures while they are being articulated by the user. The Kinect is a markerless sensor system that tracks the user's body as a skeleton structure with 20 joints. We modify and extend a recently published template-based continuous 2D gesture recognition algorithm [3] so that it can process 3D output from a Kinect sensor. In doing so we are the first to present a general bimanual gesture recognizer for the Kinect sensor that can continuously recognize arbitrarily defined gesture templates. Prior work on the Kinect have focused on pose estimation [9] and the latest Kinect Beta SDK (1.0.12) does currently not support gestures.

Gestures are natural components in human-human interaction and human neuromuscular control is well-evolved to simultaneously facilitate fast learning and accurate recall of gestures [7]. In the human-computer interaction (HCI) field, a variety of 2D gesture recognition algorithms have been developed for touchscreens and tablets. These either use a statistical model (e.g. [8]), or various forms of template matching (e.g. [1, 3, 10]). Outside the HCI field, gesture recognition typically refers to 3D gesture recognition [4]. Such gestures may be detected using a variety of sensors, such as cameras and three-axis accelerometers. Common recognition techniques include conditional density propagation, hidden Markov models, and dynamic time warping [4].

In this paper we first introduce the concept of an input zone as a gesture delimitation device for 3D full-body motion tracking sensors. We provide two reliable methods for determining whether the user's hands are inside or outside this zone. Thereafter we describe how we adapted a continuous recognition algorithm [3] for the Kinect and extended it so that it can recognize two-handed gestures. We show that our system recognizes one-handed and two-handed gestures with an accuracy of 92.7%–96.2% on held-out test data. Then we present a new interface for simultaneous bimanual gesturing and control that enables users to gesture with one hand and make selections among the predicted gesture templates with the second hand. Finally, we motivate our system by proposing a range of applications. For example, we designed a text entry method that enables users to write in thin air.

BIMANUAL CONTINUOUS GESTURE INTERACTION

We continuously track both hands of the user via the skeleton structure we obtain from the Kinect. For each hand and sample point we receive a tuple (x, y, z, t), in which x, y and z are the 3D coordinate estimates of the hand (in meters), and t is a timestamp. We smooth this signal using a moving average with an optimal window size learned from training data.

For our gesture recognition interface to work we need to be able to reliably determine the beginning and the end of the gesture articulation by the user. To perform this delimitation we use a zoning technique. When the user is interacting with the Kinect we continuously measure the distance between the user's hand and the Kinect. When this distance is below a set threshold the hand is defined to be within what we call the *input zone*. A similar approach has previously been used to delineate 3D selections [6]. We experimented with various thresholds. One solution is to use the absolute distance between the user's hand and the Kinect. We implemented this solution and used a threshold of 1.5 meters in front of the Kinect. While this solution proved to be robust, it may in some situations be advantageous to have a flexible input zone that is invariant of the distance between the user's body and the Kinect. We therefore also developed a method for determining whether the user's hand is within the input zone based on a relative measure. It uses a binary classifier that is defined as the following decision rule:

$$z(v_b, v_h, d_h) = \begin{cases} 1, & \text{if } v_b < \gamma_{vb} \wedge v_h < \gamma_{vh} \wedge d_h > \gamma_{dh} \\ 0, & \text{otherwise} \end{cases},$$

in which v_b is the speed of the user's body, v_h is the speed of the user's hand, d_h is the distance between the user's hand and the user's body, and γ_{vb}, γ_{vh} and γ_{dh} are empirically determined parameters. When $z = 1$ the user's hand is within the input zone. We set the thresholds for γ_{vb}, γ_{vh} and γ_{dh} by estimating them from data gathered from four volunteers. The participants held a wireless mouse in their right hand. They were explained the concept of an input zone and then asked to use a forward-motion to move their hand into the input zone, then move the hand laterally, and thereafter pull their hand out of the input zone. We instructed participants to press and hold down the left mouse button when they felt that their hand was within the input zone and to release the left mouse button when they felt they were outside of the zone. Based on this data we estimated the parameter values using cross-validation. We evaluated the binary classifier by investigating how accurately it could classify a sample point as being inside or outside the input zone using three tolerance thresholds: 5, 10 or 15 sample points to the left or to the right of the boundary. Cross-validation showed that the accuracy was 88.0%, 91.2% and 93.4% respectively.

There is some noise in the signal when users are entering and exiting the input zone. We therefore discard a portion of the beginning and end of the trace, a process known as de-hooking in the handwriting recognition community. The de-hooking parameters are also learned from training data.

While the hand is within the input zone the system concatenates the projected (x, y) positions of the hand into a progressively increasing input vector:

$$\mathbf{I}_i = [(x_1, y_1), (x_2, y_2), \ldots, (x_i, y_i)].$$

When a new sampling point is received the system computes a posterior probability for gesture template ω_k as:

$$P(\omega_k|\mathbf{I}_i) = \frac{P(\omega_k)P(\mathbf{I}_i|\omega_k)}{\sum_n P(\omega_n)P(\mathbf{I}_i|\omega_n)},$$

where $P(\omega_k)$ is the prior probability and $P(\mathbf{I}_i|\omega_k)$ is the likelihood. If there are reasons to believe certain gestures are more likely than others (for example, due to context), the prior can reflect this. However, in the experiments reported in this paper the prior is uniform. The likelihood is found by searching for the sub-segment of the template ω_j that maximizes the likelihood of a distance function in combination with an end-point bias [3]. The continuous recognition algorithm uses two features for the distance function: the mean Euclidean distance and the mean turning angle between two point vectors. The relative weighting between these two features is controlled via a mixture weight parameter. For details we refer the reader to the complete description of the continuous gesture recognition algorithm [3].

In this paper we extend the continuous gesture recognition algorithm so that it can also recognize two-handed gestures. In this case we have two input vectors $\mathbf{I}_i^{(l)}$ and $\mathbf{I}_j^{(r)}$ for the left- and right-hand gesture articulations respectively and we are interested in the posterior probability for a bimanual gesture $\omega_k^{(lr)}$. Assuming conditional independence under a joint model this posterior probability is:

$$P^{(lr)}\left(\omega_k^{(lr)}|\mathbf{I}_i^{(l)}, \mathbf{I}_j^{(r)}\right) = \frac{P\left(\omega_k^{(lr)}\right)P\left(\mathbf{I}_i^{(l)}|\omega_k^{(l)}\right)P\left(\mathbf{I}_j^{(r)}|\omega_k^{(r)}\right)}{\sum_n P\left(\omega_n^{(lr)}\right)P\left(\mathbf{I}_i^{(l)}|\omega_n^{(l)}\right)P\left(\mathbf{I}_j^{(r)}|\omega_n^{(r)}\right)},$$

in which $P\left(\omega_k^{(lr)}\right)$ is the prior for the bimanual gesture, and $P\left(\mathbf{I}_i^{(l)}|\omega_k^{(l)}\right)$ and $P\left(\mathbf{I}_j^{(r)}|\omega_k^{(r)}\right)$ are the likelihoods for the left- and right-hand parts of the bimanual gesture template respectively.

We also created a bimanual interface that enables users to simultaneously using the dominant hand to gesture and the non-dominant hand to modulate the recognition results. Figure 1 shows a user gesturing using this interface. In the figure the user is writing text in thin air by gesturing Graffiti letters (cf. Figure 2). While the user is gesturing the system continuously updates the four most likely predicted gesture templates to the left in the display. By moving the non-dominant hand up or down the user can select among these alternatives. We found that this style of interaction is particularly effective if a user requires very high recognition accuracy.

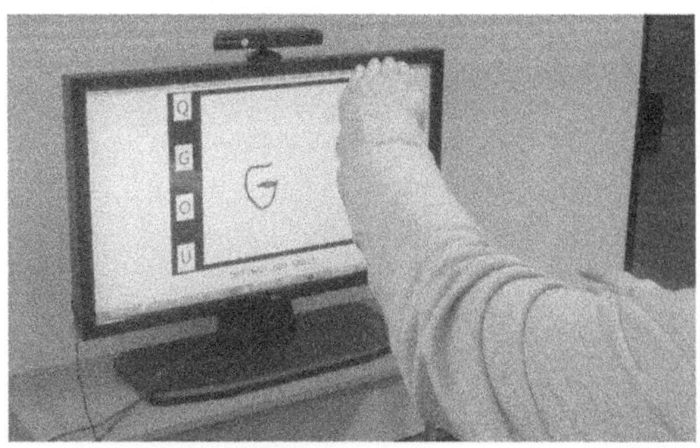

Figure 1. A user is writing in thin air by gesturing Graffiti letters and selecting among alternative predicted letters to the left of the display.

EVALUATION

We tested recognition accuracy on three gesture sets: the \$1 gesture set [10], the Graffiti gesture set, and a bimanual gesture set which we created ourselves. The \$1 gesture set and the Graffiti gesture set have been previously used in recognition experiments (e.g. [3, 10]). The gesture sets are illustrated in Figure 2.

Figure 2. The gesture sets used in the evaluation. The beginning of a gesture is indicated by a solid dot. Top: the set of one-handed gestures from the $1 gesture set [10]. Middle: the set of one-handed gestures from the Graffiti alphabet. Bottom: the set of two-handed gestures we created ourselves.

We used a Microsoft XBox 360 Kinect sensor connected to a Windows 7 laptop. Each session was divided into a practice and a testing part. In the practice part we explained to the participants the concept of the input zone and demonstrated how to articulate gestures with the Kinect. In the testing part participants were shown a series of gestures on the screen and asked to reproduce them as quickly and as accurately as possible. To ensure reproducibility we used an absolute distance of 1.5 meters between the participant's hand and the Kinect to decide whether the participant's hand was inside or outside the input zone.

We recruited 18 volunteers from our university campus. Their ages ranged between 18–35. None of the participants had any prior experience of using a Kinect sensor. The 18 participants were randomly split into two groups with nine participants each to avoid effects due to fatigue and motor learning confounding the results. Participants in the first group were asked to to articulate the gestures in the Graffiti and the bimanual gesture sets. Each Graffiti gesture was performed once and each gesture in the bimanual gesture set was performed five times. In total, each participant in this group performed 27 + 16 $\times$ 5 = 107 gestures. Participants in the second group were asked to to articulate the gestures in the $1 set. Each gesture in the gesture set was performed five times. In total, each participant in this group performed 16 $\times$ 5 = 80 gestures. This data collection task lasted approximately 20–30 minutes for each participant.

Recognizer (E,T,E+T) and input style	Accuracy	Δ
One-handed (E)	90.3%	·
One-handed (T)	92.3%	2.0%
One-handed (E+T)	92.7%	0.4%
Two-handed (E)	86.2%	·
Two-handed (T)	96.2%	10.0%
Two-handed (E+T)	96.2%	0%

Table 1. Accuracy and absolute gains in accuracy for complete one-handed and two-handed 2D gestures. One-handed gesture recognition was tested with the $1 [10] and the Graffiti gesture sets. Two-handed gesture recognition was tested with a gesture set we designed ourselves. E: Euclidean distance only, T: turning angle only, E+T: combination.

In total we collected 1683 one-handed and two-handed gestures. We split the data into a training and test set by randomly designating the gestures collected from four participants in each group (eight participants in total) as the training set and the rest of the gestures as the test set. The held-out test set was only used for final evaluations. Using the training set we searched for the optimal mixture weight for the continuous gesture recognition algorithm and the two additional parameters we have introduced in this paper: the window size of the moving average used for smoothing, and the proportion of the input gesture which is de-hooked. We used the parameter configuration that maximized accuracy on the training set and evaluated the algorithms on the held-out test set.

Table 1 summarizes the recognition results for complete gestures. The system recognized complete one-handed gestures with an accuracy of 92.7%. This is similar to prior work [3] on recognition of pen stroke gestures drawn on a Tablet PC, which found that continuous recognition of complete gestures resulted in 94.5% accuracy. Also consistent with prior work [3], the turning angle feature resulted in higher accuracy than Euclidean distance. Combining both features using an optimal mixture weight resulted in a negligible gain in accuracy.

The system recognized the two-handed gestures with an accuracy of 96.2%, which is slightly higher than the accuracy obtained for one-handed gestures. Again, the turning angle feature resulted in higher accuracy than Euclidean distance. Combining both features made no difference. Bimanual gesture recognition was easier, which is unsurprising since under an appropriate probabilistic model two simultaneous input gestures provide additional information to the recognizer.

Figure 3 plots average accuracy as a function of the proportion of a complete one-handed or two-handed gesture. The solid lines in the figure show the performance of the continuous gesture recognition algorithm. The dashed lines show the performance of a baseline algorithm that only recognizes complete gesture templates. The baseline algorithm uses optimal parameter values learned from the training set. Cross marks denote the accuracy for top-1 matches while squares denote the accuracy for top-3 matches.

As is evident in the figure, the continuous recognizer is much better at predicting the participants' intended gestures at all stages of the articulation process. As a reference point, the continuous gesture recognition algorithm was able to achieve an accuracy of 46.0% for one-handed and 55.0% for two-handed gestures when participants had gestured only 20% of the complete gesture (top-1 matches). This was an absolute gain in accuracy of 39.3% and 38.4% compared to the baseline for one-handed and two-handed gestures respectively.

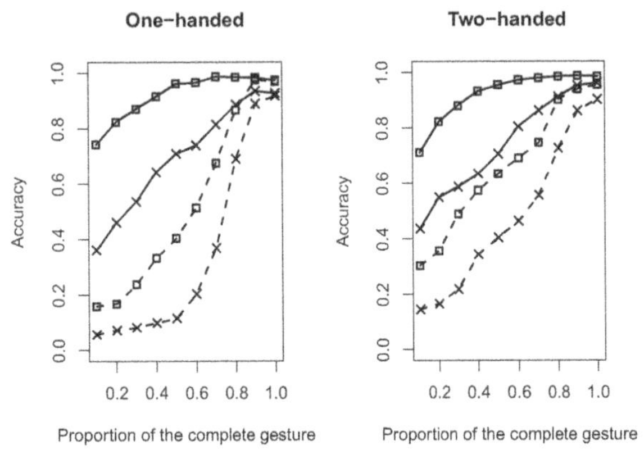

Figure 3. Accuracy for one-handed and two-handed gestures as a function of the proportion of the complete gesture for the continuous gesture recognizer (solid lines) and a baseline recognizer (dashed lines). Cross marks denote the accuracy for top-1 matches while squares denote the accuracy for top-3 matches.

DISCUSSION

As in previous work (e.g. [1, 3, 10]), we only tested a few gesture sets. Therefore, our results should be interpreted with some care. Unfortunately there is no open collection of gesture sets available for standardized comparisons.

We chose to delimit gestures via an input zone. Participants felt this was natural and they quickly adapted to it. With 92.7–96.2% accuracy for single-hand and two-handed gestures our system is directly usable as a command interface for interactions with displays at a distance, such as when users are playing video games or interacting with wall-sized displays.

A potential application of our system would be as an input technique in hospital operating rooms (ORs). ORs require hospital workers to maintain the boundary between sterile and non-sterile environments [2]. Our system enables hospital workers to access and edit information while ensuring this boundary is kept at all times. Also, unlike most gesture recognition systems, our system performs recognition continuously while the user is gesturing. This enables hospital workers to verify that the gesture will be correctly recognized as the intended command before completing it. This minimizes the risk of recognition errors as hospital workers can choose to abort the gesture if it is not properly recognized and thus prevent an unintended command from being committed.

Another application of our system is as a text entry method for writing in thin air. The 27 gestures in the Graffiti alphabet we tested suffice to perform rudimentary text entry tasks, such as writing a short message or filling out a medical form. Figure 1 shows a user writing in thin air using Graffiti. Our gesture interface makes it possible to implement freehand Graffiti input techniques for thin air that have previously only been explored via a specialized glove-based system [5].

CONCLUSIONS

We have presented a bimanual gesture recognition system for 3D full-body motion tracking sensors, such as the Kinect. Our system continuously recognizes arbitrarily defined gesture templates in real-time on a standard laptop. Our evaluation showed that the system recognizes one-handed and two-handed gestures with 92.7–96.2% accuracy.

To enable comparisons against future gesture recognition algorithms we have shared our collected data. Further, to help designers, developers and researchers we have also released the C# source code for our recognition algorithms under an open source license. Data and code can be downloaded here: `http://pokristensson.com/kinect.html`.

ACKNOWLEDGEMENTS

This work was supported by the Engineering and Physical Sciences Research Council (grant number EP/H027408/1) and the Scottish Informatics and Computer Science Alliance.

REFERENCES

1. Appert, C., and Bau, O. Scale detection for a priori gesture recognition. In *Proc. CHI 2010*, ACM Press (2010), 879–882.
2. Johnson, R., O'Hara, K., Sellen, A., Cousins, C., and Criminisi, A. Exploring the potential for touchless interaction in image-guided interventional radiology. In *Proc. CHI 2011*, ACM Press (2011), 3323–3332.
3. Kristensson, P. O., and Denby, L. C. Continuous recognition and visualization of pen strokes and touch-screen gestures. In *Proc. SBIM 2011*, ACM Press (2011), 95–102.
4. Mitra, S., and Acharya, T. Gesture recognition: a survey. *IEEE Transactions on Systems, Man, and Cybernetics, Part C: Applications and Reviews 37* (2007), 311–324.
5. Ni, T., Bowman, D., and North, C. AirStroke: bringing unistroke text entry to freehand gesture interfaces. In *Proc. CHI 2011*, ACM Press (2011), 2473–2476.
6. Poupyrev, I., Billinghurst, M., Weghorst, S., and Ichikawa, T. The Go-Go interaction technique: non-linear mapping for direct manipulation in VR. In *Proc. UIST 1996*, ACM Press (1996), 79–80.
7. Rosenbaum, D. A. *Human Motor Control*. Academic Press, San Diego, CA, USA, 1991.
8. Rubine, D. Specifying gestures by example. In *Proc. SIGGRAPH 1991*, ACM Press (1991), 329–337.
9. Shotton, J., Fitzgibbon, A., Cook, M., Sharp, T., Finocchio, M., Moore, R., Kipman, A., and Blake, A. Real-time human pose recognition in parts from single depth images. In *Proc. CVPR 2011*, IEEE Press (2011), 1297–1304.
10. Wobbrock, J. O., Wilson, A. D., and Li, Y. Gestures without libraries, toolkits or training: a $1 recognizer for user interface prototypes. In *Proc. UIST 2007*, ACM Press (2007), 159–168.

Studying User-defined iPad Gestures for Interaction in Multi-display Environment

Ekaterina Kurdyukova, Matthias Redlin, Elisabeth André
University of Augsburg
Universitaetsstrasse 6a, 56159 Augsburg, Germany
{kurdyukova, redlin, andre} @ informatik.uni-augsburg.de

ABSTRACT
The paper investigates the iPad gestures that users naturally perform for data transfer. We examine the transfer between two iPads, iPad and a tabletop, and iPad and a public display. Three gesture modalities are investigated: multi-touch gestures, performed using the iPad display, spatial gestures, performed by manipulating iPad in 3D space, and direct contact gestures, involving the physical contact of iPad and another device. We report on the user choices of modalities and gesture types, and derive critical aspects for the design of iPad gestures.

Author Keywords
User-defined gestures, tablet PC, multi-display interaction

ACM Classification Keywords
H.5.2. Information interfaces and presentation: User Interfaces – *Interaction styles, evaluation/methodology, user-centred design.*

General Terms
Design, Experimentation, Human Factors

MOTIVATION
As predicted by Mark Weiser back in 1991 [1], tablet-sized devices, such as iPad, gain an increasing importance in the modern world. Among their rich interaction possibilities, tablet devices support the convenient gestural interaction. Gestural interaction is known to be intuitive, quick, comfortable [2], as well as fun and engaging [3]. However, a great challenge remains the design of the gestures that replicate the way people interact naturally.

The goal of this work is to find the gestures that users naturally perform with iPad[1] for data transfer. By means of an experiment we study the gestures in three settings: iPad and iPad, iPad and a tabletop, iPad and a public display. We analyze the rationales behind the user choice of the gestures, and derive the guidelines for the gesture design.

IUI'12, February 14–17, 2012, Lisbon, Portugal.

STUDIES ON USER-DEFINED GESTURES
User-defined gestures have been widely studied in the domains of full body interaction [4], tabletop interaction [5, 6, 7], interaction on vertical surfaces [8, 9], as well as mobile interaction [10].

The research on natural gestures has also been done in the domains of multi-device [11, 12] and multi-display [13, 14] environments. For example, Kray et al. [2] studied user-defined mobile gestures that people perform for connection tasks between mobile devices, public displays, and tabletops.

However, not much work has been done so far to study the gestures people naturally perform with tablet-sized devices. Rekimoto [14] presented pen-based technique for the data transfer between tablet-sized devices. To enable the transfer, the technique exploits the touch screen of the tablet device. However, apart from the touch screen, a modern tablet device possesses more interaction possibilities enabled e.g. by integrated accelerometers or cameras. Therefore, there is a need for further research on tablet gestures, to understand which gestures are appreciated and found appropriate by the users.

MODALITIES OF iPAD GESTURES
Thinking of possible gestures that can be performed on the touch surfaces or with mobile devices, we can distinguish three gesture types for iPad:

- *Multi-touch gestures* are performed on the iPad screen.
- *Spatial gestures* are performed by rotating, tilting, or panning the iPad body.
- *Direct contact gestures* imply physical contact between the iPad body and the body of another device. The direct contact gestures can be also performed from a distance, imitating the real physical contact. For instance, the iPad display can reproduce the entire content of the remote display, similarly to the technique by Boring et al. [15].

[1] Here and further on we reference only to iPad. However, the discussion can be applied to any tablet PC device possessing similar physical properties and sensory equipment as iPad.

STUDYING iPAD GESTURES

In order to understand which gestures and which modalities are intuitively chosen by the users when performing the transfer tasks on multiple displays, we arranged an experiment.

The experiment involved two transfer tasks, sending and receiving, performed in three settings: *iPad-iPad, iPad-Tabletop, iPad-Public Display*. The users had to perform the transfer of a large and small object in every setting. The order of the settings was counterbalanced.

The experiment was structured into two parts. *Part 1* investigated the gestures that people perform spontaneously for the transfer in either setting. Here, the participants were free to choose any modality. However, since such spontaneous gestures may be strongly motivated by the experiences with other devices, they might not reflect the real user preferences. *Part 2* aimed to correct this effect by giving the participants a chance to explore all possible modalities. Here the participants were asked to complete the tasks in either modality, in either setting, and then to express their preferences.

The experiment was conducted as a within-group test, individually with every participant. After a short introduction, the moderator explained the basic interaction techniques on iPad, avoiding any demonstrations. Then the participants were asked to complete Part1, Part2, give their gesture preference, and explain the choice.

Important to mention, in *Part 1* two distances were examined in *iPad-Public Display* setting: closer and farther from the display. Thus, we could imitate the real life settings: often it is not possible to reach the display.

All in all, 20 persons took part in the test, 14 males and 6 females, aged between 21 and 55 (average 28,8), occupied as a carpenter, a sports teacher, law students, and IT researchers. Ten participants had experiences in the gesture-based entertainment consoles, 13 possess touch-enabled mobile devices, six participants had experiences with the tablet devices; among them only two possess an iPad; ten participants have never worked with a tabletop.

RESULTS: USER-DEFINED GESTURES

Among the gestures performed in *Part 1*, 58% included multi-touch gestures, 17% spatial gestures, and 25% direct contact gestures.

iPad-iPad Setting

Multi-touch gestures for sending of the large and the small objects were performed by 76% of the participants by *dragging the object with the finger from the participant's own iPad in the direction of the other iPad* (see Fig.1, left). Receiving with multi-touch was performed by 50% of the persons, similarly: by *dragging the object with the finger, either directly from the other iPad or only using the surface of the own iPad*. The participants usually placed their iPad in the same plane with the source iPad, organizing a common surface for dragging.

Spatial gestures for sending were performed by 20% of the participants by *pouring out of the object from the iPad* so that the object "slides" to the other iPad (see Fig. 2, left). For receiving, however, spatial gestures were generally found inappropriate. Just two participants performed them by *pulling the iPad from the source iPad in the direction of their body.*

Direct contact gestures for sending were performed by 4% of the participants by *placing or "posting" the object on the other iPad by holding the own iPad over the receiving iPad.* For receiving about 50% of the participants *placed the iPad over the other iPad to copy the object or attract it by imagined gravity* (see Fig. 3, left).

Figure 1. Sending the object with multi-touch gestures

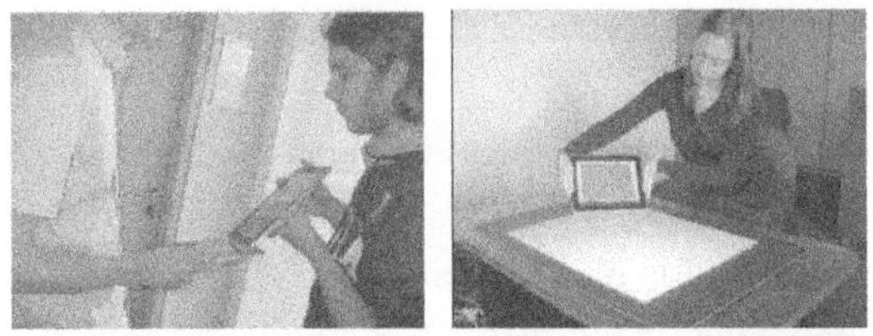

Figure 2. Sending the object with spatial gestures

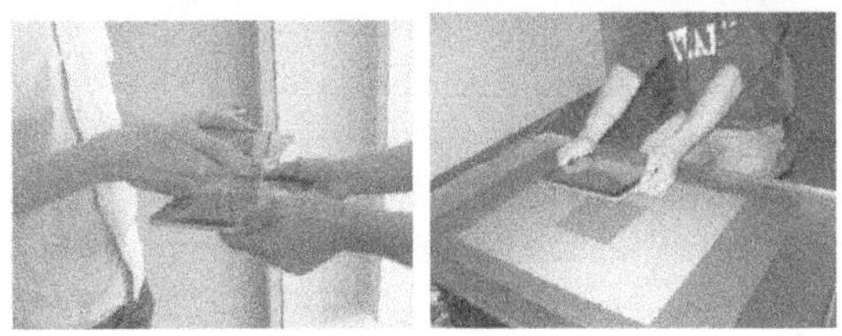

Figure 3. Receiving the object with direct contact

Figure 4. Receiving the object with multi-touch and direct contact gestures

iPad-Tabletop Setting

For sending the majority of the participants (80%) performed multi-touch gesture: *dragging the object with finger from iPad in the direction of the table* (see Fig. 1, right). Just few participants touched the table. For receiving the majority (70%) was *dragging the object from the table to iPad* (see Fig. 4, left). Most of participants touched both the table and iPad.

Spatial gestures for sending were performed by 12% of the participants. They mostly included *pouring the object out from iPad to the table* (see Fig. 2, right). Some participants shook the device additionally, to "make sure the object slides down". For receiving almost no one has performed spatial gestures, commenting that it is hard to find a good match.

Direct contact gestures for sending were performed by 8% of the participants, by *"posting" the object to the table almost placing the device physically on the surface.* For receiving, about 30% of the participants performed *holding the iPad over the table to "capture"* the small object (see Fig. 3, right) or *placing the iPad at the table to "imprint"* the large object. Seven participants placed iPad on the table before the interaction.

In both iPad-iPad and iPad-Tabletop settings, for the transfer of the large objects the participants often used several fingers. The tasks involving the small object were performed mostly with one finger. Moreover, the large objects were frequently scaled down before the transfer.

iPad – Public Display Setting

For sending the majority of the participants (75%) chose multi-touch modality by *dragging the object with the finger from iPad in the direction of the display.* For receiving, however, multi-touch gestures were found rather inappropriate. Just few participants performed *pulling the corner of iPad by multiple dragging motions*, reminding scratching movements, commenting however that the gesture is not really suitable for the transfer.

Spatial gestures for sending were performed by 15% of the participants. The gestures included *intensive jerky "throwing" of the object in the horizontal plane* or *"throwing the object" by tilting iPad from the body to the horizontal position, orthogonal to the display.* For receiving, 20% of the participants performed the gesture: *„scooping up" the object from the large display.*

Direct contact gestures for sending were performed by 10% of the persons by *"posting" or „pinning up" the object on the large display.* For receiving, direct contact gestures were performed by the majority (75%). To receive a small object the participants were *„picking up" or "capturing" the small object from the display* (see Fig. 4, right); to receive a large object they *touched an imagined marker at the large display to copy the content.*

Difference distances influenced only the sending gestures. The further the participant stayed from the display, the less multi-touch and the more spatial gestures were performed. The phenomenon can be explained by the perceived weight of the transferred object. Throwing with the finger gives the object a minor acceleration. Thus, it can "fly" only over a short distance. Throwing using the whole iPad body can produce a stronger acceleration. Therefore, the object can securely "fly" over a longer distance and not to "get lost" on the way.

Part 2 gave the inexperienced participants the chance to try all possible gesture modalities, and perhaps correct their preferences. Indeed, in *Part 2* the participants expressed more preferences for spatial and direct contact gestures, in *iPad-iPad* and *iPad-Tabletop* settings. These modalities were perceived more creative and more enjoyable than multi-touch gestures. Especially, the spatial gestures were referred as "more funny to perform". However, in *iPad-iPad* setting, even well-matching spatial gestures were often perceived as unreliable. In *iPad-Tabletop* setting, this disadvantage was diminished due to the presence of the table. Placing iPad on a solid surface, people felt they can better control the transfer.

Direct contact modality was less popular in *iPad-Tabletop* setting compared to *Part1*. The physical dimensions of iPad and the table were reported to be too different to find a well-matching metaphor for a direct transfer (in other words to "pack" the object directly to iPad).

To summarize, the participants favoured the multi-touch modality almost in all the settings. The exception were only the receiving gestures in *iPad-Public Display* setting which was most frequently performed with direct contact.

DESIGNING iPAD GESTURES

Below we emphasize the aspects important to consider when designing iPad gestures.

Physical Shape

The flat page-like shape of iPad device affects its physical disposition to the other devices, its orientation, and the set of possible spatial gestures.

The physical touch of other devices occurred mostly in *iPad-iPad* setting and especially in *iPad-Tabletop* setting. The flat shape of the iPad body invites to place it on a flat horizontal surface.

The flat shape also restricts the spatial gestures that can be performed with iPad. Thus, the usage of spatial rotations is rather provoked by the distance to the target device. The further the device, the more spatial gestures are performed. Therefore, spatial gestures were popular in *iPad-iPad* and *iPad-Public Display* settings.

Physical shape also influences the iPad orientation: during the transfer iPad is often oriented in the same plane with the display. For example, it is placed boarder to boarder to the other iPad or a tabletop arranging a continuous surface.

Thinking of Flat Metaphors

Both experienced and inexperienced users rely on real-life metaphors when thinking of well-matching gestures. The most common iPad metaphor refers to a tray (or a salver). The object on the iPad screen is associated with a flat physical object lying on the tray. The iPad is usually held with two hands; its display is associated with the top side of the tray. Therefore, iPad is almost never turned around. If iPad is manipulated in 3D space, the final position lies always in the horizontal plane, oriented by the "top of the tray". Grabbing the objects from the other surfaces is performed similarly to the collection of pieces to the tray.

The object on the tray is perceived as a physical one, having its weight and size. Therefore, the larger the object, the more effort the user needs to move it; the more power needs to be applied to throw the object away from the tray. The gestures for the larger objects require stronger acceleration and involve more fingers.

The metaphor of a flat tray is often transformed into the plate metaphor. The participants often performed pouring out gesture reminding pouring out of a liquid from a plate. Here again the size of the object was mapped onto its weight. The plates with the "heavier" objects were additionally shaken, to ensure the object slides down from the plate.

The metaphor of a spade or a shovel was often applied to receiving tasks. The participants tried to scoop up the object from the source display using iPad as a shovel. Interestingly, the metaphor was applied to both horizontal and vertical surfaces.

Privacy Matters

An important aspect in the design of iPad gestures concerns the private space. The gestures involving the touch of another private device (iPad) are seen as an intrusion into the person's private space. This concerns both the finger interaction and the direct contact of the device body. Even the contactless interaction which presumes a close proximity of two devices (see e.g. Fig. 1, left) was seen slightly privacy critical.

Another concern relates to the direct contact gestures as the demonstration of the interaction on public. Direct contact was criticized by potentially drawing public attention and by the impossibility to interact unnoticed from a distance.

CONCLUSION

The paper presented a study on iPad gestures that are naturally chosen for the data transfer in multi-display settings. The results show that the choice of the gestures is strongly influenced by the physical shape of iPad, the associated metaphors, and the privacy concerns of the users.

ACKNOWLEDGMENTS

This research is partly sponsored by OC-Trust project (FOR 1085) of the German research foundation (DFG).

REFERENCES

1. Mark Weiser. The computer for the 21st century. Scientific American Special Issue on Communications, Computers, and Networks, September, 1991.
2. Kray, C., Nesbitt, D., Dawson, J., and Rohs, M. User-defined gestures for connecting mobile phones, public displays, and tabletops. In Proc. MobileHCI 2010. ACM Press (2011), 239-248.
3. Bianchi-Berthouze, N., Kim, W. W., and Patel, D. Does Body Movement Engage You More in Digital Game Play? and Why? In Proc. ACII 2007, Springer-Verlag (2007), 102-113.
4. Shotton, J., Fizgibbon, A., Cook, M., Sharp, T., Finocchio, M., Moore, R., Kipman, A., and Blake, A. Real-time human pose recognition in parts from single depth images. In *IEEE Computer Vision and Pattern Recognition (CVPR) 2011*, IEEE.
5. Wobbrock, J.O., Morris, M.R., and Wilson, A.D. User-defined gestures for surface computing. In Proc. CHI 2009. ACM Press (2009), 1083-1092.
6. Rekimoto, J. SmartSkin: An Infrastructure for Freehand Manipulation on Interactive Surfaces. In Proc. CHI 2002, ACM Press (2002), 113-120.
7. Wu, M. and Balakrishnan, R. Multi-Finger and Whole Hand Gestural Interaction Techniques for Multi-User Tabletop Displays. In Proc. UIST 2003, ACM Press (2003), 193-202.
8. Baudisch, P., Cutrell, E., Robbins, D., Czerwinski, M., Tandler, P., Bederson, B., and Zierlinger, A. Drag-and-pop and drag-and-pick: Techniques for accessing remote screen content on touch- and pen-operated systems. In Proc. INTERACT 2003, Springer Verlag (2003), 57-64.
9. Bezerianos, A. and Balakrishnan, R. The Vacuum: Facilitating the Manipulation of Distant Objects. In Proc. CHI 2005, ACM Press (2005), 361-370.
10. Ruiz, J., Li, Y., and Lank, E. User-defined motion gestures for mobile interaction. In Proc. CHI 2011, ACM Press (2011), 197-206.
11. Lee, H., Jeong, H., Lee, J., Yeom, K., and Park, J. Gesture-Based Interface for Connection and Control of Multi-device in a Tabletop Display Environment, In *Proc. HCI 2009*, Springer Verlag (2009), 216-225.
12. Yatani, K., Tamura, K., Hiroki, K., Sugimoto, M., and Hashizume, H. Toss-it: intuitive information transfer techniques for mobile devices. In Proc. CHI 2005 Extended Abstracts. ACM Press (2005), 1881-1884.
13. Lee, J., Lee, J., Kim, H., and Kim, J. Gesture-Based Interactions on Multiple Large Displays with a Tabletop Interface, In Proc. UAHCI 2007, Springer Verlag (2007), 936-942.
14. Rekimoto, J. Pick-and-Drop: A Direct Manipulation Technique for Multiple Computer Environments, In Proc. UIST 1997, ACM Press (1997), 31-39.
15. Boring, S., Baur, D., Butz, A., Gustafson, S., and Baudisch, P. Touch projector: mobile interaction through video. In Proc. CHI 2010. ACM Press (2010), 2287-2296.

Using Intelligent Natural User Interfaces to Support Sales Conversations

Sven Gehring, Markus Löchtefeld, Florian Daiber, Matthias Böhmer, Antonio Krüger
Deutsches Forschungszentrum für Künstliche Intelligenz
Saarland University, Campus D3 2, Saarbrücken, Germany
{sven.gehring, markus.loechtefeld, florian.daiber, matthias.boehmer, krueger}@dfki.de

ABSTRACT

During sales conversations, gestures and mimics are of high importance to communicate information about a product. One prominent example for such sales gestures is the meat and cheese counter, which is one of the remaining spots in supermarkets where sales persons interact with customers. Interactions at such counters in supermarkets normally follow a simple protocol. The customer points at an item of choice. The employee takes out the item and, in most of the cases the product needs to be cut to fit the amount the customer wants to buy. Often it is ambiguous about what specific product the customer and the employees are talking about. Up to now, there are just a few efforts in HCI research to enrich communication at the point of sale. In this paper we report and analyze one scenario in which an intelligent natural user interface can support communication between customer and employee in a sales conversation. Furthermore, we report on our prototype that is able to track pointing gestures by using a depth camera and to display information about items pointed at.

Author Keywords
Gestural Interaction, Sales Conversation, Pointing.

ACM Classification Keywords
H.5.2 [Information Interfaces And Presentation]: User Interfaces - Input devices and strategies.

General Terms
Human Factors; Design

INTRODUCTION

The most crucial factor for today's retailers is to deliver true customer satisfaction and achieve superior competitive advantages despite the small margins that they have to face. For most customers the experience of shopping has become more important and the demand for exact product information has drastically increased e.g. due to food scandals. Today's customers tend to be enlightened customers. In addition, in some cases the intention for shopping is simply different: People not only go shopping when they need something; from time to time they consider shopping as a popular leisure time activity (e.g., shopping with the whole family on weekends). During sales conversations, gestures and mimics are of high importance to communicate information about a product. This especially becomes clear when considering fresh food counters. These counters are served by employees and can contain up to 500 different products. Customers often have an increased trust towards the employees compared to technology. Therefore it is of high importance to deliver exact and interesting information at such counters. The sales process at such a counter is generally a repetitive negotiation on product and amount that is supported by pointing gestures of employee and customer. Due to the physical nature of the counter that serves as a spatial separation between the customer and the products, the pointing gestures are often ambiguous. From the employee's perspective, it often remains unclear which product the customer is pointing at. The high density of items in the counter even intensifies the ambiguity. Hence, sales conversations need several iterations of pointing and confirming to disambiguate the meant product. This leads to longer service times and to a frustration of the customer. In this paper, we present an intelligent natural user interface to support the negotiation on a product during a sales conversation at a fresh food counter. A depth camera above the counter infers which products the customers are pointing at. The product is displayed to the employee on the display of the digital scale that is usually only used to weigh out and

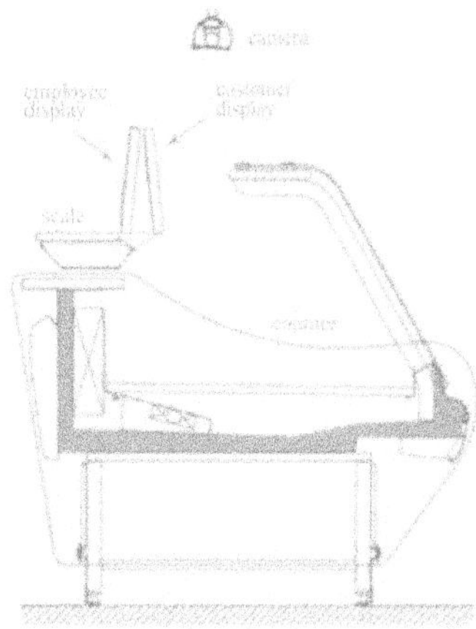

Figure 1: The application setup with the counter, a scale with two displays and a depth camera above the counter.

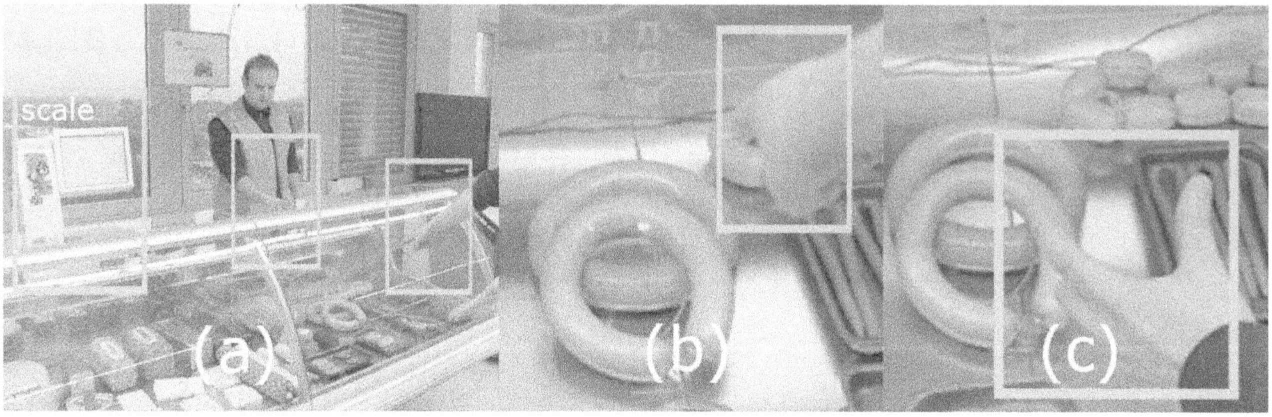

Figure 2: Pointing gestures during a sales conversation at a meat and cheese counter. The counter and the scale of our prototype implementation can be seen in (a). In (b) and (c), a customer is performing gestures above a product in the counter. In (c) a customer indicates the desired size of a certain product is shown.

label the products. Furthermore, additional information (e.g., about the origin of the product) can easily be given to even untrained employees to optimize the sales talk.

This paper is structured as follows: First, we report on common interaction problems at fresh food counters. Second, we briefly describe related work in this area. Based on this, we propose an interaction concept. Afterwards, we depict the implementation of our system. The paper concludes with an outlook and ideas for future work and use cases of such systems.

INFORMAL FIELD STUDY

In order to identify the current interaction protocol and communication problems at meat and cheese counters, we observed the meat counter in a supermarket with approximately 12,000 clients per day for one day. We continuously queued at the counter and observed regular customers during sales conversations. We focused on how customers express their desired products and how they negotiate on the desired quantities with the employees. The observers were standing in front of the meat counter and monitoring the sales conversations between customers and employees. They recorded how the customers expressed their preferences and how customers and employees negotiated on product and quantity (e.g. how many iterations the negotiation process takes) as well as how employees gave additional information on the products. During the day, approximately 350 customers visited the counter and bought 3.6 products in average (derived from the sales data of the whole day). From the observations, we obtained the following basic interaction protocol for a sale conversation at a meat and cheese counter:

1) When a customer is at his turn, he normally points at a product in the counter to indicate his preference to the employee behind the counter. 2) The employee points at the desired product and asks the customers if this certain product is the preferred one. Due to the spatial separation between customer, product and employee, this initial step often needs several iterations until customer and employee agree on a product. 3) After customer and employee agreed on the product, the employee normally asks how much the customer wants of the product. 3.1) The customer either tells the employee an amount or 3.2) he often performs a gesture to indicate the amount he wants. This can be seen in Figure 2 (c). This gesture is than mimicked by the employee to confirm the amount of the product. For example the employee points with a knife on the product to indicate how much he will cut off. The customer either agrees or corrects the employee by stating that he wants some more or less of the product. 4) After customer and employee agreed on the amount, the desired amount is cut off, packed and handed to the customer.

In addition to this basic protocol, when the costumer points to the product, we also made a second observation: On the wall behind meat and cheese counters, there are often advertisements for certain products in the counter. Customers not always point at the product in the counter but also on an advertisement asking what the advertised product is or stating that they want to buy the displayed product. To support and simplify the described interactions and to reduce the service times and the iterations we propose an application concept based on the interaction protocol we found.

RELATED WORK

The general concept of this work is inspired by the "Put-that-there" prototype by Bolt in 1980 [1]. Instead of interacting with a computer system in our case the user or customer interacts with the human employee. We track the gestures to support the discussion. More recently, Holzapfel et al. [2] focus on supporting the natural interaction and communication with a human robot using gesture tracking. In addition, they present architecture for the fusion of multimodal input streams for natural interaction. Oviatt et al. [4] provide a good overview on work in this area. In the retail domain, Wasinger et al. [5] describe a user interface that integrates multimodal input on a handheld device with

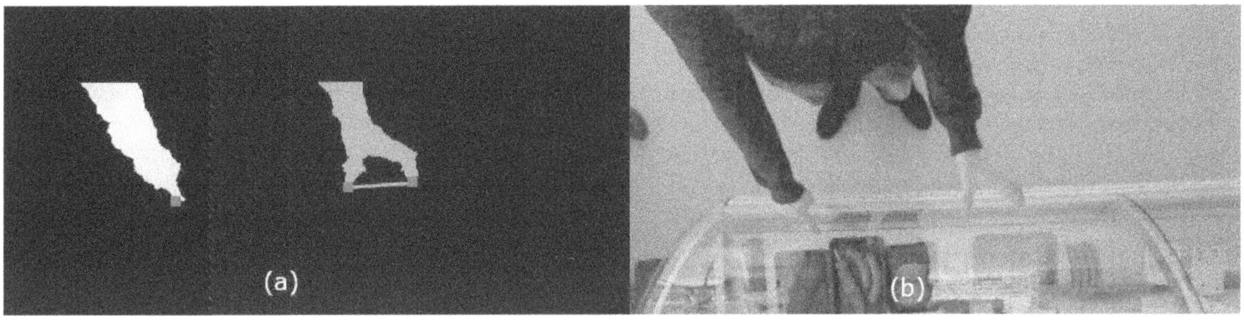

Figure 3: The filtered depth image (a) with detection of *pointing* and *size* gestures and the original image (b).

external gestures performed with products in a shelf. Spassova et al. [6] further evolve this approach. They introduced the concept of product-associated displays as a way of providing visual feedback to users interacting with physical objects in an instrumented environment. Similarly, Newcomb et al. [7] pre-sent design guidelines for a PDA based shopping assistant in a grocery store. They also state that one important aspect that has to be regarded during the design process is that shoppers often use their hands to touch and or point to the products – something we have tried to incorporate into our system and that is also a key aspect in the work of Wasinger [5]. A detailed review on literature on how gestures are used in communications is provided by Kendon [9].

Our work differs from the related work, because to the best of our knowledge, it is the first approach to use gesture recognition to improve sales conversations (i.e. human to human communication) in the retail domain.

APPLICATION SETUP

Our observations revealed that a vast amount of gesturing is already happening during sales conversations and that the protocols are already established. Therefore, instead of introducing new gestures that people would have had to learn and to not interrupt these protocols, we make use of the natural gestures that already exist. So, having the gestures already well established, we try to reduce misunderstanding and misinterpretation of the gestures to ease the sales conversation.

We implemented an application that recognizes the pointing gestures of customers and shopping assistants by using a Microsoft Kinect depth camera. It can support customers during the sales conversation by recognizing the pointing gesture and providing feedback. As can be seen in Figure 1, the scale on the counter consists of a scale unit and two displays. One display of this dual-display scale is faced towards the employee to enable weighting of the product and attaching of price labels. The second display is used to display additional information to the costumer. The layout of the displays is the same in our use-case but they are used to display additional information about the product the customer is pointing at. We provide the customer with information on origin and ingredients of the product, e.g. the fat content of a cheese. On the display facing the employee, even more information such as wine recommendations, recipes or details of the production process can be revealed. This allows the employee to give further advice and negotiation about the product. We believe that this can enhance sales conversations and with that increase customer satisfaction. An example of the setup is shown in Figure 2.

In addition, the system also allows the customer to point at an advertisement on the wall behind the counter as described in the observation section. The employee takes out the product from the presentation area of the counter and places it on a dedicated spot on the counter for cutting and preparing the products. Again the depth camera tracks the gestures of the customer, as described above in the observation section in point 3.2. This amount is again roughly highlighted on scale display on the employee's side.

IMPLEMENTATION

To test the technical feasibility of this application concept we implemented a prototype using a depth camera, a real meat and cheese counter and a dual-display scale. The setup of the scenario can bee seen in Figure 1. As proposed by Wilson [8], we use the depth image that we obtain from the camera with the OpenKinect[1] library to track the users arm. After a background subtraction only the pointing part of the user arm is left, this can be seen in Figure 3. With the depth information of the part of the image displaying the users arm, we determine the height of the pointing. By calculating the difference in the depth image between the beginning of the user's pointing arm and the pointing finger – i.e. so to say the top of the pointing gesture – we calculated the declination of the arm. By calculating the angle between the user's arm and the alignment of the image, we can then estimate the position in the counter the user is pointing at. The system automatically looks up in a database which product belongs to the estimated position. If the user points at an advertisement instead of the counter, the procedure is analogous. This pointing information is transferred via a network connection to the scale. The main restriction of our

[1] http://openkinect.org/wiki/Main_Page

system is the resolution of the Kinect. At a distance of two meters the resolution is approximately 2cm per pixel, this restrains the maximum amount of items in the shelf drastically. Furthermore we have no possibility to determine if the customer thinks that the pointing gesture is a projection of his arm or the ray casted by his hand and his eyes. This can cause severe inaccuracies and confuse the customer.

DISCUSSION

Besides the basic requirements that we extracted from the observations of customers' current interaction at fresh-food counters, we have also presented our system to various users and experts (e.g. on retail trade fairs like the EuroShop 2011[2]) and collected preliminary feedback to inform the further design of the system. We got positive feedback from customers supporting our initial observations. They agreed, that our system supports the problem of disambiguating the meant item and the desired amount. Further, they saw a benefit in the possibility of "browsing through the cheese counter while waiting in a cue" when no sales person is available. However, first tests with customers revealed that people point differently (e.g. with index finger or whole hand). So far, our system is designed for the use with stretched index finger for pointing. One solution for that might be gesture recognition that is based on a user model. A small projected curser as a visual cue might be another solution. Such a curser can easily guide the user while pointing at objects. Further, this will also support the sales person, since he will have the information what the customer is pointing at directly projected on the piece of cheese or meat. Our users also came up with the point, that our system could be useful when they buy food in foreign countries, where they do not speak the language.

We also presented our prototype implementation to experts, i.e. sales personal and retail managers. They liked the idea of unobtrusively supporting the sales talk at cheese and meat counters. Further, they suggested implementing a similar system for self-service frozen food where no sales people are available, e.g. convenience food. However, they also raised two problems that might arise when deploying such a system in the wild. On the one hand, they concerned the density of items, i.e. pieces of different sorts of cheese or meat might be a problem that might lead to inaccuracy. However, we think that we can improve the accuracy of the system by using a more precise depth camera. On the other hand, they mentioned that different pieces of cheese and meat are "traveling" during the day, i.e. when sales persons take out pieces of the counter and put it back, the size of the item changes and it might be placed a little bit apart from its previous position. However, we discussed with these experts and came to the concept of using the technique also as an input device: since the sales people know the type of cheese and meat they can point at items and update the information in the database.

[2] http://www.euroshop.de/

CONCLUSION

In this paper, we described a first concept on how to integrate intelligent natural user interfaces to ease the sales conversations at meat and cheese counters in a retail store by utilizing a depth camera and two displays attached to a scale to provide further information to both customer and employee. Our work makes the following contributions: First we identified the general communication problems that occur in such sales conversations and report on an informal field study we did in a supermarket. Second, we proposed a prototypical system to solve these communication problems with pointing gesture recognition. In addition, we reported on preliminary feedback of customers and sales people to inform a next iteration of the system.

We plan to carry out a user study in a retail store to evaluate our ideas and see how our prototype can improve the sale conversation. We want to compare the time a sales conversation takes with and without the system. Furthermore, we want to measure the effect of the proposed system on the retail sales figures at meat and cheese counters. For the future, we want to further refine the system based on the customers' and experts' feedback and investigate how we can integrate further HCI methods to support sales conversations between customer and shop assistant in retail stores.

REFERENCES

1. Bolt, R. A. Put-that-there: Voice and gesture at the graphics interface. Proc. SIGGRAPH'80, ACM (1980).
2. Holzapfel, H., Nickel, K. and Stiefelhagen, R. Implementation and evaluation of a constrained-based multimodal fusion systems for speech and 3D pointing gestures. Proc. ICMI'04, ACM (2004).
3. Oviatt, S. L. Multimodal Interfaces. In The Human-Computer Interaction Handbook: Fundamentals, Evolving Technologies and Emerging Applications. Lawrence Erlbaum Associates (2003).
4. Lalanne, D., Kohlas, J., Dumas, B. and Oviatt, S. Multimodal Interfaces: A Survey of Principles, Models and Frameworks. In Human Machine Interaction, Springer Lecture Notes in Computer Science (2009).
5. Wasinger, R., Krüger, A. and Jacobs, O. Integrating Intra and Extra Gestures into a Mobile and Multimodal Shopping Assistant. In Pervasive Computing, Springer Lecture Notes in Computer Science (2005).
6. Spassova, L., Wasinger, R., Baus, J., Krüger, A. Product Associated Displays in a Shopping Scenario. Proc. ISMAR'05. IEEE (2005).
7. Newcomb, E., Pashley, T. and Stasko, J. Mobile Computing in the Retail Area. Proc. CHI'03, ACM (2003).
8. Wilson, A. Using a Depth Camera as a Touch Sensor. Proc. ITS'10, ACM (2010).
9. Kendon, A. Do Gestures Communicate? In Research on Language & Social Interaction, 1532-7973, Volume 27, Issue 3, Pages 175 – 200 (1994).

A Glove for Tapping and Discrete 1D/2D Input

Sam A. Miller
NASA Langley Research Center
samuel.a.miller@nasa.gov

Andy Smith, Sina Bahram, Robert St. Amant
Department of Computer Science
North Carolina State University
pmsmith4 | sbahram | stamant@ncsu.edu

ABSTRACT
This paper describes a glove with which users enter input by tapping fingertips with the thumb or by rubbing the thumb over the palmar surfaces of the middle and index fingers. The glove has been informally tested as the controller for two semi-autonomous robots in a a 3D simulation environment. A preliminary evaluation of the glove's performance is presented.

ACM Classification Keywords
H5.2 [Information interfaces and presentation]: User Interfaces. - Graphical user interfaces.

General Terms
Design, Human Factors

Author Keywords
Wearable, mobile, tactile, proprioception, glove-based interaction

INTRODUCTION
Glove-based interaction can support a number of different input techniques, including finger tapping, finger flexion, hand configuration, hand orientation, and gesture [2]. Familiar examples include the chording glove [9] and commercial products from Fakespace and RallyPoint. This paper describes a glove with which users enter input by tapping a fingertip with the thumb or by rubbing the thumb over the palmar surfaces of the middle and index fingers. The glove suggests a new space of design for textile-based computing [8].

As an interaction technique, rubbing has appeared in some other devices (e.g., mobile touch interfaces [6]), but not in one of its most natural settings: between the thumb and fingers. Users can specify areas, locations, and directions by exploiting the dexterity of their finger movements as well as their proprioceptive sense, their implicit knowledge of locations on the fingers that can be touched by the thumb. Moving thumb and fingers for discrete and spatial input, independent of buttons or a fixed surface, is an expressive interaction style; users describe it as fun.

The glove is of ordinary nonconductive fabric onto which conductive fabric, thread, and wire are mounted. The result is a set of digital and analog data channels, with current supplied by a National Instruments USB-6009 device. Figure 1 shows the glove in diagram form. For clarity, we'll refer to the digits of the hand by d0 through d4, with d0 being the thumb. The tips of d0, d3, and d4 are covered in conductive fabric, and the palmar sides of d1 and d2 are covered with a grid of conductive threads, 8 on the x axis (4 threads running the length of each finger) and 10 on the y axis (10 threads crossing the width of each finger). The conductive threads on the d1/d2 grid are woven in an over-and-under pattern such that when an x thread crosses a y thread, the two are separated by nonconductive fabric.

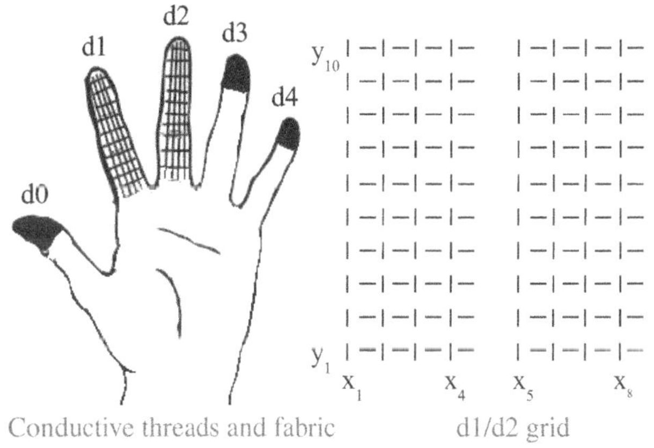

Figure 1. Notional diagrams of the glove.

From an electrical circuits perspective, the glove is a set of switches, any of which can be closed by contact with d0. This enables the glove to detect a tap on any fingertip, which closes a switch by the thumb's contact either with conductive fabric (d3 and d4) or a y_{10} thread (d1 and d2). Switches can be closed in parallel, which means the glove can detect combinations of fingertip touches (i.e., $2^4 - 1 = 15$), though not all may be ergonomically feasible. The glove detects a touch to the d1/d2 grid as a set of closed switches, $x_i \ldots x_j$ and $y_m \ldots y_n$, which define a rectangular boundary corresponding to the area of contact. This boundary changes as the thumb moves over the surface of the fingers. The glove has no independent clutch. Figure 2 shows the glove and the gestures it supports.

Input methods, including those for gloves, are typically categorized as being discrete or continuous, with discrete input for symbolic commands or characters, and continuous input for spatial information in one or more dimensions [1]. The

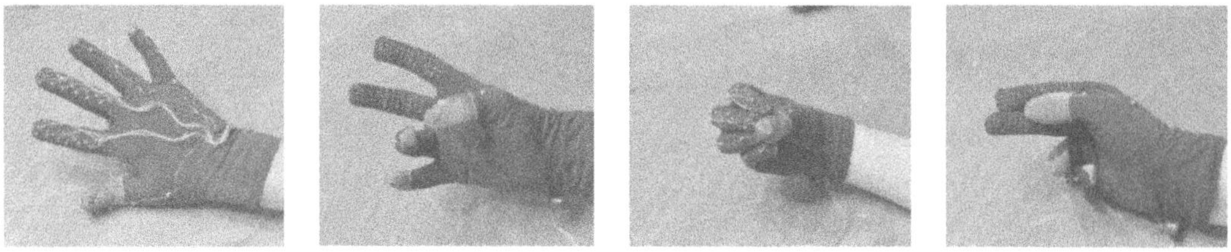

Out-of-range state | Single click | Multiple click | A rubbing gesture

Figure 2. The glove in use

Bi-linear interpolation | Proper close | Local smoothing | Exponential look-up | Centroid computation

Figure 3. Image processing of grid input

d1/d2 grid is comparable to a flexible touchpad attached to two fingers, supporting discretized spatial input. The body of this paper describes the glove's internal processing, a preliminary study of its performance, and an application we have built to explore its use in practice.

GLOVE PROCESSING

A simple approach to translating d1/d2 signals to a location or region relies on the bounding rectangle of the closed circuits. This proves to be insufficiently robust, however. The circuits are noisy—the conductive threads are prone to fraying and shorting on each other. One or two theads may sporadically fail. The glove does not fit in the same way on hands of different sizes, which introduces further noise in the touch between thumb and fingers.

Instead, we extract information using an imaging algorithm. The algorithm treats the grid as a binary image, where each x/y intersection corresponds to a pixel. The algorithm determines the location of thumb by first filtering out noise from the touch image. It then finds the energy centroid of the resulting image. Because imaging filters tend to work best on source data that is smoothly varying, the original 8×10 image is up-sampled using bi-linear interpolation to a 32×32 image. This introduces smooth edges onto the image. A "proper close" step removes small noise elements from image without disturbing the smoothed edges. A local-average filter with a 7×7 kernel is then applied to ramp all gray-scale values in the image, leaving brightest regions in the center of large regions. The dynamic range of the image is transformed by look-up in an exponential table to accentuate the brightest regions. Finally, the energy centroid is found for the entire image; this captures the point of contact with the d1/d2 grid. This is not the only possible design for an imaging algorithm for this domain, but it is the first we discovered that worked well; machine learning techniques may improve performance. The process, from binary image to final centroid, is shown by example in Figure 3.

THE GLOVE IN USE

The initial goal for the development of the glove was to support flexible one-handed interaction with a rich virtual environment, as might be provided in an augmented reality system, while the user is walking around, looking through a head-mounted display. A simulation of such an application was developed, based on a video game engine, as shown in Figure 4. The simulation contains two semi-autonomous robots, a crawler and a flyer, that follow pre-programmed paths through a rain forest. Each robot pipes its video feed and other status information to the user. The user can take control of either machine at any time to direct its actions using buttons, menus, and navigational controls.[1] The user controls the simulation with different glove gestures:

Figure 4. Control of crawler robot, in simulation.

[1]Demo video: www.youtube.com/watch?v=xx-EhsxcjJU

- *Tapping*: Some global commands are mapped to taps on fingertips: a single touch and release on one or more fingers, or repeated touches.
- *Rub positioning*: The robots can be steered by by rubbing d1. Menu navigation is through the same gesture, with selection mapped to a tap on d3. Positioning in two dimensions is also possible with rubs to the d1/d2 grid; this is used in pop-up pie menus. *Touch positioning*, in which a touch to the grid is interpreted in absolute positioning mode, is possible but was not implemented.
- *Swiping*: Some context-sensitive commands are mapped to directional "swipes" on the d1/d2 grid, to execute a command or change state in the interface.

In a formative evaluation, six participants used the simulation. Each session began with a demonstration of the glove's interactions. All participants could use the glove effectively within five minutes, the only consistent challenge being the difficulty of remembering the mapping of different gestures to commands. Qualitative feedback was positive: Participants found some gestures intuitive and enjoyable, in particular control of the movement of the robots by rubbing gestures. The glove generally met our expectations. It shows promise for controlling a simulation, with some commands and continuous actions naturally mapping to the glove gestures.

TESTING

We also carried out a preliminary experiment to test the glove for common interaction tasks. For brevity, we will concentrate on a single task in the experiment, summarizing the rest. The experiment involved 11 participants, all unpaid volunteers. Participants ranged in age from 21 to 33. Two were female, nine male. All were right-handed, with vision corrected to 20/20, and use computers daily. Each session lasted about 30 minutes.

The main task for the experiment was target selection in one dimension (Task 1a) or two dimensions (Task 1b). Task 1a was performed before Task 1b. Participants were shown a box containing a colored target region on a computer display. The spatial extent of the box was mapped in absolute terms to the d1/d2 grid. In Task 1a, the x component of touch signals was ignored.

Recall that the input resolution of the glove is much lower than that of a typical display. The goal of this task was to establish a reasonable ratio for mapping input resolution to output resolution. The box was divided into an array of $n \times 1$ elements for Task 1a and $n \times n$ elements for Task 1b (the resolution), and the target occupied $s \times 1$ elements for Task 1a, $s \times s$ elements for Task 1b (the relative target size). These divisions were not visible in the display. The specific values used for n and s are given in Table 1, based on our judgments about the difficulty of the task from a pilot study.

The participants carried out 24 trials for each task in a training phase. This was followed by 10 trials for each of the conditions in Table 1, with target locations generated at random. Each trial began with the participant's thumb out of contact with the other fingers. A target appeared in a random

s	n	*Ratio*
2	9	0.22
4	9	0.44
2	30	0.06
4	30	0.13
8	30	0.26

Table 1. Target size (s), resolution (n), and target size ratio.

location, and the participant performed a Touch positioning action, causing a cursor to appear. If the cursor did not overlap the target, the participant performed a Rub positioning action to move the cursor to the target. The participant released contact to indicate completion, and the next trial began immediately. For each trial, the duration was recorded between the release event at the end of one trial and the release event of the next trial; the time for a new target to appear was considered negligible. A trial was considered successful if the release event occurred with the cursor overlapping the target.

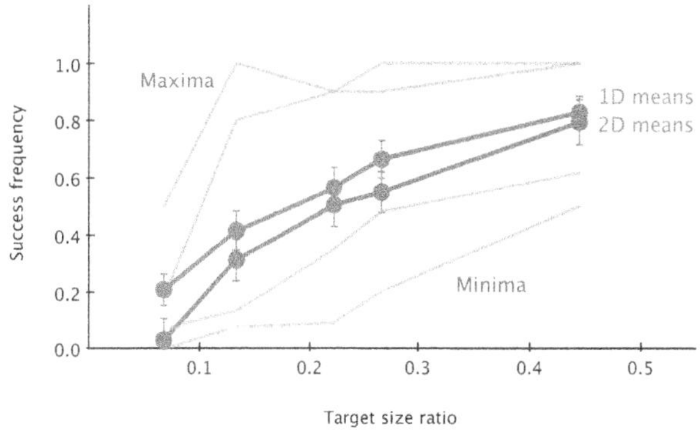

Figure 5. Task 1a/b success frequency, per target size ratio.

Some data cleaning was performed to remove outliers with durations longer than 10 seconds (less than 1% of the data for Task 1a, less than 2% of the data for Task 1b). Qualitatively, the results were largely as expected. Over all conditions, the mean duration for target selection was 1326 ms in Task 1a, 1562 ms in Task 1b. The mean duration in the fastest condition, 4/9, was 953 ms in Task 1a, 934 ms in Task 1b. The heavy lines in Figure 5 show the frequency of successful completion of a trial, which ranged from 0.21 to 0.83 across conditions for Task 1a, 0.03 to 0.79 for Task 1b. The fine lines in Figure 5 show minima and maxima over all participants.

Other tasks in the experiment produced the following results:

- Task 2a involved participants "playing the scales" on their fingers: touching d1 through d4, in order, and then in reverse order. After a practice phase of 24 trials, participants executed 50 trials. The mean duration per tap was 305 ms. Task 2b asked participants to follow a sequence of finger taps, shown a "map" of the digits on the display. In a practice phase, participants executed 24 trials using the interface, and then carried out 50 trials for the task, in which the finger to tap was determined randomly. The mean over all fingers was 575 ms, with a success frequency of 0.93.

- Task 3 was a gesture entry task, analogous to text entry tasks [4]. The gestures were single diagonal strokes, in four possible directions, from a central point on the sensor grid on the first two fingers. Four additional longer diagonal strokes were also included, from outer points on the grid (effectively the corners of the grid). Participants carried out 24 trials to practice the gestures, with a simple recognition system providing feedback about accuracy. No feedback was provided in the trials that followed, to allow users to proceed at their own speed. Unfortunately, more than half of the participants executed the gestures so quickly (averaging 150 to 400 ms per gesture) that the gesture recognizer failed. The recognition rate over all participants was 0.40. The The highest success frequency was 0.94 for one participant, whose gestures had a mean duration of 614 ms.

We view these findings as promising but not definitive. Our formative evaluation and the high performance of the glove's developers led us to an overly optimistic experiment design. For contrast, Rosenberg and Slater's evaluation of the chording glove [9] involved ten sessions of 50 minutes each for participants to reach competence in text entry (though much of that time could be attributed to learning chords). It is clear from our experiment that the glove needs further evaluation as well as improved hardware if it is to be deployed.

We find a few bright spots in our experiment: it was possible for participants to achieve good performance using the glove, even if not reliably. The authors of this paper, with more experience, significantly outperform the best of the participants; as in other glove-based work, training plays a factor in performance. Further, our results are largely consistent with other work in mobile and glove-based interaction. For example, Parhi et al. [7] give duration results for selection of targets on small touchscreens with the thumb, in one-handed use. For targets of average size on small touch screens, selection time is between 1100 and 1200 milliseconds; errors appear in almost 30% of selections. These tasks differ from those in our Task 1, but the comparable timing and error rates suggest that interaction with the glove may reach reasonable performance in the abstract.

The simulated robot application worked much better than our experiment would suggest. Failed inputs had low cost—actions could be repeated—and users found moving through linear and pie menus by rub positioning, driving and flying the robots with by rub positioning, and shifting interface modes or confirming selection by tapping, all to be effective and easy to learn. This suggests that our glove has relevance for specific application domains and interaction styles, in particular those relevant to interaction when the user's hand might be out of view.

A good deal of work remains to be done. We are currently exploring alternative sensing technology for the glove; we believe that proprioception is insufficiently exploited in input devices, with only a few examples of its explicit consideration to be found in the literature (e.g. [5]). Other application areas also appear promising; for example, given the glove's expressiveness, we have solicited input from a semi-professional musician and built a glove-controlled synthesizer application. We believe that with better hardware, the glove should offer a new avenue for interaction in wearable computing.

ACKNOWLEDGMENTS

Special thanks to Chelsea Miller, an invaluable subject matter expert who sewed the prototype glove, and to Nikunj Kela and Harshmeet Singh, who contributed to early conceptual work on the use of the glove.

REFERENCES

1. S.K. Card, J.D. Mackinlay, and G.G. Robertson. The design space of input devices. In *Proceedings of the ACM Conference on Human Factors in Computing Systems*, pages 117–124. ACM, 1990.
2. L. Dipietro, A.M. Sabatini, and P. Dario. A survey of glove-based systems and their applications. *Systems, Man, and Cybernetics, Part C: Applications and Reviews, IEEE Transactions on*, 38(4):461–482, 2008.
3. J. Fredriksson, S.B. Ryen, and M. Fjeld. Real-time 3D hand-computer interaction: optimization and complexity reduction. In *Proceedings of the Nordic Conference on Human-Computer Interaction*, NORDCHI, pages 133–141, 2008. ACM.
4. I.S. MacKenzie and R.W. Soukoreff. Text entry for mobile computing: Models and methods, theory and practice. *Human-Computer Interaction*, 17(2):147–198, 2002.
5. M.R. Mine, F.P. Brooks Jr, and C.H. Sequin. Moving objects in space: exploiting proprioception in virtual-environment interaction. In *Proceedings of the Annual Conference on Computer Graphics and Interactive Techniques*, SIGGRAPH, pages 19–26. ACM, 1997.
6. A. Olwal, S. Feiner, and S. Heyman. Rubbing and tapping for precise and rapid selection on touch-screen displays. In *Proceeding of the ACM Conference on Human Factors in Computing Systems*, CHI, pages 295–304. ACM, 2008.
7. P. Parhi, A.K. Karlson, and B.B. Bederson. Target size study for one-handed thumb use on small touchscreen devices. In *Proceedings of the Conference on Human-Computer Interaction with Mobile Devices and Services*, pages 203–210. ACM, 2006.
8. E.R. Post and M. Orth. Smart fabric, or "wearable clothing". In *Proceedings of the IEEE International Symposium on Wearable Computers*, pages 167–168. IEEE, 1997.
9. R. Rosenberg and M. Slater. The chording glove: a glove-based text input device. *IEEE Transactions on Systems, Man, and Cybernetics, Part C: Applications and Reviews*, 29(2):186–191, 1999.

Using Overlays to Support Collaborative Interaction with Display Walls

Arvind Satyanarayan
Stanford University
353 Serra Mall
Stanford, CA 94305-902, USA
arvindsatya@cs.stanford.edu

Nadir Weibel
UC San Diego
9500 Gilman Dr.,
La Jolla, CA 92093-0515, USA
weibel@ucsd.edu

James D. Hollan
UC San Diego
9500 Gilman Dr.,
La Jolla, CA 92093-0515, USA
hollan@ucsd.edu

(a) The HIPerSpace Wall Display

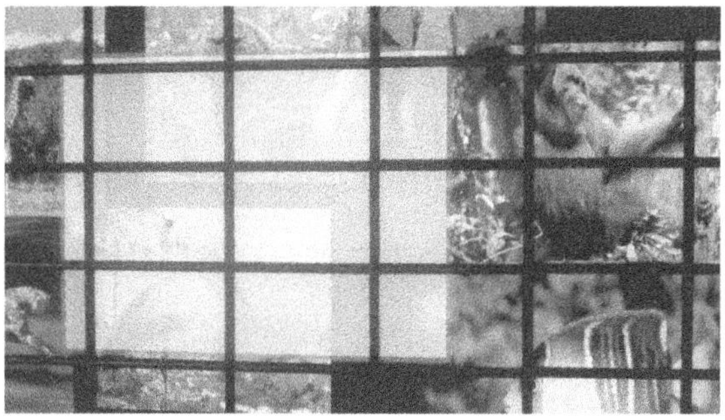

(b) The Overlay interface[1]

Figure 1. Overlays enable collaborative interaction on ultra-scale wall displays

ABSTRACT
Large-scale display walls, and the high-resolution visualizations they support, promise to become ubiquitous. Natural interaction with them, especially in collaborative environments, is increasingly important and yet remains an on-going challenge. Part of the problem is a resolution mismatch between low-resolution input devices and high-resolution display walls. In addition, enabling concurrent use by multiple users is difficult — for example, how would this large workspace be managed for multiple users and what novel collaborative interactions could occur? In this paper, we present an overlay interface element superimposed on wall-display applications to help constrain interaction, focus attention on subsections of a display wall, and facilitate a collaborative multi-user workflow.

Author Keywords
High-Resolution Ultra-Scale Displays; Multiuser Interaction; Multi-scale Interaction

ACM Classification Keywords
H.5.2 [Information Interfaces and Presentation]: User Interfaces - Interaction styles;

General Terms
Design; Human Factors; Experimentation

INTRODUCTION
As graphics processing units (GPUs) become increasingly powerful and as the cost of displays continues to fall, large display walls are likely to become widely available. High-resolution displays are especially suited for analyzing and manipulating complex datasets in multi-user multi-device collaborative environments. One such example of a tiled wall display is the CalIT2 *Highly Interactive Parallelized Display Space* (or HIPerSpace[2] — Fig. 1(a)). It employs seventy 30" Dell LCD displays tiled together, creating a 31.8 foot by 7.5 foot wall, to provide a display resolution of 35,840 x 8,000 pixels (a total of 286,720,000 pixels).

However, as highlighted by the study conducted by Rogers and Lindley [10], there are multiple interaction challenges that must be addressed for such high-resolution displays to become more widely used — in the study, users found it awkward to collaborate around a vertical display, preferring the fluid interaction afforded by horizontal tabletop displays.

An obvious problem is the resolution mismatch between low-resolution input devices and the high-resolution wall which makes it difficult for users to accomplish fine-grained manipulation of small objects on the large display. This problem is often exacerbated by providing a low-resolution image of the wall's display on the input device itself, causing users to focus their attention on their input device rather than the wall.

Another limitation of current wall display systems is reaching distant objects [3, 8] — not only can it be a slow and tedious operation but, given the larger display area, users tend

[1]The background of the Overlay has been artificially saturated to make it more visible for publication purposes.
[2]http://vis.ucsd.edu/projects/hiperspace

to compensate by accelerating mouse movements, making cursor tracking difficult [8, 9].

Finally, although large display walls are inherently multi-user and can be a useful medium for collaboration, current interfaces do little to facilitate this type of behavior [12].

In this paper, we present an *Overlay* paradigm that builds on the *Magic Lens* metaphor [1] of a movable, see-through interface superimposed on information elements. We discuss the Overlay design, its use with multitouch surfaces, touch-capable mobile devices and digital pen and paper, and describe feedback we received from initial use and plans for future work.

THE OVERLAY INTERFACE

The Overlay is a small translucent rectangle[1] that appears superimposed on a wall display. By allowing a user to only interact with objects that appear directly underneath it, it helps to focus users' attention on a small subsection of the larger display [6], and aids allocation of display space across users. As highlighted in Fig. 1(b), objects — photos in this case — are visible through the Overlay.

Design Goals

Two design goals motivated the development of the Overlay interface:

Providing compatibility with diverse devices

A variety of input devices can be coupled with display walls in order to investigate natural ways of interacting with large display walls at a distance. In contrast to existing systems such as the Active Workspace [7], a design goal for the Overlay interface was to enable compatibility with a large number of diverse input devices for object-level manipulation. Every device, by default, maps to the dimensions of the Overlay rather than the entire display wall.

Supporting multiple users

Although existing techniques such as Active Workspace and Shadow Reaching [11] discuss ways to extend the paradigm to support multiple users in collaborative environments as part of planned future work, we do not know of any concrete implementations. Our Overlay interface introduces one Overlay per user to facilitate multiple users working together and several new interaction techniques to encourage collaborative behavior.

Interactive Devices

Although our design supports compatibility with a variety of input devices, for the purposes of this paper, we will discuss using the Overlay interface with three types of devices: multitouch surfaces, touch-capable mobile devices, and digital pen and paper.

Multitouch Surfaces

Research has long demonstrated the benefits of touch-based interaction [2] and with the current proliferation of multitouch devices we expect this to be an increasingly important form of interface. We experimented with two types of multitouch surfaces. The first is the 3M M2256PW display[3], a 22-inch display capable of differentiating up to 20 touch points. One of the limitations of this display is that it is incapable of differentiating between different users. As a result, to support multiple users with the 3M display, we partition the touchscreen into multiple regions depending on the number of users (Fig. 2(a)) and each region is mapped to the correspondingly colored Overlay on the wall display (Fig. 2(b)).

[3]http://www.3m.com

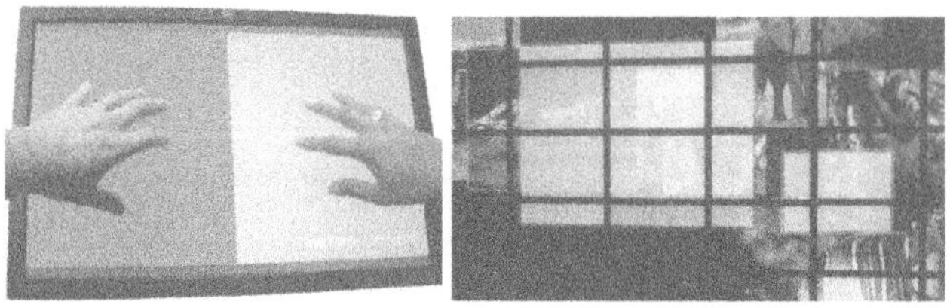

(a) Touch-based interaction (left:red, right: green) (b) Multiple Overlays (left: red, right: green)

Figure 2. Multi-user touch-based interaction with the Overlay

The DiamondTouch table[4] is the other multitouch system we used to explore use of the Overlay. It employs an array of capacitive transmitters and receivers to distinguish between multiple users [4]. Thus, we are able to easily assign one Overlay per user without manually dividing the touch surface.

Touch-capable Mobile Devices

One of the inherent limitations of the devices above is that they are positioned at a fixed location and thus restrict the movement of users. We thought mobile devices would promote different forms of interaction and exploration with the HIPerSpace wall. In order to test the use of mobile devices, we built an iOS 4 application[5] for the Apple iPhone and iPod Touch. Given that these devices are personal, likely to be only used by one user at a time and rarely shared, and given their size, we assigned one Overlay per device (shown in Fig. 3).

Figure 3. The Overlay interface: the translucent rectangle[1] is superimposed on part of the three photos displayed on the wall

Digital Pen and Paper

We conjectured that digital pen and paper interfaces might be uniquely suited for interactions with the display wall — they are mobile, offer the affordance of paper including ease of taking notes and existing user familiarity, and numerous additional interface elements may be directly printed on the paper itself.

[4]http://www.circletwelve.com

[5]http://developer.apple.com/devcenter/ios

To explore their suitability in this space, we modified the HIPerPaper interface [13] by adding an Overlay widget as as shown in Fig. 4 — the upper region of the interface maps to the entire wall display whereas the lower region represents and maps to the Overlay.

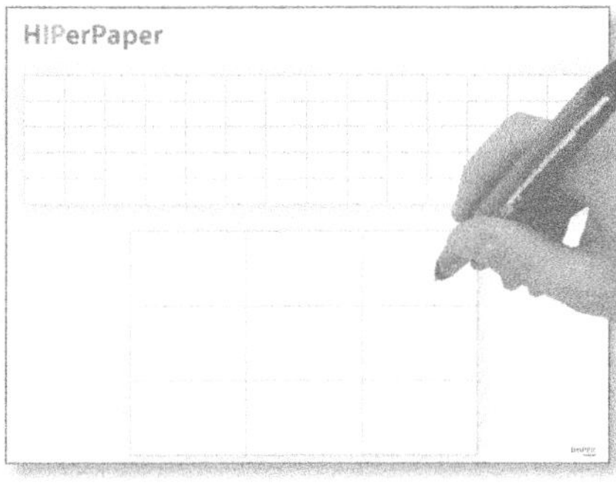

Figure 4. The HIPerPaper Overlay

Using the Overlay

The Overlay works by intercepting events transmitted to the underlying application and normalizing the event coordinates such that interaction occurs relative to the Overlay's position and dimensions rather than the entire display — i.e. the input device maps to the dimensions of the Overlay and a user is constrained to only interacting with objects that appear, at least partially, underneath their Overlay. This makes the Overlay compatible with any events that contain (x, y, z) coordinate information including selecting, dragging, zooming and rotating events.

Selecting and Zooming within the Overlay

We support the natural grammar of multitouch devices with the Overlay. When the user taps a point on the device, they select the object that is underneath the corresponding point of the Overlay. Similarly, pan, pinch and rotation gestures can be used to move, scale or rotate any selected objects. We have also implemented a two-finger double-tap gesture to be able to select multiple objects with the Overlay; the selection is then treated as a group and manipulated together. HIPerPaper's Overlay widget works in a similar fashion and maps to the dimensions of the on-display Overlay as well — users can tap an area to select an object, drag the pen to move it, trace a circle to scale it and vary the pressure with which they press the pen to select multiple objects.

We intentionally provide no local feedback on input devices as a form of (in)direct manipulation designed specifically to focus a user's visual attention on the high resolution wall over the low-resolution input device. Rather, we display interactions on the Overlay itself through small colored circles which help to orient a user and offer feedback comparable to that offered by a cursor. For example, Fig. 1(b) shows one colored circle when a finger makes contact with a touch-sensitive surface, or if a user performs a pinch gesture to zoom the selected photo, two circles would represent the motion of the user's fingers and move away from each other.

Positioning and Scaling the Overlay

To allow users to manipulate any area of the large display, the Overlay itself can be positioned at an absolute point on the display, dragged across it or scaled to take up a larger or smaller area of the display.

With touch-capable devices, the following five-finger gestures manipulate the Overlay:

- *Five-finger tap*: causes the Overlay to snap to an exact position on the display.
- *Five-finger pinch*: scales the Overlay up or down while maintaining its aspect ratio.
- *Five-finger drag*: moves the Overlay across the display, corresponding to the drag gesture.

Note that with these gestures, there is an implicit change of state — whereas previously the device mapped to the confines of the Overlay, these interactions cause the device to map to the entire display instead.

In the case of mobile devices, however, five-finger gestures may be awkward to perform and thus, we are exploring other modalities they offer to manipulate the position and size of the Overlay — for example, tilting the device towards or away from the screen to move the Overlay vertically and tilting it to either side to move it horizontally.

With HIPerPaper, users can use the main interface (top part of Fig. 4) to position the Overlay by tapping or dragging their pens to a position. By tracing a circle on this area, users can scale the Overlay up or down.

If any objects within the Overlay are selected when it is moved, they move along with it, i.e. their position remains fixed relative to the Overlay (Fig. 5).

Figure 5. Dragging the Overlay with a photo selected

Collaborative Interactions

The first step towards supporting multiple concurrent users was introducing one Overlay per user. We differentiate each user's Overlay with differently colored borders — as shown in Fig. 2(b). However, several questions remain with regard to the behavior of multiple Overlays. What happens if multiple users wish to interact with the same section of the large display? Will their Overlays intersect and overlap, or should they remain distinct? What novel collaborative interactions will multiple Overlays enable?

We are exploring two approaches to address the issue of over lapping Overlays. The first examines prohibiting overlapping Overlays by establishing a "sphere of influence" around each Overlay. An Overlay is not be able to enter another's sphere of influence, but a moving Overlay can temporarily

Figure 6. Sphere of influence

push other Overlays out of its way in a repelling fashion (see Fig. 6). Spheres of influence are only displayed when two Overlays are in danger of overlapping).

An alternative approach is to use "drop shadows" to layer Overlays. In this case a user's precedence is determined by the position of their Overlay in the pile, with the Overlay at the top having the highest precedence. Thus, if multiple users were to simultaneously interact with an object under a pile of Overlays, the user with the highest precedence would win, and other interactions would be ignored. We are also investigating allowing users to toggle between these behaviors.

CONCLUSION AND FUTURE WORK

We informally tested the Overlay interface with graduate students and researchers in our lab to gather early feedback. Each user was given a brief introduction and then given time to freely experiment with a photo application to determine if they were able to perform simple tasks including selecting, dragging, zooming and rotating photos.

Users reported that the overlay immediately drew their attention and that mappings between devices and the Overlay felt natural, noting the importance of matching the aspect ratios of the Overlay and input device. They also reported that manipulating the overlay was easy, but remarked that dragging or scaling the overlay to reach distant objects still felt tedious. None of the users expressed concerns about the (in)direct interaction, with input-only devices to control the wall display, and seemed to naturally attend to what was displayed on the wall.

Although multi-user support, particularly collaborative interaction, is still in its infancy, this early feedback suggests that introducing one overlay per user is effective — users immediately understood that they each controlled an individual overlay, and were able to work on separate tasks simultaneously. In the context of the photos application, future work will explore how the Overlay interface can support more high-fidelity collaborative interaction — for example, if one user grabbed the top-left corner of a photo while another grabbed the bottom-right and then dragged their Overlays in opposite directions, this could stretch the selected photo. To test this interface with more complex objects and data, we are also working to integrate the Overlay interface with "Shared Substance" [5], a general application framework for large display walls.

ACKNOWLEDGMENTS

We thank Falko Kuester, Kai-Uwe Doerr and So Yamaoka, members of the Gravity Laboratory at CalIT2, for assistance with CGLX and configuring simulations of the HIPerSpace Wall. This work has been funded in part by NSF Grant 0729013.

REFERENCES

1. E. A. Bier, M. C. Stone, K. Pier, W. Buxton, and T. D. DeRose. Toolglass and magic lenses: the see-through interface. In *Proc. SIGGRAPH '93*, pages 73–80, 1993.
2. W. Buxton, R. Hill, and P. Rowley. Issues and techniques in touch-sensitive tablet input. *SIGGRAPH Comput. Graph.*, 19(3):215–224, 1985.
3. M. Czerwinski, G. Robertson, B. Meyers, G. Smith, D. Robbins, and D. Tan. Large display research overview. In *CHI EA '06*, pages 69–74, 2006.
4. P. Dietz and D. Leigh. Diamondtouch: a multi-user touch technology. In *Proc. UIST '01*, pages 219–226, 2001.
5. T. Gjerlufsen, C. Klokmose, J. Eagan, C. Pillias, and M. Beaudouin-Lafon. Shared substance: developing flexible multi-surface applications. In *Proc. CHI '11*, pages 3383–3392, 2011.
6. A. Khan, J. Matejka, G. Fitzmaurice, and G. Kurtenbach. Spotlight: Directing Users' Attention on Large Displays. In *Proc. CHI '05*, pages 791–798, 2005.
7. S. Malik, A. Ranjan, and R. Balakrishnan. Interacting with Large Displays from a Distance with Vision-tracked Multi-finger Gestural Input. In *Proc. UIST '05*, pages 43–52, 2005.
8. T. Ni, G. S. Schmidt, O. G. Staadt, M. A. Livingston, R. Ball, and R. May. A Survey of Large High-Resolution Display Technologies, Techniques, and Applications. In *Proc. Virtual Reality '06*, pages 223–236, 2006.
9. G. Robertson, M. Czerwinski, P. Baudisch, B. Meyers, D. Robbins, G. Smith, and D. Tan. The large-display user experience. *IEEE Computer Graphics and Applications*, 25:44–51, 2005.
10. Y. Rogers and S. Lindley. Collaborating around vertical and horizontal large interactive displays: which way is best? *Interacting with Computers*, 16(6):1133 – 1152, 2004.
11. G. Shoemaker, A. Tang, and K. Booth. Shadow Reaching: a New Perspective on Interaction for Large Displays. In *Proc. UIST '07*, pages 53–56, 2007.
12. G. Wallace, O. J. Anshus, P. Bi, H. Chen, Y. Chen, D. Clark, P. Cook, A. Finkelstein, T. Funkhouser, A. Gupta, M. Hibbs, K. Li, Z. Liu, R. Samanta, R. Sukthankar, and O. Troyanskaya. Tools and applications for large-scale display walls. *IEEE Computer Graphics and Applications*, 25:24–33, 2005.
13. N. Weibel, A. M. Piper, and J. D. Hollan. HIPerPaper: Introducng Pen and Paper Interfaces for Ultra-Scale Wall Displays. In *Proc. UIST '10*, pages 407–408, 2010.

Virtual Stage Linked with a Physical Miniature Stage to Support Multiple Users in Planning Theatrical Productions

Yosuke Horiuchi
Graduate School of Science and Technology, Keio University
Kanagawa, Japan
yosuke@mos.ics.keio.ac.jp

Tomoo Inoue
Graduate School of Library, Information and Media Studies, University of Tsukuba
Ibaraki, Japan
inoue@slis.tsukuba.ac.jp

Ken-ichi Okada
Graduate School of Science and Technology, Keio University
Kanagawa, Japan
okada@mos.ics.keio.ac.jp

ABSTRACT
Theater is a collaborative art form that involves production team members with different specialties. Because theater involves various technical elements, such as stage design and lighting, the production team must work in cooperation among various departments to design a theatrical production. When planning a theatrical production, it is difficult to visualize the stage as a whole and to incorporate the ideas of production team members from various departments. In this paper, we propose a system for reproducing the theatrical stage by means of a virtual stage linked to a physical miniature stage. The miniature stage is presented on a tabletop interface, and the virtual stage is created by computer graphics to reflect the actions on the miniature stage in real time. By actually presenting theatrical production ideas in two spaces, users can more easily collaborate and gain a comprehensive view of the stage.

Author Keywords
Tabletop interface, tangible interface, virtual space, theater

ACM Classification Keywords
H.5.1 Information Interfaces and Presentation: Multimedia Information Systems—*Artificial, augmented, and virtual realities*

General Terms
Design, Human Factors.

INTRODUCTION
Creative activity is work where the imagination is used to produce art, such as a novel or painting. In our research, we focus on the creation of theater. Theater is a collaborative art form that involves combining various technical elements, such as set building and lighting effects, for the purpose of artistic expression. Theatrical production is proposed as an educational method because it promotes improved communication skills and a shared sense of emotion among production team members [16]. When planning a theatrical production, however, cooperative work and idea sharing are hindered by the difficulty of visualizing the stage as a whole from the perspective of different production team members. Most research into the planning of theatrical productions [1, 4, 13, 18, 23] has focused on individual work, whereas hardly any research has been devoted to cooperative work.

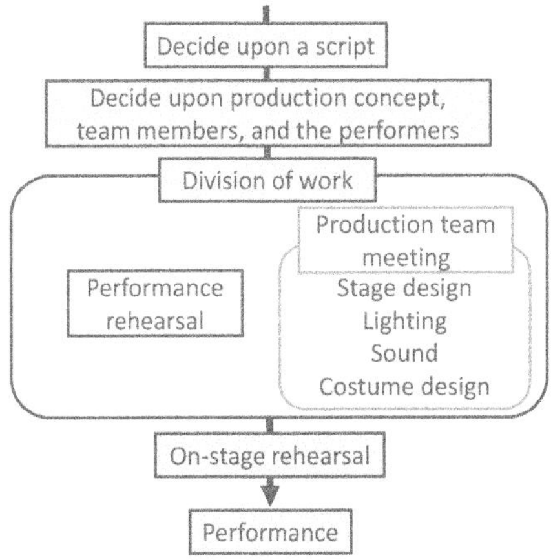

Figure 1. Workflow in theatrical production.

To solve the problem, this paper proposes a system reproducing an actual stage through two spaces for multiple users working to plan a theatrical production. One space is a miniature stage presented on a tabletop interface, and the other space is a virtual stage linked to the miniature stage. Actions occurred on the table—such as the movement of objects and the contact with operation windows projected on the table—are reflected on the virtual stage in real time; in this manner, the virtual stage presents a stage situation that includes various production elements required for theater. By actually reproducing the production ideas of each department in two spaces, it becomes easy for users to imagine the theatrical stage as a whole and to share their ideas with others.

THEATRICAL PRODUCTION PLANNING
Theatrical production includes various tasks. Figure 1 shows the typical workflow in theatrical production [11]. Our research focuses on theatrical production planning, which includes multiple production team members cooperating to dis-

cuss and decide upon the aspects of the theatrical production; this planning is described as the "Production team meeting" in Figure 1. In general, sound production, stage lighting, costume design, and set design are the elements of theater production. These elements are designed in production meetings by team members in charge of each production element. Each team member proposes their production ideas in a series of meetings in theatrical production planning. In this task, each production element must be part of a common vision shared among all of the production departments [5]. If the production lacks effective collaboration among all the departments, the entire theatrical production will suffer.

Theatrical production planning has the following problems.

- *The difficulty of visualizing the entire theatrical space*
  In the early phases of production planning, because production team members cannot reproduce and check their work on an actual stage, they must visualize the entire theatrical space in their mind. Because theater is created by cooperatively implementing each production element, the production team members must visualize a theatrical space that reproduces all the production elements, including the ones of which they are not in charge. Additionally, in order to enhance audience satisfaction, the production team members, as they design the production, must bear in mind the viewpoints of the audience members. For instance, while planning visually appealing production elements, such as lighting effects, a production team member must consider how the effects look from a variety of audience standpoints [20]. By reconstructing the miniature stage with miniature dolls and stage sets, production members can imagine the position of the actors. However, it is still difficult to create an image of the whole stage including the lighting effect and the stage backdrop, and imagine how the actual stage looks from audience. These tasks are difficult even for those with extensive experience in theater.
- *The difficulty of sharing ideas with other production team members*
  If the idea sharing is not achieved, each production team member will have difficulty carrying their production responsibilities while taking other production departments into account, and consequently overall production cooperation will suffer. Therefore, in production meetings, team members are required to share a layout of the entire theatrical space that includes the production elements designed by other departments. Lighting, for example, is designed to be placed over other production elements, such as the positions of the actors [20]. It is difficult to imagine the entire theatrical space without reproducing production elements on an actual stage. In addition, there is a possibility that each team members' visualization of the theatrical space will differ, even if each team member has experience visualizing the theatrical space. When this occurs in theatrical production planning, sharing one's vision of the entire theatrical space with other team members is difficult.
- *The task of creating a cue sheet*
  A cue sheet, used by production team members during a performance, is a chart listing the timing and production effects of a theatrical production. After all aspects of the performance are decided, each department must create a cue sheet for the actual performance. But the structure of a cue sheet is complicated; therefore, creating one is difficult for those lacking the sufficient theater experience.

REPRODUCING THEATRICAL SPACE WITH A TABLETOP INTERFACE AND VIRTUAL SPACE

Concept

Our objective is to assist users in visualizing the entire theatrical stage by presenting the theater production elements through two reproduced theatrical stages: the "mini-stage," which is a physical miniature theatrical stage presented on a tabletop surface, and the "virtual stage," which is a virtual theatrical stage linked with the mini-stage and presented through computer graphics (CG). Through the two stages, actions occurring on the real-space mini-stage are expressed.

To solve the problems in theatrical production planning, we will design the system on the basis of the following concepts.

Support for visualizing the entire theatrical stage

To help users who have *the difficulty of visualizing the entire theatrical space*, we aim to design the system that facilitates users' perception of the theatrical stage by reproducing the actual stage with both a mini-stage and a virtual stage. Users construct the mini-stage by placing miniature stage sets and dolls on the tabletop surface to reproduce the production elements; these operations are reflected on the virtual stage. Users can use the virtual stage to reproduce the theatrical stage when production elements that are difficult to represent on the physical mini-stage, such as the stage backdrop and the costume design, are required. In addition, the virtual stage allows users to change views to check how the stage appears from various positions in the audience. The virtual object's movement is synchronized with the physical doll's movement on the mini-stage. Because virtual object movement is coordinated to doll movement on the real-space tabletop, system operation is intuitive, even while moving the virtual viewpoint to any position.

Support for sharing ideas

To relieve *the difficulty of sharing ideas with other production team members*, the entire theatrical stage including each theatrical element should be constantly displayed so that each production team member checks other theatrical elements at any time. By modeling each production department's ideas on both the mini-stage and the virtual stage, the system constantly displays the entire theatrical stage design, including all the production elements. Therefore, users can comprehend the stage layout by checking the system mini-stage and virtual stage depictions, and all production team members have the same perspective of the actual stage.

Support for creating a cue sheet

To reduce the user workload of *the task of creating a cue sheet*, we will design the system automatically generating a cue sheet. By actualizing this function, the cumbersome task of creating a cue sheet will be facilitated.

System Design

On the basis of above concepts, we propose a system that supports multiple users working cooperatively to plan a theatrical production with a tabletop interface linked to an associated virtual space. With this system, users reproduce a theatrical production on the mini-stage, and obtain various perspectives of the entire theatrical stage by means of the mini-stage and virtual stage. In addition, the system automatically generates a cue sheet, which is cumbersome to create manually.

This system facilitates the users' work in visualizing and sharing layouts of the entire stage. To achieve this, the system allows three of the production elements required for theater—the position of the actors, stage effects (lighting effects and stage design), and sound effects—to be reproduced; users can then operate a movable virtual camera to view the virtual stage at various positions and to check how the stage looks from different seats in the audience.

The system facilitates the creation of a cue sheet by allowing users to store their production ideas during production planning and mini-stage setup, and then automatically generating a cue sheet using these data.

In addition, through simple operations, the system allows users to operate intuitively, even when multiple users are working simultaneously and utilizing the virtual stage. The input operations of the system are to touch the tabletop surface and to move the dolls on the table. Moreover, the system recognizes who touches the table and feeds back individual information for the user, thus contributes a smooth work environment for multiple users.

RELATED WORK

Support for Theater Production Planning

Some research has been carried out on supporting creative activity in theater by expressing the virtual theatrical space created through CG. There are some systems [18, 23] that offer users the feeling of acting on stage by coordinating the users' actions in real space with a virtual object in virtual space. Bowen Virtual Theater [13] has been developed as an environment that assists users in learning about the fundamental concepts of theater by displaying stage sets and lighting effects on a personal computer (PC) screen. Commercial systems also exist. WYSIWYG [4] aims to support the planning of lighting production, and Matrix3 [1] supports the planning of sound production. These systems are intended for individual work and have not yet considered the cooperative work of multiple users. Avatar [8] allows multiple users to plan the layout of stage sets. This system is intended for distributed collaborative work using a PC, and is therefore different from our goal of a system that assists face-to-face collaborative work.

DiamondTheater [19] supports for multiple users working to plan a theatrical production, and is similar to our present system in that users are helped to visualize a theatrical stage by actually reproducing theatrical productions on a miniature stage reconstructed on a tabletop interface. With DiamondTheater, however, reproducible production elements are not enough to visualize the stage clearly because the real-space miniature stage could express few productions such as lighting and sound effects, and positions of actor. For example, the background design and the actor costume are not reproduced with DiamondTheater. In our present system, because the virtual stage linked to the physical miniature stage is able to express various information, users become easy to visualize an actual stage by reproducing various theatrical production elements.

Support for Collaborative Work with Tabletop Interface

For multiple users to work in a face-to-face environment, tabletop interfaces that facilitate non-verbal communication in a natural manner have been developed. In the research for face-to-face collaborative work, how the tabletop system displays digital content on the table for people standing at different positions around a horizontal display has been studied, and four approaches have been devised and implemented, as described by Kruger et al. [12]: (1) a fixed orientation intended for participants sitting side-by-side [6]; (2) manual orientation that allows each user to rotate each item [21]; (3) person-based automatic orientation that provides users with the "best view" of each item by detecting which user is manipulating each item, as in InfoTable [17], with which a pointing device is used to access items on the table; and (4) environment-based automatic orientation that provides the "best view" by using person-location detection [7]. To realize flexible and smooth interaction for multiple users, we have chosen environment-based automatic orientation.

Support for Collaborative Work with Virtual Space

In recent days, virtual spaces have been used to assist distributed multiple users' work through the sharing of information. Harry et al. [9] have used a virtual space to represent the feelings of distributed multiple users. By moving the avatar that serves as a surrogate for each user to the "agree" or "disagree" area in the virtual space, the users can easily express their feelings and share ideas with one another. sTeam3D [15] supports multiple users' cooperative work by allowing them to share various products and concepts in a virtual community. In the present research, taking a different perspective, we use a virtual space to facilitate sharing of ideas among multiple users in a face-to-face environment. By modeling each user's idea, which is not able to be fully expressed in real space, the virtual space is employed as the environment to express each user's ideas.

Usage of Both the Tabletop Interface and Virtual Space

Some research has used both a tabletop interface and a virtual space. Terakawa et al. [22] adapted a tabletop interface to the operation of a three-dimensional model. To facilitate the effective utilization of the virtual space, Wu et al. [23] proposed interactions using tangible objects on a tabletop. While a tangible object is placed on a map displayed on the tabletop, the viewpoint of the object is reproduced in virtual space. Those systems, however, are designed to use a tabletop interface as the only interface to operate the virtual space, and thus their aims are different from our aim to coordinate the two spaces to express the same space—each of two presents the same theatrical situation. For children, Marco et al. [14] designed a system that allows users to operate a virtual object in virtual space by moving a tangible object on a tabletop. That research is similar to our research in that the space on the tabletop surface is regarded as virtual space, and the movement of a doll in real space is mirrored by the virtual object. Marco's work used the tabletop only to detect tangible object operation; our system, on the other hand, in order to provide users with richer functionality, uses the tabletop interface as a touch interface as well as the environment for detecting tangible object operation.

IMPLEMENTATION

System Configuration

The proposed system supports three users working simultaneously through the use of a touch panel and a tangible object, as shown in Figure 2. The users sit around a tabletop interface. In theatrical production planning, users must be able to engage in cooperative discussion; therefore the input interface is a tabletop interface suitable for cooperative work. From this, our system employs MERL's DiamondTouch table [7] which detects a user touching the surface with a capacitance sensor. When touched, the DiamondTouch detects not only the location of the touch, but also the user who touched it. The screen displaying the virtual stage is placed at one side of the table to allow all the users to see it. Dolls representing actors are placed on the tabletop to model the theatrical space and serve as tangible interface whose position, direction, and type are detected by the table. By using these dolls, along with operation windows that are projected on the table, users reproduce an actual stage and plan a theater production, as shown in Figure 3.

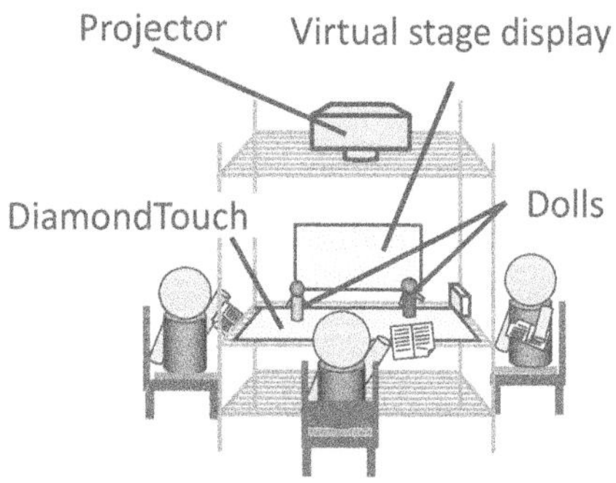

Figure 2. System architecture

Real Object Recognition

Tangible interaction bridges the gaps between cyberspace and the physical environment [10]. The DiamondTouch system has been used in some research, but not together with a tangible interface. In order to use a tangible object on the table, we have developed a real object recognition method that utilizes capacitance sensing, which is a feature of the DiamondTouch system. By sensing conductive metal plates attached to the bottom of an object, the system detects object operation on the table. Electrodes in a grid pattern are embedded in the DiamondTouch's surface at 5 mm intervals. When users touch the surface, the touch position is determined from the change

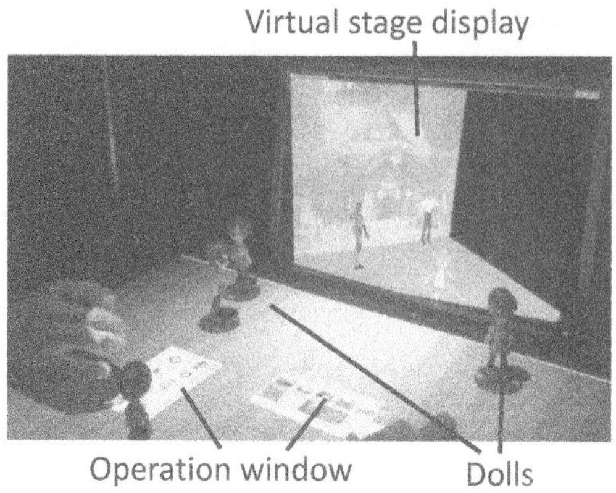

Figure 3. Aspect of actual work

in capacitance at each point on the electrode grid. By utilizing this feature, this object recognition method detects the object's position, direction, and type.

In this research, the dolls used to represent the actors are the tangible interface components. Three metallic plates (the Base Plate (BP), the Identification Plate (IP), and the Direction Plate (DP)) are attached to the bottom of each doll in a double-layered arrangement, as shown in Figure 4(i). The bottom of the doll is coated with conductive spray. When the users place dolls outfitted with these plates on the DiamondTouch unit's surface, the system detects the electrical signal from only the DP and the IP. When users place the dolls on the table, the system detects their type depending on IP shape and IP size. In addition, the system also detects their orientation in eight directions that depend on the positional relation of IP and DP. In order to prevent false recognition caused by the positional relation between IP and the electrodes arranged at intervals of 5 mm, the IP's size must differ in increments of 1 cm. In this system, we prepared two types of IP shapes: perforated and imperforated. Figure 4(ii) shows three cases of the expected value of the sensing electrodes when the same size IP is detected. As seen in this example, each IP shape has marked differences in the detected electrical signal, allowing the system to distinguish between them. In addition, by utilizing the shape of the sensing electrodes, which depends on the positional relation between IP and DP, the system detects eight directions for each doll, as shown in Figure 4(iii).

The limitation of this method is that each IP must differ in increments of 1 cm. The maximum number of the dolls concurrently detected by the DiamondTouch table is 20, and it becomes approximately 12 in light of the dolls' movement on the table. In actual theatrical performance, however, the case that more than 12 actors simultaneously act on the stage is unusual (we counted the number of the actors appeared in each scenario registered in [3], which stores 2670 scenarios in total, and brought out that the number of the actors is 12 or less in 2531 scenarios of them), therefore we think our recognition method is enough to support theatrical production planning.

To develop this object recognition method, which allows to use actual dolls as tangible interface on the DiamondTouch table, has an important advantage in our research to support multiple users working to plan a theatrical production. By achieving this, the following two system features are concurrently actualized: the system feeds back individual information for each user by utilizing the DiamondTouch's feature to detect who touches the table; and the system contributes the intuitive operation to control the virtual stage linked with the real-space mini-stage by moving the actual dolls.

Coordination of the Tabletop Interface and Virtual Space

This system aids intuitive operation by linking the virtual stage to the mini-stage arranged on the tabletop. This subsection describes how the coordination is achieved. In this research, Java3D was used to create the virtual space.

Linkage between real and virtual objects

This system uses the above object recognition method to tie virtual object movement to the information obtained from the tangible object operation on the tabletop. In Java3D, an intricately shaped virtual object consists of simple virtual object polygons that are controlled as one object. Each object has a "TransformGroup" class that allows users to operate the object's movement. Relaying the real object information to this TransformGroup class enables the operation of the virtual object's movement. The real object's movement on the tabletop is reflected by the virtual object's horizontal movement in virtual space. The virtual object's vertical movement is not enabled in this system because we do not consider midair operations on the DiamondTouch. The method employing the TransformGroup class for virtual object movement is also used to move the virtual camera to check how the stage appears from different viewpoints.

Virtual object rendering

Intricately shaped virtual objects are generated in Java3D by combining polygons that must each be specified in the virtual space coordinates by the user. However, that work is too cumbersome to generate a virtual object that depicts an actor, which requires a high level of detail. In this research, virtual objects created with Metasequoia [2], a software program specialized in generating 3D graphics, are made available in the virtual space created by Java3D. The intricately shaped virtual objects created with Metasequoia also consist of polygons. By adjusting these polygons to the coordinates of the virtual space, the system allows the virtual object created with Metasequoia to be used in the Java3D virtual space. In this way, this system assists users by allowing intricately shaped objects to be used to model the actual theatrical space, without placing undue burden on the user, even in the Java3D virtual space.

Creation of the virtual space

The proposed system allows the straightforward operation of virtual stage design by reflecting the touch operations on the tabletop. Because the virtual stage reproduces the same space as the tabletop-mounted mini-stage, the aspect ratio of the virtual stage is identical to that of the tabletop surface. The system coordinates the real object's movement to the virtual object's movement at an equal movement-to-distance ratio, thus allowing users to work intuitively.

Function for Reproducing Production Elements

This system supports multiple users working to plan a theatrical production by assisting them in visualizing the entire theatrical stage through mini-stage and virtual stage models.

Three users are in charge of the stage: the stage director, the stage effect department head, and the sound effect department head. Each user performs their functions in an operation window intended for the exclusive use of each department, as shown in Figure 5. The system allows all users to conduct doll movement operations. The system immediately reflects all operations conducted on the table to both the mini-stage and the virtual stage.

Through each operation window, each user can conduct the work as follows.

- Director's operation window
  The user in charge of stage direction can move the virtual camera, show the script window, and generate a cue sheet. The virtual camera movement and the cue sheet generation procedures are described below. The script window contains the scene that the users are going to plan. It is possible to select the scene to assign sound and lighting effects by touching the screen directly.

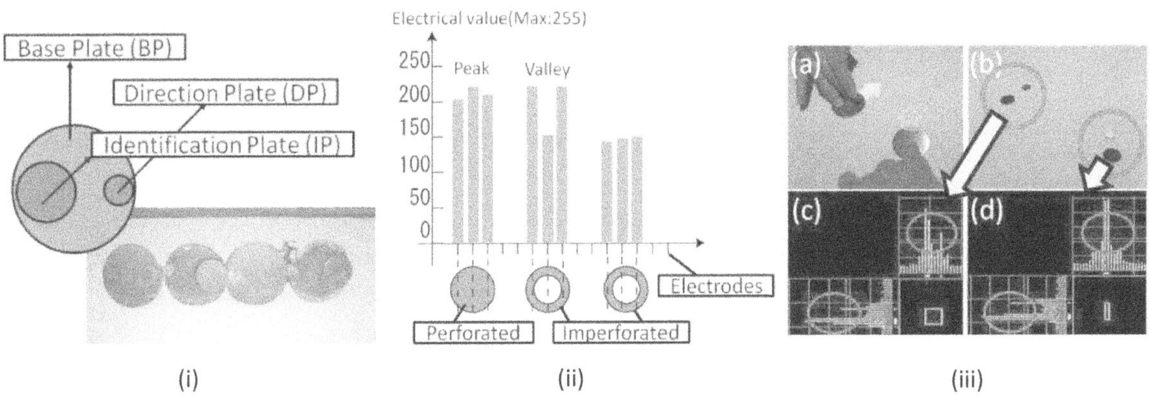

(i) (ii) (iii)

Figure 4. Object recognition method.((i) Double-layered structure with three plates. (ii) Three cases of the expected electrical signal from the sensing electrodes for a particular IP. (iii) Direction recognition of (c) upper right and (d) up. Different arrangements of electrodes allow detection of the object similarly to this case.)

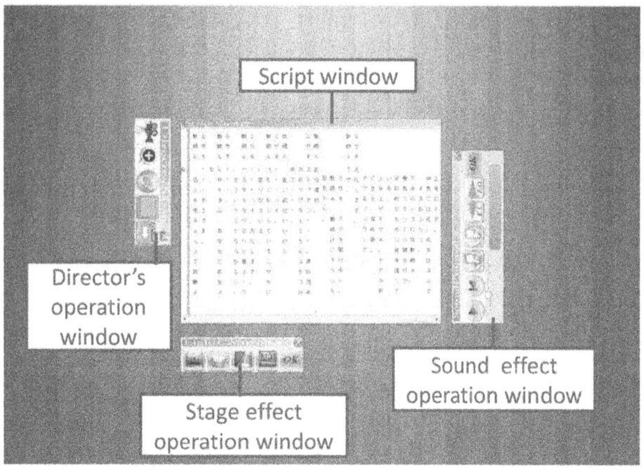

Figure 5. Operation windows displayed on the tabletop

- Stage effect operation window
  This window allows the user in charge of stage effects to reproduce the design of the stage, the stage backdrop, the global lighting effects, and the spotlight. These operations are instantly reflected to both the mini-stage and the virtual stage, with the exception of the backdrop, which the mini-stage cannot reproduce. For the stage design and the backdrop, the user simply selects items from a list and they are reproduced. For the lighting effects, the user is able not only to reproduce the lighting position, but also to control its brightness and color. With the spotlight feature, the user can select the doll to focus the light on by touching the doll directly. In addition, the user is able to assign lighting productions to a selected scene.
- Sound effect operation window
  The user in charge of sound production can control such aspects as playback, volume level, and fade-in and fade-out effects. As with the lighting effects, the sound effects are able to be assigned to a selected scene.

All users are allowed to operate the dolls. When users move a doll on the mini-stage, a virtual object corresponding to it follows it on the virtual stage.

Function for Multiple Users' Simultaneous Work

By using the DiamondTouch table which can detect who touches where, the proposed system automatically feeds back the individual information and reduces frictions in multi-user's task. For instance, when each user first touches the tabletop, only the unique user's operation window appears automatically at the contact location in an easy-to-understand state. In addition, each role's operation window allows the use by the user in charge of the same role. This function reduces the friction occurred in multi-user's task, such as "a sound effect user touched the stage effect window by mistake, and the plan designed by a user in charge of stage effect has disappeared". By these functions, multiple users can conduct their work simultaneously.

Functions for Using the Virtual Space

The following describes the usage of the virtual space that is linked to the table-mounted real space:

Reproduction of stage effects

With this system, a virtual stage that immediately reflects the users' manipulation of stage effects helps users perceive the entire theatrical stage. The virtual stage is able to reproduce various effects that are not able to be reproduced in real space, such as costumes and backdrops. Therefore, it is easier for users to imagine the theatrical stage when compared to working only with a mini-stage displayed on a tabletop.

Operation of the movable virtual camera

Operating a movable virtual camera assists users in considering various viewpoints of audience members while planning a theatrical production. The virtual camera's functions are to move to defined points (center stage, stage left and right, and overhead), zoom in and out, and fine adjustment of the camera angle. Figure 6 shows the same virtual stage viewed from four viewpoints adjusted with the virtual camera.

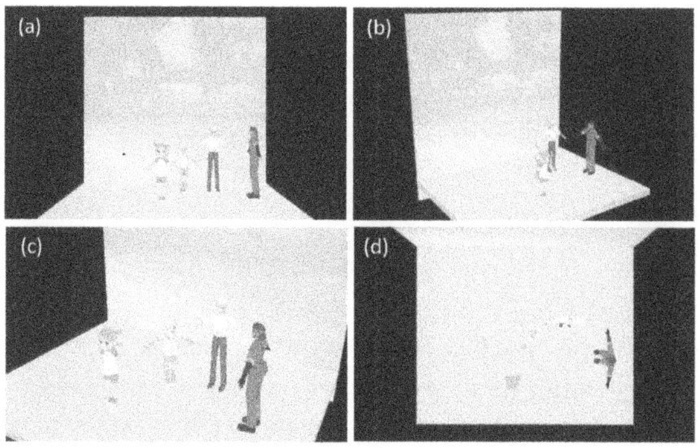

Figure 6. Examples of the operation of the movable virtual camera (each image is from a viewpoint of (a) center stage, (b) far stage left, (c) near stage right, and (d) overhead)

The operation of the virtual object

On the virtual stage, the positions of the actors can be controlled by all the users by moving the dolls placed on the mini-stage. As previously described, when users move a doll on the table, the system detects the doll's position, direction, and type, and then immediately reflects those data in the virtual object. Figure 7 shows the operation of the virtual object. As shown, the system reflects the intuitive operation of the real object in the virtual object, thereby assisting users to work with ease while operating in virtual space. In this system, we prepared four dolls to operate on the mini-stage, and prepared four virtual objects to correspond to the dolls.

Automatic Generation of the Cue Sheet

After the users' planning work is complete, the system automatically generates the sound and lighting cue sheets by organizing the production information input by the users. The sound cue sheet indicates information on each sound in the production, including the title, effect, volume, start and end scenes, and fade-in and fade-out. The lighting cue sheet shows information for each lighting effect in the production, including the lighting type, brightness, and color. Figure 8 shows an example of a sound cue sheet. Information for each sound production element is expressed by visualizing the effects in graph form; the volume is expressed by the graph's height, fade-in and fade-out are indicated by

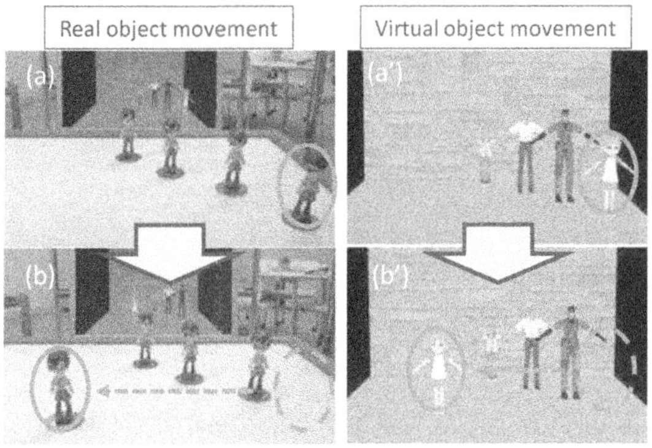

Figure 7. Virtual object movement linked to the physical object

the graph's slope, and the start and end scenes are shown at the appropriate times linked with the scene cell under the graph. Therefore, the generated cue sheets have an easy-to-understand format.

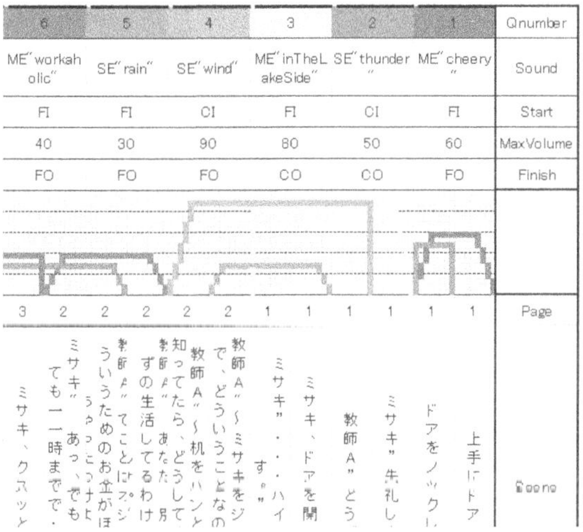

Figure 8. Example of the sound cue sheet

EXPERIMENTATION

We conducted a user study to verify whether the proposed system assisted multiple users to work cooperatively in planning a theatrical production. The most important objective of the proposed system is to assist multiple users in creating and sharing the production elements for the entire theatrical stage by reproducing the actual stage on a mini-stage and virtual stage. Therefore, this study investigated the system's contribution to the work required to model an actual theatrical stage. In addition, a questionnaire was given to all participants to evaluate the system's ease of use.

Memorizing the Layout of the Theatrical Space

Users memorize the theatrical layout more reliably if they have a clear perception of the stage. In this study, the participants actually planned theater productions for prepared scenarios using the proposed system and the previous system. Next, without these systems, the participants answered questions about the productions they had previously planned for the prepared scenario. To answer the questions, the participants had to rely on the image of the theatrical stage they memorized while working with the system. Then, we determined the differences in users' ability to memorize the theatrical stage layout between the two systems.

Groups of two participants cooperatively planned a theatrical production. The two scenarios (scenario A and scenario B) for which the participants planned productions were downloaded from a scenario download service [3]. To allow for a fair comparison, the two selected scenarios had the same length and number of actors. We selected five scenes from each scenario that we thought it would be easy to visualize, calling them "planning production scenes". The participants planned the production for these scenes.

The comparative environments in this study are the two cases that follow:

- The proposed system
  The theatrical stage is reproduced through both a virtual stage created by CG and a mini-stage displayed on a tabletop. Operating the tabletop interface and the four dolls as the tangible interface objects is allowed. All the production elements used in the study are able to be reproduced with the system.
- The previous system (The prototype of the proposed system which used Diamond Theater [19] as a reference)
  The theatrical stage is reproduced only through a table-mounted mini-stage. Operating the tabletop interface and the four dolls representing the tangible interface are allowed. The backdrop design and the virtual camera functions are not included in this system.

When planning, each participant performed a separate task, such as designing the stage effect or the viewpoint. The participant in charge of stage effects was tasked with determining the stage design, the backdrop design and the global lighting, including brightness. The participant in charge of the viewpoint was tasked with determining the best viewpoint, including the virtual camera angle and distance from the stage, from which to view the stage in each scene, to confirm that the participants could visualize the entire theatrical stage. Both participants worked together to determine the dolls' positions and directions. The participants wrote down the production plans point by point on a sheet that we prepared. After planning each scenario using the two system environments mentioned above, the participants again answered questions about the production that they had planned for each "planning production scene" without the systems.

In this study, we compared the rate of agreement between the production plans and the participants' answers. When the agreement rate was higher, we evaluated that the system assisted users more effectively to visualize the entire theatrical stage while planning their theater productions. There were 18 participants, of which 3 had experience in theater. To reduce the effect of habituation on the results, when planning productions half of all participants began with the proposed system before moving on to the previous system, while the other half began with the previous system before moving on to the proposed system.

Experimental Procedure

The participants followed the following procedure.

1. *Reading over the scenarios*
To plan their productions with the general theme of the whole scenario in mind, the participants read over the entire scenario before the experiment. Before this work, the "planning production scene" had already been specified.

2. *Planning productions*
The participants conducted their theater production planning in pairs. Before the planning began, the participants received instruction on the functions of the system, and were able to try out the system. Next, to plan their productions, the participants visualized the theatrical stage by actually reproducing the stage. During this time, the participants collaboratively planned a theater productions, even for production elements of which they were not in charge. Participants wrote down their production plans on the sheet prepared for planning the production of each scene. This sheet was used as an answer key later when the participants were quizzed about their production plans, but we did not tell them the purpose of the sheet. After the first experiment, the participants exchanged roles with their partners, and planned another scenario using the other system environment. In this way, all participants were able to experience both stage effect design and viewpoint design. These works were recorded to investigate differences in their behaviors between two conditions.

3. *Answering production plan questions and the questionnaire*
After production planning, the participants again answered questions about the productions planned in the *Plan productions* phase through their recollections of the theatrical stage. In this work, the participants relied on their memory of the theatrical stage image memorized in the planning phase, and answered questions individually to prevent discussion with other participants. The participants selected from a list of images to answer questions about stage design and backdrop design, and used only their memory to answer other production questions. To confirm that the participants had visualized the entire theatrical layout, the participants answered questions about all production elements, including the productions elements handled by their partner. In addition, to verify that the participants correctly visualized the theatrical stage, three images that did not exist during the planning phase were added to the list of stage design images, and six were added to the list of backdrop design images. The production answers were checked against the production plans, and judged to be correct if the two production elements matched. After answering another set of production questions, the participants completed a questionnaire to verify the system's ease of use and freely commented about the proposed system.

Results

Figure 9 shows the correct answer rate results from the questions answered in phase 3. The correct answers are organized in terms of system environment and production type. The stage effect category includes the virtual camera angle, the virtual camera distance to the stage, stage design, backdrop design, lighting color, and lighting brightness. To these results, we conducted the t-test. We found a significant difference between the system environments in each production element ($t(17) = 2.62, p < 0.05$ in case of the actor's position, and $t(17) = 2.13, p < 0.05$ in case of the stage effect). Because this result shows that the participants' memories of the theatrical stage were clearer when using the proposed system, the proposed system is more effective in assisting a user's visualization of the theatrical stage when compared with the previous system.

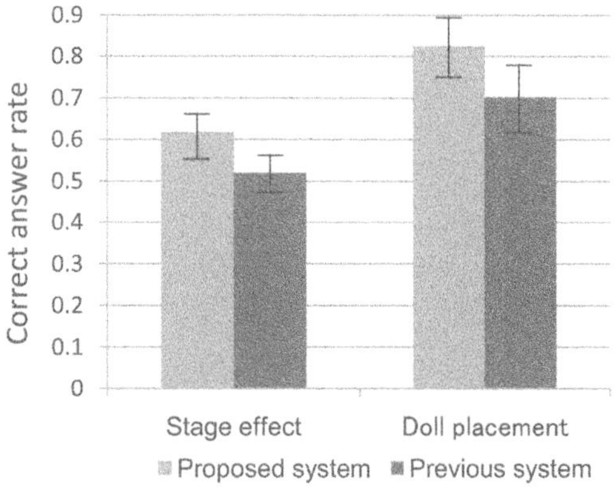

Figure 9. Correct answer rate sorted by production element (N=18)

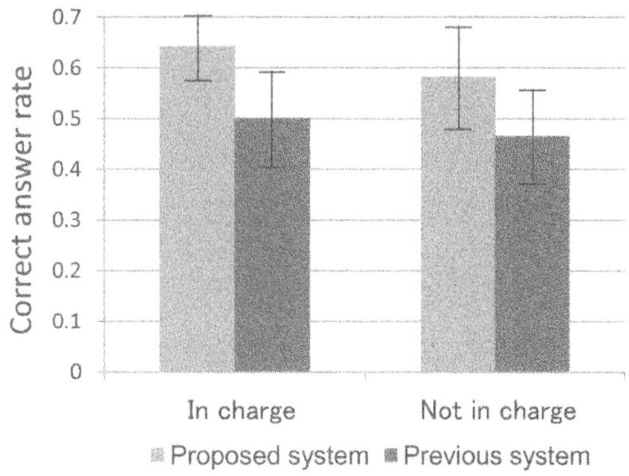

Figure 10. Correct answer rate sorted by whether the user was in charge of the production element

However, this result does not validate the assertion that production elements that are not handled by the participants become easier to visualize. The proposed system aimed to assist users in visualizing the entire theatrical layout including all production elements, even those from the departments of other users. Figure 10 shows the correct answer rate results sorted into the categories of production elements handled by the user and production elements not handled by the user. A significant difference ($t(17) = 2.17, p < 0.05$) between the proposed system and the previous system was found for production elements that the user handled, and a marginally significant difference ($t(17) = 1.85, p < 0.1$) was found for another case. This result shows that the proposed system assisted users to visualize the theatrical stage regardless of whether the participants handled the production elements.

Therefore, the proposed system aids multiple users in planning theatrical productions cooperatively by facilitating the users' visualization of the entire theatrical stage through the reproduction of various production elements.

The questionnaire (5-point scale; 5, "strongly agree") results are shown in Table 1.

Table 1. Questionnaire results

Question	Average
Operation of the virtual object was easy	4.2
Operation of the virtual space was intuitive	4.6
Multiple users' work was not cumbersome	4.8
Compared with the previous system, the viewpoint of the audience was considered	4.2
Compared with the previous system, the actual stage was easier to visualize	4.6
Compared with the previous system, other users' operations were understandable	4.6
Compared with the previous system, this system was helpful to plan productions	4.4

From the video, we found that behaviors of participants when using the proposed system differ from those when using the previous system. The differences we found in this study are as follows;

- When using the proposed system, the participants tried and checked up more production elements by actually reproducing many elements in the virtual stage.
- When using the proposed system, most of the participants' communications in the work were conducted while seeing the screen displaying the virtual stage.
- When using the proposed system, the participants sometimes spoke as an actor they controlled while planning a theatrical production.

DISCUSSION

From these results and some user comments, we discuss how the proposed system affects their work focusing on the following points;

- Support for individual task visualizing an actual stage
- Assist to collaboratively plan a theatrical production

First, how the proposed system assists users working to visualize an actual theatrical stage is discussed.

The questionnaire results shows the "*Compared with the previous system, the viewpoint of the audience was considered*" and the "*Compared with the previous system, the actual stage was easier to visualize*" received a high evaluation.

We think these are because enriched reproducible theater production elements are provided from the proposed system that uses the virtual theatrical stage. A user comment—he/she could visualize the actual stage situation clearly by checking the virtual stage which provides various theatrical elements—also describes the richness of the usable productions is helpful for the task. For instance, with "sand" selected as the stage design, the associated image became "the beach" when "ocean" was selected as the backdrop design, and the associated image became "the precincts of a shrine" when "shrine gate" was selected as the backdrop design. It became difficult for users to visualize a space that contained the backdrop, stage design and lighting elements without reproducing them.

The intuitive operation of the virtual stage, which is linked with the miniature stage reconstructed on the tabletop interface, is also important function for the task to visualize an actual stage. Because the virtual theatrical stage is easy to use, users frequently reproduce the ideas of theatrical production and then they visualize an actual stage more clearly. An example behavior found was "*When using the proposed system, the participants tried and checked up more production elements by actually reproducing many elements in the virtual stage*". In addition, from the one of the behaviors found that is "*When using the proposed system, the participants sometimes spoke as an actor they controlled while planning a theatrical production*", we found that the participants improved their ability to empathize with actors.

Secondly, we discuss about how the proposed system supports multiple users working collaboratively.

Although some previous research about theatrical production planning [1, 4, 13, 18, 23] is intended for single user's task, to support multiple users' work is required for planning a theatrical production because theater involves various theatrical elements. The questionnaire results show that the questions of "*Multiple users' work was not cumbersome*" and "*Compared with the previous system, other users' operations were understandable*" received high marks.

This is because, we think, sharing of each user's idea of theatrical production element is promoted by carrying on the task while constantly seeing the virtual stage which is a shared output space of each. This is also indicated by the users' behavior that is "*When using the proposed system, most of the participants' communications about planning production were conducted while seeing the screen displaying the virtual stage*". From this, users are facilitated comprehension of other users' idea, and then are enabled to plan a theatrical production while considering other users' work. A user comment—users came to give their views on another user's work and to take into account harmony with another elements—indicates that the collaborative work in planning a theatrical production was facilitated by the proposed system. Conversely, with the previous system, they were difficult to make consideration of other users' work because users could hardly express and share their ideas of theatrical production elements, such as the virtual camera position and the stage design.

In this experiment, most of the participants were those who had not had experience in theater. Therefore, it is conceivable that the frequency of using the virtual stage was increased because they could hardly visualize an actual stage in their head without any system. If the experts conduct this task, they might use the proposed system for different purpose with the beginners.

CONCLUSION

In creative activity in theater, production team members are required to create a vision of the entire stage and design theatrical production elements while engaging in cooperative discussions with members from different production departments. In planning a theatrical production, however, it is difficult to work cooperatively because visualizing the entire stage that includes various production elements and sharing ideas are difficult activities to accomplish.

To support multiple users working cooperatively to plan a theatrical production, this paper proposed the system that reproduces an actual stage in two spaces: the mini-stage presented on a tabletop interface and the virtual stage, which is linked to the mini-stage and reflects actions occurred on the mini-stage in real time. By actually reproducing each user's ideas of various production elements in two spaces, the system helps users to visualize the entire theatrical stage and share their ideas with others. Through the evaluation experiment and discussion, we verified that the proposed system assists multiple users in working cooperatively to plan a theatrical production by helping them create and share a vision of the entire theatrical stage.

Acknowledgments

This work was supported in part by a Grant-in-Aid for Scientific Research(B), 2011, 23300049 from the Ministry of Education, Culture, Sport, Science and Technology in Japan, and Research Projects of Graduate School of Library, Information and Media Studies, University of Tsukuba.

REFERENCES

1. Matrix3. `http://www.meyersound.com/products`.
2. metaseq.net (in japanese). `http://www.metaseq.net/metaseq`.
3. Script download service (in japanese). `http://www.haritora.net/script.cgi`.
4. WYSIWYG (in japanese). `http://www.castlighting.com`.
5. S. Asakura. *A to Z of the Theatrical Space (in Japanese)*. PARCO Ltd, 1986.
6. O. d. Bruijn and R. Spence. Serendipity within a ubiquitous computing environment: A case for opportunistic browsing. In *Proc. of UbiComp 2001*, pages 362–370. Springer-Verlag, 2001.
7. P. Dietz and D. Leigh. Diamondtouch: a multi-user touch technology. In *Proc. of UIST 2001*, pages 219–226. ACM.
8. C. Dompierre and D. Laurendeau. Avatar: A virtual reality based tool for collaborative production of theater shows. In *Proc. of CRV 2006*, pages 35–41. ACM.
9. D. Harry and J. Donath. Information spaces – building meeting rooms in virtual environments. In *Proc. of DHI EA 2008*, pages 3741–3746. ACM.
10. H. Ishii and B. Ullmer. Tangible bits: towards seamless interfaces between people, bits and atoms. In *Proc. of CHI 1997*, pages 234–241. ACM.
11. M. Kato. *The Task of Stage Direction (in Japanese)*. Rekuramu Ltd, 1999.
12. R. Kruger, S. Carpendale, S. D. Scott, and S. Greenberg. How people use orientation on tables: comprehension, coordination and communication. In *Proc. of GROUP 2003*, pages 369–378. ACM.
13. M. Lewis. Bowen virtual theater. In *ACM SIGGRAPH 2003 Web Graphics*, pages 1–1. ACM.
14. J. Marco, E. Cerezo, S. Baldasarri, E. Mazzone, and J. C. Read. User-oriented design and tangible interaction for kindergarten children. In *Proc. of IDC 2009*, pages 190–193. ACM.
15. S. Mischke, F. Goetz, R. Hinn, and T. Hampel. steam3d: bringing together virtual communities and cscw. In *Proc. of Web3D 2007*, pages 169–172. ACM.
16. Y. Nakamura and T. Hirano. The educational significance of the creation of drama -through the analysis of the practice of integrated learning, "the project of creative drama"- (in japanese). In *Bulletin of Tokyo Gakugei University, Division of Comprehensive Educational Science I, 61*, pages 57–71, 2010.
17. J. Rekimoto and M. Saitoh. Augmented surfaces: a spatially continuous work space for hybrid computing environments. In *Proc. of CHI 1999*, pages 378–385. ACM.
18. M. Slater, J. Howell, A. Steed, D.-P. Pertaub, and M. Garau. Acting in virtual reality. In *Proc. of CVE 2000*, pages 103–110. ACM.
19. T. Takeuchi, K. Watanabe, T. Inoue, and K. Okada. Diamondtheater: A system for reproducing theater and supporting creative activities. In *Proc. of HCI 2009*, pages 416–425. Springer-Verlag.
20. Y. Taki. *The Fundamental Knowledge of Theatrical Stage Design (in Japanese)*. Rekuramu Ltd, 2005.
21. P. Tandler, T. Prante, C. Müller-Tomfelde, N. Streitz, and R. Steinmetz. Connectables: dynamic coupling of displays for the flexible creation of shared workspaces. In *Proc. of UIST 2001*, pages 11–20. ACM.
22. K. Terakawa, M. Ura, T. Naka, M. Yamada, M. Endo, S. Miyazaki, and T. Yasuda. A tabletop interface for manipulating 3d human model (in japanese). In *The Institute of Image Information and Television Engineers, Vol.34, No.25*, pages 63–66, 2010.
23. Q. Wu, P. Boulanger, M. Kazakevich, and R. Taylor. A real-time performance system for virtual theater. In *Proc. of SMVC 2010*, pages 3–8. ACM.

Exploring Passive User Interaction for Adaptive Narratives

Stephen W. Gilroy, Julie Porteous, Fred Charles, Marc Cavazza
Teesside University, School of Computing
Middlesbrough, TS1 3BA, UK
{s.w.gilroy, j.porteous, f.charles, m.o.cavazza}@tees.ac.uk

ABSTRACT
Previous Interactive Storytelling systems have been designed to allow active user intervention in an unfolding story, using established multi-modal interactive techniques to influence narrative development. In this paper we instead explore the use of a form of passive interaction where users' affective responses, measured by physiological proxies, drive a process of narrative adaptation. We introduce a system that implements a passive interaction loop as part of narrative generation, monitoring users' physiological responses to an on-going narrative visualization and using these to adapt the subsequent development of character relationships, narrative focus and pacing. Idiomatic cinematographic techniques applied to the visualization utilize existing theories of establishing characteristic emotional tone and viewer expectations to foster additional user response. Experimental results support the applicability of filmic emotional theories in a non-film visual realization, demonstrating significant appropriate user physiological response to narrative events and "emotional cues". The subsequent narrative adaptation provides a variation of viewing experience with no loss of narrative comprehension.

Author Keywords
Passive interaction, interactive storytelling, physiological, entertainment computing.

ACM Classification Keywords
H.5.1 [Multimedia Information Systems]: Artificial, augmented, and virtual realities.

General Terms
Design, Experimentation.

INTRODUCTION
In Interactive Storytelling (IS) the goal is the development of systems whereby the evolution of a narrative and its presentation to a user, typically through the use of 3D graphics, are influenced in real-time by user interaction. Most approaches have assumed that users will want to *actively* engage with the interactive system. This can be seen in systems such as Façade [23], where users actively take on the role of a dinner party guest; FearNot! [4], where users take on the role of an "invisible friend"; and Gunslinger [15], where users are immersed in a virtual environment. However, another paradigm would consist of seamlessly adapting the (unfolding) of the narrative to the perceived user experience.

Considering a user's affective experience allows a richer interaction with an IS system, tapping into the empathic processes leveraged in films, games and plays. Game-like interactive experiences are commonly utilized when integrating affective concepts, with notions of "playing" a character or intervening like a ghost, manipulating the characters' interactions to affect their emotional relationships [7]. The challenge is to utilize techniques that draw on filmic properties in ways that preclude traditional interactivity, in order to create compelling affective experiences that also allow consideration of the consequences of emotional responses.

We propose that one way of achieving this is *passive* interaction, whereby implicit indicators of affective responses can be used to adapt narratives and 3D visualizations in such a way that they foster diverse affective and empathic experiences within an IS system. Filmic emotional theories such as those proposed by Smith [34] and Tan [35] appear to give credence to this approach using cinematographic techniques on film, and the success of 3D animation such as *Toy Story* clearly suggests that being computer-generated does not preclude the elicitation of affective experience [17]. Smith proposes "emotional cues" that prime viewers into accepting certain prototypical conceptualizations of film-based affective experiences, and we reason that translation of cues and cinematographic techniques into an adaptive 3D visualization and interactive narrative can be facilitated by passive interaction techniques that allow us to assess the consequences of such priming.

IUI'12, February 14–17, 2012, Lisbon, Portugal.

In this paper we outline a framework for capturing certain forms of affective responses of users of IS systems accessible through physiological signals, passive and undirected, and translating them into concepts that can form the basis of an IS system which adapts narratives compatible with translation of cinematic experiences into non-filmic 3D graphics. For example, two easily captured physiological measurements, surface electromyography (EMG) and galvanic skin response (GSR) signals can be interpreted as indicators of users' affective response [5, 19, 32] to realizations of emotional "cues" in an IS system. Responses that indicate increases and decreases in physiological arousal are used to inform appropriate narrative progression and pacing. Valenced affective responses identify potential empathic relationships between viewer and characters, and the combination of both used uncover the most effective way to present a story, in order to foster additional responses in the viewer to provide a rich empathic and affective experience.

Our approach to passive interaction has been fully implemented in a prototype system, called PINTER (Passive INTERaction). The system is presented here, along with initial experimental results with real users. PINTER features a medical drama (*Arztserie*) as a narrative setting, chosen because it is a popular genre that has been shown to elicit audience reactions to both dramatic events and character relationships (for example, the television series ER [6]).

RELATED WORK

In the area of entertainment computing, and video games in particular, there has been considerable recent interest in the use of physiological input. For instance, physiological signals have been interpreted as an indication of users' emotional state and used to trigger reactions [31], taken as a indicator of user interest in order to increase game-play challenge during periods of relative inactivity [1], and used for continuous modeling of user emotions during game interaction [22].

User studies have demonstrated the potential for "physiological games" [11], brain-computer interaction as an added modality in game design [26], truly affective video games [12] and user preference for direct physiological control in games [25]. In addition, it has been shown that skin conductance level can been used to predict user actions in games [20]. However, most computer games remain essentially task-based, the player needing to achieve specific objectives and/or complete discrete "levels". We posit that this constant user involvement and the resultant emotional response may be of a different nature than is found in IS—one that is more task and performance related and less aesthetic. In the area of IS user emotions can arise more readily from the filmic aspects rather than the task-

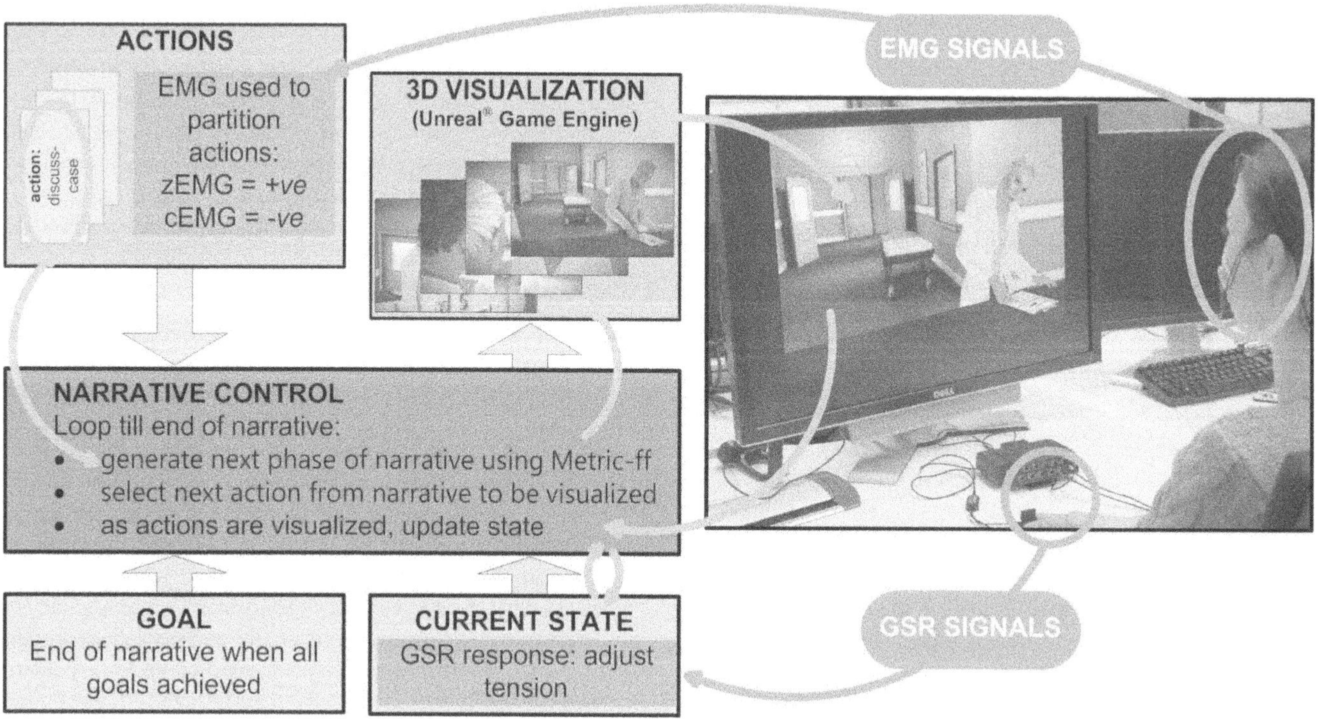

Figure 1. Overview of Passive Interaction in PINTER. An inner narrative control loop incrementally selects actions for the narrative based on the current actions, goal and state of the narrative world. They are visualized using 3D graphics and the state of the world updated to reflect the result of visualization. The users' physiological responses to the visualized narrative, measured using EMG and GSR, are fed back to the module controlling narrative generation. Positive (negative) EMG response indicates user preference (dislike) for certain actions while GSR response triggers change to the current state of the tension level.

challenge one, exhibiting a different pace to that found in games, where progress is always user-driven.

A number of approaches have emerged to identify the characteristic properties of films that match the viewer's affective experience. ELVIS [24] used a range of physiological data to categorize the most effective film summaries (by a combined *entertainment value* measure), using moving average samples of physiological data, in a unified temporal model.

In IS, story dramatization can influence both affective response and story understanding via information presentation. As an example, Jhala and Young developed an approach for building camera directives for 3D animations of a sequence of story events [16]. Their motivation was to convey "dramatic effects", which appear to be a type of affective conceptualization, through the use of a subset of Van Sijl's [36] cinematic conventions (concentrating on camera shot-based approaches). The results of their experiments showed a significant effect of the choice of shot on viewer comprehension.

Of those IS systems that feature some element of user interaction, they all adhere to the same interaction paradigm which requires the user to actively engage with the system, through the use of established multi-modal interactive techniques. For example, the anti-bullying application, FearNot! [4], and the interactive dramas Façade [23], Thespian [33], Gunslinger [15] and EmoEmma [7] all require *active* participation on the part of the user.

The starting point for our work was to challenge this dominant IS paradigm, according to which user interaction is active and the objective for our work was to explore the potential for passive interaction in interactive narratives. Our working hypothesis being that users' physiological responses to a narrative and its presentation can be used to drive narrative adaptation and evolution.

SYSTEM OVERVIEW

Figure 1 gives an overview of the passive interaction system implemented in PINTER. At the start of an interactive session the narrative control component selects initial narrative content and style parameters for presentation to the user, using real-time 3D visualization. This narrative control loop continues until a narrative end-point is reached, incrementally adjusting the next part of the narrative at each step according to the user reaction. Internal variables are constantly updated to reflect changes to characters, plot and so on as the narrative unfolds. Users are equipped with EMG and GSR sensors as an interaction device while watching the interactive narrative, which feed information back to the narrative control component to determine the way in which the narrative evolves, in terms of both its content and presentation style, thus interaction is incorporated in an affective "loop".

GSR has been shown to be a correlate of human arousal and has a quick response (onset of 1.0 to 3.0 seconds) with a longer decay period (returning to a baseline over several seconds), thus events that induce arousal will have a reinforcing effect, and also events widely spaced will not impact on arousal affect. This property is used as a reflection of the pacing of the narrative, judging when the level of narrative tension has been successfully raised, when it should be released to avoid over-saturation, and when more dramatic/different events are needed for a better arousal response. The key passive response evaluated in PINTER was the attempt to match user arousal with a cyclic pattern of narrative tension, by increasing the narrative tension level in response to sustained low levels of physiological response from the user and to decrease the narrative tension level if sustained high levels of user response are detected.

EMG information is a more instantaneous response than GSR and it does not have a decay component. The EMG information is used to partition the action set as an indication of user preference: positive user responses to narrative actions leads the system to prefer those actions and negative responses leads the system to avoid them. PINTER uses a model of congruency; repeated similar responses to categories of actions increase or decrease the perceived preference for that type of action.

The success of the affective loop, shown in Figure 2, relies on the ability of the system to trigger appropriate physiological responses through the narrative that is presented, interpret the physiological responses of the user and use them to adapt the presented narrative in ways that appropriately reflect the user responses. These are discussed in the following sections.

INDUCING PHYSIOLOGICAL RESPONSES

As mentioned in the previous section, the affective loop in PINTER requires appropriate techniques for inducing user physiological responses in a passive filmic context. Our

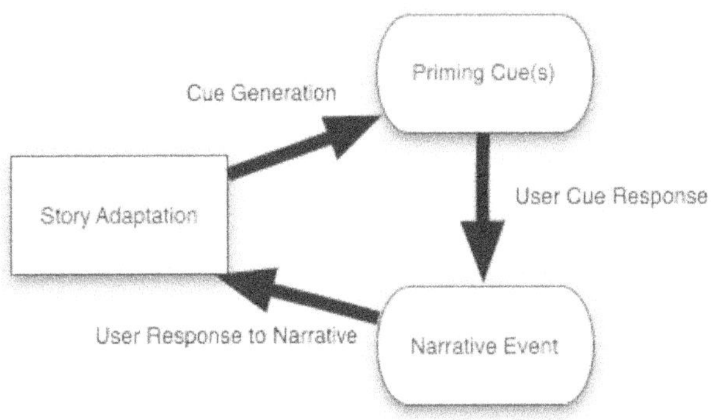

Figure 2. "Smithian" affective loop. Cues are generated to foster an emotional "priming" response using a variety of filmic techniques. This enhances the affective reaction to key narrative events. Cues and events can be combined narrative actions, or cues can stand alone.

Table 2. Example action and goal. The action preconditions specify the required tension level and relative status of the doctors in order for this action to be selected for a narrative. The dimensions intensity and dominance are set to high for use during visualization. One effect of the action is to show more of the doctors' relationship. The goal specifies the amount that must be shown about the doctors' relationship.

Action	Goal
(:action confrontation :parameters (?d1 ?d2 - doctor ?l location) :precondition (and … (≥ (tension) high)) (boss-of ?d1 ?d2)) :effect (and … (= (intensity) high) (= (dominance ?d1 ?d2) high) (increase (shown-relation ?d1 ?d2) 1)))	(:goal (and … (≥ (shown-relationship benton macnair) 5)) (…))

proposed method is inspired by Smith's emotional filmic theory [34]. Smith relates emotions to the narrative structure of films and placed emphasis on style of presentation in particular. He further argues that the emotional loop is made of multiple (and redundant) mood-inducing emotional cues, which make the viewer more likely to interpret further cues on the basis of their current mood. According to Smith it is the emotional associations provided by non-diegetic aspects, such as the mise-en-scène, cinematic idioms, color, sound, lighting and music that are crucial to triggering these filmic emotions.

Smith's theory was developed for film and not 3D graphics but our expectation was that such emotional cues would also be applicable in such a non-filmic context. Consequently we designed PINTER to utilize affective filmic principles, inspired from Smith's theory, in order to show that the theory did transfer to this context.

So that the narrative generation component of the PINTER system was able to reason about affective information, our earlier plan-based approach to narrative generation [28] was extended to include these aspects. The resulting modified narrative generator featured an implementation of the planner Metric-FF (chosen since it can plan with numeric values, a useful feature for handling physiological responses and tension levels). In adopting a plan-based approach we are following the dominant approach in IS, although taking a weaker representational stance on modeling narratives as plans. With this approach the planner generates narrative actions that can be staged in various ways according to the affective loop and affective categories. As an example, in PINTER's narrative setting of a medical drama, the actions include a confrontation between doctors resulting from pressures of work. The effects of this action include showing the viewer something of the doctors' personalities, their relationships, the working atmosphere, and so on.

The system maintains an explicit representation of the current narrative tension level and uses this to select actions

Table 1. Mapping of mood dimensions to cinematic techniques.

Dimension	Cinematographic Technique
Intensity	shot distance, lighting, point of view shots, pacing of cuts between shots environmental atmosphere, and music
Dominance	relative character position and camera angle
Menace	camera angle and lighting
Suspiciousness	camera angle, shot distance and character demeanor

and presentation style, which means that different categories of actions are brought in and out of consideration depending on the current tension level. For example, higher tension story line segments in PINTERs' medical narrative might include conflict between characters, deception, confrontation and tragic consequences for patients, whereas less dramatic story line segments could feature professional conduct, a calm hospital atmosphere and support amongst colleagues. Goals can relate to the resolution of patient cases or ensuring that aspects of a characters personality, relationships and medical style have been shown to the audience. This still ensures the existence of a baseline story, possibly made of emerging sub-plots to do with patient cases and relationships between staff, rather than a simple juxtaposition of events based on their dramatic properties. The action in Table 2 has the effect of showing something of the relationship between doctors and hence contributes to the goal shown in the table.

The actions for our medical interactive narrative were modeled to include non-diegetic aspects inspired by Smith's description of emotional cues [34] and idiomatic cinematographic techniques as discussed in [3, 37]. The action set included both *narrative* actions, which contribute to the goals of the narrative and *non-narrative* actions, which make no narrative contribution and act solely as emotional mood cues. In order to induce different levels of physiological response in the narrative the effects of actions included non-diegetic information that could be used during the visualization of the action. This information was expressed using a number of mood dimensions of relevance to the hospital domain. These dimensions were labeled Intensity, Dominance, Menace and Suspiciousness and the way they were mapped to cinematographic techniques during visualization is outlined in Table 1. Figure 3 illustrates the use of some of these cinematographic techniques in a number of narrative segments of different levels of narrative tension.

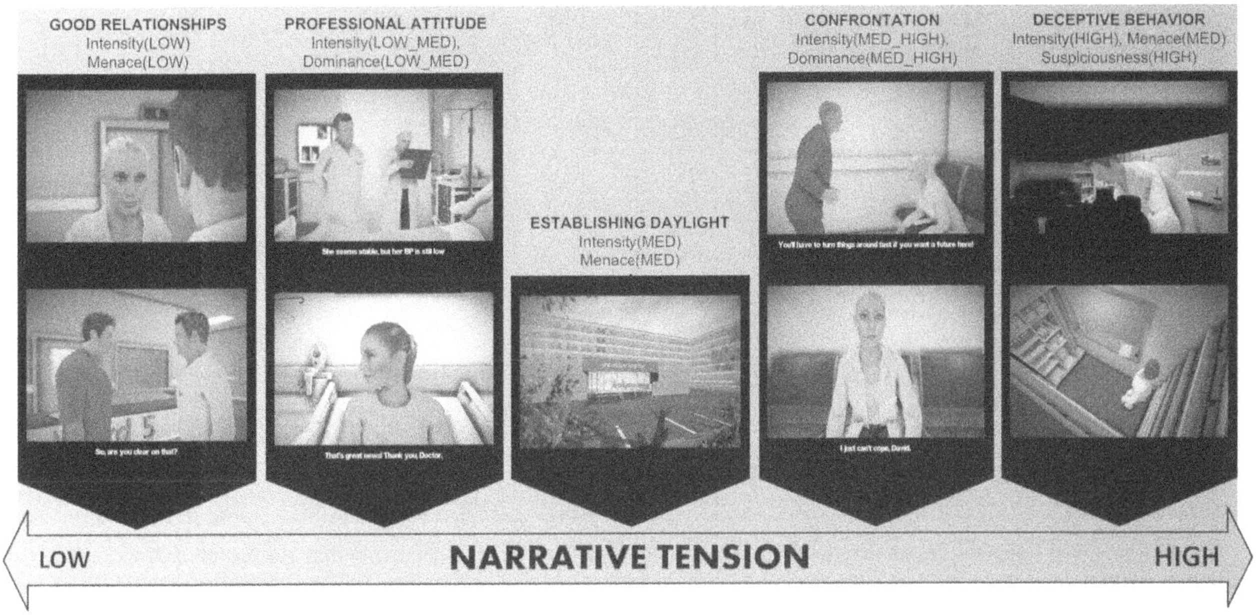

Figure 3. Example cinematic idioms applied to the hospital drama visualizations. PINTER reasons about the current level of narrative tension and selects the next segment of the narrative accordingly. It sends the narrative action along with relevant mood dimensions for visualization. For example, the high tension segment to do with deceptive behavior utilizes dramatic camera angles, lighting and character demeanor to heighten emotional cues.

PASSIVE INTERACTION AND PHYSIOLOGICAL RESPONSE

It is clear that *film* has the potential to engage viewers in a wide range of affective experiences, and creators use techniques such as those described earlier to foster empathy for characters and emotional investment in narrative development, without explicit intervention from the viewer.

We define Passive Interaction (PI) as all interaction with a system not performed intentionally through a dedicated input device. In traditional computing settings this might incorporate data from motion sensing, eye-tracking, facial recognition, and more. An application of this is as side-channel information to facilitate better experience in other interactions [14]. Certain ambient computing applications take up the idea of passive interaction in domestic and entertainment settings, where explicit sporadic inputs might break a viewer's engagement, suspension of disbelief, or concentration on other tasks, so they rely on extra "back channels" of information from the user. Of particular relevance to the system described in this paper are instances where responses are affective in nature as we are interested in utilizing mood- and emotion-based filmic characterizations. Game-like interactive scenarios come with a pre-conceived expectation of explicit interaction, to the point where periods of inactivity in games (i.e., cut scenes), are being subverted to restore an interactive experience [8]. It also has been suggested that these breaks in interactivity are still needed to invoke particular emotional engagement that involves low-arousal affective patterns [38], a feat ably performed in a filmic setting. In Entertainment Computing installations, and more latterly, domestic applications such as television, multi-modal affective information not directly related to interaction can be used to characterize the empathic viewer response to the experience. This can range from detection of implicit, uncontrolled emotional expressions (especially of an Ekmanian type) to explicit expressions of affective response to an experience [21].

Physiological signals appear an ideal candidate for an input in passive interaction system, being always available, and obtainable without further direct action on the part of the user. "Lean back" experiences, as found in traditional filmic settings, avoid problems associated with physical activity, talking or other interactions interfering with the recording/collection of physiological data. With PINTER we aim to show that such signals can be used effectively to implement passive interaction for movie-like experiences in interactive media.

Temporal Properties of Physiological Data

Previous uses of physiological data as compound proxies of affective response have integrated a variety of signal types into a single processing model. This includes conceptualizing physiological input in terms of the temporal properties of emotions and mood [22, 24]. Generally, physiologically-based systems are aiming to re-construct a discrete emotion within a window of consideration of input.

The two types of physiological input used in PINTER are the two most strongly associated with dimensions of

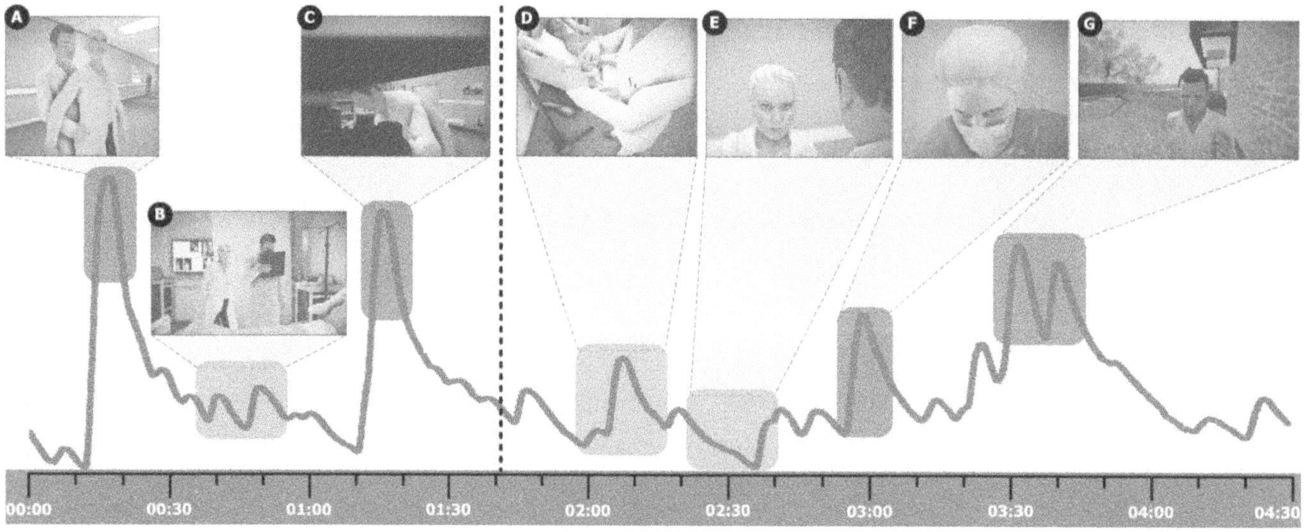

Figure 4. Physiological Response to the Interactive Narrative. A GSR signal trace is shown in blue representing the users' arousal response to narrative tension. The left-hand side of the trace shows an expected response following an alternation of higher and lower tension actions: `harass-colleague` (A), `introduce-patient` (B), `get-treatment-deceptively` (C). On the right-hand side is shown further adaptive behavior when GSR response does not increase following intended high tension events `give-treatment-deceptively` (D) and `confront-behavior` (E). PINTER adapts the story to include more high tension narrative actions, with more dramatic events, and GSR response picks up again, with `emergency-treatment` (F) and falling back into a cycle of tension with one last dramatic peak as the antagonist doctor attempts to `run-away` (G).

affective response—GSR for arousal and EMG for positive and negative valence in the *zygomaticus major* and *corrugator supercilii* muscles in the face, respectively [5, 27]. GSR is associated with a changing overall level of arousal (skin conductance level or SCL), as well as short-term changes (skin conductance responses or SCRs). These changes are not instantaneous, but have an onset of 1.0-3.0 seconds (allowing for a SCR magnitude of sufficient level to establish) and return to baseline over a number of seconds. This can be contrasted to EMG, where there is always a low level of electrical activity in muscles, but activation events occur immediately, either as spikes or bursts of electrical activity much greater than the baseline level [2].

With PINTER, instead of a single compound temporal rationalization of physiological input, we are utilizing these divergent temporal properties of EMG and GSR input to distinguish between the medium- and long- term properties of dramatic tension and pacing and the more immediate positive and negative affective response to particular types of scene or shots. Adding more physiological signals to the interaction does not necessarily guarantee a better conceptualization of true affective response to the experience. For instance, Heart Rate correlation to arousal and valence aspects of emotion is both less clear-cut and less significant as well, and furthermore, its response time does not fit well in this division of labor between EMG and GSR, with too much lag and required processing for instantaneous responses, but too much inconsistency over longer periods of time for long-term tension assessment (due to naturally varying non-affective physiological demands).

Galvanic Skin Response to the Interactive Narrative

PINTER uses SCR magnitude and frequency to calculate an arousal measure over a 30 second moving window. More SCRs of a higher magnitude indicate a higher level of arousal. We have developed an algorithm to detect SCRs in real-time without needing baseline measures. This avoids the need to handle drift in baseline SCL; these can otherwise be hard to detect when considering SCL only. The rationale behind this adaptation was the avoidance of long periods of sustained levels of arousal (either high or low)—in keeping with following a form of idealized Aristotelian curve over the course of a narrative.

Passive interaction should involve the continuous changing level of the arousal measure matching this idealized pacing curve of dramatic narrative events. If this arousal measure anticipates or lags behind the desired narrative pacing, the planner adapts the narrative actions as described in the next section. PINTER's response to a sustained period of low GSR response to low tension narrative segments is to select narrative content and presentation aimed at raising GSR response and similarly after sustained periods of high GSR response to high tension narrative segments to lower it.

If GSR still does not react in response to opposing tension narrative events, more extreme mood cues are employed and a variety of optional actions are introduced to attempt to find one that restores the natural pacing. Our experiments have shown that variation in narrative actions eventually introduces actions that the user will respond to appropriately. Figure 4 shows an example GSR trace where PINTER is adjusting dramatic tension in narratives in order to manage user arousal levels to match a model of pacing. It can be seen that arousal in terms of GSR activity starts to lag behind the anticipated pacing of major narrative events. This leads to the planner preferring more intense and varied "high-tension" actions that foster a user response and a return to the normative cycle of pacing.

Facial Electromyography Response to the Interactive Narrative

The two EMG physiological signals used in PINTER stand for discrete positively or negatively valenced passive interaction events. We are not employing a unified emotional model, so these events are not associated with an emotion concept other than valence. Higher levels of EMG signal in an event indicate a stronger valenced reaction.

We would expect a strong EMG reaction to certain mood cues within actions, for which EMG signals are used to determine the success of such cues. For the majority of the rest of dramatic narrative we aim to avoid an abundance of negative reactions to narrative events, and EMG signals are interpreted in terms of the congruence of the expected affective responses given the current discourse, and the consistency of these reactions to action categories. In other genres, such as horror, more negative reactions may be a more desirable alignment with the narrative. Therefore, both positive and negative EMG events are taken into account when deciding what categories of narrative events to show (e.g., character development, conversations, patient scenes).

Consistency and strength of EMG reactions determine how strongly preferences to particular categories of action are perceived. For example, if conflicts between characters produced a negative EMG response then the system adaptation would be to exclude this type of action from the narrative unless needed for restoration of pacing. Alternatively if the EMG response was positive then the system would prioritize the selection of this "conflict'" type action over others (e.g., flirting or joking around).

Figure 5 shows an example set of both EMG and GSR measurements against key scenes in an example narrative generated by PINTER. Two strong spikes of *zygomaticus* EMG activity can be seen which are aligned with mood cues within narrative actions and precede subsequent SCRs in the GSR activity, illustrating the difference in temporal nature of the signals.

EVALUATION

We designed a proof-of-concept study to investigate our proposed model of passive interaction. The study involved 23 subjects (7 male, 16 female), aged between 19 and 54, and the aim was to investigate the following properties of the PINTER system:

- Physiological signal levels were of a level and nature greater than random fluctuations watching neutral filmic material. (i.e., that passive interaction is not just an artifact of natural background activity.
- The narrative adaptations provided by PINTER, visualized by idiomatic cinematographic techniques provoked appropriate PI responses even though presented in non-filmic media.
- The narratives produced, whilst diverse, are also causally consistent and understandable to viewers.

Procedure

Subjects were shown 2 minutes of baseline video of a nature scene, of a kind rated as neutral in the IAPS picture set [18], while baseline physiological signal measurements were taken. They were then shown the visualization of narrative generated and adapted in real-time starting from a randomized narrative tension level. The interactive sessions lasted between 235 and 330 seconds, depending on the particular actions shown. Subjects then answered a questionnaire based on QUEST graphs [10, 13], generated from the particular narrative graph produced by PINTER during their interaction.

Physiological signals were normalized against the respective baseline per subject, and GSR measurements

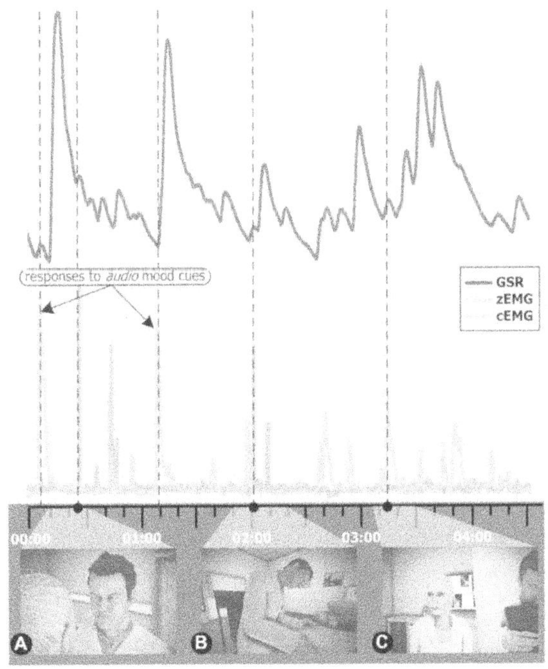

Figure 5. Combination of affective responses in story adaptations. Both zEMG and GSR are "primed" by affective audio cues, but the overriding response to actions `flirt-with-colleague` (A) and `overwhelmed-with-work` (B) are negative (cEMG), with little arousal response. When PINTER selects scenes involving the main patient story (e.g., `reflect-on-successful-treatment-arrogantly` (C)), more positive zEMG and responsive GSR results.

Table 3. Mean test(baseline) EMG activity values in peak/s. Starred values are significantly different from baseline.

Threshold	zEMG	cEMG
Low ($< 20\mu S$)	1.72 (0.51)*	0.79 (0.09)*
Med ($< 30\mu S$)	0.93 (0.28)*	0.21(0.05)*
High ($< 40\mu S$)	0.93 (0.21)*	0.10 (0.03)
Ex High ($< 50\mu S$)	0.48 (0.16)	0.05 (0.02)

were de-trended to remove effect of drifting baseline SCL over an interactive session as a whole.

Physiological Activity Compared to Baseline

GSR normalized means for baseline and test conditions show that test conditions invoke a greater average SCL than a neutral, non-dramatic baseline filmic video. A paired t-test of normalized mean GSR between baseline and test conditions across all subjects showed a significant difference ($p < 0.01$, $t = -8.8, df = 22, s.d. = 0.235$).

Both cEMG and zEMG showed difference in activity level in tests against baseline. In general there was more *zygomaticus* EMG activity than *corrugator* EMG. Mean values don't give much insight into EMG traces, due to the sporadic nature of EMG activity spikes. Instead, EMG was characterized as the number of detectable peaks in a trace, normalized for time, to give a measure of peak/s. This was evaluated at a range of threshold levels from close to the average noise floor to above what would normally be considered a significant detection level of a spike event. Lower thresholds showed better distinction between test and baseline, but obviously included more of the noise. Higher thresholds exclude noise, and still show significant difference (t-test $p < 0.05$) until you get to the highest threshold ($50\mu S$), at which point too many valid peaks are being rejected. This is illustrated in Table 3 (baseline means are in parentheses).

Whole Session GSR

Approximately 30% of whole session GSR across all subjects was matched to cue response, 50% to narrative action and 20% unattributable. This was calculated allowing a 5 second window for response to a cue or action start.

Three examples of tension adaptation to GSR response from the experiment are shown in Figure 6. Adaptation is show as a red curve characterizing the internal tension representation for the actions that were selected. Normative attempted tension response is an alternative of high and low tension. Subject 18 (top) required a sustained high tension level at the mid-point of the session to re-invoke a GSR response. Subject 4 (middle) followed a fairly successful cyclic tension curve and response, although preferences and narrative causality necessitated a period of sustained higher tension between the 2:30 and 3:00 mark. Subject 13 (bottom) involved a slow response to start with, but once the story was better adapted to pacing and preferred actions, user response followed the cycle of tension level, invoking a GSR arousal response during the dramatic finale.

These examples are representative of the kinds of experiences encountered across subjects. Generally response followed higher tension actions, and actions characterized as lower-tension engendered less response. While the characteristic cycle of tension is similar across subjects, the user response and hence experience and adapted narrative can be seen to be very individual.

Narrative Understanding

We also explored how well users could understand the interactive narratives that they viewed. To do this we used the QUEST model whereby narratives are represented as conceptual graphs that can be used to rate the relative quality of comprehension questions [10, 13, 16]. After viewing a presentation of a narrative, users are asked to assign goodness of answer (GOA) values to question-answer pairs and then the correlation with the predicted quality given by the QUEST graphs is assessed. For example, a sample pair from our experiments was:

Q: *What was the outcome for the patient?*
A: *She made a good recovery after initial treatment.*

The GOA of this pair depends on the content of the narrative that was shown to the user, i.e. whether the patient did or did not recover. For each user five questions and five answers were randomly selected from the QUEST model and subjects were asked to rate the GOA for each question

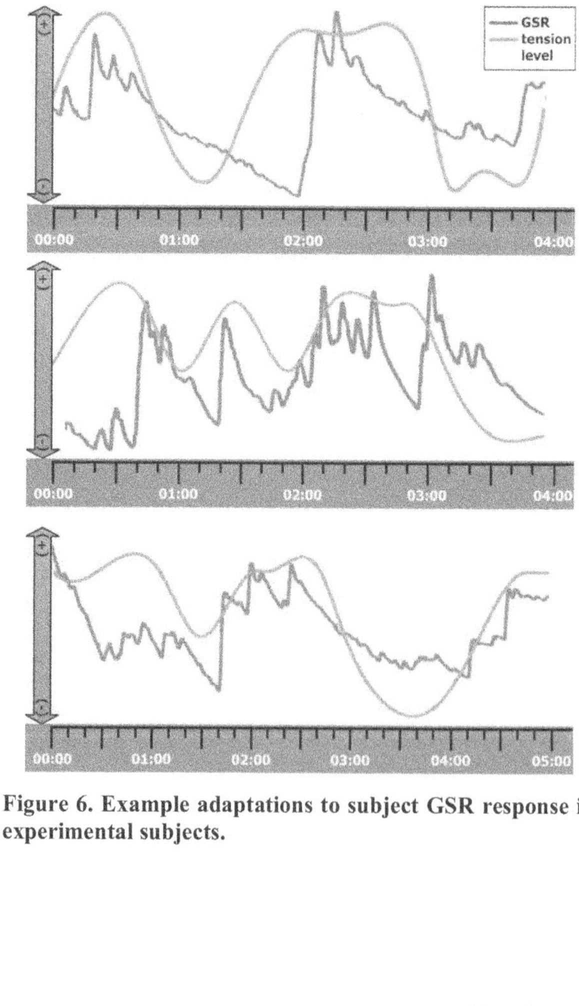

Figure 6. Example adaptations to subject GSR response in experimental subjects.

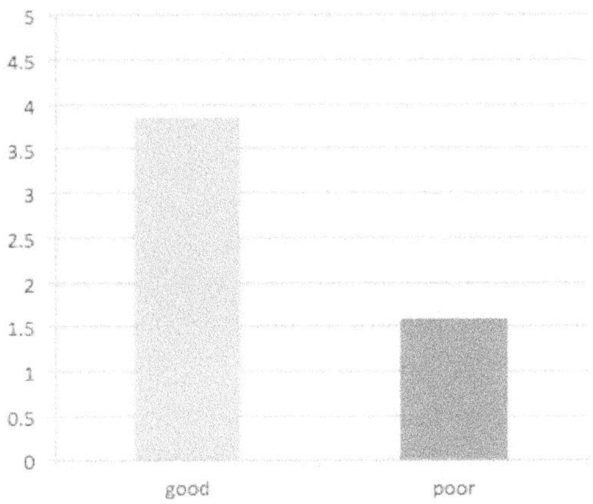

Figure 7. Bar chart showing mean Goodness of Answer for "good" and "poor" question/answer pairs. As expected, poor pairs had significantly lower GOA scores.

with a value from 1 (very bad) to 5 (very good). User responses were compared against measures of reachability and arc distance in the QUEST graph for their narrative. We set expected values for the GOA with 5 (very good) for those with arc distance 1, 4 for those with arc distance 2, and so on, with 1 (very bad) expected for question-answer pairs that were unreachable in the QUEST graph. Riedl and Young [29] partition their question space into "good" and "bad" question-answer pairs, where in a rating system of 1–5 "good" pairs have a system predicted GOA greater than the neutral, and "bad" pairs are those with a predicted GOA of less than neutral. Their general rule of thumb was understandability was indicated if the user scores for "bad" pairs were low and those for "good" pairs were high. For narratives generated by PINTER, it can be seen that this is indeed the case, as shown in Figure 7.

CONCLUSIONS

The motivation for the work presented in the paper was to demonstrate that viewers' physiological responses to the narrative could be used to drive story adaptation in a passive feedback loop. Our expectation was that filmic theories of emotion provided a suitable mechanism to induce physiological responses in viewers, despite being developed for high quality films. To show this we designed an interactive narrative using 3D graphics that featured emotional cues characteristics of these filmic theories.

Our experiments confirmed that emotional cues were applicable in a non-filmic context, with physiological responses to emotional cues significantly over the baseline. In addition to inducing physiological responses we were also able to show that narratives could be adapted on the basis of these user responses whilst preserving viewer story comprehension. This research opens the way to new paradigms for IS that could enjoy better acceptability and avoid the bottleneck of active interaction modalities such as speech and natural language input.

ACKNOWLEDGEMENTS

This work has been funded (in part) by the European Commission under grant agreements IRIS (FP7-ICT-231824) and CEEDs (FP7-ICT-258749). Visual content developed by Matthew Laverick and Catherine Dixon, Teesside University. Story ideas provided by Terry Borst, Santa Fe University of Art and Design. Character models purchased from aXYZ Design (http://www.axyz-design.com).

REFERENCES

1. Ambinder, M., Biofeedback in Gameplay: How Valve Measures Physiology to Enhance Gaming Experience. In *Procs. Game Developers Conference (GDC)*, Citeseer (2011).
2. Andreassi, J. L. 2007. *Psychophysiology: Human Behavior and Physiological Response*. Psychology Press.
3. Arijon, D. 1991. *Grammar of the Film Language.* Silman-James Press.
4. Aylett, R., Dias, J. and Paiva, A., An Affectively-driven Planner for Synthetic Characters. In *Procs. 16th Int. Conf. Automated Planning and Scheduling (ICAPS)*, AAAI Press (2006), 2-10.
5. Bradley, M. M., Codispoti, M., Cuthbert, B. N. and Lang, P. J. 2001. Emotion and Motivation I: Defensive and Appetitive Reactions in Picture Processing. *Emotion*, 1 (**3**), (2001), 276-298.
6. Bradley, S. D. 2007. Examining the Eyeblink Startle Reflex as a Measure of Emotion and Motivation to Television Programming. *Communication Methods and Measures*, 1 (2007), 7-30.
7. Cavazza, M., Pizzi, D., Charles, F., Vogt, T. and André, E., Emotional Input for Character-Based Interactive Storytelling. In *Procs. 8th Int. Joint Conf. Autonomous Agents and MultiAgent Systems, (AAMAS)*, IFAAMAS (2009), 313-320.
8. Cheng, P., Waiting for Something to Happen: Narratives, Interactivity and Agency and the Video Game Cut-scene. In *Procs. Digital Games Research Conference (DIGRA)*, Citeseer, (2007), 15-24.
9. Cheong, Y.-G. and Young, R. M., Narrative Generation for Suspense: Modelling and Evaluation. In *Procs. 1st Int. Conf. on Interactive Digital Storytelling (ICIDS 08)*, Springer (2008), 144-155.
10. Christian, D. and Young, M., Comparing Cognitive and Computational Models of Narrative Structure. In *Procs. Proc. of the 19th Nat. Conf. on Artificial Intelligence*, AAAI Press (2003), 385-390.
11. Fairclough, S. H., Psychophysiological inference and physiological computer games. In *Procs. Brainplay '07: Workshop on Brain-Computer Interfaces and Games. Advances in Computer Entertainment (ACE 2007)*, ACM (2007).

12. Gilleade, K., Dix, A. and Allanson, J., Affective Videogames and Modes of Affective Gaming: Assist Me, Challenge Me, Emote Me. In *Procs. Digital Games Research Conference (DIGRA)*, Citeseer (2005), 16-20.
13. Graesser, A. C. and Hemphill, D. 1991. Question answering in the context of scientific mechanisms. *Journal of Memory and Language*, 30 (**2**), (1991), 186–209.
14. Harrison, B. L., Fishkin, K. P., Gujar, A., Mochon, C. and Want, R., Squeeze hold tilt me! An exploration of manipulative user interfaces. In *Procs. SIGCHI Conf. on Human Factors in computing systems*, ACM Press. (1998), 17–24.
15. Hartholt, A., et al., At the Virtual Frontier: Introducing Gunslinger, a Multi-Character, Mixed-Reality, Story-Driven Experience. In *Procs. 10th Int. Conf. Intelligent Virtual Agents (IVA)*, Springer (2009), 500-501.
16. Jhala, A. and Young, R. M. 2010. Cinematic Visual Discourse: Representation, Generation, and Evaluation. *IEEE Trans. on Computational Intelligence and AI in Games*, 2 (**2**), (2010), 69–81.
17. Joly, J. Can a Polygon Make You Cry? http://www.jonathanjoly.com/front.htm
18. Lang, P., Bradley, M. and Cuthbert, B. 1997. International affective picture system (IAPS): Technical manual and affective ratings. *NIMH Center for the Study of Emotion and Attention* (1997).
19. Lang, P. J. 1995. The Emotion Probe: Studies of Motivation and Attention. *American Psychologist*, 50 (**5**), (1995), 372-385.
20. Laufer, L. and Nèmeth, B., Predicting user action from skin conductance. In *Procs. 13th Int. Conf. on Intelligent User Interfaces (IUI)*, ACM (2008), 357-360.
21. Lee, C.-H. J., Chang, C., Chung, H., Dickie, C. and Selker, T., Emotionally reactive television. In *Procs. 12th Int. Conf. on Intelligent User Interfaces (IUI)*, ACM (2007), 329–332.
22. Mandryk, R. L., Atkins, M. S. and Inkpen, K. M., A Continuous and Objective Evaluation of Emotional Experience with Interactive Play Environments. In *Procs. 24th Int. Conf. on Human Factors in Computing Systems (CHI)*, ACM Press (2006), 1027–1036.
23. Mateas, M. and Stern, A., Façade: An Experiment in Building a Fully-Realized Interactive Drama. In *Procs. Game Developers Conference*, Citeseer (2003), 82.
24. Money, A. and Agius, H. 2010. ELVIS: Entertainment-Led Video Summaries. *ACM Transactions on Multimedia Computing, Communications and Applications (TOMCCAP)*, 6 (**3**), (2010).
25. Nacke, L., Kalyn, M., Lough, C. and Mandryk, R., Biofeedback Game Design: Using Direct and Indirect Physiological Control to Enhance Game Interaction. In *Procs. Conf. on Human Factors in Computing Systems (CHI)*, ACM Press (2011), 103-112.
26. Nijholt, A., Bos, D. O. and Reuderink, B. 2009. Turning Shortcomings into Challenges: Brain-Computer Interfaces for Games. *Entertainment Computing*, 1 (2), (2009), 85-94.
27. Partala, T. 2005. *Affective Information in Human-Computer Interaction*. PhD Thesis. Department of Computer Sciences, University of Tampere, Finland.
28. Porteous, J., Cavazza, M. and Charles, F. 2010. Applying Planning to Interactive Storytelling: Narrative Control using State Constraints. *ACM Transactions on Intelligent Systems and Technology (ACM TIST)*, 1 (**2**), (2010), 1-21.
29. Riedl, M. and Young, R. M., An Objective Character Believability Evaluation Procedure for Multi-Agent Story Generation Systems. In *Procs. 5th Int. Conf. on Intelligent Virtual Agents (IVA)*, Springer (2005), 278-291.
30. Riedl, M. O. and Young, R. M. 2010. Narrative Planning: Balancing Plot and Character. *Journal of Artificial Intelligence Research*, 39 (2010), 217-267.
31. Sakurazawa, S., Yoshida, N. and Munekata, N., Entertainment feature of a game using skin conductance response. In *Procs. Int. Conf. on Advances in Computer Entertainment Technology (ACE)*, ACM (2004), 181-186.
32. Sánchez-Navarro, J. P., Martínez-Selva, J. M., Torrente, G. and Román, F. 2008. Psychophysiological, Behavioral and Cognitive Indices of the Emotional Response: A Factor-Analytic Study. *The Spanish Journal of Psychology*, 11 (**1**), (2008), 16-25.
33. Si, M., Marsella, S. and Pynadath, D. V., Thespian: using multi-agent fitting to craft interactive drama. In *Procs. 4th Int. Conf. on Autonomous Agents and Multiagent Systems (AAMAS)*, IFAAMAS (2005), 21-28.
34. Smith, G. M. 2003. *Film Structure and the Emotion System*. Cambridge University Press.
35. Tan, E. S. 1995. Film-induced affect as a witness emotion. *Poetics*, 23 (**1-2**), (January 1995), 7-32.
36. Van Sijll, J. 2005. *Cinematic Storytelling*. Studio City, CA: Michael Wiese Productions.
37. Vineyard, J. 1999. *Setting up your shots: great camera moves every filmmaker should know*. Studio City, CA: Michael Wiese Productions.
38. Zagalo, N., Torres, A. and Branco, V. Passive Interactivity, an Answer to Interactive Emotion. In *Entertainment Computing (ICEC)*, Springer, (2006) 43-52.

On Slide-Based Contextual Cues for Presentation Reuse

Moushumi Sharmin[1], Lawrence Bergman[2], Jie Lu[2], Ravi Konuru[2]
[1]University of Illinois at Urbana-Champaign, Urbana, IL, USA {sharmin2@illinois.edu}
[2]IBM T.J. Watson Research Center, 19 Skyline Drive, Hawthorne, NY, USA
{bergmanl, jielu, rkonuru}@us.ibm.com

ABSTRACT
Reuse of existing presentation materials is prevalent among knowledge workers. However, finding the most appropriate material for reuse is challenging. Existing information management and search tools provide inadequate support for reuse due to their dependence on users' ability to effectively categorize, recall, and recognize existing materials. Based on our findings from an online survey and contextual interviews, we designed and implemented a slide-based contextual recommender, ConReP, for supporting reuse of presentation materials. ConReP utilizes a user-selected slide as a search-key, recommends materials based on similarity to the selected slide, and provides a local-context-based visual representation of the recommendations. Users input provides new insight into presentation reuse and reveals that slide-based search is more effective than keyword-based search, local-context-based visual representation helps in better recall and recognition, and shows the promise of this general approach of exploiting individual slides and local-context for better presentation reuse.

Author Keywords
Contextual recommendation; slide-based search; local context; visual representation.

ACM Classification Keywords
H.5.2 [Information Interfaces and Presentation]: User Interfaces – User interaction styles, User-centered design, H.3.3 [Information Storage and Retrieval]: Information Search and Retrieval – Retrieval Models, Search process.

General Terms
Design; Human Factors.

INTRODUCTION
Presentation composition is ubiquitous among knowledge workers. One common practice in creating new presentations is to start with an existing presentation [15]. Common reuse tasks include tailoring existing presentations for different audiences, creating summary or overview presentations by collecting materials from several existing presentations, and modifying existing presentations for specific events such as conferences and client meetings. A primary challenge in presentation reuse is selecting the most appropriate material from many similar versions that exist on a user's machine.

Information management systems and search systems are commonly used for locating desired materials [12]. Information management systems facilitate retrieval by utilizing descriptive naming and hierarchical file organization. To access a presentation given in IUI 2011, for example, a user can utilize date (2011) and event (IUI) to identify the desired presentation. However, users often create multiple versions of similar presentations, use similar names to describe them, and often struggle to devise appropriate naming [13].

Desktop search systems primarily rely on user-provided keywords to retrieve desired materials. There has also been prior work on using provenance, activity history, and creation/access times for supporting personal information search [10]. However, effectiveness of these systems depends heavily on what users remember about their materials, which is often difficult to translate into a search query. For example, a user goal such as "find all slides that contain a world-map showing our office locations in green" would be extremely difficult if not impossible to describe using a keyword-based query.

A recent study conducted in a large organization confirmed the prevalence of presentation reuse among knowledge workers and pointed out the need for better reuse support systems, but offered insufficient guidelines for designing such systems [15]. In our research, we aim to gain deeper understanding of user practices and needs surrounding presentation reuse for designing effective support tools. We conducted an online survey (N=108) and a set of contextual interviews with avid presentation users (N=8). We found that users want to reuse, have specific information goals when trying to reuse, follow a specific process when reusing materials, prefer personalized organization of materials over desktop search systems, and express a need for better reuse support tools.

Based on these findings, we postulated that an intelligent assistive interface that supports presentation reuse by exploiting slide-similarity metrics and contextual information will facilitate reuse. To validate this approach and elicit both concrete reuse patterns and user feedback, we designed, implemented and evaluated a contextual recommender, ConReP, for presentation creation tasks. When a ConReP user opens a presentation and selects a

IUI'12, February 14–17, 2012, Lisbon, Portugal.

slide, the system automatically constructs a "contextual search query" by extracting text and images from the slide and uses these in conjunction with presentation attributes to find and recommend relevant slides stored on the user's machine. User feedback on ConReP is positive and indicates the potential of such systems for supporting reuse.

Our work makes the following contributions:

- Identifies specific patterns and challenges in the domain of presentation reuse.
- Presents a slide-based recommendation technique that exploits slide similarity and local context.
- Presents a novel recommender interface integrated into a presentation composition environment, which provides a local-context-based visual representation of the results to support recall and recognition.

In the next section we present related work. We then describe a survey and a set of contextual interviews we conducted to deepen our understanding of presentation reuse. This is followed by a set of system design criteria derived from the study, and a description of the resulting ConReP slide recommender. We present results of an evaluation of ConReP and conclude with possibilities for future work.

RELATED WORK

Existing research poses personal information reuse as a search and retrieval problem, namely "How can we help users to identify the best materials by building systems that assist in their retrieval?" [8]. Research in this area suggests that systems designed to support reuse need to: 1) support users' current practices [15], 2) consider what users remember about their materials to facilitate the search process [21], and 3) create novel representations of the search results to support identification of desired materials [20, 21]. A deeper understanding of users' reuse practices is the first step in designing better reuse support systems. In this research, we investigate how users reuse presentation materials and then design and evaluate the effectiveness of a slide-based contextual recommender for supporting presentation reuse tasks.

Research in the area of personal information management suggests two psychological problems associated with retrieval: difficulties in generating effective categorization and difficulties in remembering the labels that support retrieval [13]. Studies suggest that location, file type, time, keywords, and associated events are the attributes best remembered [3, 7]. However, only a subset of these attributes (e.g., file type and keywords) is utilized by current reuse support systems. In addition to these attributes, visual elements are often remembered [13] and need to be considered, since reuse of visual elements is a key factor in presentation reuse [15].

Search systems provide inadequate support for reuse due to their dependence on user-provided keywords [6, 22]. Researchers have reported that users seldom perform keyword-based search for retrieving materials from their machines [12, 19]; instead, they navigate to their search targets by utilizing contextual knowledge about the desired material [24]. Since users remember the context of use or their experience with items better than keywords, research suggests that systems should utilize these cues in the search process [5, 6]. We believe a natural way to address the problem with keyword-based search is to take a semi-automated approach, in which users' tasks lead to automatic generation of search keywords, an approach adopted in ConReP. Another problem associated with current search systems is users' failure to recall sufficient details about an item by looking at textual search results [6]. To address this problem, we utilize a set of thumbnails from each presentation to create a visual representation of the search results, which not only enables direct access to the desired slides, but also provides context that helps in identifying desired materials.

Systems utilizing semantic document models try to make atomic content units (CUs) such as paragraphs and tables reusable [17], but their success is largely dependent on user annotations of the CUs. These systems also suffer from a lack of connection between the annotation and the content creation tools [12]. While semantic systems such as CPoint mitigate the connection problem by integrating annotation capabilities in the content creation environment [12], they still suffer from users' unwillingness to spend time on annotation that may benefit future reuse [21]. To alleviate these problems, we not only integrate our system in the content creation environment but also auto-compute contextual similarity between contents, requiring little effort from the users to make contents reusable.

Several prior presentation composition systems have enabled comparison between different versions of the same presentation [4, 18, 25]. Other approaches to presentation composition have included outline matching [2], topic clustering [23], and hierarchical organization [1]. Very few researchers have investigated the design of recommender systems to support presentation composition and reuse. We extend this thread of research by investigating the effectiveness of slide-based contextual recommendation for facilitating presentation reuse.

UNDERSTANDING PRESENTATION REUSE

Method

We conducted an online survey to learn about the prevalence of presentation reuse, types of materials reused, frequency of reuse, and sources of reused materials. We also collected information about the individual, social and organizational culture of reuse. We posted the survey link in an internal company mailing list and collected 108 completed responses over the course of two weeks. Survey results regarding individual, social, and organizational aspects of reuse are reported in [15]; here we report additional findings.

Survey
Why do you reuse presentation materials?
What type of materials do you reuse (text, charts, graphs, images, template, etc.)?
How often do you start composing a presentation from scratch and from an existing presentation?
Interviews
What is your process of reusing existing presentations?
How do you find existing presentations (or slides) that you want to reuse?
What types of information and tool do you utilize when you are looking for materials for reuse?
What are the challenges (if any) you encounter during the presentation reuse process?

Table 1. Sample questions from the survey and the interviews.

Following the survey, we conducted semi-structured interviews (N=8) to learn about details of the presentation reuse process, strategies utilized for supporting reuse, and overall reuse experiences. Participants were recruited from different departments of our organization, with different job roles (managers vs. researchers) and varying degrees of presentation reuse (people who reuse frequently vs. people who reuse occasionally). Interviews consisted of open-ended questions focusing on presentation reuse practices, lasted between 30 and 60 minutes, and were audio-recorded. During each interview, we used our questions as a guide, but welcomed tangents. To ground the discussion, we asked participants to walk us through presentations they had recently created utilizing existing materials. See Table 1 for a list of sample questions.

Study Results

Prevalence of Reuse and Reasons for Reuse

Reusing existing presentation materials is common; only 3 out of 108 survey participants reported never reusing presentation content. Participants considered reusing existing materials to be a "natural practice." Repurposing existing content for different audiences, events, formats, etc. are the primary reasons mentioned by our participants for reuse. For example, people modify/update existing content to present to a different audience (retail industry vs. insurance industry), to give the presentation a different look and feel (informal vs. formal, technical vs. general), or to create a summary presentation (by combining materials from different presentations).

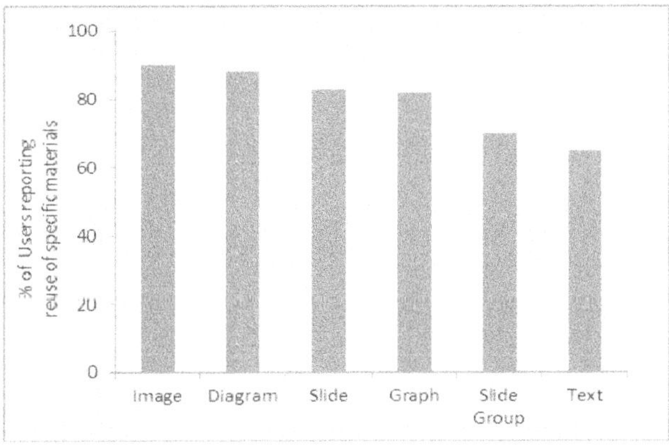

Figure 1. Reuse of different types of presentation materials.

Type and Unit of Reuse

Presentation materials that are often reused include graphical elements (e.g. images, graphs), slides, and text. Presentations are also used as sources of data, and as templates for new presentations. Figure 1, based on the survey, shows reuse of different types of presentation elements. While slides and graphical elements are the most frequently reused units, existing systems offer little support for searching for specific slides or graphical elements. Participants reported trying to collect desired materials from existing presentations by searching for a remembered slide or specific visual elements such as graphs and then locate other needed materials within that presentation.

Process of Reuse

From our contextual interviews, we learned that reuse is a complex and iterative process which often involves overlapping phases of formulating search criteria, searching and browsing existing materials, collecting the needed materials by selecting the most appropriate materials from the search and browsing phase, and finally constructing a new presentation by utilizing the collected materials. Figure 2 presents a diagrammatic representation of the main tasks involved in the reuse process. The success of reuse depends on the quality of the formulated search criteria, the success of finding relevant materials, and finally, the identification of the best available material for reuse.

Challenges in Reuse

Finding the right keywords for search is difficult

Users mentioned formulating search criteria as the most difficult among all phases of the reuse process. All of our interview participants commented on the difficulty of formulating the right keywords, which is nicely summarized by the following quote:

"I have a hard time doing it. I remember 'Oh, I had a slide I remember that looked a little like this'; I can think about this in my head but I can't type-in the right keyword for that, so that's never found. That would require me to remember a lot of keywords." – Participant 4

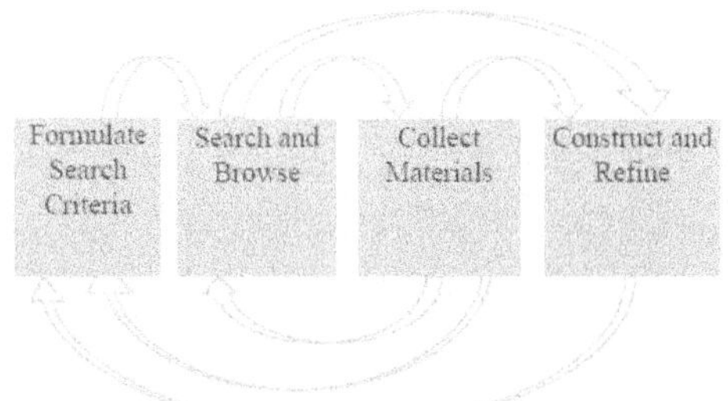

Figure 2. Process of reusing presentation materials.

This difficulty discourages users from utilizing keyword-based search tools for finding relevant presentation materials. Only one out of eight interview participants mentioned occasionally using a desktop search tool when she remembered exactly what presentations she was looking for, but described it as a very difficult process.

Gaining an overview of all relevant materials is time-consuming

Many similar versions of presentations, slides, and slide contents exist; an extremely challenging aspect of the reuse process is the accumulation and exploration of all the different versions of relevant materials. Some interview participants mentioned trying to collect the different versions before the presentation construction phase to gain an overview and to compare the differences between the versions in order to select the best version. Participants felt challenged, since it not only was time consuming but also required them to remember the names and locations of the sought-after materials. Seven out of eight interview participants mentioned that gaining an overview of the available relevant materials is the main challenge in the material collection phase. One participant stated:

"If I get a summarized variation of what I have available, then (a system) already helps me tremendously (in the reuse process)." – Participant 1

Currently, participants open presentations in sequence and browse the slides within each presentation to get a better understanding of the available materials. Two interview participants also mentioned creating "master decks" which contain all desired slides on a topic, but mentioned the difficulty of updating the deck with new materials.

Identifying the most appropriate version is non-trivial

Selecting the most appropriate version of presentation content requires recalling information about the presentation content and recognizing the difference between similar materials. Users reported struggling to correctly identify the most appropriate presentation by only looking at presentation names or thumbnails. Presentations pertaining to the same project often have similar names with content that differs slightly based on the intended audience (insurance industry vs. retail industry), the specific event type (group presentation vs. conference talk), and progression of the project (weekly project status vs. bi-yearly project status). To mitigate the challenges associated with recall and recognition, we observed that all of our interview participants are "satisficing" [22] instead of investing time and effort to identify the best version.

Personalized organization is not an effective retrieval strategy

Users predominantly use descriptive file naming and personalized directory structure when storing their presentation materials. While this behavior is common for other types of electronic documents, the unique characteristic of presentation materials (e.g. the target audience, the event) are often reflected in the directory names and presentation names that users utilize for supporting retrieval. All the interview participants reported using personalized directory and naming schemes to facilitate retrieval. The degree of difficulty associated with such location-based or name-based search and retrieval is evident from the following quote:

"(For retrieval) I use location of file. I just try to remember (where I store it). I try a combination of lot of factors I think. Titles of meetings or projects aren't that much (helpful), I have to remember what I was writing the presentation for, what the meeting was about, that kind of thing." – Participant 7

Another problem with personalized directory structure and naming schemes is that with time the names lose their effectiveness as memory cues. While a name like "speech technology 9-7-2002" indicates that this presentation contains materials regarding to speech technology project(s) and it was created in September 2002, this name does not indicate what type of materials were contained in this presentation, why this presentation was created, and whether there exist other similar presentations about similar topics. Additionally, projects expand, change directions, and new projects emerge that have overlap with past projects. However, the directory names that were used for storing the early presentations are typically not updated to reflect these changes. Presentations also get modified based on the changing direction of the projects, often making presentations stored in the same directory very dissimilar. One interview participant commented on this aspect of organization and the problems associated with this strategy:

"I name my directories meaningfully. But the meaning is never updated, that's the problem. When I start a new project, I create new directory but then the very semantic of the thing (project) changes and it evolves. I don't do any updates of my directory and I create it once and I stick with it. It grows and grows and the taxonomy that I defined in the beginning becomes meaningless as I get deeper into the project and time but I still live with it." – Participant 5

SYSTEM AND USER INTERFACE DESIGN

Design Goals

Based on our findings, we identified the following design goals for a system that facilitates presentation reuse:

1) Support reuse starting from an existing presentation. This is a common practice as shown by prior work [15] as well as our survey and interviews; users more frequently begin with an existing presentation than "from scratch."

2) Support easy identification of the "best" version of any given slide within existing presentations. As noted in our study, finding the best version is of value to users, but challenging with existing tools.

3) Support the user's ability to recognize materials. Users' ability to recognize and recall is enhanced by information

that stimulates their ability to remember the presentation's context such as purpose, audience, and event [3, 5].

4) Support users in easily locating and recognizing additional materials related to a slide in the existing presentation. Our interview findings indicate that users often remember information about co-occurrence of slides or specific materials within a presentation and use a "remembered slide" to gain access to the desired materials.

In support of these goals, we identified several key design features:

1) Slide-based recommendation. As discussed, keyword-based search is difficult for presentation materials. Rather than have the users construct queries, we chose to use the content of slides within an existing presentation as input to a recommendation algorithm. A local database containing information about similar slides and presentations stored on the user's machine is used to produce slide-specific recommendations.

2) Support for visual comparison of recommended slides. For selecting a best version, the user needs to be able to readily compare multiple similar slides.

3) Support for visual presentation of local-context for recommended slides. Single slides, particularly when multiple versions are being presented, are not adequate cues to support users in recognizing and recalling the needed materials. Furthermore, local-context-based representation provides support for finding related materials located nearby within a presentation.

System Overview

We developed the ConReP system to provide slide-level content recommendations. To closely integrate ConReP's recommendations into users' presentation creation tasks, we implemented ConReP as an add in for Microsoft PowerPoint 2003, a widely used presentation editor [16].

Figure 3 shows the architecture of ConReP. It has two main subsystems: a front end containing the ConReP UI and a recommender, and a back end containing two similarity analyzers (content and attribute analyzer), a slide information aggregator, a desktop crawler, and a presentation uploader. The recommender formulates the search query by extracting text and image from the user selected slide and then by accumulating information about the containing presentation (e.g., file attributes). The similarity analyzers match this query against a local database to extract identifiers for other similar slides and associated presentations. These are passed to the slide information aggregator, which collects slide thumbnails from the presentation repository and passes them to the recommender, which creates a visual representation of the recommendations. The desktop crawler is responsible for collecting presentations and their attributes, and for passing them to the presentation uploader and to the attribute analyzer, respectively. The presentation repository extracts

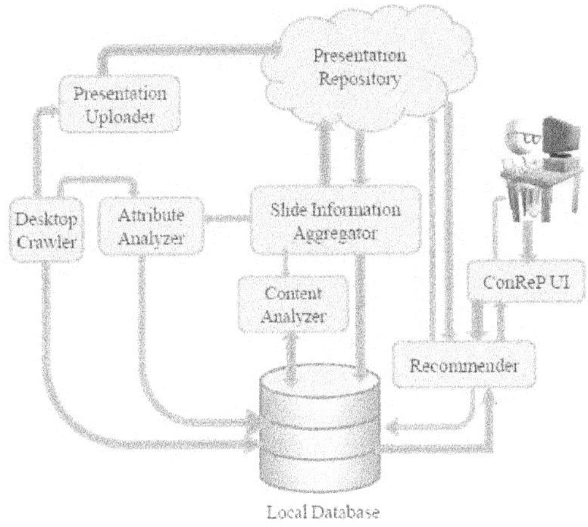

Figure 3. System Architecture.

presentation and slide contents, creates thumbnails of the slides, and passes the slide information back to the content analyzer. The content and attribute analyzers compute pairwise slide similarities and presentation similarities respectively and store the similarity scores in a database. Desktop crawling, presentation uploading, and similarity computations are executed as offline pre-processes.

A ConReP user begins by loading an initial presentation into PowerPoint, then initiates the recommendation process by selecting a presentation slide and clicking a toolbar button (Figure 4(a)). ConReP presents recommendations based on the selected slide in a separate, repositionable, and resizable window, which by default is placed near the slide thumbnails shown in PowerPoint (Figure 4(l)). The recommended slides are displayed vertically as thumbnail images (Figure 4(e)), with the most highly recommended at the top. In addition, each recommendation is flanked by local-context slide thumbnails (Figure 4(f)) – slides preceding and following the recommendation in the containing presentation. By double-clicking on any thumbnail, the user can view a popup window containing a larger slide image (comparable in size to the main PowerPoint slide view). The interface also contains controls to page through recommendation results (Figure 4(d)), as well as local-context slides (Figure 4(h) and 4(i)). Finally, the user can insert any particular slide into her presentation using the "insert" or "replace" control provided in the larger slide window (not shown in Figure 4).

User Interface Design and Preliminary Evaluation

Our study indicated that reuse of slides is common in presentations; any given slide is likely to be present in multiple files. Showing only similar slides (along with presentation name) may be inadequate to allow users to recognize particular versions, and to select the best of them. For this reason, we considered it important to include local context for each recommendation. We use the term "local-context" to refer to a small group of co-located slides from a presentation surrounding the recommendation slide.

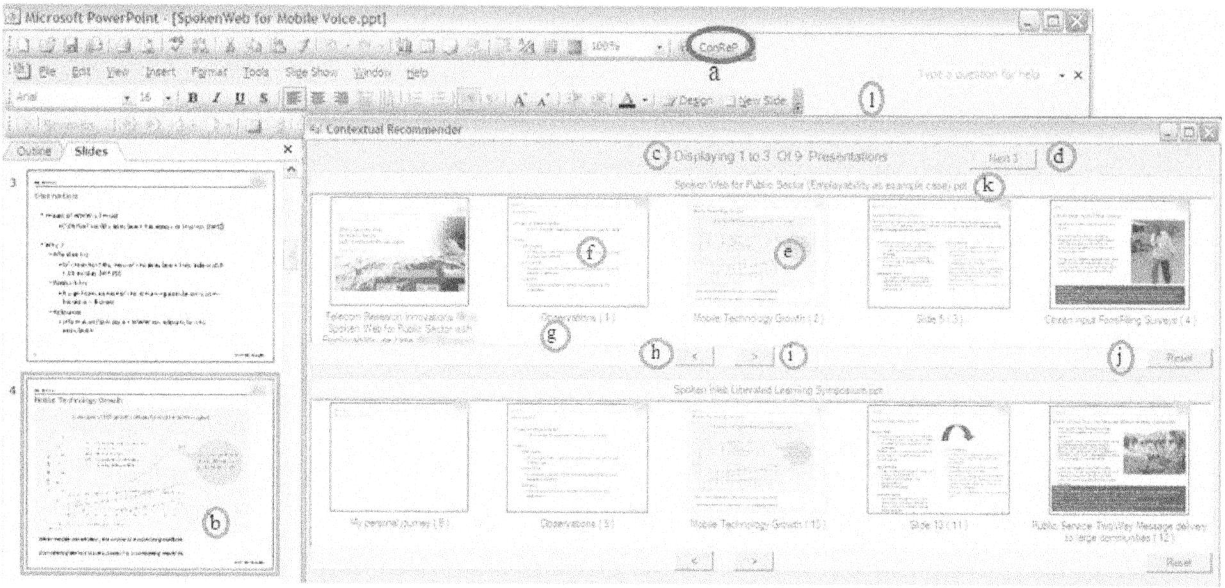

Figure 4. The ConReP system is implemented as an add-in (a) for Microsoft Power Point. User selects a slide from the active presentation (b) and clicks ConReP to view recommendations. ConReP uses a page-based recommendation interface (l) consisting of ranked thumbnail representations of multiple presentations showing - (c) total number of recommendations, (d) control for viewing next group of results, (e) recommended similar slide, (f) local-context slide, (g) slide title and location in presentation, (h and i) controls for navigating to the other slides of the presentation, (j) control for returning to the original recommendation, and (k) presentation title.

An open question remained: how much context is required for recognition, and how to best present that context. To explore this, we developed three initial prototype visualizations, each containing a different level of context. The three prototypes provided minimal-, maximal-, and local-context slides in the recommendation window. The minimal-context interface (Figure 5) shows all relevant slides in one window (one slide per presentation), but allows users to examine the other slides from a presentation on demand (double-clicking the recommendation slide opens another window showing thumbnails for the other slides from the same presentation). The maximal-context interface presents all slides from the relevant presentations in separate scrolling inner-windows, displaying the recommendation slide in the middle (Figure 6).

The local-context interface on the other hand provides a group of neighboring slides from each presentation in separate inner-windows with the recommendation slide highlighted in yellow (Figure 7). In all three interfaces, presentation names and slide titles are displayed to provide more information about the slides and their containing presentations. Providing slide titles also help to differentiate similar-looking text-heavy slides that are relatively difficult to distinguish from the thumbnail representations. We conducted a preliminary design evaluation of these three prototypes (N=5) to investigate the advantage and disadvantage of each prototype. Each participant used all three interfaces with the same set of presentation materials. We counter-balanced interface use to remove order bias.

Figure 5. Minimal-context interface.

Figure 6. Maximal-context interface.

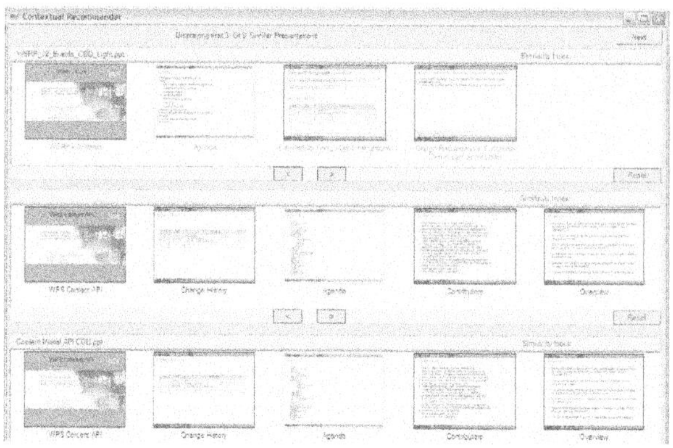

Figure 7. Local-context interface.

All of our participants preferred the local-context interface, commenting that neighboring slides made it easy to differentiate between similar presentations, especially where the recommendation slides were the same or very similar. They also liked this local-context-based interface because it rendered the recommendations faster than the maximal-context interface (due to the smaller number of slides returned) yet at the same time provided access to the slide's context to help them identify different versions. Based on the feedback received, we selected the local-context interface for our final implementation (Figure 4 shows the final design).

Recommendation Algorithm

ConReP recommends slides based on assessment of pair-wise relevance between each slide on the user's desktop and the slide selected in the main PowerPoint UI. We measure relevance between two slides by computing the similarity between the slides' contents and the similarity between their contexts (attributes of the presentation files). Below we describe how to compute each similarity, and how they are combined to determine a recommendation set.

Content similarity is computed based on two components: 1) all text (which includes slide title, bullet text, image captions), and 2) all images included on each slide. Text similarity and image similarity are computed individually for each pair of slides. We utilize a modified version of Levenshtein distance [14] for computing text similarity and Jaccard similarity [9] for images. Details of these similarity measures are reported in [15].

Contextual similarity is computed based on file attribute similarity of presentations. Since user-assigned file names (including file path) often contain important identifying information including event/project name, presentation date, or purpose, attribute similarity is computed using file names. For each presentation, a bag of words was extracted from the fully-qualified (full path) file name. The file name is split on delimiters, including the path delimiter (a slash or back-slash), and other delimiters that users typically include within file names such as periods, dashes, and underscores. The "words" that are obtained by splitting the file name were filtered by removing stop-words. The attribute similarity between two presentations is then computed as the Jaccard similarity between the resulting word bags for the two associated file names. We define the attribute similarity between two individual slides to be the attribute similarity between their containing presentations. As such, attribute similarity is calculated only once for each pair of presentations.

An overall similarity score is computed for each pair of slides on the user's desktop (a desktop crawler is utilized to find presentations and extract slides). The overall similarity score is the normalized sum of the text similarity, image similarity, and attribute similarity scores. Since each of the component similarities is in the range of [0, 1], overall normalization is accomplished simply by dividing by three. The pair-wise similarities are filtered to retain only those with a value greater than 0.5, and the resulting pairs (including slide identifier and associated presentation identifier for each pair of slides, and the overall similarity score) are stored in a local database.

Recommendations are produced by retrieving all database records containing the slide identifier of the slide selected by the user from the PowerPoint interface. This gives us the slide identifiers and the identifiers of the containing presentations for each slide similar to the query slide. The retrieved records are sorted in descending order on similarity score. The list is then filtered to ensure that only a single slide (the one with the highest similarity score) is retained from each presentation. Since our UI permits navigation to any slide within a presentation, we felt that ensuring each presentation was included only once would minimize confusion. Each slide retained in the recommendation list is enhanced with the presentation name, and a set of local-context slides. The list is presented to the user, 3 presentations at a time, in order of relevance.

EVALUATION

Our evaluation of ConReP (with the local-context interface) explored how well we met our design goals, and how well the system supports typical reuse behavior.

Method

We conducted a lab study with six users, all employed in a large organization. We recruited participants with a variety of job responsibilities – marketing directors (2), senior managers (2), and research scientists (2). We selected participants who described themselves as "avid presentation users" and affirmed their reuse practice as "extensive reuse, reusing own presentation materials for creating new presentations more than 50% of the time." We focused on participants meeting this criterion as we believe that they are likely to benefit most from a presentation reuse support system. Each of the study sessions lasted about an hour and was structured as a discussion about current reuse practice followed by a short system briefing, a presentation creation task, and finally, a post-interview. Prior to the lab session, we collected a set of presentation materials from each participant (20 presentations on average) for use during the session. These materials allowed us to simulate the effect of a personal presentation recommender system.

The goal of the system briefing was to inform participants about the functionality offered by ConReP. Next, we asked them to create a presentation similar to any of their existing presentations, but to repurpose it for a different audience (as mentioned earlier, for each participant a set of presentations was stored in the study machine). We chose this task because our survey and interview results indicated repurposing existing presentations for a different audience as the most common reuse scenario. Participants were encouraged to think-aloud during the presentation creation process. We concluded the session with a post-interview in which we asked participants to share their opinions about the search process, the quality of the recommendations, the effectiveness of the interface design, and their overall opinion of the system. We also asked what features they liked and disliked and any missing features they would like included in the system. We audio and video recorded each session. The video recordings were intended to capture interactions with ConReP, use of different features, and any system errors. The audio recordings (both the think-aloud comments and the interviews) were transcribed and later analyzed using a thematic analysis approach.

Results

Overall Opinions

Table 2 presents a summary of our participants' opinions about ConReP as a contextual recommender using a 5-point Likert scale. Four out of six participants mentioned that they are very interested in continued use and they see themselves using this system a lot (they also gave it a 5/5 in terms of overall rating and interest in continued use). The remaining two participants gave it 4/5 mentioning that they would use it on a regular basis (average score = 4.67/5.0).

Prior to the study, four out of six participants were interested but hesitant about the usefulness of an automated presentation recommender, one commenting that such systems "may not be intelligent enough to recommend anything useful." However, after using ConReP for the presentation creation task, their opinions were changed. While using the system our participants used words such as "Nice!", "Excellent!", "Great Idea!" and "Impressive!"

Users found the interface engaging and were impressed with the recommendations offered (average effectiveness of recommendation = 4.16/5.0). Five out of six participants spent most of their time exploring recommendations for a number of different types of slides (text-heavy, graphic-heavy, slides with graphic and text, slides with a single image, slides with multiple images, etc.). They also compared the slides they selected and the recommended slides while speculating the algorithm behind the recommendation. One user was "pleasantly surprised" to see two recommendations that were visually different but were created to convey the same information. Participant 1 who had concerns about the quality of automated recommender, stated:

"I am very surprised to see how well this system works for (recommending) graph-heavy slides." – Participant 1

Metric	Average Score
Overall rating	4.33
Interest in future use	4.67
Interpretability of presented information	5.00
Local context supporting recall	4.83
Recognize different versions of presentations	4.67
Relevance of recommendation	4.17
Ease of locating material within presentation	4.17
Identify different versions of similar materials	3.83

Table 2. Opinion about ConReP as a contextual recommender (Using a 5 point Likert-Scale).

All participants liked the visual representation, commenting that "the representation seems natural and intuitive." All six participants also considered the representations easily interpretable, all giving it 5/5 in the post-study questionnaire. To quote a participant:

"It's nice, it's very nice. I think what I like is the visuals, you know for slides it has to be a visually oriented operation, so I can view all the matches and context. I think this is the right idea." – Participant 6

Participants were also able to identify the different versions of similar presentations easily (average score = 4.67/5.0). While four out of six participants reported that identification of different versions of similar slides were easy, two pointed out that identifying the differences between text-heavy slides could become difficult (average score = 3.83/5.0).

Effectiveness of Slide-Based Search

ConReP uses slide-based search with the goal of freeing users from the burden of selecting appropriate keywords. All of our study participants considered slide-based search very effective, commenting on how it freed them from remembering keywords. Four out of six participants commented on the usefulness of this search technique for searching graph-heavy slides, as graphical elements are reused more often than text and forming appropriate search queries to retrieve graphical elements is extremely difficult. Figure 4 provides an example in which Participant 2 was trying to find presentations that contain materials similar to the graph marked as "b." After exploring ConReP's recommendations he commented:

"I have a slide that looked like this [pointing to b] but I can't type in the right keywords for this slide because there can be a lot of keywords. What I like about this (ConReP) is that it is using more than keywords." – Participant 2

Ability to View and Select among Multiple Versions

Five out of six participants mentioned that the visual representation of the recommendations allowed them to gain an overview of the relevant materials and helped them to examine a variety of options. To quote two participants:

"This graphic is so complex and it's a pain to find the right version. Showing all the versions are useful because otherwise you have to manually go and find the other ones." – Participant 5

"I think it is a really necessary tool, especially in our environment where you do have quite often to combine slides on demand very quickly, put them together. Just having this visual overview of multiple presentations is very useful because you can navigate and just build a picture of what you want to put together." – Participant 3

Usefulness of Local Context

For the vast majority of recommendations, the context slides flanking the recommendation slide (2 on each side) provided a unique "signature"; only 2% of the total recommended presentations had identical local-context slides. Figure 8 illustrates an example where the top three recommendations were copies of the same slide utilized in three different presentations; however, the local-context slides were different, helping the user recognize the different versions of the presentation.

User behavior seems to support the notion that local-context slides were sufficient to support recall and recognition. Users could navigate to the other slides from the recommendation slides by utilizing the left and right navigation controls, but they rarely needed to do so for recognizing the presentations; only 6% of the total slides explored during the study were not among the initial recommendations.

All of our participants considered local-context slides very effective since they provided a better way of identifying different versions of similar presentations, and helped them recall the presentations' construction story, audience, and purpose. Five out of six participants considered local-context "very useful" for supporting recall with one selecting "useful" (average score = 4.83/5.0). Participants commented on the effectiveness of local context:

"Local context is useful because it tells you, gives a sense of what presentation it was." – Participant 5

"Local context does (help in recall), it gives me more information. I can recall that I had started with this older version. I think it is useful to see it in the context." – Participant 3

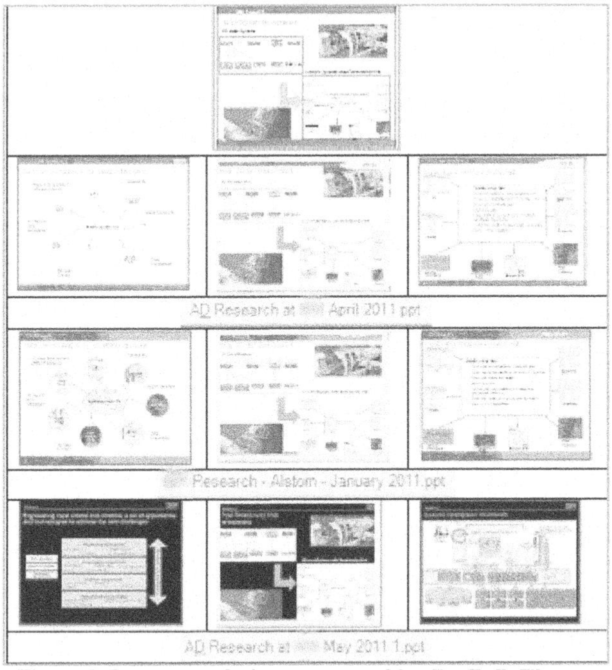

Figure 8. Recommendations generated by ConReP. The top thumbnail (row 1) represents the selected-slide and rows 2 through 4 represent recommendations. Slides are ordered based on the level of similarity (Portion of the presentation names are blurred to ensure confidentiality).

Local-context slides not only offered a better understanding of the presentation content, but also helped users understand the flow of the presentation and the context of use of specific slides. Our participants mentioned that presenting local-context slides was critical, since they helped in understanding the lead-up slides and supported understanding of slide-groups that are part of a story. To quote a participant:

"Sometimes you know you have a slide that is part of a story and just showing the thumbnail (only one thumbnail for the similar slide) won't tell you how did you get there and what lead up to it." – Participant 4

Showing multiple slides also helped in collecting nearby relevant slides. We observed that participants often used the local-context slides to select the best version of the presentation from which other desired material could be collected. Users expressed that ConReP made it easy to locate the needed materials within a presentation (average score = 4.16/5.0).

DISCUSSION

Limitation

Although our lab study involved collection of a considerable amount of materials from users, better indicators of effectiveness would be gained by a long-term deployment on users' machines. We hope to gain additional insight into the potential of contextual recommenders in assisting users in presentation reuse through such a future field deployment.

Areas of Improvement

The current ConReP system utilizes a user-selected slide as a search-key and offers recommendations based on the similarity of extracted slide content, file attributes such as file name and directory path. While we consider this to be a reasonable first step, utilization of other information is probably desirable. For example, integrating provenance information would enable the system to recommend presentations that are different in terms of content but were used by the user as a reference during the original presentation creation task. Using provenance and temporal proximity of use may shed light on relatedness among dissimilar presentations.

Currently, ConReP does not require users to provide any search keywords and instead requires users to start with an existing presentation similar to what they are looking for. However, sometimes, especially for recent presentations, users may know exactly what they are looking for and may not need to see all the variations. Allowing users to enter search keywords in addition to selecting a slide as a search-key may offer better support for some reuse scenarios.

In most cases, users were successful at comparing different versions of slides by viewing the thumbnails and commented that they did not need to utilize the larger sized view for examining slide content. During the study, however, we observed that our participants examined the details of 15% of all recommendation slides (by double-clicking on the thumbnail to view the larger image). Participants later stated that their primary motivation for doing so stemmed from a curiosity to compare the recommendation slide with the originally selected slide (used as a search-key). Additionally, we observed that all of the slides for which details were explored were text-heavy; indicating that for such slides additional measures could be taken to highlight the differences.

CONCLUSION

We have presented ConReP, a contextual recommender that enables users to gain an overview of existing relevant materials and identify the most appropriate material for reuse from several similar versions. ConReP's design is motivated by user needs surrounding presentation reuse and is guided by literature in the area of behavioral psychology, personal information management, desktop search and recommendation. We have investigated the efficacy of this system in a lab study with users exploring their own presentation materials. The study participants found ConReP to be highly usable and useful, and validated the general approach. Our semi-automated approach (search queries automatically created from user-selected slides) helps users overcome the challenges associated with traditional keyword-based search. The system aided them in locating and identifying multiple similar versions of content, as well as useful accompanying material. ConReP is valuable as both a tool for supporting reuse of existing presentation materials and as a mechanism to gain new insight in the domain of presentation reuse that can guide the design of new reuse support tools.

REFERENCES

1. Bederson, B.B. and Hollan, J.D. Pad++: a zooming graphical interface for exploring alternate interface physics. *Proc. UIST 1994*, ACM Press (1994), 17-26.
2. Bergman, L., Lu, J., Konuru, R., MacNaught, J., and Yeh, D. Outline wizard: presentation composition and search. *Proc. IUI 2010*, ACM Press (2010), 209-218.
3. Blanc-Brude, T. and Scapin, D. What do people recall about their Documents? Implications for Desktop Search Tools. *Proc. IUI 2007*, ACM Press (2007), 102-111.
4. Drucker, S.M., Petschnigg, G., and Agrawala, M. Comparing and managing multiple versions of slide presentations. *Proc. UIST 2006*, ACM Press (2006), 47-56.
5. Dumais, S., Cutrell, E., Cadiz, J., Jancke, G., Sarin, R., and Robbins, D.C. Stuff I've seen: a system for personal information retrieval and re-use. *Proc. IR 2003*, ACM Press (2003), 72-79.
6. Fuller, M., Kelly, L., and Jones, G. Applying Contextual Memory Cues for Retrieval from Personal Information Archives. *PIM Workshop at Proc. CHI*, 2008.
7. Gonçalves, D. and Jorge, J. A. Describing documents: what can users tell us?. *Proc. IUI 2004*, ACM Press (2004), 247-249.
8. Hansen, D.L. and Golbeck, J. Mixing it up: recommending collections of items. *Proc. CHI*, ACM Press (2009), 1217-1226.
9. Jaccard, P. Distribution de la flore alpine dans le bassin desDranses et dans quelques régions voisines. *Bulletin de la Société Vaudoise des Sciences Naturelles*, 37, (1901), 241-272.
10. Jensen, C. et al. The Life and times of files and information: a study of desktop provenance. *Proc. CHI 2010*, ACM Press (2010), 767-776.
11. Khoo, C. S. G., Luyt, B., Ee, C., Osman, J., Lim, H.-H, and Yong, S. How users organize electronic files on their workstations in the office environment: a preliminary study of personal information organization behaviour. *Information Research 11*, 2 (2007).
12. Kohlhase, A. and Kohlhase, M. CPoint: Dissolving the Author's Dilemma. *MKM 2594,* (2003), 175-189.
13. Lansdale, M. The psychology of personal information management. *Applied Ergonomics 19*, 1 (1988), 55-66.
14. Levenshtein, V.I. Binary codes capable of correcting deletions, insertions, and reversals. *Soviet Physics Doklady 10*, 8 (1966), 707-710.
15. Mejova, Y., Schepper, K.D., Bergman, L., and Lu, J. Reuse in the wild: an empirical and ethnographic study of organizational content reuse. *Proc. CHI 2011*, ACM Press (2011), 2877-2886.
16. Microsoft. "Microsoft PowerPoint." Accessed Oct 19, 2011, from http://office.microsoft.com/en-us/powerpoint/.
17. Nešić, S. Semantic Document Model to Enhance Data and Knowledge Interoperability, *ICWE 6*, 3(2009), 135-160.
18. Perlin, K. and Fox, D. Pad: An alternative approach to the computer interface. *Proc. SIGGRAPH*, ACM Press (2003), 57-64.
19. Ravasio, P., Schär, S.G., and Krueger, H. In pursuit of desktop evolution: User problems and practices with modern desktop systems. *Computer-Human Interaction 11*, 2 (2004), 156-180.
20. Secord, A., Winnemöller, H., Li, W., and Dontcheva, M. Creating collections with automatic suggestions and example-based refinement. *Proc. UIST 2010*, ACM Press (2010), 249-258.
21. Sharmin, M. et al. Understanding knowledge management practices for early design activity and its implications for reuse. *Proc. CHI 2009*, ACM Press (2009), 2367-2376.
22. Simon, H.A. A Behavioral Model of Rational Choice. *The Quarterly Journal of Economics 69*, 1 (1955), 99-118.
23. Spicer, R.P. and Kelliher, A. NextSlidePlease: navigation and time management for hyperpresentations. *Ext. Abstracts CHI*, 2009.
24. Teevan, J. et al. The perfect search engine is not enough: a study of orienteering behavior in directed search. *Proc. CHI*, ACM Press (2004), 415-422.
25. Zongker, D. and Salesin, D. On Creating Animated Presentations. *Proc. SIGGRAPH*, ACM Press (2003), 298-308.

Collecting Relevance Feedback on Titles and Photographs in Weblog Posts

Amy Campbell
Department of Linguistics
University of California, Berkeley
1203 Dwinelle Hall
Berkeley, CA 94720-2650
amycampbell@berkeley.edu

Christopher Wienberg and Andrew S. Gordon
Institute for Creative Technologies
University of Southern California
12015 Waterfront Drive
Los Angeles, CA 90094
cwienberg@ict.usc.edu, gordon@ict.usc.edu

ABSTRACT
We investigate new interfaces that allow users to specify topics of interest in streams of weblog stories by providing relevance feedback to a search algorithm. Noting that weblog stories often contain photographs taken by the blogger during the course of the narrated events, we investigate whether these photographs can serve as a proxy for the whole post when users are making judgments as to the post's relevance. We developed a new story annotation interface for collecting relevance feedback with three variations: users are presented either with the full post as it appears in a weblog, an embedded photograph, or only the title of the post. We describe a user evaluation that compares annotation time, quality, and subjective user experience across each of these three conditions. The results show that relevance judgments based on embedded photographs or titles are far less accurate than when reading the whole weblog post, but the time required to acquire an accurate model of the user's topic interest is greatly reduced.

Author Keywords
Weblogs; photographs; relevance feedback; user interfaces for machine learning; user study.

ACM Classification Keywords
H.5.2. User Interfaces (Interaction Styles, Evaluation).

INTRODUCTION
Machine learning algorithms are now routinely used in commercial web applications, and many enlist the users directly as providers of training data. For example, a movie rental service will incorporate a user's ratings of previous rentals when recommending new ones (e.g., Koren et al., 2009). Similarly, a personalized news service will select articles for a particular topic based on rules learned from a user's previous judgments of topic relevance (e.g., Stefik & Good, 2011). These applications and others have bolstered research interest in intelligent user interfaces that best facilitate the user's task of providing training data (Amershi et al., 2011). Successful approaches strike a balance between the user's need for a quality end-user experience and the system's need for copious amounts of quality training examples.

In this paper, we address the problem of training a system to identify weblog posts that are relevant to a user's interest. Specifically, we focus on training a system to recognize when a new weblog post is a personal story about an activity of interest to a particular user, given his or her previous relevance annotations. For example, a cardiologist may be interested in reading personal stories of people's experiences of having heart attacks. A used car salesman may be interested in reading personal stories from car buyers describing their experiences in negotiating with other salesmen. Parents of children with life-threatening diseases may be interested in reading personal stories from other parents who have gone through similar experiences of diagnosis, treatment, and recovery. More generally, people are interested in stories from other people that are relevant to their own personal lives in some direct way.

From a technology perspective, this problem is similar to that of Topic Detection and Tracking (TDT), a long-standing research challenge of developing algorithms for the automatic organization of news stories by the real-world events that they describe (Fiscus & Doddington, 2002). As with news articles, the problem of topic detection can be addressed by learning the lexical features from the documents that are predictive of topic relevance. However, the unique characteristics of personal stories in weblog posts do not lend themselves to other TDT concerns. We expect bloggers to author only one narrative about any particular event in their lives, so there is little concern for the TDT tasks of story segmentation, topic tracking, first story detection, and link detection. Conversely, the unique characteristics of weblog storytelling present different challenges and afford new opportunities.

In this paper, we seek to exploit one of the unique characteristics of weblog storytelling: stories frequently include photographs taken during the course of the narrated events. For example, a blogger telling the story of a fishing trip might include a photo of the fish that they caught, or of the damage to their boat when they crashed into a rock. Taken out of the context of the weblog story and viewed in isolation, the activity contexts of these photos are often still recognizable; a photo of a fish on the end of a fishing pole is strongly suggestive of the topic of fishing trips. If this is true often enough, then we postulate that photographs in weblog stories may serve as an effective proxy for the content of the entire post. This would allow users to quickly train a system to recognize their topic of interest by judging the relevance of photographs extracted from unlabeled posts, rather than reading the actual text of the story.

This relationship between text and images has been exploited in user interfaces of previous research. Early work on context-based multimedia retrieval (Dunlop & van Rijsbergen, 1991) sought to use the textual context to enable the retrieval of media that, at the time, could not be retrieved by content features (e.g. images). Even as content-based image retrieval has advanced, researchers have continued to use textual queries as an effective way of beginning a search for relevant images (e.g. Villa et al., 2010). Recently, Zha et al. (2010) explored a novel method for interactively improving image search by presenting a user with photographs that are exemplars of additional query terms that further disambiguate their query. In our research, we pursue an analogous approach: using images (photographs) to interactively improve the retrieval of relevant textual content. In doing so, we consider the relationship between text and images in the opposite direction than seen in context-based image retrieval. Our aim is to use images as a way to retrieve text similar to the text that surrounds them, i.e. image-based context retrieval.

In the sections that follow, we describe an experiment to determine whether the annotation of photographs appearing in weblog stories could serve as a suitable proxy for the full post when a user trains a system to recognize his or her topic of interest. We begin with a review of this genre of social media and a summary of the role of photography in existing corpora of weblog stories. We then describe a web-based user interface for annotating the relevance of weblog stories, with variants that show users only a photograph from an unlabeled post, the title of a post, or the full text of a post as it appears on the web. We describe a user evaluation to compare the effectiveness of these three variants across three different topics, and compare the time and accuracy of annotations of photos and titles to annotations of full web posts. We conclude with a discussion of the implications of these findings for future applications.

PERSONAL STORIES IN WEBLOGS

The phenomenal rise of weblogs over the last decade has created new opportunities for researchers to study personal communication on a massive scale. Within computer science, the stories that bloggers post in their weblogs have been seen as valuable sources of knowledge, both for people and computers. Gordon (2008) reviews the utility of weblog stories for organizations of people, particularly as sources of real-world experiences to serve as the basis for fictional scenarios in immersive training environments. Gordon et al. (2011) investigates the utility of weblog stories as a knowledgebase for computers, capitalizing on the causal structure of stories to guide automated reasoning systems to make causal inferences in commonsense situations. These efforts and others are predicated on the availability of very large corpora of personal stories. In this section, we describe an existing corpus of nearly one million personal stories from weblogs that we used in our experiments, along with a discussion of photographs within this dataset.

Stories in the ICWSM 2009 Spinn3r Dataset

Gordon and Swanson (2009) estimated that only 4.8% of all non-spam weblog posts are personal stories, which they define as non-fictional narrative discourse that describes a specific series of causally related events in the past, spanning a period of time of minutes, hours, or days, where the storyteller or a close associate is among the participants. Using supervised machine learning methods for text classification, these authors identified nearly one million personal stories among the 25 million English-language weblog posts from the ICWSM 2009 Spinn3r Dataset (Burton et al., 2009). We obtained this corpus of nearly one million personal stories for use in our experiments.

In our early user interface designs, we realized that it would be necessary to present users with content from these stories that is not encoded in the dataset format, e.g. a photograph that was embedded in the text of a post. For this reason, we needed to download the full post as it appears on the web. However, the posts in this corpus were nearly three years old at the time of our experiments, and many of them were no longer available. A study of 100 stories sampled at random from the corpus revealed that 26% of URLs no longer linked to the post content. For example, the popular blogging platform Vox.com had been the fifth largest source of weblog stories, accounting for 2.5% of the corpus, but had shut down entirely in September of 2010. We executed a series of scripts to identify broken links in the million-story corpus, and filtered out these items in our subsequent experiments. Additionally, we removed entries that had been marked as private, marked as containing adult content, or contained JavaScript that would prevent content from being embedded within our interface prototypes. After applying these filters, the story corpus was reduced to 627,782 stories from its original 960,098 stories (65%).

Photographs in Weblogs Stories

Ever since photography became easily accessible to the public at large, it held an important role in how we tell personal stories (Chafen, 1987). In much the same way that a physical photograph can be a catalyst for storytelling in face-to-face communication, digital photography contributes an element of immersion to the textual stories that people write on their weblogs and in other social media. In our examination of the million-story corpus of Gordon and Swanson (2009), we were struck by the sheer frequency of photographs that appeared in weblogs, and how often these photographs had been taken in the context of the narrated events. To investigate the use of photographs in more detail, we conducted a series of analyses to quantify the relevance of photograph content to stories in which they were embedded.

First, we sought to determine the ratio of photographs to other types of images embedded in corpus documents. We began by extracting every image tag (`<img>`) in the HTML of every story in our corpus. As prepared by Spinn3r.com, the weblog posts in this corpus are presented with all extraneous "chrome" HTML removed, including sidebars, advertising, and navigation structure. Consequently, the image tags in the corpus HTML are only those included by the author as a part of a given post. However, only a subset of these images consisted of photographs of real life events. We randomly sampled 100 image links where the image was still available on the web, and labeled each as either a photograph or a non-photographic image. Of these, 71% of the images were photographs, with others consisting largely of navigation icons, computer generated images, and images used to track hits on a page.

Second, using the same random subset of 100 images, we considered several simple heuristics for automatically distinguishing between photographs and non-photographs. We found that simply establishing a minimum width and height for images served as an effective photograph filter. Requiring that an image was at least 50 pixels wide by 50 pixels tall yielded 0.90 precision and 1.0 recall of photographs. An even better heuristic was to check the aspect ratio of the image to see if it matches common aspect ratios of photographs. We compared the ratio of the length of an image's shorter edge to its longer edge to the ratios 2:3, 3:4 and 9:16, corresponding to three of the most popular aspect ratios for still photography. By permitting a 5% deviance from these pre-set aspect ratios, this heuristic achieves a precision of 1.0 and recall of 0.94 in identifying photographs in the random sample. We then applied this heuristic to every image still available in our corpus of personal stories, identifying 534,514 photographs.

Third, we investigated the variations in how these photographs were distributed across the stories still available on the web. Only 13% of the stories still available on the web contained photographs that were also still available. In these stories, the mean number of photographs was five, and 40% had only one photograph. Assuming that stories with and without photographs disappear from the web at the same rate, we estimate that 19.5% of stories included a photograph when they were originally posted.

Fourth, we investigated the relevance of photographs to the narrated events of the story. We observed that not all of the photographs contained in weblog posts of personal stories had a direct relationship to the text of the post, e.g. a story about living in a retirement community might include a photo of the author's grandchildren. To determine what percent were relevant, we selected a random sample of 100 photographs from the set identified using our photograph heuristic. We annotated each as to whether it was relevant to the story in which it was embedded. Here we defined relevance to mean that the photograph depicted or was likely to have been taken in the context of the events that are narrated in the story. In cases where our heuristic failed or the post was not a personal story, we marked the photograph as non-relevant. In this sample, 82% of photographs were relevant to the stories in which they were embedded.

Fifth, we sought to develop a heuristic for selecting the most likely relevant photograph in stories that contained more than one. That is, we wondered whether the first, middlemost, or last photograph embedded in a personal story most often depicted the events that were narrated in the text. We randomly selected 100 stories that contained at least two photographs, then annotated each photograph as either relevant or irrelevant to the story surrounding it. In total, we annotated 672 photographs in this sample, and found 530 photographs (79%) in this sample to be relevant to the story in which they appear. We then compared the relevance of the first photograph, the middlemost photograph, or the last photograph. We found that 79% of stories on our sample have a relevant first photograph, 79% have a relevant photograph in the middlemost position of all photographs in the story, and 77% of stories have a relevant final photograph. Given no clear preference, we selected a heuristic that agreed with our intuition, and selected the middlemost photograph as the one most likely to be central to the story. We then applied this heuristic to each of the 105,456 available stories that contained photographs, selecting a single photograph for each that best represented its content.

In the course of these analyses, we saw several different ways that people use photographs in weblog storytelling. We made several qualitative observations that we feel are important to understanding the character of weblog story photography. The most common way authors present their photography was to interweave them with the text of the story. When posts are written in this style, the photographs often carry at least as much burden of telling the story as the narrative text. In some cases the photographs constitute the narration, with nearly all of the text consisting of photograph captions. These cases of photographs interwoven with narrative text are analogous to sitting around the family photo-album, or watching the slides of a friend's vacation. Here photographs provide a visual storytelling experience, where the author presents the photographs with enough description to bind them together into a coherent narrative, but allows the photographs to provide the details.

The analogy to physical photo albums breaks down when considering the topics of the stories containing photographs. Although stories with photographs are often compelling, the events that are narrated in weblogs tend to be more mundane than those that might be documented in a family photo album. Owing perhaps to the medium of weblogs and to the proliferation of digital photography, photographs in weblog stories often depict events common in everyday life. While a family album might be reserved for photographs from vacations, holidays, and other extraordinary moments in life, a weblog story is at least as likely to have photographs from the author's daily walk around their neighborhood, the leaky pipe under their kitchen sink, or their halfway finished art project.

Nearly all of the photography we encountered was taken in the context of leisure time, with almost none depicting the professional lives of the authors. This is to be expected; it is often inappropriate to take photographs in a work environment. However, there are many stories without photographs that describe situations related to work, such as the author complaining about his or her boss or celebrating an accomplishment. This observation reveals a more general point about weblog story photography: stories featuring photography are not representative of all weblog stories as a whole. Rather, weblog stories with photography over-represent stories that are particularly photogenic, where photography is not only appropriate, but illuminative of the activity. For instance, stories without photographs may be more likely to describe daily commutes and writing novels, i.e. things that are not particularly visual. Some stories about these topics will have photographs, but these stories generally have an additional, visual component, e.g. a daily commute where a stone had cracked the windshield of the author's car.

Photographs that are not relevant to the story are generally relevant to the author's life in some other direct way. In these cases, the author generally includes a statement cross-referencing another story to which the photograph relates. Generally, the author implies that his or her readers will have enough knowledge about the author's life—knowledge gained from either previous posts or personal acquaintance—to understand the photographs and the context in which those photographs were taken.

The author of the post is almost always the one who originally took the photograph, as indicated by his or her own descriptions.

ANNOTATION INTERFACES FOR STORY RELEVANCE

The central aim of our research effort was to develop and evaluate new interfaces that would allow end-users to train a machine learning algorithm to recognize weblog stories that are relevant to their specific interests. As a user interface design project, our primary concerns were to minimize the time required to gather copious amounts of high quality training data from the user, while maximizing the quality of the subjective user experience. We designed and implemented three story annotation interfaces, and paired them with a back-end story retrieval system so as to evaluate the effectiveness of these interfaces in situations that approximate those found in web-scale search applications.

In each of the three interfaces, a user would be presented with content from weblog stories selected by the back-end system as relevant to the user's interest, and asked to rate them as either relevant or not relevant to this interest. Relevance judgments would then be used to adjust the system's relevance model, and additional materials would be selected. The three interfaces varied primarily on the type of content that was presented to the user. In the "full text" condition, the full weblog post would be presented to the user as it appears on the web. In the "photo-only" condition, a photograph from the post would be shown, selected using the heuristic described in the previous section. In the "title-only" condition, the title of the post would be the only content presented to the user. In each condition, the full text of the annotated weblog story was used as relevance feedback. For example, if a photograph was annotated as relevant to the user, the full text of the story in which it was embedded would be used to adjust the system's relevance model.

Our hypothesis was that users would be able to quickly and accurately judge the relevance of embedded photographs to their topic of interest. Given that not all photographs are relevant to the events narrated in the story, we expected that a user's relevance feedback would contain inaccuracies. However, we anticipated that noise in this feedback would be overcome by the quantity of training data that could be annotated by a user in a given period of time, as compared to the full text interface. Our third condition, the "title-only" interface, provided an alternative to photographs that could also be quickly judged by users. However, we expected that titles alone would not provide sufficient information to make correct relevance judgments often enough to overcome the noise that was introduced.

Our designs were implemented as a Django (Python-based) web application with two back-end services for database access and textual search. We used the Terrier IR Platform (Ounis et al., 2007) as our back-end text search engine, using the default Divergence from Randomness retrieval model on an index of each of the 627,782 stories in the collection. Beginning with an initial topic description, the system employed a simple relevance-feedback method to update the query after each user annotation (Rocchio, 1971). The updated query is then run against the corpus, yielding an updated list of search results from which new content is chosen for display and annotation. This type of interactive, example-based machine learning is known to be a promising approach when dealing with large, unstructured data sets (Amershi et al., 2011), and is well suited to our goal of finding clusters of related stories in a large corpus of weblog posts.

Design Principles

Our interface design choices were guided by a small set of general principles. First, we limited ourselves to using *readily available, weblog author-supplied content*. This principle informed our choice of content items to be annotated in each interface. An interface displaying the full text of each story was necessary to establish baseline performance. In determining which sub-story content items could serve as potential proxies for the full text we chose story titles because they are tagged in the ICWSM 2009 Spinn3r Dataset, and photographs because they are easily stripped from the full story HTML. We ruled out an interface that would ask users to annotate query-based summarizations, for instance, because it would require additional processing to generate that content.

A second principle that informed our design was *user choice*. We display multiple content items on a single screen and do not require users to annotate them in any particular order; in fact, we instructed experimental users to work at their own pace in any order they choose. The title- and photo-based interfaces display six content items in a grid arrangement. While there isn't sufficient screen space for a grid in the full text interface, we retain the ability for users to choose among content items by including a set of six tabs along the side of the page that control which story is displayed in the main frame (see Figure 1 below). In all three interfaces we allow users to skip content items, rather than forcing them to make a decision about every item.

The final principle we employed in designing our system was *consistency of appearance and functionality* across interfaces. Shneiderman (1998) urges to "strive for consistency" as the first golden rule of interface design. Specifically, in similar situations the terminology used, controls displayed, and actions required should be kept as consistent as possible. This principle was important to us because each subject in our user study would be using three different interfaces. A consistent interaction mechanism across each interface, with a similar look and feel, allowed the user to focus on the primary annotation task, rather than on the interface itself.

Learning algorithm

To support the comparative evaluations of our interface designs, we implemented a standard query-refinement algorithm based on relevance feedback (Rocchio, 1971). Beginning with an initial query, each user annotation updates the query by combining query terms with the terms in the annotated document, following a weighted mixture scheme. Following common practice, Rocchio parameters were set to $\alpha = 1$, $\beta = 1$, and $\gamma = 0$, which weights the initial query and relevant documents equally, and effectively ignores negative feedback. In order to maintain query times that supported real-time interaction, it was necessary to restrict refined queries to the 50 most information-laden terms, as indicated by their tf-idf scores computed over the entire corpus. Queries were updated after each annotation

Figure 1. Full-text annotation interface

Figure 2. Photo-only annotation interface

Figure 3. Title-only annotation interface

using this approach, and the highest-ranking story that had not yet been annotated by the user was selected to replace the item just annotated in the user interface.

Three annotation interfaces

In the full-text interface (Figure 1) users see the full text versions of weblog stories that match the search query, as they would appear on the authors' weblogs. These stories usually contain titles and may contain embedded photos. A set of tabs at the left side of the page allows users to change the displayed story. The tab corresponding to the current story is visually distinguished by its color and by the appearance of the annotation icons. Users are instructed to click thumbs-down if the story is not relevant to the search topic, skip if they aren't sure, and thumbs-up if the story is relevant. Once a story is annotated its text is used to revise the query and search the collection, and then the item is replaced by the highest-ranking story without an annotation.

The photo-only interface (Figure 2) displays photographs embedded in the matching stories. Although the overall look of the page is consistent with the full text system, the photo panels are arranged in a grid to maximize user choice. The annotation icons used in this interface are the same as those used in the full text interface. Users are instructed to consider a photograph relevant if it was taken in the context of the activity denoted by the search topic.

The title-only interface (Figure 3) displays only the titles of the weblog stories matching the search query. The page layout and the annotation controls are identical to those of the photo-based interface. Users are instructed to consider a title as relevant if it seems to be the title of a relevant story.

EVALUATION

In order to evaluate our system we designed an experiment to measure the effects of using titles or photographs as proxies for full stories in the annotation task. Objectively, we wondered how system accuracy would change with respect to annotation time and number of annotations in each of the three annotation interfaces. Subjectively, we wanted to determine how users perceived each interface's ease of use and enjoyment, as well as their confidence levels in the accuracy of each interface.

Participants

We recruited 18 people to participate in a user study; all but one were employees of the University of Southern California's Institute for Creative Technologies. There were 8 male and 10 female participants, and their ages ranged between 20 and 61. At a minimum, all participants had attended some college; 5 held a Bachelor's degree and 11 held a Master's or Doctoral degree. Job titles were diverse, with research and technical occupations being the most common, though administrative jobs were represented as well. 15 of the participants reported being "experienced" or "very experienced" computer users, 11 described themselves as regular readers of weblogs, and 4 stated that they maintain their own weblog. Each participant was paid $20 for approximately 45 minutes of participation.

Experimental Design and Procedures

All 18 participants used all three interfaces during the experiment. Subjects used the photo-only and title-only interfaces for exactly five minutes each. Subjects used the full-text interface for exactly 15 minutes, which allotted them enough time to read and annotate a suitable number of weblog posts. Subjects were asked to use each interface for the full amount of allotted time without stopping, but otherwise annotated at their own pace.

Since all users interacted with all interfaces, we needed to ensure that a user would not encounter the same content in different interfaces. For instance, if a user read a story in the full text interface, it would bias the results if the same user later annotated the title of the same story in the titles-

Topic	Initial "boring story" search query
Topic 1: Sailing	We went sailing. We motored our sailboat out of our slip in the harbor. We raised the main sail and the jib with the halyards, and trimmed the sails with the lines. The wind was blowing some knots, and the waves were good. We tacked into the wind, then jibed away from the wind. We sat on the deck of the boat and enjoyed the weather. At the end of the day, we returned to the harbor.
Topic 2: Car accidents	I crashed my car. I was driving in heavy traffic and the visibility wasn't very good. Out of nowhere this other car came at me and smashed into the side of the car. The airbag blew up in my face, but the seatbelt worked. I checked to see that I was okay, then got out of the car to see the damage. The other driver was pretty shaken up. The police showed up and an ambulance came, but everyone was okay. I got the insurance information from the other driver, and a tow truck came to pick up my car.
Topic 3: Doctor visits	I had a doctor's appointment. I went to the medical offices and checked in with the receptionist and sat in the waiting room. When it was my turn I went to the exam room and a nurse took my blood pressure took a blood sample using a syringe. I changed into an examination gown. The doctor came in and asked me about my health. The doctor listened to my heart using a stethoscope. The doctor said I needed to watch my cholesterol level. When my appointment was over, I went to the receptionist and gave them my insurance information.

Table 1. Initial "boring story" queries for the three topics used in the experiment

only interface. For this reason, we developed three queries for the user study and planned for each participant to use a different query for each of the three interfaces.

The queries were formulated as short stories that contained vocabulary typical of a particular activity context. This style follows the "boring story" format advocated by Gordon and Swanson (2008) for searching indexed story collections. Table 1 lists the search topics and "boring story" queries that we used. Query 1 is a simple story about the activity of sailing, query 2 is about a car accident, and query 3 is about a visit to the doctor's office.

Subjects were randomly sorted into three experimental groups that differed in the mapping of queries to interfaces. Within each group we counterbalanced for the order in which interfaces were used. There are six possible orders of use of the three interfaces, and we assigned one participant in each group to each order. Each experimental group thus comprised 6 participants, for 18 participants total.

RESULTS

During the experiment we collected two types of data suitable for quantitative analysis. First, the annotation system itself logs information about each interaction session and all of the user's actions therein. Second, after each interaction session participants were asked to rate several aspects of their interaction using paper and pencil rating scale measurements.

Objective measures

The system logs captured the following information about each user session: interface type (full text, titles-only, or photos-only), user ID, start time, and initial query. For each user annotation the system recorded the story ID, the query that resulted in the story being delivered and the associated confidence score, the user-assigned annotation value ("yes", "no", or "skip"), and a time stamp. This information was later used to reproduce the user's search results at various points in their session, allowing us to evaluate our objective measures: accuracy over time and over number of annotations.

Our first task in analyzing the system data was to check the level of inter-rater agreement in the full text interface, which we expected to yield the most accurate annotations because users had access to all of the story information.

In calculating inter-rater agreement we disregarded stories skipped by users and looked only at positive or negative relevance annotations, a decision motivated by the heterogeneous nature of the skip category. Participants were instructed to skip for a number of reasons (if they weren't sure whether the content was relevant or not, if an error message loaded instead of the live weblog story, etc.) and so two users' "skip" annotations could not be said to "agree" in any meaningful way. Skip annotations accounted for about 4% of annotations in the full text interface (21 skips in 269 total annotations), 19% of annotations in the titles-only interface (278/1484), and 8% of annotations in the photos-only interface (144/1853).

Table 2 presents the inter-rater agreement measures for each of the three interfaces. Pairwise agreement is based on all items that two annotators both rated, and here we report raw agreement (a) as well as agreement normalized for chance (Cohen's Kappa) (b). Scores are aggregated across all three topics. Results indicate that inter-rater agreement was not perfect, even in the full text interface. It appears that much of the disagreement was due to genuine subjectivity in story interpretation. For instance, the topic "car accidents" included one story that many participants viewed where the author had been hit by a car while riding a bicycle. It is reasonable to think that some readers would consider this to be a story primarily about a bike ride (with the collision being an important sub-event), while others would consider it to be primarily about the collision (with the bike ride being background context).

In order to evaluate the accuracy of the titles-only and photos-only interface we generated a "gold standard" – the definitive set of relevance annotations for a particular search topic – from the full text annotations. The gold set included all stories annotated as relevant or not relevant in the full text interface (again omitting "skip" annotations). We dealt with inter-rater disagreement for a particular story by majority rule: if the positive annotations outnumbered the negative annotations then the gold standard annotation for that story was "relevant". The gold set for query 1 contained 47 stories (43 relevant, 4 not relevant), 67 stories for query 2 (35 relevant, 32 not relevant), and 49 stories for query 3 (46 relevant, 3 not relevant), for a total of 163 stories.

Table 2, row C, lists the raw agreement of annotations from the photo-only and title-only interfaces with the gold-standard annotations, averaged across subjects. As we expected, users were more likely to assign correct relevance annotations to photographs than to titles, although neither interface achieved high levels of accuracy.

Our system and experimental design afforded a novel

Measure	Full-text	Photo-only	Title-only
a. Average pairwise raw agreement	<u>0.84</u>	0.82	0.73
b. Average pairwise Cohen's Kappa	0.42	<u>0.65</u>	0.50
c. Average raw agreement with full-text gold standard		<u>0.65</u>	0.56

Table 2. Annotation agreement measures for full-text, photo-only, and title-only interfaces

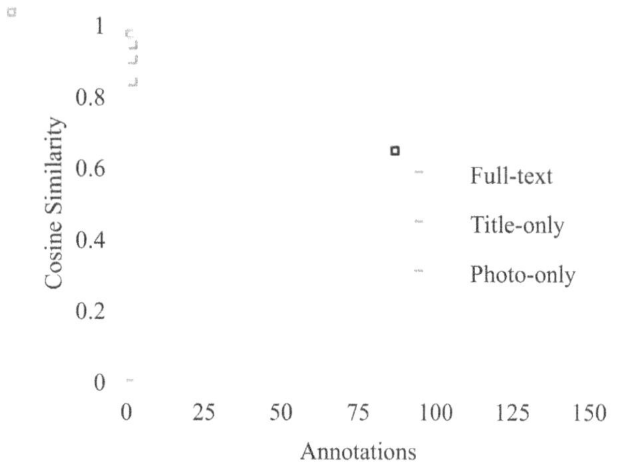

Figure 4. Average cosine similarity by number of annotations

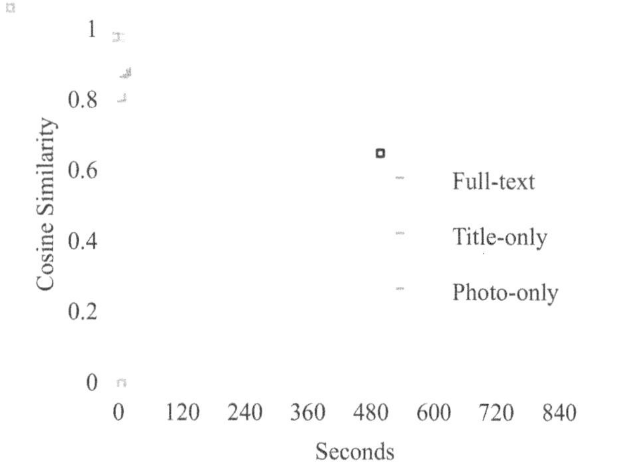

Figure 5. Average cosine similarity by annotation time (300 second limit in title-only and photo-only interfaces)

method of assessing the objective quality of queries across the three interfaces as they evolved over time and with the addition of new annotations. At any given moment in the use of an interface, the current query is represented as a weighted vector of 50 query terms. Using a simple similarity measure (Cosine distance), we can assess the quality of the query by calculating its similarity to a gold-standard query. We constructed three gold-standard term vectors (one for each topic) using the tf-idf weighted terms in each of our gold-standard annotation sets. In this post-hoc analysis, we excluded the initial "boring-story" query from both the evolving queries and the gold-standards, and truncated only the evolving queries to the top 50 most information-laden terms.

Figure 4 plots the average cosine similarity between the evolving queries and its corresponding gold-standard term vector for each interface, for increasing numbers of user annotations (skips included). As expected, the full-text interface requires fewer annotations to approach the gold-standard than either the photo-only or title only condition, although this result is confounded somewhat by the higher degree of overlap between the evolving full-text queries and the gold-standards. Surprisingly, the titles-only condition outperforms the photos-only interface.

This result shows that one is better off judging the full text of a story than a photo or title, given the same number of annotations. However, the results are markedly different when we consider how the annotations evolved over time. Across the three interfaces, the time required to judge an item as relevant, not relevant, or skip varied substantially. On average, judgments were made in the photo-only interface every 2.90 seconds ($\sigma^2 = 9.18$ seconds). The title-only interface was only slightly slower ($\mu = 3.63$ seconds, $\sigma^2 = 8.17$ seconds). The full-text interface was nearly ten times slower, with a judgment made every 30.09 seconds on average, with huge variation ($\sigma^2 = 885.81$ seconds).

To see the impact of this time disparity between interfaces, Figure 5 plots the average cosine similarity between the evolving queries and gold-standard queries over the duration of user interaction. Results show that both the photo-only and title-only conditions outperform the full-text interface when given limited time. Again, we were surprised to find a slight benefit to the title-only interface over the photo-only interface.

Subjective measures

After each use of one of the three interfaces, participants were asked to fill out a six-item questionnaire. The interface evaluation questionnaire asked users to respond to the following questions. The first three items were answered on a ten-point percentage scale (10% being the lowest and 100% being the highest), as follows:

a) What percentage of the stories were about the search topic?

b) What percentage of the stories did you find interesting?

c) What percentage of the stories do you think you were able to annotate accurately?

The next three questions were answered on a five-point Likert scale, with 5 denoting "strongly agree."

d) It is easy to use.

e) I enjoyed using it.

f) If I needed to search for personal stories on weblogs, I would use it again.

After answering these questions, participants were given an opportunity to provide us with open-ended qualitative feedback about the interface they had just used. At the very end, participants were asked one final question:

g) Which of the three interfaces you used (full text, titles only, and photos only) did you prefer?

Table 3 gives the response value for each questionnaire item, averaged over all 18 users of each interface with the exception of item g, where one user did not indicate a

Measure	Full-text	Photo-only	Title-only
a. Percent relevant (10-100)	87.7	64.7	46.4
b. Percent interesting (10-100)	69.2	53.6	38.6
c. Percent annotated accurately (10-100)	95.3	83.1	62.5
d. Ease of use (1-5)	4.58	4.53	4.36
e. Enjoyment (1-5)	3.97	4.14	3.31
f. Would use again (1-5)	4.03	3.64	2.19
g. Preferred interface (fraction expressing preference)	12/17	5/17	0/17

Table 3. Subjective measures from participant questionnaire

preference. The full-text interface scored the highest in every subjective measure except enjoyment. The title-only interface scored the lowest in every subjective measure.

If we examine interface preference (g) across different queries, some interesting complexity emerges. Participants annotating sailing stories expressed a 66.7% preference for the full text interface; for car accidents the preference for full-text was only 40%, and for doctor's visits it was 100%. These data suggest that some topics are more suited than others for a particular interface, and this affects how users feel about the interface overall.

Table 3 shows a clear rejection of the titles-only interface, and some of the open-ended, qualitative responses help to illuminate the reasons for this. Users indicated that the titles-only interface displayed "too much vague and irrelevant information" and that "just a title is not enough to determine" relevance. These comments agree well with the quantitative data in several ways. Users of the title interface skip the greatest number of items (19% of titles were skipped, as opposed to 8% of photos and 4% of full text stories). Also striking is the low level of annotation confidence reported by participants (c). It appears to be important to users that they have enough information to be reasonably confident that they are making the "right" decision when they annotate. Absent an adequate level of confidence they skip stories more often and feel less comfortable using the interface.

A final point brought out by the qualitative feedback is that users are sensitive to the tradeoff between speed and accuracy. Participants who preferred the photos interface reported enjoying the greater speed with which they were able to annotate content. Those who preferred the full text interface reported feeling satisfied because even though each annotation took more time, they were sure they had all the available information and could make an accurate judgment. So while there does seem to be a qualitative, subjective, enjoyment-based aspect to interface preference, it is also clear that the ability to provide accurate responses was crucial to interface preference. Although users on average enjoyed using the photos interface the most (e), they felt most confident about their annotations in the full-text interface (c), and preferred the full-text interface overall (g).

DISCUSSION

There are several dichotomies seen in these results. Participants prefer the full-text interface, but it is more efficient to use the title-only or photo-only interface. Participants are more confident and more accurate in their annotations in the photo-only interface over the title-only interface, but the title-only interface is more efficient overall. Participants find the photo-only interface most enjoyable, but much prefer the full-text interface.

We conclude that the experience of reading personal stories is more rewarding than the labor of annotating photos or titles, particularly when users are not given enough information to be confident of their judgments. When the accuracy of individual annotations is the paramount concern, the full text interface is the best choice. However, it takes ten times longer to make a relevance judgment based on reading the full-text of a story. When time is a limiting factor, users are far better off training a topic-detection system by annotating titles or photos, and would much prefer to annotate photos.

However, we estimated that only 19.5% of stories included a photo when they first appeared on the web. In the corpus we used in this study, a smaller fraction of stories (13%) still available on the web also had photographs that were also still available. As a consequence, users of the photo-only interface were making relevance judgments that were, on average, further away from the current query than those in the title-only interface. Inaccurate annotation of photos (false positives) slowed the progress of the aggregate query vector toward the gold-standard. This is reflected in Figure 5, particularly in the latter half of the use of the photo-only interface, when items without annotations would be furthest down in the results list. Titles, in contrast, are included on nearly every weblog post. Although users were particularly bad at judging the relevance of titles (only 56% correct), these inaccuracies were outweighed by the volume of annotations that could be collected on items close to the current query vector.

The surprising success of the title-only interface in this evaluation suggests that a hybrid approach would be best when efficiency is the primary concern. Users could be provided with the titles of weblog posts along with a photo from the story in cases where one is available (13% of the time). Our results indicate that the addition of photos would both make the task more enjoyable and increase annotation accuracy.

The overall utility of the photo-only interface, balancing efficiency and enjoyment, might be best exploited in innovative new user interfaces that are divorced from language altogether. Using a photo-only interface, users need not even be fluent in the language of the authors in order to train a high-quality topic model, e.g. an English speaker could just as easily use this interface to identify weblog stories about a given topic written in Spanish, Japanese, or Arabic. While these users may not be able fully to enjoy the stories of the target language, such a tool might be interesting as a way to see, through pictures, how things are done across the world's language barriers.

ACKNOWLEDGMENTS

The authors would like to acknowledge the important contributions and suggestions of Sinhwa Kang, Kenji Sagae, Don Metzler, and Anton Leuski during the course of this research project. The projects or efforts depicted were or are sponsored by the U. S. Army. The content or information presented does not necessarily reflect the position or the policy of the Government, and no official endorsement should be inferred.

REFERENCES

1. Amershi, S., Fogarty, J., Kapoor, A., and Tan, D. (2011) Effective End-User Interaction with Machine Learning. In Proceedings of the 25th AAAI Conference on Artificial Intelligence, August 7-11, San Francisco, CA.
2. Burton, K., Java, A., and Soboroff, I. (2009) The ICWSM 2009 Spinn3r Dataset. In Proceedings of the Third Annual Conference on Weblogs and Social Media (ICWSM 2009), May, San Jose, CA.
3. Chafen, R. (1987) Snapshot Versions of Life. Bowling Green, OH: Bowling Green State University Popular Press.
4. Dunlop, M. and van Rijsbergen, C. (1993) Hypermedia and free text retrieval. Information Processing and Management 29(3):287-298.
5. Fiscus, J. and Doddington, G. (2002) Topic Detection and Tracking. Norwell, MA: Kluwer Academic Publishers.
6. Gordon, A., Bejan, C., and Sagae, K. (2011) Commonsense Causal Reasoning Using Millions of Personal Stories. In Proceedings of the 25th AAAI Conference on Artificial Intelligence, August 7-11, San Francisco, CA.
7. Gordon, A. and Swanson, R. (2009) Identifying Personal Stories in Millions of Weblog Entries. In Proceedings of the Third Annual Conference on Weblogs and Social Media (ICWSM 2009), Data Challenge Workshop, May, San Jose, CA.
8. Gordon, A. and Swanson. R. (2008) StoryUpgrade: Finding Stories in Internet Weblogs. Proceedings of the Second Annual Conference on Weblogs and Social Media (ICWSM 2008), March 31-April 2, Seattle, WA.
9. Koren, Y., Bell, R., and Volinsky, C. (2009) Matrix Factorization Techniques for Recommender Systems. IEEE Computer 42(8):30-39.
10. Ounis, I., Lioma, C., Macdonald, C., and Plachouras, V. (2007) Research Directions in Terrier: a Search Engine for Advanced Retrieval on the Web. Upgrade 7(1):49-56.
11. Rocchio, J. (1971) Relevance Feedback in Information Retrieval. In Salton: The SMART Retrieval System: Experiments in Automatic Document Processing. Prentice Hall, 313-323.
12. Shneiderman, B. (1998) Designing the User Interface. Addison, Wesley, and Longman.
13. Stefik, M. and Good, L. (2011) The News that Matters to You: Design and Deployment of a Personalized News Service. Proceedings of the 23rd Innovative Applications of Artificial Intelligence Conference, August 7-11, San Francisco, CA.
14. Villa, R., Halvey, M., Joho, H., Hanna, D., and Jose, J. (2010) Can an intermediary collection help users search image databases without annotations? Proceedings of the 10th Annual Joint Conference on Digital Libraries (JCDL-10).
15. Zha, Z., Yang, L., Mei, T., Wang, M., Wang, Z., Chua, T., and Hua, X. (2010) Visual Query Suggestion: Towards Capturing User Intent in Internet Image Search. ACM Transactions on Multimedia Computing, Communications and Applications, Vol. 6, No. 3, Article 13.

Effective Browsing and Serendipitous Discovery with an Experience-Infused Browser

Sudheendra Hangal **Abhinay Nagpal** **Monica S. Lam**
Computer Science Department
Stanford University
{hangal, abhinay, lam}@cs.stanford.edu

ABSTRACT

In the digital age, users can have perfect recall of their digital experiences. In this paper, we explore how this recall can be leveraged during web browsing.

We have built a system called the Experience-Infused Browser that indexes a user's digital history from email and chat archives. As the user browses the web, it observes the contents of pages viewed, and highlights named entities on the page that the user has encountered in the past. This browser has two benefits. First, it highlights terms on the page that occur frequently in the user's archive, effectively personalizing the page for the user. Second, the system can remind the user of names that she has encountered in the past but may not remember.

We evaluated how users reacted to the browser during organic web browsing. Our users have reported that it was useful on crowded web pages to surface content that they otherwise may have missed, and in recalling serendipitous connections to people that they had forgotten. Most of our users said they would use the browser beyond the experimental study, indicating that they derived clear benefit from it.

Author Keywords

Web browsing, Personal Digital Archives, Email, Annotation, Personalization

ACM Classification Keywords

H.5.2 Information Interfaces and Presentation: Miscellaneous—*Optional sub-category*

INTRODUCTION

In the digital age, the memories of our lives are etched in silicon. Eventually everybody's digital life experiences can be captured in his or her personal archive, leading to the promise of "Total Recall" [4, 7]. This paper explores the question of how we might use this ability of recall to help users in routine tasks, and specifically, in the task of web browsing.

Users are overwhelmed today by the massive amount of information in pages they encounter on the web, such as crowded news portals, social networking feeds, long web pages, and even entire books. In response, they frequently resort to rapid skimming and selective reading of web pages. We propose to improve web browsing efficacy by exploiting a simple observation: when skimming a piece of text, whether online or offline, terms we know jump out at us and grab our attention, based on factors such as our experiences, memories, interests and cultural background. The same content can evoke very different reactions from different users, based on their personal context.

We propose to enhance a user's browsing experience by infusing the browser with her archive of digitally captured experiences. This approach allows terms of special interest to her to be automatically identified from the archive and to be quickly brought to her attention if they are on a page. In this way, an experience infused browser can enhance the effect of a user noticing personally relevant terms on a page, and scale it to long pieces of content that are difficult to skim manually. As an additional benefit, the browser can help revive memories from the personal archive related to the web page that the user may have been forgotten.

Personal Digital Archives

A personal digital archive, especially of social interactions, reflects a great deal about the owner of the archive. People use email to communicate with friends or use instant messaging to chat with them. Reportedly, many users spend more time connecting with people on online social networks than in real life [21]. These interactions can often be implicitly and continuously captured in personal archives with no additional effort needed by a user. Over a period of time, the archive captures many entities, such as the names of people, places, and organizations associated with the user. It also contains signals that indicate the relative strength of the user's relationship with these friends or entities [8]. Therefore, the archive captures in some sense a detailed profile of the user, which he can exploit for his own benefit. There are many uses for these archives from reminscence to recollecting information and remembering events [25].

In this paper, we focus specifically on textual digital archives. A major advantage of a textual archive is that it is highly granular and searchable. Therefore automatic tools working on behalf of the user can use the archive to effectively augment and illuminate any information encountered by the user.

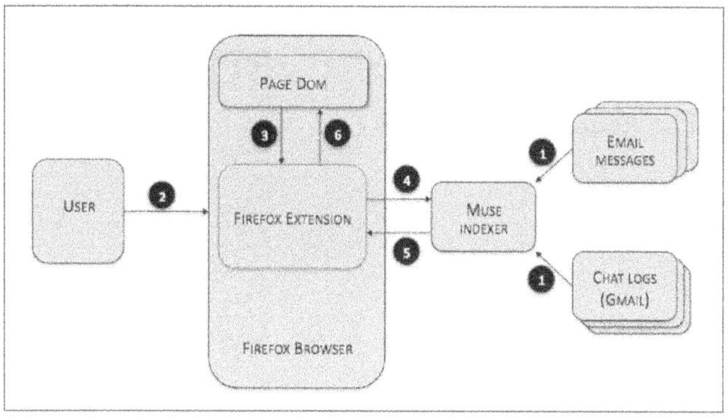

Figure 1. Prototype system design. 1) The MUSE program accesses the user's email archive and chat logs, and creates an index. This index is created once. 2) The user initiates a page load. 3) Our browser extension extracts text from the page Document Object Model (DOM) and 4) posts it to the MUSE index. 5) The MUSE index looks up and ranks named entities in the posted text, and returns them to the extension. 6) The browser extension modifies the page DOM to highlight terms of interest, insert a call-out, and provide links to the actual message contents behind a hit on the page.

In the archiving context, email is particularly significant since it is used by nearly 2 billion people [22] and much of it is frequently archived, especially with the advent of the "Never Delete Anything!" mindset. Email is used as a tool of record, and people often use their email accounts as an informal backup device. It contains rich records in the form of names of friends and interesting people, shopping receipts, travel history, ticket confirmations, movie rental history through services like Netflix, and so on. Tools to analyze this archive can generate a detailed list of terms important to the user, and moreover, can keep the list updated on an ongoing basis with no burden on the user.

Infusing a Browser with the User's Experience

In this paper, we introduce the notion of a browser, *infused* with a user's experience as captured by her personal digital archives. The browser annotates every web page, helping her identify terms of interest without any explicit action on her part. Of course, the user may not always be receptive to annotation, so it is important to minimize interfere with normal browsing, to the extent possible.

Our browser brings users' attention to terms of interest by highlighting them on the page, making their background yellow, as if someone intimately familiar with the user's background and interests had prepared the page for the user and marked it up with a highlighter. This allows users to notice these terms easily as they skim and scroll around the page. In addition, the user can see at a glance all highlighted terms on the page in a subtle call-out row at the bottom of the page. This functionality is especially useful on busy web pages, where a user may be interested in only a fraction of the available content. Of course, highlighted terms are linked back to the text in the archive that contains them, so users can always explore the original messages in case they have forgotten about the terms. Especially for users with long-term archives, this functionality can serendipitously help them recall connections to their past life experiences that have been forgotten.

We note that our current system is limited to highlighting and promoting terms that a user has already seen in the past; in other words, it does not help in discovering new or related content.

Privacy Preserving Personalization

Fig. 1 illustrates the working of a prototype system that we have created to experiment with the concept of an experience-infused browser. The primary components are a Firefox browser plugin and a specialized version of MUSE, a program that analyzes the user's email messages (and instant messaging logs, if available). Both these components run entirely on the user's own computer. This design offers users the benefits of a highly personalized experience without compromising privacy, since no third party is involved.

Privacy is one of the major concerns people have with commercial personalization mechanisms. Apart from allaying privacy concerns, client-side personalization has two major benefits: a) It can be relatively complete, since only the user has the entire view of all his data and b) It removes the burden on each web page or service of implementing personalization.

We invite interested readers to try out our system which is publicly available at the URL:
http://mobisocial.stanford.edu/exp-browser/.

Contributions

The contributions of this paper include the following:

- We propose the concept of an experience-infused browser that brings a user's entire digital archives (perhaps accumulated over a long-term) to bear on the task of web browsing. The browser automatically annotates visited pages by highlighting terms of potential interest to the user. Our approach honors users' privacy by running locally on their own computer, yet provides the benefits of personalization.
- We have created a publicly available prototype of our approach, and report on design and implementation tradeoffs discovered while building this prototype.
- We show that our system is fairly effective in achieving its goals. Seven out of the nine users in our user study indicated that they were interested in using the system beyond the duration of the study. While our study is relatively small and preliminary, we provide qualitative examples to show that a simple engine, infused with a massive amount of personal information, can be useful in many different ways.

RELATED WORK

Total Recall

Recently, the idea of Total Recall has popularized the notion that a lifetime's worth of digital experiences can be recorded and stored [4, 7]. However, most research focuses on the capture, preservation and explicit use of this personal data. Our research goal is to investigate scenarios and techniques to make implicit use of this data for ordinary tasks such as web browsing.

Web browsing

A closely related system to ours is Rhodes's Margin Notes [24]. Margin Notes takes the paragraph currently being viewed on a web page and tries to find messages in an archive that have similar words in them. While our system employs a broadly similar architecture, our goals and techniques are different, and our primary motivation is in some sense almost the opposite of that of Margin Notes. Margin Notes aims to suggest related material from the archives that a user may have missed. In contrast, we aim to help users rapidly select the few parts of long pages that they may be interested in. Further, the context tested for Margin Notes was to supplement the more or less linear reading of a document; our context is one of skimming rich websites that agglomerate all kinds of names, events and stories on a page, laid out in an arbitrary manner and difficult to pick out manually.

Our differences with Margin Notes's design goals lead to different design decisions in the relevance matching algorithm and user interfaces. Margin Notes tries to find the most closely related message to the words in a paragraph. As we will describe later, our experience-infused browser looks for named entities, which potentially makes our analysis less sensitive to the language used in the text. While Margin Notes shows a sidebar of related content, we use in-place highlighting of terms on the page, so the user can identify them without affecting the normal flow of reading. Our browser inserts a call-out at the bottom with a summary of terms highlighted throughout the web page; this is often used by users as an index to the personally relevant content on the page.

There are several other systems that attempt to display documents similar in content to the page a user is browsing [27]. The Google related toolbar (http://google.com/related) suggests content on other pages that may be related. Another method to focus a user's attention within a page is to highlight the content that has changed on the page since the user's previous visit [1]. There has been research on enhancing browsing experience by flagging irrelevant links and suggesting useful links based on browsing patterns [16]. Tools like SparTag.us [13] let users manually highlight text snippets in-situ and allow them to refer to these tags easily. Semantic web browsers like Magpie use ontologies to find out related concepts and point the user to such content [5]. However, none of these systems exploit users' personal archives.

A lot of work has gone into making web browsing effective by considering how users generally browse a particular website and then analyzing this information to guide users in browsing (e.g., [14]). The YouPivot system facilitates searching for contextually associated activities on a desktop computer [10].

Personalization

Many web services attempt to personalize content for a user (e.g. [17]). Gauch et al. survey techniques and related work in this area [6]. While the mechanisms used for personalization are generally opaque to users, these services need to either build up a profile of users' behavior on that site, or ask people to enter coarse-grained profile information up-front. Though personalization can be very useful, users are often hesitant to participate in such services, or provide incorrect data in their profiles, due to the privacy issues and the additional burden of providing information.

Our approach of client-side personalization has benefits in that it does not necessarily require the user to identify himself to the website, and give up personal details. In addition, the personal history used to illuminate the web page can be relatively complete, since it is under the user's control and may aggregate different sources of personal data.

Email analysis

The MUSE system has been shown to be effective in reviving memories using long-term email archives [11]. Systems like Xobni and Rapportive bring in specific content from the web (like a public profile of the message sender) to supplement messages in the inbox; our system can be viewed as an inversion of this model, where email archives are used to illuminate web pages instead.

There has been work done to show emails containing the URL of the currently visited page to the user [18]. However this is limited by the fact that, more often than not, an email message may not contain the exact URL of the page being visited. In contrast, in this paper we present a technique to "intersect" the terms on a web page with the actual contents of the user's email archive and highlight terms that may potentially interest the user. We use standard natural language processing and information retrieval techniques to achieve this goal. Thus our experience-infused browser overcomes some of the limitations of earlier work.

Serendipity

It is known that serendipitous discoveries are important, and moreover that they entertain and captivate users [15, 9]. But it is also acknowledged that serendipity is hard to define, let alone engineer [2], and therefore somewhat hard to study formally. However, in an indicative experiment, Andre et al. found that users rated 1 in 5 results of web searches "interesting", even when they were not "directly relevant".

Ramakrishnan et al. outline the data mining techniques that could be used to discover serendipitous events [23]. Meerkat and Tuba are recent systems designed for promoting serendipity, and the authors make the intriguing observation that *"the design for serendipitous experiences has to some extent disappoint as well in order to be effective"* [12]. Beale presents techniques to model serendipity and interest based on pages recently viewed by the user; the author uses this prior information to highlight interesting links on the page using special coloring mechanisms [3].

USER EXPERIENCE

Our browser augments every page browsed to bring the users' attention to potential points of interest, without interfering with the normal reading of the page. The user can always

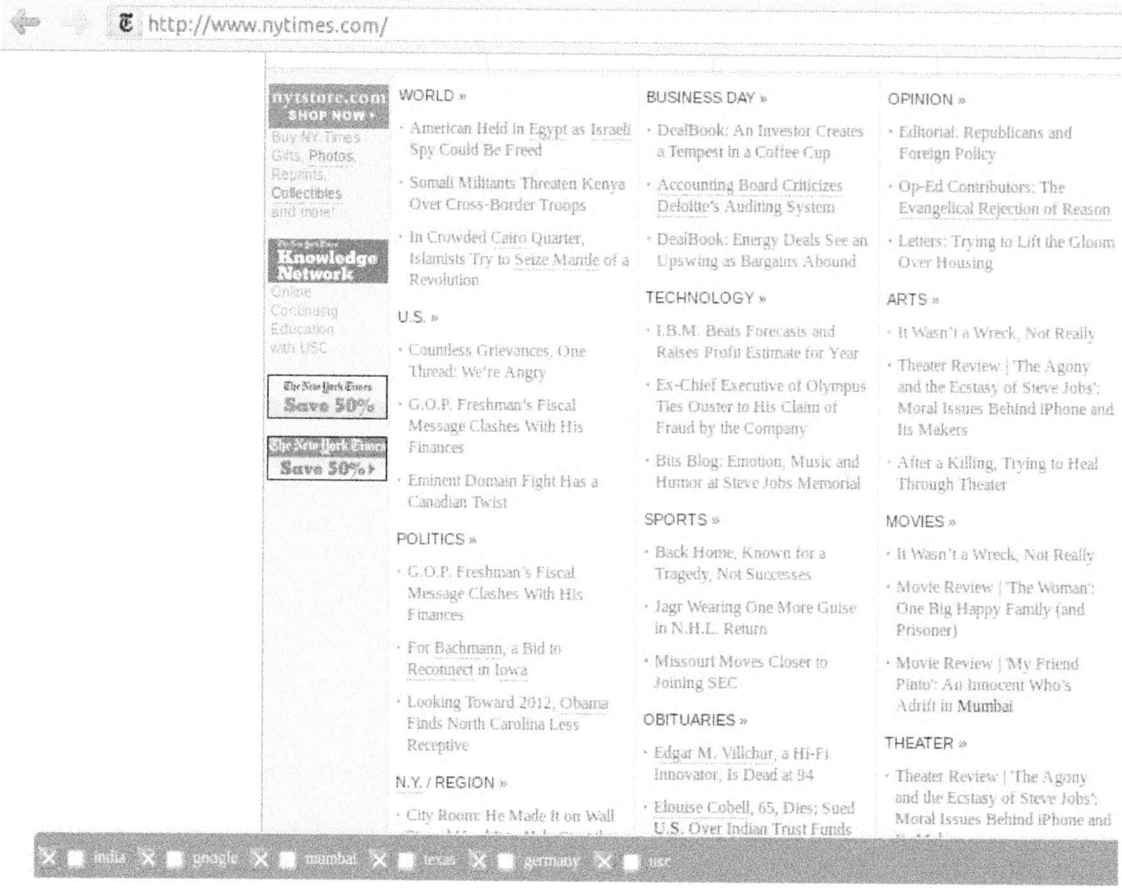

Figure 2. Highlighted terms and a summary of terms in the call-out bar at the bottom of the page.

ignore the highlight and read the page as usual. This experience can be likened to watching a game of American football on television, where the line of scrimmage and the first-down line are highlighted in the field virtually.

Our browser brings the user's attention to terms that are likely to be meaningful to him. Examples of such terms are proper nouns and names of friends or places that appear in the user's email archive. Figure 2 shows a screenshot of the browser on the New York Times home page for one of the participants in our study. Here the terms *Mumbai* and *USC* are highlighted; it turned out that this user comes from the city of Mumbai and had applied to USC for admission.

Even for terms that appear on the page and in the archive, users may have varying degrees of interest and association with them. We attempt to capture the strength of the user's relationship with each term and convey it in the interface; stronger terms can be highlighted more prominently. Our current implementation employs only two levels of highlighting, strong and weak. Terms are scored according to their entity type on the page and their frequency in the corpus, and classified as having either strong or weak interest. Strong-interest terms are highlighted in bright yellow, making them hard to miss as the user scrolls around the page. Weak-interest terms are highlighted in light yellow, allowing the user to see the terms if they are so inclined, but they do not jump out as prominently at the reader. While we currently highlight all matching terms at one of these two levels, it is easy to implement ranking algorithms to avoid highlight overcrowding in case it occurs. The next section describes how scores for a term are computed.

The browser also displays at the bottom of the screen a call-out listing all the terms found in the page that also match the archive. This call-out serves as an index to convey to users what is on the page without requiring them to scroll through the page. This feature is particularly useful for long web pages. One of our users has commented that it feels like a personalized tag-cloud of the terms on the page. As shown in Figure 2, the call-out is shown in a fairly unobtrusive way at the bottom of the page. The user can easily ignore the display of terms if so inclined, or hide it. In addition, the user can dismiss a term by clicking the cross icon next to it, and the browser will remove the term from consideration in subsequent pages.

The browser also lets users find out why it highlighted the terms shown. By simply clicking any highlight terms or a term in the call-out, the user can see a preview of the email messages that contain the terms of interest. This is very important especially for people with long-term email archives,

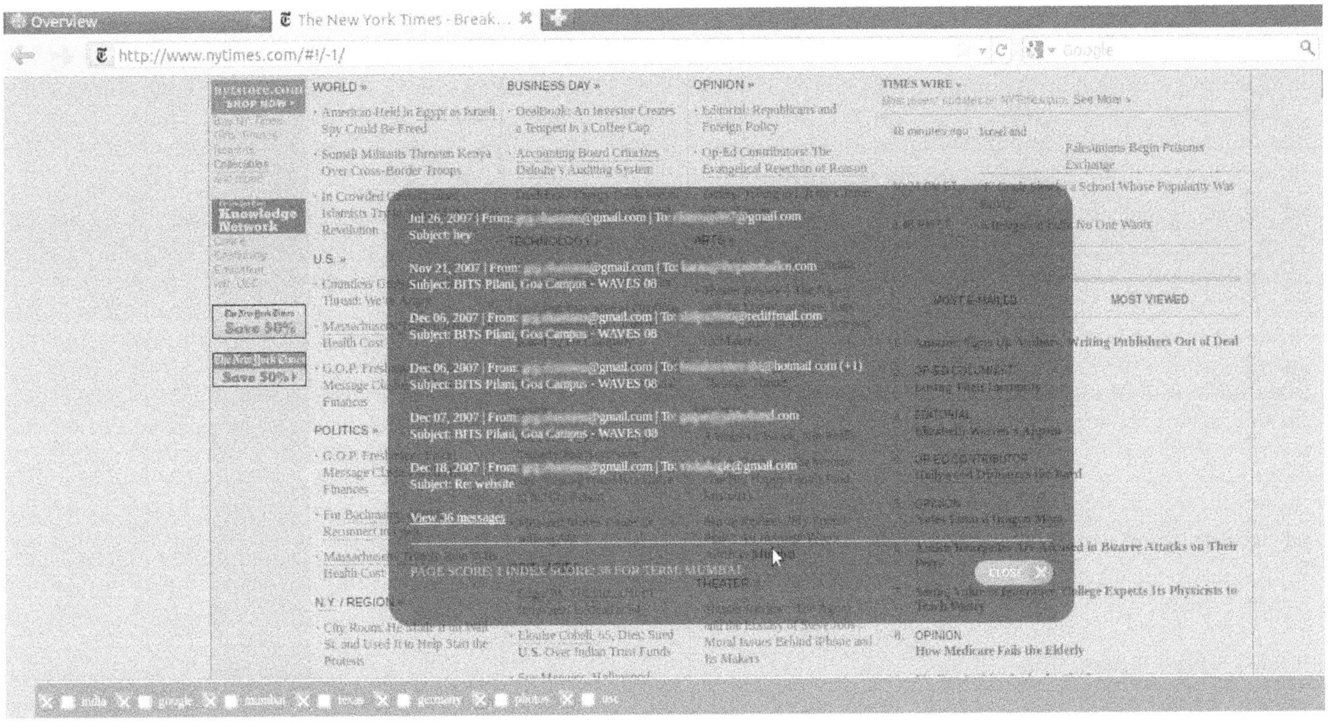

Figure 3. The browser lets users click on a highlighted term to display content in the archive that is related to that term. Each entry can be clicked to view the full message containing the term. Some details are blurred in this screenshot to preserve user privacy.

because they may have forgotten their encounter with the highlighted term. In this way, users can discover old connections and recall forgotten facts. As shown in Figure 3, the browser displays snippets for up to 5 messages. For more, the user has to click on "view messages" and go to a new browser tab. Clicking on any of the message snippets will show the entire message.

The brower applies the highlights immediately after a page is loaded. If page scripts subsequently change its contents, the user has the option to click a refresh button, which re-highlights the page. Users can also hide the call-out box if they find it distracting.

SYSTEM DESIGN

Our system consists of two parts – a background service that accesses and indexes the user's personal history from email files or online email accounts, and a Firefox browser plugin that performs user interface tasks. We chose this separation because the indexing component needs to be highly performant due to the size of personal archives, often running into tens of thousands of messages and spanning hundreds of megabytes of text. The background service is implemented in Java. The front-end part is implemented in Javascript, and is kept relatively lightweight so it can be ported to other browsers in the future. Fig. 1 illustrates the components of the system and the flow when a typical web page is loaded.

The background service is built upon MUSE [11], a system that accesses and indexes email message contents (and chat archives if available through an IMAP interface such as that of Gmail). MUSE processes loosely organized email archives – for example, it can access multiple sources of email (accessed online or stored locally), perform data cleaning and entity resolution, and eliminate duplicate messages. The indexer runs in the background on the user's own computer. It has to run only once, and for most users, indexing is a one-time operation that takes less than 30 minutes. The index is serialized and saved to disk, so that it can be quickly loaded after a computer or browser restart.

To allow easy experimentation, we implemented our browser extension as a Greasemonkey user script[1], in about 1,000 lines of Javascript. After the web page is completely loaded by the browser, the user script extracts page contents and posts it to MUSE that is running on the same machine in the background. We extended MUSE by enabling it to look up the textual contents of a web page in its index. For most web pages, the lookup completes in about a second. The results of the lookup are used to inject Javascript into the page to highlight the relevant terms. In any case, users can begin to interact with the page as soon as it is loaded, without waiting for the highlights to appear.

Named Entities

From our early experimentation, we realized that by blindly matching terms on the page with terms in the archive, it is easy to inundate users with terms of little or no interest. A key design decision we made is to focus on named entities. This is a useful heuristic – while names are a relatively small

[1] `http://www.greasespot.net`

fraction of the text on the page, they capture a large number of personal associations as compared to ordinary words. Therefore, the use of named entities reduces the number of hits on a page to a manageable number, improving precision and reducing noise, while still allowing a relatively high degree of recall.

We extract named entities from the page text using the Stanford NLP toolkit [26]. The named entity recognizer can identify names from a piece of text, and also classify them as likely to belong to a person, place or organization. We have to format contents appropriately in preparation for the recognizer, since it depends on signals such as capitalization, nearby words and whether the term appears at the start of sentence. Therefore, we traverse all HTML elements in the web page, extract text from them, and concatenate them to form the page text. As a special case, we insert full stops if needed after the text extracted from division elements (<div>), list elements (<li>), paragraphs (<p>) and headers (<h1>, . . . , <h6>) since it is unlikely that normal sentences would span across these elements.

Ranking and Filtering Hits

To determine the importance of each term that hits in the personal archive, we assign it a score. Through experimentation, we observed that users almost always find people names more interesting than other named entities (such as names of places and countries, which can be fairly generic). We therefore bias the scoring based on entity type. The scoring formula for a term t on the page is:

$$score(t) = w(Type_t) \times |\{d|t \in d\}|$$

where $Type_t$ is the weight assigned to the name type of t, and d is a document in the archive that contains t (whether in its headers or in its body). Our default weight is 1,000 for the person type, and 1 for all other types, strongly boosting the score of person names. To decide whether to highlight the term strongly or weakly, we check whether its score is above or below a threshold (the default threshold is 5). The call-out at the bottom displays terms in order of decreasing score. We expect this scoring function may become more sophisticated in future implementations.

An additional filtering step we found necessary was due to false hits generated by common single-word names (e.g., names like *James* and *Mary*). We eliminate single-word names that belong to the list of each of the 1000 most common (English language) last names, male first names and female first names.

RESULTS FROM A USER STUDY

We designed our browsing system by conducting formative studies with a few lead users and by using it ourselves for routine browsing for a few weeks. When our design was reasonably stable, we conducted a formal round of studies by inviting 9 users (3 female) to test out our system. The users were in the age group 23-29. We deployed the system on the participants' own machines to assure them about privacy. We asked the participants to download MUSE and run it on email folders of their choice, which were typically sent message folders, chat messages if available (via Gmail), and other folders that they thought contained messages interesting or important to them.

Our users had between 2,600 and 21,835 emails and chat logs. We helped them with the retrieval and indexing of their archives which typically took between 2-3 hours. Participants were then asked to install our browser extension. They were given a tour of the features of the system and asked to browse normally for an hour and report any interesting terms that the browser highlighted for them that they otherwise might have missed. They reported these terms by clicking a check-box presented in the call-out at the bottom of the page. They were also told that they could remove any term deemed noisy or irrelevant by clicking the cross icon next to it. After an hour, we collected their browsing logs and gave them a questionnaire asking for their opinion about various aspects of the browser.

We chose this setup to give our experiment broad ecological validity, and because we wanted to learn about the utility of the system on a diverse range of web pages. While the fact that users were aware that their browsing was being logged may have slightly altered their normal browsing behavior, we do not think these changes were significant enough to change our conclusions.

The overall results of this user study were very encouraging. When asked if they would want to continue to use the browser beyond the study period, 7 of 9 users replied in the affirmative. One participant replied "not sure" whereas another wanted to keep using the system "on search and news websites".

Qualitative feedback

The primary goal with this user study was to obtain qualitative user feedback at an early stage of development. We therefore asked users for their detailed impressions of the system, as well as specific examples that did or did not perform well for them. We present and categorize below some examples that are representative of their experiences. Users in the controlled study are referred to as P1 to P9, though we have also included feedback from other users (including the authors) who have informally used the system outside the context of this study.

People names

A common theme was for users to discover the names of someone they either knew directly or whose name they had encountered in the body of an email message. One user, while reading an op-ed article on a news site, found that it mentioned the president of his university. This name was mentioned in the bottom half of the article ("below the fold"), so the user would have missed it had it not been presented in the browser call-out. In this instance, the user had not directly exchanged email messages with the president of the university, but his name was present in email conversations with friends.

P4 was looking at a company website and found a person's name highlighted by the browser. On exploring further, the user discovered that the person had given a talk some years

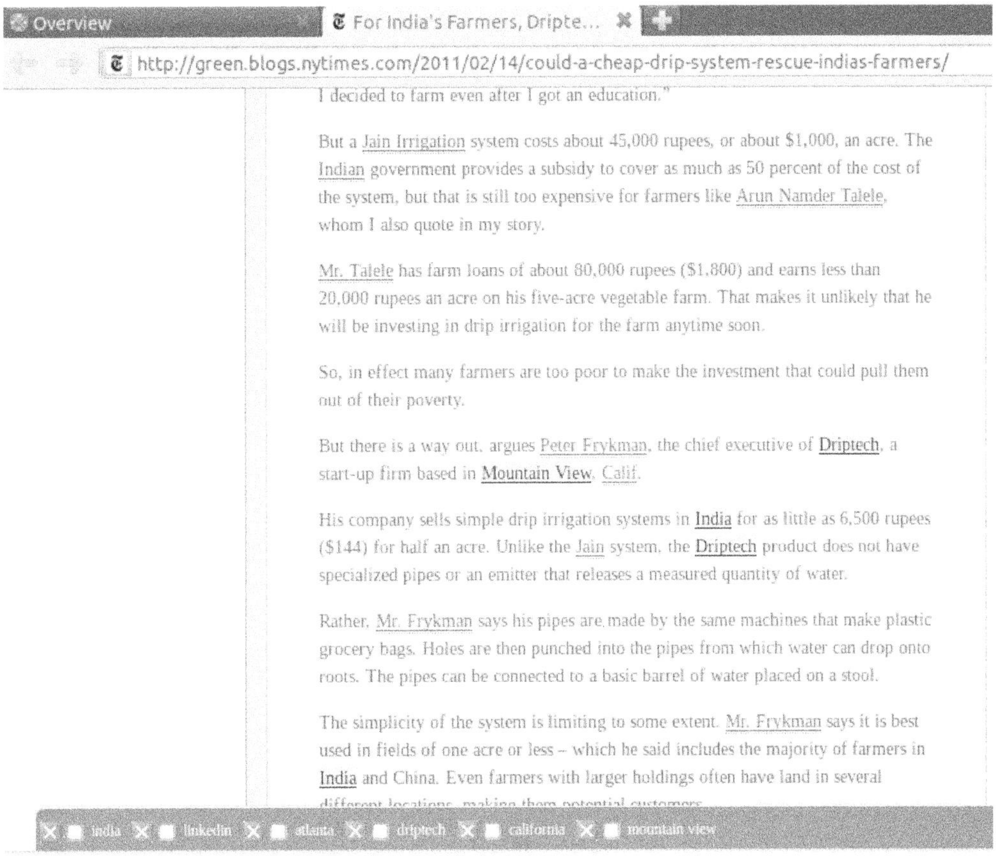

Figure 4. Example of a highlight of a company name that a user had interned at the previous summer.

ago which he had attended. He remarked, *"I would like to have such a tool present everywhere which helps me reach for such hidden information, which I have forgotten about."*

One user who is a professor, while attending a conference and browsing its program web page, found several highlighted occurrences of a person whose name was not familiar to her at all. By examining the relevant email messages, she discovered that the person had applied to her university years ago and was turned down for an interview despite her recommendation. The university should have considered the candidate after all! This story demonstrates that our browser can be effective in illuminating the serendipitous re-crossing of paths.

P2 was browsing a website for applying to a foreign internship and found a testimonial on the website by a person he knew and responded *"I would not have noticed this name had it not been highlighted."*

P9 was reading a page with a list of startup companies that had recently been incorporated when she was surprised to find highlighted the name of a former customer of hers with whom she had interacted 3 years ago.

Yet another user found that the name of the teaching assistant for a course that he was considering was highlighted. Examining the related messages reminded him that the TA had emailed him in response to a campus classified advertisement.

The above examples show that highlighting previously encountered person names, along with the messages in which they were encountered, can be useful in a variety of contexts: personal or professional, either directly known or merely discussed, and well known to the user or forgotten about after a chance encounter.

Products and commerce

P1 found the browser useful as he was browsing an airline's website and found its loyalty program named *Skywards* highlighted. The user responded *"The airlines had emailed me that I have accumulated sufficient miles to get a discount and I had almost forgotten about it."*

Another user found an article on a news site about the car *Toyota Prius*, that he owned. This indicates that personalization based on products owned by a user is possible using names present in ordinary email conversations or in email receipts.

Interestingly, our browser sometimes highlighted relevant words in page advertisements as well. This indicates that it may be effective in highlighting relevant ads without compromising user privacy.

Organization and place names

One user found that a news blog happened to mention Driptech, the name of the company he had interned at the previous summer, and it helped him notice its presence (See Fig. 4.) Yet another user (who was from India) discovered an article that mentioned Indian cooking in the cooking section of a news site, to which he ordinarily does not pay any attention.

In these examples, users were surprised to find the particular name on a page, and were happy that our browser helped surface information that they otherwise might have missed.

General comments

Participants in the study found our browsing extension an effectively way of viewing a web page through a uniquely personal lens. They found it especially compelling on sites that they usually only skimmed, or that had a lot of content or listings of people names.

P5 said *"I feel like this almost presents me with a personal synopsis of the (web) page."*

P8 also responded along the same lines: *"This tool lets me skim through websites faster."*

P6 mentioned *"I like how it recognizes certain topics that I am interested in–the highlight helps me walk through the site better."*

Users generally liked how the browser helped them find interesting material to read when they were skimming through certain websites. For a particular news site, P9 also remarked, *"After I've got used to it, and know what to expect for this site, it's easy for me to see that there's no new news on it for me today."*

Most users liked the fact that the browser ran completely locally on their own computer, and hence their private information was not being shared with anyone else. P3 said, *"I like the idea of personalization without giving my data to anyone."*

DISCUSSION

Users spend a significant portion of their time browsing the Internet. This browsing activity may be focused on a particular transaction or it may involve exploratory or casual browsing. Many users spend more Internet time on social networking sites and blogs than on reading news [19]. One reason for this may possibly be that social networking feeds are inherently tailored for the user, since a user's friends often reflect his interests. In contrast, most generic news sites are curated by editors for a wide audience, and hence they may fail to get articles of interest across to specific users. We believe that the principle of supplementing organic web browsing with color gleaned from personal history can be very useful in many settings.

One way of thinking about our browsing system is that it effectively creates lightweight "alerts" for thousands of terms in the personal index. When any of these terms are present on the current web page, the browser tries to ensure that the user notices their presence.

We have found that experience-infused browsing is particularly useful for reading news or long blog posts. For instance, the website of The New York Times typically has over 120 stories on its front page. A small number of these are likely to be interesting to any particular user. Our browser can help users identify news stories particularly relevant to them. Often these are stories related to particular places, people and organizations that the user is interested in or affiliated with. Similarly, the browser can be useful for the news site of a small community (such as a campus newspaper) because there is a chance that the user knows specific people in the community who may be mentioned on a particular day. It can also be used to highlight interesting items in social network feeds like those from Twitter and Google Plus.

The results of experience-infused browsing depend on the quality of data present in the personal archive. For example, we recommend that users index both incoming and outgoing e-mail with MUSE. It is useful to include folders containing receipts of transactions such as shopping records, tickets booked, etc. Instant messenging logs are also useful as they reflect real-time discussions among people and encompass a wide range of information, from restaurant reviews to buying a car. We envision that in the future, users will actively enhance and manage their own digital archive. For example, a user can declare interest in all his classmates by importing the class directory into the corpus (perhaps just by emailing it to himself), or a professor could ensure that the names of all the students she has taught over the years are available in her personal index. Similarly, people can save business cards or LinkedIn profiles of their contacts in their digital archive. Now, whenever the name of any of these people is on the web page being browsed, the user will not miss noticing it. This often turns out to useful when looking at a page containing a lot of names – for example, attendees at a large event.

Along the same lines, users may wish to import a curated set of blogs or pages that they trust into the archive. Then they would not need to read and remember them entirely, but the browser could surface connections from the current page to the imported content as a reminder to the user. Perhaps users could subscribe to high-quality mailing lists related to their broader interests that they do not necessarily read manually, but that are used only to build up a corpus of terms related to the topic that can be used to highlight related text on web pages. Students could import the class materials for all their courses into their personal archive, so that when they visit any related web page at any time in the future, the browser can insert a link back to their original class material. Researchers can import their own papers into the personal index, so they can spot related material when reading other papers. These scenarios indicate that total recall is not only possible, it can be very useful in a wide range of applications.

We found that over time, users built up a mental model of the kind of things our browser was good at highlighting on a particular site (for example, a news site that they visited daily). They used our index to quickly guess when there was no useful content, which saved them time.

The experience-infused browsing technique would be particularly useful on mobile devices where screen area is limited and it is relatively difficult to browse a large amount of text. We would like to explore this use case in future work.

LIMITATIONS AND FUTURE WORK

We now discuss the limitations of our current browser, which need to be addressed in future work. Our current implementation has a slight speed impact when the browser is loading a heavy page. One user complained to us about this sluggishness during the user studies. We plan engineering improvements to address this issue in the future.

More importantly, the browser is relatively easily fooled by noise. For example, a relatively common name like *Michael Scott* may result in false hits, unless the user marks and dismisses the term. One way of solving this problem is to filter more terms; another is to look for co-occurring names to disambiguate each other. For example if the personal index contains messages from a certain *Michael Scott* working at *Dunder Mifflin* (and therefore both names frequently appear together in the archive), the browser could highlight the name *Michael Scott* on a page only if *Dunder Mifflin* also appears on it. Similarly, place names can be broad and non-specific; highlighting names like *U.S.A.* is probably not useful in most circumstances.

While email and chat logs are conveniently accessible and capture a rich fraction of personal history for many users, a more comprehensive archive would incorporate more social streams such as those from Facebook and Twitter. Eventually, one could also consider importing a subset of web pages the user has visited (and perhaps spent a minimum amount of time on) in a browser into the archive. Needless to say, maintaining the security of a comprehensive personal digital archive is essential. Studying ways to integrate and score terms encountered via disparate sources and at different times in such an archive is likely to be an interesting challenge.

Currently our browser does not change page layout in any way. It also accesses content only within the current page. This could be expanded to items that may be of interest to the user but are hidden deeper down on related pages. Some of our users commented to us that they would like the browser to chase navigation links from the front page of a news portal into its various sections to uncover stories that they might be interested in. A useful approach might be to identify relevant articles for the user from a news feed of all articles, and then generate a customized newspaper by laying out just the relevant articles on a single page.

Of course, not everything that the browser highlights, even if accurate, is necessarily useful, and it may not always be desirable to only promote terms that the user has already encountered in the past. Personalization can lead to online "filter bubbles" [20]. More work is needed to determine how, when, and to what extent an experience-infused browser should intervene. We hope that deploying systems such as ours will shed more light on this problem.

CONCLUSIONS

We have found that the experience-infused browser is useful to let users efficiently browse textual content by highlighting personally relevant named entities in web pages. Our approach of using personal archives as a way to capture a user's experiences and interests appears to be effective, and the technique of matching named entities on web pages is a useful heuristic. From our user studies we see that deploying these archives in the context of web browsing can be a valuable tool for improved personalization and web browsing using purely client-side mechanisms. This is a significant departure from personalization based on user profiling by specific services.

The prototype we have developed appears to strike a good balance between surfacing interesting information and not being obtrusive. Users may not find interesting highlights on every page, but every so often it augments the browsing experience in interesting ways. Users find material that they may have missed, notice friends where they did not expect and recall people that they have long forgotten. This notion of infusing everyday tools with our digital life experiences can potentially be used in many other settings.

Serendipity is, by definition, rare [2], so how does one build a tool that surfaces potential serendipitous facts without inundating users with irrelevant or obvious information? Instead of just listing all possible connections, our tool uses the information in the archive to highlight terms familiar to a user, thus providing the primary benefit of more efficient browsing while imposing little cognitive overhead. Users can click on highlighted terms only if they are curious about the connections to those terms. The general idea of supporting serendipitous discovery in everyday tools can be applied to other contexts.

ACKNOWLEDGEMENTS

We thank Peter Chan for useful discussions, our study participants, and the anonymous IUI reviewers for excellent feedback. This research was partially funded by the NSF POMI 2020 Expedition Grant 0832820 and the Stanford MobiSocial Computing Laboratory.

REFERENCES

1. E. Adar, J. Teevan, and S. T. Dumais. Resonance on the web: web dynamics and revisitation patterns. In *Proceedings of CHI '09*, pages 1381–1390. ACM, 2009.
2. P. André, M. C. Schraefel, J. Teevan, and S. T. Dumais. Discovery is never by chance: Designing for (un)serendipity. In *C&C 09: Proceedings of the seventh ACM conference on Creativity and Cognition*. ACM, 2009.
3. R. Beale. Supporting serendipity: Using ambient intelligence to augment user exploration for data mining and web browsing. *International Journal of Human-Computer Studies*, 65(5):421–433, 2007.
4. G. Bell and J. Gemmell. *Total Recall: How the E-Memory Revolution Will Change Everything*. Dutton Adult, 2009.

5. M. Dzbor, J. Domingue, and E. Motta. Magpie towards a semantic web browser. In D. Fensel, K. Sycara, and J. Mylopoulos, editors, *The Semantic Web - ISWC 2003*, volume 2870 of *Lecture Notes in Computer Science*, pages 690–705. Springer Berlin / Heidelberg, 2003.

6. S. Gauch, M. Speretta, A. Chandramouli, and A. Micarelli. User profiles for personalized information access. In P. Brusilovsky, A. Kobsa, and W. Nejdl, editors, *The Adaptive Web*, volume 4321 of *Lecture Notes in Computer Science*, pages 54–89. Springer Berlin / Heidelberg, 2007.

7. J. Gemmell, G. Bell, and R. Lueder. MyLifeBits: a personal database for everything. *Communications of the ACM*, 49(1), 2006.

8. E. Gilbert and K. Karahalios. Predicting tie strength with social media. In *Proceedings of CHI '09*. ACM, 2009.

9. J. Gritton. Of serendipity, free association and aimless browsing:do they lead to serendipitous learning? `http://www.education.ed.ac.uk/e-learning/gallery/gritton_serendipitous_learning/conclusion/assets/assignment_print_version.pdf`.

10. J. Hailpern, N. Jitkoff, A. Warr, K. Karahalios, R. Sesek, and N. Shkrob. Youpivot: Improving recall with contextual search. In *Proceedings of CHI '11*. ACM, 2011.

11. S. Hangal, M. S. Lam, and J. Heer. MUSE: Reviving memories using email archives. In *Proceedings of UIST '11*. ACM, 2011.

12. J. Helmes, K. O'Hara, N. Vilar, and A. Taylor. Meerkat and tuba: Design alternatives for randomness, surprise and serendipity in reminiscing. In *Proceedings of the 13th IFIP TC 13 International Conference on Human-Computer Interaction*, INTERACT'11. Springer-Verlag, 2011.

13. L. Hong, E. H. Chi, R. Budiu, P. Pirolli, and L. Nelson. Spartag.us: A low cost tagging system for foraging of web content. In *Proceedings of the working conference on Advanced Visual Interfaces*, AVI '08. ACM, 2008.

14. T. Joachims, D. Freitag, and T. Mitchell. Webwatcher: A tour guide for the world wide web. In *Proceedings of the 1997 IJCAI*, August 1997.

15. J. Lawley and P. Tompkins. Maximising Serendipity: The art of recognising and fostering unexpected potential - A Systemic Approach to Change. `http://www.cleanlanguage.co.uk/articles/articles/224/1/Maximising-Serendipity/Page1.html`.

16. H. Lieberman, C. Fry, and L. Weitzman. Exploring the web with reconnaissance agents. *Communications of the ACM*, 44:69–75, August 2001.

17. J. Liu, P. Dolan, and E. R. Pedersen. Personalized news recommendation based on click behavior. In *Proceedings of IUI '10*. ACM, 2010.

18. M. Mesarina, J. Jain, C. Sayers, T. Close, and J. Recker. Evaluating a personal communication tool: Sidebar. In *Proceedings of the 13th International Conference on Human-Computer Interaction. Part I: New Trends*, pages 490–499, Berlin, Heidelberg, 2009. Springer-Verlag.

19. Nielsen. Social Media Report: Q3 2011. `http://blog.nielsen.com/nielsenwire/social/`.

20. E. Pariser. Beware online "filter bubbles", March, 2011. `http://www.ted.com/talks/eli_pariser_beware_online_filter_bubbles.html`.

21. B. Quinn. Social network users have twice as many friends online as in real life, May 08, 2011. `http://www.guardian.co.uk/media/2011/may/09/social-network-users-friends-online`.

22. Radicati Group Inc. Email Statistics Report, 2010-2014. `http://www.radicati.com/?p=5282`.

23. N. Ramakrishnan and A. Grama. Data mining: from serendipity to science. *Computer*, 32(8):34 –37, Aug 1999.

24. B. J. Rhodes. Margin notes: building a contextually aware associative memory. In *Proceedings of IUI '00*. ACM, 2000.

25. A. J. Sellen and S. Whittaker. Beyond total capture: a constructive critique of lifelogging. *Communications of the ACM*, 53:70–77, May 2010.

26. The Stanford Named Entity Recognizer. `http://nlp.stanford.edu/software/`.

27. D. Wolber, M. Kepe, and I. Ranitovic. Exposing document context in the personal web. In *Proceedings of IUI '02*. ACM, 2002.

Towards an Intelligent Reviewer's Assistant: Recommending Topics to Help Users to Write Better Product Reviews

Ruihai Dong, Kevin McCarthy, Michael P. O'Mahony, Markus Schaal, Barry Smyth
Clarity - Centre for Sensor Web Technologies,
School of Computer Science and Informatics,
University College Dublin, Belfield, Dublin 4, Ireland
{firstname.lastname}@ucd.ie

ABSTRACT
User opinions and reviews are an important part of the modern web and all major e-commerce sites typically provide their users with the ability to provide and access customer reviews across their product catalog. Indeed this has become a vital part of the service provided by sites like Amazon and TripAdvisor, so much so that many of us will routinely check appropriate product reviews before making a purchase decision, regardless of whether we intend to purchase online or not. The importance of reviews has highlighted the need to help users to produce better reviews and in this paper we describe the development and evaluation of a *Reviewer's Assistant* for this purpose. We describe a browser plugin that is designed to work with major sites like Amazon and to provide users with suggestions as they write their reviews. These suggestions take the form of topics (e.g. product features) that a reviewer may wish to write about and the suggestions automatically adapt as the user writes their review. We describe and evaluate a number of different algorithms to identify useful topics to recommend to the user and go on to describe the results of a preliminary live-user trial.

Author Keywords
Intelligent user interfaces; text mining; writer's assistance; browser plugin.

ACM Classification Keywords
H.5.2. Information Interfaces and Presentation: User Interfaces; H.3.1. Information Storage and Retrieval: Content Analysis and Indexing

General Terms
Design; Algorithms; Experimentation.

INTRODUCTION
Increasingly, in the world of the social web and user-generated content, users who had previously played the role of content consumers are now increasingly involved in the creation of content whether through creating our own web pages or blogs or simply commenting on the articles/posts of others. One segment of user generated content that has experienced incredible growth over the last 5 years is user reviews. Today millions of users contribute their opinions of products and services on sites like TripAdvisor, Hotels.com, Amazon, BestBuy, IMDB, and countless more. In fact, user reviews are routinely providing an important and unique service to buyers every day. Indeed for many of us it is all but unthinkable that we would book a hotel without checking out its TripAdvisor reviews. And millions of shoppers every day use Amazon as a source of product review data even if they are planning to purchase elsewhere.

The growing importance of this type of user-generated content has highlighted a number of interesting research challenges. First and foremost, considerable research attention has recently been paid to better understanding the quality and fairness of user-generated reviews. For example Mahony and Smyth [9] uses reviewer's reputation and Liu et al.[7] uses reviewer's genre familiarity to predict the quality or helpfulness of a review. In addition, review length and unigram distribution, cf. Kim et al. [6], or recency of reviews, cf. Liu et al. [7], have also shown good performance as predictive classifiers for review quality. The power of combining multiple criteria has been investigated by Wu et al. [12]. Wu et al. [13] also investigated distortion as a validation measure for the classification of suspicious reviews.

In this paper we are also interested in ensuring review quality but we adopt a very different, albeit complementary, approach. Rather than evaluating the quality of reviews that have already been written, we support the process of writing good reviews. Inspired by the GhostWriter system [4, 5], we have developed the *Reviewer's Assistant* system to work with sites like TripAdvisor and Amazon and to make suggestions to users as they start to write a review. These suggestions are optional and of course the user may choose to ignore them. The sugges-

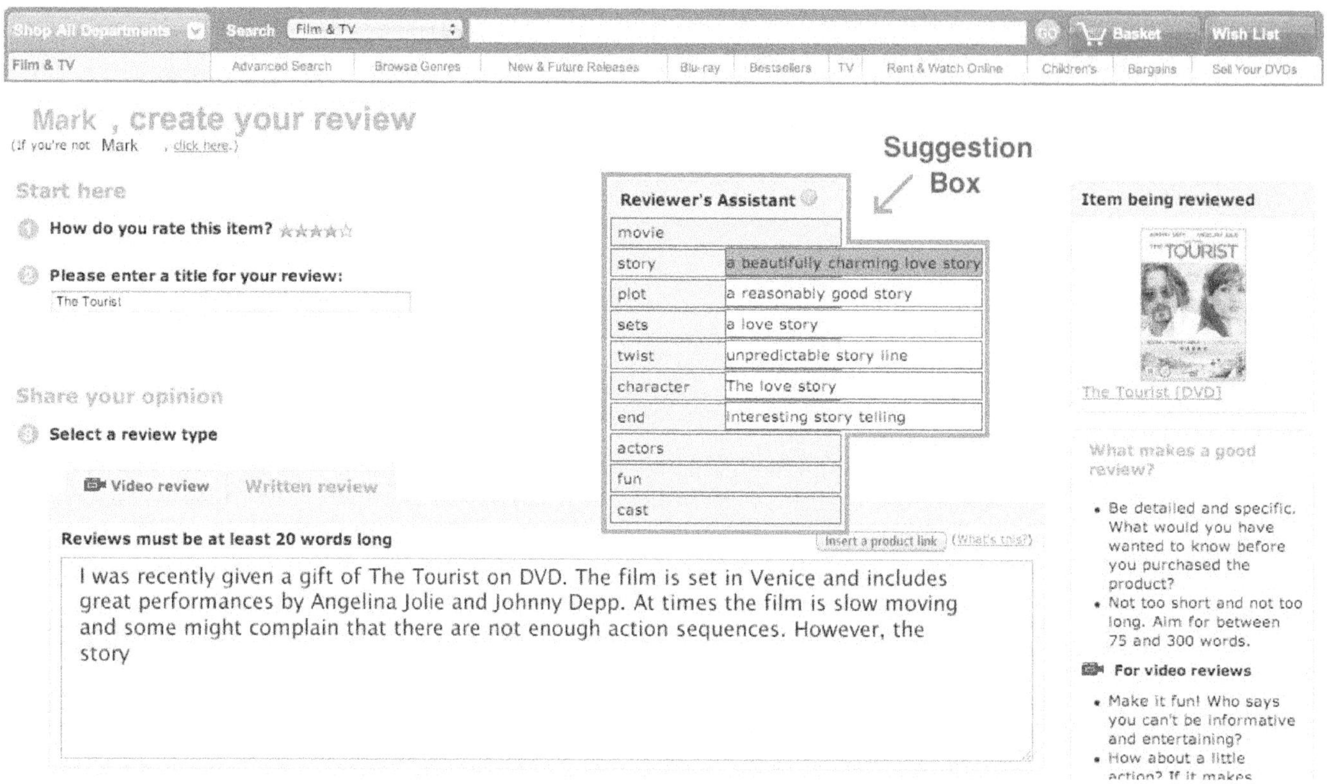

Figure 1: The *Reviewer's Assistant* browser plugin

tions take the form of a set of words that are designed to highlight key features/topics related to the product or service that the user is writing about, which have been extracted from other related reviews. As they write their review these suggestions change in response to what they write. For example, in reviewing a Nikon D90 SLR camera on Amazon, initial suggestions to the user might encourage them to discuss the *price* of the camera or its *resolution*; and via the assistant tool, the user can always see what other users have written about these features if they wish. Moreover, as the review becomes more complete, these suggestions will change. Features that have already been covered will fall away and new, possibly more niche features, will be suggested. For example, the reviewer might be encouraged to discuss the camera's *battery* life or the *weight* of the body or even its *shutter* type. Of course these suggestions are entirely optional. At all times it is up to the user whether they choose to write about particular suggestions but because they are available our hope is that some users will benefit some of the time and that this will lead, in due course, to a greater number of high quality, helpful reviews. An example screen shot of the Reviewer's Assistant is presented in Figure 1. Briefly it shows the Reviewer's Assistant's suggestions box with a number of suggested topics related to the review that the user has started to write; in this case it is a review about the movie The Tourist starring Angelina Jolie and Johnny Depp. As indicated, if the user mouses over one of these suggestions then they see a short list of review fragments from related reviews that have touched on this topic. We will return to this example later and discuss the various techniques that have been used to extract these recommendations from review content in real-time.

The main contribution of this paper is as follows. First we review the GhostWriter work and propose that its focus on noun-phrase suggestions is not ideal when it comes to providing review-writing assistance because it can lead to a cut-and-paste type reviewer behavior. Rather, we propose a focus on extracting *topics* (nouns) from related reviews and suggesting these topics to users to encourage them to form their own opinion on these topics. We describe a number of different recommendation strategies based on this idea and evaluate them on a range of real-world data sets. In addition, we describe the development of the *Reviewer's Assistant* browser plugin and describe the results of a preliminary live-user trial on Amazon.

THE GHOSTWRITER SYSTEM

The GhostWriter system was first proposed by Bridge et al. [4] and Healy and Bridge [5] as an approach to guide users in the construction of short snippets of user generated content. Originally, this took the form of guiding users during the creating of classified adverts for products they wished to sell/exchange. Subsequently, the GhostWriter researchers turned their attention to helping users produce review content on Amazon.

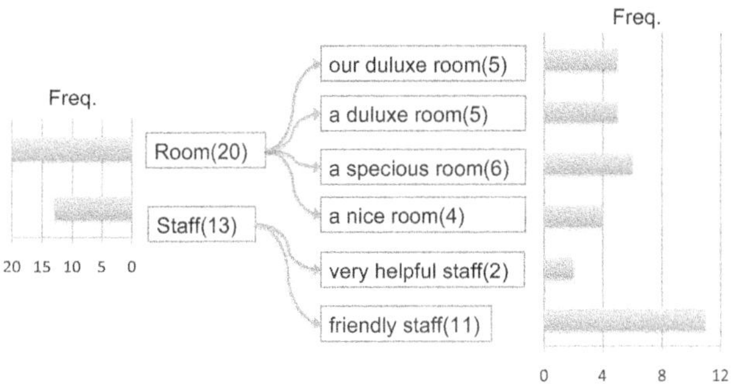

Figure 2: *Multiple noun phrases representing the same topic*

The system is inspired by Conversational Case-Based-Reasoning (CCBR) techniques [3] where existing reviews are treated as past cases and the current review fragment as a query. Currently GhostWriter 2.0 [5] extracts noun phrases from these past product reviews (cases), and suggests these phrases directly to the reviewer/user. At the beginning of our work on providing a similar type of assistance to budding reviewers we had in mind two important questions about the GhostWriter approach. Are noun phrases really the right type of objects to guide a writer of reviews? How can we measure (and improve) the quality of suggestions presented to the user?

The noun phrases suggested by the GhostWriter system to the editor of a review typically carry two types of information: highly structured knowledge from prior reviews which are presented as sentence fragments; and topical knowledge contained in those fragments. And the primary aim of GhostWriter was to provide a set of useful fragments that could be copied directly into an evolving review. However, there are two problems with this approach. Very often the review fragment (phrase) that is suggested does not make for a clear talking point for the reviewer; the central topic can be somewhat hidden in the larger review fragment. Moreover, the intent to remove review friction by facilitating a copy-and-paste approach can inevitably lead to reviews that lack novelty and interest.

Concretely then there are two key issues with GhostWriter that are considered as opportunities for improvement in this paper:

1. Nouns might be represented by multiple noun phrases, as illustrated in Figure 2. Assuming there are two features hidden in the reviews: *room* and *staff*. *room* is mentioned 20 times and *staff* is mentioned 13 times. If we only recommend one feature based on the frequency from the noun words point of view, *room* is the best choice. However, if we extract the feature from the noun phrase directly, *friendly staff* is a best choice based on the frequency calculation.

2. The relationship between current writing and topics to be covered in the remainder of the writing process is not sufficiently considered by GhostWriter 2.0. In particular, association rule mining, which is generally useful for discovering interesting relationships hidden in large data sets, may help to reduce this inaccuracy. For example, in market basket analysis, $\{Bread, Milk\}$ is an example of a frequent itemset. It indicates that a relationship exists between the sale of *bread* and *milk* because many customers who buy *bread* also buy *milk*.

THE REVIEWER'S ASSISTANT

The *Reviewer's Assistant* has been developed as a browser plugin so that it can integrate directly with review systems across a wide variety of web sites. In this paper we focus on its application to Amazon but it will work in a similar manner with sites such as Best-Buy, Hotels.com, TripAdvisor etc. As mentioned previously the Reviewer's Assistant takes the form of an additional recommendation module that appears on the review-creation pages of Amazon as shown in Figure 1. Quite simply the module presents an updating list of topic recommendations to the user as they write their review. These suggestions are extracted from the texts of related reviews in real-time and based on the review content that the reviewer has provided so far. As such the suggestions adapt to the review as the reviewer writes it: as topics are covered, these suggestions fall away and are replaced with additional suggestions. The module is fully interactive and the user can, for example, hover over a suggestion to see additional information, such as the review fragments from related reviews that discuss the topic. One simple difference between the Reviewer's Assistance and GhostWriter, that is worth highlighting at this stage, is that the former recommends nouns (topics) to the user in the first instance, with noun phrases (review fragments) available on request, whereas the latter recommends noun phrases directly.

This move from noun phrases to nouns, while simple, is important. It is motivated by the observation that many words in noun phrases do not carry the actual meaning and can distract from the topic in question. Also, it is less attractive to use nouns for a cut and paste writing style, and we hope to increase the quality of the review authors by shifting the focus from *coverage* (What do I need to write about?) to *evaluation* (How good is feature xyz?).

In what follows we will describe the techniques that the Reviewer's Assistant users to extract, recommend, and rank review topics.

System Overview

The overall Reviewer's Assistant system architecture is presented in Figure 3 and can be best understood with reference to the following core components:

1. *Filtering*. Select *good quality* User Generated Content (UGC) as knowledge base. UGC is created by common users without supervision. These common users are

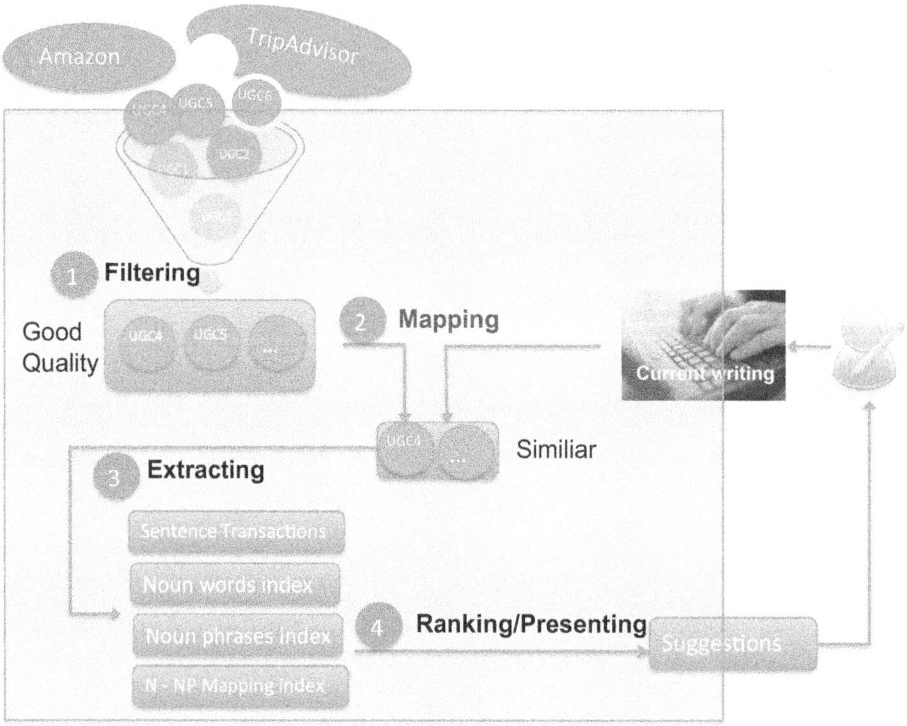

Figure 3: *High level system view of the Reviewer's Assistant*

not professional or technical writers. Therefore the quality of UGC is an issue.

2. *Mapping.* Assuming good quality UGC is identified, the similarity between the current writing of the user (in progress) and similar texts in the knowledge base is computed to identify *relevant* UGC. For example, when a user writes a camera review, books reviews might be not useful for her writing even though these reviews have a good quality.

3. *Extracting.* Extracting features from relevant and good quality UGC is the basis for generating and ranking suggestions. Features can be manifold, including indices to nouns or noun phrases, transactions for association rule mining, or mappings between topics (nouns) and noun phrases.

4. *Presenting.* In order to present topics to the user, suggestions must be generated from the extracted features and ranked in order to pick top N suggestions.

While being an important system component to ensure quality, *Filtering* is not investigated here. For our experimental knowledge bases we used review helpfulness.

For *Mapping*, all system variants investigated here use the Jaccard similarity coefficient to measure the similarity between the current user's writing and similar texts in the knowledge base, and the top 50 reviews have been selected consistently for further processing.

Let c_i, c_t be two texts, then the Jaccard similarity coefficient is calculated by equation 1; where $|c_i \cap c_t|$ is the number of words (ignoring stopwords) that both pieces of text have in common.

$$sim(c_i, c_t) = \frac{|c_i \cap c_t|}{|c_i \cup c_t|} \quad (1)$$

Note, the topics that can be presented to the user are limited by the broadness of the knowledge base. We have considered the exploitation of related knowledge bases for cases of insufficient coverage, but we consider this to be beyond the scope of this work.

Extracting for Reviewer's Assistant

We use OpenNLP[1] to split reviews into sentences, and to extract noun words and noun phrases from each sentence. For noun phrases, we record the frequency and the length of noun phrases. For noun words, only frequency is recorded. For association rule mining, we also generate transactions from sentences. A transaction is simply the set of noun words without stop words that is contained in a sentence. Figure 4 shows an example of converting a review to a group of sentence transactions.

Strategies for Generating Suggestions

We will compare the noun phrase selection strategy of Ghostwriter 2.0 with various noun selection strategies of

[1]OpenNLP: http://incubator.apache.org/opennlp/

Case$_i$	Sentences	Sentence transaction
The **room** was spacious with a comfortable **bed**. The **pillows** were really fluffy and everything you would expect with a **stay** at the **Bellagio**. The **bathroom** was spacious as well, with a separate **bath** and **shower**.	The **room** was spacious with a comfortable **bed**.	{room,bed}
	The **pillows** were really fluffy and everything you would expect with a **stay** at the **Bellagio**.	{pillows,stay, Bellagio}
	The **bathroom** was spacious as well, with a separate **bath** and **shower**.	{bathroom, bath, shower}

Figure 4: *Example of sentence transactions*

Reviewer's Assistant. All strategies propose exactly 10 (topical) suggestions to the user.

The following algorithm simulates the Ghostwriter generation of noun phrase suggestions (*gw*− denotes GhostWriter, *np* denotes noun phrase):

1. *gw-np* is an approximation of the GhostWriter 2.0 system. It generates noun phrases as suggestions and ranks these suggestions by the product of frequency and length of the noun phrase, e.g. if s is the suggested noun phrase and $freq(s)$ the total count of occurrences of the noun phrase in the similar reviews, then

$$score(s) = freq(s) \times length(s).$$

Some suggestions share the same score. To break ties, the GhostWriter 2.0 system (and *gw-np*) sums and compares the helpfulness of the reviews that contain the two suggestions.

Algorithm 1: The $ra - ans - n$ Algorithm

Input: T, $CurrWriting$
Output: S
$S = \emptyset$;
F_3 =k-itemsets($T, k = 3, min\_support = 2$);
$Rules$ =rules($F_3, min\_confidence = 0.5$);
$count = 0$;
while $Rules \neq \emptyset$ **do**
  select $r \in Rules$ with highest confidence;
  $Rules = Rules \setminus \{r\}$;
  if *left side of r in CurrWriting* **then**
    $S = S \cup \{$right side of $r\}$;
    $count++$;
  end
end
if $count < 10$ **then**
  fill-up S from $tf - n$;
end

Four different new algorithms for extracting the Top 10 topical nouns were evaluated (*ra*− denotes Reviewer's Assistant, *ans* denotes a-priori for nouns with sentence transactions):

1. *ra-n* is the baseline for noun word suggestions. It works like the original GhostWriter, but ranks nouns instead of noun phrases, e.g. if s is the suggested noun, then $freq(s)$ is the total count of occurrences of the noun in the similar reviews. Note, nouns are considered as noun phrases of length one, so the score is identical to the frequency.

2. *ra-ans-n* uses Association Rule Mining [10, 1] to search for missing topics once topical nouns have been identified. For the Reviewer's Assistant, we deployed the efficient a-priori association rule mining algorithm by Agrawal and Srikant [2]. Algorithm 1 shows the entire *ra-ans-n* Algorithm. It takes the sentence transactions (T) and the current writing as input and produces a set of 10 suggestions (S) as output. First we generate frequent 2- and 3-itemsets from *sentence transactions* with fixed minimum support of 2[2]. We then generate the rules for a minimum confidence of 0.5, and add the right sides of applicable rules to our suggestion set S until we have 10 suggestions. If the algorithm does not generate sufficient noun words, it uses *ra-n* as a fall-back strategy, i.e. the remaining noun word suggestions are generated from *ra-n*.

3. *ra-df* uses document frequency of noun words instead of term frequency, e.g. if s is the suggested noun, then $freq(s)$ is the total count of reviews (documents) in which the suggestion occurs.

4. *ra-ans-df* is identical to *ra-ans-n*, except it uses *ra-df* as fall-back strategy if less than 10 noun words are generated.

EXPERIMENTAL EVALUATION: OFF-LINE STUDY

So far we have motivated the Reviewer's Assistant as a tool to help users during product review tasks. Our central hypothesis is that by extracting key topics from past related reviews we can provide new reviewers with a series of hints or suggestions about the type of topic that they may wish to cover in their own review. In this section we will describe a two-part evaluation of the Reviewer's Assistant. First we will focus on an off-line, leave-one-out style evaluation of the different topic extraction techniques that we have described in order to assess their potential effectiveness when it comes to identifying topics that are likely to be written about by reviewers. Of course for a system such as the Reviewer's Assistant and off-line study such as this only tells part of the story and the real test is whether users find the service useful and whether it helps them to write better reviews. Therefore, we also describe a live-user trial in which a group of users spent time using the Reviewer's Assistant in a realistic setting as they wrote product reviews. We will describe their observations and summarize their assessment of the utility of the system, leaving the question of whether it helped them create better reviews as part of future work.

[2]The value for the maximum itemset size has been determined, then we chose a pareto-optimal combination of minimum support and minimum confidence by means of prior experiments across the entire set of possible parameter values.

Off-Line Datasets

The data for our experiments originally consisted of two different product review data sets from Amazon and TripAdvisor. Each data set was produced by mining review content directly from Amazon and TripAdvisor. In addition, for the purpose of this evaluation we also created a second Amazon data set that focused on a small set of six frequently reviewed products; the purpose of this was to look at the evaluation in the context of a mixture of sparsely populated and more densely populated review data sets.

A summary of the data contained in these three data sets is presented in Tables 1, 2, and 3. In the case of the Amazon data sets the reviews cover a range of products and product types (books, consumer electronics, DVDs etc.) as shown. In the case of the first Amazon data set (Amazon I) there are 100 randomly chosen reviews for each product category and reviews were selected only if they received at least 5 positive votes for helpfulness according to the Amazon review data. As per Table 1 each review contains from 6-9 sentences and includes about 30-50 noun words as candidate topics. The second Amazon data set (Amazon II) focused on a particular set of 6 popular products and for each product we have included from 57-100 reviews. Similar statistics are presented for the number of sentences and nouns in these more focused review data, cf. Table 2.

The TripAdvisor data set is based on a randomly selected set of 100 reviews for each class of hotels as shown in Table 3. As shown the TripAdvisor reviews tend to be a lot longer than their Amazon equivalents, ranging in length from 13-20 sentences. In terms of content focus, the TripAdvisor data set is more focused than the Amazon I data set, but broader than the Amazon II data set.

Category	#Rev	#Sen	#Words	#NW
books	100	7.85	182.77	49.23
electronices	100	9.23	174.83	42.1
camera	100	7.61	144.81	34.71
dvd	100	8.61	199.85	52.83
music	100	6.58	146.95	39.12

Table 1: Amazon I data set (categories, broad)

Item	#Rev	#Sen	#Words	#NW
The Kindle	99	16.23	407.40	85.65
A Vacuum Clean.	100	7.16	158.23	34.11
A Book on Chin.	57	4.56	96.18	21.09
The Nikon D90	77	6.88	156.84	36.84
A Samsung TV	66	4.55	99.76	22.97
The Tourist DVD	65	6.21	142.34	35.8

Table 2: Amazon II data set (products, focussed)

Experimental Setting

For evaluation purposes, we have adapted a standard leave-one-out methodology. For each of the review data sets we temporarily remove each review in turn; this is the *target review* and plays the role of the review that is currently being constructed in this evaluation. In turn we remove content from this review to reflect the review at various stages of completion. For example, we use different ablation levels from 20%-80% such that, for example, at the 80% ablation level it means that only 20% of the original review is available for use. The remaining review, denoted by Q (for query) is then used as the basis for the Reviewer's Assistant recommender engine to generate suggestions. The removed review is not used for the generation of suggestions, i.e. neither for the computation of frequency counts nor for the generation of frequent item sets. The ablated portion of the review is denoted as T and is used to test these suggestions.

Hotel Class	#Rev	#Sen	#Words	#NW
2.5 of 5	100	14.29	258.65	63.04
3.0 of 5	100	13.84	275.65	67.86
3.5 of 5	100	19.87	364.95	90.2
4.0 of 5	100	20.26	408.33	101.32
4.5 of 5	100	18.38	361.99	91.63
5.0 of 5	100	20.77	392.85	97.68

Table 3: Tripadvisor data set

We use each of the different generation/ ranking strategies described previously in turn to generate 10 suggestions, denoted by S per strategy for Q. To evaluate these suggestions we turn to two common metrics, *Precision* and *Recall* by comparing the suggestions from Q to the remainder of the review T. The intuition here is that if many of the suggestions are contained within the remainder of the review then this is good because the suggestions were actually written about by the original reviewer. This precision is the percentage of suggestions that are contained in T. Conversely, if many of the nouns in T are contained in the suggestions S then this is also good because it implies that the suggestions provide good coverage of the topics that were important to the original reviewer. Thus recall is the percentage of nouns present in T that are contained within the suggestions set S.

$$precision = \frac{|T \cap S|}{|S|} \qquad (2)$$

$$recall = \frac{|T \cap S|}{|T|} \qquad (3)$$

In the experiments, there are two kinds of suggestions, *single noun words* and *noun phrases*. For single noun words, $n \in T \cap S$ is easy to decide. A suggestion is in the ablated part of the review, if and only if it appears there. For noun phrase suggestions, the situation is slightly more complex. We therefore define a range of precision and recall for noun phrases in the following way:

- All (Min. Precision/ Recall): We consider a suggestion to be in the ablated part of the review iff *all* of its nouns are present.
- Any (Max. Precision/ Recall): We consider a suggestion to be in the ablated part of the review iff *at least one* of its nouns is present.

Ablation Experiment
Even though a quantitative comparison between GhostWriter and Reviewer's Assistant is impossible, due to the natural differences between nouns and noun phrases, we have tried to illustrate the differences in a qualitative manner.

In Figure 5, we show the comparison of precision and recall for each of the 3 data sets (6 sub-figures). Each of the sub-figures provides a comparison between GhostWriter (precision range from $gw - np(min)$ to $gw - np(max)$) and different strategies of Reviewer's Assistant (denoted by $ra - X$). For some of the data sets, there was no visual difference between some of the strategies. In these cases we represented multiple methods by a single line of mean values.

The following qualitative observations motivated us to do the Pilot Study with the Reviewer's Assistant plugin:

- Reviewer's Assistant (nouns) is consistently better than the minimum of the GhostWriter (noun phrases) precision range, i.e. at least nouns are a reasonable candidate for topical suggestions instead of noun phrases.
- Reviewer's Assistant consistently improves for higher ablations relative to the maximum of the GhostWriter precision range
- For the Amazon I data set and for the Trip Advisor data set, Reviewer's Assistant is best. For the Amazon II data set, Reviewer's Assistant is not stronger than Ghostwriter, but improves for higher ablations and is equally good as the maximum of the GhostWriter precision range for 80% ablation.

EXPERIMENTAL EVALUATION: LIVE-USER STUDY
In the previous section we described the results of an off-line ablation study to illustrate the relative effectiveness of our different recommendation strategies across 3 different data sets. The true test of a system like Reviewer's Assistant however is clearly how it performs in a real-world setting with live users. To that end we describe a preliminary live-user study in this section.

Study Setup
The purpose of this study is to evaluate the performance of the Reviewer's Assistant in a realistic setting in which users are asked to write reviews for particular products. In this case we focused on Amazon and configured the Reviewer's Assistant to generate its suggestions using the $ra - ans - n$ technique described earlier.

In total there were 19 participants, recruited from the School of Computer Science and Informatics in University College Dublin. Each user was instructed to install the Reviewer's Assistant Browser plugin in their browser (Google Chrome in this case) and they were asked to write reviews for a particular set of products that were familiar to them. Only 4 out of the 19 users had previously written an Amazon review prior to the study and in total the 19 users produced 40 different reviews.

During the study we logged the suggestions provided by the Reviewer's Assistant and the reviews produced as they were written. The participants also completed a post-study questionnaire. We were interested in understanding a number of key aspects of the system. First and foremost, was there evidence that the suggestions made by the system were useful to the reviewers; was there any evidence that they preferred the noun-based approach to the noun-phrase refinements? And ultimately, having used the system did users find it to be useful and would they use it in the future if available?

Suggestion Relevance
To evaluate the suggestions made to the user (S) we use an indirect measure of relevance by comparing these suggestions to the noun content of the review the user actually wrote (N). This provides precision- and recall-like measures as follows; in a technical sense we are measuring *precision* and *recall* of our suggestions against the complete review written by the user.

- $\frac{|S \cap N|}{|S|}$ or Precision: The percentage of suggestions the user actually wrote into the review.
- $\frac{|S \cap N|}{|N|}$ or Recall: The percentage of suggestions among the nouns written by the user.

Of course strictly speaking it is not possible to be fully confident that just because a suggestion was made by the system and written about by the user does mean that the user was influenced by the suggestion. Perhaps they did not notice the suggestion but wrote about the feature anyway. This is certainly a limitation but since our participants were generally paying attention to the suggestions made by the Reviewer's Assistant during this study we can be somewhat confident in our measures, and even if a particular reviewer did not notice a suggestion, the fact that they subsequently wrote about it still speaks to the effectiveness of the recommendation strategy.

The results are presented in Figure 6 as a graph of precision and recall (as defined above) versus review length (number of words), averaged over the 40 reviews produced by the 19 users; note that the x-axes also indicates the number of actual reviews. Overall we can see that the Reviewer's Assistant performs well across different length of reviews. As expected precision improves with review length, since longer reviews have a greater opportunity to include suggested topics. For example, we can see that shorter reviews (up to 40 words) contain

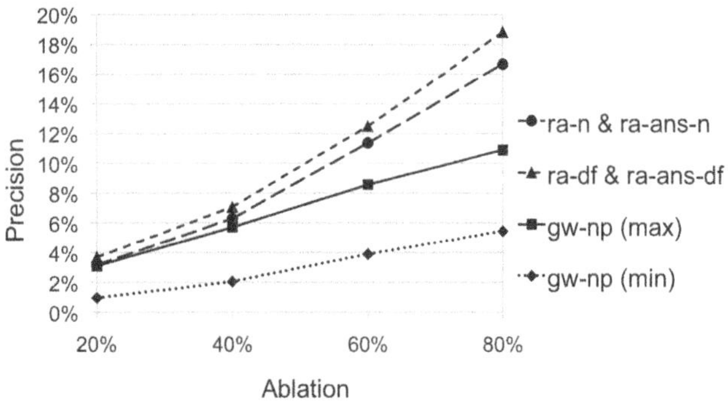

(a) Amazon I (5 categories) - precision

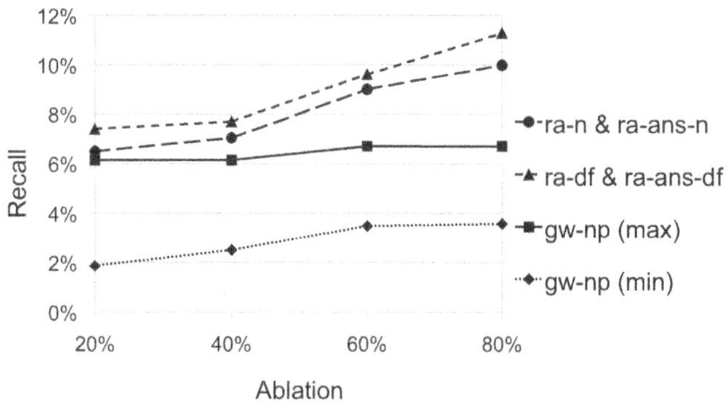

(b) Amazon I (5 categories) - recall

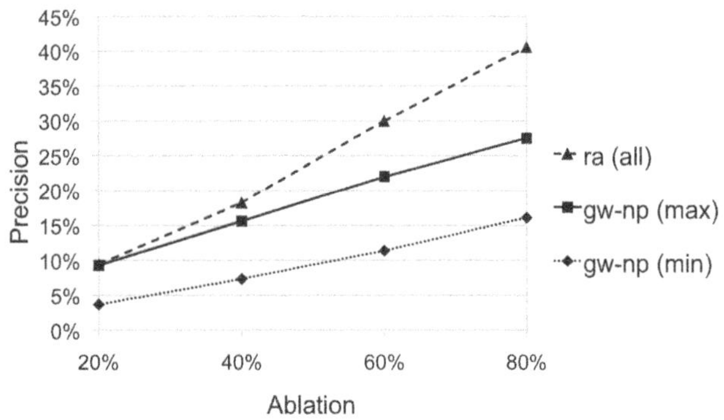

(c) Trip Advisor - precision

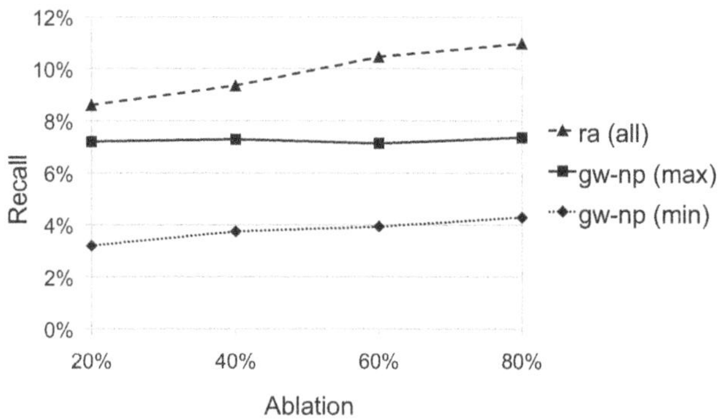

(d) Trip Advisor - recall

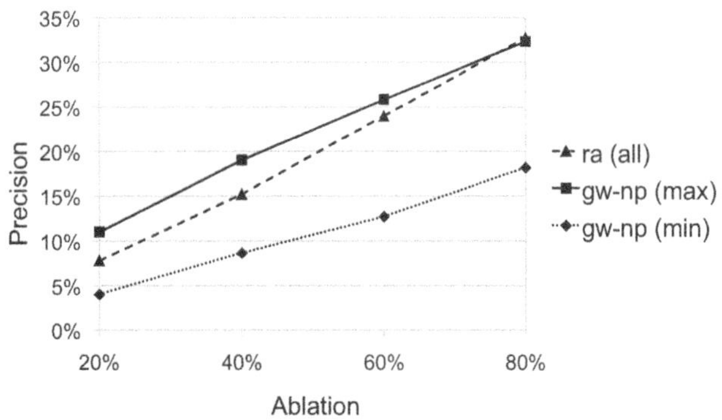

(e) Amazon II (6 products) - precision

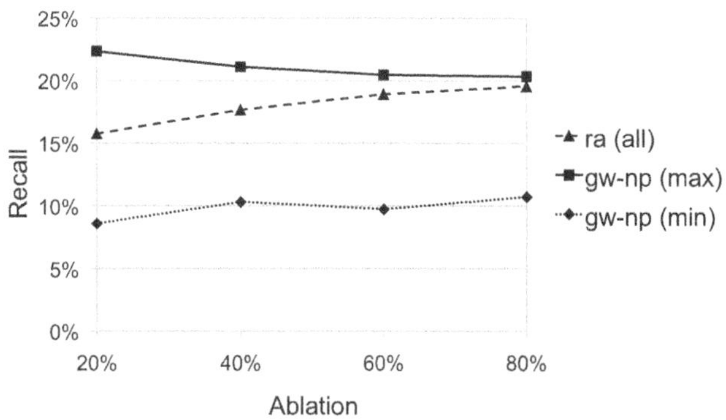

(f) Amazon II (6 products) - recall

Figure 5: Comparison

about 25% of the topics suggested during their construction and this rises to more than 40% for longer reviews with more than 120 words. Likewise recall is seen to fall as review length increases indicating that proportionally fewer suggestions are being used in longer reviews: for short reviews recall approaches 60% and falls to just over 30% for longer reviews.

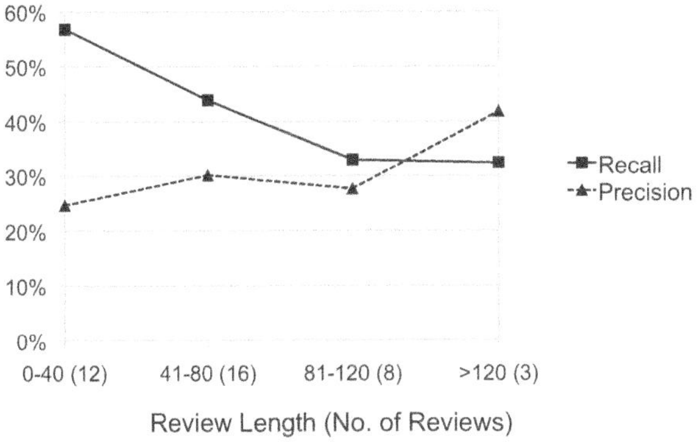

Figure 6: *Suggestion relevance*

Nouns vs. Noun Phrases

As described previously, the Reviewer's Assistant allows users to move from noun-based suggestions to noun-phrases that represent review fragments. In the study, noun-based suggestions were presented by default, but participants were reminded that they could see further details and review fragments and we were interested to see how often users would make this switch and when they did, whether they would continue to use noun-phrases. In fact, in only 10 out of the 40 reviews created did users ever switch to noun phrases. The total time they spent on average an noun phrases and nouns during each review is illustrated in Figure 7 as opposed to the average time the other 30 users spent on their reviews in total (on nouns).

Interestingly, even those 10 users who explored *noun phrases* as suggestions, switched back to *nouns* after an average time of 25 seconds, while they stayed for an average of 44 seconds with *nouns* even after they discovered *noun phrases* as an alternative.

User Feedback

As mentioned previously, upon completion of the study each user was asked to complete a short questionnaire to provide feedback on the Reviewer's Assistant. In particular we asked each participant to indicate their agreement/disagreement on four key statements:

1. The suggestions made by the Reviewer's Assistant were relevant to the product you were reviewing.
2. The suggestions made were helpful with respect to the review you were writing.
3. Taken together the suggestions made provided good coverage of the product you were reviewing.

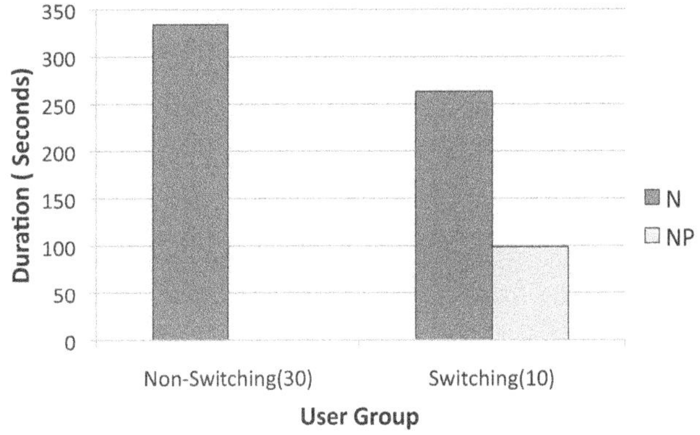

Figure 7: *Time spent on nouns vs. noun phrases*

4. You were satisfied with the utility of the Reviewer's Assistant and would use it again if available.

The results are summarized in Figure 8 and show the strong levels of support expressed by the participants. For example, we can see that more than 90% of users agreed that the suggestions being made were relevant to the product they were reviewing. About 75% of users found these suggestions to be helpful and comprehensive. And overall, more than 70% of users expressed a level of satisfaction with the Reviewer's Assistant that would lead them to use the tool in the future if available.

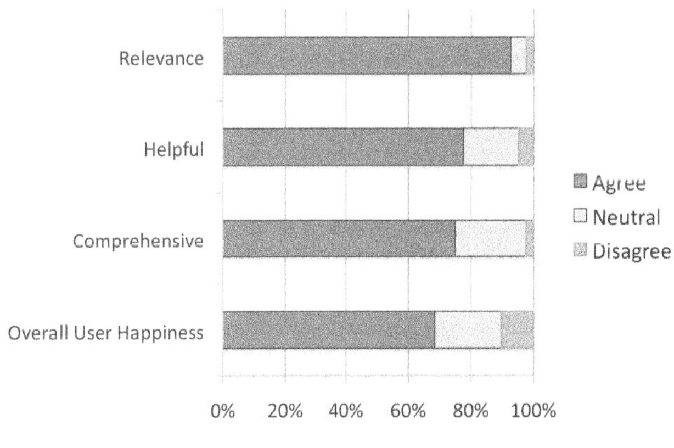

Figure 8: *User feedback*

CONCLUSIONS AND FUTURE WORK

As more and more users become producers of online content there is a need for a new generation of supporting tools, especially to help to guide users during their initial forays into user-generated content. This seems particularly relevant when it comes to producing reviews, which more users are inclined to do, and which are proving to be an increasingly important repository of decision informing opinions.

In this paper we have described the Reviewer's Assistant tool that is designed to support users as they write product reviews. We have described an initial set of techniques for automatically extracting useful suggestions from past reviews which can be recommended to new reviewers as they write. We have evaluated these strategies and demonstrated their practical usefulness in a live-user trial.

Undoubtedly there is still much to do in relation to this area of research. And certainly this paper represents an initial foray, presenting a set of benchmark techniques, and proving some preliminary evaluation results. These results indicate the the noun-based approach used by the Reviewer's Assistant performs better than previous approaches that have proposed a noun-phrase based approach. Overall, user feedback indicates that the Reviewer's Assistant is capable of making relevant, helpful, and comprehensive suggestions to reviewers as they write and the majority of users indicated that that they would use the system in the future. An open question is the quality of the resulting reviews, i.e. is it true that user satisfaction with the Reviewer's Assistant is reflected in higher review quality?

There is a obvious opportunity to improve the sophistication of the recommendation techniques used in the Reviewer's Assistant and as a next step, we plan to explore related methods for the improvement of topical suggestions with nouns. In particular, we will look into topic detection and topical relationships among nouns. Discovering conceptual relationships from text corpora, cf. e.g. Maedche and Staab [8], may help to extract topical features after mapping is completed. Topic discovery, e.g. the identification of descriptive terms for a set of texts, cf. e.g. Schaal et al. [11], may help to select the right nouns, especially if combined with word sense disambiguation.

ACKNOWLEDGMENTS

This work is supported by Science Foundation Ireland under grant 07/CE/I1147.

REFERENCES

1. R Agrawal, Tomasz Imieliński, and A Swami. Mining Association Rules between Sets of Items in Large Databases. *ACM SIGMOD Record*, 22(May):207–216, 1993.
2. Rakesh Agrawal and Ramakrishnan Srikant. Fast Algorithms for Mining Association Rules in Large Databases. In *Proceedings of the 20th International Conference on Very Large Data Bases*, VLDB '94, pages 487–499, San Francisco, CA, USA, 1994. Morgan Kaufmann Publishers Inc.
3. David W Aha, Leonard A Breslow, and Héctor Muñoz-Avila. Conversational Case-Based Reasoning. *Applied Intelligence*, 14(1):9–32, 2001.
4. Derek Bridge and Aidan Waugh. Using experience on the read/write web: The ghostwriter system. In Derek Bridge, Enric Plaza, and Nirmalie Wiratunga, editors, *Procs. of WebCBR: The Workshop on Reasoning from Experiences on the Web (Workshop Programme of the Eighth International Conference on Case-Based Reasoning)*, pages 15–24, 2009.
5. Paul Healy and Derek Bridge. The GhostWriter-2.0 System: Creating a Virtuous Circle in Web 2.0 Product Reviewing. In Derek Bridge, Sarah Jane Delany, Enric Plaza, Barry Smyth, and Nirmalie Wiratunga, editors, *Procs. of WebCBR: The Workshop on Reasoning from Experiences on the Web (Workshop Programme of the Eighteenth International Conference on Case-Based Reasoning)*, pages 121–130, 2010.
6. S.-M. Kim, P. Pantel, T. Chklovski, and M. Pennacchiotti. Automatically assessing review helpfulness. In *Proceedings of the Conference on Empirical Methods in Natural Language Processing (EMNLP 2006)*, pages 423–430, Sydney, Australia, July 22-23 2006.
7. Y. Liu, X. Huang, A. An, and X. Yu. Modeling and predicting the helpfulness of online reviews. In *Proceedings of the 2008 Eighth IEEE International Conference on Data Mining (ICDM 2008)*, pages 443–452, Pisa, Italy, December 15-19 2008. IEEE Computer Society.
8. Alexander Maedche and Steffen Staab. Discovering Conceptual Relations from Text. In *ECAI'00*, pages 321–325, 2000.
9. M. P. O'Mahony and B. Smyth. Learning to recommend helpful hotel reviews. In *Proceedings of the 3rd ACM Conference on Recommender Systems (RecSys 2009)*, New York, NY, USA, October 22-25 2009.
10. Gregory Piatetsky-Shapiro. *Discovery, Analysis, and Presentation of Strong Rules*, volume 229, pages 229–248. AAAI/MIT Press, 1991.
11. Markus Schaal, Roland M. Müller, Marko Brunzel, and Myra Spiliopoulou. RELFIN - Topic Discovery for Ontology Enhancement and Annotation. In *ESWC'05*, pages 608–622, 2005.
12. G. Wu, D. Greene, and P. Cunningham. Merging Multiple Criteria to Identify Suspicious Reviews. In *Proc. 4th ACM Conference on Recommender Systems (RecSys'10)*, 2010.
13. Guangyu Wu, Derek Greene, Barry Smyth, and Pádraig Cunningham. Distortion as a Validation Criterion in the Identification of Suspicious Reviews. In *Proceedings of the First Workshop on Social Media Analytics*, SOMA '10, pages 10–13, New York, NY, USA, 2010. ACM.

Are Explanations Always Important? A Study of Deployed, Low-Cost Intelligent Interactive Systems

Andrea Bunt
Computer Science Department
University of Manitoba
bunt@cs.umanitoba.ca

Matthew Lount
Computer Science Department
University of Manitoba
matthew.lount@gmail.com

Catherine Lauzon
Computer Science Department
University of British Columbia
catherine.lauzon@gmail.com

ABSTRACT
Intelligent interactive systems (IIS) have great potential to improve users' experience with technology by tailoring their behaviour and appearance to users' individual needs; however, these systems, with their complex algorithms and dynamic behaviour, can also suffer from a lack of comprehensibility and transparency. We present the results of two studies examining the comprehensibility of, and desire for explanations with deployed, low-cost IIS. The first study, a set of interviews with 21 participants, reveals that i) comprehensibility is not always dependent on explanations, and ii) the perceived cost of viewing explanations tends to outweigh the anticipated benefits. Our second study, a two-week diary study with 14 participants, confirms these findings in the context of daily use, with participants indicating a desire for an explanation in only 7% of diary entries. We discuss the implications of our findings for the design of explanation facilities.

Author Keywords
Explanations, comprehensibility, transparency, qualitative evaluations, diary studies, recommender systems

ACM Classification Keywords
H.5.2 [User Interfaces]: Evaluation/methodology;

INTRODUCTION
When equipped with the right underlying reasoning mechanisms, Intelligent Interactive Systems (IIS) have enormous potential to improve the manner in which users interact with technology, including providing individualized instruction (e.g., [10]), helping users complete tedious tasks efficiently (e.g., [12]), and helping them cope with large information spaces (e.g., [17]). Potential downsides of incorporating more machine intelligence within an application, however, include an extra layer of complexity and diminished predictability, both of which can make it difficult for end users, particularly those with low technical expertise, to form sufficiently accurate *mental models* (i.e., an internal representation of how a system works [16]). In fact, a lack of comprehensibility or transparency is often viewed as a key usability challenge for IIS, or even an inherent disadvantage of these systems (e.g., [9, 18]).

One strategy for improving transparency is to provide users with information on why and how a system generates its intelligent behaviour. A number of studies have shown such explanations to be beneficial (e.g., [4, 7, 8, 11, 15, 25]). Given the various benefits, one might infer that all systems should include an explanation facility, however, explanations are also difficult to design effectively (e.g., [2, 8]), require time and effort on behalf of the user to consume, and may even lead to lower decision quality for some users [5]. In other words, explanations can be beneficial, but at a potential cost at design time and/or during application use. Consequently, it is important to determine when explanation facilities are most needed.

Despite the large body of work on explanations in IIS, there is still limited information on what properties of an IIS and usage scenarios result in users having information needs that cannot be met through application use alone. This is for two primary reasons. First, most work on explanation utility has focused on complex domains and/or systems that assist users in making relatively high-stakes decisions. There are many examples, however, of what we call "everyday" IIS, such as Google (Fig. 1, right) and YouTube (Fig. 1, left), which assist users in making low-cost decisions, and provide assistance in a generally unobtrusive manner. Many of these systems do not include explanation facilities and the need for such facilities remains largely unexplored. Second, most evaluations have been conducted using research prototypes in a laboratory setting. These types of settings make it difficult to i) assess users' information needs when given the opportunity to interact with an IIS over extended periods of time, and ii) explore realistic cost vs. benefit scenarios, where explanation viewing takes time away from real-world tasks.

Through two primarily qualitative studies, an interview study with 21 participants and a diary study with 14 participants, we examine users' information needs with deployed, low-cost IIS that they interact with on a day-to-day basis. These systems are low-cost in that their recommendations have limited financial, time, and/or safety consequences, in comparison to, for example, a decision-support system for medical diagnoses, where lives could be at stake. Our studies reveal that i) despite having no real explanations available, our participants view the IIS that

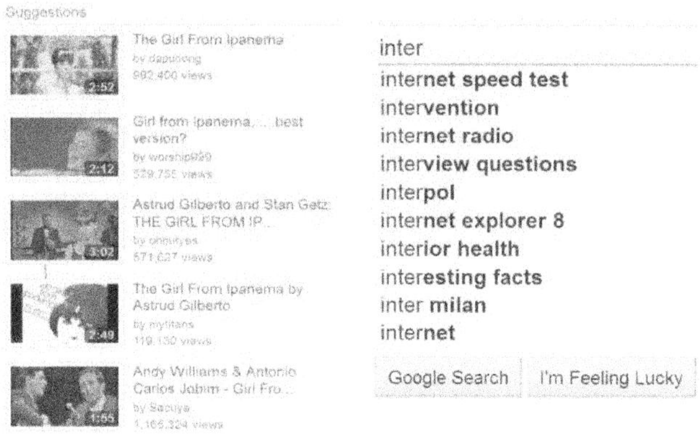

Figure 1. Two low-cost IIS at work: YouTube Suggestions while watching a video and Google Suggest while searching.

they use in a positive light; ii) most participants have formed plausible mental models, although these models are often lacking in detail; and iii) while some users are interested in learning more about how the systems work for general interest or in hopes of improving system behaviour, most feel that the effort to view an explanation would outweigh any potential personal benefit. Together, our findings suggest that explanations are not always necessary to achieve at least operational transparency, and similarly, that not all users need a detailed understanding of how a system works to derive utility from it.

Our studies provide three primary contributions: (1) we describe users' attitudes towards increased transparency in a prevalent class of IIS that has received little attention to date; (2) we present findings based on users' real-world experiences with deployed IIS, used over extended periods of time, to complete real tasks, under real time constraints; and (3) we report qualitative data describing *why* users want or do not want to view explanations.

The remainder of the paper is structured as follows. We first review related work in the area. This is followed by a description of our two studies, including their methods and findings. We then discuss implications for design, study limitations, and promising directions for future work.

RELATED WORK

In this section we review work related to IIS comprehensibility and transparency. We structure our review according to the type of domain studied: expert or knowledge-based systems, ubiquitous systems, complex task assistants, and low-cost recommenders.

Expert or Knowledge-Based Systems

The largest body of work advocating the need for transparency within IIS has been in the domain of decision-support systems and knowledge-based product recommender systems, where explanations are often viewed as a critical component of their success (e.g., [15, 19, 20, 22, 25]). According to Gregor and Benbasat's survey of a number of studies in this domain [7], explanations can improve user performance, helping users make faster and better decisions. Explanations can also improve perceptions of the systems, in particular by increasing levels of trust. The authors suggest, however, that for a user to access an explanation, there must be a specific trigger (e.g., an anomalous result) or a true need to learn how the system works. There is also preliminary evidence that explanations might negatively impact decision quality for some users when the recommender accuracy is low [5].

Ubiquitous Systems

While studies of expert and knowledge-based systems date back to the early 1980s, more recently work has investigated the role of explanations in the domain of ubiquitous computing, or with sensor-based systems (e.g., [3, 13, 14, 24]). Lim and Dey conducted two large-scale Mechanical Turk experiments examining users' information needs with a range of hypothetical ubiquitous applications [13, 14]. Their results indicated that the majority of users wanted more information on how the systems worked, and that when given the experimental task of understanding the system, explanations did improve comprehensibility.

Also in the area of sensor-based systems, and one of the few examples of a relevant field study, Tullio *et al.* [24] conducted a six-week qualitative field study of an interruption management system. Using a set of semi-structured interviews, the study focused primarily on how participants' mental models of the system evolved. The study found that most users had reasonable mental models from the outset, which did not tend to evolve throughout the course of the study, even when provided with explanations.

Complex Task Assistants

In the domain of intelligent task assistants, Glass *et al.* [6] performed a field study evaluating information needs and perceptions of trust of the CALO system, a complex task assistant for a range of office-related tasks. After using the system for a period of 1 day to 2 weeks, participants expressed only a moderate desire for information on why the system behaved a certain way (~3.4 on a 5-point scale), but did indicate transparency as the number one factor influencing their trust in the system. While data gathered in this type of field setting is invaluable, some of the participants in this particular study were highly technically literate, and "several" were CALO developers, which may impact the generalizability of the findings.

Stumpf *et al.* [21] conducted a related study on using explanations to help increase comprehensibility of a machine learning algorithm. Analysis of coded think-aloud statements revealed that certain explanations were preferable to others, but the study did not test whether explanations were needed at all.

Low-Cost Recommenders

The systems described above are either complex, or support high-cost or high-stakes decisions (e.g., large potential impacts on finances, time, or health). We are aware of only two studies focusing on comprehensibility of and explanations in IIS that support low-cost decisions. Herlocker *et al.* [8] studied the impact of explanations in a movie recommender through two experiments: a laboratory evaluation, and a one-month field study. The laboratory evaluation revealed that certain explanations did significantly improve users' perceived likelihood of viewing a fictitious movie, while others significantly lowered perceptions. The field study revealed that the explanations did not significantly impact users' movie-going behaviour, but that the majority of users wanted the explanations to be included in future versions of the system. A second example can be found in Bunt *et al.*'s study of a system that recommends GUI customizations [2]. While the study revealed that the majority of users appreciated the explanations and wanted them present in the system, there were also users for whom the explanations had little value, and there was no significant impact on user behaviour.

Summarizing Prior Work

In summarizing the above work, we note two main trends. First, the predominant focus has been on complex IIS for which understandability is likely to be most difficult to acquire solely through interactions, and on IIS that support users in making high-cost decisions. The extent to which explanations are needed in lightweight, low-cost IIS has received comparatively much less attention. Second, the majority of evaluations have been laboratory-based, often with the explicit experimental task of understanding how the system works and/or viewing example scenarios instead of interacting with a system. Consequently, their findings do not necessarily generalize to real-world situations, where users both are time-pressured, and have the opportunity to understand and trust a system through long-term use.

STUDY 1: INTERVIEW STUDY

To understand users' desire for explanations in lightweight, low-cost, "everyday" IIS, our first step was to conduct a set of semi-structured interviews with 21 participants (7 male and 14 female).

Study Method

Participants

To understand IIS information needs of an "average" population, we recruited participants who had little formal computer training through a low-level computer usage course and by distributing posters across a university campus (with the exception of the computer science building). The majority of the 21 participants were full-time undergraduate students, with three exceptions: P12 was a civil servant; P13 was a child care worker; and P21 was working in the area of data management. None of the participants had any formal computer training outside of a basic introductory class. Students from the computer usage class received course credit as compensation; the others were given a $10 gift certificate.

Applications Discussed

The focus of our interviews was on eliciting information on IIS that our participants use. If participants couldn't think of any relevant examples, we would then ask if they used a number of applications from a list of popular applications, including: Windows Start Menu, Google Suggest, YouTube recommended videos, Amazon, iTunes Genius, Facebook, and cell phone text messaging. While not an exhaustive list of all deployed IIS, the above list includes a range of system complexities and domains (e.g., GUI customization, low-cost product recommenders, music or video recommenders, and word predictors). Participants were given a second opportunity to describe any other relevant applications after viewing our list.

Explanation facilities within all applications discussed were either extremely shallow or difficult to find without extensive searching, which no participant reported doing. Thus, our findings pertain to systems without a detailed or prominent explanation facility. Table 1 summarizes the capabilities and explanation facilities of all applications discussed by more than two participants.

Study Questions

For each application used, we sought to answer the following:

- To what extent does the participant want to know more about how the system generates its intelligent behaviour?

To further understand factors influencing these information needs, we also sought to answer:

- How does the participant use the application and how does s/he perceive its usefulness?
- How does the participant think the application generates its intelligent behaviour?

Interviews typically lasted from 30 minutes to one hour, and were all recorded. Afterwards, each interview was transcribed in full. We analyzed the transcripts using qualitative analysis techniques from *Contextual Inquiry* [1]. In particular, we created affinity diagrams to identify themes common in the pattern of use and thoughts of participants. In creating the affinity diagrams, participant quotes were clustered based on similarity using a bottom-up, inductive analysis approach. These clusters were then examined for emergent themes. These themes were revised during data interpretation sessions held among the paper authors where we continually revisited the raw data to ensure that the data were consistent with the themes.

Study Findings

To contextualize our findings, we begin by considering whether or not our participants find their "everyday" IIS useful. We then discuss the mental models that our participants have acquired through interacting with the systems. This is followed by a discussion of whether or not our participants desire information on how the IIS work.

Code	Application	Description	Explanation Facilities	Discussed By
YT	YouTube	Recommends videos related to the current video.	Uses the phrase 'because you watched' beside a previously watched video.	P4, P5, P6, P7, P8, P10, P11, P12, P13, P14, P15, P16, P17, P18, P19
CP	Cell Phone	Automatic word corrections or suggestions.	None. Information only available through searching online or through cell phone manual.	P1, P2, P3, P6, P7, P10, P11, P13, P14, P16, P18, P19, P20
AM	Amazon	Recommends products for purchase.	Uses the phrase: 'Customers who bought this item also bought'.	P6, P7, P10, P12, P13, P14, P17
IT	iTunes Genius	Creates playlists from music in a library and suggests music for purchase.	None. Information only available through searching online or through help menus.	P3, P17, P19
FBF	Facebook Friend Finder	Suggests friends for a user's profile on the social media website, Facebook.	Uses the phrases: '# mutual friends' and lists any 'networks' that they share.	P11, P12, P13, P14, P15, P16, P18, P19, P20
FBP	Facebook Page Suggestions	Suggests pages for a user's profile on the social media website, Facebook.	Uses the phrase 'people who like X also like Y'.	P10, P14, P17, P20
GS	Google Suggest	While typing a search into Google, a list of searches is listed that start with the current keystrokes.	None. Information only available through searching online	P4, P5, P7, P8, P9, P10, P12, P13, P14, P15, P16, P17, P18, P19, P20, P21
SM	Start Menu	In Windows, a list of programs that changes according to use.	None. Information only available through searching online or through help menus.	P3, P5, P8, P9, P11, P12, P13, P14, P15, P16, P17, P18, P19, P20

Table 1: Applications that our participants reported using (with >2 discussants) in Study 1.

Perceived Utility

Participants' comments suggest that they generally perceive the low-cost IIS that they use in a positive light, with the primary advantages being time savings and assistance with domain exploration. For example, P18 describes how Google Suggest streamlines his web browsing, and goes so far as to declare speed to be his most pressing concern:

> At some point if you want to go to YouTube, you just hit 'y'; it's the first one... It's always about going quicker and faster when you're browsing the internet. [P18, GS]

In terms of domain exploration, P3 explains how iTunes Genius helps her find available music:

> Actually, it's good because there are a lot of songs that I never knew was [sic] out. I don't listen to the radio as much anymore because of the iPod. [P3, IT]

While most participants find their IIS to be useful and accurate, a number of limitations were discussed. Some feel that the systems lack the sophistication necessary for true personalization. For example, P11 feels that YouTube's suggestions are often redundant, failing to recognize equivalent content between videos:

> If I select one song from one band [...] usually on that recommendation list is just different versions of the same song. [P11, YT]

Others were concerned that recommendations are commercially motivated rather than being personalized:

> Maybe those company [sic] pay money to advertise. [P6, AM]

Thus, participants' comments indicate that they find value in the IIS, but that they aren't uniformly content. None of our participants, however, commented directly on a lack of comprehensibility or transparency as being usability flaws.

Nature of Mental Models

We examine the issue of comprehensibility by describing the mental models that participants have acquired through their interactions with the systems. Our assessments of the accuracy of participants' mental models are based on any explanations found in help menus of the target applications or on-line searching.

Our participants' descriptions of how the systems work suggest a number of mental models (~20%) that are both highly plausible and relatively detailed. For example, in the quotes below, P10 describes how his cell phone makes word suggestions, while P11 talks about YouTube's suggested videos. Both descriptions discuss what sources of data the system considers and P10 also describes how this data is being used:

> It stores a dictionary of words and tries to intelligently guess which word you're going for, based on the grammar and stuff like that – where you're going with the sentence. Words that you use most frequently come up first, and so on. [P10, CP]

> [...] different videos have titles, so it's based on text, rather than the content of the video, because I think audio, like the sound and the picture, are much more difficult to capture than the text. [P11, YT]

Other descriptions (~10%) were extremely vague, incorrect, or expressed a great deal of uncertainty. For example, in the quotes that follow, P5 and P15 feel that there is something sophisticated going on, but are not sure exactly what:

> Yeah, what was it... We looked at it in [a computer usage class]. How does it go...? Jeez, I can't remember. Is it the P2P thing? [P5, GS]

> This kind of algorithm that they use, [a] searching algorithm, [...] it's like, the strongest algorithm. Probably they can search thousands of data at a time within a second or a millisecond or something. But that's all I know. [P15, GS]

The majority of participants' descriptions (~70%), however, fell somewhere between the above two extremes; plausible explanations, but lacking in detail, and/or uncertain about how different sources of data are combined:

> When watching a video, it will get something similar related to what you are watching. Like if I'm watching something – another video related to that concept, I get more information about what the stuff I was watching [sic]. More information comes up. ... Yeah. The topic. [P8, YT]

> Probably what other people have searched [...] Probably what's on the websites, maybe? I guess sometimes when you searched words before, they usually come up first. [P20, GS].

In the above examples, P8 and P20 have working understandings of what the IIS are trying to do, but not of the details as to how things like "topic" and "similarity" are determined, or exactly what sources of data the system is using to make suggestions. Common sources of confusion were: i) exactly which factors or attributes are considered; ii) how complex factors are assessed; and iii) when multiple factors or attributes are considered, how they are combined.

To summarize, most participants have at least a basic or plausible understanding of how their IIS work, but in most cases, this understanding could be improved through explanations. We next look at whether or not participants are interested in obtaining additional information.

Desire for Additional Information

When initially asked whether they wanted more information on how the IIS they use work, participants' responses were almost evenly divided. Variability in responses tended to relate more to the individual than the application, with certain participants generally interested in more information and others not. As we describe below, reasons behind these initial responses, however, reveal few concrete reasons for wanting additional information, and illustrate some potential challenges for explanation facilities in these types of IIS.

More Knowledge is Never a Bad Thing: Of those instances where participants did want more information, most didn't describe tangible ways in which this knowledge would improve either their interactions with or perceptions of the system. Instead, they indicated that they generally like to know things or thought that the knowledge might help them in future employment. Examples of such sentiments are expressed below:

> In this life you need information. You need to know a lot of things or else you will be left behind. [P8]

> It would be good to know how it works, just like for personal reasons. Just general knowledge. [P2]

> I can tell the kids when they ask me. [P13]

> Because I think there's a very broad market for it in the future, so, maybe I can find a job in it someday. [P11]

Potential for Improved Interactions: The other primary reason for wanting access to an explanation was a hope that viewing one could lead to improved interactions:

> I like to know how things work, and I might find out how to use it better in the future as well. [P10]

> I guess it could help me in my own choice of search terms – to choose the most appropriate thing – if I knew how it worked. [P12]

> Maybe it would help me understand why it doesn't work the greatest. It might help me trick it into recommending better videos. [P10]

In the above quotes, P12 and P10 wish that information on how the system works could help them manipulate the system. P11, on the other hand, hoped that she could use this knowledge to choose to use a product whose reasoning mechanism better suited her needs:

> The next time I choose my cell phone I [could] choose a better one. I will ask which program it's using. [P11]

Two participants also commented on a desire to use the information to maintain their privacy. For example:

> Can I avoid or at least try to avoid things that I don't want known about me to be known? [P21]

Understanding Anomalous Behaviour and Increasing Trust: Two additional justifications for wanting access to more information included helping to understand anomalous behaviour, but for good behaviour as opposed to system errors, and for reasons of trust:

> I would be interested in how it works if they got accurate to the point that it was exactly what I was looking for. [P18]

> I just think it is sort of creepy how it can find things that are just so 'on'. [P17]

> It might affect my opinion of things, and maybe make me trust them more. [P12]

Given findings from prior work, however, we were surprised at the lack of comments relating explanations to trust. P12's comment above was one of only two quotes to directly refer to this issue.

Transparency not Important When it Works: In terms of why participants did not want more information, the most prevalent reason involved only the bottom line mattering:

> I don't really care how things work, just that they do. [P17]

> It wouldn't really bother me if I didn't know, as long as it works. [P15]

> As long as it's working then it's fine. [P1]

In other words, for many participants, detailed transparency is not considered to be important when the system does its job effectively.

Sufficiently Transparent without Explanations: The second major reason for not wanting more information was participants feeling like they already knew how the system works, or at least knew enough:

> Not that interested. Yeah maybe they will just explain what I said in more complicated terms. [P19]

> I cannot explain very clearly, but I think it is like, common sense. [P11]

Examining the mental models of those who indicated they already knew enough revealed a mix in accuracy. Some had quite accurate descriptions, while others had plausible, but incomplete mental models. None, however, gave descriptions that were outright inaccurate. Thus, while some of these participants would likely be able to improve their comprehension by viewing an explanation, none had significant misconceptions that needed repair.

Undesirable Cost vs. Benefit Trade-off: The final reason for not wanting more information involved costs and perceived lack of benefit. A number of participants commented on the time and effort necessary to consume the information. For example, P19 was concerned that any explanation would be overly technical:

> I might find, like, too much technical information about the process. [P19]

For others, there was a lack of apparent benefit:

> I just don't HAVE to know it. [P13]

> Are there options for me after I know this information? Like, I know how it works, so I can adjust them, so then it works better for me. Without the second step, it doesn't make any sense. [P11]

> [Knowing more] doesn't matter that much. If understanding that would help me type faster, but I think [my] typing speed is already fast. [P16]

In the quotes above, both P11 and P16 indicate that viewing the explanations would have to directly lead to improving their performance with the system either through faster use or making higher quality decisions, with P11 suggesting that he would like the explanation only if he could modify the system to make it better suit his needs.

Discussion

Study 1's findings suggest three primary themes: (1) a high appreciation of these "everyday" IIS despite limited or no explanation facilities available; (2) IIS comprehensibility is not necessarily dependent on explanations; and (3) the cost of explanations is not often perceived to be worth any benefits. We elaborate on these themes below.

High Perceived Value Despite Lack of Explanations

Our participants generally spoke fondly of the IIS they use, with the lack of explanation facilities not negatively impacting general perceptions. Our study does not fully isolate the reason for these positive perceptions, which are likely based on numerous factors, including effective interaction design, commercial success, and the fact that these systems generally work. It could be that explanation facilities are more critical in systems attempting to establish a user base, where accuracy is more difficult to achieve, or with less usable interfaces; however, these results provide encouraging support that if IIS are well designed, users can derive benefit without reading explanations.

Comprehensibility without Explanations

Most users have at least some plausible understanding of how the IIS work. This understanding, while often incomplete, tends to be reasonable enough that it limits many participants' desire for further information. Our study results imply that for at least some IIS, users can acquire workable mental models without the presence of explanations, confirming the generalizability of Tullio *et al.'s* findings [24]. While it is possible that participants could benefit more from IIS with more accurate mental models, a lack of transparency was not perceived to be an inherent limitation despite previous concerns (e.g., [18]). We note, however, that our results do not speak to the perceived utility of explanations in systems where users are not able to build up accurate mental models either because of limited exposure to the system or system complexity.

High Perceived Cost vs. Uncertain Benefits

When using certain IIS as part of their daily lives, our participants indicated that they tend to be more focused on getting their tasks accomplished than on improving their mental models. In fact, a primary attraction of these IIS for our participants is the ability to perform tasks more efficiently than they could autonomously. Consequently, they are wary of explanations that require time and substantial cognitive effort, particularly since they are unsure as to what tangible benefits such additional knowledge might bring.

Gregor and Bensabat [7] indicate that users are not likely to access explanations without a specific trigger, such as anomalous system behaviour. Our results support this notion and raise the question of whether these triggers exist within low-cost IIS. Our participants felt fairly positive about the systems, and ignored the system (or found alternative programs) when it performed poorly. While a couple of participants indicated an interest in seeing explanations for truly amazing behaviour, one might question the likely prevalence of such scenarios.

A second trigger discussed by Gregor and Benbasat [7] is a need to learn how a system works. In a high-cost domain such as medical diagnosis, explanations might be needed to help users explain or justify decisions that they make with the help of the systems to others. The same is not likely to be true of the decision to visit a website or watch a short video. Several participants in our study indicated that there would have to be clearly apparent personal benefit for them to view an explanation. For most of our participants, simply learning about the system was not enough; they wanted it to enhance their use of the system, for example, by making it more accurate, or by increasing the speed gains.

STUDY 2: DIARY STUDY

A potential limitation of Study 1 is that participants' self-reflections might not be representative of their true day-to-day information needs. Thus, to gauge desire for explanations in the context of daily use, we conducted a two-week diary study with 14 participants.

Method

Participants

Participants were recruited through posters distributed around campus. All 14 participants (7 male, 7 female) were either full-time or part-time undergraduate students. None had any formal computer science training beyond an introductory class and none had participated in Study 1. Participants received a $100 gift certificate.

Procedure

Study 2 took place in three stages. In the first stage participants took part in a semi-structured pre-interview, with a format similar to that in Study 1. This was then followed by a 14-day field study, where participants completed one on-line diary entry for each IIS that they used that day. Questions in a diary entry included:

- How useful was the application (scale of 1-7)
- How accurate was the application (scale of 1-7)?
- Did the application behave according to the participant's expectations? Why/why not?
- When interacting with the application, did the participant want more information on how the application works? Why/why not?

Upon completion of the 14-day field portion of the study, participants took part in a post-interview, where further detail on the diary entries was solicited.

Applications

Table 2 lists the applications used by our participants in Study 2 along with the total number of diary entries for each application. Two new applications introduced by participants in this study were: the movie/program recommender in Netflix, and Beatport, an on-line music store with a recommender. Like in Study 1, none of the applications had any explanation facilities to speak of.

Results

In the interest of space, we concentrate our reporting on the diary entries since the pre-interview transcripts revealed attitudes and mental models similar to those in Study 1. Our analysis focuses on the quantitative data present in each diary entry (i.e., the yes/no and Likert-scale questions). We also coded two types of qualitative data. The first was the reasons for why an application matched or did not match expectations. After inspecting the data, we chose a two-level coding scheme: behaved better than expected and behaved worse than expected. The second source was any reasons for wanting more information, which were coded using the themes identified in Study 1 as a starting point.

Application	Discussed By	# Diary Entries
YouTube	P3, P4, P5, P7, P8, P9, P10, P12, P13, P14	35
Cell Phone	P1, P2, P3, P4, P5, P6, P7, P8, P10, P12	51
Amazon	P3, P7, P11	5
Facebook Friend Finder	P1, P3, P5, P7, P8, P12, P13	9
Facebook Page Suggestions	P2, P7	4
Google Suggest	P2, P3, P4, P5, P6, P8, P9, P11, P13, P14	31
Windows Start Menu	P3, P4, P5, P6, P8, P13, P14	15
iTunes Genius	P5, P7, P13, P14	6
Netflix	P2, P3, P4, P5	8
BeatPort	P3	3

Table 2: Applications used in Study 2.

Across all 14 participants, there were a total of 167 diary entries, where each entry represented an entire day's use for a given application. The mean number of entries per person was 11.9 (sd: 4.73). An individual entry reflected anywhere from 1 to greater than 8 uses of the IIS that day, for a combined duration of between 5 minutes and 6 hours. Table 2 shows the breakdown of the entries according to application. Text messaging with cell phones was the most frequently reported application (51 entries), followed by YouTube (35 entries) and Google Suggest (31 entries).

Utility, Accuracy and Matching Expectations

Figure 2 shows the mean ratings for accuracy and usefulness for each application. Means for usefulness ranged from 4.44 to 5.69, whereas means for accuracy were between 4.56 and 6.00. These ratings suggest that participants were generally positive about the systems and that the recommendations tended to be accurate. However, there were also a number of low or neutral ratings (21% of all ratings for usefulness and 23% for accuracy) indicating that there is still room for improvement.

Participants also tended to report that the applications' behaviour matched their expectations (82% or 137/167 entries). Figure 3 (Left) shows the breakdown by application; instances where the application did not match expectations were generally distributed across the applications. Responses for how the application behaved unexpectedly revealed that it was most often because the application was behaving worse than expected (80% or 24/30 instances).

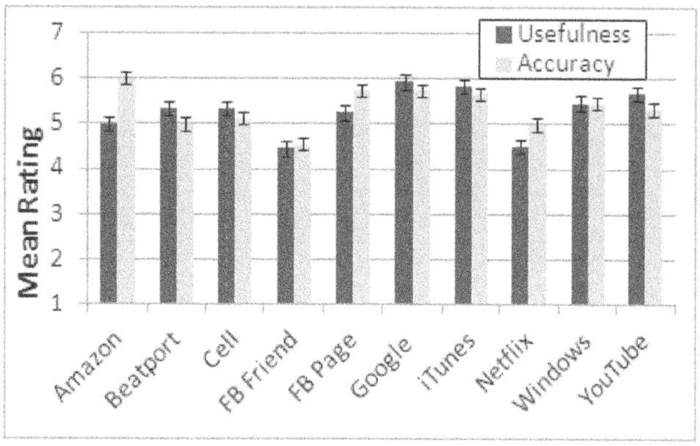

Figure 2. Mean ratings for usefulness and accuracy for each application. Error bars represent the standard error.

Desire for More Information

Participants expressed a desire for more information in only 7% of the diary entries (11 entries). Figure 3 (Right) shows the breakdown by application, indicating that the desire for more information was limited to five applications. These responses also came from only 4 participants; the participant with the largest number of instances of wanting more information (5 of 11) was one of two participants in a more technical field (Electrical Engineering).

We looked at possible triggers for participants' desire for more information. In five of the 11 entries, the participant had reported that the application did not behave as expected, and in all cases, participants comments indicated that the application behaved worse than expected; however, these cases correspond to only 17% (5/30) of the total number of times where participants reported unexpected behaviour.

We also examined accuracy and usefulness ratings to see if poor system behaviour in general was a potential trigger. To do so, we divided the diary entries into two groups: entries where participants wanted more information (*Yes-Entries*) and entries where they did not (*No-Entries*). Usefulness ratings were significantly lower for the *Yes-Entries* according to a 2-tailed independent samples t-test (*Yes-Entries*: 4.6, sd. 2.07; *No-Entries*: 5.51, sd 1.53; p=0.049).

For the difference in accuracy ratings, there was also a trend for the ratings for the *Yes-Entries* to be lower (*Yes-Entries*: mean 4.6, sd 1.86; *No-Entries*: mean 5.39, sd 1.48; p = 0.073). Thus, when participants did want more information they were likely to be less satisfied with the application than when they did not. There were many instances, however, where participants were not enthusiastic about the system behaviour, and did not want more information. This was true for 83% (29/35) and 86% (33/38) of usefulness and accuracy ratings, respectively, that were at or below 4 (on the 7-point scale).

Confirming the above analysis, participants' stated reasons in their diary entries for wanting more information were spread fairly even across four main categories: (1) wanting to understand poor or inconsistent behaviour; (2) a desire for improved interactions (even if that meant disabling the feature); (3) wanting to understand atypically good behaviour; and (4) general curiosity.

In the post-interviews, we probed for participants' reasons for *not* wanting more information, which was the case in 93% of diary entries. Responses were reflective of the themes uncovered in Study 1: participants didn't feel like the information would be of personal benefit, didn't want to take any additional time, cared only that the application worked, felt that they already had sufficient understanding gained through interactions with the system, or had built up a high level of trust through interactions. The following quotes illustrate some of the above reactions:

> I kind of figured it out just as I went. [...] I didn't have the time to go and look for it, but I guess I learned as I go [sic]. [P7]

> I think it's mostly because I don't really feel like it affects my life that much. [P1]

> I've been using these things so long that I just generally tend to trust them, or not. [P5]

> I don't generally care about how things work as long as it does work. Like if it ain't broke, don't fix it, kind of thing. [P5]

Study 2 Discussion

The results of the diary study reveal that participants very rarely wanted more information on these deployed,

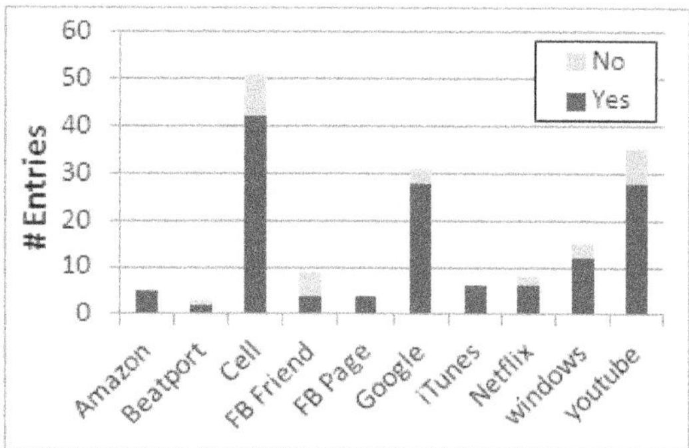

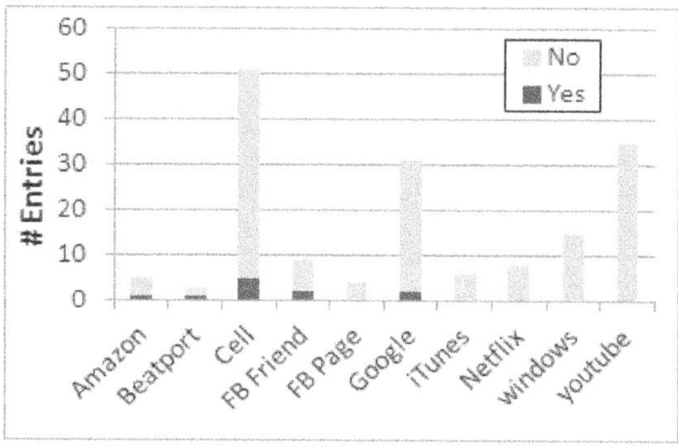

Figure 3. Left: Whether or not the application behaved as expected. Right: Whether or not the participant wanted more information.

lightweight, low-cost systems during the course of their daily use. In fact, in only 7% of the total number of entries did participants express a desire for more information. Those instances tended to have lower usefulness and accuracy ratings than when participants did not want more information; however, in approximately 80% of instances of poor or anomalous system behaviour, participants did not want to know why. Participants' reasons for wanting or not wanting information mirror those in Study 1, providing additional evidence of the validity of those findings.

IMPLICATIONS FOR DESIGN

Our studies help define the boundaries of explanation utility for certain classes of IIS that are used in real-world environments. Without a deeper understanding of when and why explanations are seen as necessary, designers are unable to assess tradeoffs as to where to focus their design/development effort, and how much to promote detailed explanations within their interfaces. While most work on explanations in IIS has advocated their inclusion, our results suggest that explanations are not, in fact, critical in certain systems. Our participants were not overwhelmed by the complexity of the IIS that they use, nor were they confused to the point of not being able to derive benefit.

While our results suggest that explanations are not critical for low-cost, lightweight IIS, there is room to improve the precision of some participants' mental models, and it is possible that improved understanding could lead to enhanced interactions. Our results, however, point to a tension between making explanations highly visible or making them accessible only "on demand". Given our participants' lack of overwhelming interest in obtaining more information, explanations that take attention away from users' primary tasks are not likely to be well perceived. On the other hand, this same reluctance is not likely to result in on-demand explanations being frequently accessed.

In terms of content to include in an explanation facility, the findings from Study 1 point to a number of promising avenues for further study. First, participants doubted that they could personally benefit from viewing an explanation. Therefore, to encourage participants to view explanations, it may be helpful to make any anticipated benefits of viewing an explanation highly visible and within the explanation itself, including information that fosters users' ability to enhance their use of the system. Alternatively, rather than requiring users to use their newly acquired knowledge to adapt their behaviour, an explanation facility could allow users to modify the system's behaviour, or the sources of information that it uses. Second, we found that most users understood the general idea behind the systems, but lacked knowledge on the details, such as how complex concepts (interest, similarity, relevance, etc.) are assessed, or when multiple factors are considered, the manner in which they interact. Thus, if the goal of the explanation facility is to improve mental models beyond what can be derived from interactions alone, a general description is not likely to be sufficient. Finally, participants' desire to invest effort to read and comprehend explanations was low and there was apprehension that the explanations would be too technical. Consequently, it is likely important to keep explanations brief and to use layperson's terms.

LIMITATIONS AND FUTURE WORK

In this section we acknowledge some of the limitations of our studies. First, even the diary study required some degree of self-reflection, since entries were completed once per day as opposed to during system use. Experience sampling would be useful to further validate our findings, by polling users for information needs during system use.

A second limitation of our studies is that participants' reluctance for additional information may have been biased by their pre-conceived notions of what form this information would take. We chose not to introduce any experimental manipulations to gather data on deployed systems used on a regular basis, which happened to have either very minimal or no real explanation facilities, and to avoid a novelty or Hawthorne effect. We feel our results on attitudes towards these deployed "everyday" systems serve as important complements to prior work that has examined different potential formats, but typically in a more controlled and consequently less ecologically valid setting (see [23] for a summary of related work in this area). Viewing different explanation variants, however, might have prompted further discussion and participants might have been more enthusiastic about certain styles of explanations than others.

Finally, our studies indicate that there are systems for which explanations are not crucial, but did not isolate system or user properties that lead to this perception. First, we did not incorporate user expertise into our analysis since we did not screen or test for this factor. Our studies provide initial evidence that some users are more interested in explanations than others, with further evaluations required to understand which user characteristics influence this need. We would also like to explore the impact of the manner in which intelligent support is delivered, focusing on the level of obtrusiveness. For example, the IIS studied here are fairly unobtrusive, whereas IIS with more proactive or interrupting behaviour could require more detailed transparency. Other potential contributing factors to explore are application popularity, commercial success and the level of actual system accuracy.

SUMMARY

In this paper, we described two studies aimed at assessing users' information needs, and consequently the role of explanations in deployed IIS that support users in making low-cost decisions. In doing so, this work is one of the few to examine this class of system and to gather data on non-technical user attitudes towards transparency in IIS based on their real-world experiences.

Our results raise questions as to the importance of, and consequently anticipated usage of, explanation facilities within this type of system. We found that our participants generally perceive these IIS in a positive light despite the lack of meaningful or accessible explanation facilities, and have constructed plausible mental models from their day-to-day interactions with the systems. While some users were interested in accessing more information, the dominant responses were that the applications were sufficiently transparent, or that the cost of viewing an explanation would outweigh the benefit. In combination with prior work on IIS in high-cost domains, our results help define when and why explanations are necessary.

ACKNOWLEDGMENTS

This work was supported by the GRAND Network Centre of Excellence. We would also like to thank Kasia Muldner for her comments on drafts of the paper.

REFERENCES

1. Beyer, H., and Holtzblatt, K. *Contextual Design: Defining Customer-Centered Systems*. Morgan Kaufmann, San Francisco, CA, USA, 1988.
2. Bunt, A., McGrenere, J., and Conati, C. Understanding the utility of rationale a mixed-initiative system for GUI customization. *Proc. UM,* (2007), 147-156.
3. Cheverst, K., Byun, H.E., Fitton, D., Sas, C., Kray, C., and Villar, N. Exploring issues of user model transparency and proactive behaviour in an office environment control system. *User Modeling and User-Adapted Interaction, 15,* 3-4, (2005), 235–273.
4. Dzindolet, M.T., Peterson, S.A., Pomranky, R. A., Pierce, L. G., and Beck, H. P. The role of trust in automation reliance. *Int. J. of Human-Computer Studies 58,* (2003), 697-718.
5. Erlich, K., Kirk, S., Patterson, J. Rasmussen, J., Ross, S., and Gruen, D. Taking advice from intelligent agents: The double-edged sword of explanations. *Proc IUI,* (2011), 125-134.
6. Glass, A., McGuinness, D.L., and Wolverton, M. Toward establishing trust in adaptive agents. *Proc. IUI,* (2008), 227-236.
7. Gregor, S. and Benbasat, I. Explanations from intelligent systems: theoretical foundations and implications for practice. *MIS Quarterly 23*, 4 (1999), 497-530.
8. Herlocker, J.L., Konstan, J.A., and Rield, J. Explaining collaborative filtering recommendations. *Proc. CSCW, (2000)*, 241-250.
9. Jameson, A. Understanding and dealing with usability side effects of intelligent processing, *AI Magazine 30,* 4, *(2009),* 23-40.
10. Koedinger, K.R., Anderson, J.R., Hadley, W.H., and Mark, M. Intelligent tutoring goes to school in the big city. *Int. J. of AIED 8,* (1997), 30–43.
11. Lee, J.D. and See, K.A. Trust in automation: Designing for appropriate reliance. *Human Factors 46*, 1, (2004), 50–80.
12. Leshed, G., Haber, E.M., Matthews, T., and Lau, T. CoScripter: automating & sharing how-to knowledge in the enterprise. *Proc. CHI*, (2008), 1719-1728.
13. Lim, B.Y. and Dey, A.K. Assessing demand for intelligibility in context-aware applications. *Proc. UbiComp*, (2009), 195-204.
14. Lim, B.Y., Dey, A.,K., and Avrahami, D. Why and why not explanations improve the intelligibility of context-aware intelligent systems. *Proc. CHI,* (2009), 2119-2128.
15. Pu, P. and Chen, L. Trust building with explanation interfaces. *Proc. IUI*, (2006), 93–100.
16. Norman, D.A. Some observations on mental models. In D. Gentner & A. Stevens (Eds.) *Mental Models*, Hillsdale, NJ: Erlbaum, (1983), 7-15.
17. Resnick, P., Iacovou, N., Sushak, M., Bergstrom, P., and Riedl, J. GroupLens: An open architecture for collaborative filtering of Netnews. *Proc. CSCW*, (1994), 175–186.
18. Shneiderman, B. and Maes, P. Direct manipulation vs. interface agents. *Interactions 4*, 6, (1997), 42–61.
19. Stylianou, A.C., Madey, G.R., and Smith, R.D. Selection criteria for expert systems shells: A sociology technical framework. *CACM*, 35, 10, (1992), 30–48.
20. Suermondt, H.J. and Cooper, G.F. An evaluation of explanations of probabilistic inference. *Proc. Computer Applications in Medical Care*, (1992), 579-585.
21. Stumpf, S., Rajaram, V., Li, L., Wong, W., Burnett, M., Dietterich, T., Sullivan, E., and Herlocker, J. Interacting meaningfully with machine learning systems: three experiments. *Int. J. of Human-Computer Studies 67,* (2009), 639-662.
22. Teach, R.L., and Shortliffe, E.H. An analysis of physician attitudes regarding computer-based clinical consultation systems. *Computers and Biomedical Research 14*, (1981), 542–558.
23. Tintarev, N. and Masthoff, J. Designing and evaluating explanations for recommender systems. In F. Ricci, L. Rokach, B. Shapira & P. Kantor, (Eds.) *Recommender Systems Handbook,* Dordrecht, Netherlands: Springer, (2011), 479-510.
24. Tullio, J., Dey, A.K., Chalecki, J., and Fogarty, J. How it works: A field study of non-technical users interacting with an intelligent systems. *Proc. CHI*, (2007), 31-40.
25. Wang. W. and Benbasat, I. Recommendation agents for electronic commerce: Effects of explanation facilities on trusting beliefs. *J. of Management Information Systems 23*, 4, (2007), 219–249.

Modeling Topic Specific Credibility in Twitter

Byungkyu Kang, John O'Donovan,
Tobias Höllerer
Department of Computer Science
University of California Santa Barbara
{bkang, jod, holl}@cs.ucsb.edu

ABSTRACT
This paper presents and evaluates three computational models for recommending credible topic-specific information in Twitter. The first model focuses on credibility at the user level, harnessing various dynamics of information flow in the underlying social graph to compute a credibility rating. The second model applies a content-based strategy to compute a finer-grained credibility score for individual tweets. Lastly, we discuss a third model which combines facets from both models in a hybrid method, using both averaging and filtering hybrid strategies. To evaluate our novel credibility models, we perform an evaluation on 7 topic specific data sets mined from the Twitter streaming API, with specific focus on a data set of 37K users who tweeted about the topic "Libya". Results show that the social model outperfoms hybrid and content-based prediction models in terms of predictive accuracy over a set of manually collected credibility ratings on the "Libya" dataset.

Author Keywords
Credibility, Trust, Microblogs, Data Mining, Social Networking

ACM Classification Keywords
H.3.3 Information Storage and Retrieval: Information Search and Retrieval

INTRODUCTION
Twitter's micro-blogging service is a free forum for the provision of all sorts of information, bringing together many millions of users, from individuals to large corporations. Twitter enables uploads and dissemination of short messages called "tweets" from an increasingly diverse number of client devices such as cellphones and tablets. For example, Apple's recent release of iOS 5 supports "tweeting" natively from millions of iOS 5 enabled devices[1], for both text and image content. All of these mechanisms make it easy for people to post facts, opinions, statements or any other arbitrary tweet in this melting pot of information. The primary focus and contribution of this paper is on an evaluation and comparison of three novel approaches for predicting credible information for specific topics on Twitter –an important challenge given the abundance of useless information in the forum. We first model social credibility, then focus on content-based (tweet-only) credibility, and lastly on a hybrid of features from both approaches. This aims to maximize the available window of information from the social web site upon which we can base a credibility assessment. The paper focuses on two core questions: 1) how well can we assess credibility in Twitter using our proposed models? 2) how do social, content-based and hybrid models perform at identifying credible information? Analysis of our methods is performed on a range of metrics, from credibility-based predictions of simple features from available metadata, to prediction on thousands of tweets with manually labeled credibility assessments. Our evaluations also consider the contextual nature of credibility on Twitter, from the perspective that credibility can vary with perceived context. Results from a user study assessing credibility on a set of tweets with varying credibility indicators (context) are presented and discussed. We will begin by describing the Twitter domain in terms of social links and information flow, and define what we mean by "credibility" in this context, then follow with a discussion of relevant research in this area.

[1]http://blog.twitter.com/2011/10/twitter-and-ios-5-sharing-made-simple.html

Information Flow
Propagation of information on Twitter is largely based on a "friends and followers" model, making it a suitable forum for the spread of news and other trends. Tweets and profiles are public and anyone can see a user's posts. Propagation of content generally occurs via posts from people you follow that are streamed proactively to your personalized twitter feed, and conversely your posts are streamed to your followers' feeds. Text-based search is also supported, along with a ranked list of "trending topics", which are tweets containing a topic keyword labeled with "#", such as "*#LondonRiots*" for instance. Trending topics are ranked both globally and by geographic area. Users can reference others in their tweets through the "mention" tag "@", as in "thanks @bob2011". Interpersonal communication is facilitated through a "reply" function, where a user can click a button and reply to the author of any tweet. Information flow is further enabled through a "retweet" mechanism, whereby a user can click a button and post another user's tweet to his/her own profile, and therefore broadcast it to his/her followers. "Credible" tweets contain factual, newsworthy or otherwise useful information, for example, "Libya names new armed forces chief

aje.me/AcOXz4". Conversely, less credible tweets contain false, malicious or simply no useful information, for example, "I am Dajjal Mahmood commander w/ NATO in Libya. Hold this secret help secure 2m dinars I recover in the house of Gaddafi", or highly personal information such as "I like Mexican food!!!". With more than 200 million users contributing up to 5000 tweets per second through the above methods, a thriving and highly dynamic social network exists, along with an abundance of meta-data and text-based content, which we believe is a suitable domain for a hybrid (social and content-based) prediction strategy.

Defining Credibility.

The classic problem of the social web: information overload, abounds in Twitter. This paper examines several strategies for distinguishing "credible" information (and information sources) about a topic of interest from the abundance of useless, false or nonsensical information available through the Twitter services. For the purpose of our discussion, we define two types of "credibility" in the context of a target topic of interest:

Definition 1. *Tweet-Level Credibility: A degree of believability that can be assigned to a tweet about a target topic, i.e.: an indication that the tweet contains believable information.*

Definition 2. *Social Credibility: The expected believability imparted on a user as a result of their standing in the social network, based on any and all available metadata.*

Tweet-level credibility is similar to Castillo's definition in [4], with the addition of the topic level constraint. Tweet level credibility can also be summed/propagated to the user level by averaging over a profile of tweets. Conversely, a user's social credibility is attached to all of his/her tweets.

BACKGROUND

The primary contribution of this paper is the design and analysis of credibility models for microblogs. Since the proliferation of the social web as a platform for user provided content, a large amount of research effort has focused on modeling trust and credibility of content producers. In this discussion of related work we focus on a handful of the most relevant works. Our analysis falls into three broad categories: research in the general area of trust and credibility on the web; research in the microblog domain; and finally an overview of relevant works from the field of recommender systems, particularly those works that have guided the models and methods presented in this paper.

Credibility and Trust on the Web

Research on trust and credibility in a social context has been popular for many decades, from Kochen & Poole's experiments [20] and Milgram's famous small worlds experiment [16], trust has been shown to play an important role in social dynamics of a network. With social web API's, researchers now have many orders of magnitude more data at our fingertips, and we can experiment and evaluate new concepts far more easily. This is evident across a variety of fields, for example, social web search [13], semantic web [6] [8], online auctions [10] [22] [19], personality and behavior prediction [11] [1], political predictions [7] and many others.

Credibility on Twitter

Scale, network complexity and rich content make twitter an ideal forum for research on trust and credibility. Some approaches, for example [23] rely on content classifiers or the social network individually, while others harness information from both sources. Canini et al. [3] present a good example of the latter, to source credible information in Twitter. As with the methods in this paper, they concentrate on topic-specific credibility, defining a ranking strategy for users based on their relevance and expertise within a target topic. Based on user evaluations they conclude that there is "a great potential for automatically identifying and ranking credible users for any given topic". Canini et al. also evaluate the effect of context variance on perceived credibility. Later in this paper, we provide a brief overview of a similar study performed on our data, correlating with the findings in [3] that both network structure and topical content of a tweet have a bearing on perceived credibility.

Twitter has been studied extensively from a media perspective as a news distribution mechanism, both for regular news and for emergency situations such as natural disasters for example [4][15][12]. Castillo et. al. [4] describe a very recent study of information credibility, with a particular focus on news content, which they define as a statistically mined topic based on word co-occurrence from crawled "bursts" (short peaks in tweeting about specific topics). They define a complex set of features over messages, topics, propagation and users, which trained a classifier that predicted at the 70-80% level for precision/recall against manually labeled credibility data. While the three models presented in this paper differ, our evaluation mechanism is similar to that in [4], and we add a brief comparison of findings in our result analysis. Mendoza et. al [15] also evaluate trust in news dissemination on Twitter, focusing on the Chilean earthquake of 2010. They statistically evaluate data from the emergency situation and show that rumors can be successfully detected using aggregate analysis of Tweets. Our evaluation of Follower / Following relations from our crawled data (shown in Figures 5 and 6 yields a very similar pattern to their result.

Credibility in Recommendation

Recommender systems have been the focus of research attention for many years, and reputation metrics (such as credibility) [18] have been shown to play an important role in the process of content prediction. They can be applied in social filtering to augment user similarity metrics in the recommendation process. [18]. They have also been shown to increase robustness of prediction algorithms in cases where bad (malicious / erroneous) ratings exist [2][17]. Models that include explicit distrust have recently been shown to produce better predictions, for example, Victor et. al [24] highlight the advantage of combining trust and distrust metrics to compute predictions over multiple network paths, while a recent study by Golbeck shows that distrust metrics can be used to predict hidden trust edges in a network with very high accuracy [5]. In this paper, we are not propagating credibility values around the network, or computing direct interpersonal trust at the dyadic level, however, the authors believe that distrust metrics can potentially improve credibility predictions in Twitter.

MODELING CREDIBILITY

Traditional recommendation strategies such as content-based [14] or collaborative filtering [9] [21] typically compute a *personalized* set of recommendations for a target user based on some derivation from that user's profile of item preferences. An important distinction between these techniques and the approaches presented here is that personalization is only performed at the topic level in our algorithms. That is, personalized preferences for a single target user are not considered, only those for a target group who are interested in a specific topic. While we believe that traditional personalization does play an important role for predicting credible content, the focus here is on predicting credible information within a target group centered around a topic of interest, and moreover on the prediction of credible content for target users beyond that group, where preference information is commonly inaccessible.

Given these goals and constraints, we now present three computational models for assessing credibility of information within a specific microblog topic. We begin with by defining nomenclature for the domain:

Definition 3. *The Twitter domain can be represented as a quintuple* (U, F_o, F_e, T, X), *where* F_o *and* F_e *are two* $U \times U$ *matrices representing binary mappings* $f \in F_o, F_e \mapsto 0, 1$ *between users in* U *(termed "follower" and "following" groups, respectively).* T *is the set of tweets, distributed over* U, *and* X *is the set of topics in* T.

By this definition, Twitter is rich in both text content and social network links. Research in recommender systems has long argued the benefits of combining content based and collaborative approaches to recommendation to maximize information gain in the prediction process [14] [9] [21]. For example, while content-based methods tend to predict narrowly, in that they must match a text description of an item already in a target user's profile, collaborative techniques have the potential to provide more serendipitous predictions since they are based on subjective opinions of groups of similar users.

Since our domain is rich in both text content and network links, we propose the following three approaches for identifying credible information, borrowing from the content and collaborative synergies identified by the recommender system community.

1. *Social Model*: A weighted combination of positive credibility indicators from the underlying social network.
2. *Content Model*: A probabilistic language-based approach identifying patterns of terms and other tweet properties that tend to lead to positive feedback such as retweeting and/or credible user ratings.
3. *Hybrid Model*: A combination of the above, firstly by simple weighting, and secondly through cascading / filtering of output.

Social Model

Complex network structure and feed-based information flow make dissemination of information on Twitter highly dynamic and ephemeral in nature. Accordingly, the task of detecting factors of credibility is inherently difficult. Consider internet pioneer Tim Berners-Lee for example: Tim follows 83 people, but has almost 54,000 followers, compared to the global average of 126 followers. Former US House speaker Newt Gingrich has over 1.5 million followers, however a recent report[2] revealed that only 8% of these are real people, and the remainder are automatically generated profiles used to create a false impression of popularity. Another example outlier is the user "@Twitter", which has 6.4 million followers, since it shares useful news about the forum itself. Furthermore, direct marketing companies commonly follow users to collect information solely for target advertising, and don't behave as "regular" followers. There are also a large number of fake profiles that have become very popular, for instance CNET's analysis[3] revealed dozens of popular profiles for talk show host Stephen Colbert, all but one of which are fake. Our social model attempts to mitigate these problems by weighting a diverse range of *positive credibility indicators* within a target topic.

We first consider the "retweet" as an indication of credibility. Equation 1 gives a value for credibility based on the deviation of a user $u \in U$'s retweet rate RT_u from the average retweet rate $\overline{RT_x}$ in a target topic $x \in X$. In practice, values from the following equations are mapped to a log-log scale to handle large outliers in the data. Notation has been left out for simplicity.

$$Cred_{RT}(u, x) = |RT_u - \overline{RT_x}| \quad (1)$$

Keeping with retweet analysis, Equation 2 considers retweet rate but factors in usage rate and number of followers F_o, in other words, a utility metric from the potential number of retweets.

$$Utility_{RT}(u, x) = |\frac{RT_{u,x} \times F_o(u)}{t_{u,x}} - \frac{\overline{RT_x} \times \overline{F_{o,x}}}{t_x}. \quad (2)$$

Retweet metrics function over both the content of a collection of tweets and the underlying network. We believe that the network topology itself can also provide insights into credibility of a user. Equation 3 computes a social credibility score as the deviation in the number of user u's followers from the mean number of followers in the domain, again normalized by number of tweets.

$$Cred_{social}(u) = |\frac{F_o(u)}{t_u} - \frac{\overline{F_o}}{t}| \quad (3)$$

Assuming that a "follow" request is usually an indication of credibility, we can now also weight Equation 3 by factoring

[2] http://gawker.com/5826645

[3] http://news.cnet.com/8301-17939_109-10218926-2.html

in the ratio of friends to followers as a deviation from the norm for a given topic. For example, an information gathering agent for a direct marketing company is likely to follow many profiles, but have few followers. Equation 4 describes the social balance of a user u as the ratio of follower (F_o) to following (F_e) group size.

$$Balance_{social}(u) = |\frac{F_o(u)}{F_e(u)} - \frac{\overline{F_o}}{\overline{F_e}}| \quad (4)$$

There are cases where the opposite is true however, for example, a popularity-hungry politician may pay to have automated agents create accounts and follow his profile, but these profiles are not likely to have strong social connectivity, and can be discounted by other filters in this model, such as Equation 2 for example.

We also consider social connections within a given topic as a positive indication of credibility, both in the F_o and F_e groups. Consider a user who has tweeted frequently about a topic, lets say "#IUI2012". If that user has few or no followers with associations to that topic, this should raise suspicion about that user's credibility in the topic. Our findings indicate that network data is frequently too sparse within a specific topic for this metric to yield useful results, but we include it in the model because it leverages social connections in a potentially useful way.

$$Cred_{social}(u,x) = |\frac{F_o(u,x)}{t_{u,x}} - \frac{\overline{F_{o,x}}}{t_x}| \quad (5)$$

The final metric in our social credibility model addresses the focus of a target user within a given topic space as a function of their global profile. For example, many people have set up Twitter accounts solely for business or research purposes, and thereby have a more constrained number of topics that they tweet about, potentially indicating an increased level of credibility, since the likelihood of recurring topics is higher. A practical nugget being that the authors of this paper have tweeted about "#IUI2012" many times, and it appears as a peak in their personalized topic-distribution graphs. Equation 7 computes this metric as the sum of the tweets for a user u on topic x as a percentage of their total number of tweets t_u.

$$Focus(u,x) = |\frac{\sum_{t \in T} t_{u,x}}{\sum_{t \in T} t_u}| \quad (6)$$

Weighting Scheme

Now that we have described an array of potential credibility indicators in the microblog domain, we incorporate them into a single predictive mechanism that can be used to make inferences about credible sources. There are a variety of utility functions that can be applied to train the weighting scheme, for example, prediction of manually labeled "ground-truth" data, prediction of empirical "retweet" data. We will discuss these in detail in our evaluation section. For the purpose of the discussion here, we provide the simple weighted combination below:

$$C_u = \alpha(Focus(u,x) + \beta(Balance(u) \times Cred_{social}(u)) + \gamma(Utility_{RT}(u,x) \times Cred_{RT}(u,x)) \quad (7)$$

Content-based Model

We have described how the social provenance of a piece of information can have a bearing on its credibility. However, credibility can be assigned both to the information source, and to the information itself in an intrinsic way. Accordingly, our second credibility model focuses in on tweet content, isolated from the underlying social network. Following this discussion, we will describe integration strategies that harness strengths of both approaches.

We begin by representing all tweets in our topic-specific data sets as a set of salient credibility indicators (12 numeric and 7 binary). Approximately half of the these features are taken from a 2011 study by Castillo et al. [4]. However, their work defined a much larger set that incorporated features for Tweet, Topic, User and Propagation scopes, in a multiple topic setting. In this model, we are interested in tweet content only, for a single topic, and hence other features are not included.

Numeric Indicators:

1. *Positive Sentiment Factor*: Number of positive words (matching our lexicon)
2. *Negative Sentiment Factor*: Number of negative words
3. *Sentiment Polarity*: Sum of sentiment words with intensifier weighting (x2) ('very', 'extremely' etc)
4. *Number of intensifiers*: 'very', 'extremely' etc., based on our lexicon.
5. *Number of swearwords*: Simple count, based on lexicon.
6. *Number of popular topic-specific terms*: Simple count, based on lexicon.
7. *Number of Uppercase Chars*: Simple Count
8. *Number of Urls*: Simple Count
9. *Number of Topics*: Number of topics '#' (All have at least 1)
10. *Number of Mentions*: Number of user's mentioned with '@'
11. *Length of Tweet (Chars)*: simple count.
12. *Length of Tweet (Words)*: simple count.

Binary Indicators:

1. *Is Only Urls*: No text, only links.
2. *Is a Retweet*: From metadata
3. *Has a Question Mark*: '?' or contains any of Who/What/Where/Why/When/How
4. *Has an Exclamation Mark*: '!'
5. *Has multiple Questions/Exclamations*: '??' '???' '!!' '!!!' etc.
6. *Has a positive emoticon*: :) :-) ;-) ;)
7. *Has a negative emoticon*: :(:-(;-(;(

To evaluate the utility of this model for predicting credible/useful information, we train a range of classifiers using 5000 manually annotated tweets from a user evaluation. Details and results of this analysis are presented in the evaluation section.

Hybrid Model

So far we have focused our discussion on credibility indicators at the user level and the tweet level individually. A logical progression is to combine aspects from both methods to maximize the information upon which we can base credibility decisions. Both models contain many variables, making it infeasible to conduct an exhaustive analysis of possible hybrid strategies in this paper. As a representative sample, we now present four novel methods for combining facets from the earlier models that aim to improve their ability to predict credible information and credible information sources. Since our earlier models compute credibility at different levels of granularity (user and information level), so also do the following hybrid strategies.

Content-based Ranking

This strategy predicts credibility at both the user and tweet levels. The hybrid algorithm first performs a filtering step based on the user level (social) credibility score from model 1, passing profiles with a credibility score above a threshold S_{min} to the second model. The content based model extract features from each tweet and computes a credibility score which is used to re-rank tweets from the set of credible users. $u \in U\ where\ S_u < S_{min}$.

Weighted Combination

This simple combination of output from the two earlier models predicts at the user level only. Credibility scores from the content-based model are aggregated over each $u \in U_t$. The resultant user-level score C_u is combined with the social credibility S_u using a harmonic mean weighting strategy to minimize outlier values: $C_{weighted} = \frac{2}{C_u + S_u}$.

Feature Combination

This strategy computes a credibility at the tweet level, and is designed to use all available data to generate a prediction. Feature lists from both the social model, the content based model, and a collection of other user metadata from the Twitter API are used to train a J-48 decision tree to generate a prediction model.

Content-boosted Social Credibility

The final hybrid method predicts at the user level, incorporating the aggregated content-based score for a user into the social model. This approach is similar to the Weighted Combination with the exception that the content-based credibility factor is considered at the same level as the $Cred_{RT}$ and $Cred_{social}$ scores from Equations 1 and 2 respectively.

EVALUATION SETUP

Ultimately, we would like to incorporate the models presented in this paper into a real world system for recommending credible information and information sources from a microblog to collect rich preference feedback. Meanwhile, we evaluate our methods using 7 topic-specific data sets from Twitter. Our evaluation is organized as follows: Firstly we describe the data collection process and provide an overview of each topic-specific collection. Next, a brief statistical analysis of the data is presented to highlight core trends across each set, with specific focus on our larger data set on the topic "#Libya". Following this, we describe an online user study of 150 participants wherein ground truth credibility assessments were collected on the Libya data set. Lastly, we describe a set of predictive accuracy experiments performed for each of the three models and provide a detailed discussion and comparative analysis of the results.

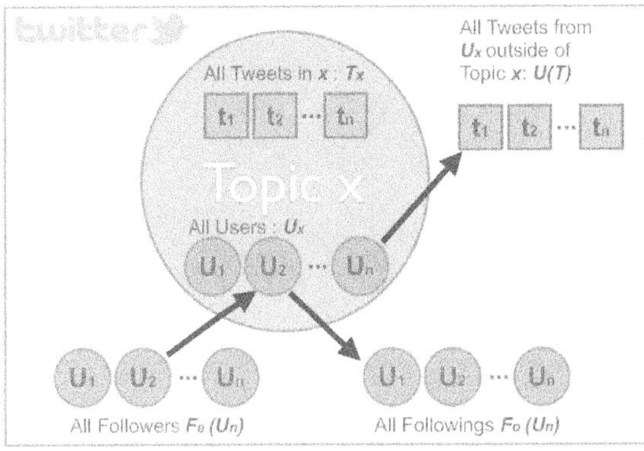

Figure 1. Illustration of the scope of crawled data for each of 7 current topics.

Set Name	*Core Tweeters*	*Core Tweets*	F_o *and* F_e (overlapped)	F_o *and* F_e (distinct)
Libya	37K	126K	94M	28M
Facebook	433K	217K	62M	37M
Obama	162K	358K	24M	5M
Japanquake	67K	131K	25M	4M
LondonRiots	26K	52K	30M	4M
Hurricane	32K	116K	35M	5M
Egypt	49K	217K	73M	36M

Table 1. Overview of 7 topic-specific data collections mined from the Twitter streaming API.

Data Gathering and Analysis

We ran a python-based crawler[4] for 8 weeks from a cluster of 12 machines using 14 different Twitter authentications. Data was crawled from the Twitter streaming API[5] and stored in a relational database. Our choice of topics was guided by two factors: firstly we required popular topics that would create a flurry of activity in the network, yet we were also interested

[4]The authors have made this crawler and data sets publicly available at www.wigis.net/twitterdata

[5]https://dev.twitter.com/docs/streaming-api

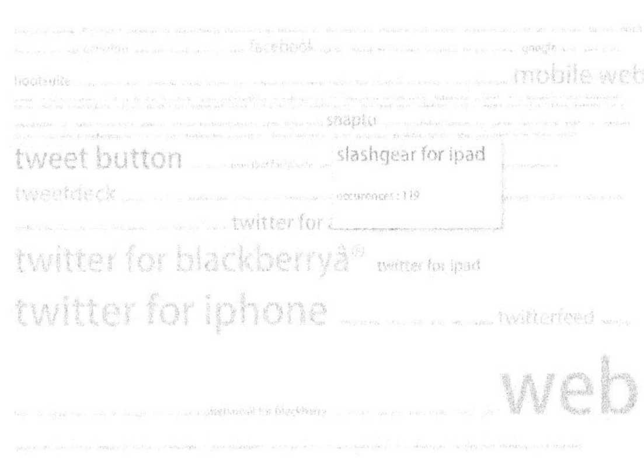

Figure 2. Word cloud showing origin of tweets in the Libya data set.

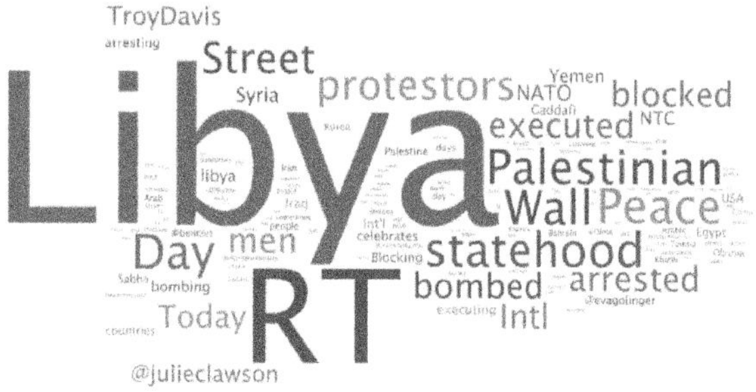

Figure 3. Word cloud showing distribution of popular terms in the Libya data set.

in topics which would yield significant interconnections in the underlying social networks of the users within the topics. Figure 1 is an illustration of the crawling algorithm. Starting at a topic keyword such as '#Libya' for instance, all tweets containing the tag were collected. Additionally, all users who tweeted with this tag were crawled and their tweets (with or without) the topic tag were stored, along with all available metadata from the API. For each of these "core users" information on their Follower and Following groups was also collected. We did not store the tweets of these users, only metadata such as number of following and followers, number of retweets etc. The main challenge in this process was rate limitation and 403-503 range error codes returned by the API, giving an approximate download rate of 350 queries per hour with approximately 200 tweets per query. As shown in Table 1, the second order social groups are exponentially larger, ranging in size from 25 to 94 million profiles across the 7 collections. Core users collections ranged from 26k to 433k. A small world effect is evident in these data sets, since there is very significant overlap in the F_o and F_e groups, as shown by the last two columns in Table 1. A visual overview of originating devices for the tweets in or Libya data set is given in Figure 2, and distribution of popular terms is shown in Figure 3.

User Study: Credibility and Context

An online study was set up for two purposes: Firstly to collect ground truth credibility assessments of the crawled tweets from real users, for the purpose of evaluating our prediction models. However, we were also interested in analyzing the effects of Twitter context on perceived credibility, so we performed a within subjects study, varying source context (dependent variable), with the goal of examining the effect on perceived credibility rating (independent variable). 145 participants took the online study, which lasted about 10 minutes. Participants were 39% female, 61% male, varying in age from 19 to 56 with an average age of 26 (median 28). Participants were generally familiar with Twitter (4 out of 5 rating on average). In total, credibility ratings on 5025 tweets were collected, excluding those that were rated as "can not answer". Participants were all asked to leave comments and insights in a feedback form. Comments varied widely, but there was a consensus that information provenance (i.e: links to other sources) produced a sense of credibility. One participant reported the opposite: "that social network activity should have no bearing on credibility". Each participant was shown four groups of 10 tweets and asked to provide a credibility rating for each tweet on a scale of 1 to 5, with an option to click a "can't answer" response. Following from the analysis in [4], the general statement "likely to be credible" was removed. Group 1 contained just the raw tweet, with no context information about the tweeter. Group 2 contained statistically poor credibility features for the tweeter (few followers, few retweets), while Group 3 contained statistically "good" context (many followers, many retweets). The final group was shown the true context, i.e: the user's real number of retweets and followers. It is important to note that only ratings from the "true" context were used in the evaluation of our prediction models. Figure 4 shows the average perceived credibility rating for each group. A one-way ANOVA showed a significant difference between each the groups ($p = 0.039$). Results indicate that context does have an effect on perceived credibility, with the positive context achieving an average rating of 2.34, and the negative context a score of 1.58. This reveals a relative rating shift of 0.76 or 26% between the extreme contexts.

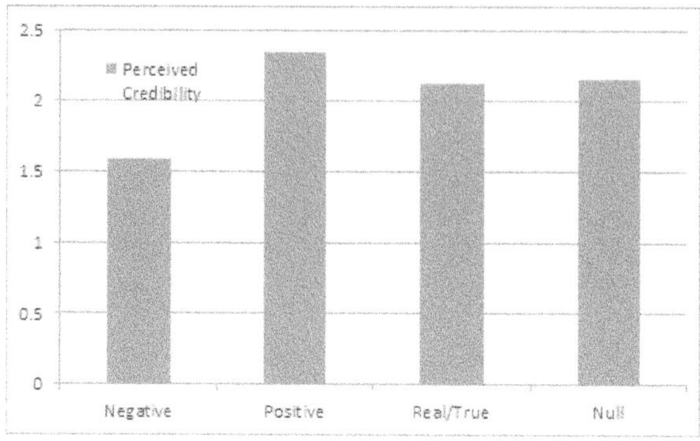

Figure 4. Plot showing perceived credibility in each of four Twitter contexts (Negative, Positive, True, Null).

EVALUATION

Now that we have presented our models for predicting credibility, and our ground truth collection process, we must assess and compare performance of each model. Given our available resources, substantial credibility assessment data could only be collected on the Libya data set, so we focus on that set for most of the following evaluation, namely, where comparisons against user provided assessments are performed.

Data Analysis

Before we describe our evaluation of predictive accuracy, we first take a broader statistical view of the collected data sets to gain insights about trends, clusters and any interesting anomalies about the data sets. A detailed comparison and discussion of every feature in our models is not feasible here, so we focus in on a selection of features that influence the models most (F_o, F_e, links and retweets), based on a best-first feature analysis performed using WEKA[6]. Figure 8 shows a comparative analysis of a selection of features from both social and content-based models. In this figure, lighter (red)

[6]www.cs.waikato.ac.nz/ml/weka/

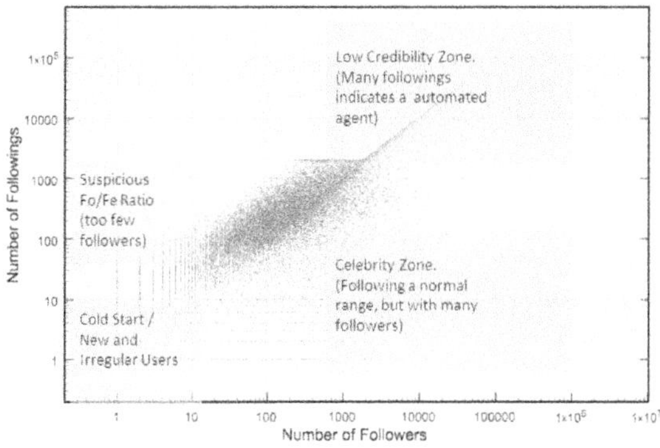

Figure 5. Plot showing number of followers to number of following profiles for the Libya data set. Areas of particular interested are shaded in grey and labeled accordingly.

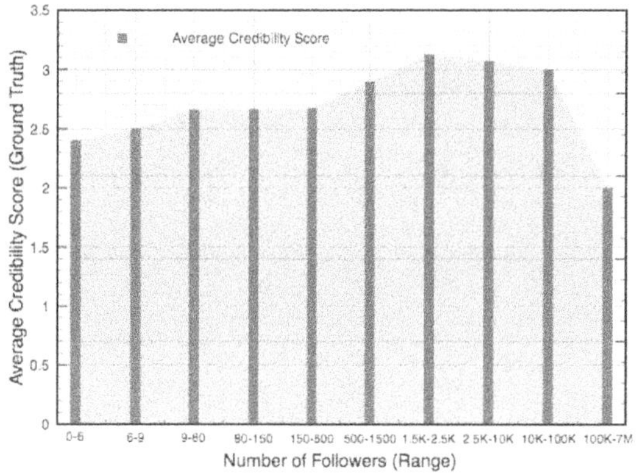

Figure 7. Average credibility rating from the web survey versus number of followers for the tweet authors (binned).

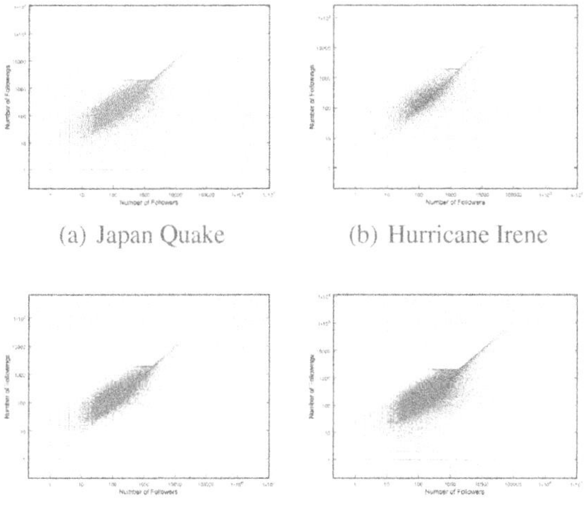

(a) Japan Quake (b) Hurricane Irene

(c) Enough is Enough (d) Facebook

Figure 6. Friend to Follower patterns across four of our topic-specific data sets. All other sets exhibited a similar distribution.

nodes indicate positive credibility and darker (blue) nodes indicate negative credibility assessments from the user study. Clusters appear in some of the scatter plots, indicating that the feature does have some bearing on assessed credibility. For example, looking at the features for "char" and "word", it is clear that longer tweets tend to be assigned more credibility than shorter ones. Number of tweets (status-count) and number of listings (listed-count) also align well with reported credibility.

Friend to Follower Analysis

Figure 5 shows a comparison of the number of followers F_o to the number of following users F_e over the 37,000 core users in our Libya data set. The shaded areas in the resulting distribution reveal areas that have a potentially negative impact on credibility. For example, at a threshold where users are following more than approximately 5000 others, the data appears to form a straight line. However, on the log-log scale, this is evidence of the long tail of a power law distribution. This is marked as low credibility zone since the group size is abnormally high for a human user, and we must therefore assume that the profiles are based on automated agents or "bots". Vice-versa, small sized F_o and F_e groups indicate new or irregular users. This is a low credibility group because we do not have sufficient social information (and by correlation, content information) to perform a reasonable assessment of credibility. This is analogous to the cold start problem in the recommender system literature [21]. Groups along the other extremities of this graph are also interesting: those with very few followers but larger following groups are (again by correlation) likely to tweet less and be leaf nodes in retweet chains, while conversely, the "celebrity" group (high F_o and low F_e tend to be higher in retweet chains, and have many retweets. The latter two groupings do not necessarily bear on credibility, but the other shaded areas of Figure 5 do indicate negative credibility. Accordingly, the "balance" component of our social credibility model, shown in Equation 4 is weighted to penalize these groups. Figure 6 shows similar distributions of follower to following groups across the JapanQuake (67k users), Hurricane Irene(32k users), Enough is Enough(65k users), and Facebook (433k users) topics. We found similar distributions for all of the other sets in Table 1.

Followers and Credibility

Figure 7 shows an analysis of the average credibility reported for tweets in the user study compared with number of followers. Binning of followers was applied to highlight the distribution. There is a significant correlation between reported credibility and number of followers up to a network size of approximately 1500 followers, after which, reported credibility drops off steeply. This result aligns well with our earlier analysis of follower to following groups. The reported drop in credibility past this threshold is likely due to the "bot" effect shown in Figures 5 and 6.

Retweets, Links and Other Credibility Indicators

The hybrid approaches proposed in this paper rely on a variety of different features from the social network, tweets and from user metadata. Once again a discussion of the benefits and merits of all features tested is not possible here, as a sample, we now discuss interesting findings from our analysis. The distribution graph in Figure 8 shows an overview of a subset of features. Links (presence of urls in tweets) were

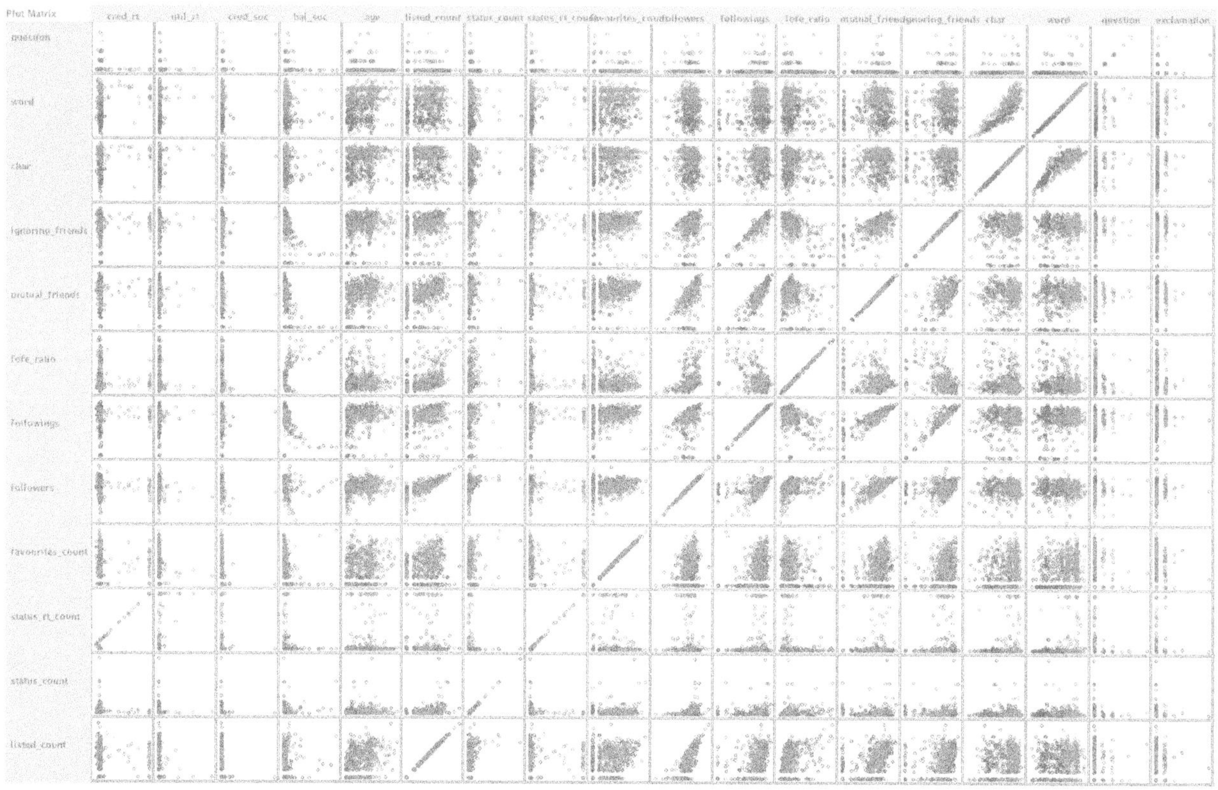

Figure 8. Comparisons of each feature used in computing the social credibility model. In this plot, lighter (red) areas indicate high credibility and darker (blue) areas indicate low credibility assessments.

found to be a very positive of credibility and were more frequently used in older profiles. Users who provided links frequently tended to be listed more often, and added to other users' "favorite" groups. Presence of links in tweets was found to correspond to sentiment (presence of positive or negative sentiment keywords) in an interesting way: if the sentiment metric was polarized, either negatively or positively, links were far more common, and users tended to assess credibility more highly. Tweets containing links were also found to be retweeted more frequently. Retweets were generally reported as credible in our study, and were also more frequent in older user profiles. Interestingly, emoticons (both positive and negative) were found to be an indicator of retweeting. Additionally, longer tweets were retweeted more frequently than shorter ones.

Predicting Credibility

Treating each hybrid strategy independently, a total of 6 credibility prediction strategies were tested. Each strategy was represented as a set of weighted features and loaded as an input file to WEKA machine learning toolkit. Our goal was to accurately predict the user-provided credibility scores from the online study. Preliminary experiments were performed using Bayesian classifiers (and a range of others) to learn a model based on the features of each prediction strategy. For the full experiment a J48 tree-based learning algorithm was used, firstly since it performed well in preliminary tests, and secondly to allow for comparison of results with Castillo et. al's similar evaluation in [4]. Predictions were run on a train-

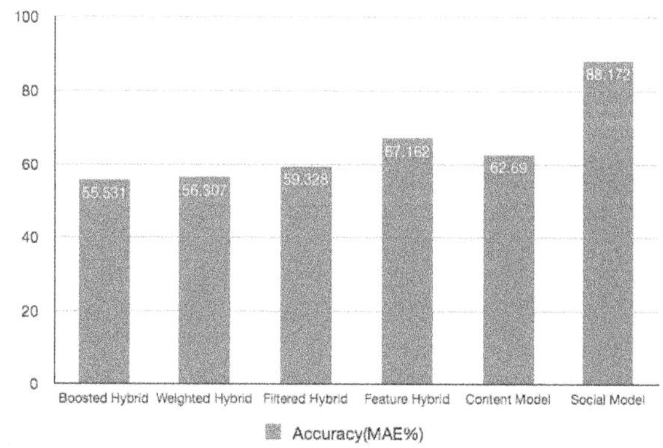

Figure 9. Comparison of predictive accuracy over the manually collected credibility ratings for each model.

ing set of 591 tweets with annotated credibility scores. A 10-fold cross-validation was applied, and training sets were separate from test sets. The algorithm attempted to classify each test instance into one of two credibility classes. To clarify, we note that all predictions were made at the tweet level, that is, if a strategy (such as the standalone social model) predicts credibility at the user level, the evaluation applied this approach to predicting credibility of a tweet by that user. Class instances were evenly distributed in the training sets. For each strategy, the mean absolute error between the predicted rating and the user provided rating was recorded.

Figure 9 shows the results of this evaluation for each strategy. The content-based and hybrid models performed reasonably at the prediction task, but were far outperformed by the social model, which achieved an accuracy of 88.17%, an improvement of 11% over the feature hybrid which was the next best performer (statistical analysis shown in Figure 10. The content-based approach scored an accuracy of 63% while the hybrid approaches ranged from 56% to 67%. Our initial expectations were that the simple rule of "more features, better prediction" would apply across this study, but in this case our findings have indicated otherwise, since the social model outperform the hybrid and content-based methods significantly. The relatively poor performance of the content based model (67%) can perhaps be attributed to the fact that tweet text is short and does not always contain sufficient information to make a credibility judgement. The feature-hybrid method exhibited a small improvement in accuracy ($\tilde{1}0\%$) over the next best hybrid strategy, which was the filtered approach. An overview of the statistical output from the J48 learner process is provided in Figure 10 for our best performing method, showing a correct classification of 902 of the 1023 instances, yielding 88.172% accuracy. The content-based (and therefore, hybrid) approaches rely on tweet text, whereas our social model relies on rich interconnections in the twitter network, including dynamic information flow metrics (retweets). Our findings indicate that the underlying network and dynamics of information flow are better indicators of credibility than text content.

Castillo et. al's examination of credibility in Twitter produced similar accuracy scores to the above (8% less accurate than our best performing social model result), with "precision and recall in the range of 70-80%". Several key differences make it infeasible to perform a fair comparison of classification accuracy however. For example, [4] analyses groups of "newsworthy" tweets, whereas our analysis focuses on "credible" individual tweets or users, as per our earlier definition. Furthermore, our analysis are focused in a topic-specific domain consisting of a different set of users and tweets.

DISCUSSION AND FUTURE WORK

The study of credibility models presented here is my no means exhaustive, and we believe that there are still better prediction strategies to be found. It appears from our evaluations that while stand alone social or content-based approaches fair reasonably well at predicting user provided credibility ratings, they are outperformed by hybrid methods which combine features from both, ultimately basing credibility assumptions on a larger window of information. Our evaluation answers the research question posed in the introduction, that credible tweets can be automatically detected with high accuracy (88% for our social model). Accurate detection of credible information in Twitter has many practical implications. For example, automatic filtering/ranking of twitter feeds based on credibility, spam detection, automatic recommendation of credible information [18] and identification of key players in information dissemination, which can be useful in assessing/predicting situations of social unrest such as the "occupy" movements and the London riots for instance.

```
=== Stratified cross-validation ===
=== Summary ===

Correctly Classified Instances         902               88.172 %
Incorrectly Classified Instances       121               11.828 %
Kappa statistic                          0.8222
Mean absolute error                      0.0771
Root mean squared error                  0.2162
Relative absolute error                 22.8584 %
Root relative squared error             52.6661 %
Total Number of Instances             1023

=== Detailed Accuracy By Class ===

               TP Rate   FP Rate   Precision   Recall  F-Measure   ROC Area  Class
                 0.901     0.009      0.966     0.901     0.932      0.966    1.0
                 0.946     0.061      0.924     0.946     0.935      0.965    2.0
                 0.896     0.083      0.816     0.896     0.854      0.936    4.0
                 0.214     0.02       0.387     0.214     0.276      0.876    5.0
Weighted Avg.    0.882     0.054      0.872     0.882     0.875      0.952

=== Confusion Matrix ===

   a   b   c   d   <-- classified as
 200  21   1   0 |   a = 1.0
   5 424  17   2 |   b = 2.0
   2  12 266  17 |   c = 4.0
   0   2  42  12 |   d = 5.0
```

Figure 10. Statistical results from a J48 tree learner for the best performing credibility prediction strategy (Social Model)

There are a significant number of possible next-steps for this research. We believe that improvements could be made by incorporating interpersonal factors such as the credibility that exists between users, also known as a trust relation. Such metrics can be incorporated both at the positive and negative levels (distrust), and have been shown to be useful for finding credible information in microblog domain. Furthermore, we are interested in evaluating the mechanisms presented here in a real world system, to elicit significant user feedback on the credibility of information in a real-world information consumer context, as opposed to the simple user survey approach presented here. This includes considering the role of interfaces and interactions that communicate credibility to, and elicit credibility data from real users.

CONCLUSION

As with most interactions on the Social Web, the window of information upon which we can make credibility judgement on Twitter is limited. As this forum becomes more popular, it becomes increasingly important to investigate new models for assessing credibility of the information it distributes. This paper presented three computational models for assessing such credibility, using social, content-based and hybrid strategies. The models were evaluated on 6 collections of tweets about current topics, including the associated social network information for each tweeter, as provided by the Twitter streaming API. An automated analysis of the predictive ability of each model was performed, predicting on both empirical "retweet" data, and on a collection of manually assessed tweets collected in an online user survey. Results showed that the social model outperformed both content-based and hybrid models, achieving a predictive accuracy of 88.17%, compared with 62% and 69% for content-based and the next best performing hybrid (weighted strategy) respectively.

ACKNOWLEDGEMENTS
The authors would like to thank Cha Lee and Sibel Adali for their input on analysis methods and credibility indicators for microblogs, respectively. This work was partially supported by the U.S. Army Research Laboratory under Cooperative Agreement No. W911NF-09-2-0053; by NSF grant IIS-1058132; by the Intelligence Advanced Research Projects Activity (IARPA) via Air Force Research Laboratory contract number FA8650-10-C-7060; and by the U.S. Army Research Laboratory under MURI grant No. W911NF-09-1-0553; The views and conclusions contained in this document are those of the authors and should not be interpreted as representing the official policies, either expressed or implied, of ARL, AFRL, IARPA, NSF, or the U.S. Government. The U.S. Government is authorized to reproduce and distribute reprints for Government purposes notwithstanding any copyright notation here on.

REFERENCES
1. Adali, S., Escriva, R., Goldberg, M. K., Hayvanovych, M., Magdon-Ismail, M., Szymanski, B. K., Wallace, W. A., and Williams, G. T. Measuring behavioral trust in social networks. In *ISI* (2010), 150–152.
2. Burke, R., Mobasher, B., Zabicki, R., and Bhaumik, R. Identifying attack models for secure recommendation. In *Beyond Personalisation Workshop at the International Confevece on Intelligent User Interfaces*, ACM Press (San Deigo, USA., 2005), 347–361.
3. Canini, K. R., Suh, B., and Pirolli, P. L. Finding credible information sources in social networks based on content and social structure. In *Proceedings of the third IEEE International Conference on Social Computing (SocialCom)* (2011).
4. Castillo, C., Mendoza, M., and Poblete, B. Information credibility on twitter. In *WWW* (2011), 675–684.
5. DuBois, T., Golbeck, J., and Srinivasan, A. Predicting trust and distrust in social networks. In *Proceedings of the third IEEE International Conference on Social Computing (SocialCom)* (2011).
6. Golbeck, J. *Computing with Social Trust*. Springer Publishing Company, Incorporated, 2010.
7. Golbeck, J., and Hansen, D. L. Computing political preference among twitter followers. In *CHI* (2011), 1105–1108.
8. Haifeng Zhao, William Kallander, T. G. F. W. Read what you trust: An open wiki model enhanced by social context. In *Proceedings of the third IEEE International Conference on Social Computing (SocialCom)* (2011).
9. Herlocker, J. L., Konstan, J. A., and Riedl, J. Explaining collaborative filtering recommendations. In *Proceedings of ACM CSCW'00 Conference on Computer-Supported Cooperative Work* (2000), 241–250.
10. Houser, D., and Wooders, J. Reputation in auctions: Theory, and evidence from ebay. *Journal of Economics and Management Strategy 15*, 2 (2006), 353–369.
11. Jennifer Golbeck, Cristina Robles, M. E. K. T. Predicting personality from twitter. In *Proceedings of the third IEEE International Conference on Social Computing (SocialCom)* (2011).
12. Kwak, H., Lee, C., Park, H., and Moon, S. What is twitter, a social network or a news media? In *WWW '10: Proceedings of the 19th international conference on World wide web*, ACM (New York, NY, USA, 2010), 591–600.
13. McNally, K., O'Mahony, M. P., Smyth, B., Coyle, M., and Briggs, P. Towards a reputation-based model of social web search. In *Proceedings of the 15th international conference on Intelligent user interfaces*, IUI '10, ACM (New York, NY, USA, 2010), 179–188.
14. Melville, P., Mooney, R., and Nagarajan, R. Content-boosted collaborative filtering. In *In Proceedings of the Eighteenth National Conference on Artificial Intelligence* (2002).
15. Mendoza, M., Poblete, B., and Castillo, C. Twitter Under Crisis: Can we trust what we RT? In *1st Workshop on Social Media Analytics (SOMA '10)*, ACM Press (July 2010).
16. Milgram, S. The small world problem. *Psychology Today 1* (May 1967), 61–67.
17. Mobasher, B., Burke, R., Bhaumik, R., and Williams, C. Toward trustworthy recommender systems: An analysis of attack models and algorithm robustness. *ACM Trans. Inter. Tech. 7*, 4 (2007), 23.
18. O'Donovan, J., and Smyth, B. Trust in recommender systems. In *IUI '05: Proceedings of the 10th international conference on Intelligent user interfaces*, ACM Press (2005), 167–174.
19. O'Donovan, J., Smyth, B., Evrim, V., and McLeod, D. Extracting and visualizing trust relationships from online auction feedback comments. In *IJCAI* (2007), 2826–2831.
20. Pool, D., and Kochen, M. Contacts and influence. *Social Networks 1*, 1 (1978), 5–51.
21. Resnick, P., Iacovou, N., Suchak, M., Bergstrom, P., and Riedl, J. Grouplens: An open architecture for collaborative filtering of netnews. In *Proceedings of ACM CSCW'94 Conference on Computer-Supported Cooperative Work* (1994), 175–186.
22. Resnick, P., and Zeckhauser, R. Trust among strangers in internet transactions: Empirical analysis of ebay's reputation system. *The Economics of the Internet and E-Commerce. Volume 11 of Advances in Applied Microeconomics.* (December 2002).
23. Suzuki, Y. A credibility assessment for message streams on microblogs. In *3PGCIC* (2010), 527–530.
24. Victor, P., Cornelis, C., Cock, M. D., and Herrera-Viedma, E. Practical aggregation operators for gradual trust and distrust. *Fuzzy Sets and Systems 184*, 1 (2011), 126–147.

Summarizing Sporting Events Using Twitter

Jeffrey Nichols, Jalal Mahmud, Clemens Drews
IBM Research – Almaden
650 Harry Rd, San Jose, CA 95120
{jwnichols,jumahmud,cdrews}@us.ibm.com

ABSTRACT
The status updates posted to social networks, such as Twitter and Facebook, contain a myriad of information about what people are doing and watching. During events, such as sports games, many updates are sent describing and expressing opinions about the event. In this paper, we describe an algorithm that generates a journalistic summary of an event using only status updates from Twitter as a source. Temporal cues, such as spikes in the volume of status updates, are used to identify the important moments within an event, and a sentence ranking method is used to extract relevant sentences from the corpus of status updates describing each important moment within an event. We evaluate our algorithm compared to human-generated summaries and the previous best summarization algorithm, and find that the results of our method are superior to the previous algorithm and approach the readability and grammaticality of the human-generated summaries.

Author Keywords
Implicit Crowdsourcing, Journalism, Social Media, Status Updates

ACM Classification Keywords
H.5.2. [Information Interfaces and Presentation]: User Interfaces; H.2.8. [Database Management]: Database applications - Data mining.

General Terms
Algorithms, Experimentation, Human Factors

INTRODUCTION
Everyday, people are posting millions of status updates to social networks, such as Twitter and Facebook. As of June 2011, more than 200 million updates were being posted to Twitter each day [1]. Some of these updates describe events that people are participating in or watching through a media source such as television, including natural disasters [25], political debates [21], and sporting events [11]. These updates provide important information about what is happening in real-time, but this information must be summarized or visualized in order to be accessible to human viewers. If automated summaries could be generated, breaking information could be presented more quickly without waiting for a journalist to manually generate a summary and news stories could be written for smaller events that journalists are not able to cover.

IUI'12, February 14–17, 2012, Lisbon, Portugal.

In this paper, we explore an automated method for *implicitly crowdsourcing* summaries of events using only status updates posted to Twitter as a source. We focus on summarizing sporting events, specifically World Cup soccer matches, because each event takes place over a short defined period of time, there is a substantial volume of tweets about each event, and there is press coverage of each event to serve as a gold standard. Specifically we make the following contributions:

- An unsupervised algorithm for generating a textual summary of events, especially sporting events from status updates in Twitter.
- Evaluation of our algorithm's results compared to human-generated summaries using the standard automated ROUGE method [12] and human evaluators that rated summaries in terms of readability and grammaticality. The results of both demonstrations show that our algorithm works reasonably well and outperforms the best-known algorithm for micro-blog summarization [24].

RELATED WORK
A substantial amount of work on text summarization exists in the literature [9]. Unfortunately, techniques developed for summarizing large text documents, such as blogs [30], are not readily applicable for summarizing large sets of status updates, which have very different qualities (e.g., small amounts of text, highly repetitive, and very noisy). Prior work on micro-blog summarization includes summarization of a set of status updates by Sharifi et al. [23, 24] and event summarization by Chakrabarti et al. [7].

Our work leverages a word frequency-based technique, based on the phrase graph technique proposed by Sharifi et al. [23, 24]. Unlike their work, which focused on generating a single sentence from a set of tweets, we broaden the scope to look at an entire event and generate multiple sentences that describe each important moment within an event.

Chakrabarti et al. [7] use Twitter to generate summaries of long running, structure rich events, where multiple events share the same underlying structure. They looked specifically at multiple American football games, and used a modified Hidden Markov Model (HMM) that learns the structure and vocabulary of the event. However, the assumption of the availability of multiple similar events may not be possible in practice, especially at the granularity of the moments they considered within their events. For example, an HMM is unlikely to capture all possible sequences of sub-events (e.g., interception, touchdown in American football) in an event. Also, certain vocabulary items, such as the names of participants, cannot be learned unless the same two teams have played multiple times, which is not common in some sports or in non-sporting events. Our algorithm is not limited by the availability of multiple similar events. Our approach is also unsupervised, whereas supervision is required to train an HMM model.

Several other systems aggregate tweets on a topic into visual summaries, such as TweetMotif [8], the Visual Backchannel [10], TwitInfo [13], and others [11, 21, 22]. These visualizations must be interpreted by users and do not include sentence-level textual summaries. Although each of these systems has various differences, most label important moments within the Twitter stream with single word labels or word clouds. A common thread across many of these systems is the need to detect important moments within the Twitter stream.

The use of rapid increases (or "spikes") in status update volume over time is a common technique across many systems, and is used in our algorithm as well, however the particular method in which volume is used differs. TwitInfo [13] has an algorithm based on TCP congestion detection that uses the weighted moving average, variance, and the absolute value of volumes to find spikes. Weng et al. [27] describe an event detection algorithm from tweets based on clustering of wavelet-based signals. They use wavelet analysis on the frequency based signals of the words from tweets, filter words which have low signal-auto correlations, and cluster the remaining words to form events with a modularity-based graph partitioning technique. Shamma et al. [21, 22] use a slope-based method similar to ours, but also extend this method to operate on the volume changes in specific topics rather than just the overall volume of recording. Petrovic et al. describe an algorithm that detects events that have not occurred previously [14].

Other systems use domain knowledge or manual supervision to guide their event detection, whereas our algorithm does not rely on any domain knowledge. Hannon et al. use a set of keywords provided by the user along with volume information to determine what events to include in an automatically generated video highlight reel [11]. SportSense (http://www.sportsense.us) uses domain knowledge of American football games (e.g., touchdown, fumble) to visually display the major events that occurred in a game and rate fans' excitement level. Sakaki et al. use a domain specific classifier to detect earthquake events from Twitter status updates [19]. Becker et al. use a supervised classifier to detect events [5]. Popescu et al. detect events from twitter using knowledge of known entities [16, 17].

Our work on detecting and summarizing events using only Twitter data is related to other work that performs the same function using different data sources. For example, Piriou et al. [15] detect events using computer vision from video sources. Baillie et al. [3] use crowd noise from an audio recording to detect important moments within a sporting event, which is analogous to our use of Twitter volume for the same purpose. Xu et al. [28] experimented with both a hybrid audio and video approach to detect moments within a sporting event, and using webcast text to perform the same function. This latter work did not have to consider noise in the text however, because the webcast text was much cleaner than typical Twitter data.

DATASET

For the design and evaluation of our algorithm, we collected a dataset of tweets from 36 games of the 2010 World Cup. Tweets for this dataset were recorded through Twitter's Streaming API using a track stream that receives tweets based on keyword query. Most games were recorded using the keywords "worldcup" and "wc2010" that were promoted by FIFA (www.fifa.com) and Twitter for World Cup games. Note that the Twitter API matches keywords without case-sensitivity and also matches hashtags. Some games occurred simultaneously with others, and for these we used keywords such as the names of the countries, any country abbreviations, and any distinct team names (e.g. "socceroos" for Australia). Due to various technical difficulties, many recorded games contained gaps of 5 minutes or longer where tweets were missed.

Evaluation of the algorithm, as you will see, requires substantial human effort to identify important moments, create manual summaries, and rate automated summaries, so we reduced the set of 36 games to just 3. These 3 games can be seen in Table 1, and were selected randomly from the set of games with complete recordings.

Game	Tweets	Max Tweets/Min
US vs. Slovenia	113189	3992
Germany vs. Serbia	72335	1810
Australia vs. Serbia	77517	8235

Table 1. Summary of World Cup Dataset

SUMMARIZING SPORTING EVENTS

Sporting events consist of a sequence of moments, each of which may contain actions by players, the referee, the fans, etc. Our algorithm relies on Twitter users to collectively identify the important moments within an event and also describe those moments. At a high level, our algorithm relies on two properties of the Twitter stream:

- Sudden increases, or "spikes," in the volume of tweets in the stream suggest that something important just happened because many people found the need to comment on it.

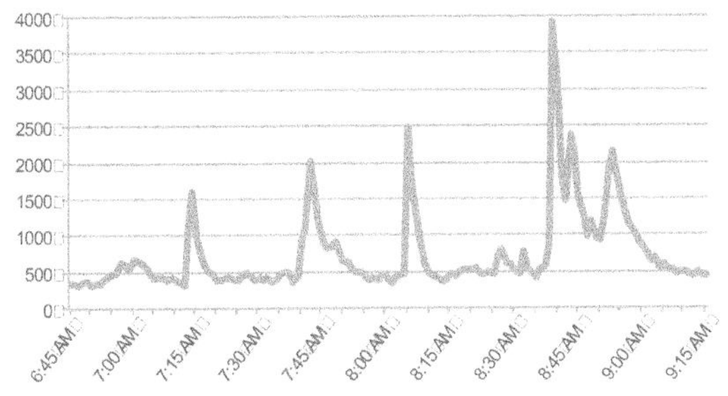

Figure 1. Twitter volume graph for the 2010 World Cup game of US vs. Slovenia. The x-axis is time and the y-axis is volume as measured in tweets/minute.

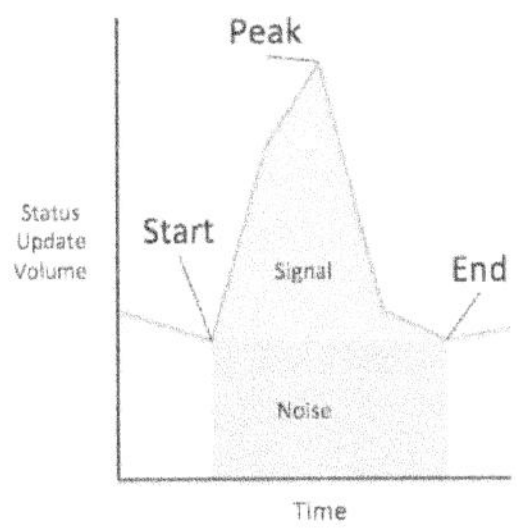

Figure 2. The anatomy of a spike, showing start, peak, and end times.

- A high percentage of the contents of the tweets at a "spike" in volume contain text describing what happened in the moment, and this text often contains repetitive elements, such as the names of players involved, the type of the event, etc.

Our algorithm breaks the problem of generating a summary of an event into the following steps, which are described in more detail in the following sub-sections:

- Status updates are collected using basic keyword filtering.
- The important moments within an event are detected by searching for extreme changes in update volume on a per minute basis.
- Status updates from each important moment are identified.
- Several noise reduction algorithms are used to eliminate spam and off-topic status updates.
- A word frequency table is calculated using the longest sentence in each status update.
- Sentences from the status updates are ranked using the phrase graph, and the top *n* sentences containing no overlapping tokens are returned.

Detecting Important Moments

Shamma et al. [21, 22] and Marcus et al. [13] have noted that important moments can often be detected in Twitter streams when the volume of status updates increases sharply. Over the course of a sporting event, this may happen many times (for example, see Figure 1).

We could have used a moment detection algorithm that relies on the absolute value of the volume, however we discovered two problems with this approach. First, sometimes the stream volume may stay high for several minutes and have multiple localized peaks. Second, some moments generate significantly less traffic than others and might be missed by a technique that relies on absolute values. To avoid the above problems, we chose to use a detection algorithm based on the change in volume (i.e. the slope of the volume graph). In this paper, we measure tweet volume at the granularity of tweets/minute.

Our algorithm is motivated by spike detection as described in [21]. In particular, we have implemented both an offline version and an online version of our algorithm for moment detection. When our algorithm is used offline (i.e. tweets from the entire event are available), it computes a threshold for the entire event from basic statistics of the set of all slopes for that event. For example, a threshold for a particular soccer match may be computed from the tweets recorded for that entire match. In the online approach, we compute this threshold from the tweets in a moving window with start time and end time, where the size of the moving window is a parameter. The experiments reported in this paper use the offline approach to detect this threshold from the entire event.

We tried several different formulas for computing the slope threshold. The first threshold we tried was median + 2 * standard deviation, in order to include only extreme outliers in the set. Unfortunately, we found that for events with very large spikes the standard deviation in the slope is too large to find the smaller but still meaningful spikes. After some experimentation, we settled on a threshold of 3 * median, which produced results that closely matched a visual inspection of spikes across our larger 36 game data set. In future work, we plan to examine this heuristic to see how it applies to other types of sporting events not in our data set.

After identifying all slopes that exceed the threshold, we generate a list of "spikes" that correspond to the important moments in the event. Each spike can be defined as the tuple of <Start Time, Peak Time, End Time>. For each slope above threshold, we calculate the start time by searching backwards in time until we find the point where the slope began going up. The peak time is calculated by searching forward until we find the point where the slopes start decreasing. Finally, we calculate the end time by searching forward from the peak time to find the point where the slope begins increasing again (see Figure 2). Before returning the list of spikes, we remove any duplicates, which may happen for large spikes that include multiple above threshold slopes.

Selecting Updates for Moments

Given an important moment, as described by a spike tuple, we need to select a set of status updates that are representative of that moment. We could, for example, choose to select all status updates sent between the start and end time of the spike, but we have found in practice that this option is not desirable. This is because there is often a relatively constant amount of noise throughout the stream, whereas the "signal" is greatest at the peak and goes to zero at the start and end of the spike (see Figure 2). Thus, our goal is to select the largest possible set of status updates within the spike that also have a high signal-to-noise (SNR) ratio. This is a multi-variable optimization problem [26].

We use a heuristic approach to select a time range that optimizes both SNR and G, the number of signal tweets that can be extracted. This time range can be calculated for a time interval given knowledge of the noise over that interval. We approximate the noise over a time interval as the tweets arriving per unit time (e.g., minutes, as in our implementation) at the time the spike begins or ends (see Figure 2) multiplied by the length of the time interval. We start with the peak time T_p, calculate SNR and G for time intervals $(T_p, T_p + \Delta t)$, $(T_p - \Delta t, T_p)$ and $(T_p - \Delta t, T_p + \Delta t)$, and iteratively increase the value of Δt (1 min, 2 min, etc.). We select a time interval where the SNR for that interval is above a threshold θ_{SNR} and the ratio of the number of signal tweets within the interval to the total signal tweets over the entire spike is above a threshold θ_G. If there are multiple such intervals, we select the one that yields the most status updates. The thresholds are set experimentally, and we found that $\theta_{SNR} = 0.7$ and $\theta_G = 0.6$ work reasonably well for our dataset.

Noise Elimination

Once we detect important moments and the status updates corresponding to those moments using the previous step, we use several noise elimination techniques to filter out spam and off-topic tweets. First, we use a language detector from the Apache Nutch project (http://nutch.apache.org/) in combination with the language information reported by Twitter to detect the languages of each update and remove those that are non-English. Note that the information provided by Twitter is unreliable and often reports that English is the language of a tweet when it is not, necessitating the use of another language detector. Second, we use a set of heuristics to filter out spam and types of tweets that we have generally found to not be useful. Spam is filtered using a dictionary of common terms that we found in spam tweets. Other heuristics include removing tweets that are replies to other users and tweets that contain URLs. In general, our algorithm will ignore most spam anyway, provided the signal from the tweets in the spike dominates the noise (generally true). Next, we perform a normalization process where we eliminate repeating characters from a term, e.g., gooooooal becomes goal as a result of normalization.

Extracting Summary Sentences

The final step is to find the N sentences contained in our set of status updates that best summarize the set. Sentences are extracted from tweets using heuristics, primarily by splitting on punctuation symbols. Our approach is to construct a phrase graph from the longest sentence in each status update, weight the graph according to frequency of words and a few other heuristics, and then to score the longest sentence using the phrase graph. The use of a phrase graph and the weighting scheme is borrowed from Sharifi [23, 24], however unlike their technique that only generated a single sentence per topic, we generate multiple sentences that describe each of the important moments within an event. In addition, our approach incorporates several important differences from Sharifi's algorithm that we will describe in detail.

The intuition for using a phrase graph is that many words and short phrases are repeated by status update authors, either intentionally through mechanisms such as Twitter's ReTweet feature or unintentionally because there are common elements in the moment to which authors refer (e.g., "goal" or the name of a key player). The phrase graph consists of a node for each word appearing in any status update, and an edge between each set of two words that are used adjacently in any status update (see Figure 3).

Repetition is represented through weights assigned to the nodes, and optionally the edges, that reflect the frequency with which the word occurs in the set of status updates. We have experimented with several methods of weighting, described later, and settled on the basic approach of using a weight equal to just the number of occurrences of the word. The weight of stop words and hashtags are set to 0. For example, Figure 3 shows the phrase graph that would be generated from these status updates: *Landon Donovan scores!*, *Donovan scores a brilliant strike*, *Landon Donovan is brilliant.*

We construct the phrase graph from only the longest sentence in each status update, rather than using the entire update. This helps to ensure that our generated summaries are well formed and eliminates some of the noise found in updates. We also remove hashtags from the beginning and end of each extracted sentence, which often are meta-data descriptors for the update rather than meaningful language that should be included in the sentence. The language is still often noisy, and we may consider other techniques for cleaning the sentences in future work. Note that we did not include a virtual END symbol in our phrase graph because we are scoring existing sentences rather than generating new ones.

Sharifi's algorithm uses a phrase graph to generate a single sentence summary [23]. In contrast, we leverage the phrase graph to score the input sentences, each extracted from one

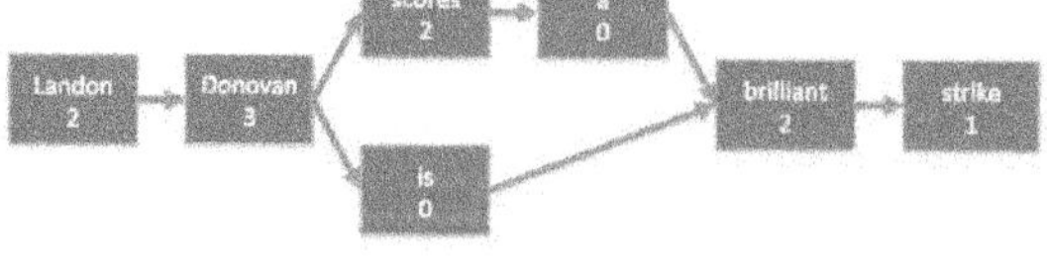

Figure 3. An example phrase graph. Words and their respective weights are shown in each box.

Game	Actual Events	Detected		R	P
		Moments	Events		
US vs. Slovenia	13	9	8	0.62	0.89
Germany vs. Serbia	16	8	11	0.69	0.92
Australia vs. Serbia	11	9	10	0.91	0.91

Table 2. Recall/Precision Performance of Moment Detection

status update, and find the best scoring sentences. To score a sentence, we tokenize the sentence, remove any duplicate tokens, and sum the weights of all nodes matching a token to generate a score. Duplicate tokens are removed so that tokens that appear multiple times only contribute to the score once. We also tried a variant of this algorithm that included edge weights in the score, but we found that node weights alone were sufficient to generate good summaries. We also considered normalizing the score by the number of tokens in the sentence, however normalized scores seem to favor shorter sentences made up of a few high scoring terms whereas not normalizing favors longer sentences with more information.

Given the list of scored sentences, we then output the top N sentences that *do not share any non-stop word stemmed tokens*. This ensures that the sentences each include different information, although this is sensitive to the quality of the stemming algorithm (we use the Porter stemmer [18]) and the tweet normalization applied during noise elimination. The value N may be chosen based on the summarization application; we find that choosing N=3 seems to work well.

EVALUATION

Here we describe our evaluation metrics, experimental setup, and our quantitative and qualitative results.

Evaluation of Important Moment Detection

To evaluate the performance of our moment detection algorithm, we compare the counts of various types of key moments detected by our algorithm to counts extracted from reading several recap articles about each game. We chose the following categories of key events in a soccer game: goals, penalties, red cards, yellow cards, disallowed goals, game start, game end and half time.

To establish event counts for our algorithm, one author manually examined all of the status updates selected to represent each important moment and identified the number and type of the events described in that moment. Note that an important moment may contain multiple key events, e.g., a red card followed by a penalty, or a goal followed by half time. An important moment may not contain a reference to any key event, and we consider these "noisy" moments.

To establish actual event counts for these games, one author examined game recap articles from four sources: FIFA.com, ESPN.com, New York Times and Yahoo! Sports. The first two sources were also used for our summarization evaluation later. We used multiple sources to ensure that no key events were missed.

Recall (R) of moment detection is defined as the ratio of the number of key events detected by our algorithm and the total number of key events in the entire game. Precision (P) has the same numerator, but the denominator is the sum of the total number of key events detected by our algorithm plus the number of "noisy" moments.

Table 2 shows overall performance in terms of precision and recall. Observe that precision performance is very high for each game, which means that when our algorithm detects an important moment it likely contains at least one key event.

Recall performance is somewhat low for the first two games. To further examine this, we computed recall for each key event type. Table 3 shows that our algorithm can accurately identify goals, red cards, penalties, game ends, and disallowed goals. This makes sense, because these key events cause significantly large spikes in tweet volume during these games. However, yellow cards, game starts, and half times did not cause sufficient increases in tweet volume in our data set and are thus harder to detect. Note that detection of game ends was better than game start events. We have observed that people often tweet their reactions to the game immediately after the game ends. For example, at the end of the US vs. Slovenia game there are many complaints about the referee and a disallowed goal.

Key Event Type	Recall
Goal	1.0
Red Card	1.0
Yellow Card	0.53
Penalty	1.0
Game Start	0.67
Game End	1.0
Half Time	0.33
Disallowed Goals	1.0

Table 3. Recall of Key Event Detection

Evaluation of Summarization

For the second experiment, we use two methods:

- The ROUGE-N metric to compare our summaries to gold standards generated by humans [12].
- Human evaluation of the summaries for readability, grammatical correctness and meaning in comparison to the gold standards.

We use two gold standards:

Game	Spike	Manual Summary	Our Summary	TF-IDF Summary
US vs. Slovenia	1	In the first 15 mins of the soccer game between USA and Slovenia, Slovenia is leading with a goal by Birsa. Birsa scored an easy goal from midfield to the right of the goal, as USA left that shot wide open. Terrible defense by USA team, too much space left open.	Good goal for Slovenia and the USA once again starts a game terrible. Birsa gives #SVN 1-0 lead with smart shot. Howard didn't even look like he saw that one coming.	The Slovenians strike first, #USA standing around waiting for a whistle, or a bus, or something. vs #SVN 0-1 '15 GOAL by Birsa #USMNT defende looked hipnotized, Howard questionable positioning was a factor too. #usa playing like high skool kids in a practice match with no game plan.
Germany vs. Serbia	3	Klose argues with referee, gets second yellow cards and is out of the game. Germany down to 10 men. 1-0 Serbia.	Germany screwed by the refs and a red card for Klose; seconds later, a pretty goal by the Serbs. yellow seems to be a very popular colour in this game.	So first I didn't make my bet on a red card, then Germany conceed meaning I lose points for TWO defenders in my fantasy team. This Ref is absolutely insane, just 35 mins in, 7 bookings & already #GER star Miroslav Klose is sent off on a bullshit challenge. Mick McCarthy claiming the referee is 'a clown' = best line of the world cup so far.
Australia vs. Serbia	9	Serbia Australia match ends with 2-1. With a result of 1:0 between Germany and Ghana this means that Ghana and Germany will advance to the knock out rounds and serbia and australia will be out.	Australia won 2-1 on serbia, Germany won 1-0 vs Ghana, Germany and Ghana goes on to the next round. Great win by #aus but not good enough to go through. Final score #Aus 2 #Srb 1.	Kalo timnas kita pake pelatih luar spt AUS & GHA ini, apkh kita bs masuk Piala Dunia. Germany beats Ghana, Australia beats Serbia, which means, Germany and Ghana continue on, and Ghana will face the United States. Socceroos leading 2-1, Gillard leading Rudd, crowds on either sides of earth gather with vuvuzelas.

Table 4. Sample summaries for each game in our data set

- Game "recap" articles written by FIFA.com and ESPN.com.
- Manual summaries generated by humans from our Twitter corpus for each important moment detected by our algorithm.

The recap articles allow us to evaluate our overall summary of the game, although these articles are longer than the summaries generated by our algorithm. The manual summaries generated by humans for each spike allow us to evaluate our summaries of each important moment separately. To generate the manual summaries, we recruited six humans and randomly assigned each to summarize one game (2 subjects for each game). Each subject was given a list of tweets for each moment as identified by our algorithm and asked to generate summaries for each moment of at most three sentences using only words that appeared in the tweets. Our subjects were busy researchers from our lab, so to keep the task manageable we provided them with a randomly generated subset of at most 750 tweets for each moment and limited them to an hour to generate all summaries. Pilot studies showed that subjects were able to generate high quality and representative summaries given these constraints.

We chose the ROUGE-N method to compare summaries because it is widely used in the summarization community, it is automated, and its results have been shown to correlate strongly with human judgments of summary quality [12]. ROUGE-1, which compares the similarity of summaries at the level of unigrams, has been shown to work well for short summaries, such as headlines, and used for evaluating tweet-sized summaries [24]. ROUGE-2, which uses bigrams, has been shown to work well for longer summaries. We use ROUGE-1 to compare our summaries of important moments, because they are relatively short, and ROUGE-2 to compare the full game summary with the recap articles. The automated nature of ROUGE allows us to easily compare many different variations of our algorithm. We also compare our results to the modified TF-IDF algorithm of Sharifi et al. [24], which is the best tweet summarization algorithm of which we are aware.

Automated summary evaluations are not perfect however, and so we conducted a human evaluation of the automated summaries generated by the best variants of our algorithm and Sharifi's modified TF-IDF algorithm. Each summary was evaluated by 3 humans. They were shown both the automatically generated summary and the human-generated summaries for each important moment. Each evaluator then used a 7-point Likert scale to rank the automatically generated summaries on three dimensions: readability, grammatical correctness, and inclusion of content found in the manual summaries. To provide a baseline and to assess the quality of the manual summaries, we also asked the evaluators to rate the readability and grammatical correctness of the manual summaries.

Automated Summary Evaluation Results

Table 4 shows a selection of summaries generated by our algorithm and the modified TF-IDF algorithm. We start by examining the performance of our algorithm relative to the manual summaries generated for each important moment in a game. This evaluation compares our summary generation to Sharifi's modified TF-IDF algorithm and a human generated gold standard. Figure 4 shows the results.

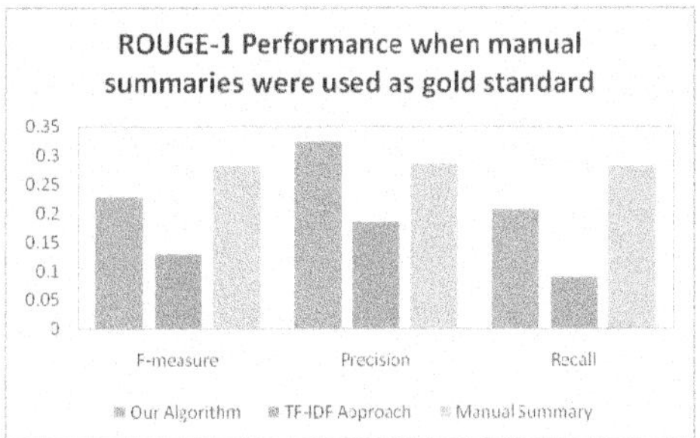

Figure 4. ROUGE-1 comparison of our algorithm, modified TF-IDF algorithm and manual summaries for important moments within an event.

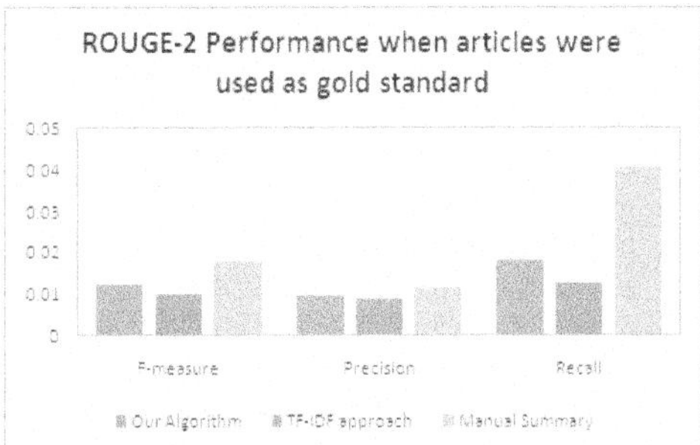

Figure 5. ROUGE-2 comparison of our algorithm, modified TF-IDF, and the manual summaries using recap articles as the gold standard.

These results show that there is fairly large variation between the two manual summaries for each game, which is reflected in the relatively low numbers for their comparison using ROUGE-1. Our algorithm performs just below this high bar, and even achieves a higher precision than the manual summary comparison. This indicates that our summaries at least occasionally must contain elements of both manual summaries that are not shared between the manual summaries. We find no significant difference between the summaries generated by our algorithm and the manual summaries ($p \sim= 0.684$, paired t-test, $n=26$). Our algorithm significantly outperforms the modified TF-IDF algorithm ($p < 0.001$, paired t-test, $n=26$).

The summaries for each important moment can then be concatenated together to form a full game summary. To evaluate the quality of these summaries, we compare them to press articles using the ROUGE-2 algorithm. Figure 5 shows the results. Note that the manual summary evaluation is different for articles than it was for moments. Here we concatenate the manual summaries generated for important moments into a full game summary, and use ROUGE-2 to compare with the two recap articles. As before, the numbers for the manual summaries represent an upper bound of what we expect our automated algorithms to accomplish. Note that the manual summaries and all algorithms have low performance on the ROUGE 2 test, largely because the recap articles are substantially longer than the concatenated summaries. There were also mismatches in word use, perhaps because journalists typically use different words than Twitter users. The recap articles also contain post-game quotes from players and coaches, which are not contained in the datasets available to our summarization algorithms. Still, we find it instructive that our algorithm appears to perform better than the modified TF-IDF approach, although n is too small ($n=3$) to test for statistical significance.

	Mean	Median	Std. Dev.
Readability	6.01	6	1.00
Grammaticality	5.60	6	1.19
Content	5.19	5	1.39

Table 5. Results from 3 human evaluators for our algorithm using a 7-point Likert scale

	Mean	Median	Std. Dev.
Readability	3.75	3.66	1.62
Grammaticality	3.8586	3.5	1.7872
Content	3.5754	3.3333	1.8763

Table 6. Results from 3 human evaluators for TF-IDF algorithm using a 7 point Likert scale

	Mean	Median	Std. Dev.
Readability	6.53	7	0.59
Grammaticality	6.37	6.67	0.73

Table 7. Results from 3 human evaluators for manual summaries using a 7-point Likert scale

Human Evaluation Results

Results of the human evaluation of the summaries are shown in Table 5, Table 6, and Table 7. Note that ratings for inclusion of content from the manual summaries are only available for the algorithm-generated summaries. These results suggest that our human evaluators found the summaries generated by our algorithm to be understandable and contain much of the same information as the manual summaries, thus confirming the automated evaluation. The similar readability and grammaticality ratings for our results compared to the manual summaries suggest that our summaries may be of suitable quality for human consumption.

ALGORITHM VARIANTS

During our algorithm design process, we considered several variants to our algorithm. These included the use of a keyword filtering method, clustering, and several weighting schemes for the phrase graph. In this section, we describe these variants and the results of experiments comparing these variants to our final algorithm. We include these negative results to assist future researchers in creating new tweet summarization algorithms.

Keyword Filtering

During the noise elimination phase of our algorithm, we considered using a keyword filtering approach to eliminate off-topic tweets using a two-stage process. This is conceptually similar to the centroid-based content selection method proposed by Becker et al. [6]. We start by identifying the top-M keywords for each important moment using TF-IDF [20]. Here the value M is determined experimentally. For computing IDF required by the TF-IDF approach, we use a different approach for offline and online summarization. If we have access to all of the status updates for an event (offline), we build a corpus using status updates from every important moment. In the online case, we use a corpus of status updates collected from important moments found in previous similar events, e.g., other World Cup games. In either case, each moment corresponds to a Document and IDF is calculated across moments for a given match. Keywords identified using this approach represent those that are unique to the current important moment but do not appear evenly across all moments. We eliminate all status updates that do not contain any of these keywords under the assumption that these updates are likely off-topic.

To assess the effect of keyword filtering, we tested both our summarization algorithm and Sharifi's TF-IDF algorithm with and without this feature. We observe that the performance of our algorithm drops with keyword filtering (about a 5% decrease on average for both summary types), perhaps because some of the tweets removed for being off-topic do contain topical information that positively affects the phrase graph weighting. Keyword filtering improves the performance of the modified TF-IDF algorithm however (about a 50% increase on average for both summary types). Perhaps the TF-IDF technique's topically important term selection is sensitive to noise and filtering removes some of that noise. The results presented in the Evaluation section were computed using the best choice for each algorithm; filtering was turned off for our algorithm, but was turned on for the modified TF-IDF algorithm.

Clustering

Clustering would seem to be an intuitive method for sets of tweets describing different aspects of an important moment. For example, in a soccer game a goal moment might be described both in terms of the goal scorer (e.g., brilliant strike to the top of the net) and the goalkeeper's reaction (e.g., caught flatfooted).

We tried a number of clustering algorithms, such as EM and KMEANS from WEKA [2], but through experimentation we observed that none of these methods were more effective than our non-overlapping token sentence selection method. At the important moment level using manual summaries as the gold standard, we observed approximately a 10-15% performance drop when clustering was used. When articles were used as the gold standard, we observed a performance increase of 5-10%, though this may be meaningless given the overall low performance. A visual inspection of the clusters suggests that the algorithms we tried do a poor job of creating clusters that are topically different. This leads to similar updates existing in multiple clusters, which results in a final summary that includes several similar sentences. In contrast, our non-overlapping token method relies on selecting sentences from the scored list that are demonstrably different because they do not share any keywords. This latter option guarantees diversity, which seems to improve the final result.

Different Sentence Scoring Approaches

To determine the best sentence scoring method using the phrase graph, we varied different factors such as a penalty for distance from the term with maximum frequency [23] and the inclusion of edge weights. We tried two edge-weighting options: weights on all edges based on frequency and weights only on edges between non-stop words. We computed summarization performance for each of those cases.

We found the penalty for distance from the term with maximum frequency hurt performance in all cases, which differs from the Sharifi's results. This may be because Sharifi's work focused on generating summaries for tweets selected based on a single keyword, which is not true for our dataset.

We also found that the weighting scheme that did not use any edge-weights performed the best, though only slightly better than version that used edge weights on non-stop word edges. Thus the best variant is, unfortunately, the same as basic frequency scoring, which would not require the creation of the phrase graph. While it is disappointing that the phrase graph does not significantly improve the results of summarization, it is useful to note that simple approaches can yield quality results. The very close performance with and without non-stop word edge weights also suggests that there may be ways to use of the phrase graph in more beneficial ways, and we plan to examine this in future work.

No.	Add Penalty?	Add Edge Weight?	F
1	Yes	Yes	0.2058
2	Yes	No	0.21111
3	Yes	No stop word weights	0.2107
4	No	Yes	0.2198
5	No	No	0.2274
6	No	No stop word weights	0.2273

Table 8. Performance comparison for different sentence scoring options using the phrase graph

APPLICATION TO OTHER SPORTING EVENTS

We have presented the evaluation of our summarization algorithm for World Cup soccer matches, however we have also experimented with applying our algorithm to other types of sporting events, such as baseball. We collected tweets for two major league baseball games during the summer of 2011: Boston vs. Seattle and Boston vs. Kansas. Tweets were recorded using a similar method with the

Spike 7: Boston Red Sox vs. Seattle Mariners
Josh reddick homerun puts the red sox up 5-4 on seattle. #redsox take a 5 to 4 lead and put Lackey in position to win despite sucking. You hear all those cheers following # red sox

Table 9. Sample summary for a spike from a baseball game

keywords "baseball," "mlb," the names of the teams, the cities the teams were from, and the last names of the starting pitchers.

When we applied our algorithm to detect important moments from those games, it detected 11 moments from the first game and 9 moments from the second game. We conducted a similar important moment evaluation as before, using baseball-specific events such as run, home run, single, double, stolen base, hit, game start, game end, and inning break. For manual annotation, we used game recap articles from ESPN. We found that our algorithm could detect key events such as game start (100% recall), game end (100% recall) and home runs (approximately 75% recall). Those key events are typically associated with large number of tweets. Our algorithm also detected some runs (approximately 60% recall), however it showed poor performance (20-25% recall) for detecting detailed events such as singles, doubles, and inning breaks. These events typically contain lower tweet volumes than home runs or game start and hence our moment detection algorithm fails to detect them. In the future, we could use domain knowledge such as use of certain keywords to search tweets for these key events, perhaps employing a topic method similar to Shamma et al. [22]. We also examined precision and found that 2/11 moments from the first game and 1/9 moments did not correspond to any key event.

We also examined the summaries generated by our algorithm for important moment (see Table 9 for an example). Summary quality appeared to be comparable to the World Cup results, provided that the moment being summarized referenced some key event.

CONCLUSION AND FUTURE WORK

Our summarization algorithm seems to produce reasonable sentence-level summaries of important moments, and then these moment summaries can be concatenated to produce an event summary of a few paragraphs. We believe these event summaries could communicate what happened during an event to a person who could not follow it in real-time.

One question we have not addressed is the inclusion of bias in our generated summaries. For a sporting event, status updates often include an opinion in favor or against one of the teams that is competing, and we would like to take this bias into account. One option would be to generate summaries from only neutral status updates. Alternately, it might be desirable to include updates with just a single bias. Developing automated methods of detecting bias would be key to this work.

We would also like to improve the quality of the generated summary sentences. Our approach produces reasonable sentences from tweets, however we are curious to try other approaches, such as lattice-based paraphrase generation [4].

We have presented the evaluation of our algorithm in detail for soccer matches, with a brief discussion of an evaluation with baseball games. A key question is how our algorithm might apply to different, possibly longer term, events. We believe it should be possible to apply our technique to longer-term events because projects, such as TwitInfo [13], have used techniques similar to ours to detect sub-events as part of visualizing longer-term events. One feature that might be needed for other event types is the inclusion of domain information. In this paper, we have explicitly avoided using domain information about sports and soccer in particular, but this may be necessary for some events. For example, events in baseball are sometimes dependent on each other, and detecting the manner in which a run scored may require knowledge of baseball to extract a reasonable summary of a run-scoring event.

To support smaller scale events, which would be needed to generate journalistic descriptions of events that journalists do not cover, we will need to understand what the signal/noise and volume requirements are for our algorithm. It seems that our algorithm generates summaries with less consistent quality for smaller spikes, where the signal/noise ratio is worse than for larger spikes. Our algorithm also depends on repetition in status updates, and it is unclear what volume will be needed to get sufficient repetition to generate a reasonable summary. We plan to explore these issues in future work.

We believe this work represents a unique step towards crowdsourcing journalism. Unlike previous attempts, which have explicitly recruited participants, our method *implicitly crowdsources* a journalistic description from information that users are posting for their own reasons. We are excited to explore how this technique might change the way journalists do their work.

REFERENCES

1. http://blog.twitter.com/2011/06/200-million-tweets-per-day.html
2. WEKA, http://www.cs.waikato.ac.nz/ml/weka/
3. Baillie, M., Jose, J. M. An Audio-based Sports Video Segmentation and Event Detection Algorithm, In *Proc. CVPRW'04*.
4. Barzilay, R. and Lee, L. Learning to Paraphrase: An Unsupervised Approach Using Multiple-Sequence Alignment, In *Proc. HLT-NAACL 2003*.
5. Becker, H., Naaman, M. and Gravano, L. Beyond Trending Topics: Real-World Event Identification on Twitter. In *Proc. ICWSM 2011*.
6. Becker, H., Naaman, M. and Gravano, L. Selecting Quality Twitter Content for Events. In *Proc. ICWSM 2011*.

7. Chakrabarti, D. , Punera, K, Event Summarization using Tweets, In *Proc. ICWSM 2011.*

8. Connor, B. O'., Krieger, M., Ahn, D. TweetMotif: Exploratory Search and Topic Summarization for Twitter. In *Proc. ICWSM 2010.*

9. Das, D., Martins, A.F. T. A survey of automatic text summarization, CMU technical report. http://www.cs.cmu.edu/~nasmith/LS2/das-martins.07.pdf

10. Dörk, M., Gruen, D., Williamson, C., and Carpendale, S. A. Visual Backchannel for Large-Scale Events, *IEEE Transactions on Visualizatoin and Computer Graphics*, 16(6):1129-38, 2010.

11. Hannon, J., McCarthy, K., Lynch, J., Smyth, B. Personalized and Automatic Social Summarization of Events in Video, In *Proc. IUI 2011.*

12. Lin, C. ROUGE: A Package for Automatic Evaluation of Summaries. Prof. of the Workshop on Text Summarization Branches Out, post conference workshop of *ACL 2004.*

13. Marcus, A., Bernstein, M. S., Badar, O., Karger, D. R., Madden, S., Miller, R. C., TwitInfo: Aggregating and Visualizing Microblogs for Event Exploration. In *Proc. of CHI 2011.*

14. Petrovi´c, S., Osborne, M., and Lavrenko, V., Streaming first story detection with application to twitter. In *Proc. of NAACL 2010.*

15. Piriou, G., Bouthemy, P., Yao, J. Learned probabilistic image motion models for event detection in videos, In *Proc. ICPR 2004.*

16. Popescu, A., Pennacchiotti, M., Paranipe, D., Extracting events and event descriptions from Twitter, In *Proc. of WWW 2011.*

17. Popescu, A. , Pennacchiotti, M., Detecting Controversal Events from Twitter, In *Proc. of CIKM, 2010.*

18. Porter, M.F., An Algorithm for Suffix Stripping, *Program*, 14(3): 130–137, 1980

19. Sakaki, T., Okazaki, M., Matsuo, Y. Earthquake Shakes Twitter Users: Real-time Event Detection by Social Sensors, In *Proc. WWW 2010.*

20. Salton, G., Wong, A. , Yang, C.S. A vector space model for automatic indexing. *Comm. of the ACM*, 18(11): 613–620, 1975.

21. Shamma, D. A., Kennedy, L., and Churchill, E. F. Tweet the debates: Understanding Community Annotation of Uncollected Sources, In *Proc.* WSM 2009.

22. Shamma, D.A., Kennedy, L., Churchill, E.F. Peaks and persistence: modeling the shape of microblog conversations. In *Proc. of CSCW 2011.*

23. Sharifi, B., Hunton, M.A.,and Kalita, J. Summarizing Microblogs Automatically: In *Proc. ACL-HLT 2010.*

24. Sharifi, B., Hunton, M.A., and Kalita, J. Experiments in Microblog Summarization. *IEEE Second International Conference on Social Computing, 2010.*

25. Starbird, K., Palen, L., Hughes, A., and Vieweg, S. Chatter on The Red: What Hazards Threat Reveals about the Social Life of Microblogged Information. In *Proc. of CSCW 2010.*

26. Steuer, R.E., *Multiple Criteria Optimization: Theory, Computations, and Application*. New York: John Wiley & Sons, Inc., 1986

27. Weng, J., Lee, F. Event Detection in Twitter, In *Proc. of ICWSM 2011.*

28. Xu, M., Duan, L.Y., Xu, C.S., Tian,Q., Fusion Scheme of Visual and Auditory Modalities For Event Detection In Sports Video, In. *Proc.* of *ICME 2003.*

29. Xu, C., Zhang, Y.F., Zhu, G., Rui, Y., Lu, H., and Huang, Q. Using Webcast Text for Semantic Event Detection in Broadcast Sports Video, *IEEE Transactions on Multimedia,* Vol 10 No 7, Nov, 2008.

30. Zhou, L., and Hovy, E. On the summarization of dynamically introduced information: Online discussions and logs, In *AAAI-2006 Spring Symposium on Computational Approaches to Analyzing Weblogs.*

EPIC: A Multi-Tiered Approach to Enterprise Email Prioritization

Jie Lu Zhen Wen Shimei Pan Jennifer Lai
IBM T. J. Watson Research Center
19 Skyline Drive, Hawthorne, NY 10532 USA
{jielu, zhenwen, shimei, jlai}@us.ibm.com

ABSTRACT
We present Enterprise Priority Inbox Classifier (EPIC), an automatic personalized email prioritization system based on a topic-based user model built from the user's email data and relevant enterprise information. The user model encodes the user's topics of interest and email processing behaviors (e.g. read/reply/file) at the granularity of pair-wise interactions between the user and each of his/her email contacts. Given a new message, the user model is used in combination with the message metadata and content to determine the values of a set of contextual features. Contextual features include people-centric features representing information about the user's interaction history and relationship with the email sender, as well as message-centric features focusing on the properties of the message itself. Based on these feature values, EPIC uses a dynamic strategy to combine a global priority classifier with a user-specific classifier for determining the message's priority. An evaluation of EPIC based on 2,064 annotated email messages from 11 users, using 10-fold cross-validation, showed that the system achieves an average accuracy of 81.3%. The user-specific classifier contributed an improvement of 11.5%. Lastly we report on findings regarding the relative value of different contextual features for email prioritization.

Author Keywords
Email, prioritization, priority inbox, enterprise, user model.

ACM Classification Keywords
H.5.2 [Information Interfaces and Presentation]: User Interfaces—User interaction styles; H.4.1 [Information Systems Applications]: Office Automation—Time management.

General Terms
Algorithms, Design, Experimentation.

1. INTRODUCTION
To help alleviate the problem of "email overload", we have developed Enterprise Prioritize Inbox Classifier (EPIC), a system that automatically identifies high-priority emails in a user's inbox and displays them in a separate section from other emails in the interface, with the goal of assisting the user in his/her daily triage of incoming messages. The prioritization is informed by a user model automatically created from the user's email data along with relevant enterprise information (e.g. organizational structure). Information encoded in this user model is used in conjunction with the message metadata and content to compute the values of a set of contextual features. Based on these contextual features, the system then determines the priority of the incoming message using a multi-tiered approach, which dynamically determines how to combine a global priority classifier (established from labeled training data of multiple users) with a user-specific classifier built from ongoing feedback.

EPIC differs from previous work on email prioritization in two primary aspects. First, we derive a set of contextual features from each message based on a topic-based user model. This user model encodes granular information about the user's interaction with different people on different topics, and the user's relationship with each of his/her email contacts in an enterprise environment. Second, we have implemented a multi-tiered approach to priority classification. Instead of simply combining a global classifier and a user-specific classifier with fixed weights (e.g. [1]), our system uses instance-based matching between a new message and messages for which the user has provided one-click feedback to dynamically determine the best strategy to combine the two classifiers. This approach enables the system to quickly incorporate user-specific criteria for determining email priority without sacrificing the reliability provided by a global classifier, which has been created using pooled training data from multiple users.

2. RELATED WORK
Prior studies show that the action a user takes on an email message (e.g. read, reply, file, delete) largely depends on the user-perceived importance of this message [2, 9]. The user's relationship with the email sender, recency of contact, the history of communication between them, and the type of message content were found to be the main characteristics that influenced users' perceptions of message importance [2, 7, 9].

Previous works on redesigning email interfaces help users quickly identify important emails in their inbox by automatically grouping emails into conversational threads [1, 4, 8], displaying the social metadata associated with each email [5],

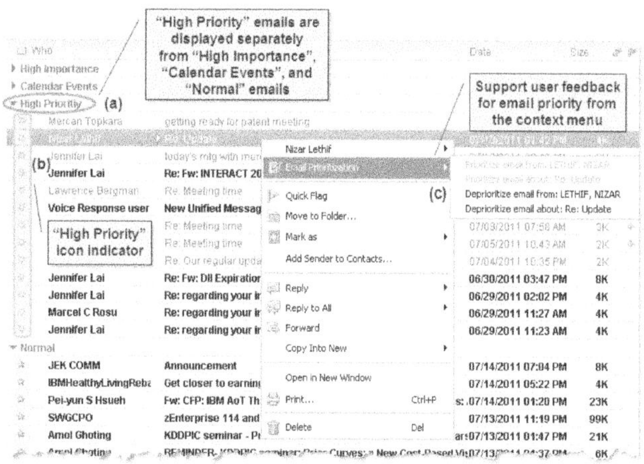

Figure 1. EPIC user interface

or allowing users to sort emails based on metrics that measure the social importance of the user's email correspondents [7]. In comparison, EPIC automatically groups emails into high-priority vs. normal categories displayed at the interface, and incorporates threading and social information into the contextual features it uses for determining email priority.

Existing approaches to automatic email prioritization mostly prioritize emails based on the classifier learned using supervised learning algorithms [1, 3, 10]. The content-based features used for classifier learning are simply words that occur in email content. By contrast, EPIC includes high-level features such as the importance of the topic discussed in email content (inferred based on a user model) to increase the robustness of prioritization. For user feedback, existing approaches either only learn the classifiers through one-time processing of labeled training data and do not consider dynamic user feedback [3, 10], or simply use user feedback to incrementally update the feature weights of the existing classifiers [1]. In comparison, EPIC dynamically combines a global classifier learned from training examples aggregated across multiple users with a user-specific classifier created based on ongoing user feedback to achieve a balance between robustness and responsiveness.

3. SYSTEM OVERVIEW

3.1 System Architecture

EPIC consists of five main modules. The *user modeling* module creates a model for each user based on his/her email data and relevant enterprise organizational information (Section 4). The *feature extraction* module takes an email message and the user model as input, and computes the values of a set of contextual features (Section 5). The *batch learning* module creates a global priority classifier using supervised learning based on labeled messages from multiple users (Section 6.1), and the *feedback learning* module collects dynamic user feedback about the priority of individual messages, and analyzes them to create a user-specific classifier (Section 6.2). Both modules call the feature extraction module to extract contextual features from the messages used for learning. Finally, the *classification* module combines the result from applying the global classifier and that from the user-specific classifier to classify each message as either high-priority or not (Section 6.3).

3.2 User Interface

Figure 1 shows the interface of EPIC developed as an extension to an IBM Lotus Notes 8 email client. Lotus Notes 8 supports two types of inbox view: a sort-ordered view with messages sorted by sender name, subject, date, or size, and a grouped view in which messages are automatically organized into different categories: "High Importance" for messages marked highly important by senders (which does not mean they are of high priority to the receiver), "Calendar Events" for messages related to calendar activities, and "Normal" for all other messages. All messages within each category are ordered by date.

EPIC extends this email interface by adding a new category of "High Priority" (Figure 1a) to display messages classified as high-priority by its automatic email prioritization. In addition, a "High Priority" icon is added to the display of each high-priority email in the inbox view (Figure 1b) so that even when a user uses a sort-ordered view instead of a grouped view, s/he can still easily identify high-priority emails based on the icon indicator. To support user feedback, an email prioritization menu item was added to the context menu triggered when a user right mouse buttons down on a message highlighted in the inbox view. The user can indicate to the system to de-prioritize a high-priority message or to prioritize a message currently in the "Normal" category while supplying the reason for such de-prioritization or prioritization (e.g. whether it is because of the sender and/or the subject of the message, see Figure 1c).

4. USER MODEL

EPIC creates a user model for each user. It encodes information about the user's interaction history with each email contact and their relationship, two characteristics that have been shown to be influential of the user's assessment of message importance [2, 7, 9]. It extends the multi-tiered, topic-based user model proposed in [6] to record finer-grained information about the user's behaviors in his/her interactions with different people, and the user's relationships with them in an enterprise environment. Below we describe in detail *interaction* and *relationship*, two of the main data structures in EPIC's user model.

4.1 Interaction

The interaction between the user and an email contact consists of the set of messages exchanged between them (sent to and copied on), the statistical topic model generated from the aggregate content of this set [6], as well as relevant statistics derived from these messages and associated user actions. Specifically, the statistics include: the number of incoming/outgoing messages from/to this person; the number of incoming messages from this person that have been read, replied, or filed by the user; the average time taken by the user to reply a message from this person; the time of the most recent message exchanged between them.

4.2 Relationship

The relationship between the user and an email contact consists of one or more connections between the two. The connections fall into four categories: *communicational* connections derived from email senders/recipients and calendar meeting participants; *organizational* connections based on organizational structure (e.g. managing, managed, same manager); *social* connections derived from activities in enterprise online social networks (e.g. community co-membership, wiki co-editing, file sharing); *academic* connections as a result of academic activities such as paper/patent co-authoring. Different connections are assigned different weights to reflect their inherently different strengths (e.g. organizational connections are typically stronger than social connections). The overall relationship strength between the user and an email contact is the weighted sum of all their connections.

5. CONTEXTUAL FEATURES

The contextual features used for prioritization are developed based on previous study findings and our own observations about the influential characteristics in determining message importance, which include people-centric features and message-centric features.

5.1 People-Centric Features

People-centric features represent aggregate information about the user's interaction and relationship with the sender of the message, including: *incoming_freq* and *outgoing_freq* (the frequency of incoming/outgoing messages from/to this person); *read_rate*, *reply_rate*, and *file_rate* (the percentage of incoming messages from this person that have been read, replied, or filed by the user); *reply_lapse* (the average time taken by the user to reply a message from this person); *interaction_recency* (the recency of interaction calculated based on the time lapse between current time and the time of the most recent message exchanged between the user and this person); *relationship_type* (the type of the highest weighted connection between the user and this person); *relationship_strength* (the overall relationship strength between the user and this person, see Section 4.2).

5.2 Message-Centric Features

Message-centric features focus on the properties of the message itself, which include: *message_scope* (whether the message is sent exclusively to the user, or to a small group, or to a large group); *message_type* (whether the message is a regular mail, or a meeting notice such as invite or reschedule that requires user action, or a meeting notice such as confirm that does not require user action, or something else such as automatic out-of-office reply); *content_type* (if the message content contains a request, time-critical words, keywords prespecified by the user, file attachments); *threading* (if the message belongs to an email thread, if the user has taken any action on previous messages from the same thread); *topic_likelihood* (the likelihood that the message content is about the topic inferred by the system, calculated based on LDA's document-topic distribution as LDA is used to derive the topics contained in the user model [6]); *topic_importance* (the importance of the topic to the user inferred from the message content, which is computed using a weighted combination of the percentage of the user's emails about this topic, the percentage of the emails about this topic that were read, and the percentage of the emails about this topic that were forwarded, replied, or filed).

6. PRIORITIZATION

6.1 Global Priority Classifier

EPIC uses linear regression (chosen for its efficiency and robustness) to create a global priority classifier based on labeled training messages collected from multiple users. The priority score of an email message is a weighted linear combination of the message's contextual features. To determine the priority of a message using this classifier, the system calculates the message's priority score and classifies it as high-priority if the score is greater than a classification threshold t_c. The value of t_c can be determined based on application needs or user preferences (e.g. a smaller t_c value for low false-negative rate but potentially high false-positive rate).

6.2 User-Specific Priority Classifier

A user-specific classifier is dynamically learned based on ongoing user feedback. Currently EPIC focuses on using explicit user feedback to obtain more accurate and reliable ground truth data for creating user-specific classifiers. When a user provides priority feedback for a message (e.g. through the email prioritization context menu item described in Section 3.2), the system records the priority label (e.g. high-priority or low-priority because of the sender, the subject, or both) along with the contextual features of the message to create a feedback *instance*. When enough feedback instances are collected for this user, linear regression is used to learn a user-specific classifier. The classifier is updated as the number of feedback instances grows.

6.3 Priority Classification

Priority classification is based on a combination of the global classifier and the user-specific classifier. We propose three methods, described below.

Basic Linear Combination (BASIC)

This method linearly combines the priority scores from the global classifier s_g and the user-specific classifier s_u as:

$$s = w \times s_g + (1 - w) \times s_u$$

We experimented with different values of w to investigate how w affects prioritization performance.

Dynamic Linear Combination with Instance Matching on Contextual Features (DYNAMIC+FEATURES)

Given a new message M, this method dynamically assesses the quality of the user-specific classifier to decide if it is a reliable choice for determining M's priority. The quality is estimated based on the distance d between M and previous feedback instances used to train the user-specific classifier:

$$d = \min_j\left(\sum_{i=1}^{n}(f_{M,i} - f'_{j,i})\right)$$

where $f_{M,i}$ is the value of M's i^{th} contextual feature as defined in Section 5, and $f'_{j,i}$ is the value of the ith contextual feature

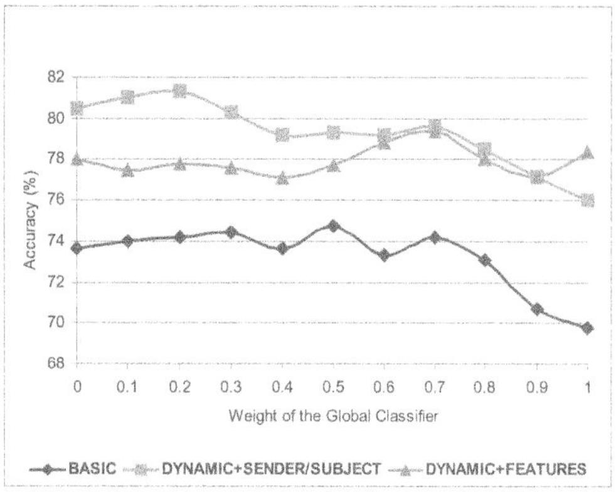

Figure 2. Accuracy results of three priority classification methods in different weight settings

in the jth feedback instance. If d is below a certain threshold (empirically set to 0.5), it indicates that previous feedback instances contain message(s) similar to M, which implies that the user criteria of determining the priority of a message similar to M have been encoded in the classifier. As a result, the user-specific classifier is expected to perform well in predicting M's priority, so the system sets the weight of the global classifier to 0 in linear combination, essentially utilizing the user-specific classifier only. If d value is above the threshold, the basic linear combination of the two classifiers, as described in the first method, is used.

Dynamic Linear Combination with Instance Matching on Sender/Subject (DYNAMIC+SENDER/SUBJECT)

This method utilizes information about the factors (e.g. because of the sender and/or the subject) indicated by users in explicit priority feedback. If a new message matches one previous feedback instance on these factors, the message is given the same priority as this feedback instance. If it matches multiple feedback instances, then the message is assigned the priority of the most recent feedback instance. Otherwise, the basic linear combination method is used to determine the message's priority.

7. EVALUATION

We recruited 11 people within a large organization for the evaluation. Each participant was asked to annotate the priority (high-priority or low-priority because of the sender, the subject, or both) of a set of messages (100–303 in number) randomly selected from his/her previously received messages (on average 5,050 in number). A total number of 2,064 labeled messages were collected. We compared the three priority classification methods described in Section 6.3. The classification threshold t_c (see Section 6.1) was set to 0. We conducted 10-fold cross-validation and report here the *accuracy* (percentage of messages that were correctly classified) averaged over all folds and study participants.

Figure 2 depicts the accuracy results for the three methods when different weights were used to combine the global classifier and the user-specific classifier. The figure shows that the two DYNAMIC methods consistently outperformed the BASIC method in all weight settings, and the method of DYNAMIC+SENDER/SUBJECT worked better than DYNAMIC+FEATURES in most settings. The study results demonstrate that 1) a combination of the global classifier and the user-specific classifier yielded better performance than either classifier alone, 2) the instance matching-based quality assessment of the user-specific classifier worked reasonably well, and 3) the additional information gathered in priority feedback from users (i.e. because of the sender and/or the subject) helped further improve accuracy.

To investigate the relative value of different contextual features for email prioritization, we compared the weights of different features in the learned (global and user-specific) classifiers. A large absolute weight value for a feature indicates the predicting power of this feature in determine email priority. A feature that has a small variance in its weights across multiple user-specific classifiers indicates its robustness in determining email priority. Based on these two criteria (large absolute value and small variance), the eight "most important" contextual features are *incoming_freq*, *outgoing_freq*, *file_rate*, *reply_lapse*, *relationship_strength*, *message_scope*, *threading*, and *topic_importance*.

8. CONCLUSION

In this paper, we present Enterprise Priority Inbox Classifier, a system that automatically prioritizes a user's incoming email messages in his/her inbox using a topic-based user model and a multi-tiered approach to priority classification. The evaluation results showed the effectiveness of our approach for personalized email prioritization.

REFERENCES

1. Aberdeen, D., Pacovsky, O., & Slater, A. The learning behind Gmail Priority Inbox. In *NIPS 2010 Workshop on Learning on Cores, Clusters and Clouds*.
2. Dabbish, L., Kraut, R., Fussell, S., & Kiesler, S. Understanding email use: predicting action on a message. In *CHI 2005*.
3. Horvitz, E., Jacobs, A., & Hovel, D. Attention-sensitive alerting. In *UAI 1999*.
4. Kerr, B. & Wilcox, E. Designing REMAIL: reinventing the email client through innovation and integration. In *CHI 2004*.
5. Lockerd, A. Understanding implicit social context in electronic communication. MIT Master's Thesis.
6. Lu, J., Pan. S., Lai, J., & Wen, Z. Information at your fingertips: contextual IR in enterprise email. In *IUI 2011*.
7. Neustaedter C., Brush, A., Smith, M., & Fisher, D. The social network and relationship finder: social sorting for email triage. In *CEAS 2005*.
8. Venolia, G. & Neustaedter, C. Understanding sequence and reply relationships within email conversations: a mixed-model visualization. In *CHI 2003*.
9. Wainer J., Dabbish, L., & Kraut, R. Should I open this email?: inbox-level cues, curiosity and attention to email. In *CHI 2011*.
10. Yang, Y., Yoo S., & Lin, Frank. Personalized email prioritization based on content and social network analysis. *IEEE Intelligent Systems*, 25(4):12–18, 2010.

Finding Someone in My Social Directory Whom I Do not Fully Remember or Barely Know

Michelle X. Zhou[1] Wei Zhang[1] Barton Smith[1] Erika Varga[2] Martin Farias[3] Hernan Badenes[3]
[1]IBM Research – Almaden [2]IBM Software Group – Collaboration Solutions [3]IBM Argentina
{mzhou, zhangwe, basmith, evarga}@us.ibm.com {fariasm, hbadenes}@ar.ibm.com

ABSTRACT

REACH is an intelligent, people-finding system that helps users to find someone in their social directory, especially those whom they do not fully remember or barely know. It analyzes a user's communication and social networking data to automatically extract all the contacts and derive multiple facets to characterize each contact in relation to the user. It then employs a personalized, faceted search to retrieve and present a ranked list of matched contacts based on their properties. A preliminary evaluation shows the effectiveness of our approach.

ACM Classification Keywords
H.5.2 [Information Interfaces and Presentation]

Author Keywords
Social directory, multifaceted people finding, contact.

INTRODUCTION

As one becomes more connected, his *social directory* of *all* the people with whom he has ever associated, volitionally (e.g., Facebook friends) or unintentionally (e.g., email co-recipients), grows rapidly. Here we use *anchor* to refer to the owner of a social directory, and *contact* to denote an entry (person) in the directory. With the growing number of social contacts, finding the right contact becomes more challenging for several reasons. First, one's contacts may be scattered in multiple places (e.g., email and LinkedIn) and the contact information may be outdated or missing. As a result, the user may be unaware of all the contacts, let alone the current status of the contacts (e.g., job changes or out of office). This lack of awareness prevents the user from assessing the fitness of a contact. Second, the user may not remember the full details of every contact (e.g., full name), especially those infrequently contacted. In such cases, she must wade through the directory to find the contact. Third, the user may want to contact a group of people but such a group may not exist *a priori* in the social directory. This would require the user to manually find the individuals.

To address the above challenges, we are building an intelligent, people-finding system, called REACH (REIationship

Figure 1. REACH results for query "Karen Ronnie".

Analytics for Connecting Humans), which helps people automatically create a unified, personalized social directory of all contacts, and easily find desired contacts in such a directory. Since a user interacts frequently with only a small number of people in her social directory [3], she may not fully remember or barely know the majority of her contacts. REACH thus currently focuses on helping users to quickly find their unfamiliar contacts from two aspects.

First, REACH allows a user to express his people-finding needs using the clues that he remembers. Figure 1 shows a user query for finding someone named "Karen" whose last name the user does not remember. However, the user recalls that "Karen" is closely related to "Ronnie"; so he puts "Ronnie" as a clue in the query. To support this type of inquiry, REACH analyzes a user's online communication (e.g., emails) and social networking data (e.g., LinkedIn) to automatically extract all contacts and derive multiple facets to characterize each contact in relation to the user. In the above example, REACH analyzes the emails between the user and Karens to derive a set of facets to describe them, including the topics and others involved in the email exchanges. It then retrieves the desired contacts by matching the query terms to the facets of a contact.

Second, REACH tailors the presentation of retrieved contacts to a user's personal context, which in turn helps the user recall and select whom to contact. Currently, REACH ranks and presents the retrieved contacts based on their properties. In Figure 1, Karen B ranks higher than Karen O because Karen B has more recent contact with the user and a closer relationship with Ronnie. Furthermore, since the user has infrequent contact with both Karens, REACH provides several cues for the user to recall their connections, including the key topics discussed and key people involved. In contrast, REACH displays current status and updates about Ronnie, who is a close contact of the user.

RELATED WORK

Our work is closely related to two areas of research. First, our work is related to social relationship analysis, which mines one's communication or social networking data to extract and characterize one's personal social network [10, 2, 3]. However, most existing works focus on characterizing the structure of a personal social network, including connectivity [10, 3] and grouping patterns [3, 2, 6]. In contrast, we characterize the pair-wise relationships between a user and each of his contact, including their interaction patterns and context, such as the topic and people involved in such interactions. The other related area of work is people-finding or people-recommender systems [8, 4, 5, 7]. Most such systems are on finding/recommending people (experts) outside one's social network. Compared to these works, ours is to find people in one's social directory by taking into account the fine-grained properties of contacts in direct relation to the user, such as their contact patterns (e.g., one-on-one versus group interaction), content, and partners (i.e., who else were involved).

OUR APPROACH

We first give an overview of REACH, and then describe its two key aspects: (1) analysis of a person's communication and social networking activities to extract the contacts and derive a multi-faceted model that characterizes each contact in relation to the person; and (2) use of a personalized, faceted search to retrieve, rank, and present the matched contacts for a given user's input.

REACH Overview

Figure 2 shows the key components of REACH. To bootstrap a person's social directory, REACH collects a person's contacts from multiple data sources (e.g., a person's email and LinkedIn account) through a *data interface*. It automatically extracts a person's contacts from these data

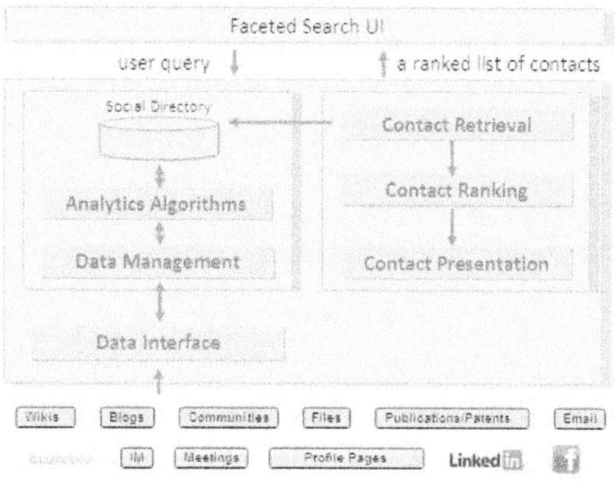

Figure 2. REACH Overview.

sources and then uses a set of *analytic algorithms* to derive multiple facets that characterize each extracted contact, including his/her full name, job title, organization, and interaction patterns with the anchor. The extracted contacts along with their properties are then stored in the social directory database. Given a user query, the *contact retrieval* and *ranking* component finds and ranks the matched contacts. Finally, the *contact presentation* component decides how to display the ranked contacts based on their matched facets and relationships to the user. A user interacts with REACH through a *faceted search UI* where simple, keyword-based queries, e.g., "Karen Ronnie" and "Lisa relocation", are entered to obtain a ranked list of matched contacts. Like Google, REACH supports auto-completion and auto-suggestion while the user is entering the search terms.

Multifaceted Characterization of Each Contact

To help a user find contacts using the clues that he remembers, REACH analyzes multiple data sources related to the user (e.g., emails, calendar, and social networking data). It derives multiple facets to characterize each contact. By their semantics, the facets can be classified into three categories to describe: (1) a contact's profile, (2) communication patterns between the contact and the user (anchor); and (3) communication context between the two.

Deriving Profile of a Contact

A contact's profile includes various personal information, including photo, name, organization, and contact information. REACH derives a profile mainly from three sources: our company directory, personal web pages/profiles posted on the intranet or internet (e.g., LinkedIn), and email signature block. If a contact is within our company, his profile is mainly extracted from our company directory. Otherwise, REACH uses the contact's external profile if one exists (e.g., LinkedIn profile) or parses the email signature block to derive such information. If a contact is connected to the anchor through multiple channels (e.g., email and LinkedIn), multiple profiles are merged into one. Currently REACH takes a conservative approach to merge the profiles by asking the user when conflicts or ambiguities arise.

Deriving Communication Patterns with a Contact

Since users care most about how their contacts are connected to them [2], they are most likely to use the properties of such connections to recall a contact. For example, one may use "Bob email" to find Bobs whom he has interacted with mostly via email. To characterize the connections between a user and his contacts, currently REACH mines the user's email and calendar data to extract communication patterns by a set of features, including contact *frequency*, *recency*, *form* (e.g., one-to-one email exchanges or group meetings), and *channel* (e.g., email and teleconference). Such information is used directly in two ways: (1) allowing an anchor to find contacts by communication patterns (e.g. "Friday meeting" to find a group of contacts who meet with the anchor on Fridays); and (2) suggesting the preferred channel to reach a contact (e.g., emailing a contact if he normally responds to emails promptly).

Moreover, REACH uses communication patterns to estimate the *importance* of a contact, since a user usually organizes his contacts by their importance [2]:

$$R \times \sum_i w_i \times F_i(freq, rec, f) \qquad \text{(Formula 1)}$$

Here, R is the relationship between the contact and the anchor (e.g., employee-manager); for the ith interaction channel, w_i is the weight and F_i is the function that takes the frequency (freq), recency (*rec*), and form (*f*) to compute the *closeness* between the anchor and the contact. Intuitively, the more frequent, recent, and intimate interactions (e.g., one-on-one) they have, the closer they are, and more important the contact is. In our current measure, the relationship R is extracted from the company directory. We weigh *form* the most, followed by *recency* and *frequency*, to promote important but infrequent contacts who have been in touch with the anchor more recently.

Deriving Communication Context with a Contact

Just like a user who uses various contextual cues to locate a document [1], one is also likely to use the context of their interactions to recall a contact whom he does not fully remember. Currently, REACH focuses on extracting three contextual cues: *key topics* that they discussed before, *others* who were involved in their interaction, and the *time frame* when such interactions took place. It mines several data sources, including emails, calendar, and social networking data, to extract these three features.

REACH adopts the method in [9] to extract a set of keywords (tags) to describe the topics discussed by the anchor and a contact. Each topic keyword T_i is associated with a score S_i, indicating the salience of T_i—how often it was talked about and how unique it was to the pair-wise interactions. Figure 3 shows an example of using a topic ("DARPA") to retrieve a contact ("David").

Similarly, REACH extracts other people related to the pair-wise interactions. It uses additional information, such as our company directory, to further rank the extracted people.

Figure 3. REACH results for "David DARPA".

Figure 4. REACH results for "GTO 2011", organized by location.

Currently, we consider several types of relationships captured by the company directory, including peers, manager-employee, and assistant-principal relation. Such additional information helps relate the contact and the extracted people. In Figure 1, when REACH extracts "Ronnie" as a person related to both Karens, the company directory also indicates the assistant-principal relationship between Karen B and Ronnie. This increases the salience score of Ronnie for Karen B, signaling their closer relationship.

Time is another useful clue for the anchor to recall an unfamiliar contact or a group of contacts. Currently, REACH mines the anchor's communication and social networking data to identify the time periods during which the interactions between the anchor and the contact are most active. Figure 4 shows an example where the user wants to find a group of contacts related to the "GTO" topic in year 2011. In this case, since "GTO" is an annual topic in the anchor's interaction with many different groups, the time criterion helps distinguish one "GTO" group from the other.

Personalized, Faceted People Search

As described above, REACH analyzes multiple data sources to derive a multi-faceted model that characterizes each contact in a social directory. More formally, each contact is represented by a vector of facets, each of which is associated with a value and a salience score: $\{\ldots, \langle f_i, v_i, s_i \rangle, \ldots\}$. Given a user query, REACH matches the query terms with the facets in each contact. Currently, it only retrieves contacts that match all the query terms. It then ranks and presents the retrieved contacts.

Personalized Ranking of Retrieved Contacts

REACH ranks the retrieved contacts by three criteria: (1) the salience of the matched facets, (2) the number of matched facets, and (3) the importance of the matched contact. Since both criteria (1) and (3) are anchor-specific, the result is personalized for the anchor.

The more important a facet is, the better the facet characterizes the contact. The first criterion favors contacts who match the query with more salient facets, since a user is more likely to refer to a contact by such facets. In Figure 3, "DARPA" matches the *topic* facet of both David B (s=0.8) and David L (s=0.3). By criterion 1, David B ranks higher, since the user is more likely to relate "DARPA" to him. The second criterion favors the contacts that produce more matches, since more matches increase the probability for the contacts to be accepted. In Figure 1, Karen B has three matched facets (*name*, *job title*, and *relation*) compared to Karen O with two matches (*name* and *relation*). The third criterion favors contacts that are more important to the anchor (Formula 1), since users are more likely to seek someone important to them albeit infrequently contacted.

Customized Presentation of Matched Contacts

To help a user better assess the retrieved contacts especially the unfamiliar ones, REACH currently tailors the presentation of a contact based on their closeness to the user. REACH first classifies all the contacts into three categories based on their *closeness* to the user (F in Formula 1): closest contacts (normally the top 10%), known contacts (the next 20%), and the rest (70%). For closest contacts whom the user knows well, REACH displays their status and status updates without the personal details (e.g., organization or job role unless they are changed). For the second category, REACH shows their profile and the topic facets to remind the user how they are connected. For the last category of people, REACH shows their profile, and communication pattern and context, including topic, time, relation, and form of communication (Figure 2). The additional information helps users recall the unfamiliar contacts.

IMPLEMENTATION AND PRELIMINARY EVALUATION

We have implemented REACH on top of Solr (http://lucene.apache.org/solr/). All server-side components are in Java, and the web-based client components are in JavaScript and Dojo. For privacy reasons, a user must give explicit permission to REACH as which data source can be mined to extract the contacts. REACH does not store the original data (e.g., emails) but stores the extracted contacts on a secured server, accessible only by the user using his intranet authentication. Currently, the user must request to update his social directory explicitly by re-connecting to the desired data sources.

To evaluate the effectiveness of our approach, we conducted a preliminary evaluation. We recruited five users and asked them to submit a set of queries on paper to find someone whom they could not remember fully or barely know. They were *not* allowed to use REACH when writing the queries. The number of contacts in their social directories ranged from 402 to 4610. We collected a total of 100 queries and then ran the queries in REACH using the respective user's social directory. Among the queries, the top-3 search criteria used were: first name (67%), topic (62%), and relationship (19%). While 94% of queries seek an individual, 6% looked for a group of contacts.

For each query, we computed the precision of finding the target being the top-Kth match in the ranked list. We calculated two average precision scores, 76.3% (K=1) and 80% (K=5), respectively. We further examined the results and observed the following: (1) REACH did well for personalized search. For example, query "database" was to find someone who discussed databases with the user recently. Although there were many matches, the person who interacted with the user recently ranked very high. (2) REACH retrieved a group of contacts easily, which can be used to support *dynamic* grouping by any user-defined criteria. (3) REACH did poorly when personal information was used as a clue (e.g., "Joe's wife"). In these cases, REACH simply did not have the information.

CONCLUSION

We have presented REACH, a people-finding system that helps users find the desired contacts in their social directory. We focused on how REACH helps find contacts with whom a user is unfamiliar in two steps. It first analyzes a user's communication and social networking data to derive a multi-faceted model that characterizes each contact. Using this model, it uses a personalized, faceted search to match a user query against the facets of each contact. The matched contacts are ranked and presented based on their properties (e.g., their relationships to the user). Our preliminary evaluation demonstrated that REACH achieved 76% precision with the target being the top match.

REFERENCES

1. Blanc-Brude T. and Scapin D. What do people recall about their documents: Implications for desktop search tools. *Proc IUI' 07*, pp 102-111.
2. Farnham, S., Portnoy, W., Turski, A., Cheng, L., and Vronay, D. Personal Map: Automatically modeling the user's online social network. *Proc INTERACT'03*, pp 567-574.
3. Fisher, D. Using Egocentric Networks to Understand Communication. *IEEE Internet Computing* 9(5): 20-28, 2005.
4. Guy I., Ronen I., and Wilcox E.: Do you know: Recommending people to invite into your social network. *Proc IUI' 09*, pp 77-86.
5. Lin, C.-Y., Ehrlich, K., Griffiths-Fisher, V., and Desforges, C. SmallBlue: People Mining for Expertise Search. *IEEE Multimedia* 15(1) pp 78-84, 2008.
6. MacLean D., Hangal S., Teh S., Lam M., and Heer J. Groups without tears: mining social topologies from email, *Proc IUI' 2011*, pp 83-92.
7. Reichling, T. and Wulf, V. Expert Recommender Systems in Practice: Evaluating Semi-automatic Profile Generation. *Proc. of CHI '09* pp 59-68.
8. Terveen, L. and Mcdonald, D.W. Social Match-ing□: A Framework and Research Agenda. *TOCHI* 12 (3), 2005, pp 401-434.
9. Vig J., Sen S., and Riedl, J., Navigating the tag genome, *Proc. IUI 2011*, pp 93-102.
10. Whittaker S., Jones Q., Nardi B., Creech M., Terveen L., Isaacs E., and Hainsworth J. ContactMap: Organizing Communication in a Social Desktop. *TOCHI*, 11(4), 2004, pp 445-471.

A Visual Programming Language for Designing Interactions Embedded in Web-based Geographic Applications

The Nhan Luong, Patrick Etcheverry, Christophe Marquesuzaà and Thierry Nodenot
T2i - LIUPPA - Université de Pau et des Pays de l'Adour
IUT de Bayonne et du Pays Basque, 2 Allée du Parc Montaury, 64600 Anglet, France
{thenhan.luong, patrick.etcheverry, christophe.marquesuzaa, thierry.nodenot}@iutbayonne.univ-pau.fr

ABSTRACT
Visual programming languages (VPLs) provide notations for representing both the intermediate and the final results of a knowledge engineering process. Whereas some VPLs particularly focus on control flow and/or data flow of a software, very few VPLs stress on the interactive dimension of application (dialogue flow). This paper focuses on a VPL allowing designers to specify interactions between a user and a system, in the field of Web-based geographic applications. We first present the underlying interaction model that the VPL is based on, and then the detailed characteristics of the VPL. We show how this VPL has been integrated in a graphical design framework allowing designers to immediately assess their specification. Then we illustrate the way to use the framework from the design step to the final code generation step. Last, we detail an experimentation aiming at evaluating the strengths and the weaknesses of our VPL.

Author Keywords
Visual design language, interaction design, geographic application design, visual authoring tools.

ACM Classification Keywords
H.5.m. Information Interfaces and Presentation (e.g. HCI): Miscellaneous

General Terms
Design, Languages.

INTRODUCTION
Visual programming languages (VPLs) aim at facilitating software design and implementation by minimizing or avoiding complex coding steps. The visual nature of these languages is characterized by the use of graphic elements that can be combined and connected within a two (or more) dimensional design workspace. The expressive power of these languages explain their attractiveness for simplifying the description of complex things. This richness can also be a constraint when it comes to interpreting the meaning of diagrams in order to automatically generate executable code.

Our research consists in promoting VPLs to empower designers developing interactive applications. Depending on the domain, such VPL-based prototyping tools are more or less difficult to produce. Our challenge is to focus on an ill-structured domain that addresses (on a medium-term) the design of applications promoting "Engaged reading interactive scenarios that make use of geographic information". We chose such a domain for three main reasons. Firstly, geographic information promoting engaged reading can be quite informal, but its semantics, once captured by automatic or semi-automatic analysers, can be exploited to promote rich interactive scenarios. Secondly, there is a real need for some VPLs to design applications for touristic, cultural or educational purposes. Lastly, deploying such interactive applications from a VPL is a challenging task because the required VPL must stress on the interactive dimension of the application (dialogue flow) and not only on the control flow and/or the data flow.

In this paper we present a VPL that does not address computer-science companies with structured teams of developers but people (with some computer-science background) from firms or organisations who are interested in deploying interactive applications without having to manage all the complexity of the technology. This visual language only focuses on human computer interactions and proposes specific descriptor elements allowing designers to quickly specify and assess what happens (from a system reaction viewpoint) when a user carries out an action.

The paper is structured as follows: Section 2 ("Related Work") defines more precisely the concept of VPL and positions our contribution according to similar and related work. Section 3 ("Geographic Application Modelling") describes the underlying model on which the VPL is based on. This three-part model allows designers to define the contents that will be handled, how they will be displayed on the screen and the possible interactions allowed within these contents. Section 4 ("Visual Specification of Interactions") presents the main contribution of the paper: we describe the characteristics of the VPL that will allow designers to specify interactions according to the model described in Section 3. Section 5 ("Application Design with WINDMash") illustrates the operational nature of the proposed VPL through a graphical design environment called WINDMash. This design environment integrates our VPL and allows designers to visually specify Web-based geographic applications from an interactive viewpoint and then to generate the corresponding executable code. Section 6 ("Evaluation") presents a first experimentation aiming at evaluating the main strengths and weaknesses of our VPL. Finally, we conclude this paper by summing up the results and presenting our plans for future work.

RELATED WORK

This paper intends to offer a VPL allowing designers to graphically describe human computer interactions and to generate the corresponding Web-based application. The contribution focus on a VPL adapted to the description of interactions. Focusing on interaction is particularly interesting because it is generally the most complex thing to describe, to specify and to implement in a program. In this paper, the underlying code generation process is not considered as a scientific contribution but as an engineering work based on existing model transformation techniques (MDA).

In next sections, we use visual programming to mean the construction of a program starting from a graphical representation of its behaviour. We define a VPL in the same way as [15, 19, 20, 22]: any graphical language that lets programmers create programs by handling program elements represented graphically rather than textually. According to the classification described in [3] (which compiles the viewpoint of authors such as [6, 7, 22]), we offer a hybrid text and visual language: programs are visually created and then translated into an underlying high-level textual language, which is then translated into executable source code.

Integrating VPLs in Geographic Information Systems (GIS) is not a new idea: ArcGIS, Mapinfo, AutoCAD Map3D are sophisticated GIS restricted to specialists. VPLs try to make these systems available to standard users. As shown in [9], the two recurring problems addressed by VPLs in such systems relate to the creation/selection/aggregation of data and to the manner of representing this data on a map or textually. To our knowledge, there is no VPL allowing designers to define user interactions with displayed data, except the default interactions provided by the displayer (e.g. changing the background of the map that displays the data). Moreover, default interactions provided by displayers cannot (generally) be set up or disabled by designers.

Similar problems can be highlighted with Mashup systems such as Google Mashup or IBM mashup center which allow designers to graphically create/aggregate data (from feeds for example) and to display it in a specific way (on a map with Google Mashup, using widgets with IBM mashup center). However, these tools do not allow designers to create new interactions with displayed data: interactive possibilities are predefined by displayers (sorting data in a spreadsheet widget for example) and designers have little control over these predefined interactions.

The underlying programming approach is also very important. We can identify two main approaches [9, 25] that use VPLs in GIS: The traditional programming approach and the programming by demonstration approach. The first approach deals with using a visual language to describe what the program must do (*cf.* ModelBuilder in ArcGIS or the Workflow Designer in AutoCAD Map3D). The resulting description is then compiled or interpreted and run. The second approach consists in creating a program by showing an existing system how to carry out a specific task: The system memorizes each step of the process as a new program. Each step is graphically represented to allow designers checking the features of the program they are elaborating (see for example the C-SPRL system in [25]).

In these two approaches, VPLs are used to specify which data must be handled and what must be done with this data. There is also a continuous feedback which allows designers to control/correct the program they are elaborating. However, designers activity is quite different: In a traditional programming approach, designers carry out a specification/formalization activity of the program to elaborate whereas in a programming by demonstration approach, designers carry out a "tutor" activity by showing an existing system how to execute a specific task. The VPL we propose aims at elaborating geographic application from scratch and so, designers will use our language to design their program in a traditional way.

The interaction programming language we propose is based on UML which provides several models to describe interactions in an application. As shown in [1, 14, 26], UML can be used as a visual programming language to generate Java code starting from classes and statechart diagrams. Generally, the interactive aspect of the application is described using statechart diagrams that specify the reactions of a system according to the actions of a user. Statechart diagrams allow designers to describe the interactive dimension of an application globally but this global description can be complex if the application includes many interactive possibilities.

The sequence diagram-like VPL we propose allows designers to decompose the global interaction of a system into several separate interactions. The design is facilitated because each diagram describes only one interaction. The global view and the coherence of the interactive possibilities of the system can be reconstituted by merging the set of sequence diagrams to produce a state chart diagram as presented in [14] and in [26].

GEOGRAPHIC APPLICATION MODELLING

We offer to guide the design process considering the contents presented to users and the interactive possibilities given to them. With such an approach, designers' work involves defining the contents to be manipulated, how they will be displayed and the interactions handling these contents.

We offer design tools allowing designers to focus on the application's interactive dimension. To achieve this goal, we rely on operational models to be elaborated and integrated in design environments. These environments should assist the designer from the specification step to the deployment step.

This section defines the main key concepts that we offer to describe the interactions within an application. Figure 1 presents an overview of these concepts. The model may be divided into three parts (*Content*, *Interface* and *Interaction*) articulated around the concept of geographic contents (*geo-contents*) which represents the central concept of our model

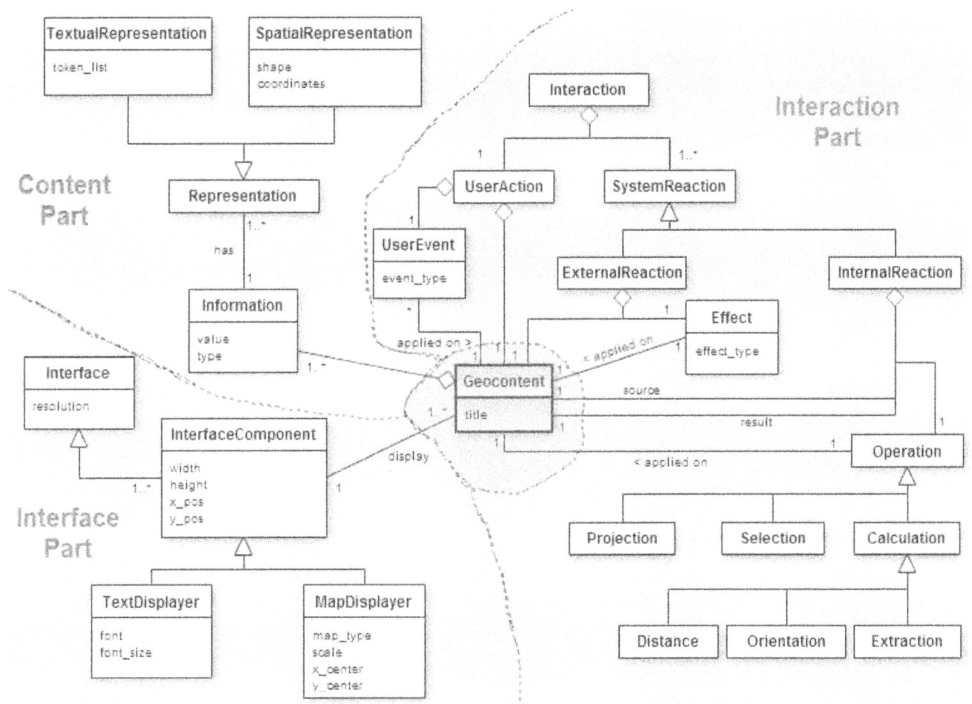

Figure 1. Global model for describing geographic applications

because our design approach mainly focuses on emphasizing geographic data [16].

In the content part, geocontents are defined by a set of structured information; each one has a type (absolute or relative spatial entity), a value (e.g. "*Mauléon-Licharre*") and one or more possible representations of this value (e.g. 9th token of the first paragraph in the text or *POINT(2, 45)* in the map). Each considered representation allows a geocontent specific dimension (textual or spatial) to be emphasized.

The application interface is a visualization layer allowing geocontents to be displayed in various forms [8].

In our approach, design is guided by interactions to emphasize contents specified by the designer. As proposed by [10, 24], the vocabulary used for designing interactions is based on user action and system reaction. An interaction is defined as a communication between a user and the system. This communication is always initiated by the user and ends when the application has visually reacted to the user request. An interaction is implemented by a user action triggering a system (external or internal) reaction.

To automatically generate a Web-based application according to this model, we have implemented a design environment. Each model's part is instanciated into an RDF file [17] which lists the characteristics of geographic contents / interface / interactions. Merging these RDF descriptions constitutes a structured specification which is used to automatically generate the final application thanks to MDA techniques.

We will now define how to instantiate the interaction model part with a visual specification language allowing designers to specify interactions according to previously defined concepts.

VISUAL SPECIFICATION OF INTERACTIONS

To use the interaction model during the design activity, we offer a visual language [4, 23] allowing designers to describe the characteristics of the interactions to set up. For an interaction, it is necessary to specify: the user action triggering the interaction, the system reactions, and the geocontents which are visually modified by the interaction.

As mentioned in Related Work, we offer a visual language inspired from UML sequence diagrams. Sequence diagrams are often used as a graphic language to describe interactions between a user and a system and also between system components [12, 5]. [13] proposed specific uses of these diagrams to describe interactions according to graphic components displayed on the interface. We also agree with this approach since our objective is to describe interactions according to what the user sees on the screen (interface components) but also contents displayed by these components.

[11] proposed an approach dedicated to interaction design based on the nature of the contents to emphasize. This approach was already based on the traditional UML sequence diagrams. We currently offer a language derived from the sequence diagrams which is both simplified and partially specialized for the description of interactions on geographic contents. It is not an extension of traditional sequence diagrams but only a resumption of their graphic formalism in order to describe interactions according to our interaction model.

In the following subsections we present the interaction elements of the visual language that we offer to specify interactions. Each interaction is described by a diagram specifying the user action initiating the interaction as well as the system reactions. Geocontents involved in the interaction are represented on these diagrams and are defined according to the model presented in the previous section or calculated during the interaction via internal reactions.

Specification of a user action

A user action is initiated by a specific event (e.g. *click*, *mouse-over*, ...). This event is applied on contents which are displayed on an interface component. As an interaction is triggered by a user event, a user action is represented by an arrow going from the user toward the system and labelled with the name of this triggering event (Figure 2).

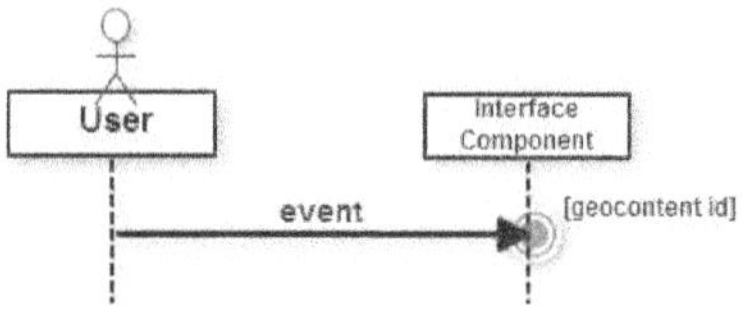

Figure 2. Specification of a user action

The arrow destination refers to the contents involved in the interaction and the interface component used to display them. The contents have an automatically generated identifier that can be renamed by the designer. This identifier allows the designer to handle the same contents into several interactions.

Specification of an external system reaction

This reaction is always visible by the user. It results in a visual modification of contents displayed on the interface. This modification is carried out by the system by applying one or some visual effects on the contents to emphasize.

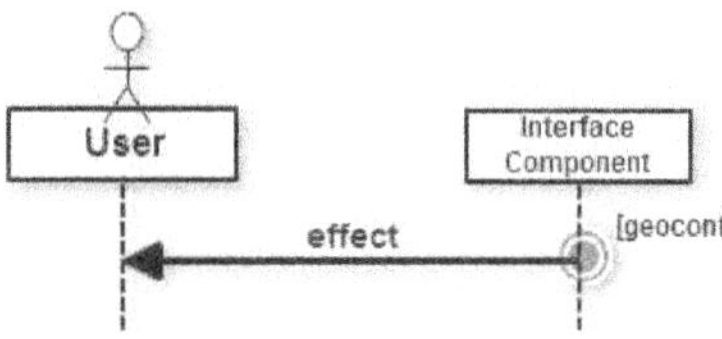

Figure 3. Specification of an external system reaction

Since an external reaction is applied on contents and can be seen by the user, it is represented by an arrow going from the contents to emphasize toward the user (Figure 3). The arrow label specifies the effect applied to emphasize these contents.

Specification of an internal system reaction

We consider three distinct internal reactions: *projection*, *selection* and *calculation*.

Projection

The projection operation involves transferring contents on a given interface component. Thereafter, the transferred contents can either be displayed on the target interface component or be used to calculate new contents on this interface component. The arrow origin (Figure 4) specifies the contents that must be projected and the destination defines the interface component where the contents is projected.

Selection

A selection is an operation allowing the designer to specify contents by selecting a subset of displayed contents. This

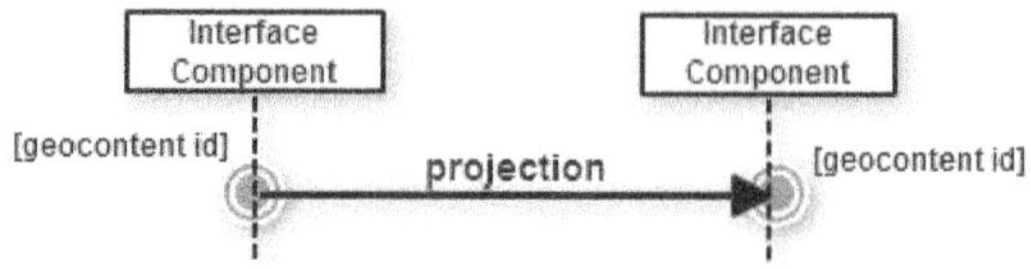

Figure 4. Specification of a projection operation

subset becomes new contents that can be emphasized in the continuation of the interaction.

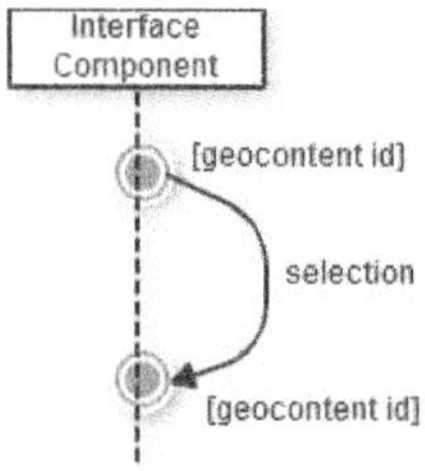

Figure 5. Specification of a selection operation

The selection operation is graphically represented by an arrow going from the initial contents toward the subset contents designated by the user (Figure 5). The selected contents belong to the interface component displaying the initial contents. Thenceforth, these new created contents can be displayed via another external reaction or can be transferred on another interface component with a projection operation.

Calculation

This operation allows designers to create new contents by applying a calculation operation on specific contents. As the contents are in a geographic nature, the authorized operations are also in a geographic nature: distance calculation, orientation, surface, etc. A calculation operation is represented by an arrow labelled with the calculation service to apply. The arrow connects the input and output contents (Figure 6).

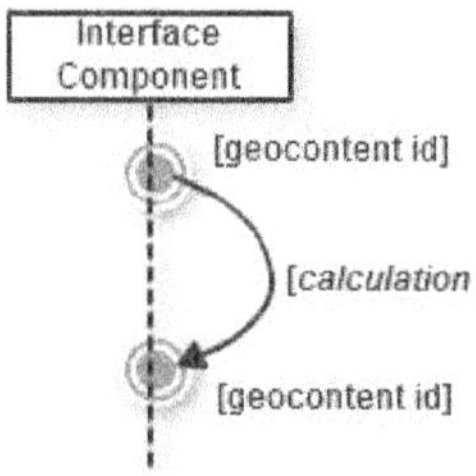

Figure 6. Specification of a calculation operation

The calculation parameters must be defined during the design activity. The calculation operations must also be pertinent with the input contents. These consistency checks can only be carried out if the design activity is supported by an adapted software environment.

APPLICATION DESIGN WITH WINDMASH

In order to illustrate our approach, we use the WINDMash[1] prototype allowing a designer to elaborate in a visual way Web-based geographic applications.

[1] `http://erozate.iutbayonne.univ-pau.fr/Nhan/windmash4/`

Starting from a text and a map presenting some towns located on the French Atlantic and Mediterranean coasts, the main goal of the application to design is to learn the concept of "*département*"[2]. The behaviour of the application (Figure 7) is as follows: When the user clicks on a town written on the text (located on the left part of the screen) or displayed on the map zone (located on the right part of the screen), then the name of the corresponding "*département*" is automatically displayed (in a dedicated zone in the top centre of the screen) and the border of the "*département*" are highlighted (in a dedicated zone in the bottom centre of the screen). The name of the clicked town in the main text and the border of this town in the main map will also be highlighted.

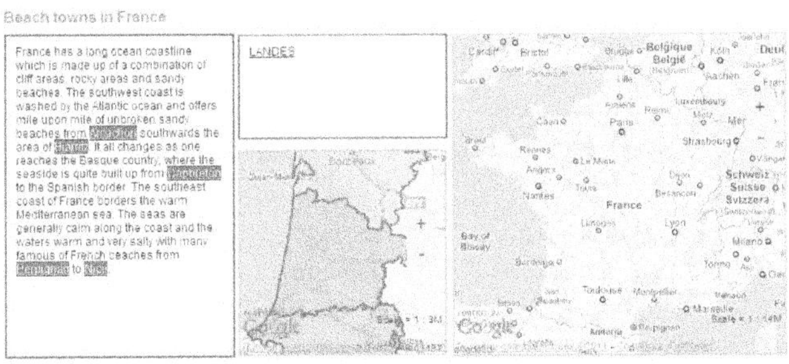

Figure 7. Screenshot of the final application

A designer may use three complementary workspaces on the WINDMash environment. These workspaces respectively deal with defining the geocontents to be handled (*Data* workspace), organizing the presentation layout of the application (*Interface* workspace) and specifying how end-users will be able to interact with the application (*Interaction* workspace). Each workspace corresponds to the instanciation of its specific part of the global model presented in Figure 1. Each workspace allows designers to specify a particular viewpoint of the application, and each specification leads to the instanciation of a specific part of the global model.

Defining geocontents of the application

In order to build the geocontents that will be handled in the final application, designers use the *Data* workspace (Figure 8) which provides (on the left side) a set of services allowing to automatically extract geocontents from a text or a geographic database.

We have used the following text to illustrate the example described above: "*France has a long ocean coastline which is made up of a combination of cliff areas, rocky areas and sandy beaches. The south-west coast is washed by the Atlantic ocean and offers mile upon mile of unbroken sandy beaches from Arcachon southwards the area of Biarritz. It all changes as one reaches the Basque country, where the seaside is quite built up from Capbreton to the Spanish border. The south-east coast of France borders the warm Mediterranean sea. The seas are generally calm along the coast and the waters warm and very salty with many famous of French beaches from Perpignan to Nice.*"

[2] A "*département*" is an administrative and geographic French concept corresponding to a region. Each place, town, city belongs to one (and only one) of 95 "*département*" (except overseas territories).

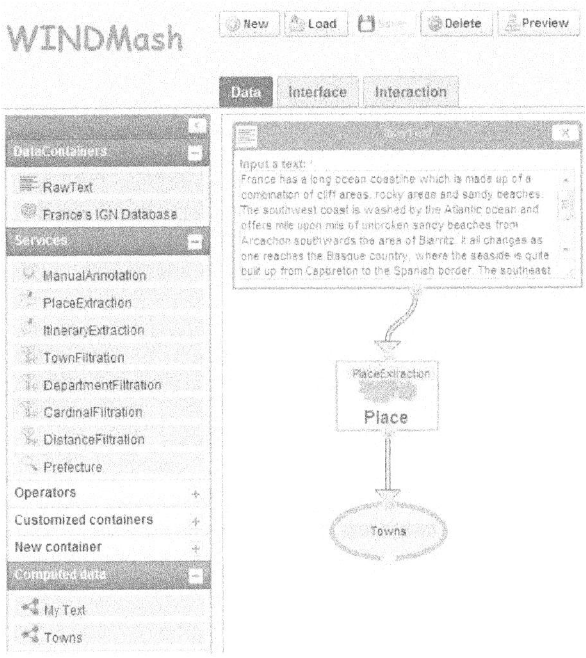

Figure 8. *Geocontents* designed with WINDMash

Figure 8 presents a simple processing chain which corresponds to the presented example. The design of such processing chain is based on drag and drop. Starting from the `RawText` presented above, the designer can use a service named `PlaceExtraction` which automatically extracts all places quoted in the text. These extracted places become a new set of geocontents (named here "`Towns`") which are added in the geocontent library of WINDMash.

Organizing presentation layout of the application

The *Interface* workspace of WINDMash enables designers to organize the presentation layout of their Web-based geographic application. WINDMash supports many ways to represent geographic contents such as `TextDisplayer`, `MapDisplayer`, `ListDisplayer`, `CalendarDisplayer`, `TimelineDisplayer` and `PhotoDisplayer`. Indeed, in this phase, designers have to decide how previously defined geocontents will be displayed on the screen. This choice is done by selecting specific displayers that will define the appearance of the geocontents.

In our example, designers have to create a graphic interface composed of a main left `TextDisplayer` showing the text and a main right `MapDisplayer` showing spatial information of the towns quoted in this text. Final application also needs a bottom centre secondary `MapDisplayer` showing the department border of the selected town and a top centre secondary `TextDisplayer` showing the name of the corresponding department. For more reader-friendliness, designers decide also to highlight all towns quoted in the primary text.

Figure 9 illustrates how designers can build the corresponding graphical interface of the final application. Designers have to

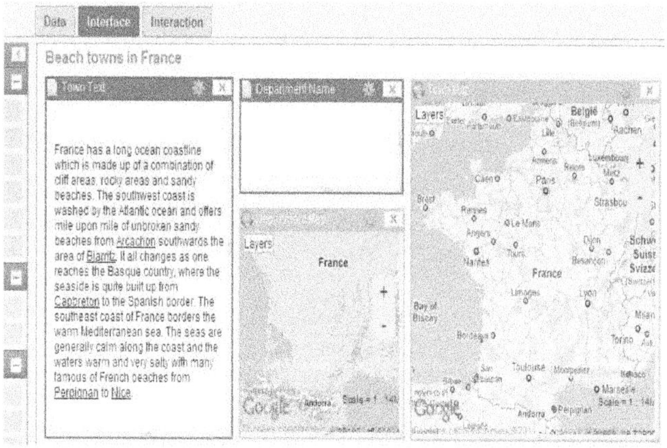

Figure 9. ***Interface*** **designed with WINDMash**

drag and drop two `TextDisplayers` and two `MapDisplayers` onto the central workspace. Designers can easily position and resize these displayers in order to build the final interface of the application. They can set up the name of the primary text displayer "`Town Text`", the name of the primary map displayer "`Town Map`", the name of the secondary text displayer "`Department Name`" and the name of the secondary map displayer "`Department Map`".

Then, designers select the set of geocontents that must be initially appeared in each one of these displayers. From the geocontents library in the left menu of WINDMash, they drag the set of annotations named "`Towns`" and drop it into the displayer "`Town Text`" as well as the displayer "`Town Map`". Two displayers named "`Department Name`" and "`Department Map`" do not hold geocontents yet, they will show computed geocontents when interactions are triggered.

Thus, the *Interface* phase involves positioning displayers into the interface and then dragging and dropping a set of geocontents into each displayer. Next subsection will show how to make geocontents interactive in the *Interaction* phase.

Specifying user interactions of the application

WINDMash allows designers to specify the interactions of their application using the VPL presented in the previous main section. In our example (Figure 10):

When the user selects a town in the text displayer named "`Town Text`" (A, B), this town (C) is highlighted in this displayer (D) as well as in the map displayer named "`Town Map`" (E, F). In addition, the text displayer named "`Department Name`" will show the name of the department of the selected town (G, H, I, J) and the map displayer named "`Department Map`" will zoom in on the department (G, H, K, L).

The second interaction triggered from towns selected in the map can be designed in the same way.

The diagram construction is carried out rather simply: when a designer drags and drops created displayers into the *Interaction* workspace, they become lifelines. Then, the designer has to drag the necessary interaction elements (*user action*, *selection*, *projection*, *calculation* or external *system reaction*) and drop them on the adequate lifeline.

The five interaction elements defined for our VPL allow designers to build complex interactions as we see in Figure 10.

A demonstration video of the complete design process is available at: **`http://youtu.be/3uxR8euHPwM?hd=1`**.

EVALUATION

We conducted a first test protocol in order to assess if our visual language allows designers to correctly design the interactive behaviour of their geographic Web-based application. To prepare and to carry out this evaluation, we focused on three research papers [2, 18, 21]. The goal was to assess the cognitive dimensions of our VPL notations. We wanted to concretely evaluate if designers understood the VPL components but also their underlying advantages and drawbacks.

[21] suggested that syntactic and semantic density were the main standards to evaluate visual languages. [2] proposed new dimensions with different refinement levels such as consistency, visibility, viscosity, hidden dependencies, creative ambiguity or abstraction management. As more recently presented by [18], we used a set of nine principles for evaluating the cognitively effective visual notation of our VPL. This approach uses a combination of craft and scientific knowledge.

Participants, Procedure, and Measurement

We invited thirty two volunteers in second year "DUT Informatique" (High National Diploma in Computer Science) to participate in this evaluation. None of the students had any significant academic experience of the UML sequence diagram. The evaluation procedure was organized into six steps.

Example presentation

We gave a 35 minutes presentation on a simple but complete example of how to design a Web-based geographic application. Within this example, we specified an application helping the user to know the "*préfecture*"[3] of a list of given cities.

The example application (Figure 11) displays both a list of towns and cities and a map initially displaying a visible point for each town/city. The application behaviour is presented as follows: When the user clicks on any place name in the top list, the application computes the "*préfecture*" of this place and the map zooms in on this "*préfecture*" (see **`http://bit.ly/uwAZne`**).

Describing this interaction can be done in several equivalent ways. For example, a sequence of projection and calculation operations or the inverse sequence produces two different diagrams, but the resulting behaviour is identical.

During this presentation, we focused on the *Interaction* phase in order for the participants to understand the role of our VPL components.

Oral presentation of the test application

Then, during ten minutes, we presented the application that participants had to design (Figure 7).

[3] A "*préfecture*" is a French administrative city corresponding to the main city of a "*département*".

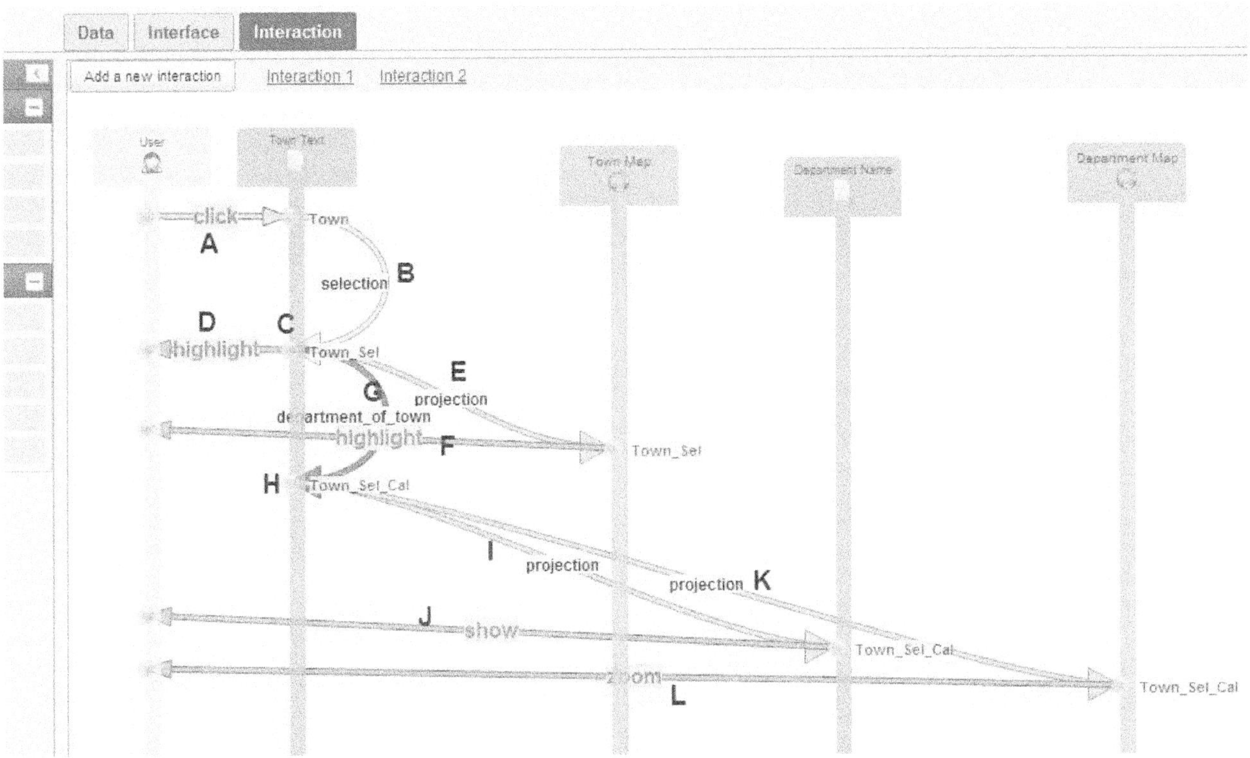

Figure 10. `Interaction` designed with WINDMash

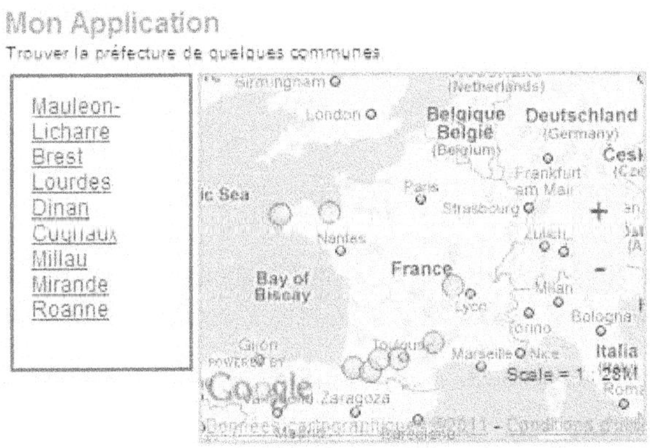

Figure 11. Screenshot of the example application

Guided creation of the Content and Interface phases

We have co-designed during ten minutes the two phases corresponding to the design of embedded geocontents (*Content* phase) and the design of the graphical user interface (*Interface* phase).

Hand-made production of the Interaction phase

Then, we made a break with the WINDMash environment in order for the participants to focus on the design of the interactive abilities of the final application. During fifteen minutes, they produced, without any help nor answer to their questions, paper interaction diagrams using our VPL.

This preparatory work allowed them to focus on the VPL independently from the WINDMash environment.

Implementation and assessment of the Interaction phase

During fifteen minutes, participants had to translate their interaction diagrams and then to generate the executable code in order to assess the final application.

Evaluation

Last we asked participants to give us their hand-made paper interaction specifications and to tell us if they had to make some changes within the WINDMash environment.

To conclude, we spent ten minutes with the participants to fill in an evaluation form composed of eleven questions (presented in a colloquial wording in French) relative to the nine cognitive dimensions [18] used to evaluate our VPL:

- **Semiotic clarity** (**SC1**: Is there redundancy between semantic constructs and graphical symbols? **SC2**: Is there deficit between semantic constructs and graphical symbols?)
- **Perceptual Discriminability** (**PD**): Is any symbol clearly distinguishable to each other?
- **Semantic Transparency** (**ST**): Does visual representation appearance suggest its meaning?
- **Complexity Management** (**CM**): Does visual language include explicit mechanisms for dealing with complexity?
- **Cognitive Integration** (**CI**): Does visual language include explicit mechanisms to support integration of information from different diagrams?

- **Visual Expressiveness (VE)**: Does visual language use the full range and capacities of visual variables?
- **Dual Coding (DC)**: Does visual language use text to complement graphics?
- **Graphic Economy (GE)**: Is the number of different graphical symbols cognitively manageable?
- **Cognitive fit** (**CF1**: Is visual language handled similarly on paper and within the WINDMash environment? **CF2**: Is visual language handled well by designers unfamiliar with UML sequence diagrams?)

For any question, four possible answers were available (Strongly Agree, Agree, Disagree, Strongly Disagree). Moreover, participants had the options to justify their answer with a short open comment.

Results and Discussion

Figure 12 resumes the participants' answers:

	Strongly Agree	Agree	Disagree	Strongly Disagree	
SC1	0%	0%	13%	88%	☺
SC2	0%	0%	63%	38%	☺
PD	38%	50%	0%	13% ☹	☺
ST	50%	38%	13%	0%	☺
CM	38%	63%	0%	0%	☺
CI	13% ☹	13% ☹	25% ☺	50% ☺	: –
VE	13%	50%	38%	0%	: –
DC	0%	13%	38%	50%	☺
GE	25%	75%	0%	0%	☺
CF1	75%	25%	0%	0%	☺
CF2	0%	63%	13%	25%	: –

Figure 12. Result table of the experimentation

From a global viewpoint, the evaluation results are encouraging as illustrated by smileys added in the above result table.

However, some specific points still need to be improved. Relating to Cognitive Integration, it should be interesting to define mechanisms allowing designers to reuse interaction parts of a diagram in other diagrams. This traditional software engineering approach (black box vs. glass box) would increase reuse abilities of the VPL. Another interesting perspective relates to the Visual Expressiveness principle. We should improve the usability of each interaction element, and specially its visual representation, to better suggest its role. The underlying design environment may also better check connection possibilities between graphic elements in order to reduce some possible designers errors.

Moreover, for the test application, participants have produced two different artifacts/deliverables. We may raise some patterns to their strengths and weaknesses. They first produced a hand-made production of the interaction specification phase. During this step, 81% of the participants have produced a "fully-correct" proposal. Other 19% have syntactic problems which may be overcome with the WINDMash environment. 6% of the participants have described the application's interactive possibilities with 4 diagrams whereas 94% used 2 diagrams. This result shows the flexibility of the VPL that allows designers to specify interactions according to several level of complexity: it is possible to decompose the description of a complex interaction into some simple interactions whose behaviour is equivalent to the one of the complex interaction. For example, a participant proposed the four following diagrams (Figure 13) that are equivalent to the diagram presented in Figure 10:

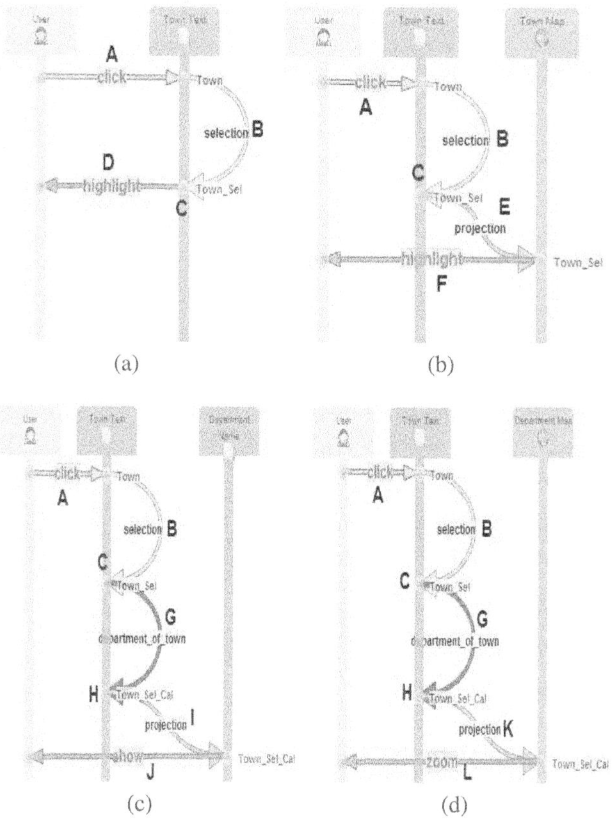

Figure 13. Interaction diagram in Figure 10 divided into four diagrams

- the first for describing the highlight of the "`Town`" clicked in the displayer named "`Town Text`" (Figure 13(a))
- the second for describing the highlight in the displayer named "`Town Map`" of the "`Town`" clicked in the displayer named "`Town Text`" (Figure 13(b))
- the third for computing the department of the selected "`Town`", then sending and showing the result of this calculation in the displayer named "`Department Name`" (Figure 13(c))
- the fourth for computing the department of the selected "`Town`", then sending and zooming in on the result of this calculation in the displayer named "`Department Map`" (Figure 13(d))

The interaction elements used in Figure 10 (A, B, C, ..., L) can also be found in Figure 13 but they are dispatched into four diagrams.

Lastly, the participants had to transfer their hand-made proposal into the WINDMash environment and to generate their application to immediately check their design. As WINDMash is still a prototype, most of participants encountered problems when they wanted to correct or to modify a diagram. Our system is still in development and each correction requires participants to restart their diagram. Some participants (a quarter) could not achieve their design in time. However, among those who had syntactic problems with their hand-made proposal, all could correct some or all of their "mistakes".

CONCLUSION AND FUTURE WORK

In this paper we have offered a VPL allowing designers to specify and to implement interactions into Web-based geographic applications. Our VPL has been integrated in a graphic design framework called WINDMash for designing applications according to three main views:

- Which data (geocontents) must be emphasized?
- How this data must be visually displayed?
- What kind of interactions are available to handle this data?

The considered interactions focus on users and are always described in terms of user action triggering system reactions. We gave priority to this "simple" vision of interactions for two main reasons:

- to facilitate designers' work by describing "simple" processes rather than a global and complex process;
- to favour the elaboration of operational models that can be exploited to generate executable code from visual specifications thanks to model transformation techniques.

Interactions diagrams resulting from our VPL highlight the exchanged flow between the user and the system but also between the interface elements composing the system. We have chosen to describe interactions according to data presented on the interface. We think that it is a natural way to describe:

- the interface elements that may trigger an interaction;
- how the system will react from a visual viewpoint.

The resulting interaction diagrams may be simple but these diagrams are always described with high level abstraction elements that increase the expressive power and the meaning of the diagram: The designer may define what happens when a user selects a town, without defining what is a town. Designating something on the interface is easy to describe / understand from a graphical viewpoint, even if the designated element is something complex (any town).

Our VPL is mostly independent from the geographic field we work on because interactions are described according to:

- user actions which deal with designating data presented on a displayer;
- internal system reactions which deal with computing what has been selected by the user, transferring data toward specific displayers or computing new data (in this work calculation operations are the only elements that are specific to the geographic area);
- external system reactions which deal with emphasizing (*highlight*, *show*, *hide*, etc.) specific or computed data.

As shown on the experimentation presented in this paper, our VPL offers sufficient flexibility to manage the complexity of an interaction. According to their expertise level, designers may choose to describe a complex interaction (composed of multiple system reactions) with a single diagram or with several diagrams, each one specifying a system reaction part of the global interaction.

First evaluation results about our VPL are very encouraging. Of course, the evaluation task is still a work in progress and we must elaborate new test protocols to evaluate our interaction language according to other criteria such as those presented in [2]. However, this first experimentation has shown that our visual language is rather easy to master for designers specialists knowing UML sequence diagrams. We have noted that sequence diagrams seem particularly adapted when it deals with describing interactions thought in terms of flow exchanges between a user and the system but also between system components.

Future work deals with elaborating mechanisms allowing designers to check the consistency of the designed interactions. As seen in this paper, describing interactions in a separate way is of course an advantage when it deals with designing a complex interactive system. However, this advantage can also become a problem when designers need to evaluate the consistency of all the system's interactive possibilities. Currently, interactions are specified separately by a set of diagrams but there is no mechanism control that checks the global coherence of the described interactions. The interactions described below introduce an example of two ambiguous specifications that can lead to an incoherent system reaction:

- When the user clicks on a town in the text, the map zooms in on this town;
- When the user clicks on a town in the text, the map displays the corresponding administrative province of this town.

Currently, each specified interaction is encoded using RDF. We plan to exploit the underlying merging and querying mechanisms of RDF to try to detect possible inconsistencies between all interactions specified by the designer. This hard task deals with specifying rules that must been verified to ensure the consistency between two diagrams. The idea is to integrate these checking rules into WINDMash in order to provide a first assistance level allowing designers to keep control over the global behaviour of the elaborated application.

ACKNOWLEDGEMENTS

This work has been supported by the ANR MOANO (`http://moano.liuppa.univ-pau.fr`) project.

REFERENCES

1. Barbier, F. Supporting the uml state machine diagrams at runtime. In *Model Driven Architecture Foundations and Applications*, I. Schieferdecker and A. Hartman, Eds., vol. 5095 of *Lecture Notes in Computer Science*. Springer Berlin / Heidelberg, 2008, 338–348.
2. Blackwell, A., and Green, T. R. A Cognitive Dimensions Questionnaire Optimised for Users. In *Proceedings of 12th Workshop of the Psychology of Programming Interest Group* (Corigliano Calabro, Cosenza, Italy, 2000), 137–154.
3. Boshernitsan, M., and Downes, M. S. Visual programming languages: a survey. Tech. Rep. UCB/CSD-04-1368, EECS Department, University of California, Berkeley, Dec 2004.
4. Botturi, L., and Stubbs, T., Eds. *Handbook of Visual Languages for Instructional Design - Theories and Practices*. Information Science Reference, 2007.
5. Bowles, J. Decomposing interactions. In *Algebraic Methodology and Software Technology*, M. Johnson and V. Vene, Eds., vol. 4019 of *LNCS*, Springer Berlin / Heidelberg (2006), 189–203.
6. Burnett, M. M., and Baker, M. J. A classification system for visual programming languages. *J. Vis. Lang. Comput. 5*, 3 (1994), 287–300.
7. Chang, S.-K., Ed. *Principles of visual programming systems*. Prentice-Hall, Inc., 1990.
8. Cooper, A. *About Face: The Essentials of User Interface Design*, 1st ed. John Wiley & Sons, Inc., 1995.
9. Dobesova, Z. Visual programming language in geographic information systems. In *Proceedings of the 2nd international conference on Applied informatics and computing theory*, AICT'11, World Scientific and Engineering Academy and Society (WSEAS) (Stevens Point, Wisconsin, USA, 2011), 276–280.
10. Engels, G., Hausmann, J. H., Heckel, R., and Sauer, S. Dynamic meta modeling: a graphical approach to the operational semantics of behavioral diagrams in UML. In *Proceedings of the 3rd International Conference on the Unified Modeling Language: advancing the standard*, UML'00, Springer-Verlag (2000), 323–337.
11. Etcheverry, P., Marquesuzaà, C., and Corbineau, S. Designing suited interactions for a document management system handling localized documents. In *Proceedings of the 24th annual ACM international conference on Design of communication*, SIGDOC '06, ACM (2006), 188–195.
12. Harel, D., and Marelly, R. *Come, Let's Play: Scenario-Based Programming Using LSC's and the Play-Engine*. Springer-Verlag New York, Inc., 2003.
13. Hennicker, R., and Koch, N. Modeling the user interface of web applications with UML. In *Workshop of the pUML-Group held together with the "UML"2001 on Practical UML-Based Rigorous Development Methods - Countering or Integrating the eXtremists* (2001), 158–172.
14. Khler, H.-J., Nickel, U., Niereand, J., and Zndorf, A. Using UML as visual programming language. *Technical Report tr-ri-99-205* (1999).
15. Koegel, J. F., and Heines, J. M. Improving visual programming languages for multimedia authoring. In *ED-MEDIA '93, World Conference on Educational Multimedia and Hypermedia* (1993), 286–293.
16. Luong, T. N., Laborie, S., and Nodenot, T. A framework with tools for designing web-based geographic applications. In *ACM Symposium on Document Engineering* (2011), 33–42.
17. Manola, F., and Miller, E. RDF Primer. Recommendation, W3C, February 2004. `http://www.w3.org/TR/rdf-syntax/`.
18. Moody, D. The physics of notations: Toward a scientific basis for constructing visual notations in software engineering. *IEEE Trans. Softw. Eng. 35* (November 2009), 756–779.
19. Myers, B. A. Taxonomies of visual programming and program visualization. *Journal of Visual Languages and Computing 1* (March 1990), 97–123.
20. Narayanan, N. H., and Hübscher, R. *Visual language theory: towards a human computer interaction perspective*. Springer-Verlag New York, Inc., New York, NY, USA, 1998, 87–128.
21. Raymond, D. R. Characterizing visual languages. In *Proc. 1991 IEEE Workshop on Visual Languages. (Kobe*, Society Press (1991), 176–182.
22. Shu, N. C. Visual programming: Perspectives and approaches. *IBM Systems Journal 38*, 2/3 (1999), 199–221.
23. Stubbs, T., and Gibbons, A. The power of design drawings in other design fields. In *Handbook of Visual Languages in Instructional Design; Theories and Practice* (2007).
24. Stühmer, R., Anicic, D., Sen, S., Ma, J., Schmidt, K.-U., and Stojanovic, N. Lifting events in RDF from interactions with annotated web pages. In *Proceedings of the 8th International Semantic Web Conference*, Springer-Verlag (2009), 893–908.
25. Traynor, C., and Williams, M. G. *End users and GIS: a demonstration is worth a thousand words*. Morgan Kaufmann Publishers Inc., San Francisco, CA, USA, 2001, 115–134.
26. Ziadi, T., Blanc, X., and Raji, A. From requirements to code revisited. In *Proceedings of the 2009 IEEE International Symposium on Object/Component/Service-Oriented Real-Time Distributed Computing*, ISORC '09, IEEE Computer Society (Washington, DC, USA, 2009), 228–235.

Automatic Reverse Engineering of Interactive Dynamic Web Applications to Support Adaptation across Platforms

Federico Bellucci, Giuseppe Ghiani, Fabio Paternò, Claudio Porta
CNR-ISTI, HIIS
Via Moruzzi 1, 56124 Pisa, Italy
{federico.bellucci, giuseppe.ghiani, fabio.paterno, claudio.porta}@isti.cnr.it

ABSTRACT
The effort and time required to develop user interface models has been one of the main limitations to the adoption of model-based approaches, which enable intelligent processing of user interface descriptions. In this paper, we present a tool to perform reverse engineering of interactive dynamic Web applications into a model-based framework able to describe them at various abstraction levels. We indicate how information in HTML, HTML 5, CSS, Ajax and JavaScript is transformed into such logical framework, which facilitates adaptation to other types of interactive devices. We also discuss how this reverse engineering tool has been exploited in an environment for run-time adaptation or migration of interactive Web applications to various devices in ubiquitous use cases.

Author Keywords
User interface reverse engineering, Web applications, Model-based user interface descriptions.

ACM Classification Keywords
H.5 Information Interfaces and Presentation; H.5.2 User Interfaces

General Terms
Design, Human Factors.

INTRODUCTION
Model-based approaches have been considered in order to aid user interface design and development by providing abstractions useful to manage the increasing complexity of user interface implementations. They have been used for many purposes (for example in [11] a model-based tool to guide early interface design has been proposed), and are also currently under consideration by the W3C for standardization purposes [4]. One of their main applications is for supporting design and development of multi-device user interfaces, since each device has specific interaction resources and implementation languages to execute such user interfaces. The basic idea is to provide a universal small conceptual vocabulary to support user interface design, which can then be refined into a variety of implementation languages with the support of automatic transformations, without requiring developers to learn all the details of such implementation languages. However, the effort and time required to develop user interface models has been one of the main limitations to the adoption of model-based approaches.

In order to overcome such limitation, we propose a tool that performs reverse engineering of interactive Web applications into MARIA [9], a model-based framework for describing interactive applications at two abstraction levels. In particular, the MARIA framework is composed of one abstract (platform-independent) language and various concrete (platform-dependent) languages. We use the platform concept to indicate groups of devices that share similar interaction resources (desktop, smartphone, vocal, ...). The concrete languages add to the abstract language refinements that depend on the class of devices to which they correspond. Thus, they still provide descriptions that are independent of the final implementation languages. The advantage of transforming the implementation into a concrete MARIA description is that in this way it is then easier to adapt it to a different platform, since all the platform-dependent descriptions share the same core set of concepts that are derived from the abstract description. In addition in this way the adaptation rules can be independent of the implementation languages used for the interactive applications.

The reverse engineering tool is able to create logical descriptions of the whole implementation of Web pages into the MARIA language, managing HTML as well as CSS and most JavaScript, and thus preserving the aspect and functionality of the original pages. A logical description of the page is easier to manipulate than the original page itself: the interactive application elements can be more easily transformed according to predefined rules for specific target devices before re-implementing the page starting with the modified logical description. This will result in a more compact user interface that better suits the limited screen of a mobile device.

The Reverse engineering tool supports several steps, each of which manages an aspect of the input page. It is able to analyse the DOM of the current page, thus any effect of dynamic changes can be immediately detected. The analysis includes both the styles defined within the HTML document and the external CSS files. JavaScript code is also extracted from the document and the referenced external files. The events related to HTML elements (such as *onclick*, *onload*, …) are mapped in the MARIA specification, which provides the possibility to describe events and event handlers as well.

In the paper, after discussing some related work we provide some background information on the MARIA framework in order to allow readers unfamiliar with it to better understand how our reverse tool works. Then, we move on to describe the algorithm and the rules that allow the tool to transform the implementation of Web applications into MARIA specifications. We show an example application of the approach proposed and report on some work to validate it and show its generality. We discuss what results this reverse engineering tool can enable by describing how it has been integrated in a platform supporting interactive application adaptation. Lastly, we provide some concluding remarks and some indications for future work.

RELATED WORK

In recent years, interest in user interface reverse engineering has received strong impetus from the advent of mobile technologies and the need to support multi-device applications. To this end, a good deal of work has been dedicated to user interfaces reverse engineering in order to identify corresponding meaningful abstractions (see for example [1, 2, 13]). Other studies have investigated how to derive the task model of an interactive application starting with the logs generated during user sessions [5]. However, this last approach is limited to building descriptions of the actual past use of the interface, which is described by the logs, but is not able to provide a general description of the tasks supported, which includes even those not considered in the logs. A different approach [3] proposes re-engineering Java graphical desktop applications to mobile devices with limited resources, without considering logical descriptions of the user interface. Hwang et al. [6] have introduced Web transcoding techniques, based on heuristics, that take into account the structure of the page, the main components and their semantics. The page is then automatically rearranged in order to be accessible from handheld devices.

Solutions for adaptation of Web interfaces to specific target devices also directly involving end users have being investigated as well. For example, a support for crowdsourced adaptation is presented in [14]: the end user is seen both as a consumer and as a contributor, and is provided with a visual environment to easily adapt the application to different contexts (e.g. mobile devices).

In the area of user interface reverse engineering, a model-based architecture to reverse event handlers of applications developed with RAD (Rapid Application Development) environments is presented in [15]. The aim is to convert existing legacy applications into Web-based ones by exploiting platform-independent representations for the original code, in particular for the event handlers. In particular, the authors of this work have focused on the case of Oracle Forms converted into Web applications with Ajax.

Memon et al. [8] describe an application called GUI Ripping, which consists in a dynamic process that transverses a GUI by opening all its windows and extracting all the widgets (GUI objects) and their information. GUIsurfer [13] defines a framework for tools capable of analysing the source code of applications written in Java/Swing, and generating behavioural models of their user interfaces, which can be useful for supporting formal reasoning. Another tool, Swing2Script [12], supports conversion of Java-Swing applications to Web applications implemented in XUL.

One of the main areas of interest has been how to recover semantic relations from Web pages. An approach based on visual cues is presented in [16], in which semantic relations usually apply to neighbouring rectangle blocks and define larger logical rectangle blocks. However, previous work in the reverse engineering of interactive Web applications (such as ReversiXML [2] for UsiXML, ReverseAll [1] for TERESA, …) has mainly addressed the possibility of reversing HTML tags. Unfortunately, the way to write Web applications has changed considerably in recent years and the HTML part is only a small fraction of Web applications. Usually a Web application is a set of resources (style sheets, scripts, …), which can be dynamically loaded, linked by the HTML core, and the corresponding DOM tree can be modified at runtime within the browser. In general, there is a lack of approaches able to address all such resources at runtime and build the corresponding logical descriptions, which can be exploited in multi-device and multimodal environments. This also implies the ability to analyse the JavaScript parts of Web applications. This is a difficult task given the wide variety of ways in which JavaScript can be used. An example JavaScript analysis was done with Feedlack [7], a tool that explores Web applications' behaviours to identify missing feedback. This processing is performed by enumerating control flow paths originating from user input, identifying paths that lack output-affecting code. FeedLack was applied to 330 applications; of the 129 that contained input handlers and did not contain syntax errors, 115 were successfully analysed (which is about one third of the original set of applications considered, indicating how complex this type of analysis is).

MARIA FRAMEWORK

As mentioned before, MARIA is composed of one abstract language and various concrete languages that refine it. The Abstract User Interface (AUI) level describes a UI only through the semantics of the interaction, without referring to a particular device capability, interaction modality or implementation technology.

An AUI is composed of various Presentations that contain model elements, which are presented to the user simultaneously. There are two types of model elements:

Interactor or InteractorComposition. The former represents every type of user interaction object, the latter groups together elements that are logically associated. According to its semantics an interactor belongs to one of the following subtypes:

- Selection. Allows the user to select one or more values among the elements of a predefined list. It contains the selected value and the information about the list cardinality. According to the number of values that can be selected, the interactor can be a Single Choice or a Multiple Choice.
- Edit. Allows the user to manually edit the object represented by the interactor, which can be text (TextEdit), a number (NumericalEdit), a position (PositionEdit) or a generic object (ObjectEdit).
- Control. Allows the user to switch between presentations (Navigator) or to activate UI functionalities (Activator).
- Onlyoutput. Represents information that is submitted to the user, not affected by user actions. It can be a text, a Description that represents different types of media, an Alarm, a Feedback or a generic Object.

The different types of interactor compositions are:

- Grouping: a generic group of interactor elements.
- Relation: a group where two or more elements are related to each other.
- CompositeDescription: represents a group aimed to present contents through a mixture of Description and Navigator elements.
- Repeater: used to repeat the content according to data retrieved from a generic data source.

MARIA allows describing not only the presentation aspects but also the interactive behaviour. For this purpose it has various features:

- Data Model. The user interface definition contains descriptions of the data types that are manipulated by the user interface. The interactors can be bound with elements of the data model, which means that, at runtime, modifying the state of an interactor will also change the value of the bound data element and vice-versa. This mechanism allows the modelling of correlations between UI elements, conditional layout, conditional connections between presentations, input values format. The data model is defined using the standard XML Schema Definition constructs.
- Generic Back End. The interface definition contains a set of ExternalFunctions declarations, which represents functionalities exploited by the UI but implemented by a generic application back-end support (e.g. web services, code libraries, databases etc.). One declaration contains the signature of the external function that specifies its name and its input/output parameters.
- Event Model. Each interactor definition has a number of associated events that allow the specification of UI reaction triggered by the user interaction. Two different classes of events have been identified: the Property Change Events that specify the value change of a property in the UI or in the data model (with an optional precondition), and the Activation Events that can be raised by activators and are intended to specify the execution of some application functionalities (e.g. invoking an external function).
- Dialog Model. The dialog model contains constructs for specifying the dynamic behaviour of a presentation, specifying what events can be triggered at a given time. The dialog expressions are connected using CTT operators in order to define their temporal relationships.
- Continuous update of fields. It is possible to specify that a given field should be periodically updated by invoking an external function.
- Dynamic Set of User Interface Elements. The language contains constructs for specifying partial presentation updates (dynamically changing the content of entire groupings) and the possibility to specify conditional navigation between presentations.

This set of new features provides, already at the abstract level, a model of the user interface that is not tied to implementation layout details, but it is sufficiently complete for reasoning on how the UI supports both the user interaction and the application back end.

A Concrete User Interface (CUI) in MARIA provides platform-dependent but implementation language-independent details of a UI. A platform is a set of software and hardware interaction resources that characterize a given set of devices. MARIA currently supports the following platforms:

- Desktop CUIs model graphical interfaces for desktop computers.
- Mobile CUIs model graphical interfaces for mobile devices.
- Multimodal Desktop CUIs model interfaces that combine the graphical and vocal modalities for desktop computers.
- Multimodal Mobile CUIs model interfaces that combine the graphical and vocal modalities for mobile devices.
- Vocal CUIs interfaces with vocal message rendering and speech recognition.

Each platform-dependent meta-model is a refinement of the AUI specifying how a given abstract interactor can be represented in the current platform. For instance, if we consider the abstract Single Choice interactor, it can be implemented (on a graphical desktop platform) with a radio button, a drop down list or a list box, while on the vocal platform it can be rendered with a list of vocal messages, one for each option associated to a given keyword.

The same applies to the interactor compositions: in a desktop platform a grouping can be implemented using background colours, borders, etc., while in a vocal platform it is possible to use sounds at the beginning and the end of a group of elements. The model definition can be exploited for creating (or deriving with a code generator) final implementations in different target languages. Indeed, it is possible to exploit the same mobile concrete user interface description for representing an App for the iPhone or an Android device.

THE OVERALL ALGORITHM IN THE REVERSE PROCESS

As already stated in the introduction, our reverse tool takes an HTML page, and the associated files (with stylesheets and scripts) as input and produces a CUI as output. The tool is able to directly access the DOM (Document Object Model) of the page to be reversed if it was previously created (e.g., for preprocessing purposes). Otherwise, the HTML file is passed to the Reverse tool, which exploits an HTML parser, named Tidy[1], to build the DOM. We have extended the Tidy parser in order to also manage the new tags introduced by HTML5. This parser also allows us to manage Web pages that are not well-formed according to the (X)HTML or HTML5 languages by correcting tags that are missing, improperly positioned or misspelled.

The Reverse main procedure consists of translating the HTML document, i.e. the actual page implementation, into a MARIA concrete, implementation-independent representation. The first check is to see whether JavaScript nodes exist in the DOM, in this case all their content is stored in an external file with extension ".js". The next check is whether there are CSS nodes in the DOM, in this case their information is stored in a cache memory. Then, the document is analysed through a deep first visit of the DOM tree. Each node is analysed and its CSS properties are managed by looking into the cache memory to see whether there are any CSS selectors referring to the currently analysed HTML node; in this case its content is used to specify attributes of the corresponding MARIA elements.

As mentioned before, CSS properties are reversed for all the elements present in the page and stored within their respective CUI representations. So some CSS rules may be lost in this process if there are no elements referring to those rules in the version of the page considered when the reverse is performed. This can be a problem when reversing dynamic Web pages that can add new elements at runtime or simply change the style properties of existing elements. To deal with this issue we make a static analysis of the JavaScript code to spot assignments to class attributes, which are largely responsible for the changes in style elements in dynamic pages. Then, the CSS content is analysed to see whether there are attributes referring to the classes identified. If they exist their content is included in the CUI.

[1] http://tidy.sourceforge.net/

In a next step, the algorithm checks whether there are events associated with the current DOM node. There are two possibilities: one is that an event is indicated (e.g. onclick, onmouseover, onfocus, onload, ...) along with the corresponding function call; in the other case, instead of a function call there is some code including functions definitions, declarations, variable instantiations. In the former case we add an event handler in the MARIA specification to indicate the JavaScript function that should be called. In the latter case, a function is created and is associated with the code contained in the event handler. Such code is included in the list of external functions and it is called by the corresponding event handler. Indeed, in MARIA a user interface can be associated with a list of external functions.

REVERSING HTML CODE

This phase of the Reverse process considers each single occurrence of HTML tags within the document and converts them into CUI elements, according to the specifications of the MARIA language. An excerpt from the conversion rules used for this purpose is shown in Table 1.

The document analysis starts from the *body* element, and the CUI is built while the visit proceeds in depth down to the leaves of the HTML tree.

For example, the table shows that the HTML INPUT tag is mapped onto various concrete MARIA elements depending on its type attribute, which substantially determines it semantics.

The Reverse primary output is an XML file containing the logical description of the input Web page in the MARIA language and a file containing the associated JavaScripts that can thus be reused in case of generation of an adapted version for another platform.

The Reverse is able to manage HTML 5 tags as well. Some conversion rules are listed in Table 2. In the case of TIME and METER tags the Reverse creates a MARIA element and in addition a corresponding data type in the data model. Various HTML 5 tags mainly provide an indication of the type of content associated with some presentation techniques (e.g. ARTICLE, HEADER, NAV, FIGCAPTION). This distinction is mainly captured through the role attribute in the MARIA specification.

REVERSING CSS

Two modules are involved in the CSS reverse phase: *CSS Handler* and *CSS Cache*. The CSS Handler is in charge of parsing the CSS information of the input page, extracting it and storing it in the CSS Cache. It is worth noting that any style information is considered in the CSS processing phase, including:

- External CSS files referred by *link* tags
- Internally defined *style* tags containing CSS code
- Content of style attributes within HTML tags

X(HTML) element		MARIA CUI element (desktop)
Tag name	*Attribute(s)*	
A	-	Navigator
	any event attribute	Activator
P	-	CompositeDescription (description | navigator | activator)
DIV	-	Grouping
IMG	-	Image
FORM	-	Relation
INPUT	type = null | text | password	TexEdit
	type = checkbox	MultipleChoiceType(Checkbox, Choiceelements++)
	type = radio	SingleChoiceType(RadioButton, ChoiceElements++)
	type = hidden	Object
	type = reset | submit	ActivatorButton
	type = submit	SubmitButton
BUTTON	type = reset | submit	Activator(Button)
	type != reset, type != submit	Navigator(Button)
TEXTAREA		TextEdit
SELECT	multiple = null	SingleChoice(DropDownList, ChoiceElements++)
	multiple != null	SingleChoice(ListBox, ChoiceElements++)
OL, UL, LI	-	Grouping
IFRAME	-	Grouping
COMMAND	-	Grouping

Table 1. HTML to MARIA conversion rules.

The first two cases are managed by a CSS parser (CSSOMparser) that builds an object Java structure, which facilitates its processing. The third case does not require any parser and is managed directly within the HTML analysis phase (because the content of a style attribute is already in HTML).

The CSS Cache is a data structure implemented as a Hash Table, with CSS selectors as keys and CSS properties as values. The data structure hosts in memory any CSS information until CUI elements creation begins. Thus, the CSS information is not immediately used because it defines properties that depend on the document structure. Indeed, the binding between attributes and elements is done according to the CSS selectors.

HTML5 element		MARIA CUI	
Tag name	*Distinctive element*	*Element*	*Attribute*
TIME	-	Description(text) + DataType containing the data	
METER	-	Description(text) + DataType containing the values max, min, val	
ARTICLE	If only output children or links	Composite description (description|navigator|activator)	role = article
	not only output or link children	Grouping	
FIGURE	only output children or link	Composite description (description|navigator|activator)	role = figure
	not only output or link children	Grouping	
COMMAND	-	Activator(button)	
MARK	-	Composite description (description|navigator|activator)	
ASIDE	-	Grouping	role = aside
FOOTER	-	Grouping	role = footer
HEADER	-	Grouping	role = header
HGROUP	-	Grouping	role = hgroup
NAV	-	Grouping	role = nav
SECTION	-	Grouping	role = section
MENU	-	Grouping	role = menu
DETAILS	-	textType	role = details
FIGCAPTION	-	textType	role = figcaption
OUTPUT	-	text	role = output

Table 2. HTML 5 to MARIA conversion rules.

INTEGRATION OF JAVASCRIPT IN MARIA

Scripting languages are becoming more and more common, not only within Web pages, but also in servers (e.g. the NodeJS JavaScript library) and in standalone applications (e.g. ActionScript-AIR applications). When the MARIA language was designed it was provided with some basic constructs to represent generic programming statements such as assignments, conditions, loops, etc. When we started to extend the Reverse module to support reverse engineering of dynamic Web applications we realized that it was not worth reimplementing a new abstract programming language within MARIA. So we decided to add the possibility to include scripts in MARIA using JavaScript itself. This type of solution mainly works for Web languages, but within them it could work with different interaction modalities (graphical, vocal, multimodal, ...).

To make the original JavaScript compliant with the CUI generated by the reverse process, the JavaScript code is parsed and modified. For instance, since the MARIA language does not implement a *name* attribute for its elements, the Reverse concatenates the *name* to the *identifier* (eventually generated), and modifies every related *identifier* in the JavaScript. The modifications are applied to the Abstract Syntax Tree (AST), which is created by a specific procedure starting from the JavaScript code. The modified AST is then stored in XML format along with the CUI.

In the case of an adaptation of the HTML page to a mobile platform, the XML representation of the JavaScript can be used to regenerate the original JavaScript, along with an adapted version of the original HTML, disabling or modifying any undesired part of the JavaScript code. An even more challenging scenario is the adaptation towards a vocal platform, such as a VoiceXML voice browser, which usually integrates a limited JavaScript interpreter that cannot access the DOM of the VoiceXML document. An example of a tool supporting desktop-to-vocal adaptation is reported in [9], which produces a simplified VoiceXML adaptation of the original Web page. In order to improve it, the JavaScript XML representation produced by the Reverse module can be translated into native VoiceXML constructs (such as VAR, ASSIGN, IF) and integrated into the VoiceXML adapted version of the Web application. Thereby, it reproduces part of the dynamic behavior of the source Web application in the generated vocal application.

VALIDATION

The Reverse tool has been successfully applied to various existing Web sites. An excerpt from a validation exercise is shown in Table 3.

The input was a set of pages belonging to the 100 most highly ranked well-known international Web sites (according to http://www.alexa.com).

Before triggering the Reverse, each page was downloaded and annotated through our proxy server. The annotation consisted of two steps:

- converting every URL on the page into an absolute address including the proxy server, in order to enable the Reverse to find every resource referred to by the page (e.g., external CSS and JavaScript)
- insertion of the scripts for automatically forwarding the currently visited document to the Reverse Web service.

The URL conversion is needed because the Reverse procedure runs locally and is not able to resolve relative addresses; thus, any reference within the original HTML page has to be extended as an absolute URL.

The input pages were classified by HTML depth and size, as well as the size of externally referred CSS. Each input page was also validated through the W3C Markup Validator Service (http://validator.w3.org/) in order to detect the number of errors and/or warnings. The validation was carried out on the (X)HTML version of the page, which was automatically detected by the W3C validator.

All the trials were successful (i.e. there were no failures in building the corresponding CUI), and the output obtained from the Reverse was classified by size and number of lines of the generated CUI file, and by the time taken to perform the Reverse.

The results do not reveal any correlation between the Reverse performance and a particular aspect of the page. For example, the three pages that took the longest time, which are #2, #4 and #10 in Table 3) are among the ones with the greatest amount of HTML and CSS. Nevertheless, #9 also has quite a large amount of HTML and CSS but took less than 2 seconds to be reversed. However, it is worth noting that, while #2, #4 and #8 contain more than 100 validation errors, #7 was totally correct. Thus, a combination of parameters, such as page size and errors, seems to affect the Reverse time.

The more elements the page has, the more time is needed by the Reverse to translate the page into the MARIA language, because every element has to be analyzed before being converted. Unfortunately, most of the Web pages are affected by validation errors (see the column "Errors/Warnings" on Table 3). Validation errors also impact negatively on the Reverse time, because every inconsistency, missing attribute or invalid character may raise an exception on the parsing procedure, which is performed according to W3C HTML specifications. All such issues have to be fixed in some way by the parser, thus having a negative impact on the overall Reverse time.

A quality indicator for the pages back-generated starting with the MARIA concrete description obtained by the reverse tool is reported in Table 3. The values listed in the "Generation" column refer to the level of consistency with the layout and the functionalities of the original page. The generation of the new pages was obtained from MARIA concrete descriptions adapted to a mobile device (i.e., to a device with limited screen size). We have defined the following three quality levels:

- A: The layout of the page as well as the functionalities are maintained.
- B: The layout is mostly maintained, while a few functionalities are not fully accessible, but can be easily corrected.

- C: The layout is mostly maintained and it would enable the user to interact with the page, but the regenerated JavaScript does not support all of the original functionalities.

Most of the generated Web pages received the intermediate score "B" because of some layout inconsistencies and/or some small lack in the original functionalities. In the "B" level, lacking functionalities are typically caused by issues in the dynamic query formulation, when the actual URL of the page is different from the one expected by the JavaScript. This type of issue can be solved by a minimal manual intervention.

The "C" score was given to those pages that, even while maintaining an acceptable layout to potentially preserve the interaction, had some underlying functional inconsistencies. For instance, in pages with dynamic JQuery management of the event handlers, the environment was unable to correctly restore to the adapted implementation the event handlers previously associated to the interactive elements.

APPLICATION TO ADAPTATION AND MIGRATION

We have integrated our tool for reverse engineering in an environment for adaptation or migration of interactive applications. This adaptation environment is server-based (see Figure 1). The adaptation server includes a proxy so that when users navigate Web pages, the links therein are modified to force them to pass through the server. The accessed Web pages are downloaded in the server, including the external resources that they refer to (JavaScripts, CSS files, …). These are passed to the reverse engineering tool, which performs the processing described in the previous sections. The resulting MARIA specifications can be passed to one of the possible adaptation engines. The choice of which adaptation transformation to apply depends on the device currently used by the user. So far, we have considered the possibility to adapt to mobile devices, characterised by smaller screens and lower processing capabilities, and to vocal devices, in which case there is a complete change of interaction modality. These adaptation tools are complex and their description is beyond the scope of this paper, whose focus is on the reverse engineering tool that enables such adaptation possibilities. However, it is worth pointing out that they are based on the features of the MARIA language, since they exploit concrete languages for the target platforms (vocal devices, mobile devices). Since such languages share the same core structure (the abstract MARIA language) it is easier to define and implement the adaptation rules. Indeed, when such transformations find a graphical element (e.g. a radio button), then they look at the corresponding abstract semantic effect (in this case a single selection), and lastly inspect how they are supported in the target concrete language (for example in the vocal concrete language there is a vocal choice).

In addition to adaptation, another feature that we have found useful in ubiquitous environments is migration. It allows mobile users to dynamically change the interaction device and migrate the interactive application from the source to the target device while preserving its state. In a Web application this means that users can find on the target device the interactive application at the point in which it was left off and also still find the input they entered in the forms, the JavaScript in a consistent state, the same cookies and session variables. This allows users to freely move about, change device and still be able to continue their activities in a seamless manner.

Input								*Output MARIA CUI*		*Reverse Time (s)*	*Generation*
#	*Domain*	*Page*	*Size (B)* HTML	*Size (B)* CSS	*DOM Depth*	*Version*	*Errors / Warnings*	*Size (B)*	*Lines*		
1	www.ebay.com	Home	211.015	69.120	18	HTML 4.01 transitional	359 / 16	569.045	9.307	3,736	A
2	motors.shop.ebay.com	25 items search result	456.398	123.767	30	HTML 4.01 transitional	175 / 1	978.707	18.144	12,703	C
3	www.google.com	Home	91.595	13.045	22	HTML 5	35 / 2	55.460	940	4,390	B
4	www.yahoo.com	Home	391.897	209.311	18	HTML 5	130 / 8	281.694	3.517	12,172	A
5	www.youtube.com	Home	374.195	232.526	18	HTML 5	130 / 2	357.385	4.801	10,892	B
6	www.youtube.com	24 videos search result	268.423	232.518	16	HTML 5	97 / 3	544.135	7.189	10,453	B
7	www.msn.com	Home	226.549	177.212	19	XHTML 1.0 strict	0 / 0	220.129	5.532	1,797	B
8	www.linkedin.com	User Home	388.518	192.542	20	HTML 5	117 / 118	1.007.023	15.828	11,920	C
9	www.bbc.co.uk	Business News	198.135	327.400	20	XHTML + RDFa	0 / 0	543.858	9.016	6,484	B
10	en.wikipedia.org	Technology	246.725	98.459	15	XHTML 1.0 transitional	2 / 0	541.514	10.731	4,188	B
11	www.amazon.com	Kindle eBooks	462.143	104.257	31	XHTML 4.01 transitional	433 / 157	463.086	8.147	8,875	C
12	wordpress.org	Forum	52.514	66.871	18	XHTML 1.0 transitional	1 / 0	180.140	3.524	2,563	A
13	www.bing.com	10 items search result	119.816	4.310	20	XTHML 1.0 transitional	6 / 0	147.909	2.511	1,297	B

Table 3. Validation test results.

The output of the adaptation components are MARIA specifications in the concrete language of the target platform. Then, there are generators for various corresponding implementation languages. For example, for vocal interfaces we have generators into VoiceXML, for Web applications we have generators in HTL+CSS+JavaScripts or JSP, if Web service access is required.

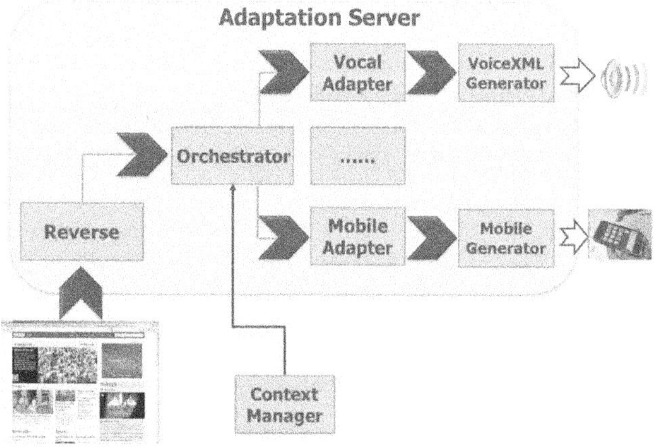

Figure 1. Adaptation Platform Exploiting our Reverse Engineering Tool.

EXAMPLE

To provide an example of what our Reverse produces when applied to a dynamic Web page, and how the generated elements relate to the original HTML, we can consider the reverse home page of altavista.com. The input page is shown in Figure 2, highlighting some of the components of the original page. An example of dynamic feature is the possibility to show suggestions of possible terms depending on what characters the user types. The management of such events is not specified in the HTML code but is dynamically added through JavaScrips that modify the DOM. With respect to Figure 2, the component of the page circled in yellow (5) is converted (see Figure 2) into a *Grouping*; the one circled with blue dots (3) becomes an *Activator*; the one highlighted with red lines/dots (2) turns into a *Text Edit*; the components circled with green dashed lines (1, 4) turn into *Navigators*.

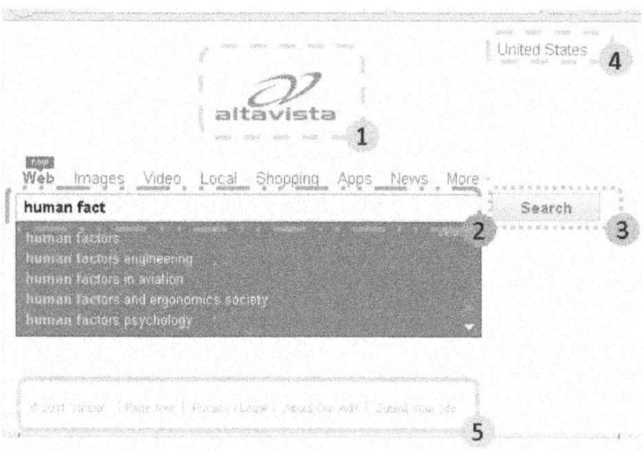

Figure 2. An example of input page highlighting some components.

For the sake of clarity, only some components are considered in this example because the actual Reverse deals with an input HTML page of about 24 kB. Figure 3 shows the sections of the output CUI related to the highlighted parts of Figure 2. Note that most of the CUI MARIA specification has been cut or collapsed, in order to make it more legible. Such CUI can be adapted for mobile access, and then from the adapted CUI it is possible to generate the corresponding implementation.

```
...
<composite_description id="Obj_2">
    <navigator focus="false" id="link_4">
1       <link><label><image alt="Image: " source="http://a.l.yimg.com/a/i/us
    </navigator>
</composite_description>
...
<relation id="sf" padding-right="0" padding-left="0" padding-bottom="0" padd
        ...
            <text_edit id="yschsp.p">
2               <text_field password="false" length="8" text=""/>
            </text_edit>

            <activator focus="false" id="yschbt">
3               <button margin-left="6px">
                    <label><text><string>Search</string></text></label>
                </button>
            </activator>
        ...
    <relation_settings/>
</relation>
...
<navigator focus="false" id="link_43">
4   <link>
        <label><text role="normal"><string>United States</string> <font_sett
    </link>
</navigator>
...
<grouping padding-right="0" padding-left="0" padding-bottom="0" padding-top=
5   <grouping margin-right="10px" id="Obj_67">
        <description focus="false" id="ShowText_68">
            <text role="normal"><string>© 2011 Yahoo!</string></text>
        </description>
        <properties position="column" />
    </grouping>
        ...
            <navigator focus="false" id="link_69">
                <link><label><text role="normal"><string>Page Tour</string><
            </navigator>
        ...
    <properties position="row"><font_settings decoration="none" weight="norm
</grouping>
...
```

Figure 3. An excerpt of the CUI produced by the Reverser.

In Figure 4 the Web page version resulting from the adaptation to a smartphone is shown. The adaptation support receives as input the MARIA CUI of the page and a set of constraints (device height/width, interactors transformation rules, tolerance to scrolling, ...). The output of the adaptation support is an adapted MARIA CUI, which describes a new version of the page optimized for the destination device (smartphone): the components have been rearranged in order to better exploit the screen space of the mobile device, and the page width has been reduced so that the need for horizontal scrolling is minimized. The actual implementation of the page is produced by a MARIA-to-HTML + JavaScript generator.

The Web page implementation generated from the CUI adapted for smartphones devices (Figure 4), with a slightly different layout, maintains the initial interactive functionalities. Indeed, the generated search form has the original attributes values (action, name and id of the input elements), and the page generated for mobile access is able to perform a Web search through the submit button.

It is worth noting that almost all the page elements have maintained the original id, and that the JavaScript support is still able to access those elements. Thus, thanks to the ability to reverse and restore the JavaScript functions, the generated page for smartphones also provides the real-time dynamic suggestion of the terms while the user is typing in the text field as in the original version of the page.

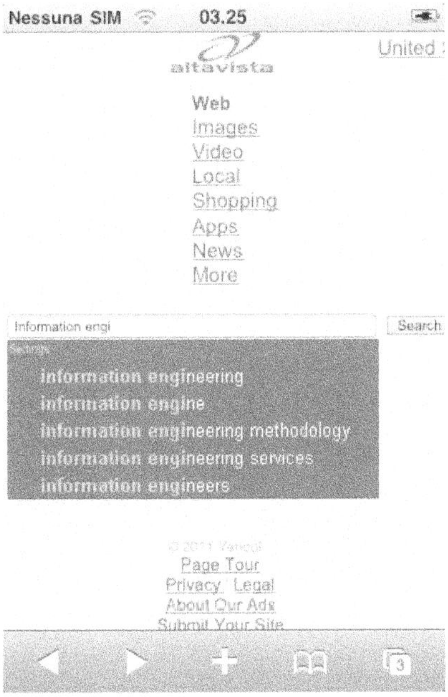

Figure 4. The resulting UI adapted to the smartphone.

CONCLUSIONS AND FUTURE WORK

In this paper we have presented a reverse engineering tool for interactive dynamic Web applications able to transform them into model-based specifications. Such model-based descriptions can be used for various purposes (adaptation tools for multi-device environments, documentation, support to usability evaluation, …). In particular, we have discussed how the Reverse tool has been integrated into a run-time platform where it allows the dynamic adaptation of the pages that users can access through various devices.

The desktop version of the tool is available for download at http://giove.isti.cnr.it/tools/ReverseMARIA/download

Future work will be dedicated to further improving the reverse engineering tool in order to address some cases that are not yet addressed related to JQuery and dynamic modifications, such as when JQuery scripts dynamically add event handlers to the DOM. Another possible extension is to provide the possibility to derive higher-level abstraction descriptions from the MARIA specification, such as task models that describe the activities performed by users to reach their goals, and that allow reasoning about their performance in intelligent environments.

ACKNOLEDGEMENTS

This work has been partly supported by the EU SERENOA STREP project (EU ICT FP7-ICT N.258030).

REFERENCES

1. Bandelloni, R, Paternò, F., Santoro, C. Reverse Engineering Cross-Modal User Interfaces for Ubiquitous Environments, Proceedings EIS'07, Salamanca, LNCS 4940, 285-302, Springer Verlag, March 2007.
2. Bouillon, L., Limbourg, Q., Vanderdonckt, J., and Michotte, B. Reverse engineering of web pages based on derivations and transformations. In In: Proceedings of third Latin American web congress LA-Web'05. IEEE Computer Society Press, 2005.
3. Canfora, G., Di Santo, G., Zimeo, E. Toward Seamless Migration of Java AWT-Based Applications to Personal Wireless Devices, Proceedings WCRE'04, 1-9.
4. Fonseca, J.M.C. (ed.), W3C Model-Based UI XG Final Report, May 2010, available at http://www.w3.org/2005/Incubator/model-based-ui/XGR-mbui-20100504/.
5. Hudson, S., John, B., Knudsen, K., Byrne, M. A Tool for Creating Predictive Performance Models from User Interface Demonstrations. Proceedings UIST'99, 93-102, ACM Press, 1999.
6. Hwang, Y., Kim, J., and Seo, E. Structure-Aware Web Transcoding for Mobile Devices. Proc. IEEE Internet Computing, pp. 14-21.
7. Ko, A. J., Zhang, X. Feedlack detects missing feedback in web applications. Proceedings CHI 2011, 2177-2186, ACM Press, Vancouver, 2011.
8. Memon, A., Banerjee, I., and Nagarajan, A.. Gui ripping: Reverse engineering of graphical user interfaces for testing. In WCRE '03: Proceedings of the 10th Working Conference on Reverse Engineering, page 260, Washington, DC, USA, 2003. IEEE Computer Society.
9. Paternò, F., Santoro, C., Spano, L.D. MARIA: A Universal Language for Service-Oriented Applications in Ubiquitous Environment. ACM Transactions on Computer-Human Interaction, Vol.16, N.4, November 2009, 19:1-19:30, ACM Press.
10. Paternò, F., Sisti, C. Model-Based Customizable Adaptation of Web Applications for Vocal Browsing, ACM SIGDOC, pp.83-90, ACM Press, Pisa, October 2011.
11. Puerta, A. R., Micheletti, M., Mak, A. The UI pilot: a model-based tool to guide early interface design. IUI 2005, 215-222.

12. Samir, H., Stroulia, E., Kamel, A. Swing2Script: Migration of Java-Swing Applications to Ajax Web Applications. WCRE 2007, 179-188.

13. Silva, J. C., Silva, C. E., Gonçalo, R- D., Saraiva, J., Campos, J. C.. The GUISurfer tool: towards a language independent approach to reverse engineering GUI code. EICS 2010, 181-186, ACM Press.

14. Nebeling, M., and C. Norrie, M. Tools and architectural support for crowdsourced adaptation of web interfaces. In Proceedings of the 11th international conference on Web engineering (ICWE'11). Springer-Verlag, Berlin, Heidelberg, 243-257.

15. Sánchez Ramón, O., Sánchez Cuadrado, J., García Molina, J. Reverse Engineering of Event Handlers of RAD-Based Applications. Proc. Of WCRE 2011. IEEE, 293-302.

16. Xiang, P., Shi, Y. Recovering semantic relations from web pages based on visual cues, Proceedings of the 11th international conference on Intelligent user interfaces, January 29-February 01, 2006, Sydney, Australia, 342-344.

Towards Automatic Functional Test Execution

Pablo Pedemonte
IBM Argentina
Ing. Butty 275 – C1001AFA
Buenos Aires, Argentina
ppedemon@ar.ibm.com

Jalal Mahmud
IBM Research – Almaden
650 Harry Rd.
San Jose, CA 95120
jumahmud@us.ibm.com

Tessa Lau
IBM Research – Almaden
650 Harry Rd.
San Jose, CA 95120
tessalau@us.ibm.com

ABSTRACT

As applications are developed, functional tests ensure they continue to function as expected. Nowadays, functional testing is mostly done manually, with human testers verifying a system's functionality themselves, following hand-written instructions. While there exist tools supporting functional test automation, in practice they are hard to use, require programming skills, and do not provide good support for test maintenance. In this paper, we take an alternative approach: we semi-automatically convert hand-written instructions into automated tests. Our approach consists of two stages: first, employing machine learning and natural language processing to compute an intermediate representation from test steps; and second, interactively disambiguating that representation to create a fully automated test. These two stages comprise a complete system for converting hand-written functional tests into automated tests. We also present a quantitative study analyzing the effectiveness of our approach. Our results show that 70% of manual test steps can be automatically converted to automated test steps with no user intervention.

Author Keywords

Manual Test Automation; Natural Language Processing; Supervised Learning

ACM Classification Keywords

H.5.2 Information Interfaces and Presentation: User Interfaces—*Natural Language*;

INTRODUCTION

Testing can be an expensive task [9] whose effectiveness is crucial to a project's success. One way to achieve an effective testing process is by means of test automation. By automating some or all of the work necessary to execute a test, testers can focus on verifying complex cases and key features instead of dedicating time to repetitive, tedious execution tasks. Automated execution excels on repetitive tasks like unit testing [6]. But there are other testing disciplines where automated execution is hard to achieve with existing tools.

Functional testing poses a case where test automation is difficult to achieve. Functional tests verify that a system complies with its specifications and requirements, ignoring internal details such as code, design or architecture. According to our experience in large organizations, functional testing is done mostly manually: system functionality is verified by human testers, following hand-written instructions detailing how to feed a system with some input, and the expected outputs. This situation is particularly problematic for large, long-lived projects, which might carry hundreds of legacy functional tests. Periodically executing such tests by manual means can take a considerable amount of time and resources. Our work aims to automate functional test execution, thus helping to alleviate this problem.

In practice, the approach to functional test automation consists of deriving a program from a test. One can derive such a program either by coding it (which puts the automation burden on the developers) or by means of a recording tool [8]. At first glance, recording looks like a good solution for automating functional tests. At the price of manually following the test instructions during a recording session, one obtains a script that can be executed later without incurring further automation overhead. But there are limitations to recording. First, testers still need to manually execute the test during recording. Second, software artifacts resulting from recording consist of generated code, which is not easy to maintain. If a test needs to be changed one has to modify the resulting program. This requires programming skills, and might not be a simple task. Alternatively one could re-record, which implies manually executing the test again. While end-user programming systems such as CoScripter [13] could reduce the programming requirement, the recording barriers remain. In contrast, we propose a semi-automated approach that eliminates the need to do any recording at all.

We address functional test automation with a two stage approach:

1. Converting a manual functional test into an intermediate representation amenable for automated execution.

2. Interpreting the intermediate representation with user guidance.

Our approach processes a test step by step, converting and interpreting each step in turn. The key problem with understanding natural language is that it is imprecise, so the meaning of a hand written instruction might not be unambiguously determined. We handle such cases by asking for user guidance: if while executing a test we find an instruction whose meaning can not be precisely determined, we ask the user how to proceed. We use this feedback to create a modified manual test based on the original, which can be automatically executed using our system. Our approach is especially suited for periodic functional test execution, which is the norm in test organizations, as functional tests are used during development to ensure a system continues to work as specified. After a first run of a test requiring user intervention to handle ambiguous instructions, our approach enables fully automatic execution by a returning a new test defining the same actions as the original, but requiring no user assistance to execute.

This approach frees programmers from the tedious task of writing code for functional tests, and testers from the burden of manual step execution (provided the interpreter does not require user intervention at every step). But why is it better than recording? Like recording, our approach requires effort from the user only for the first execution of a test, and future runs will not need user intervention. But unlike a recording session, our first execution requires user intervention sporadically, only when the interpreter finds an ambiguous instruction. Furthermore, since our approach generates written manual tests instead of code, it reduces the cost of maintaining these tests over time.

Specifically, we make the following contributions:

- A machine learning-based algorithm for converting a test into an intermediate representation suitable for automated execution.
- A semi-automated algorithm for interpreting the intermediate representation derived from a test, requesting feedback from the user if the intermediate representation can not be unambiguously interpreted, and using this feedback to create an equivalent test with no ambiguous steps.
- An implemented system for automatic manual test execution, based on our conversion and interpreter algorithms.
- A quantitative study evaluating the performance of our algorithms. Our results show that we can execute more than 70% of the instructions in a test without user intervention.

We start with a formulation of our approach to functional test automation, then we describe the stages of our approach. After that, we present the quantitative study analyzing the effectiveness of our approach. Finally, we discuss key aspects of our approach and future research directions, and conclude with an overview of related work.

PROBLEM DEFINITION

A manual test is an ordered sequence $\{s_i\}$, $i \geq 1$, of test steps (or instructions). A *value-free* manual test is a pair (M, vs), where M is a manual test whose literal values (such as "10" in `type quantity 10`) have been replaced by variables, and vs is an ordered set of values. The idea is that a value-free test is a parametrized test that can be executed many times with different values, by providing distinct sets. We transform a manual test into its value-free version by a manual *value replacement* stage which we will describe later.

Given a value-free manual test (M, vs), $M = \{s_i\}$, our system executes the steps s_i in order of occurrence and returns a new test $M' = \{s'_i\}$ that defines the same actions as M, but *does not* require user intervention when executed. In this way we materialize the benefits of our approach: executing M might require user intervention, but after that we will have a manual test M' equivalent to M, requiring no effort from the user to execute. Fig. 1 (a) depicts the complete process.

Executing a step involves two stages: converting it to an intermediate representation, and interpreting that representation on the application under test. Fig. 1 (b) shows how these two stages interact in order to execute a single step.

Converting Test Steps

Based on existing work about interpreting hand-written instructions [13, 12], we view test steps as entities denoting *actions* to perform on *target* GUI elements of the application. Hence, in order to execute a step, we need to identify:

- The actions denoted by the step.
- The target for each action in the step.
- Any data required by the actions. For example, the "enter" action requires a value to be entered into a text field.

Fig. 2 shows a sample real-world test about reinstating lapsed insurance policies. The actions in step 1 are "enter" and "press", and their respective targets are two GUI elements labeled "policy number" and "search". Moreover, the "enter" action has a policy number template as associated data. Targets can be specified either by a label alone (e.g., "search" in step 1) or by a label and a target type (like "save button" in step 4). Targets specified only by a label are *implicit*.

Therefore, we define the intermediate representation of a test step to be a tuple combining the action intended by the step, the target of the action, and any associated data if present. We will refer to these as (A, T, D) tuples.

We define the current application state st to be the combined state of all the GUI elements of the application at the present time. Performing an action on the application (e.g., entering some text) might change the GUI, and hence, the current state. Our conversion algorithm is then defined as a function taking a pair (st, s) representing the current application state and a test step to convert, and returning an ordered list of one or more tuples $\{(A_i, T_i, D_i)\}$, $i \geq 1$, one for each operation denoted by a step. From now on, we will refer to the conversion algorithm as *tuple extraction*.

Fig. 3 shows the (A, T, D) tuples obtained from the example test (a "•" in the data component means that the tuple carries no data). Note that a test step can be converted into multiple tuples. Note also that there is no translation for step 5 in Fig. 2. That step does not denote an action to apply on the application's GUI, but rather a verification step we know nothing about (even a tester attempting to execute this step might have trouble trying to find out what are the "operational and referral rules" that the system should follow). Processing such instructions is an area for future work.

Interpreting Test Steps

We define the interpreter algorithm to be a function taking the current application state st, the textual representation s of

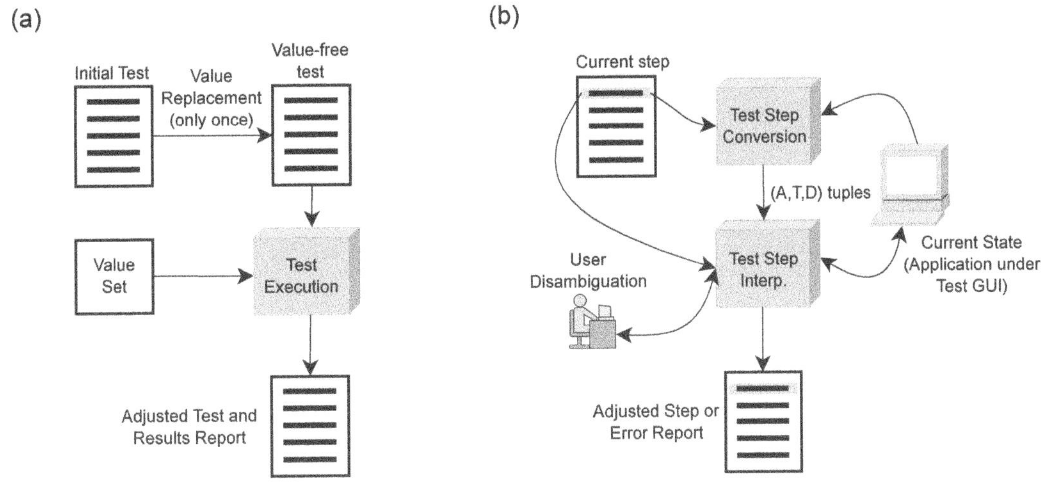

Figure 1. (a) Complete manual test automation process – (b) Execution of a single step

the current step, and a tuple (A, T, D) to interpret, obtained from converting s. The result will be a pair (st', s'), where st' is the new application state resulting from interpreting the tuple, and s' an unambiguous version of the step s, based on the user's feedback if disambiguation took place. If user intervention was not needed, s' will be equal to s. Therefore, the result of running the interpreter on each step of a test M is a new test, M', whose steps have been fully disambiguated.

Interpreting an (A, T, D) tuple requires applying the action A to the target denoted by T. The crucial step is resolving the target, i.e., finding a GUI element matching T. There can be multiple elements matching T. For example, consider a page having a search link and a search icon. Both elements will match the target in the tuple (*click*, *search*, •). It is likely that clicking either element will have the same effect, but we can not assume that in general. When the target of a tuple can not be uniquely determined, we say that the tuple's target is *ambiguous*. In some cases, this ambiguity can be overcome by inspecting the tuple to interpret. But in general, there may not be enough information to select the intended target.

Let $T.l$ be the label in the target specification, and $T.t$ the type (which will be the undefined value "•" if T is implicit). Let $label$ be a function that given the application state and an GUI element computes its label, and $type$ a function that returns an element's type. Then, the set of elements e matching the target specification T is:

$$\{e \in st \mid T.l = label(st, e) \land (T.t = \bullet \lor T.t = type(e))\}$$

Note that in order to find the candidate targets matching T we need the application state to be up to date, i.e., reflecting the effects of the steps interpreted previously. This means that when we try to interpret the tuples obtained from a step s_i, the application under test must be in a state reflecting the effect of the tuples for the steps $s_1 \dots s_{i-1}$. One way to achieve this is to "thread" the state through the interpreter, passing the current state to the function and returning a new state resulting from interpretation of the tuple.

```
1. enter the policy number as xxx-xxx-xxxx
     then press search
2. press reinstate button
3. enter the following
     effective date as mm-dd-yyyy
     paid indicator as "y"
     comments as "payment done"
4. press save button
5. validate system follows operational
     and referral rules
```

Figure 2. A real-world manual test

1 (**enter**, *policy number*, *xxx-xxx-xxxx*)
(**press**, *search*, •)
2 (**press**, *reinstate button*, •)
3 (**enter**, *effective date*, *mm-dd-yyyy*)
(**enter**, *paid indicator*, *y*)
(**enter**, *comments*, *payment done*)
4 (**press**, *save button*, •)

Figure 3. Tuples for manual test in Fig. 2

From now on, we will refer to the algorithm interpreting the intermediate representation of a test step (i.e., a sequence of (A, T, D) tuples) as the *tuple interpreter*.

VALUE REPLACEMENT

In practice, functional tests are executed many times with different values. This might have an impact on the way that tests are written. For example, step 1 in Fig. 2 tells us to enter a policy number following the pattern "xxx-xxx-xxxx", but it says nothing about the valid values we could pass to the system in order to move on to step 2. This is because the test is expected to be executed with different policy numbers. For example, one could verify that the system correctly processes different classes of policies, e.g., car accident and credit card insurance.

This complicates repeated test execution: every time we execute a test, we might need to modify it in order to provide new values. We overcome this complication by introducing a mechanism to abstract out values from a functional

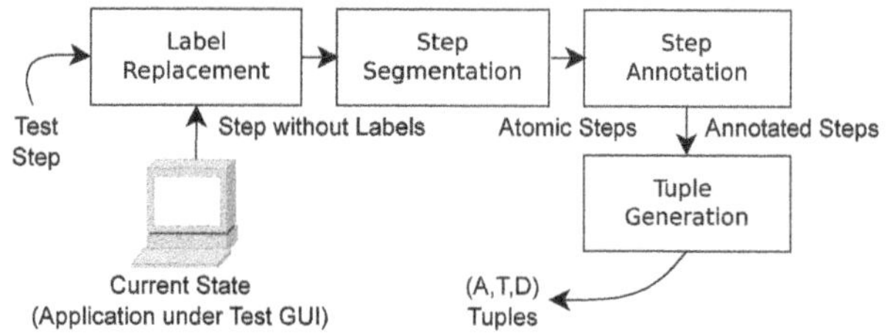

Figure 4. Tuple extraction process

test, namely *value variables*. Value variables have the form $VALUE(i)$, referring to the ith value in an ordered set of values available at text execution. This way, step 1 in Fig. 2 would change to:

```
enter policy number as VALUE(0)
  then press Search
```

where the test must be run with an ordered set of values holding a policy number at position 0. Value variables are useful in other cases where values are often missing, such as login instructions. A step like `enter user name and password` can be converted into `enter user name VALUE(0) and password VALUE(1)`, thus making the values explicit.

In the value replacement stage users replace values in a test with variables and define one or more value sets. Like user disambiguation, value replacement will be necessary only for the first execution of a test. Although this represents a slight overhead for the tester, it facilitates repeated test execution. If we need to execute a test several times with different values, we only need to re-execute with a different value set. The test remains unchanged. Automatic value replacement is an area for future work.

TUPLE EXTRACTION

We extract a sequence of (A, T, D) tuples from a step by a succession of fully automatic transformations (depicted in Fig. 4). We start with an example, then we describe all the transformations in detail. For the example we will use the first step of the test in Fig. 2. After value replacement, we have:

```
enter policy number VALUE(0) then press search
```

We start by replacing target labels with label variables. This is similar to introducing value variables, but since we can query the current state of the application for the available labels in the GUI, it is possible to automatically enumerate all the labels and remove their occurrences in the step. This *label replacement* stage leaves us with a simplified, less verbose test step. Our example test step becomes:

```
enter LABEL(policy number) VALUE(0)
  then press LABEL(search)
```

Note that this step denotes two actions. Our next stage, *step segmentation*, decomposes such a *composite* step into steps containing *exactly one action verb*, i.e., a verb that can act as the A component of a tuple. We call such steps *atomic*. Segmentation gives us two atomic steps: `enter LABEL(policy number) VALUE(0)` and `press LABEL(search)`.

The next stage, *step annotation*, identifies the tokens in each atomic step referring to the action, target and data of the tuples we intend to obtain. In our first atomic step we identify "enter" as the action, the label as the (implicit) target, and the value as the associated data. In the second atomic step, "press" is the action and the label the (again implicit) target. Based on this information, in the final *tuple generation* step we compute the two tuples as shown in Fig. 3: (***enter**, policy number*, $VALUE(0)$) and (***press**, search*, •).

Label Replacement

There are cases where different instructions have the same underlying structure. Consider the steps:

```
click Add item to shopping cart icon
click Search button
```

What if we replace target labels with variables, like we did with values? If we write label variables as $LABEL(l)$, where l is the replaced target label, the example becomes:

```
click LABEL(Add item to shopping cart) icon
click LABEL(Search) button
```

Replacing labels with variables has has the desirable effect of inducing a notion of a test step normal form that allows us to focus on the *structure* of the step. After label replacement, seemingly different steps end up having the same structure. This simplifies the remaining stages of the extraction process, by reducing the number of forms that test steps can take. Besides, label replacement results in shorter instructions where it is simpler to identify the components of the (A, T, D) tuples to extract. For example, in its original form the first step has 7 tokens; after label replacement it has been reduced to 3 tokens ("click", a *LABEL* variable, and "icon") which directly correspond to the step's action, target label, and target type. Later, we will see that label replacement also allows us to avoid tricky labels that might prove problematic for later stages of our tuple extraction algorithm.

Label replacement starts by tokenizing and POS tagging [3] the current step. Then, we identify target labels with the aid of a table holding all currently available labels. We compute the table by collecting the labels of all the elements in the application's GUI. Once we have this table, we calculate all n-grams in the step using suffix arrays [14]. Then, for each n-gram, we query the table to check if it is a label. We have implemented a few strategies to ensure that we don't have false positives, e.g.: discard candidate unigrams POS-tagged as verbs if they belong to a list of typical actions (e.g., click, select, type, enter, etc.), and ignore n-grams that are included in another candidate n-gram. Finally, we replace each matching n-gram l with a variable $LABEL(l)$ POS-tagged with the *NN* tag (i.e., a noun).

Step Segmentation

The latter stages of the tuple extraction algorithm work on atomic test steps, i.e., steps including exactly one action verb. The step segmentation phase does the work of computing the atomic constituents of a possibly composite test step. If the input step is already atomic, then this stage reduces to the identity function.

A possible approach to segmentation is to define a set of delimiter words (e.g., "and" or "then"), using them to obtain the atomic instructions in a step. For example:

```
enter user admin and password admin01
  and click login
```

This naïve approach would result in the steps `enter user admin`, `password admin0`, and `click login`. But note the second step: it does not include an action verb, so it is not atomic. We could determine that the action is "enter" by inspecting the previous step, but this introduces dependencies on previous actions in the test.

We decided to avoid such backward dependencies by an alternative criteria based on action verbs instead of delimiter words. The action verbs in the example step are "enter" (applied to two input fields) and "click" (applied to a button). These two action verbs map to the atomic instructions `enter user admin and password admin0`, and `click login`. Note that these steps are atomic, and that atomic steps might denote more than one action (although they include only one action verb). This new criteria complicates the naïve segmentation strategy: separator words like "and" will not always be delimiters. Simply looking for delimiter tokens is no longer a reliable strategy for segmentation.

Sentence chunking [1] (also known as shallow parsing) is a technique for assigning labels to tokens in a text, typically used to divide text into syntactically related non-overlapping groups of words. Sentence chunking is a well known problem in the natural language processing community (see the CoNLL-2000 shared task [22]), and there are several solutions to it. If we use special labels to delimit atomic instructions in composite steps, then we can reduce the decomposition problem to sentence chunking with these labels. A convenient form for such delimiter labels is the BIO tagging scheme [15]. Under this scheme, a token either starts a step, is inside, or outside an atomic step. So we only need three tags: *B-CMD*, *I-CMD* and *O*, respectively. The example instruction should be chunked like this:

```
enter             B-CMD
LABEL(user)       I-CMD
admin             I-CMD
and               I-CMD
LABEL(password)   I-CMD
admin01           I-CMD
and               O
click             B-CMD
login             I-CMD
```

Notice the labels for the "and" tokens: the first one is *inside* an atomic action, since `password admin01` is not an atomic step. But the second one is a delimiter for the two atomic instructions in the composite step.

Step Annotation

The previous stage transformed a possibly composite test step into a sequence of atomic instructions. In order to derive (A, T, D) tuples from an atomic step, we must identify the regions corresponding to the action, targets and additional data in the step. For that purpose, we will annotate atomic steps using again sentence chunking. But this time, we will have a richer set of labels. From analysis of a comprehensive set of manual steps written by professional testers, we decided to use the following labels:

- *ACT*: action part of the step
- *TGT*: target part of the step
- *VAL*: data part of the step, if any
- *LOC*: location information, explains how to reach a target
- *DSC*: description of step's intention or effect, usually not useful for computing tuples.

The following instruction exemplifies how we annotate test steps:

```
In the LABEL(Sender Data) tab,
enter anonymous in the LABEL(name) textbox
for anonymous feedback
```

Note that this step is atomic, as it features a single action (enter some text). This is the labeling we expect to obtain:

```
In                    B-LOC
the                   I-LOC
LABEL(Sender Data)    I-LOC
tab                   I-LOC
,                     O
enter                 B-ACT
anonymous             B-VAL
in                    O
the                   B-TGT
LABEL(name)           I-TGT
textbox               I-TGT
for                   B-DSC
anonymous             I-DSC
feedback              I-DSC
```

We have the `enter` token marked as the action, and `the name textbox` as the target. We also have a value to enter in the text box, `anonymous`. Finally, we identify location information (the target is in the `Sender Data tab`), and a verbose explanation of the instruction's intent.

Tuple Generation

Having a sequence of annotated atomic steps, we have to derive a set of tuples from this data. Based on the output obtained from the step annotation stage, we discovered that the following rules suffice to generate tuples from an annotated step:

1. *Single target*: generate a single tuple.
2. *Multiple targets, no values*: distribute the action across the targets, generating as many tuples as targets in the step.
3. *Multiple (target,value) pairs*: generate a tuple for every target; using the corresponding value as the data component of the tuple.

The first option is the trivial case. With a single target, we only need to group it with the action and any data (i.e., a value chunk) present in the step. For example, for the step `click ok` the resulting tuple will be (***click***, *ok*, •).

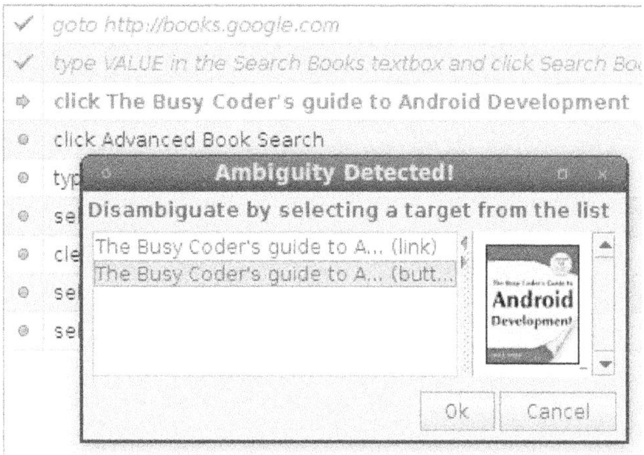

Figure 5. Disambiguation dialog

Rule 2 refers to steps with multiple targets and no data, such as `click remember me and login`. In this case we distribute the action across all the available targets, to get (***click***, *remember me*, •) and (***click***, *login*, •).

When we find a sequence of targets, some or all of them paired with a following data region, it means that we are processing a multiple data entry step. Instructions to fill in a form follow usually follow this pattern. For example:

```
enter
  first name as John,
  last name as Doe
```

According to rule 3, we generate one tuple for each (target, value) pair in the instructions. That gives us the tuples (***enter***, *first name*, *John*) and (***enter***, *last name*, *Doe*).

These three rules define how to map a single action plus multiple targets and values to a sequence of tuples. What about location regions? They specify spatial relations that help to locate targets. The two relations that we identify are containment (for example, `click the ok button inside the checkout tab`) and relative placement (for example, `click the search button next to the settings link`).

Containment relations result in an extra tuple to select the target's container before performing an action on the target. For the containment example above, we will obtain the tuples (***click***, *checkout tab*, •) and (***click***, *ok button*, •). The first tuple ensures the container for the "ok" button has focus, while the second one performs the intended "click" action on the "ok" button.

Relative placement relations can be useful for avoiding ambiguity. If we had two buttons with label "b", one next to a panel "p" and another besides a panel "q", we could say `click the b button next to panel p` to unambiguously refer to the first one. At the expense of requiring user intervention due to ambiguities that could have been avoided otherwise, we are still not using relative placement relations in our tuple extraction algorithm. Processing relative placement information so we can reduce target ambiguity is a topic for future work.

TUPLE INTERPRETATION

After converting a step into its intermediate representation, we must interpret the resulting tuples against the application under test. Our tuple interpretation algorithm is defined by the following pseudo-code:

```
procedure interpret (st, s, (A, T, D)):
  es ← {e ∈ st | label(st, e) = T.l ∧
                 (T.t = • ∨ T.t = type(e))}
  if |es| = ∅
    error ("Invalid tuple")
  if |es| > 1
    es ← heuristicDisamb (es, (A, T, D))
  if |es| > 1
    (e, s') ← userDisamb (es, s)
  else
    e ← the only element in es
    s' ← s
  st' ← apply ((A, T, D), e)
  return (st', s')
```

Here, st is the current application state, s is the textual representation of the current step, and (A, T, D) is the tuple to interpret. We start by resolving the target denoted by T. For that, we collect the set es of all the available GUI elements from the application state for which the tuple applies. If es is empty, the tuple is invalid. If there are multiple candidate elements, we try to narrow down the set by a heuristic disambiguation procedure. If we still have multiple elements we ask for user disambiguation, using the user's choice to compute a new textual step s'. If user feedback was not required, s' will be equals to s. Once we compute the GUI element e denoted by T, we apply the tuple (A, T, D) to it, resulting in state st'. We return st' and the step s'.

The heuristic disambiguation procedure uses the (A, T, D) tuple to narrow down the candidate set to a single element. For example, if we have a tuple (***enter***, *Search*, *books*) and the candidates are an input field and a button, we must be referring to the former, since entering some text applies to input fields, not buttons. Hence, we can discard the button, ending up with a single candidate element.

If we still have multiple candidates, we ask the user to disambiguate. Our interpreter presents a dialog to the user with the list of candidate elements. Fig. 5 depicts the execution of a test doing a book search on a web application. The user is being asked to pick between the title or an image of the cover of the book for the instruction `click the Busy Coder's Guide to Android Development`. Once the user picks an alternative, the interpreter can proceed to apply the action to the user's selection. But equally important, the user's answer is used to compute a new test step s' reflecting the answer. In our example, if the user picks the link option, the step will be adjusted to `click the Busy Coder's Guide to Android Development` **`link`**.

SVM			CRF		
Prec.	Rec.	F_1	Prec.	Rec.	F_1
97.32	96.29	96.80	97.83	95.76	96.78

Table 1. Step segmentation results

Applying an (A, T, D) tuple to a GUI element e requires programmatically emulating the action A on e. For example, if $A =$ "click" we will generate a click event on e, and if $A =$ "type", we will set e's value to D. The set of available actions is the same as in CoScripter [13], plus synonyms for them (e.g., "press" for "click", or "type" and "fill in" for "enter").

EVALUATION

We conduct a series of experiments to analyze the effectiveness of the segmentation and annotation stages of our tuple extraction algorithm. We also determine how much label replacement contributes to step annotation, by repeating our experiments with the label replacement stage turned off. In addition, we measure how much user intervention our approach needs to create a fully automatable test.

Experiment 1: Step Segmentation

For this experiment, we used a corpus of 27 real world manual tests, written by professional testers. These tests comprise a total of 154 test steps. We manually annotated the test steps with the corresponding *CMD* and *O* labels, and trained two chunk annotators on this data: Yamcha[1] (based on Support Vector Machines [5], or SVM for short), and CRF++[2] (based on Conditional Random Fields [11], or CRF for short). We evaluated the resulting models using a 10 fold cross-validation experiment on the training data, calculating precision, recall, and the F_1 measure for each run.

We calculate precision P, recall R, and F_1 measure for a tag t as follows: let N be the number of occurrences of t in a test corpus, O the number of occurrences of t reported by an annotator, and C the number of true positives (i.e., the number of correct occurrences reported by the annotator). Then, $P = C/O$, $R = C/N$, and $F_1 = 2PR/(P + R)$.

In Table 1 we present the results for the 10 runs in the experiment. The training set includes 189 *CMD* regions. The SVM annotator found 187 regions, with 182 true positives. The CRF annotator found 185 regions, with 181 true positives. Both performances are practically the same, as the similar F_1 scores show.

Experiment 2: Step Annotation

We conducted two 10 fold cross-validations. One was on a training corpus consisting of the 182 atomic instructions correctly identified in the step segmentation experiment by the SVM annotator. The other was on a corpus of 200 atomic instructions, collected from the documentation of an industrial application server giving step by step instructions for several administrative tasks. We manually labeled both training corpora with *ACT*, *TGT*, *VAL*, *LOC* and *DSC* labels. As in step segmentation, we experimented with SVM and CRF-based chunking. We present precision, recall and F_1 for both chunkers in Table 2 and 3.

[1] `http://chasen.org/~taku/software/yamcha`
[2] `http://crfpp.sourceforge.net/`

	SVM			CRF		
	Prec.	Rec.	F_1	Prec.	Rec.	F_1
ACT	99.45	99.45	99.45	99.44	98.35	98.90
DSC	86.05	77.08	81.32	88.64	81.25	84.78
LOC	93.33	66.67	77.78	88.89	76.19	82.05
TGT	88.21	93.94	90.99	88.89	88.89	88.89
VAL	87.01	84.81	85.90	90.53	85.15	87.76
Total	91.65	91.98	91.81	92.65	90.16	91.39

Table 2. Step annotation (corpus #1)

	SVM			CRF		
	Prec.	Rec.	F_1	Prec.	Rec.	F_1
ACT	99.00	99.50	99.25	98.51	99.50	99.00
DSC	70.97	57.89	63.77	65.62	55.26	60.00
LOC	73.08	82.61	77.55	67.86	73.08	70.37
TGT	93.03	92.57	92.80	92.96	91.58	92.27
VAL	93.43	94.52	93.88	93.15	93.15	93.15
Total	93.06	92.02	92.54	92.13	91.28	91.71

Table 3. Step annotation (corpus #2)

On the first corpus, our SVM annotator correctly chunked 164 of the 182 atomic commands (90.11%). The CRF annotator correctly chunked 158 of 182 (86.81%). Overall results are similar in both cases. Individually, results are generally good for each region except location, which shows a low recall (66.67% with SVM chunking, and 76.19% with CRF). This means that we are missing approximately one third of the locations in the test corpus. Of all these missed location tokens, approximately 60% were mislabeled as targets. This happens because in some cases targets "take precedence" over locations. For token sequences of the form {*preposition*, "the", *LABEL*, *type*} (e.g., `in the save dialog`), the preposition is discarded (labeled as *O*), so the chunker sees a sequence denoting a target: {"the", *LABEL*, *type*}. We believe that the reason is that there are much more targets than location regions in our test corpus (the locator/target ratio is 0.092%), so our model lacks enough training to properly detect all location regions. We plan to continue our experiments with training data featuring a higher locator occurrence ratio.

Results are similar on the second corpus. The SVM annotator chunked correctly 183 out of 200 steps (91.5%); the CRF annotator 181 out of 200 (90.5%). The ratio of correctly annotated steps is above 91%; and precision, recall and F_1 measure are high for the *ACT*, *TGT*, and *VAL* labels. We are missing locations, which is reflected in low precision and recall for the *LOC* regions. Again, we are annotating some locations as targets: approximately 70% of the missed locations were misclassified as targets. Descriptions show a particularly low performance. Given that this corpus was extracted from a book, descriptions explaining instructions are very verbose in some cases, complicating their recognition.

	SVM			CRF		
	Prec.	Rec.	F_1	Prec.	Rec.	F_1
ACT	99.45	99.45	99.45	99.45	99.45	99.45
DSC	85.37	72.92	78.65	87.18	70.83	78.16
LOC	86.67	65.00	74.29	63.64	33.33	43.75
TGT	81.40	83.47	82.43	80.33	81.70	81.01
VAL	72.31	60.26	65.73	88.06	75.64	81.38
Total	86.79	83.87	85.30	87.92	83.87	85.84

Table 4. Step annotation, no label replacement (corpus #1)

	SVM			CRF		
	Prec.	Rec.	F_1	Prec.	Rec.	F_1
ACT	94.87	95.85	95.36	94.90	96.37	95.63
DSC	43.75	18.92	26.42	84.62	29.73	44.00
LOC	72.73	76.19	74.42	71.43	47.62	57.14
TGT	82.41	83.67	83.04	78.95	84.18	81.48
VAL	82.19	83.33	82.76	83.10	81.94	82.52
Total	85.54	82.76	84.13	83.10	81.94	82.52

Table 5. Step annotation, no label replacement (corpus #2)

Experiment 3: Contribution of Label Replacement

To get a measure of how much label replacement contributes to good performance in step annotation, we repeat the step annotation experiments, skipping the label replacement stage. We give the results from this experiment in Tables 4 and 5.

On the first corpus, the SVM annotator correctly chunked 141 of the 182 instructions (77.47%). The CRF annotator correctly chunked 144 of the 182 instructions (79.12%). As expected, the performance in target recognition dropped noticeably. We move from a F_1 around 90 with label replacement, to approximately 80 in this experiment.

We get similar results for the second corpus. The SVM annotator chunked correctly 153 of the total 200 instructions (79.27%); the CRF annotator chunked properly 155 of the total (77.50%). One noticeable result is the very low recall and precision we obtain for descriptions from both annotators. For the same reason as in the previous experiment, recognizing descriptions is challenging for book instructions, and even more in face of target labels, which can also be long chunks of tokens. Therefore, we conclude that label replacement significantly increases the performance of our tuple extraction algorithm.

Experiment 4: Interpreting Tuples

Our manual test automation procedure should keep user intervention low. Otherwise, it degrades to step by step execution or recording approaches. Our last experiment aims to find out how much user intervention is required in practice to execute a test. For this, we execute with our tuple interpreter the 164 (out of 182) correctly annotated steps obtained from our step annotation experiment on the first corpus.

We measure how many steps could be executed without user intervention, relative to the number of correctly annotated steps (i.e., 164) and also relative to the number of total atomic steps (i.e., 182). Table 6 summarizes the results. Out of the 164 properly annotated test steps, our system executed 129 (i.e., 78.66% of them) without any kind of user intervention. The remaining 35 steps referred to ambiguous targets that required user intervention in order to be executed. Relative to the total number of atomic steps, we could execute 70.88% of them without aid from the user.

Total test steps	182		
Properly labeled	164	(90.11%)	
	#	% properly labeled	% total
Executed	129	78.66%	70.88%

Table 6. Tuple execution without user intervention

Given the total 182 atomic instructions, our procedure correctly processed and executed 70.88% (more than two thirds) without any user intervention. And furthermore, user intervention will not be needed in future executions. Recording, on the other hand, would require executing all the steps in a test manually, one by one, before having a script that could be executed without user intervention. Our approach leads to the same results with one third of the work, and the resulting artifacts are more easily maintainable than the programs or scripts obtained with traditional recording.

DISCUSSION AND FUTURE WORK

Our approach requires users to transform a manual test into a value-free test by manually replacing values with variables. Although value replacement needs to be done only once, it still poses an overhead to the test automation process. But how much? Our corpus of 154 instructions required 49 replacements, roughly 1/3 of the instructions. We believe this overhead is acceptable for a do-only-once task. However, we would like to automate value replacement as much as possible.

Label replacement looks like an arbitrary stage. But besides normalizing seemingly different steps, replacing labels can help us to avoid tuple extraction mistakes. Consider the step `click Click Here and win an IPod`. This step just instructs the user to press a (suspicious) "Click Here and win an IPod" button. But this label will fool the segmentation stage, resulting in two tuples: (***click***, *Click Here*, •) and (***win***, *IPod*, •). By replacing this step's label we get `click LABEL(Click Here and win an IPod)`, from which we can extract the expected (***click***, *Click Here and win an IPod*, •) tuple.

Tuple extraction might deliver the wrong results occasionally. Our tuple extraction algorithm does not attempt to do error detection, instead we simply assume that extraction errors will surface at execution time. Our experiments show that this is the case. All the errors we found manifested as non-existent or ill-formed targets. Our interpreter is prepared to report inexistent targets as well as unrecognized actions (which besides an error, might signal that the action set needs to be extended). Although possible, we have not encountered steps wrongly converted to tuples denoting another valid or ambiguous instruction.

Our approach has a number of limitations that we plan to address in future work. The most immediate are:

- Processing arbitrary position relations (as in `click the activate checkbox in the 10th row`), and using such relations to adjust ambiguous test steps.
- Interpreting instructions not referring to actions on the GUI, such as verification steps.
- Handle high-level steps representing multiple actions without stating them explicitly (e.g., `add item to shopping cart`). There is work in this area that we plan to use as a starting point for this task [2].

In addition, we would like to add more variety to our training data, since writing styles can vary wildly among testers. The more and diverse the training data, the better our chunk annotators will handle such variance. We also plan to work on a more robust algorithm for label replacement, based on named entity recognition – despite being unlikely in practice, there are pathological cases that challenge label replacement, e.g., a step like `click the "click the"`. A similar entity recognition-based strategy could help to automate the value replacement stage as well.

RELATED WORK

Thummalapenta et al. [20] describe an approach for functional test automation based on brute force search. They implemented a heuristic procedure that tries all the possible interpretations of an instruction until one can be executed, backtracking in case of failure. But using heuristics can be problematic for tests including "unseen" instructions, since they will need to modify their heuristics in order to adapt to new cases. Our machine learning-based tuple extraction algorithm is easier to extend. We simply have to enrich our training set with new examples and retrain, without any need to modify our algorithm. We believe that the two approaches can be combined to get a more robust and easily extensible test automation system.

Lau et al. [12] experiment with 3 approaches (keyword, grammar and machine learning-based) to compute (A, T, D) tuples from a corpus of written how-to instructions. The corpus was obtained by crowdsourcing the task of writing how-to instructions on Amazon's Mechanical Turk. Our tuple extraction algorithm aims to solve the same problem, but with some important differences. Our algorithm utilizes domain knowledge about the application to identify labels in an instruction. In addition, we do step segmentation, while their work assume that how-to instructions are already segmented. Finally, we bridge the gap between tuple extraction and execution by providing an interactive tuple interpreter algorithm.

Branavan et al. [2] present a system to execute hand-written instructions. The salient feature of their work is the distinction between low-level and high-level instructions (i.e., instructions specifying a goal to achieve without explicitly stating all the required steps). The authors process low-level instructions by means of reinforcement learning, using a log-linear policy function to map instructions to actions. For high-level instructions, the authors map them into a sequence of low-level instructions by means of an extension to the original reinforcement learning model. Adopting these ideas for processing high-level instructions would be enormously beneficial to our approach. For example, we could process a high-level instruction like `login as Admin` by mapping it into the low-level steps `enter username Admin`, `enter password Admin`, and `click Login`.

Other authors also explore the use of machine learning techniques to process natural language navigation instructions. Chen and Mooney [4] discuss a system that transforms natural language directions into an executable plan. They use a corpus of (instruction, actions, world state) tuples to learn a parser translating instructions into navigation plans. Kollar et al. [10] present a system that follows natural language directions. They use conditional random fields [11] to derive a linguistic structure (spatial direction clauses) from a set of directions. Their system uses these spatial direction clauses to infer an optimal path in a map, according to a model based on the meaning of spatial prepositions. Shimizu [16] uses machine learning to chunk a sequence of instructions in natural language, inferring the action taken by each step from the chunk labels. This scheme is later improved by Shimizu and Haas [17], introducing the notion of "template" labels which can be parametrized with so-called slot fillers. In these two systems, the goal is to guide a robot to some destination. The domain of discourse is limited to moving straight to the end of a hallway, turning right or left, or entering some door. We rely on similar techniques for extracting tuples from a test step, but on a larger scale: we handle several kinds of actions and a broader variety of targets.

There is a large body of work proposing techniques for generating software artifacts from textual descriptions. Tichy et al. [21] argue that progress in natural language processing will leverage the construction of tools for deriving test cases, UML models and source code from natural language input. Fantechi at al. [7] utilizes natural language analysis to perform quality evaluation of use cases. Sinha et al. [19] present an engine for use case translation and analysis. This linguistic engine is used to implement Text2Test [18], a platform for authoring and verifying test cases.

The idea of interpreting manual tests described using natural language stems from CoScripter [13], a system for recording and automating actions taken on a web application. Our machinery for identifying labels in test steps and resolving targets at runtime is based on CoScripter's label finding algorithms and heuristics.

CONCLUSIONS

We presented an approach to functional test automation, consisting of an algorithm for extracting the actions denoted by a test step and an interpreter for executing such actions with user guidance. We performed a series of experiments on our prototype in order to quantify the effectiveness of our approach, as well as to analyze how much user intervention our approach requires in practice.

With an F_1 measure above 90% in the step segmentation and annotation stages, we believe that our tuple extraction algorithm can be useful in practice. Our last experiment shows that approximately 70% of the 182 test steps of our test corpus can be executed without user intervention. We think that these are good indicators of the feasibility and potential usefulness of our approach.

For many organizations manual functional testing is a nuisance they are used to, mainly because of the shortcomings in current tools for test automation. We believe that the contributions in this paper constitute a step towards improving current functional test automation technology.

ACKNOWLEDGMENTS
We thank S. Tummalapenta for his help and the anonymous reviewers for their insightful comments.

REFERENCES

1. Abney, S. P. Parsing by chunks. In *Principle-Based Parsing: Computation and Psycholinguistics* (1991), 257–278.
2. Branavan, S. R. K., Zettlemoyer, L. S., and Barzilay, R. Reading between the lines: learning to map high-level instructions to commands. In *Proc. of the 48th Annual Meeting of the Association for Computational Linguistics*, ACL '10 (2010), 1268–1277.
3. Brill, E. A simple rule-based part of speech tagger. In *Proc. of the third conference on Applied natural language processing*, ANLC '92 (1992), 152–155.
4. Chen, D. L., and Mooney, R. J. Learning to interpret natural language navigation instructions from observations. In *Proc. of the Twenty-Fifth AAAI Conference on Artificial Intelligence* (2011).
5. Cortes, C., and Vapnik, V. Support-vector networks. *Mach. Learn. 20* (1995), 273–297.
6. Dustin, E., Rashka, J., and Paul, J. *Automated software testing: introduction, management, and performance*. Addison-Wesley Longman Publishing Co., Inc., 1999.
7. Fantechi, A., Gnesi, S., Lami, G., and Maccari, A. Application of linguistic techniques for use case analysis. In *Proc. of the 10th Anniversary IEEE Joint intl. conf. on Requirements engineering*, RE '02 (2002), 157–164.
8. Gouveia, D., Davis, C., Saracevic, F., Bocarsly, J., Chirillo, D., and Quesada, L. *Software Test Engineering with IBM Rational Functional Tester: The Definitive Resource*. IBM Press, 2009.
9. Kit, E., and Finzi, S. *Software testing in the real world: improving the process*. ACM Press/Addison-Wesley Publishing Co., 1995.
10. Kollar, T., Tellex, S., Roy, D., and Roy, N. Toward understanding natural language directions. In *Proc. of the 5th ACM/IEEE intl. conf. on Human-robot interaction*, HRI '10 (2010), 259–266.
11. Lafferty, J. D., McCallum, A., and Pereira, F. C. N. Conditional random fields: Probabilistic models for segmenting and labeling sequence data. In *Proc. of the 18th intl. conf. on Machine learning*, ICML '01 (2001), 282–289.
12. Lau, T., Drews, C., and Nichols, J. Interpreting written how-to instructions. In *Proc. of the 21st intl. joint conf. on Artificial intelligence* (2009), 1433–1438.
13. Leshed, G., Haber, E. M., Matthews, T., and Lau, T. CoScripter: automating & sharing how-to knowledge in the enterprise. In *Proc. of the 25th annual SIGCHI conf. on Human factors in computing systems*, CHI '08 (2008), 1719–1728.
14. Manber, U., and Myers, G. Suffix arrays: a new method for on-line string searches. *SIAM J. Comput. 22* (1993), 935–948.
15. Ramshaw, L. A., and Marcus, M. P. Text chunking using transformation-based learning. In *Proc. of the Third Annual Workshop on Very Large Corpora* (1995), 82–94.
16. Shimizu, N. Semantic discourse segmentation and labeling for route instructions. In *Proc. of the 21st intl. conf. on Computational linguistics*, COLING ACL '06 (2006), 31–36.
17. Shimizu, N., and Haas, A. Learning to follow navigational route instructions. In *Proc. of the 21st intl. joint conf. on Artificial intelligence* (2009), 1488–1493.
18. Sinha, A., Jr., S. M. S., and Paradkar, A. Text2Test: Automated inspection of natural language use cases. In *Proc. of the 2010 3rd intl. conf. on Software Testing, Verification and Validation*, ICST '10 (2010), 155–164.
19. Sinha, A., Paradkar, A. M., Kumanan, P., and Boguraev, B. A linguistic analysis engine for natural language use case description and its application to dependability analysis in industrial use cases. In *DSN* (2009), 327–336.
20. Thummalapenta, S., Sinha, S., Mukherjee, D., and Chandra, S. Automating test automation. Tech. Rep. RI11015, IBM Research, 2011.
21. Tichy, W. F., and Koerner, S. J. Text to software: developing tools to close the gaps in software engineering. In *Proc. of the FSE/SDP workshop on Future of software engineering research*, FoSER '10 (2010), 379–384.
22. Tjong Kim Sang, E. F., and Buchholz, S. Introduction to the CoNLL-2000 shared task: chunking. In *Proc. of the 2nd workshop on Learning language in logic and the 4th conf. on Computational natural language learning - Volume 7*, ConLL '00 (2000), 127–132.

Lin-spiration: Using a Mixture of Spiral and Linear Layouts to Explore Time Series

Eduardo Graells
Web Research Group
Universitat Pompeu Fabra
Barcelona, Spain
egraells@yahoo-inc.com

Alejandro Jaimes
Yahoo! Research Barcelona
Barcelona, Spain
ajaimes@yahoo-inc.com

ABSTRACT
Time series data is pervasive in many domains and interactive visualization of such data is useful for a wide range of tasks including analysis and prediction. In spite of the importance of visualizing time series data and the fact that time series data is often easily interpretable, traditional approaches are either very simple and limited, or are aimed at domain experts. In this paper, we propose a novel interactive visualization paradigm for exploring and comparing multiple sets of time series data. In particular, we propose a focus+context approach, where a "focus" segment of a time series is zoomed into and visualized using a linear layout at one scale, while the remaining segments of the time series (i.e., the context) are visualized using spiral data layouts. Our paradigm allows the user to dynamically select and compare different sections of each time series independently, facilitating the exploration of time series data in a fun and engaging way.

Author Keywords
Visualization, Time Series, Visual Interfaces, Focus + Context

ACM Classification Keywords
H.5.2 Information Interfaces and Presentation: Miscellaneous

General Terms
Design, Human Factors

INTRODUCTION
A great number of datasets in a wide variety of application domains have a temporal component. For instance, all data obtained from sensors, and from activity logging on the web has *timestamps* associated with it. Time information plays a major role in many contexts, including economics, finance, environment analysis, medicine, and web activity among many others. Time series in these domains are in turn used for many purposes, such as trend analysis, forecasting, identification of cycles and seasonal effects, among others.

Research on visualization and visual analysis of time-series, however, has focused either on aiding domain experts via special tools, or in creating simple, but limited visualizations for non-expert users. In addition, in recent years, interactive visualization has gained importance, not just for specific data mining purposes, but also in popular, widely accessed on-line publications. Several news outlets, most notably The New York Times and The Guardian often feature special interactive visualization features on specific topics. Interest in fun, and informative visualizations is therefore increasing, and yet, there are many open research challenges.

Considering this context, we are working on creating interactive visualization paradigms that are useful and engaging, and potentially appealing to non-experts. Time-series data has enormous potential in narrative visualization, and is often easily interpretable by non-experts.

With these motivations, we present a new focus+context interaction paradigm to explore and compare one or more time-series, inspired by the current trends in narrative visualization and the need for interactive visualizations for non-experts. This interaction paradigm is called *Lin-spiration* because it presents a mixture of linear visualization, spiral visualizations and dynamic scrollbars to present the information in a visual way. Our main contributions can be summarized as follows:

1. The combination of spirals and linear layouts in visualization to provide an organic, engaging feel from the spiral interaction while providing the perceptual benefits of linear layouts.
2. The dynamic usage of different scales in the different parts of the layout, in order to enhance the focus+context nature of the interaction paradigm.

Our framework is general and can be applied to any type of time-series data. We use stock market data as an example in a prototype we have implemented which is easily embeddable in web pages, making it suitable for use in a variety of scenarios accessed by non-experts.

The rest of the paper is organized as follows. Section 2 briefly explains related work, Section 3 describes our design principles, and Section 4 describes our proposed interaction mechanisms. Section 5 discusses an example implementation, and conclusions and future work are discussed in Section 6.

RELATED WORK

The most common techniques to visualize time-series are line plots and area charts. Other techniques include *stacked graphs* [3], *horizon graphs* [5], among several others (see review by Aigner et al. [1]). Applications for analyzing, exploring, and mining time-series include VizTree by Lin et al. [7] and KronoMiner by Zhao et al. [12]. VizTree implements a decomposition of time-series in sequences that are displayed using trees (hence the name of the application). KronoMiner allows the user to select different ranges in one or more time-series, arrange those ranges in a radial tree layout, and perform diverse analytical operations in a visual and interactive way. Both applications are designed for expert users.

In visualization of time-series, spirals have been a popular choice because of their organic appearance and the potential of identification of periodic structures in the data, as shown by Weber et al. [11]. However, a problem that several authors, such as Lin et al. [7], have identified is that when the period of the time-series is unknown or the data isn't periodic, spirals are not effective.

Most focus+context time-series visualizations are made using *dual scale* charts, which are visualizations that use two different scales for different parts of the visualization: one scale for the focused part and another for the context part. Isenberg et al. [8] present a study on how different dual scale charts allow users to understand time-series. According to their results, the most useful chart is the *cut-out chart*, which outperformed the other charts in elementary graphical perception tasks. The cut-out chart presents two linear visualizations, one on top of the other, where one of them displays the full time-series and the other displays the focused time range.

An interesting trend in visualization research is narrative visualization, which aims at the use of visualization techniques as narrative device to tell a story. Segel and Heer [9] propose a taxonomy of techniques and approaches in narrative visualization and list 58 examples available on the Web. They define seven narrative visualization types (which can be combined) and two approaches: *reader-driven*, where the visualization is fully interactive, and *author-driven*, where the visualization is controlled automatically through a play button or by automatic startup.

Our proposed approach is different from previous work in that we combine the strengths of two paradigms, which, with additional interactive features, aim at providing rich functionality for interactively exploring and comparing time-series data. In particular, our approach benefits from the combination of a linear layout that zooms into a user-selected rage in the time-series, and the spiral layouts that represent the context that surrounds the focused range. Our approach combines different scales (for the linear and spiral components, respectively) following the principles of fisheye views by Furnas [4]. In addition, when the framework is used to compare multiple time series, each one has its own independent controls, allowing the user to compare different segments at multiple scales.

DESIGN PRINCIPLES

Traditional linear layout charts are very effective, but for large datasets the user has to constantly use scrollbars or similar interaction controls to examine data that falls outside of the viewing window. Typical scrollbars allow the user to know what part of the dataset he is exploring, and whether there is more data before and after that part. There is no information about the shape of the data outside of the viewing area, which creates a loss of context and makes it difficult for the user to decide which way to explore (e.g., left or right). In order to address these limitations, we defined the following design principles:

- Create a visualization that maintains context (i.e., avoid losing of "sight" of parts of the dataset).
- Encourage interaction with the data set by using multiple interactive controls.
- Clearly define which part of the visualization represents the focused data and which part represents the context.

In accordance to these principles, we propose a design that retains a linear visualization in the center, as a focused area that displays a certain rage of the dataset, and that is linked with two spirals, one at each side, that represent the context that surrounds the focused range (Figure 1). Since the context is clearly visible, the user can reason about it while focusing on an interesting range in the dataset. We emphasize this difference by applying a different time scale in the linear part than in the spiral parts: the linear part should display a small range of the data, while each turn in the spiral should display a wider period of time. Figure 2 shows a detailed view of this behavior.

Our design allows us to show different time-series in parallel, using a *small multiples* approach as described by Tufte [10], which means that, in the presence of multiple time-series, instead of plotting them together in a shared space, we plot them in parallel, splitting the space by the number of time-series. As result, in the linear part the different datasets are juxtaposed, and in the spiral parts, each datasets keeps following its own spiral path, without intersecting the others, as shown by Weber et al. [11] with their *parallel spirals*. We decided to use small multiples based on the results in perception of time-series by Javed et al. [6]. Their results indicate that split space techniques are better for dispersed discrimination tasks, typical in comparison of time-series, than shared space techniques.

This way of juxtaposing different time-series requires data-specific computations of the size of the spirals, in

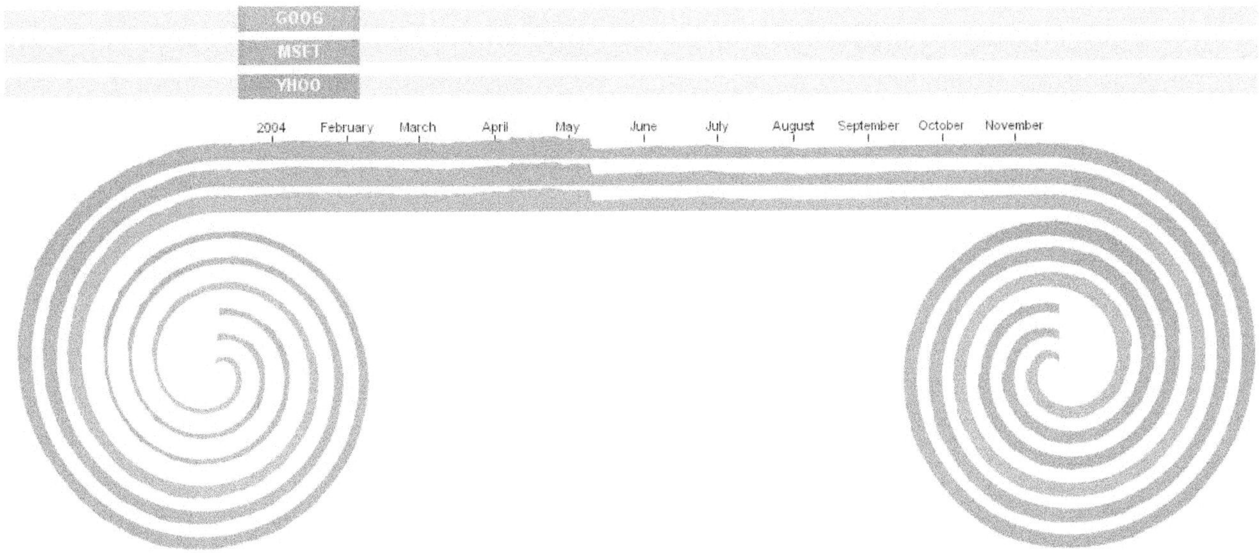

Figure 1. A prototype implementation of Lin-spiration. The linear part shows the focused area of the data, while the spiral parts shows the context. Note that the horizontal scale for the linear part is different from the scale of the spirals, and the horizontal sliders at the top indicate the segment that is "zoomed in" by the linear section of the visualization. The user can set each of the two selections independently and the visualization changes dynamically, allowing the user to compare different segments of the time series at different scales.

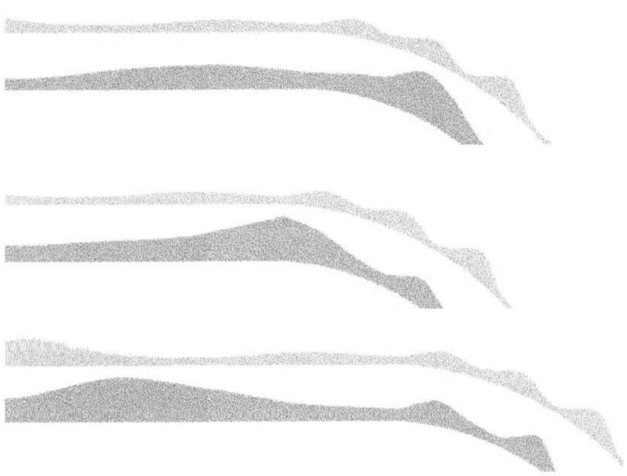

Figure 2. Detail of differences in time scale between linear and spiral sections of the visualization. The context, displayed using spirals, has a time scale in which time is condensed in comparison to the linear part. In the top pair of data streams, a bump is visible in the lower data segment. Note how that bump in the lower two pairs is shifted to the left, and note that the scale of the bump is different. In this particular example, the user has scrolled the lower time series to the left, while keeping the top time series fixed.

particular their max radius and the number of cycles that the visualization of the dataset should have in each spiral. Depending on those values, the visualization will have a blank space below the linear part, which can be used to display details on demand about the focused part of the dataset or event about a specific point in time selected by the mouse pointer.

The system considers an optional intelligent component based on time-series analysis, such as Fourier transform, to determine: *a)* interesting time ranges for the focused and context parts, *b)* the number of cycles for each spiral, and *c)* whether to use the same height scaling for all the time-series being visualized, which should be useful for volume comparison, or a normalized scaling in each one, which should be useful to explore trends.

INTERACTION MECHANISMS

The presence of typical scrollbars indicates to the user that there is something to interact with. Taking advantage of this, we extend the scrollbar controls to indicate the selected (i.e., "focused") range, as shown on Figure 3 in the top image. Thus, the user can move or modify the range and see how the visualization updates. Changing of the range by moving either the left or right selection edges, creates a re-scaling of the data. In traditional linear visualization, the user would simply see the time series shift left or right, but not re-scale. We believe this interaction control motivates exploration, because it gives the user a joyful interaction with the dataset, where a visual effect denotes the entrance and exit into the focused area because the elements that change from a spiral part to a linear one, and the other way around, are re-scaled.

When two or more time series are juxtaposed, for each dataset there is a different scrollbar with its own range. Each range spans the same period of time, and the user is able to move one or more ranges simultaneously. It is possible to move only one range first, and then move the others, to create a fixed separation within different datasets, which can be helpful in the comparison of cross-correlated time-series. We also support the variation of the scale in the selected time range as depicted on Figure 3.

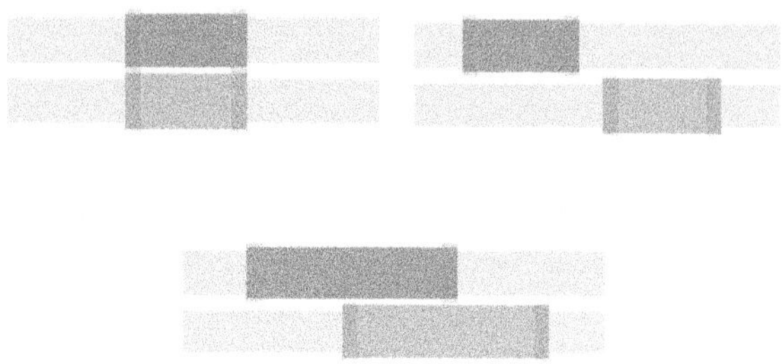

Figure 3. Three different ways to interact with the scrollbars. Each scrollbar has a movable slider that represents the focused time range. The top left image shows the default state of the scrollbars, where both focus the same time-range. The top right image shows that one scrollbar can be moved independently from the other. The bottom image shows that is possible to enlarge or decrease the focused time range.

IMPLEMENTATION

One of our goals is to use this interface inside embedded widgets in web sites to support narrative visualization. For this purpose, we have built a prototype using Javascript and SVG. We use the D3 library by Bostock et al. [2].

In order to test Lin-spiration, we present an example of the exploration of stock data, retrieved from Yahoo! Finance. We have retrieved stock data for three stock symbols, shown on Figure 1. We display a range of one year for the linear part and one year for each spiral cycle, displaying two cycles in each spiral. A focused time-period is displayed over the linear part. In the example we are searching for drops in the closing value for each stock during the year. We have found a significant drop in the three stocks at the same day in one year. This is an opportunity to fix the position for one or two stocks and search for another similar price drop in another date. This example can be used in a narrative visualization context to compliment a set of news articles about the related companies.

Since the example time-series spans several years, our prototype helps the user focus on one month to make the comparison between trends in different time periods. A direct benefit of our interaction paradigm is that users can quickly identify, by looking at the spirals, one or more sections of large differences between the time-series, and quickly zoom-in/move to those dates to examine the data in detail.

CONCLUSIONS AND FUTURE WORK

We presented *Lin-spiration*, a novel interaction paradigm, which defines a focus+context approach to explore and interact with time-series, based on linear and spiral layouts of visualizations juxtaposed in parallel along with horizontal sliders to interact with the visualizations. This interaction paradigm is aimed at narrative visualizations and designed for non-expert users. We implemented this paradigm in a prototype to compare trends in stock data. We believe that this is an initial step into building a framework of novel visualizations, interfaces and interaction mechanisms to support narrative visualization in a more engaging way than current approaches.

Future work includes user studies with defined tasks and different configurations to evaluate the framework in comparison with traditional approaches in a similar way to the work of Isenberg et al. [8]. The evaluation should include an analysis of the interaction mechanisms, scaling techniques, and will determine the engaging qualities of the proposed approach, possibly using eye and mouse tracking.

ACKNOWLEDGEMENTS

The authors thank the anonymous reviewers for their comments that helped to improve this paper. This work was partially funded by Grant TIN2009-14560-C03-01 of the Ministry of Science and Innovation of Spain.

REFERENCES

1. Wolfgang Aigner, Silvia Miksch, Wolfgang Müller, Heidrun Schumann, and Christian Tominski. Visual methods for analyzing time-oriented data. *IEEE Transactions on Visualization and Computer Graphics*, 14:47–60, January 2008.
2. Michael Bostock, Vadim Ogievetsky, and Jeffrey Heer. D3: Data-driven documents. *IEEE Trans. Visualization & Comp. Graphics (Proc. InfoVis)*, 2011.
3. Lee Byron and Martin Wattenberg. Stacked graphs – geometry & aesthetics. *IEEE Transactions on Visualization and Computer Graphics*, 14:1245–1252, November 2008.
4. G. W. Furnas. Generalized fisheye views. In *Proceedings of the SIGCHI conference on Human factors in computing systems*, CHI '86, pages 16–23, New York, NY, USA, 1986. ACM.
5. Jeffrey Heer, Nicholas Kong, and Maneesh Agrawala. Sizing the horizon: The effects of chart size and layering on the graphical perception of time series visualizations. In *ACM Human Factors in Computing Systems (CHI)*, 2009.
6. Waqas Javed, Bryan McDonnel, and Niklas Elmqvist. Graphical perception of multiple time series. *IEEE Transactions on Visualization and Computer Graphics*, 16:927–934, November 2010.
7. J. Lin, E. Keogh, and S. Lonardi. Visualizing and discovering non-trivial patterns in large time series databases. *Information visualization*, 4(2):61, 2005.
8. Petra Isenberg and Anastasia Bezerianos and Pierre Dragicevic and Jean-Daniel Fekete. A Study on Dual-Scale Data Charts. *Transactions on Visualization and Computer Graphics*, 17(12):24692478, December 2011.
9. Edward Segel and Jeffrey Heer. Narrative visualization: Telling stories with data. *IEEE Transactions on Visualization and Computer Graphics*, 16:1139–1148, November 2010.
10. Edward R. Tufte. *The visual display of quantitative information*. Graphics Press, Cheshire, CT, USA, 1986.
11. M. Weber, M. Alexa, and W. Müller. Visualizing time-series on spirals. In *Infovis*, page 7. Published by the IEEE Computer Society, 2001.
12. Jian Zhao, Fanny Chevalier, and Ravin Balakrishnan. Kronominer: using multi-foci navigation for the visual exploration of time-series data. In *Proceedings of the 2011 annual conference on Human factors in computing systems*, CHI '11, pages 1737–1746, New York, NY, USA, 2011. ACM.

Intelligent Pairing Assistant for Air Operation Centers

Jeremy Ludwig
Stottler Henke Associates
San Mateo, CA
Ludwig@stottlerhenke.com

Eric Geiselman
Air Force Research Laboratory
Dayton, OH
Eric.Geiselman@wpafb.af.mil

ABSTRACT
Within an Air Operations Center (AOC), planners make crucial decisions to create the air plan for any given day. They are expected to complete the plan in part by pairing targeting or collection tasks with the available platforms. Any assistance these planners can acquire to help create the plan in a timely manner would make the entire process more efficient and effective. This paper describes the Intelligent Pairing Assistant (IPA) prototype, which would provide pairing recommendations at specific decision points in the planning process. IPA is designed as a plug-in for software systems already in use within AOCs. The primary contribution described in this paper is the application of existing research in intelligent user interfaces to a novel domain.

Author Keywords
Air operations center, intelligent user interface, reinforcement learning, pairing.

ACM Classification Keywords
H.4.1. Office Automation: Workflow management

INTRODUCTION
The role of an Air Operation Center (AOC) in the United States Air Force is to provide command and control of air operations. Simply put, the AOC receives a high-level description of tasks and effects and generates a plan of how to best execute them. Within an AOC, planners make crucial decisions to create the overall air plan for any given day. They are expected to complete the plan in a limited amount of time, in part by pairing collection or targeting tasks with the available platforms and weapons. Any assistance these planners, especially the less experienced ones, can obtain to help create the air plan in a timely manner would make the entire process more effective.

One major challenge is in orchestrating the target list; designing packages to strike more than one target at a time makes efficient use of resources and improves survivability. Making the best use of available resources presents another challenge. For instance, rather than assigning a unmanned aerial vehicle to a collection task, it may be more expedient to further task a manned aircraft that is already operating in the area. Hurried human planners often overlook opportunities to take advantage of relationships between tasks.

IUI'12, February 14–17, 2012, Lisbon, Portugal.
Copyright 2012 ACM 978-1-4503-1048-2/12/02...$10.00.

The idea behind the Intelligent Pairing Assistant (IPA) is to help AOC planners make more efficient and effective use of resources. One existing system allows planners to use a "wizard" system to walk through the planning process. This system helps focus the user on particular parts of the user interface for different planning decisions. However, there is still a wide array of possibilities within each wizard page. The prototype framework illustrates how data already contained in the existing planning system would be used to make *recommendations* to planners in the context of a particular wizard page. That is, IPA provides an intelligent user interface that highlights preferred decisions and certain types of optimizations in order to assist planners in making efficient and effective decisions. Given the potential consequences of these decisions, attempting to foster trust in the recommendations is an important part of the interface. The prototype framework also illustrates how planners can enter *annotations* to specific items on the target and collection lists. This allows planners to associate information not already available electronically with a task, which can be used to help refine the recommendations supplied by the pairing assistant.

The remainder of the introduction is devoted to describing related work. In the next section we identify requirements for IPA. Following this are descriptions of the interface and implementation of the IPA prototype. Next is a section on the annotation interface. The conclusion summarizes this paper and outlines directions for future work.

Related Work
The work described in this paper relies heavily on existing research. This includes representing expert knowledge [e.g. 4], interactive/adaptive recommendation systems [1, 3, 6, 10], and especially research in the area of building trust in recommendation systems [2, 5, 7, 8, 9, 11, 12]. The primary contribution described in this paper is the application of prior research in these areas to a novel domain.

RECOMMENDATION REQUIREMENTS
As stated previously, one of the challenges facing IPA is to build trust within the AOC planning community. Several of the system-level requirements stem directly from attempts to address this challenge. First, the model used to make recommendations needs to be in a human-readable format and small enough that a human could understand it [8].

This requirement was used as a guideline throughout the prototype with an emphasis on maintaining simplicity. Second, an explanation facility needs to be incorporated into the user interface so planners understand why recommendations were made [2, 5, 7, 8, 9, 11, 12]. Third, the interface should be responsive to the planner and adjust recommendations based on implicit and explicit feedback [10]. Fourth, the user should have the chance to verify any decisions made as a result of recommendations [7].

The design of the user interface should also take into account existing guidelines for recommendation systems [6]. These guidelines include limiting the number of recommendations, which ensures that they are relevant to the decision being made, and that at least some of the recommendations are "good". Based on these guidelines, we developed two additional requirements for the recommendation table: fifth, the recommendations need to be limited in number, and sixth, recommendations with little utility should not be shown at all.

USER INTERFACE FOR RECOMMENDATIONS

The IPA prototype illustrates how IPA would function as a plug-in to an existing wizard-based planning toolkit. The wizard walks users through the planning process via a number of customized screens that expose only the relevant portion of the tool to the planner as they go about fulfilling planning requests. Generally, IPA is an unobtrusive toolbar that resides on the bottom of the screen. When recommendations are available on the current wizard page, the user can bring up a panel that displays the recommendation interface.

The recommendation interface is based on a common table that displays recommendations created by IPA in a similar format across recommendation types for different decision points. An example table is shown in Figure 1. The beginning and ending columns are always the same, with the intervening columns specific to the particular decision being made. The remainder of this section includes details on the recommendation table and on providing explanations and making user of user feedback.

The first column contains the accept/reject buttons. If accept was clicked, the existing AOC software would be expected to be updated with the actions associated with the selected recommendation, the text color turn green, and the buttons become grayed out, as shown in the first row. At this point, the planner could look at the proposed decisions in the existing AOC to verify the result. If reject were clicked, the recommendation would be removed from the table and the user given a chance to explain the rejection by selecting one of a number of available options from a list. Accepting/rejecting will adjust future recommendations even if no explicit feedback is given, by adjusting the relative ranking given to the recommendations. Explicit rejection will be used to manually improve the model

The second to last column is the relative ranking of the recommendations. This is presented to the user as a value of 1 (best), 2, or 3 (worst) in order to maintain similarity to existing priority ranking within AOCs. Note that while relative rank is always seen as 1, 2, or 3, recommendations are sorted based on the actual rank. Therefore, a recommendation with rank of 1.25 would appear before one with 1.33, even though they both appear to have a rank of "1" to the planner. Recommendations with a rank > 3 (significant negative feedback) would not be displayed in the table at all, and those with a rank < 1 (positive feedback) would be shown as having a 1.

The last column is the explanation for the recommendation. This is an English description of the rule or rules that fired to create the recommendation. The point of the explanation column is to allow the user to quickly scan the rationale behind each of the recommendations. The explanation column also includes popups that allow the user to quickly display the complete explanation when it is too large for the table area. Currently, the form of popup interaction is click to show, click to release, though other options would be investigated as part of future work. Ideally, most of the time, the planner should be able to see all of the recommendations and all of the explanations simultaneously. Based on the length of actual explanations in a deployed system, and the expected number of recommendations, we may adjust row height, column width, etc. to minimize the situations in which popups are needed.

DEVELOPING RECOMMENDATIONS

This section describes our investigation into the technology responsible for creating and ordering recommendations. Two particular areas were investigated. The first is knowledge representation – how to represent the state of the world and subject matter expertise in making pairing

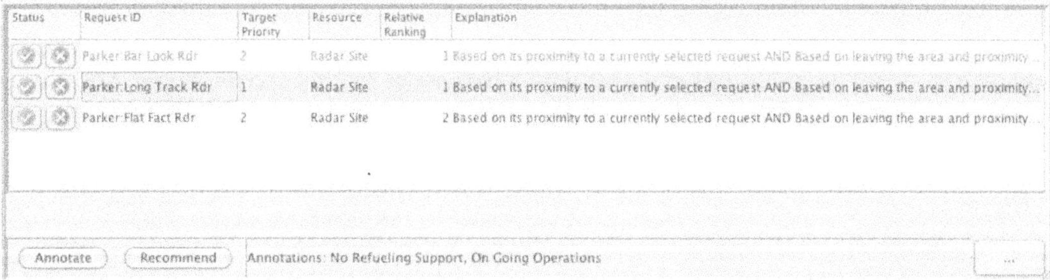

Figure 1. IPA recommendation table. The columns headers in this recommendation example are: Status, Request ID, Target Priority, Resource, Relative Ranking, and Explanation.

decisions. The second is developing the feedback algorithm, which empowers individual planners by allowing them to alter the shape of future recommendations.

Knowledge Representation

The reasoning engine is the system that is responsible for creating recommendations by applying a model of expert knowledge to a data model that contains all of the required details of the current planning problem (collection list, resources, weather, etc.). For this project, we decided to use the representation of production (IF-THEN) rules to meet the project requirements:

- Sufficiently powerful to represent decision policies, while still allowing for efficient inference.
- Can be used to provide clear explanations to the user about the rationale behind decision-making.
- Can be verified by subject matter experts prior to deployment. This is especially true in the case of IPA, where the problem is divided into a number of non-interacting rule-bases for specific decision points, and each individual rule-base will contain a relatively small number of rules.
- Can be created manually (working with subject matter experts) or be learned (from compiled knowledge).

As part of the prototype research effort, we modeled a small portion of the rules developed by subject matter experts using the commercial off-the-shelf Jess rule-based reasoning engine (http://www.jessrules.com). The main aspects of the prototype are: a simple data model created in Java, rules created in Jess, running the Jess engine to generate recommendations, and finally, gathering recommendations and supplying them to the user interface. Each recommendation also includes a simple explanation that is constructed by the rules that create the recommendation.

Influencing Recommendations based on User Feedback

In the user interface, the planner will have three options with a provided recommendation: ignore, accept, and reject. Each of these options provides feedback that will be used to adjust the ranking of recommendations, which will in turn affect the ordering and visibility of recommendations in the user interface. Additionally, one of the requirements is that the planner needs to see that their feedback is being used quickly and correctly, in order to help build trust in the recommendations made by IPA. The rank-updating algorithm is designed to respond quickly to feedback, with a goal that the recommendations from a rule should stop being displayed after only three rejections (three strikes and it is out).

Ranking of recommendations is performed by associating weights with the rules that are used to create the recommendations. If only one rule creates a recommendation, then its relative rank is equal to the weight of the rule. In cases where more than one rule is responsible for a recommendation, the recommendations relative rank is determined by averaging the weights of the associated rules.

The approach we took to learning how to adjust the weights associated with rules based on the user's feedback falls into the category of reinforcement learning problems [13]. The proposed algorithm for rule weight update is $V(a) = V(a) + r$, where $V(a)$ is the value associated with a particular rule, a, and r is the positive or negative feedback given by the user based on the reward function. The initial $V(a)$ is 1, the minimum -3 (performing well), and the maximum 5 (performing poorly) This algorithm is designed to be easy to understand relative to the 1-2-3 ranking already used in AOCs, maintain responsiveness to user feedback and support the desired three strikes functionality.

The amount and direction of the reward r is:

1. (Accept recommendation.) Set $r \leftarrow -1$
2. (Reject recommendation without detailed feedback.) Set $r \leftarrow +1$
3. (Reject recommendation with detailed feedback.) Set $r \leftarrow +0.75$
4. (Implied rejection.) Set $r \leftarrow +0.25$

Accepting a recommendation improves the ranking of associated rules (lower is better) while rejection for no reason decrements the ranking by the same amount. If a recommendation is rejected for a particular reason, the associated rules are decremented by a lesser amount, with the idea that they may be generally useful even if they were rejected in this particular context. Finally, an implied rejection occurs when a recommendation is selected that has a worse ranking than another recommendation that was not selected.

ANNOTATION INTERFACE

A second objective of the prototype was to identify how additional information associated with targeting and collection tasks, the "why" behind planning decisions, could be captured. This is information that is not currently available in a computer-friendly format but is required to make good decisions. That is, IPA needs to allow the planner to quickly encode information they might have received verbally, from online chat discussion, or from Word / PowerPoint documents so that the pairing assistant can provide the best possible recommendations.

Figure 2 shows the annotation interface implemented in the prototype, where the actual annotation names and categories have been replaced with placeholders. The interface is designed to be quick and easy to use, with a small number of annotations (less than 50) divided across a set of tabs with familiar names that form distinct categories. In most cases, the planner needs only to check the appropriate boxes to indicate the annotation. Based on the results of our knowledge engineering efforts, this relatively simple interface should be able to cover a majority of the needs usually associated with a task. Additionally, the prototype supports a flexible system that allows planners to

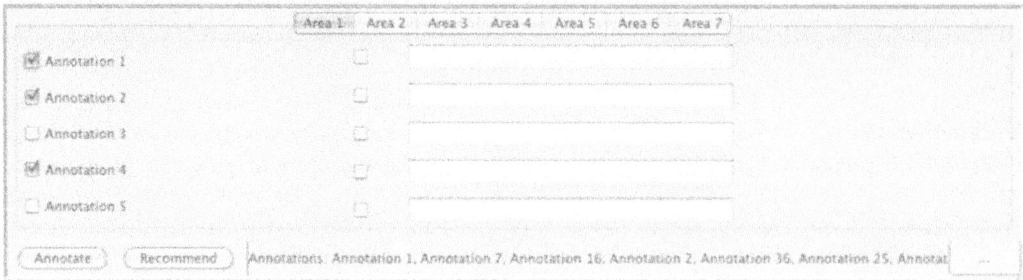

Figure 2. Annotation interface. The annotation categories are browsed via tabs (top) while the annotations themselves are selected via checkboxes. A summary of the selected annotations is shown along the bottom, even when the annotation pane is not visible.

suggest new annotations by typing in new annotation names. These new annotations would be recorded and could be used in future recommendation rules.

CONCLUSION

To summarize, this paper presents a prototype of an Intelligent Pairing Assistant designed to allow planners in Air Operations Centers to complete their jobs more efficiently and effectively. We describe the requirements that were developed, the underlying technologies and algorithms, and the assistive user interface.

As this work is in a preliminary state, there is significant future work starting to get underway on nearly every aspect of the system; for example: performing additional knowledge engineering, adding more flexible explanation capabilities, and meeting the technical challenge of integrating the developed system with the actual AOC system. Significant research questions and technical challenges that were not addressed in the prototype exist in each of these areas.

ACKNOWLEDGMENTS

We would like to thank Todd Cloutier, Drew Decker Donald Hulten, Bart Presnell, Beverly Sanford, and Milt Waddell. This material is based upon work supported by the United States Air Force Research Laboratory under Contract No. FA8650-10-M-6082. The views, opinions, and/or findings contained in this article/presentation are those of the author/presenter and should not be interpreted as representing the official views or policies, either expressed or implied, of the AFRL. DISTRIBUTION STATEMENT A: Approved for Public Release, Distribution Unlimited

REFERENCES

1. Adomavicius, G. Toward the next generation of recommender systems: A survey of the state-of-the-art and possible extensions. *IEEE Transactions on Knowledge and Data Engineering 17,* 6, 734–749.
2. Arnold, V., Clark, N., Collier, P.A., Leech, S.A., & Sutton, S.G. The Differential Use and Effect of Knowledge-Based System Explanations in Novice and Expert Judgment Decisions. *MIS Quarterly, 30*, 1 (March 2006), 79-97.
3. Berry, P., Donneau-Golencer, T., Duong, K., Gervasio, M., Peintner, B., & Yorke-Smith, N. Evaluating user-adaptive systems: Lessons from experiences with a personalized meeting scheduling assistant, in *Proceedings of IAAI'09* (Pasadena CA, July 2009), AAI Press.
4. Buchanan, B. and Shortcliffe, E. *Rule-Based Expert Systems: The Mycin Experiments of the Stanford Heuristic Programming Project*. Addison Wesley Publishing Company, Reading MA, 1984.
5. Ehrlich, K., Kirk, S.E., Patterson, J., Rasmussen, J.C., Ross, S.I., & Gruen, D.M. Taking advice from intelligent systems: the double-edged sword of explanations. In *Proceedings of IUI '11* (Palo Alto CA, Feb 2011), ACM Press, 125-134.
6. Gervasio, M.T., Moffitt, M.D., Pollak, M.E., Taylor, J.M., & Uribe, T.E. Active preference learning for personalized calendar scheduling assistance, in *Proceedings of IUI '05* (San Diego CA, Jan 2005), ACM Press.
7. Glass, A., McGuinness, D.L., & Wolverton, M. Toward establishing trust in adaptive agents. In *Proceedings of IUI '08* (Gran Canaria, Canary Islands, Spain, Jan 2008), ACM Press, 227-236.
8. Fleischmann, K.R. and Wallace, W.A. A covenant with transparency: opening the black box of models. *Commun. ACM 48*, 5 (May 2005), 93-97.
9. Gregor, S. and Benbasat, I. Explanations From Intelligent Systems: Theoretical Foundations and Implications for Practice. *MIS Quarterly 23*, 4 (December 1999), 497_530.
10. Langley, P. User modeling in adaptive interfaces. In *Proceedings of UM '99* (Banff, Canada, June 1999), Springer Wien, 357–370.
11. Lim, B.Y., Dey, A.K., & Avrahami, D., Why and why not explanations improve the intelligibility of context-aware intelligent systems. In *Proceedings of CHI '09* (Boston MA, April 2009), ACM Press, 2119-2128.
12. Pu, P. and Chen, L. Trust building with explanation interfaces. In *Proceedings of IUI '06* (Sydney, Australia, Jan-Feb 2006), ACM Press, 93-100.
13. Sutton, R. and Barto, A, *Reinforcement Learning: An Introduction*. MIT Press, Cambridge MA, 1998.

CAVIAR: A Vibrotactile Device for Accessible Reaching

Sina Bahram, Arpan Chakraborty, Robert St. Amant
Department of Computer Science
North Carolina State University
sbahram | achakra | stamant@ncsu.edu

ABSTRACT
CAVIAR is designed to aid people with vision impairment in locating, identifying, and acquiring objects in their peripersonal space. A mobile phone, worn on the chest, captures video in front of the user; the computer vision component locates the user's hand and objects in the video stream. The auditory component informs the user about the presence of objects. On user confirmation, the reaching component sends signals to vibrotactile actuators on the user's wristband, guiding the hand to a specific object. This paper describes an end-to-end prototype of CAVIAR and its formative evaluation.

ACM Classification Keywords
H5.2 [Information interfaces and presentation]: User Interfaces. - Haptic I/O.

Author Keywords
Mobile, haptic, tactile, accessibility.

INTRODUCTION
The Computer-vision Assisted Vibrotactile Interface for Accessible Reaching (CAVIAR) is a wearable tactile system designed to aid people with vision impairment (PWVI) in locating, identifying, and acquiring objects in their peripersonal space (i.e., the space within their reach). The prototype relies on a mobile phone for video input/processing and a wristband with four vibrating actuators. The mobile phone processes video input to recognize objects within its field of view and makes these known to the user via audio. On voice command, directional guidance to a chosen object is given as a sequence of continuous signals to the actuators on the user's wristband. A brief scenario illustrates the use of CAVIAR.

The user is sitting at a work table, wearing a mobile phone in a harness on his chest (running CAVIAR*) and a wristband on his wrist. The phone's camera scans items on the desk. The phone informs the user of distinct objects it identifies. On user confirmation,* CAVIAR *sends vibrotactile signals using the wristband to guide the user's hand to the object.*

Work in this area—using modern technology to make the world more accessible to people with vision impairment—is important. Hundreds of thousands of PWVI live in the U.S. alone, and a lightweight, low-cost system like CAVIAR could significantly improve their lives. PWVI have strategies for retrieving nearby objects, relying on common sense knowledge about object locations, grid search techniques, and the sense of touch. But many modern objects are difficult to distinguish based on touch alone; consider a store display of DVDs or packaged food. Computer vision plus guidance techniques can provide useful missing information.

Researchers have developed wearable vibrotactile feedback systems for motor tasks (e.g. [3, 5]); CAVIAR shares some of the goals of such systems. We have implemented a prototype of CAVIAR, running on a mobile phone, with the following:

- *Communication:* Voice recognition, based on an existing online service, for issuing commands to the device and speech generation for system feedback.
- *Computer vision:* Object recognition from video on the phone and tracking of objects and the location of the hand.
- *Tactile guidance:* The wristband, with its vibrotactile actuators, and the embedded software to generate signals to guide the user's hand. The wristband is directed via bluetooth from a mobile phone or other similar device.

This paper focuses on the design and formative evaluation of the computer vision and tactile guidance capabilities of the prototype, tested as separate components from the integrated system. To identify relevant design parameters and estimates for their values, we have carried out a non-interactive study with a fixed camera and an interactive, single-participant study using video from an overhead camera. The vision component can locate objects with a Euclidean distance error of 6.1 cm, which is adequate for the constraints of the task. Guided, linear movement is possible, though speed varies across different conditions, ranging from about 7 to 20 cm/s. We find lower deviations from guided paths in rectilinear versus diagonal movements. For rectilinear movement, response times to vibrotactile signals average 700 ms for changes of direction and 300 ms for stopping at a target location. These formative findings were influential on the development of CAVIAR.

SYSTEM
In CAVIAR, a wristband with small coin-type vibrators serves the purpose of generating continuous stimuli for guiding the user. The vibrators are governed by a microcontroller strapped

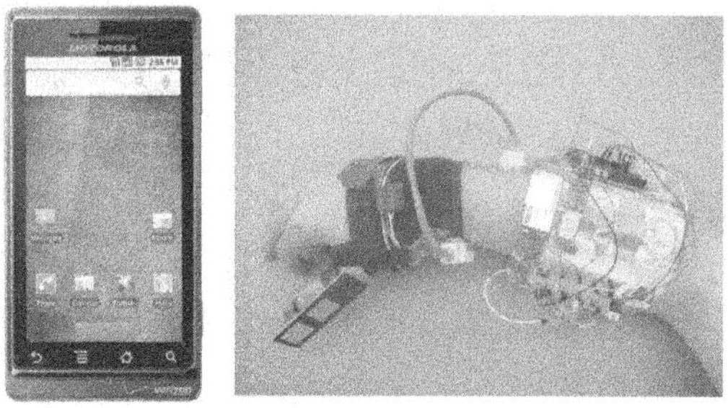

Figure 1. Mobile phone, wristband and controller

to the arm, which communicates with the phone over Bluetooth. These physical components are shown in Figure 1.

Computer vision

The vision component is a finite state machine for image processing and supporting functions. A master controller receives frames from the phone's camera, dispatches them to other appropriate components, and orchestrates user interaction. It maintains a common data store. The other parts of the vision system are as follows.

Calibration. CAVIAR reasons about spatial quantities, which requires a calibration step to obtain real-world equivalents of information in the system's image space. Camera calibration techniques exist for robust computation of parameters [2], e.g., to to use a planar pattern with distinctive features on it, such as a chessboard, and compute the intrinsic and extrinsic camera parameters from different views of the pattern.

In CAVIAR, two colored squares are placed a known distance apart on the thumb. The centroids of the two detected squares are used in lieu of absolute points. The known and observed distances between these two points (in pixels) can be used to obtain a relative measure of the distance from the hand to the phone's camera. This information, along with the assumption that a table-top surface is flat and level with the ground, lets us compute the vertical distance of the camera's line of view from the table's surface. We assume that the camera's line of view is parallel to the surface.

Formally, if the projection of a real point $\vec{p}$ on a plane surface S is a point $\vec{p'}$ on the image plane, and $\vec{O}$ is the focal point of the camera, then the $\vec{p}$ is the point of intersection of the line L (passing through $\vec{O}$ and $\vec{p'}$) and plane S. Any two-dimensional plane S can be characterized by a point $\vec{p_0}$ lying in it and a unit normal vector $\hat{n_s}$, such that all points $\vec{p}$ lying in the plane satisfy the equation:

$$(\vec{p} - \vec{p_0}) \cdot \hat{n_s} = 0$$

Similarly, the equation for a line L passing through two points, say $\vec{O}$ and another point $\vec{p}$ is

$$\vec{p} = d \cdot \widehat{n_l} + \vec{O}.$$

Here d is the Euclidean distance between $\vec{O}$ and $\vec{p}$, and $\widehat{n_l}$ is the unit vector representing the direction of L. Given any point $\vec{p'}$ on the line, $\widehat{n_l}$ can be computed as

$$\widehat{n_l} = \frac{\vec{p'} - \vec{O}}{\left|\vec{p'} - \vec{O}\right|}.$$

Given the observed separation between the two calibration points on the image plane r_{obs} and the known real separation r_{real}, d can be estimated as $k \times r_{real}/r_{obs}$, where k is a constant of proportionality. Following that, the intersection point $\vec{p}$ is simply $\vec{p} = d \cdot \widehat{n_l} + \vec{O}$. If $\vec{O}$ is taken to be the origin, then the vertical coordinate of $\vec{p}$ is the distance between the line of view of the camera and the surface, or in other words, how far the table-top is below the phone's camera.

Target Acquisition. This component integrates speech recognition, robust object detection, and affine-invariant recognition. Target acquisition is simplified by a smoothed background model and detection of foreground regions associated with changes over time. These regions are analyzed to extract colored connected components to detect object boundaries.

Hand Location and Tracking. Locating a familiar object is much more straightforward than detecting unknowns. There are several techniques for detecting known objects that usually require some form of limited training. In our current prototype, the user's hand is located simply by performing a template match to look for a known marker. We re-use one of the squares from the calibration stage for this purpose. The user gets appropriate messages via the speech output system to know what is to be done at different points of time. In this case, the user needs to keep his hand in view. Once the user's hand is located, we extract the color histogram of the region where the marker is present, and use that as our primary observation for tracking. At each frame processed from then on, we essentially look for image regions with the same histogram composition and find the most likely current position. This process is optimized by the position filtering component.

Position Filtering. Tracking can be enhanced if we have a model for the expected movement of objects. We use a particle filter to smooth out the information generated by the tracking step, which can be quite noisy. We initialize several *particles* in and around the initial location of the marker. The positions of these particles are predicted using the limited motion model and updated using observations made from the frames being processed. Each of these particles is then weighed by the similarity of a histogram extracted around it to the initial object histogram. The weighted sum of the particles' position is used as the current position of the object. Resampling is done as necessary when particle locations degenerate. The detected hand location is then transformed into world coordinates using the transformation parameters from calibration.

The Wristband

The CAVIAR wristband has four 10mm shaftless vibrating motors. Each is connected via an NPN 2N3904 transistor and a 1K Ohm resistor to its own pin on an Arduino board. The wristband puts the vibrating motors in contact with the center of the dorsal (top), ventral (bottom/palm), inner and outer

Figure 2. Two experiment environments

lateral sides of the wrist. Assuming that the reaching is carried out with the palm of the hand facing downward, the vibrations felt by the user map to the direction indicated by the system: the wristband can signal movement to the right or left (which we'll refer to as the x axis) and forward or backward (the z axis); activation of two adjacent motors signals a diagonal movement. These conventions help reduce cognitive load in translating vibrotactile feedback to hand movement. PWVI need their hands, especially their fingers, for exploration and interaction with their environment. A wristband does not restrict or prevent movement of the fingers. Justification for wristband guidance can also be found in models of movement in HCI: the hand defines a frame of reference and dominates the effectiveness of movement. Unfortunately, it is known [1] that the sensitivity that the user may receive from the four quadrant regions of the wrist, as discussed above, is much less than in areas such as the knuckles or other parts of the hand closer to the fingers and fingertips; nevertheless wristbands are still commonly used in vibrotactile systems (e.g. [4]). This issue is explored below.

EVALUATION

Our formative evaluation covered two areas: computer vision for object localization and interaction with the wristband.

Computer vision

Figure 2, left, shows the camera, mounted on a tripod, and a sampling of objects within its field of view. This experimental set-up more closely approximates the intended use of the system. For a set of objects, a marker standing in for the hand was used for calibration, in particular to establish the distance of the surface. Other objects for testing included an iPhone, a coffee mug, a water bottle, and a pair of scissors.

In the coordinate system of the camera, the line of sight is parallel to the surface, with the x^+ axis to the right, y^+ down, and z^+ directly away from the camera. In this work, we are interested in estimates of z and x values for objects; however, CAVIAR is not limited to this plane for operation. We tested the computer vision component by comparing estimated locations against the actual measured locations of 18 objects, treated singly. Three cases resulted in failure due to image segmentation. Figure 3 diagrams the estimated locations of the remaining objects (shown as filled circles) with arrows pointing to actual locations.

The mean error in Euclidean distance for successful cases is 6.1 cm (in Manhattan distance, 8.1 cm), which can clearly be improved. Manhattan distance is provided because of its importance when discussing rectalinear cardinal directions without diagnal supercardinal directions. Estimation errors are due to two main sources. In some cases only the upper part of an object was captured; in other cases, shadows and other lighting effects influenced estimation. These problems are well-understood, if not completely resolved, in the computer vision literature, and we expect to improve these results.

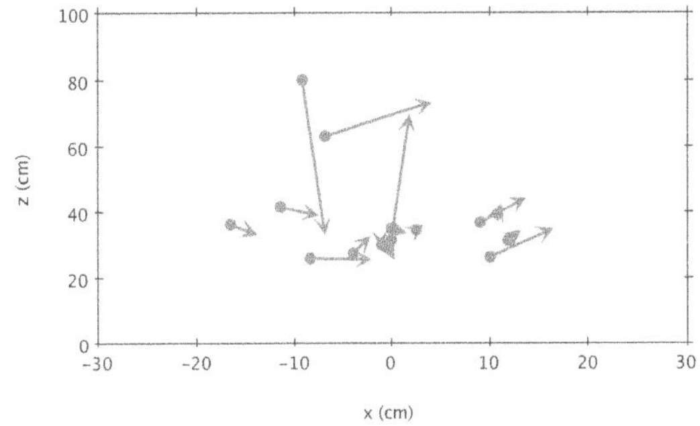

Figure 3. Object location estimates

Interaction

A set of interaction studies was carried out with a PWVI, one of the authors of this paper, acting as the single participant. An overhead camera tracked a visual marker on the wristband; Figure 2, right, shows the camera view. All signals during the experiment were based on processing of video data from the camera, as was the computation of user performance metrics after the experiment. The target of the movement was a virtual object, a square 24×24 pixels (6.4 cm) in size. A trial was completed when overlap is detected between the wristband marker and the target.

Our initial experimentation was with a beacon approach. The participant was instructed to treat the wristband as a beacon sending signals to move in any of the cardinal directions or diagonals, with the signalled direction changing based on the location of the hand relative to the target. Figure 4 shows the movement of the hand in one representative trial. The green dot indicates the starting point, the red square in the dotted circle the target. The pattern in the movement indicates that a beacon approach is impractical. A stair-stepping pattern and many movement irregularities can be seen; one 18-second trial involved over a dozen changes in direction. The problems are error from so many direction changes, and higher frustration and cognitive load.

Through further experimentation we developed a refined approach for guidance. The separation between the current location of the hand and the target is decomposed into its rectilinear components, and the components are reduced in alternation: first the x direction, then z, then x, and so forth. Movement in a given direction is continuously signaled until the system detects that a threshold distance from the target has been passed, and then the alternate direction is signaled. Alternation is also triggered when excessive movement away from the target is detected in the non-signaled direction. This approach effectively eliminated stair-stepping.

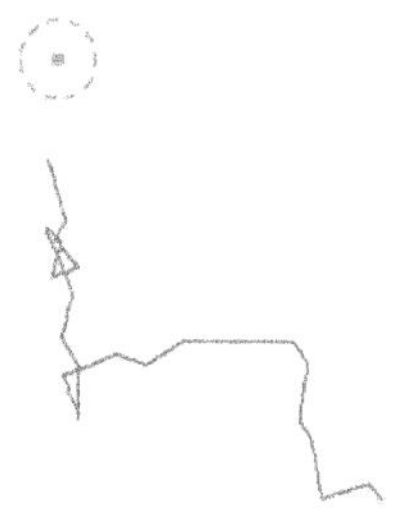

Figure 4. Sample path traversal, beacon guidance

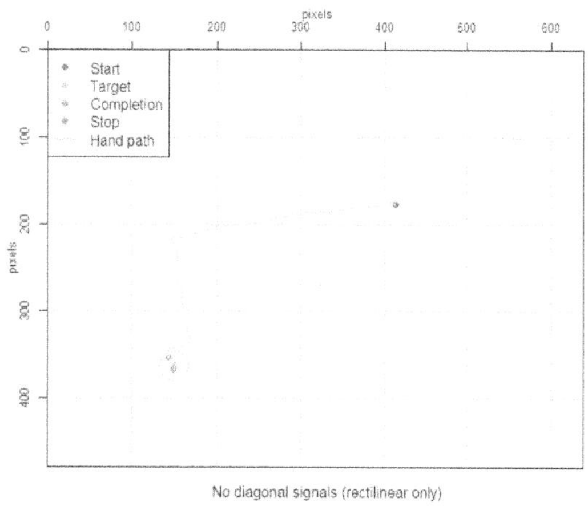

Figure 5. Sample path traversal, iterative reduction guidance

We ran a study in which the participant moved his hand to a virtual target, in two blocks. In the *Rectilinear* block, only rectilinear movements were signaled; in the *Diagonal* block, diagonal signals were also included. The participant carried out 100 trials in the Rectilinear block and 50 trials in the Diagonal block. Distances ranged from 27 to 103 cm, with a mean of 52 cm. Trial duration ranged from 516 ms to 41 s, with a mean of 12 s. Camera tracking failed in four of the Rectilinear trials and two of the Diagonal trials; the remaining trials contained only one diagonal failure to reach the target.

The resulting interaction was much improved. Figure 5 shows a representative path in a Rectilinear trial. The blue dot shows the start of a movement, the pink dot the point at which a stopping signal was issued, and the red dot overshoot. Statistics are shown in Table 1, the top row for the Rectilinear block and the bottom row for the Diagonal trials. T_{change} shows the response time to a signal for a new direction. T_{end} is the interval between a signal to stop and the actual stopping of the hand; *Over* is the distance moved (overshoot) during that time. $Speed_i$ is the instantaneous speed along the path followed by the hand. Dev_a is the instantaneous angular deviation from the signalled direction, *#Ch* the mean number of changes in direction signaled, and *Miss* the percentage of those signals for which a response was not detected (via $Deviation_a$). The new guidance strategy produced fewer directional changes and was much easier to follow.

T_{change}	T_{end}	*Over*	$Speed_i$	Dev_a	*#Ch*	*Miss*
0.691s	0.303s	1.6cm	6.7cm/s	26.0°	1.84	13%
0.969s	0.375s	3.2cm	8.2cm/s	45.7°	1.38	11%

Table 1. Study movement characteristics

Our formative evaluation suggests guidelines for future development: rectilinear signals show shorter response times, smaller overshoot, and lower deviation. We attribute the differences to lower cognitive effort for interpreting signals in the Rectilinear block and a subtle form of vibrotactile masking: Diagonal and Rectilinear signals can overlap in the actuators they use, which delays the recognition of a signal change. Diagonal speed is 20% higher than straight speed, surprisingly; in principle, diagonal movement also results in shorter paths. The higher speed does not entirely account for the increase in overshoot, however.

Our work suggests that movement with vibrotactile guidance is feasible. Speed of movement is variable, even for a single user, with single sessions under different conditions varying between 6 and 18 cm/s. Response times are also variable, but higher for changes of direction than for stopping. These numbers change with practice, and individual differences will doubtless appear in more extensive experiments, but the results give us preliminary guidelines for the use of CAVIAR. Narrow corridors of movement are impractical and movement along rectilinear paths appears to be more reliable than movement along diagonals. If CAVIAR is to support movement to targets while avoiding obstacles, its signals must be predictive, given the speed of movement and delays in response to signal changes. Prediction of movement at least 300 ms into the future appears to be a reasonable requirement for CAVIAR. Qualitative feedback indicates that CAVIAR is workable, though not quite ready for practical application.

ACKNOWLEDGMENTS

This work was supported by a gift from Google.

REFERENCES

1. K.S. Hale and K.M. Stanney. Deriving haptic design guidelines from human physiological, psychophysical, and neurological foundations. *Computer Graphics and Applications*, 24(2):33–39, 2004.
2. R. Hartley and A. Zisserman. *Multiple view geometry in computer vision*. Cambridge University Press, 2003.
3. J. Lieberman and C. Breazeal. Tikl: Development of a wearable vibrotactile feedback suit for improved human motor learning. *IEEE Transactions on Robotics*, 23(5):919–926, 2007.
4. M. Matscheko, A. Ferscha, A. Riener, and M. Lehner. Tactor placement in wrist worn wearables. In *Proceedings of the International Symposium on Wearable Computers (ISWC)*, pages 1–8, 2010.
5. J. Van Der Linden, E. Schoonderwaldt, and J. Bird. Good vibrations: Guiding body movements with vibrotactile feedback. In *Proceedings of the International Workshop on Physicality*, pages 13–18, 2009.

Clustering Web Pages to Facilitate Revisitation on Mobile Devices

Jie Liu **Chun Yu** **Wenchang Xu** **Yuanchun Shi**
Department of Computer Science and Technology, Tsinghua University,
Beijing, P.R. China
{liujiejesse, yc2pcg, wencxu}@gmail.com; shiyc@tsinghua.edu.cn

ABSTRACT
Due to small screens, inaccuracy of input and other limitations of mobile devices, revisitation of Web pages in mobile browsers takes more time than that in desktop browsers. In this paper, we propose a novel approach to facilitate revisitation. We designed AutoWeb, a system that clusters opened Web pages into different topics based on their contents. Users can quickly find a desired opened Web page by narrowing down the searching scope to a group of Web pages that share the same topic. Clustering accuracy is evaluated to be 92.4% and computing resource consumption was proved to be acceptable. A user study was conducted to explore user experience and how much AutoWeb facilitates revisitation. Results showed that AutoWeb could save up a significant time for revisitation and participants rated the system highly.

Author Keywords
Mobile Web, Clustering, Revisitation.

ACM Classification Keywords
H5.m. Information interfaces and presentation (e.g., HCI): Miscellaneous.

General Terms
Human Factors, Algorithms

INTRODUCTION
People spend more time surfing the Internet on mobile devices nowadays. However, user experience on mobile Web browsing is still affected by many factors, such as small screens and low CPU performance. Small screens make it difficult to get a normal view of what is displayed and also affect the accuracy of input via pen taps or direct finger touches. When users want to revisit an opened Web page among a large number of previous pages, they have to scroll the long history list vertically or horizontally to find the desired one, which makes the revisitation frustrating.

IUI'12, February 14–17, 2012, Lisbon, Portugal.

To facilitate revisitation, searching scope should be reduced. We can put opened Web pages into groups with different topics according to their contents. When a user wants to revisit a previous Web page, s/he can first choose the group with the related topic and then in this group find the target. The scope of searching is narrowed down greatly. In that case, revisitation becomes topic-specific that needs less scrolling and navigation changes from one layer to two layers.

If we simply apply classification to mobile browsers in the same way as desktop browsers [8, 12], users have to classify opened Web pages manually, which in turn increases the input complexity. Instead, classification can be performed by browsers themselves, which is clustering. As a result, we design AutoWeb (Figure 1) to cluster opened Web pages into different groups on their contents to facilitate the revisitation. In AutoWeb, at revisitation, users first step into Group Level to choose a group, and then in In-Group Level, find the desired Web page.

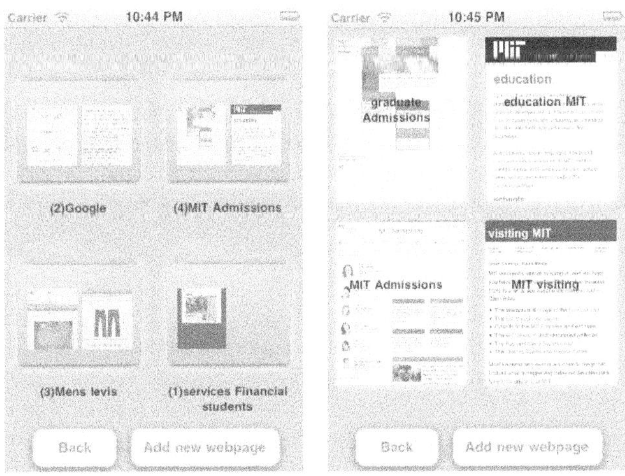

Figure 1. Revisitation in AutoWeb
(Left: Group Level, Web pages are clustered into groups. Right: In-Group Level, similar Web pages are in one group)

RELATED WORK
Various studies have been conducted to investigate mobile Web browsing and how to facilitate revisitation. We discuss them in both existing revisitation methods and clustering algorithms for Web pages.

Revisitation Methods

Usually, users resort to history lists, back buttons and bookmarks for revisitation. However, these tools can only help to revisit Web pages in a specific context [3, 7]. Many novel tools try to facilitate revisitation. Session Highlights [6] arranged Web page thumbnails in chronological order besides browser. Visual Snippets [11] presented a compact representation of Web pages to re-find previous pages. MacKay [8] and Wang [12] designed browser plugins to support multi-session tasks. Users manually managed tasks and Web pages.

Clustering Algorithms for Web Pages

Many algorithms have been proposed for clustering Web pages, such as link-based analysis algorithms, content-based analysis algorithms and usage-based algorithms. Link-based analysis algorithms use hyperlink information inside Web page source. If one page has a link to another page, these algorithms infer that these two Web pages are relevant to each other. But linkage information cannot show the sematic meaning of Web pages [5]. Content-based analysis algorithms use information retrieval methods to extract keywords from a set of Web pages and figure out the similarity among them. It is more accurate than the link-based analysis algorithms [9]. We use content-based analysis algorithm for clustering in AutoWeb.

AUTOWEB

We design AutoWeb to achieve the goal of facilitating revisitation for mobile browsing. In AutoWeb, we use two levels to represent opened Web pages. Group Level holds all groups of topics, and In-Group Level contains opened Web pages in each group sharing the same topic.

Considerations in Design

We choose iPhone as the platform. A recent report in May, 2011 reveals that iPhone tops first in mobile phones' network traffic in 10 out of 13 main countries [4]. Besides, it is easy for development using Xcode and distribution via App Store.

To help users identify Web pages quickly, an appropriate Web page representation is necessary. We use a hybrid way by combining thumbnails and text. Thumbnails give users visual cues and provide large touch areas for selection. Words used for clustering are also displayed on top of thumbnails to help users find the target. In Group Level, we use a folder as metaphor for a group of clustered Web pages. Smaller thumbnails also appear in the folder to indicate the content of this group.

As with the order of each opened Web page, we adopt the recency-based approach to sort groups and opened Web pages in each group. Recency is a strong reuse pattern when browsing the Web. It needs less cognitive effort when users search for newly visited sites on top of the list. When a Web page is loaded, a pop-up window will show the topic of this Web page for one second to give users first impression. It guide users match their mental models with clustering results during revisitation later on.

Clustering Algorithm in AutoWeb

Clustering is a computation intensive task. In consideration of limited computing resources on mobile phones, an efficient clustering algorithm is necessary.

We use vector-space model (VSM) to represent each Web page source as vectors in a multidimensional Euclidean space. The frequency of each word is counted. AutoWeb uses TF-IDF algorithm [1]. Term frequency $TF(d,t)$ is the number of times term t occurs in document d, which is $n(d,t)$. So, $TF(d,t) = \frac{n(d,t)}{\sum_{\tau} n(d,\tau)}$.

For Inverse document frequency $IDF(t)$, if D is the document collection and D_t is the set of documents containing t, $IDF(t) = \log \frac{|D|}{1+|D_t|}$.

Web page source is in a relatively structured format. HTML tags and metatags indicate different significance of terms. So we assign weights to them. Title, keywords and description in metatags weigh the highest. The first level headings have a medium weight, and bold words, headings in second level and below weigh the lowest. Hence, in vector space, the coordinate of document d in axis term t is given by $d_t = w_t TF(d,t) IDF(t)$, where w_t is the weight of t. Let $\vec{d}$ represent document d in vector space, then each Web page can be represented as $vec(d) = \{i : w_i TF(d,i) IDF(i)\}$.

After calculating TF-IDF value of an incoming Web page source, we apply single-pass incremental clustering to it. Although for each calculated Web page, its D and D_t may change by 1. This doesn't affect the clustering result greatly. So we don't re-calculate IDF values for the consideration of efficiency. The similarity of incoming Web page with existing pages in each cluster is computed. We calculate inter-document similarity $s(\vec{d_i}, \vec{d_j})$ using cosine measure, which is $s(\vec{d_i}, \vec{d_j}) = \frac{\vec{d_i} \bullet \vec{d_j}}{|\vec{d_i}||\vec{d_j}|}$.

If the similarity value is above a given threshold, this Web page belongs to this cluster. If more than one cluster pass the threshold, all these clusters will contain this Web page so as to increase the hit rate of revisitation. A new cluster will be created when no existing clusters go beyond the threshold.

Clustering Procedure

When users input a URL or touch a link, a request for a Web page is issued. After getting the requested Web page, AutoWeb extract Web source and parse it in several steps.

Figure 2 shows the detailed procedure of clustering. We parse the source for text components using Document Object Model (DOM). Given the limited computing resources on mobile phones, we choose the most significant parts of text components, which are titles, keywords, description, bold words and headings. We remove stop words in these components. Porter Stemming algorithm [10] is employed to map words to the same stem. Then we assigned different weights to different components and calculate TF-IDF values for each selected terms in this Web page. After single-pass clustering, results are stored and ready for revisitation. Users interact with the system by a designed UI as illustrated in Figure 1.

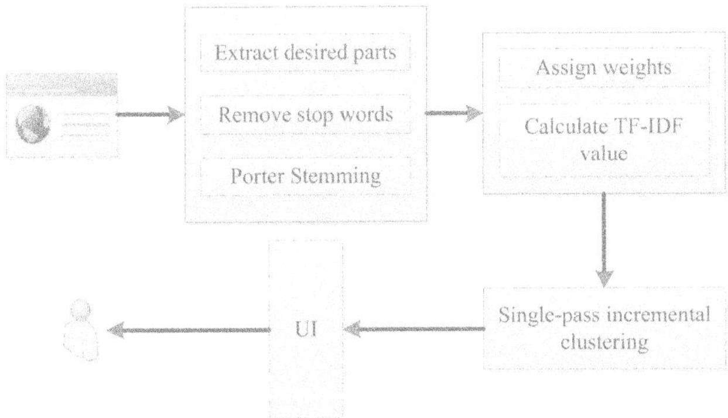

Figure 2. The Procedure of Clustering Web Pages

SYSTEM EVALUATION

We evaluated the system by processing Web pages related to four kinds of most frequent activities [2], that is *local services*, *travel*, *trivia* and *work/studies/hobbies*. We did these activities in AutoWeb with at least 50 related Web pages opened for each activity. We recorded the numbers of Web pages that were clustered into one correct group, more than one correct group, and wrong group. In the case that the Web page was clustered into several groups but not all these groups should hold this Web page, we considered it was clustered into wrong group.

Accuracy of Clustering

Figure 3 shows the results of evaluation. In every activity, about 80% of Web pages can be correctly clustered into one group of topic. Plus more than one correct group clustering, the accuracy is 92.4%. It also indicates that the kinds of activities don't exert a great influence on clustering accuracy. But, there are 7.6% of Web pages that were not placed into correct groups. We analyzed these Web page sources and found that they contained few feature words and less descriptive titles and headings, which were difficult for clustering. This is the drawback suffered by content-based analysis algorithms.

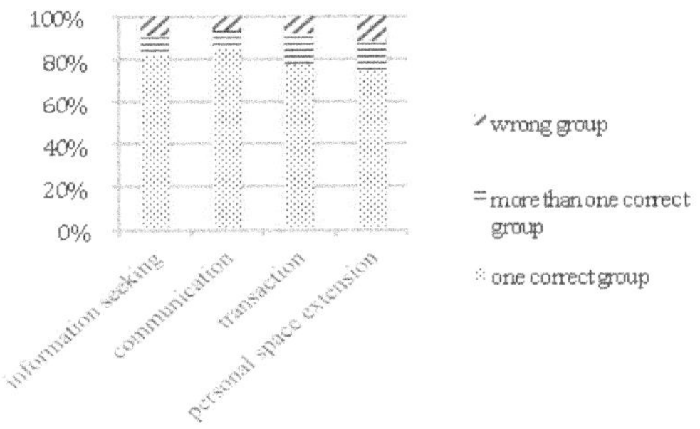

Figure 3. Clustering Accuracy in Each Activity

Computing Resources Consumption

We also validate the time and space consumption of AutoWeb. We use debug tool Instruments in Xcode to trace the memory usage at each load of Web pages. The elapsed time along with memory consumption is illustrated in Figure 4. In iPhone 3GS, time consumption is 119ms at the beginning and grow up to 181ms when 50 Web pages were opened. iPhone 4 has a faster CPU frequency so the time consumption started at 87ms and ended in 131ms. This latency isn't large enough to be noticed. At beginning, the system takes up 11300KB (11.0 MB) memory space and memory consumption increases with 80KB per Web page approximately. With 50 Web pages opened, the system used 15500KB (15.1MB) memory. So the system latency introduced by clustering and memory consumption of AutoWeb is acceptable.

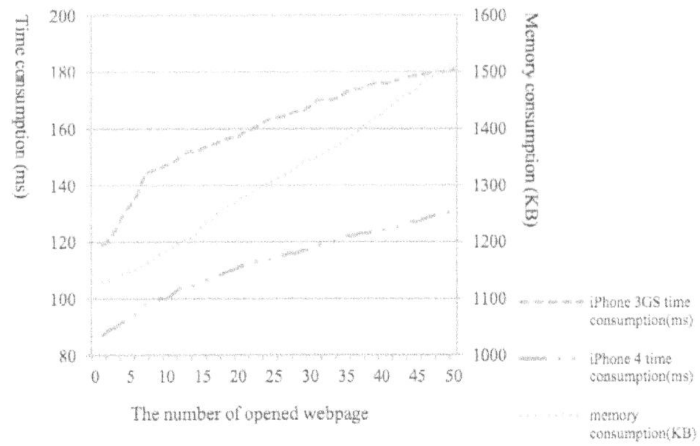

Figure 4. Time and Memory Consumption

USER STUDY

We compare AutoWeb with a conventional mobile browser called PlainWeb to log events. It only has back button and traditional history list for revisitation. We recruited 26 participants (9 females). Ages ranged from 21 to 32 years (*mean* = 22.4, *SD* = 4.5). They are active mobile Web users with iPhone. Before experiments, all participants were instructed how to use AutoWeb and PlainWeb. They practiced browsing Web pages with these browsers for at least half an hour until they got used to them.

To conduct the experiment in a controlled way, we designed three typical sets of tasks according to existing studies about mobile browsing content [2]. All participants fulfilled tasks using both AutoWeb and PlainWeb. 13 participants used AutoWeb first, and the others used PlainWeb first to receive counterbalanced results.

We investigate the average revisitation time in different tasks and browsers. The average revisitation time is the average time participants spent in re-finding each opened Web page. Figure 5 illustrated every participant's average revisitation time in two passes. There is a significant difference in AutoWeb and PlainWeb in terms of average revisitation time ($F(1, 24)=6.53$; $p<.001$). The result suggests that participants were able to revisit previous Web pages more quickly using AutoWeb. The average revisitation time of AutoWeb is 5.52sec (SD=.96sec), while the average revisitation time of PlainWeb is 7.83sec (SD=1.10sec). AutoWeb saves up to overall 29.5% revisitation time.

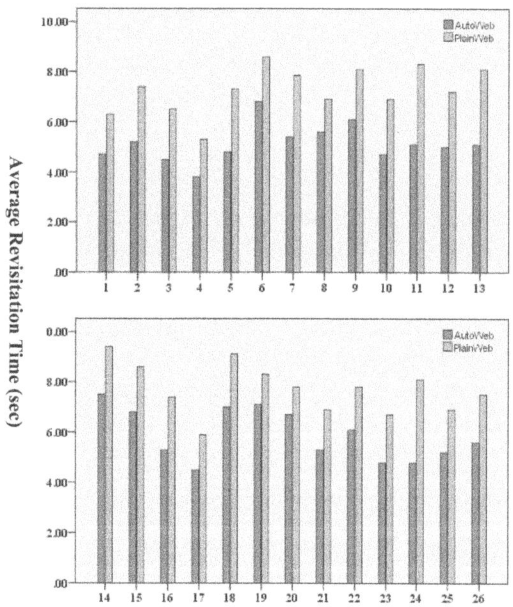

Figure 5. Average Revisitation Time for Each Participant

We also investigated participants' browsing experience with AutoWeb and PlainWeb. After finishing these three tasks, Participants filled out a questionnaire to rate AutoWeb and PlainWeb in a 5-point Likert scale.

As with ease of use, AutoWeb received an average rating of 4.13, while PlainWeb received 4.08. There is no obvious difference in ease of use between these two browsers. With the question, "Which browser do you like", AutoWeb received an average rating of 4.50, and PlainWeb receive 3.12. Mann-Whitney U Test show a significant differences between AutoWeb and PlainWeb (z=4.13, $p<.001$). It reveals that participant prefer AutoWeb.

CONCLUSION AND FUTURE WORK

Results presented in user study confirm that AutoWeb is easy to use and facilitates the revisitation for browsing mobile Web pages. AutoWeb introduces the concept of clustering according to Web topics into mobile browsers. This method proves effective and conducive to revisitation.

Future work includes adding the features that users can intervene in clustering process for more satisfactory results. Besides, a more extensive user study should be conducted.

ACKNOWLEDGEMENTS

This work is supported by National Natural Science Foundation of China, No. 61003005.

REFERENCES

1. Chakrabarti S. Mining the Web: Discovering Knowledge from Hypertext Data. 2002. pp. 56-57
2. Church, K., and Smyth, B. Understanding the Intent Behind Mobile Information Needs. In Proc. IUI 2009, pp. 247-256
3. Cockburn, A. and McKenzie, B. What do Web Users do? An Empirical Analysis of Web Use. In IJHCS, 2001(54), pp.903-922.
4. Device Essentials. http://www.comscore.com/Press_Events/Press_Releases/2011/6/comScore_Introduces_Device_Essentials
5. Dourisboure, Y., Geraci, F., et al. Extraction and classification of dense implicit communities in the Web graph. In ACM Trans. Web 2009;3(2)
6. Jhaveri, N. and Räihä, K. The Advantages of a Cross-Session Web Workspace. In Proc. CHI EA, 2005, pp. 1949-1952
7. Kellar, M., Watters, C. and Shepherd, M. A Goal-Based Classification of Web Information Tasks. In Proc. the American Society for Information Science and Technology, 2006, 43(1), pp. 1–22
8. MacKay, B. and Watters, C. Building support for multi-session tasks. In Proc. CHI 2009, pp. 4273-4278.
9. Nikolaev, K., Zudina, E., and Gorshkov. A. Combining anchor text categorization and graph analysis for paid link detection, In Proc. WWW 2009.
10. Porter, M., An algorithm for suffix stripping. 1980 http://tartarus.org/~martin/PorterStemmer/
11. Teevan, J., Cutrell, E.,et al. Visual Snippets: Summarizing Web Pages for Search and Revisitation. In Proc. CHI 2009, pp. 2023-2032.
12. Wang, Q., and Chang H. Multitasking Bar: Prototype and Evaluation of Introducing the Task Concept into a Browser, In Proc. CHI 2010, pp. 103-112

Out of the Bubble - Serendipitous Event Recommendations at an Urban Culture Festival

Andreas Forsblom[1,2], Petteri Nurmi[1,2], Pirkka Åman[2], Lassi Liikkanen[2]
[1] Helsinki Institute for Information Technology HIIT
PO Box 68, FI-00014 University of Helsinki, Finland
firstname.lastname@cs.helsinki.fi
[2] Helsinki Institute for Information Technology HIIT
PO Box 19800, FI-00076 Aalto University, Finland
firstname.lastname@hiit.fi

ABSTRACT
Advances in positioning technologies have resulted in a surge of location-based recommendation systems for mobile devices. A central challenge in these systems is to avoid the so-called filter bubble effect, i.e., that people are not only exposed to information that is in line with their personal ecosystem, but that they can also discover novel and otherwise interesting content. We present results from a field study of a mobile recommendation system that has been aimed to support serendipitous discovery of events at an urban culture festival. Results from the study indicate that suitably designed recommendations together with access to relevant external information sources can lead to serendipitous discovery of new content, such as new artists, bands or individual songs. Our results also indicate that proximity has little effect on the effectiveness of serendipitous recommendations.

Author Keywords
Mobile Recommendations, Serendipity, Urban Computing

ACM Classification Keywords
H.5.m. [Information Interfaces and Presentation (e.g. HCI)]: Miscellaneous; H.4.2. [Information Systems]: Information Systems Applications

General Terms
Human Factors, Experimentation

INTRODUCTION
Increased sensing capabilities of smartphones combined with advances in positioning technologies have resulted in a widespread interest in mobile recommender systems that tailor their content based on the user's current location, personal profile, activity or other situational factors; see, e.g., [1, 4, 7, 8]. A central challenge in these systems is how to avoid the so-called *filter bubble*[1], i.e., that people are only exposed to content that is in line with their personal ecosystem. Another major challenge is avoiding the *popularity bias*, i.e., that recommendations and consumption tend to concentrate on popular items instead of enabling people to easily find novel and serendipitous content [3]. To explore how mobile recommender systems can support serendipitous discovery in an urban context, we have developed Sounds of Helsinki (SoH), a novel mobile recommendation system. To evaluate the effectiveness of SoH in supporting serendipitous discovery, we have conducted a field study with 15 participants during an urban culture festival in Helsinki, Finland. In the study, SoH was used to recommend cultural events in the urban environment. The recommendations were augmented with additional media whenever possible. The results of the study demonstrate that suitably designed recommendations can lead to serendipitous discovery of new content, such as artists, bands or individual songs. As part of the study we also evaluated whether proximity to recommended events had an influence on the effectiveness or perceived relevance of the presented recommendations.

SOUNDS OF HELSINKI
Sounds of Helsinki is a mobile recommendation system for supporting serendipitous discovery of events in an urban environment. Sounds of Helsinki has been implemented following a client-server architecture. The server-side is responsible for generating event recommendations, managing event information and maintaining information about the location of the user. The server-side also acts as repository for any additional media that is available about the performers related to the events. The client-side of the system is web-based and operates in the browser of the mobile phone. The client-side additionally consists of a background script that periodically sends the GPS location of the user to the server. The script is also responsible for triggering notifications about new recommendations whenever they become available. The notifications are given using vibro-tactile feedback and playing an

[1] http://www.ted.com/talks/eli_pariser_beware_online_filter_bubbles.html

Figure 1. The user interface displaying part of a recommendation on a Nokia N900.

audio alert. To avoid unwanted disruptions, the notifications conform with the current profile of the client device.

The web based user interface is designed to run on a Nokia N900 smartphone, which has a 3.5" touch screen. The interface has two main views, a recommendation listing and an event view. The recommendation listing shows all of the user's recommendations in reverse chronological order, with previously unseen ones marked as new. This view is opened automatically by the client when a new recommendation becomes available. This view can also be opened manually at any time using a shortcut on the phone's desktop. The recommendations can be viewed by tapping on the corresponding item on the listing, which leads to the event view. The event view shows the name of the event and the performer(s), the address of the venue where the event takes place and distance from the user's current position, static maps centered on the user and on the event, and an overview map displaying both; see Fig. 1. In addition, the time and date of the event is shown. For recurring events, all future showings or performances are also listed. If the event is sold out, this is also indicated. For events that we were able to locate suitable media for, the event view enabled the user to listen to music samples of the artist, or to view embedded YouTube videos of the artist.

Sounds of Helsinki currently integrates two different recommendation techniques. Both recommendation techniques restrict the recommendations to events that take place during the current day and which have not yet started. We refer to the events satisfying these criteria as the *candidate pool*. Both recommendation techniques assign a weight w_i for each of the events i in the candidate pool C and select the event to recommend through weighted random sampling. The first technique, `RANDOM`, assigns uniform weights for all events in the candidate pool. The second technique, `LOCATION-BASED`, assigns the weight based on proximity to the event. Specifically, if d_i denotes the distance in kilometers to the event i from the user's current location, the `LOCATION-BASED` recommender uses $\exp(-d_i)$ as the weight of event i. As sold-out events would be associated with information about artists and potentially also with media, we did not filter out sold-out events from the candidate pool before generating recommendations.

FIELD STUDY

To evaluate the effectiveness of Sounds of Helsinki in supporting serendipitous discovery, we have conducted a field study during the Helsinki Festival 2011, a yearly cultural festival taking place in Helsinki, Finland. The duration of the festival is approximately two weeks, during which numerous cultural events, such as music, dance, cinema and theater performances take place at different locations throughout the city. For conducting the user evaluation, we recruited two groups of people that described themselves as active listeners of mobile music and avid event-goers. The participants were aged between 24 and 45. The first group ($N = 8$) participated in the study for two days, while the second group ($N = 7$) participated for three days that did not overlap with the days of the first group. The participants were provided with Nokia N900 smart phones equipped with prepaid SIM cards for the duration of the study, and they were rewarded with tickets to one of two selected events during the festival. The reward events were excluded from being recommended by our system.

To avoid disrupting participants during night or working hours, recommendations were only generated between 2 p.m. and 10 p.m. To preserve battery of the client device, GPS location updates were sent to the server at five minute intervals. The time between successive recommendations was randomly sampled between 40 and 80 minutes. The algorithm that was used to generate recommendations was chosen randomly each time a new recommendation was made. For each recommendation, the participant had the option of rating the recommendation using *thumbs up* and *thumbs down* buttons.

To supplement the thumbs up/down ratings, at the end of the field study we collected post-hoc survey responses. Specifically, for each participant, we replayed the event recommendations that were shown to him/her during the study. For each recommendation, the participant was asked to respond to a six item questionnaire that measured whether the participant saw the recommendation, how good and serendipitous the recommendation was, and whether the recommendation influenced the participant's behavior or not. The question items that were included were adapted from the user-centric recommendation evaluation framework proposed by Pu et al. [6]; see Table 1 for the items that were included in the questionnaire. Responses for all items were elicited using a 5-point Likert scale that was anchored at "completely disagree" (=1) and "completely agree" (=5). After completing the questionnaire for each event recommendation, the participant was asked to complete a ten item end-questionnaire measuring the overall usefulness of the system and its capability to support serendipity; see Table 2.

RESULTS

Events and Recommendations

In total, 241 recommendations were made in the field study. Most of the recommendations (212, 88%) were viewed by the participants, which indicates that the system was effective in increasing awareness of available events. In total, recommendations were made for 68 different events. Out of 241 recommendations, 95 (39%) had either streaming music or a YouTube video associated with them. The media was consumed at least once in 50 of the 95 cases (53%), but more than once only in 5 cases. Of the recommendations that were viewed, 74 (35%) were rated as good (thumbs up), 46 (22%) as poor (thumbs down), and 92 recommendations (43%) were not rated. No statistically significant differences were observed in the ratings between the `RANDOM` or the `LOCATION-BASED` recommendations. The median distance to events recommended using the `RANDOM` technique was 2.9 kilometers from the user's current location. For the `LOCATION-BASED` recommendations the median distance was 2.0 kilometers.

Influence of Recommendations

Table 1 summarizes responses elicited to questions measuring the relevance and goodness of individual event recommendations. We used non-parametric ANOVA to compare the responses to the recommendations generated with the `RANDOM` method and the `LOCATION-BASED` method. The comparison revealed no statistically significant differences between the two recommendation methods. We separately evaluated whether distance to recommended events influenced any of the responses. This analysis was conducted using one sided t-tests assuming unequal variance. Before analysis, the distance values were normalized by applying a logarithmic function on them. The analysis did not return any statistically significant effects, which suggests that proximity had no influence on perceived relevance or effectiveness of recommendations in our study.

The responses to the questionnaire indicate, first of all, that most of the recommendations were for artists/performers that were previously unknown to the participant and for events that the participant had not heard of before. Together with the high consumption rate of additional media, the results thus indicate that SoH was effective in supporting serendipity. However, the responses also indicate that the event recommendations were considered neither interesting nor uninteresting, implying a trade-off between relevance of recommendations and support for serendipity.

The recommendations that were presented were considered neither good or bad in terms of their timeliness. The responses also suggest that the recommendations had little impact on the behavior of the participants. Comments of the participants suggest that one of the main reasons for the limited impact of the recommendations on their behavior was related to pre-planning of the day's schedule before being exposed to the event recommendations. Some of the recommended events that the participants considered interesting had already been sold out which prevented them from having an influence on the participant's behavior.

Table 2 summarizes the responses to the questionnaire measuring the overall goodness of the system. The responses indicate, first of all, that, while individual event recommendations were not considered particularly relevant, overall the participants were satisfied with the system and the support it provided for determining which events to attend. Similarly to the responses to the individual event recommendations, the participants did not consider the system to have a significant influence on their behavior.

DISCUSSION AND CONCLUSIONS

We have presented Sounds of Helsinki, a mobile recommendation system for supporting serendipitous discovery of events in an urban environment. Results from a field study with 15 participants, conducted during an urban culture festival, indicate that SoH is effective in supporting serendipity. However, the results also indicate that the recommendations were not considered particularly interesting or relevant. While personalization techniques could be used to improve the interestingness of recommendations, this would easily decrease the effectiveness of SoH in supporting serendipity. A potential solution would be to use personalization techniques not only for determining what to recommend, but to determine when the user is more likely to be interested in novel and serendipitous content.

The results of the study also indicated that proximity to events had no influence on the perceived goodness of the recommendations. The city of Helsinki, where the study was conducted, has a good public transportation system and many central culture venues are within walking distance from each other in the city centre. For a person located outside the city center, this means that it will take him or her approximately equally long to get to any venue. On the other hand, for someone already in the city centre, most culture venues can be reached within 15 minutes by foot or by public transportation. Given this, the effort required to get to an event is likely to be similar for events that are recommended using either of the recommendation techniques. The similar rate of positive and negative responses for the two recommendation techniques further supports this interpretation. This finding is in line with results from studies in location-based personal information management [5] and mobile marketing [2] which have shown that user preferences regarding location are complex, extending beyond geographic proximity and depending on a multitude of factors ranging from user plans to movement routines and social geography of an area.

Acknowledgments

The authors wish to thank Helsinki Festival for providing the reward tickets. This work was supported by Aalto MediaFactory and EIT ICT Labs.

REFERENCES

1. Bellotti, V., Begole, B., Chi, E. H., Ducheneaut, N., Fang, J., Isaacs, E., King, T., Newman, M. W., Partridge, K., Price, B., Rasmussen, P., Roberts, M., Schiano, D. J., and Walendowski, A. Activity-based serendipitous recommendations with the Magitti mobile leisure guide. In *Proceeding of the 26th annual SIGCHI conference on Human factors in computing systems*, ACM (2008), 1157–1166.

2. Drossos, D., Giaglis, G. M., Lekakos, G., Kokkinaki, F., and Stavraki, M. G. Determinants of effective SMS

	RANDOM	LOCATION-BASED
	Median (IQR)	Median (IQR)
I am sure that I saw this recommendation.	5 (2)	5 (1)
The recommendation was interesting.	3 (2)	3 (2)
I was already familiar with the artist.	1 (3)	1 (2)
I had already heard about the recommended event.	1 (1)	1 (1)
The recommendation was presented at a suitable time.	3 (2)	3 (3)
The recommendation affected my behaviour.	1 (1)	1 (1)

Table 1. Summary of per-recommendation questionnaire results. The questions have been translated from Finnish.

	Median (IQR)
I enjoyed the [listening to or watching] the artists/bands of the recommended events (through media samples or attending the events).	3 (1.0)
The recommendations helped me find new artists.	3 (1.5)
The artists/bands related to the recommended events were not previously familiar to me.	3 (2.0)
I found the recommended events interesting.	4 (0.5)
The recommended events did not interest me.	2 (1.0)
The recommended events were similar to each other.	2 (0.5)
The recommendations were timely	4 (1.0)
The recommendations affected my decisions to attend events.	2 (2.0)
When I use the service, I feel that it supports me in trying to find content or events that I like.	4 (1.0)
Overall, I am satisfied with the recommendations made by the system.	4 (1.0)

Table 2. Summary of end-questionnaire results. The questions have been translated from Finnish.

advertising: An experimental study. *Journal of Interactive Advertising 7*, 2 (2007), 16–27.

3. Fleder, D. M., and Hosanagar, K. Recommender systems and their impact on sales diversity. In *Proceedings of the 8th ACM conference on Electronic commerce*, ACM (2007), 192–199.
4. Krüger, A., Baus, J., Heckmann, D., Kruppa, M., and Wasinger, R. Adaptive mobile guides. In *The Adaptive Web*, P. Brusilovsky, A. Kobsa, and W. Nejdl, Eds., vol. 4321. Springer, 2007, 521 – 549.
5. Ludford, P. J., Frankowski, D., Reily, K., and Terveen, L. Because I carry my cellphone anyway: Functional Location-Based Reminder Applications. In *Proceedings of the SIGCHI conference on Human factors in computing systems (CHI'06)* (2006).
6. Pu, P., Chen, L., and Hu, R. A user-centric evaluation framework for recommender systems. In *Proceedings of the 2011 ACM Conference on Recommender Systems (RecSys)*, ACM (2011), 157–164.
7. Tintarev, N., Flores, A., and Amatrain, X. Off the beaten track - a mobile field study exploring the long tail of tourist recommendations. In *Proceedings of the 12th International Symposium on Human-Computer Interaction with Mobile Devices and Services (MobileHCI)* (2010).
8. Zheng, V. W., Zheng, Y., Xie, X., and Yang, Q. Collaborative location and activity recommendations with GPS history data. In *Proceedings of the 19th international conference on World wide web*, ACM (2010), 1029–1038.

Image Registration for Text-gaze Alignment

Pascual Martinez-Gomez
The University of Tokyo
pascual@nii.ac.jp

Chen Chen
The University of Tokyo
chenchen@is.s.u-tokyo.ac.jp

Tadayoshi Hara
National Institute of Informatics
harasan@nii.ac.jp

Yoshinobu Kano
PRESTO, Japan Science and Technology Agency
kano@nii.ac.jp

Akiko Aizawa
National Institute of Informatics
aizawa@nii.ac.jp

ABSTRACT
Applications using eye-tracking devices need a higher accuracy in recognition when the task reaches a certain complexity. Thus, more sophisticated methods to correct eye-tracking measurement errors are necessary to lower the penetration barrier of eye-trackers in unconstrained tasks. We propose to take advantage of the content or the structure of textual information displayed on the screen to build informed error-correction algorithms that generalize well. The idea is to use feature-based image registration techniques to perform a linear transformation of gaze coordinates to find a good alignment with text printed on the screen. In order to estimate the parameters of the linear transformation, three optimization strategies are proposed to avoid the problem of local minima, namely Monte Carlo, multi-resolution and multi-blur optimization. Experimental results show that a more precise alignment of gaze data with words on the screen can be achieved by using these methods, allowing a more reliable use of eye-trackers in complex and unconstrained tasks.

Author Keywords
text-gaze alignment; error correction; image registration

ACM Classification Keywords
H.5.2 Information Interfaces and Presentation

INTRODUCTION
Tracking user's eye movements when reading a text can be specially interesting [12, 3] for the observation of the on-line cognitive processing [8] and to build the user's model of the world. However, captured data is still noisy and there is a severe misalignment between positions of words in text and positions of gaze samples obtained with the device [4]. Error-correction methods proposed in the literature [4, 6, 5, 12] either introduce strong constraints in the task or are too specific to the task to be considered as general methods. In the past three decades there have been important advances in understanding reading behavior [10] and reading models for eye-movement have been developed [11]. These linguistic and psychological models have been applied for predicting future gaze points, in that models with better prediction imitate better the cognitive process of language understanding at lexical level. Our research is motivated by recently emerging applications of eye-trackers such as user-oriented document summarization [12], and relevance segments filtering [3]. While conventional studies usually rely on carefully contrived experimental settings in a laboratory, these new applications present us a challenge to handle the gaze data collected in an open environment as well as the necessity of considering different types of reading behavior.

Based on this, the objective of this paper is to propose robust and formalized unsupervised techniques for error correction of gaze data for unconstrained tasks. Specifically, the method introduced in this work is based on the concept of feature-based image registration, which performs a spatial transformation of gaze coordinates to find a good correspondence with the image representation of a text. This method works independently of the reading behavior of the user since it performs the alignment only by using the distribution of the gaze samples and the geometric characteristics of the text. As far as we know, there have been only few studies dedicated to a theoretical framework of model-based error correction of gaze data with textual information, and although still in its preliminary stage, our investigation in this paper is intended to be an initiating work towards this direction.

PROBLEM FORMULATION
Given a temporal sequence of gaze points on a text, the goal is to identify the fixations done by the reader and align them with the words in the text so that the *reading sequence* of the words can be identified. Since words have an irregular shape, we will use word bounding boxes as a simplification to describe the basic features of the text such as the layout, the width of words, the height of lines, etc. There are two types of errors in a normal eye-tracking session [4]. The first one is a variable error and can be corrected by aggregating gaze samples into fixations. The second type is a systematic error, usually in the form of a particularly significant vertical drift [5] and its correction is not obvious. There are also two important types of reading behaviors depending on the task and goal. The first type is *careful reading*, where the reader

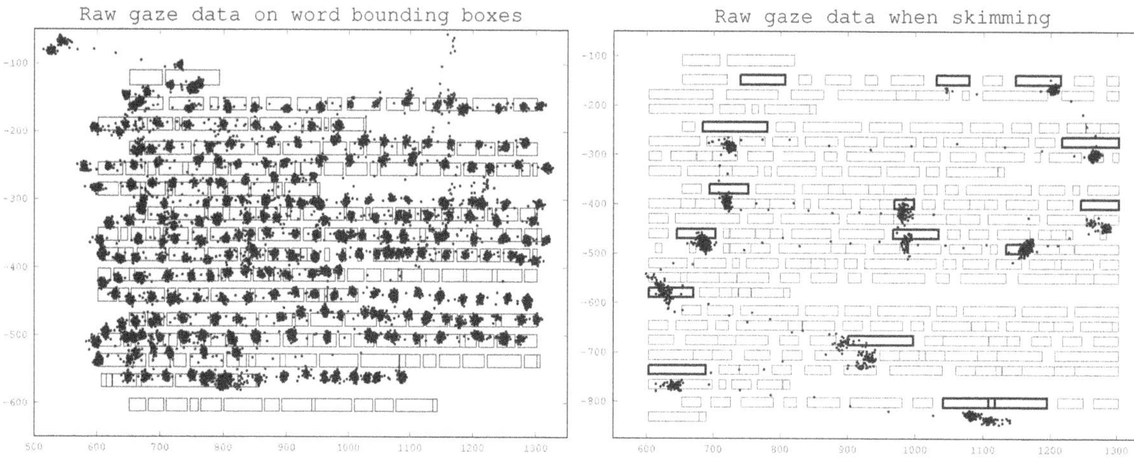

Figure 1. On the left, careful reading gaze data superimposed to word bounding boxes. On the right, skimming gaze data on word bounding boxes. On the right plot, fixated words during the skimming simulation are represented by bounding boxes with thicker contours. Gaze samples are represented by points. A small but important vertical mismatch between gaze data and word bounding boxes can be observed.

reads sequentially from left to right in a line by line basis. The second type is *skimming*, where the reader may look for key words that can be randomly spread all over the text. To preserve generality, no assumptions on the reading behavior are made in this work. An example of the effect of measurement errors on gaze samples when reading and skimming can be found in fig. 1. Although there is no assumption on a certain reading behavior, it is reasonable to think that fixations are produced on the structure or content (i.e. words) of the text and that the goodness of the alignment can be measured by some evaluation function either directly or indirectly.

IMAGE REGISTRATION FOR TEXT-GAZE ALIGNMENT

Image registration [7, 2] is a well studied technique that plays a crucial role in the analysis of medical images captured in different conditions. The goal is to align two images by doing a spatial transformation of the source image to match a certain target image. In this paper, image registration can be seen as a procedure that performs a spatial transformation of gaze coordinates to find a good correspondence with the image representation of a text. The key is to define a spatial transformation that solves the problem while keeping under control the number of transformation parameters. The systematic error in the form of a vertical drift reported in [4] (see fig. 1) motivates the decision of constraining spatial transformations to translations (constant shifts) and scalings on y-coordinates, considerably simplifying the problem by reducing the number of parameters governing the resulting linear transformation. Thus, a mapping (transformation) $g_{a,b}$ from eye-coordinates (x, y) into text-coordinates can be defined as:

$$g_{a,b} : (x, y) \rightarrow (x, y \cdot b + a) \quad (1)$$

where a (translation) and b (scaling) are the transformation parameters of the y-coordinates that have to be estimated by means of an optimization strategy. To complete the formalization of an optimization problem, the design of an objective function is essential. The ideal alignment locates every gaze sample into its corresponding word bounding box. Let $\mathbf{G}_{a,b}$ be the image representation of the mapped gaze samples, where pixel $\mathbf{G}_{a,b}(i, j)$ has a low value if there is a gaze sample in coordinates (i,j). And let $\mathbf{W}$ the image representation of word bounding boxes in a text, where pixel $\mathbf{W}(i, j)$ has a low value if it falls inside a bounding box. A measure of alignment between the two image representations can be defined as the sum of absolute differences of pixels (i,j):

$$f(\mathbf{G}_{a,b}, \mathbf{W}) = \sum_i \sum_j |\mathbf{G}_{a,b}(i, j) - \mathbf{W}(i, j)| \quad (2)$$

The intention is then to estimate the values $(\hat{a}, \hat{b})$ of the transformation parameters that minimize the objective function f:

$$\begin{aligned}(\hat{a}, \hat{b}) &= \operatorname*{argmin}_{a,b} f(\mathbf{G}_{a,b}, \mathbf{W}) & (3)\\ &= \operatorname*{argmin}_{a,b} \sum_i \sum_j |\mathbf{G}_{a,b}(i, j) - \mathbf{W}(i, j)| & (4)\end{aligned}$$

The solution space is not convex and finding the optimal parameter values that minimize the objective function depends greatly on the initialization values. Thus, methods to escape local minima are necessary. Three alternative optimization strategies to overcome the problem of the local minima are described, and examples of their effects can be found in fig. 2.

Monte Carlo sampling

Optimizing a function using the Monte Carlo method [9] consists in performing a repeated random sampling of transformation parameters and select the assignment of values that provides the minimum value of the objective function. Since the dimensionality of the solution space, the domain of reasonable values and the computational cost of evaluating the function are small, a large amount of random samples can be drawn to increase the chances of finding the global minimum.

Multi-resolution optimization

A different strategy is to smooth the solution space to transform it into a convex space such that a standard optimization algorithm would find the optimal parameter values regardless of the initialization. Then, those optimal values are used as initial estimations in the optimization of a less smoothed solution space. This process is repeated for progressively less

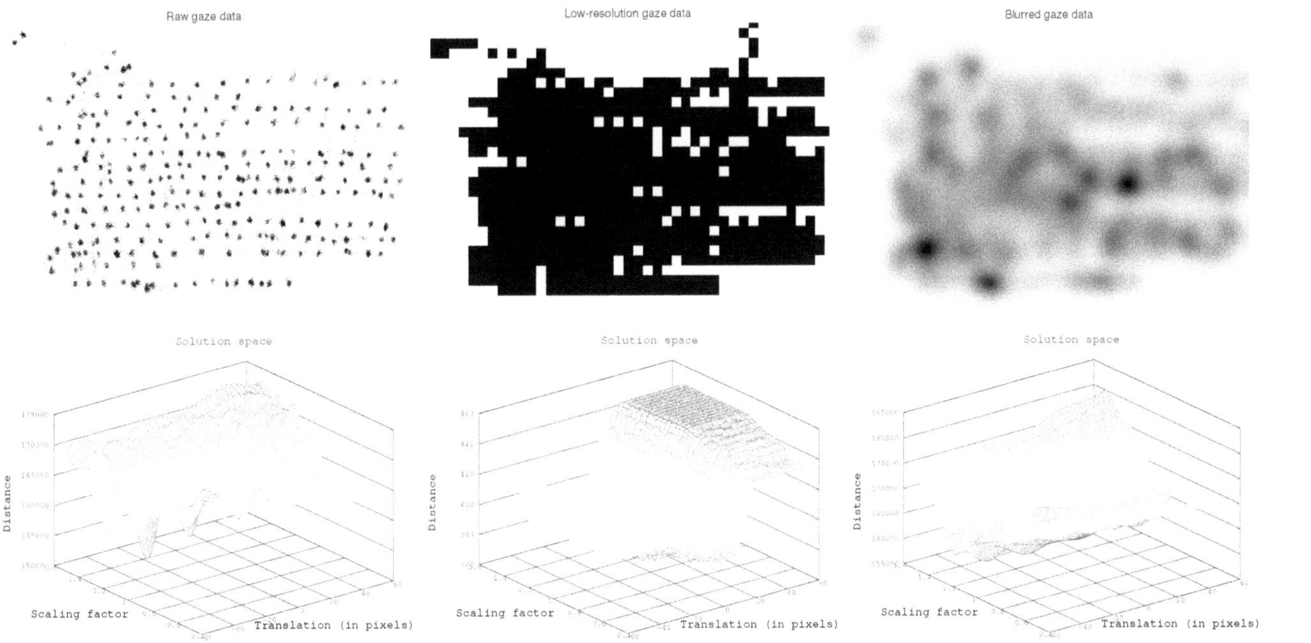

Figure 2. On top row, from left to right, image representations of raw gaze data, lower resolution and blurred gaze data. On the bottom, their respective solution spaces. For lower image resolutions and higher blurs, standard optimization algorithms have higher chances to find the global minimum.

smoothed solution spaces, re-using the estimations of the previous iteration. In the final iteration, the optimization algorithm is run on the original solution space using informed initial estimations. The smoothing of the solution space is achieved by decreasing the resolution of the image representations of gaze samples and word bounding boxes.

Multi-blur optimization

Multi-blur optimization is also an iterative optimization technique that blurs images by convolving them with an isotropic gaussian filter with spread σ. The resolution of the images is left unchanged, allowing for a more reliable re-use of estimations from previous iterations of the optimization process. The disadvantage of this technique is the cost of performing linear transformations, clearly more computationally expensive than in the multi-resolution optimization strategy.

After finding the optimal parameter values in each optimization strategy, gaze coordinates are mapped into the space of the words. Then, every gaze sample is assigned to the word with the closest bounding box and all gaze samples that follow a temporal sequence and are assigned to the same word are aggregated into the same fixation. Finally, fixations with a number of samples below a certain threshold are filtered out.

EXPERIMENTS

Performance was evaluated in two tasks simulating careful reading and skimming behavior. Data for the first task was obtained by instructing subjects to read in sequence all words in a text, trying not to skip words nor make regressions. Although these instructions are not realistically representative of careful reading, this setup allows to assume that the real word sequence T that subjects followed is known and has length $|T|$ equal to the number of tokens in the text. Readers were also told that understanding the text was not required but fixating every word was important. The evaluation metric was a similarity measure $\text{eval}(T, E) = 1 - \frac{\text{lev}(T,E)}{|T|}$ related to the levenshtein distance between T and the sequence of recognized words E. When skimming, fixated words are not random but they can be randomly spread all over the text. To simulate skimming in this worst case, words were turned into the same color as the background and some randomly selected words were kept visible. Readers were asked to fixate once in all visible words, following their most preferred order. The evaluation metric was the F-score $F = 2 \cdot \frac{\text{precision} \cdot \text{recall}}{\text{precision} + \text{recall}}$, a weighted average between precision and recall of visible words that subjects read and the recognized words.

For data collection, Tobii TX300 was used to capture gaze samples at a rate of 300 Hz in a 23" screen at a resolution of 1920 x 1080. The top-most left position of the text was located at pixels (600px, 10px) and the bottom-most right position was located at (1300px, 960px). Words were displayed in a web browser using Text2.0 framework [1] allowing to easily format the text using CSS style-sheets and to recover the geometric boundaries of the words. The font family was Courier New of size 16px and line height 30px, in black on a light gray background. A chin rest was used to reduce error introduced by readers. Text on the screen was short enough not to require any action to entirely visualize it. There were 6 subjects participating in two tasks from the first set of experiments and in two other tasks from the second set, alternating them. The eye-tracker was calibrated only once per subject.

According to preliminary experimentation using a disjoint data set, the threshold on the number of samples used to filter out fixations with small evidence was 8, the number of random samples drawn in the Monte Carlo method was set to 2400,

Table 1. Performance on the careful reading task was measured using the average Levenshtein similarity and for the skimming task it was measured using the average F-score among all readers.

	Careful reading (avg. Levenshtein sim.)	Skimming (avg. F-score)
baseline	.43	.29
Monte Carlo	.46	.35
Multi-resolution	.47	.38
Multi-blur	**.53**	**.43**
gold recognition	.75	–

the width of successive resolutions in the multi-resolution optimization was $60, 59, \ldots, 1$ and, for computational reasons, the σ in the multi-blur optimization was $30, 20, 10, 5, \epsilon$, for a very small positive ϵ. We did not find in the literature a general method to retrieve the reading word sequence in unconstrained tasks. For this reason, a naïve error-correction method was used as a baseline, where no mapping is performed. Results of the comparison of every method for the careful reading and skimming simulation are in table 1. The highest recognition accuracy was achieved when using multi-blur optimization in both types of reading behavior, significantly higher than the baseline. In general, recognition accuracy for the careful reading task is higher than recognition accuracy achieved in the skimming task. Text-gaze alignment by multi-blur optimization method was found to be good in a subjective evaluation. A manual word sequence recognition for the careful reading task led to an accuracy of about 75%, which we consider to be an upper bound of the automatic recognition accuracy. There are several reasons for this accuracy not to be 100%, e.g. the impossibility for subjects to control their eye-movements at word level or the existence of signal losses by the sensor. Thus, the best performing method achieves a recognition accuracy of about 70% relative to the gold recognition accuracy. Note that manually retrieving words fixated when skimming cannot be reliably performed due to the high ambiguity.

CONCLUSION AND FUTURE WORK

We have formalized error-correction of gaze measurements as a feature-based image registration problem with three optimization strategies. We proved that using information about the shape of words and the structure of the text to guide text-gaze alignment leads to an increased recognition accuracy without making assumptions on user's reading behavior.

While multi-blur optimization strategy was the method with the highest recognition accuracy, Monte Carlo sampling was the worst performing strategy. However, Monte Carlo optimization was the method that more often found global minimums for text-gaze alignment, but such estimations did not lead to a better recognition accuracy. This demonstrates a flaw in the objective function since a good text-gaze alignment does not necessarily mean a good recognition accuracy. Multi-resolution and multi-blur optimization strategies successfully overcome this problem. The automatic evaluation metric was validated using a subjective evaluation and we found that the reading word sequence accuracy is a good indicator of appropriate fits of gaze samples into focused words. The reason for image registration methods to perform worse in the skimming task is probably due to the small amount of captured gaze samples and the possibility of finding an inappropriate linear transformation that achieves a good alignment of gaze samples with wrong words. In the design of the mapping function, there is a trade-off between its complexity and the accuracy of estimations. Thus, an implicit assumption in the design of the mapping function was that y-error is constant horizontally but linear vertically. Counter-examples are not common but they are not negligible either. For this reason, non-rigid transformation should also be considered in the future. Finally, when on-line error-correction is required, Kalman and particle filters might be good candidates.

REFERENCES

1. Biedert, R., Buscher, G., Schwarz, S., Möller, M., Dengel, A., and Lottermann, T. The text 2.0 framework - writing web-based gaze-controlled realtime applications quickly and easily. In *Proc. of the International Workshop on Eye Gaze in Intelligent Human Machine Interaction (EGIHMI)* (2010).
2. Brown, L. G. A survey of image registration techniques. *ACM Computing Surveys 24* (1992), 325–376.
3. Buscher, G., and Dengel, A. Gaze-based filtering of relevant document segments. In *International World Wide Web Conference (WWW)* (2009).
4. Hornof, A., and Halverson, T. Cleaning up systematic error in eye-tracking data by using required fixation locations. *Behavior Research Methods 34* (2002), 592–604. 10.3758/BF03195487.
5. Hyrskykari, A. Utilizing eye movements: Overcoming inaccuracy while tracking the focus of attention during reading. *Computers in Human Behavior 22* (2005), 657–671.
6. Kennedy, A., and Pynte, J. Parafoveal-on-foveal effects in normal reading. *Vision Research 45* (2005), 153–168.
7. Lucas, B. D., and Kanade, T. An iterative image registration technique with an application to stereo vision (1981). 674–679.
8. McDonald, S. A., and Shillcock, R. C. Eye movements reveal the on-line computation of lexical probabilities during reading. *Psychological Science 14*, 6 (2003), 648–652.
9. Metropolis, N., and Ulam, S. The monte carlo method. *Journal of the American Statistical Association 44*, 247 (Sept. 1949), 335–341.
10. Rayner, K. Eye movements in reading and information processing: 20 years of research. *Psychological Bulletin 124* (Nov. 1998), 372–422.
11. Reichle, E., Rayner, K., and Pollatsek, A. The e-z reader model of eye-movement control in reading: Comparisons to other models. *Behavioral and brain sciences 26* (2003), 445–526.
12. Xu, S., Jiang, H., and Lau, F. C. User-oriented document summarization through vision-based eye-tracking. In *International Conference on Intelligent User Interfaces (IUI)* (2009).

Music Listening History Explorer

An alternative approach for browsing Music Listening History Habits

Ricardo Dias, Manuel J. Fonseca, Daniel Gonçalves
Department of Information Systems and Computer Science
INESC-ID/IST/Technical University of Lisbon
Lisbon, Portugal
ricardo.dias@ist.utl.pt, mjf@inesc-id.pt, daniel.goncalves@inesc-id.pt

ABSTRACT
Nowadays, people spend time using services to track their music listening history. Although these services provide statistics and small graphics/charts, they are mainly used to record and to allow direct access to the information, not providing any visualization and exploration functionality. In this paper we describe a new approach for browsing and visualizing music listening histories, which combines a timeline-based visualization, with a set of synchronized-views and an interactive filtering mechanism to provide a flexible and easy to use solution. This was complemented with brushing and highlighting techniques that allow users to observe trends on artists, albums and tracks listening. Experimental evaluation with users revealed that they were able to complete all the proposed tasks with a low error rate, and that they found the solution easy to use. Moreover, users liked our approach for browsing and exploring listening histories, emphasizing its flexibility and effectiveness, and founding the full experience engaging and rewarding.

ACM Classification Keywords
H.5.2 Information Interfaces and Presentation: Graphical User Interfaces - GUI

General Terms
Design, Experimentation

Author Keywords
Listening History, Interactive Browsing, Visualization

INTRODUCTION
Nowadays, millions of people spend their time using online services to track different aspects of their lives. Moods[1], the places they go[2] or the songs they ear[3], are just a few examples. This data contains intrinsic information about users' habits and behaviors, and most of it can be tracked without user intervention. As a consequence, it quickly becomes quite complex to understand and visualize this type of personal information.

[1]http://www.moodstats.com
[2]https://foursquare.com
[3]http://www.last.fm

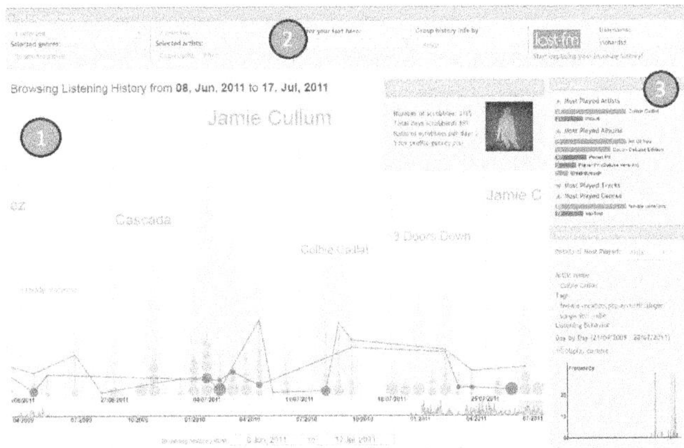

Figure 1: Prototype user interface.

These services often enrich the available data with statistics and small graphics, but their main use is still to record and allow direct access to the information. This raises the opportunity to create visualizations using this type of personal information. Some visualization techniques and solutions have already been developed, being the most relevant those developed by Byron and Wattenberg, the *StreamGraph* [4], and those created by Baur et al, *LastHistory*[3], and the *Tangle, Strings and Knots*[2] visualizations. Other community-created static visualizations, such as the *Scrobbling Timeline*[4], the *Last.fm Explorer*[5] and the *LastGraph*[6], represent the fans effort to visualize this information, besides creating entertainment visualizations. However, these approaches present some limitations, such as: they are more concerned about creating general overviews and statically pleasing visualizations of listening histories, instead of providing interactive browsing and filtering mechanism; input data limitation, regarding the number of songs listened to; and finally, some rely on external software plugins or are OS dependent.

In this paper we describe a new approach for interactively

[4]http://playground.last.fm/demo/timeline
[5]http://alex.turnlav.net/last_fm_explorer/
[6]http://lastgraph.aeracode.org

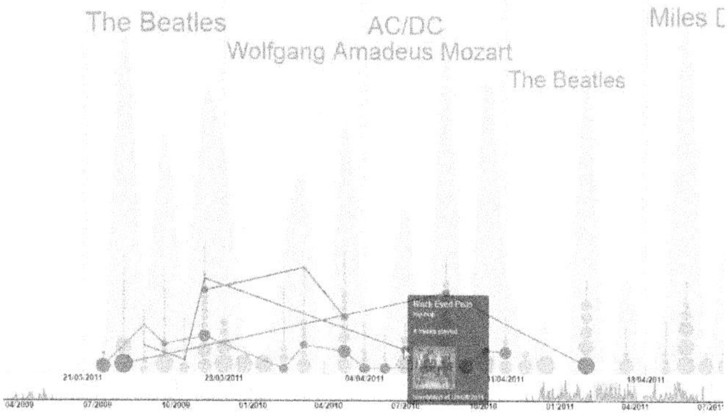

Figure 2: Multiple selection in main visualization.

browsing and filtering music listening histories that addresses the described concerns. Our solution uses data collected from the *Last.fm* service to create a compound visualization using a zoomable timeline and a set of synchronized views (see Figure 1). This solution provides not only an overview of the entire music listening history, but also an interactive mechanism to inspect a specific time period or *data element* (artist, album, track). It also supports listening histories up to thousands of tracks, and was built as a web application, so it could be available from anywhere.

Experimental evaluation shows that users were able to complete all the tasks with a very low error rate (<3%), and that they enjoyed using our solution and found it very easy to use. They also pointed that the solution was very flexible providing an engaging and rewarding experience. Results also revealed the users' awareness for this type of personal information, and the need to make use of it to personalize and improve music recommendation algorithms. The interactive exploration and filtering mechanisms were considered as the greatest advantage of our approach.

In the remainder of this document, we start by describing our solution and its design rational, providing insight about its main features and interaction. Later, we describe the conducted evaluation and present the main results. Finally, we conclude with our contributions and limitations, and present some directions for future work.

OUR SOLUTION

Our solution is a novel approach for exploring and visualizing music listening histories. On a timeline-based visualization users can browse their listening history in three different ways: *artists, albums and tracks*. Listening data can also be grouped by time and be filtered using the available criteria.

The developed prototype is shown in Figure 1. It includes three areas of interaction: main visualization area (1), filtering area (2) and statistics and details area (3).

Main Visualization

The visualization area (1) contains the *timeline* and the *stacked dot* visualizations for exploring the listening histories. As listening history data is inherently time based, temporal and timeline-based techniques were chosen to visualize this information (see [1] and [5] for a context).

The *doted* visualization is the main visualization over the users' listening histories. In this technique, much alike the ones Viégas developed in [6] and [7], each bar of *stacked dots* encode a time slice of the selected time period, and each dot represents a *data element* (artist, album or track) listened in that time slice. For example, in Figure 1, each column represents a day, and each dot an artist listened in that day.

Listening history data can be grouped by *day, week, month or year*. Depending on the amount of data contained in the selected period, the visualization will change accordingly. As the user starts to increase the selected time period, the amount of data to be displayed in the same space also increases, making the size of the dots smaller. However, as this cannot continue until the visualization becomes imperceptible, whenever the dots maximum size is about to decrease above a determined minimum size, the group operation is changed to one higher level in the temporal hierarchy. In the given example, it would change from day to week, making the visualization perceptible again. This feature enables users to interactively browse the listening history by time, always using the best suitable visualization over data. Nevertheless, users always have control over the applied zoom and can switch between group modes whenever they need more precise details.

The size of the dots and their order are mapped by a function that uses the listening frequency of the encoded *data element*, and its relevance in the full listening history. The color of the dot, unlike what other solutions do, instead of representing the genre of the element, introduces a new concept to characterize the users: it represents how recent or how old the tracks listened are (regarding to the release date of the track/album). The colors range from *strong and warm* ones (e.g. red tones), representing recently release tracks/albums, to colder colors (e.g. blue tones), representing older elements. This property allows users to get insights about their listening habits, for example, *"Do I hear more recent musics than old ones?"*, or *"Last month I heard old tracks from Bon Jovi, but now I move forward to listen just the new albums! Didn't realize that!"*, something that cannot be answered using current state-of-the-art solutions.

As for interaction, whenever the user *highlights* a dot, additional information is displayed, and a line appears, connecting all the dots that represent the same *data element*. This property makes it possible to visually follow the evolution of that element's listening. By clicking over it (or pressing the *CTRL* key for multiple selection, see Figure 2), a filter is applied using the dot's data, and the visualization dynamically adapts to show the filtered information. The line colors are mapped by the ones used in the *user statistics* details, explained bellow.

Filtering and Browsing

The filtering area (2), contains the interface for the interactive filtering mechanism. Users can filter the main visualization using three different filters: *genre, artist name* and *free text*. These filters can be combined and results are *dynamically highlighted* in the visualization. Although the filters limit the information we will see, they have different behaviors over the main visualization.

Genre filter makes the dots in the visualization to fade if they do not encode data from one of the selected genres, or to maintain its color otherwise. Although using this method users lose the ability to clearly identify the genre of each element, it gives them the ability to infer about the listened tracks/artists in that period and for that genre: "Were they recent or old?". When only one genre is selected, this fact becomes even clear, giving users the possibility to track their behavior for that genre over time.

As for artists filter, picking them from the set of listened artists in the selected time period, makes the respective dots to be get connected in the main visualization. Connecting the dots in the visualization acts as a visual clue to help users to track the trend of a specified artist, album or track listening (when in track/album visualization, artist filtering makes all the albums/tracks in the visualization to be individually connected, so users can follow the progress of a specific album/track listening). Although an increase in the line slope mean a decrease in frequency, during evaluation this did not prove to be a problem.

Text filter is a regular text input control where users can enter free text to filter data. It searches in the available tags and element information for matches (or partial matches), and then filters the visualization much alike the two filters above describe.

Statistics and Details

To provide an interactive environment to explore and filter users listening histories, our solution uses a synchronized-views paradigm. Besides the main visualization, two other provide statistic information and details about user listening history: the first one contains information about the most frequently played artists, albums, tracks and genres; and the other provides details about the most frequently played elements.

Statistics region displays general statistics about the most played artists, albums, tracks and genres, in the selected time period. By default, users can always keep track of the top five elements; however, by filtering the main visualization, they can obtain detailed information for less or more elements than those in the initial value. This visualization uses a *bar chart* encoded with the frequency an element was played, and a color mapping, from *green to dark red* (not collapsing with main visualization schema color), to indicate the most played element, and allow users to visually link with the other panels. These colors also map to the *brushing lines* that connect the dots in the main visualization.

In the details panel, users can obtain generic information, such as the release date of an album or the duration of the track, but also aggregated information specific to the user and the selected element. Two visualization techniques are used: a *day-by-day* and a hourly visualization (see figure 3). The day-by-day visualization consists in a *bar chart* where each bar represents a day in the selected time period when the element was listened to (see figure 3a), and the hourly visualization in a *dot chart*, where each dot represents an element listened at a specific time (day, hour-minutes). For these two visualizations, the overall context can be displayed, see figure 3b, showing the total listening history for that element and highlighting the selected time period. These visualizations provide insights about how the user listened to that particular artist, album or track, answering questions like "*Which days did I play Colbie's music (and how much) and at what time? Do I hear it a lot? Always at morning?*".

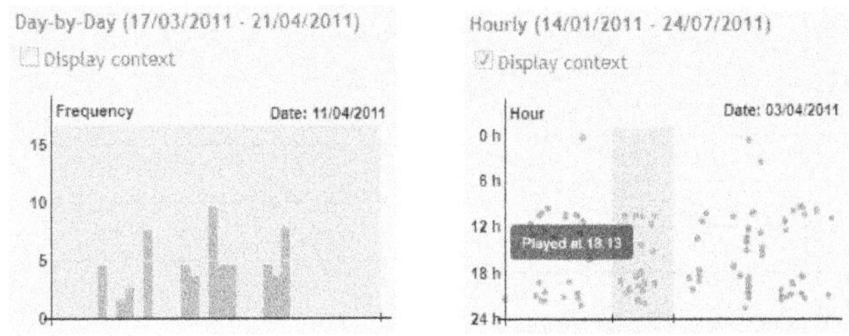

(a) Day-by-day with no context

(b) Hourly with surround context

Figure 3: Day-by-day and hourly visualizations.

EXPERIMENTAL EVALUATION

In order to evaluate our approach we conducted a set of user tests. We intended to evaluate the users' ability to complete all the proposed tasks, the error rate, and finally their satisfaction and experience about using our solution.

Users

We conducted tests with 10 users (2 females and 8 males), 7 of them aged between 20 and 30 years, and the remaining between 30 and 50 years. 7 out of 10 listen to music every day and have different backgrounds: four were graduate computer science students, two were software engineers (one being an amateur musician), one was a journalist, another was a human science student, and the remaining two were undergraduate computer science students (one worked as a saleslady in a local supermarket). 9 users reported listening to music at home, 8 at work and while driving. They all listen to music in computer and 8 of them using radios, and 7 use *smartphones* when moving around.

Procedure

Each test session lasted in average 30 minutes, and was performed using users' personal computers. The only requirement about the setup was that an Internet connection was available. To establish a baseline for all tests, a common *Last.fm* account was used for all sessions. Although this data was not personal to users, we adopted this solution because in these tests we do not intend to evaluate personal issues.

First, we started with a brief description about the test, thanking the person and explaining our objectives and what we were going to do. Next we introduced our application, explaining its main features and how to use them. At this time we gave a practice time for users to get familiar with the solution. A video was used in this part to present the interaction and main features of the solution. Next, users performed a set of tasks using the application. Tasks covered different objectives as explained bellow. When authorized, user's interaction with the application was recorded, using a screen capture software for later post-analysis. Finally, users answered a satisfaction survey and an informal interview was conducted to get feedback from users about the experience.

Tasks and Objectives

Based on the analysis of related work (see [3]), we designed 10 tasks, grouped into two sets accordingly to our main objectives. In the first group, we tried to evaluate if users could use our approach to effectively explore the listening history. Tasks ranged from direct use of the applications interface (e.g., getting information about most played artists, or the period with more intense music listening activity), to others where combining filtering (with genre and artist information) was mandatory. On the second group, we intended to assess if users could find and use information that would lead them to get insights about *listening trends*, and to understand *statistics* about the user's profile. Tasks covered describing the listening evolution of a song (e.g., if it increased/decreased or was constant, etc.), or trying to understand some facets of the user's profile, such as, "*Does he listens to complete albums, or he prefers to hear isolated tracks?*".

Main Results

In short, all users were able to finish the required tasks in the given time period, and they did not found any relevant difficulty in executing them.

On average, 9 out of 10 users found the execution of the required tasks *very easy* (using a 5-point Likert scale ranging from *Very Difficult* to *Very Easy*), and only user 1, in task 5 about browsing found it to be tricky. This issue was due to a temporary confusion with the brushing lines concept.

Task success rate was very high for 9 of the 10 tasks. A task was considered successfully completed if the user finished it and gave a correct answer (when required). Indeed, only task 3 got an error rate of 40% against the average error rate of 3% for the remaining tasks. To complete this task, users should infer about the most intense listening period. This suggests that improvements should be made to provide more detailed information when necessary.

Satisfaction survey revealed some interesting results. 9 out of 10 users were able to use the application and understand the information presented. 4 of them had difficulties in executing task 7 (describing the listening history evolution of a song), but their main concern was about giving a wrong answer, as this was a subjective and interpretative question. When asked to classify the experience and the evaluation using semantic scales, 8 users described it as engaging and rewarding. They all felt that they were learning something about the other user's listening history, and wanted to use the application to explore their own listening history.

All users said that it was important to understand the listening history, but only three have previously tried it. They tried to obtain global statistics about the most played tracks/artists, and only one failed to get the desired information. They all said it would be easy to obtain it using our solution. When inquired about using this information to improve recommendation systems, for example, to suggest songs or generate playlists, they all agreed that this is essential, as this data encodes their tastes and listening patterns.

In general, users enjoyed using our solution and they intended to use it to explore their own listening history. One user even said: "*This tool is very nice. I would like to use it to browse my listening history. I wonder which my personal patterns are and how my behavior changes over time!*".

CONCLUSIONS AND FUTURE WORK

In this paper we described an alternative solution for exploring and filtering music listening histories. The solution used a timeline-based visualization and a set of synchronized-views to allow users to perform an interactive exploration of their music listening histories. Results from user evaluation showed that the developed solution was easy to use, with users completing all the tasks with a low error rate.

As for future work, we are willing to follow two paths: the first one is to conduct a further user evaluation to assess if users can get insights about their personal patterns and habits, while browsing and filtering their personal listening histories; next, we intend to apply data mining techniques to this information to create a set of user profiles (for example, the users that always seek the tops, the ones that enjoy mostly female voices or that listen to classic music in the morning, etc.), and then use them to improve and personalize music recommendation and automatic playlist generators.

ACKNOWLEDGEMENTS

This work was supported by FCT (INESC-ID multiannual funding) through the PIDDAC Program funds, and through the Crush project, PTDC/EIA-EIA/108077/2008.

REFERENCES

1. Aigner, W., Miksch, S., Müller, W., Schumann, H., and Tominski, C. Visualizing time-oriented data - a systematic view. *C&G* (June 2007).
2. Baur, D., and Butz, A. Pulling strings from a tangle: visualizing a personal music listening history. IUI (2009).
3. Baur, D., Seiffert, F., Sedlmair, M., and Boring, S. The streams of our lives: Visualizing listening histories in context. *IEEE TVCG* (2010).
4. Byron, L., and Wattenberg, M. Stacked graphs geometry & aesthetics. *IEEE TVCG* (2008).
5. Muller, W., and Schumann, H. Visualization methods for time-dependent data - an overview. In *Simulation Conference* (2003).
6. Viegas, F., Boyd, D., Nguyen, D., Potter, J., and Donath, J. Digital artifacts for remembering and storytelling: posthistory and social network fragments. In *HICSS '04* (2004).
7. Viégas, F. B., Golder, S., and Donath, J. Visualizing email content: portraying relationships from conversational histories. CHI (2006).

LogicPad: A Pen-Based Application for Visualization and Verification of Boolean Algebra

Bo Kang
Interactive Systems and User Experience Lab
University of Central Florida
Orlando, Florida 32816
bkang@cs.ucf.edu

Joseph J. LaViola Jr.
Interactive Systems and User Experience Lab
University of Central Florida
Orlando, Florida 32816
jjl@eecs.ucf.edu

ABSTRACT
We present LogicPad, a pen-based application for boolean algebra visualization that lets users manipulate boolean function representations through handwritten symbol and gesture recognition coupled with a drag-and-drop interface. We discuss LogicPad's user interface and the general algorithm used for verifying the equivalence of three different boolean function representations: boolean expressions, truth tables, and logic gate diagrams. We also conducted a short, informal user study evaluating LogicPad's user interface, visualization techniques, and overall performance. Results show that visualizations were generally well-liked and verification results matched user expectations.

Author Keywords
Pen-based User Interface, Sketch Understanding, Boolean Algebra, Logic Verification

ACM Classification Keywords
H.5.2 Information Interfaces and Presentation: User Interfaces—*Interaction Styles*; G.4 Mathematics of Computing: Mathematical Software—*User Interfaces*

General Terms
Design, Human Factors

INTRODUCTION
Boolean Algebra [8] is a fundamental concept in computer science and digital system design. Many problems in digital logic design and testing, artificial intelligence, and combinatorics can be expressed as a sequence of boolean operations and boolean variables. A boolean function can be represented as an expression, truth table, or logic gate diagram; the three different representations of the same boolean function are considered equivalent.

Traditional complex computer-aided design applications are important tools for designing logic circuits. Nevertheless, for novices, such as students who are learning the fundamentals of boolean algebra, simple and quick prototyping is important. Most students still find using pen and paper to quickly sketch out boolean expressions, truth tables, and logic gate diagrams to be useful. Therefore, we made LogicPad (see Figure 1), a new pen-based application that combines the ease-of-use of pen and paper with the automation of computer-aided design applications. LogicPad focuses on the relationship between three different representations of boolean functions. Users can quickly sketch a boolean function and visualize the function in each representation simultaneously. In addition, we provide a general method for verifying the equivalence of two boolean functions.

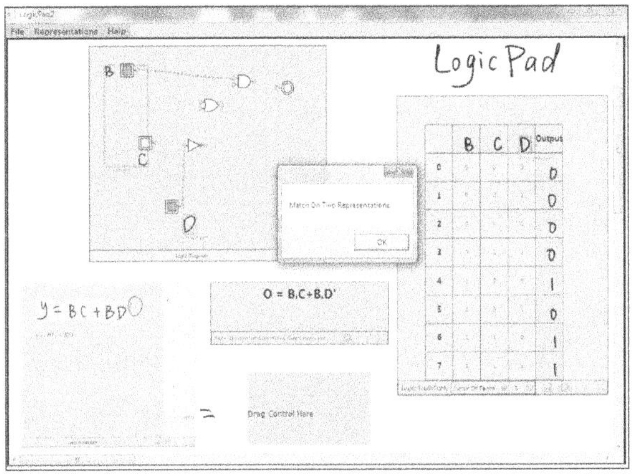

Figure 1. LogicPad's main window with three boolean function representations.

RELATED WORK
Computer aided design applications for undestanding logic circuits have been previously developed, such as LogicAid, which lets users develop boolean functions using representations such as truth tables, state tables, and state graphs [9]. LogicAid is similar in spirit to our work, but LogicAid does not make use of a pen-based interface.

Logic gate diagrams are well-suited for pen-based sketching environments. SketchREAD describes a multi-domain sketch recognition engine capable of recognizing hand-drawn diagram sketches [1]. Wais' user study explored critical sketch recognition user interface issues with logic gate diagrams [10]. Alvarado also analyzed how students created freely-drawn logic gate diagrams in class over the course of a full semester [2]. However, these works use user interfaces that are entirely sketch-based, while our work uses a combination of sketching and a drag-and-drop interface.

Besides sketching diagrams, research in the recognition, evaluation, and visualization of mathematical expressions has also been conducted previously. MathPad^2 is a mathematical sketching tool for solving mathematics problems [5]. MathBrush is a mathematics recognition tool that supports mathematical transformations and problem solving through the use of a back-end Computer Algebra System [4]. Our work expands upon the notion of mathematical sketching, extending it by combining mathematical expressions and logic gate diagrams.

USER INTERFACE

LogicPad provides a sketching area for the user to write on as they normally would using pen and paper. Instead of sketching the various boolean function representations on a single canvas, a separate widget with its own canvas is created for each representation, which can be added to the sketching area.

Users write gestures on the sketching area in order to create widgets. For instance, drawing an 'E' will create a boolean expression widget. Truth table widgets and logic gate diagram widgets are created using 'T' and 'D', respectively. A scribble erase gesture is used to erase both ink and user interface elements, because it mimics natural erasing.

CONCEPTUAL MODEL

As previously discussed, boolean functions have three basic representations: truth tables, boolean expressions, and logic gate diagrams. The three representations in LogicPad provide visualization cues to help the user understand the boolean function they are working with.

Logic Gate Diagram Widget

With a sketching interface, the user needs to know the shape of each type of logic gate, which can be a cognitive burden for students who are still learning about boolean algebra. Therefore, we try to ease the burden by using a drag-and-drop radial menu [3] showing the different types of logic gates. Figure 2 shows a logic gate diagram widget with a radial menu showing the six basic logic gates.

Users can hold down the stylus on the tablet screen for 3 seconds in order to trigger the radial menu and drop a gate from it on the sketching area. Gates can also be freely moved around the sketching area. We provide a sketching interface for this widget; after gates are dragged and dropped on the canvas, a user can sketch a line to connect any two gates. If a stroke starts at one gate and ends at another, it is recognized as a wire and the stroke is removed and replaced with a wire.

A user can sketch a label near each gate. Label association is decided by checking whether an ink stroke falls within a threshold distance from a gate. Any strokes that fall within the threshold are analyzed by the Microsoft Ink Analyzer as typeset notations underneath strokes and used as the gate's label. In addition, after the user connects two gates with a wire, the widget animates current flowing through the wire.

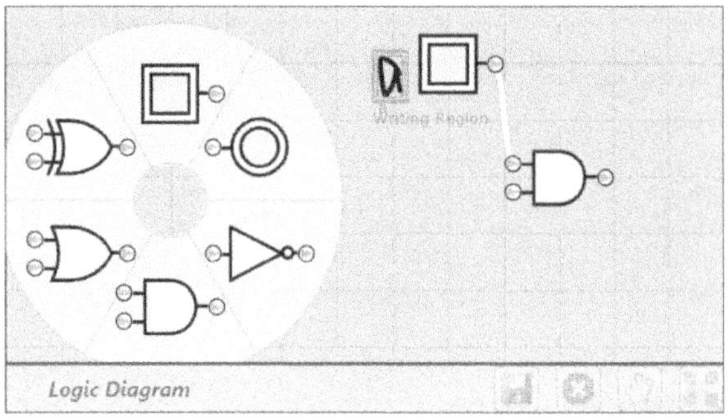

Figure 2. A logic gate diagram widget with a radial menu open showing the six kinds of logic gates: AND, OR, NOT, XOR, Input, and Output.

Handwritten Symbol	Boolean Operator	Example
$+$	OR	$A+B$
$\cdot$	AND	$A \cdot B$ or AB
$'$	NOT	A'
$\oplus$	XOR	$A \oplus B$

Table 1. Mapping between handwritten symbols and boolean operators.

Boolean Expression Widget

Since sketching mathematics is natural, LogicPad's boolean expression widget is a canvas that interprets the user's handwritten math and converts it to a typeset notation. After recognizing alphabetical letters, numbers and numerical operators using StarPad [11], four handwritten boolean operators can be interpreted by LogicPad, which are summarized in Table 1.

During expression construction, a user can circle strokes and select alternate recognition options from an alternates bar in case the default recognition does not match the user's expectation. In addition, expressions can be selected and moved around the widget.

Truth Table Widget

The truth table widget presents a table for the user to fill out with the expected output of the boolean function they are working with. The user can change the number of variables; each variable can be renamed by erasing the old name and writing a new one, then the handwritten symbol is analyzed by the Microsoft Ink Analyzer as the typeset notation underneath it. In comparison to pen and paper, LogicPad helps the user by creating a table with variables and the factorial combinations of their input values, which can be an onerous step when working with many variables. Thus, the user can concentrate on working out the output values for the truth table.

MAPPING

LogicPad can determine the boolean function each widget represents and minimize the function. The other two function representations can also be created from any type of widget.

Figure 3. Process for converting a widget in order to determine whether two widgets represent the same boolean function.

Verifying the equivalence of two boolean functions is essential to LogicPad, because it lets users compare the different representations, which can help them to understand boolean algebra and boolean function representations.

Each kind of widget stores data in a different format; when the user wants to see the widget's function in another representation, the widget converts its data to a parse tree that stores a variable name or boolean operator at each node. Logic gate diagram widgets use XML to represent the gates and wires, expression widgets use a binary tree to represent the mathematics, and truth table widgets use a tabular array to store the input values, output values, and variable names.

Looking at two boolean functions, it can be ambiguous whether they are equivalent. For instance, $F = X + 0$ and $F = X$ are equivalent, as are $F = XY' + XY$ and $F = X$. In order to determine the equivalence of two boolean functions, we apply the steps shown in Figure 3.

The tree rewriting phase always changes the structure of the parse tree. It includes five sub-steps. First, boolean identity laws are checked. For instance, the parse tree that represents $X + 0$ is reduced to X. Second, the XOR operator is substituted for its equivalent form. For example, the parse tree that represents $A \oplus B$ is converted to $AB' + A'B$. Third, the parser will make sure that all NOT operator nodes are located as deep in the tree as possible. Fourth, boolean functions are formulated as a sum-of-products expansion. Fifth, boolean complement laws are checked.

The goal of the tree segmentation phase is to convert the parse tree to an ordered array of 0-1 bitstrings. In this phase, the parse tree changes each sum-of-products expansion to an array-of-products expansion, and variable names are analyzed as a one or zero depending on the presence of a NOT operator parent node.The final phase is to minimize the boolean function. We use the Quine-McCluskey algorithm [6] to simplify the ordered array of bitstrings.

FEEDBACK

We use two approaches to verify the user's logic construction, both of which can be seen in Figure 1. Our first approach is an explicit feedback mechanism. When a user designs a boolean function using one type of representation, the other two can be generated from the representation menu.

Our second approach is a gesture-based mechanism which can be seen as an implicit feedback mechanism. A user can draw an equals sign on the sketching area between two widgets. When the equals sign is recognized, LogicPad will check if there is a widget on either side of the equals sign. If there is no widget on one side, then a rectangle will be drawn on the sketching area to give the user a hint to drag a widget to that area. Finally, LogicPad parses the two widgets and tells the user whether the boolean functions represented by the widgets are equivalent using a pop-up window.

INFORMAL USER STUDY

To gain insight into the perceived utility of LogicPad for domain users, we conducted an informal user study.

We recruited 6 participants (1 female and 5 males, aged 18-25, 2 left-handed) from the undergraduate electrical engineering department at the University of Central Florida. Participants all had basic knowledge of boolean algebra. The study was conducted in the lab, using an HP Compaq tc4400 12.1 inch tablet PC. We informed participants of minor bugs when possible, as our goal was to evaluate system design rather than implementation and recognition issues.

Users were asked to practice a set of tasks in order to get familiar with the system. The practice tasks consisted of creating and manipulating boolean expressions, truth tables and logic gate diagrams. Finally, users were asked to design two boolean functions and to verify the equivalence between corresponding representations.

After the practice phase, participants were required to solve a list of tasks using LogicPad. Pen and paper were also provided in case the participant needed to write down their thinking process. The tasks were divided into two categories. In the first category, one boolean function representation was provided and participants were then asked to sketch one of the other two corresponding representations of the same function and to verify their equivalence using LogicPad. In the second category, two boolean function representations were provided and participants were then required to manually determine if the representations were logically equivalent before using LogicPad to verify the result.

At the completion of the study (which lasted approximately 50 minutes), participants completed a questionnaire inquiring if the tool was useful for boolean function verification and if it was helpful for logic problem solving.

Observations

Triggering Widgets

Five out of six participants preferred our gestural method to add widgets. One participant argued that it would be better to give a option to select the widget from a menu. Two users were frustrated by the difficulty of triggering widgets by writing gestures due to incorrect handwriting recognition results obtained from the recognizer.

Diagram User Widget

All participants preferred the method for triggering the radial menu, noting that it reduced the learning time and augmented the retention time in drawing logic gates. Only one participant said that it would be better to make the radial menu visible longer than the given time interval.

All became accustomed to the drag-and-drop interface of applying the gate to the canvas. One participant suggested that it may be better to simply tap each gate on the radial menu to make the gate visible in the widget. From our observations, we believed that other participants would have the same preference. After participants triggered the radial menu, their first instinct was to use the stylus to target one specific gate and wait for response from the system. We also found one mode-switching issue. For instance, some users would unintentionally trigger the radial menu when trying to change the position of logic gates already present in the sketching area. We conjecture that using a mode inference approach [7] could reduce this ambiguity.

Expression User Widget

Four out of six participants found it easy to manipulate. However, one participant reported being frustrated by wrong recognition results when writing expressions. For example, when he wrote apostrophes as negation operators, they were always falsely recognized as another notation, requiring him to select an alternative recognition result. He recommended to use a hat symbol as the negation operator.

Truth Table User Widget

All of the participants appreciated not having to draw the entire truth table. One participant said, "I like how I could add variables easily with the menu at the bottom." Another participant commented that it would be better to initialize all of the output values to zero first and then scribble out non-zero values, replacing them with ones.

Feedback

All participants preferred our two approaches, as both of them provided intuitive ways to visualize and comprehend boolean functions.

Overall, every participant preferred having separate widgets, and one of them commented that it was a natural way to represent boolean functions. Another user commented "I did like LogicPad but I think you should be able to have the choice on if you want separate widgets or not." All participants who used LogicPad thought that it was a good verification tool for problem solving, but two commented that it would be better if LogicPad was faster and more reliable.

CONCLUSION AND FUTURE WORK

We have presented LogicPad, a pen-based tool that support boolean function visualization and verification. It provides different sketching areas to write boolean function representations and parses user's logic representations in order to generate other boolean function representations. In the logic gate diagram widget, we illustrated one mixed sketch-drag-and-drop approach. We also conducted an informal study, where we found that our boolean function knowledge representation approach was well liked by the participants. We also found that participants wanted tools to help them to verify their problem solving results in general. In the future, we plan to continue to explore under what circumstances should a sketching interface or drag-and-drop interface be chosen, how LogicPad could be used to aid students, and understanding LogicPad's pedegogical implications.

ACKNOWLEDGMENTS

This work is supported in part by NSF CAREER award IIS-0845921 and NSF awards IIS-0856045 and CCF-1012056. We would also like to thank the members of the ISUE lab for their support and the anonymous reviewers for their useful comments and feedback.

REFERENCES

1. Alvarado, C., and Davis, R. Sketchread: A multi-domain sketch recognition engine. In *Proc. of the 17th annual ACM symposium on User interface software and technology* (Santa Fe, New Mexico, USA, 2004), 23–32.
2. Alvarado, C., and Lazzareschi, M. Properties of real-world digital logic diagrams. In *Proceedings of the First International Workshop on Pen-Based Learning Technologies*, PLT '07, IEEE Computer Society (Washington, DC, USA, 2007), 1–6.
3. Callahan, J., Hopkins, D., Weiser, M., and Shneiderman, B. An empirical comparison of pie vs. linear menus. In *Proceedings of the SIGCHI conference on Human factors in computing systems*, CHI '88, ACM (New York, NY, USA, 1988), 95–100.
4. Labahn, G., Lank, E., MacLean, S., Marzouk, M., and Tausky, D. Mathbrush: A system for doing math on pen-based devices. In *Document Analysis Systems, 2008. DAS '08. The Eighth IAPR International Workshop on* (sept. 2008), 599 –606.
5. LaViola, Jr., J. J., and Zeleznik, R. C. Mathpad^2: a system for the creation and exploration of mathematical sketches. In *ACM SIGGRAPH 2004 Papers*, SIGGRAPH '04, ACM (New York, NY, USA, 2004), 432–440.
6. McCluskey, E. J., and Schorr, H. Minimization of boolean functions. *Bell System Technical Journal 35*, 5 (November 1956), 1417–1444.
7. Negulescu, M., Ruiz, J., and Lank, E. Exploring usability and learnability of mode inferencing in pen/tablet interfaces. In *Proceedings of the Seventh Sketch-Based Interfaces and Modeling Symposium*, SBIM '10, Eurographics Association (Aire-la-Ville, Switzerland, Switzerland, 2010), 87–94.
8. Nelson, V. P., Nagle, H. T., Carroll, B. D., and Irwin, J. D. *Digital logic circuit analysis and design*. Prentice-Hall, Inc., Upper Saddle River, NJ, USA, 1995.
9. Roth, C. *Logicaid, CAD Software for Logic Design, Version 3.0 for Windows: Users Guide and Reference Manual*. Cengage Learning, 1995.
10. Wais, P., Wolin, A., and Alvarado, C. Designing a sketch recognition front-end: User perception of interface elements. In *SBM*, M. van de Panne and E. Saund, Eds., Eurographics Association (2007), 99–106.
11. Zeleznik, R., Miller, T., Li, C., and Laviola, Jr., J. J. Mathpaper: Mathematical sketching with fluid support for interactive computation. In *Proceedings of the 9th international symposium on Smart Graphics*, SG '08, Springer-Verlag (Berlin, Heidelberg, 2008), 20–32.

Interactive Uncertainty Analysis

Pedro Szekely, Rajiv T. Maheswaran, Yu-Han Chang, Yan Wang, Huihui Cheng and Karan Singh
Information Sciences Institute
University of Southern California
{pszekely, maheswar, ychang}@isi.edu
{wang79, huihuich, karans}@usc.edu

ABSTRACT

Humans have difficulty evaluating the effects of uncertainty on schedules. People often mitigate the effects of uncertainty by adding slack based on experience and non-stochastic analyses such as the critical path method (CPM). This is costly as it leads to longer than necessary schedules, and can be ineffective without a clear understanding of where slack is needed. COMPASS is an interactive real-time tool that analyzes schedule uncertainty for a stochastic task network. An important feature is that it concurrently calculates stochastic critical paths and critical tasks. COMPASS visualizes this information on top of a traditional Gantt view, giving users insight into how delays caused by uncertain durations propagate down the schedule. Evaluations with 10 users show that users can use COMPASS to answer a variety of questions about the possible evolutions of a schedule (e.g., what is the likelihood that all activities will complete before a given date?)

Author Keywords

Visualization, Uncertainty Analysis, Plan Understanding, Schedule Visualization, Gantt Chart, Monte Carlo Simulation.

ACM Classification Keywords

I.6.6 Simulation and Modeling: Simulation Output Analysis; I.6.6 Simulation and Modeling: Types of Simulation—*Monte Carlo*

General Terms

Human Factors

INTRODUCTION

Uncertainty is inherent when scheduling tasks but unfortunately humans are poor at calculating its effects. The problem is exacerbated in task networks of non-trivial size as nonlinear effects (e.g., when a task depends on the completion of multiple tasks) cascade. Given a task network, a user will have multiple questions of different types that they want answered. This can range from questions about the given plan, such as when it's expected to finish or the likelihood of making a deadline, to what-if scenarios (e.g., what happens if it rains? what if everything takes two days longer than anticipated?). Our goal is to support real-time interactions to answer these questions to help users get an overall understanding of how uncertainty affects their plans.

While others have worked on various aspects of the problem (see Related Work), none have provided real-time what-if capabilities over multiple aspects of the plan, a visual representation of uncertainty and its effects on the entire plan, nor a validation through user studies. Our contribution is COMPASS (see Figure 1), a tool which (1) performs stochastic analysis of schedules, (2) enables real-time interactivity and feedback, (3) provides a comprehensive and intuitive visualization of the entire plan, and (4) includes diverse types of what-if capabilities. In addition, we (5) conducted a user study that shows significant improvements in the accuracy of and confidence in the participants' answers involving stochastic schedules.

INTERACTIVE UNCERTAINTY ANALYSIS

We describe COMPASS and its capabilities in the context of a user study we performed to evaluate its effectiveness. Users were given a plan to build a house involving 40 tasks (partially shown in Figure 1) with 11 agents and 30 enablement dependencies. They were then asked to answer questions such as determining the expected plan completion time, 90% confidence interval for the completion times, and what-if questions that involved changing the uncertainty distributions. We modeled task durations using beta distributions ($\beta(2,10)$). With these skewed bell-curves, durations range from 80% to 200% of the mean, and 99% of the durations are between 80% and 140% of the mean. Users can see and modify the distributions by selecting the tasks in the display.

To help users answer these questions, COMPASS performs thousands of Monte Carlo simulations of schedule execution (typically between 2 and 10 thousand simulations) satisfying all constraints in the temporal network and using a execution policy where agents perform tasks as soon as they can (agent is free and all task constraints are satisfied). The COMPASS visualizations consist of layers that summarize the information gathered in these simulations.

When will it be done? We asked the users to answer deeper variants of the question "when will a given task be complete?":

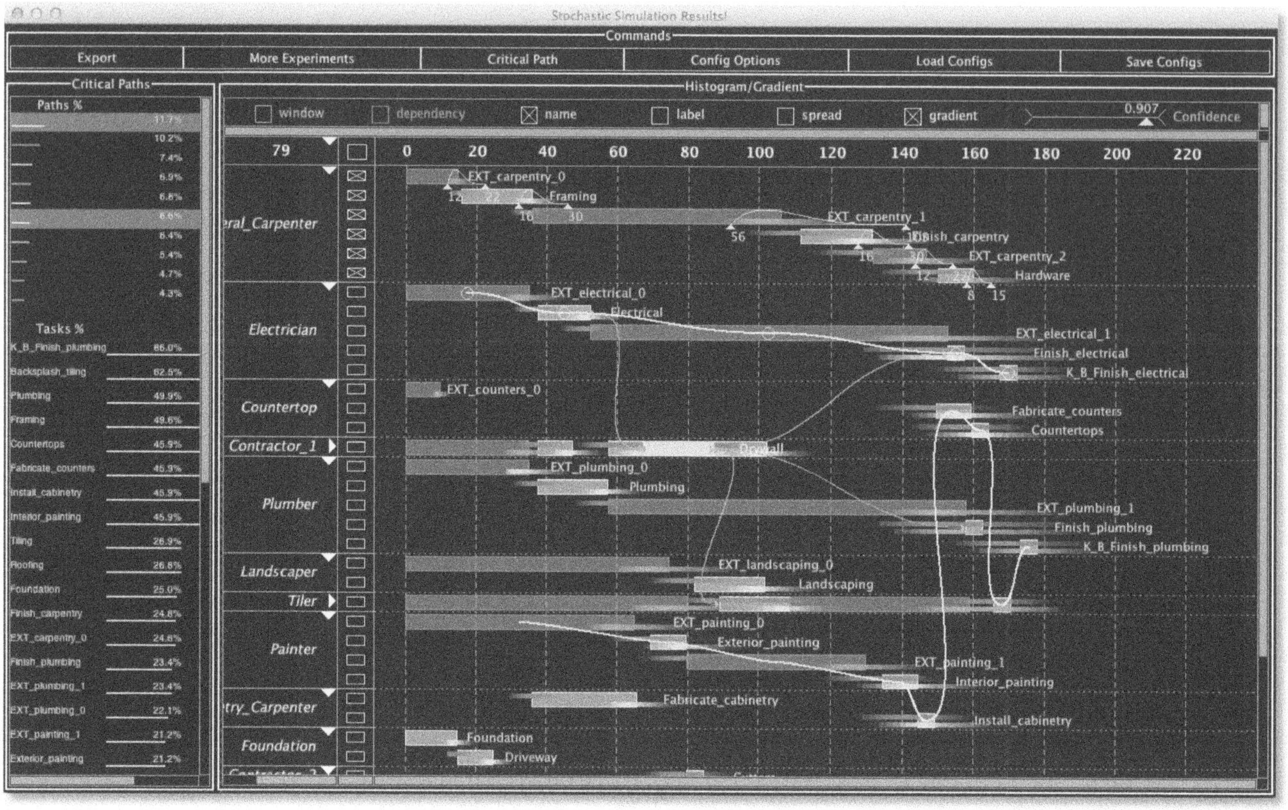

Figure 1. Visualization of schedule uncertainty analysis using COMPASS.

1. What is the expected time when the house will be finished?
2. At what day will we be 90% confident that the house will be done? (i.e., 90% of the time, the house will be finished before this day).
3. What is the probability that our house will be finished within 180 days?
4. How wide is the uncertainty window for completing a task if we want to be 90% confident that the task completes within that window?

Users can answer the questions above using the *window* and *gradient* layers, and the *confidence* slider (see Figure 2). The time windows enable users to specify earliest and latest desired times for task completion, and are shown as thin rust color lines behind the task boxes. The gradients layer displays histograms constructed from the Monte Carlo simulations of the schedule execution. The histograms for each task are visualized as color gradients on the time line, one for the start time and one for the end time. The intensity of the color at each time point is proportional to the number of simulation runs that started and ended at the given time point. The gradients for start-times are blue, and the gradients for end-times are green or red depending on the time windows and the value V of the confidence slider (between 0 and 1): If the fraction of the area of an end-time histogram that falls within the time window is larger than V, then the gradient is green, otherwise it is red.

In Figure 2, the left panel shows the histograms at 80% confidence: finish_carpentry and EXT_Carpentry_2 are expected to complete within their time windows with 80% confidence, while the other two tasks are not. When users drag the confidence slider, the colors update dynamically, enabling users to see the interplay between confidence and the time windows, seeing histograms change to red as they increase the desired confidence threshold. In Figure 2), the right panel shows the state when the user drags the confidence slider until the histogram for EXT_Carpentry_2 turns red, indicating that there is only a 90% confidence that this task will complete within the desired time window.

The user can answer the first two questions by manipulating the confidence slider, and moving the mouse to appropriate positions on the visualization and reading the time marker. The third question can be answered by defining the time windows for tasks and then moving the confidence slider until the corresponding histogram changes color (see Figure 2). For the fourth question, users can turn on the *spread* layer, which shows the spread window for the start and end-time of all tasks. Users can manipulate the confidence slider and see how the spreads change as a function of it. In schedules that use beta distributions, spreads increase dramatically as confidence approaches one.

To help users understand how uncertainty propagates, when users move the mouse over a task, COMPASS draws purple arrows from the enabling tasks to the enabled tasks. Figure 1 shows the enablement lines for the Drywall task in the middle

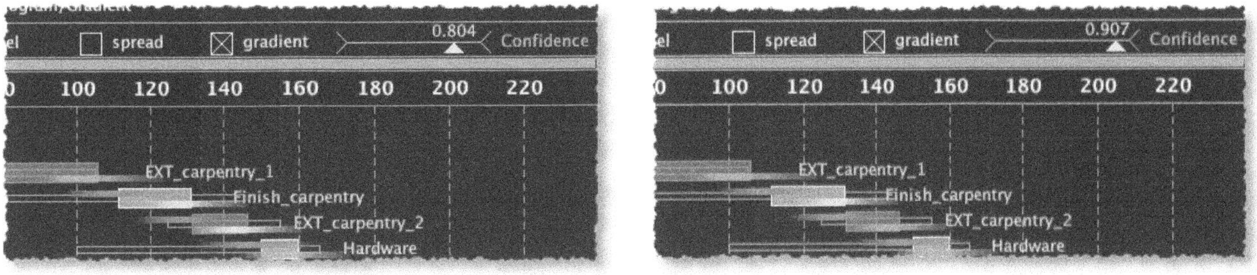

Figure 2. Time window, gradients and confidence sliders to analyze the uncertainty of task completion.

of the screen.

Which are the most critical tasks? In the traditional, non-stochastic Critical Path Method, a critical path consists of the set of tasks with the property that if any of these tasks are delayed, it will delay the completion of the schedule. Here the answer to the question is simple: the most critical tasks are those in the critical path, since any delay in these tasks will cause the schedule to slip (their slack is zero). If task durations are uncertain, the traditional definition is not appropriate because tasks can have a range of durations, and it is not clear which one should be used in the computation of the critical path.

To answer the question in the model with uncertainty, COMPASS computes the critical path of each simulation run, and then builds a histogram of all critical paths. Figure 1 shows the visualization of critical paths. The left panel lists the different critical paths and the percentage of traces where they occur. Users can compare critical paths visually by selecting them and seeing the curves that connect the tasks in each path. In our example, the most common critical path occurs 11.7% of the time, involving tasks for the painter, carpenter, counter-top installer and the plumber. Below the list of critical tasks is a list of tasks sorted by the likelihood that they lie on some critical path. This helps users understand the criticality of tasks and focuses their attention on the tasks that are more likely to cause schedule delays. For example, even though the most critical path occurs only 11.7% of the time, the most critical task is part of 86% of all critical paths.

What will happen if . . . ? Many interesting what-if questions can be expressed in terms of changes to the duration distributions of sets of tasks. For example:

1. If it rains, and every task affected by rain becomes twice as uncertain (e.g., the worst-case time doubles), when will we be 90% certain that our house is done?
2. If we believe the electrician underestimates his duration estimates by two days, when will our house be completed on average if we shift all his estimates upwards by two days?

COMPASS offers several ways to select tasks and alter distributions. Users can select tasks individually by clicking on them, and they can select all the tasks performed by an agent by clicking on the agent. A more sophisticated selection mechanism uses the *label* layer, where users can see and associate arbitrary labels (keywords) with tasks. Users can select all tasks with a given label by clicking on any of the labels. When tasks are selected, their duration distributions appear. Users can simultaneously modify all the distributions for the selected tasks by editing the distribution of any one of them. They can shift the distribution in either direction, and all other distributions are shifted by the same amount. They can drag the minimum or maximum time while keeping the other constant, and other distributions are scaled by the same amount. Figure 3 shows an example where the labels layer was activated, and the user selected all tasks labeled rain.

Using COMPASS, users can answer the first question by selecting all the tasks labeled rain, and then dragging the right edge of any of the distributions so that the distribution becomes twice as wide. When users release the mouse COMPASS re-runs the Monte Carlo simulations and within 2 seconds updates the display, showing how the new distributions affect the schedule. Similarly, users can answer the second question by clicking on the electrician to select all its tasks, dragging them two days to the right, and seeing the effect on the whole schedule.

Together, these features enable users to visualize how uncertainty affects the schedule, to investigate how external events that affect multiple tasks affect the whole schedule (e.g., rain), and to investigate the effects of alternative resources with different characteristics (e.g., faster, more reliable). Video: http://youtu.be/vmT86VXTN9Y

EVALUATION

Our evaluation, conducted with ten subjects, consisted of three 30-minute parts. In part 1, we familiarized users with the house schedule by giving them hardcopies of the Gantt chart and task dependency graphs, and explaining the schedule to them. In part 2, we trained users on COMPASS using a small sample plan consisting of 3 agents, 5 tasks, and 4 enablement dependencies. We introduced the COMPASS features one at a time, and asked users to practice it on the sample schedule before introducing the next feature. In part 3, we asked users to answer "when", "criticality" and "what-if" questions similar to those shown in the previous sections. We gave users 30 minutes to answer 20 questions.

Subjects answered 81% of the questions correctly. If we omit data from two users who had trouble with the direct manipulation techniques, the top 8 users answered 91% of the questions correctly. Based on exit surveys, the other major source of error was the users' general misunderstanding of the notion of spread.

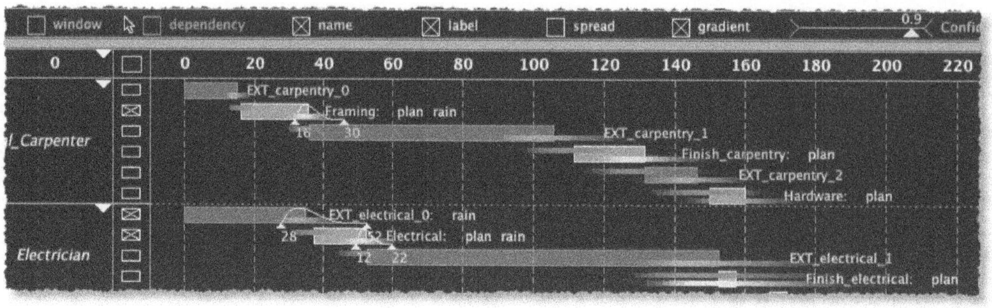

Figure 3. Tasks labeled *rain* are selected; their duration distributions can be simultaneously edited.

RELATED WORK

Clark and Gantt [4] published their seminal work on Gantt charts in 1923. This early work is noteworthy not only because it introduced Gantt charts, but also because it describes several variants of the basic Gantt chart that use additional symbols and annotations to encode additional information for decision making. While they did not address the issue of uncertainty, our work on embellishing Gantt charts to encode information useful for understanding uncertainty, follows the same approach. Our work is most similar to the work on Planning Lines [1] that also embellishes the basic Gantt charts to encode uncertainty by using shades of color to denote different intervals of uncertainty. Planning Lines focuses on conveying information about minimum and maximum duration times and earliest and latest start and completion times, and thus uses only a fixed number of colors. Tory et al. [6] also augment Gantt charts to show task delays and aid with schedule comparison. Our work quantifies the uncertainty using histograms, which we encode using color gradients.

Work on understanding uncertainty in schedules also has a long tradition. PERT [5] focused on "most likely time", "optimistic time", and "pessimistic time". More recent work [3, 2] focused on quantifying uncertainty using Monte Carlo techniques. This work focused on the mechanics of valid stochastic simulations, without paying heed to the need for user comprehension and interaction. For example, Lee [8] and Lana [7] introduced software that performs stochastic simulation and simple criticality analysis. After providing the plan parameters and assumptions through dialog boxes, the user is simply given the resulting distribution of plan completion times, without any insight about where the delays begin, how they propagate, where slack is helpful, or where to focus efforts to improve completion confidence. Our work visualizes the results of the simulations. However, the main difference between the previous work and our work is that the COMPASS visualizations are active. We use the dynamic query techniques first introduced by Shneiderman [9] to enable users to ask questions of the visualization, and thereby ask what-if questions about schedules.

CONCLUSIONS

The user study suggests that users understand the COMPASS visual language and can use it to answer questions regarding uncertainty. A surprising aspect of this work is that informal demonstrations to engineers and researchers revealed that they are unable to answer the questions in the user study without the system. COMPASS made them realize they had ignored an important issue in their reasoning. Our initial user study revealed that some users had trouble manipulating the small graphic elements of our visualization. We are working to refine the visualization and the interaction techniques, and on techniques to compare schedules so users can better understand the before and after states of their what-if scenarios.

Acknowledgements This research was sponsored by the Army Research Laboratory and was accomplished under Cooperative Agreement Number W911NF-11-2-0007. The views and conclusions contained in this document are those of the authors and should not be interpreted as representing the official policies, either expressed or implied, of the Army Research Laboratory or the U.S. Government. The U.S. Government is authorized to reproduce and distribute reprints for Government purposes notwithstanding any copyright notation herein.

REFERENCES

1. Aigner, W., Miksch, S., Muller, W., Schumann, H., and Tominski, C. Visual methods for analyzing time-oriented data. *IEEE Transactions on Visualization and Computer Graphics 14* (2008), 47–60.
2. Bowman, R. A. Efficient estimation of arc criticalities in stochastic activity networks, 1995.
3. Burt, J. M., and Garman, M. B. Conditional monte carlo: A simulation technique for stochastic network analysis. *Management Science 18*, 3 (1971), 207–217.
4. Clark, W., and Gantt, H. L. *TThe Gantt chart, a working tool of management*. New York, Ronald Press, 1923.
5. Fazar, W. Program evaluation and review technique. *The American Statistician 13*, 2 (1959), 646–669.
6. Huang, D., Tory, M., Staub-French, S., and Pottinger, R. Visualization techniques for schedule comparison. *Computer Graphics Forum 28*, 3 (2009), 951–958.
7. Lana, E. H. Stochastic critical path. In *Crystal Ball User Conference* (2006).
8. Lee, D.-E. Probability of project completion using stochastic project scheduling simulation. *Journal of construction engineering and management 131*, 3 (March 2005), 310–318.
9. Schneiderman, B. Dynamic queries for visual information seeking. *IEEE Software 11* (1994), 70–77.

The Quest for Validated Personality Trait Stories

Matt Dennis, Judith Masthoff, Chris Mellish
Computing Science, University of Aberdeen
King's College, AB24 3UE, Aberdeen, UK
{m.dennis, j.masthoff, c.mellish}@abdn.ac.uk

ABSTRACT
This paper describes how a set of stories, each conveying a personality trait from the Five Factor Model at a high or low level, were developed using Amazon's Mechanical Turk. These stories will be used to develop interfaces that adapt to personality using a User as Wizard method. The paper shows how difficult it is to construct stories that convey a single personality trait. It also shows how such stories can be constructed for most cases, and how Mechanical Turk can aid to achieve this.

Author Keywords
Personality, validation, adaptation, user stories

ACM Classification Keywords
H.1.2 User/Machine Systems: Human Factors

General Terms
Design, Experimentation, Human Factors, Measurement

INTRODUCTION
AI researchers have been interested in personality for a long time [2]. Within the Intelligent User Interface field, there has been considerable research on personality, for example: detecting personality for recommender systems [3], how personality affects users' attitudes to technology and adaptive strategies [4], how it affects goals while learning [5] and how it can be used in conjunction with existing preference elicitation methods [6].

Many theories of personality have been developed, of which the trait model is seen as a convenient way to model and measure personality for computer systems [7]. There are several trait models; the Five Factor Model (FFM) [1] is the most popular among psychologists [8]. In this paper, the five traits are referred to as: Extraversion (Ext), Agreeableness (Agr), Conscientiousness (Cons), Emotional Stability (ES) and Openness (Op). These traits are relatively easy to identify and measure, due to the prevalence of validated questionnaires.

To design an intelligent system which adapts to personality, we can utilize the User as Wizard method [9]. This method suggests that studies are conducted in which participants take the role of the system, to investigate and model how they adapt to a user, in this case to a user's personality.

To use this method, participants (playing the part of the "system") would need to be provided with an indication of the personality of the "user". A first option is to use real users. However, it is hard to ensure participants adapt to personality instead of for example affective state. Also, participants would have to spend considerable time with the user to fully understand their personality. A second option is to ask participants to "imagine a user with personality X" or provide a statement such as "John is confident". This approach has been tried unsuccessfully: saying "John is confident" as part of other data about the user was easily overlooked and ignored [10]. A third option is to provide a story about the user which conveys their personality. This approach was taken successfully in [10], which investigated whether Generalized Self-Efficacy was taken into account by teachers when giving feedback. This option implicitly made the users' personality more prominent, without giving away what was being investigated.

This paper describes an investigation into the creation of validated stories for each of the five traits in the FFM, for use by those investigating the role of personality in intelligent systems. It also shows how Mechanical Turk [12] can be used to run the many studies required.

STUDIES
The goal was to develop and validate, for each trait, a pair of stories about a student: one story conveying a high level of the target trait, and the other conveying a low level of that trait. We also wanted the stories in each pair to only vary the level of the target trait. So, for example, we wanted a story conveying high extraversion and a story conveying low extraversion, but conveying other traits similarly and in a neutral fashion. We ran a series of studies; each focusing on one target trait, all using the same design.

Design

Experimental Design
We used a between-subject design, where each participant was presented with a story about a student, with the story predicted to convey a particular target trait at either a high or low-level. Participants then assessed this student's personality using the big 5 Mini-Markers scale [11].

Trait			Ext		Agr		Cons		ES		Op	
Normal range			4.75 – 7.63		5.10 – 7.96		4.48 – 7.10		3.72 – 6.08		4.99 – 7.45	
Story	Target trait	Story type	Perceived Trait Levels									
			Ext		Agr		Cons		ES		Op	
	Ext	Low	1.78 (0.76)	***	**4.85 (1.31)**	***	6.08 (1.04)		4.90 (0.52)	***	5.47 (1.35)	
		High	8.25 (0.42)		7.47 (0.62)		5.52 (1.04)		**6.1 (0.85)**		5.77 (0.65)	
	Agr	Low	7.10 (0.73)		1.71 (0.88)	***	4.91 (0.57)		**2.80 (1.01)**	***	**4.96 (0.77)**	
		High	6.37 (0.88)		8.48 (0.49)		5.67 (0.96)		**7.28 (0.96)**		5.20 (0.50)	
	Cons	Low	**4.79 (0.45)**	*	**4.75 (0.45)**	***	2.00 (0.76)	***	4.93 (0.37)		**3.44 (1.14)**	*
		High	5.73 (0.57)		6.3 (1.06)		8.13 (0.98)		5.73 (0.89)		5.30 (1.13)	
	ES	Low	**3.92 (0.76)**	***	**5.05 (0.37)**	***	**4.25 (0.94)**	***	3.07 (0.47)	***	5.23 (1.14)	
		High	5.96 (1.08)		6.57 (0.83)		6.64 (1.34)		7.73 (0.94)		5.44 (0.70)	
	Op	Low	**4.70 (0.92)**	***	**3.92 (1.42)**	*	6.22 (0.97)		4.76 (1.35)		2.76 (1.54)	***
		High	**7.75 (0.82)**		5.67 (1.11)		5.43 (1.20)		5.67 (1.22)		7.48 (1.61)	

Table 1. Perceived levels of traits for the constructed stories, T-test significance values between low and high stories, Bonferroni corrected, *=p<.05, **=p<.01, ***=p<.001. Grey cells indicate level of target trait. Non-target trait value in bold = outside normal range. Significance value in bold = undesirable difference between non target traits. Target trait score underline = score not outside normal range.

Participants

We first compared results of on-site participants with those found by using Mechanical Turk and found that they were similar. Following this, participants were found using Mechanical Turk and paid $0.40. Participants were adults and based in the US. Only people with a high level of English fluency (tested through the Cloze Test [13]) could participate. Participants were excluded if their response was incomplete or they rated each descriptor identically at the middle of the scale (to avoid including spammers).

Materials

The stories were adapted from the NEO-IPIP 20-item scales [14]: combining the phrases into sentences to form a short story, with the addition of a name picked from the most common male names [15]. Table 2 shows an example.

NEO-IPIP Phrases for ES Low	Often feel blue. Dislike myself. Am often down in the dumps. Have frequent mood swings. Panic easily. Am filled with doubts about things. Feel threatened easily. Get stressed out easily. Fear for the worst. Worry about things.
Story Generated for ES Low	Josh often feels sad, and dislikes the way he is. He is often down in the dumps and suffers from frequent mood swings. He is often filled with doubts about things and is easily threatened. He gets stressed out easily, fearing the worst. He panics easily and worries about things.

Table 2: Example of story construction.

Independent Variables

The independent variable was the story, in two levels: high and low. The high story was constructed to portray a high level of the target trait, and the low story a low level.

Dependent Variables

The dependent variables were the perceived levels of the target trait and non-target traits, as rated by the participants.

Hypotheses

H1: There will be a significant difference in the perceived level of the target trait between the high and low story.

H2: The perceived level of the target trait will be outside the trait's normal range, with the perceived level being higher than the normal range for the high story, and lower than the normal range for the low story.

H3: There will be no significant difference in the perceived level of the non-target traits between the high story and the low story.

H4: The perceived level of the non-target traits will be within normal range both for the high and low story.

Procedure

Participants read a story about a student and then rated the Mini-Marker's 40 adjectives on how well they applied to that student, using a scale from 1 (extremely inaccurate) to 9 (extremely accurate). They were instructed to use 5 if they hadn't got enough information to decide. Results were scored as outlined by [11], resulting in a rating for each trait on a scale from 1 (extremely low) to 9 (extremely high). To decide on the traits' normal range, we used the ratings of a liked peer from the norms for mini-marker scale [11]: we used the range of the mean minus standard deviation till the mean plus standard deviation (see Table 1).

Results

Table 1 shows the results of the original stories. There were 10 participants per story (67% female).

In correspondence with Hypothesis H1, between all 5 pairs of stories there was a significant difference in the perceived trait values for the target trait between the high story and the low story. In support of hypothesis H2, for all but one personality trait (Openness), the perceived target trait values were outside the normal range and in the correct direction. The perceived target trait value for Openness is outside the normal range and in the correct direction for the low story. The high story varied the trait correctly in the high direction, but failed to make it high enough to be outside the normal range. In contrast to H3, there were many significant differences between the perceived non target trait values as outlined in Table 1. Several perceived non-target trait values were also outside the normal range, showing H4 did not hold for these stories.

Discussion & Mitigation

The stories did not meet our objectives as set out by our hypotheses. The following problems occurred between the pairs of stories:

P1. Perceived trait values on a non-target trait differ significantly

P2. Perceived trait values on a non-target trait are outside normal range

P3. Perceived target trait values are within normal range

Problems P1 and P2 often appeared together. That is, one (or both) of the perceived values for a non-target trait were outside normal range and thus significantly different from the other. We therefore tried to address P1 and P2 together.

For example, in the story for Low Extraversion, the student was perceived to be less agreeable than normal. The story correctly conveyed that they had low extraversion and the scores for the remaining non target traits was within the normal range. Thus we hypothesised that the following approaches could be taken in an attempt to mitigate problems P1 and P2:

S1. Add a statement to the story which implied a semi neutral stance on the problem trait. For example "Jack is quite a nice person" to mitigate low Agreeableness.

S2. Remove a statement which may be causing the interaction. For example, removing "Jack has little to say to others" may increase agreeableness.

S3. Add a statement from a story targeting the non-target trait that is causing the problem. For example, we could add "Jack has a good word for everyone" from the High Agreeableness story to increase agreeableness.

We used S1 as we wanted to avoid removing statements from the stories wherever possible, as this may affect their ability to convey the target trait. We rejected S3 as it may alter the non-target trait score too much and bring it out of range in the other direction.

The results from the original stories show that most undesired non-target trait scores occurred in the Low stories, with scores lower than normal range. To mitigate, we constructed slightly positive statements (see Table 3).

For the High variants of the stories, only two non-target traits needed to be modified: Extraversion in the Openness High story, and Emotional Stability in the Extraversion High and Agreeableness High stories.

For the Extraversion High story, the score for Emotional Stability was 6.10, and the normal range ends at 6.08. Because this was so close, and there was no significant difference between that and the Low variant's ES score, we decided not to modify it as doing so may affect other traits. In the case of the Agreeableness High story, the value for

Non-target trait	Statement to add if below normal
Extraversion	tends to enjoy talking with people
Agreeableness	quite a nice person
Conscientiousness	tends to do his work
Emotional Stability	tends to be calm
Openness	quite likes exploring new ideas

Table 3. Mitigating statements

ES was 7.28. So we again utilized S1, adding a mildly negative statement "He is occasionally a bit anxious".

The Openness High story was a special case as it did not convey its target trait convincingly, so the original story required modification any way. So, approach S2 was used in this case, removing statements such as "[he can] express himself beautifully" as shown in Table 4.

Original Op High story	Oliver believes in the importance of art and has a vivid imagination. He tends to vote for liberal political candidates. He likes to carry the conversation to a higher level, enjoying hearing new ideas. He enjoys thinking about things and can express himself beautifully. He enjoys wild flights of fantasy, getting excited by new ideas. He has a rich vocabulary.
Changed version	Oliver believes in the importance of art and has a vivid imagination. He tends to vote for liberal political candidates. He enjoys hearing new ideas and thinking about things. He enjoys wild flights of fantasy, getting excited by new ideas.

Table 4: Two stories for high openness

Round 2 results

Table 5 shows the results of the modified stories. Solution S1 was successful in most cases in mitigating problems P1 and P2. Exceptions to this were in the Agreeableness stories, the undesired non-target trait scores still remain, with the Low story expressing low ES and the High story expressing high ES (problems P1 and P2). In the Conscientiousness stories, problem P1 occurred for Openness, despite both values being in the normal range. For Emotional Stability, S1 was not effective for bringing the perceived trait value into normal range for Extraversion in the low story, with problems P1 and P2 still extant.

S2 was successful in solving P2 for Openness High; the Agreeableness value is now in normal range. However it was not successful in solving P3 for Openness high; the score for the target trait is still within normal range.

CONCLUSIONS

We partially achieved our goals; we have a set of stories[1] which convey each trait from the five factor model at high and low levels. The challenge was to have them express a target trait at a polarized level, whilst expressing non target traits as normal, however this was always going to be difficult. While the traits are supposed to be orthogonal, several studies have shown they are intercorrelated [8].

In the case of Agreeableness versus Emotional Stability, this interaction was too strong for our statements to fix.

[1] See www.abdn.ac.uk/~r06md9/stories for the stories.

Trait			Ext		Agr		Cons		ES		Op	
Normal range			4.75 – 7.63		5.10 – 7.96		4.48 – 7.10		3.72 – 6.08		4.99 – 7.45	
	Target trait	Story type	Perceived Trait Levels									
			Ext		Agr		Cons		ES		Op	
Story	Ext	Low	2.00 (0.64)	***	5.91 (1.04)	***	5.64 (0.88)		5.05 (1.00)		5.48 (1.18)	
		High†	8.25 (0.42)		7.47 (0.62)		5.52 (1.04)		6.10 (0.85)		5.77 (0.65)	
	Agr	Low	6.65 (1.08)		1.78 (0.77)	***	5.01 (1.43)		**2.94 (1.45)**	***	5.11 (1.10)	
		High	5.84 (1.07)		8.21 (0.62)		5.64 (0.68)		**6.26 (1.17)**		5.21 (0.69)	
	Cons	Low	6.59 (0.69)		5.93 (0.86)		2.16 (0.91)	***	5.67 (1.01)		5.06 (1.03)	***
		High†	5.73 (0.57)		6.3 (1.06)		8.13 (0.98)		5.73 (0.89)		5.30 (1.13)	
	ES	Low	**4.49 (1.59)**	**	6.38 (0.67)		5.77 (1.00)		3.35 (0.71)	***	5.97 (0.76)	
		High†	5.96 (1.08)		6.57 (0.83)		6.64 (1.34)		7.73 (0.94)		5.44 (0.70)	
	Op	Low	6.39 (0.78)		5.77 (1.13)		5.59 (0.91)		5.38 (0.99)		2.91 (1.44)	***
		High	6.89 (1.04)		6.60 (1.18)		5.00 (1.32)		5.92 (1.24)		7.28 (0.93)	

Table 5. Perceived levels of traits for the revised stories, T-test significance values between low and high stories Bonferroni corrected, **=p<.01, ***=p<.001. Grey cells indicate level of target trait. Non-target trait value in bold=outside normal range. Significance value in bold = undesirable difference between non-target traits. Target trait value underlined = score not outside normal range.

Adding a stronger statement to the story to attempt to bring Emotional Stability into the normal range may cause more interactions with the other three non-target traits.

For the two stories targeting Conscientiousness, the score for Openness significantly differed despite being in the normal range (P1). We may need to relax our requirements and accept stories as long as the perceived score for the non-target trait is in the normal range for the two stories.

Problem P3 was not solved in the case of High Openness. Openness may be the most difficult trait to immediately conceptualise, incorporating culture and art as well as political beliefs [8]. The perceived score was at the high end of the scale, however, it was the only trait that scored so highly. It is likely therefore that it was expressing Openness highly, just not outside the range we devised.

The fact that the statements which the stories were based on do not only express information about their target trait may cast doubt about the effectiveness of the five factor model and its measurement methods. However, it is possible that when participants read the stories about one trait, they draw on their life experiences of people who displayed these traits, and score the other traits in line with this.

Validating material can be resource intensive, particularly as the evaluation of adaptive systems may require a lot of different materials to represent different types of users. Our research shows that Mechanical Turk can be effectively used for validation. It proved to be a reliable source for recruiting participants, with $0.01 per question seeming reasonable. Results could be previewed before payment, allowing spam to be filtered out. Spam was more frequent if multiple studies were running simultaneously, so studies were ran one at a time. Random button pressing did not occur, as results always identified the target trait.

ACKNOWLEDGEMENTS

We thank Helen Pain for her suggestions. The studies were funded by EPSRC platform grant EP/E011764/1.

REFERENCES

1. Goldberg, R. (1993). The structure of phenotypic personality traits. *American Psychologist, 48*(1), 26-34.
2. Carbonell, J. (1980). Towards a Process Model of Personality Traits. *Artificial Intelligence, 15*, 49-74.
3. Dunn, G., Wiersama J., Ham, J. & Aroyo L. (2009). Evaluating Interface Variants on Personality Acquisition for Recommender Systems. *UMAP 2009*, 259-270.
4. Graziola, I., Pianesi F., Zancanaro M, & Goren-bar, D. (2005). Dimensions of Adaptivity in Mobile Systems: Personality and People's Attitudes. *IUI'05*, 223-230.
5. Zhou, X. and Conati, C. (2003). Inferring User Goals from Personality and Behavior in a Causal Model of User Affect. *IUI'03*, 211-218.
6. Hu, R. & Pu, P. (2009). A comparative user study on rating vs. personality quiz based preference elicitation methods. *IUI'09*, 367-372
7. Nunes, M. A. S. N. (2008). Recommender system based on personality traits. PhD Thesis. Université Montpellier.
8. Chamorro-Premuzic, T. (2011). *Personality and Individual Differences*, 2nd Ed. Oxford: BPS Blackwell
9. Paramythis, A. et al. (2010). Layered evaluation of interactive adaptive systems: framework and formative methods . UMUAI, 20, 383-453.
10. Dennis, M., Masthoff, J., Pain, H., & Mellish, C. (2011). Does self-efficacy matter when generating motivational feedback? AIED, 444-446.
11. Saucier, G. (1994). Mini-markers: A brief version of Goldberg's unipolar big-five markers. *Journal of Personality Assessment, 63*(1), 506-516.
12. Amazon Mechanical Turk, (http://www.mturk.com).
13. Taylor, W.L. (1953). Cloze procedure: A new tool for measuring readability. *Journalism Quarterly, 30*, 415–433
14. International Personality Item Pool (ipip.ori.org/).
15. Top baby names of 2008, (guardian.co.uk)

Audio Cloud: Creation and Rendering

Jitendra Ajmera, Om D Deshmukh, Anupam Jain,
Amit Anil Nanavati, Nitendra Rajput, Saurabh Srivastava
IBM India Research Lab
4, Block C, ISID Campus, Vasant Kunj, New Delhi, India
jajmera1,odeshmuk,anupamjain,namit,rnitendra,saurabhsrivastava@in.ibm.com

ABSTRACT
Word clouds are extensively used to present a summary of the prominent words in a document on the World Wide Web. Such clouds give the user an idea about the content of the document. In this paper we present a mechanism to create and render an audio cloud for audio content. Such audio clouds are expected to provide a similar summary of the audio documents. They have wide applicability in various domains, especially for low-literate users who currently do not use the Internet but interact with audio-based systems.

Detecting words from an audio content is challenging, especially if the audio is in languages for which a speech recognition system does not exist. We present a language-independent mechanism to detect frequently occurring words within an audio document. We then present four ways to render these words that form an audio cloud. The four prototypes for rendering the audio cloud are based on varying the amplitude, the voice quality, echo and the repetition of audio words. An evaluation study conducted across 32 users suggests that literate and low-literate users easily understand the concept of audio cloud.

Author Keywords
Audio cloud, low-literate, language independent

ACM Classification Keywords
H.5.2 Information Interfaces and Presentation: User Interfaces—*Voice I/O*.

General Terms
Design, Experimentation, Human Factors

INTRODUCTION
With increasing amount of text on the world wide web, summarization techniques [5] and the concepts of keywords and tags [2] started to develop for representing a large text document. Recently, Word Clouds [11] have emerged as a very powerful and intuitive way to represent the content of a document. These word clouds present the most frequently occurring words in a larger font (example Figure 1) so that the user gets not only the keywords but also their relative occurrences in the document.

Figure 1. A word could of the abstract in this paper

Wide adoption of word clouds on the Internet suggests that they are able to provide a good representation of the content and that the users are able to perceive the representation. In this paper we wish to replicate the concept of word clouds for audio content. The goal is to create an audio cloud of a spoken document. A user should be able to determine the keywords and their level of importance in a speech by listening to the audio cloud. We therefore define an audio cloud to be an audio utterance that contains different words spoken in different styles such that each word can represent a different level of prominence. While it is clear that large font size can suggest an increased prominence of the text based word cloud, such features need to be explored in the audio world. We wish to determine such features through the work presented in this paper.

A visual illustration of an audio segment and its corresponding audio cloud is shown in Figure 2. Figure 2(a) has the 100 second long audio signal. The color coding represents words that are repeated in the audio. Four prominent words that are repeated often enough are used to form the audio cloud that is shown in Figure 2(b). Detection of repetitive prominent parts in an audio of any language and then rendering them to generate the audio cloud is the focus of this paper.

Paper Contribution
The high-level contribution of this paper is to present the concept of audio cloud that can be used to represent prominent words in any spoken content. As with the case of word cloud,

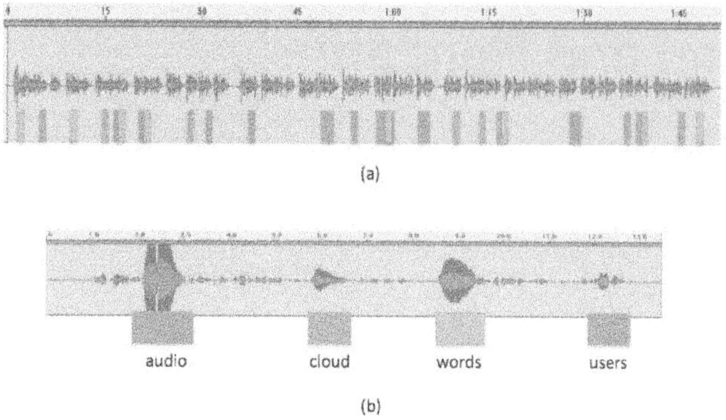

Figure 2. (a) The audio corresponding to the abstract of this paper. The vertical marks represent the location of the most frequent words in this segment. (b) The audio cloud of the four words, each with different amplitude, corresponding to the frequency of occurrence in the above audio document.

the audio content could be of any length. However, it is challenging to determine the frequency of repetitions of words in an audio content, unlike the case of text. An audio needs to be converted to text using speech recognition techniques before applying such frequency based counting techniques. However, such speech recognition systems do not exist for a large number of languages in developing countries.

Our second main contribution is in the space of being able to detect the repetitive audio words or phrases in a language-independent manner. We present a subword-unit based method to detect frequently occurring patterns from audio content, without having to perform speech recognition. *The third contribution of the paper is with respect to presenting these words in the audio cloud.* We develop and evaluate four prototypes of presenting audio clouds: changing volume, changing voice quality, echoing words and changing word repetition frequency.

The motivation for this work stems from the fact that while word clouds are very popular on the Internet, the Internet penetration in rural developing regions is still below 2% [3]. This coupled with the fact that ninety eight percent of all non-literates live in developing countries [10] suggests that providing oral information over mobile devices has the potential to reach the 3 billion users who are currently not accessing any information technology services.

CLOUD CREATION: AUDIO PATTERN MINING

One of the obvious choices to detect prominent audio patterns is to employ a large-vocabulary continuous speech recognition (LVCSR) system. A significant drawback of this approach is that it cannot deal with out-of-vocabulary (OOV) words. Many of these OOV words are proper nouns such as place and people names which are very likely to be the desired prominent patterns. To allow for the detection of these OOVs we explore an approach based on phoneme lattices.

Our approach is based on using a phonetic speech recognizer to generate phonetic lattices. Phonetic lattices essentially represent N-best phonetic strings. An efficient method for indexing these lattices and searching for a given query is presented in [8]. This method is efficient as it allows for searching for a given query with a single composition operation between an index WFST [8] and the query acceptor. The index WFST maps every possible phonetic substring present in the data to the set of utterances where the substring is found. The weight on each arc corresponds to the expected number of counts of the substring in any particular utterance for a given query. Once the target utterances are idenfitied, the next step is to get the timing information and corresponding ASR confidence of the resulting segments. This is acheived by converting the phonetic lattices of the utterances into WFSTs where for every input phoneme label the output label is the timing information and the weight is the posterior probability associated with the phoneme. The WFST implementation is based on the OpenFST toolkit [1].

To establish the effectiveness of this phonetic approach, first set of evaluations were conducted on 15 English query terms and 15 hours of indexed Indian English data. The Acoustic Model (AM) associated with the phonetic recognizer was trained on 300 hours of Indian English data. The phonetic Language Model (LM) was trained on the phone-level transcription of this data where each word is considered as individual training utterance. The P@10 (precision at 10) accuracy was 88% in this case which establishes the efficacy of the proposed approach.

The approach also has the advantage of working for languages where the available data is not enough to train an ASR system for that language. To demonstrate that, we indexed 15 hours of Gujarati data using the Indian English AM mentioned above. The P@10 accuracy for 15 Gujarati terms is 45%. Note that all of these 15 Gujarati terms are OOV with respect to the Indian English AM. A significant improvement was obtained by using a phone-level LM trained on Gujarati data. The Gujarati data was obtained from local online news sites. The Gujarati text was first transliterated into Roman script and then a Grapheme-to-Phoneme (G2P) system was used to obtain phone level transcription of these Gujarati words. The G2P system was trained on Hindi for which we have enough pairs of words and their phonetic transcription. Note that we chose Hindi (over India English) for G2P training as Hindi is phonetically and orthographically similar to Gujarati and the phoneset in our Hindi data is identical to that of the Indian English phonset. The P@10 accuracy for this revised system is 65%.

CLOUD RENDERING

After detecting the prominent words (or segments of audio) within an audio document, as shown in the previous section, the next step is to present these audio words to the user in a fashion that makes it convenient to perceive the relative prominence of the words.

As one would imagine, there can be a number of ways to render an audio cloud to the user. Since the end users (especially the low-literate population) may have never seen or may not know the concept of a word cloud, it is critical to determine the most intuitive and usable rendering of an audio cloud. Marzano's information processing theory [6] claims that a short term acoustic memory can be held longer than iconic memory. Studies in cognitive psychology have found that people have a higher ability to hold sound than images if there are up to seven pieces of independent information [7]. Therefore we restrict our audio cloud design to contain not more than eight words. That said, the inherently sequential nature of audio makes the interaction design of an audio cloud even more challenging than a word cloud since the rendition is parallel in the latter. To remove the transitory nature of the audio, we presume that a user can listen to the audio cloud more than once till s/he is able to determine which words are more prominent than others.

The rich nature of audio signals allow for a range of features to be modulated to contrast the relative prominence of different words. The features modulated in this study to generate the audio cloud from a given set of words are: (a) amplitude, (b) voice-quality, (c) word-echo, (d) word repetitions. We will now describe our basis for choosing these four features for rendering the audio cloud.

Amplitude: Formal studies to evaluate the effect of various speech parameters on perceived dominance rate amplitude as one of the strong correlates of perceived dominance. For example, authors in [9] report that *'results indicated that mean amplitude and amplitude standard deviation were positively associated with dominance judgments'*. Our hypothesis is that words with higher amplitude would be perceived as more prominent ones as compared to the words with lower amplitudes.

Voice Quality: Studies in Psychology (c.f., [4]) have shown that for both men and women, a male voice is perceived to be more dominant in establishing trust and authority. It is therefore reasonable to expect that variations in pitch (largely indicative of the human gender) and variations in formant frequencies (largely indicative of the vocal tract size and hence the overall size of the speaker) can be utilized to encode the relative prominence of the words. In the current study, we recorded speech signals from two male and two female speakers with different voice qualities.

Echo: The third rendition is based on echoing the individual audio segments. In the Indian culture, especially among the low-literates, there is a general conception that any message from God or an expression from a 'superlative' human is announced in the form of an echo.

Repetition: In the fourth prototype of the audio cloud, we represent the prominence of a word by the number of times it is repeated. When a user listens to an audio cloud continuously, more prominent words would occur more frequently in this rendition.

EXPERIMENTS AND RESULTS

The goal of the experiment was to measure the accuracy with which participants determine the auditory prominence of the words in the audio cloud. Through a performance test (described later) we tested whether the difference between the participants' order of tags was significantly different form the expected order. To keep things simple and to remain within the Millers magic number, we designed the first experiment with four words in the audio cloud.

Rendering Prototype	Words	Variable Feature
Amplitude	Ahmedabad	24 dB
	Shaakbhaaji	18 dB
	Baraber	12 dB
	Utpadan	6 dB
Voice-Quality	Jamnagar	$f_0 = 108; f_1 = 425$
	Jagdish	$f_0 = 195; f_1 = 499$
	Kisaan	$f_0 = 151; f_1 = 450$
	Namaskar	$f_0 = 237; f_1 = 499$
Echo	Kapas	4 echo
	Jantunashak	3 echo
	Magnesium	2 echo
	Khatarnak	1 echo
Repetitions	Gujarat	4 times
	Adhunik	3 times
	Prasaran	2 times
	Karykram	1 time

Table 1. The different audio cloud prototypes and the corresponding words in them.

Table 1 shows the four prototypes, the corresponding words in them and the value of the variable feature for each prototype. As is seen in the table, no words are repeated across prototypes - to ensure there is no bias introduced due to repeated listening of the same word.

Participants were asked to listen to the four audio clouds one after the other, in no particular order. A participant was allowed to listen to a particular audio cloud more than once, till they were confident of the order. The number of times an audio was played was noted and verbal feedback were collected. This process was repeated for all the four prototypes. Finally, participants were asked to rank the four prototypes in order of their preference.

Figure 3. Researcher interacting with different participants during the course of the study.

The experiment was conducted with 32 participants in North India. Out of these, sixteen participants were literate (with more than 16 years of formal education) and 16 were low literate (with less than 10 years of formal education). All were Hindi speaking and aged from 22 to 46. Out of these 32 participants, 5 were female and rest were male. Each participant was met individually, was introduced to the study and the prototype and was explained the steps for conducting the task.

We use two different metrics to quantify the comparisons across the ground-truth rank and the user-estimated rank. The Average Rank Mismatch (ARM) is defined as the average of the absolute difference between the ground-truth rank and the user-estimated rank. ARM is 0 when the user-estimated rank is exactly the same as the ground-truth rank for all the words and increases steadily as the rank differences increase. The Discounted Cumulative Gain (DCG) measure factors in the

	ARM		DCG	
	mean	std-dev	mean	std-dev
	Literate participants			
Amplitude	**0.406**	0.417	**8.114**	1.379
Voice-Quality	**0.438**	0.443	**7.813**	1.602
Echo	0.813	0.479	6.527	1.583
Repetition	0.594	0.664	7.222	2.220
	Low-literate participants			
Amplitude	**0.719**	0.446	**7.151**	1.347
Voice-Quality	**0.656**	0.598	**7.216**	2.037
Echo	1.063	0.479	6.180	1.505
Repetition	1.031	0.670	5.977	2.235
	All participants			
Amplitude	**0.563**	0.453	**7.632**	1.427
Voice-Quality	**0.547**	0.529	**7.515**	1.828
Echo	0.938	0.488	6.353	1.530
Repetition	0.813	0.693	6.599	2.281

Table 2. Mean and standard deviation of ARM and DCG measures for the four prototypes

ground-truth rank of the individual words while evaluating the user-estimated ranks. The gain values are 10, 7, 3 and 0 for *Exact Match*, *Approximate Match*, *Possible Match*, and *Clear Mismatch*, respectively.

Table 2 compares the mean and standard deviation values for the ARM and DCG measures for the four prototypes described earlier. The *Amplitude* performed the best for the literate speakers on both the ARM and the DCG measures while the *Voice-Quality* prototype is a close second. Optimal performance on both the measures implies that the *Amplitude* prototype not only leads to minimum number of aggregate rank mismatches but the number of mismatches on words with high ground-truth ranks is also low for this prototype. In the case of low-literate speakers, the *Voice-Quality* prototype performed the best on both the measures while the *Amplitude* prototype is a close second. Overall, the *Amplitude* prototype and the *Voice-Quality* prototype are better than the other two prototypes.

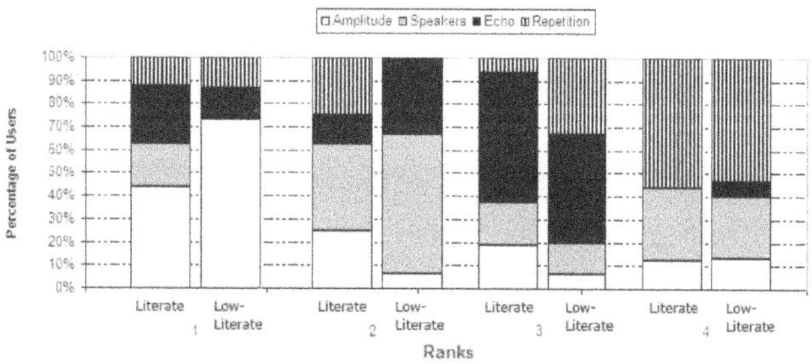

Figure 4. Ranked preferences of participants for the four prototypes.

Figure 4 shows the rank that participants assigned to the four prototypes. The literate users clearly prefer the *Amplitude* and the Voice-Quality prototype in their qualitative assessment of the different audio clouds. Low-literate users also have a clear preference for the *Amplitude* prototype in their qualitative assessment. However the second most-preferred prototype is not clearly *Voice-Quality* audio cloud, but it is the most prominent one. These qualitative results of the ranks correlate with the quantitative results mentioned above, which rate the *Amplitude* and the *Voice-Quality* audio cloud as the best.

From the qualitative and quantitative analysis, it is safe to infer that Amplitude and Voice-Quality prototypes are more promising in terms of rendering the prominence of words.

CONCLUSION

To our knowledge this is the first paper to introduce the concept of audio clouds. Generating audio cloud from an audio document is a non-trivial extension from the text domain. We present a novel method to detect frequent words from a given audio. This technique is language-independent as it uses sub-word units based pattern matching within the audio document. We then present four different ways to render the frequent words based on their prominence. We believe the paper opens up research avenues in the domain of audio clouds and establishes a novel audio summarization technique.

Audio clouds have immense potential for the call-center industry where operators deal with millions of calls but analyzing these calls becomes difficult due to lack of accurate speech recognizers. The music industry provides another potential use-case where audio clouds can be used to generate a thumbnail of songs for a pre-purchase review to customers.

REFERENCES

1. Allauzen, C., Riley, M., Schalkwyk, J., Skut, W., and Mohri, M. Openfst: A general and efficient weighted finite-state transducer library. *CIAA* (2007), 11–23.
2. Furnas, G. W., Fake, C., von Ahn, L., Schachter, J., Golder, S., Fox, K., Davis, M., Marlow, C., and Naaman, M. Why do tagging systems work? In *CHI '06 extended abstracts*, CHI EA '06 (2006), 36–39.
3. Internet Usage World Wide by Country. http://www.infoplease.com/ipa/a0933606.html, Last accessed on October 10, 2011.
4. Legg, L., and Gilbert, P. A pilot study of gender of voice and gender of voice hearer in psychotic voice hearers. *Psychology and Psychotherapy: Theory, Research and Practice* (2006), 517–527.
5. Liddy, E. Advances in automatic text summarization. *Inf. Retr. 4* (April 2001), 82–83.
6. Marzano, R. J. A theory-based meta-analysis of research on instruction. *Mid-continent Aurora, Colorado: Regional Educational Laboratory.* (2000).
7. Miller, G. A. The magical number seven, plus or minus two: Some limits on our capacity for processing information. *The Psychological Review* (1956), 81–97.
8. Parada, C., Sethy, A., and Ramabhadran, B. Query-by-example spoken term detection for oov terms. *Proc. of Automatic Speech Recognition and Understanding* (2009).
9. Tusing, K., and Dillard, J. The sounds of dominance. *Human Communication Research 26*, 1 (2000), 148–171.
10. UNESCO Institute for Statistics. Global education digest 2010: Comparing education statistics across the world, 2010.
11. Vigas, A. B., Wattenberg, M., and Feinberg, J. Participatory visualization with wordle. *IEEE Transactions on Visualization and Computer Graphics 15* (2009).

Pointing at Responsive Objects Outdoors

Yang-Lei Zhao, Arpan Chakraborty, KyungWha Hong, Shishir Kakkaradi, and Robert St. Amant
Department of Computer Science
North Carolina State University
yzhao11 | achakra | khong | achakra | smkakara | stamant@ncsu.edu

ABSTRACT
In this paper we analyze pointing techniques for simple remote control of nearby and distant objects in an outdoor environment, using a mobile phone. In an experiment we determine the accuracy of pointing at targets from a few meters to a few hundred meters away, either by focusing the phone's camera on a target or holding the phone at waist level in the direction of the target. We describe a simulated network application in which users can activate and control one or more responsive objects using either interaction technique.

Author Keywords
Pointing devices, ubiquitous computing

ACM Classification Keywords
H5.2 Information interfaces and presentation: User Interfaces—*Input devices and strategies*

General Terms
Human Factors, Performance

INTRODUCTION
In this paper we explore the possibilities for interaction with "responsive" objects in a large-scale environment: objects that users can see and that respond visibly to commands. For example, imagine adjusting the view of a motor driven security camera placed high on a building or a spotlight on an outdoor stage; imagine testing a computer networking box mounted on an light pole or selectively adjusting the lighting in some areas at a nighttime party; imagine controlling an active art exhibit placed outside a museum. Such environments are not common today, but we expect them to appear in the future, as examples of ubiquitous computing [4].

It is possible to query and control remote objects by conventional means, viewing a list or a map of targets on a laptop or mobile screen, and choosing appropriate commands to send. Another possibility exists, however: Users might simply point at a target, real or virtual, and give it commands. The advantage of such interaction is its naturalness. Rather than concentrating on virtual objects in a computer display (generally no more than several inches across), users can focus their attention on the physical objects they are interacting with. We would expect some forms of situation awareness to be improved, in that users' attention can remain on the larger, real environment.

People are surprisingly good at pointing in specific directions at targets. Wong and Gutwin [6] show that users can point to visible targets with a laser pointer (turned off during the pointing gesture) with an accuracy of 2° or less. Cockburn et al. [2] find that users can point at invisible targets on a display two meters away with average error less than 1°, depending on the amount of visual feedback.

Sensing the direction of pointing outside the laboratory, however, is challenging. Nickel and Stiefelhagen [3] describe a variety of camera-based techniques for estimating pointing direction, achieving a minimum error of 16.9°. Breuer et al. [1] report an average error angle of 7.28°, for the identification of pointing directions in the context of human-robot interaction. The first author of this paper [7] describes a glove provides estimates of pointing directions in three dimensions, with error of 6.25° in the horizontal and 4.18° in the vertical.

This is a small sampling of work on mid-air pointing. Such studies tend to have a few limitations: they are often carried out indoors; measurements are made with specialized equipment that does not translate to practical use; users are most often asked to point at targets directly in front of them. We address these issues in this paper with a study of pointing outdoors using a mobile phone, in which users point at nearby and distant targets on a 180° arc in front of them.

In our experiment, users indicate targets in different ways, by focusing the phone's camera or simply turning with the phone held about waist level. From the results of our experiment we derive distributions of pointing direction. The parameters of these distributions are used as input to probabilistic models of pointing at targets in different locations. The models are implemented in a simulation environment of responsive objects, which we have built to test our models, communication prototocols, and information management.

POINTING WITH A MOBILE PHONE
Our study replicates Zhao's earlier study with a glove for pointing [7]; ours relies on a mobile phone. We used as targets everyday objects within sight of a fixed location: the top of a street lamp, an electrical tower, a sign, an antenna, and a fire alarm, as shown in the photo in Figure 1. Targets ranged

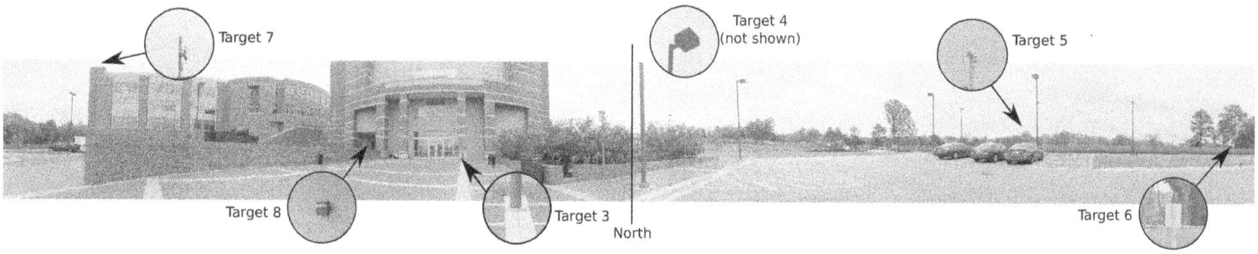

Figure 1. Panorama of test location

from a few meters to several hundred meters distant. True directions to the targets were provided by two professional surveyors. The height of the instrument for the measurements was 1.5 meters. All target objects occupied less than 2° of the horizontal visual field. Table 1 shows the directions of the targets from the fixed location; we use Zhao's labeling conventions but do not include his Targets 1 and 2, which were for calibration.

Target	*Horizontal*	*Vertical*
3	−46°	−3°
4	10°	46°
5	113°	5°
6	174°	0°
7	−151°	23°
8	−74°	2°

Table 1. Target locations

Fourteen volunteers, students in the authors' computer science department, participated in the experiment. They received a small gift in compensation for their time. Seven participants were male and seven were female, ranging in age from 23 to 33. All participants were right-handed, and all used their right hand for pointing. Their self-reported height ranged from 1.52 meters (5 feet) to 1.85 meters (6 feet, 3 inches). All participants used the same Motorola Droid (A855), with a gyroscope, accerometer (ST Microelectronics, LIS331DL), and magnetic compass (AKM AK8973).

Participants carried out trials in three separate *Gesture type* conditions, in order. In the *Point* condition, participants held the phone in their hand and pointed to targets, arm outstretched. In the *Focus* condition, participants focused the phone camera on the targets.[1] In the *Hold* condition, participants held the phone flat between waist and chest height, so that they could see the screen. Unlike the other conditions, in the Hold condition participants were told to orient the phone in the horizontal plane, like a compass.[2]

[1]No crosshairs or other visual indication of the center of the screen was provided. We did not perform analysis of the images captured by the camera, but pilot testing for this condition showed that participants tend to center the camera image on targets, within a few pixels. This is an unmodeled source of variance in this condition, but we believe it is relatively small.

[2]Our analysis covered all three gesture type conditions, but the data for the Point condition were extremely noisy; our discussion leaves out this condition for space considerations—results are unchanged.

Participants pointed at the six targets in succession, maintaining their pointing direction for eight seconds in each trial. Each such block was repeated four times in each condition. In all trials, participants began facing north and did not move their feet; in realistic scenarios, people are sometimes interested in targets that are not directly in front of them. This constraint allows us to test pointing in several different directions, relative to the direction the participant is initially facing.

Gesture duration

Our first question deals with the duration of a pointing gesture. None of the conditions included a clutch, i.e., a button press to indicate the completion of the gesture; the easiest gesture, in our view, is simply to point, letting the system determine when the gesture is complete. Figure 2 shows an example, for a single trial, of the instantaneous changes over time of the directional components (horizontal pointing angle, or azimuth; vertical pointing angle, or pitch; and rotation about the pointing axis, or roll). In this case, changes settle out around 3000 ms, indicating a stable gesture.

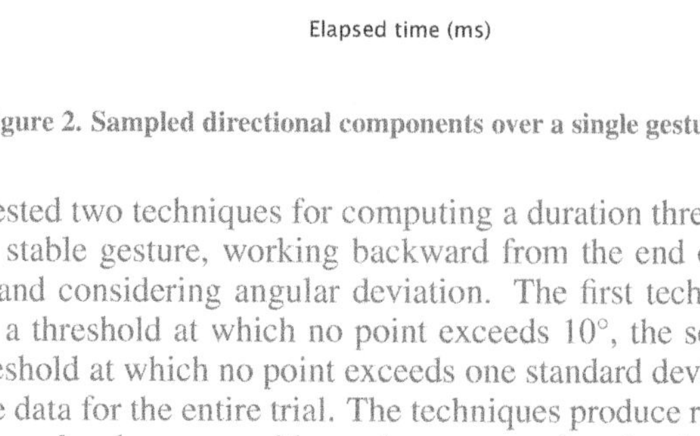

Figure 2. Sampled directional components over a single gesture

We tested two techniques for computing a duration threshold for a stable gesture, working backward from the end of the data and considering angular deviation. The first technique finds a threshold at which no point exceeds 10°, the second a threshold at which no point exceeds one standard deviation of the data for the entire trial. The techniques produce results that are closely comparable, and we report data for the second. Hold is faster than Focus, at 1,536 ms versus 2,475 ms. In an analysis of variance, with *Gesture type* modeled as a

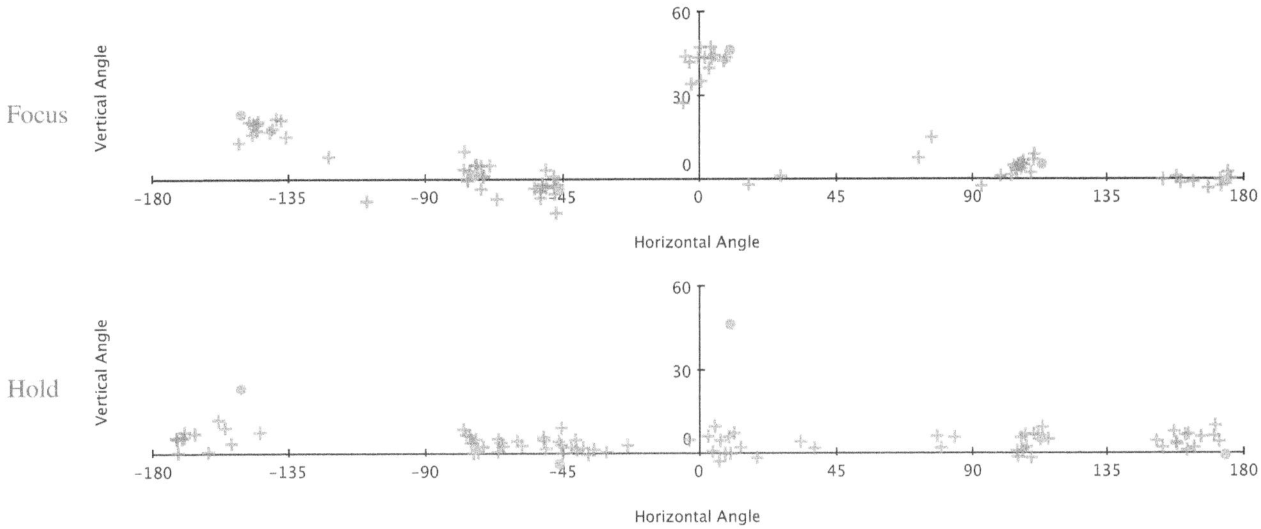

Figure 3. True directions (red) with North at origin, and pointed directions (purple or blue)

fixed effect and *Target* and *Participant* being random effects, Gesture type is highly significant ($F(2) = 343$).

Gesture accuracy

Once a stable gesture is achieved, a direction can be computed. The scatter plots in Figure 3 shows the mean pointing direction for each participant and each target. A red circle shows the true direction of a target; blue crosses show the direction as measured by the pointing device. As expected, both conditions show clusters around the targets. The mean absolute error over all targets is 9.9° in the horizontal plane for the Focus condition, with an identical value for the Hold condition. In the vertical plan, the Focus condition gives a mean absolute error over all targets of 3.9°.

In mid-air pointing systems (e.g. [3]), adjustments to measured directions are typically carried out to account for bias. For example, if one is pointing at a target with the right index finger, the direction as measured along the arm or finger will be slightly to the left and above the actual target, because the shoulder is to the right and below eye level. Non-zero bias is found in both the Focus and Hold conditions, as determined by parametric and non-parametric tests showing that the horizontal and vertical estimates are significantly different from zero. Measured pointing directions are thus adjusted by a constant offset in the horizontal and vertical components. For the Focus condition the offsets are $-2.3°$ and $-1.6°$, producing an adjusted absolute error of 6.4° in the horizontal and 3.7° in the vertical. Analogously, a horizontal offset for the Hold condition of $-4.2°$ produces an adjusted error of 9.4°.

We are interested in more than characterizing comparative accuracy of pointing gestures; for our purposes we need explicit models of accuracy, especially in the horizontal. We begin by observing that significant outliers exist in the experimental data. If we eliminate trials for which the magnitude of the difference between a measured direction and a target exceeds 45°, assuming these to be user errors, 12 points are removed from the Focus condition and 10 from the Hold condition (about 3% of the trials in both cases). The result is the distributions shown in the top row of Figure 4.

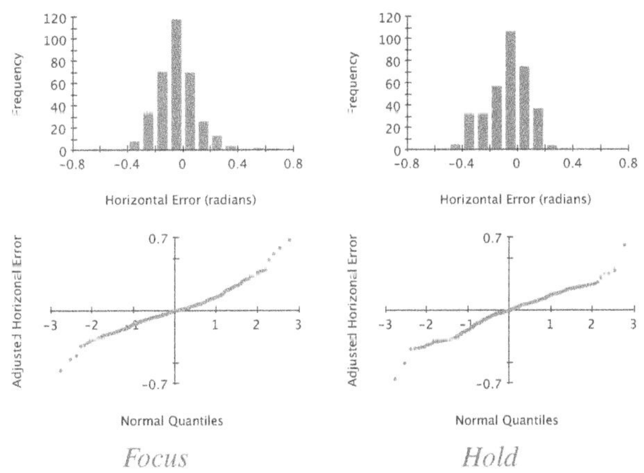

Figure 4. Normal quantiles for horizontal pointing error

Parametric and non-parametric tests show no difference in variance between the distributions for the Focus and Hold conditions; this result is unchanged whether outliers are included or not. This is slightly surprising. It might seem that focusing a phone camera on a target would produce greater accuracy than simply holding the phone in the appropriate direction about waist level. Accurately focusing a camera on a target, however, does not necessarily imply that the other sensors will be as accurate in indicating direction. Two other factors may contribute. One is errors in target selection by the participants; this possibility was not measured in our experiment, but the removal of outliers should have ameliorated such an effect. Another is that focusing a camera on a target involves variability in the position of the camera with respect to the participant's line of sight to the target, another aspect not measured in our experiment. Further work would be needed to distinguish these cases.

There is reason to believe that the pointing gestures in our experiment are Fitts' Law tasks, which would lead us to expect the distributions to be Gaussian [5] (though we cannot go as far as to predict the parameters of the distribution in advance). The distributions for the Focus and Hold conditions do not pass tests of normality; deviations in the tails of both distributions can be seen in their normal quantile plots, even though outliers have been removed. Nevertheless the deviations are small. A reasonable Gaussian approximation for the horizontal directions in the Focus condition is $\mathcal{N}(-0.041, 0.023)$, with $\mu = -0.041$ being the horizontal offset and $\sigma^2 = 0.023$ the variance of the fitted distribution. The corresponding approximation for the Hold condition is $\mathcal{N}(-0.074, 0.026)$.

POINTING IN A LARGE-SCALE ENVIRONMENT

We have developed a simple scheme to enable a user to select an object by pointing in the horizontal plane, along with a demonstration application that works in simulation. The application is a gesture-based controller for lamps. The system consists of two main components: a mobile phone for the pointing device and a remote computer that sends object state information to the phone. Probability computations and object selection are performed on the computer.

In this context, the phone acts as a sensor server, implemented as an Android application. It obtains realtime information including GPS coordinates and device orientation, and makes it available via simple TCP/IP communication. The computer runs a client program that connects to the device and polls it periodically for this information. The coordinates of objects along with their present state (in this case, simply "on" or "off") are stored on the computer. Effectively, the behavior of the lamps is simulated by the client.

Figure 5 shows a snapshot of the phone's display when the computer detects a pointing gesture in the direction of a known object. The interface is deliberately simple; also shown is status information for event tracking, which would be be hidden in a deployed version. A display is also maintained on the computer, to show information about the user and the locations and states of objects.

The logic used to determine which object is selected is straightforward. For each object O within a maximum distance λ from the device, the probability that the object is the one being pointed at is evaluated using the device's current location L and heading H (plus other system parameters). Among all objects that have probability above a threshold value, the one that maximizes this probability is chosen as the one selected. If no object crosses the threshold, then none is selected and this information is communicated to the phone.

In this work, we have presented an approach towards modeling the activity of pointing outdoors using a mobile phone. Empirical results indicate that pointing uncertainty can be approximated using a normal distribution, with non-zero mean, and that mean and variance are similar whether the user is treating the phone as a camera or using it as a compass.

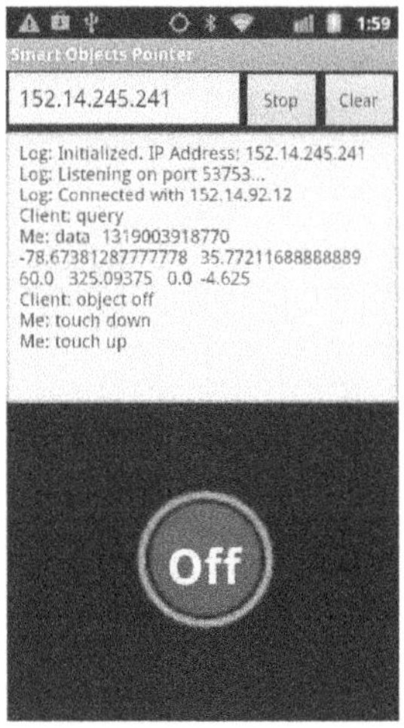

Figure 5. Snapshot of the phone's display

Our simulation, though still in a preliminary stage, demonstrates a setting in which our work can be put to use. Because object selection is performed by pointing, the user's attention need not be on the device until an object has been identified, and the device's interface has more room for other capabilities and information. Future directions for this work include control of objects more complex than two-state lamps; we are working on communicating and visualizing information from outdoor network boxes, as mentioned above. Rich outdoor environments that contain different types of responsive objects are not yet commonplace; our work may make such environments more usable.

REFERENCES

1. Breuer, T., Ploeger, P., and Kraetzschmar, G. Precise pointing target recognition for human-robot interaction. In *Proceedings SIMPAR* (2010), 229–240.

2. Cockburn, A., Quinn, P., Gutwin, C., Ramos, G., and Looser, J. Air pointing: Design and evaluation of spatial target acquisition with and without visual feedback. *International Journal of Human-Computer Studies* (2011), 401–414.

3. Nickel, K., and Stiefelhagen, R. Visual recognition of pointing gestures for human-robot interaction. *Image and Vision Computing 25*, 12 (2007), 1875–1884.

4. Weiser, M. Some computer science issues in ubiquitous computing. *Communications of the ACM 36*, 7 (1993), 75–84.

5. Wobbrock, J., Cutrell, E., Harada, S., and MacKenzie, I. An error model for pointing based on Fitts' law. In *Proceedings of CHI* (2008), 1613–1622.

6. Wong, N., and Gutwin, C. Where are you pointing?: the accuracy of deictic pointing in CVEs. In *Proceedings of CHI* (2010), 1029–1038.

7. Zhao, Y. Gibbon: A wearable device for pointing gesture recognition. Master's thesis, Department of Computer Science, North Carolina State University, 2011.

Towards Recognizing "Cool": Can End Users Help Computer Vision Recognize Subjective Attributes of Objects in Images?

William Curran[1], Travis Moore[1], Todd Kulesza[1], Weng-Keen Wong[1], Sinisa Todorovic[1], Simone Stumpf[2], Rachel White[1], and Margaret Burnett[1]

[1]Oregon State University, School of EECS
Corvallis, OR 97331, USA
{curranw, moortrav, kuleszto, wong, sinisa, white, burnett} @eecs.oregonstate.edu

[2]City University, London
London, UK
Simone.Stumpf.1@city.ac.uk

ABSTRACT

Recent computer vision approaches are aimed at richer image interpretations that extend the standard recognition of objects in images (e.g., cars) to also recognize object attributes (e.g., cylindrical, has-stripes, wet). However, the more idiosyncratic and abstract the notion of an object attribute (e.g., "cool" car), the more challenging the task of attribute recognition. This paper considers whether end users can help vision algorithms recognize highly idiosyncratic attributes, referred to here as *subjective attributes*. We empirically investigated how end users recognized three subjective attributes of cars—"cool", "cute", and "classic". Our results suggest the feasibility of vision algorithms recognizing subjective attributes of objects, but an interactive approach beyond standard supervised learning from labeled training examples is needed.

Author Keywords

Computer vision, interactive machine learning, classification, human factors.

ACM Classification Keywords

H.1.2 Models and Principles: User/Machine Systems; I.4.m Image Processing and Computer Vision. Miscellaneous, I.2.6 Learning

General Terms

Design, Human Factors, Experimentation

INTRODUCTION

Computer vision research on image interpretation has been primarily focused on *naming objects* occurring in an image. A common approach is to use machine learning techniques on features extracted from the image (e.g., textured patches, edges, or segments) to detect occurrences of an object class of interest (e.g., cars). Recently, computer vision has also developed methods to describe objects' *measurable attributes* (e.g., cylindrical, has-stripes, wet) that can be quantified directly from pixel values [3,4]. (Note that attributes of *objects* are different from features of *images*: attributes are descriptive characteristics of object appearance, such as has-stripes, whereas features are perceptually salient image parts, such as corners and edges.) Attribute recognition algorithms operate in a similar manner as object recognition algorithms -- by classifying a vector of image features. The classifier learns natural variations of object attributes from training examples with the attributes annotated.

This paper explores recognizing *subjective attributes*. For example, given an image of a car, can an algorithm recognize whether the car is "cool", "cute", or "classic"? Before addressing the feasibility of using computer vision for this task, however, we must first understand how *people* distinguish between such subjective attributes. This problem has not yet been addressed in computer vision or human-computer interaction research.

Why Subjective Attributes are Challenging

One possibility is that subjective attributes can be expressed in terms of concrete image features, and machine learning algorithms may be able to recognize such subjective attributes. In order to express these attributes as image features, we need to understand how people reason about subjective attributes like "cool". Then, in order for machine learning algorithms to recognize these attributes, we need to address at least three challenges to such recognition.

The first challenge is that subjective attributes may be vaguely defined in end users' minds. End users may not be able to communicate their personalized definition of an attribute in a "language" understood by a computer vision algorithm. Vision algorithms can operate only on observable, semantically low-level image features (e.g., two image regions share a boundary) but because human visual perception is largely an unconscious process, these low-level image features are often meaningless to end users.

Second, prior work [3,4] has shown that simply tagging an entire training image with an attribute name is insufficient for learning the attribute. Richer annotations, such as placing a bounding box around an example object and tagging the region with the attribute name, can improve attribute recognition but are extremely time-consuming for humans to provide.

Third, because a *specific* end user's own definition of the subjective attribute is the gold standard, the amount of training data available is inherently limited, especially when the algorithm is first deployed. The amount of training data cannot be increased by simply pooling together training examples of attributes labeled by different annotators. Even for non-subjective attributes, related work [3,6] has shown that this pooling decreases performance because annotators differ to a large degree in their visual perceptions of an attribute even though they may have a similar mental model of that attribute. These differences introduce labeling noise that we expect to be even more pronounced in the case of subjective attributes.

	Example from participant transcript	**Code**
Cool	"Mostly it's very aerodynamic, it's very cool in design"	Aerodynamic
Cute	"Cute ones are usually smaller."	Small
Classic	"I guess if they're not built in and they're really round shape, so I would actually label classic" [he circles headlights].	Headlights-Round, Headlights-External

Table 1: Three examples of how one participant's feedback was coded.

Together, these issues indicate that algorithms that recognize subjective attributes need to extend beyond standard supervised learning from labeled training examples. Our results suggest the need for a rich form of interaction wherein an end user can guide the learning algorithm to be able to find cool cars according to *that* user's definition.

Research Questions

To investigate the issues we have raised in this section, we conducted an empirical study in which we asked end users to explain how to classify images of cars as "cool", "cute", or "classic". Our research questions were:

RQ1: What visual image properties do end users use to identify subjective attributes of objects?

RQ2: Can these visual image properties be mapped to low-level image features used by vision algorithms?

RQ3: How consistent are these visual image properties for subjective attributes across multiple users?

RQ4: How distinct are these visual image properties for different types of subjective attributes?

STUDY SET-UP

To investigate the viability of computer vision algorithms for recognizing subjective attributes, we conducted an empirical study in which participants explained how they reasoned about "cool", "cute", and "classic" subjective attributes of cars in images. We chose cars because they are widely used in computer vision and they present challenges pertinent to subjective attributes such as large variations in shape, arbitrary color patterns, and differences in sizes.

Participants and Procedures

We recruited 12 participants (7 males and 5 females) from the local community. These participants had little or no programming experience, no machine learning experience, and none were computer science majors. Participants were compensated $20 for their time.

We introduced participants to the idea of "thinking-aloud" by reasoning about cars. Participants were asked to describe prominent areas that stand out in a car by verbalizing their thoughts and marking up a printed image. Participants practiced this skill before the main study began.

The participants' task for the study was to describe which visual properties make (or do not make) a car "cool", "cute", or "classic" from a set of 15 car images. To avoid forced classifications, participants were asked to perform the task only on images that sparked their interest. This task lasted 20 minutes, which we observed to be suitable in our pilot runs. We video-recorded all sessions and transcribed the participants' verbalizations and image mark-ups for detailed analysis.

The Images

We obtained 67 images of cars from the PASCAL 2010 database [2], a well-known collection of images for object recognition. From these we selected a subset of images in which an entire car was in the center of the image and the image contained few background objects (e.g., pedestrians). Three researchers manually classified these as "cool", "cute", or "classic". We used the majority's decision to resolve any disagreements. For the study, we used 15 images, four for each subjective attribute, and three that did not clearly represent the subjective attributes.

RESULTS

Which Visual Image Properties Matter to End Users?

Subjective attributes rely on tacit knowledge, so it could be difficult for end users to precisely describe them as concrete visual properties [6]. We thus investigated how end users described the "cool", "cute", and "classic" subjective attributes, with particular attention to the concrete visual properties they discussed.

We used a fine-grained code set to characterize participants' feedback about "cool", "cute", and "classic" cars. The codes were words we extracted directly from the participant transcripts from part one of the study. Each code represents a visual property that the coders believed expressed a low-level image feature. We coded feedback as *part-property* when the focus was on a specific car part, or simply *property* when the participants' feedback was about the entire car. Table 1 shows an example for each code.

The primary purpose of this code set was to group synonyms together. Thus, if a participant described a car's headlights as "not built in" (Table 1), we applied the code "headlight-external". Two researchers iteratively built a list of such codes, refining the set to include each part and property participants discussed. The final code set had 37 codes for parts, 99 codes for properties of these parts, and 229 unique part-property combinations.

Figure 1: Tag clouds showing the frequency of participants' feedback for the subjective attributes "Cool,", "Cute," and "Classic."

To validate our code set's reliability, the two researchers independently coded 187 transcript samples (representing 40% of the total number of transcript samples). We computed reliability using the Jaccard index, where the number of agreeing codes (size of the intersection) was divided by the total number of applied codes (size of the union). Part codes and property codes were treated independently. For example, if Researcher 1 coded a segment as "headlight-round" while Researcher 2 coded the same segment as "headlight-external", agreement would be 1/3 because "headlight" agreed but "round" and "external" did not. The two researchers achieved a reliability of 80% over their 187 transcript samples. Despite the large number of codes, high reliability was achieved relatively easily as the code set functioned as a look-up dictionary for part and property synonyms. Given this acceptable level of reliability, one researcher independently coded the remaining transcripts.

Figure 1 shows how often each code occurred in participants' explanations about why a car was "cool", "cute", or "classic". The size of each code represents its popularity across all participants, i.e., between-participant consistency. (We did not analyze within-participant consistency because participants almost never explained the same things twice; for example, once they explained to us that aerodynamics was important to "coolness", they did not explain it again.) Participants consistently used certain visual properties of each subjective attribute. For example, in Figure 1, the property *Small* dominates the "cute" attribute. The most common descriptions applied to the entire car (e.g., *Aerodynamic* or *Boxy*), rather than part of a car, suggesting that participants focused on the whole *gestalt* before examining individual sub-objects.

Participants used a wide range of properties to explain subjective attributes but each attribute differed in the variety of properties (Figure 2). For instance, participants used nearly three times as many image properties to describe "cool" as they did for "cute". The degree of dominance also differed (e.g., *Small* was more dominant for "cute" than *Aerodynamic* was for "cool"). Most importantly, the participants' descriptions of properties had very little overlap between the attributes, as shown in Figure 2. In fact, only eight codes (4.5% of the total) were shared by all three attributes.

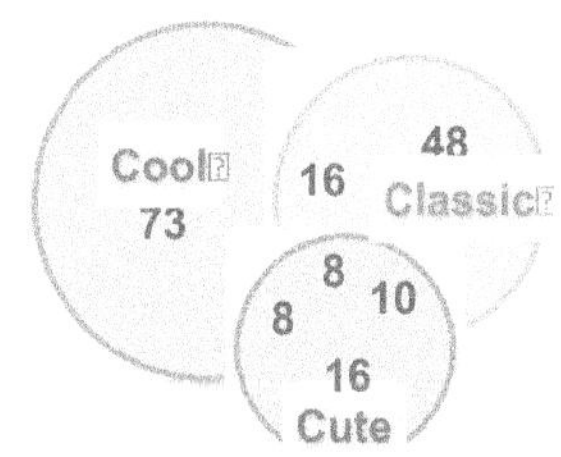

Figure 2: The number of codes for each attribute and their overlap.

Implications for Attribute Recognition Algorithms

As seen in Figure 1, the most common codes participants discussed, specifically 67% of them, involved shapes, sizes, and textures – all of which could be expressed using the types of low-level image features commonly used in computer vision. For example, "boxy" can be captured by shape descriptors. Codes referring to car parts, such as "tires", can also be readily detected in images using off-the-shelf part detectors available in open-source computer vision libraries. A compound code such as "headlights-round" can be detected using a combination of part and shape detectors. An interesting code for "cool" pointed out by most participants was "aerodynamic", which can be interpreted as a simpler object attribute that defines the more complex attribute "cool". This hierarchical approach to attribute recognition, however, would require new theoretical formulations in computer vision.

The diffuse yet distinct nature of these subjective attributes has implications for attribute recognition algorithms. On one hand, the lack of overlap between the codes, as well as the presence of a core set of primary image properties, suggest that learning algorithms can learn the main concept defining the subjective attribute. On the other hand, while the primary properties can be identified as the amount of training data grows, identifying the subtler secondary image properties that define the attribute for a *specific* user is more challenging. The personalized definition of the subjective attribute for a specific user is much smaller than the diffuse set seen in Figure 1. Using the secondary properties collected from *all* the participants makes the concept noisier and harder to learn. A better alternative to supervised learning of the subjective attribute is to employ a richer form of interaction between the specific user and the learning algorithm, such as active learning [5], feature labeling [7] and interactive concept learning [1].

Altogether, our results strongly suggest that participants' descriptions of subjective attributes may be of real use to computer vision algorithms. Participants generally agreed on the core properties about *what* made a car "cool", "cute", or "classic", with little overlap between these attributes, and in terms that vision algorithms could readily leverage.

DISCUSSION

These results suggest two open issues for attribute recognition algorithms.

First, participants in our study viewed the shape of cars as the most prominent property defining "cool", "cute", and "classic". For example, Figure 1 shows that shape properties such as "round", "boxy", and "aerodynamic" were more relevant for recognition of the three car attributes than a car's material or color. This raises an open question regarding the relative importance of visual properties (shape versus color and texture)—a fundamental and as yet unanswered question for computer vision algorithms.

Second, participants were asked whether they thought properties for "cool", "cute", and "classic" cars could be applied to objects other than cars. For example, could the property "Small" apply equally to cute cars and cute cats? Most participants said the properties were independent of the object itself: *"I think so. I think the same criteria in general can be followed for bikes or clothes, tables, chairs, etc."* These responses suggests new theoretical developments in computer vision, which currently treat attributes as tightly related to specific objects, and thus tie object recognition to attribute recognition. Our study suggests it might be possible to develop more general algorithms for recognizing attributes that transcend individual objects (e.g., an algorithm that recognizes "cuteness" regardless of whether the image shows cars or cats or cartoon characters).

CONCLUSION

This work is a first step toward expanding the scope of vision systems to include subjective, user-defined attributes—from simply "is there a car?" to "is this car *cool*?" Participants in our study consistently relied upon shapes, sizes, and textures to describe subjective attributes (RQ1). These image properties can be readily mapped to low-level image features commonly used by computer vision algorithms (RQ2). Participants agreed on a core set of primary image properties defining each subjective attribute but some attributes were more conceptually diffuse than others (RQ3). The properties participants identified for a specific subjective attribute did not substantially overlap, suggesting discriminative power for computer vision algorithms (RQ4). Overall, these results provide evidence that end users could interact with computer vision algorithms to recognize subjective attributes of objects in images.

ACKNOWLEDGMENTS

This work was supported in part by NSF grant IIS-0803487.

REFERENCES

1. Amershi, S., Fogarty, J., Kapoor, A. and Tan, D. Overview-based examples selection in mixed-initiative interactive concept learning. In *Proc. UIST*, ACM (2009).
2. Everingham, M., Van Gool, L., Williams, C., Winn, J., Zisserman, A. The PASCAL Visual Object Classes Challenge 2010 Results. http://www.pascalnetwork.org/challenges/VOC/voc2010/workshop/index.html
3. Farhadi, A., Endres, I., Hoiem, D., and Forsyth, D. A. Describing objects by their attributes. In *Proc. CVPR*, IEEE (2009), 1778-1785.
4. Farhadi, A., Endres, I. and Hoiem, D. Attribute-centric recognition for cross-category generalization. In *Proc. CVPR*, IEEE (2010), 2352-2359.
5. Vijayanarasimhan, S. and Grauman, K. What's it going to cost you? Predicting effort vs informativeness for multi-label image annotations. In *Proc. CVPR*, IEEE (2009), 2262-2269.
6. Welinder, P., Branson, S., Belongie, S., and Perona, P. The multidimensional wisdom of crowds. *Advances in NIPS 23*, (2010), 2424-2432.
7. Wong, W-K., Oberst, I., Das, S., Moore, T., Stumpf, S., McIntosh, K., and Burnett, M. End-user feature labeling: A locally-weighted regression approach. In *Proc. IUI*, ACM (2011), 115-124.

Where do Facebook Intelligent Lists Come From ?

Fatoumata Camara[1,2], Gaelle Calvary[1]
Laboratoire d'Informatique de Grenoble[1]
385 avenue de la Bibliothque 38400 Saint Martin d'Heres
Firstname.Lastname@imag.fr

Rachel Demumieux[2], Nadine Mandran[1]
Orange Labs[2]
2 Avenue Pierre Marzin 22300 Lannion
Firstname.Lastname@orange.com

ABSTRACT
On September 19th 2011, Facebook introduced "Intelligent Lists" which are Friends Lists (FL) automatically created and pre-filled based on users' and their contacts' profiles information (education, work, city of living, kin, etc.). In early 2011, we conducted a study on contact management in Facebook in order to understand users' real needs. Outcomes from this study suggest several recommendations, some of which can be found today in the Facebook Intelligent Lists.
This paper provides explanations on the recent evolution in Facebook contact management. The user study involved 148 participants. From their Facebook accounts, we retrieved 340 Friends Lists and 347 family ties. In the overall, the study has led to numerous interesting outocomes. In this paper, we focus on those related to Friends Lists and, particularly, on recommendations that have not yet been implemented in Facebook.

Author Keywords
SNS, Facebook, contact management, recommendations.

ACM Classification Keywords
H.5.2 Information Interfaces And Presentation: Miscellaneous

General Terms
Human Factors.

INTRODUCTION
Until recently, Social Network Sites (SNS) have ignored the diversity of social ties. All of the network nodes were mixed in a single encompassing group and referred to under the general headings "contacts" or "friends". Yet, existing studies [5, 8, 9] show that the building of an online social network follows an offline-to-online directionality that remains consistent over time [9]. Thus, as in the offline reality, not all online contacts are equal : some are family members ; some others are best friends, just friends or classmates and so forth.

Recent studies have highlighted contacts segmentation as essential in SNS. Binder and al. [2] state the problem of conflicting social spheres as an immediate consequence of the lack of compartmentalization in SNS. Jones and O'Neill [7] demonstrated the feasibility of segmenting Facebook contacts into groups of information sharing. Less recently (i.e. in 2003), Boyd [3] has noted that, even at the simplest levels, people often do not want certain groups of friends to be able to reach out and connect with their other groups of friends.

Major changes have occurred regarding contact management in SNS. For example, Windows Live provides five predefined categories of contacts (family, friends, colleagues, favorites and others) and also makes it possible to create personalized categories. In 2008, Facebook introduced Friends Lists as a means for organizing online contacts. Later on, there was a noted focus on human relationships, allowing users to create the different types of existing kinship (mother, brother, grandson, ect.) and reveal information about to their intimate life (e.g. in a relationship, married).
However, it is worth noting that, in the specific case of Facebook, the integrated contact management features are not extensively used. Marc Zuckerberg, himself, admitted that nobody wants to make lists [1]. Moreover, in the study presented in [7], the contacts sorting task lasted approximately 27 minutes. In the end, the overwhelming consensus among participants of this study was that "organizing contacts requires too much time and effort to be worthwhile". From the same study, it appeared that participants had placed only 20% of friends into predefined groups that were available in that previous Facebook. Participants typically regarded those groups as "too incomplete to be useful".

Indeed, little is known about contact management in SNS and related issues. Only few qualitative studies examined the topic. To tackle our lack of perspective, we conducted a quantitative study (148 participants) on contact management in Facebook. Our goal was to explore users' needs in order to propose recommendations that could possibly improve the contact management User Interface (UI) and task. The study used actual usage data and, unlike previous relevant studies, has not been carried out in specialized contexts. For instance, in [10], the authors focused on the workplace. In [7], the concern was about privacy. To our knowledge, this is the first quantitative study of the kind. Jones and O'Neil investigated Facebook usage collection as well. However, their sample was limited to 15 participants.

This paper reports our study : protocol, participants, data, and analysis, as well as results. It also presents a list of recommendations for an intelligent contact management system.

OUR STUDY

Protocol

The study consisted of an online survey followed by usage data collection. To access participants' Facebook accounts for usage data collection, we have created a Facebook application using the Graph API (PHP version). To access the questionnaire, participants had to log in to the application through Facebook. The questioning covered demographic information and different aspects of Facebook use (e.g. context, duration, and frequency of use ; numbers of contacts and Friends Lists). Within an average of ten days from the day of participation, we proceeded to data collection from participants' Facebook accounts. During the period of the survey, we paid attention to Facebook in order to be aware of any evolution that could introduce a bias. No change affecting our study occurred.
Still during that period, we kept participants' Facebook IDs in order to avoid multiple participations. Once the data collection completed, IDs were replaced by numerical ordered numbers in order to guarantee anonymity promised to participants.

Participants

One hundred and forty eight people (148), 75 males (51%), 72 females (49%), and 1 unknown (because the participant did not answer the question related to gender) responded to the online survey, and provided access to their Facebook accounts. Most of them were students or senior executives. Twenty five percent (25%) of our participants had more than 350 contacts on Facebook. There was an average of 315.2 contacts (std : 429.7), which is very high (more than the double of Dunbar's number [4]). So unsurprisingly, most of them were seasoned and frequent Facebook users. Our participants were mostly native to Europe (75%) and Africa (41%). The total number of participants native to the other continents did not exceed 10.

Tables 1 and 2 give more information about participant profiles.

16-20	14 (9%)
21-23	34 (23%)
24-26	32 (22%)
27-30	38 (26%)
Older than 30	30 (20%)

Table 1. Participants' age

Students	69 (47%)
Senior executives	46 (31%)
Employees	19 (13%)
Middle management	6 (4%)
Unemployed	2 (1%)
No response	3 (2%)

Table 2. Participants' occupation

Results

We collected 340 Friends Lists from 81 (55%) participants' accounts.
We have examined the names of Friends Lists simultaneously using a classification by synonym and by theme. The classification by synonym involves associating FL labels with the same meaning (for example, the French word "famille" and the English word "family"). The classification by theme involves grouping the FL labels linked to the same topic (for example, all of the Friends Lists labels corresponding to a particular educational establishment, a class at a school, etc. fell under the same heading "Studies").
The classification procedure resulted in 17 groups. Due to space constraints, we focus on the most important of them : the four (4) representing social spheres that are generally mentionned in works on social networks [6] ("Family" (26 FL), "Friends" (27), contacts related to "Studies" (70) and "Work" (19)), the group representing places which was one the largest groups (36), and the group of FL that were obviously aimed at controlling privacy and online presence.
These 6 groups of FL have been examined according to age and occupation. Findings are respectively reported on next two sections. For each age group, as well as for each occupation group, percentages were calculated considering the total number of participants who created the Friends Lists of the particular group.

Analysis of the six groups of Friends Lists according to age

Figure 1 shows results of the analysis of the six groups of Friends Lists according to age.
First, we note the absence of FL in the group "Family" among

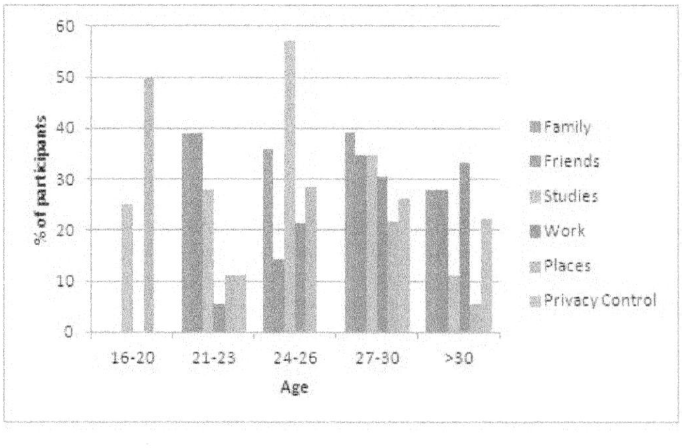

Figure 1. Percentages of participants who created the FL in each group, according to age.

the 16-20 year olds. In this young age group, the lists created are solely related to school life and to geographic locations. We also note a slight increase in the percentage of participants creating "Studies" FL among the 21-23 years old. Next, we note a significant increase in this percentage among the 24-26 year olds. At the same time, among the 24-26 year olds, there is a notable decrease in the percentage of participants creating "Friends" FL. This trend can most likely be explained by the offline phenomena that, during higher-education years, school life is very important to individuals. Indeed, we can observe that the percentage of participants who created studies-related FL significantly decreases right after the university years (i.e. among the 27-30 years old and older) while an increase in the percentage of participants having created "Friends" and "Work" FL is notable. We notice as well that participants older than 30 years mostly created FL related to work.

Family related FL are present in all four age groups over than 20 years old.

Apparently, older participants are most concerned by privacy : 22.2% of the participants older than 30 and 26% of the 27-30 years old created FL intended to control privacy. Only 11.1% of the 21-23 years old created such FL and none of the 16-20 and 24-26 years old created a FL related to privacy control.

Analysis of Friends Lists according to occupation

Figure 2 shows results of the analysis of the six groups of Friends Lists according to occupation.

First, we note that 30% of students created FL related to studies. But, more surprisingly, we observe that even more senior executives (37.5%) had such FL linked to studies. FL related to studies were also created by participants of the other occupations. The last two observations show the strength of ties one makes in higher education years, which may remain throughout life. We can also note that none of the participants in the other occupations created FL related to geographic locations. Yet, this group of FL is one the largests groups. In our opinion, this can be most likely explained by the phenomena that, senior executive positions and student life offer more opportunities for travelling (business trips, internships, conferences, etc.), and thus living in different places.

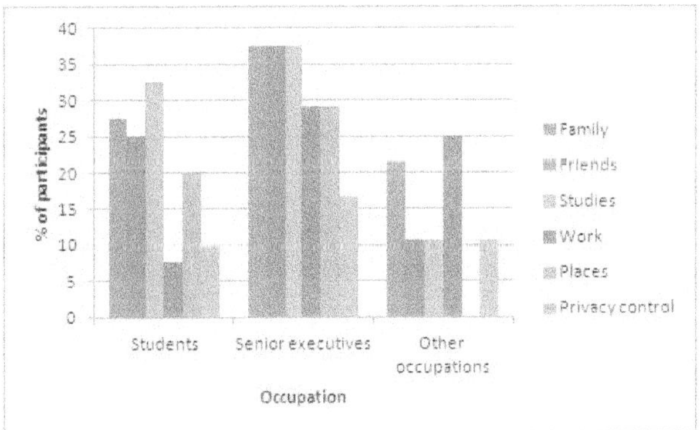

Figure 2. Percentages of participants who created the FL according to occupation.

Senior executives seem to be concerned with privacy. The percentage of participants in this category creating such FL is the highest.

Kin

We have collected 347 declared kin from 75 (51%) participants' accounts, of which 96% created direct kinship (father, mother, brother, sister) and 30.60% indirect kinship (cousin, nephew, grandmother, etc.).

We have examined many aspects linked to kin. Here, we report a summary of the resulting findings.

Natives from Africa appeared to be the most active in kinship creation. Among the 75 participants who created kinships, 37 were native to Africa versus 29 native to Europe.

Intra-generational family ties (e.g. brother, sister, cousin) appeared to be those mostly created by participants compared to inter-generational ones (e.g. mother, uncle, niece).

A participant had explicitly declared two mothers. Further examinations in this participants' information revealed that this last one was from Africa.

Eighty-two (82) kin, or 23.6 %, were organized in groups by 25 participants. We have noted that almost half of kin were placed in a FL of the group "Family".

IMPACT ON DESIGN : RECOMMENDATIONS

This section presents, based on the aforementioned results, a number of recommendations for contact management in Facebook.

It is important to mention that, despite the quantitive aspect of the study, recommendations listed below should be cautiously considered as they are solely based on Facebook data. Further investigations may be required before applying them to other systems.

- **Predefined Lists**

  Most of the existing social spheres involved in an individual's life emerged from the analysis of Friends Lists. With the exception of the 16-20 years old, who created FL only related to studies and geographical locations, and the participants other than students and senior executives, who had not created any FL in the group "Places", we found FL related to family, friends, studies and work in the accounts of the all other participants having created some Friends Lists. Moreover, we have found Friends Lists, of which one was explicitly labeled "other", that seem to be intended for people with no defining qualities.

  Based on the aforementioned observations, **we propose that the contact management UI in Facebook comes with 5 predefined lists named :** "Family", **"Friends", "Studies", "Work", and "Other"**.

  More than half of the kin that were organized were placed in a FL of the group "Family". Based on this observation, we suggest, for any user, automatically placing any contact explicitly declared as a kin in the list "Family". This recommendation has been implemented and Facebook goes even further by placing inferred kin in the list "Family" as well.

- **Adaptive and Personalized Lists**
  A large number of Friends Lists were related to places, studies, and work. These Friends Lists probably represent important entities for users such as cities/countries of born or living, current or former work institution. Based on this observation, we suggest taking into account the personal story of each Facebook user during the automatic process of lists creation and pre-filling. We suggest automatically creating a list corresponding to each institution (related to studies and work) to which the user has declared to be linked. Initially, names of such lists can be set to the institutions names. The system should take advantage of information of the user's contacts for pre-filling automatic lists related to studies and work. For a given institution, the system should place all of the user's contacts who have declared being attached to this last one and follow the same logic for pre-filling Friends Lists related to places.
  This recommendation has been implemented in Facebook as well. However, we suggest to go further **by automatically proposing Friends Lists corresponding to cities in which a user's institutions are located**.
  In addition, we propose that contact management UI supports personalized lists creation and allows control over the automatically created ones (e.g. change of labels, deletion of contacts or lists, move of contacts).

- **Hierarchical Organization**
  A large majority of participants had more than one Friends List. Like in Jones and O'Neil's study [7], some of FL that the participants created seem to be subgroups of larger groups. Based on this observation, **we suggest a hierarchal organization of lists**. In other words, we suggest supporting subgroups creation.
  To go further, we propose **considering all of the Friends Lists corresponding to instutions (study, work) as subgroups of the top-level lists "Studies" and "Work". However, we propose considering Friends Lists related to cities of instutions as top-level lists**.

CONCLUSION AND FUTURE WORK

This work investigated users' contact management needs in Facebook and proposes a list of set-ups for an intelligent contact management system. Adaptations concern automatic creation and pre-filling of Friends Lists, according to users' and their contacts' profiles information.

Future work will follow two directions. On the one hand, we will focus on the contact management UI, itself, with the goal to design a more convenient and less time-consuming one. On the other one hand, we will investigate an adaptive visualization of contacts that integrates recommendations presented in this paper.

ACKNOWLEDGEMENT

The work was funded by Orange Labs. We also warmly thank the national SYSEO project (ANR 2010-2014) for its support.

REFERENCES

1. Zuckerberg : "guess what ? nobody wants to make lists.". http ://techcrunch.com/2010/08/26/facebook-friend-lists/, August 2010.
2. J. Binder, A. Howes, and A. Sutcliffe. The problem of conflicting social spheres : effects of network structure on experienced tension in social network sites. In *Proceedings of the 27th international conference on Human factors in computing systems*, CHI '09, pages 965–974, New York, NY, USA, 2009. ACM.
3. D. Boyd. Reflections on friendster, trust and intimacy. http ://cite-seerx.ist.psu.edu/viewdoc/summary ?doi=10.1.1.82.466, 2003.
4. R. I. M. Dunbar. Co-evolution of neocortex size, group size and language in humans. *Behavioral and Brain Sciences*, 16(4), 1993.
5. N. B. Ellison, C. Steinfield, and C. Lampe. The benefits of facebook "friends :" social capital and college students' use of online social network sites. *Journal of Computer-Mediated Communication*, 12(4) :1143–1168, July 2007.
6. C. S. Fischer. *To Dwell Among Friends. Personal Networks in Town and City*. University of Chicago Press, Chicago, 1982.
7. S. Jones and E. O'Neill. Feasibility of structural network clustering for group-based privacy control in social networks. In *Proceedings of the Sixth Symposium on Usable Privacy and Security*, SOUPS '10, pages 9 :1–9 :13, New York, NY, USA, 2010. ACM.
8. C. Lampe, N. Ellison, and C. Steinfield. A face(book) in the crowd : social searching vs. social browsing. In *Proceedings of the 2006 20th anniversary conference on Computer supported cooperative work*, CSCW '06, pages 167–170, New York, NY, USA, 2006. ACM.
9. C. Lampe, N. B. Ellison, and C. Steinfield. Changes in use and perception of facebook. In *Proceedings of the 2008 ACM conference on Computer supported cooperative work*, CSCW '08, pages 721–730, New York, NY, USA, 2008. ACM.
10. M. M. Skeels and J. Grudin. When social networks cross boundaries : a case study of workplace use of facebook and linkedin. In *Proceedings of the ACM 2009 international conference on Supporting group work*, GROUP '09, pages 95–104, New York, NY, USA, 2009. ACM.

Machine Listening: Acoustic Interface with ART

Benjamin D. Smith
University of Illinois at Urbana-Champaign
bdsmith3@illinois.edu

Guy E. Garnett
University of Illinois at Urbana-Champaign,
Illinois Informatics Institute
garnett@illinois.edu

ABSTRACT
Recent developments in machine listening present opportunities for innovative new paradigms for computer-human interaction. Voice recognition systems demonstrate a typical approach that conforms to event oriented control models. However, acoustic sound is continuous, and highly dimensional, presenting a rich medium for computer interaction. Unsupervised machine learning models present great potential for real-time machine listening and understanding of audio and sound data. We propose a method for harnessing unsupervised machine learning algorithms, Adaptive Resonance Theory specifically, in order to inform machine listening, build musical context information, and drive real-time interactive performance systems. We present the design and evaluation of this model leveraging the expertise of trained, improvising musicians.

Author Keywords
Artificial intelligence, unsupervised machine learning, machine listening, music, adaptive resonance theory.

ACM Classification Keywords
H.5.m [Information Interfaces and Presentation (e.g. HCI)]: Miscellaneous

General Terms
Algorithms, Human Factors, Performance, Theory

INTRODUCTION
On-line machine learning (ML) continues to gain increasing application as the problems of real-time interactive system control become more and more approachable and better understood [4]. In particular, the promise of the transparent union of live performer and complex multi-media performance through intelligent interfaces is alluring to many, and has been the focus of continuing research over the last several decades. With the development of on-line ML algorithms and the computing power required for real-time operation, such performances are rapidly becoming reality. Yet, most musical ML applications developed to-date use pre-trained neural networks or other supervised models, typically requiring extensive pre-performance training.

This presents an unusual challenge to the improvising performer, as once the training is complete the musician is constrained to the pre-selected material. Yet, what if the computer could effectively participate as an intelligent partner, listening to the musical development and making informed choices and mappings *as the improvisation unfolds?* Musical context, the consciously and unconsciously perceived relationships between musical events within a given work, informs human perception of a piece through the formation of expectations [9]. Building a similar model of context and expectations for a computer promises parallel comprehension and the potential for truly intelligent interactions and responses.

In order to privilege the creativity and intuition of an improvising performer qua user we propose a system that listens as a trained human might, extracting relevant information from the music as it unfolds. The resulting data in turn can be mapped to the control inputs of any interactive system. This model employs an on-line, unsupervised machine learning implementation, based on Adaptive Resonance Theory (ART, [1]) algorithms to efficiently process any musical improvisation or input.

BACKGROUND
The applicability of ML methods to problems in interactive musical performance is evidenced by the number and variety of applications and cases (see for example [14, 15]). Recent systems, such as the work of [4], focus both on "real-time" training, in order to better match the musician's work process, as well as the use of ML to discover new musical expressions. Rather than attempt to exactly duplicate preconceived mappings they encourage the exploration of unexpected results stemming from active training during a performance.

However, all of these implementations require that the user define both their input material as well as the desired outputs before use, relying heavily on the acuity of the users in defining appropriate control spaces. Yet, if the user is inspired to take the musical improvisation in a new direction the connection to the computer becomes challenged, as the content of the music moves away from the domain that the system was trained for.

The potential to capture the informational content without pre-performance training is presented in unsupervised, online ML models, which have seen virtually no application in interactive performance to date. These models allow the system to discover classifications and find groupings and patterns across inputs based on relationships inherent in the data, rather than training on preconceived, external knowledge of the inputs. Effectively, the computer is allowed to build its own interpretation of the musical work, listening in a fashion analogous to the human listener [2]. Unsupervised methods lend themselves naturally to sequential input processing, which is a prominent aspect of human perception models, rather than all-at-once training.

By giving the computer the capability to discern musical priorities and relationships on-the-fly, mappings can be constructed that serve to expose the musical development (and potentially emotional cues [7]) of the improvisation. This minimizes user cognitive load and allows the improvisor to focus on playing and creating a compelling musical work, speaking a language of melodic and textural relationships without worrying about the computational details. The capabilities of unsupervised learning to analyze musical material is shown by [5] and [12]. While our work focuses on interactive computer music, the same models can be applied to other intelligent, interactive computer control systems with high dimensional, real-time input.

ART

Basing our machine listening implementation on contemporary theories of human perception and audition [10], we employ a multi-layer design to parse melodic input streams. The human model comprises both a short-term memory (STM), to retain the last several seconds of sound input, and a long-term memory (LTM); grouping, relating, and categorizing inputs for later retrieval. Both of these memory functions feed into higher level processes that discern patterns, extract knowledge, and make decisions.

Spatial encoding [3], a method employed in natural language parsing, is employed to characterize sequential input data, transforming melodic context into a twelve-dimensional spatial representation (one dimension for each pitch-class in 12-tone equal-tempered tuning). Spatial encoding employs an unordered single layer Neural Network (NN), with one node for every token in the input set. When a token is presented to the NN the associated node is fully activated and the activity of the network x is attenuated by a small amount α: $x_t = \alpha x_{t-1}$. This model preserves the ordering of inputs by creating a vector encoding, where α may be variably set to control the length of the "memory" (typically to retain 5-9 tokens, based on Miller's Law [8]). This system is used in [5], for example, to successfully recognize formal relationships in early Mozart piano works.

The biggest limitations of the standard spatial encoding are the inability to describe repetitions and the generic nature of the activation. Two sequences, such as AABC and BABC, can produce the same encoded vector, yet in musical contexts sound distinctly different. Additionally, it has been shown that the human ear weights sonic input differently based on accents of agogic, dynamic, and metric inflection [11]. However, spatial encoding treats all tokens equally.

We propose a modification to the spatial encoding NN to dynamically adjust the node activation levels based on the perceived attention a particular token warrants, which we term Dynamic Encoding. The update rate is now set at a rapid sample rate (~20hz) and the activation level is set nominally to increment by a small value (such as 0.05, to avoid oversaturating the network). In practice this gives proportionally more weight (a more active node) to longer notes, while short notes only appear in the network for a few update cycles. Other types of accents are incorporated by increasing and decreasing the activation value appropriately (i.e. louder notes get more activation and softer notes receive less).

The activation level (l) for dynamic accents is calculated based on the amplitude of the current sample (a_t) and a running average (of length k, typically 16) of the amplitudes of previous samples.

$$l = \frac{a_t k}{\sum_{i=1}^{k} a_{t-1}} \quad (1)$$

Thus $l = 1$ for equal amplitude notes, $l > 1$ for louder notes, and $l < 1$ for quieter notes. The activation level is then scaled to account for the rapid update rate (by 0.05 in our tests below).

Finally, the STM decay function has a significant impact on the shape derived from the melodic input. The standard model is a linear function, $x = x_{t-1} - b$, or exponential. We also consider a sigmoid curve, $x = x_{t-1}^c$, where c controls the effective temporal length of the memory module.

Long-Term Memory

Once the STM is created, the resulting vectors are fed to an ART module for classification. The ART is a competitive NN that trains in an unsupervised manner, discovering categories based on an ordered sequence of input vectors. Different orderings of the same data will produce divergent classifications and while this lack of consistency is typically seen as a limitation, here it is an asset. Just as a human listener relates later melodic development (such as a sonata-form development section, or recapitulation) to earlier auditions (i.e. the exposition) based on the meaningful ordering of music, so does the ART algorithm. The details of the ART algorithm are described at length by [1]. Two parameters of significance are the category size limit, or "vigilance" parameter (p), and the learning rate (β), which allows the network to both train new inputs immediately and still adapt gradually, retaining the identity of older categories. Setting the learning rate high causes categories to fully incorporate new inputs while setting it low causes the categories to adjust slowly, settling into an average area of the category space.

EVALUATION

We describe the ART analysis of an improvised solo by violinist Jean-Luc Ponty, "No Strings Attached," from the album *Le Voyage*. This recording was chosen due to its commercial availability, evident virtuosity, and range of harmonic and melodic content. The digitization involved running the recording through a pitch tracker to produce a stream of paired pitch and amplitude values (one sample approximately every 50 milliseconds for 6892 samples total). This ensured comparability between tests by removing any variability in the pitch reduction process. The recording selected is ~5' 56" in duration, consisting of a gradual exposition of material with

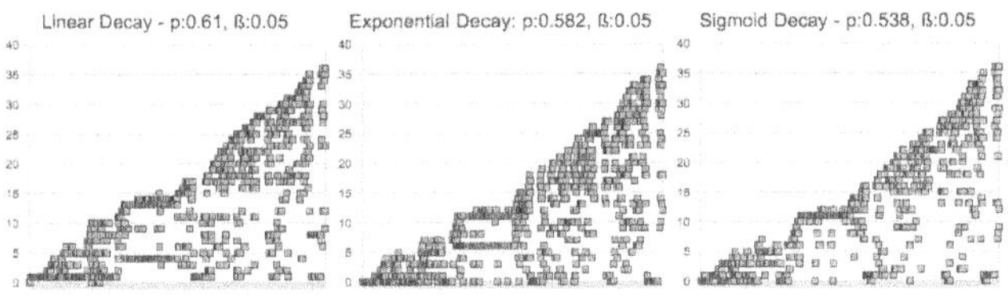

Figure 1. Categorizations with Spatial Encodings (linear, exponential, sigmoid) of *No Strings Attached* (category ID vs. time).

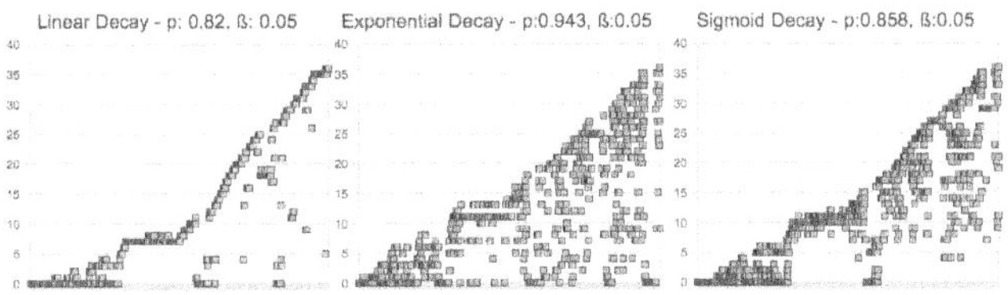

Figure 2. Categorizations with Dynamic Encodings (linear, exponential, sigmoid) of *No Strings Attached* (category ID vs. time).

several sections dominated by looped drones and rhythmic ostinati. We focus solely on melodic material, incorporating rhythmic duration and dynamics, as this is the primary index for pattern identification in human musical cognition [6].

For comparison we employ six STM models: spatial encoding and dynamic encoding each with three decay models (linear, exponential, and sigmoid). Decay rates were set so that each model effectively retains 7 ± 2 inputs at each update. Using slower decay rates tends towards gradually increasing category creation (as more context information is retained), while quicker decay rates produce far fewer categories (only twelve at the limit). Both of these extremes lead to problems building a useful understanding of musical context.

ART Classification

Next we feed each of these STM outputs into ART modules to produce categorizations and find patterns in the feature vectors. Fig. 1 and 2 show the categories generated over the course of the recording for each STM setting noted above (ART vigilance, p, and learning rates, β, are set to ensure a comparable number of categories—36—are identified for each encoding model). Note that the vigilance settings need to vary greatly to ensure the same total category creation for the very different STMs. This further emphasizes the impact of each encoding model on the characterization of the feature data.

The unfolding of the work produces gradual category creation for all encodings, which is appropriate to this free improvisation. The impact of the different encoding schemes can be seen. Some encodings, the dynamic encoding with linear decay for example, suffer from overfitting, creating new categories with few returns to old material. Others, such as the spatial encoding with exponential decay, are more reductive, showing apparently random repetition without sufficiently accounting for context. However, all indicate a move to a second musical section near the middle (esp. the dynamic sigmoid encoding), and hint at brief returns to the initial material in the middle and near the end (category 0 at the bottom of each graph).

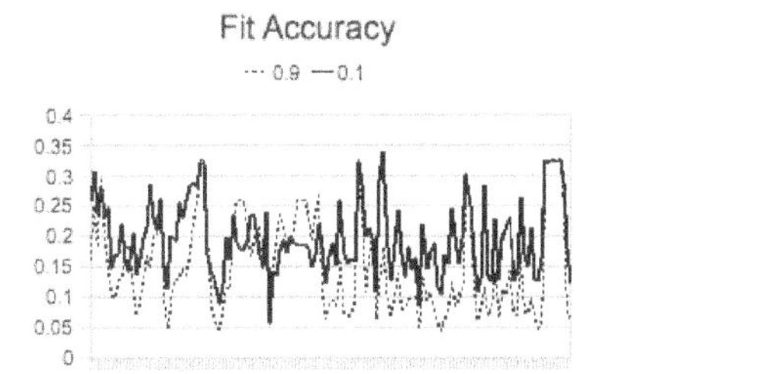

Figure 3. Accuracy of fit, *No Strings Attached*, spatial encoding, sigmoid decay, $c = 2.0$, $p = 0.9$.

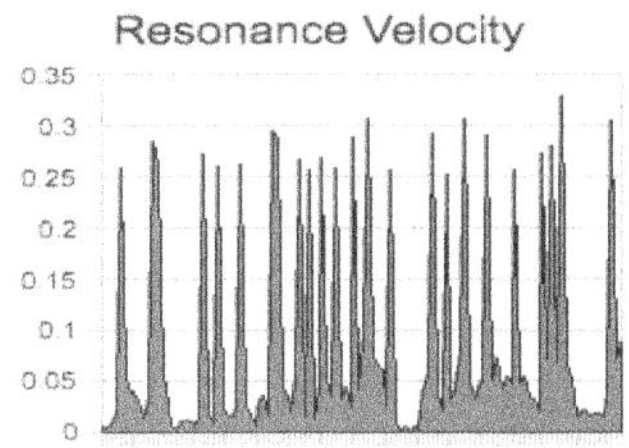

Figure 4. Euclidean distance between resonance vectors, *No Strings Attached*, 2' 53" to the end. [Dynamic encoding, sigmoid decay, $c = 1.10409$, $p = 0.858$, $\beta = 0.05$]

The vigilance parameter was set in order to produce a comparable number of categories. The effect of the vigilance on the category generation rate is roughly exponential in nature, resulting in $\sim$50 at $p = 0.9$, $\sim$180 at 0.75, and $\sim$1100 at 0.95 (for our chosen example with a spatial encoding and sigmoid decay). The learning rate parameter indirectly affects the rate of category creation (varying from a total of 8 categories when $\beta = 0.01$, with a dynamic, sigmoid decay, $p = 0.9$, to 40 when $\beta = 1$). Distinctly different inputs are still recognized as such, regardless of the learning rate. The learning rate parameter is also visibly at work in the "accuracy" measure of the input classification. This is calculated by taking a simple Euclidean distance measure for each input vector to the center of the matched category (fig. 4). The higher learning rate (0.9) results in more accurate fits generally while the lower rate (0.1) is looser, adapting to new inputs more slowly. The tradeoff is between the nature of the information sought: rapid, accurate categories, or slower, more general categories.

Resonance

Given the STM and LTM above, the extraction of information regarding musical relationships is now possible. Sectional movement can be identified by large movements in encoded feature space, resulting from changes in pitch material (modulations and transpositions). As fig. 4 shows, the distance between successive resonance vectors varies dramatically, indicating movement between different musical sections. Short periods of relative stasis are followed by sudden shifts to different areas of the category space, denoting the same shift in the source musical material.

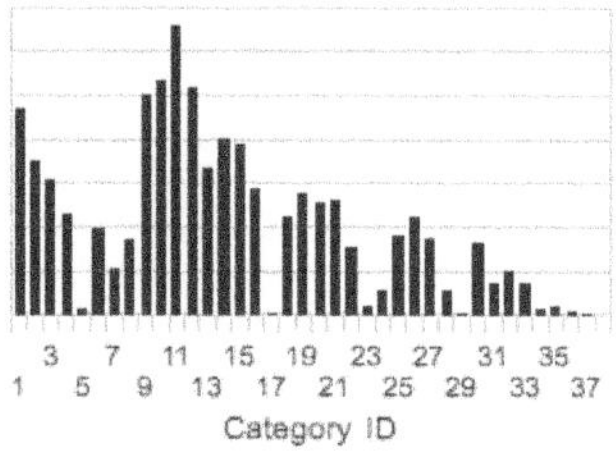

Figure 5. Total occurrences of each category at a resonance of 0.96 or greater. ***No Strings Attached,*** **Dynamic Encoding with sigmoid decay, $c = 1.10409$, $p = 0.858$, $\beta = 0.05$.**

Additionally, counting the number of matches for each category can be translated as a measure of the importance of each category. Taking the resonance vectors, and thresholding the resonances of each category observation, it is possible to compute a relative import for each category. Fig. 5 shows the ratio of category resonances observed with a value over 0.96. Certain categories appear with much greater frequency, while others (categories 5, 17, 23, 29, and 37, for example) only appear rarely. Using this knowledge the computer could decide to map significant outputs to strongly recurring categories, or the converse, highlighting the fleeting, unexpected categories.

Analyzing the resonance vector for these types of shifts and changes is the goal of this process. They are readily apparent to the trained human ear, and through statistical processing they can be appreciated by the computer "ear" as well.

FUTURE DIRECTIONS

The STM and LTM models set forth above provide an analysis of a live improvisation, extracting context information through the categorization of melodic feature data and the measure of relationships and movements within the melodic feature space. At the moment, the task of mapping this data to an interactive performance system remains predominantly in the hands of the technician or composer. Automating this process will require additional analyses of the fit data (both the resonance vectors and accuracy) over time, locating significant categories, tracking the movements in feature space, and mapping their inputs to desirable outputs. Both neural-network type dynamic mapping systems as well as ARTMAP may lead to viable solutions. This promises rich mapping possibilities that might match the perceptive complexity of the musical improvisation.

The models discussed thus far are currently being further evaluated and employed in a suite of pieces, transforming the musical improvisation of a live violinist into animations and audio through a granular synthesis engine [13].

ACKNOWLEDGEMENTS

The National Center for Supercomputing Applications at the University of Illinois at Urbana-Champaign, the Institute for Advanced Computing Applications and Technology, and the Illinois Informatics Institute.

REFERENCES

1. Carpenter, G. A., Grossberg, S., and Rosen, D. B. Fuzzy ART: fast stable learning and categorization of analog patterns by an adaptive resonance system. *Neural Networks 4* (1991), 759–771.
2. Collins, N. *Towards Autonomous Agents for Live Computer Music: Realtime Machine Listening and Interactive Music Systems*. PhD thesis, University of Cambridge, Cambridge, UK, 2006.
3. Davis, C. J., and Bowers, J. S. Contrasting five different theories of letter position coding: Evidence from orthographic similarity effects. *Journal of Experimental Psychology: Human Perception and Performance 32*, 3 (2006), 535–557.
4. Fiebrink, R., Cook, P. R., and Trueman, D. Play-along mapping of musical controllers. In *Proceedings of the International Computer Music Conference* (2009).
5. Gjerdingen, R. O. Categorization of musical patterns by self-organizing neuronlike networks. *Musical Perception* (1990).
6. Hébert, S., and Peretz, I. Recognition of music in long-term memory: are melodic and temporal patterns equal partners? *Memory & Cognition 4* (1997), 518–533.
7. Krumhansl, C. An exploratory study of musical emotions and psychophysiology. *Canadian Journal of Experimental Psychology/Revue canadienne de psychologie expérimentale 51*, 4 (1997), 336.
8. Miller George, A. The magical number seven, plus or minus two: some limits on our capacity for processing information. *The Psychological Review 63* (1956), 81–97.
9. Pearce, M., and Wiggins, G. Expectation in melody: The influence of context and learning. *Music Perception* (2006), 377–405.
10. Peretz, I., and Zatorre, R. J. Brain organization for music processing. *Annual Reviews Psychology*, 56 (2005), 89–114.
11. Pfordresher, P. The role of melodic and rhythmic accents in musical structure. *Music Perception* (2003), 431–464.
12. Piat, F. G. P. *Artist: Adaptive resonance theory to internalize the structure of tonality*. PhD in human development and communication sciences, University of Texas, Dallas, Aug. 1999.
13. Smith, B., and Garnett, G. The self-supervising machine. In *New Interfaces for Musical Expression* (2011).
14. Thom, B. Interactive improvisational music companionship: a user-modeling approach. *User Modeling and User-Adapted Interaction 13* (2003), 133–177.
15. Wessel, D. Connectionist models for musical control of nonlinear dynamical systems. *The Journal of the Acoustical Society of America* 92, 4 (Oct. 1992), 2402.

1F: One Accessory Feature Design for Gesture Recognizers

Radu-Daniel Vatavu
University Stefan cel Mare of Suceava
13 Universitatii
Suceava, Romania
vatavu@eed.usv.ro

ABSTRACT
One Feature (1F) is a simple and intuitive pruning strategy that reduces considerably the amount of computations required by Nearest-Neighbor gesture classifiers while still preserving the high recognition rate. Performance results are reported for 1F by analyzing a large set of candidate features showing recognition rates of 99% with a peak reduction in computations of 70%. 1F is easy to implement, flexible with respect to the choice of the feature, and exploits the intuition of the designer by exposing clear innerworkings.

Author Keywords
Gesture recognition; nearest neighbor; feature selection; pruning; training set; classification; comparing classifiers; gesture descriptors

ACM Classification Keywords
H.5.2 Information Interfaces and Presentation (e.g. HCI): User Interfaces - Input devices and strategies; I.5.2 Pattern recognition: Design methodology - Classifier design and evaluation, Feature evaluation and selection

General Terms
Algorithms, Design, Experimentation.

INTRODUCTION
The Nearest-Neighbor rule (NN) is a simple and commonly used technique for pattern recognition as all it needs are a metric and a set of previously classified samples. The NN classifier works by computing the distance between the candidate pattern and all the samples provided in the training set and outputs the class of the closest sample. The amount of computations is therefore determined exclusively by the size of the training set and the cost of computing the metric. Despite its simplicity, the NN classifier was shown to deliver high performance for recognizing stroke gestures [3, 6, 7].

As the problem of finding the nearest neighbor is a classic algorithmic challenge, many solutions exist (not necessarily coming from the pattern recognition community) that introduce and make use of complex specialized data structures, most of them tree-like: kD-tree, M-tree, the slim tree, Burkhard-Keller tree, vantage point tree, bisector tree, BBD tree, etc. [8]. Such structures work by partitioning the hyperspace and exploiting the way data points organize themselves into relative distinct regions. However, all these approaches, although promising in terms of low theoretic complexity, may prove difficult to implement by a practitioner or a user-interface designer trying to speed-up a gesture recognizer. Even for experienced practitioners and developers, the above data structures may present challenges in implementation which detract from rapid prototyping and testing. To the best of the author's knowledge, such advanced techniques have not found their way in the HCI community simply because of the above reasons although speed improvements are needed in many cases.

The article describes a speed-up of the NN classification rule which consists in pruning the training set with the help of just one extra feature. Using this feature only, a first approximation is obtained for the classification of a candidate gesture. As shown by experimental findings, the correct classification is *not far* from this initial guess and therefore a local search is sufficient to deliver the correct answer with considerably less computations than running the entire NN procedure. 1F is very simple to implement for its performances and offers flexibility in selecting the feature.

THE 1F STRATEGY
For all following discussion, a gesture is a series of 2D points:

$$g = \{p_i = (x_i, y_i) \in \mathbb{R}^2\}$$

If gestures g and q are sampled into the same number of points, the dissimilarity between g and q may be estimated using the sum of the individual Euclidean distances between pairs of corresponding points taken in order [1, 2, 6, 7]:

$$\|g - q\| = \sum_{i=0}^{n-1} \sqrt{(g_i - q_i) \cdot (g_i - q_i)^T}$$

The recognition performance of the Euclidean metric was analyzed in the context of the $1 recognizer [7] while the sampling resolution n was previously investigated by [6].

In order to formulate the classification problem, let m be the number of distinct gesture types (or classes) and let $\mathcal{T}$ be a training set composed of $|\mathcal{T}|$ gesture samples for which the classification is already known:

$$\mathcal{T} = \{(g_i, c_i) \mid c_i \in \{1..m\}\} \quad (1)$$

where c_i represents the class of sample g_i, $i = 1..|\mathcal{T}|$. A NN classifier will perform $O(|\mathcal{T}|)$ calls to the metric it relies on. For example, the classifier will perform $O(|\mathcal{T}| \cdot n)$ computations when using the Euclidean distance.

In order to gain computation speed, two options are available: either reduce the sampling rate n or the size of the training set $\mathcal{T}$. The effect of sampling rate on classifier performance has recently been studied by Vatavu [6]. The 1F technique takes the other route by filtering the training set down to the most relevant samples. The idea is to use an accessory feature[1] that describes each gesture globally. If we denote by f such a feature, the set $\mathcal{T}$ can now be ordered in accordance with f:

$$\mathcal{T}(f) = \{(g_i, c_i, f_i) \mid c_i \in \{1..m\}, f_i \le f_{i+1}\} \quad (2)$$

where $f_i = f(g_i)$ is the feature evaluation for sample g_i. For example, f may be gesture length, bounding box, or any other geometric or kinematic descriptor that can be imagined.

Let $f(g)$ be the value of the feature computed for a candidate gesture g. This value can be used in order to obtain an initial approximation for the classification of g. Let g_j be the training sample from $\mathcal{T}(f)$ for which the difference $|f_j - f(g)|$ is minimized. Using the feature only, one can simply draw the conclusion that g belongs to the same class as g_j. Although this could work at the intuition level, one feature is not enough in practice as it does not exhibit sufficient discrimination power and therefore sets of features need to be employed [5]. However, *the hypothesis behind 1F is that the correct sample (i.e. the real closest neighbor that NN would return) is not too far away from this initial suggestion.* In order to find the correct sample, a local search can be performed around g_j as $T(f)$ is already sorted by f. The relevant question is how far should one search around g_j to make sure that the correct classification would not be missed? The answer lies in computing a probability distribution function (pdf) that models how far the correct classification is located from the initial $f(g)$ guess. The pdf is constructed during the training procedure taking place for each sample $g_i \in \mathcal{T}$:

1. Remove g_i from the training set $\mathcal{T}$;
2. Obtain the initial guess for g_i using its feature value f_i. Let g_j be the sample for which f_j is closest to f_i;
3. Let g_k be the correct classification as outputted by NN using exhaustive search over the entire set $\mathcal{T}$;
4. Compute the error in terms of how far (in index distance) the initial estimate is from the correct sample: $\epsilon = k - j$;
5. Update $pdf(\epsilon) \leftarrow pdf(\epsilon) + 1$.

Classification of a candidate gesture g proceeds as follows:

1. Compute the feature value $f(g)$;
2. Find the initial approximation using the closest feature in $\mathcal{T}(f)$ (let that be located at index j);
3. Perform NN search in the vicinity of j: $\{j - |l|...j + |r|\}$.

[1]hence the name 1F

The two values l (left) and r (right) that actually filter the training set are chosen such that the cumulative sum of frequencies in the pdf between l and r is above 99%:

$$\sum_{i=l}^{r} pdf(i) > 0.99 \cdot \sum pdf(i)$$

The reason we do this is to eliminate pdf outliers that would cause unnecessary computations.

Classifying g requires a binary search in $\mathcal{T}(f)$ in order to find the initial suggestion on top of which we superimpose the pdf distribution. The final classification is obtained by performing $O(r - l + 1)$ comparisons. Therefore, we have $O(log(|\mathcal{T}|) + (r - l + 1) \cdot n)$ for $1F^2$ vs. $O(|\mathcal{T}| \cdot n)$ for NN working with the Euclidean distance. 1F will outperform NN in classification speed when $r - l + 1$ is smaller than $|\mathcal{T}|$.

PERFORMANCE ANALYSIS OF 1F

The amount of computations 1F performs is likely to depend on the feature being used. Therefore, a set of 20 features was compiled for the analysis by borrowing from previous works on feature-based gesture recognition [5] and designing new descriptors. The set of features was selected by following several criteria:

i. The set should cover a wide range of shape descriptors including lengths and angles defined both locally and globally on the gesture motion;
ii. The set should borrow descriptors already proposed and used in the literature;
iii. The features should preferably be easy to compute and, if possible, posses intuitive meanings (such as length) that could give hints on their workings and suggest expected performance for 1F;
iv. In accordance to the author's intuition, some features were chosen for their presumed better performance (such as *Total energy*) while others were specifically designed for bad results (*SignXY*) in order to test 1F in extreme cases.

Table 1 lists the set of features. As most of the feature definitions should be clear, we only mention that the Hu moments borrowed from image processing are shape invariants defined using the normalized unscaled central moments [4]:

$$U(\alpha, \beta) = \sum_{i=0}^{n-1} (x_i - \overline{x})^{\alpha} \cdot (y_i - \overline{y})^{\beta}$$

$$V(\alpha, \beta) = U(\alpha, \beta) \cdot n^{-\frac{\alpha+\beta}{2}}$$

For example, the first two Hu moments are defined as:

$$hu_1 = V(2,0) + V(0,2)$$

$$hu_2 = (V(2,0) - V(0,2))^2 + 4 \cdot V(1,1)^2$$

(see [4] for the description of the 7 Hu invariants and their properties).

[2]assuming the feature can be computed in linear time $O(n)$ which is a sufficient upper limit in most practical cases (see next section discussing many geometric descriptors)

Feature	Definition
Production Time	time measured in ms necessary to produce the gesture
Length	$\sum_{i=0}^{n-2} \|\|p_{i+1} - p_i\|\|$
Radium	$\frac{1}{n}\sum_{i=0}^{n-1} \sqrt{x_i^2 + y_i^2}$
R_1	$\frac{\|\|p_0 - p_{n-1}\|\|}{\|\|p_0 - p_{n/2}\|\| + \|\|p_{n/2} - p_{n-1}\|\|}$
R_2	$\frac{Length}{\|\|p_0 - p_{n/2}\|\| + \|\|p_{n/2} - p_{n-1}\|\|}$
R_3	$\frac{Length}{2 \cdot \pi \cdot Radium}$
Angle Middle	$\angle(\overline{p_0 p_{n/2}}, \overline{p_{n/2} p_{n-1}})$
Angle Center	$\angle(\overline{p_0 O}, \overline{O p_{n-1}})$ where $O = (0,0)$
Total curvature	$\int k(s)ds = \sum_{i=0}^{n-2} \frac{k_i + k_{i+1}}{2} \cdot (x_{i+1} - x_i)$
Total energy	$\int k^2(s)ds = \sum_{i=0}^{n-2} \frac{k_i^2 + k_{i+1}^2}{2} \cdot (x_{i+1} - x_i)$
SumXY	$\frac{1}{n}\sum_{i=0}^{n-1} x_i \cdot y_i$
Atan2XY	$\frac{1}{n}\sum_{i=0}^{n-1} atan2(y_i, x_i)$
Hu invariants $hu_1, hu_2..hu_7$	see [4](p.606-607) for full description
SignXY	$\frac{1}{n}\sum_{i=0}^{n-1} sign(x_i \cdot y_i)$

Table 1. Features used with 1F. NOTE: A gesture is represented as a series of n points $\{p_i = (x_i, y_i), i = 0..n-1\}$. $||a - b||$ is the Euclidean distance between points a and $b \subset R^2$. $\angle(\overline{ab}, \overline{cd})$ is the angle between line segments ab and cd.

Gesture set and experiment design

The performance of 1F was measured on the $1 gesture set of Wobbrock et al. [7]. The set contains 16 gestures acquired from 10 participants which repeatedly executed each gesture for 10 times[3]. As a preprocessing step, each gesture was normalized without distortion in the $[-1,1] \times [-1,1]$ square, centered to origin $(0,0)$, and resampled uniformly into $n = 16$ points (resampling is needed in order to compute the Euclidean metric and represents a common preprocessing operation [1, 2, 6, 7]).

Recognition rates were computed using the procedure described in [6, 7] for the set of 20 features while varying the size of the training set T from 2 to 9 samples for each gesture type. In total, 10 (participants) × 16 (gestures) × 21 (classifiers[4]) × 8 (T) × 100 (repetitions) = 2,688,000 individual recognition tests were performed.

[3] http://depts.washington.edu/aimgroup/proj/dollar/
[4] 20 instances of 1F + the unmodified NN

The effect of feature type on recognition rate

Figure 1 shows the recognition rates obtained using each feature from the set as well as the performance of the unmodified NN technique. Friedman's ANOVA showed significant differences between all 1F classifiers and NN ($\chi^2(20) = 557.693, p < .001$) as well as a significant influence of feature type among 1F ($\chi^2(19) = 380.208, p < .001$).

The recognition rate obtained for unmodified NN was 99.6%. All the 1F classifiers had lower rates (a result to be expected when working with a smaller training set) but, with only one exception, all the rates were above 98.3%. The top 3 features with the highest rates were R_1, *Angle Center*, and *Angle Middle*, all above 98.9% (at less than 1% distance from the ideal performance exhibited by NN). No significant difference was detected between the top 3 features ($\chi^2(2) = 2.214, n.s.$). However, the rates of NN and the best feature R_1 were significantly different (at $p < .001$). As expected, *SignXY* had the lowest (but still substantial) recognition rate of 96.1%.

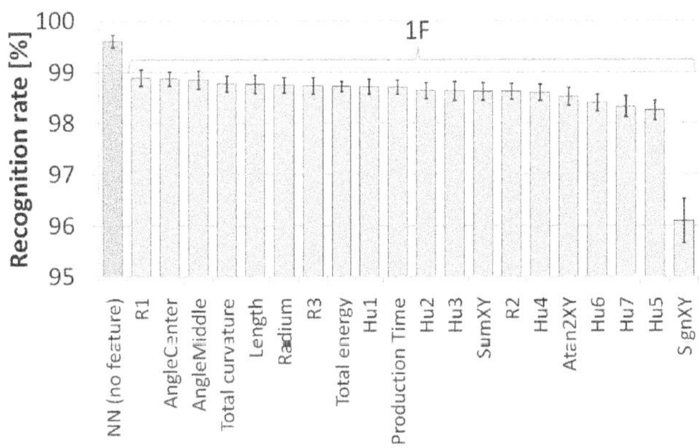

Figure 1. Recognition rate versus feature type. NOTE: Features are shown in descending order of their recognition rate.

The effect of number of samples in the training set over recognition performance is displayed in Figure 2. The average recognition rate of 1F starts from 97.9% for $T = 2$ samples and rises above 98.3% for $T \geq 3$ while reaching the peak (98.8%) for $T \in \{5, 6\}$. Note that the rates are averaged for all the features. At the same time, the rate of NN starts with 99.5% for $T = 2$ samples and reaches its peak (99.6%) for $T \in \{8, 9\}$. A significant effect of the number of training samples T over recognition performance was detected for both 1F ($\chi^2(7) = 1032.830, p < .001$) and unmodified NN ($\chi^2(7) = 1072.571, p < .001$). Figure 3 shows the effect of T over each feature from which the poor choice of *SignXY* clearly stands out.

1F classification speed-up

As NN works by comparing the candidate gesture with all the samples from the training set, the computations rate C_r was defined as the ratio between the number of comparisons needed by 1F and the total number of comparisons performed by the unmodified version of NN. Figure 4 shows the amount of computations needed for each feature. Friedman's ANOVA showed that C_r was significantly affected by the feature type, $\chi^2(19) = 1221.699, p < 0.001$. The top 3 best

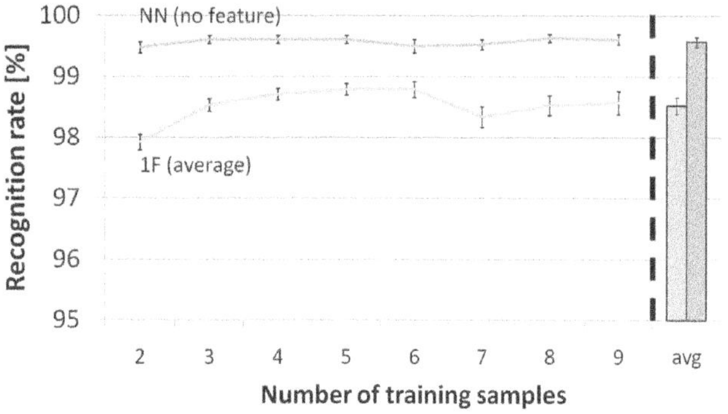

Figure 2. Recognition rate versus number of training samples (average performance across all features).

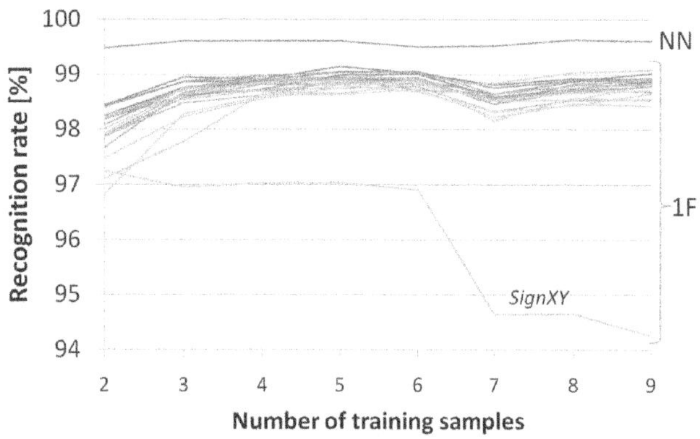

Figure 3. Recognition rate versus number of training samples (individual features). NOTE: Legend not shown to save chart space. NN performance shown at top. Except *SignXY*, all features form a single group exhibiting similar variation.

features for which 1F required the smallest amount of computations were *Angle Center* (28.6% of the total amount of computations that NN would require), *Angle Middle* (30.8%), and *Total curvature* (32.0%). No significant difference was detected between *Angle Center* and *Angle Middle* ($\chi^2(1) = 2.649, n.s.$) and a marginally significant difference appeared between the top 3 features ($\chi^2(2) = 6.490, p = .04$). The top 3 worst features (the ones that required the largest amount of computations) were Hu_5 (71.1%), *Atan2XY* (72.4%), and Hu_7 (75.7%).

It is surprising how a conventional simple measurement such as *Length* only required 39% computations showing that a 2 : 5 reduction ratio was achieved just by sorting the training samples by their length! The same can be said for the R_1 and R_3 that, despite being simple ad-hoc ratios, managed to reduce the computations with 63%.

CONCLUSION

The 1F technique for pruning the training set of template-based NN gesture recognizers was introduced and its performance analyzed. Using one feature only, 1F managed to reduce the computations of NN with more than 70% while still maintaining the high recognition rate (> 98%). The implementation of 1F is straightforward as it only consists in sorting the 1D array of features followed by local search. Even

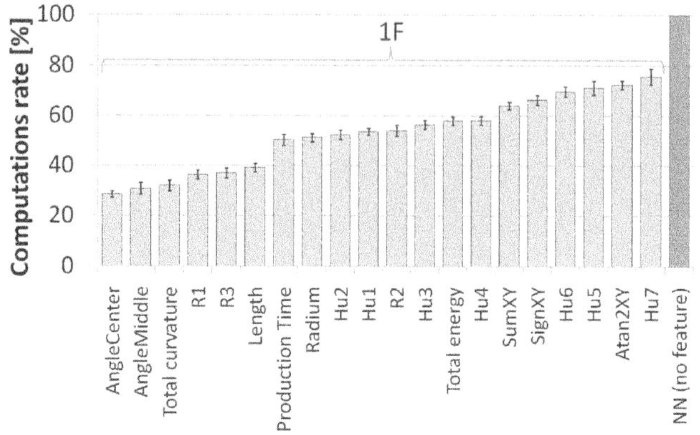

Figure 4. Computation rate versus feature type. NOTE: Features are shown in ascending order of their computation rate. Small is better.

simple features such as the length of a gesture lead to non-negligeable reduction rates (60%). It is the author's hope that 1F will prove useful for practitioners of gesture-based recognizers to help reduce the computational load for real-time applications.

ACKNOWLEDGMENTS

This paper was supported by the project "Progress and development through post-doctoral research and innovation in engineering and applied sciences- PRiDE - Contract no. POSDRU/89/1.5/S/57083", project co-funded from European Social Fund through Sectorial Operational Program Human Resources 2007-2013.

REFERENCES

1. Cao, X., and Zhai, S. Modeling human performance of pen stroke gestures. In *CHI '07*, ACM (2007), 1495–1504.
2. Kristensson, P.-O., and Zhai, S. Shark2: a large vocabulary shorthand writing system for pen-based computers. In *UIST '04* (2004), 43–52.
3. Li, Y. Protractor: a fast and accurate gesture recognizer. In *CHI '10*, ACM (New York, NY, USA, 2010), 2169–2172.
4. Pratt, W. K. *Digital Image Processing, 3rd Edition (pp. 606-607)*. John Wiley and Sons, New York, 2001.
5. Rubine, D. Specifying gestures by example. *SIGGRAPH Comput. Graph. 25* (July 1991), 329–337.
6. Vatavu, R.-D. The effect of sampling rate on the performance of template-based gesture recognizers. In *ICMI '11*, ACM (New York, NY, USA, 2011), 271–278.
7. Wobbrock, J. O., Wilson, A. D., and Li, Y. Gestures without libraries, toolkits or training: a $1 recognizer for user interface prototypes. In *UIST '07*, ACM (New York, NY, USA, 2007), 159–168.
8. Zezula, P., Amato, G., Dohnal, V., and Batko, M. *Similarity Search. The Metric Space Approach*, vol. 32. Springer, 2006.

Activity-Aware Recommendation for Collaborative Work in Operating Rooms

Afsaneh Doryab, Julian Togelius and Jakob E. Bardram
The Pervasive Interaction Technology Laboratory
IT University of Copenhagen, Denmark
{adoryab, juto, bardram}@itu.dk

ABSTRACT
This paper presents a recommender system for teams of medical professionals working collaboratively in hospital operating rooms. The system recommends relevant virtual actions, such as retrieval of information resources and initiation of communication with professionals outside the operating rooms. Recommendations are based on the current state of the ongoing operation as recognised from sensor data using machine learning techniques. The selection and non-selection of virtual actions during operations are interpreted as implicit feedback and used to update the weight matrices that guide recommendations. A pilot user study involving medical professionals indicates that the adaptation mechanism is effective and that the system provides adequate recommendations.

Author Keywords
Information Retrieval, Collaborative Work, Hospitals, Operating Room, Context-Aware, Recommendation

ACM Classification Keywords
H.5.2 Information Interfaces and Presentation: User Interfaces—*Evaluation/methodology*; J.3 Computer Applications: Life and Medical Science—*Medical information systems*

General Terms
Algorithms, Design, Experimentation

INTRODUCTION
Context-aware information retrieval refers to systems that help providing resources that are relevant to the current situation of users [3]. In many work environments, carrying out a task demands massive information access and management, while at the same time sharing and coordinating this information with co-workers. Context-aware computing in such settings can reduce the need for manual information retrieval and assist users in bringing forward relevant resources. So far, research in context-aware computing has mainly focused on adapting systems and services to an individual user [3, 2, 5, 4]. However, in a collaborative work environment such as a hospital, adaptive information retrieval goes beyond covering the needs of individuals, as medical procedures often involve multiple users working concurrently, sharing systems, devices, and documents.

This paper presents a novel approach in context-aware information adaptation and retrieval in shared collaborative settings. The approach is based on principals of recommendation systems [6]. The main contribution is an adaptation mechanism that (i) incrementally builds and updates its model of relevant information for every situation based on similar past situations, and (ii) incorporates users' information choices as implicit feedback and adapts the model to provide better information assistance. This research focuses on work inside an operating room (OR), where surgical procedures are performed by a team of co-located clinicians who have different information needs. This means that the information resources presented on e.g. a wall display in the OR should adapt to several people's need concurrently.

This research is rooted in a series of detailed, video-recorded observations of more than 25 surgical operations in two hospitals, combined with numerous semi-structured interviews. In these operations, several clinicians with different specialities collaborate on parallel, overlapping tasks. Based on what distinguishes surgical actions from each other, we have identified a set of 17 main tasks which we refer to as physical actions (pa), such as anesthesia, intubation and incision. Some actions follow a specific order while others do not. And at any time, complications might occur. There is a huge demand for consultation, discussion, and rapid information retrieval in case of complications and emergency in patient cases.

THE OVERALL APPROACH
Activity-aware recommendation in multi-user shared setting of an OR is supported by an overall architecture containing a Context Acquisition Component, a Physical-Action Recognition Component, a Virtual-Action Discovery Component, and a Recommender Surface. The contextual information, e.g., the location of a person acquired from sensors or other sources is used for recognition of physical actions (pas) performed by clinicians (ps). The collection of recognized pas is used by the Virtual-Action Discovery component which finds and adjusts a set of relevant virtual actions (vas) to be presented on the Recommender Surface. We apply machine learning techniques on the data obtained from sensors to recognize concurrent actions spread over time and space. The process of learning these actions is out of the scope of this paper and is presented in [1].

Virtual Action Adaptation

The adaptation mechanism responds to each detected pa with a set of *virtual actions* (va) which are associated with a collection of information resources and services (r). An example of a virtual action is showing and updating the patient's medical record (r_1) with information obtained from monitoring devices (r_2) during the operation.

Each task can be composed of several steps spread in different spaces. This means that even when changing the situation, a virtual action (va) which has been relevant in the last situation can still be either highly relevant, less relevant, or irrelevant. During the sequence of a task, a va can be relevant during the whole task (e.g., access to the medical record) or only during part(s) of it (e.g., during the phases of anesthesia or instrument checking). Any number of vas can be relevant during any particular pa, though the relative weight of the urgency or importance of vas for any given pa may vary.

Similar situations in the physical setting entail similarity in the information need and thus similarity in adaptation mechanism. For example, the treatment process for patients with similar diseases are typically very similar. Although there are differences in new situations, past patterns can still suggest an initial collection of vas that might be of interest in the new situation. The primary set of vas is created from a co-occurrence matrix which keeps track of relevance weights of the vas in accordance to pas. The relevance weight is the probability of action va_i while occurring pa_j and is adjusted according to physical actions and users' interactions with vas.

Hence, during each task, there are two adaptation steps as presented in figure 1. At step A, the initial set of potentially relevant vas is collected by applying similarity measures using three sources (Profile Pr, Community C, and Domain D). The profile is used as a pre-filtering source to further identify the community and domain knowledge source.

During the process, those vas whose resources relate to procedures and domain knowledge (e.g., guidelines) are customized by looking at the D source, while other vas with content related to similar cases are customized in C. Step B is dynamic where the presented collection of the vas from step A is updated based on changes in e.g., current pas. Change in the set of pas, triggers the adaptation algorithm to update the collection of presented vas. Each va can have a different relevance weight to a different pa.

The weight of vas is updated by incorporation of *implicit feedback* that is given to the presented collection on the surface by e.g., the users. In this case, the implicit feedback mainly includes visible interactions with the vas, e.g., in form of a click. The feedback updates two co-occurrence matrices $pa - va$ and $va - va$. The former keeps relevance weights between pa and vas and the latter updates co-occurrence weights for pairs of vas.

Our design integrates the collaborative filtering concept [6] which suggests that the interest of a user can be predicted by collecting information from many other users. We generalize this definition by saying that the behaviour of an entity (human or object) can be predicted by collecting behaviour patterns of similar entities. In this case, what 'interests' a situation in terms of relevant vas might also have been of interest in other past situations. Hence, the algorithm finds relevant vas by looking at past situations using entity's profile as the filtering vector, and then, it presents them on the surface as a set of recommendations for current situation. The users' interactions with the suggested vas indicate whether the presented set has been of any interest or use in the situation. The generated set is then updated based on the feedback.

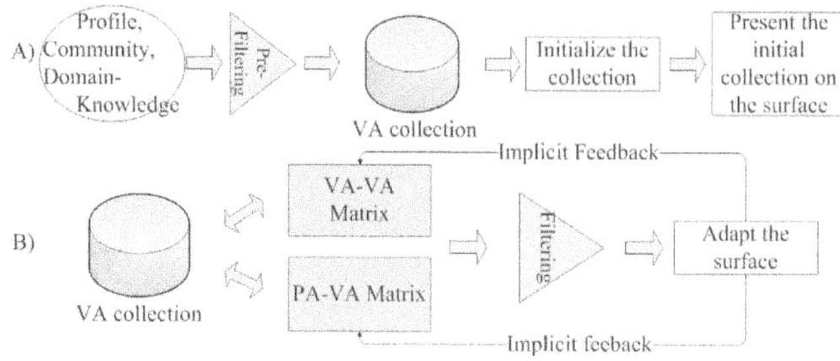

Figure 1. Adaptation steps for virtual actions related to each situation

RECOMMENDATION PROCESS

Figure 2 illustrates that vas can be in three states; *created*, *updated*, or *maintained* based on changes in the situation.

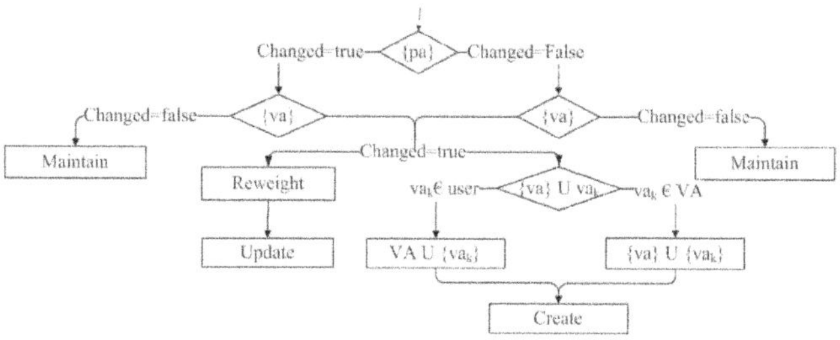

Figure 2. The flow of system actions based on different combinations of physical and virtual actions at each time step.

Creation of a va occurs in both steps when it is attached to the current task for the first time. After pre-filtering, the primary set of vas is created from matrices. A va is also created during the second step either by the users in form of a complete new collection of resources or from an existing set of vas which is not currently presented by the recommender. Every time the set of currently active pas changes, the collection of vas is *updated*. The updated collection can be completely different from the previous one, have some common vas with different or same weights, or have identical set of elements with different weights. After suggesting the collection, the weights of presented vas is changed via implicit feedback from the user.

Finding and suggesting relevant virtual actions ($\{va\}$) in a time series of physical actions ($\{pa\}_t$) is done as described in algorithm 1. As mentioned, we use two matrices to keep weights. The first matrix is:

$$M_{pa-va} = [m_{ij}], i = 0...|PA|, j = 0...|VA|,$$
$$m_{ij} = w_{va_j|pa_i}$$

where w is the current relevance weight between pa_i and va_j. The second matrix is the co-occurrence matrix for virtual actions defined as:

$$M_{va-va} = [n_{ij}], i = 0...|VA|, j = 0...|VA|\,,$$
$$n_{ij} = w_{va_i,va_j}$$

where w is the co-occurrence weight between va_i and va_j. The following steps present the algorithm:

Initialization: The set of top-n similar candidates in Community (C) and top-m relevant candidates in Domain (D) with least distance to current situation and task are chosen using a weighted similarity metric applied on profile vectors. The weight indicates the importance of an attribute. For instance, the value of the disease attribute is a stronger filter for irrelevant operations than the patient's gender. All distance values are normalized.

Filtering and Adaptation: In the beginning, i.e., at time $t = 0$, the set of vas generated by the initialization algorithm is presented to the users on the surface. This collection is then adapted based on changes in the set of pas observed at each time step. In the filtering step, the recommended set of items is updated by finding the top-k weighted va candidates in M_{pa-va} and then choosing top-k vas in M_{va-va} matrix which are different from the set that was already chosen. (In our experiments, $k = 6$.)

Implicit Feedback Incorporation: The weight of recommended virtual actions is updated based on the users' interactions with the suggested vas (e.g., in form of clicks), and each use is considered a positive feedback which increases the relevance weight of the corresponding va. The weights are then updated in both matrices and the filtering process is repeated.

Updating Matrices: The process of updating two matrices M_{pa-va} and M_{va-va} is as follows: Let $PA_t = \{pa_k, 0 \leq k \leq |PA|\}$ be the set of physical actions being performed at time t and $VA_t = \{va_s, 0 \leq s \leq |VA|\}$ be the set of virtual actions suggested at time t. While updating M_{pa-va}, for each $pa_i \in PA_t$ and $va_j \in VA_t$, $m_{ij} = m_{ij} + \alpha$, where α is an aggregate value or in the simplest case a constant, e.g., $\alpha = 1$. In M_{va-va}, $\forall va_i, va_j \in VA_t$, and $w_{va_i}, w_{va_j} > 0$:

$$w_{va_i,va_j} = min(w_{va_i}, w_{va_j}) \text{ and } n_{ij} = max(w_{va_i,va_j}, n_{ij})$$

Decay After the end of each sequence, the weights of items in the M_{pa-va} matrix are decreased by multiplying them by a decay value, e.g. 0.9. This is done in order to bound the weights in the matrix, so that new feedback can have a practical effect even after a large number of update cycles.

EXPERIMENTAL EVALUATION

To evaluate our approach, we implemented the algorithm in a simple user interface and conducted an experiment with a group of 16 clinicians in 3 different hospitals. Our hypotheses were that (1) the system can find a collection of relevant vas based on a set of pas, and (2) adjust and improve the relevance model over time based on the users' interactions.

We used the data streams of 10 real-world surgical operations that were annotated and used for activity recognition. The op-

Algorithm 1 Activity-aware recommendation

1: *Initialization:*
2: *set* $pr_{sP} = (at_1, ..., at_n)$ /* profile vector
3: *set* $pw_{sP} = (pw_1, ..., pw_n)$ /* priority vector
4: **for all** $c_i \in C$ **do**
5: $dist(pr_{sp}, pr_{c_i}) = (d_{i1}, ..., d_{in})$ /* distance vector
6: *normalize* $d_{i1}, ..., d_{in}$
7: *add* priority weights (pw_{sp}) to $dist(pr_{sp}, pr_{c_i})$
8: *calculate* $dist_{sp,c_i} = \sqrt{\sum_{j=1}^{n} d_{ij}}$
9: *set* $sim_{sp,c_i} = \frac{1}{1+dist_{sp,c_i}}$
10: *choose top-n* c_is with $max(sim_{sp,c_i})$
11: **end for**
12: **for all** $e_j \in D$ **do**
13: $dist(pr_{sp}, pr_{e_j}) = (d_{j1}, ..., d_{jn})$ /* distance vector
14: *normalize* $d_{j1}, ..., d_{jn}$
15: *add* priority weights (pw_{sp}) to $dist(pr_{sp}, pr_{e_j})$
16: *calculate* $dist_{sp,e_j} = \sqrt{\sum_{k=1}^{n} d_{jk}}$
17: *set* $sim_{e_j} = \frac{1}{1+dist_{e_j}}$
18: *choose top-m* candidates e_js with $max(sim_{e_j})$
19: **end for**
20: *initialize* M_{pa-va}, M_{va-va} with $\{c_i\}$ and $\{e_j\}$ collection
21: ---
22: *Filtering:*
23: let R be the set of recommended vas
24: if $t \neq 0$, *set* $R = \emptyset$
25: *set* $PA_t = \{pa_k, 0 \leq k \leq |PA|\}$ /* at time t
26: **for all** $pa_i \in PA_t$ **do**
27: *find top* $- k$ values for m_{ij} in M_{pa-va}, $m_{ij} = w_{pa_i|va_j}$
28: *add* va_js to R
29: **end for**
30: In M_{va-va} *find top* $- k$ values for n_{ij}, $n_{ij} = w_{va_i,va_j}$
31: **if** $va_i, va_j \notin R$ **then**
32: *add* va_i and va_j to R
33: **else**
34: *repeat* 30
35: **end if**
36: *suggest* R on the surface
37: ---
38: *Implicit Feedback Incorporation:*
39: **while** $PA_t \neq \emptyset$ **do**
40: on $f_{va_i} > 0$, /* feedback value given to va_i
41: $w_{va_i} = w_{va_i} + f_{va_i}$
42: **end while**
43: **if** $PA_{t+1} \neq PA_t$ **then**
44: *update* M_{pa-va} and M_{va-va}
45: **end if**
46: ---
47: *Updating Matrices:*
48: *set* $VA_t = \{va_s, 0 \leq s \leq |VA|\}$ /* at time t
49: **for all** $pa_i \in PA_t$ and $va_j \in VA_t$ **do**
50: $m_{ij} = m_{ij} + \alpha$
51: **end for**
52: **for all** $va_i, va_j \in VA_t$, and $w_{va_i}, w_{va_j} > 0$ **do**
53: $w_{va_i,va_j} = min(w_{va_i}, w_{va_j})$
54: $n_{ij} = max(w_{va_i,va_j}, n_{ij})$
55: **end for**
56: ---
57: *Decay:*
58: **if** $PA_t = \emptyset$ **then**
59: **for all** $m_{ij} \in M_{pa-va}$ **do**
60: $m_{ij} = m_{ij} * d$, $d < 1$ (e.g., 0.9)
61: **end for**
62: **end if**

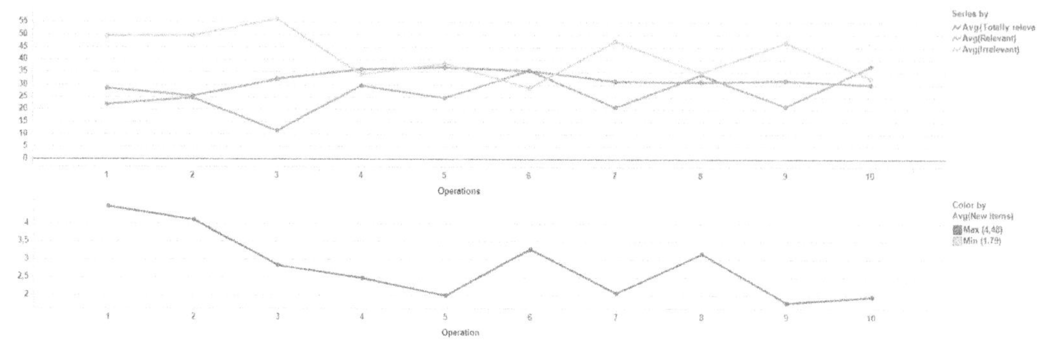

Figure 3. The upper diagram shows the development in presenting relevant virtual actions from operation 1 to 10. The lower diagram presents the average number of new items added by users in different operations.

erations were of the same type (open hernia), but they varied slightly in the set of physical actions being performed. The total collection of virtual actions used during the experiment was selected in cooperation with the medical staff. The system was designed to apply the recommendation algorithm on streams of physical actions and recommend the set of top 6 most relevant virtual actions on the surface. We also used a schema where we listed the flow of that typical operation and asked 6 participants (out of 16) with different specializations to rate the relevance of each va to each pa as well as add new vas if they were missing in the schema.

Ten out of 16 clinicians volunteered to rate the system suggestions for relevant vas to current pas. The experiment started with no training, and the system thus suggested a random va collection to the user in the first operation. Each subsequent operation used the updated matrices from previous operations. The users were asked to put themselves in the situation of that particular operation and imagine what kind of information would be useful as the operation was simulated.

Results

For testing our hypotheses, the experiment was designed to show whether the number of recommended items would stabilize towards the last operation. The expectation was that after each simulated operation, the number of relevant vas suggested by the system would increase, resulting in a decrease in the number of irrelevant items suggested, as well as reduction in the number of new items added by the users.

We calculated the average weights given by the users to the vas suggested by the system during each operation. We also computed the number of new items added by clinicians as relevant items to current pas. The results are summarized in Figure 3. Despite the variations, the average number of totally relevant items seems to stabilize, the average number of relevant vas shows a slight increase resulting in reduction of irrelevant items. The number of new added items (lower diagram) is decreasing from $\sim$ 4.5 items in the first operation to $\sim$ 1.8 in the end, implying that more of the relevant actions were already part of the recommendation set in the latter operations compared to the earlier operations. 73% of the relevance rates between virtual and physical actions obtained by the system at the end of the experiment were identical or close to the rates given by clinicians in the schemas.

CONCLUSION

We have presented our approach to context-aware information retrieval and filtering in shared environments by developing a recommender system based on collaborative filtering and implicit feedback techniques. The method was employed in an activity-aware recommender system inside an operating room. Data collected from real surgical operations was used as context to which the display adapts. The results of an experiment with clinicians showed a stabilization tendency in the set of relevant recommended items based on current physical actions being performed during surgical operations. This shows that the algorithm is able to incorporate the users' interactions with virtual actions as feedback and gradually obtain the same knowledge as intended by the users. However, more thorough testing should be carried out, for example conducting a study by testing the adaptive recommendation against a non-adaptive approach where all or a fixed set of virtual actions are presented to the users.

REFERENCES

1. Afsaneh Doryab. *Context-aware Information Adaptation In Collaborative Settings*. PhD thesis, IT University of Copenhagen, Denmark, October 2011.
2. J. E. Bardram. Applications of Context-Aware Computing in Hospital Work - Examples and Design Principles. In *Proceedings of the 2004 ACM Symposium on Applied Computing*, pages 1574–1579. ACM Press, 2004.
3. A. Dey, G. D. Abowd, and D. Salber. A conceptual framework and a toolkit for supporting the rapid prototyping of context-aware applications. *Human-Computer Interaction*, 16:97–166, 2001.
4. A. N. Dragunov, T. G. Dietterich, K. Johnsrude, M. McLaughlin, L. Li, and J. L. Herlocker. Tasktracer: a desktop environment to support multi-tasking knowledge workers. In *IUI '05: Proceedings of the 10th international conference on Intelligent user interfaces*, pages 75–82, New York, NY, USA, 2005. ACM.
5. T. Rattenbury and J. Canny. Caad: an automatic task support system. In *CHI '07: Proceedings of the SIGCHI conference on Human factors in computing systems*, pages 687–696, New York, NY, USA, 2007. ACM.
6. F. Ricci, L. Rokach, B. Shapira, and P. B. Kantor. *Recommender Systems Handbook*. Springer-Verlag New York, Inc., New York, NY, USA, 1st edition, 2010.

Universal Earphones: Earphones with Automatic Side and Shared Use Detection

Kohei Matsumura[1&2], Daisuke Sakamoto[2&3], Masahiko Inami[2&4], and Takeo Igarashi[2&3]

[1]Japan Advanced Institute of Science and Technology
1-1 Asahidai, Nomi, Ishikawa 923-1211, Japan

[2]JST ERATO Igarashi Design Interface Project
1-28-1-7F Koishikawa, Bunkyo, Tokyo 112-0002 Japan

[3]The University of Tokyo
7-3-1, Hongo, Bunkyo, Tokyo 113-0033, Japan

[4]Keio University
4-1-1 Hiyoshi, Kohoku, Yokohama 223-8526 Japan

matsumur@acm.org, sakamoto@is.s.u-tokyo.ac.jp, inami@kmd.keio.ac.jp and takeo@acm.org

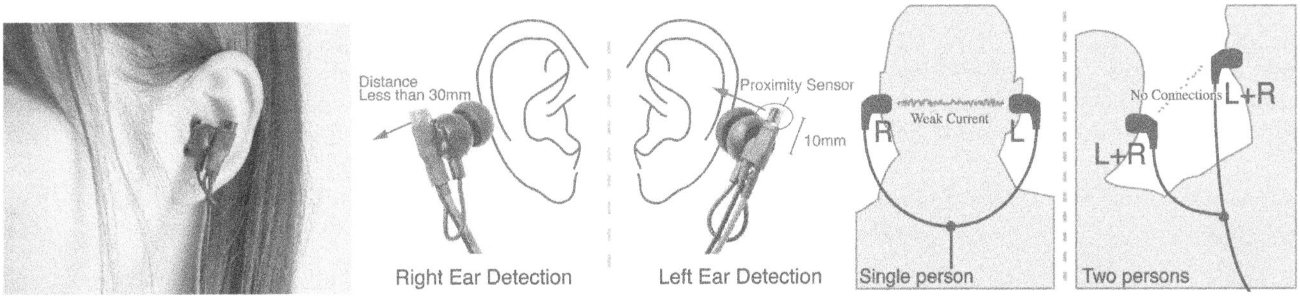

Figure 1 Left: Universal earphone in use. Center: Side detection. Right: Shared use detection.

ABSTRACT

We present universal earphones that use both a proximity sensor and a skin conductance sensor and we demonstrate several implicit interaction techniques they achieve by automatically detecting the context of use. The universal earphones have two main features. The first involves detecting the left and right sides of ears, which provides audio to either ear, and the second involves detecting the shared use of earphones and this provides mixed stereo sound to both earphones. These features not merely free users from having to check the left and right sides of earphones, but they enable them to enjoy sharing stereo audio with other people.

Author Keywords

Earphones, implicit interaction, intelligent interface.

ACM Classification Keywords

H.5.m. Information interfaces and presentation (e.g., HCI): Miscellaneous.

General Terms

Design, Human Factors.

INTRODUCTION

Even though interfaces have been widely prevalent and intuitively used by everyone, they present several problems. For example, when we are using earphones and headphones, we sometimes have problems in using them, i.e., in placing them on the wrong ears. This might be a small problem, but it demonstrates the possibility of refining traditional interfaces, especially in making them more intelligent. We consider that good interfaces and interactions are implicit, and users should not have to worry about them. If interfaces have intelligence to capture the contexts of users, no matter how small, and users do not know about these contexts, the interfaces and interactions will be much better than the previous ones.

We therefore present a device called universal earphones (UEs) that automatically detect the left and right sides of the ears and provide stereo audio to the most suitable side. The single greatest obstacle when using earphones is matching each earphone to the most suitable side of ears as this is necessary to enjoy audio experiences, particularly in professional audio production and modern 3D audio environments like those for 3D games and movies. The UEs not only free users from having to check the sides of earphones, but they also support detection when a single set of earphones is being shared by two people. In such cases, commercially available earphones force users to divide output into two audio channels, i.e., each person is able to hear either the left or right channel. The UEs mix stereo sound and present it to both sides of the earphones. These two features engender implicit interaction between the user and the UEs, and they enable the UEs to act as a good music communication medium.

SIDE DETECTION

We embedded a proximity sensor in a single side of the UEs to detect the left and right sides of the ears, and we measured the distance between the center of the earphones and the pinna (external ear). When this distance is less than 30 mm, the UEs activate the right channel; otherwise, the channel is changed to the left. We referred to the Anthropometrical Database [5] to determine the threshold for the distance. The channel for the other side of the earphones was automatically changed to the opposite channel. We attached a sensor to the inside of the ear pads of the headphones and the sensor measured the distance from the ear pads to the outside of the pinna. To enable these features, we embedded both a proximity sensor and an analog switch IC into the earphones (Figure 2).

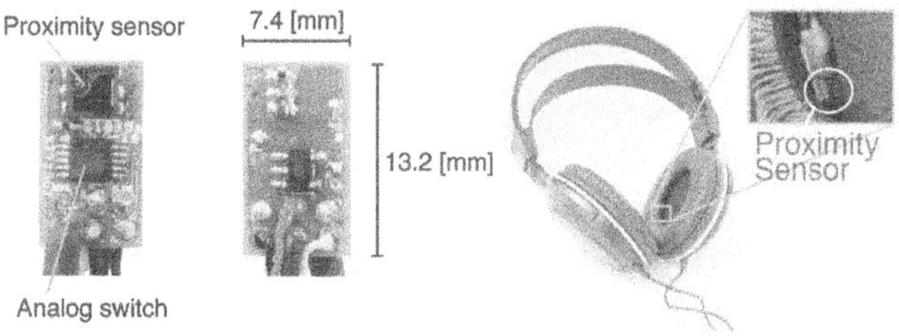

Figure 2 Left: Sensor unit. Right: Photograph of headphones.

RELATED WORK

Buxton proposed classifying human-computer interactions into two categories of foreground and background interactions [1]. He defined foreground interaction as "activities which are in the fore of human consciousness" and background interaction as "tasks that take place in the periphery 'behind' those in the foreground." According to this, our UEs can be categorized as background interaction. There have been several studies on background interaction. Ju et al. proposed a framework for background interaction and they developed an interactive whiteboard based on the framework [4]. Hinckley et al. integrated sensors into a mobile device and they demonstrated several features that engaged sensors such as recording memos when the device was held like a cell phone and automatically powering the device up when a user picked it up [3]. Dietz et al. proposed a device that sensed when a phone was removed from the ear and that buffered the incoming audio [2]. When the phone was returned, the missed incoming audio was played back at a rate faster than that in real time. Users did not need to operate these devices, which sensed the situation and worked unobtrusively in the background. Our UEs were aimed at working in this way to help users with background interaction, which enabled them to focus on foreground work.

FUTURE WORK

We focused on both single-user and dual-user utilization of our earphones and implemented two features in the earphones, i.e., ear-side and shared-use detection. However, if we could focus on either single-user or multi-user utilization, we would be able to make the design of background interaction for the earphones explicit. This section discusses future work on UEs with respect to either single-user or multi-user utilization. On the one hand, skin conductance sensors can be used to determine if the earphones are attached to the ears or not when focusing on single-user utilization. When earphones are detached from the ears, they could automatically pause music. This feature would free users from having to push play/pause buttons. On the other hand, the feature to detect shared use could be utilized to provide two sets of music separately to both earphones when focusing on multi-user utilization. Two users would be able to enjoy listening to music by sharing both the earphones and the music player.

REFERENCES

1. Buxton, W. 1995. Integrating the Periphery and Context: A New Model of Telematics. In *Proceedings of Graphics Interface '95*, 239-246.
2. Dietz, H.P. and Yerazunis, S.W. 2001. Real-time audio buffering for telephone applications. In *Proceedings of the 14th annual ACM symposium on User interface software and technology* (UIST '01). ACM, New York, NY, USA, 193-194.
3. Hinckley, K., Pierce, J., Sinclair, M., and Horvitz, E. 2000. Sensing techniques for mobile interaction. In *Proceedings of the 13th annual ACM symposium on User interface software and technology* (UIST '00). ACM, New York, NY, USA, 91-100.
4. Ju, W., Lee A.B., and Klemmer, R.S. 2008. Range: exploring implicit interaction through electronic whiteboard design. In *Proceedings of the 2008 ACM conference on Computer supported cooperative work* (CSCW '08). ACM, New York, NY, USA, 17-26.
5. National Institute of Advanced Industrial Science and Technology, Anthropometrical Database, http://riodb.ibase.aist.go.jp/dhbodydb/properties/s/index-e.html.

A Demo of a Facial UI Design Approach for Digital Artists

Pedro Bastos
Instituto Telecomunicações
Fac. Engenharia Univ. Porto
ptbbastos@gmail.com

Xenxo Alvarez
Instituto Telecomunicações
Fac. Ciências Univ. Porto
xenxo3d@gmail.com

Verónica Orvalho
Instituto Telecomunicações
Fac. Ciências Univ. Porto
veronica.orvalho@dcc.fc.up.pt

ABSTRACT

In the character animation industry, animators use facial UI's to animate a character's face. A facial UI provides widgets and handles that the animator interacts with to control the character's facial regions. This paper presents a facial UI design approach to control the animation of the six basic facial expressions of the anthropomorphic face. The design is based in square shaped widgets [5] holding circular handles that allow the animator to produce the muscular activity relative to the basic facial expressions [1]. We have implemented a prototype of the facial UI design in the Blender open-source animation software and did a preliminary pilot study with three animators. Two parameters were evaluated: the number of clicks and the time taken to animate the six basic facial expressions. The study reveals there was little variation in the values each animator marked for both parameters, despite the natural difference in their creative performance.

Author Keywords

Facial animation, user interfaces, widgets, handles.

ACM Classification Keywords

B.5.1 Design: Control Design

INTRODUCTION

Producing character facial animation in the entertainment industry is a serious bottleneck for character animators [7]. A character's face assumes complex expressions [3] which the animator needs to produce in tight production schedules. To animate the character's expressions a facial user interface, or a facial UI, is used. This UI has widgets and handles that the animator manipulates to control the character's expressions.

We present a facial UI design approach to animate the six basic facial expressions defined in [1] for the anthropomorphic face: surprise, fear, disgust, anger, happiness and sadness. An anthropomorphic face is any face with the anatomical characteristics of a human face (e.g. number, symmetry and position of facial regions). The goal was to realize if the UI design averaged the animators' performance posing the expressions. We did a prototype (Fig. 1) and a pilot study with 3 animators.

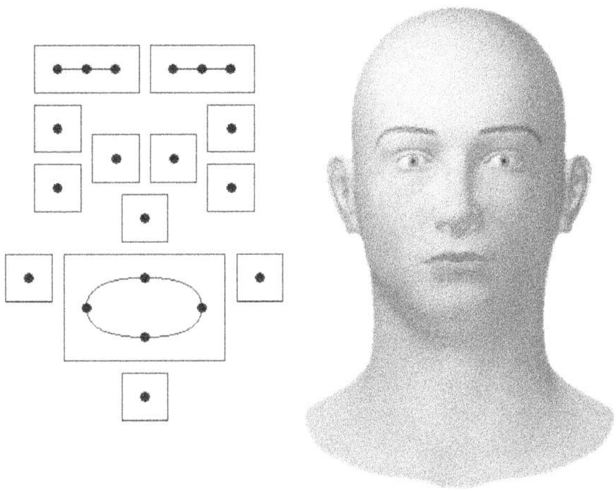

Figure 1. The design approach of the facial UI.

The animators were introduced to the interface controls and to the guidelines defined by Ekman and Friesen [1] to animate the expressions. Following they were asked to reproduce the six basic facial expressions without any further guidance. To evaluate their performance using the controls we analyzed three parameters: the quality of the expressions, the number of clicks performed and the time taken to animate them.

THE FACIAL UI DESIGN APPROACH

The facial UI design is based in the widgets and handles found in Parke and Waters [5] work, which we adapted using the muscular activity information of the face, categorized by Ekman and Friesen [2] into Action Units, Action Descriptors and Gross Behavior Codes. We filtered the muscular activity relative to the six basic facial expressions to reach a behavioral classification [6] of the handles and prevent the usual complexity found in this kind of animation interfaces [4].

We considered the information on skin deformation described by Ekman and Friesen [1] for each facial expression. For instance, the fact that the eyebrows appear curved during surprise, or the upper lip is raised during disgust, or the nose wrinkles and the cheeks raise during anger, or the corners of the lips are drawn back and slightly up during happiness.

The result is an interface paradigm with 10 square shaped and 3 rectangle shaped widgets and a total of 20 handles. Each handle can be moved horizontally to change one parameter and vertically to change another. The handles control the eyebrows, eyelids, nose, cheeks, lips and jaw, which were defined by Ekman and Friesen [1] as the facial regions that allow the six basic facial expressions to be perceived.

		The Six Basic Facial Expressions						TOTAL
		Surprise	Fear	Disgust	Anger	Happiness	Sadness	
	Optimal Clicks	7	9	4	8	2	4	34
Animator 1	Clicks	9	9	6	8	2	4	38
	Time	27	30	15	15	4	10	101
Animator 2	Clicks	7	13	5	8	2	4	39
	Time	17	32	17	24	5	11	106
Animator 3	Clicks	8	9	5	12	2	6	42
	Time	31	28	20	57	8	20	164

Table 1. Statistics of the animators' interaction with the facial UI.

THE PILOT STUDY

Three animators were asked to test a prototype of the facial UI design approach. The animators' interaction was evaluated by the number of clicks performed and the time taken to produce the six basic facial expressions defined by Ekman and Friesen [1]. Table 1 shows the results of the animators' interaction.

Animator 1 did 38 clicks in 101 seconds. Animator 2 did 39 clicks in 106 seconds. Animator 3 did 42 clicks in 164 seconds. The number of clicks each animator did is very similar to each other and close to the optimal number of clicks (34). The time taken was similar for animators 1 and 2. Animator 3 required more time to place the controls thus achieving the most accurate expressions, as seen in Fig. 2. Despite Animator 3 required more time, the number of clicks performed did not change significantly from Animators 1 and 2.

Fig. 2 illustrates, in the top row, the optimal poses we built for each facial expression following the guidelines defined by Ekman and Friesen [1]. We registered our performance as the optimal number of clicks seen in Table 1. The animators were given these guidelines as well and their results are shown in Fig. 2. In overall, the animators were able to simulate the six basic facial expressions with increased accuracy.

CONCLUSION AND FUTURE WORK

We designed a facial user interface paradigm that approximattes the number of clicks and time that animators require to animate the six basic facial expressions defined by Ekman and Friesen [1] for the anthropomorphic face. The paradigm successfully averaged the number of clicks for the simulation of the six basic facial expressions.

Fig. 2 shows that fear was the single facial expression that the animators could not simulate as well as its corresponding optimal expression. We believe this is because animators did not consider that the middle portion of the eyebrows should raise only during surprise [1], whereas during fear the eyebrows should appear straightened [1]. For this reason, the animators ended up doing an expression of fear which is somewhat similar to that of surprise.

We continue working to improve and extend the interface design to go beyond the six basic expressions and into the entire behavioral set for the anthropomorphic face defined in the Facial Action Coding System [2]. We are also working to provide animators the possibility to customize each handle according to the target emotion to be expressed.

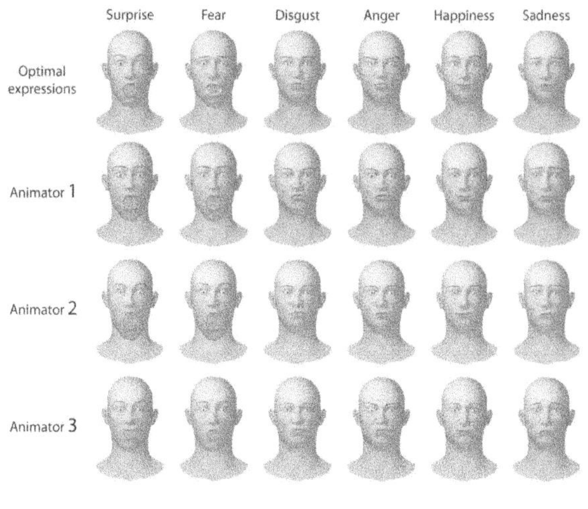

Figure 2. Comparison of the animators' results.

We provide an audiovisual format of the user interface prototype running in the latest version of the Blender open-source animation software.

ACKNOWLEDGMENTS

This paper is financially supported by Fundação para a Ciência e a Tecnologia (FCT), grant SFRH/BD/69878/2010, by Instituto de Telecomunicações (IT) and partially by the European Union FP7 Integrated Project VERE (No. 257695). The face shown in the figures was generated in the MakeHuman© open-source modeling software, licensed under the GNU General Public License. We thank the animators that tested the prototype: José Ricardo Silva, Nuno Vasco Costa and Pedro Marques Pereira. We also thank José Serra for his support.

REFERENCES

1. Ekman, P., and Friesen, W. V. *Unmasking the Face: A Guide to Recognizing Emotions from Facial Clues.* Prentice-Hall, 1975. pp. 34-128.
2. Ekman, P., and Friesen, W. V. *Manual of the Facial Action Coding System.* Consulting Psychologists Press, Stanford University, 1977. pp. 15-347.
3. Hauser, T. *The Pixar Treasures.* Disney Editions Deluxe Scrapbook, 2011.
4. Matejic, L. LOG: Building 3D User Interface Widgets by Demonstration. *Technical Report for the Department of Computer Science, Brown University Providence, p. 2* (1993).
5. Parke, F., and Waters, K. *Computer Facial Animation.* A.K. Peters, 2008. p. 153.
6. Wang, L. J., Sajeev, A. S. M., and Inchaiwong, L. A Formal Specification of Interaction Widgets Hierarchy Framework. *Proc. 3rd International Conference on Information Technology: New Generations. IEEE Computer Society, p. 1* (2006).
7. Williams, R. *The Animator's Survival Kit.* New York University, 2001. pp. 246-250.

Simple, Fast, and Accurate Clustering of Data Sequences*

Luis A. Leiva and Enrique Vidal
Institut Tecnològic d'Informàtica, Universitat Politècnica de València
{luileito,evidal}@iti.upv.es

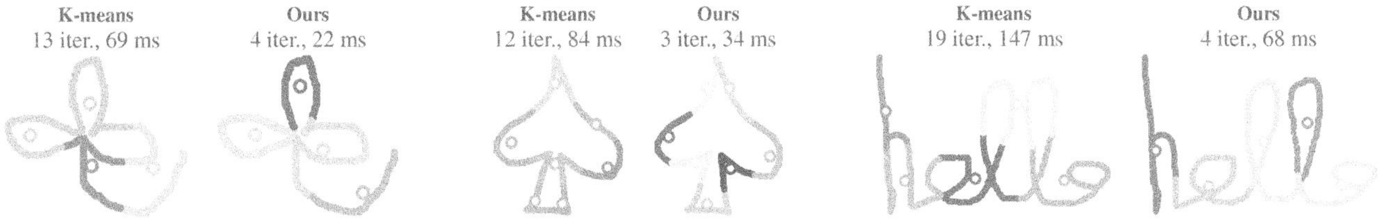

(a) Trifolium: 467 points, 4 classes **(b) Pica**: 484 points, 7 classes **(c) Hello**: 836 points, 5 classes

Figure 1: *Continuous* handwriting HTML5 canvas-based experiments performed on an i686 dual core CPU @ 1GHz running Firefox 3.6. (1a) Identifying drawing parts. (1b) Discovering symmetries. (1c) Isolating characters. As observed, our proposal provides better solutions in terms of performance (less computation time) and accuracy (well-formed segmentations).

ABSTRACT

Many devices generate large amounts of data that follow some sort of sequentiality, e.g., motion sensors, e-pens, or eye trackers, and therefore these data often need to be compressed for classification, storage, and/or retrieval purposes. This paper introduces a simple, accurate, and extremely fast technique inspired by the well-known K-means algorithm to properly cluster sequential data. We illustrate the feasibility of our algorithm on a web-based prototype that works with trajectories derived from mouse and touch input. As can be observed, our proposal outperforms the classical K-means algorithm in terms of accuracy (better, well-formed segmentations) and performance (less computation time).

Author Keywords

Sequential data, clustering, trajectory segmentation

ACM Classification Keywords

H.5.2 User Interfaces: Input devices and strategies; I.5.3 Clustering: Algorithms

INTRODUCTION

There is a notably increasing spectrum of devices that capture dense volumes of sequentially-generated information (e.g., active RFID tags, e-pens, eye trackers, etc.). Therefore, a clear interest exists in new compression techniques and methods to simplify the structure of this kind of data, so that original objects can be represented by more compact structures that are better tailored for classification, storage, and retrieval purposes. This can be approached as a clustering problem, i.e., organizing such an object sequences into subgroups whose members are similar in some way.

When clustering sequential data there exists a strong constraint, often related to time, that can be exploited to a great advantage. Nonetheless, by ignoring this constraint, classical clustering techniques fail to cope with the underlying sequential data structure, as illustrated in Figure 1. What is more, previous research on sequential data clustering considered the objects to cluster as whole data sequences or previously determined subsequences thereof, c.f. [3, 4]. Instead, we are interested in discovering *subtrajectories* within a single trajectory, so that we can obtain a simplified data structure preserving the underlying data sequentiality. From this point of view, approaches based on Hidden Markov Models (HMMs) have been proposed; e.g., [1]. The downside of HMMs, however, is that they require a complex training, and also can be prohibitive if processing power is a restriction, e.g., working on mobile devices. As such, we propose here a closed-form solution having a *low computational cost* in terms of performance, which translates to really fast convergence times, and providing *consistent results* in terms of accuracy: each run for a given number of classes always yields the same (well-formed) sequential clustering configuration.

SYSTEM OVERVIEW

In our prototype, the user can draw on a browser canvas with any pen-based device, including a traditional computer mouse or a touchscreen. The desired number of clusters can be either specified by the user or estimated by the system. The generalized workflow is shown in Algorithm 1.

*Work supported by MIPRCV (CSD2007-00018) and MITTRAL (TIN2009-14633-C03-01) projects, and grant Prometeo/2009/014.

IUI'12, February 14–17, 2012, Lisbon, Portugal.
ACM 978-1-4503-1048-2/12/02.

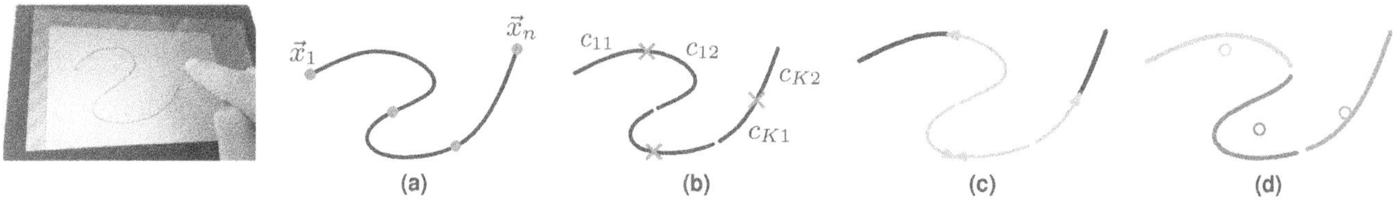

Figure 2: Graphical overview of Algorithm 1 for $K = 3$ clusters. (2a) Key points identification: the first and last key points always match the first and last data points ($\vec{x}_1$ and $\vec{x}_n$); (2b) Initial segmentation: crosses mark the K segments' middle points; (2c) Point visiting order for reallocation: notice that chunks c_{11} and c_{Kn} do not need to be inspected; (2d) Final clustering configuration: circles represent each segment's centroid.

Method Rationale

Given a data sequence (or *trajectory*) X of n points and the number of clusters (or *segments*) K, the system provides a *sequential* clustering configuration that minimizes the sum of quadratic errors (or *distortion*) criterion. To this end, the increment in the overall distortion that would be caused by reallocating a point $\vec{x}$ from cluster j to cluster k is incrementally computed as [2]:

$$\Delta J(\vec{x}, j, k) = \frac{n_k}{n_k + 1} \parallel \vec{x} - \vec{\mu}_k \parallel^2 - \frac{n_j}{n_j - 1} \parallel \vec{x} - \vec{\mu}_j \parallel^2 \quad (1)$$

where $\vec{\mu}_j$ and $\vec{\mu}_k$ are the means of the two clusters involved. Point $\vec{x}$ is reallocated when this increment is negative. This way of reallocating data points is inspired by Duda and Hart's K-means algorithm [2], which allows an incremental computation of the new cluster means, and has been shown to perform better than the popular K-means version [5]. As discussed below, we follow Duda and Hart's reallocation strategy but, in contrast to K-means, we capitalize on the data sequentiality to produce well-defined partitions.

Algorithm pseudo-code

Input: Trajectory $X = \vec{x}_1, \ldots, \vec{x}_n$; No. Clusters $K \geq 2$
Output: Minimum Error Segmentation of X

```
Interpolate K + 1 points from X
Initialize K segments
repeat
    for j = 1 to K do
        Inspect the first chunk of segment j
        Inspect the second chunk of segment j
until no reallocations
```

Algorithm 1: The steps of our sequential clustering algorithm.

Method Description

To begin with, a series of key points must be initialized in an ordered way (Figure 2a). This can be achieved by using any interpolation method (e.g., piecewise constant, linear, nonlinear, etc.) over the input data set. Such ordered points are then used to build the initial segments. Next, each segment is divided into two chunks around its middle point (Figure 2b), and both are sequentially inspected. Points belonging to the first chunk in segment j can only be reassigned to the second chunk of segment $j - 1$, and points in the second chunk of segment j can only be reassigned to the first chunk of segment $j + 1$ (Figure 2c). If and only if a point reassignment (Equation 1) contributes to decrease the overall clustering distortion, then the point is finally reallocated. Otherwise, the next chunk is inspected, in order to preserve the clustering sequentiality. In sum, three key features differentiate our approach from other K-means based algorithms: initialization, visiting order, and sequentiality constraints.

ENVISIONED APPLICATIONS

Besides the illustrative web-based system for freehand drawing described before[1], we depict here some usage scenarios where our approach suitably fits.

Online Handwriting. Our clustering technique can be used as a preprocessing step for online text recognition. As illustrated in Figure 1c, the obtained (well-formed) segments capture pen-stroke or even full-character regularities which can be advantageously exploited by existing handwritten recognition approaches to increase character recognition accuracy.

Eye/Mouse Tracking. This algorithm entails a reliable contribution to clustering eye movements on aggregated data; e.g., both heatmaps and areas of interets (AOIs) are computed by distance-based clusters, and therefore they do not distinguish between long-time fixations of a single person or short-time fixations of a group of people.

Motion Segmentation. The storage and transmission of motion tracking content is a problem due to their tremendous size and the noise caused by imperfections in the capture process. Thus, one could use our method for a more compact representation of these (large) data.

In general, any discipline that would handle ordered data sequences could benefit from our approach; e.g., human motion classification from surveillance cameras or automatic video key frame extraction.

REFERENCES

1. Bashir, F. I., Khokhar, A. A., and Schonfeld, D. Object trajectory-based activity classification and recognition using hidden markov models. *IEEE Trans. on Image Processing* (2007), 1912–1919.
2. Duda, R. O., Hart, P. E., and Stork, D. G. *Pattern Classification*, 2nd ed. John Wiley & Sons, 2001.
3. Guralnik, V., and Karypis, G. A scalable algorithm for clustering sequential data. In *Proc. ICDM* (2001), 179–186.
4. Lee, J.-G., Han, J., and Whang, K.-Y. Trajectory clustering: a partition-and-group framework. In *Proc. SIGMOD* (2007).
5. Leiva, L. A., and Vidal, E. Warped K-Means: An algorithm to cluster sequentially-distributed data. *Pattern Recognition Letters* (2012). To be published.

[1] Available at **`http://personales.upv.es/luileito/wkm/`**.

Interaction-based User Interface Redesign*

Luis A. Leiva
ITI – Institut Tecnològic d'Informàtica
Universitat Politècnica de València
llt@acm.org

ABSTRACT
This paper demonstrates a general framework to restyle UI widgets, in order to adapt them to the user behavior. Different implementation examples illustrate its feasibility. The value of this methodology comes from the fact that it is suited to any application language or toolkit supporting structured data hierarchies and style sheets; e.g., interfaces created in HTML, XUL, Flex/AIR (ActionScript), or Java. As described in the paper, an explicit end user intervention is not required, and changes are gradually applied so that they are not intrusive for the user.

Author Keywords
Adaptive Interfaces, Implicit Interaction, Redesign

ACM Classification Keywords
H.5.2 User Interfaces: User-centered design

INTRODUCTION
In computing systems, technology alone cannot survive without adequate user interfaces. To maximize the benefits that usable interfaces bring to users, often developers try to target as many people as possible. However, attempting to create UIs by following the *one-size-fits-all* approach is doomed to fail if an application is intended to be exposed to an arbitrary audience — take for instance web pages or mobile applications. As such, proposals that involve active end user manipulation have been considered to adapt the appearance of UIs (e.g., [1]). Nonetheless, user-driven customization requires to perform additional activities beyond the main purpose of using the application. Claypool et al. [2] observed that every user interaction can contribute to an *implicit interest indicator*; therefore alternative adaptation approaches without burdening the user can be derived. What is more, as stated by Gajos and Weld [3], the rendering of an interface should reflect the needs and usage pattern of individual users. This work is inspired by these ideas.

It is commonly agreed that adaptive systems should accommodate the UI to the user, but also that doing so automatically is a non-trivial problem. Adaptation should be predictable, transparent, and discreet, so that the changes introduced to the UI do not confuse the user. Also, adaptation should not interfere with the structure of the application.

The rationale of this approach follows the Attentive UIs concept [5], i.e., weigh the importance of the information supplied with estimated priorities in user activity. This way, by leveraging information that is submitted with little or no awareness (e.g., mouse movements, clicks, key strokes) those elements (*widgets* from here onwards) where users focus their interaction are incrementally mutated. Specifically, due to the fact that exertions are preceded by attention most of the time, the importance of an interaction towards a specific widget is measured as the proportion of UI-generated events on that widget between consecutive sessions, as shown in Figure 1 and described in Implementation.

SYSTEM OVERVIEW
With the growing popularity of web-based applications, the Cascading Style Sheets (CSS) paradigm has been widely adopted by several programming environments beyond the browser. For instance, it is possible to use CSS in Java[1], GTK+[2], and Qt[3]. CSS allows attaching styles to the application, decoupling the data model and its presentation. This way, in this system, adaptation operates by automatically overriding the rendering of widgets, by simply modifying their CSS. The technique was first introduced in [4], which has been now reformulated to generalize to structured applications (e.g., document object models and scene graphs).

Adaptation Protocol
Initially, the developer indicates which widgets and which properties can be restyled by the system, by using a straightforward JSON notation. Later, when the application is loaded, event listeners will track such widgets in the background. While working with the application, the system "learns" from the user interactions, so that the next time the application is loaded, the visual appearance of the widgets the user has interacted most is subtly modified. Finally, when the user leaves the application, interaction data are serialized and stored on a local database. Figure 2 summarizes the architecture of this framework.

*An accompanying video submission is available. This work is supported by the Spanish research programme Consolider Ingenio 2010: MIPRCV (CSD2007-00018).

[1] http://weblogs.java.net/blog/2008/07/17/introducing-java-css
[2] http://gnomejournal.org/article/107/styling-gtk-with-css
[3] http://doc.qt.nokia.com/4.3/stylesheet.html

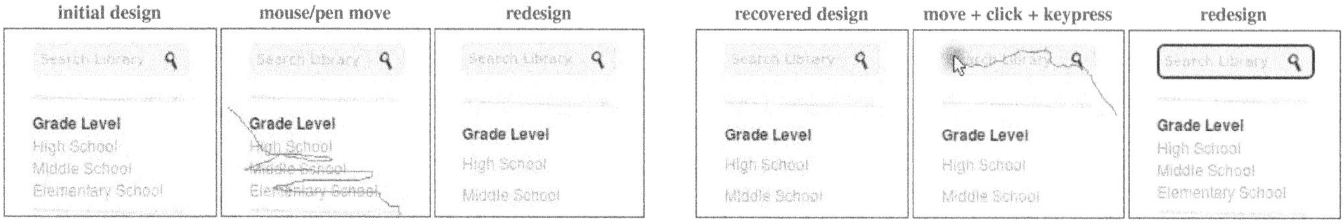

(a) Session #1 (b) Session #2

Figure 1: This adaptation technique is tightly coupled to the user interactions, but also delimited by the UI developer. In this example, the system is allowed to modify the **border-width** and **border-color** properties of the search box, and the **padding-top** property of the list items. In the first session (1a) the list is hovered, and hence the padding is increased accordingly. In the second session (1b) the previous redesign is recovered from the local database. Since this time the user does not interacted with the list items, the padding is therefore decreased.

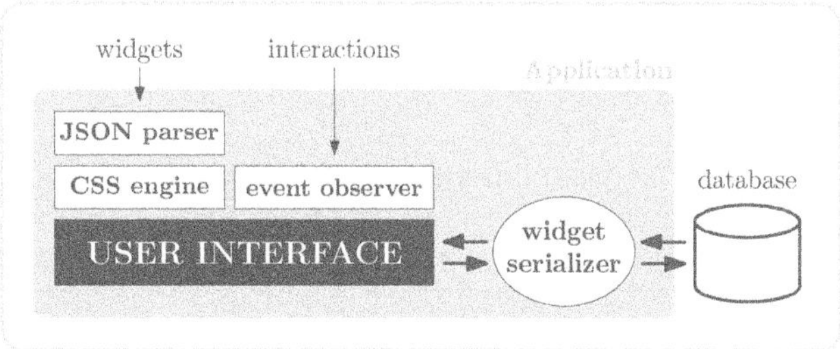

Figure 2: System architecture. Adaptable widgets are indicated by the developer, which will be modified according to how users interact.

Implementation

The API exposes a single method to invoke the system (Figure 3), which takes a configuration object as mandatory argument. Note that such an object notation is dramatically less verbose than the syntax envisioned in [4], and that it can support as many combination of selectors as the underlying CSS engine can implement. This reverts in a wide range of adaptation possibilities, as shown in Figure 1.

```
interface UIAdapt {
  void setWidgets(Object config, Object context);
};
```

```
import org.[illegible].classes.Adapt;
public static void main(String[] args) {
  Adapt.setWidgets({
   "#title": ["font-size", "color"],
   "JFrame > JSlider": ["top", "margin"]
  }, this);
}
```

Figure 3: API definition in Interface Description Language (top) and a conceptual Java Swing implementation example (bottom).

Once the JSON configuration is parsed, object keys are used to select the marked widgets (eg., a button, a table cell, or a text paragraph). Additionally, a series of event lists (hash tables) are created to log interaction data at runtime (e.g., **mousemove**, **click**, or **keydown** event lists). Such an event lists are thus composed of a serialized widget representation as keys and an interaction score as values — the more the user interacts with a widget during a session, the higher the score and vice versa. Scores are not cumulative but differential, following a non-linear distribution (using sigmoid functions) bounded to the interval $]-1.0, 1.0[$ in order to ensure that adaptations will be incrementally applied [4]. Take for instance a button that is allowed to adapt its size by scaling, having a design value of, say, 20px. If the computed score is 0.3, the new size will be $20(1 + 0.3) = 26$px. Conversely, if afterwards the computed score is -0.1, the new font size will be $26(1 - 0.1) = 23.4$px. Event lists are the only user information stored in the local database.

EVALUATION

In terms of system performance, adaptation takes just a few milliseconds to complete (5 ms on average for 50 defined elements with 10 CSS properties each on a traditional computer). Regarding human assessment, an informal study involving 12 users revealed that adaptation works adequately, being also not perceived as distracting most of the time (9 users). These results indicate that this technique supports their intended goals. Nonetheless, I will report on a systematic user evaluation in future papers, to ensure its validity.

DISCUSSION

Building interfaces for each type of device and every kind of user is not scalable for human programmers, therefore, an automated solution is necessary [3]. I have presented an alternative to redesign interface widgets that operates unobtrusively both for the user and the application structure. Substantial improvements can be made at no cost, since the system is the only responsible of performing the adaptation, being delimited by the (implicit) user interactions and the restrictions imposed by the developer (so that not all events affect all styling). A limitation of this framework is that only *numerical* CSS properties can be adapted, i.e., those related to *dimensions* and *colors*. Therefore, more advanced adaptation strategies such as re-arranging several UI components (beyond alignment) or inserting/removing contents would require a technically more sophisticated approach.

REFERENCES

1. Bolin, M., Webber, M., Rha, P., Wilson, T., and Miller, R. C. Automation and customization of rendered web pages. In *Proc. UIST* (2005), 163–172.
2. Claypool, M., Le, P., Waseda, M., and Brown, D. Implicit interest indicators. In *Proc. IUI* (2001), 33–40.
3. Gajos, K. Z., and Weld, D. S. SUPPLE: Automatically generating user interfaces. In *Proc. IUI* (2004), 93–100.
4. Leiva, L. A. Restyling website design via touch-based interactions. In *Proc. mobileHCI* (2011), 91–94.
5. Vertegaal, R. Attentive user interfaces. *Commun. ACM 46*, 3 (2003), 31–33. Editorial note.

Explain-a-LOD: Using Linked Open Data for Interpreting Statistics

Heiko Paulheim
Technische Universität Darmstadt
Hochschulstrasse 10, 64283 Darmstadt
paulheim@ke.tu-darmstadt.de

ABSTRACT
While statistics are omnipresent, e.g., depicting the corruption in different countries, it is often not trivial to find the explanation for a statistical effect, e.g., *why* the corruption is higher in some countries than in others. The necessary facts that can explain a statistic are often not contained in the statistics file itself. This demo shows *Explain-a-LOD*, a tool for generating possible explanations for statistics from Linked Open Data. The tool accepts statistical data as input, and it automatically retrieves data from the Linked Open Data cloud and generates possible explanations.

ACM Classification Keywords
H.2.8 Database Management: Database Applications—*Data Mining, Statistical Databases*; I.2.1 Artificial Intelligence: Applications and Expert Systems

General Terms
Algorithms, Design

Author Keywords
Linked Open Data, Statistics, Semantic Web, Data Analysis

INTRODUCTION
Statistical data is very wide-spread in the media. In many cases, those statistics only contain a few attributes, e.g., a country's name and its corruption index. When asking for an explanation for the phenomenon depicted by the statistics, such as *why* is the corruption higher in country A than in country B, additional information is needed.

Explanations for such phenomena are usually found based by analyzing the correlation of the target attribute with other attributes: for example, the corruption in a country may be negatively correlated with the GDP (gross domestic product) per capita. Such correlations can be found with statistical methods. However, those methods can only be applied if the corresponding attribute (in this case: GDP per capita) is contained in the statistics, which is often not the case. Especially when there are no initial hypotheses, it is difficult to select relevant data for performing the analysis.

In this paper, we introduce *Explain-a-LOD*[1], a tool for automatically generating hypotheses for interpreting statistics. Given a statistic, which may consist only of two columns, such as a country and an indicator of interest, it automatically retrieves information about that country from Linked Open Data (LOD) [1], a large collection of semantically annotated data sets, and creates hypotheses based on that information.

PROTOTYPE
Figure 1 depicts a high-level view of Explain-a-LOD. The statistical data to examine, usually a tabular CSV (comma separated values) file, is loaded into the feature generation toolkit *FeGeLOD* [2]. That toolkit performs three steps:

1. Recognizing corresponding entities in the LOD cloud. For example, an entry about Germany would be tagged with `http://dbpedia.org/resource/Germany`, which serves as an entry point to the LOD cloud for retrieving further information about Germany.

2. Generating attributes (or *features*, as they are commonly called in data mining) for the corresponding entities. FeGeLOD has six different generation strategies that may be combined for creating features: using type information, data properties, and qualified as well as unqualified incoming and outgoing relations.

3. For being able to process the data further in reasonable time, a simple pre-selection of features is performed to reduce the complexity of the data set.

The result of running FeGeLOD on the data set is an enriched data set which contains more attributes. That data set is then processed in two different ways. A simple correlation analysis is performed to find simple correlations of the generated features and the target value under examination. Rule learning is used for discovering more complex explanation patterns that involve more than one feature.

Both the correlated attributes and the discovered rules are presented to the user in the user interface of Explain-a-LOD in a verbalized way. In order to allow the user to quickly grasp the significance of an explanation (the absolute correlation or the rule learner's confidence in a rule, respectively), the

[1] `http://www.ke.tu-darmstadt.de/resources/explain-a-lod`

IUI'12, February 14–17, 2012, Lisbon, Portugal.
ACM 978-1-4503-1048-2/12/02.

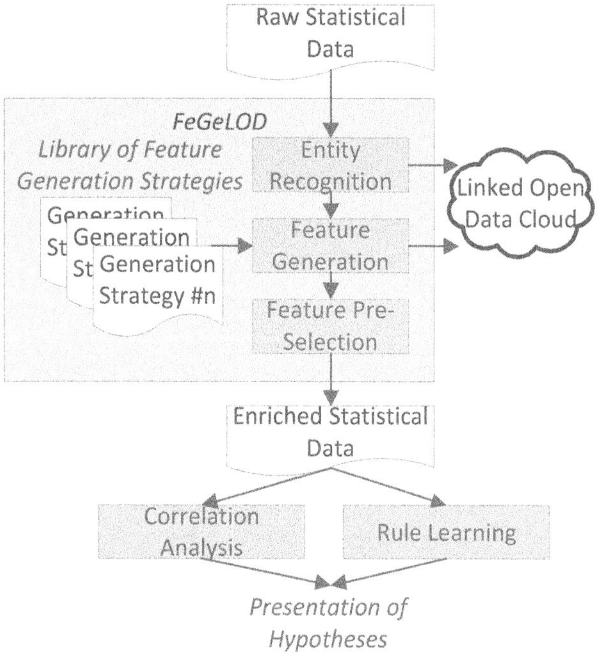

Figure 1. Architecture of Explain-a-LOD. The tool enriches a raw statistics file, using different generators extracting information from Linked Open Data. Correlation analysis and rule learning are employed on the enriched statistics file for creating possible explanations for the statistics.

hypotheses are color coded, using green for high-confidence hypotheses, going over to red for low-confidence hypotheses, as shown Figure 2.

EXPERIMENTS

We have tested our approach on different datasets, such as the 1999 Mercer quality of living survey[2] and the 2010 Corruption Perceptions Index by Transparency International[3]. The first observation is the that the hypotheses that are ranked highest are always useful concepts. Examples for such hypotheses include: *Member states of the EU (European Union) have a low corruption index*, or *Capitals of Africa have a low perceived quality of living*. It is important to notice that the information that a country is an EU member state or that a city is a capital of Africa is not included in the input dataset, but extracted from Linked Open Data.

Some observations from our first set of experiments hint to a set of current limitations of our approach. First, the data quality in LOD is not always good, and information may be inequally distributed. For example, in the hypotheses stating *Cities which are the headquarter of many companies have a high quality of living*, the condition should be more carefully read as *Cities for which the information is stored that they are the headquarter of many companies that have an entry in the LOD cloud*. Furthermore, many data sets in LOD have regional (mostly US-centric) bias, which may be propagated into the generated hypotheses.

[2]http://across.co.nz/qualityofliving.htm
[3]http://www.transparency.org/policy_research/surveys_indices/cpi/2010/results

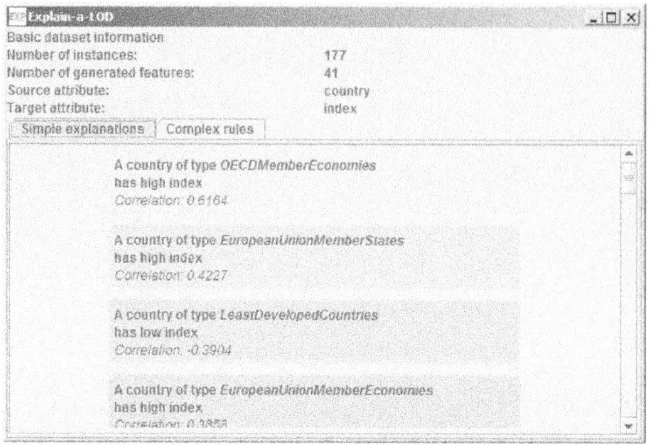

Figure 2. Screenshot of the Explain-a-LOD tool, showing possible explanations for a statistics coded with different colors.

Second, the quality of labels in Linked Open Data sometimes makes it hard to verbalize the hypotheses. Although Linked Open Data follows the structure of subject, predicate, and object, the labels for predicates are often not proper verbs.

Third, the approach can only present correlations to the user, but it is not capable of telling about the causality. In the example shown above, it is not known whether the low corruption of a country was a prerequisite for becoming an EU member state, if its low corruption is a consequence of the country being an EU member state, or if both have a common cause.

CONCLUSION AND FUTURE WORK

With this demo, we have introduced a first prototype of *Explain-a-LOD*, a tool for finding possible explanations for statistical phenomena. For a given statistics, we extract additional information from LOD, and we use statistical as well as rule learning methods for producing hypotheses.

We plan to improve both the generation of hypotheses as well as the presentation of those hypotheses. On the generation side, we aim at using more sophisticated algorithms within the feature generation component *FeGeLOD*, such as the use of different rule learning algorithms for creating interesting hypotheses, as well as the exploitation of more data sets in Linked Open Data. On the presentation side, we aim at visual clustering of hypotheses, allowing for interactive refinements of explanations, as well as more intuitive, non-textual presentation of rules.

ACKNOWLEDGEMENTS

The work presented in this paper was supported by the German Science Foundation (DFG) project FU 580/2 "Towards a Synthesis of Local and Global Pattern Induction (GLocSyn)".

REFERENCES

1. C. Bizer, T. Heath, and T. Berners-Lee. Linked Data - The Story So Far. *International Journal on Semantic Web and Information Systems*, 5(3):1–22, 2009.

2. H. Paulheim and J. Fürnkranz. Unsupervised Feature Generation from Linked Open Data. Technical Report TUD-KE-2011-2, Technische Universität Darmstadt, 2011.

Smart Interface for Reshaping Photos in 3D

Rui Nóbrega
CITI, Departamento de Informática,
Faculdade de Ciências e Tecnologia, FCT,
Universidade Nova de Lisboa
2829-516 Caparica Portugal
rui.nobrega@di.fct.unl.pt

Nuno Correia
CITI, Departamento de Informática,
Faculdade de Ciências e Tecnologia, FCT,
Universidade Nova de Lisboa
2829-516 Caparica Portugal
rui.nobrega@di.fct.unl.pt

ABSTRACT
In this work we present an interactive prototype for an interface that supports the interaction with virtual objects integrated in a real life scenario. The user can reshape or re-design a real space with virtual objects using several pictures of the desired space. The images are analyzed for known features such as surfaces, edges, floor location and room orientation. Using these elements, it is possible to devise an augmented reality system where the user can add virtual objects to the scenario. The smart interface attaches the objects to the scene elements (e.g., floor) automatically. The current demo loads images from user files or takes a snapshot directly from the camera. The high-level features are automatically detected, but can be manually adjusted. A use-case example of an augmented reality application is presented.

Author Keywords
Image Recognition, HCI, Computer Vision, Augmented Reality.

ACM Classification Keywords
H.5.1 Multimedia Information Systems - Artificial, augmented, and virtual realities.

General Terms
Design, Experimentation, Algorithms.

INTRODUCTION
The goal of this work is to develop a design tool that uses real photos as background and lets the user experiment with virtual objects as if they were in the scene [4,5]. The main motivation is to enable the creation of augmented reality applications [8] that interact with real life elements using only camera images. This excludes the use of marks or extra hardware such as depth-sensing cameras.

To implement the concept, the application has to recover the spatial layout [1] of the photographed scene in order to be able to merge the two realities. To interact with the scene several features are extracted from the single photo [6] such as: vanishing points [3], surfaces (floor and walls) [2,7] and room orientation [3].

The interface goal is to simplify the introduction of 3D models in the scene. The user simply lays the objects and pushes them around back and forth or left and right on the floor, avoiding the extra burden of having to worry about the third dimension.

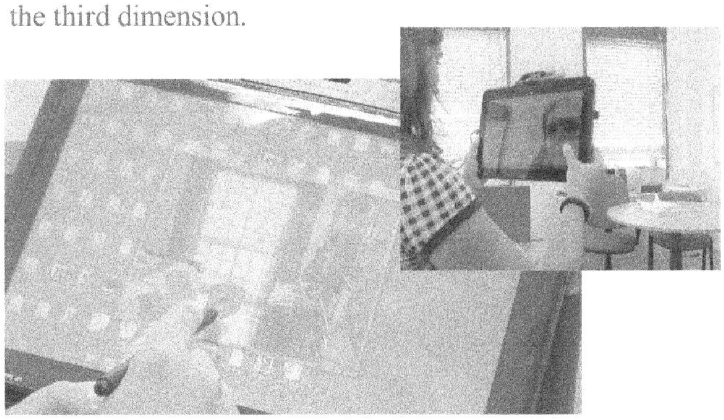

Figure 1. The user takes a photo of a space using a device such as a tablet with a camera. Using the photo she can add virtual augmented objects that react to elements of that image, such as floor or room orientation.

Figure 2. Image analysis to detect vanishing points, room orientation and floor.

CURRENT PROTOTYPE
In the current prototype the user holds a tablet in the room and takes a picture of the desired space (as seen in Figure 1). The system automatically informs the user if the image has enough scene elements for an optimal detection. The image is then preprocessed to search for the scene elements [4]. The system does a series of line and edge detection algorithms with different thresholds (Figure 2). A value of a likelihood function is given to each parameter configuration. Using a weighted voting system the most

probable vanishing points and floor orientation matrix are extracted. The interface uses the calculated features to present the user with guidelines to properly insert the augmented objects in the photographed scene (Figures 3 and 4).

Figure 3. Prototype screenshot presenting the snapping system. When the user drags the object down, the floor attracts it, showing yellow guidelines. When the object is rotated it snaps every 90 degrees when its orientation is aligned with the scenario, showing the green guidelines.

SYSTEM IMPLEMENTATION

The current demo is implemented using openFrameworks (http://www.openframeworks.cc/) as a graphics framework and OpenCV (http://opencv.willowgarage.com/) for computer vision algorithm support. The main algorithm in this system is the automatic detection of the vanishing points, as seen in Figure 2. This algorithm relies on the detection of lines using Canny filters, Erode and Dilate operations and Hough-Transform line detectors. The voting system uses Random Sample Consensus (RANSAC) to compare all lines in pairs, to discover intersections. These intersection points are grouped in clusters through a local nearest neighbor implementation algorithm. The most important clusters are analyzed to verify if they are suitable vanishing points. Using the detected vanishing points it is possible to rotate the camera in order to align it with the horizon of the camera. These high-level features can be used in augmented reality applications such as the ones in Figure 3 and 4, to superimpose objects that have the appearance of being part of the scene.

Regarding future work, new high-level features are being explored, and applications and games are being devised to take advantage of the techniques described here.

ACKNOWLEDGMENTS

This work was funded by FCT/MCTES, through grant SFRH/BD/47511/2008 and partly funded by Centro de Investigação em Informática e Tecnologias da Informação (CITI/FCT/UNL)through grant PEst-OE/EEI/UI0527/2011.

Figure 4. Augmented objects positioned on the detected 3D model of the room.

REFERENCES

1. Hedau, V., Hoiem, D., Forsyth, D.A. Recovering the spatial layout of cluttered rooms. In *Proc. ICCV 2009*, IEEE Computer Society, (2009), 1849 - 1856.
2. Klein, G. and Murray, D. Parallel Tracking and Mapping for Small AR Workspaces. In *Proc. Symposium on Mixed and Augmented Reality 2007*. IEEE Computer Society, (2007), 1-10.
3. Lee, D.C., Hebert, M., and Kanade, T. Geometric reasoning for single image structure recovery, In *Proc. CVPR 2009*. IEEE Computer Society, (2009), 2136-2143.
4. Nóbrega, N. and Correia, N. Design your room: adding virtual objects to a real indoor scenario. In *Ext. Abstracts CHI 2011*, ACM Press, (2011), 2143-2148.
5. Nóbrega, N. Modeling places for interactive media and entertainment applications. In *Ext. Abstracts CHI 2011*, ACM Press, (2011), 1081-1084.
6. Saxena, A., Min Sun, and Andrew Y. Ng. Make3D: Learning 3D Scene Structure from a Single Still Image. *IEEE Transactions on Pattern Analysis and Machine Intelligence*, IEEE Computer Society, (2009), 824-840.
7. Simon, G. Automatic online walls detection for immediate use in AR tasks. In *Proc. Symposium on Mixed and Augmented Reality 2006*. IEEE Computer Society, (2006), 39-42
8. Wagner, D., Reitmayr, G., Mulloni, A., Drummond, T., and Schmalstieg, D. Real-Time Detection and Tracking for Augmented Reality on Mobile Phones. IEEE Transactions on Visualization and Computer Graphics, IEEE Computer Society, (2010), 355-368.

RadSpeech's Mobile Dialogue System for Radiologists

Daniel Sonntag, Christian Schulz, Christian Reuschling and Luis Galarraga
German Research Center for AI - DFKI
Stuhlsatzenhausweg 3
Saarbrücken, 66123, Germany
Firstname.lastname@dfki.de

ABSTRACT
With RadSpeech, we aim to build the next generation of intelligent, scalable, and user-friendly semantic search interfaces for the medical imaging domain, based on semantic technologies. Ontology-based knowledge representation is used not only for the image contents, but also for the complex natural language understanding and dialogue management process. This demo shows a speech-based annotation system for radiology images and focuses on a new and effective way to annotate medical image regions with a specific medical, structured, diagnosis while using speech and pointing gestures on the go.

Author Keywords: Speech Dialogue, Mobility, Healthcare

ACM Classification: H.5.2 [Information Interfaces And Presentation]: User Interfaces - Interaction styles;

General terms: Management, Reliability, Human Factors

INTRODUCTION
In radiology, computed tomography (CT) or magnetic resonance imaging (MRI) images are used to both diagnose and treat diseases visualised within the human body. Clinical research partners, such as the University Hospital Erlangen in Germany, produce a lot of patient images and have a total of about 65 TB of medical images. The problem with current technology is that a clinician cannot directly create a structured report while scanning the images: in this *eyes-busy* setting, he or she can only dictate the finding to a tape-recorder. After the reading process, he or she can replay the dictation to manually fill out a patient's finding form or delegate other personnel. But since the radiologist has to check the form again, task delegation does not save time. With our technology developed over the last 5 years, we implemented the first mobile dialogue system on the iPad and iPhone, which is tuned for the radiology domain and makes the complete system unique. Our solution not only provides more robustness compared to speech-to-text systems (we use a rather small, dedicated, and context-based speech grammar which is also very robust to background noise), it also fits very well into new radiology reporting processes which will be established in Germany and the U.S. over the next several years: in *structured reporting* you directly have to create database entries instead of text.

RadSpeech (www.dfki.de/RadSpeech/) is the design and implementation of a multimodal dialogue system for structured radiology reports. With traditional user interfaces, users may browse or explore patient data, but little to no help is given when it comes to the interpretation of what is being displayed or structuring the input. In order to allow a radiologist to annotate special image regions in a database format and to search for similar cases, we developed a Desktop-based manual annotation tool called RadSem [3]. Anatomical structures and diseases can be annotated while using the auto-completion combo-boxes with a search-as-you-type functionality. The resulting annotation is accurate but very time-consuming.

In addition, RadSem did not fulfill the special requirement that clinicians have: to have access to a coherent view of image data within their particular diagnosis or treatment context in the radiology department while they are skimming many image series and thousands of pictures in a minute's time. Although it is widely reductive to put it this way, a senior radiologist has three main goals: (1) access the images and image (region) annotations, (2) complete them, and (3) refine existing annotations. We argued that these tasks can best be fulfilled while using a multimodal dialogue system, and first we experimented with a large touchscreen installation [1, 2]. Since the results with speech interaction were very promising, we tried to opt for the mobile context. Our mobile system is expected to provide the radiologist with the ability to review images when outside the laboratory, and to make diagnosis without having to be back at the workstation,
see www.youtube.com/watch?v=uBiN119_wvg.

The semantic dialogue system presented in this demo should be used to ask questions about the image annotations while engaging the clinician in a natural speech dialogue. Different semantic views of the same medical images (such as structural, functional, and disease aspects) can be explicitly stated, integrated, and asked for. This is the essential part of the knowledge acquisition process [3]. Two aspects are implemented and shown in the demo. First, the inspection of and navigation through the patient's data, and second, the annotation of radiology images by use of speech and gestures.

EXAMPLE DIALOGUE

A radiologist treats a lymphoma patient. The patient visits the doctor after chemotherapy for a follow-up CT examination. The focus of the speech-based interactions is the following sub-dialogue (for simplicity, the cancer annotation is replaced by a simple anatomy annotation).

- U: "Show me the CTs, last examination, patient XY."
- S: Shows corresponding patient CT studies as DICOM picture series and MRI images and MRI videos.
- U: "Annotate this picture with 'Heart' (+ pointing gesture) and 'Heart chamber'" (+ pointing gesture)
- S: Shows the new annotations on the image and confirms a database update.

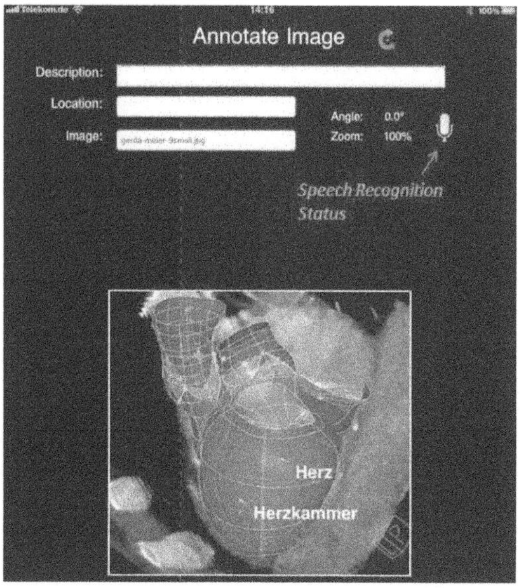

Figure 1. Screenshot of the Speech-based Image Annotation Screen

Figure 1 shows the screenshot of the annotation screen. Upon touching a region in the white square, the speech recognition system is activated. After recognition, the speech and gesture modalities are fused into a complex annotation using a combination of medical ontologies. For disease annotations for example, the complete Radlex (http://www.radlex.org/) terminology can be used. More complex interactions can be seen in the demo video at http://www.youtube.com/watch?v=uBiN119_wvg, where a set of multi-touch gestures to control the image selection and manipulation phase without the usage of distracting screen buttons is shown as well.

SYSTEM ARCHITECTURE

We implemented a middleware that invokes the MEDICO backend server directly. This middleware is implemented by means of the Ontology-based Dialogue Platform (ODP): the central *Event Bus* is responsible for routing message between the *Dialogue System* and other connected components. Such components include a speech recogniser (*ASR*) and a speech synthesis (*TTS*) module. On the client, e.g., an iPad, only a slim application is needed to encode the speech and gesture input and receive the speech synthesis to be played (Figure 2, details are explained in [2]). New clients can be added easily by, e.g., downloading an iPad app.

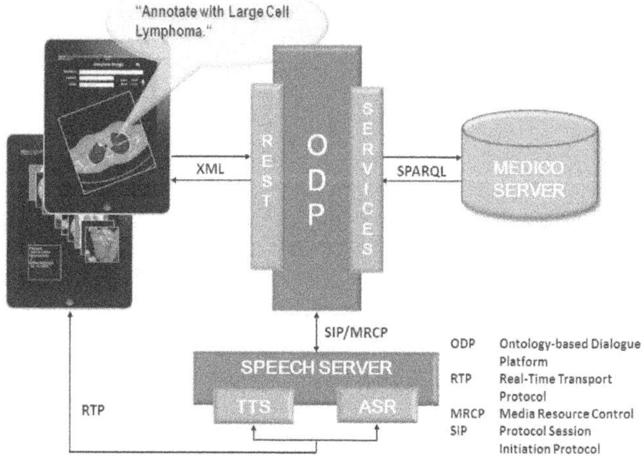

Figure 2. Technical Architecture of RadSpeech

CONCLUSION

Today, medical images have become indispensable for detecting and differentiating pathologies, planning interventions, and monitoring treatments. We have presented a mobile semantic speech dialogue system for the radiologist. Our new prototypical dialogue system provides the radiologist with the ability to review images when outside the laboratory, to annotate important image regions while using speech and gestures, and to make a *structured* diagnosis without having to be back at the workstation. Our experts predict that mobile dialogue technology will dominate mobile healthcare in just a few short years. The speech-based dialogue system RadSpeech is currently a part of a larger clinical study about the acquisition of medical image semantics at Siemens Healthcare, the University Hospital in Erlangen, and the Imaging Science Institute (ISI).

ACKNOWLEDGEMENTS This research has been supported by the research programme THESEUS, which is funded by the German Federal Ministry of Economics and Technology under the grant number 01MQ07016.

REFERENCES

1. Cohen, P.R., Oviatt, S. The role of voice input for human-machine communication. Proc. Natl. Sci. USA (1995)
2. Sonntag D., Reithinger N., Herzog G. and Becker T. A Discourse and Dialogue Infrastructure for Industrial Dissemination. Proceedings of IWSDS, Lee et al. (Eds.): LNAI 6392, Springer (2010)
3. Sonntag, D. Intelligent Interaction and Incremental Knowledge Acquisition for Radiology Images. Proceedings of SAMT, Springer (2010)

Airwriting: Demonstrating Mobile Text Input by 3d-Space Handwriting Recognition

Christoph Amma
Karlsruhe Institute of Technology
76131 Karlsruhe, Germany
christoph.amma@kit.edu

Tanja Schultz
Karlsruhe Institute of Technology
76131 Karlsruhe, Germany
tanja.schultz@kit.edu

ABSTRACT
We demonstrate our airwriting interface for mobile hands-free text entry. The interface enables a user to input text into a computer by writing in the air like on an imaginary blackboard. Hand motion is measured by an accelerometer and a gyroscope attached to the back of the hand and data is sent wirelessly to the processing computer. The system can continuously recognize arbitrary sentences based on a predefined vocabulary in real-time. The recognizer uses Hidden Markov Models (HMM) together with a statistical language model. We achieve a user-independent word error rate of 11% for a 8K vocabulary based on an experiment with nine users.

Author Keywords
Gesture recognition, handwriting recognition, human computer interaction, wearable computing, accelerometers

ACM Classification Keywords
H.5.2. Information Interfaces and Presentation: User Interfaces; I.5.4 Pattern Recognition: Applications

General Terms
Performance, Algorithms, Experimentation

INTRODUCTION
Gestures have the potential to facilitate hands-free mobile interaction. Instead of forcing a user to manually operate a device, hand gestures allow operation with empty hands and without the need to focus on tiny screens and keys. Current systems focus on the use of a small set of emblematic gestures which can be mapped on commands. We introduce a demonstration system which can compensate the limited expressive power of such small sets of gestures by enabling complex textual input through handwriting gestures.

The paper describes a wearable gesture recognition system based on inertial sensors that is capable of continuously recognizing whole sentences written in the air, i.e. no pauses are necessary, users can write in one single continuous movement. We build upon the work in [2], where we introduced a character recognition and a preliminary word recognition system. We evaluate the system on a data corpus recorded from nine subjects and achieve high accuracies for the person-independent case.

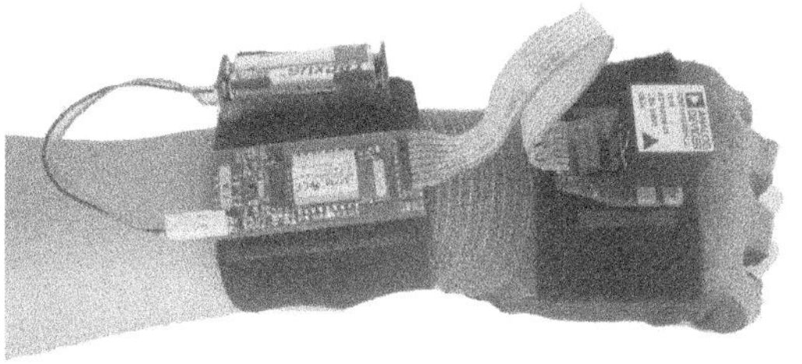

Figure 1. Prototypical wireless data glove for signal acquisition.

Abandoning the need to hold an extra device in ones hand raises the problem how to present visual output to the user. The Sixth Sense project [5] proposes a small projector worn like a necklace to project the screen on arbitrary surfaces in front of the user. Baudisch et al. propose to drop the screen at all and use a mental representation of an imaginary interface screen on which the user spatially interacts [3]. We follow the same idea and our experiments and demonstration system show that users do not rely on visual feedback to perform machine recognizable handwriting motion. Systems to recognize 3d-space handwriting with inertial sensors integrated in a pen-like controller or a mobile phone have been proposed but rely on artificial pauses between strokes [1] or are limited to single characters or short words [4].

SYSTEM OVERVIEW
Figure 2 shows an overview of the systems components. Hand-motion is measured with a self-developed prototypical data glove, equipped with an inertial measurement unit attached to the back of the hand shown in figure 1. The sensor contains a 3-dimensional accelerometer and a 3-dimensional gyroscope to measure acceleration and angular rate. Data is transmitted wirelessly to a laptop via Bluetooth where all further processing takes place.

As the next step data is segmented into parts which contain handwriting motion and parts that don't. First, this avoids the need to constantly perform computationally costly HMM decoding for implicit segmentation during operation. Second, due to the large variance of human everyday motion, it will be hard to build appropriate models for the null-class. Segmentation is realized as a binary classificator, which classifies each window as writing motion or non-writing motion. Whenever

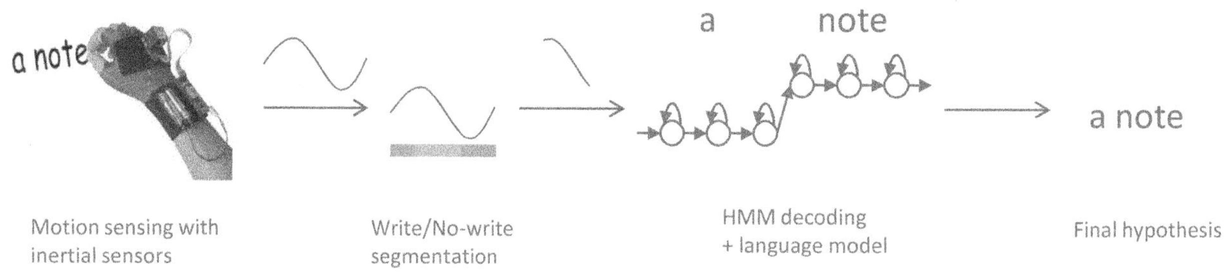

Figure 2. Overview of the complete system. The steps show the data flow through the stages of the system. After acquisition, the segmentation stage cuts the signal in parts that likely contain handwriting motion. These signals are then decoded by HMMs in combination with a language model to produce the final hypothesis.

the segmenter classifies the incoming signals as handwriting motion, the original signals of the segment are passed to the recognition stage.

We use continuous density HMMs for the recognition of the handwriting motion. As features we use the normalized and smoothed sensor signals. Normalization involves mean and variance normalization. This compensates the effect of gravitational force and differences in speed of the individual users. We use one HMM for every character and concatenated character HMMs to model whole words. The search space for sentences is specified by a predefined vocabulary. The architecture allows the use of arbitrary vocabularies. In addition we use a 3-gram language model to increase performance by incorporating statistical information on word sequence frequencies.

The decoder constantly produces hypothesis considering all signals seen so far. The current hypothesis is shown on the screen of the laptop in regular intervals of time. A user can therefore control the correctness of the hypothesis during operation. When the segmentation stage signalizes the end of the handwriting motion segment, the final hypothesis is printed. The system is running in an always on mode, whenever handwriting motion is detected the recognizer starts decoding the signals in real-time.

EXPERIMENTS

To evaluate the performance of our system and to collect training data for the HMMs we conducted experiments with nine subjects, each of them writing 80 defined sentences in the air in front of them. Every subject contributed 366 words to the data set. We asked the users to write in block capital letters and with fixed wrist at arbitrary speed. We further asked them to repeat sentences if they noticed they made an error. The systems performance is measured by the word error rate. The reference sentence is aligned with the hypothesis by computing the minimal edit distance on word level. This gives the number of word insertions (I), deletions (D) and substitutions (S). The word error rate is then computed by $WER = 100 \cdot \frac{S+I+D}{N}$ where N is the total number of words in the reference. The experiments took approximately 30min for each participant, including pauses. After several sentences the participants usually had to make a short pause due to fatigue of the writing arm. For input of longer texts, airwriting input doesn't seem to be suitable.

In all experiments the same 3-gram language model was used. The model contains 60K unigrams and 7M bi- and 8M trigrams with an OOV of zero. It was originally created for a speech recognition system and no optimization towards our test set was performed. We use a vocabulary of 8k words for the experiments. A per person cross-validation was performed to assess the user independent recognition performance. We reach a WER of 11% averaged over the nine participants.

For two subjects, the performance was much lower than the average. This is probably due the differences in the individual writing style. Our character level experiments in [2] showed that even for the case of block capital letters, people do write characters very differently. We observed five different variants of writing an "E" in [2], mainly distinguished in the order and direction of strokes. If one writer has a very different writing style compared to the majority we would expect the system to have a much lower performance. On the other hand, for some users very high accuracies are reached on our dataset.

CONCLUSION

We demonstrate a wearable hands-free text input system, which recognizes 3d-space handwriting. Motion is measured with inertial sensors. We achieve a user-independent word-error-rate of 11% for an 8K vocabulary, i.e. arbitrary users can expect a good system performance with few errors. The recognition engine works in real-time, feedback to the user can be shown immediately.

REFERENCES

1. Agrawal, S., Constandache, I., Gaonkar, S., Roy Choudhury, R., Caves, K., and DeRuyter, F. Using mobile phones to write in air. In *Proc. of MobySys '11*, ACM (2011), 15–28.
2. Amma, C., Gehrig, D., and Schultz, T. Airwriting recognition using wearable motion sensors. In *Proc. Augmented Human Conf.*, ACM Press (2010).
3. Gustafson, S., Bierwirth, D., and Baudisch, P. Imaginary interfaces: spatial interaction with empty hands and without visual feedback. In *Proc. of UIST '10*, ACM (2010), 3–12.
4. Kim, D., Choi, H., and Kim, J. 3d space handwriting recognition with ligature model. In *Ubiquitous Computing Systems*, vol. 4239/2006 of *LNCS*, Springer Berlin / Heidelberg (2006), 41–56.
5. Mistry, P., and Maes, P. Sixthsense: a wearable gestural interface. In *ACM SIGGRAPH ASIA Sketches*, ACM (2009), 11.

Wheeling around with Wanteat: Exploring Mixed Social Networks in the Gastronomy Domain

Fabrizio Antonelli (2), Giulia Biamino (1), Francesca Carmagnola (1), Federica Cena (1), Elisa Chiabrando (1), Luca Console (1), Vincenzo Cuciti (2), Matteo Demichelis (2), Franco Fassio (3), Fabrizio Franceschi (2), Roberto Furnari (1), Cristina Gena (1), Marina Geymonat (2), Piercarlo Grimaldi (3), Pierluigi Grillo (1), Elena Guercio (2), Silvia Likavec (1), Ilaria Lombardi (1), Dario Mana (2), Alessandro Marcengo (2), Michele Mioli (1), Mario Mirabelli (2), Monica Perrero(1,2), Claudia Picardi (1), Federica Protti (1,2), Amon Rapp (2), Roberta Sandon (3), Rossana Simeoni (2), Daniele Theseider Dupré (1), Ilaria Torre (1), Andrea Toso (1), Fabio Torta (3), Fabiana Vernero (1)
University of Turin (1), Telecom Italia (2), University of Gastronomic Sciences (3)
C.so Svizzera 185, Torino (1) - Via Reiss Romoli 274, Torino (2) - Piazza Vittorio Emanuele 9, Bra (3)
vernerof@di.unito.it (corresponding author: F. Vernero)

ABSTRACT
Wanteat is a framework and a suite of applications which allow users to interact with and explore mixed social networks of smart objects and people in the gastronomy domain, thus promoting the cultural heritage of a territory. Wanteat interaction model is based on the concept of a "wheel" [1].

Author Keywords
Social Web of Things, Smart Objects, Playful Interaction, Cultural Heritage, Gastronomy, Mobile Applications.

ACM Classification Keywords
H.5.m. [Information Interfaces and Presentation (e.g. HCI)]: Miscellaneous;

INTRODUCTION
Food-related issues are attracting growing interest, as demonstrated by the flourishing of systems which support users in making decisions about eating (see for example [5]). However, food is also an important part of cultural heritage: if food items such as a cheese or an apple could interact with people, they could tell them about the territory they come from, the people who produced them, the recipes which use them as ingredients, other products with similar organoleptic qualities, and so on. Moreover, they could listen to the experiences of the people interacting with them, and learn new knowledge from their comments and actions: for example, a cheese could discover that many people tasted it together with a certain type of wine, and that the two make an excellent matching. Wanteat [4] is a framework and a suite of applications which apply these ideas, based on the following concepts:

- *Smart objects.* They can a) create and manage links with one another and with the users they interacted with, maintaining a "Social Web" of things and people [3]; b) share knowledge about themselves and the world around them; c) personalize their interaction with users.
- *Here and now interaction.*
- *No infrastructuring.* Image recognition technologies are used to identify food items based on their product labels.
- *Playful and entertaining interaction.*
- *Relationship centrality.* WantEat interaction model bases on the possibility to discover related objects whenever a certain object is chosen as a focus of interest. Relationships can be inferred from an ontology representing the domain knowledge, or derived from the behavior and social actions of users.

WANTEAT SUITE OF APPLICATIONS
WanEat consists in a suite of applications. WantEat Mobile is a smartphone application for final users such as tourists or foodies [1] and it is especially suited for here and now interaction with things which are physically present. WantEat Web supports a continuum of experience with WantEat Mobile when users are at home. WantEat Video is an application for knee-top devices which allows users to watch videos related to things in the gastronomy domain [2]. WantEat Backshop is a Web application for stakeholders such as producers that allows them to register themselves and their products as things in the system.

An example flow of interaction
Let us imagine Mr Lami, a cold cuts producer, registers for WantEat using WantEat Backshop, indicating that he produces "Salampatata", a pork and potato salami. Tourists who

meet Mr Lami's "Salampatata" (for example, at a local farmers market) interact with it using WantEat mobile: they make it tell stories about the territory it comes from, about well-matching wines, about recipes which use it as an ingredient and about Mr Lami himself. They also comment on the product and its stories, tag, rate or bookmark them. As a result of users' social actions, new relationships can be established among Mr Lami's "Salampatata" and other things in WantEat system: for example, "Salampatata" can be related to a new restaurant, if several users said they tasted it there. Accessing WantEat Backshop again, Mr Lami can examine what users said about "Salampatata" and discover its new relationships.

INTERACTION MODEL

The interaction model we developed for WantEat supports experience rather than goal-driven interaction, drawing inspiration from the concept of a "wheel" [1] (see Figure 1). From a conceptual point of view, an object which has been identified represents the center of the world users are going to explore: in our wheel model, the object in the center represents the current focus, while objects arranged along the wheel circumference clearly appear to be related to it. Moreover, the wheel radiuses can embody the relations among objects. A simple form of spatial categorization is also provided by partitioning the area surrounding the center in four sectors corresponding to four broad macro-categories (for example, "Territory", "Products"). Items in the four sectors can be explored by making them rotate, as in an old style telephone dialing selector. When users change the wheel focus by dragging an object from a sector to the wheel center, the whole wheel is recomputed and displayed to the user.

NOTES ON ARCHITECTURAL DESIGN

WantEat has been designed as a partially distributed system. The *server side* is constituted by a number of agents. The ontology manager is in charge of maintaining an ontological representation of the application domain, defining all the concepts in the domain and the relations among them. This includes a taxonomy of gastronomic products, linking them to actors (e.g. producers) and to places in a geographic ontology. Inferences on the ontology allow the system to associate inferred properties to objects and to create links between objects. Other important agents are the social network manager and the personalization and recommendation module, which maintains an explicit user model and tailors content ranking to user interests.
The *client side* is available on mobile smartphones, on knee-top devices and on the Web. It is in charge of managing the interaction between people, objects and networks.

EVALUATION WITH USERS

Having adopted a user-centered approach, we performed a series of evaluations starting at an early stage of the project: at the requirement phase we carried out an early evaluation aimed at stakeholders; at the preliminary evaluation phase, we carried out a small-scale user evaluation of the first interface design with the wheel metaphor. At the final evaluation phase, we carried out an extensive quantitative user evaluation on the first complete prototype of WantEat Mobile

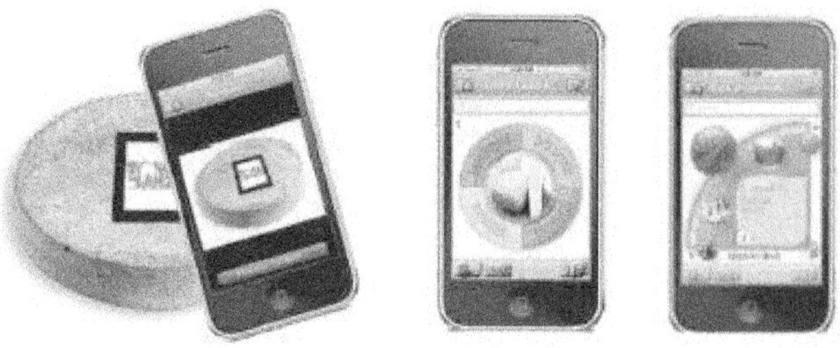

Figure 1. WantEat Mobile: the wheel model

application, which was introduced to, and tested by 684 subjects at Salone Internazionale del Gusto 2010 (October 2010), a huge event dedicated to the exposition and tasting of high quality food, which is organized by Slowfood in Torino. Results showed a very high level of acceptance with respect to every tested dimension: ease of use (average evaluation of 3,42 on a Likert-like scale ranging 1-4), comprehensibility (3,46), pleasantness (3,43) and usefulness (3,12). In September 2011, during the international food fair Cheese 2011, we made a user field test, installing WantEat Mobile on the iPhones of 157 users, to monitor the patterns of usage of the application. We are currently analyzing the gathered data.

CONCLUSION

In this paper we presented WantEat, a framework and a suite of applications which allow users to interact with and explore mixed social networks of smart objects and people in the gastronomy domain. We are planning to extend WanEat to let all users register new products in the system.

ACKNOWLEDGMENTS

The project has been partially supported by Regione Piemonte, grant ICT Converging Technologies 2007. We thank Adriano Design (`www.adrianodesign.it`) for their support in the graphic design.

REFERENCES

1. Biamino, G., Grillo, P., Lombardi, I., Marcengo, A., Rapp, A., Simeoni, R., and Vernero, F. "The Wheel": an innovative visual model for interacting with a social web of things. In *Proceedings of Workshop on Visual Interfaces to the Social and Semantic Web, held in conjunction with IUI 2011 (VISSW 2011)*, ACM Press (2011), 1–5.
2. Chiabrando, E., Franceschi, F., Furnari, R., and Vernero, F. Questing for videos: a user-centric model for exploring the gastronomy domain. In *Proceedings of Networked & Electronic Media Summit 2011*, Eurescom GmbH (2011), 100–105.
3. Console, L., Lombardi, I., Picardi, C., and Simeoni, R. Toward a Social Web of Intelligent Things. *AI Communications 24*, 3 (2011), 265–279.
4. PIEMONTE Team. Wanteat: interacting with "social" networks of intelligent things and people in the world of enogastronomy. In *Proceedings of Workshop on Interacting with smart objects, held in conjunction with IUI 2011*, ACM Press (2011), 1–6.
5. van Pinxteren, Y., Geleijnse, G., and Kamsteeg, P. Deriving a recipe similarity measure for recommending healthful meals. In *Proceedings of the 16th international conference on Intelligent user interfaces*, IUI '11, ACM (New York, NY, USA, 2011), 105–114.

KMulE: A Framework for User-Based Comparison of Recommender Algorithms

Alan Said, Ernesto W. De Luca, Benjamin Kille, Brijnesh J. Jain, Immo Micus, Sahin Albayrak
DAI Lab
Technische Universität Berlin
{alan, deluca, kille, jain, immo, sahin}@dai-lab.de

ABSTRACT

Collaborative Filtering Recommender Systems come in a wide variety of variants. In this paper we present a system for visualizing and comparing recommendations provided by different collaborative recommendation algorithms. The system utilizes a set of context-aware, hybrid, and other collaborative filtering solutions in order to generate various recommendations from which its users can pick those corresponding best to their current situation (i.e. context). All user interaction is fed back to the system in order to additionally improve the quality of the recommendations. Additionally, users can explicitly ask the system to treat certain recommenders as more important than others, or disregard them completely if the list of recommended movies is not to their liking.

ACM Classification Keywords

H.3.3 Information Search and Retrieval: Retrieval models; H.3.5 Online Information Services: Web-based services

General Terms

Algorithms, Design, Experimentation, Human Factors, Performance

Author Keywords

Recommender systems, human factors, evaluation, analysis, personalization, user-centric evaluation, context-awareness, movie recommendation

INTRODUCTION

Recommender Systems (RS) have been a central part of the World Wide Web for as long as it has existed, online RSs actually pre-date the Web itself [2]. One of the most popular recommendation techniques, Collaborative Filtering (CF), analyses users' historical data in order to find items which could be of interest now.

In this paper, we present a system which utilizes several CF techniques to find movie recommendations for users, and presents them on a per-algorithm basis allowing the user to give feedback on which recommender is preferred at a certain point in time (i.e. in a certain situation). The demonstration shows a movie RS built to evaluate different types of recommendation algorithms providing users with descriptions of why they are being recommended certain movies, allowing the user to implicitly change the context [1] by selecting a different recommender.

IUI'12, February 14–17, 2012, Lisbon, Portugal.
ACM 978-1-4503-1048-2/12/02.

CONTEXT-BASED MULTIMEDIA RECOMMENDER

The Context-based Multimedia Recommender System (KMulE) consists of several recommender algorithms developed within the project providing recommendations for a movie recommendation demo website. Users can either register and create persistent profiles for multiple use which allows storing their movie ratings for personalized recommendations, or create profiles offhand by rating a smaller set of movies for instant, personalized recommendations. In addition to their ratings, the systems also keeps track of users' ages, genders, locations (where they live), etc. If users have persistent profiles, additionally data on which recommender algorithms were used at which point in time and what type of recommendation was rated is stored in order to help model the users' contexts.

The system performs recommendations using several types of algorithms including variants of context-aware and hybrid ones, additionally a standard CF baseline recommender is used for comparison. The majority of the implemented algorithms have been described in closer detail in related publications, the context-aware approaches, e.g. interaction-based, event-based, user-based in [4, 5, 8] and combinations of hybrid recommenders, e.g. popularity-based, tag-based in [6, 7]. Additional similar approaches have been presented in [3]. We refer to these publications for detailed information on how the recommender algorithms and approaches work and perform.

RECOMMENDER UI

The user interface used in the KMulE system is a website which presents its users with several options on how to obtain recommendations for interesting movies. First, a user either has to create a persistent user profile, or create a one offhand in order to test the system before registering. However, persistent profiles contain more information, and thus allow for more personalized and accurate recommendations.

Both the offhand user creation page as well as the persistent user creation page asks the users to provide some basic data about themselves (age, gender, location, etc). After filling this out (offhand users), or logging in (persistent users), users

Figure 1. The list of recommendations shown to users. Each column corresponds to one recommender algorithm. Users can choose to rate the movies or the list of recommendations itself.

are met by a page containing movie recommendations. For offhand users, this list contains the most popular movies for different contexts and user profiles (e.g. popular movies in the user's age group). Additionally, there is a search function which the users can use for rating specific movies not presented by the recommenders.

Having rated a set of movies, the recommenders begin to provide personalized recommendations, shown in Figure 1. Each column corresponds to one of the recommenders implemented in the system. Being presented with a set of recommended lists of movies, users can choose to give feedback on the list of recommended movies (as shown in Figure 2) or click a link to show more lists of recommendations by other recommendation algorithms. Users can choose to either not show or increase the importance of recommendations from a certain recommender. In doing so, the system can obtain more knowledge on whether users perceive certain recommenders to be positive or not. Additionally, by rating movies in any of the columns, the system collects information on whether a certain recommender generated a successful recommendation (a rating was performed), or not (no rating performed).

The system which has been presented in this paper allows for a user-based evaluation of specific recommendation algorithms. The feedback obtained from the user can be used directly by the system to provide better recommendations, and give relevant insights into what items and contexts are important at which points in time.

ACKNOWLEDGMENTS

The work in this paper was conducted in the scope of the KMulE project which was sponsored by the German Federal Ministry of Economics and Technology (BMWi). The authors would like to express their gratitude to the Moviepilot team for their relevant insights and support.

Figure 2. The explanation to why a certain list of recommendations is shown to a user.

REFERENCES

1. Dey, A. K. Understanding and using context. *Personal Ubiquitous Computing 5* (01/2001).
2. Needham, C. IMDb history. `http://www.imdb.com/help/show_leaf?history` - 12/2009.
3. Said, A., Berkovsky, S., De Luca, E. W., and Hermanns, J. Challenge on context-aware movie recommendation: CAMRa2011. In *Proc. of the 5th ACM Conf. on Recommender systems*, RecSys '11, ACM (2011).
4. Said, A., De Luca, E. W., and Albayrak, S. Inferring contextual user profiles - improving recommender performance. In *Proc. of the 3rd Workshop on Context-Aware Recommender Systems*, CARS '11 (2011).
5. Said, A., De Luca, E. W., and Albayrak, S. Using social and pseudo social networks to improve recommendation. In *Proc. of the 9th Workshop on Intelligent Techniques for Web Personalization and Recommender Systems (ITWP'11)* (2011).
6. Said, A., Jain, B., and Albayrak, S. Analyzing weighting schemes in collaborative filtering: Cold start, post cold start and power users. In *Proc. of the 2012 ACM symposium on Applied computing*, SAC '12, ACM (2012).
7. Said, A., Kille, B., De Luca, E. W., and Albayrak, S. Personalizing tags: a folksonomy-like approach for recommending movies. In *Proc. of the 2nd Intl. Workshop on Information Heterogeneity and Fusion in Recommender Systems*, HetRec '11, ACM (2011).
8. Said, A., Plumbaum, T., De Luca, E. W., and Albayrak, S. A comparison of how demographic data affects recommendation. In *Adjoint Proc. of the 19th international conference on User modeling, adaption, and personalization* (2011).

A prototype for Interactive Speech Transcription Balancing Error and Supervision Effort

Isaias Sanchez-Cortina, Nicolás Serrano, Alberto Sanchis, Alfons Juan
DSIC/ITI, Universitat Politècnica de València
Camí de Vera, s/n, 46022 València, Spain
{isanchez,nserrano,josanna,ajuan}@dsic.upv.es

ABSTRACT
A system to transcribe speech data is presented following an interactive paradigm in which both, the system produces automatically speech transcriptions and the user is assisted by the system to amend output errors as efficiently as possible. Partially supervised transcriptions with a tolerance error fixed by the user are used to incrementally adapt the underlying system models. The prototype uses a simple yet effective method to find an optimal balance between recognition error and supervision effort.

Author Keywords
Computer-assisted speech transcription, confidence measures, speech recognition, interactive machine learning

ACM Classification Keywords
H.5.2 Information Interfaces and Presentation: User Interfaces

INTRODUCTION
Speech transcriptions produced by human transcribers can provide high quality results. However, the overall process is slow and usually expensive. An effective approach is to manually correct (i.e. supervise) the automatically recognized transcriptions. In this way, supervision should reduce the user effort in producing a qualified result. However, correcting a very faulty text might eventually require more effort than manually transcribing the whole speech.

Interactive Speech Transcription (IST) aims at benefiting from the user cooperation to amend the output of an automatic speech recognizer (ASR) system. In IST, the user is introduced in the core of a ASR system so that the system and the user interact with each other to minimize the effort in producing a satisfactory output. Different approaches have been proposed to improve interaction efficiency for the purpose of obtaining completely accurate transcripts of speech [2, 3]. Here, however, we present a prototype to IST in which the user decides the quality required for the task. The more tolerated proportion of errors, the less effort will be needed. We call this "balancing error and supervision effort".

In this supervision scenario, successfully applied to handwriting transcription [4], the main goal is to significantly reduce the supervision effort by deciding a maximum tolerance error in the speech transcriptions. Word-level confidence measures [8] computed over the recognition word-graph are used to suggest which words should be supervised. The supervision is performed while an estimation of the transcription errors is higher than the tolerance error. Moreover, supervised and high-confidence parts of the transcriptions are used to improve incrementally the underlying statistical speech recognizer models. This will likely improve the subsequent recognitions lowering the necessary number of corrections.

SYSTEM OVERVIEW
The IST prototype has been implemented on the *Transcriber tool* [1]. A transcription is fulfilled iteratively by performing the following three steps, accessible from the "ASR" menu (Fig. 1): Recognize, Semi-supervise and Re-train . First, the user activates "Recognize". Once recognized a part of the speech, the minimum acceptable quality of the final transcript is established by a maximum tolerated Word Error Rate (WER), W^* using a slider (Fig. 1, bottom). Then, the user starts "Semi-supervise" to be assisted. Additionally, at anytime, the user can make the system to "Re-train" the ASR model in order to improve subsequent recognitions.

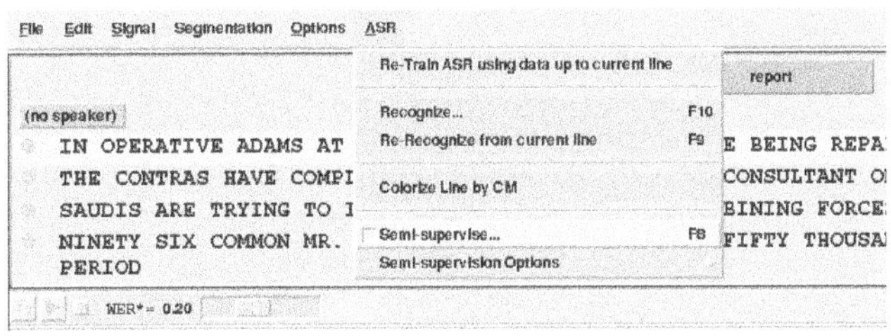

Figure 1. Screenshot showing IST prototype menu.

Recognize
ASR is performed based on a state-of-the-art statistical speech recognizer [6]. The IST prototype asks for a configuration file to read the location of audio samples and different parameters of the ASR system. Automatic transcriptions of a batch of utterances are obtained along with word-level confidence measures computed over word-graphs [8].

Semi-supervise using Balacing Method

The supervision of the automatically obtained transcriptions is performed sequentially from the first to the utterance in a word by word basis:

- The error, $\hat{W}^-$, of the unsupervised parts of the transcriptions up to the current utterance under revision is estimated (calculation is detailed in [4]). If $\hat{W}^- > W^*$:
  - The system asks the next lowest-confidence word in the utterance. The corresponding audio (obtained using the time alignment provided during recognition), is played once. The audio portion is enlarged by fixed margin of 15ms to avoid chopping. Some extra audio context would help the user in understanding. However, this is left as a future work.
  - The user can replay the audio, validate the word or type the proper correction (fig. 2).
  - $\hat{W}^-$ is updated accordingly. If $\hat{W}^- < W^*$ it proceeds to next utterance.
- Add new samples to the training data using the supervised and high-confidence parts of the utterance.

Figure 2. Screenshot of a recognized utterance under revision. Underlined text shows performed corrections. In green, a word to be supervised (it flashes for a moment in this striking color to attract attention). In maroon, low-confidence parts which are candidates to supervision.

Re-Train models

Acoustic and language models can be re-estimated any time after a new utterance is supervised. The system uses HTK [9] and SRILM [5] to train new acoustic and language models, respectively. Initial ASR models can be obtained from external sources similar to the task. Since this is not usually feasible a small part of the speech must be initially fully transcribed. The recognition of the non-supervised utterances can be performed every time the recognizer models are re-trained since it is expected to progressively adapt and perform better.

CASE STUDY

The prototype has been evaluated for the task of transcribing the whole WSJ1 training set of the Wall Street Journal (WSJ) speech database [7]. This corpus is composed of about 66 hours (approximately $624k$ running words) of speech data uttered by 200 speakers. Two tolerance values have been tested: $W^* = 6\%$ and 12%. Re-training of acoustic and language models have been carried out approximately each 1000 utterances (i.e. about 2 hours). Initial models were obtained using the correct transcriptions of the first 1000 utterances.

Figure 3 shows supervision effort and residual accumulated WER after the transcription of WSJ1 training data for both tolerance errors. Results are shown for each time the re-training of the models is carried out. It should be highlighted that an important decrease in the user effort is achieved for both tolerance errors. For a tolerance error of $W^* = 6\%$, final output resulted lower than 2% of WER by supervising about the 65% of the running words. And a WER lower than 4% by supervising about the 50% of the running words for $W^* = 12\%$.

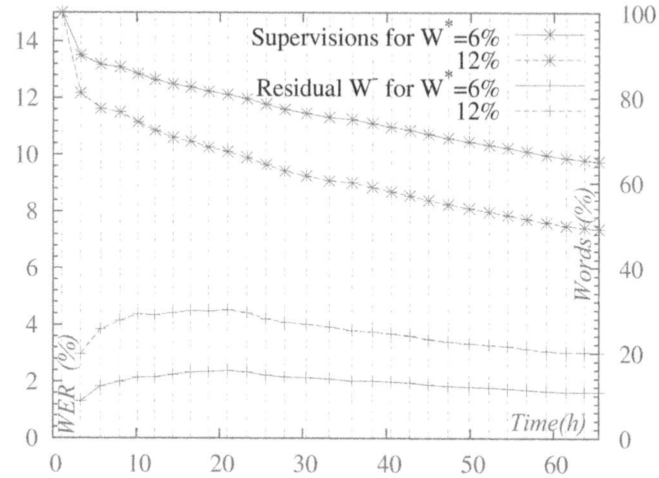

Figure 3. Transcription of WSJ1 training data for a tolerance of $W^* = 6\%$ and 12%. Reduction of the user effort in terms of the number of supervisions relative to the recognized words (at top). Residual accumulated WER after semi-supervision (at bottom). Vertical dotted lines show the time when model re-training is carried out.

Acknowledgements

Work supported by the EC (FEDER/FSE) and the Spanish MEC/MICINN under the MIPRCV "Consolider Ingenio 2010" program (CSD2007-00018), iTrans2 (TIN2009-14511) and MITTRAL (TIN2009-14633-C03-01) projects and the FPI Scholarship BES-2010-033005. Also supported by the Spanish MITyC under the erudito.com (TSI-020110-2009-439) project and by the Generalitat Valenciana under grant Prometeo/2009/014 and GV/2010/067, and by the "Vicerrectorado de Investigación de la UPV" under grant UPV/2009/2851 (grant 20080033).

REFERENCES

1. Barras, C., Geoffrois, E., Wu, Z., and Liberman, M. Transcriber: a free tool for segmenting, labeling and transcribing speech. In *Proceedings of LREC* (1998), 1373–1376.
2. Luz, S., Masoodian, M., and Rogers, B. Interactive visualisation techniques for dynamic speech transcription, correction and training. In *Proceedings of CHINZ* (2008), 9–16.
3. Rodríguez-Ruiz, L., Casacuberta, F., and Vidal, E. Computer assisted transcription of speech. In *Proceedings of the IbPRIA* (2007), 241–248.
4. Serrano, N., Sanchis, A., and Juan, A. Balancing error and supervision effort in interactive-predictive handwriting recognition. In *Proceedings of the IUI* (2010), 373–376.
5. Stolcke, A. Srilm - an extensible language modeling toolkit. In *ICSLP* (2002).
6. Luján-Mares M. et al. iATROS: A speech and handwritting recognition system. In *Proceedings of the JTH* (2008), 75–78.
7. Pallett D.S. et al. 1993 benchmark tests for the arpa spoken language program. In *Proceedings of the workshop on HLT* (1994), 49–74.
8. Wessel, F., Schlüter, R., Macherey, K., and Ney, H. Confidence measures for large vocabulary continuous speech recognition. *IEEE Trans. on Speech and Audio Processing 9*, 3 (2001), 288–298.
9. Young, S., Woodland, P., and W.J.Byrne. *HTK: Hidden Markov Model Toolkit V1.5*. Cambridge Univ. Eng. Dept. and Entropic Research Labs Inc., Cambridge, UK, 1993.

Seamless Online/Offline Shopping Experience Design for In-store Customers

Udana Bandara
Rakuten Institute of Technology, Rakuten Inc.
Tokyo, Japan
udana.bandara@mail.rakuten.com

ABSTRACT
Over the last few years, the conventional brick and mortar business model has been challenged by the proliferation of smartphone-based shopping apps, which exploit the weaknesses of this conventional model. As an alternative to these apps, we have developed *Ubira* [1], a patent-pending service platform that allows healthy online/offline competition rather than merely exploiting the weaknesses. This business model provides brick and mortar shops a fair chance to compete with online stores while creating a seamless shopping experience for in-store customers based on an online/offline partnership. The main design challenge in *Ubira* has been to promote serendipity in shopping rather than bargain hunting, and integrate the legacy inventory systems of brick and mortar businesses into the platform. To overcome these challenges, we have made some critical design choices based on context awareness and seamful design methods.

Author Keywords
Mobile Shopping Interface, Retailers, Context Awareness.

ACM Classification Keywords
Human factors, Prototyping, User-centered Design.

General Terms
Design, Economics, Human Factors.

INTRODUCTION
Undoubtedly, we already live in a contemporary ubiquitous computing environment [2] in which a smartphone user could literally carry an online shop into a brick and mortar store. As a result, more and more users mix online and offline (brick and mortar) shopping services according to their needs to optimize their shopping experience. While offline retail allows hands-on evaluation of products, online stores are far superior in detailed product research and offer better prices. Indeed, a recent survey [3] shows that 66% of smartphone users use their phones to compare prices of products or services while shopping in-store.

This trend has clearly disrupted the conventional business model of offline stores. In fact, there are already many customers who use the offline stores merely as showrooms before purchasing products online later-on. Furthermore, smartphone apps such as ShopSavvy [4] and Amazon Price Check [5] exploit this opportunity by providing easier ways to input product information via barcode scanning or image processing. However, we believe that discarding the contribution of the offline store in the overall process of buying a product is neither a fair nor a sustainable business model. Therefore, we propose the patent-pending Ubira [1] platform as an alternative service platform. *Ubira* provides an inclusive business model that allows offline shops to compete with their online counterparts within the same mobile platform by issuing context-aware coupons. Furthermore, it allows offline shops to receive an affiliation fee for all online purchases made by customers in-store.

UBIRA SYSTEM DESIGN & IMPLEMENTATION
As described in the referenced paper [1], the Ubira platform allows offline shops to run a coupon issuing service (CIS) to users who are "checked-in"(GPS-based) to the offline store. The CIS receives real time information about user-scanned products including the selected online price information through Ubira server. Based on received data, algorithms of CIS conduct real time calculations that determine whether the offline shop should issue a discount coupon to a specific user. The coupon is issued through the Ubira app just before the user makes an online purchase. When a user scans a product from the offline shop and buys it from an online shop, the transaction is marked as an affiliate sale. Therefore, an offline shop will be able to obtain an affiliation fee for every online purchase made inside its premises. Based on the above two approaches, Ubira platform enables fair competition between online and offline shops. Here, when the user is "checked-in" to a physical store, the priority to reach the user is given to the offline shop, and even when the user is buying online, the offline shop is credited with an affiliation fee.

The Ubira platform consists of three main parts: Users front-end, Offline Shop Front-end and Ubira Back-end. These components communicate via the Internet and offline shops share their inventory with Ubira backend servers. In the prototype implementation, three versions of user front-end are implemented, namely OS native, iOS+HTML5 hybrid and Android+HTML5 hybrid. The shop front-end is implemented as a web service and the back-end is implemented based on web server.

IUI'12, February 14–17, 2012, Lisbon, Portugal.
ACM 978-1-4503-1048-2/12/02.

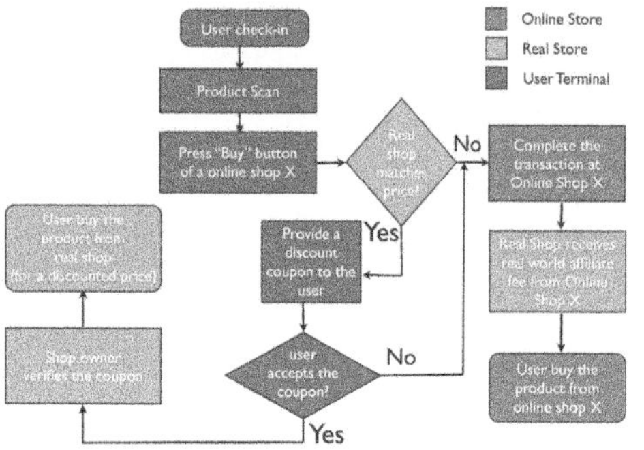

Figure 1. Ubira Main Functionality Flow

USER EXPERIENCE CHALLENGS & APPROACH

The main design challenges we faced in providing a seamless in-store online/offline shopping experience are: 1) integrating the legacy inventory systems into the Ubira platform and 2) creating serendipity in discount coupon issuing. More specifically, the owners of brick and mortar businesses are sometimes reluctant to make a huge initial investment, which makes the implementation of CIS a commercially not viable option. To overcome these design problems we have taken the following two approaches:

Seamful System Integration

We have applied the seamful system design concepts [6] to the legacy inventory system integration problem. The main requirement for implementing the CIS is comparing user-selected online prices with in-store prices. However, due to the huge investment needed for extracting in-store prices from the inventory databases of some offline stores, we came up with an alternative procedure (as discussed below) to provide discount coupons without implementing CIS. This can be done by not having to display in-store prices within the mobile app since it is already displayed in the showroom.

This alternative procedure is based on the fact that all online shops using the Ubira platform are legitimate online stores, so their prices might be slightly less than in-store prices but not dramatically different. Therefore, taking the median online price, the offline shop can have a very good understanding of the product. Based on this price, offline shops can run a selectively price-matching algorithm taking into account the limit of the coupon budget and gap between the user-selected online price and the online median price. The offline shop owners are given a real time web interface (in the cashier booth) to keep track of provided discounts and are able to intervene in the coupon providing process. Each time a customer redeems a coupon, the shop owner/assistant inputs their in-store price into the system and the Ubira server keeps track of the grand total of discounts. In addition, the offline shop has the ability to stop the course of coupon giving algorithm anytime using the web interface.

With this seamful system integration, we were able to implement the system without a large initial investment and test it's effectiveness. Furthermore, we were able to maintain the seamless user experience as originally designed without any compromising.

Serendipity in Discount Coupon Issuing

The second major design choice was not enabling end users to actively search for discounts. Instead, we wanted the discount receiving to be a serendipity. Therefore, the users are provided with all the available online/offline price options and are allowed to choose. However, even in case the user chooses an online offer, offline stores may match the online price with a discount coupon. Then, the user can claim the discount at the cash register and receive the product directly from the offline shop. In the mobile app, coupons are issued as an alert given after the user presses the 'buy button' of an online offer. Therefore, the discount coupon has a serendipity factor encoded in its design. In this case, the user welcomes the serendipity rather than be disappointed with not receiving any coupons after actively looking for one.

CONCLUSION

As explained above, we describe an initial Ubira implementation that could be deployed in an offline store without the need of a large initial investment. The main contribution of the above-explained approach is that the lesser expensive version does not have to compromise the seamless user experience of the initial system, and at the same time finds a way to bypass the initial investments of the system with seamful system design methods. We have implemented a prototype system with two versions of the user front-end: 1) HTML 5 technologies as well as 2) iOS native application, and demonstrated these to several merchants. Currently, we are discussing the possibility of a field study with several partners.

REFERENCES

1. U. Bandara, J. Chen, "Ubira: a mobile platform for an integrated online/offline shopping experience" Proceedings of the 13th international conference on Ubiquitous computing, 2011
2. P.Dourish et al, "DivingaDigitalFuture"page117-136, MIT press, 2011
3. Chadwick Martin Bailey, "How Smartphones Are Changing the Retail Shopping Experience" March 9, 2011
4. ShopSavvy: http://shopsavvy.mobi/
5. AmazonPriceCheck http://www.amazon.com/gp/pricecheck_iphone_mobile/
6. M. Chalmers et al, "Seamful interweaving: heterogeneity in the theory and design of interactive systems" Proceedings of the 5th conference on Designing interactive systems: processes, practices, methods, and techniques, 2000

icAuth: Image Color Based Authentication System

Pramod Verma
Johns Hopkins University
Baltimore MD, 21218
pramod@cs.jhu.edu

ABSTRACT
Authentication interfaces are GUIs that provide the protection for an application or system. In this paper, we present **icAuth**: a novel image and color based authentication interface for the authentication process. We enhance the existing Image Based Authentication (IBA) with an additional interactive method. In our approach, the user not only chooses image(s) as a key during the registration process, but also clicks on various regions on the image to generate an additional key. This additional key is in the form of a sequence of colors that correspond to the clicked areas. In essence, the user chooses a color sequence along with the selected images. During the next authentication process, the user has to produce the same color sequence on the recognized images. The user is required to remember the same switching sequence among the images, without having to memorize the precise location of the initial clicks during setup.

Author Keywords
IBA, Security, Usability

ACM Classification Keywords
H.5.m. Information Interfaces and Presentation (e.g. HCI): Miscellaneous

INTRODUCTION
Image Based Authentication (IBA) is more usable than Text Based Authentication (TBA)[1]. In a basic IBA, during the registration process, the user has to choose images from a given set of images and recognize them during the authentication process[2]. Researchers also experimented to select and recognize objects or patterns in the given image for the authentication process. We extend the basic IBA process by using an interactive approach described in next section.

ARCHITECTURE
icAuth system needs a pointing device to click or some kind of interactive technique such as a touch screen to click or touch the images. The system has two components: Client and Server. Client gets user credentials and the server does authentication based on authentication protocol described below.

Figure 1. An example of icAuth system where two images were used as key images and color key can be produced by clicking on region A, B, C, D, E to generate sequence $W_i B_i B_j G_j B_i$ where i is top and j is bottom image and W, B, G are key-letter for color white, blue and green.

Protocol: During the registration process, the user first chooses images as a key. Then user produces an additional key by clicking on the image regions. The user can switch to any image during the clicking process, but needs to memorize both the color sequence and switching sequence. The key is a sequence of colors related to the clicked areas of the respective images. Colors are sampled to a few levels to reduce complexity. During the authentication process the user has to reproduce the key. To make it more usable, in a given image, the user is not required to click on the exact locations to generate the desired color sequence. The protocol described here is a generalized version that can be customized according to one's requirements.

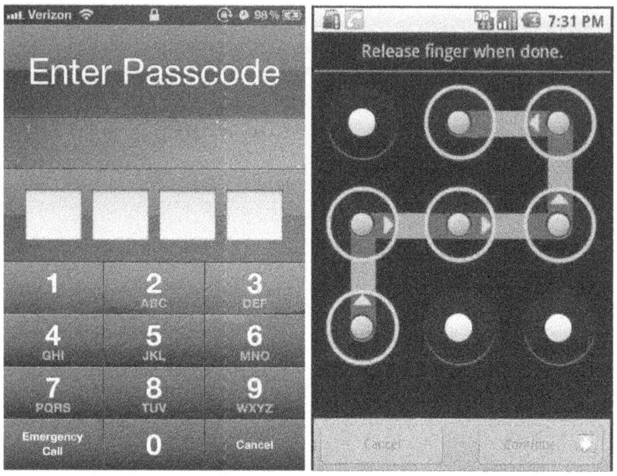

Figure 2. Example of a authentication interfaces on handheld devices such as iPhone™(Left) and Android™(Right).

GRAPHICAL USER-INTERFACE

GUI for **icAuth** has two interfaces. First GUI helps the user to register a color key. The user selects images and generates a key. To assist the user, we display the key sequence underneath the key-image. In the second GUI on the Client side, the user enters a token or user name and submits the request. Afterwards, the Server sends sets of images back to Client GUI. The user then selects appropriate images and generates the color key sequence to complete the authentication.

IMPLEMENTATION

We implemented the **icAuth** system for the authentication of a website using aforementioned protocol and GUIs. Interfaces were built using PHP and AJAX on the Apache2 web server.

We also implemented the **icAuth** system on an iPhone4G handheld device. The login page contains an image(s) on which user has to produce a key-color sequence for a successful authentication. Most of these handheld devices have touch screen capabilities, where it may be easier to generate key sequences by tapping than by typing using a virtual keyboard.

To address the precision and fuzziness of colors matching we set following equation.

$$\alpha \leq \frac{\vec{c}_1.\vec{c}_2}{\|\vec{c}_1\|\|\vec{c}_2\|} = \cos\theta \leq 1 \qquad (1)$$

Where $\vec{c}_1$ and $\vec{c}_2$ are two color vectors with $c_i[R_i, G_i, B_i, I_i]$ and they are treated the same if their dot product (or cosine similarity) is greater than or equals to a predefined threshold α such as 0.99. $\vec{c}_1$ and $\vec{c}_2$ can be estimated by averaging the color vectors or pixels values of clicked areas with a small radius r.

DISCUSSION

Our approach is easy to implement and adds an additional layer of security in IBA. The system can be used at various

Figure 3. Demonstration of icAuth interface on a handheld device. User selects [red, green, blue, blue, green] color sequences to unlock the device.

places where small PIN like identification is required via keyboard entry on handheld devices, where a user frequently enters the passcode to unlock the device. For example, Google's Android uses a pattern based authentication interface.

One another advantage of the **icAuth** system is that it creates an associative memory in the user's brain regarding the password. For instance, in Figure 3, the password can be easily remembered by viewing objects such as red leaves, green grass, blue sky, etc.

It has similar drawbacks as IBA, such as brute force attack. However, it can be used with combination of other robust methods. In addition, the system has a limitation that users with color blindness are unable to use the icAuth system. Furthermore, sometimes users may have trouble distinguishing precise colors in specific light conditions. But, we can choose appropriate images to overcome these issues.

icAuth relies not only on a sequence of different regions in one image but on a sequence of different colors in a sequence of images; therefore, the system would utilize images that can be fully or partially segmented into few sections of colors.

CONCLUSION AND FUTURE WORK

We present a novel idea for image and color based authentication. Future work may involve designing and performing a detailed user study comparing authentication methods using desktop and handheld interfaces.

REFERENCES

1. Dhamija, R., and Perrig, A. D ej a vu: A user study using images for authentication. *proceedings of USENIX Security Symposium* (Aug. 2000).
2. Newman, R. E., Harsh, P., and Jayaraman, P. Security analysis of and proposal for image-based authentication. *proceedings of IEEE ICCST* (Oct. 2005), p. 141.

A Web-Based User Interface for Interaction With Hierarchically Structured Events

Sven Buschbeck and Anthony Jameson
DFKI, German Research Center for Artificial Intelligence
Saarbrücken, Germany
Sven.Buschbeck@dfki.de, jameson@dfki.de

Tanja Schneeberger and Robin Woll
Saarland University
Saarbrücken, Germany
tanjaschneeberger89@googlemail.com,
robin_woll@web.de

ABSTRACT

Intelligent technologies have been used in various ways to support more effective representation and processing of media and documents in terms of the events that they refer to. This demo presents some innovations that have been introduced in a web-based interface to a repository of media and documents that are organized in terms of hierarchically structured events.

Author Keywords

Events, visualization, interaction

ACM Classif cation Keywords

H.5.1 Information Systems and Presentation: Multimedia Information Systems

SCIENTIFIC AND PRACTICAL CONTEXT

In recent years, researchers in several communities, including (intelligent) multimedia retrieval and the semantic web (see, e.g., [3]), have begun to realize the potential benef ts of assigning an important role to *events* in the representation and organization of knowledge and media.

Intelligent technology is being applied to several aspects of this enterprise, such as the automatic detection and classif - cation of events. A question that has been less intensively studied is that of how to provide user interfaces that enable users to interact with and benef t from event-oriented representations. This demo presents a web-based user interface[1] which was developed to address this question within the 7th Framework EU Integrating Project GLOCAL.[2] The user interface is implemented with the GOOGLE WEB TOOLKIT. It makes use of REST services to access media and event structures.

The following scenario is a typical one for the deployment of this user interface: There exists a web-based repository of media, documents, and commentary concerning complex sets of interrelated events, ranging from highly prestructured events like soccer tournaments to spontaneously emerging events like political uprisings. Content for this repository is provided and accessed by professional users such as employees of news agencies and nonprofessional users ranging from "citizen reporters" to casual visitors.

The following section sketches three innovative aspects of this user interface.

INNOVATIVE ASPECTS

1. Going beyond timelines to capture the hierarchical structure of complex events

The most familiar way of visualizing sets of events is with timelines, and there are a number of sophisticated web-based implementations of timelines, such as TIMELINE[3] and the recently introduced FACEBOOK timeline mode. But there are limitations to timelines' ability to capture the hierarchical structure of events. André et al. (in [1]) showed how some hierarchical structure could be introduced into a timeline visualization, but this method is not generalizable to hierarchies of essentially arbitrary depth.

Hierarchical structure is often an essential part of event-based organization. For example, the signif cance of a goal in a soccer tournament or a debate in a presidential campaign can often be understood only in terms of the larger event of which it is a part. Therefore, as shown in Figure 1–1, the GLOCAL user interface explicitly visualizes a complex event as a hierarchy based on a *subevent* relation (symbolized by the light-grey icon); subevents on the same level are shown on a simple timeline where appropriate.

2. Providing collapsing and f ltering functionality for f exible access to the various types of content that are associated with events

Any interface that represents events is likely to associate with each event various types of content such as media depicting the event, information about participants in the event, comments about the event, information about purchase options, and various types of metadata. The most straightforward approach for linking these items to an event is to have them appear in a separate display area when the user selects the event and requests display of the additional content. This method has limitations when the user wants to get an overview of a number of events and their related content at once. On the other hand, making all of the available content visible makes it diff cult for users to focus on types of content that interest them. The GLOCAL interface addresses these limitations by

[1] `http://www.dfki.de/glocal/latest`

[2] GLOCAL: Event-based Retrieval of Networked Media, grant agreement 248984, `http://www.glocal-project.eu/`

[3] `http://www.simile-widgets.org/timeline/`

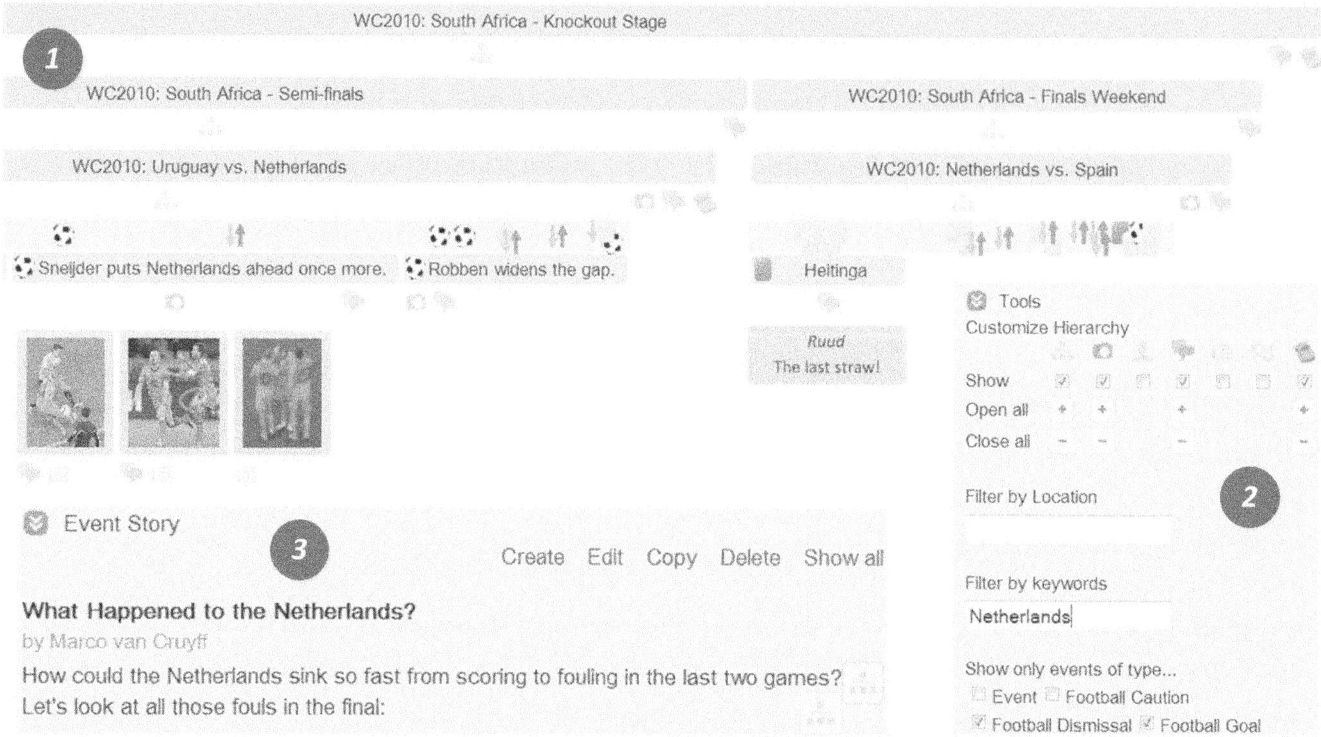

Figure 1. Partial screenshot of the GLOCAL user interface, cropped and rearranged for compactness, illustrating the three innovative aspects discussed in the text.

(a) representing the related items via links of different types within the visualization of the event hierarchy (e.g., for media and for users' comments, as shown in Figure 1–1); and (b) providing powerful and flexible mechanisms for expanding and collapsing particular subtrees of the hierarchy and for filtering the visible content (see Figure 1–2). Some of these mechanisms were suggested by functionality offered by mind-mapping tools (e.g., Mindjet's MINDMANAGER), whose functionality is seldom found in web-based systems.

3. Support for view sharing in the context of event-related stories

There are various situations in which a user may want to create or read some sort of *story* concerning a set of events. For example, a Dutch soccer fan may want to discuss why his team committed so many fouls in the final game of the 2010 World Cup; or a professional journalist may want to explain the fall from power of Colonel Gaddafi. These needs are similar to those addressed in a different context by the *sense.us* system of Heer et al. (see [2]), which enables users to (among other things) share and discuss saved *views* of visualizations of data.

The GLOCAL user interface satisfies these needs by (a) making it possible to save a view of an event hierarchy just by storing the current page URL; and (b) providing an intuitive interface with which the user can read or compose a text that includes links to such views. Each view shows a subset of the content which the author of the story has interactively created using the various collapsing and filtering methods mentioned earlier (see, e.g., the view in Figure 1–1, which is linked to the first sentence of the story in Figure 1–3). The reader of the story can interact with each of these views using the same interface functionality.

Two of the ways in which this interface solution differs from that in *sense.us* are that (a) a given piece of text can contain any number of links to views and (b) the visualization shows where stories are available by including backward pointers from events to stories which refer to them (e.g., the icon in the upper right of Figure 1).

REFERENCES

1. André, P., Wilson, M. L., Russell, A., Smith, D. A., and schraefel, m. Continuum: Designing timelines for hierarchies, relationships and scale. In *Proceedings of UIST 2007* (2007), 101–110.

2. Heer, J., Viégas, F. B., and Wattenberg, M. Voyagers and voyeurs: Supporting asynchronous collaborative information visualization. In *Human Factors in Computing Systems: CHI 2007 Conference Proceedings*, B. Begole, S. Payne, E. Churchill, R. S. Amant, D. Gilmore, and M. B. Rosson, Eds. ACM, New York, 2007.

3. van Erp, M., van Hage, W. R., Hollink, L., Jameson, A., and Troncy, R., Eds. *Proceedings of the ISWC 2011 Workshop on Detection, Representation, and Exploitation of Events in the Semantic Web*. CEUR, Aachen, Germany, 2011. Available from http://ceur-ws.org/Vol-779/.

PINTER: Interactive Storytelling with Physiological Input

Stephen W. Gilroy, Julie Porteous, Fred Charles, Marc Cavazza
Teesside University, School of Computing
Middlesbrough, TS1 3BA, UK
{s.w.gilroy, j.porteous, f.charles, m.o.cavazza}@tees.ac.uk

ABSTRACT
The dominant interaction paradigm in Interactive Storytelling (IS) systems so far has been active interventions by the user by means of a variety of modalities. PINTER is an IS system that uses physiological inputs—surface electromyography (EMG) and galvanic skin response (GSR) [1]—as a form of passive interaction, opening up the possibility of the use of traditional filmic techniques [2, 3] to implement IS without requiring immersion-breaking interactive responses. The goal of this demonstration is to illustrate the ways in which passive interaction combined with filmic visualisation, dialogue and music, and a plan-based narrative generation approach can form a new basis for an adaptive interactive narrative.

Author Keywords
Interactive Storytelling, Physiological Input.

ACM Classification Keywords
H.5.1 [Multimedia Information Systems]: Artificial, augmented, and virtual realities.

General Terms
Design, Experimentation.

INTRODUCTION
The central idea in Interactive Storytelling (IS) is the modification of an unfolding narrative in response to the behaviour of spectators. Since early research in interactive cinema, the dominant paradigm has been one where spectators *actively* influence the story through increasingly sophisticated interfaces, from remote controls to speech understanding systems [4]. In our current work, we challenge this approach, by introducing a *passive* mode of interaction based on users' physiological response to the narrative (this is a companion paper to our IUI paper [7]).

The basic mechanisms for narrative generation are common to both active and passive versions of interactive storytelling: based on a user's reaction to displayed narrative actions, compute the future evolution of the story, using a planning algorithm to propagate causality and maintain semantic consistency. However, the main difference between active and passive interaction is that in the latter, user input is essentially continuous, which makes it possible to adapt the story using both short-term responses to individual events and longer-term overall reactions to the perceived evolution of the story (including dramatic tension, pace and suspense).

IUI'12, February 14–17, 2012, Lisbon, Portugal.
ACM 978-1-4503-1048-2/12/02.

DEMONSTRATION SCENARIO
The demonstration system PINTER features an underlying narrative that consists of a medical drama (*Arztserie*) which combines aspects of medical practice with the evolution of personal relationships between lead characters. The narratives generated by the system and their 3D visualizations which are shown to users, utilize the notion of "Smithian" cues [5], where the atmosphere of actions is used to "prime" user responses to important narrative events. The presentation of the narratives to viewers feature different dramatic visualizations of narrative events such as patients being in critical medical situations or arguments between characters, as well as having a different overall feel depending on the target level of user response for phases of the narrative.

The demonstration scenario features three medical characters and a patient character whose condition and treatment form the main plot. This provides an opportunity to highlight how the visualisation of the unfolding of narrative elements is adapted to the on-going physiological reactions of the user as they are gathered by the system.

DEMONSTRATION SYSTEM OVERVIEW
The overall installation setup of the PINTER demonstration system is illustrated in Figure 1. The user sits in front of one screen viewing the real-time visualisation of the 3D contents from the unfolding medical drama, including text subtitles from character dialogues and a soundtrack enhanced with musical effects. To gather continuous passively interactive feedback, they are equipped with two types of physiological sensors: Galvanic Skin Resistance (GSR) and facial surface electromyography (EMG), which are attached with electrodes on the hand and face respectively. On a second screen (not shown to the user) are displayed details of the internal components of the PINTER system and interpretation of physiological input.

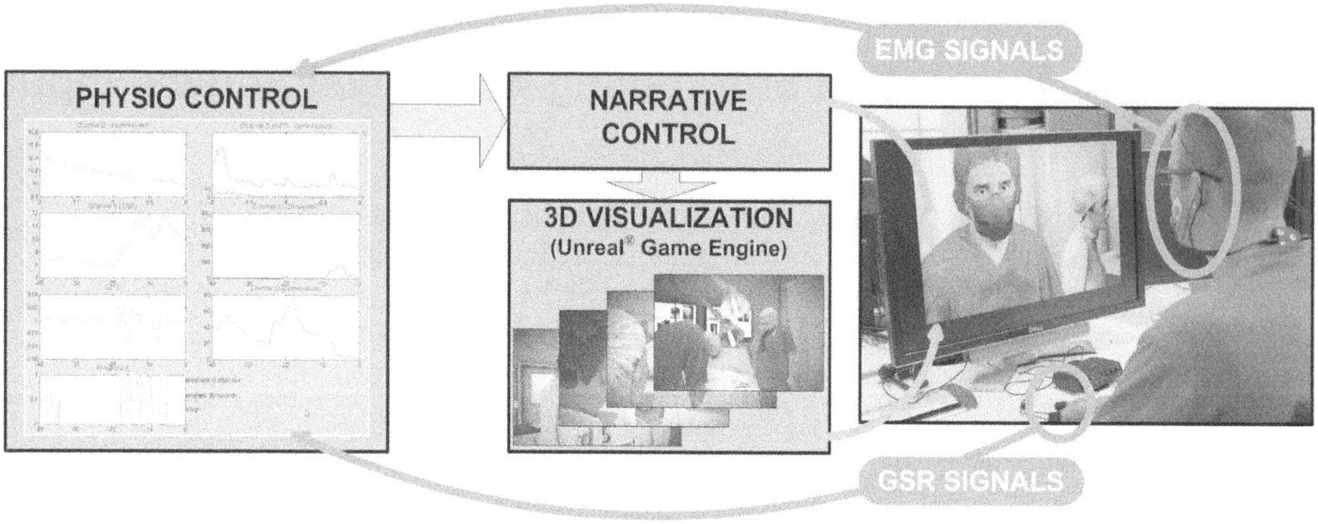

Figure 1. PINTER demonstration installation setup.

Visualisation is driven by a self-adaptive narrative whereby physiological inputs influence the process of narrative generation (using a variant of the Metric-FF planner [6]), which selects actions based on a projected progression of dramatic events. The tension and suspense of the core narrative are determined by the intensity of measured arousal of the user through GSR, while the system manages the overall pacing of the narrative by inserting a variety of re-orderable and re-combinable scenes illustrating plot background and character relationships.

The system smooths variations in user response according to a cycle of narrative tension and release, avoiding both incongruent proximate action selection and unwanted biofeedback of simplistic physiological adaptation. EMG signals are used to measure positive and negative response to categories of actions, which are selectively preferred or avoided in future narrative adaptation.

INTERACTING WITH *PINTER*

Typical user sessions with the demonstration system last between 5–7 minutes. The variation in duration of the user sessions depends on the spontaneity of the user's emotional responses. Viewers should ideally not be acquainted with the baseline narrative of the scenario they watch, so as to guarantee the spontaneity of their response.

Also displayed during a user session are details of the internal components of the PINTER system working together in real-time, particularly the interpretation of physiological input. As arousal levels change in response to visualisations, different filmic techniques are used to best fit the desired narrative tension, which then engender future responses. In the demonstration, different narratives will be generated and adapted for different users depending upon variations in the real-time physiological feedback.

ACKNOWLEDGEMENTS

This work has been funded (in part) by the European Commission under grant agreement IRIS (FP7-ICT-231824) and grant agreement CEEDs (FP7-ICT-258749). Visual content was developed by Catherine Dixon and Matthew Laverick of Teesside University. Story ideas provided by Terry Borst, Santa Fe University of Art and Design. Character models were purchased from aXYZ Design (http://www.axyz-design.com).

REFERENCES

1. Andreassi, J. L. *Psychophysiology: Human Behavior and Physiological Response*. Psychology Press, 1997.
2. Arijon, D. *Grammar of the Film Language*. Silman-James Press, U.S., 1991.
3. Van Sijll, J. *Cinematic Storytelling*. Studio City, CA: Michael Wiese Productions, 2005.
4. Cavazza, M., Pizzi, D., Charles, F., Vogt, T. and André, E. Emotional Input for Character-based Interactive Storytelling. *Proc. of the 8th Int. Conf. on Autonomous Agents and Multiagent Systems (AAMAS)*, IFAAMAS, (2009), 313–320.
5. Smith, G. *Film Structure and the Emotion System*. Cambridge University Press, 2003.
6. Hoffmann, J. The Metric-FF Planning System: Translating "Ignoring Delete Lists" to Numeric State Variables. *Journal of Artificial Intelligence Research*, 20 (2003), 291-341.
7. Gilroy, S., Porteous, J., Charles, F., and Cavazza, M. Exploring Passive User Interaction for Adaptive Narratives. *Proc. of the Int. Conf. on Intelligent User Interfaces (IUI),* ACM, (2012).

A Flexible Platform for Developing Context-Aware 3D Gesture-based Interfaces

Ali Bigdelou* **Loren Arthur Schwarz*** **Tobias Benz** **Nassir Navab**
Computer Aided Medical Procedures (CAMP)
Technische Universität München, Germany
{bigdelou,schwarz,benzt,navab}@cs.tum.edu
* Joint corresponding and first authors.

ABSTRACT

In this paper, we introduce a flexible framework that can facilitate the definition of 3D gesture-based interfaces. Highlighting the need for context awareness in complex domains, such as the operating room, we argue how the proposed architecture can overcome integration challenges. Through a real-life scenario, an intra-operative medical image viewer, we demonstrate how the proposed framework can be used in practice to define user interfaces in collaborative environments, where the behavior and the system response can be adapted based on the current workflow stage and individual user requirements. Finally, we demonstrate how the defined interface can be manipulated using a high-level visual programming interface. The extensibility of the proposed architecture makes it applicable to a wide range of scenarios.

Author Keywords

Gesture-based Interaction; Context Awareness; Framework

ACM Classification Keywords

H.5.2 Information Interfaces and Presentation (e.g. HCI): User Interfaces; J.3 Life and Medical Sciences: Health

INTRODUCTION

Contactless interfaces utilizing 3D gestures are studied intensively [1, 4] and are of particular interest for domains where classical touch-based interfaces are not applicable, such as the operating room [3]. The operating room (OR) is a highly complex environment where surgical staff often use various types of assistive computerized medical systems, for instance to visualize patient data. However, sterility regulations restrict the use of classical mouse-driven or touch-based user interfaces [3, 5]. Typical solutions, such as delegating physical control to less-skilled assistants, increase the amount of verbal communication, raising the chance of human error and adversely affecting efficiency [3]. On the other hand, context awareness is an important factor for intra-operative user interfaces [2]. Additionally, since the OR is a collaborative environment where several users are sharing the control over different target systems, the proposed interface should be able to cope with these requirements as well. In this work we introduce a framework to facilitate the definition of customizable and context-aware 3D gesture-based interfaces for collaborative environments and show its usage in the OR scenario.

IUI'12, February 14–17, 2012, Lisbon, Portugal.
ACM 978-1-4503-1048-2/12/02.

GESTURE RECOGNITION

Our gesture interaction framework builds upon machine learning techniques for gesture recognition that provide simultaneous categorical and spatio-temporal control [1, 5]. These methods learn a set of gestures from training data recorded with a modality of choice, such as body-worn inertial sensors or the Kinect. Internally, dimensionality-reduced models of the gestures are learned. After training, the type of gesture is automatically recognized (categorical control), as well as the relative body pose within this gesture (spatio-temporal control). Using these two types of information, users can simultaneously select features to be controlled and fine-tune continuous parameters with their gestures. Figure 1 shows the usage of the proposed framework in the OR.

FRAMEWORK ARCHITECTURE

A framework for incorporating the recognized gesture parameters into the user interface should satisfy certain architectural requirements. Such a framework should be extensible, since gestures can be utilized to control different types of target systems using different types of input modalities. Moreover, the used architecture should also be customizable, due to the fact that the real end user requirements are not usually known in advance and strongly depend on the end usage context.

Component Model. To achieve the desired extensibility and customizability, we propose a framework with a component-based architecture. In this model, components expose their functionalities to the framework as a set of signals, an abstraction of typical properties, methods and events. We define four main kinds of components. 1) *Sensor components* encapsulate the interface to input devices such as inertial sensors or Kinect. 2) *Gesture recognition components* contain the implementation of a gesture recognition method. 3) *Target components* wrap the interface of a target application, such

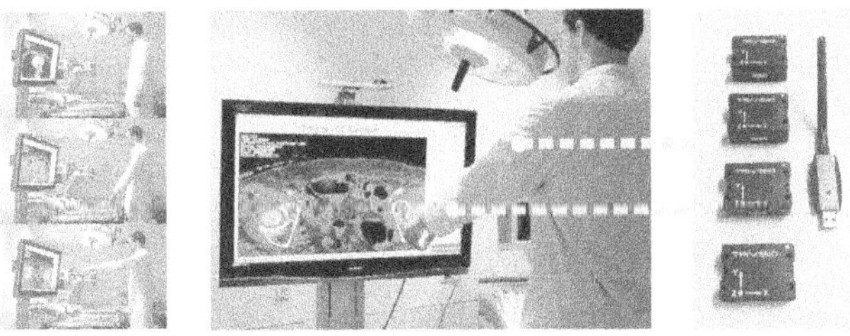

Figure 1. Gesture-based interaction in the OR, using the inertial sensors.

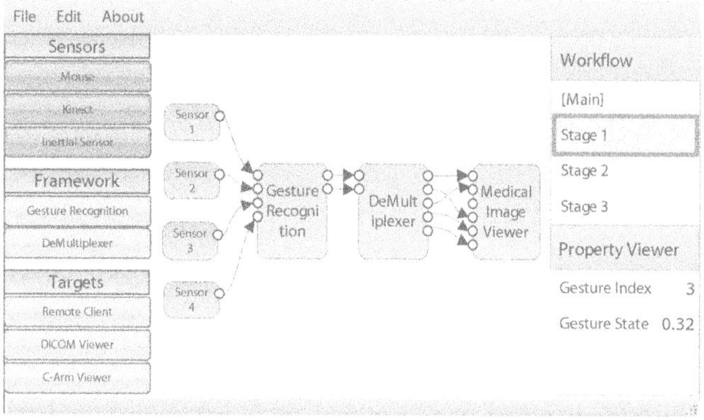

Figure 2. GUI of a visual editor for defining interaction pipelines.

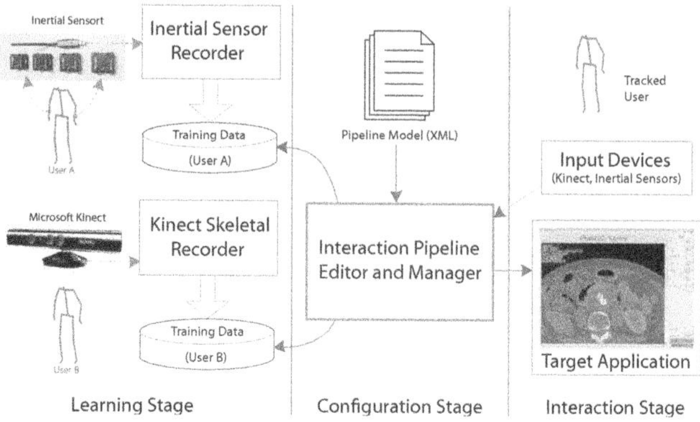

Figure 3. Practical stages for deploying a 3D gesture-based interface.

as an intra-operative image viewer. 4) *Demultiplexer components* act as a switch between the *gesture recognition components* and *target components*, forwarding the recognized gesture value to the relevant feature of the target component.

Bindings and Data Flow. In order to set up a data connection among signals exposed from different components, we extend the framework with the data flow model. Such a data pipeline can be achieved by synchronizing signal values which are bound either directionally or bi-directionally. Once such a binding is defined, at runtime, the framework propagates values of all the changed signals to all the dependent properties in the other components, by updating their values.

Customizing System Behavior. The pipeline model, including a list of composed components and their interconnections (bindings), can be serialized in an XML file. Having such a persistent pipeline model, the behavior of the system can be defined and retrieved, as required for a specific usage scenario, without extra programming. The configuration of the pipeline model can be facilitated using a visual programming interface, such as illustrated in Figure 2. This enables the end users to further customize the system behavior at runtime.

CONTEXT-AWARENESS

The proposed architecture can be used to create and adapt a 3D gesture-based interface, based on a given usage context.

Collaborative Environment. In collaborative domains, such as the OR [2], the interaction with a target application may be distributed between multiple human roles. Since the input sensors are uniquely identified each with a seperate component, the underlying data pipeline can be rewired properly to provide the required control for each individual user.

Multiple Targets. Our modular architecture enables simultaneous control of different target applications. By encapsulating each target application in a corresponding *target component*, several of such targets can be included in a pipeline.

Workflow Awareness. At any given time during the usage workflow, typically only a small subset of features of a target application is practically needed, e.g. in the OR [2]. With proper understanding of the workflow, a separate pipeline configuration can be defined for each workflow stage, hence the same set of gestures can be used for different purposes.

PRACTICAL USAGE

The proposed framework can be deployed in practice within three stages: learning, configuration and interaction, as shown in Figure 3. 1) During the *learning* stage, a recorder application is used to collect the training data, consisting of one example per gesture. This enables users to customize gestures. 2) Within the *configuration* stage, the pipeline editor, presented in Figure 2, is used to set up the data flow within the framework separately for each workflow stage. 3) In the *interaction* stage, the system can be used while the framework continuously reads the sensor values, runs the gesture recognition method and updates the target devices based on the recognized gestures and the defined pipeline. The system behaviour can be further customized at runtime, using the visual editor or by changing the current workflow stage.

CONCLUSION

We presented a framework for integration of categorical and spatio-temporal gesture recognition approaches into the application logic. The proposed software framework enables a dynamic association of learned gestures to arbitrary target systems. The architecture is flexible and both, the gestures and the target parameters to be controlled, can be customized based on runtime requirements. This enables the application to customize its behaviour in a context-aware manner.

REFERENCES

1. Bigdelou, A., Schwarz, L., and Navab, N. An adaptive solution for intra-operative gesture-based human-machine interaction. In *ACM IUI* (2012).
2. Bigdelou, A., Sterner, T., Wendler, T., Matthes, F., and Navab, N. OR specific domain model for usability evaluations of intra-operative systems. *IPCAI* (2011).
3. Johnson, R., O'Hara, K., Sellen, A., Cousins, C., and Criminisi, A. Exploring the potential for touchless interaction in image-guided interventional radiology. *Human Factors in Computing Systems* (2011).
4. Mitra, S., and Acharya, T. Gesture recognition: A survey. *IEEE Transactions on Systems, Man, and Cybernetics, Part C: Applications and Reviews 37*, 3 (2007), 311–324.
5. Schwarz, L., Bigdelou, A., and Navab, N. Learning gestures for customizable human-computer interaction in the operating room. In *MICCAI* (2011).

First Demonstration of the Intelligent Reviewer's Assistant

Ruihai Dong, Kevin McCarthy, Michael P. O'Mahony, Markus Schaal, Barry Smyth
Clarity - Centre for Sensor Web Technologies,
School of Computer Science and Informatics,
University College Dublin, Belfield, Dublin 4, Ireland
{firstname.lastname}@ucd.ie

ABSTRACT
User opinions and reviews are an important part of the modern web and all major e-commerce sites typically provide their users with the ability to provide and access customer reviews across their product catalog. The importance of reviews has driven the need to improve the review quality by providing interactive support for the reviewer and we will demonstrate the first version of an *Intelligent Reviewer's Assistant* for this purpose. Our browser plugin is designed to work with major sites like Amazon and to provide users with suggestions as they write their reviews. In particular, these suggestions take the form of topics (e.g. product features) that a reviewer may wish to write about and the suggestions automatically adapt as the user writes their review.

ACM Classification Keywords
H.5.2. Information Interfaces and Presentation: User Interfaces

INTRODUCTION
Today millions of users contribute their opinions of products and services on sites like Trip Advisor, Hotels.com, Amazon, IMDB, and countless more. The growing importance of this type of user-generated content has highlighted a number of interesting research challenges. First and foremost, considerable research attention has recently been paid to better understanding the quality and fairness of user-generated reviews.

For our *Intelligent Reviewer's Assistant,* we adopted a very different approach. Inspired by the GhostWriter system [1, 2], we propose to help users to write more meaningful and insightful reviews in the first place. Specifically, we have developed our system to work with sites like Trip Advisor and Amazon and to make suggestions to users during the writing process. The suggestions take the form of noun words that are chosen to highlight key features/topics related to the product or service that the user is writing about, and which have been extracted from other related reviews. As they write their review these suggestions change in response to what they write. For example, in reviewing a Nikon D90 SLR camera on Amazon, initial suggestions to the user might encourage them to discuss the *price* of the camera or its *resolution*; and via hovering over the suggestions, the user can always see what other users have written about these features if they wish. Moreover, as the review becomes more complete, these suggestions will change. Features that have already been covered will fall away and new, possible more niche features, will be suggested. For example, the reviewer might be encouraged to discuss the camera's *battery* life or the *weight* of the body or even its *shutter* speed.

Of course these suggestions are meant as an optional guidance. At all times it is up to the user whether they choose to write about particular suggestions but because they are available our hope is that some users will benefit some of the time and that this will lead, in due course, to a greater number of high quality, helpful reviews. An example screenshot of the Intelligent Reviewer's Assistant is presented in Figure 1. Briefly it shows the Intelligent Reviewer's Assistant's suggestions box with a number of suggested topics related to the review that the user has started to write; in this case it is a review about the movie *The Tourist* starring Angelina Jolie and Johnny Depp. As indicated, if the user mouses over one of these suggestions then they see a short list of review fragments from related reviews that have touched on this topic.

SYSTEM OUTLINE
The Intelligent Reviewer's Assistant system architecture comprises four base components:

1. *Filtering* Select *good quality* User Generated Content (UGC) as knowledge base. In the current version of the demo, the first hundred reviews are scraped from Amazon for that product.
2. *Mapping* Assuming good quality UGC is identified, the similarity between the current writing of the user (in progress) and similar texts in the knowledge base is computed to identify *relevant* UGC. In the current version of the demo, Jaccard similarity after Stop-Word-Removal and Stemming is applied to pick the 50 reviews that are most similar to the current writings.
3. *Extracting* Extracting features from relevant and good quality UGC is the basis for generating and ranking suggestions. For the current version of the demo, noun words are extracted as topic descriptors and corresponding noun phrases from UGCs are linked with those noun words.
4. *Presenting* In the current version of the demo, users see a list of Top-10 noun words in the suggestion box. Hovering over the suggestions will show noun phrases containing those nouns.

IUI'12, February 14–17, 2012, Lisbon, Portugal.
ACM 978-1-4503-1048-2/12/02.

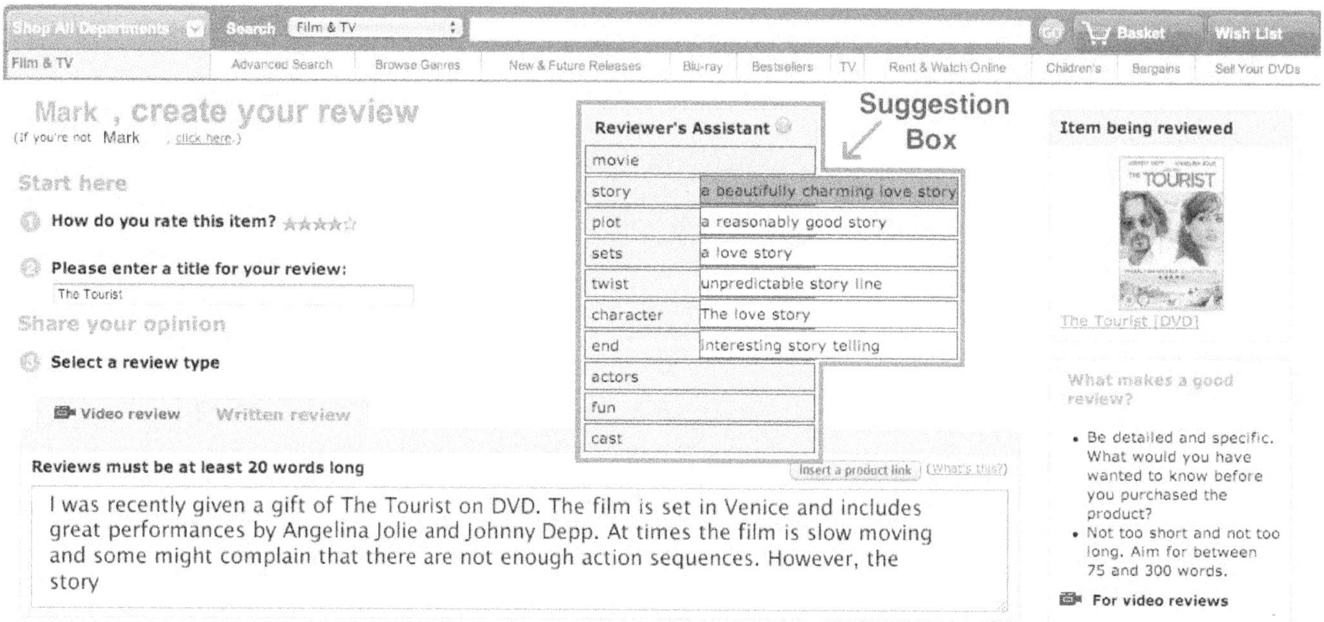

Figure 1: The *Reviewer's Assistant* Browser Plugin

RELATED WORK

The GhostWriter system was first proposed by Bridge et al. [1] and Healy and Bridge [2] as an approach to guide users in the construction of short snippets of user generated content. Originally, it was applied to the writing of classified adverts for products users wished to sell/exchange. Subsequently, the GhostWriter researchers turned their attention to helping users produce review content on Amazon. Currently GhostWriter extracts noun phrases from past product reviews (cases), and suggests these phrases to the reviewer/user as fragments to be copied directly into an evolving review.

Our Reviewer's Assistant differs from the Ghostwriter system in the following ways:

1. We suggest nouns instead of noun phrases, thus users are not guided towards a particular sentiment contained in the phrase. Rather, noun words guide the user towards covering topics that other users have covered before or topics that were covered for other products.

2. We use association rule mining instead of word frequencies, i.e. we try to follow the user's intent while he is writing up his review. Preliminary expert assessment seems to indicate that the suggestions generated by association rule mining provide better guidance for quality reviews.

TECHNICAL ASPECTS

The *Reviewer's Assistant* has been developed as a browser plugin so that it can integrate directly with review systems across a wide variety of web sites. The current version of the demo works with Amazon but it will work in a similar manner with sites such as BestBuy, Hotels.com, TripAdvisor etc. As mentioned previously the Reviewer's Assistant takes the form of an additional recommendation module that appears on the review-creation pages of Amazon as shown in Figure 1. Quite simply the module presents an updating list of topic recommendations to the user as they write their review. These suggestions are extracted from the texts of related reviews in real-time and based on the review content that the reviewer has provided so far. As such the suggestions adapt to the review as the reviewer writes it: as topics are covered, these suggestions fall away and are replaced with additional suggestions. The module is fully interactive and the user can, for example, hover over a suggestion to see additional information, such as the review fragments from related reviews that discuss the topic.

ACKNOWLEDGMENTS

This work is supported by Science Foundation Ireland under grant 07/CE/I1147.

REFERENCES

1. Derek Bridge and Aidan Waugh. Using experience on the read/write web: The ghostwriter system. In Derek Bridge, Enric Plaza, and Nirmalie Wiratunga, editors, *Procs. of WebCBR: The Workshop on Reasoning from Experiences on the Web (Workshop Programme of the Eighth International Conference on Case-Based Reasoning)*, pages 15–24, 2009.

2. Paul Healy and Derek Bridge. The GhostWriter-2.0 System: Creating a Virtuous Circle in Web 2.0 Product Reviewing. In Derek Bridge, Sarah Jane Delany, Enric Plaza, Barry Smyth, and Nirmalie Wiratunga, editors, *Procs. of WebCBR: The Workshop on Reasoning from Experiences on the Web (Workshop Programme of the Eighteenth International Conference on Case-Based Reasoning)*, pages 121–130, 2010.

Collecting Multimodal Data in the Wild

Michael Johnston
AT&T Labs Research
Florham Park, NJ, USA
johnston@research.att.com

Patrick Ehlen
AT&T
San Francisco, CA, USA
patrick.ehlen@att.com

ABSTRACT
Multimodal interaction allows users to specify commands using combinations of inputs from multiple different modalities. For example, in a local search application, a user might say "gas stations" while simultaneously tracing a route on a touchscreen display. In this demonstration, we describe the extension of our cloud-based speech recognition architecture to a Multimodal Semantic Interpretation System (MSIS) that supports processing of multimodal inputs streamed over HTTP. We illustrate the capabilities of the framework using Speak4it[SM], a deployed mobile local search application supporting combined speech and gesture input. We provide interactive demonstrations of Speak4it on the iPhone and iPad and explain the challenges of supporting true multimodal interaction in a deployed mobile service.

Author Keywords
multimodal, speech, gesture.

ACM Classification Keywords
H.5.2 [Information Interfaces And Presentation]: User Interfaces - Input devices and strategies (e.g., mouse, touchscreen);

INTRODUCTION
Commercial speech recognition and natural language processing systems have become commonplace over the past decade, and can now be accessed in places where speech recognition was not available before. Likewise, the capabilities of gesture recognition systems are now more compact and inexpensive, and used in people's personal devices and homes. Combining these two technologies may help to create a new era of computer interaction in which people will at last be able to interact with computers using many of the same behaviors and methods they use to interact with each other, using language, gesture, and other natural methods of signaling [1].

This prospect of true multimodal interaction has motivated expansion of our speech recognition platform [4] to support processing, recognition, and interpretation, not just of speech, but of multimodal input streams. The resulting Multimodal Semantic Interpretation System (MSIS) is designed to handle and process both low-level and high-level speech and gesture input signals, and to output semantic interpretations of these signals separately or in combination. Here we illustrate its use by demonstration in Speak4it, the first commercially deployed multimodal application using the system.

IUI'12, February 14–17, 2012, Lisbon, Portugal.
ACM 978-1-4503-1048-2/12/02.

MULTIMODAL SEMANTIC INTERPRETATION SYSTEM
MSIS was developed using AT&T's Watson platform, fostered in part by two advances: a streaming HTTP API that supports cloud-based recognition, and a plug-in development environment that supports complex chains of diverse processing for signal streams. While cloud-based speech recognition of streamed audio has become commonplace, Watson's MSIS can handle complex HTTP data streams that comprise not only audio, but also gesture, vision, or context data, or any other type of data one might wish to process. These data can be multiplexed into a single threaded data stream sent from a client application, including standardized data signal protocols like InkML [6] or EMMA [7], alongside custom protocols. Thus, an HTTP data connection to the cloud service has become a versatile pipe through which many types of data can be streamed simultaneously (Figure 1).

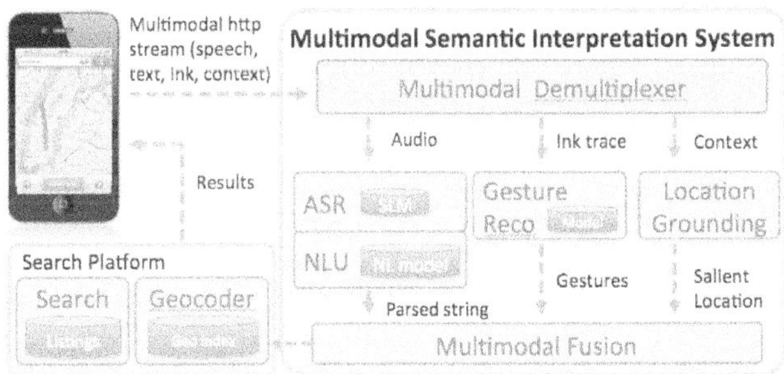

Figure 1. Multimodal architecture

At the other end of the HTTP connection, MSIS supports a chain of processing plug-ins that handles these streams of multiplexed data. The first stop for any stream is a de-multiplexing plug-in, which scans the HTTP input stream packets for different types of data and the boundaries that separate them. As these data arrive, they are passed on to buffers for handler plug-ins that begin the processing chain for the required type of data. Arrival of new data types triggers events that launch handlers for the new data. Thus de-multiplexed streams of data can undergo "sidechain" processing that handles one or more types of data, such as vision or gesture data, or a combination of the processing results from those data, such as composing lattices of semantic hypotheses of both ASR and gesture recognition.

To handle these different types of data, each plug-in can load its own set of models, developed either using the tools provided with the recognizer, or using third-party tools (Watson supports plug-ins developed in C/C++ or Python). In addition to the acoustic and language models standard to ASR systems, there are now models for natural language understanding, gesture recognition, multimodal integration, context grounding, and disambiguation. Thus complex sets of combined streams of user interaction data can be processed in parallel and produce an integrated semantic interpretation of diverse and simultaneous signals. How does an application use this system to foster natural user interaction? To answer that question, we will demonstrate Speak4it, a multimodal business search application [8].

Speak4it Demo: Multimodal Local Search

Speak4it performs simultaneous recognition of user speech and deictic finger gestures performed on a digital map. In addition to providing this combined interpretation of speech and gesture, Speak4it also collects user context data gathered by the client device to help make disambiguation judgments about important but potentially ambiguous referents, like the user's intended location context. These data are streamed in real-time along with the user's speech and finger gesture data, and analyzed by a context resolution plug-in in combination with the semantic output of both speech and gesture recognition.

Demonstration attendees will see how Speak4it uses multimodal interaction to enhance search. They have a hands-on opportunity to speak any natural language combination of U.S. business name, business category, and U.S. geographic locations or landmarks, such as "real estate attorneys in Detroit, Michigan" or "bicycle repair shops near the Golden Gate Bridge," and see the map zoom to the intended location to display the search results. They will also be able to manipulate the map view using drag (pan) and pinch (zoom) touch gestures, or using spoken commands, and use multimodal commands where the location is specified directly by drawing on the map while speaking [5], such as "Italian restaurants near here," in conjunction with a point or area gesture.

As a user performs one of these multimodal commands, their speech audio, finger gesture movements, and device context data are multiplexed on the client and streamed over HTTP to the Watson MSIS, which de-multiplexes it and begins processing even as the user is still interacting with the device. The user's finger traces are passed to a gesture recognizer, which classifies the traces as a point, a line, or an area (in this case, an area). The audio stream is recognized using a statistical language model whose output is then passed to a natural language understanding plug-in (NLU) [3] that parses the query into semantic slots that include a topic phrase for the user's desired search subject (e.g., "Italian restaurants") and, if applicable, a location phrase (like "San Francisco") or a deictic location (like "here") that designates a desired location. In cases where there is an explicit location phrase (e.g. "pizza restaurants in San Francisco"), the location phrase is geo-coded so search results from the topic phrase may be sorted and displayed according to their proximity to the location. If the location is ambiguous, the location grounding plug-in receives context data streamed from the device and uses it in conjunction with semantic interpretation hypotheses from ASR and gesture to determine the user's intended search location [2]. At the end of the semantic processing chain, the intended search location is geocoded and sent with the search topic to a local search engine. The locations of relevant businesses are then displayed on the map. This local search system integrates simultaneous collection and processing of multiple streams of input data, and combines those behaviors from different types of user signals into a single semantic interpretation.

Equipment

Speak4it functions on an iPhone or iPad over a reasonably reliable wireless network connection. We will demonstrate on an iPad, and no other equipment is required.

REFERENCES

1. Clark, H. H. and Krych, M. A., "Speaking While Monitoring Addressees for Understanding", *J. of Memory and Language, 50*, 1 (2004), 62-81.
2. Ehlen, P. and Johnston, M., Location Grounding in Multimodal Local Search. *Proc. of ICMI-MLMI* (2010).
3. Feng, J., Bangalore, S., and Gilbert, M., "Role of Natural Language Understanding in Voice Local Search", *Proc. of Interspeech* (2009), 1859-1862.
4. Goffin, V., Allauzen, C., Bocchieri, E., Hakkani-Tür, D., Ljolje, A., Parthasarathy, S., Rahim, M., Riccardi, G., and Saraclar, M., "The AT&T Watson Speech Recognizer", *Proc. of ICASSP* (2005), 19-23.
5. Johnston, M., Bangalore, S., Vasireddy, G., Stent, A., Ehlen, P., Walker, M., Whittaker, S., and Maloor, P, "MATCH: An Architecture for Multimodal Dialogue *Systems. Proc. of ACL, 4* (2002) 376-383.
6. http://www.w3.org/2002/mmi/ink
7. http://www.w3.org/TR/emma/
8. http://speak4it.com/

Deducing Parameters for Personalizing Maps from Map Interaction Patterns

Beate Weninger
HafenCity University Hamburg
Hebebrandstraße 1, 22297 Hamburg, Germany
beate.weninger@hcu-hamburg.de

ABSTRACT

Interactive maps on the internet have become frequently used means to convey spatial information to the public. However, many maps are not developed to suit a variety of users and thus lead to frustration. To user-center maps we therefore recommend to personalize them to individual users. As many parameters that can be used as a trigger for personalization are not easy to be logged on the internet, we suggest user-map interaction. Interaction can be easily tracked and gives comprehensive information about map use. Since no interpretation of user-map interaction is available it is the aim of this PhD to observe interaction, and to evaluate and interpret it. We hypothesize that there are map interaction patterns, means recurring sequences of consecutive actions which are necessary to complete a task. Our goal is to deduce parameters for personalization from these map interaction patterns.

Author Keywords

Interaction, interactive maps, personalization, adaptive maps.

ACM Classification Keywords

H.5.2. [Information interfaces and presentation]: User interfaces – Theory and methods;

CONTEXT AND MOTIVATION

Interactive maps are popular to convey spatial information to the public. Through the internet they are suitable to inform a broad mass of people about spatial developments in cities or about environmental issues, such as noise, energy, or land use. Therefore they are frequently used as information platforms for spatial topics on the internet.

However, maps on the internet have their drawbacks: different map users with varied interests, experiences with digital maps and previous knowledge are provided with the same map content, functions and interaction modes. Wilson [13] gives an example of the consequences: "Presenting all users with maps containing default feature content can easily hinder individual users' particular task goals by including irrelevant spatial feature content". Given the small attention span of users to convince them of a product and the risk of a high rate of disappointment caused by unsuitable maps this approach of one for all has to be scrutinized. The interface and interaction of the map needs to be user-centered and "intelligent technology" that increases usability has to be implemented.

To user-center maps we suggest personalizing them by adapting them to the needs and preferences of individual users. By personalization we understand the adaptation of content, functions, appearance, technology in use, or information demand to individual users. This could for example mean to change the color scheme according to the cultural background of the user, or to change the presentation or points of interest according to the season (winter landscape and places for ice skating versus summer landscape and places for fishing). Also recommendations on the basis of interaction with the map are possible. People who frequently request information about cultural events and therefore click on respective symbols might be interested in special offers. A lot of commercial websites and applications are personalized already, but in practice only a few maps use very simple approaches of personalization. *Google Maps* is an example for a map that uses "localization", which is the adaptation to the region, where the map is used. This adaptation, however, has to be much more comprehensive and advanced to suit successful map interaction and understanding.

To personalize maps, parameters have to be defined that trigger the adaptation process. We assume that considering user-map interaction is a reliable approach because results from classical web analytics methods, such as information about the operating system, plug-ins, adjustments, access time, and number of page views etc. have proven to be not sufficient to characterize individual users and to be basis for personalization [12]. The arguments for our approach are: firstly user-map interaction can be easily logged with non-invasive methods while map-usage. Secondly, according to our hypothesis, map-user interaction characterizes individual users and interaction patterns can be identified. Interaction patterns are recurring sequences of consecutive actions which are necessary to complete a task.

Usually the user group is considered to design maps according to users' need, such as experts as user group for scientific maps. The problem for interactive maps for the fuzzy user group "public" is that the parameter "user group" is too vague. In that case user-map interaction is the only parameter that characterizes map use of individual users, which can be used for personalization.

Interaction for this work is defined by two attributes: first there has to be an exchange of data between the user and the map. This can for example be the user clicking on a button. Secondly the map has to react on users' input to be defined as interactive and e.g. show a layer after the user clicked on a button.

RELATED WORK

A taxonomy of adaptive interfaces [9] that defines different parameters of the adaptation process such as what can be adapted, to what is it adapted, when is it to happen, and who controls the process, builds the very basis of this work and helps to understand the complexity of options within an adaptation process.

Work about adaptive maps has especially been done for mobile purposes. Usability issues and thus the need for adaptation stem from the small display size and limited transfer rates. Examined have been adaptive maps for mobile use in tourism [10, 15], usability of adaptive maps [6, 11], adapting map symbols [11], and user-adaptive mobile guides [6, 10, 14, 15]. Only recent articles describe the use of adaptation and personalization techniques for web mapping [7, 13].

The difference between existing work mentioned above and the presented work is that most examples which track interaction, infer on users' interest and thus provide users with feature content that is supposed to be interesting for them [7, 13]. We see a lack in basic research on map-user interaction with internet maps, because we suppose that this is necessary to develop strategies for personalization and to provide users with suitable functions, help and content. Considering just the content that interests users is not enough, as map functions have to be suitable for the respective tasks as well.

A considerable number of work has been done on map interaction in general. Starting with discussions about what makes maps interactive and listing prevalent kinds of interaction [e.g. 1]. Existing typologies describe the steps that are done to complete a task, the different kinds users navigate through data [5] or classify interaction into levels beginning with the least interactive functions and ending with the most interactive ones [3]. These typologies do not seem ample for the aim of this work, because the classification has to be suitable to deliver data that is appropriate to build map interaction patterns.

Van Elzakker's [2] model of geographic problem solving gives an overview how to proceed in map use research. The suggested approach is to decide for the map type first. This is essential as tasks vary very much with the map type. An example would be "exploratory cartography", where cartographic visualization adds to explore unknown geographic data to get an overview. Then he clarifies the overall objective of the task, such as "getting information about noise in my district". Next he defines map use tasks to reach the objective, which consist of answering basic geographic questions (e.g. What is here?) and analytical tasks (e.g. How many subjects are here?). Map operations, which are physical actions, such as zooming, result from the objective and map use tasks.

STATEMENT OF THESIS

The superior hypothesis of this work is that personalized maps that adapt automatically to users' needs are better for a big and thus fuzzy user group on the internet. This hypothesis is based on the problem that public information maps do often not suit a plurality of users.

Our theory is that comprehensive knowledge about the interaction with maps is needed to personalize them to individual users. Therefore we hypothesize the following:

- There are interaction patterns in map use. These are recurring sequences of consecutive actions which are needed to complete a task (e.g. choose a map, choose a layer, zoom in...).
- These interaction patterns classify users in different user groups. We assume that users are characterized by their interaction behavior and that e.g. experts and laymen can be identified because of their unique interaction style respectively. Therefore the follow-up of single actions, which are necessary for a task, is decisive. Research questions to gain insight into user-map interaction are: "In which groups can map users be classified according to their map interaction patterns? How is their interaction characterized?"
- Patterns and groups that will be found are appropriate to develop a strategy for personalization. The corresponding research question is: "Which parameters for personalization can be derived from interaction patterns? How are they to interpret for personalization?"

RESEARCH GOALS AND METHODS

Since no work has been done that evaluates and interprets user-map interaction to serve as basis for personalization it will be done within this work. The objective is to derive map interaction patterns, which are recurring sequences of single user actions. The **goal** of this work is to contribute by developing a theoretical concept to define parameters for personalization on the basis of map interaction patterns. They will be derived from an empirical study of user-map interaction.

As the research focus is on interaction with maps, observation is a suitable **method** to gain insights, which for example questionnaires could not give. For observation, eye tracking and screen recording are useful. Additionally, interaction can be logged and the "think aloud" method can be applied to get insights on what users think while interaction.

We will conduct a laboratory study with standardized tasks based on the aforementioned model [2]. To guarantee general applicability a sample as representative as possible is to be chosen for the study. Additionally „one should often aim to study more than one task: if the same phenomenon is seen under widely varying task conditions, one can tentatively conclude that the phenomenon is a general one.“ [4]

Preliminary work for the study is first the definition of the map type that will be examined. Because the exploration of unknown geographic data is a popular use case on the internet, "exploratory cartography" is chosen as map type. In a next step the objectives of map use and map use tasks will be examined and defined, "as the analytical tasks, their relative importance and the possible orders in which they are executed [...] may differ considerably, because of differences in the overall objectives of the spatial data exploration. It is clear, for instance, that task scenarios will differ when a user is exploring a spatial dataset in order to find a suitable place to live or when he/she is doing that in order to gain insight into the geographical aspects of the results of elections. " [2].

As the observed interactions will consist of many single actions it will be necessary to filter them according to relevance and weight them to derive interaction patterns. Therefore the data will be aggregated, which means combined into single units, according to defined characteristics. This is a crucial step to extract relevant information and derive knowledge. The **map-based interaction types** listed below are inspired by Mac Aoidh's mouse movement hierarchy [8]. They will be used for the aggregation of single actions and are thought to weight actions to distinguish necessary from unnecessary information.

Map perception:

Map perception can be observed with eye tracking. It is according to our definition no real interaction, but it shows the area of attention.

Functional interaction:

- Functional software operations:
  Interaction which is necessary to operate an interactive map, such as adjusting windows, saving bookmarks etc.
- Not appropriated interaction:
  Interaction that is "a means to an end", e.g. the mouse movement to a button. The click on the button would be intentional interaction; the movement to the button is only functionally necessary and thus functional interaction.

Intentional interaction (explicit interaction):

- Interaction with thematic content:
  Interaction that is appropriated to reach a goal and done consciously, e.g. to toggle map layers.
- Interaction with spatial content:
  General navigation, such as map adjustment, zooming, panning etc.

Unintentional interaction (implicit interaction):

Interaction, such as moving the mouse cursor along a line while reading, which happens subconsciously.

Users' input in personalized maps happens implicitly and unintentional as well. The user interacts with the map, which adapts in many cases automatically. The users do, in case of automatic adaptation, not know what triggered the adaptation.

Accidental interaction:

Interaction that is carried out by mistake, such as accidentally moving the map, or mixing up zoom in and zoom out.

Results will consist firstly of observed interaction patterns. These patterns will be derived from an observation with the help of the above mentioned map-based interaction types. The patterns will be the basis for recommendations for map personalization. To illustrate these recommendations a mock up of a personalized map will be developed.

DISSERTATION STATUS

An already achieved result is the elaboration on a user typology of eParticpation users [12]. The survey provided insights into the given possibilities to build user types with data from web analytics tools. The outcome is that building user groups based on this data, does not work, therefore map use and interaction have to be examined in detail.

We did an extensive literature research about map personalization, interaction and human-computer interaction with focus on maps and GIS and developed preliminary map-based interaction types to derive interaction patterns that will be enhanced after studies.

As the map type for the observation has already been defined in the near future possible objectives of map users, the concrete map use tasks and possible physical actions have to be clarified. Based on them hypotheses for the interaction patterns will be developed to produce or choose appropriate map examples for the user study. As soon as we have a clearer idea about objectives and map use tasks we will conduct pre-tests to approve our interaction typology. To get a first insight into map interaction we will explore screen recordings of a map usability survey. These maps were very simple, no functions like zoom, etc. were offered, but we suppose to be able to identify patterns in map reading (e.g. some users move the mouse cursor along the text of the legend while reading). In 2012 experiments to derive map interaction patterns are planned that will be evaluated and published.

OPEN QUESTIONS

Especially the methodology needs additional work. We got a broad overview, but need to adapt the methods better to our goals. Firstly the methods for the observation of map interaction and the tasks which are observed have to be clarified. Open questions therefore are:

- What are the objectives using exploratory maps? What are the map use tasks and physical actions?
- What kind of tasks is representative to guarantee general applicability of results?
- Are eye tracking and screen recording sufficient methods to gain results, or are additional methods like interaction logs and the "think aloud method" necessary?

Secondly it has to be defined how the data is evaluated and further exploited for the personalization strategy. This is supposed a very important step, as actions will be weighted for further usage. An open question concerning the evaluation is: Are the map-based interaction types sufficient for weighting and aggregating actions?

Also the format of the strategy for personalization is not defined yet. In this context especially an exchange with experts from the broad area of intelligent user interfaces would be enriching, to get feedback on the research of interaction and to discuss the evaluation and interpretation of data to use it for personalization.

REFERENCES

1. Crampton, J.W. Interactivity Types in Geographic Visualization. In *Cartography and Geographic Information Science*, Vol. 29, No. 2 (2002), (pp. 85-98).
2. Elzakker, C.P.J.M. van. Map use tasks in regional exploratory studies. In Mapping the 21st Century. *Proceedings of the 20th International Cartographic Conference*, Beijing, (2001), (pp. 2496-2505).
3. Elzakker, C.P.J.M. van. The use of maps in the exploration of geographic data. In *Netherlands Geographical Studies* 326. Utrecht/Enschede, (2004).
4. Davies, C. and D. Medyckyj-Scott. Feet on the Ground: studying User-GIS Interaction in the workplace. In Nyerges, T.L. et al. (eds.) Cognitive Aspects of Human-Computer Interaction for Geographic Information Systems. Kluwer Academic Publishers, (1995), (pp. 123-139).
5. Haak, J. Interaktivität als Kennzeichen von Multimedia und Hypermedia. In Issing, L.J. and Klimsa, P. (Hrsg.). Information und Lernen mit Multimedia, (1997), (pp. 152-166).
6. Nivala, A.-M. and L.T. Sarjakowski. User Aspects of Adaptive Visualisation for Mobile Maps. In *Cartography and Geographic Information Science*, Towards Ubiquitous Cartography, 34 (4), (2007), (pp. 275-284).
7. Mac Aoidh, E. , McArdle, G. , Petit, M. , Ray, C. , Bertolotto, M. , Claramunt, C. and D. Wilson. Personalization in adaptive and interactive GIS. In *Annals of GIS*, 15: 1, (2009a), (pp. 23- 33).
8. Mac Aoidh, E., Wilson, D.C. and M. Bertolotto. A Study of Spatial Interaction Behaviour for Improved Delivery of Web-Based Maps. In Carswell, J.D. et al. (eds.) W2GIS 2009, LNCS 5886, Springer, Berlin Heidelberg, (2009b), (pp. 120-134).
9. Malinowski, U., Kühme, T., Dieterich, H. and M. Schneider-Hufschmidt. A taxonomy of adaptive user interfaces. In Monk, A., Diaper, D. and M.D. Harrison (eds.). *HCI'92, People and Computers VII*. Cambridge University Press (1992), (pp. 391-414).
10. Reichenbacher, T. Adaptive Methods for Mobile Cartography. Proceedings of the *21st International Cartographic Conference* (ICC), (2003), (pp.1311-1322).
11. Sarjakowski, L.T. and A.-M. Nivala. Adaptation to Context - A Way to Improve the Usability of Mobile Maps. In Meng, L., Zipf, A. and T. Reichenbacher (eds.). Map-based Mobile Services, Theories, Methods and Implementations, Springer, NY, (2005), (pp. 107-123).
12. Weninger, B., Krek Poplin, A. and J. Petrin. Developing a Typology of Public Participation 2.0 Users: an Example of Nexthamburg.de. In Schrenk, M., Popovich, V., Engelke, D. and P. Elisei (eds.). *REAL CORP 2010 Proceedings*, (2010).
13. Wilson, D., Bertolotto, M. and J. Weakliam. Personalizing map content to improve task completion efficiency. In *International Journal of Geographic Information Science*, Vol. 24, No. 5, May, (2010), (pp. 741-760).
14. Zimmermann, A. and A. Lorenz. LISTEN: a user-adaptive audio-augmented museum guide. In *User Modeling and User-Adapted Interaction*, Vol. 18, No. 5, (2008), (pp.389-416).
15. Zipf, A. User-Adaptive Maps for Location□Based Services (LBS) for Tourism. *ENTER 2002 – International Congress on Tourism and Communication Technologies in Tourism*, Innsbruck, (2000).

Evaluating an Organic User Interface for Learning Mathematics

Wong Bee Suan
Victoria University of Wellington
RH506 – SIM
P.O. Box 600
New Zealand 6140
Suan.wong@vuw.ac.nz
+6012 286 8003

ABSTRACT

The current formats used for presenting mathematics either on paper or in electronic form have usability limitations that make learning mathematics challenging. The concept of an Organic User Interface, promises a natural interface that blends with the human ecology system and therefore affords smoother transition and improved usability. This research aims to examine how the affordances of an Organic User Interface influence users learning of important mathematical concepts. The relationship between learning time and the usability factors, or affordances of an Organic User Interface will be determined and contrasted with those of Graphical User Interfaces.

Author Keywords

Organic User Interface; Affordance; Usability; learning time

ACM Classification Keywords

H.1.2 User/Machine System: Human Information Processing

General Terms

Learnability; Graphical User Interface; Organic User Interface

INTRODUCTION

Computer applications, handheld devices, and other specific tools like MathPad[2] are created with the same aim, to make complex subjects like mathematics easy to learn [10]. All these tools in the past were bounded by planar surfaces that have usability limitations but this trend is changing with the availability of the concept of an Organic User Interfaces. This non-planar interface has clear affordances and is deformable, which make it a potentially good tool for learning mathematics. This research aims to establish the usability factors that an Organic User Interface has with focus on affordance as compare to Graphical User Interface, which may reduce learning time of users.

RELATED WORK

Learning mathematics involves the manipulation and understanding of different diagrams, sketches, equations and formulas and the visualization of several of these being presented together [2,6]. Different applications and methods have been developed to address different needs of learning mathematics but the aim is always to make learning an easier task [2,6]. Normally these solutions have been deployed on computers using Graphical User Interfaces.

Recently, it has been proven empirically that human problem solving reasoning, including mathematical is "based in tacit spatial-temporal simulated action" [1]

Studies have been done on human-centered design that advocates modeling users' natural behavior so that interfaces can be designed to be more intuitive and natural, and freer of performance errors [7]. This natural interface design has the potential to shorten the learning time for users.

An Organic User Interface is defined as a computer interface that uses a non-planar display as input as well as output and has the ability to deform through manipulation and interaction with users [5,8]. There are three main principles of an Organic User Interface: input equals output, form equals function, and form follows flow [5,8]. The advances in user interface incorporated in Organic User Interfaces are made possible by breakthroughs in display, sensor, input and other technologies. Commercial products such as the iPhone, Nike running shoes, among others are some of the early forms of the Organic User Interface [5, 8].

The affordance of a user interface contributes to the usability of that interface. Hartson further clarified the concept by categorizing it according to cognitive, physical, sensory and functional affordances [4,9].

One of the greatest advantages of Organic User Interface is its affordance. The study in this area is still not being fully explored as most studies are focusing on the technical aspects of Organic User Interface. With its affordance and usability, it provides an interface that enables users to interact intuitively with minimum learning time.

STATEMENT OF THESIS OR PROBLEM

To date, the potential of using a natural interface such as the Organic User Interface to learn mathematics has not been investigated in the field.

It is the aim of this research to investigate this potential as compare to solutions that have been done by using Graphical User Interface. The problem statement:

Establish a usability framework for the affordances of an Organic User Interface to learn mathematics and to explore the relationship between the framework and learning time.

a. Establishing a usability framework that identifies the usability factors for an Organic User Interface with a focus on the affordances of that interface.

b. Measuring with a range of learnability metrics interaction of a user with an Organic User Interface compared with a Graphical User Interface.

RESEARCH GOALS AND METHODS

The main research goal is to establish the usability framework for an Organic User Interface by:

a. Developing a theoretical framework – examining previous work focusing on the User Action Framework and establishing the Usability Framework for an Organic User Interface.

b. Conducting lab experiments – comparing the time a user takes in learning mathematics using the Graphical User Interface or an Organic User Interface. The results collected will be analyzed using a range of learnability metrics.

c. Conducting a Survey – After the lab experiments, users will be requested to do a survey. The survey will ask usability related questions exploring the users' perception of the interface. This is to strengthen the findings in a. & b.

Lab experiments & the survey (b. & c.) will help to triangulate and justify the theoretical framework (a.).

DISSERTATION STATUS

I am currently researching, preparing, and starting to write the proposal, which includes sections on the research problem & objectives, literature review, methodology, details on data collection and how the data is going to be being analyzed. There will be a presentation for my proposal and I can start with the data collection once the proposal is accepted and the University Human Ethics Committee has approved it. I hope to be able to present the proposal by mid 2012.

I have found a substantial literature on learning mathematics using different applications and methods such as MathPad2, handheld devices and applications based.

Also, I have found much literature on the Organic User Interface relating to the technical aspects including e-Ink, OLED, or kinetic energy and others.

Most of my writing is in rough draft and on isolated but related topics. My future plans are to continue looking in-depth into usability frameworks and Organic User Interfaces and also to produce some possible sample experiments for testing purposes. I anticipate this may take another 6 months. Since this is an emerging area, I hope to gain greater insight from the **IUI 2012 Doctoral Consortium** and also to look for opportunities to work with people who have already developed interfaces that I can utilize. In this way, I am able to contribute on the cognitive aspects of Organic User Interface, which is to learn mathematics. I also hope that there will be stimulated exchanges and brainstorming sessions that further promote this area of study.

OPEN QUESTIONS

Organic User Interface is still being developed in the technical aspects and not much has been explored in the cognitive area yet. It is therefore challenging to carry out empirical study in this area at the moment, as there is limited fully developed organic interface. Some of the questions are:

i) How to create the "Organic" interface and in what form?

ii) Whether it is viable to compare the learning time between Graphical User Interface and Organic User Interface? This question arises as it maybe difficult to obtain results that have sufficient distinction to draw conclusion at the later stage.

iii) Further discussion on the Mathematic related case study to be used during the lab experiments and selection of metrics to measure learnability.

CONCLUSION

In conclusion, this research aims to measure with a range of learnability metrics interaction of a user with an Organic User Interface compared with a Graphical User Interface. Also, to establish usability framework that identifies the usability factors for an Organic User Interface with a focus on affordances of that interface.

REFERENCES

[1] Abrahamson, D., & Trninic, D. Toward an Embodied-Interaction Design Framework for Mathematical Concepts. in *Proc. IDC,* (2011)

[2] Dragunov, A. N., & Herlocker, J. L. Designing intelligent and dynamic interfaces for communicating mathematics. In *Proc. IUI*, (2003).

[3] Hartson, H. R. Cognitive, physical, sensory, and functional affordances in interaction design. *Behaviour and Information Technology*, 22(5), (2003), 315-338.

[4] Holman, D., & Vertegaal, R. Organic user interfaces: designing computers in any way, shape, or form. *Commun. ACM*, (2008), 51(6), 48-55.

[5] Joseph J. LaViola, J., & Zeleznik, R. C. (MathPad2: a system for the creation and exploration of mathematical sketches. In *ACM SIGGRAPH* (2006).

[6] Oviatt, S. Human-centered design meets cognitive load theory: designing interfaces that help people think. In *Proc. ACM on Multimedia*, (2006).

[7] Poupyrev, R. V. a. I. Organic User Interfaces. *Organic User Interfaces: A Special Issue of Communicationa of the ACM*, (2008), 51(6).

[8] Vyas, D., Chisalita, C. M., & Veer, G. C. v. d. (2006). Affordance in interaction. In *Proc. CE*, (2004).

Generation Y Interactions

Wei Liu
ID-StudioLab
Delft University of Technology
wei.liu@tudelft.nl

ABSTRACT
Information technology (IT) support of office work has increased rapidly in functionality, but the interaction styles have evolved more slowly. This project explores interaction design opportunities of IT supported tools in the context of office work. A series of (contextual) interviews was conducted with Generation Y office workers, aiming to identify their interaction qualities. Three interactive prototypes were built to map these interaction qualities and to demonstrate future ways of working. This project resulted in a set of design guidelines, aiming to support Generation Y interactions in future office work. Designers and researchers who focus on understanding (rich interactions in) the work context would benefit from the result of this project.

Author Keywords
Generation Y office worker, interaction qualities, interactive prototyping, design guidelines.

ACM Classification Keywords
H.5.2. User Interfaces: User-centered design.

CONTEXT AND MOTIVATION
Today's workplace is dominated by a workforce who has grown up interacting with computers through the ubiquitous set-up of keyboard, display, and mouse. Being somewhat reluctant when it comes to using new technology, they have adapted themselves as well as possible to this set-up, more or less quietly accepting its limitations. However, a new generation of workers is now quickly entering the market. They are called "Generation Y" office workers [1,4,6]. They are digital natives [7], who have been experiencing digital technology their entire lives. Thus they have developed new ways and habits of interacting with their digital world, putting very high demands on the applications, services, devices, and networks that enable and support these interactions. While previous generations waited a week for a film to be returned from the photo lab, "Generation Y" snaps digital pictures with their camera phones, e-mails them to friends, sends them to their Flickr account, and puts them on their Facebook page within minutes. They personalize their Yahoo home pages to get local headlines and weather, choose which news stories to read based on topic and create their own greatest hits collections by downloading their favorite songs. Songs that they share through social networks with a large community of virtual friends, with whom they have frequent and immediate contact through email, instant messaging, and cell phones.

IUI'12, February 14–17, 2012, Lisbon, Portugal.

STATEMENT OF THESIS OR PROBLEM
"Generation Y" fully embraces new and innovative technologies. They are tech-savvy multi-taskers, who are very demanding when it comes to their working equipment [6]. But in today's workplace, rich interactions between office workers and work context are still missing. The problem lies in the conflicts through how they interact with artefacts. Besides, advanced and visionary interaction techniques from telerobotics and computer games, as for example portrayed in movies such as Minority Report, are beginning to find their way into serious applications (e.g. multi-touch in the Apple iPhone or Microsoft Surface), but the balance falls through to completely visual interaction. Studies of human cognition, however, show that both visual and verbal thinking modes are important in creative work, and that different people use different styles, sometimes for different work [4,5]. To cater to this new generation of workers, future business applications and services should thus fit in with richer ways of interaction that go beyond keyboard, mouse, and display. The goal of this project is therefore to explore "Generation Y" interactions within the context of office work, to develop new tools and applications that support these interactions and to study how they could affect future ways of working.

RESEARCH QUESTIONS
The main research question deals with the intersections of my research framework: how can new interactions assist "Generation Y" office workers efficiently and pleasantly in their work? The sub-questions include:

- What are the characteristics/classifications of "Generation Y" office workers?
- What are the relevant trends/opportunities in interaction design?
- How to map these characteristics into the development of "Generation Y" interfaces?
- How well do the new interfaces improve work?

RESEARCH FRAMWORK

Figure 1 shows our research framework, which distinguishes three major components: "Generation Y" (people), information technology (IT) and work context. On the intersections of these three components lie the interactions we want to understand. Literature research provided us with an overview of current knowledge, trends, and the state-of-the-art for each component, but also revealed that not much has been published on the intersections. Therefore, in a series of (contextual) interviews, we tried to gain insights at these intersections. In further studies we intend, mainly through prototyping and case studies, to explore interaction design opportunities with our understanding of these intersections, and ultimately to come to guidelines for supporting "Generation Y" interactions in office work situations.

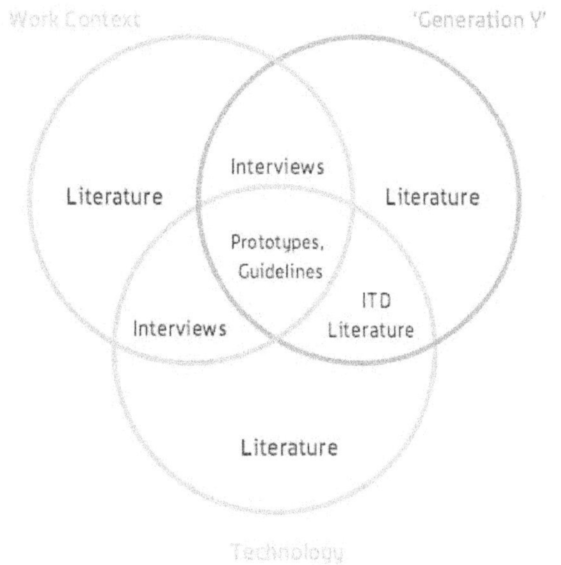

Figure 1. Research framework.

RESEARCH GOALS

The main goal of this project is to explore and develop new "Generation Y" interactions and to study how they affect future ways of working. The detailed goals include:

- To acquire a thorough understanding of the classifications/characteristics of "Generation Y" office workers, specifically on how they interact in their (digital) working environments.
- To investigate relevant trends/opportunities in new media and user interface design.
- To apply "Generation Y" characteristics into the development of new interactive tools, techniques and/or applications that assist "Generation Y" workers in their (digital) work.
- To evaluate these new interactive tools, techniques and/or applications on usability and user experience aspects.

RESEARCH APPROACH

Our research and design activities are intertwined in an iterative "Research through Design" cycle [10,11], so new concepts can be quickly visualized and tested, ensuring a high flow of thoughts, ideas, and knowledge. Our design and research is combined in the process of generating new insights and artefacts. Therefore from the beginning and throughout the whole project, prototypes that are rich in aesthetic, expressive, and experiential quality will be built and tested in real contexts. In the first phases of the project the emphasis will be on the exploration of new ways of interacting, while later on in the project the focus will shift to applying these new techniques within the domain of business applications.

Horvath (2007) describes three distinct phases in design inclusive research:

- Explorative Research
- Creative Design Actions
- Confirmative Research Actions

These phases should not be considered as separate steps in my research process. Instead, these different phases are rather intertwined and iterative. Approaches that will be applied are literature review, prototyping, target group interviews, case studies, and evaluations.

DISSERTATION STATUS

Besides literature review, four interviews with "Generation Y" workers have taken place at four companies in spring 2010. We found that this type of office workers put very high demands on the applications, services, devices, and networks that enable and support collaborative work. They expressed that some (online) collaborative tools that assist them efficiently and pleasantly in their private life were not available or did not meet their expectation in their work settings. From these interviews, we have identified six key interaction qualities [2,8,12] typical for "Generation Y" (table 1).

Qualities	Private Life	Work
Instant	Use Twitter to tweet	Check email
Collaborative	Game with virtual friends	Discuss in group
Playful	Send emoticon in Skype	Watch a video in a PPT
Expressive	Shake iPhone to shuffle	Present a PPT
Responsive	Tap to wake up a device	Answer a phone
Flexible	Telework besides office	Work in office

Table 1. Examples of Qualities of Interactions in Private Life and Work.

A prototyping study took place in spring 2011, aiming to demonstrate novel Generation Y interactions by mapping interaction qualities (instant, playful, collaborative, expressive, responsive and flexible) identified in the private and work contexts. In an interactive prototyping course three prototypes were built in which these qualities are demonstrated [11]. DropBall is one of the three prototypes. DropBall is an explorative concept for fun and easy file transfer (see Figure 2). With DropBall users can transfer files by throwing a physical and familiar object: a stress ball. Colleagues are enabled to share digital files and links on this ball through an easy user interface. A squeeze in the ball triggers a desktop application to pop up, and while squeezing the ball the user can drag and drop files into the digital representation of the ball. Now the fun starts. Pick out a colleague you would like to share the information with, and throw the ball towards him/her. Once received, the colleague only needs to squeeze the ball to make the files appear on screen, and clear the data ready for next use.

Figure 2. Workflow of DropBall.

In summer 2011, a series of contextual interviews has been conducted involving "Generation Y" office workers from different work domains and backgrounds, focusing on the way in which they interact with IT supported home and work activities [9]. From learning and comparing these user interactions in the six interaction qualities (instant, playful, collaborative, expressive, responsive and flexible), we found that the office workers experienced the interaction qualities in their home context as generally richer than the interactions in their work context. They regarded instant, collaborative, and expressive as more important interaction qualities in work context. They experienced the interactions in home context as more playful, expressive, responsive, and flexible than in work context. They also expressed the wish to experience the same interaction qualities in work context. The instant and collaborative qualities were exceptions. They experienced these interactions as equally instant in home and work contexts. They experienced the interactions in home context as less collaborative. These findings have implications on the development of future office services that should utilize the power and advantages of the interaction qualities, yet integrate the rich interaction qualities from home context to work context. This study resulted in a set of design guidelines for supporting "Generation Y" interactions, specifically focused on new ways of working. Many of these design guidelines can also be used in the development of other office services and/or tools for conceptualization. Especially the latter draws attention to IT supporting alternative ways of interacting that are currently emerging from organizing, mixing, and separating work and private life. Below are the guidelines:

- **Promote instant (mobile) communication when working -** the interaction has to allow the office worker to experience working seamlessly and regardless of locations.
- **Endow playfulness in physical office services -** playfulness is highly valuable, but is only appreciated when the office worker does low-attention office tasks. Attention should be therefore directed towards the context of use, which has to be organized and presented in a playful way.
- **Design collaborative group interactions among offices** - today's offices are often geographically spread in one company. Therefore the interaction should be designed to support information exchange for collaborative working.
- **Enable expressive user input actions for commonly used office services** - the interaction should focus on adding expressiveness to input actions, instead of falling into visual effects (e.g. pretty icons).
- **Provide immediate and responsive feedback for all interactions in the office** - the interaction should afford a high degree of responsiveness to provide the office worker with immediate user feedback.
- **Keep work content flexible and customizable -** the interaction should possess a highly flexible character, enabling the office worker to fully concentrate on the workflow. The customization should allow the office worker to set personal preferences in a high degree (e.g. customize settings and reorganize the interface).
- **Switch modes between home and work tasks –** the office worker should be able to switch between home and work modes. The interaction should provide a natural way to switch the two modes, because they are increasingly merging.

We have argued that to successfully support the generation of office workers that is now currently entering the market, future business tools and services should fit in with richer ways of user interactions. The challenges lie in further supporting "Generation Y" interactions within the context of office work, developing new tools that support these interactions, and studying how they could affect future ways of working. We need to do further studies to determine these challenges fit into concrete work contexts on interaction qualities in industrial practice. Conducting more qualitative research studies to further identify and formulate design guidelines as well as designing and testing, through a "research through design" cycle [10,11], prototypes in which these guidelines are implemented, will thus be critical to support "Generation Y" interactions in a work context. Our next step is to design prototypes of office services in which these design guidelines are implemented. These prototypes will demonstrate how the design guidelines can be used, and will also assess how well the design guidelines can benefit the future office work. Designers and researchers who focus on understanding work context would benefit from the result of our study.

OPEN QUESTIONS

We would like to pose the following open questions to the expert audience that will be at the panel of the doctoral consortium:

- How can we improve the research framework?
- How can we move from research data to prototype building?
- How can we structure the studies done so far into thesis writing?

We would like to gain the following experiences from attending the doctoral consortium:

- Peer review.
- Knowledge exchange on methods and skills.

REFERENCES

1. Accenture. *Millennial are at the Gates.* High Performance IT Research (2008).
2. Arvola, M. *Interaction Design Qualities: Theory and Practice.* Proceedings of the 6th Nordic Conference on Human-Computer Interaction: Extending Boundaries, New York: ACM Press (2010).
3. Horvath I. *Comparison of Three Methodological Approaches of Design Research.* In Proceedings of International Conference on Engineering Design ICED '07, Paris, France, (2007), 28-31.
4. Litmus. *Decoding the Digital Millennials.* Colombus, OH: Resource Interactive (2006).
5. Oblinger, D. G., Oblinger, J. L. *Educating the Net Generation.* EDUCAUSE (2005). http://www.educause.edu/educatingthenetgen/
6. Oxygen Report. *Generation Y and the Workplace Annual Report 2010.* Johnson Controls (2010).
7. Prensky, M. *Digital Natives, Digital Immigrants.* On the Horizon, 9, 5 (2001).
8. Ross, P. R., Wensveen, S. A. G. *Designing Aesthetics of Behavior in Interaction: Using Aesthetic Experience as a Mechanism for Design.* International Journal of Design 4, 2 (2010), 3-13.
9. Sleeswijk Visser, F. *Context Mapping: Experiences from Practice.* International Journal of CoCreation in Design and the arts 1, 2 (2005), 119-149.
10. Stappers, P. J. *Doing Design as a Part of Doing Research.* Design Research Now: Essays and Selected Projects. Birkhauser Verlag AG (2007), 81-91.
11. Stappers, P. J., Hekkert, P., etal. Consolidating the *User-Centered Design Focus in Industrial Design Engineering.* The 9th Conference on Engineering & Product Design Education. New Castle (2007), 69-74.
12. Taylor, S. J., Bogdan, R. *Introduction to Qualitative Research Methods (3rd ed.).* New York: John Wiley (1998).

Active Forms for Responsive Environments

Simon Scott-Harden
School of Design,
Northumbria University,
87 New Bridge Street,
Newcastle upon Tyne, E1 2SW. UK.
simon.scott-harden@northumbria.ac.uk

ABSTRACT

Active Forms are interactive artefacts that are a focal point of attention for the user. Such devices are interactive and can change shape. They are embedded with both sensors and actuators and are a visualisation and embodiment of some application or service. To be more specific, Active Forms are defined as interactive products or devices that can render content thanks to perceptible changes to their physical form and appearance. We see Active Forms as ideal gateway for the interaction with and the control of Responsive Environments (RE) as defined in [1].

Tangible interaction is the precursor of Active Forms, it was essentially about coupling digital content and physical elements of an interface in an integrating combination. The content is about the internal state of the products and about some of the application(s) and service(s) they support. The tangible interaction focuses on the interface or systems that are physically embodied in the physical artifact. Tangible User Interfaces (TUI) are reactive devices that require a user input to change shape. Active Forms, on the other hand are interactive devices that change shape and appearance. The changes in the Active Forms are a result of either, user actions or internal actuators, both the physical form, such as shape or size, and the appearance, such as colour or temperature, can change.

Within Active Forms, there is a balance to be had between the cognitive load on the user, the selection of modalities, the media bandwidth and the user attention. The aim being to have the Active Forms as the user focus of interaction and attention. We have listed below some of the key features of Active Forms:

- Active Forms are interactive devices that are both reactive to user actions and proactive in displaying information.
- Active Forms are a gateway to applications or services within the RE and there is a change to the internal state of the device.
- The user actions and the device reactions of an Active Form are merged and are spatially co-located.
- Active Forms act as their embodiment, as physical objects, Active Forms also have aesthetic value per se.
- The changes in the Active Forms are a result of either, user actions or internal actuators, both the physical form, such as shape or size, and the appearance, such as colour or temperature, can change.

AUTHER KEYWORDS

Tangible interaction, smart objects, user experience, embedded interaction, merged modalities, interactive products.

ACM CLASSIFICATION KEYWORDS

H.5.2. Information interfaces and presentation: User Interfaces.

GENERAL TERMS

Design; Experimentation.

CONTEXT AND MOTIVATION

A definition of RE is one of physical spaces enhanced with a system that deliver context awareness, ubiquitous computing, natural interaction and a pre-defined user experience (UX). A particular point of interest when it comes to RE is the gateway between people and the environment; the connection between the RE as a system and the people as users. We are keen to investigate the gateway as an interactive artifact that is an embodiment of the RE and a focal point of attention of the user, where the embodiment of the RE is in an interactive gateway. We intend to investigate such a gateway as interactive and changing forms that are embedded with both sensors and actuators and are a visualisation and embodiment of the RE.

My prime motivation behind my PhD is to undergo research on Active Forms as gateways to RE, another motivation is to conduct this proposal as an Empirical Research through Design Method [2], by making prototypes, models and running experiments. The benefits of this process will be to create a collection of working devices to demonstrate the concept of Active Forms as RE embodiments and to demonstrate some causal relationships between design decisions and some features of the Active Forms. My research will be set up to deliver explanations about which design of Active Forms delivers what usability and what UX. Therefore I intend to develop causal explanations, arguing that certain design choices will affect certain aspects of usability and of the UX. The user experience is a combination of interaction, perception and aesthetic experiences. An Active Form is the focal point of attention for the user and encapsulates the user's attention; it is the gateway to the application, services and contents. I will start with observations and use inductive reasoning to derive a theory from these observations. This theory will describe a causal relationship between design choices, usability, as well as UX; and will make sense of the observations. It is therefore a *post-factum* theory. The explanatory research that I intend to conduct will focus on highlighting the different design choices that can be made and their effect on the usability of the Active Forms developed as well as the UX that results from it.

Active Forms are interactive products or devices that can render content thanks to perceptible changes to their physical form and appearance. The content is about the internal state of the products and about some of the application(s) and service(s) they support. The changes are a result of either user actions or internal actuators, both the physical form, such as shape or size, and the appearance such as colour or temperature can change. As devices with form, Active Forms have a requirement for aesthetics, affordance [3] and context suitability. As active devices, technology such as sensors and actuators have to be integrated and merged into the interaction. Finally as Active Forms, user experience, information bandwidth, and integration into a context all have to be considered. Active Forms are interactive devices that change shape and appearance as a result of user actions or because of a change to the internal state of the device (such as a phone battery running out) or to the embodied application. Active Forms are both reactive to user actions and proactive in displaying information. There is a balance to be had between the cognitive load on the user, the selection of modalities, the media bandwidth and the user attention handling. As physical objects, Active Forms also have to have an aesthetic value, they have to be designed as well as engineered. Aesthetics, appearance and style are to be considered if the form is to be adopted in everyday context and environments. Inspiration for the form has to come from our surroundings, notably nature; this is to ensure we end up with an intuitive device, where physical properties suggest usage.

Affordance is detrimental and fundamental to the success of the Active Form. It is the quality the Active Form possesses as a device to help the user identify possible actions and it is about the suitability of the afforded interaction in relation to the services and applications supported. However, as the Active Form changes shape or form, the affordance of the device may change to suit the situation and/or context. The integration of the Active Form in its environment is very important, in line with the work on calm and ambient technology [4]. We believe that Active Forms need to be compatible with its environment in terms of domain, genre and design.

The interaction is embedded in the technology, sensors, actuators and processors that are optimised for the interaction proposed. Similarly, the technology, modalities and media are matched to the technology relied on. The user actions and the device reactions of an Active Form are merged and are spatially co-located, what action the user performs is met with a feedback in the same modality and same location (obviously whenever appropriate). There is also a temporal co-location, whereby a user action immediately triggers a feedback through the device, although the start of the feedback needs to be instantaneous, its completion however can be delayed.

RELATED WORK

Rauterberg, Salem and van de Mortel [5] first introduced the notion of Active Forms in their paper "From passive to Active Forms" where they discussed how to design the feedback of the internal state of the interactive products in a intuitive and straightforward way through new approaches notably a change of shape and appearance.

Beyond this initial work, the literature review into this area produced a number of publications relating to the area of research, amongst others: AmI, Ubiquitous computing, TUI and Interaction Design. Weiser [6] has defined the concept of ubiquitous computing as an environment where users are continually interacting with hundreds of nearby wirelessly interconnected computers. These computers are organised around human needs and functions, and they are in a way, invisible to the users. Cooperstock et al. [7] developed a reactive environment, the "Reactive Room", to tackle the burden of controlling simultaneously and seamlessly a myriad of complex devices. They propose that an ICT system should be appropriately designed to infer user's intentions. Similarly Wisneski and colleagues [4] developed the Ambient Room, turning an environment into an interface between users and digital content, mostly through ambient displays. Ishii and Ullmer [8] introduced the concept of "Tangible Bits", allowing users to grasp and manipulate information, by merging interaction and information in everyday objects and architectural surfaces. Ullmer and Ishii [9] introduce the MCRpd (model-control-representation (physical and digital)) interaction model for tangible interfaces, which relates the role of physical and digital representations, physical control, and underlying digital models which all serve as a foundation for identifying and discussing several key characteristics of tangible user interfaces. Ross and Keyson [10] explored interaction design within ambient system control, and suggest the design of tangible interfaces with a shift from technology user to technology presence, as well as a transition, from task-oriented to experience-drive interaction. Farella [11] outlines the recent advances in microelectronics and related fields have made the dream of intelligent spaces and objects come true and identifies significant examples of ongoing research on smart environments, sensitised tangible interfaces applied to smart spaces and assistive technologies are presented. Finally, Alves Lino et al. [1] published their paper on "Responsive Environments: user experiences for ambient intelligence" is of high relevance as it contains an extensive review of the field and defining the concept of Responsive Environment.

STATEMENT OF PHD THESIS OR PROBLEM

We hope to produce new knowledge in the area of Active Forms as a gateway to RE. This should be relevant to both designers and other practitioners interested in interaction design and the development of RE. I also intend to establish research practices in the area of Active Forms and some of their interaction principles. Here are the project actions:

- Preparation into the field of study will require a complete review of Active Forms (as well as some TUI), AmI systems and RE currently being researched and practiced.
- The technology requirements for the Active Forms needs to be identified and sourced such as Information Displays, Light, Sound, Tracking, Sensors and Actuators.
- Infrastructure for RE installation is required to carry out the research. Specifications will be established on how the Active Forms will represent the environment it will be tested in. Any tracking/sensing/actuating equipment required as well as software will also be specified.
- Design and building of the Active Forms within the RE installation using all the technology specified.
- The artifact will be tested within the RE and the analysis will be based on descriptive statistics, analytical statistics using SPSS.
- Data from the analysis will be used as the basis for possible further iterations of the design, build experiment cycles.

In summary, my aim is to develop the concept of Active Forms and demonstrate their suitability as interactive devices acting as gateways to RE. The value of the PhD will be through the production of new knowledge that will help understand the relationship between physical actuated objects, affordance and interaction, furthermore, new knowledge will also be produced about the evaluation of design choices in relation to usability and UX.

The key research question being asked within this thesis is the following; is the combination of user action, system feedback, and system information used within current Tangible Interaction configurations intuitive? Do TUI provide the user with the ability to grasp and manipulate the information? In essence, are Active Forms better than tangible interface?" In this context better is assessed in terms of usability and user experience

RESEARCH METHODOLOGY

The proposed research will combine a comprehensive literature review and the building of an initial collection of prototypes that will allow for the investigation of various design directions that could be taken at later stages of the PhD. The design of the initial prototypes will be informed by the literature review and an awareness of the state of the art in the field of Active Forms including TUI, physical computing and RE.

The main thrust of the research will then come through further iterative design cycles, whereby we propose to develop prototypes that will undergo a series of tests and experiments. These will help establish causal relationships between the designs choices and the usability of the Active Forms as well as the resulting UX, thus contributing to the core of the PhD. The research is therefore mainly practice based, with the intention to deliver up to three iteration stages for the duration of the PhD (i.e. three cycles of designing, producing, testing and analysing Active Forms).

Currently there are no specific theories about the interaction paradigms and principles suitable for Active Forms as gateways to Ambient Intelligence (as this goes beyond ubiquitous computing), and in particular when there is a focus on the UX (i.e. in the case of RE). Therefore, it is proposed that an evaluation and a systematic description of the interaction issues within AmI and specifically the UX will be studied, to eventually establish relationships and patterns between various implementations of interaction paradigms (via the proposed Active Forms) to finally formulate a theory of interaction. The research will be conducted inductively, with a collection of individual instances of Active Forms, and then hopefully proceed to a generalisation that would yield a theory (e.g. Grounded Theory [12]). To assist in this approach, established standards for usability evaluation (e.g. ISO 9241-11 and ISO 25010) will be used as guidance, we will refine further to focus its relevance to Active Forms within the context of RE.

I will start the Empirical Research through Design Method by formulating a hypothesis based on input from the literature review and inspiration from current commercial products. Iteratively, various prototypes of Active Forms will be developed, based on design choices. The prototypes proposed should include both conventional design (aesthetics, form), industrial design (materials, mechanics, rapid prototyping), electronics and ICT. Initial prototypes, and in line with literature, will be based on one of the following:

1. An interactive lamp for the home, that is both intuitive and natural to use, it will fit into the environment and is configurable to the different scenarios that can happen. (e.g. Ross & Keyson [10])
2. A responsive medical device that, post operation, helps the patient understands his/her general condition and visualise signs of recovery through ambient technologies. (Bayer Contour Blood Glucose Meter [13])
3. A household product that is designed to alert the user to an action or an event through interaction of the senses (sight,

hearing, smell, taste, touch, balance and acceleration, temperature, kinesthetic sense, pain and also other internal senses). (Lindam Clarity Digital Video Monitor [14])

The prototypes will be produced in house at the Northumbria University School of Design facilities, relying on the extensive experience available in: rapid prototyping techniques, CNC, CAD, materials, mechanics, engineering, manufacturing knowledge, craftsmanship, and traditional workshop model making techniques.

The prototypes will then be tested based on the underlying hypotheses of causal relationship, important findings will fed into the following design iteration to improve and refine the design choices of the Active Form. This procedure will be repeated at least three times until the right prototype is developed by which the hypothesis of a causal relationship between the design choices and the usability and the UX can be tested. The final prototype will then be used to run an experiment by which the user's perspective will be a fully functional prototype of an Active Form running in context in an RE; as the research question and resulting prototype involves some longitudinal usage (e.g. learnability) it should be tested in a simulated RE (field).

This is research through design, it will involve an increased degree of integration of technology in the successive prototypes of the Active Forms. Embedding sensors in these Active Forms allows the gathering of objective measurements. However, in the preliminary iterations of the research, Wizard of Oz settings will be used, therefore both objective measurements in addition to the subjective data obtained from questionnaires will be recorded. The experiments proposed will be conducted under controlled conditions, there will be both within-subjects (for repeated measurements, and measurements under different conditions) and between-subjects test conditions (for measurements of one condition). During the project, a relevant set of criteria will be selected for the analysis to measure usability and user experience. Inspiration from ISO 9241-11 and ISO 25010 will be used for usability and from Beven [15], Hassenzahl [16] for user experience.

DISSERTATION STATUS

The PhD started in September 2011. The main contribution will be in the generation of new knowledge related to Active Forms and their implementation within the context of Ambient Intelligence. The particular context would be on RE, Ambient Intelligence installations that focuses on the delivery of pre-determined user experiences. The concept of Active Forms and how they could be implemented within a RE will both be at the core of the contribution, which will take the form of publications.

OPEN QUESTIONS

The PhD proposal is truly multidisciplinary in nature, encompassing product design, interaction design, CHI and usability studies, there are some key issues that would need to be addressed in a limited way, within the scope of the research. The PhD main thrust will be about addressing the following topics and they should be raised during the doctoral consortium:

- How to design, measure and assess the user experience?
- What will the embedded interaction be and how to couple it with the affordance of the Active Form?
- How to effectively merge the modalities afforded by the Active Form
- What algorithms for user adaptation should be investigated to ensure a tailored interaction (one that is refined when the user is gaining expertise).

The main reason behind applying to the IUI 2012 Doctoral Consortium is to develop an understanding of designing and evaluating a range of intelligent and innovative interactive systems and user Interfaces with multiple methods and from multiple disciplinary perspectives. This will have a direct relevance to the PhD, there is also interest in how IUI theories can in practice inform the design and evaluation of the work. Using the opportunity to interact and network with other PhD students will be a great benefit to the field of research.

REFERENCES

[1] Alves Lino J., Salem B., Rauterberg M., Responsive Environments: user Experience for Ambient Intelligence, Journal of Ambient intelligence and Smart Environments, 2010, Vol 2, No 4, 347-367.

[2] Keyson D.V., Bruns Alonso, M., Empirical Research Through Design, In Proc. IASDR 2009, 4585-4594.

[3] Gibson, J. J., The ecological approach to visual perception. Lawrence Erlbraum (1979), 235-236. ISBN 0-89859-958-X.

[4] Wisneski, C., Ishii, H., Dahley, A., Gorbet, M., Brave, S., Ullmer, B., Yarin, P., Ambient Displays: Turning architectural space in an interface between people and digital information, Proc. Intl. Workshop on Cooperative Buildings CoBuild'98 (Darmstadt), 1998, DE: Springer.

[5] Rauterberg, M., Salem, B., van de Mortel, D., From passive to Active Forms. In: L. Feijs, S. Kyffin and B. Young (eds.) Proceedings of Design and semantics of form and movements, 2005, DeSForM.

[6] Weiser, M., Some Computer Science Issues in Ubiquitous Computing, Communication of the ACM, 1993, Vol 36, No7, pp.75-84.

[7] Cooperstock., J.R., Fels., S.S., Buxton., W., Smith, K.C., Reactive Environments: Throwing Away your keyboard and Mouse, Communication of the ACM, 1997, Vol 40 No 9, pp. 65-73.

[8] Ishii H, Ullmer B., Tangible bits: towards seamless interfaces between people, bits, and atoms. In:

Proceedings of the CHI'97 conference on human factors in computing systems, 1997, pp 234–241.

[9] Ullmer, B., Ishii, H., Emerging frameworks for tangible user interfaces, IBM Systems Journal, 2000, Vol 39, No 3&4, pp. 915-931.

[10] Ross, P., Keyson, D.V., The Case of Sculpting atmospheres: towards design principles for expressive tangible interaction in control of ambient systems, Personal Ubiquitous Computer, 2007, Vol 11, pp. 69-79.

[11] Farella, E., Ambient Intelligence, Smart Objects and Sensor Networks: practical experiences, IEEE/IFIP International Conference on Embedded and Ubiquitous Computing, 2010, pp. 416-421.

[12] What is Grounded Theory: www.groundedtheoryonline.com/what-is-grounded-theory.

[13] Bayer Contour Blood Glucose Meter: http://www.bayerdiabetes.co.uk/sections/products-for-my-diabetes/meters/bayer-contour-meter/bayer-contour-overview.

[14] Lindam Clarity Digital Video Monitor: http://www.lindam.com/product/monitors/monitors/clarity-digital-video-monitor.html.

[15] Bevan, N., What is the difference between the purpose of usability and user experience evaluation methods? UXEM Workshop at INTERACT 2009.

[16] Hassenzahl, M., User experience (UX): Towards an experiential perspective on product quality, IHM'08 (2008), Proc. Intl. Conf. of the Association Francophone d'Interaction Homme-Machine.

Using Theories of Intrinsic Motivation to Support ICT Learning for the Ageing Population

Tanya Goldhaber
Cambridge University Engineering Department
Engineering Design Centre
Cambridge CB2 1PZ
United Kingdom
tg313@cam.ac.uk
(+44) 7597 711779

ABSTRACT

Access to Information and Communication Technology (ICT) has the potential to improve the quality of life for many members of the ageing population. However, some older users lack the intrinsic motivation to learn to use this technology, and poor user interface design is partly to blame. The research presented here investigates how motivation theory can be applied to interface design in order to encourage older users to learn to use ICT. In addition to a brief literature review, an overview of methods, research goals, and current research status are presented.

Author Keywords
Intrinsic motivation, Ageing population, Inclusive design, Information and Communication Technology (ICT)

ACM Classification Keywords
H.5.2 [Information Interfaces and Presentation]: User Interfaces – User-centred design;

Acknowledgements
The author would like to first and foremost acknowledge her supervisor and co-supervisor, Professor John Clarkson and Dr. Patrick Langdon at the Engineering Design Centre, who were integral to the development of this work. The author would also like to thank British Telecom, in particular BT Retail, for supporting this research.

CONTEXT AND MOTIVATION

As more individuals worldwide are reaching an advanced age, Information and Communication Technology (ICT) systems provide an increasingly promising platform with which to improve the efficiency and effectiveness of healthcare, particularly in a preventative context (Blaschke, Freddolino, & Mullen, 2009; Gupta, Chotard, Ingporsson, Bastos, & Borges, 2009; Rechel, Doyle, Grundy, & McKee, 2009). For example, ICT can enable better communication with carers and medical professionals, allow individuals to better manage their own care, increase independence for older individuals, and reduce some of the problems of social isolation associated with old age (Blaschke et al., 2009; Chaffin & Harlow, 2005). Unfortunately, older people have persistently been slow to adopt ICT and consequently miss out on many of the benefits that could drastically improve their well-being (Czaja et al., 2006; Czaja & Hiltz, 2005; Mynatt, Melenhorst, Fisk, & Rogers, 2004; Wagner, Hassanein, & Head, 2010; Wherton & Prendergast, 2009). Moreover, poor user interface (UI) design is partially responsible for some of the problems with ICT adoption in the ageing population (Czaja et al., 2006; Dickinson, Eisma, Gregor, Syme, & Milne, 2005; Hawthorn, 2000, 2007).

The problems with interface adoption and use in the ageing population are partially problems of motivation: older adults are not necessarily motivated to learn to use existing or new ICT interfaces (Ofcom, 2006). However, while both motivation in older adults (Lawton, Moss, Winter, & Hoffman, 2002; Melenhorst, Rogers, & Bouwhuis, 2006) and the application of motivation theory to UI design (Jung, Schneider, & Valacich, 2010; Williams, Lynch, & Glasgow, 2007) have been studied to some extent, the direct application of motivation theory to UI design for the ageing population has not. Because ICT will continue to present opportunities for improved healthcare and independence for the ageing population, motivating use of ICT is essential. The present research aims to apply psychological theories of motivation, particularly of intrinsic motivation, to UI design in order to create interfaces that inherently motivate learning through increased user interest and engagement.

RELATED WORK

In general, older people are less likely to engage in activities that they do not find enjoyable. As explained by Melenhorst et al. (2001): "Even if they are relatively healthy, older adults realize their place in the life cycle, and experience their lifetime as limited, and, consequently, as precious. They tend to be present-oriented and are reluctant to spend their time in an unpleasant way" (Melenhorst, Rogers, & Caylor, 2001). According to Socioemotional Selectivity Theory (SST), imposed time constraints, including ageing, can lead to a change in overall goals (Carstensen, Isaacowitz, & Charles, 1999), and many older users do not see modern ICT as related to their interests or goals (Hawthorn, 2007). In addition, they may not find the use of an initially difficult and confusing interface enjoyable and may therefore be reluctant to learn to use it even if they are aware of the potential benefits (Melenhorst et al., 2006).

Intrinsic motivation is undertaking a task because it is inherently interesting or enjoyable, not for a separable reward. Because older adults are less likely to engage in activities they do not find enjoyable, creating more intrinsically motivating user interfaces has the strong potential to remove some of the motivational barriers that older adults face when learning to use unfamiliar ICT. Intrinsic motivation has been well-studied in the field of psychology, and there are several prominent theories of intrinsic motivation that give a good framework for thinking about potential design modifications. These are summarised briefly below.

Self-Determination Theory
Self-Determination Theory (SDT) is based on "the hypothesis that there is a set of universal psychological needs that must be satisfied for effective functioning and psychological health" (Deci & Ryan, 2008). Importantly, the fulfilment of these needs predicts not only overall well-being but also the extent to which motivation becomes internalized - intrinsic motivation being the mostly highly internalized form of motivation (Ryan & Deci, 2000) - and the consequent potential for learning (Deci, Vallerand, Pelletier, & Ryan, 1991). These core needs are defined by Deci and Ryan as autonomy, relatedness, and competence (Deci & Ryan, 2000). Earlier literature by White (1959) and Bandura (1977) indicates that competence should be a key area of focus in the present research (Bandura, 1977; White, 1959).

Flow
Another theory of intrinsic motivation is the theory of Flow. Csíkszentmihályi, the researcher who first wrote widely on the Flow experience, identifies three main components of an activity that lead to Flow. The first is a challenge level that is matched to the skill set of the user. Second, an activity must have clear and bounded goals such that the person involved has a direction for their activity. Third, there must be immediate feedback so that the user or actor knows how they are doing. It is essential in order to experience Flow that someone knows that they are accomplishing the goals that have been laid out. (Csikszentmihalyi, 1990). Many non-game interfaces currently lack appropriate challenge level, goals, and feedback, potentially making them less intrinsically motivating to users.

Theory of Intrinsically Motivating Instruction (TIMI)
In the early 1980's, Thomas Malone studied different educational games, both interviewing students about their reactions, likes, and dislikes, also modifying the interfaces in various ways in order to try to isolate motivating properties (Malone, 1981). As the result of this research, he identified three factors that appear to facilitate intrinsically motivating instruction within educational interfaces: challenge, fantasy, and curiosity. Malone's experimental methods also provide a good framework for future experimental work in this area.

The 2 x 2 Achievement Goal Framework
The 2 x 2 Achievement Goal Framework deals with two dimensions of motivation: performance-mastery and approach-avoidance. This framework comprises four achievement goals: "mastery-approach (focused on attaining task-based or intrapersonal competence), performance-approach (focused on attaining normative competence), mastery-avoidance (focused on avoiding task-based or intrapersonal incompetence), and performance-avoidance (focused on avoiding normative incompetence" (Cury, Elliot, Da Fonseca, & Moller, 2006). In general, mastery goals prove more intrinsically motivating than performance goals, and approach goals more so than avoidance goals. It is important that user interfaces try to cultivate a mastery-approach mentality in users.

Positive Design Theory
Ping Zhang (Zhang, 2007, 2008) identifies the need to take a motivational approach to ICT design, explaining that "understand[ing] technology use behaviour and eventually feed[ing] this understanding into technology design...naturally calls for a motivational approach because motivation explains what gives behaviour its energy and direction" (Zhang, 2007). Zhang's papers provide good overviews of how various theories of motivation relate to different design problems.

Funology and Gamification
The idea that non-game interfaces should be fun is often overlooked in the field of Human-Computer Interface (HCI) design (Monk, Hassenzahl, Blythe, & Reed, 2002). While it is obviously not always a desirable feature to have interfaces be fun, particularly when those interfaces are a means to an end, Draper (1999) identifies three scenarios in which fun is an important consideration in design: (1) when fun is the main purpose of the interface, such as a game; (2) when learning is the main function of the interface; and (3) when "learnability is considered as an important secondary requirement of software with some other main function" (Draper, 1999). This third category is applicable to the current research. Monk et al. (2002) proposes the term "Funology" to refer to the study of making interfaces fun for purposes including but not limited to games, the importance of which is recognised in the literature, if not pervasively (Draper, 1999; Rieber, Smith, & Noah, 1998).

STATEMENT OF THESIS OR PROBLEM
Several questions are motivated in the context of this research:

1. Can existing methods of measuring intrinsic motivation (which have largely been normalised on younger individuals) be used with the ageing population?
2. If so, do the principles of intrinsic motivation apply equally well to older people?
3. If so, how can interfaces be made more intrinsically motivating?

Answering the first two questions is essential to the investigation of the third, in which inventories developed in response to the first research question will be used to measure user reaction to UI modifications based on the exploration of the second research question.

RESEARCH GOALS AND METHODS

The present research has several goals. The first goal is the development of a reliable way of measuring older user engagement with ICT. Motivation researchers have developed several methods of measuring intrinsic motivation in user interaction. The first is a standard questionnaire. An initial experiment will combine the SDT-inspired Intrinsic Motivation Inventory (Deci, Egharri, Patrick, & Leone, 1994; Plant & Ryan, 1985; Ryan, 1982; Ryan, Connell, & Plant, 1990; Ryan, Koestner, & Deci, 1991; Ryan, Mims, & Koestner, 1983; University of Rochester Department of Clinical & Social Sciences in Psychology) and the Player Experience of Need Satisfaction inventory (Przybylski, Rigby, & Ryan, 2010; Ryan, Rigby, & Przybylski, 2006) into one questionnaire that will be tested on older users engaged in one of three tasks: a boring task, an interesting skill-matched task, and an overly challenging task. An additional measure of user engagement will be seeing if the subject continues doing the task if the experimenter leaves the room and lets the subject know that it is voluntary to continue (Ryan et al., 1991). These methods were chosen because they have already been used broadly and successfully in the intrinsic motivation literature. There will be a minimum of ten participants per condition, with older users (those over age 60) making up one tested population and younger users (those under age 30) making up another as a control group.

The results of the first experiment will inform a standard method for the rest of the research for measuring user engagement. Research will then focus on modifying user interfaces, likely on a tablet device, and measuring user response. The focus of experiments will be to generate engagement through positive initial experiences and frequent, relevant feedback during use. User engagement and intrinsic motivation as a result of different interface modifications can be measured using the tool developed in the first set of experiments.

These experiments will provide both a set of recommendations for an intrinsically motivating interface design and a method that designers can use to measure the intrinsic motivation of users during the design process.

DISSERTATION STATUS

The research is currently in its second year, having moved beyond the first year assessment procedure, which included a detailed literature review and outlining of methods. At the time of the submission of this report, the author is engaged in pilot studies for the initial set of experiments testing motivation inventories. The three experimental tasks have been set, the questionnaires are being modified and the experimental conditions are being finalised. Pilot work indicates that subjects do indeed find the tasks boring, interesting, or overly challenging according to condition, but not enough subjects have been tested to attribute statistical significance to these findings or to anticipate the significance of any results.

A key goal is to produce a questionnaire that can be used to assess user engagement with various ICT devices and interfaces in order to discern which interface modifications result in more intrinsic motivation in older users. It is anticipated that data for the first set of experiments will be collected by early 2012, and subsequent experiments will take up to a year, leaving the latter half of 2013 for data analysis and dissertation write-up.

At present, a paper adapted from the literature review of the author's first year report has been accepted to and will be presented at the 2012 Cambridge Workshop on Universal Access and Assistive Technology (CWUAAT) (Goldhaber, Langdon, & Clarkson, in press).

OPEN QUESTIONS

While the method for the first set of experiments is almost completed, design modifications for the second phase of the research have not been finalised. Feedback from expert interface designers and other design researchers would be very helpful in order to design the best possible set of experiments to test user engagement and motivation based on interface modifications. In addition, it would be useful to know how the research could be modified to be most useful to designers. Finally, it would be helpful to gain feedback on the data that will be gathered by early 2012, including ideas for analysis and preliminary conclusions.

REFERENCES

1. Bandura, A. (1977). Self-efficacy: Toward a Unifying Theory of Behavioral Change. *Psychological Review, 84*(2), 191-215.
2. Blaschke, C. M., Freddolino, P. P., & Mullen, E. E. (2009). Ageing and Technology: A Review of the Research Literature. *British Journal of Social Work, 39*(4), 641-656.
3. Carstensen, L. L., Isaacowitz, D. M., & Charles, S. T. (1999). Taking time seriously - A theory of socioemotional selectivity. *American Psychologist, 54*(3), 165-181.
4. Chaffin, A. J., & Harlow, S. D. (2005). Cognitive Learning Applied to Older Adult Learners and Technology. *Educational Gerontology, 31*, 301-329.
5. Csikszentmihalyi, M. (1990). *Flow : the psychology of optimal experience*. New York: Harper & Row.
6. Cury, F., Elliot, A. J., Da Fonseca, D., & Moller, A. C. (2006). The social-cognitive model of achievement motivation and the 2x2 achievement goal framework. *Journal of Personality and Social Psychology, 90*(4), 666-679.
7. Czaja, S. J., Charness, N., Fisk, A. D., Hertzog, C., Nair, S. N., Rogers, W. A., et al. (2006). Factors predicting the use of technology: Findings from the center for research and education on aging and technology enhancement (CREATE). *Psychology and Aging, 21*(2), 333-352.
8. Czaja, S. J., & Hiltz, S. R. (2005). Digital aids for an aging society. *Communications of the Acm, 48*(10), 43-44.
9. Deci, E. L., Egharri, H., Patrick, B. C., & Leone, D. R. (1994). Facilitating Internalization - the Self-Determination Theory Perspective. *Journal of Personality, 62*(1), 119-142.
10. Deci, E. L., & Ryan, R. M. (2000). The "what" and "why" of goal pursuits: Human needs and the self-determination of behavior. *Psychological Inquiry, 11*(4), 227-268.
11. Deci, E. L., & Ryan, R. M. (2008). Self-Determination Theory: A Macrotheory of Human Motivation, Development, and Health. *Canadian Psychology-Psychologie Canadienne, 49*(3), 182-185.
12. Deci, E. L., Vallerand, R. J., Pelletier, L. G., & Ryan, R. M. (1991). Motivation and Education: The Self-Determination Perspective (Vol. 26, pp. 325 - 346): Routledge.
13. Dickinson, A., Eisma, R., Gregor, P., Syme, A., & Milne, S. (2005). Strategies for teaching older people to use the World

Wide Web. *Universal Access in the Information Society, 4*(1).
14. Draper, S. W. (1999). Analysing fun as a candidate software requirement. *Personal and Ubiquitous Computing, 3*(3), 117-122.
15. Goldhaber, T., Langdon, P. M., & Clarkson, P. J. (in press, March 2012). *Intrinsic Motivation and Design of ICT for the Ageing Population.* Paper presented at the Cambridge Workshop on Universal Access and Assistive Technology, Cambridge, United Kingdom.
16. Gupta, M., Chotard, L., Ingporsson, O., Bastos, J., & Borges, I. (2009). Health@Home - An e-Service Model for Disease Prevention and Healthcare in the Home. In *Electronic Healthcare* (Vol. 1, pp. 17-24). New York: Springer.
17. Hawthorn, D. (2000). Possible implications of aging for interface designers. *Interacting with Computers, 12*(5), 507-528.
18. Hawthorn, D. (2007). Interface design and engagement with older people. *Behaviour & Information Technology, 26*(4), 333-341.
19. Jung, J. H., Schneider, C., & Valacich, J. (2010). Enhancing the Motivational Affordance of Information Systems: The Effects of Real-Time Performance Feedback and Goal Setting in Group Collaboration Environments. *Management Science, 56*(4), 724-742.
20. Lawton, M. P., Moss, M. S., Winter, L., & Hoffman, C. (2002). Motivation in later life: Personal projects and well-being. *Psychology and Aging, 17*(4), 539-547.
21. Malone, T. W. (1981). Toward a theory of intrinsically motivating instruction. *Cognitive Science, 5*(4), 333-369.
22. Melenhorst, A. S., Rogers, W. A., & Bouwhuis, D. G. (2006). Older adults' motivated choice for technological innovation: Evidence for benefit-driven selectivity. *Psychology and Aging, 21*(1), 190-195.
23. Melenhorst, A. S., Rogers, W. A., & Caylor, E. C. (2001). The Use of Communication Technologies by Older Adults: Exploring the Benefits from the User's Perspective. *Human Factors and Ergonomics Society Annual Meeting Proceedings, 45*(3), 221-225.
24. Monk, A., Hassenzahl, M., Blythe, M., & Reed, D. (2002). *Funology: designing enjoyment.* Paper presented at the CHI '02 extended abstracts on Human factors in computing systems.
25. Mynatt, E. D., Melenhorst, A. S., Fisk, A. D., & Rogers, W. A. (2004). Aware technologies for aging in place: Understanding user needs and attitudes. *Ieee Pervasive Computing, 3*(2), 36-41.
26. Ofcom. (2006). *Older people and communications technology*: Ofcom Consumer Panel.
27. Plant, R. W., & Ryan, R. M. (1985). Intrinsic Motivation and the Effects of Self-Consciousness, Self-Awareness, and Ego-Involvement - an Investigation of Internally Controlling Styles. *Journal of Personality, 53*(3), 435-449.
28. Przybylski, A. K., Rigby, C. S., & Ryan, R. M. (2010). A Motivational Model of Video Game Engagement. *Review of General Psychology, 14*(2), 154-166.
29. Rechel, B., Doyle, Y., Grundy, E., & McKee, M. (2009). *How can health systems respond to population ageing?* Copenhagen, Denmark: World Health Organization
30. Rieber, L. P., Smith, L., & Noah, D. (1998). The Value of Serious Play. *Educational Technology, 38*(6), 29-37.
31. Ryan, R. M. (1982). Control and Information in the Intrapersonal Sphere - an Extension of Cognitive Evaluation Theory. *Journal of Personality and Social Psychology, 43*(3), 450-461.
32. Ryan, R. M., Connell, J. P., & Plant, R. W. (1990). Emotions in non-directed text learning. *Learning and Individual Differences, 2*, 1-17.
33. Ryan, R. M., & Deci, E. L. (2000). Self-determination theory and the facilitation of intrinsic motivation, social development, and well-being. *American Psychologist, 55*(1), 68-78.
34. Ryan, R. M., Koestner, R., & Deci, E. L. (1991). Varied forms of persistence: When free-choice behavior is not intrinsically motivated. *Motivation and Emotion, 15*, 185-205.
35. Ryan, R. M., Mims, V., & Koestner, R. (1983). Relation of Reward Contingency and Interpersonal Context to Intrinsic Motivation - a Review and Test Using Cognitive Evaluation Theory. *Journal of Personality and Social Psychology, 45*(4), 736-750.
36. Ryan, R. M., Rigby, C. S., & Przybylski, A. (2006). The motivational pull of video games: A self-determination theory approach. *Motivation and Emotion, 30*(4), 347-363.
37. University of Rochester Department of Clinical & Social Sciences in Psychology. (09 Aug 2011). Self-Determination Theory: An approach to human motivation & personality. *Questionnaires* Retrieved 09 Aug 2011, from http://www.psych.rochester.edu/SDT/questionnaires.php
38. Wagner, N., Hassanein, K., & Head, M. (2010). Computer use by older adults: A multi-disciplinary review. *Computers in Human Behavior, 26*(5), 870-882.
39. Wherton, J., & Prendergast, D. (2009). The Building Bridges Project: Involving Older Adults in the Design of a Communication Technology to Support Peer-to-Peer Social Engagement. *HCI and Usability for e-Inclusion. Proceedings 5th Symposium of the Workgroup Human-Computer Interaction and Usability Engineering of the Austrian Computer Society, USAB 2009*, 111-134.
40. White, R. W. (1959). Motivation Reconsidered - the Concept of Competence. *Psychological Review, 66*(5), 297-333.
41. Williams, G. C., Lynch, M., & Glasgow, R. E. (2007). Computer-assisted intervention improves patient-centered diabetes care by increasing autonomy support. *Health Psychology, 26*, 728-734.
42. Zhang, P. (2007). Toward a Positive Design Theory: Principles for Designing Motivating Information and Communication Technology. In M. Avital, R. Bolland & D. Cooperrider (Eds.), *Designing Information and Organizations with a Positive Lens*: Elsevier.
43. Zhang, P. (2008). Motivational Affordances: Reasons for ICT Design and Use. *Communications of the ACM, 51*(11), 145-147.

Virtual Marionette

Luís Leite
FEUP
Rua Roberto Frias, 4200-465 Porto
luis.grifu@gmail.com

ABSTRACT
Virtual Marionette is a research on digital puppetry, an interdisciplinary approach that brings the art of puppetry into the world of digital animation. Inspired in the traditional marionette technology our intention is to study novel interfaces as an interaction platform for creating artistic contents based on computer animated puppets. The overall goal of this thesis is to research and deploy techniques and methods for the manipulation of articulated puppets in real-time with low-cost interfaces to establish an interaction model for digital puppetry.

Author Keywords
Digital Puppetry; Virtual Marionette; Real-time animation; Computer Kinematics; Interactive Animation; Performance Animation; Human Computer Interaction.

ACM Classification Keywords
H.5.2 [Information Interfaces And Presentation]: User Interfaces - Interaction styles.

CONTEXT AND MOTIVATION
Sometimes we just want to tell a story with simple character animation, but then, we take so much time producing the animation that we forgot the story line.

Digital character animation based on key-frame techniques is laborious and time consuming, especially for non-expert animators that have to lead with complex concepts like time and space in animation for building motion. In other hand, traditional puppetry techniques presents a natural and intuitive interaction between the manipulator and the puppet. With digital puppetry the animation is produced in real-time focusing the performer improvisation, which is great for live shows and storytelling. An interactive way for working with narratives turning story time into life.

Some digital puppetry techniques like motion capture are a common practice for character animation in high-end industry, like film productions that spend a high budget in technology. With today low-cost technologies, like Microsoft Kinect, Nintendo WII, Sony Playstation Move, or multi-touch surfaces, digital puppetry became a hot topic opening new targets like the home entertainment industry. As a result, a new research domain related to the interaction methods opens the door for different ways of interacting with puppets using low-cost devices, which must be explored.

With these novel interfaces the human to computer interaction (HCI) paradigm is changing raising new questions, like multi-user interaction or gesture recognition.

We intend to study the interaction possibilities with puppets using digital interfaces with different users like, animators, puppeteers and non-export artists.

Our main focus is the pedagogical environment, developing a prototype to be used as a learning tool for children. An application for story telling that let children explore the magical and fascinating world of puppets in a simpler manner and easy to control system. A learning tool, that brings the creative and inventive world of puppets into the computer animation.

In this way, we can measure and evaluate how children respond to the interaction with the puppets and the success of these applications as learning tool.

Another contribution will be for the entertainment industry, building a model for a virtual live TV puppet show, making use of the cinematic language, using lights and cameras. The evaluation of this model with animators and puppeteers will show the potential of digital puppetry in television.

Artistic performances using digital puppetry are also part of this research; understating how live performers can interact with digital puppetry. We will work with performers to explore the relation between analog and digital interaction.

Our final contribution is to disseminate digital puppetry through different areas as an interaction platform for puppet animation.

RELATED WORK
Digital puppetry experiments started in early 1960s, using analog circuits to animate figures in real-time conducted by Lee Harrison III [16]. The interaction with the character was made with analog sliders and knobs. In 1967 he presented the first approach to mechanical motion capture using a rig of potentiometers inside an armature that was

used by a performer to control a video character in real-time. But it was only in 1988 that arrived the live animated computer graphics characters rendered in real-time. Thanks to the combination of the Silicon Graphics 4D workstation with real-time computer graphics (CG) and Waldos, mechanical controllers made by deGraf/Wharman and Pacific Data Images (PDI), digital puppetry was born. Mike the Talking Head was the result of this combination, a real-time animated head controlled by a puppeteer. In the same year, PDI brought the first successful real-time digital animated figure for television. Waldo C. Graphic was built for Jim Henson productions [5]. Performed and rendered in real-time with a low-resolution model for "The Jim Henson Hour" TV series for later post-production; Waldo was manipulated trough a mechanical arm controlled by a puppeteer. In 1991, Medialab presents Mat the Ghost, a fully real-time CG animated puppet for a television production. A multimodal system, using data-gloves, joysticks, motion capture and midi devices used by puppeteers to control Mat [14]. A very interesting solution for mapping performer movements to animated characters is presented by Kyun et al. [9]. They describe a method for transferring motion capture data to animated characters whose size and proportion may differ from the performer. Using the notion of dynamic importance of an end-effector applied to the inverse kinematic solver preserving the main motion aspects of the performance. Since then, many researches and developments have been made on digital puppetry, from motion capture technologies to film production companies [11]. Henson Digital Puppetry Studio is an example of this evolution, a system that provides performance animation with CG characters using a mechanical hand controls that can be broadcast for television. Sid the Science Kid is an example of the recent Jim Henson production for television that combines motion capture with hand controls.

The most common approaches to create animations using digital puppetry include: digital strings to control the puppets using a digital glove [2]; computer vision for tracking color marks in a object that controls the marionette movements [10]; using a multi-touch surface for direct manipulation of bi-dimensional shape puppets [13]; hand gesture recognition to use fingers to move the marionette simulating a string controller [7] a multi-modal interface to simulate different marionette techniques in a virtual puppet show [6]; a motion capture system for performance-driven with gesture recognition to trigger behavior animation for virtual theater, using an extra joystick for expanding the movement area [12].

These researches contributed to a greater knowledge on character animation using digital puppetry, but some are complex to use or to implement, and others use expensive equipment. We propose easy to use affordable systems to be used in different environments and different users.

STATEMENT OF THESIS

Digital Character animation is complex and time consuming. Based on this question we propose using puppetry as an interaction and rigging model to simplify character animation using affordable interfaces as controllers, which could be used for content generation as a story telling technique in educational and entertainment.

Our main goal is to build an interaction model for digital puppetry using traditional marionette methods as a starting point. Seeking new ways for a user to interact with performing objects in real-time.

A model that can be abstract from the interaction interface, which simply map different inputs into a single or multiple outputs converting and scaling the input data to the desire animation values. In this way, a multi-model interaction solution could contribute to a more expressive result in performance animation.

It is important to establish digital puppetry taxonomy. Looking at traditional puppetry taxonomy approaches we found that Alexandre Passos [8] presented a simple classification based on the available manipulations systems. Upper, medium and lower manipulation level are the divisions to classify from were the puppets are manipulated. But this classification doesn't fit completely in the digital medium, which presents other methods of interaction. A different approach is presented by Stephen Kaplin [3], based on distance and objects/performers ratio. Kaplin describes "distance" as the contact and separation level between the performer and the manipulated object. Starting with absolute contact, were the performer and the object are just one, to the opposite scale based on physical and psychological body factors, and temporal contact levels. With objects/performers ratio, Stephen Kalplin refers to the number of performing objects compared to the number of performers. We can build a digital puppetry taxonomy based on this two classification systems assuming the performer as the main interaction platform. To describe a methodology for digital puppetry performance animation we propose three parts:

1. Performing objects structure, describing the rigging system, shape and materials, like if they are rigid or deformable.

2. User interaction methods, which defines the way users interacts with the puppet, describing the performer expressions, interaction interfaces and joint mapping.

3. Animation, which defines the motion of the puppets using performance, pre-recorded, procedural or physics based animation.

Rigging the puppet defines his behavior with bones connecting joints; the mapping is the correspondence of the performer joints to the puppet, which can be direct or indirect mapping, like the hand of the performer to control the head of a monster; the input interface establish the controlling method, using a perceptual input which doesn't require any physical contact with the device or a non-perceptual input which requires physical contact like a mouse; in animation, puppet responds to the performing animation, use pre-recorded animation to produce actions, physics to create enhanced and natural motion, and procedural that can be trigger by the performer.

To understand how this model works in a pedagogical, artistic and entertainment environment we intend to develop three proofing tools. Each approach will be focus on the particularities of each environment. For the pedagogical approach the intention is to work with groups of children creating a virtual marionette play for storytelling. A complete virtual play, with performing puppets, animated scenery and props. For the artistic environment the main objective is to create a live performance in which the puppet interacts with the performer. The entertainment approach is for live television or film productions in which the performer controls mainly characters that interact with images from other sources.

By the end of this research we expect to achieve the following results:

- An Interaction Model to be used in digital puppetry.
- Prototype of a Virtual Puppet Show as a learning tool.
- Evaluation and validation of the interaction model.
- Classification of digital puppetry.
- Dissemination of results in scientific journal and conferences of high impact.
- Digital puppetry demonstrations in different fields.

The Prototype of the Virtual Puppet Show will be evaluated with a pilot experiments. Using a focus group of children in a school environment for a live story telling experiment. This experiment needs to be validated with a survey and statistical analysis of puppet interactions.

Beyond the study of marionette mechanics we will also seek the cultural and artistic aspects related to the marionette, like the puppet theatre. Search for similarities and differences between marionette motion and digital character animation; for instance, an important difference between frame-by-frame animation and real-time animation is the improvisation of the puppeteer.

We will explore the various expressions of the marionettes, in particular their different ways of handling and its particular language, studying the anthropological and cultural side. Two examples of this study are "Os bonecos de Santo Aleixo" from the Portuguese *Bonecreiros* [12] and the silhouette puppets (shadow theatre) *Wayang Golek* [4] of Java in Indonesia. Ancient puppetry presenting different ways of handling, which we will explore and compare with digital interfaces:

- Multi-touch interfaces for multiple control points manipulation;
- Computer Vision methods for the use of body language;
- The use of sensors like accelerometer to simulate rod or string controllers;
- Computer Sound Analysis for generating facial expressions;
- Networks for multiuser manipulation

DISSERTATION STATUS

It is intended to follow up the previous studies, published in the Master's thesis "Marionetas Virtuais" [10] with the prototype "ANIMATIC" [1] and thus further research in the areas of interaction and in the real-time animation.

For the PhD we have built new prototypes, created a poster for I Interactive Multimedia Group Symposium, and conducted an experiment with a survey, which was published in ACE 2011 with the name "Anim-Actor".

Research prototypes:

"Virtual Silhuette" and "reActor" are two examples of 2D and 3D real-time rigid puppet animation using low-cost motion capture systems published in the online support site [15].

"Kine-Puppet Show" a 3D virtual puppet shows with deformable puppets, using Microsoft Kinect as a motion capture system.

"IPADATA" is an experiment of digital puppetry simulating a direct puppet manipulation. A multi-touch interaction method using the Apple Ipad as interface. The system can work with several devices at the same time and compromise three parts: Input, mapping and animation. The input device sends the finger coordinates via wireless network through the Tangible User Interface (TUIO) framework. Then, a middleware software, OSCulator, acts like a bridge between the input and output mapping the messages to be interpreted by the animation package sending them via network. Finally the animation software, which defines the shape and the bone structure, animates the joints.

"WIIDATA" is a similar experiment as "IPADATA" but works with the Nintendo *WIImotes* that are used to simulate the rod puppet manipulation.

For future work we intend to build and evaluate the three puppet tools that were mentioned, based on digital puppetry techniques with different puppets and performing objects.

As a result of the experiments we intend to build a classification map to identify different interaction methods.

OPEN QUESTIONS

Digital puppetry is subject of debate within the puppetry and animation communities since a long time and differs from conventional puppetry techniques, because there is no tangible puppet and from conventional computer animation because it involves performing characters, rather than frame by frame animation.

This undefined border of digital puppetry being integrated in puppetry or in animation raises some questions that we will explore through this research.

The main Question:

- Virtual Marionette can be considered a Marionette in terms of behaviors and characteristics and in terms of its proximity with the puppeteer/user?

Secondary Question:

- Can performance animation achieve the same or better results as traditional puppetry in storytelling?

REFERENCES

1. ANIMATIC Prototype. http://www.grifu.com/animatic/.
2. Bar-Lev, A., Bruckstein, A., Elber, G.: Virtual marionettes: A System and Paradigm for Real-time 3D Animation. *The Visual Computer, Vol. 21*, (2005), (pp. 488-501).
3. Bell, J.: Puppets, Masks and Performing Objects, Londres, Mit Press, (2001).
4. Currell, D.: The Complete Book of Puppet Theatre, A & C Black, London, (1985).
5. Graham, W.: The Story of Waldo C. Graphic. *Course Notes: 3D Character Animation by Computer*. ACM SIGGRAPH, Boston, (1989), (pp. 6-79).
6. Leite, L.: Marionetas Virtuais – Animação interactiva em tempo real, Master Thesis in Multimedia Communication Technologies, Engineering Faculty of the University of Porto (FEUP), Porto, (2006).
7. Ninomiya, D., Miyazaki, K., Nakatsu, R.: Networked Virtual Marionette Theater. In *Proceedings of the 3rd international conference on Technologies for E-Learning and Digital Entertainment (Edutainment '08)*. Springer-Verlag, Berlin, Heidelberg (2008), (pp. 619-627).
8. Passos, A.: Bonecos de Santo Aleixo, Adágio, Évora (1999).
9. Shin, H., Lee, J., Shin, S., Gleicher, M.: Computer puppetry: An importance-based approach. In *ACM Trans. Graph. 20, 2* (2001), 67-94.
10. Sirota, A., Sheinker, D., Yossef, O.: Controlling a Virtual Marionette using a Web Camera, Technion - Israel Institute of Technology, Israel (2003).
11. Sturman, D.J.: Computer puppetry. In *Computer Graphics and Applications, IEEE, vol.18, no.1*, (1998), (pp. 38-45).
12. Sturman, D.: The State of Computer Animation. In *ACM SIGGRAPH Comput. Graph.* ACM Press, New York. (1998), (pp. 57-61).
13. Takeo, I., Yuki, I.: Implementing As-Rigid-As-Possible Shape Manipulation and Surface Flattening. In *Journal of Graphics, GPU, and Game Tools*, A.K.Peters, Volume 14, Number 1, (2009), (pp. 17-30).
14. Tardif, H.: Character animation in real time. In *Panel Proceedings: Applications of Virtual Reality I*, ACM SIGGRAPH, 1991.
15. Virtual Marionette http://www.grifu.com/vm/.
16. Wu, Q.,Boulanger, P, Kazakevich, M., Taylor, R.: A Real-time Performance System for Virtual Theater. In *Proceedings of the 2010 ACM workshop on Surreal media and virtual cloning (SMVC '10)*. ACM, New York, USA. (2010), (pp. 3-8).

Eliciting Evaluative Comments from Users in Web 2.0 Scenarios

Richard C. Gomer
Web Science DTC, University of Southampton
SO17 1BJ, Southampton, UK
rcg1v07@soton.ac.uk

ABSTRACT
In recent years, we've seen a huge growth in the level of user-supplied reviews posted online. These reviews range from feedback on eBay or comments on sites such as YouTube, to social bookmarking sites like StumbleUpon that allow users to comment on almost any page on the web.

I'm interested in how these comments are incorporated into evaluative judgements by the users that read them, and how we can improve them through better user interfaces in order to maximise their value to other users. The work draws on psychology and neurology, as well as ideas around credibility from information science, to design and test the impact of intelligent interface changes and behaviour on review composition and ascertain how the composition of a review can make it more or less useful.

ACM Classification Keywords
H.5.2 User Interfaces

Author Keywords
comment, review, feedback, nudge, qualitative

CONTEXT AND MOTIVATION
The characteristics of Web 2.0 include an increased level of discourse around, or annotation of, online content. This is evident in social bookmarking sites such as StumbleUpon, delicious and Reddit, which allow users to review web resources, as well as sites such as YouTube or Flickr which provide the facility for users to leave comments on the uploaded videos and photos.

However, it is, as yet, unclear why many people write these reviews, how people use them and to whom they are most useful. The degree to which these comments provide a resource in themselves, how they can inform evaluative judgements by other users and how we can maximise their potential are areas still to be explored.

As the amount of information available increases and as the barriers to publishing new materials are lowered, the ability of users to identify credible information is important. Search engines can help to overcome the volume of information that is available, but do not provide much support to users in determining the credibility of the information that they find. Given that some users already post reviews of the material that is available, these reviews provide a potential means of helping users to make these credibility judgements.

Despite the increasing prevalence of these user reviews in Web 2.0 scenarios, the quality of the reviews is varied and often low. The ability to review resources is a combination of evaluation and communication, both of which have been identified as aspects of digital literacy [1]. I propose that user interface design may play a role in supporting and fostering the evaluative and communicative skills related to writing reviews.

This work is of relevance in a number of domains. Health and finance are obvious candidates, given the importance of accurate information in these areas. E-commerce is another domain in which interface designs could be deployed to foster evaluative comments, given that users seek reviews in order to inform their purchasing decisions.

RELATED WORK
When users encounter information on the web, they must make judgements about the credibility of the information that they find, based on various criteria [2-6]. These judgements form an evaluation of the resource, and aspects of this evaluation will generally be reflected in a user's review of that resource. These judgements are usually made in the context of a particular task and may be influenced by the credibility of the source itself (including the URL or author) [2, 7], characteristics of the information object itself, such as aesthetics [8], the judgements of other users [6] and a user's existing knowledge or beliefs [7].

According to Rieh and Hilligoss, the importance of credibility to users varies based on the information seeking task in which they are engaged, with credibility being more important when seeking information about health or finance [6]. Some groups of users have difficulty making or articulating relevance and credibility judgements on information that they find [6] and that some groups are more likely to judge information as more credible than others [9]. Whilst this suggests that encouraging critical evaluation of information may be achieved by improving

IUI'12, February 14–17, 2011, Lisbon, Portugal.

digital and/or information literacy in general, it also raises the possibility that these groups may benefit from more effective communication of judgements by other users who are better able to perform the evaluation.

Other researchers have attempted to improve the credibility judgements that users make by intervening during the users' information seeking process. Schwarz and Morris [10] developed a series of visualisations that were designed to help users judge source credibility based upon factors such as usage by experts, and then tested the effectiveness of these augmented search results on the accuracy of users' credibility judgements compared to "ground truth" judgements obtained from domain experts.

Yanbe et al have used user-generated reviews from social-bookmarking sites to augment search results [11].

From an interaction design perspective, eliciting reviews from users requires that the breadth and depth of the review is balanced against the cognitive effort required on the part of the user in writing that review. Increasing the cognitive effort required to complete a task in a social-bookmarking context has been shown to reduce participation [12].

A series of nudges, corresponding theory and an associated political framework called "liberal paternalism" are presented in Thaler & Sunstein's influential 2008 book, "Nudge: Improving decisions about health, wealth and happiness" [13]. A nudge is an aspect of a choice architecture "that alters people's behaviours in a predictable way without forbidding any options or significantly changing their economic incentives." [13] Effectively, a nudge anticipates and uses cognitive biases to influence a person's decision. Thaler and Sunstein use psychological work, such as that of Asch [14], relating to social influences on decision making, and research into how people can be "primed" to answer questions [15], to provide explanations for how various nudges influence decisions.

Outside the domain of information evaluation and communication, nudges have been used to influence behaviour successfully in numerous domains, including health care [16, 17], diet [18] and charity fundraising. This work spans both online contexts such as social networks [20, 21] as well as work in offline settings.

It is noteworthy, however, that the use of nudges has not been welcomed unanimously and has been criticised as indistinct from other interventions and supported by a weak evidence base [22, 23].

STATEMENT OF THESIS OR PROBLEM

My thesis may be described as "Developing user interfaces to elicit evaluative judgements in a web 2.0 context." At present, many websites that support user comments or reviews take a fairly naïve approach to eliciting reviews from users, effectively presenting the content alongside a box into which comments can be typed. In many cases the comments that are elicited by these sites are often of low quality, which reduces their value to other users as an aid to their own evaluations and undermines the potential for these reviews to help users to locate credible resources.

I aim to develop interface automation techniques that could be applied in real-world scenarios such as social bookmarking sites to influence judgement elicitation and improve the usefulness of the supplied reviews for other users seeking to evaluate resources, either during searching or when forming evaluative judgements about a previously encountered resource.

I plan to generalise these techniques beyond just reviews of web or information resources, to encompass, for instance, reviews of products or more abstract things like weight-loss diets.

RESEARCH GOALS AND METHODS

G1 Identify trends in the composition of existing reviews in web 2.0 contexts: This will involve qualitative analysis of existing review corpuses from, for example, social bookmarking sites, using coding techniques. Qualitative analysis will be supplemented by quantitative analysis of the coded resources in order to determine common features of the reviews.

G2 Understand the motivations behind reviewers and review-readers: In answering this goal, I aim to describe the reasons for which people write and/or seek reviews. Do reviewers write reviews with the aim of informing other users, as a tool to aid their own reflection or for other reasons? Do people seek out the opinions of other users through reviews, and if so, why? Are these motivations the same in all domains, or do the motivations in seeking reviews of a web page differ to the motivations for reading reviews of a physical product?

This goal will be approached using qualitative techniques such as interviews and focus groups.

I also aim to determine whether we can attribute "roles" to various contributors in a review scenario, in a similar manner to work that has been done on tele-deliberative democratic discourse [24] or online forums, and explain how each of these roles contributes. Some literature already exists in this space, for instance [25].

G3 Suggest and test which aspects of reviews are most helpful to users when searching for or evaluating information or other resources in particular domains: A core part of this research, especially with regard to broadening the applicability beyond just web resources, will be to identify which aspects of the object under review are most useful and which can be successfully elicited from reviewers using various techniques; and to propose methods by which these criteria may be identified prior to the design or implementation of particular user interface factors.

Aspects of a review (for instance a reference to a particular property of the subject) that are likely to be found useful may be inferred from the literature surrounding models of cognitive processing, as well as identified from qualitative study of users making evaluations. Aspects identified using these methods will then be tested through user studies, to see, for instance, whether they have a positive impact on the accuracy of users' evaluative judgements of information credibility when compared to ratings of expert users.

G4 Design and test a range of nudges that can be deployed in a social-bookmarking context to improve the composition of user reviews: Nudges will be designed based on research into cognitive bias from psychology and neurology, and these nudges will be tested experimentally in user trials to determine if they significantly and predictably alter the characteristics of the supplied reviews. These nudges may be "intelligently" tailored to individual users, based on their previous reviews.

These experiments will, where possible, emulate the scenario in which they are designed to be deployed. For instance, nudges designed for a social bookmarking context will be tested in an experimental system that emulates the behaviour of such a system.

G5 Understand if and how reviews impact upon the decisions made by other users: This will involve identifying the ways in which people are influenced by comments when searching for and evaluating information or other resources. One aspect of this goal will be to ascertain how reviews affect the search phase (predictive evaluations) relative to evaluations made during an encounter with a resource.

I will also aim to answer the question of whether the process of writing better reviews helps the author to form a more complete evaluation of the resource, and whether they become better at reviewing resources in general.

Research towards this goal will be largely experimental, making use of online user studies, but will be supplemented by qualitative feedback from users through interviews and questionnaires.

DISSERTATION STATUS & PLAN

At present, I have demonstrated the effectiveness of two nudges in a social-bookmarking context related to the review of online health-related information. This contributes towards Goal 4 above. The study was run online with a group of participants who were recruited via social media. The nudges encouraged users to mention particular "target criteria" (such as trustworthiness, accuracy or appearance) of the resources in their reviews. These nudges can be integrated into existing comment scenarios in order to alter user behaviour, without denying users a choice. Importantly, this should be possible with only a modest increase in the cognitive effort required on behalf of users, a factor which has been shown to reduce participation in a social-bookmarking context [12].

Year 1

I am currently working on a study based on the methodology that was used by Schwarz and Morris to test the effect of augmented search results on credibility judgements [10] in order to test whether reviews containing references to the target criteria improve credibility judgements of those resources by other users, and which of those target criteria are the most useful. This will continue working towards Goal 4 and contribute to Goal 5.

This study will be run across two groups of users. One group of users, the parents of disabled children, have a necessary interest in finding relevant information (for instance about social care). The second group, users interested in health and fitness, have a casual interest in a topic. By splitting the study across two groups, I aim to determine whether the impact of the target criteria differs across these domains.

I also aim to carry out qualitative evaluation of reviews from existing and nudged scenarios, working towards Goals 1, 2 and 5.

Year 2

In my second year, I will focus on refining identified nudges and understanding the broader psychological and social influences that they have, as well as understanding more about the review qualities that are most important to readers. I will, for instance, investigate whether nudges affect the social norms within a community of reviewers and whether improve the credibility judgement of the reviewers themselves. This work will contribute to Goals 2, 3 and 5.

Year 3

In my final year, I plan to study how the techniques developed during my earlier work could be applied in broader contexts to scenarios that have not previously been studied. This could include reviews of products as well as information resources, or usage within specialist communities, for instance healthcare professionals.

OPEN QUESTIONS

The domains into which I will expand the research are still not clearly defined. Although my work currently focuses on health, I plan to examine how insight gained in this domain can be used in other areas. These areas could include online purchasing or more subjective areas such as video reviews.

It is, as yet, unclear how interaction design that is supportive of evaluative comments might best be achieved, both in terms of encouraging such comments and in delivering them to the users who may benefit from them. Whilst contemporary social bookmarking sites require that the user visit another website to view comments on the resource that they're interested in, other techniques such as delivering comments via extensions to the web browser itself may prove more valuable. I will not be able to focus on particular approaches to delivery until I better understand the scenarios in which users seek reviews and their motivations for doing so.

REFERENCES

1. O. Erstad, "Citizens navigating in literate worlds," in Deconstructing Digital Natives: Young people, technology and the new literacies, M. Thomas, Ed. New York: Routledge, 2011, pp. 99-118.
2. B. R. Bates, S. Romina, R. Ahmed, and D. Hopson, "The effect of source credibility on consumers' perceptions of the quality of health information on the Internet.," Medical informatics and the Internet in medicine, vol. 31, no. 1, pp. 45-52, 2006.
3. Z. Liu, "Perceptions of credibility of scholarly information on the web," Information Processing & Management, vol. 40, no. 6, pp. 1027-1038, Nov. 2004.
4. C. Marton, "Quality of health information on the Web: user perceptions of relevance and reliability," New Review of Information Behaviour Research, vol. 4, no. 1, pp. 195-206, Dec. 2003.
5. S. a Rains and C. D. Karmikel, "Health information-seeking and perceptions of website credibility: Examining Web-use orientation, message characteristics, and structural features of websites," Computers in Human Behavior, vol. 25, no. 2, pp. 544-553, Mar. 2009.
6. S. Y. Rieh and B. Hilligoss, "College students' credibility judgments in the information-seeking process," in Digital Media, Youth, and Credibility, M. J. Metzger and A. J. Flanagin, Eds. Cambridge, MA: The MIT Press, 2007, pp. 49–72.
7. S. Y. Rieh, "Judgment of information quality and cognitive authority in the Web," Journal of the American Society for Information Science and Technology, vol. 53, no. 2, pp. 145-161, 2002.
8. F. Alsudani, "The effect of aesthetics on web credibility," Proceedings of the 23rd British HCI Group, pp. 512-519, 2009.
9. Q. Liao, "Effects of Aging and Individual Differences on Credibility Judgment of Online Health Information," in Proceedings of the 33rd Annual Meeting of Cognitive Science Society, 2011, pp. 384-389.
10. J. Schwarz and M. Morris, "Augmenting web pages and search results to support credibility assessment," in Proceedings of the 2011 annual conference on Human factors in computing systems, 2011, pp. 1245–1254.
11. Y. Yanbe, A. Jatowt, S. Nakamura, and K. Tanaka, "Can social bookmarking enhance search in the web?," Proceedings of the 2007 conference on Digital libraries - JCDL '07, p. 107, 2007.
12. J. Li, B. Whitworth, and B. Jones, "Interface and Feedback Factors in Social Bookmark Usage." pp. 1-16, 2010.
13. R. H. Thaler and C. R. Sunstein, Nudge: Improving Decisions About Health, Wealth and Happiness. New Haven & London: Yale University Press, 2008.
14. S. E. Asch, "Effects of group pressure upon the modification and distortion of judgments," in Groups leadership and men, vol. 27, no. 3, H. Guetzkow, Ed. Carnegie Press, 1951, pp. 177-190.
15. F. Strack, L. L. Martin, and N. Schwarz, "Priming and communication: Social determinants of information use in judgments of life satisfaction," European Journal of Social Psychology, vol. 18, no. 5, pp. 429-442, 1988.
16. G. C. Harewood, K. Clancy, J. Engela, M. Abdulrahim, K. Lohan, and C. O'Reilly, "Randomised clinical trial: a 'nudge' strategy to modify endoscopic sedation practice.," Alimentary pharmacology & therapeutics, vol. 34, no. 2, pp. 229-34, Jul. 2011.
17. S. Munson, "Beyond The Share Button: Making Social Network Sites Work For Health And Wellness," IEEE Potentials, no. September, 2011.
18. P. Rozin, S. Scott, M. Dingley, J. K. Urbanek, H. Jiang, and M. Kaltenbach, "Nudge to nobesity I: Minor changes in accessibility decrease food intake," Judgment and Decision Making, vol. 6, no. 4, pp. 323–332, 2011.
19. A. Breman, "Give more tomorrow: Two field experiments on altruism and intertemporal choice," Journal of Public Economics, May. 2011.
20. S. A. Munson, D. Lauterbach, M. W. Newman, and P. Resnick, "Happier Together : Integrating a Wellness Application into a Social Network Site," Lecture Notes in Computer Science, vol. 6137, pp. 27-39, 2010.
21. D. Foster, S. Lawson, M. Blythe, P. Cairns, and B. Pool, "Wattsup ?: Motivating reductions in domestic energy consumption using social networks," October, pp. 178-187, 2010.
22. C. Bonell, M. McKee, A. Fletcher, P. Wilkinson, and A. Haines, "One nudge forward, two steps back," BMJ, vol. 342, no. jan25 3, p. d401-d401, Jan. 2011.
23. E. Selinger and K. Whyte, "Is There a Right Way to Nudge? The Practice and Ethics of Choice Architecture," Sociology Compass, vol. 5, no. 10, pp. 923-935, Oct. 2011.
24. S. Wylie and A. R. Marri, "Teledeliberative democratic discourse: a case study of high school students' use of Web 2.0," Campus-Wide Information Systems, vol. 27, no. 4, pp. 193-209, 2010.
25. C.-C. Lin and C.-C. Tsai, "Applying social bookmarking to collective information searching (CIS): An analysis of behavioral pattern and peer interaction for co-exploring quality online resources," Computers in Human Behavior, vol. 27, no. 3, pp. 1249-1257, May. 2011.

Graph based User Modeling

Amit Tiroshi
Information Systems Department, University of Haifa
Mount Carmel, Haifa 31905, Israel
atiroshi@is.haifa.ac.il

ABSTRACT

An overload in service applications and websites induced by ubiquitous connectivity has brought the need for personalization, as a way to cope with it. However, the need for providing every service with a user model calls for interoperable user models, since user details are scattered in many different systems (e.g., online services such as mail/banking/healthcare/ecommerce sites/social networks), each storing the user's details, preferences and history in different representations and data formats. Various approaches for user modeling interoperability were studied from different perspectives (general ontologies, personalized ontologies, mediation), but so far the challenges are yet to be met. This paper proposes a new way for representing user models, an abstracted graph based one, which will support both interoperability and advanced user modeling features.

Author Keywords

Ubiquitous User Modeling, Graphs, Personalization

ACM Classification Keywords

H.5.m. Information interfaces and presentation (e.g., HCI): Miscellaneous.

CONTEXT AND MOTIVATION

Today's digital services are becoming ubiquitous - being almost everywhere in our daily lives; we either interact with them directly (as in: ATMs, movies/transportation tickets purchasing kiosks, medical information kiosks, etc.) or they are being operated in the background (e.g., food ordering in a restaurant, medical treatment in the hospital, flight boarding in the airport, shopping, etc.). They are required to adapt to their users in order to overcome information overload problems. These may include: which books/movies/music to present to users? Where to dine? What hotel to select? Where to buy a specific product? Helping users finding people whom they might know in a social network and many more. To carry out such adaptations, information about the users is required: what are the users' preferences, interests and other personal characteristics (e.g., if a library system would have known which courses a student is taking, it could have offered relevant books). These user characteristics are also known (and represented) as a user model. Naturally, every service needs to build its own user model and this may result in tedious, repetitive task for the users. If individual services would have been able to share user model parts (while preserving the user's privacy), the need for querying users for details they have probably already provided before to another system could have been eliminated; thus, time and hassle on both sides (services providers and clients) would have been saved (also information would have passed in a more accurate way). Providing an approachable and easy user modeling interoperability option to such services can make them serve our needs better and thus affect our lives. However, effective and easy sharing of user models is yet to be achieved, mostly because there is no common standard for storing user models (representation/ formats/ types/ protocols) as well as commercial competition. Methods for bridging different representations have already been studied, but with limited adoption (as reviewed in the next section). In the proposed research a new approach for representing and reasoning about user models is suggested. It will support interoperability without requiring a user modeling standard to be dictated to service providers.

RELATED WORK

A recent user modeling interoperability survey [1] shows that there is still no universal solution for exchanging user model parts between systems (applications/services) and users (P2P). One of the approaches mentioned in the survey is a general user modeling ontology (GUMO) [2], that defined a standard user modeling ontology, hoping it will be commonly adopted and will make each system's user model parts understandable to all. The success of such an approach relies on its potential clients' willingness to adopt a new standard with all the limitations it imposes. So far GUMO has not been adopted as a standard. Another approach surveyed, that is detailed in [3] is user model mediation, where knowledge stored in user models of different types (e.g., collaborative filtering vs. content based filtering) or domains (movies vs. music) can be mediated from one to another. However, for each pair of user models a dedicated mediation mechanism has to be developed. The above-mentioned limitations are possible reasons why ideas like GUMO and mediation have not been widely adopted yet (as well as others, as surveyed by [1]). In an earlier study [4] the possibility of having a single centralized user modeling server has also been suggested, but it was also mentioned that it is unlikely to be seen in the near future.

There is little research on graph based representations of user models, besides its usage in ontology based approaches. Overlay [5] based user modeling took ontological knowledge graphs and added a layer of ratings on its elements, representing the individual user's interest/familiarity with the concepts. The limitation of overlay user models that is intended to be addressed in the proposed approach is in being bounded to the underlying ontology. In a generic graph-based representation, ratings could be overlaid to concepts imported from more than a single ontology, or from a non ontological representation at all. Other semi related fields that use graphs are social network analysis and recommender systems; a recent study for example used graphs to analyze folksonomies and represent both social and semantic data in a graph. Other works such as [6] and [7] used graph based representation to enhance collaborative filtering recommendation based approaches. Conceptual networks for the purpose of graph based knowledge representation were studied in many works which are summarized in [8]. Those works explore various reasoning and modeling approaches on graphs that resemble ontologies (annotated links), however none are specifically oriented towards the modeling of user preferences and attributes. In the proposed research it is intended to adopt part of the reasoning methods defined for conceptual graphs and adapt them to nowadays challenges such as interoperability in the field of user modeling.

STATEMENT OF THESIS OR PROBLEM

As mentioned in the previous sections, there is currently no user modeling approach that allows easy sharing of user model parts on one side, and that can easily be integrated into legacy services as well as to new services on the other side (both legacy and new services would like to make as few changes as possible in their design to support user model sharing). Previous studies have proposed various ways to handle this problem but their success is limited for different reasons. This research will build upon those studies and try to use a new and generic representation approach along with graph based methods (e.g., strongly connected components finding, shortest weighted paths, etc.) to cope with the challenges they have faced: *existence of non standard user model representations, and a need for generic means to mediate between domains*.

RESEARCH GOALS AND METHODS

The goals of the proposed research are to: A. Be able to represent user data in a way that will support multiple user model vendors (along with their changing formats/data types/accuracy). B. define the methods for maintaining this new representation and servicing its stored knowledge to different consumer applications with their changing needs (context, format) C. Address issues of scalability and distribution. The research will be conducted using quantitative research methods. The first goal will be pursued by building upon previous user modeling approaches such as ontologies and conceptual networks, and abstracting from them to a generic graph based representation. The main issue with ontologies is that there is no commonly accepted standard that everyone adheres to. In the proposed graph based user model (as illustrated in Figure 1), all previous hierarchies given by ontologies are flattened into a single graph, that also embeds the user details in it. Definitions, attributes, and their values are all node elements linked to each other based on their relations.

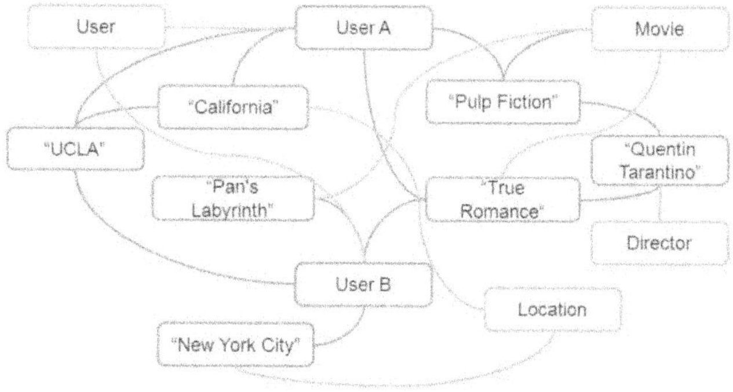

Figure 1. A partial graph based representation of User A's user model. Nodes and routes colored Green are ontological definitions that are now represented as graph elements and linked to their values thus achieving a level of abstraction that will better support graph based algorithms. The graph also embeds other non ontological data related to User A, and User A herself as a node.

For example if a movie based ontology specifies that each movie has an attribute named "starring" under which all actors that have played in the movie are listed, in the graph based representation all relevant actor entities would be linked to the movie name, a "movie" element would also be linked to the movie name, and an "actor" element would be linked to all actors. This abstracted view of the ontology will allow graph based algorithms to traverse the nodes in a generic way and will also support linking elements from different ontologies or even non ontological representation using simple heuristics (such as string comparison). The ability to apply graph based algorithms on the abstracted ontology will also provide new tools for implicitly inferring user's preferences and interests. Users and their details (e.g., location, social connections, etc) will be added to the graph using the same principles and would also be linked to the graph elements that were imported from the ontologies. In Figure 2 an example for how such link prediction could work in a graph based user model is given. Since all user model attributes in such a representation are abstracted to the same level, finding a schema for inferring links between users and their preferences will be relevant to all domains (movies/music/reading/etc.). Graph elements that were imported from ontologies will not permanently lose their ontological overlay; their ontological representation will be saved in a different layer, thus keeping an option to explore hybrid graph-based-to-ontologies algorithms.

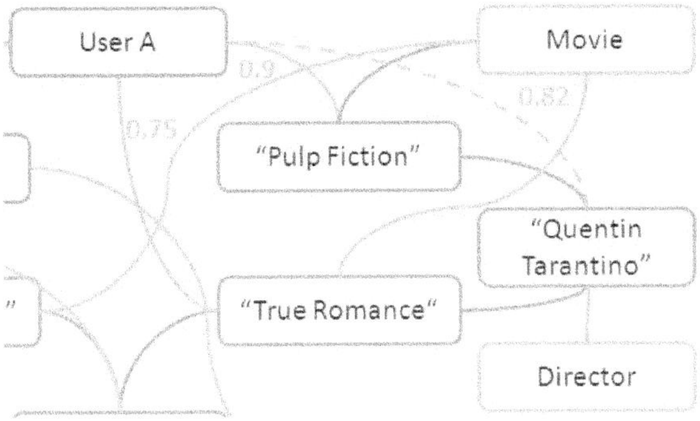

Figure 2. An overlay of weights on the graph links. High value links to two movies that are linked to the same director can be used to infer a high value link between the user and the director (aiding in finding additional movies of that director which might interest the user).

The goal of switching to a graph based user modeling representation will be achieved by bootstrapping several graphs, both from actually online sources such as social web services (Facebook/Twitter) and from available data sets. The second goal will be carried out by first trying to find weighting schemas to reflect each graph element relevance to the user. A single graph serves several users using different weights overlays. An initial weighting schema can be a representation of the occurrences of each element in the source datasets (element being anything that was represented as an ontology instance in previous ontology based approaches). The next step in this goal's evaluation would be to implement classic personalization algorithms which will be ran on the graph based user model. Their results will then be compared to those of a non-graph based implementation. One example is of a Collaborative Filtering graph based variation running on the MovieLens[1] data set compared to a regular CF implementation results. In Figure 3 a partial user model graph is presented, given that graph and the following query: ("Person", "User A", "Movie") a domain independent collaborative filtering algorithm can be implemented by: 1. Finding all nodes that are connected to "User A" and are also connected to a "Movie" node 2. On 1's results find all nodes that are connected to a "Person" node 3. On 2's results find all nodes that are connected to a "Movie" node 4. Subtract from 3's results 1's results, and return them. This algorithm can then be used to make collaborative based recommendations for any domain and it can also be extended to make cross domain recommendations and mediations (e.g., make music recommendations to User A based on his/her shared movies with other users and their links to music related elements).

[1] http://www.grouplens.org/node/73

Additional methods for inferring links and handling temporal aspects in the graph (e.g., How would link weights decay to reflect things that used to define the user but no longer do) will be researched, implemented and evaluated in a similar way. Those methods will be based on graph algorithms such as: clique finding, strongly connected components finding, shortest paths, etc. Scalability and distribution related metrics will be benchmarked and analyzed to know the proposed approach limitations and compare them to previous approaches, however developing new methods for storing graphs is out of this research scope.

A key tool to be used in this research is a NoSQL graph database management system for the purpose of storing the user model. NoSQL database management systems differ from relational ones in that they do not require fixed table schemas and join operations, thus being ideal for storing graphs. Graph database systems also support dedicated graph query languages and distributed graph processing methods. A list of currently available graph based database frameworks can be found at [9], those frameworks are being evaluated and one of them will be used in this research's development process.

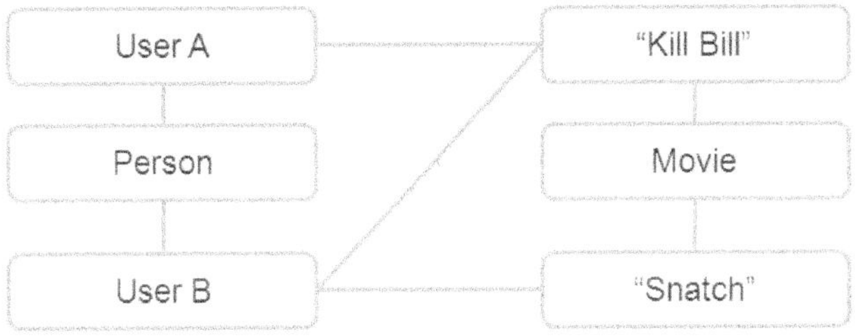

Figure 3. A partial user model graph pruned for the purpose of making collaborative filtering like recommendations (pruning nodes from multiple domains, such as movies and music, would allow making cross domain recommendations)

DISSERTATION STATUS

To this moment a literature survey about user modeling interoperability and ubiquitous user modeling was conducted. Through this survey information about the requirements, previous approaches, and challenges in this field have been gathered. A paper was published at AUM'11 (workshop at UMAP'11) [10], offering a mapping between information available in online social web service and how it could aid classic user modeling approaches (some of those presented concepts would be used to bootstrap the graph based user model from social web services). Also a framework for exchanging user model parts between clients and services that require personalization has been designed and partially implemented. The framework uses a common available communication interfaces (QR codes in mobile smart phones) in a novel way to exchange user model parts. A key part that will empower this framework, once implemented and integrated, will be the new graph based representation.

A research proposal detailing the ideas presented in this paper is being drafted nowadays. During which the graph based user modeling representation schema is being continuously developed while emphasizing the need to evaluate against multiply usage scenarios and supporting issues such as scalability/distribution.

OPEN QUESTIONS

Current open questions are related to the evaluation process of the proposed representation and methods. Several social web data sets (e.g., Facebook/Twitter) have been listed as potential bootstrapping sources for the graph based user model; Where can additional related datasets be found (such that are: heterogeneous, span over time and different locations)? What scales of graphs (quantities of nodes and edges per entity category e.g., users/attributes/ semantic data) would be considered as significant for the domain and evaluations? What are possible methods to evaluate aspects such as "user model interoperability"?

REFERENCES

1. Carmagnola, F., Cena, F., Gena, C.: User model interoperability: a survey. User Modeling and User-Adapted Interaction, 1-47 (2011)
2. Heckmann, D., Schwartz, T., Brandherm, B., Schmitz, M., Wilamowitz-Moellendorff, M.: Gumo--the general user model ontology. User modeling 2005, 428-432 (2005)
3. Berkovsky, S., Kuflik, T., Ricci, F.: Mediation of user models for enhanced personalization in recommender systems. User Modeling and User-Adapted Interaction 18(3), 245-286 (August 2008)
4. Kobsa, A.: Generic user modeling systems. User modeling and user-adapted interaction 11(1), 49-63 (2001)
5. Carr, B. P., Goldstein, I. P.: Overlays: A theory of modelling for computer aided instruction. (1977)
6. Aggarwal, C. C., Wolf, J. L., Wu, K. L., Yu, P. S.: Horting hatches an egg: A new graph-theoretic approach to collaborative filtering. In : ACM, pp.201-212 (1999)
7. Huang, Z., Chung, W., Chen, H.: A graph model for E-commerce recommender systems. Journal of the American Society for information science and technology 55(3), 259-274 (2004)
8. Sowa, J. F.: Conceptual graphs summary. In : Ellis Horwood, pp.3-51 (1992)
9. Wikipedia: Graph Database. In: Wikipedia. (Accessed November 2011) Available at: http://en.wikipedia.org/wiki/Graph_database
10. Tiroshi, A., Kuflik, T., Kay, J., Kummerfeld, B.: Recommender Systems and the Social Web. Augmenting User Models with Real World Experiences to Enhance Personalization and Adaptation (AUM '11), UMAP 2011.

An Explanation-Centric Approach for Personalizing Intelligent Agents

Todd Kulesza
Oregon State University
Corvallis, Oregon
kuleszto@eecs.oregonstate.edu

ABSTRACT

Intelligent agents are becoming ubiquitous in the lives of users, but the research community has only recently begun to study how people establish trust in and communicate with such agents. I plan to design an explanation-centric approach to support end users in personalizing their intelligent agents and in assessing their strengths and weaknesses. My goal is to define an approach that helps people understand when they can rely on their intelligent agents' decisions, and allows them to directly debug their agents' reasoning when it does not align with their own.

Author Keywords

Interactive machine learning, mental models, trust, end-user programming.

ACM Classification Keywords

H.5.m. Information interfaces and presentation (e.g., HCI): Miscellaneous.

CONTEXT AND MOTIVATION

Intelligent agents have moved beyond mundane tasks like filtering junk email. Search engines now exploit pattern recognition to detect image content (e.g., clipart, photography, and faces); Facebook and image editors take this a step further, making educated guesses as to *who* is in a particular photo. Netflix and Amazon use collaborative filtering to recommend items of interest to their customers, while Pandora and Last.fm use similar techniques to create radio stations crafted to an individual's idiosyncratic tastes. Simple rule-based systems have evolved into agents employing complex algorithms. These *intelligent agents* are computer programs whose behavior only becomes fully specified *after* learning from an end user's training data. Advances in machine learning and pattern recognition continue to unlock new applications for intelligent agents, but two challenges prevent end users from more fully utilizing the automated decisions and recommendations from these tools.

First, end users of intelligent agents need to understand when they can trust, their agent's work. Such trust is highly contextual—some of the agent's predictions may not matter at all to an end user, while others may matter a great deal. Further, the agent's reasoning is constantly changing as it learns from the user's behavior, so a system that was reliable yesterday may not be trustworthy today.

The second challenge is about personalization. When an intelligent agent's reasoning causes it to perform unexpectedly in the field, only the end user is in a position to personalize, or more accurately, *to debug*, the agent's flawed reasoning. Here, debugging refers to *mindfully and purposely* adjusting the agent's reasoning (after its initial training) so it more closely matches the user's expectations. Recent research has made inroads into supporting this type of functionality [1,8,10,13], but debugging can be difficult for even trained software developers—helping end users, who have knowledge of neither software engineering nor machine learning, is no trivial task.

I believe these two challenges—establishing contextual trust in an agent, and aligning its reasoning with a specific end user's—are inherently linked. My thesis work aims to understand how people reason about intelligent agents, how people communicate with intelligent agents, and how intelligent agents can improve their reasoning given these communications. I hypothesize that explaining an agent's reasoning to end users will enable them to form better judgments of the agent's reliability, and to provide feedback that can substantially improve the agent's future predictions, as illustrated in Figure 1.

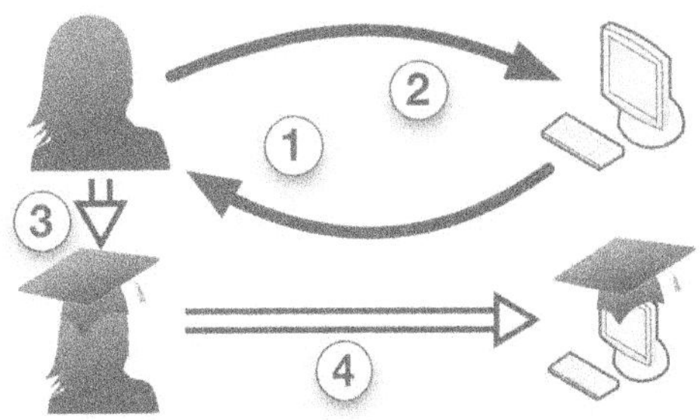

Figure 1: I envision a cyclic, explanation-based approach for users to learn about the agent's reasoning (1) and interactively adjust it (2). In the process, the user learns more about how to effectively steer the agent (3), with the eventual outcome of "more intelligent" intelligent agents (4).

RELATED WORK

Mental Models

Mental models are internal representations that people build based on their experiences in the real world. There are two main types of mental models: *Functional* (shallow) models provide the ability to use a system, whereas *structural* (deep) models provide a detailed understanding of how and *why* it works. These models do not have to be entirely *complete* to be useful, but they must be *sound* (i.e., accurate) enough to support effective interactions. Many instances of unsound mental models guiding erroneous behavior have been observed [15].

When things go wrong, the richness of a mental model can also have an effect. While a structural model can help someone deal with unexpected behavior and fix the problem, a purely functional model does not provide the abstract concepts required for such interactions [7]. Knowing how to *use* a computer, for example, does not mean you can *fix* one that fails to power on.

Because much of this thesis rests upon end users' ability to understand and adjust an intelligent agent's reasoning, an understanding of how users build mental models of this reasoning is foundational. Outside the realm of intelligent agents, it has been argued that users should be exposed to transparent, intuitive systems and appropriate instructions to build mental models [18]. *Scaffolded instruction* is one method that has been shown to contribute positively to learning to use a new system [16], but has not been explored in the context of machine leaning.

To date, very little work has investigated end users' mental models of an intelligent system. One study found prolonged use of such a system induced plausible models of its reasoning, but these models were surprisingly hard to shift, even when people were aware of contradictory evidence [21]. My preliminary work has found that users will change their mental models for an intelligent agent when it makes its reasoning transparent [10], but some explanations by agents may lead to only shallow mental models [19].

Interactive Machine Learning

There has been recent interest in supporting the debugging of intelligent agents' reasoning [1,8,10,12,13,19]. This debugging consists of two components: explanations about the agent's current reasoning, and end-user corrections to align this reasoning with his or her own.

For users to debug an intelligent agent's reasoning, they must first be able to see it. Explanations of intelligent agent's reasoning have taken a variety of forms, such as relating user actions and the resulting predictions [3], detailing why a program made a particular prediction [14], or explaining how an outcome resulted from user actions [21,22]. However, these explanations are limited to account for the intelligent agent's past behavior and do not extend to accepting user corrections to adapt *future* behavior.

The second component of interactive machine learning consists of users debugging faults in the machine's reasoning. One such system, EnsembleMatrix [20], provides a visualization of a classifier's accuracy and the means to adjust its logic, but is targeted at machine-learning experts *developing* complex ensemble classifiers, rather than end users *working with* the resulting classifiers. ManiMatrix [8] provides an interactive visualization of a classifier's accuracy, but user interactions are restricted to modifying a classifier's cost matrix. Most closely related to my own work, Stumpf et al. have explored potential end-user debugging techniques for intelligent agents, finding that even simple corrections from end users have the potential to increase the accuracy of an agent's predictions [19]. Some participants' corrections, however, decreased the quality of the agent's predictions; there were barriers that prevented them from successfully debugging the agent. I conducted a study [11] building upon this work, identifying and categorizing these barriers and the information participants requested to overcome them.

Contextual Trust

Existing work has investigated how end users establish trust in intelligent agents [6], identifying a number of themes (e.g., transparency, user expectations) that impact users' trust in such systems. Other researchers have identified a positivity bias toward trusting intelligent agents (i.e., people trust the agent without initial proof that it is trustworthy) [5]; this same bias is well-established among human interactions [4].

Dzindolet et al. found that end users quickly lose trust in agents once even a handful of agent mistakes are observed [5]. One explanation for this erosion of trust comes from theories on expectations, or *schemas*, in which unexpected situations stand out as individual events in memory, while expected situations are lumped together as a single schema [2] (e.g., someone is unlikely to remember the specifics of brushing his or her teeth this morning, but everyone can likely recall a time they dropped their toothbrush someplace they did not want it to land). Thus, after only a few mistakes on the part of the intelligent agent, an end user may be unduly influenced by the memory of these aberrations, and so form a lesser degree of trust in the system than may be warranted. My preliminary work has also found evidence of this phenomenon—in a 10-minute assessment task that involved identifying an agent's mistakes, participants consistently reported that the agent was less reliable than it actually was [9].

STATEMENT OF THESIS

The purpose of my dissertation research is to improve peoples' experiences with intelligent agents in two specific ways: (1) by helping people correct errant agents, and (2) by helping people establish appropriate levels of trust in their agent's work. My central thesis is that two-way communication between the user and the intelligent agent will be necessary for each of these tasks; thus, much of my research will investigate explanations (both from the agent to the user and from the user to the agent), their potential content, and the impact this content may have on user's mental models and the agent's reasoning.

RESEARCH GOALS AND METHODS

Because replicating experiments over the diverse range of intelligent agents is a prohibitively large undertaking, I propose to focus on the domain of music recommendation systems. Music recommendation embodies two of the components of intelligent agents I care most about—they are widely used, and their work is *beneficial* without being *critical* to their end users. This is a more challenging problem than studying agents that perform critical tasks, because non-critical systems cannot assume a high level of attention and effort from their users. Further, low-cost solutions to these problems are likely to applicable to high-criticality systems, whereas high-cost solutions are unlikely to be useful for non-critical domains.

RQ1.1 (cost/benefit): How much will end users assess and provide feedback to intelligent agents when the perceived benefits are relatively low?

RQ1.2 (cost/benefit): How can interfaces lower the cost of assessing and providing feedback when the perceived benefits are relatively low?

I plan to study RQ1.1 via a longitudinal study of a deployed recommender system, while using low-fidelity prototypes to iteratively explore RQ1.2 in a laboratory setting.

My hypothesis is that sound structural mental models of the agent's reasoning will be critical to both assessment and feedback, so I will explore how mental models impact trust in and corrections of intelligent agents. Because this work will inform the design of explanations of an agent's reasoning, I will also explore how different attributes of explanations (salience, visibility, concreteness, etc.) influence the feedback users provide intelligent agents. I plan to develop a taxonomy of these attributes and the various trade-offs associated with them.

RQ2.1 (mental models): Do sound structural mental models of an intelligent agent's reasoning lead to more appropriate perceptions of its reliability?

RQ2.2 (mental models): Do sound structural mental models of an intelligent agent's reasoning lead to improved end-user debugging of its reasoning?

RQ2.3 (explanation attributes): What are common attributes of machine-generated explanations, and how do they influence the feedback provided by end users?

I plan to investigate RQ2.1 with a Wizard-of-Oz study. One of my goals for the Doctoral Consortium is to discuss methods for reliably exploring RQs 2.2 and 2.3. RQ2.3 seems particularly suited to a grounded theory approach, and will hopefully lead to a vocabulary and methodology for evaluating explanations.

I next intend to investigate methods for end users to communicate, either implicitly or explicitly, which of an agent's decisions matter most. Current work on active learning [17] views end users as tireless oracles—the main goal of such techniques is to shore up "fuzzy" decision boundaries by eliciting more details from the end user. I hypothesize the converse is attainable—end users could tell agents which of their decisions or decision boundaries need to be reliably accurate, so that any information the agents ask users to provide is directly related to what the user most needs the agent to get right.

RQ3.1 (evaluation abstraction): At what level of abstraction do users prefer to assess an agent's reasoning (e.g., decision boundaries, individual predictions, etc.)?

RQ3.2 (evaluation prioritization): Can end users tell intelligent agents which predictions matter to them in a way that allows the agent to apply active learning techniques to focus on particular classes or decision boundaries?

RQ3.1 will be investigated via a formative lab study involving low-fidelity intelligent agent prototypes. During this study I expect to gather participant feedback in a manner that will permit me to run offline studies exploring RQ3.2 via modifications to active learning techniques.

To conclude my dissertation research, I plan to use the results of RQs 1-3 to inform an approach for end users to assess and debug the reasoning of intelligent agents. This will be followed with a summative user study to evaluate the overall success of (and individual strengths and weaknesses inherent in) the approach. In essence, I will be attempting to answer these final research questions:

RQ4.1 (effectiveness): Can end users reliably assess the accuracy of an intelligent agent via an explanation-centric approach?

RQ4.2 (effectiveness): Can end users reliably improve the accuracy of an intelligent agent via an explanation-centric approach?

DISSERTATION STATUS

I am currently studying RQs 1 and 2 via a longitudinal study of end users steering a customizable music recommendation system. The preliminary results suggest that end users are initially willing to spend time and effort debugging an agent's reasoning, and that the more they learn about how the agent while debugging it, the more beneficial they view these debugging efforts. I have previously investigated parts of RQ 2 via both a qualitative study and a summative quantitative study, identifying a vocabulary end users wanted to employ when explaining corrections to an intelligent agent, and finding that presenting "run-time" debugging explanations to end users helped them debug the agent's reasoning more than "static" explanations of the agent's logic [10]. I have also begun exploring RQ3 with a statistical study exploring how end users responded to a systematic approach for assessing an agent's decisions, and testing a technique for leveraging user assessments to test similar agent predictions [9].

I plan to use qualitative studies to explore RQs 1.2, 2.3, 3.1, and 3.2, which I hope to complete in the next 18 months. These results will iteratively inform an explanation-centric debugging and assessment approach and prototype. This approach and prototype will be evaluated by a final summative study approximately two years from now.

OPEN QUESTIONS

I have three primary questions to discuss with the researchers at the IUI Doctoral Consortium.

First, capturing mental models is not trivial [15]. I would like to discuss other researchers' experiences capturing mental models, including methods others have found useful and potential drawbacks to be aware of.

Second, I am still uncertain of how to design formative studies to answer RQ2, and would like to discuss design ideas with researchers who have performed similar formative work.

Finally, I am looking for different levels of abstraction to use when investigating RQ 3.1. The two I have in mind are general decision boundaries and individual predictions, but would like to hear ideas from researchers who have more extensive machine learning backgrounds than my own.

My dissertation research is gathering momentum, and with approximately two years left, I feel this is an ideal time to discuss my work at the IUI Doctoral Consortium. I have enough experience with human-computer interaction research to constructively discuss the work of fellow students, but am not yet too far along to integrate their advice into my own research.

REFERENCES

1. Amershi, S., Fogarty, J., Kapoor, A. and Tan, D. 2010. Examining multiple potential models in end-user interactive concept learning. *Proc. CHI*, 1357–1360.
2. Ashcraft, M.H. 1994. *Human memory and cognition.* Harpercollins College Div.
3. Billsus, D. and Hilbert, D. 2005. Improving proactive information systems. *Proc. IUI*, 159-166.
4. Bruner, J.S. and Tagiuri, R. 1954. The Perception of People. *Handbook of Social Psychology*. G. Lindzey, ed. Addison-Wesley.
5. Dzindolet, M.T., Peterson, S.A., Pomranky, R.A., and Pierce, L.G. 2003. The role of trust in automation reliance. *International Journal of Human-Computer Studies*. 58, 6 (Jun. 2003), 697–718.
6. Glass, A., McGuinness, D. and Wolverton, M. 2008. Toward establishing trust in adaptive agents. *Proc. IUI*, 227-236.
7. Johnson-Laird, P.N. 1983. *Mental Models: Towards a Cognitive Science of Language, Inference, and Consciousness*. Cambridge University Press.
8. Kapoor, A., Lee, B., Tan, D. and Horvitz, E. 2010. Interactive optimization for steering machine classification. *Proc. CHI*, 1343-1352.
9. Kulesza, T., Burnett, M., Stumpf, S., Wong, W., Das, S., Groce, A., Shinsel, A., Bice, F. and McIntosh, K. 2011. Where Are My Intelligent Assistant's Mistakes? A Systematic Testing Approach. *Proc. IS-EUD*, 171–186.
10. Kulesza, T., Stumpf, S., Burnett, M., Wong, W.-K., Riche, Y., Moore, T., Oberst, I., Shinsel, A. and McIntosh, K. 2010. Explanatory Debugging: Supporting End-User Debugging of Machine-Learned Programs. *Proc. VL/HCC* (2010), 41–48.
11. Kulesza, T., Stumpf, S., Wong, W.-K., Burnett, M., Perona, S., Ko, A. and Obsert, I. 2011. Why-Oriented End-User Debugging of Naive Bayes Text Classification. *ACM Transactions on Interactive Intelligent Systems*. 1, 1 (Oct. 2011).
12. Kulesza, T., Wong, W.-K., Stumpf, S., Perona, S., White, R., Burnett, M., Oberst, I. and Ko, A. 2009. Fixing the program my computer learned: barriers for end users, challenges for the machine. *Proc. IUI.*
13. Lim, B. and Dey, A. 2010. Toolkit to support intelligibility in context-aware applications. *Proc. Ubicomp*, 13-22.
14. Lim, B., Dey, A. and Avrahami, D. 2009. Why and why not explanations improve the intelligibility of context-aware intelligent systems. *Proc. CHI*, 2119-2128.
15. Norman, D. 1983. Some Observations on Mental Models. *Mental Models*. D. Gentner and A. Stevens, eds. Psychology Press.
16. Rosson, M. and Carrol, J. 1990. Smalltalk scaffolding: a case study of minimalist instruction. *Proc. CHI*, 423-429.
17. Settles, B. 2009. *Active learning literature survey*. University of Wisconsin-Madison.
18. Sharp, H., Rogers, Y. and Preece, J. 2007. *Interaction Design*. John Wiley & Sons Inc.
19. Stumpf, S., Rajaram, V., Li, L., Wong, W., Burnett, M., Dietterich, T., Sullivan, E. and Herlocker, J. 2009. Interacting meaningfully with machine learning systems: Three experiments. *International Journal of Human-Computer Studies*. 67, 8 (Aug. 2009), 639–662.
20. Talbot, J., Lee, B., Kapoor, A. and Tan, D. 2009. EnsembleMatrix: Interactive visualization to support machine learning with multiple classifiers. *Proc. CHI*, 1283-1292.
21. Tullio, J., Dey, A., Chalecki, J. and Fogarty, J. 2007. How it works: a field study of non-technical users interacting with an intelligent system. *Proc. CHI*, 31-40.
22. Vig, J., Sen, S. and Riedl, J. 2009. Tagsplanations: explaining recommendations using tags. *Proc IUI*, 47-56.

Design for Reflection on Health Behavior Change

Feng Gao
University of Southampton
Southampton, SO17 1BJ, United Kingdom
fg3g09@ecs.soton.ac.uk

ABSTRACT
Although the persuasion-based health behavior change systems have achieved certain success particularly in motivating physical activity, researchers now start criticizing that persuasion-based systems have problems in taking over too much control, paying not enough attention to people's thinking, and failing in acknowledging external constraints and exploring resources. The alternative notion of reflection has been supported by different researchers' views, and in my thesis work I aim to explore this notion in the context of dietary change. The main goal of my thesis work is to explore what people think in the different food-related activities and apply those understandings into system designs to foster and assist people's reflection on everyday dietary change.

Author Keywords
Behavior change, dietary change, reflection.

ACM Classification Keywords
H5.m. Information interfaces and presentation (e.g., HCI): Miscellaneous.

General Terms
Human Factors

CONTEXT AND MOTIVATION
It is predicted by the World Health Organization [13] that in 2015, 41 million people will die due to various chronic diseases: such as heart diseases, diabetes, obesity and cancer. Chronic diseases are reported to be highly linked to three health-related behaviors: unhealthy eating, physical inactivity and tobacco use. Encouraging people to change those unhealthy behaviors is one reasonable way to prevent chronic diseases.

On the other hand, considering the role of design in our world, Papanek argues that one job of design is "to transform man's environment and tools and, by extension, man himself" [10]. Based upon this argument and the rapid development of Information and communication technology, it is not surprising that technology could be designed to achieve motivating and assisting humans' positive health-related behavior change. My thesis work thus is motivated by this big background to explore how to design technology for health-related behavior change and particularly focus on the notion of reflection which is discussed below.

RELATED WORK: FROM PERSUASTION TO REFLECTION
Persuasive Technology [4] , which is defined as technology to change attitudes or behaviors of the users through persuasion, has inspired several successful research projects to change health-related behavior. One basic feature of persuasive technology is to simplify certain tasks and convey persuasive messages to users. Successful systems like Ubifit [2] take advantage of Ubicomp technology to collect behavior data by various sensors. Such so called self-monitoring or quantified-self notion is popular in today's design and it does offer both researchers and users a good opportunity to collect enough data about an individual's behavior and assess those behavior based on quantitative standards like daily calorie amount. In addition, those systems also try to offer feedbacks based upon users' progress, for example, the Fish 'n' Steps [6] introduced animated fish as a reward for users who make progress on having more steps. Such reward as a feedback motivates users to keep being engaged in the process of change. Social support also has been taken into account to support behavior change. Application like MAHI [8] established a patient-expert network to help new diabetes patients receive feedbacks from experts based upon their continuous self-monitoring data.

Those persuasion-based systems, even though they have achieved certain success, mainly focusing on simplifying behavior change. However, as [11] pointed out, while those systems make certain actions such as monitoring behavior more simpler, they also take the opportunity that people could proactively engage in understanding, practicing and maintaining behavior change from users. In other words, current behavior change system design follows the design philosophy that aims to make people more efficient when carrying out tasks. The design philosophy was developed in the context of office and business, in which people expect that systems could improve their productive and reduce cognitive loads [5]. But in behavior change, even people dream of efficient and fast change, the reality is different.

As we discussed before, behavior change is a complicated process and requires people to proactively engage in the whole process of change for a long term. The slowness in learning, practicing and maintaining a new behavior is the nature of behavior change and it is not bad at all. In fact, such slowness gives people the opportunity to know themselves, the environment and other people much better. It expects people could slow down their pace to reflect on what they did and what they could achieve. The slowness, therefore, should be acknowledged by system design and be harnessed in technology-based intervention. The slow technology [5] thus could be introduced to help us re-consider how we design behavior change technology. Unlike fast technology (e.g. the persuasive technology we described above) that compresses time to achieve given tasks, the slow technology aims to provide people with time to reflect on what they do, what resources they have and what they could achieve. For example, instead of simplifying how people evaluate food by providing auto or semi-auto calorie counting, the system could create opportunity for people to proactively engage in the evaluation of food to help people reflect on their food choice and understand what is healthy food.

In addition to the slow technology, the mindful technology [1] also supports the notion of reflection in the process of behavior change:

"Mindful technologies focus on engagement with one's mental and emotional state as a medium for behavior change and well-being. This focus on technology-mediated reflection is contrasted by many health technologies that are reactive in nature: technologies that prescribe behavior change."

Indeed, those persuasion-based technologies try to prescribe behavior change in a way that technologies encapsulate existing behavior change theories or guidelines into a digital agent. But those existing behavior change theories are usually static and inflexible [12], thus persuasion-based technologies can not make frequent iterative adjustment on the intervention to meet new requirements. Therefore, similar with the Don Norman's view [9] that users usually blame themselves when computer interface can not work, our view is that users likely attribute blame to themselves instead of the digital agents when users fail in the process of behavior change. Even though such failure might be due to constraints that can not be overcame by the individual, users will still feel guilty of the failure and likely give up trying changes and stop the interaction with the technology.

Unlike persuasion-based technologies, personal trainers, even though they also design interventions based on those static behavior change theories, have the ability to tailor intervention based on their experience and the interaction with their clients in which they could know the progress the individual makes and understand constraints the individual faces. The interaction here means the process of negotiation between the client and the personal trainer; it means they need to sit down and work together on the behavior change plan. In Maitland's PhD thesis [7], Maitland further argues that technology could be designed in a new way that help people to exploit, highlight or develop resources or acknowledge constraints. In terms of acknowledging constraints, Maitland suggests technology should acknowledge that people have different constraints and appraise small progresses users make under those constraints. Moreover, while technology interventions impossibly give people more money to buy healthy food or build a new store to provide more healthy food, technology does have the ability to help people reflect on how they could organize and use available resources. For example, a shopping planner could be developed to help people make reasonable shopping plan on a tight budget and tight schedule by highlighting cheap stores or farm markets and planning convenient route for shopping.

RESEARCH GOALS, QUESTIONS AND METHODS

In my thesis work, I will reflect on the success and problems of systems in persuasive technology category and try to explore the notion of reflection. Particularly, since our group has special interest in the relation of food to dietary change, this thesis work will explore the notion of reflection in the context of dietary change to

(1) Understand what people think while they are engaged in activities including discovering, planning, shopping, eating and assessing food in everyday life,

(2) Understand what people think while interacting with technologies supporting above activities, and

(3) Mapping above understandings into intervention and interaction design in order to foster and assist reflection on dietary behavior change.

More specific, this thesis work will explore how to design systems to foster and support two different type of reflection that occurs in different dietary change activities: reflection-on-action (logging and assessing how healthy you eat) and reflection-in-action (discovering, planning and shopping foods).

Reflection-on-Action: Design for Reflection on How Healthy You Eat

In terms of reflection-on-action, I will aim to develop novel system/user interface to assist people in making meaningful assessment of how healthy they ate.

The specific design challenges with respect to my thesis aim are:

(1) How to engage people in assessing how healthy they ate?

The notion of gamification could be adopted to develop game-like systems to provide users with incentives that could motivate people to assess foods' healthiness. In addition, social influence, social facilitation and social support mechanisms could be introduced to make people engage in evaluation of foods' healthiness with other people.

(2) How to design user interfaces to map people's thought on foods' healthiness into an evaluation interface?

To investigate this design challenge, one research question should be first asked is how people evaluate everyday foods' healthiness without technology support. A qualitative research method could be adopted to collect data of what foods' attributes people mention and what strategies they use when they are asked to evaluate the healthiness of a real foods. The results of the study could provide a framework on what and how attributes/strategies could be abstracted or directly mapped into the interface design to help people express their thoughts and foster discussion and reflection.

(3) How to design user interfaces to support people's better interpretation of evaluation results?

The specific challenge here is what information the system should present to help a specific person interpret the result from several aspects: whether my understanding is right, which part I do well, and what action I might take based upon the result. The key open question here is how the system could tailor the information and presentation/visualization based upon the specific person's various contexts such as diet knowledge, diet type, and eating history.

Reflection-in-action: Design for Reflection in the Process of Discovering, Planning and Shopping for Food

The first part of my work more focuses on the after-thought and tries to improve people's skill of evaluation of food. In the second part of my work, I will further explore how the system could assist people in making real changes. The particular focus will be on how the system could help people make better choice when discovering, planning and shopping food. The system, in terms of reflection, will ask thought-provoking questions and presenting information in a thought-provoking way to guide people re-think about their food choice. Particularly, the system is expected to have the ability to tailor its questions and visualizations to a particular user's particular contexts. Therefore, The specific design challenges with respect to my thesis's aim are:

(1) How different contexts might influence people's food choice?

The system needs a model to describe what type of contexts might influence people's food choice then the system could possibly know how to ask right questions to collect necessary contexts from user or how to provide right information based upon those contexts. The model could be developed based upon previous literature in health domain and possible interview/survey studies we might conduct.

(2) How the system could collect the contexts?

The system is expected to be able to determine what context information it needs based upon current particular scenario and then determine how information should be collected. For example, a person who wants to build muscle just finished workout and now is going to have a lunch before the next lecture starting 30 minutes later. How the system could be aware of all those contexts -- the goal (building muscle), the physical activity status (finished workout), and the constraint (30 minutes) -- is a real challenge. Two open questions are asked: How the system could determine what type of contexts it needs based upon data it has now? And how the system could collect all data without requiring user to explicitly input everything?

(3) How the system tailor its visualizations of information motivate people make better decisions?

Finally, the last challenge is on how food resources data will be visualized with the annotation of contexts such as dietary goals and specific constraints in order to provide a specific user with a clear view on what they could do under specific constraints. Particularly this is about how the system could personalize its output to meet a specific person's goals and needs.

This part research will aim to design two example systems to support people's lunch discovering and planning on campus and people's grocery planning and shopping in the city. This part research will also employ qualitative research method to solicit food determinants information and the process of food-related decision making from people and then apply understandings I gain into real system design to look at how a model could be developed. User studies will be conducted to collect data on how people interact with the system particularly on how they have the conversation with the system to provide data and collect data on how the system might engage people in reflection on what they could achieve under specific constraints.

DISSERTATION STATUS

Thus far, I have completed two research studies and one application design, which all focus on reflection-in-action. The first research study, as an exploratory study, tried to understand (1) what prevent people from achieving successful change while they are given certain supports and (2) how they seek and give help in a community. In the study, I selected two online communities as targets: Tweetwhatyoueat and Precision Nutrition. Each community offers two kind of supports: guidance on what is good dietary and tools to track diet. The research method I adopted is qualitative analysis of two communities' forum posts. By analyzing those posts about issues people have in practicing dietary change and summarizing the way they ask and offer help, I reported four key findings in the poster [3] presented at Pervasive Health 2011:

(1) People describe contextual information and personal condition to point out barriers to dietary change

(2) People like to connect with people who share similar conditions or who have similar experience

(3) People need the community support to review and verify own understandings and opinions

(4) People share and discuss their emotional attitudes to food and dietary change

The second study I conducted tried to understand how people evaluate food's healthiness. I conducted a survey study to ask participants rate 15 food photos and give explanations. In this survey study, I successfully identified 8 approaches/attributes people use to evaluate food's healthiness: *Brand, Comparison&Relation, Nutrient Use, Health Effect, Quality, Portion Size, Uncertainty and Equivalence Labeling.*

Another exploratory design I have done is an iPhone application that is called "GoodFood". This application encourages people to take pictures of what they eat and assess foods' healthiness based upon five heuristics. The application currently is available on App store and a field study will be conducted later.

At my next stage of work, the focus will be mainly on supporting food discovery, planning and shopping. One planned study is to develop and study a system that could assist university students in discovering and planning their lunch on the campus. I will first investigate design opportunities and challenges based upon the review of theoretical frameworks of food choice. Then I will apply the understandings into real system design. This work is expected to aim for top conference in HCI area.

OPEN QUESTIONS

My open questions here are mainly related to my second part of research and I expect to get feedback from other researchers on what methodology I could use to tackle those challenges:

1. How does context influence decisions around the food choices? And how the system could develop a model to describe it?
2. How will these contexts be identified without the person having to say explicitly this is what I'm doing?
3. How will that context affect delivery of food-related information? How will this content be pushed to the user depending on that context?

REFERENCES

1. Chen, F. What is a Mindful Technology? Design Mindfulness.http://www.designmindfulness.com/2011/04/what-is-a-mindful-technology/. Last Accessed:10/12/2011
2. Consolvo, S., Klasnja, P., McDonald, D.W., et al. Flowers or a robot army? Flowers or a robot army?: encouraging awareness & activity with personal, mobile displays. *UbiComp (2008)*, 54-63.
3. Feng, G. and Schraefel, M. Social interaction around diet applications: An initial study. *PervasiveHealth* (2011), 262-265.
4. Fogg, B.J. *Persuasive technology: using computers to change what we think and do.* Morgan Kaufmann Publishers Inc., 2002.
5. Hallnas, L. and Redstrom, J. Slow Technology - Designing for Reflection. *Personal and Ubiquitous Computing 5*, 3 (2001).
6. Lin, J.J., Mamykina, L., Lindtner, S., Delajoux, G., and Strub, H.B. Fish'n'Steps: encouraging physical activity with an interactive computer game. *Ubicomp (2006), 261-278.*
7. Maitland, J. From persuasion to negotiation in health promoting technology. 2009. Doctoral Thesis, University of Glasgow.
8. Mamykina, L., Mynatt, E., Davidson, P., and Greenblatt, D. MAHI: investigation of social scaffolding for reflective thinking in diabetes management. *CHI (2008).*
9. Norman, D.A. *The Psychology of Everyday Things.* Basic Books, 1988.
10. Papanek, V. *Design for the Real World: Human Ecology and Social Change.* Academy Chicago Publishers, 1985.
11. Purpura, S., Schwanda, V., Williams, K., Stubler, W., and Sengers, P. Fit4Life□: The Design of a Persuasive Technology Promoting Healthy Behavior and Ideal Weight. *CHI (2011)*, 423-432.
12. Riley, W.T., Rivera, D.E., Atienza, A.A., Nilsen, W., Allison, S.M., and Mermelstein, R. Health behavior models in the age of mobile interventions: are our theories up to the task? *Translational Behavioral Medicine 1*, 1 (2011), 53-71.
13. World Health Organization. *Preventing chronic diseases: a vital investment.* 2005.

Managing Implicit Assumptions In Natural Language Interfaces

Dustin Arthur Smith
MIT Media Lab
E15-358; 77 Massachusetts Ave
Cambridge, MA 02139; USA
dustin@media.mit.edu

ABSTRACT

A person's choice of what to communicate and how to communicate it depends on the information he or she believes is shared with the audience. This presents a challenge for natural language interfaces, because it is hard for people to predict what information they share with the interface and how it will use this information to interpret their text. This is especially difficult for pragmatic-level assumptions supplied by the interpreter that go beyond the information in the surface text, because these assumptions are negotiated in dialogue and frequently revised or redacted.

We have built a calendaring interface that allows users to communicate English event descriptions. This constrained task gives us a clear criteria for communication success and failure. Failures are opportunities to acquire and revise assumptions: to collect lexical and semantic knowledge from a variety of users. By lowering the interaction barrier so end users can contribute to the linguistic interpretation process, we can collect culture-specific lexical and semantic knowledge directly from the members of the cultural group who possess it. This knowledge is essential for the pragmatic task of deriving what a speaker *meant* from what they *said*.

The goal of this research is to make the assumptions involved with interpreting natural language explicit to the user. Using a model of language generation and interpretation based on planning and plan recognition, we capture, through user contributions, word definitions and commonsense assumptions–and we represent both as belief-changing actions. Using visualizations and a direct manipulation interface, users can access the interpretation status, inspect which assumptions were made, and suggest or modify existing assumptions. With the aim of providing the functionally equivalent of the negotiation stage in interpersonal dialogue, we evaluate the interface by how it allows users to revise and extend assumptions toward successful interpretation.

Author Keywords

Natural Language Interfaces; Knowledge Acquisition; End-User Programming; Commonsense; Event Management

ACM Classification Keywords

H.5.2 Information Interfaces and Presentation: User Interfaces—*Natural language*; I.2.6 Artificial Intelligence: Artificial Intelligence—*Knowledge acquisition*; I.2.6 Artificial Intelligence: Artificial Intelligence—*Language acquisition*

CONTEXT AND MOTIVATION

When people communicate using natural language, we rely on shared information; for example by using words with shared meanings, referring to entities in the environment that were jointly perceived, and assuming commonsense knowledge. When we communicate with a computer, it's harder, because we don't necessarily know *what* the computer knows nor *how* it will interpret our message. The distinctions people choose to communicate and the words we use to do so are influenced by what we expect our audience knows. Sometimes computers know too little: your phone will correctly respond to "call Mom" but not "call her back". Sometimes it seems they know too much: "call José" presents you with 5 guys, some of whom you haven't talked with in years. If you say "meet at Pastéis de Belém", and the words "Pastéis de Belém" activated a Lisbon café in your listener's mind, it is because that was a convention you and he shared.

Suppose you say "dinner at 6" to Google Calendar. It will create a new event and correctly populate the starting time to 6 pm. However, if you enter "dinner at 9", it will misinterpret the time reference as the inaccurate 9 *am*. If you say this to a person, he will cooperatively supply an assumption that you meant 9 *pm* and not *am*; but, will just as easily revise this assumption later if you gave him the additional information that "9" is the name of a nearby restaurant that you enjoy. In both cases, the human listener supplied assumptions that went beyond your utterance in an effort to fill in all of the information he thought you *intended* to communicate.

When interpreting language, a human listener will offer his own assumptions, which we can think of as joint actions toward a shared communication goal. Linguists call these implicit, pragmatic-level assumptions **conversational implicatures** [7]. Conversational implicatures are prone to errors and are characterized by their defeasability or negotiability [3]: a listener can ask the speaker for confirmation or clarification, and in turn revise or redact his assumption. Assumptions are shared and circulate among individuals and their social groups and can become commonsense. When we talk to people or a natural language interface, the assumptions they use to understand what we say are beyond our control. An interpreter may over-cooperate and make assumptions that we did not expect or think were justified; for instance, imagine if Google Calendar also chose *whom* to invite to your dinner tomorrow morning!

We take the position that interpretation failures, particularly at the pragmatic level, are an inescapable part of the communication process. Currently, when a computer interprets natural language, the human user is excluded from the interpretation process, or can only interact using a single modality (natural language: spoken or written). How can users interact with these underlying assumptions? How can we make it easier to repair interpretation failures when they inevitability occur, ideally so that the computer does not make the same mistake again? My research goal is to uncover how best to reveal the assumptions involved with language interpretation to end-users in a way that is analogous to a good debugging tool, which allows programmers to quickly track down and correct the root cause of a problem—in our case, the problem is a misunderstanding.

To keep this paper succinct, I first explain a constrained communication task and then review linguistic terminology to confirm my words are in the **common ground**[1].

Task: communicating English event descriptions

Our interface is part of a personal calendaring application, where the user's communication task is to describe a concrete event representation to a computer. The interface's communication goal is to recover the same concrete event that the user intended to convey with her description; moving it into the common ground. We represent the result of an event interpretation using four **event components**; and so our communication task can be translated into four selection tasks:

1. Picking a **starting time** from a set of 1440 minutes in a day.
2. Picking a **starting day** from the set of $365n$ days in the next $n = 5$ years.
3. Picking a **location** from the set of all locations in a Point of Interest database, e.g., Yahoo! Local API.
4. Picking a **group of people** from the set of 2^n subgroups of an n-person social network, e.g. Facebook or Google Contacts.

Any combination of multiple choices (subsets) for each component forms a potential **belief state**, which initially represents all of the possible events that can be communicated. For our task domain, the collaborative goal is for the computer and user to establish a definite reference for an event's starting time, starting day, location and attendees. Communication progresses from a state of maximal uncertainty about each of the event's components, to complete certainty, when each event component contains one member and thus the combined size of the event's belief state is 4.

[1]Common ground is sum of beliefs thought to be mutual knowledge among communicating parties.

Users can communicate the event using two modalities: written natural language and direct manipulation. Analogous to a direct manipulation selection task, the linguistic task of individuating specific items from a set is called **generating** a **referring expression** [12]. To do this, the user must first select words that discriminate the intended referents from the possible referents. For example, the referring expression "tomorrow" selects an individual starting day from a set of possible days. The intended referent, e.g. November 8th, is called the **target set** and is selected from possible referents called the **context set**, whose non-target set members comprise the **contrast set**.

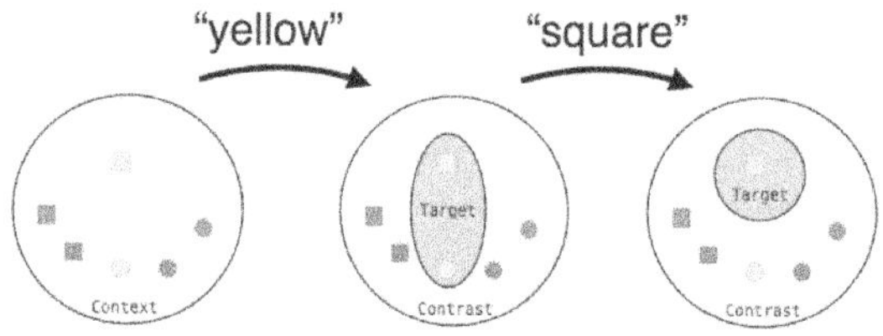

Figure 1. Starting with a *context set* (leftmost circle) containing 6 members, the referring expression "yellow square" incrementally generates a *target set* with one member and a *contrast set* with 5. The progression from left to right shows two actions segments of the interpretation process.

Because our event communication task is constrained, it gives us clear criteria of when the communication goal has been met; or, to use another term from sociolinguistics, when both participants' **grounding criteria** (GC) has been met [5]—there is a single member in all of the four target sets.

GC: Does the set of referents (*target set*) specify a concrete event description?

In this view, a single interpretation of an event description is a sequence of interleaved belief state refinement actions, which can either be caused by the user, using language or direct manipulation, or by the interpreter putting forth assumptions. This is conveyed in figure 2:

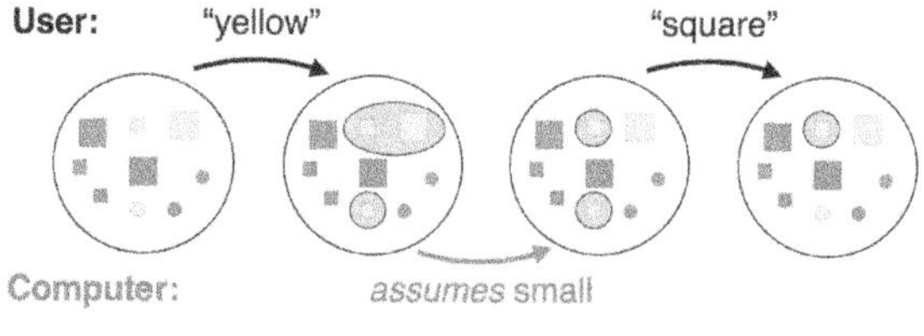

Figure 2. Here we have added three additional objects (large squares) to the context set of figure 1, and show an example of the interpreter cooperatively adding an assumption toward the joint goal deriving an interpretation.

In figure 2, the interpreter offers the assumption that the user intended to specify *small* items. For concreteness, imagine that the items represent profiteroles at a dessert buffet, and a friend is asking you to pass him one. You know that your friend is on a diet, so when he begins to describe a sugary dessert item, saying "yellow...", you cooperatively provide the assumption that he wants a smaller portion.

Each action, either corresponding to a word or an implicit assumption, an *action* in the overall belief state plan to achieve the communication goal. Following [3, 8], controlling which assumptions and word-producing actions are deployed can be construed as a planning problem, where the goal is to find the interpretation path(s) with the lowest cost.

Any interpretation is a specific plan, and we use a subway map as a visual metaphor to represent the plan's progress (figure 3). As the plan progresses toward the joint goal of the GC, we extend the line from starting belief state (containing the full contrast set) to the right, a goal state, where the set size is 1.

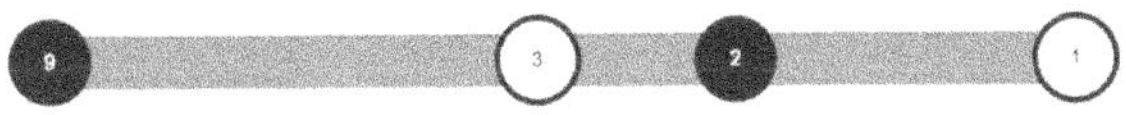

Figure 3. This subway visualization shows the interpretation plan from figure 2 that a user could to see the status of the interpretation task and alter its decisions. The line colors convey which event component is being represented. Circles represent action's effects and the current size of the target set after the action. User actions, denoted by white circles ③, are observed words or interface actions; assumptions that the computer made are filled circles ❷. The numbers indicate the size of the current target set, progressing from left to the rightmost goal state: ❶ or ①. We use a logarithmic scale because the last refinements tend to involve very small belief states.

Research from automated planning has argued that goal recognition can be viewed as planning in reverse [1] and demonstrated how to use the representations of actions and goal states from classical planning models to implement goal recognition [11]. Just as generating a referring expression can be modeled using planning [2, 10, 15], an interpretation is an inverted plan: a particular path through a belief refinement space.

RESEARCH GOALS AND RELATED WORK

This thesis developed from the position that commonsense can be seen through pragmatic lenses. Pragmatics offers theoretical frameworks to build upon, which requires broadening the picture of commonsense to include the communicational contexts which depend on it. The broader aim of this work is not simply to make interpretations more predictable, but to make the interaction more natural and engaging for the user; by improving human interaction, by giving the user real control in the interaction in a way that they would not be able to when communicating with people.

My long-term research vision is to build easy-to-use language debugging interfaces with the ultimate goal of overcoming the lexical and commonsense knowledge acquisition bottleneck. The goal of my Ph.D thesis is to uncover the best strategies for recognizing and repairing assumptions for natural language interpretation of event descriptions.

The scope of this problem is subsumed by the broad research program of building spoken dialogue systems. Modern dialogue systems (e.g. [16]) are capable of generating requests for acknowledgement or clarification in order to solicit more information from the user when there is uncertainty about an interpretation. I suspect that the medium of natural language is not the best way to deal with failures in understanding natural language, because it forces the user to continue using a modality that has just demonstrated it has flaws. Only allowing the user to continue interacting using the same buggy medium is a sure path to user frustration. This thesis takes a different approach, by providing a direct manipulation interface that the user can use to debug and edit the interpretation directly; however, as [6] noted, the strengths and weaknesses of natural language and direct manipulation interfaces are complementary.

For this project, the communication goal is to interpret the referring expressions for event components. This focused goal makes the set of communication failures much more constrained than open dialogue. Very similar work reported in [14], describes approaches for acquiring knowledge by generating referring expressions to match examples using a fixed contrast set; and shares the same spirit of our work, with the author realizing "any tools that help in formalizing this new knowledge, no matter how simple, will be advantageous." While Stone's work contains valuable theories about how to detect contrast set discrepancies given a referring description, it does not describe or test any user interface for acquiring such knowledge.

Finally, several projects have crowdsourced the acquisition of commonsense knowledge [13]; however, none of these collect it in a context in which it is used.

PROBLEM STATEMENTS

Natural language communication is a collaborative, coordinated, iterative process, in which participants work together to ensure that information is understood by all participants. NLP presents a number of interaction challenges that should be of interest to the HCI community.

Conventional menu and icon-based interfaces can give the user access and control to the full information state of a computer program, but regrettably can only present a small number of choices to the user at any one time. On the other hand, **natural language interfaces** (NLI) such as Google Calendar's *Quick Add* feature, allows users to interact using natural language, which gives the user the freedom to choose what to say and at which levels of granularity. The main virtue of an NLI is that a speaker doesn't have to include all details in the message; she can rely on the interpreter to unpack all of the information she intended to convey. This transfers the burden of using assumptions to resolve ambiguities and fill in missing details onto the interpreter. Until NLP is fully capable of dealing with this burden, we take the position of [6] that the problem is best solved through a multi-modal approach which combines the contributions of a natural language interface with traditional, direct-manipulation interface. Given the current state of technology, we believe natural language itself (e.g. dialogue systems) is not the best medium to attempt to repair natural language interpretation failures.

NLI work in opposition to the human-computer usability principles of transparency and predictability. Natural language interfaces are opaque, so when interpretation goes wrong, and it inevitably does, the human is left without recourse. Recall the anecdotes about the earliest users of Joseph Weizenbaum's ELIZA program, who thought his simple rule-based NLI had great intellect. Sometimes this does not work in the computer's favor, and users will mistake the interface's ignorance for unhelpful and unfriendly behavior [4]. Because users' human-level expectations for NLIs appear to be unavoidable, HCI could provide a much needed characterization of which factors are most important for conveying natural interaction.

More broadly than NLP, this research is relevant to the HCI problem of putting assumptions into an interface. Traditionally default assumptions of programs are made by the programmer at the time of program design. Users can't ask a program what its assumptions are, force it to use new assumptions, nor critique existing assumptions. Ideally, users would negotiate these assumptions, and be aware of what assumptions are embedded, and change them if necessary. Moreover, it would be desirable to create a process whereby end-users share assumptions with their social groups, and in doing so exchange assumptions among members of a community.

RESEARCH QUESTIONS AND METHODS

This thesis work seeks to uncover the key properties that bring transparency to natural language interfaces. Specifically, it looks at how assumptions can be made plain to end-users such that the user can revise and teach the computer assumptions when necessary in the context of describing common events. Here are several more specific research questions that we can ask using this interface:

- How does the interpreter's transparency affect the interface's overall usability? How does the transparency affect the work the user perceives the interface to be doing? How satisfied were users with the interaction? What interfaces components modulate the usability of the interface: Does knowing the status of the overall interpretation help the user achieve the communication goal? Does having control over the interpretation decisions help the user achieve the communication goal?

- Are users able to successfully teach the computer lexical and commonsense knowledge? Given a shared task of contributing commonsense or lexical knowledge about an event, how similar are different users' contributions?

- Which of types of failures are harbingers of assumption-level problems? Given an interpretation (a plan containing a sequence of assumptions and observations through the belief space) can we use redundant actions to at least partly automate the detection of problematic assumptions? Word-production actions that do not contribute toward the goal of meeting the GC may imply discrepancies between the communicators' assumptions—an opportunity for the interface to direct the user's attention toward modifying or acquiring assumptions. Is this actually the case? Is there any salient distinction between cases in which assumptions need to be refined versus cases where assumptions need to be acquired?

To answer these questions, we will conduct a large-scale online user study. Subjects will communicate an event to the interface and then will be tested on how quickly they were able to refine the event to their intended specification. Next, subjects will be asked to articulate a variation on the same event. In other experiments, users will be asked to predict the outcome of the interfaces' predictions, and then we will compare them with the actual outcomes. As a follow up, subjects will be evaluated on their subjective experience using the interface.

DISSERTATION STATUS

So far we have built a prototype of the transparent natural language interface (see figures 4 and 5).

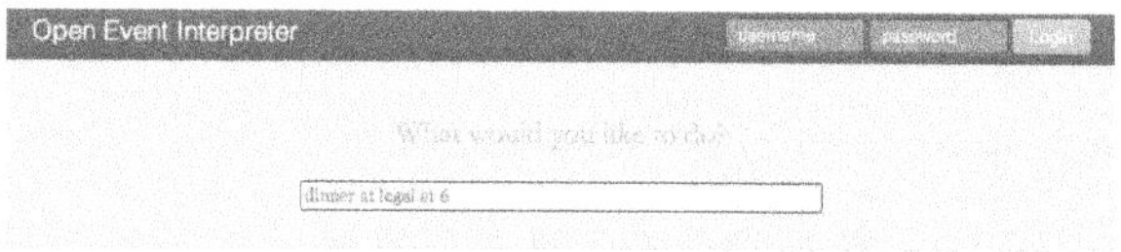

Figure 4. The user enters a description into the interface.

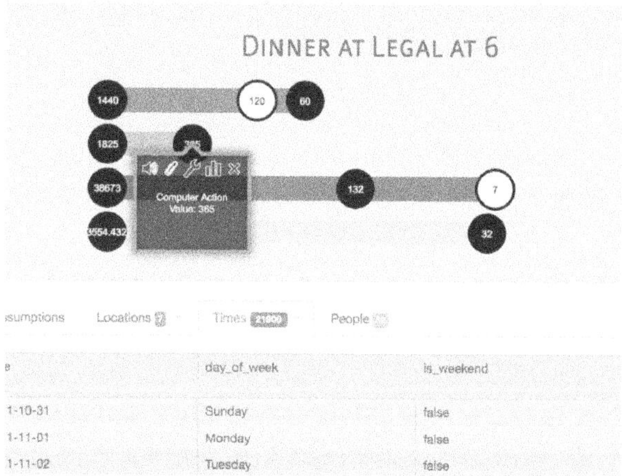

Figure 5. A prototype of the interface, showing the overall progress toward the interpretation goal.

When a user clicks on an action (represented as a circle) they are given the option to remove or revise it. After modifying an action, the interface will adjust the contrast set and change the status of the overall interpretation process, removing or adding words to the input description if necessary. When the user edits the contrast set or target set, the system determines if this action conflicts with previous assumptions, and otherwise adds it to the interpretation and adjusts the corresponding interpretation status.

The next step is to debug and revise the interface so that we can conduct a large-scale user experiment to approach centered around the above questions.

OPEN QUESTIONS

I believe that good user interfaces can solve a lot of NLP problems; and, given the current limitations of natural language processing, the process of negotiating and debugging assumptions is better served by a direct-manipulation approach than spoken dialogue, and best served by an approach that includes both modalities. At the IUI Doctoral Consortium, I would like to learn from others who have worked on interdisciplinary research efforts and try to hone and refine the contributions into portions that can be more easily digested and disseminated. In addition, there are several questions that remain open in this research project, including:

1. How do we represent actions? How should we define the syntactic and semantic preconditions and effects of each action (word or assumption)? Should I follow the approach of [9] and use lexicalized[2] tree adjoining grammar (LTAG) to represent the entries in the lexicon? LTAG appears to represent one point in a large space of possible design decisions.
2. How to divide the contributions of a word from the contributions of an assumption? We foresee a challenge with distinguishing whether lexical units, larger states of the interpretation, or potentially unlimited contextual information will trigger an assumption. If an assumption is triggered by only one lexical unit (e.g., word), how do we decide whether it should become part of the semantic component of the lexical unit, or if it should exist independently as an assumption?
3. How can we extend the classical planning approach to deal with a dynamic planning domain? Not all of the referents and their properties are available at beginning of the planning problem. Traditional classical planners, even when generalized to deal with incomplete domains, assume that the number of entities in the domain is fixed at the start of the planning process. We will need to extend our belief state planning approach to accommodate a dynamic domain.

REFERENCES

1. Baker, C., Tenenbaum, J. B., and Saxe, R. Goal inference as inverse planning. *Proceedings of the 29th annual meeting of the Cognitive Science Society* (2007).
2. Bauer, D. Statistical natural language generation as planning. Master's thesis, Department of Computational Linguistics, Saarland University, Saarbrücken, Germany, 2009.
3. Benotti, L. *Implicature as an Interactive Process*. PhD thesis, Université Henri Poincaré, INRIA Nancy Grand Est, Francia, 2010. Examined by Patrick Blackburn, Nick Asher, Bart Geurts, Alexander Koller and Claude Godart.

[2]A **lexicalized grammar** takes the approach that syntactic constraints are defined locally for each word sense, rather than expressed in global, abstract syntactic rules.

4. Benotti, L., and Blackburn, P. Classical planning and causal implicatures. *Modeling and Using Context* (2011), 26–39.
5. Cahn, J. A psychological model of grounding and repair in dialog. *AAAI Symposium on Psychological Models of Communication in Collaborative Systems* (1999).
6. Cohen, P. The role of natural language in a multimodal interface. In *Proceedings of the 5th annual ACM symposium on User interface software and technology*, ACM (1992), 143–149.
7. Grice, H. Logic and conversation. *1975* (1975), 41–58.
8. Hobbs, J., Stickel, M., Appelt, D., and Martin, P. Interpretation as abduction. *Artificial Intelligence* (1993).
9. Koller, A., and Petrick, R. Experiences with planning for natural language generation. *Computational Intelligence 27*, 1 (2011), 23–40.
10. Koller, A., and Stone, M. Sentence generation as a planning problem. In *Association for Computational Linguists*, vol. 45 (2007), 336.
11. Ramırez, M., and Geffner, H. Plan recognition as planning. In *Proceedings IJCAI* (2009), 1778–1783.
12. Reiter, E., and Dale, R. *Building natural language generation systems*. Cambridge University Press, New York, NY, USA, 2000.
13. Singh, P. The public acquisition of commonsense knowledge. In *Proceedings of AAAI Spring Symposium: Acquiring (and Using) Linguistic (and World) Knowledge for Information Access* (2002).
14. Stone, M. Specifying generation of referring expressions by example. In *Proceedings of the AAAI Spring Symposium on Natural Language Generation in Spoken and Written Dialogue* (2003), 133–140.
15. Stone, M., Doran, C., Webber, B. L., Bleam, T., and Palmer, M. Microplanning with communicative intentions: The spud system. *Computational Intelligence 19*, 4 (2003), 311–381.
16. Williams, J., and Young, S. Partially observable markov decision processes for spoken dialog systems. *Computer Speech & Language 21*, 2 (2007), 393–422.

Quantitative Analysis and Inference on Gaze Data Using Natural Language Processing Techniques

Pascual Martinez-Gomez
Graduate School of Information Science and Technology
The University of Tokyo
National Institute of Informatics (NII)
pascual@nii.com

ABSTRACT
Eye-tracking devices find applications in human-machine interaction, hypothesis testing in psycholinguistic and usability studies, relevant feature extraction when designing models related to human behavior and to build user-centered information systems. We aim at providing a general and robust framework to do quantitative analysis and inference using data collected by eye-trackers when users read text. To achieve this objective, first the accuracy of eye-trackers has to be increased beyond sensor capabilities by using information from the content or the structure of the text. Then, natural language processing techniques will be used to process text appearing on the screen and the recognized reading word sequence. Within this framework, it will be possible to better understand user's intentions, record knowledge acquisition and predict information needs. The intention is to build a user model and user model of the World from texts that users have read. This opens the door to more personalized systems with on-line adaptation capabilities.

Author Keywords
eye-tracking, natural language processing, quantitative approaches, user-centered systems

ACM Classification Keywords
H.5.2 Information Interfaces and Presentation

CONTEXT AND MOTIVATION
Using eye-tracking systems to improve machine perception on human behavior has obvious advantages. Eye-movements are strongly correlated to focus of attention and provide invaluable information in understanding user's intentions without requiring explicit human actions. However nowadays, eye-trackers are simply used to detect gaze on predefined Areas of Interest (AOI). Moreover, systems that try to detect gaze on small elements that appear dynamically on the screen fail at producing a reliable and useful detection.

Eye-trackers have also intensively been used in psycholinguistic studies, resulting in interesting fundamental insights into the complex process of *reading*. Although eye-movements potentially reflect on-line cognitive processing [4], only lexical processing has been carefully studied in very constrained tasks [5]. These studies were based on qualitative analysis of a small amount of observations because experts were needed to manually label the gaze data and it is an expensive and time consuming task.

The human reading process is a complex task that involves perceptions and actions at several levels derived from a personal cognitive processing. However, with eye-trackers we can only observe eye movements in the form of gaze data. Gaze data when reading text can be used to observe and extract useful features and to create models that predict eye movements [6]. The extraction of these features had some limits in the literature due to the difficulty of creating models that include higher-level information beyond lexical processing. To observe the impact of syntactic and semantic load in reading behavior, more advanced techniques are needed.

Recently, there have been some works aiming at integrating gaze data into user-centered information systems. Eye-trackers are a constant source of information on user's focus of attention and information systems can be more fine-grained personalized and constantly adapted. Examples of works in this direction are recommender systems [7], document summarization [8] and query expansion [1]. These works are the first attempt in combining natural language processing techniques with obtained gaze data from an eye-tracker. Although these works used gaze data in their systems with a certain level of success, accuracy of eye-trackers when used to identify words in a text is still not good enough. This fact forces the introduction of multiple constraints into the task and real applications can seldom benefit from these ideas.

All previously described fields using eye-trackers would greatly benefit from significant increases in recognition accuracy. Standard webcams that can be acquired with a reasonable price are still far from providing an acceptable recognition accuracy. Modern eye-trackers are still expensive and recognition at word level in common texts is not yet reliably possible. But even if eye-trackers suddenly succeed at providing an acceptable recognition accuracy at word level, the error introduced by users still needs to be corrected to achieve a good gaze-text alignment.

Solving the gaze-text alignment problem opens the door to a more interesting problem. From a sequence of fixation points on words, we want to obtain the information acquired by the reader. In the long run, the user model and the user model of the World can be built and the prediction of information needs can be more reliable.

STATEMENT OF THESIS

The hypothesis behind this thesis in progress is that using gaze data obtained from eye-trackers, user-centered information systems can be fine-grained personalized. With this level of personalization, it is possible to do more accurate inference on user's intentions, goals, knowledge acquired and information needs.

To satisfy this hypothesis, two major issues need to be addressed. First, the sequence of fixated words have to be identified. Second, useful information about the reader has to be extracted using the sequence of fixated words and the texts the user has been exposed to. On the way, solutions to smaller problems should be designed and verified through realistic gaze-language applications such as predicting the level of understanding given a certain reading behavior or classifying users according to their language ability or knowledge profile. Solving these problems allows the design of adaptive proactive systems using gaze data obtained from eye-trackers.

RESEARCH GOALS AND METHODS

In this section, we state the goals to achieve during the pursue of this thesis.

Data collection

During this thesis, solutions have to be developed to attain the goals explained in this section. In order to evaluate the level of success of the solutions, data that simulates real scenarios has to be collected and methods have to be tested on this data in a controlled environment.

Data collection greatly depends on the task. As a general guideline, we are planning to collect data using different cameras (standard webcam, Wii camera, Kinect camera, etc.) together with a high-quality sensor (Tobii TX300 was recently acquired). The purpose is to obtain gaze data collected using sensors with different accuracies and investigate the performance of methods and algorithms when using different devices. Gaze and text data can then be made available to the eye-tracking community to stimulate a faster progress. The goal is to obtain gaze data from at least 15 users participating in more than 10 different tasks.

Gaze-text alignment

Recognizing the reading word sequence of a user when reading a common text is still not possible. Although modern eye-trackers have high quality cameras, the error introduced by the machine is considerable and fixated words are difficult to identify. The error incurred by low-quality eye-trackers (e.g. webcams) is more severe and can be aggravated with errors introduced by the user. It can be said that, in general, there is a need of improving recognition accuracy far beyond sensor capabilities.

Due to a lack of sensor precision or errors introduced by users, there is a misalignment between gaze data and text appearing on the screen. This gaze-text misalignment is mainly produced by variable and systematic errors [2]. While variable errors can be corrected by aggregating gaze samples into fixation points, systematic errors are more difficult to correct. There are several approaches in the literature to handle these errors, but they are either very task-specific [8] or force the introduction of constraints on the eye-tracking task [3].

In the first stage of this research, we aim at designing general error-correction methods for gaze-text alignment that can be used in unconstrained tasks. For that purpose, we are exploring the use of information on the content or the structure of the text appearing on the screen to increase recognition accuracy. This idea can be implemented using image registration techniques between the image representation of gaze and text data. Linear transformations have been successfully used, achieving a relative recognition accuracy of about 70% in unconstrained reading and skimming tasks, when compared to manual alignment. Further improvements are expected using non-rigid transformations and Self Organizing Maps. Image registration allows for an easy implementation of multimodal error-correction via image representations of linguistic features of the text appearing on the screen, and it will be explored soon.

In certain applications, an on-line tracking of fixation points might be necessary. We are also planning to develop general error-correction methods for these applications, where Kalman and particle filters are good candidate techniques.

The objective by the end of the first half of this PhD thesis is to achieve a recognition accuracy in unconstrained batch and on-line applications higher than 90%.

Extracting information from reading word sequence

Once the gaze-text alignment problem has been solved, fixated words can be identified in a reading sequence. A sequence of words in a text differ from a sequence of fixated words in a reading sequence. In the former, words appear in the order the author decided to express him/herself. In the latter, words appear in the order the reader analyzes and understands the text. The reading word sequence may reflect multiple aspects from the user when reading a text. Examples are the interest of the user in the text or the incremental acquisition of information that results in knowledge construction during the reading act.

As it has been previously stated, the intention is to build more personalized user-centered systems that can be constantly adapted to the user. This can be achieved by building the user model and the user model of the World. In the user model, we try to represent user's interests, goals, desires and other properties related to the user. In the user model of the World, we try to represent the knowledge the user has about the reality. Both models can be learned from the comparison and combination of the words appearing in the text and the recognized reading word sequence. The goal is to find a good strategy to process both words in the text and words in the reading sequence to extract useful information and enrich the reading act. This goal can be pursued by using natural language processing techniques to recognize named entities, find meaningful chunks in the stream of words, parse sentences to find dependencies, etc. Ultimately, we have to integrate and find an appropriate representation of the information present in the text and the information acquired by the user to unlock an eventual reasoning over human knowledge.

Representing information and knowledge in a computable form is not trivial. Concepts, ideas or desires have to be automatically extracted and connected to each other in a meaningful way. From a recognized reading word sequence, automatically extracted ontologies or graph-based representations are possible candidate techniques to represent knowledge acquired by users. These representations may also have the advantage of allowing reasoning and complex inference on what the user knows and may want to know.

We cannot see an obvious way to directly measure the level of achievement of this goal. Instead, it can be measured the effect on tasks dependent on personalized information systems. Thus, we can evaluate what is the improvement in document summarizers, recommender systems and other user-centered information systems when using user models and user models of the World built from gaze data.

Hypothesis testing and feature extraction

The development of good and general error-correction methods has another advantage. In psycholinguistic and usability studies, hypotheses are usually tested using a qualitative analysis of fixation points in previously defined areas of interest. However, computers and statistical models allow us to perform quantitative analysis to test hypotheses. If a reading word order can be reliably recognized, we can formalize a framework to ease quantitative hypothesis testing when using eye-trackers.

The procedure that we propose is first to build a model representing common knowledge on a fact. Then, to build a model including the hypothesis that has to be tested. This hypothesis is expected to better explain the gaze evidence. Finally, the perplexity of both models is measured on test sets. The hypothesis is rejected if there is no significant reduction in perplexity.

Relevant features can be extracted by using a similar procedure. A model representing the knowledge we have about the reality has to be build. Then, features can be added to the model and we can observe whether or not there is a reduction in perplexity. If there is a significant reduction, we can say that such a feature helps to better explain the data. Finally, gaze data can be discarded and the feature can be used to increase the expressivity of the model.

DISSERTATION STATUS

The main problem that we are addressing at this moment is the alignment between gaze and text data. Linear transformations of gaze data have been successfully applied to map gaze samples into the space of text coordinates, achieving a relative recognition accuracy of 70%. Before focusing on information extraction from gaze data, we want to improve the error-correction method to achieve around 90% of recognition accuracy. We plan to implement a non-rigid transformation image registration method to improve gaze-text alignment before the end of 2011 and we expect this method to allow us to proceed to the next stage of this PhD thesis.

OPEN QUESTIONS

Once general and robust error-correction methods have been developed and information on reading word sequence is extracted from gaze data, it is not clear how to integrate such information with the actual text appearing on the screen and how to find an appropriate representation. This representation should allow for on-line adaptation and inference on it.

I also would like the panel of experts to advice me on how to transform my current PhD thesis into a research work that maximizes the contribution and reusability in the scientific community from intelligent user interfaces and information systems.

REFERENCES

1. Buscher, G., Dengel, A., and van Elst, L. Query expansion using gaze-based feedback on the subdocument level. In *ACM Special Interest Group on Information Retrieval (SIGIR)* (2008).
2. Hornof, A., and Halverson, T. Cleaning up systematic error in eye-tracking data by using required fixation locations. *Behavior Research Methods 34* (2002), 592–604. 10.3758/BF03195487.
3. Hyrskykari, A. Utilizing eye movements: Overcoming inaccuracy while tracking the focus of attention during reading. *Computers in Human Behavior 22* (2005), 657–671.
4. McDonald, S. A., and Shillcock, R. C. Eye movements reveal the on-line computation of lexical probabilities during reading. *Psychological Science 14*, 6 (2003), 648–652.
5. Rayner, K. Eye movements in reading and information processing: 20 years of research. *Psychological Bulletin 124* (Nov. 1998), 372–422.
6. Reichle, E., Rayner, K., and Pollatsek, A. The e-z reader model of eye-movement control in reading: Comparisons to other models. *Behavioral and brain sciences 26* (2003), 445–526.
7. Xu, S., Jiang, H., and Lau, F. C. Personalized online document, image and video recommendation via commodity eye-tracking. In *ACM Recommender Systems (RecSys)* (2008).
8. Xu, S., Jiang, H., and Lau, F. C. User-oriented document summarization through vision-based eye-tracking. In *International Conference on Intelligent User Interfaces (IUI)* (2009).

IUI 2012 2nd Workshop on Location Awareness for Mixed and Dual Reality (LaMDa'12)

Tim Schwartz
Cluster of Excellence - Multimodal Computing & Interaction
Campus E1_1
66123 Saarbruecken, Germany
schwartz@cs.uni-saarland.de

Gerrit Kahl
German Research Center for Artificial Intelligence
Campus D3_2
66123 Saarbruecken, Germany
gerrit.kahl@dfki.de

Petteri Nurmi
Helsinki Institute for Information Technology HIIT
P.O. Box 68
FI-00014 University of Helsinki, Finland
ptnurmi@cs.helsinki.fi

Teemu Pulkkinen
Helsinki Institute for Information Technology HIIT
P.O. Box 68
FI-00014 University of Helsinki, Finland
teemu.pulkkinen@cs.helsinki.fi

Eyal Dim
MIS Department
The University of Haifa
Mount Carmel, Haifa, Isreal
dimeyal@bezeqint.net

Sally Applin
Centre for Social Anthropology and Computing
University of Kent
Canterbury, UK
sally@sally.com

ABSTRACT

The workshop explores the interactions between location awareness and Dual/Mixed Reality in smart environments and the impact on culture and society. The main scope of this workshop is: How can the Dual Reality paradigm be used to improve applications in smart environments and which new possibilities are opened up by these paradigms? This includes positioning methods and location-based services using the DR paradigm, such as navigation services and group interaction services (location-based social signal processing). The workshop is also open to discuss sensor and actuator technologies that may help to realize the synchronization of the virtual and real world.

The main scope of this workshop is: How can the Dual Reality paradigm be used to improve location-based and socially-aware services and other applications in smart environments?

Author Keywords

Dual Reality; Mixed Reality; Positioning; Location-Based Services; Social Anthropology

ACM Classification Keywords

H.5.2 Information Interfaces and Presentation: User Interfaces; H.5.3 Information Interfaces and Presentation: Group and Organization Interfaces

MOTIVATION AND OBJECTIVES OF THE WORKSHOP:

Dual Reality (DR) and Mixed Reality (MR) gained a lot of interest over the last years, as both concepts enable the development of new applications and new intuitive user interfaces. To represent the current real-world state in a virtual model and to bring changes from the virtual world into the real world, both worlds have to be synchronized, so that each action in the real world has an effect on the virtual model and vice versa. This concept is referred to as Dual Reality (DR). Using the sensors of smart environments, recognized actions can be used for adapting the current state of the virtual model and effectors can be used to bring changes in the virtual world into the real world. Location awareness and positioning of users as well as objects where identified as an important *enabling technology* during the first LaMDa workshop, which was held in conjunction with IUI 2011. On the other hand, a synchronous virtual representation of the real world could also help to improve the accuracy of such real world positioning systems.

Generally, many applications already use virtual representations of the real world, which are restricted, or modeled according to the application's needs. For example, a navigation system uses a map to indicate the position of the user; a steerable projector needs a three-dimensional model to find appropriate presentation areas and to be able to accomplish distortion-free projections. Assuming that a synchronized virtual model of the real world exists, many applications could use that model to gain the required representation. Moreover, a virtual model can also be used for simulation and it is valuable for development and testing. Some applications, for example a product finder in a retail environment, need up-to-date information about recent changes in the real world, e.g. relocation of products by customers or staff. Even simulation results from the virtual world could have a benefit on the real world by proactively transmitting the relevant changes into the real world. For example, a simulation might yield to the conclusion that assigning more staff to the cashiers will lead to optimized queue behavior.

Since DR also offers interfaces from the virtual world to the real one, information measured and calculated in the virtuality can be used to adapt assistant systems in the real world. For instance, if the system calculates in the virtual model that a user cannot see a specific product from his or her current position because it is hidden behind a bigger one, it can adapt the assistant system in the real world. A further example of the interoperability of the virtual and real world is a scenario in which a shopper may consult a friend in the virtual world or in the real world.

In many cases, services and applications depend both on the social context and on the location context. Since positioning methods are crucial for location-based services and DR or MR systems, one focus will be on indoor and outdoor positioning methods. The social context requires detection and representation of the social situation gained through Social Signal Processing.

In regards to the location context, a wide variety of indoor positioning technologies have been proposed in the literature ranging from tag-based systems (e.g., RFID) to radio wave technologies (e.g., WLAN or ultrawideband). The aforementioned technologies vary in accuracy (ranging from a few meters to centimeters) and in the deployment costs. The development of different technologies has been mainly motivated by the trade-off between positioning accuracy and deployment costs, but from the application and user perspective, the main issues typically are whether the positioning accuracy is sufficiently good for the target application and whether the positioning errors are predictable and consistent in different areas. As part of the workshop, we discuss how accurate indoor positioning has to be for different applications and if/how the accuracy can be enhanced using a detailed virtual model in the sense of DR and MR.

As for the social context, people are often part of a group like family, colleagues or friends. The social group may exist in the real world, in the virtual world or in both of them. Interaction with group mates should be based on the group structure, the group members' locations and orientations, the proximity, the social characteristics of the group, etc. The situational awareness requires social signal sensing, processing, representation and visualization.

Another interesting aspect is the impact DR and MR technology could have on society in general. This includes questions about privacy issues as well as changes in the communication behavior, as can already be observed by the impact of email, Facebook, Twitter and the like.

The first LaMDa workshop was rated as very interesting and inspiring by the participants. This was mainly due to the moderated discussion-blocks that were held in the middle and at the end of the workshop. During these discussions, a mindmap was created by the participants, which aimed to put the different contributions into context and to identify similarities as well as synergy potential. We will continue to do this during this iteration of the workshop. Another highly rated aspect was the contribution and participation of Sally Applin and Michael Fischer, two anthropologists, who gave an interesting new point of view on social aspects of Dual Reality and introduced the concept of PolySocial Reality. Their contribution to LaMDa was even discussed by Bruce Sterling, a science fiction novelist and one of the founders of the cyberpunk genre, on the Wired magazine 'beyond the beyond' blog. With Sally Applin being an organizer in the second LaMDa Workshop will broaden this interdisciplinary approach.

WORKSHOP TOPICS

The workshop explores the interactions between location awareness and Dual/Mixed Reality in smart environments and the impact on culture and society. The main scope of this workshop is: How can the Dual Reality paradigm be used to improve applications in smart environments and which new possibilities are opened up by these paradigms? This includes positioning methods and location-based services using the DR paradigm, such as navigation services and group interaction services (location-based social signal processing). The workshop is also open to discuss sensor and actuator technologies that may help to realize the synchronization of the virtual and real world.

POTENTIAL PARTICIPANTS AND WORKSHOP ATTRACTION:

The workshop invites submissions of position papers that address one or more of the target research questions. Each paper will be peer-reviewed by at least two members of the international program committee (potential members listed at the end of the proposal). The workshop proceedings, which comprise of the accepted papers together with summaries of the discussions at the workshop, will be published by the Cluster of Excellence for Multimodal Computing & Interaction, Saarbrücken. Depending on the number and quality of submissions, selected papers might develop into a special issue of a suitable journal, such as IEEE Pervasive Computing.

We expect to have between 20 and 30 participants from academia and industry. Potential participants will be attracted by disseminating the call for papers to relevant mailing lists and research groups. Relevant mailing lists for disseminating the call for papers include IUI announcements, the User Modeling mailing list, Ubicomp announcements and SIGCHI announcements.

FORMAT

The workshop is planned as full-day and sessions will be centered around specific research questions. Each session will start with short presentations of position papers (10 to 15 min each) and the presentations will be followed by an interactive discussion phase that attempts to identify open issues and potential future directions for the corresponding research question. During each session, one of the workshop organizers will act as a moderator for the discussions and another will record the outcomes of the discussion. The discussion notes will be reviewed at the end of the workshop and the final, revised notes will be made publicly available on the workshop web page.

More specifically, the workshop will address the following research questions:

- Location: What level of accuracy is required for location-based services in smart environments? How can a detailed virtual model help to improve real world positioning systems?
- Mixed and Dual Reality: How can Mixed or Dual Reality paradigms be used to enhance applications? Which new possibilities are opened up through the paradigms?
- Group interactions: What kind of information and interfaces are useful for supporting interactions between group members in location-enhanced Dual or Mixed Reality applications?
- Social Anthropology: What impact could Mixed or Dual Reality have on the communication behavior and other social/anthropological aspects?

ORGANIZATION

Sally Applin
Sally A. Applin is a Ph.D. Candidate at the University of Kent at Canterbury, UK, in the Centre for Social Anthropology and Computing (CSAC). She holds a Masters degree from the graduate Interactive Telecommunications Program (NYU/ITP) within New York University's Tisch School of the Arts, and a BA in Conceptual Design from San Francisco State University. Sally has had a 20 year career in the science museum design, computer software, telecommunications, and product design/definition industries working as a Senior UX Designer, Ethnographic Researcher and Senior Consultant. Sally is a founding member of AnthroPunk and is currently researching the impact of technology on culture, and the consequent inverse: specifically the reifications of Virtual Space in Personal Space.

Eyal Dim
Eyal Dim is a researcher at the University of Haifa. He is currently working on his PhD thesis on the topic "Exploring the Potential of Social Signal Processing Technology for Supporting Leisure Activities: the Museum Group Visit Experience", which deals with indoor sensors and processing methods for detection and analysis of group social context.

Gerrit Kahl
Gerrit Kahl is a researcher at the German Research Center for Artificial Intelligence (DFKI) in Saarbrücken. He is also working at the Innovative Retail Laboratory, a living lab representing an instrumented shopping environment. He is currently working on his PhD thesis on the topic "Applying the Dual Reality Paradigm to Instrumented Shopping Environments". In this context, he is studying the visualization of simulator in- and outputs in a virtual model.

Petteri Nurmi
Petteri Nurmi is a researcher at the Helsinki Institute for Information Technology HIIT. He has studied computer science at the University of Helsinki, where he obtained a M.Sc. in 2006 and a Ph.D. in 2009. Currently, he is the co-leader of the Adaptive Computing research group at HIIT. His research interests focus on intelligent mobile systems, including personalization, context recognition and novel interaction techniques. He has published over 40 scientific articles and served as a reviewer and program committee member for several conferences and journals. He was the workshop co-chair for Pervasive 2010 and he is a program committee member for IUI 2011. He has previously participated in the organization of four workshops, most recently the Pervasive User Modeling and Personalization workshop held at the UMAP 2010 conference.

Teemu Pulkkinen Teemu Pulkkinen is a project researcher at the Helsinki Institute for Information Technology HIIT. He has studied computer science at the University of Helsinki, where he received his M.Sc. in 2010. His research has focused on indoor positioning systems, as well as the design of a cohesive and easy-to-use framework for ubiquitous positioning.

Tim Schwartz
Tim Schwartz is a researcher at DFKI (German Research Center for Artificial Intelligence) and is associated to the Cluster of Excellence for Multimodal Computing and Interaction at the Saarland University. His main research interests lie in the field of indoor positioning methods, which follow the 'Always Best Positioned' paradigm.

1st International Workshop on User Modeling from Social Media

Jalal Mahmud
IBM Research - Almaden
650 Harry Rd, San Jose, CA
jumahmud@us.ibm.com

Jeffrey Nichols
IBM Research - Almaden
650 Harry Rd, San Jose, CA
jwnichols@us.ibm.com

Michelle Zhou
IBM Research - Almaden
650 Harry Rd, San Jose, CA
mzhou@us.ibm.com

ABSTRACT
Massive amounts of data are being generated on social media sites, such as Twitter and Facebook. People from all walks of life share data about social events, express opinions, discuss their interests, publicize businesses, recommend products, and, explicitly or implicitly, reveal personal information. This workshop will focus on the use of social media data for creating models of individual users from the content that they publish. Deeper understanding of user behavior and associated attributes can benefit a wide range of intelligent applications, such as social recommender systems and expert finders, as well as provide the foundation in support of novel user interfaces (e.g., actively engaging the crowd in mixed-initiative question-answering systems). These applications and interfaces may offer significant benefits to users across a wide variety of domains, such as retail, government, healthcare and education. User modeling from public social media data may also reveal information that users would prefer to keep private. Such concerns are particularly important because individuals do not have complete control over the information they share about themselves. For example, friends of a user may inadvertently divulge private information about that user in their own posts. In this workshop we will also discuss possible mechanisms that users might employ to monitor what information has been revealed about themselves on social media and obfuscate any sensitive information that has been accidentally revealed.

Author Keywords
User Modeling; Social Media;

ACM Classification Keywords
H.1.2. User/Machine Systems; H.2.8. Database Applications [Data Mining]

General Terms
Human Factors; Design; Experimentation; Algorithm.

BACKGROUND AND MOTIVATION
Massive amounts of data are being generated on social media sites, such as Twitter and Facebook. People from all walks of life share data about social events, express opinions, discuss their interests, publicize businesses, recommend products, and, explicitly or implicitly, reveal personal information. Many research projects and commercial products have used this information to drive a variety of services, such as recommending local news stories [3], detecting and summarizing events [4, 5], and determining group sentiment of products and brands [1, 2]. The majority of this work, however, has focused on aggregating data across many users.

This workshop will focus on the use of social media data for creating models of individual users from the content they publish. This has been an active area of research recently and a number of papers in this topic appeared in related conferences and workshops [6, 7, 8, 9, 10, 11, 12, 13, 14]. User modeling techniques have been applied to infer users' home location [10, 11, 12], gender [6, 10], age [6], regional origin [6], ethnicity [8], political orientation [6, 8, 9], finding potential experts in a question-answering community [13], place-naming preferences [14], etc. Deeper understanding of user behavior and associated attributes can benefit a wide range of intelligent applications, such as social recommender systems and expert finders [7], as well as provide the foundation in support of novel user interfaces (e.g., actively engaging the crowd in mixed-initiative question-answering systems). These applications and interfaces may offer significant benefits to users across a wide variety of domains, such as retail, government, healthcare and education.

User modeling from public social media data may also reveal information that users would prefer to keep private. Such concerns are particularly important because individuals do not have complete control over the information they share about themselves; friends of a user may inadvertently divulge private information about that user in their own posts. For example, a friend writing the message "Happy Birthday!" to another user has just revealed that user's birthday and might also give away that user's age in a subsequent post. In this workshop we will also discuss possible mechanisms that users might employ to monitor what information has been revealed about themselves on social media and obfuscate any sensitive information that has been accidentally revealed.

In this workshop, we will discuss related topics:

- What aspects of an individual can be modeled from their public social media postings?
- What aspects cannot be modeled?
- What aspects should not be modeled?
- How accurate are the models that can be extracted?
- What are the best techniques for creating models?
- How might the creation of such models be thwarted? (e.g. to preserve privacy while still allowing participation on a social network)

We hope to bring together researchers and practitioners from diverse areas, such as user modeling, intelligent user interaction, social media analysis, natural language processing, data mining, machine learning, privacy and security, to discuss these issues and share results.

OBJECTIVES

This workshop aims to achieve three main objectives:

1) Identify key research issues and challenges in designing and developing techniques for user modeling from social media; and

2) Establish and grow a community that consists of researchers and practitioners from multiple disciplines to tackle the difficult problems of user modeling from social media; and

3) Initiate proper collaboration (e.g., creating and sharing public datasets) among different teams.

In addition to the questions above, topics of interest may include:

- Domain-specific user modeling using public social media including twitter, facebook, myspace, social Q&A sites, and Amazon.com reviews for
  - Retail
  - Government
  - Healthcare
  - Education
  - Sports
  - News
- Domain-independent user modeling using public social media such as twitter, facebook, myspace, and foursquare to derive a wide variety of user traits including:
  - Locations
  - Behaviors
  - Demographics
  - Age
  - Gender
- Enterprise-focused user modeling using social media data on public social networks and communications (e.g., emails and blogs) within an enterprise
  - Employees' social and collaboration patterns in a workplace
  - Work-related personality traits such as innovativeness, flexibility, and adaptiveness
- Task-specific user modeling for
  - Information recommendation
  - Crowd-sourcing
  - Expert finding
  - Social Q&A

ORGANIZERS

Jalal Mahmud

https://researcher.ibm.com/researcher/view.php?person=us-jumahmud

Jalal Mahmud is a research staff member at IBM Almaden Research Center. He received his MS. and PhD degree from Department of Computer Science, Stony Brook University in 2006 and 2008 respectively. His PhD thesis was focused on developing web accessibility models from click stream analysis and machine learning. He has published over 20 papers in top rated conferences and also received several best paper nominations in WWW conference (the premier conference on World Wide Web) for his work in Web accessibility. He has also served as program committee member and reviewer in major conferences such as WWW, IUI, IJCAI. His current research interests include intelligent user interface, web mining, social media analysis and applied machine learning.

Jeffrey Nichols

http://www.jeffreynichols.com/

Jeffrey Nichols is a Research Staff Member at IBM Research – Almaden. His research interests are in the field of human-computer interaction, with a specific focus on crowd-sourcing, social media, automated design, mobile computing, and end-user programming. He received his Ph.D. in December 2006 from the Human-Computer Interaction Institute in Carnegie Mellon University's School of Computer Science. His thesis described the first system to automatically generate interfaces that are consistent with a user's previous experience and provided the first evidence from user studies that automatically generated interfaces can be more usable than human-designed interfaces in certain situations.

Michelle Zhou

https://researcher.ibm.com/researcher/view.php?person=us-mzhou

Michelle Zhou manages the User Systems and Experience Research (USER) group at IBM Almaden Research Center. She received a Ph.D. in Computer Science from Columbia University in 1999. Her expertise is in the interdisciplinary areas of intelligent user interaction, including automated generation of multimedia responses, smart visual text analytics, and people-centric information systems. Her work received the best paper award at ACM IUI 2005 and was nominated for the best paper award at CIKM 2009. Zhou is active in several communities. She was the general conference co-chair for ACM IUI 2007 and is the technical program co-chair for ACM MM 2009 and IUI 2010. She serves on the editorial board of two major journals: ACM Transactions on Multimedia Computing, Communications, and Applications, and ACM Transactions on Intelligent Systems and Technology.

REFERENCES

1. http://twittersentiment.appspot.com/
2. http://twitrratr.com/
3. Owen Phelan, Kevin McCarthy, and Barry Smyth. (2009). Using Twitter to Recommend Real-time Topical News. *RecSys 2009 - The Proceedings of the 3rd ACM Conference on Recommender Systems*.New York, NY, USA October.
4. T. Sakaki, M. Okazaki, and Y. Matsuo. Earthquake shakes twitter users: real-time event detection by social sensors. In WWW, 2010.
5. Chakrabarti, D. , Punera, K, Event Summarization using Tweets, In *Proc. of ICWSM 2011.*
6. Delip Rao, David Yarowsky, Abhishek Shreevats, Manaswi Gupta, Classifying Latent User Attributes in Twitter, In *Proc. of* SMUC '10.
7. Fabian Abel, Qi Gao, Geert-Jan Houben, Ke Tao, Analyzing User Modeling on Twitter for Personalized News Recommendations, In *Proc. of* UMAP'11.
8. Marco Pennacchiotti and Ana-Maria Popescu, A Machine Learning Approach to Twitter User Classification, In *Proc. of* ICWSM'11.
9. Jack Lindamood, Raymond Heatherly, Murat Kantarcioglu, Bhavani Thuraisingham, Inferring Private Information Using Social Network Data, In *Proc. of* WWW'09.
10. Popescu, A. and Grefenstette, G. Mining User Home Location and Gender from Flickr Tags. *ICWSM '10.*
11. Brent Hecht, Lichan Hong, Bongwon Suh, Ed H. Chi, Tweets from Justin Bieber's Heart: The Dynamics of the "Location" Field in User Profiles, CHI 2011.
12. Zhiyuan Cheng, James Caverlee, Kyumin Lee, You Are Where You Tweet: A Content-Based Approach to Geo-locating Twitter Users, CIKM 2010.
13. Aditya Pal, Rosta Farzan, Joseph A. Konstan, and Robert E. Kraut. Early Detection of Potential Experts in Question Answering Communities, In *Proc. of* ICWSM'11.
14. Jialiu Lin, Guang Xiang, Jason I. Hong, Norman Sadeh, Modeling People's Place Naming Preferences in Location Sharing, In *Proc. of UbiComp* '10.

3rd Workshop on Semantic Models for Adaptive Interactive Systems (SEMAIS)

Tim Hussein
University of Duisburg-Essen, Germany
tim.hussein@uni-due.de

Stephan Lukosch
Delft University of Technology, The Netherlands
s.g.lukosch@tudelft.nl

Heiko Paulheim
TU Darmstadt, Germany
paulheim@ke.tu-darmstadt.de

Jürgen Ziegler
University of Duisburg-Essen, Germany
juergen.ziegler@uni-due.de

Gaëlle Calvary
Grenoble INP, CNRS, LIG, France
gaelle.calvary@imag.fr

ABSTRACT
The International Workshop on Semantic Models for Adaptive Interactive Systems (SEMAIS 2012) aims to identify emerging trends in interactive system design using semantic models.

Author Keywords
Semantic Models, Interface Design, Model-driven User Interfaces, Usability, Adaptive Interactive Systems.

ACM Classification Keywords
H.5.2. [Information Interfaces and Presentation]: User Interfaces – Graphical User Interfaces, User-centered Design.

General Terms
Design, Human Factors

INTRODUCTION
Semantic technologies and, in particular, ontologies as formal and shareable representations of a domain play an increasingly important role in computer science, especially for the design, development and execution of interactive systems. Semantic models can serve a number of different purposes in this context. They can be used as functional core or user interface models *in model-driven analysis, design, generation*, and *adaptation* of user interfaces [1,3,4,6,8,9]. Ontologies may enhance the functional coverage of an interactive system as well as its visualization and interaction capabilities in various ways, e.g., by providing input assistance, intelligently clustering information, guiding collaborative interaction [6], or adapting the user interface according to the user's context [10]. Especially in the latter case, ontologies can be applied for representing the various kinds of context information for context-aware and adaptive systems [2,11]. In particular, they have promised to provide a technique for representing external physical context factors such as location, time or technical parameters, as well as 'internal' context such as user interest profiles or interaction context in a consistent, generalized manner [5,7]. Owing to these properties, semantic models can also contribute to bridging gaps, e.g., between user models, context-aware interfaces and model-driven UI generation.

There is, therefore, a considerable potential for using semantic models as a basis for adaptive interactive systems. The range of potential adaptations is wide comprising, for example, context- and user-dependent recommendations, interactive assistance when performing application-specific tasks, adaptation of the application functionality, adaptation of the collaboration process, or adaptive retrieval support. Furthermore, a variety of reasoning and machine learning techniques exist, that can be employed to achieve adaptive system behavior.

Following up the successful SEMAIS Workshops at IUI 2010 and IUI 2011, the workshop addresses the following research issues:

- Representing user models, systems and their behavior, domain knowledge and user interaction by means of semantic models
- Cognitively or neurally founded reasoning techniques such as activation spreading for semantic user models
- Context-aware interaction based on semantic models
- Adaptation strategies and techniques based on semantic models, e.g for. recommender systems, adaptive retrieval, collaboration support systems and others
- Generating explanations or visualizations to increase user confidence and support traceability
- Scalability and performance of semantic model-based interactive systems
- Semantic model-driven UI development
- Semantic models to foster designers' creativity

- Semantic models for dynamic composition of user interfaces, e.g. for guiding collaborative user interaction
- User interfaces of/for semantic models
- Generation and evolution of semantic models for interactive systems
- Bringing ontologies together with current UI modeling languages, such as UsiXML
- Evaluation approaches for semantic models based adaptive interactions and the quality of semantic models

In this year's workshop, we especially encourage contributions that

- focus on intuitive interaction
- dynamically adapt to the user and/or group over long time periods
- leverage information contained in Linked Open Data

The workshop generally aims at sharing experience and identifying a set of shared research issues that need to be addressed in future research. Specifically, we intend to

- bring together researchers within the IUI, HCI and Semantic Web communities to initiate future collaboration
- identify and structure challenges, approaches and techniques for semantic model-based interaction and adaptation with the aim of developing a conceptual framework that covers all the stakeholders (e.g., designer, end-user, system)
- identify the potential for building and sharing ontologies or semantic model-based components for adaptive user interfaces and, possibly, to start an initiative for developing them
- identify evaluation methods and criteria for semantic model-based interactive systems.

POTENTIAL PARTICIPANTS

The target audience for this workshop are researchers from the HCI and AI communities and the intersecting area of intelligent user interfaces which is the focus of the conference. We intend to attract persons from the Semantic Web community with an interest in user interface issues such as the SWUI group. We further expect the workshop to be of interest for researchers in the area of ubiquitous and context-aware systems, context-adaptive collaboration as well as for designers interested in semantic models based creativity.

We will solicit contributions using all usual channels incl. announcements in mailing lists, conferences and personal contacts. The participants of the 1st and 2nd SEMAIS workshops will be also invited.

ORGANIZERS

Tim Hussein works as a researcher at the University of Duisburg-Essen. He leads a group of researchers exploring intelligent user interfaces. His main research interests include context-aware interaction and recommendation techniques based on semantic models. He co-organized workshops at IUI, Interact, ACM RecSys, and national German conferences and regularly serves as reviewer for these conferences.

Stephan Lukosch is associate professor at the Delft University of Technology. His current research interests include collaborative design and engineering, context-adaptive collaboration support, collaborative storytelling and design patterns for computer-mediated interaction. He is a steering committee member of the special interest group on Computer-Supported Cooperative Work (CSCW) of the German computer science society and serves on the editorial board of the Journal of Universal Computer Science (J.UCS) and the International Journal of Cooperative Information Systems (IJCIS). Since 2010, he regularly co-organizes workshops at ACM IUI and CHI.

Heiko Paulheim works as a researcher at Technische Universität Darmstadt, with a focus on machine learning, semantic web, and linked open data. His current research interests encompass the building of intelligent systems using ontologies, creating user interfaces to the semantic web, as well as topics such as ontology matching machine learning on Linked Open Data. He is active as a PC member and reviewer for various conferences and workshops in the fields of semantic web, artificial intelligence, and user interface engineering.

Jürgen Ziegler is professor for interactive systems and interaction design at the University of Duisburg-Essen. His main areas of research are context-adaptive interaction, information visualization and user interfaces for semantic data. Recent work in the CONTici project addresses ontology-based context models for adaptive cooperation support. He has served in many functions for leading HCI conferences and has also been a workshops chair for CHI twice.

Gaëlle Calvary is professor in computer science at Grenoble INP. She is deputy director of the Laboratory of Informatics of Grenoble. Her research area is about UI Plasticity, ie UIs capable of adaptation to the context of use while preserving user-centered properties. She explores model-driven engineering as well as artificial intelligence, and claims for models alive at runtime to support opportunistic user needs and unforeseen contexts of use. This opens her research area on creativity. She co-chaired CADUI'06 and ACM SIGCHI EICS'09.

Tim Hussein, Stephan Lukosch, and Jürgen Ziegler have successfully organized the 1st SEMAIS Workshop at IUI 2010 in Hong Kong. The 2nd SEMAIS Workshop at IUI 2011 additionally included Heiko Paulheim and Gaëlle Calvary.

REFERENCES

1. Bauer, M. and Baldes, S. An Ontology-based Interface for Machine Learning. In *Proc. IUI* 2005. ACM Press (2005), 314-316.
2. Chen, H., Finin, T., and Joshi, A. An Ontology for Context-aware Pervasive Computing Environments. *The Knowledge Engineering Review, 18,3* (2003), 197–207.
3. Crampes, M. and Ranwez, S. Ontology-supported and Ontology-driven Conceptual Navigation on the World Wide Web. In *Proc. Hypertext 2000,* ACM Press (2000), 191–199.
4. Gurevych, I., Merten, S., and Porzel, R. Automatic Creation of Interface Specifications from Ontologies. In *SEALTS 2003*, Association for Computational Linguistics (2003), 59-66.
5. Hussein, T. and Ziegler, J. Adapting Web Sites by Spreading Activation in Ontologies. In *Proc. ReColl 2008.*
6. Haake, J. M., Hussein, T., Joop, B., Lukosch, S., Veiel, D. and Ziegler, J. Modeling and Exploiting Context for Adaptive Collaboration. *International Journal for Cooperative Information Systems (IJCIS),* 2010, 19, 71-120
7. Lukosch, S., Veiel, D., and Haake, J.M. Enabling Context-adaptive Collaboration for Knowledge-intense Processes. In *Proc. ICEIS 2009*, Springer (2009), 34-41
8. Masson, D., Demeure, A., Calvary, G. Magellan, an evolutionary system to foster user interface design creativity, *EICS '10 Proceedings of the 2nd ACM SIGCHI symposium on Engineering interactive computing systems*, 2010, pp 87-92
9. Paraiso, E. C. Ontology-based Utterance Interpretation for Intelligent Conversational Interfaces. In *SAC 2008*, ACM Press (2008), 1578–1582.
10. Paulheim, H. Ontologies for User Interface Integration. In *Proc. ISWC 2009*, Springer (2009), 973-981.
11. Paulheim, H. and Probst, F. Ontology-Enhanced User Interfaces: A Survey. In: Int. J. on Semantic Web and Information Systems (IJSWIS), 2010, 6(2), 36-59.

Developing Intelligent User Interfaces for e-Accessibility and e-Inclusion

Pradipta Biswas*, Pat Langdon
Engineering Design Centre
Department of Engineering
University of Cambridge, UK
{pb400,pml24}@cam.ac.uk

Christoph Jung, Pascal Hamisu
Fraunhofer-Institut für Graphische
Datenverarbeitung IGD,
Germany
{chjung,phamisu}@igd.fraunhofer.de

Carlos Duarte
Departamento
de Informática
Faculdade de Ciências
University of Lisbon,
Portugal
cad@di.fc.ul.pt

Luis Almeida
Centro de
Computação
Gráfica,
Portugal
Luis.Almeida@ccg.pt

**Primary contact*

Abstract
This workshop aims to gap the bridge between mainstream research on intelligent systems and accessibility researchers by presenting papers and demonstrations on developing adaptable multimodal systems for elderly and disabled users. The workshop is organized in the context of EU GUIDE project and focus on Web and Digital TV applications. However the research and applications are also relevant for different platforms like computers, tablet and ubiquitous devices. The workshop consists of a keynote speech on standardization of developing intelligent and accessible systems followed by six paper and demonstration presentations. A set of papers from this workshop will later appear at the International Journal of Digital Television.

Categories and Subject Descriptors
D.2.2 [Software Engineering]: Design Tools and Techniques – *user interfaces;* **K.4.2 [Computers and Society]:** Social Issues – *assistive technologies for persons with disabilities*

General Terms
Algorithms, Experimentation, Human Factors, Measurement

Keywords
Human Computer Interaction, Assistive Technology, Usability Evaluation, User Model, e-Inclusion.

1. Motivation
Modern research in intelligent interactive systems can offer valuable assistance to elderly and disabled population by helping them to engage more fully with the world. However, many users find it difficult to use existing interaction devices either for physical or aging-related impairments, though researches on intelligent voice recognition, adaptable pointing, browsing and navigation, affect and gesture recognition can hugely benefit them. Additionally, systems and services developed for elderly or disabled people often find useful applications for their able bodied counterparts – a few examples are mobile amplification control, which was originally developed for people with hearing problem but helpful in noisy environment, audio cassette version of books originally developed for blind people, standard of subtitling in television for deaf users and so on. Further many important technical achievements could not yet be implemented at industrial level, mostly due to lack of awareness among industrial developers, and missing software and guidelines support during design and development. Existing research on intelligent systems often works for 'average' users and excludes a certain portion of the population who finds it difficult to use existing systems and may benefit from intelligent adaptation of the interface. Lack of knowledge about the problems of disabled and elderly users has often led designers to develop non inclusive systems. On contrary accessibility research often focus on developing tailor-made products for certain type of disability and lacks portability across different platforms and users.

This workshop aims to be one of first platforms to reduce gap between existing mainstream research on intelligent systems and researches in accessibility. In this workshop, we shall try

- to identify existing problems in providing accessibility in mainstream electronic interface development,
- to look at prospective solutions in terms on multimodal interfaces, user modeling and simulation
- to sketch vision for future of accessibility and electronic interface design by creating new international standards or contributing to existing ones.

Rest part of the document is organized as follows. We point out objectives of the workshop in next section. Section 3 provides background information of the workshop through discussing the EU GUIDE project. Section 4 presents the detail of participation and list of papers followed by a brief

IUI'12, February 14–17, 2011, Lisbon, Portugal.

detail of workshop organizers.

2. Objectives

This workshop will take a broader approach than existing ones for improving the quality of interaction experience for a wide range of users. It will explore the applicability of different modalities of interaction (like speech, gesture, haptic interface, and so on) and investigate ways to develop intelligent adaptation systems that meet accessibility criteria and personalized according to the range of abilities of the user. A particular focus will be given on interoperability though the adherence to standards for Accessibility such as WAI-ARIA and ISO standards. We shall expand on existing efforts for developing guidelines like WCAG and investigate how accessibility researchers and intelligent system developers can follow accessibility standards for more applications besides web based systems. For example, the guidelines are not enough to develop intelligent adaptation systems to customize interfaces based on a range of abilities of users and as an alternative we shall explore the possibility of an interoperable user modeling and simulation standard.

The objectives of this workshop are

- Providing an interdisciplinary platform for discussing research on intelligent user interfaces and multimodal interaction,
- Investigate how intelligent user interfaces can support inclusive design
- Finding ways to use multimodality to improve quality of life, especially focusing on elderly and disabled people.
- Broadening the applications of both multimodal interaction and assistive technology
- Involving different stakeholders, especially the industry as the bridge to the end users, in developing accessible intelligent systems and fostering standards in development and design.
- Investigating ways to develop new standards for accessibility and interoperable user modelling.
- Initiating an effort to bridge the gap between assistive technology researchers and main stream HCI and AI researchers.
- Present and demonstrate latest results and prototypes from intelligent user interface research.

3. Context

The workshop is organized in the context of the EU GUIDE project. The research project is partly funded by the European Commission under the Seventh (FP7 - 2007-2013) Framework Programme for Research and Technological Development. It is creating a software framework and design tools which allows developers to efficiently integrate accessibility and personalisation features into their applications, minimizing intervention with existing development process and tools. It also involves developing a set of references applications (home automation, video conferencing, tele-learning, media access) that can help elderly citizens to simplify their daily life, stay connected in their social network and enhance their understanding of the world. More detail about the project can be found from the project website at http://www.guide-project.eu/. This workshop will demonstrate a few technologies developed in the GUIDE project like

- browsing an Electronic Program guide through gestures,
- simulating interaction patterns of disabled and elderly users and
- adapting interfaces and interaction based on range of abilities of users.

4. Participation

This workshop will provide a multi-disciplinary platform for combining research in the fields of

- Multimodal human computer interaction
- Intelligent and adaptable systems
- Universal and inclusive design
- Assistive technology
- Standardization

The following is a tentative set of papers and demonstrations to be presented at the workshop.

Keynote Speech

- How can intelligent interfaces make a difference to accessibility?

Papers

1. Developing accessible and adaptive digital TV applications through user modeling and simulation
2. Evaluating Fusion Engines through Simulation of Interaction Scenarios
3. An open-source software framework for adaptive multi-modal user interfaces in Web TV applications
4. From low to high fidelity prototypes: Challenges when developing for elderly users
5. Accessibility in dynamic Web TV applications

Demonstrations

1. GUIDE Simulator - simulation of interaction pat-

terns of disabled and elderly

2. Gravity Well Adaptation algorithm

3. Multimodal TV controller

These papers and demonstrations focus on the emerging Web & TV platforms and services as these platforms have the potential to become the main media terminals in the users' homes, due to their convenience and wide acceptance. They cover a wide variety of topics like standardizing accessibility, developing adaptation algorithms to personalize interfaces for elderly users, fusing multiple streams of input channels and developing an open access framework for connected TV applications. Most of these papers are even relevant outside the domain of digital TV as these algorithms were evaluated using both set top boxes and computers. For example the fusion and adaptation algorithms can be used for standard pointing devices with laptop or PCs and the framework can be used in both set top box and standard computers or Tablet devices.

A set of papers from this workshop will be selected for publication at the International Journal of Digital Television (http://www.intellectbooks.co.uk/journals/view-journal,id=175/), probably in the Autumn issue.

4. Format

The workshop will consist of one keynote speech, followed by about ten paper, poster and demonstration presentations and panel discussion involving all participants.

Mr. Peter Olaf Looms from Danish Broadcasting Corporation will deliver the keynote speech. He is currently chairman of the ITU-T Focus Group on Audiovisual media Accessibility that aims to produce a roadmap for digital media accessibility actions by the end of 2012. Previously he was involved in setting up the DTV4ALL consortium that assisted the European Commission in promoting e-inclusion and television across Europe. Using examples from current work to make digital media accessible at the International Telecommunications Union, this Keynote will provide a framework for discussing the context in which intelligent interfaces can make a difference to persons with disabilities.

Besides a regular question answering session after each paper presentation, the workshop will promote interaction by offering participants hands on experience on interacting with state-of-the-art intelligent interfaces for accessibility. It will include adaptive interfaces involving gesture recognition, eye gaze tracker and scanning interfaces. The workshop will also have a one-hour slot for open discussion on existing problems and future vision about intelligent system design for accessibility. A tentative agenda is as follows

9.30-10.30	Keynote speech
10.30-10.45	Discussion
10.45-11.00	Coffee break
11.00-12.30	Paper presentations
12.30-14.00	Lunch
14.00-15.00	Paper presentation
15.00-15.30	Coffee break and demo preparation
15.30-16.30	Poster and demo presentation
16.30-17.30	Panel Discussion and Conclusion

6. Organization

This section provides a brief biography of the organizers. They were previously involved in organizing AccessibleTV workshop (http://www.accessibletv.eu/index .html) in AMI 2010.

Pradipta Biswas is a Research Associate at the Engineering Design Centre and Trinity Hall of University of Cambridge. His research aims to make the interfaces of modern digital devices accessible to elderly users and people with different ranges of abilities. In particular, he works on developing user models that help to reflect problems faced by people with different range of abilities in using interactive systems. He has published about 30 journal and conference papers in Human Computer Interaction and Assistive Technology. He has a PhD in Computer Science from University of Cambridge. He was awarded a Gates-Cambridge Scholarship in 2006. He previously undertook a first degree in Information Technology at the University of Kalyani and a master degree at the Indian Institute of Technology, Kharagpur. He is a working group coordinator of the International Telecommunication Union's (ITU) focus group on Audio Visual Media Accessibility, committee member of British Standardization Institute, and member of the EU task force on Standardization of User Models, Higher Education Academy, British Computer Society and Royal Society of Medicine.

Carlos Duarte holds a PhD (2008) in Computer Science, from the University of Lisbon, and an MsC in Electronic and Computers Engineering from the Instituto Superior Técnico, Technical University of Lisbon, where he also graduated in Electronic and Computers Engineering. He is currently a Professor at the Department of Informatics, Faculty of Sciences of the University of Lisbon, and a senior researcher at LaSIGE, as a member of the HCIM Group since 2000. His main research interests include multimodal and adaptive interfaces, with a special emphasis on accessibility, usability evaluation, mobile devices, UI design, hypermedia, digital books, and eLearning. He has published over 30 refereed technical and scientific papers and book chapters, and has supervised several undergraduate projects and master dissertations, and is currently supervising PhD thesis. He is a member of several program committees for international and national conferences and a reviewer of international conferences and journals. He participated in several research projects, European and national. He is a member of ACM SIGCHI.

Pat Langdon's experimental doctoral and post-doctoral research has contributed to cognitive science, artificial intelligence, robotics and psychophysical studies of the human visual system. His experimental PhD researched the psychological reality of certain Artificial Intelligence-based theories of vision and he was employed by an Artificial Intelligence Vision Research Unit at the University of Sheffield working on the area of robotics. Subsequently, he moved into Engineering Design Research at the University of Lancaster EDC, working on the application of user centred design principles to complex engineering design systems. Since 1998 Pat Langdon has been employed at the Cambridge EDC, where he has pursued a number of research directions. He is currently External Examiner for the Kings College London and Guy's Hospital Intercollegiate MSc in Assistive Technology.

Christoph Jung works as a project- and technology manager in Fraunhofer IGD since 2007. He has been involved in several European research projects, such as "hArtes" (audio signal processing on heterogeneous reconfigurable embedded platforms) and "ANSWER" (Content-based video analysis for work flow automation in movie post-production). Christoph is coordinator of the European Research project "GUIDE", which develops adaptive multimodal interfaces for Connected TV services, based on speech, gestures and context awareness. He further leads a project on adaptive/interactive advertisement and audience measurement for digital-out-of-home systems utilizing visual sensors. He supervises the lecture on Image Processing at the University of Technology Darmstadt. Christoph is also currently involved in standardisation activities in the European VUMS (Visual User Modelling & Simulation) Cluster.

Pascal Hamisu received his Dipl-Ing (MSc) degree in Electrical Engineering and Information Technology from Technische Universität Darmstadt, Germany in 2006. In 2004 he received a certificate for an International Program for New Media Technologies and Business Practices at IMEDIA, Providence RI, USA. Prior to his current posit ion at Fraunhofer Institute for Computer Graphics IGD, he gained experience in several research projects as a student research associate. Since 2007, has been involved in both German national and EU R&D projects in the areas of Ambient Assisted Living and E-inclusion for people with limited interaction affordances; especially elderly users. His research interests include open software frameworks supporting multimodal interaction, inter –sensory interfaces to integrate vision, speech and gesture modalities for augmented computing via intuitive user interfaces. Other interests are semantic modelling of wireless sensory data in an AmI environment for human behavioral analysis and scene reconstruction.

Luis Almeida received a five-year degree in Mathematics (specialization in Computer Graphics and Applications) from the Science and Technology faculty of Coimbra University, Portugal. Since July 1994, for two years, he was a computer graphics researcher and application programmer at Marine Technology and Engineering Department from Technical University of Lisbon. Since end of 1996, for three years, he was a researcher for computer graphics at CCG - Centro de Computação Gráfica (Portugal). Since 2000 he assumed the role of senior project manager. His research interests are now primarily concerned with Information Visualisation and Management, Mobile Multimedia, Virtual and Augmented Reality for Cultural Heritage preservation, in the context of national and European projects. He has also been participating, on behalf of CCG, for projects where interaction techniques and technologies are designed and developed targeting users with special needs, like for example elderly people at home. He is author and co-author of several publications, short communications and seminars. He was the author and principal manager of several R&D projects with particular emphasis in the area of the application of technology and its transfer to end-user solutions. He was also a member of the internal review Board of the INI-GraphicsNet Foundation and a member of EUROGRAPHICS - the European association for computer graphics.

Program Committee

The workshop papers have been reviewed by the following program committee.

- Pradipta Biswas, Pat Langdon & John Clarkson, University of Cambridge, UK
- Christoph Jung & Pascal Hamisu, Frauhofer IGD, Germany
- Carlos Duarte, University of Lisbon, Portugal
- Per Ola Kristensson, University of St Andrews, UK
- Mari Feli Gonzalez, INGEMA, Spain
- Luis Almeida and Ido Iurgel, CCG, Portugal
- Peter Olaf Looms, Danish Broadcasting Corporation, Denmark

2nd Workshop on Context-awareness in Retrieval and Recommendation

Ernesto W. De Luca
Technische Universität Berlin
Berlin, Germany
deluca@dai-lab.de

Matthias Böhmer
DFKI GmbH
Saarbrücken, Germany
matthias.boehmer@dfki.de

Alan Said
Technische Universität Berlin
Berlin, Germany
alan@dai-lab.de

Ed Chi
Google Inc.
Mountain View, CA, USA
chi@acm.org

ABSTRACT

Context-aware information is widely available in various ways and is becoming more and more important for enhancing retrieval performance and recommendation results. The current main issue to cope with is not only recommending or retrieving the most relevant items and content, but defining them ad hoc. Other relevant issues include personalizing and adapting the information and the way it is displayed to the user's current situation and interests. Ubiquitous computing further provides new means for capturing user feedback on items and providing information.

ACM Classification Keywords

H.3.4 Information Technology and Systems Applications: Decision support; H.3.3 Information Storage and Retrieval: Information Filtering, Relevance feedback, Retrieval models, Search process, Selection process

General Terms

Algorithms, Design, Experimentation, Human Factors.

CONTENTS AND MAIN GOALS

The first installment of the CaRR workshop [2] received enthusiastic feedback from the context-awareness community with a total of 15 submitted papers and more than 30 attendees at IUI 2011 in Palo Alto. A total of 9 papers were accepted for presentation at the workshop and publication in the proceedings [1]. An indication that *context-awareness in retrieval and recommendation* is a very interesting and timely topic. Among the issues discussed at the workshop were: how context-awareness has changed the goal of retrieval and recommendation, e.g. drifting from recommendations that fit to the general user interest to ad-hoc recommendations that fit to the user's context. Additional topics covered were new emerging areas where the role of retrieval and recommendation increases, e.g. recommending places to go, activities to take, or apps to use.

The 2nd edition of the CaRR workshop[1] continued focussing on the integration of context for retrieval and recommendation. The contexts focused on were a general content context and a user-centric content context. The general content context is a common case defined by time, weather, location and many similar other aspects whereas the user-centric content context is given by user profiles, e.g. language, interests, devices used for interaction, etc.

Other important issues addressed included the importance of developing context-aware systems that can generate and present situation-specific information. The need of personalizing and adapting information is accentuated when we consider this kind of device- and interaction-based context.

The aim of the CaRR Workshop was to invite the community to a discussion in which we tried to find new creative ways to handle context-awareness. Furthermore, the workshop aimed at exchanging new ideas between different communities involved in research, such as HCI, machine learning, information retrieval and recommendation.

RESEARCH QUESTIONS

The workshop was especially intended for researchers working on multidisciplinary tasks, to discuss problems and synergies. Ideas on creative and collaborative approaches for context-aware retrieval and recommendation were of special interest.

The participants were encouraged to address the following questions:

- What is context?
- Is context-awareness in retrieval and recommendation necessary?
- Which benefits come from context-aware retrieval and recommendation systems?
- How do user interfaces handle context?

[1] http://carr-workshop.org

- In what ways can context improve HCI?
- How can we combine general- and user-centric context-aware technologies?
- How should context affect the way information is presented?
- Which new means for collecting user feedback does UbiComp provide?
- What new type of items (beyond books, news and movies) are worth recommending by means of context-aware systems (e.g. places, friends, apps)?

TOPICS

The topics of interest included, but were not limited to:

- Context-aware information retrieval
- Context-aware profiling, clustering and collaborative filtering
- Machine learning for context-aware information retrieval and ontology learning
- Ubiquitous and context-aware computing
- Use of context-aware technologies in UI/HCI
- Context-aware advertising
- Recommendations for mobile users
- Context-awareness in portable devices

WORKSHOP ORGANIZERS

Ernesto William De Luca is Head of the Competence Center for Information Retrieval and Machine Learning at the DAI Lab, Technische Universität Berlin. He is the author of more than 60 papers on national and international conferences and journals in the fields of Computational Linguistics, Information Retrieval, Adaptive Systems and other related areas. He has chaired a number of workshops on semantic personalization, context-awareness in recommender systems and related topics.

Matthias Böhmer is a researcher at the Innovative Retail Laboratory of the German Research Center for Artificial Intelligence (DFKI) in Saarbrücken, Germany. His main research focus is on context-aware recommender systems that suggest mobile applications. He is interested in deducing the contextual relevance of particular apps from a users device interaction, e.g. usage patterns or icon arrangement.

Alan Said is a research associate at the Competence Center for Information Retrieval and Machine Learning at the DAI Lab, Technische Universität Berlin. He has authored papers on national and international conferences in the fields of recommender systems, social networks, context-awareness and other related areas. He has organized and been involved in workshops on recommender systems and related topics.

Ed H. Chi is a Research Scientist at Google. Until very recently, he was the Area Manager and a Principal Scientist at Palo Alto Research Center's Augmented Social Cognition Group. He led the group in understanding how Web 2.0 and Social Computing systems help groups of people to remember, think and reason. Ed completed his three degrees (B.S., M.S., and Ph.D.) in 6.5 years from University of Minnesota, and has been doing research on user interface software systems since 1993. He has been featured and quoted in the press, including the Economist, Time Magazine, LA Times, and the Associated Press.

PROGRAM COMMITTEE MEMBERS:

- Omar Alonso, Microsoft, USA
- Hideki Asoh, AIST, Japan
- Linas Baltrunas, Telefonica Research, Spain
- Toine Bogers, RSLIS, Denmark
- Robin Burke, DePaul University, USA
- Li Chen, Hong Kong Baptist University, China
- Karen Church, Telefonica Research, Spain
- Marco Degemmis, University of Bari Aldo Moro, Italy
- Ido Guy, IBM, Israel
- Qi He, IBM, USA
- Tim Hussein, University of Duisburg-Essen, Germany
- Brijnesh-Johannes Jain, TU-Berlin, Germany
- Dietmar Jannach, TU-Dortmund, Germany
- Alexandros Karatzoglou, Telefonica Research, Spain
- Carsten Kessler, University of Münster, Germany
- Alfred Kobsa, University of California, Irvine, USA
- Antonio Krüger, DFKI, Saarbrcken, Germany
- Michael Kruppa, DFKI, Berlin, Germany
- Martha Larson, TU-Delft, The Netherlands
- Ulf Leser, Humboldt-Universität zu Berlin, Germany
- Pasquale Lops, University of Bari Aldo Moro, Italy
- Petteri Nurmi, HIIT, Finnland
- Till Plumbaum, Technische Universität Berlin, Germany
- Francesco Ricci, Free University of Bozen-Bolzano, Italy
- Markus Schedl, Johannes Kepler University, Austria
- Armando Stellato, University of Tor Vergata, Rome, Italy
- Domonkos Tikk, Gravity R&D, Hungary

ACKNOWLEDGEMENTS

The organizers would like to thank all the authors for contributing to CaRR 2011 and all the members of the program committee for ascertaining the scientic quality of the workshop.

REFERENCES

1. *CaRR '11: Proceedings of the 2011 Workshop on Context-awareness in Retrieval and Recommendation*, New York, NY, USA, 2011. ACM.

2. E. W. De Luca, A. Said, M. Böhmer, and F. Michahelles. Workshop on context-awareness in retrieval and recommendation. In *Proceedings of the 16th international conference on Intelligent user interfaces*, IUI '11, pages 471–472, New York, NY, USA, 2011. ACM.

Author Index

www.ingramcontent.com/pod-product-compliance
Ingram Content Group UK Ltd.
Pitfield, Milton Keynes, MK11 3LW, UK
UKHW051511290926
15471UKWH00008B/1556

9 781450 313704